FRANK NORRIS

FRANK NORRIS

NOVELS AND ESSAYS
Vandover and the Brute
McTeague
The Octopus
Essays

THE LIBRARY OF AMERICA

The paper used in this publication meets the
minimum requirements of the American National Standard
for Information Sciences—Permanence of Paper for
Printed Library Materials, ANSI z39.48–1984.

Distributed to the trade in the United States
and Canada by the Viking Press.

Published outside North America by the Press Syndicate
of the University of Cambridge,
The Pitt Building, Trumpington Street, Cambridge CB2IRP, England
ISBN 0 521 32485 8

Library of Congress Catalog Card Number: 85–23133
For cataloging information, see end of *Notes* section.
ISBN 0–940450–40–2
_____
First Printing

Manufactured in the United States of America

DONALD PIZER
WROTE THE NOTES AND SELECTED
THE TEXTS FOR THIS VOLUME

Grateful acknowledgement is made to the National Endowment for the Humanities and the Ford Foundation for their generous financial support of this series.

Contents

VANDOVER AND
THE BRUTE

Chapter One

IT WAS ALWAYS a matter of wonder to Vandover that he was able to recall so little of his past life. With the exception of the most recent events he could remember nothing connectedly. What he at first imagined to be the story of his life, on closer inspection turned out to be but a few disconnected incidents that his memory had preserved with the greatest capriciousness, absolutely independent of their importance. One of these incidents might be a great sorrow, a tragedy, a death in his family; and another, recalled with the same vividness, the same accuracy of detail, might be a matter of the least moment.

A certain one of these wilful fillips of memory would always bring before him a particular scene during the migration of his family from Boston to their new home in San Francisco, at a time when Vandover was about eight years old.

It was in the depot of one of the larger towns in western New York. The day had been hot and after the long ride on the crowded day coach the cool shadow under the curved roof of the immense iron vaulted depot seemed very pleasant. The porter, the brakeman and Vandover's father very carefully lifted his mother from the car. She was lying back on pillows in a long steamer chair. The three men let the chair slowly down, the brakeman went away, but the porter remained, taking off his cap and wiping his forehead with the back of his left hand, which in turn he wiped against the pink palm of his right. The other train, the train to which they were to change, had not yet arrived. It was rather still; at the far end of the depot a locomotive, sitting back on its motionless drivers like some huge sphinx crouching along the rails, was steaming quietly, drawing long breaths. The repair gang in greasy caps and spotted blue overalls were inspecting the train, pottering about the trucks, opening and closing the journal-boxes, striking clear notes on the wheels with long-handled hammers.

Vandover stood close to his father, his thin legs wide apart, holding in both his hands the satchel he had been permitted to carry. He looked about him continually, rolling his big

3

eyes vaguely, watching now the repair-gang, now a huge white cat dozing on an empty baggage truck.

Several passengers were walking up and down the platform, staring curiously at the invalid lying back in the steamer chair.

The journey was too much for her. She was very weak and very pale, her eyelids were heavy, the skin of her forehead looked blue and tightly drawn, and tiny beads of perspiration gathered around the corners of her mouth. Vandover's father put his hand and arm along the back of the chair and his sick wife rested against him, leaning her head on his waistcoat over the pocket where he kept his cigars and pocket-comb. They were all silent.

By and by she drew a long sigh, her face became the face of an imbecile, stupid, without expression, her eyes half-closed, her mouth half-open. Her head rolled forward as though she were nodding in her sleep, while a long drip of saliva trailed from her lower lip. Vandover's father bent over her quickly, crying out sharply, "Hallie!—what is it?" All at once the train for which they were waiting charged into the depot, filling the place with a hideous clangor and with the smell of steam and of hot oil.

This scene of her death was the only thing that Vandover could remember of his mother.

As he looked back over his life he could recall nothing after this for nearly five years. Even after that lapse of time the only scene he could picture with any degree of clearness was one of the greatest triviality in which he saw himself, a rank thirteen-year-old boy, sitting on a bit of carpet in the back yard of the San Francisco house playing with his guinea-pigs.

In order to get at his life during his teens, Vandover would have been obliged to collect these scattered memory pictures as best he could, rearrange them in some more orderly sequence, piece out what he could imperfectly recall and fill in the many gaps by mere guesswork and conjecture.

It was the summer of 1880 that they had come to San Francisco. Once settled there, Vandover's father began to build small residence houses and cheap flats which he rented at various prices, the cheapest at ten dollars, the more expensive at thirty-five and forty. He had closed out his business in the

East, coming out to California on account of his wife's ill health. He had made his money in Boston and had intended to retire.

But he soon found that he could not do this. At this time he was an old man, nearly sixty. He had given his entire life to his business to the exclusion of everything else, and now when his fortune had been made and when he could afford to enjoy it, discovered that he had lost the capacity for enjoying anything but the business itself. Nothing else could interest him. He was not what would be called in America a rich man, but he had made money enough to travel, to allow himself any reasonable relaxation, to cultivate a taste for art, music, literature or the drama, to indulge in any harmless fad, such as collecting etchings, china or bric-à-brac, or even to permit himself the luxury of horses. In the place of all these he found himself, at nearly sixty years of age, forced again into the sordid round of business as the only escape from the mortal *ennui* and weariness of the spirit that preyed upon him during every leisure hour of the day.

Early and late he went about the city, personally superintending the building of his little houses and cheap flats, sitting on saw-horses and piles of lumber, watching the carpenters at work. In the evening he came home to a late supper, completely fagged, bringing with him the smell of mortar and of pine shavings.

On the first of each month when his agents turned over the rents to him he was in great spirits. He would bring home the little canvas sack of coin with him before banking it, and call his son's attention to the amount, never failing to stick a twenty-dollar gold-piece in each eye, monocle fashion, exclaiming, "Good for the masses," a meaningless jest that had been one of the family's household words for years.

His plan of building was peculiar. His credit was good, and having chosen his lot he would find out from the banks how much they would loan him upon it in case he should become the owner. If this amount suited him, he would buy the lot, making one large payment outright and giving his note for the balance. The lot once his, the banks loaned him the desired amount. With this money and with money of his own he would make the final payment on the lot and would begin the building itself, paying his labour on the nail, but getting his material, lumber, brick and fittings on time. When the building was half-way up he would negotiate a second loan from the banks in order to complete it and in order to meet the notes he had given to his contractors for material.

He believed this to be a shrewd business operation, since the rents as they returned to him were equal to the interest on a far larger sum than that which he had originally invested. He said little about the double mortgage on each piece of property "improved" after this fashion and which often represented a full two-thirds of its entire value. The interest on each loan was far more than covered by the rents; he chose his neighbourhoods with great discrimination; real estate was flourishing in the rapidly growing city, and the new houses, although built so cheaply that they were mere shells of lath and plaster, were nevertheless made gay and brave with varnish and cheap mill-work. They rented well at first, scarcely a one was ever vacant. People spoke of the Old Gentleman as one of the most successful realty owners in the city. So pleased did he become with the success of his new venture that in course of time all his money was reinvested after this fashion.

At the time of his father's greatest prosperity Vandover himself began to draw toward his fifteenth year, entering upon that period of change when the first raw elements of character began to assert themselves and when, if ever, there was a crying need for the influence of his mother. Any feminine influence would have been well for him at this time: that of an older sister, even that of a hired governess. The housekeeper looked after him a little, mended his clothes, saw that he took his bath Saturday nights, and that he did not dig tunnels under the garden walks. But her influence was entirely negative and prohibitory and the two were constantly at war. Vandover grew in a haphazard way and after school hours ran about the streets almost at will.

At fifteen he put on long trousers, and the fall of the same year entered the High School. He had grown too fast and at this time was tall and very lean; his limbs were straight, angular, out of all proportion, with huge articulations at the elbows and knees. His neck was long and thin and his head large, his face was sallow and covered with pimples, his ears were big, red and stuck out stiff from either side of his head. His hair he wore "pompadour."

Within a month after his entry of the High School he had a nickname. The boys called him "Skinny-seldom-fed," to his infinite humiliation.

Little by little the crude virility of the young man began to develop in him. It was a distressing, uncanny period. Had Vandover been a girl he would at this time have been subject to all sorts of abnormal vagaries, such as eating his slate pencil, nibbling bits of chalk, wishing he were dead, and drifting into states of unreasoned melancholy. As it was, his voice began to change, a little golden down appeared on his cheeks and upon the nape of his neck, while his first summer vacation was altogether spoiled by a long spell of mumps.

His appetite was enormous. He ate heavy meat three times a day, but took little or no exercise. The pimples on his face became worse and worse. He grew peevish and nervous. He hated girls, and when in their society was a very bull-calf for bashfulness and awkward self-consciousness. At times the strangest and most morbid fancies took possession of him, chief of which was that every one was looking at him while he was walking in the street.

Vandover was a good little boy. Every night he said his prayers, going down upon his huge knees at the side of his bed. To the Lord's Prayer he added various petitions of his own. He prayed that he might be a good boy and live a long time and go to Heaven when he died and see his mother; that the next Saturday might be sunny all day long, and that the end of the world might not come while he was alive.

It was during Vandover's first year at the High School that his eyes were opened and that he acquired the knowledge of good and evil. Till very late he kept his innocence, the crude raw innocence of the boy, like that of a young animal, at once charming and absurd. But by and by he became very curious, stirred with a blind unreasoned instinct. In the Bible which he read Sunday afternoons, because his father gave him a quarter for doing so, he came across a great many things that filled him with vague and strange ideas; and one Sunday at church, when the minister was intoning the Litany, he remarked for the first time the words, "all women in the perils of child-birth."

He puzzled over this for a long time, smelling out a mystery beneath the words, feeling the presence of something hidden, with the instinct of a young brute. He could get no satisfaction from his father and by and by began to be ashamed to ask him; why, he did not know. Although he could not help hearing the abominable talk of the High School boys, he at first refused to believe that part of it which he could understand. For all that he was ashamed of his innocence and ignorance and affected to appreciate their stories nevertheless.

At length one day he heard the terse and brutal truth. In an instant he believed it, some lower, animal intuition in him reiterating and confirming the fact. But even then he hated to think that people were so low, so vile. One day, however, he was looking through the volumes of the old Encyclopædia Britannica in his father's library, hoping that he might find a dollar bill which the Old Gentleman told him had been at one time misplaced between the leaves of some one of the great tomes. All at once he came upon the long article "Obstetrics," profusely illustrated with old-fashioned plates and steel engravings. He read it from beginning to end.

It was the end of all his childish ideals, the destruction of all his first illusions. The whole of his rude little standard of morality was lowered immediately. Even his mother, whom he had always believed to be some kind of an angel, fell at once in his estimation. She could never be the same to him after this, never so sweet, so good and so pure as he had hitherto imagined her.

It was very cruel, the whole thing was a grief to him, a blow, a great shock; he hated to think of it. Then little by little the first taint crept in, the innate vice stirred in him, the brute began to make itself felt, and a multitude of perverse and vicious ideas commenced to buzz about him like a swarm of nasty flies.

A certain word, the blunt Anglo-Saxon name for a lost woman, that he heard on one occasion among the boys at school, opened to him a vista of incredible wickedness, but now after the first moment of revolt the thing began to seem less horrible. There was even a certain attraction about it. Vandover soon became filled with an overwhelming curiosity, the eager evil curiosity of the schoolboy, the perverse craving for the knowledge of vice. He listened with all his ears to everything that was said and went about through the great city with eyes open only to its foulness. He even looked up in the dictionary the meanings of the new words, finding in the cold, scientific definitions some strange sort of satisfaction.

There was no feminine influence about Vandover at this critical time to help him see the world in the right light and to gauge things correctly, and he might have been totally corrupted while in his earliest teens had it not been for another side of his character that began to develop about the same time.

This was his artistic side. He seemed to be a born artist. At first he only showed bent for all general art. He drew well, he made curious little modellings in clayey mud; he had a capital ear for music and managed in some unknown way of his own to pick out certain tunes on the piano. At one time he gave evidence of a genuine talent for the stage. For days he would pretend to be some dreadful sort of character, he did not know whom, talking to himself, stamping and shaking his fists; then he would dress himself in an old smoking-cap, a red table-cloth and one of his father's discarded Templar swords, and pose before the long mirrors ranting and scowling. At another time he would devote his attention to literature, making up endless stories with which he terrified himself, telling them to himself in a low voice for hours after he had got into bed. Sometimes he would write out these stories and read them to his father after supper, standing up between the folding doors of the library, acting out the whole narrative with furious gestures. Once he even wrote a little poem which seriously disturbed the Old Gentleman, filling him with formless ideas and vague hopes for the future.

In a suitable environment Vandover might easily have become an author, actor or musician, since it was evident that he possessed the fundamental *afflatus* that underlies all branches of art. As it was, the merest chance decided his career.

In the same library where he had found the famous encyclopædia article was "A Home Book of Art," one of those
showily bound gift books one sees lying about conspicuously
on parlour centre tables. It was an English publication calculated to meet popular and general demand. There were a
great many full-page pictures of lonely women, called "Reveries" or "Idylls," ideal "Heads" of gipsy girls, of coquettes,
and heads of little girls crowned with cherries and illustrative
of such titles as "Spring," "Youth," "Innocence." Besides
these were sentimental pictures, as, for instance, one entitled
"It Might Have Been," a sad-eyed girl, with long hair, musing
over a miniature portrait, and another especially impressive
which represented a handsomely dressed woman flung upon
a *Louis Quinze* sofa, weeping, her hands clasped over her
head. She was alone; it was twilight; on the floor was a heap
of opened letters. The picture was called "Memories."

Vandover thought this last a wonderful work of art and
made a hideous copy of it with very soft pencils. He was so
pleased with it that he copied another one of the pictures and
then another. By and by he had copied almost all of them.
His father gave him a dollar and Vandover began to add to
his usual evening petition the prayer that he might become a
great artist. Thus it was that his career was decided upon.

He was allowed to have a drawing teacher. This was an
elderly German, an immense old fellow, who wore a wig and
breathed loudly through his nose. His voice was like a trumpet and he walked with a great striding gait like a colonel of
cavalry. Besides drawing he taught ornamental writing and
engrossing. With a dozen curved and flowing strokes of an
ordinary writing pen he could draw upon a calling card a
conventionalized outline-picture of some kind of dove or bird
of paradise, all curves and curlicues, flying very gracefully and
carrying in its beak a half-open scroll upon which could be
inscribed such sentiments as "From a Friend" or "With Fond
Regards," or even one's own name.

His system of drawing was of his own invention. Over the
picture to be copied he would paste a great sheet of paper,
ruling off the same into spaces of about an inch square. He
would cut out one of these squares and Vandover would copy
the portion of the picture thus disclosed. When he had copied

the whole picture in this fashion the teacher would go over it himself, retouching it here and there, labouring to obviate the checker-board effect which the process invariably produced.

At other times Vandover copied into his sketch-book, with hard crayons, those lithographed studies on buff paper which are published by the firm in Berlin. He began with ladders, wheel-barrows and water barrels, working up in course of time to rustic buildings set in a bit of landscape; stone bridges and rural mills, overhung by some sort of linden tree, with ends of broken fences in a corner of the foreground to complete the composition. From these he went on to bunches of grapes, vases of fruit and at length to more "Ideal heads." The climax was reached with a life-sized Head, crowned with honeysuckles and entitled *"Flora."* He was three weeks upon it. It was an achievement, a veritable *chef-d'œuvre.* Vandover gave it to his father upon Christmas morning, having signed his name to it with a great ornamental flourish. The Old Gentleman was astounded, the housekeeper was called in and exclaimed over it, raising her hands to Heaven. Vandover's father gave him a five-dollar gold-piece, fresh from the mint, had the picture framed in gilt and hung it up in his smoking-room over the clock.

Never for a moment did the Old Gentleman oppose Vandover's wish to become an artist and it was he himself who first spoke about Paris to the young man. Vandover was delighted; the Latin Quarter became his dream. Between the two it was arranged that he should go over as soon as he had finished his course at the High School. The Old Gentleman was to take him across, returning only when he was well established in some suitable studio.

At length Vandover graduated, and within three weeks of that event was on his way to Europe with his father. He never got farther than Boston.

At the last moment the Old Gentleman wavered. Vandover was still very young and would be entirely alone in Paris, ignorant of the language, exposed to every temptation. Besides this, his education would stop where it was. Somehow he could not make it seem right to him to cut the young man adrift in this fashion. On the other hand, the Old Gentleman had a great many old-time friends and business acquaintances in Boston who could be trusted with a nominal supervision of his son for four years. He had no college education himself, but in some vague way he felt convinced that Vandover would be a better artist for a four years' course at Harvard.

Vandover took his father's decision hardly. He had never thought of being a college-man and nothing in that life appealed to him. He urged upon his father the loss of time that the course would entail, but his father met this objection by offering to pay for any artistic tuition that would not interfere with the regular college work.

Little by little the idea of college life became more attractive to Vandover; at the worst, it was only postponing the Paris trip, not abandoning it. Besides this, two of his chums from the High School were expecting to enter Harvard that fall, and he could look forward to a very pleasant four years spent in their company.

Out at Cambridge the term was just closing. The Old Gentleman's friends procured him tickets to several of the more important functions. From the gallery of Memorial Hall Vandover and his father saw some of the great dinners; they went up to New London for the boat-race; they gained admittance to the historic Yard on Class-day, and saw the strange football rush for flowers around the "Tree." They heard the seniors sing "Fair Harvard" for the last time, and later saw them receive their diplomas at Sander's Theatre.

The great ceremonies of the place, the picturesqueness of the elm-shaded Yard, the old red dormitories covered with ivy, the associations and traditions of the buildings, the venerable pump, Longfellow's room, the lecture hall where the minute-men had barracked, all of these things, in the end, appealed strongly to Vandover's imagination. Instead of passing the summer months in an ocean voyage and a continental journey, he at last became content to settle down to work under a tutor, "boning up" for the examinations. His father returned to San Francisco in July.

Vandover matriculated the September of the same year; on the first of October he signed the college rolls and became a Harvard freshman. At that time he was eighteen years old.

Chapter Two

THERE WAS LITTLE of the stubborn or unyielding about Vandover, his personality was not strong, his nature pliable and he rearranged himself to suit his new environment at Harvard very rapidly. Before the end of the first semester he had become to all outward appearances a typical Harvardian. He wore corduroy vests and a gray felt hat, the brim turned down over his eyes. He smoked a pipe and bought himself a brindled bull-terrier. He cut his lectures as often as he dared, "ragged" signs and barber-poles, and was in continual evidence about Foster's and among Leavitt and Pierce's billiard-tables. When the great football games came off he worked himself into a frenzy of excitement over them and even tried to make several of his class teams, though without success.

He chummed with Charlie Geary and with young Dolliver Haight, the two San Francisco boys. The three were continually together. They took the same courses, dined at the same table in Memorial Hall and would have shared the same room if it had been possible. Vandover and Charlie Geary were fortunate enough to get a room in Matthew's on the lower floor looking out upon the Yard; young Haight was obliged to put up with an outside room in a boarding house.

Vandover had grown up with these fellows and during all his life was thrown in their company. Haight was a well-bred young boy of good family, very quiet; almost every morning he went to Chapel. He was always polite, even to his two friends. He invariably tried to be pleasant and agreeable and had a way of making people like him. Otherwise, his character was not strongly marked.

Geary was quite different. He never could forget himself. He was incessantly talking about what he had done or was going to do. In the morning he would inform Vandover of how many hours he had slept and of the dreams he had dreamed. In the evening he would tell him everything he had done that day; the things he had said, how many lectures he had cut, what brilliant recitations he had made, and even what food he had eaten at Memorial. He was pushing, self-

13

confident, very shrewd and clever, devoured with an inordinate ambition and particularly pleased when he could get the better of anybody, even of Vandover or of young Haight. He delighted to assume the management of things. Vandover, he made his protégé, taking over the charge of such business as the two had in common. It was he who had found the room in Matthew's, getting it away from all other applicants, securing it at the eleventh hour. He put Vandover's name on the waiting list at Memorial, saw that he filled out his blanks at the proper time, helped him balance his accounts, guided him in the choice of his courses and in the making out of his study-card.

"Look here, Charlie," Vandover would exclaim, throwing down the Announcement of Courses, "I can't make this thing out. It's all in a tangle. See here, I've got to fill up my hours some way or other; *you* straighten this thing out for me. Find me some nice little course, two hours a week, say, that comes late in the morning, a good hour after breakfast; something easy, all lectures, no outside reading, nice instructor and all that." And Geary would glance over the complicated schedule, cleverly untangling it at once and would find two or three such courses as Vandover desired.

Vandover's yielding disposition led him to submit to Geary's dictatorship and he thus early began to contract easy, irresponsible habits, becoming indolent, shirking his duty whenever he could, sure that Geary would think for the two and pull him out of any difficulty into which he might drift.

Otherwise the three freshmen were very much alike. They were hardly more than boys and full of boyish spirits and activity. They began to see "college life." Vandover was already smoking; pretty soon he began to drink. He affected beer, whisky he loathed, and such wine as was not too expensive was either too sweet or too sour. It became a custom for the three to go into town two or three nights in the week and have beer and Welsh rabbits at Billy Park's. On these occasions, however, young Haight drank only beer, he never touched wine or spirits.

It was in Billy Park's the evening after the football game between the Yale and Harvard freshmen that Vandover was drunk for the first time. He was not so drunk but that he knew he was, and the knowledge of the fact so terrified him that it kept him from getting very bad. The first sensation soon wore off, and by the time that Geary took charge of him and brought him back to Cambridge he was disposed to treat the affair less seriously. Nevertheless when he got to his room he looked at himself in the mirror a long time, saying to himself over and over again, "I'm drunk—just regularly drunk. Good Heavens! what *would* the governor say to *this?*"

In the morning he was surprised to find that he felt so little ashamed. Geary and young Haight treated the matter as a huge joke and told him of certain funny things he had said and done and which he had entirely forgotten. It was impossible for him to take the matter seriously even if he had wished to, and within a few weeks he was drunk again. He found that he was not an exception; Geary was often drunk with him, fully a third of all the Harvard men he knew were intoxicated at different times. It was out of the question for Vandover to consider them as drunkards. Certainly, neither he nor any of the others drank because they liked the beer; after the fifth or sixth glass it was all they could do to force down another. Such being the case, Vandover often asked himself why he got drunk at all. This question he was never able to answer.

It was the same with gambling. At first the idea of playing cards for money shocked him beyond all expression. But soon he found that a great many of the fellows, fellows like young Haight, beyond question steady, sensible and even worthy of emulation in other ways, "went in for that sort of thing." Every now and then Vandover's "crowd" got together in his room in Matthew's, and played Van John "for keeps," as they said, until far into the night. Vandover joined them. The stakes were small, he lost as often as he won, but the habit of the cards never grew upon him. It was like the beer, he "went in for it" because the others did, without knowing why. Geary, however, drew his line at gambling; he never talked against it or tried to influence Vandover, but he never could be induced to play "for keeps" himself.

One very warm Sunday afternoon in the first days of April, when the last snows were melting. Vandover and Geary were in their room, sitting at opposite ends of their window-seat,

Geary translating his Monday's "Horace" by the help of a
Bohn's translation, Vandover making a pen and ink drawing
for the next *Lampoon*. A couple of young women passed
down the walk, going across the Yard toward the Square.
They were cheaply and showily dressed. One of them wore a
mannish shirtwaist, with a high collar and scarf. The other
had taken off her gloves and was swinging a bright red cape
in one of her bare hands. As the couple passed they stared
calmly at the two young fellows in the window; Vandover
lowered his eyes over his work, blushing, he could not tell
why. Geary stared back at them, following them with his eyes
until they had gone by.

All at once he began laughing and pounding on the window.

"Oh, for goodness sake, quit!" exclaimed Vandover in great
alarm, twisting off the window-seat and shrinking back out of
sight into the room. "Quit, Charlie; you don't want to insult
a girl that way." Geary looked at him over his shoulder in
some surprise, and was about to answer when he turned to the
window again and exclaimed, grinning and waving his hand:

"Oh, just come here, Skinny; get on to this, will you? Ah,
come here and look, you old chump! Do you think they're
nice girls? Just take a *look* at them." Vandover peered timidly
around Geary's head and saw that the two girls were looking
back and laughing, and that the one with the red cape was
waving it at them.

At supper that night they saw the girls in the gallery of
Memorial. They pointed them out to young Haight, and
Geary at length managed to attract their attention. After supper the three freshmen, together with two of their sophomore
acquaintances, strolled slowly over toward the Yard, lighting
their pipes and cigarettes. All at once, as they turned into the
lower gate, they came full upon the same pair of girls. They
were walking fast, talking and laughing very loudly.

"Track!" called out one of the sophomores, and the group
of young fellows parted to let them pass. The sophomore exclaimed in a tone of regret, "Don't be in such a hurry, girls."
Vandover became scarlet and turned his face away, but the
girls looked back and laughed good-naturedly. "Come on,"
said the sophomore. The group closed around the girls and
brought them to a standstill; they were not in the least

embarrassed at this, but laughed more than ever. Neither of them was pretty, but there was a certain attraction about them that pleased Vandover immensely. He was very excited.

Then there was a very embarrassing pause. No one knew what to say. Geary alone regained his assurance at length, and began a lively interchange of chaff with one of them. The others could only stand about and smile.

"*Well*," cried the other girl after a while, "I ain't going to stand here in the snow all *night*. Let's take a walk; come along. I choose *you*." Before Vandover knew it she had taken his arm. The sophomore managed in some way to pair off with the other girl; Haight had already left the group; the two couples started off, while Geary and the other sophomore who were left out followed awkwardly in the rear for a little way and then disappeared.

Vandover was so excited that he could scarcely speak. This was a new experience. At first it attracted him, but the hopeless vulgarity of the girl at his side, her tawdry clothes, her sordid, petty talk, her slang, her miserable profanity, soon began to revolt him. He felt that he could not keep his self-respect while such a girl hung upon his arm.

"Say," said the girl at length, "didn't I see you in town the other afternoon on Washington Street?"

"Maybe you did," answered Vandover, trying to be polite. "I'm down there pretty often."

"Well, I guess yes," she answered. "You Harvard sports make a regular promenade out o' Washington Street Saturday afternoons. I suppose I've seen you down there pretty often, but didn't notice. Do you stand or walk?"

Vandover's gorge rose with disgust. He stopped abruptly and pulled away from the girl. Not only did she disgust him, but he felt sorry for her; he felt ashamed and pitiful for a woman who had fallen so low. Still he tried to be polite to her; he did not know how to be rude with any kind of woman.

"You 'll have to excuse me," he said, taking off his hat. "I don't believe I can take a walk with you to-night. I—you see—I've got a good deal of work to do; I think I'll have to leave you." Then he bowed to her with his hat in his hand, hurrying away before she could answer him a word.

He found Geary alone in their room, cribbing "Horace" again.

"Ah, you bet," Geary said. "I shook those chippies. I sized them up right away. I was clever enough for that. They were no good. I thought you would get enough of it."

"Oh, I don't know," said Vandover after a while, as he settled to his drawing. "She was pretty common, but anyhow I don't want to help bring down a poor girl like that any lower than she is already." This saying struck Vandover as being very good and noble, and he found occasion to repeat it to young Haight the next day.

But within three days of this, at the time when Vandover would have fancied himself farthest from such a thing, he underwent a curious reaction. On a certain evening, moved by an unreasoned instinct, he sought out the girl who had just filled him with such deep pity and such violent disgust, and that night did not come back to the room in Matthew's. The thing was done almost before he knew it. He could not tell why he had acted as he did, and he certainly would not have believed himself capable of it.

He passed the next few days in a veritable agony of repentance, overwhelmed by a sense of shame and dishonour that were almost feminine in their bitterness and intensity. He felt himself lost, unworthy, and as if he could never again look a pure woman in the eyes unless with an abominable hypocrisy. He was ashamed even before Geary and young Haight, and went so far as to send a long letter to his father acknowledging and deploring what he had done, asking for his forgiveness and reiterating his resolve to shun such a thing forever after.

What had been bashfulness in the boy developed in the young man to a profound respect and an instinctive regard for women. This stood him in good stead throughout all his four years of Harvard life. In general, he kept himself pretty straight. There were plenty of fast girls and lost women about Cambridge, but Vandover found that he could not associate with them to any degree of satisfaction. He never knew how to take them, never could rid himself of the idea that they were to be treated as ladies. They, on their part, did not like him; he was too diffident, too courteous, too "slow." They preferred the rough self-assertion and easy confidence of Geary, who never took "no" as an answer and who could chaff with them on their own ground.

Vandover did poor work at Harvard and only graduated, as Geary said, "by a squeak." Besides his regular studies he took time to pass three afternoons a week in the studio of a Boston artist, where he studied anatomy and composition and drew figures from the nude. In the summer vacations he did not return home, but accompanied this artist on sketching tours along the coast of Maine. His style improved immensely the moment he abandoned flat studies and began to work directly from Nature. He drew figures well, showed a feeling for desolate landscapes, and even gave promise of a good eye for colour. But he allowed his fondness for art to interfere constantly with his college work. By the middle of his senior year he was so loaded with conditions that it was only Geary's unwearied coaching that pulled him through at all—as Vandover knew it would, for that matter.

Vandover returned to San Francisco when he was twenty-two. It was astonishing; he had gone away a pimply, overgrown boy, raw and callow as a fledgling, constrained in society, diffident, awkward. Now he returned, a tall, well-formed Harvardian, as careful as a woman in the matter of dress, very refined in his manners. Besides, he was a delightful conversationalist. His father was rejoiced; every one declared he was a charming fellow.

They were right. Vandover was at his best at this time; it was undeniable that he had great talent, but he was so modest about it that few knew how clever he really was.

He went out to dinners and receptions and began to move a little in society. He became very popular: the men liked him because he was so unaffected, so straightforward, and the women because he was so respectful and so deferential.

He had no vices. He had gone through the ordeal of college life and had come out without contracting any habit more serious than a vague distaste for responsibility, and an inclination to shirk disagreeable duties. Cards he never thought of. It was rare that he drank so much as a glass of beer.

However, he had come back to a great disappointment.

Business in San Francisco had entered upon a long period of decline, and values were decreasing; for ten years rents had been sagging lower and lower. At the same time the interest on loans and insurances had increased, and real estate was brought to a standstill; one spoke bitterly of a certain great monopoly that was ruining both the city and state. Vandover's father had suffered with the rest, and now told his son that he could not at this time afford to send him to Paris. He would have to wait for better times.

At first this was a sharp grief to Vandover; for years he had looked forward to an artist's life in the Quarter. For a time he was inconsolable, then at length readjusted himself good-naturedly to suit the new order of things with as little compunction as before, when he had entered Harvard. He found that he could be contented in almost any environment, the weakness, the certain pliability of his character easily fitting itself into new grooves, reshaping itself to suit new circumstances. He prevailed upon his father to allow him to have a downtown studio. In a little while he was perfectly happy again.

Vandover's love for his art was keen. On the whole he kept pretty steadily to his work, spending a good six hours at his easel every day, very absorbed over the picture in hand. He was working up into large canvases the sketches he had made along the Maine coast, great, empty expanses of sea, sky, and sand-dune, full of wind and sun. They were really admirable. He even sold one of them. The Old Gentleman was delighted, signed him a check for twenty dollars, and told him that in three years he could afford to send him abroad.

In the meanwhile Vandover set himself to enjoy the new life. Little by little his "set" formed around him; Geary and young Haight, of course, and some half dozen young men of the city: young lawyers, medical students, and clerks in insurance offices. As Vandover thus began to see the different phases of that life which lay beyond the limits of the college, he perceived more and more clearly that he was an exception among men for his temperance, his purity, and his clean living.

At their clubs and in their smoking-rooms he heard certain practices, which he had always believed to be degrading and abominable, discussed with shouts of laughter. Those matters which until now he had regarded with an almost sacred veneration were subjects for immense jokes. A few years ago he would have been horrified at it all, but the fine quality of this first sensitiveness had been blunted since his experience at college. He tolerated these things in his friends now.

Gradually Vandover allowed his ideas and tastes to be moulded by this new order of things. He assumed the manners of these young men of the city, very curious to see for himself the other lower side of their life that began after midnight in the private rooms of fast cafés and that was continued in the heavy musk-laden air of certain parlours amid the rustle of heavy silks.

Slowly the fascination of this thing grew upon him until it mounted to a veritable passion. His strong artist's imagination began to be filled with a world of charming sensuous pictures.

He commenced to chafe under his innate respect and deference for women, to resent and to despise it. As the desire of vice, the blind, reckless desire of the male, grew upon him, he set himself to destroy this barrier that had so long stood in his way. He knew that it was the wilful and deliberate corruption of part of that which was best in him; he was sorry for it, but persevered, nevertheless, ashamed of his old-time timidity, his ignorance, his boyish purity.

For a second time the animal in him, the perverse evil brute, awoke and stirred. The idea of resistance hardly occurred to Vandover; it would be hard, it would be disagreeable to resist, and Vandover had not accustomed himself to the performance of hard, disagreeable duties. They were among the unpleasant things that he shirked. He told himself that later on, when he had grown older and steadier and had profited by experience and knowledge of the world, when he was stronger, in a word, he would curb the thing and restrain it. He saw no danger in such a course. It was what other men did with impunity.

In company with Geary and young Haight he had come to frequent a certain one of the fast cafés of the city. Here he met and became acquainted with a girl called Flossie. It was the opportunity for which he was waiting, and he seized it at once.

This time there was no recoil of conscience, no shame, no remorse; he even felt a better estimation of himself, that self-respect that comes with wider experiences and with larger views of life. He told himself that all men should at one time see certain phases of the world; it rounded out one's life. After all, one had to be a man of the world. Those men only were perverted who allowed themselves to be corrupted by such vice.

Thus it was that Vandover, by degrees, drifted into the life of a certain class of the young men of the city. Vice had no hold on him. The brute had grown larger in him, but he knew that he had the creature in hand. He was its master, and only on rare occasions did he permit himself to gratify its demands, feeding its abominable hunger from that part of him which he knew to be the purest, the cleanest, and the best.

Three years passed in this fashion.

Chapter Three

VANDOVER HAD DECIDED at lunch that day that he would not go back to work at his studio in the afternoon, but would stay at home instead and read a very interesting story about two men who had bought a wrecked opium ship for fifty thousand dollars, and had afterward discovered that she contained only a few tins of the drug. He was curious to see how it turned out; the studio was a long way downtown, the day was a little cold, and he felt that he would enjoy a little relaxation. Anyhow, he meant to stay at home and put in the whole afternoon on a good novel.

But even when he had made up his mind to do this he did not immediately get out his book and settle down to it. After lunch he loitered about the house while his meal digested, feeling very comfortable and contented. He strummed his banjo a little and played over upon the piano the three pieces he had picked up: two were polkas, and the third, the air of a topical song; he always played the three together and in the same sequence. Then he strolled up to his room, and brushed his hair for a while, trying to make it lie very flat and smooth. After this he went out to look at Mr. Corkle, the terrier, and let him run a bit in the garden; then he felt as though he must have a smoke, and so went back to his room and filled his pipe. When it was going well, he took down his book and threw himself into a deep leather chair, only to jump up again to put on his smoking-jacket. All at once he became convinced that he must have something to eat while he read, and so went to the kitchen and got himself some apples and a huge slice of fresh bread. Ever since Vandover was a little boy he had loved fresh bread and apples. Through the windows of the dining-room he saw Mr. Corkle digging up great holes in the geranium beds. He went out and abused him and finally let him come back into the house and took him upstairs with him.

Then at last he settled down to his novel, in the very comfortable leather chair, before a little fire, for the last half of August is cold in San Francisco. The room was warm and snug, the fresh bread and apples were delicious, the good tobacco in his pipe purred like a sleeping kitten, and his novel was interesting and well written. He felt calm and soothed and perfectly content, and took in the pleasure of the occasion with the lazy complacency of a drowsing cat.

Vandover was self-indulgent—he loved these sensuous pleasures, he loved to eat good things, he loved to be warm, he loved to sleep. He hated to be bored and worried—he liked to have a good time.

At about half-past four o'clock he came to a good stopping-place in his book; the two men had got to quarrelling, and his interest flagged a little. He pushed Mr. Corkle off his lap and got up yawning and went to the window.

Vandover's home was on California Street not far from Franklin. It was a large frame house of two stories; all the windows in the front were bay. The front door was directly in the middle between the windows of the parlour and those of the library, while over the vestibule was a sort of balcony that no one ever thought of using. The house was set in a large well-kept yard. The lawn was pretty; an enormous eucalyptus tree grew at one corner. Nearer to the house were magnolia and banana trees growing side by side with pines and firs. Humming-birds built in these, and one could hear their curious little warbling mingling with the hoarse chirp of the English sparrows which nested under the eaves. The back yard was separated from the lawn by a high fence of green lattice-work. The hens and chickens were kept here and two roosters, one of which crowed every time a cable-car passed the house. On the door cut through the lattice-fence was a sign, "Look Out for the Dog." Close to the unused barn stood an immense windmill with enormous arms; when the wind blew in the afternoon the sails whirled about at a surprising speed, pumping up water from the artesian well sunk beneath. There was a small conservatory where the orchids were kept. Altogether, it was a charming place. However, adjoining it was a huge vacant lot with cows in it. It was full of dry weeds and heaps of ashes, while around it was an enormous fence painted with signs of cigars, patent bitters, and soap.

Vandover stood at a front window and looked out on a rather dreary prospect. The inevitable afternoon trades had been blowing hard since three, strong and brisk from the ocean, driving hard through the Golden Gate and filling the city with a taint of salt. Now the fog was coming in; Vandover could see great patches of it sweeping along between him and the opposite houses. All the eucalyptus trees were dripping, and occasionally there came the faint moan of the fog-horn out at the heads. He could see up the street for nearly two miles as it climbed over Nob Hill. It was almost deserted; a cable-car now and then crawled up and down its length, and at times a delivery wagon rattled across it; but that was about all. On the opposite sidewalk two boys and a girl were coasting downhill on their roller-skates and their brake-wagons. The cable in its slot kept up an incessant burr and clack. The whole view was rather forlorn, and Vandover turned his back on it, taking up his book again.

About five o'clock his father came home from his office. "Hello!" said he, looking into the room; "aren't you home a little early to-day? Ah, I thought you weren't going to bring that dog into the house any more. I wish you wouldn't, son; he gets hair and fleas about everywhere."

"All right, governor," answered Vandover. "I'll take him out. Come along, Cork."

"But aren't you home earlier than usual to-day?" persisted his father as Vandover got up.

"Yes," said Vandover, "I guess I am, a little."

After supper the same evening when Vandover came downstairs, drawing on his gloves, his father looked over his paper, saying pleasantly:

"Well, where are you going to-night?"

"I'm going to see my girl," said Vandover, smiling; then foreseeing the usual question, he added, "I'll be home about eleven, I guess."

"Got your latch-key?" asked the Old Gentleman, as he always did when Vandover went out.

"Yep," called back Vandover as he opened the door. "I'll not forget it again. Good-night, governor."

Vandover used to call on Turner Ravis about twice a week; people said they were engaged. This was not so.

Vandover had met Miss Ravis some two years before. For a time the two had been sincerely in love with each other, and though there was never any talk of marriage between them, they seemed to have some sort of tacit understanding. But by this time Vandover had somehow outgrown the idea of marrying Turner. He still kept up the fiction, persuaded that Turner must understand the way things had come to be. However, he was still very fond of her; she was a frank, sweet-tempered girl and very pretty, and it was delightful to have her care for him.

Vandover could not shut his eyes to the fact that young Haight was very seriously in love with Turner. But he was sure that Turner preferred him to his chum. She was too sincere, too frank, too conscientious to practise any deception on him.

There was quite a party at the Ravises' house that evening when Vandover arrived. Young Haight was there, of course, and Charlie Geary. Besides Turner herself there was Henrietta Vance, a stout, pretty girl, with pop eyes and a little nose, who laughed all the time and who was very popular. These were all part of Vandover's set; they called each other by their first names and went everywhere together. Almost every Saturday evening they got together at Turner's house and played whist, or euchre, or sometimes even poker. "Just for love," as Turner said.

When Vandover came in they were all talking at the same time, disputing about a little earthquake that had occurred the night before. Henrietta Vance declared that it had happened early in the morning.

"*Wasn't* it just about midnight, Van?" cried Turner.

"I don't know," answered Vandover. "It didn't wake me up. I didn't even know there was one."

"Well, I know I heard our clock strike two just about half an hour afterward," protested young Haight.

"Oh, it was almost five o'clock when it came," cried Henrietta Vance.

"Well, now, you're *all* off," said Charlie Geary. "I know just when she quaked to the fraction of a minute, because it stopped our hall clock at just a little after three."

They were silent. It was an argument which was hard to contradict. By and by, young Haight declared, "There must have been two of them then, because ——"

"How about whist or euchre or whatever it is to be?" said Charlie Geary, addressing Turner and interrupting in an annoying way that was peculiar to him. "Can't we start in now that Van has come?" They played euchre for a while, but Geary did not like the game, and by and by suggested poker.

"Well—if it's only just for love," said Turner, "because, you know, mamma doesn't like it any other way."

At ten o'clock Geary said, "Let's quit after this hand round—what do you say?" The rest were willing and so they all took account of their chips after the next deal. Geary was protesting against his poor luck. Honestly he hadn't held better than three tens more than twice during the evening. It was Henrietta Vance who took in everything; did one ever *see* anything to beat her luck? "the funniest thing!"

They began to do tricks with the cards. Young Haight showed them a very good trick by which he could make the pack break every time at the ace of clubs. Vandover exclaimed: "Lend me a silk hat and ninety dollars and I'll show you the queerest trick you ever saw," which sent Henrietta Vance off into shrieks of laughter. Then Geary took the cards out of young Haight's hands, asking them if they knew *this* trick.

Turner said yes, she knew it, but the others did not, and Geary showed it to them. It was interminable. Henrietta Vance chose a card and put it back into the deck. Then the deck was shuffled and divided into three piles. After this Geary made a mental calculation, selected one of these piles, shuffled it, and gave it back to her, asking her if she saw her card in it; then more shuffling and dividing until their interest and patience were quite exhausted. When Geary finally produced a jack of hearts and demanded triumphantly if that was her card, Henrietta began to laugh and declared she had forgotten *what* card she chose. Geary said he would do the trick all over for her. At this, however, they all cried out, and he had to give it up, very irritated at Henrietta's stupidity.

Vexed at the ill success of this first trick, he retired a little from their conversation, puzzling over the cards, thinking out new tricks. Every now and then he came back among them, going about from one to another, holding out the deck and exclaiming, "Choose any card—choose any card."

After a while they all adjourned to the dining-room and

Turner and Vandover went out into the kitchen, foraging among the drawers and shelves. They came back bringing with them a box of sardines, a tin of *paté*, three quart bottles of blue-ribbon beer, and what Vandover called "devilish-ham" sandwiches.

"Now do we want *tamales* to go with these?" said Turner, as she spread the lunch on the table. Henrietta Vance cried out joyfully at this, and young Haight volunteered to go out to get them. "Get six," Turner cried out after him. "Henrietta can always eat two. Hurry up, and we won't eat till you get back."

While he was gone Turner got out some half-dozen glasses for their beer. "Do you know," she said as she set the glasses on the table, "the funniest thing happened this morning to mamma. It was at breakfast; she had just drunk a glass of water and was holding the glass in her hand like this"— Turner took one of the thin beer glasses in her hand to show them how—"and was talking to pa, when all at once the glass broke right straight around a ring, just below the brim, you know, and fell all ——" On a sudden Turner uttered a shrill exclamation; the others started up; the very glass she held in her hand at the moment cracked and broke in precisely the manner she was describing. A narrow ring snapped from the top, dropping on the floor, breaking into a hundred bits.

Turner drew in a long breath, open-mouthed, her hand in the air still holding the body of the glass that remained in her fingers. They all began to exclaim over the wonder.

"Well, did you ever in all your *life*?" shouted Miss Vance, breaking into a peal of laughter. Geary cried out, "Cæsar's ghost!" and Vandover swore under his breath.

"If that isn't the strangest thing I ever saw!" cried Turner. "*Isn't* that funny—why—oh! I'm going *to try it with another glass*!" But the second glass remained intact. Geary recovered from his surprise and tried to explain how it could happen.

"It was the heat from your fingers and the glass was cold, you know," he said again and again.

But the strangeness of the thing still held them. Turner set down the glass with the others and dropped into a chair, letting her hands fall in her lap, looking into their faces, nodding her head and shutting her lips:

"Ah, *no*," she said after a while. "That *is* funny. It kind of scares one." She was actually pale.

"Oh, there's Dolly Haight!" cried Henrietta Vance as the door bell rang. They all rushed to the door, running and scrambling, eager to tell the news. Young Haight stood bewildered on the door mat in the vestibule, his arms full of brown-paper packages, while they recounted the marvel. They all spoke at once, holding imaginary beer glasses toward him in their outstretched hands. Geary, however, refused to be carried away by their excitement, and one heard him from time to time repeating, between their ejaculations, "It was the heat from her fingers, you know, and the glass was cold."

Young Haight was confused, incredulous; he could not at first make out what *had* happened.

"Well, just come and *look* at the broken *glass* on the *floor*," shouted Turner decisively, dragging him into the dining-room. They waited, breathless, to hear what he would say. He looked at the broken glass and then into their faces. Then he suddenly exclaimed:

"Ah, you're joking me."

"No, honestly," protested Vandover, "that was just the way it happened."

It was some little time before they could get over their impression of queerness, but by and by Geary cried out that the *tamales* were getting cold. They settled down to their lunch, and the first thing young Haight did was to cut his lip on the edge of the broken glass. Turner had set it down with the others and he had inadvertently filled it for himself.

It was a trifling cut. Turner fetched some court-plaster, and his lip was patched up. For all that, it bled quite a little. He was very embarrassed; he kept his handkerchief to his mouth and told them repeatedly to go on with their lunch and not to mind him.

As soon as they were eating and drinking they began to be very jolly, and Vandover was especially good-humoured and entertaining. He made Henrietta Vance shout with laughter by pretending that the olive in his *tamale* was a green hen's egg.

About half-past ten young Haight rose from the table saying he thought it was about time to say good-night. "Don't

be in a hurry," said Turner. "It's early yet." After that, however, they broke up very quickly.

Before he left Vandover saw Turner in the dining-room
alone for a minute.

"Will I see you at church to-morrow?" he asked, as she held
his overcoat for him.

"I don't know, Van," she answered. "You know Henrietta
is going to stay all night with me, and I think she will want
me to go home with her to-morrow morning and then stay
to dinner with her. But I'm going to early communion to-
morrow morning; why can't you meet me there?"

"Why, I can," answered Vandover, settling his collar. "I
should like to very much."

"Well, then," she replied, "you can meet me in front of the
church at half-past seven o'clock."

"Hey, break away there!" cried Geary from the front door.
"Come along, Van, if you are going with us."

Turner let Vandover kiss her before they joined the others.
"I'll see you at seven-thirty to-morrow morning," he said as
he went away.

The three young men went off down the street, arm in
arm, smoking their cigars and cigarettes. As soon as they were
alone, Charlie Geary began to tell the other two of everything
he had been doing since he had last seen them.

"Well, sir," he said as he took an arm of each, "well, sir, I
had a fine sleep last night; went to bed at ten and never woke
up till half-past eight this morning. Ah, you bet I needed it,
though. I've been working like a slave this week. You know I
take my law-examinations in about ten days. I'll pass all right.
I'm right up to the handle in everything. I don't believe the
judge could stick me anywhere in the subject of torts."

"Say, boys," said Vandover, pausing and looking at his
watch, "it isn't very late; let's go downtown and have some
oysters."

"That's a good idea," answered young Haight. "How
about you, Charlie?"

Geary said he was willing. "Ah," he added, "you ought to
have seen the beefsteak I had this evening at the Grillroom."
And as they rode downtown he told them of the steak in

question. "I had a little mug of ale with it, too, and a dish of salad. Ah, it went great."

They decided after some discussion that they would go to the Imperial.

Chapter Four

THE IMPERIAL was a resort not far from the corner of Sutter and Kearney streets, a few doors below a certain well-known drug store, in one window of which was a show-case full of live snakes.

The front of the Imperial was painted white, and there was a cigar-stand in the vestibule of the main entrance. At the right of this main entrance was another smaller one, a ladies' entrance, on the frosted pane of which one read, "Oyster Café."

The main entrance opened directly into the barroom. It was a handsome room, paved with marble flags. To the left was the bar, whose counter was a single slab of polished red-wood. Behind it was a huge, plate-glass mirror, balanced on one side by the cash-register and on the other by a statuette of the Diving Girl in tinted bisque. Between the two were pyramids of glasses and bottles, liqueur flasks in wicker cases, and a great bouquet of sweet-peas.

The three bartenders, in clean linen coats and aprons, moved about here and there, opening bottles, mixing drinks, and occasionally turning to punch the indicator of the register.

On the other side of the room, facing the bar, hung a large copy of a French picture representing a *Sabbath*, witches, goats, and naked girls whirling through the air. Underneath it was the lunch counter, where clam-fritters, the specialty of the place, could be had four afternoons in the week.

Elsewhere were nickel-in-the-slot machines, cigar-lighters, a vase of wax flowers under glass, and a racing chart setting forth the day's odds, weights, and entries. On the end wall over the pantry-slides was a second "barroom" picture, rep-resenting the ladies of a harem at their bath.

But its "private rooms" were the chief attraction of the Im-perial. These were reached by going in through the smaller door to the right of the main vestibule. Any one coming in through this entrance found himself in a long and narrow passage. On the right of this passage were eight private rooms, very small, and open at the top as the law required.

Half-way down its length the passage grew wider. Here the rooms were on both sides and were much larger than those in front.

It was this part of the Imperial that was most frequented, and that had made its reputation. In the smaller rooms in front one had beer and Welsh rabbits; in the larger rooms, champagne and terrapin.

Vandover, Haight, and Geary came in through the ladies' entrance of the Imperial at about eleven o'clock, going slowly down the passage, looking into each of the little rooms, searching for one that was empty. All at once Vandover, who was in the lead, cried out:

"Well, if here isn't that man Ellis, drinking whisky by himself. Bah! a man that will drink whisky all *alone*! Glad to see you just the same, Bandy; move along, will you—give a man some room."

"Hello, hello, Bandy!" cried Geary and young Haight, hitting him in the back, while Geary added: "How long have you been down here? *I've* just come from making a call with the boys. Had a fine time; what are you drinking, whisky? *I'm* going to have something to eat. Didn't have much of a lunch to-day, but you ought to have seen the steak I had at the Grillroom—as thick as that, and tender! Oh, it went great! Here, hang my coat up there on that side, will you?"

Bancroft Ellis was one of the young men of the city with whom the three fellows had become acquainted just after their return from college. For the most part, they met him at downtown restaurants, in the foyers and vestibules of the theatres, on Kearney Street of a Saturday afternoon, or, as now, in the little rooms of the Imperial, where he was a recognized habitué and where he invariably called for whisky, finishing from three to five "ponies" at every sitting. On very rare occasions they saw him in society, at the houses where their "set" was received. At these functions Ellis could never be persuaded to remain in the parlours; he slipped up to the gentlemen's dressing-rooms at the earliest opportunity, and spent the evening silently smoking the cigars and cigarettes furnished by the host. When Vandover and his friends came up between dances, to brush their hair or to rearrange their neckties, they found him enveloped in a blue haze of smoke, his feet on a chair, his shirt bosom broken, and his waistcoat unbuttoned. He would tell them that he was bored and thirsty and ask how much longer they were going to stay. He knew but few of their friends; his home was in a little town in the interior and he prided himself on being a "Native Son of the Golden West." He was a clerk in an insurance office on California Street, and had never been out of the state.

For the rest he was a good enough fellow and the three others liked him very much. He had a curious passion for facts and statistics, and his pockets were full of little books and cards to which he was constantly referring. He had one of those impossible pocket-diaries, the first half dozen pages loaded with information of every kind printed in blinding type, postal rates to every country in the world, statistics as to population and rates of death, weights and measures, the highest mountains in the world, the greatest depths of the ocean. He kept a little book in his left-hand vest pocket that gave the plan and seating capacity of every theatre in the city, while in the right-hand pocket was a tiny Webster's dictionary which was his especial pride. The calendar for the current year was pasted in the lining of his hat, together with the means to be employed in the resuscitation of a half-drowned person. He also carried about a "Vest Pocket Edition of Popular Information," which had never been of the slightest use to him.

The room in which they were now seated was very small and opened directly upon the passage. On either side of the table was a seat that would hold two, and on the wall opposite the door hung a mirror, its gilt frame enclosed in pink netting. The table itself was covered with a tolerably clean cloth, though it was of coarse linen and rather damp.

There were the usual bottles of olives and pepper sauce, a plate of broken crackers, and a ribbed match-safe of china. The sugar bowl was of plated ware and on it were scratched numberless dates together with the first names of a great many girls, "Nannie," "Ida," "Flossie."

Between the castor bottles was the bill of fare, held by a thin string between two immense leather covers which were stamped with wine merchants' advertisements. Geary reached for this before any of the others, saying at the same time, "Well, what are you going to have? *I'm* going to have a Welsh rabbit and a pint of ale." He looked from one to the other as if demanding whether or no they approved of his choice. He assumed the management of what was going on, advising the others what to have, telling Vandover not to order certain dishes that he liked because it took so long to cook them. He had young Haight ring for the waiter, and when he had come, Geary read off the entire order to him twice over, making sure that he had taken it correctly. "That's what we want all right, all right—isn't it?" he said, looking around at the rest.

The waiter, whose eyes were red from lack of sleep, put down before them a plate of limp, soft shrimps.

"Hello, Toby!" said Vandover.

"Good evening, gentlemen," answered Toby. "Why, good evening, Mr. Vandover; haven't seen you 'round here for some time." He took their order, and as he was going away, Vandover called him back:

"Say, Toby," said he, "has Flossie been around to-night?"

"No," answered Toby, "she hasn't shown up yet. Her running-mate was in about nine, but she went out again right away."

"Well," said Vandover, smiling, "if Flossie comes 'round show her in here, will you?"

The others laughed, and joked him about this, and Vandover settled back in his seat, easing his position.

"Ah," he exclaimed, "I like it in here. It's always pleasant and warm and quiet and the service is good and you get such good things to eat."

Now that the young fellows were by themselves, and could relax that restraint, that good breeding and delicacy which had been natural to them in the early part of the evening at the Ravises', their manners changed: they lounged clumsily upon their seats, their legs stretched out, their waistcoats unbuttoned, caring only to be at their ease. Their talk and manners became blunt, rude, unconstrained, the coarser masculine fibre reasserting itself. With the exception of young Haight they were all profane enough, and it was not very long before their conversation became obscene.

Geary told them how he had spent the afternoon promenading Kearney and Market streets and just where he had gone to get his cocktail and his cigar. "Ah," he added, "you ought to have seen Ida Wade and Bessie Laguna. Oh, Ida was rigged up to beat the band; honestly her *hat* was as broad across as that. You know there's no use talking, she's an awfully handsome girl."

A discussion arose over the girl's virtue. Ellis, Geary, and young Haight maintained that Ida was only fast; Vandover, however, had his doubts.

"For that matter," said Ellis after a while, "I like Bessie Laguna a good deal better than I do Ida."

"Ah, yes," retorted young Haight, "you like Bessie Laguna too much anyhow."

Young Haight had a theory that one should never care in any way for that kind of a girl nor become at all intimate with her.

"The matter of liking her or not liking her," he said, "ought not to enter into the question at all. You are both of you out for a good time and that's all; you have a jolly flirtation with her for an hour or two, and you never see her again. That's the way it ought to be! This idea of getting intimate with that sort of a piece, and trying to get her to care for you, is all wrong."

"Oh," said Vandover deprecatingly, "you take all the pleasure out of it; where does your good time come in if you don't at least pretend that you like the girl and try to make her like you?"

"But don't you see," answered Haight, "what a dreadful thing it would be if a girl like that came to care for you seriously? It isn't the same as if it were a girl of your own class."

"Ah, Dolly, you've got a bean," muttered Ellis, sipping his whisky.

Meanwhile, the Imperial had been filling up; at about eleven the theatres were over, and now the barroom was full of men. They came in by twos and threes and sometimes even by noisy parties of a half dozen or more. The white swing doors of the main entrance flapped back and forth continually, letting out into the street puffs of tepid air tainted with the smell of alcohol. The men entered and ordered their drinks, and leaning their elbows upon the bar continued the conversation they had begun outside. Afterward they passed over to the lunch counter and helped themselves to a plate of stewed tripe or potato salad, eating it in a secluded corner, leaning over so as not to stain their coats. There was a continual clinking of glasses and popping of corks, and at every instant the cash-register clucked and rang its bell.

Between the barroom and the other part of the house was a door hung with blue plush curtains, looped back; the waiters constantly passed back and forth through this, carrying plates of oysters, smoking rarebits, tiny glasses of liqueurs, and goblets of cigars.

All the private rooms opening from either passage were full; the men came in, walking slowly, looking for their friends; but more often, the women and girls passed up and down with a chatter of conversation, a rattle of stiff skirts and petticoats, and a heavy whiff of musk. There was a continual going and coming, a monotonous shuffle of feet and hum of talk. A heavy odorous warmth in which were mingled the smells of sweetened whisky, tobacco, the fumes of cooking, and the scent of perfume, exhaled into the air. A gay and noisy party developed in one of the large back rooms; at every moment one could hear gales of laughter, the rattle of chairs and glassware, mingled with the sounds of men's voices and the little screams and cries of women. Every time the waiter opened the door to deliver an order he let out a momentary torrent of noises.

Girls, habitués of the place, continued to pass the door of the room where Vandover and his friends were seated. Each time a particularly handsome one went by, the four looked out after her, shutting their lips and eyes and nodding their heads.

Young Haight had called for more drinks, ordering, however, mineral water for himself, and Vandover was just telling about posing the female models in a certain life-class to which he belonged, when he looked up and broke off, exclaiming:

"Well, well, here we are at last! How are you, Flossie? Come right in."

Flossie stood in the doorway smiling good-humouredly at them, without a trace of embarrassment or of confusion in her manner. She was an immense girl, quite six feet tall, broad and well-made, in proportion. She was very handsome, full-throated, heavy-eyed, and slow in her movements. Her eyes and mouth, like everything about her, were large, but each time she spoke or smiled, she disclosed her teeth, which were as white, as well-set, and as regular as the rows of kernels on an ear of green corn. In her ears were small yellow diamonds, the only jewellery she wore. There was no perceptible cosmetic on her face, which had a clean and healthy look as though she had just given it a vigorous washing.

She wore a black hat with a great flare to the brim on one side. It was trimmed very dashingly with black feathers, imitation jet, and a little puff of plush—robin's-egg blue. Her dress was of rough, black camel's hair, tailor-made, and but for the immense balloon sleeves, absolutely plain. It was cut in such a way that from neck to waist there was no break, the buttons being on the shoulder and under the arm. The skirt was full and stiff, and without the least trimming. Everything was black—hat, dress, gloves—and the effect was of a simplicity and severity so pronounced as to be very striking.

However, around her waist she wore as a belt a thick rope of oxidized silver, while her shoes, or rather walking slippers, were of white canvas.

She belonged to that class of women who are not to know one's last name or address, and whose hate and love are equally to be dreaded. There was upon her face the unmistakable traces of a ruined virtue and a vanished innocence. Her slightest action suggested her profession; as soon as she removed her veil and gloves it was as though she were partially undressed, and her uncovered face and hands seemed to be only portions of her nudity.

The general conception of women of her class is a painted and broken wreck. Flossie radiated health; her eyes were clear, her nerves steady, her flesh hard and even as a child's. There hung about her an air of cleanliness, of freshness, of good nature, of fine, high spirits, while with every movement she exhaled a delicious perfume that was not only musk, but that seemed to come alike from her dress, her hair, her neck, her very flesh and body.

Vandover was no longer the same as he had been during his college days. He was familiar now with this odour of abandoned women, this foul sweet savour of the great city's vice, that quickened his breath and that sent his heart knocking at his throat. It was the sensitive artist nature in him that responded instantly to anything sensuously attractive. Each kind and class of beautiful women could arouse in Vandover passions of equal force, though of far different kind. Turner Ravis influenced him upon his best side, calling out in him all that was cleanest, finest, and most delicate. Flossie appealed only to the animal and the beast in him, the evil, hideous brute that made instant answer.

"What will you take, Flossie?" asked Vandover, as she settled herself among them. "We are all drinking beer except Ellis. *He's* filling up with whisky." But Flossie never drank. It was one of the peculiarities for which she was well known.

"I don't want either," she answered, and turning to the waiter, she added, "You can bring me some Apollinaris water, Toby."

Flossie betrayed herself as soon as she spoke, the effect of her appearance was spoiled. Her voice was hoarse, a low-pitched rasp, husky, throaty, and full of brutal, vulgar modulations.

"Smoke, Flossie?" said Geary, pushing his cigarette case across to her. Flossie took a cigarette, rolled it to make it loose, and smoked it while she told them how she had once tried to draw up the smoke through her nose as it came out between her lips.

"And honestly, boys," she growled, "it made me that sick that I just had to go to bed."

"Who is the crowd out back?" asked Geary for the sake of saying something. Flossie embarrassed them all a little, and conversation with girls of her class was difficult.

"Oh, that's May and Nannie with some men from a banquet at the Palace Hotel," she answered.

The talk dragged along little by little and Flossie began badgering young Haight. "Say, you over there," she exclaimed, "what's the matter with you? You don't say anything."

Young Haight blushed and answered very much embarrassed: "Oh, I'm just listening." He was anxious to get away. He got up and reached for his hat and coat, saying with a good-natured smile: "Well, boys and girls, I think I shall have to leave you."

"Don't let me frighten you away," said Flossie, laughing.

"Oh, no," he answered, trying to hide his embarrassment, "I have to go anyhow."

While the others were saying good night to him and asking when they should see him again, Flossie leaned over to him, crying out, "Good night!" All at once, and before he knew what she was about, she kissed him full on the mouth. He started sharply at this, but was not angry, simply pulling away from her, blushing, very embarrassed, and more and more anxious to get away. Toby, the waiter, appeared at their door.

"That last was on me, you know," said young Haight, intercepting Vandover and settling for the round of drinks.

"Hello!" exclaimed Toby, "what's the matter with your lip?"

"I cut it a little while ago on a broken glass," answered young Haight. "Is it bleeding again?" he added, putting two fingers on his lips.

"It is sure enough," said Geary. "Here," he went on, wetting the corner of a napkin from the water bottle, "hold that on it."

The others began to laugh. "Flossie did that," Vandover explained to Toby. Ellis was hastily looking through his pockets, fumbling about among his little books.

"I had something here," he kept muttering, "if I can only *find* it, that told just what to do when you cut yourself with glass. There may be glass *in* it, you know."

"Oh, that's all right, that's all right," exclaimed young Haight, now altogether disconcerted. "It don't amount to anything."

"I tell you what," observed Geary; "get some court-plaster at the snake doctor's just above here."

"No, no, that's all right," returned young Haight, moving off. "Good night. I'll see you again pretty soon."

He went away. Ellis, who was still searching through his little books, suddenly uttered an exclamation. He leaned out into the passage, crying: "The half of a hot onion; tie it right on the cut." But Haight had already gone. "You see," explained Ellis, "that draws out any little particles of glass. Look at this," he added, reading an item just below the one he had found. "You can use cigar ashes for eczema."

Flossie nodded her head at him, smiling and saying: "Well, the next time I have eczema I will remember that."

Flossie left them a little after this, joining Nannie and May in the larger room that held the noisy party. The three fellows had another round of drinks.

All the evening Ellis had been drinking whisky. Now he astonished the others by suddenly calling for beer. He persisted in drinking it out of the celery glass, which he emptied at a single pull. Then Vandover had claret-punches all round, protesting that his mouth felt dry as a dust-bin. Geary at length declared that he felt pretty far gone, adding that he was in the humour for having "a high old time."

"Say, boys," he exclaimed, bringing his hand down on the table, " what do you say that we all go to every joint in town, and wind up at the Turkish baths? We'll have a regular *time*. Let's see now how much money I have."

Thereat they all took account of their money. Vandover had fourteen dollars, but he owed for materials at his art dealer's, and so put away eight of it in an inside pocket. The others followed his example, each one reserving five dollars for immediate use.

"That will be one dollar for the Hammam," said Geary, "and four dollars apiece for drinks. You can get all we want on four dollars." They had a last claret-punch and, having settled with Toby, went out.

Coming out into the cold night air from the warm interior of the Imperial affected Vandover and Geary in a few minutes. But apparently nothing could affect Ellis, neither whisky, claret-punch nor beer. He walked steadily between Vandover and Geary, linking an arm in each of theirs.

These two became very drunk almost at once. At every minute Vandover would cry out, "Yee-ee-*ow*! Thash way I feel, jush like that." Geary made a "Josh" that was a masterpiece, the success of the occasion. It consisted in exclaiming from time to time, "Cherries are ripe!" This was funny. It seemed to have some ludicrous, hidden double-meaning that was irresistible. It stuck to them all the evening; when a girl passed them on Kearney Street and Geary cried out at her that "Cherries were ripe!" it threw them all into spasms of laughter.

They went first to the Palace Garden near the Tivoli Theatre, where Geary and Vandover had beer and Ellis a whisky cocktail. The performance was just finishing, and they voted that they were not at all amused at a lean, overworked girl whom they saw performing a song and dance through a blue haze of tobacco smoke; so they all exclaimed, "Cherries are ripe!" and tramped out again to visit the Luxembourg. The beer began to go against Vandover's stomach by this time, but he forced it down his throat, shutting his eyes. Then they said they would go to the toughest place in town, "Steve Casey's"; this was on a side-street. The walls were covered with yellowed photographs of once-famous pugilists and old-time concert-hall singers. There was sand on the floor, and in the dancing room at the back, where nobody danced, a jaded young man was banging out polkas and quick-steps at a cheap piano.

At the Crystal Palace, where they all had shandy-gaff, they met one of Ellis's friends, a young fellow of about twenty. He was stone deaf, and in consequence had become dumb; but for all that he was very eager to associate with the young men of the city and would not hear of being separated and set apart with the other deaf mutes. He was very pleased to meet them and joined them at once. They all knew him pretty well and called him the "Dummy."

In the course of the evening the party was seen at nearly every bar and saloon in the neighbourhood of Market and Kearney streets. Geary and Vandover were very drunk indeed. Vandover was having a glorious time; he was not silent a minute, talking, laughing, and singing, and crying out continually, "Cherries are ripe!" When he could think of nothing else to say he would exclaim, "Yee-ee-*ow*! Thash way I feel."

For two hours they drank steadily. Vandover was in a dreadful condition; the Dummy got so drunk that he could talk, a peculiarity which at times had been known to occur to him. As will sometimes happen, Geary sobered up a little and at the "Grotto" bathed his head and face in the washroom. After this he became pretty steady, he stopped drinking, and tried to assume the management of the party, ordering their drinks for them, and casting up the amount of the check.

About two o'clock they returned toward the Luxembourg, staggering and swaying. The Luxembourg was a sort of German restaurant under a theatre where one could get some very good German dishes. There Vandover had beer and sauerkraut, but Ellis took more whisky. The Dummy continued to make peculiar sounds in his throat, half-noise, half-speech, and Geary gravely informed the waiter that cherries were ripe.

All at once Ellis was drunk, collapsing in a moment. The skin around his eyes was purple and swollen, the pupils themselves were contracted, and their range of vision seemed to stop at about a yard in front of his face. Suddenly he swept glasses, plates, castor, knives, forks, and all from off the table with a single movement of his arm.

They all jumped up, sober in a minute, knowing that a scene was at hand. The waiter rushed at Ellis, but Ellis knocked him down and tried to stamp on his face. Vandover and the Dummy tried to hold his arms and pull him off. He turned on the Dummy in a silent frenzy of rage and brought his knuckles down upon his head again and again. For the moment Ellis could neither hear, nor see, nor speak; he was blind, dumb, fighting drunk, and his fighting was not the fighting of Vandover.

"Get in here and help, will you?" panted Vandover to Geary, as he struggled with Ellis. "He can kill people when he's like this. Oh, damn the whisky anyhow! Look out— don't let him get that knife! Grab his other arm, there! now, kick his feet from under him! Oh, kick hard! Sit on his legs; there now. Ah! Hell! he's bitten me! Look out! here comes the bouncer!"

The bouncer and three other waiters charged into them while they were struggling on the floor. Vandover was twice knocked down and the Dummy had his lip split. Ellis struggled to his feet again and, still silent, fought them all alike, a fine line of froth gathering at the corners of his lips.

When they were finally ejected, and pulled themselves together in the street outside, Geary had disappeared. He had left them during the struggle with Ellis and had gone home.

Ah, you bet he wasn't going to stay any longer with the crowd when they got like that. If Ellis was fool enough to get as drunk as that it was his own lookout. *He* wasn't going to stay and get thrown out of any saloon; ah, no, you bet he was too clever for that. He was sober enough now and would go home to bed and get a good sleep.

The fight in the saloon had completely sobered the rest of them. Ellis was tractable enough again, and very sorry for having got them into such a row. Vandover was horribly sick at his stomach.

The three locked arms and started slowly toward the Turkish baths. On their way they stopped at an all-night drug store and had some seltzer.

Vandover had about three hours' sleep that night. He was awakened by the attendant shaking his arm and crying:

"Half-past six, sir."

"Huh!" he exclaimed, starting up. "What about half-past six? I don't want to get up."

"Told me to call you, sir, at half-past six; quarter to seven now."

"Oh, all right, very well," answered Vandover. He turned away his face on the pillow, while a wretched feeling of nausea crept over him; every movement of his head made it ache to bursting. Behind his temples the blood throbbed and pumped like the knocking of hammers. His mouth would have been dry but for a thick slime that filled it and that tasted of oil. He felt weak, his hands trembled, his forehead was cold and seemed wet and sticky.

He could recall hardly anything of the previous night. He remembered, however, of going to the Imperial and of seeing Flossie, and he *did* remember at last of leaving word to be called at half-past six.

He got up without waking the other two fellows and took a plunge in the cold tank, dressed very slowly, and went out. The stores were all closed, the streets were almost deserted. He walked to the nearest uptown car-line and took an outside seat, feeling better and steadier for every moment of the sharp morning air.

Van Ness Avenue was very still. It was about half-past seven.

The curtains were down in all the houses; here and there a servant could be seen washing down the front steps. In the vestibules of some of the smaller houses were loaves of French bread and glass jars of cream, while near them lay the damp twisted roll of the morning's paper. There was everywhere a great chittering of sparrows, and the cable-cars, as yet empty, trundled down the cross streets, the conductors cleaning the windows and metal work. From far down at one end of the avenue came the bells of the Catholic Cathedral ringing for early mass; and a respectable-looking second girl hurried past him carrying her prayer-book. At the other end of the avenue was a blue vista of the bay, the great bulk of Mount Tamalpais rearing itself out of the water like a waking lion.

In front of the little church Turner was waiting for him. She was dressed very prettily and the cold morning air had given her a fine colour.

"You don't look more than half awake," she said, as Vandover came up. "It was awfully good of you to come. Oh, Van, you look dreadfully. It is too bad to make you get up so early."

"No, no," protested Vandover. "I was only too glad to come. I didn't sleep well last night. I hope I haven't kept you waiting."

"I've only just come," answered Turner. "But I think it is time to go in."

The little organ was muttering softly to itself as they entered. It was very still otherwise. The morning sun struck through the stained windows and made pretty lights about the altar; besides themselves there were some half dozen other worshippers. The little organ ceased with a long droning sigh, and the minister in his white robes turned about, facing his auditors, and in the midst of a great silence opened the communion service with the words: "Ye who do truly and earnestly repent you of your sins and are in love and charity with your neighbours——"

As Vandover rose with the rest the blood rushed to his head and a feeling of nausea and exhaustion, the dregs of his previous night's debauch, came over him again for a moment, so that he took hold of the back of the pew in front of him to steady himself.

Chapter Five

Iᴺ ᴛʜᴇ ᴀꜰᴛᴇʀɴᴏᴏɴꜱ Vandover worked in his studio, which was on Sacramento Street, but in the mornings he was accustomed to study in the life-class at the School of Design.

This was on California Street over the Market, an immense room partitioned by enormous wooden screens into alcoves, where the still-life classes worked, painting carrots, grapes, and dusty brown stone-jugs.

All about were a multitude of casts, the fighting gladiator, the discobulus, the Venus of Milo, and hundreds of smaller pieces, masks, torsos, and the heads of the Parthenon horses. Flattened paint-tubes and broken bits of charcoal littered the floor and cluttered the chairs and shelves. A strong odour of turpentine and fixative was in the air, mingled with the stronger odours of linseed oil and sour, stale French bread.

Every afternoon a portrait class of some thirty-odd assembled in one of the larger alcoves near the door. Several of the well-known street characters of the city had posed for this class, and at one time Father Elphick, the white-haired, bare-headed vegetarian, with his crooked stick and white clothes, had sat to it for his head.

Vandover was probably the most promising member of the school. His style was sketchy, conscientious, and full of strength and decision. He worked in large lines, broad surfaces and masses of light or shade. His colour was good, running to purples, reds, and admirable greens, full of bitumen and raw sienna.

Though he had no idea of composition, he was clever enough to acknowledge it. His finished pictures were broad reaches of landscape, deserts, shores, and moors in which he placed solitary figures of men or animals in a way that was very effective—as, for instance, a great strip of shore and in the foreground the body of a drowned sailor; a lion drinking in the midst of an immense Sahara; or, one that he called "The Remnant of an Army," a dying war horse wandering on an empty plain, the saddle turned under his belly, his mane and tail snarled with burrs.

Some time before there had come to him the idea for a

great picture. It was to be his first masterpiece, his salon picture when he should get to Paris. A British cavalryman and his horse, both dying of thirst and wounds, were to be lost on a Soudanese desert, and in the middle distance on a ridge of sand a lion should be drawing in upon them, crouched on his belly, his tail stiff, his lower jaw hanging. The melodrama of the old English "Home Book of Art" still influenced Vandover. He was in love with this idea for a picture and had determined to call it "The Last Enemy." The effects he wished to produce were isolation and intense heat; as to the soldier, he was as yet undecided whether to represent him facing death resignedly, calmly, or grasping the barrel of his useless rifle, determined to fight to the last.

Vandover loved to paint and to draw. He was perfectly contented when his picture was "coming right," and when he felt sure he was doing good work. He often did better than he thought he would, but never so well as he thought he *could*.

However, it bored him to work very hard, and when he did not enjoy his work he stopped it at once. He would tell himself on these occasions that one had to be in the mood and that he should wait for the inspiration, although he knew very well how absurd such excuses were, how false and how pernicious.

That certain little weakness of Vandover's character, his self-indulgence, had brought him to such a point that he thought he *had* to be amused. If his painting amused him, very good; if not, he found something else that would.

On the following Monday as he worked in the life-class, Vandover was thinking, or, rather, trying not to think, of what he had done the Sunday morning previous when he had gone to communion with Turner Ravis. For a long time he evaded the thought because he knew that if he allowed it to come into his mind it would worry and harass him. But by and by the effort of dodging the enemy became itself too disagreeable, so he gave it up and allowed himself to look the matter squarely in the face.

Ah, yes; it was an ugly thing he had done there, a really awful thing. He must have been still drunk when he had knelt in the chancel. Vandover shuddered as he thought of this, and told himself that one could hardly commit a worse sacrilege, and that some time he would surely be called to account for it. But here he checked himself suddenly, not daring to go further. One would have no peace of mind left if one went on brooding over such things in this fashion. He realized the enormity of what he had done. He had tried to be sorry for it. It was perhaps the worst thing he had ever done, but now he had reached the lowest point. He would take care never to do such a thing again. After this he would be better.

But this was not so. Unconsciously, Vandover had shut a door behind him; he would never again be exactly the same, and the keeping of his appointment with Turner Ravis that Sunday morning was, as it were, a long step onward in his progress of ruin and pollution.

He shook himself as though relieving his shoulders of a weight. The model in the life-class had just been posed for the week, and the others had begun work. The model for that week was a woman, a fact that pleased Vandover, for he drew these nude women better than any one in the school, perhaps better than any one in the city. Portrait work and the power to catch subtle intellectual distinctions in a face were sometimes beyond him, but his feeling for the flesh, and for the movement and character of a pose, was admirable.

He set himself to work. Holding his stick of charcoal toward the model at arm's-length, he measured off the heads, five in all, and laid off an equal number of spaces upon his paper. After this, by aid of his mirror, he studied the general character of the pose for nearly half an hour. Then, with a few strokes of his charcoal he laid off his larger construction lines with a freedom and a precision that were excellent. Upon these lines he made a second drawing a little more detailed, though as yet everything was blocked in, angularly and roughly. Then, putting a thin flat edge upon his charcoal, he started the careful and finished outline.

By the end of an hour the first sketch of his drawing was complete. It was astonishingly good, vigorous and solid; better than all, it had that feeling for form that makes just the difference between the amateur and the genuine artist.

By this time Vandover's interest began to flag. Four times

he had drawn and redrawn the articulation of the model's left shoulder. As she stood, turned sideways to him, one hand on her hip, the deltoid muscle was at once contracted and foreshortened. It was a difficult bit of anatomy to draw. Vandover was annoyed at his ill success—such close attention and continued effort wearied him a little—the room was overheated and close, and the gas stove, which was placed near the throne to warm the model, leaked and filled the room with a nasty brassy smell. Vandover remembered that the previous week he had been looking over some old bound copies of *l'Art* in the Mechanics Library and had found them of absorbing interest. There was a pleasant corner and a huge comfortable chair near where they were in the reading-room, and from the window one could occasionally look out upon the street. It was a quiet spot, and he would not be disturbed all the morning. The idea was so attractive that he put away his portfolio and drawing things and went out.

For an hour he gave himself up to the enjoyment of *l'Art*, excusing his indolence by telling himself that it was all in his profession and was not time lost. A reproduction of a picture by Gérôme gave him some suggestions for the "Last Enemy," which he noted very carefully.

He was interrupted by a rustle of starched skirts and a voice that said:

"Why, hello, Van!"

He looked up quickly to see a young girl of about twenty dressed in a black close-fitting bolero jacket of imitation astrakhan with big leg-of-mutton sleeves, a striped silk skirt, and a very broad hat tilted to one side. Her hair was very blond, though coarse and dry from being bleached, and a little flat curl of it lay very low on her forehead. She was marvellously pretty. Vandover was delighted.

"Why, *Ida!*" he exclaimed, holding her hand; "*it's* awfully nice to see you here; won't you sit down?" and he pushed his chair toward her.

But Ida Wade said no, she had just come in after a new book, and of course it had to be out. But where had he kept himself so long? That was the way he threw off on her; ah, yes, he was going with Miss Ravis now and wouldn't look at any one else.

Vandover protested against this, and Ida Wade went on to ask him why he couldn't come up to call on her that very night, adding:

"We might go to the Tivoli or somewhere." All at once she interrupted herself, laughing, "Oh, I heard all about you the other night. *'Cherries are ripe!'* You and the boys painted the town red, didn't you? Ah, Van, I'm right on to *you!*"

She would not tell him how she heard, but took herself off, laughing and reminding him to come up early.

Ida Wade belonged to a certain type of young girl that was very common in the city. She was what men, among each other, called "gay," though that was the worst that could be said of her. She was virtuous, but the very fact that it was necessary to say so was enough to cause the statement to be doubted. When she was younger and had been a pupil at the Girls' High School, she had known and had even been the companion of such girls as Turner Ravis and Henrietta Vance, but since that time girls of that class had ignored her. Now, almost all of her acquaintances were men, and to half of these she had never been introduced. They had managed to get acquainted with her on Kearney Street, at theatres, at the Mechanics' Fair, and at baseball games. She loved to have a "gay" time, which for her meant to drink California champagne, to smoke cigarettes, and to kick at the chandelier. She was still virtuous and meant to stay so; there was nothing vicious about her, and she was as far removed from Flossie's class as from that of Turner Ravis.

She was very clever; half of her acquaintances, even the men, did not know how very "gay" she was. Only those—like Vandover—who knew her best, knew her for what she was, for Ida was morbidly careful of appearances, and as jealous of her reputation as only fast girls are.

Bessie Laguna was her counterpart. Bessie was "the girl she went with," just as Henrietta Vance was Turner's "chum" and Nannie was Flossie's "running-mate."

Ida lived with her people on Golden Gate Avenue not far from Larkin Street. Her father had a three-fourths interest in a carpet-cleaning establishment on Howard Street, and her mother gave lessons in painting on china and on velvet. Ida had just been graduated from the normal school, and often substituted at various kindergartens in the city. She hoped soon to get a permanent place.

Vandover arrived at Ida's house that night at about eight o'clock in the midst of a drenching fog. The parlour and front room on the second floor were furnished with bay windows decorated with some meaningless sort of millwork. The front door stood at the right of the parlour windows. Two Corinthian pillars on either side of the vestibule supported a balcony; these pillars had iron capitals which were painted to imitate the wood of the house, which in its turn was painted to imitate stone. The house was but two stories high, and the roof was topped with an iron cresting. There was a microscopical front yard in which one saw a tiny gravel walk, two steps long, that led to a door under the front steps, where the gas-meter was kept. A few dusty and straggling calla-lilies grew about.

Ida opened the door for Vandover almost as soon as he rang, and pulled him into the entry, exclaiming: "Come in out of the wet, as the whale said to Jonah. *Isn't* it a nasty night?" Vandover noticed as he came in that the house smelt of upholstery, cooking, and turpentine. He did not take off his overcoat, but went with her into the parlour.

The parlour was a little room with tinted plaster walls shut off from the "back-parlour" by sliding doors. A ply carpet covered the floor, a cheap piano stood across one corner of the room, and a greenish sofa across another. The mantelpiece was of white marble with gray spots; on one side of it stood an Alaskan "grass basket" full of photographs, and on the other an inverted section of a sewer-pipe painted with daisies and full of gilded cat-tails tied with a blue ribbon. Near the piano straddled a huge easel of imitation brass upholding the crayon picture of Ida's baby sister enlarged from a photograph. Across one corner of this picture was a yellow "drape." There were a great many of these "drapes" all about the room, hanging over the corners of the chairs, upon an edge of the mantelpiece, and even twisted about the chandelier. In the exact middle of the mantelpiece itself was the clock, one of the chief ornaments of the room, almost the first thing one saw upon entering; it was a round-faced timepiece perversely set in one corner of an immense red plush palette;

the palette itself was tilted to one side, and was upheld by an easel of twisted brass wire. Out of the thumb-hole stuck half a dozen brushes wired together in a round bunch and covered with gilt paint. The clock never was wound. It went so fast that it was useless as a timepiece. Over it, however, hung a large and striking picture, a species of cheap photogravure, a lion lying in his cage, looking mildly at the spectator over his shoulder. In front of the picture were real iron bars, with real straw tucked in behind them.

Ida sat down on the piano stool, twisting back and forth, leaning her elbows on the keys.

"All the folks have gone out to a whist-party, and I'm left all alone in the house with Maggie," she said. Then she added: "Bessie and Bandy Ellis said they would come down to-night, and I thought we could all go downtown to the Tivoli or somewhere, in the open-air boxes, you know, way up at the top." Hardly had she spoken the words when Bessie and Ellis arrived.

Ida went upstairs to get on her hat at once, because it was so late, and Bessie went with her.

Ellis and Vandover laughed as soon as they saw each other, and Ellis exclaimed mockingly, "Ye-e-ow, thash jush way I feel." Vandover grinned:

"That's so," he answered. "I *do* remember now of having made that remark several times. But *you*—oh, you were fearful. Do you remember the row in the Luxembourg? Look there where you bit me."

Ellis was incensed with Geary because he had forsaken their party.

"Oh, that's Charlie Geary, all over," answered Vandover.

As they were speaking there came a sudden outburst of bells in various parts of the city and simultaneously they heard the hoarse croaking of a whistle down by the waterfront.

"Fire," said Vandover indifferently.

Ellis was already fumbling in his pockets, keeping count of the strokes.

"That's one," he exclaimed, pulling out and studying his list of alarm-boxes, "and one-two-three, that's three and one-two-three-*four*, one thirty-four. Let's see now! That's Bush and Hyde streets, not very far off," and he returned his card to the inside pocket of his coat as though he had accomplished a duty.

He lit a cigar. "I wonder now," he said, hesitating. "I guess I better not smoke in here. I'll go outside and get a mouthful of smoke before the girls come down." He went out and Vandover sat down to the cheap piano and played his three inevitable pieces, the two polkas and the air of the topical song; but he was interrupted by Ellis, who opened the door, crying out:

"Oh, come out here and see the *fire*, will you? Devil of a blaze!" Vandover ran out and saw a great fan-shaped haze of red through the fog over the roofs of the houses.

"Oh, say, girls," he shouted, jumping back to the foot of the stairs; "Ida, Bessie, there's a fire. Just look out of your windows. Hark, there go the engines."

Bessie came tearing down the stairs and out on the front steps, where the two fellows were standing hatless.

"Where? Oh, show me where! O-o-oh, sure enough! That's a *big* fire. Just *hear* the engines. *Oh, let's go!*"

"Sure; come on, let's go!" exclaimed Vandover. "Tell Ida to hurry up."

"Oh, Ida," cried Bessie up the stairs, "there's an awful big fire right near here, and we're going."

"Oh, wait!" shouted Ida, her mouth full of pins. "I had to change my waist. Oh, *do* wait for me. Where is it *at*? Please wait; I'm coming right down in just a minute."

"Hurry up, hurry up!" cried Vandover. "It will be all out by the time we get there. I'm coming up to help."

"No, no, no!" she screamed. "Don't; you rattle me. I'm all mixed up. Oh, *darn* it, I can't find my czarina!"

But at last she came running down, breathless, shrugging herself into her bolero jacket. They all hurried into the street and turned in the direction of the blaze. Other people were walking rapidly in the same direction, and there was an opening and shutting of windows and front doors. A steamer thundered past, clanging and smoking, followed by a score of half-exhausted boys. It took them longer to reach the fire than they expected, and by the time they had come within two blocks of it they were quite out of breath. Here the excitement was lively; the sidewalks were full of people going in the same direction; on all sides there were guesses as to where the fire was. On the front steps of many houses stood middle-aged gentlemen, still holding their evening papers and cigars, very amused and interested in watching the crowd go past. One heard them from time to time calling to their little sons, who were dancing on the sidewalks, forbidding them to go; in the open windows above could be seen the other members of the family, their faces faintly tinged with the glow, looking and pointing, or calling across the street to their friends in the opposite houses. Every one was in good humour; it was an event, a fête for the entire neighbourhood.

Vandover and his party came at last to the first engines violently pumping and coughing, the huge gray horses standing near by, already unhitched and blanketed, indifferently feeding in their nosebags. Some of the crowd preferred to watch the engines rather than the fire, and there were even some who were coming away from it, exclaiming "false alarm" or "all out now."

The party had come up quite close; they could smell the burning wood and could see the roofs of the nearer houses beginning to stand out sharp and black against the red glow beyond. It was a barn behind a huge frame house that was afire, the dry hay burning like powder, and by the time they reached it the flames were already dwindling. The hose was lying like a python all about the streets, while upon the neighbouring roofs were groups of firemen with helmets and axes; some were shouting into the street below, and others were holding the spouting nozzles of the hose. "Ah," exclaimed an old man, standing near to Ida and Vandover, "ah, *I* was here when it first broke out; you ought to have seen the flames then! Look, there's a tree catching!"

The crowd became denser; policemen pushed it back and stretched a rope across the street. There was a world of tumbling yellow smoke that made one's eyes smart, and a great crackling and snapping of flames. Terribly excited little boys were about everywhere whistling and calling for each other as the crowd separated them.

They watched the fire for some time, standing on a pile of boards in front of a half-built house, but as it dwindled they wearied of it.

"Want to go?" asked Vandover at last.

"Yes," answered Ida, " we might as well. Oh, where's Bessie and Ellis?" They were nowhere to be seen. Vandover whistled and Ida even called, but in vain. The little boys in the crowd mimicked Ida, crying back, "Hey! Bessie! Oh, *Bes-see*, mommer wants you!" The men who stood near laughed at this, but it annoyed Vandover much more than it did Ida.

"Ah, well, never mind," she said at length. "Let them go. Now shall *we* go?"

It was too late for the theatre, but to return home was out of the question. They started off aimlessly downtown.

While he talked Vandover was perplexed. Ida was gayly dressed and was one of those girls who cannot open their mouths nor raise a finger in the street without attracting attention. Vandover was not at all certain that he cared to be seen on Kearney Street as Ida Wade's escort; one never knew who one was going to meet. Ida was not a bad girl, she was not notorious, but, confound it, it would look queer; and at the same time, while Ida was the kind of girl that one did not want to be seen with, she was not the kind of girl that could be told so. In an upper box at the Tivoli it would have been different—one could keep in the background; but to appear on Kearney Street with a girl who wore a hat like that and who would not put on her gloves—ah, no, it was out of the question.

Ida was talking away endlessly about a kindergarten in which she had substituted the last week.

She told him about the funny little nigger girl, and about the games and songs and how they played birds and hopped around and cried, "Twit, twit," and the game of the butterflies visiting the flowers. She even sang part of a song about the waves.

> "Every little wave had its night-cap on;
> Its white-cap, night-cap, white-cap on."

"It's more *fun* than enough," she said.

"Say, Ida," interrupted Vandover at length, "I'm pretty hungry. Can't we go somewhere and eat something? I'd like a Welsh rabbit."

"All right," she answered. "Where do you want to go?"

"Well," replied Vandover, running over in his mind the places he might reach by unfrequented streets. "There's Marchand's or Tortoni's or the Poodle Dog."

"Suits *me*," she answered, "any one you like. Say, Van," she added, "weren't you boys at the Imperial the other night? What kind of a place is that?"

On the instant Vandover wondered what she could mean. Was it possible that Ida would go to a place like that with him?

"The Imperial?" he answered. "Oh, I don't know; the Imperial is a sort of a nice place. It has private rooms, like all of these places. The cooking is simply out of sight. I think there is a bar connected with it." Then he went on to talk indifferently about the kindergarten, though his pulse was beating fast, and his nerves were strung taut. By and by Ida said:

"I didn't know there was a bar at the Imperial. I thought it was just some kind of an oyster joint. Why, I heard of a very nice girl, a swell girl, going in there."

"Oh, yes," said Vandover, "they do. I say, Ida," he went on, "what's the matter with going down *there*?"

"The *Imperial*?" exclaimed Ida. "Well, I guess *not!*"

"Why, it's all right, if I'm with you," retorted Vandover, "but if you don't like it we can go anywhere else."

"Well, I guess we *will* go anywhere else," returned Ida, and for the time the subject was dropped.

They took a Sutter Street car and got off at Grant Avenue, having decided to go to Marchand's.

"That's the Imperial down there, isn't it?" asked Ida as they reached the sidewalk. Vandover made a last attempt:

"I say, Ida, come on, let's go there. It's all right if I'm with you. Ah, come along; what's the odds?"

"*No—no—*NO," she answered decisively. "What kind of a girl do you think I am, anyway?"

"Well, I tell you what," answered Vandover, "just come down *by* the place, and if you don't like the looks of it you needn't go in. I want to get some cigarettes, anyhow. You can walk down with me till I do *that*."

"I'll walk down with you," replied Ida, "but I shan't go in."

They drew near to the Imperial. The street about was deserted, even the usual hacks that had their stand there were gone.

"You see," explained Vandover as they passed slowly in front of the doors, "this is all quiet enough. If you pulled down your veil no one would know the difference, and here's the ladies' entrance, you see, right at the side."

"All right, come along, let's go in," exclaimed Ida suddenly, and before he knew it they had swung open the little door of the ladies' entrance with its frosted pane of glass and had stepped inside.

It was between nine and ten o'clock, and the Imperial was quiet as yet; a few men were drinking in the barroom outside, and Toby, the red-eyed waiter, was talking in low tones to a girl under one of the electric lights.

Vandover and Ida went into one of the larger rooms in the rear passage and shut the door. Ida pushed her bolero jacket from her shoulders, saying, "This seems nice and quiet enough."

"Well, of course," answered Vandover, as though dismissing the question for good. "Now, what are we going to have? I say we have champagne and oysters."

"Let's have Cliquot, then," exclaimed Ida, which was the only champagne she had ever heard of besides the California brands.

She was very excited. This was the kind of "gay" time she delighted in, tête-à-tête champagne suppers with men late at night. She had never been in such a place as the Imperial before, and the daring and novelty of what she had done, the whiff of the great city's vice caught in this manner, sent a little tremor of pleasure and excitement over all her nerves.

They did not hurry over their little supper, but ate and drank slowly, and had more oysters to go with the last half of their bottle. Ida's face was ablaze, her eyes flashing, her blond hair disordered and falling about her cheeks.

Vandover put his arm about her neck and drew her toward him, and as she sank down upon him, smiling and complaisant, her hair tumbling upon her shoulders and her head and throat bent back, he leaned his cheek against hers, speaking in a low voice.

"No—no," she murmured, smiling; "never—ah, if I hadn't

come—no, Van—please——" And then with a long breath she abandoned herself.

About midnight he left her at the door of her house on Golden Gate Avenue. On their way home Ida had grown more serious than he had ever known her to be. Now she began to cry softly to herself. "Oh, Van," she said, putting her head down upon his shoulder, "oh, I am so *sorry*. You don't think any less of me, do you? Oh, Van, you must be true to me now!"

Chapter Six

EVERYBODY IN San Francisco knew of the Ravises and always made it a point to speak of them as one of the best families of the city. They were not new and they were not particularly rich. They had lived in the same house on California Street for nearly twenty years and had always been comfortably well off. As things go in San Francisco, they were old-fashioned. They had family traditions and usages and time-worn customs. Their library had been in process of collection for the past half century and the pictures on the walls were oil paintings of steel engravings and genuine old-fashioned chromos, beyond price to-day.

Their furniture and ornaments were of the preceding generation, solid, conservative. They were not chosen with reference to any one style, nor all bought at the same time. Each separate piece had an individuality of its own. The Ravises kept their old things, long after the fashion had gone out, preferring them to the smarter "art" objects on account of their associations.

There were six in the family, Mr. and Mrs. Ravis, Turner, and her older brother, Stanley, Yale '88, a very serious young gentleman of twenty-seven, continually professing an interest in economics and finance. Besides these were the two children, Howard, nine years old, and his sister, aged fourteen, who had been christened Virginia.

They were a home-loving race. Mr. Ravis, senior, belonged to the Bohemian Club, but was seldom seen there. Stanley was absorbed in his law business, and Turner went out but little. They much preferred each other's society to that of three fourths of their acquaintances, most of their friends being "friends of the family," who came to dinner three or four times a year.

It was a custom of theirs to spend the evenings in the big dining-room at the back of the house, after the table had been cleared away, Mr. Ravis and Stanley reading the papers, the one smoking his cigar, the other his pipe; Mrs. Ravis, with the magazines and Turner with the *Chautauquan*. Howard

59

and Virginia appropriated the table to themselves where they played with their soldiers and backgammon board.

The family kept two servants, June the "China boy," who had been with them since the beginning of things, and Delphine the cook, a more recent acquisition. June was, in a way, butler and second boy combined; he did all the downstairs work and the heavy sweeping, but it was another timeworn custom for Mrs. Ravis and Turner to spend part of every morning in putting the bedrooms to rights, dusting and making up the beds. Besides this, Turner exercised a sort of supervision over Howard and Virginia, who were too old for a nurse but too young to take care of themselves. She had them to bed at nine, mended some of their clothes, made them take their baths regularly, reëstablished peace between them in their hourly quarrels, and, most arduous task of all, saw that Howard properly washed himself every morning, and on Wednesday and Saturday afternoons that he was suitably dressed in time for dancing school.

It was Sunday afternoon. Mrs. Ravis was reading to her husband, who lay on the sofa in the back-parlour smoking a cigar. Stanley had gone out to make a call, while Howard and Virginia had forgathered in the bathroom to sail their boats and cigar boxes in the tub. Toward half-past three, as Turner was in her room writing letters, the door-bell rang. She stopped, with her pen in the air, wondering if it might be Vandover. It was June's afternoon out. In a few minutes the bell rang again, and Turner ran down to answer it herself, intercepting Delphine, who took June's place on these occasions, but who was hopelessly stupid.

Mrs. Ravis had peered out through the curtains of the parlour window to see who it was, and Turner met her and Mr. Ravis coming upstairs, abandoning the parlour to Turner's caller.

"Mamma and I are going upstairs to read," explained Mr. Ravis. "It's some one of your young men. You can bring him right in the parlour."

"I think it's Mr. Haight," said Turner's mother. "Ask him to stay to tea."

"Well," said Turner doubtfully, as she paused at the foot of the stairs, "I will, but you know we never have anything to speak of for Sunday evening tea. June is out, and you know how clumsy and stupid Delphine is when she waits on the table."

It *was* young Haight. Turner was very glad to see him, for next to Vandover she liked him better than any of the others. She was never bored by being obliged to entertain him, and he always had something to say and some clever way of saying it.

About half-past five, as they were talking about amateur photography, Mrs. Ravis came in and called them to tea.

Tea with the Ravises was the old-fashioned tea of twenty years ago. One never saw any of the modern "delicacies" on their Sunday evening table, no enticing cold lunch, no spices, not even catsups or pepper sauces. The turkey or chicken they had had for dinner was served cold in slices; there was canned fruit, preserves, tea, crackers, bread and butter, a large dish of cold pork and beans, and a huge glass pitcher of ice-water.

In the absence of June, Delphine the cook went through the agony of waiting on the table, very nervous and embarrassed in her clean calico gown and starched apron. Her hands were red and knotty, smelling of soap, and they touched the chinaware with an over-zealous and constraining tenderness as if the plates and dishes had been delicate glass butterflies. She stood off at a distance from the table making sudden and awkward dabs at it. When it came to passing the plates, she passed them on the wrong side and remembered herself at the wrong moment with a stammering apology. In her excess of politeness she kept up a constant murmur as she attended to their wants. Another fork? Yes, sir. She'd get it right away, sir. Did Mrs. Ravis want another cuppa tea? No? No more tea? Well, she'd pass the bread. Some bread, Master Howard? Nice French bread, he always liked that. Some more preserved pears, Miss Ravis? Yes, miss, she'd get them right away; they were just over here on the sideboard. Yes, here they were. No more? Now she'd go and put them back. And at last when she had set the nerves of all of them in a jangle, was dismissed to the kitchen and retired with a gasp of unspeakable relief.

Somewhat later in the evening young Haight was alone

with Turner, and their conversation had taken a very unusual and personal turn. All at once Turner exclaimed:

"I often wonder what good I am in the world to anybody. I don't *know* a thing, I can't *do* a thing. I couldn't cook the plainest kind of a meal to *save* me, and it took me all of two hours yesterday to do just a little buttonhole stitching. I'm not good for anything. I'm not a help to anybody."

Young Haight looked into the blue flame of the gas-log, almost the only modern innovation throughout the entire house, and was silent for a moment; then he leaned his elbows on his knees and, still looking at the flame, replied:

"I don't know about that. You have been a considerable help to *me*."

"To *you*!" exclaimed Turner, surprised. "A help to *you*? Why, how do you mean?"

"Well," he answered, still without looking at her, "one always has one's influence, you know."

"Ah, lots of influence *I* have over anybody," retorted Turner, incredulously.

"Yes, you have," he insisted. "You have plenty of influence over the people that care for you. You have plenty of influence over me."

Turner, very much embarrassed, and not knowing how to answer, bent down to the side of the mantelpiece and turned up the flame of the gas-log a little. Young Haight continued, almost as embarrassed as she:

"I suppose I'm a bad lot, perhaps a little worse than most others, but I think—I hope—there's some good in me. I know all this sounds absurd and affected, but *really* I'm not posing; you won't mind if I speak just as I think, for this once. I promise," he went on with a half smile, "not to do it again. You know my mother died when I was little and I have lived mostly with men. You have been to me what the society of women has been to other fellows. You see, you are the only girl I ever knew very well—the only one I ever wanted to know. I have cared for you the way other men have cared for the different women that come into their lives; as they have cared for their mothers, their sisters —and their wives. You have already influenced me as a mother or sister should have done; what if I should ever ask you to be—to be the *other* to me, the one that's best of all?"

Young Haight turned toward her as he finished and looked at her for the first time. Turner was still very much embarrassed.

"Oh, I'm very glad if I've been a help to—to anybody—to you," she said, confusedly. "But I never knew that you cared—that you thought about me—in that way. But you mustn't, you know, you mustn't care for me in that way. I ought to tell you right away that I never could care for you more than—I always have done; I mean care for you only as a very, very good friend. You don't know, Dolly," she went on eagerly, "how it hurts me to tell you so, because I care so much for you in every other way that I wouldn't hurt your feelings for anything; but then you know at the same time it would hurt you a great deal more if I *shouldn't* tell you, but encourage you, and let you go on thinking that perhaps I liked you more than any one else, when I *didn't*. Now wouldn't that be wrong? You don't know how glad it makes me feel that I have been of some good to you, and that is just why I want to be sincere *now* and not make you think any less of me—think any worse of me."

"Oh, I know," answered young Haight. "I know I shouldn't have said anything about it. I knew beforehand, or thought I knew, that you didn't care in that way."

"Maybe I have been wrong," she replied, "in not seeing that you cared so much, and have given you a wrong impression. I thought you knew how it was all the time."

"Knew how what was?" he asked, looking up.

"Why," she said, "knew how Van and I were."

"I knew that Van cared for you a great deal."

"Yes, but you know," she went on, hesitating and confused, "you know we are engaged. We have been engaged for nearly two years."

"But *he* don't consider himself as engaged!" The words were almost out of Haight's mouth, but he shut his teeth against them and kept silence—he hardly knew why.

"Suppose Vandover were out of the question," he said, getting up and smiling in order not to seem as serious as he really was.

"Ah," she said, smiling back at him. "I don't know; that's a hard question to answer. I've never *asked* myself *that* question."

"Well, I'm saving you the trouble, you see," he answered, still smiling. "I am asking it *for* you."

"But I don't want to answer such a question off-hand like that; how can I tell? It would only be *perhaps*, just now."

Young Haight answered quickly that "just now" he would be contented with that "perhaps"; but Turner did not hear this. She had spoken at the same time as he, exclaiming, "But what is the good of talking of that? Because no matter what happened I feel as though I could not break my promise to Van, even if I should want to. Because I have talked like this, Dolly," she went on more seriously, "you must not be deceived or get a wrong impression. You understand how things are, don't you?"

"Oh, yes," he answered, still trying to carry it off with a laugh. "I know, I know. But now I hope you won't let anything I have said bother you, and that things will go on just as if I hadn't spoken, just as if nothing had happened."

"Why, of course," she said, laughing with him again. "Of *course*, why shouldn't they?"

They were both at their ease again by the time young Haight stood at the door with his hat in his hand ready to go.

He raised his free hand over her head, and said, with burlesque, dramatic effect, trying to keep down a smile:

"Bless you both; go, go marry Vandover and be happy; I forgive you."

"Ah—don't be so *utterly* absurd," she cried, beginning to laugh.

Chapter Seven

O N A CERTAIN EVENING about four months later Ellis and Vandover had a "date" with Ida Wade and Bessie Laguna at the Mechanics' Fair. Ellis, Bessie, and Ida were to meet Vandover there in the Art Gallery, as he had to make a call with his father, and could not get there until half-past nine. They were all to walk about the Fair until ten, after which the two men proposed to take the girls out to the Cliff House in separate coupés. The whole thing had been arranged by Ellis and Bessie, and Vandover was irritated. Ellis ought to have had more sense; rushing the girls was all very well, but everybody went to the Mechanics' Fair, and he didn't like to have nice girls like Turner or Henrietta Vance see him with chippies like that. It was all very well for Ellis, who had no social position, but for *him*, Vandover, it would look too confounded queer. Of course he was in for it now, and would have to face the music. You can't tell a girl like that that you're ashamed to be seen with her, but very likely he would get himself into a regular box with it all.

When he arrived at the Mechanics' Pavilion, it was about twenty minutes of ten, and as he pushed through the wicket he let himself into a huge amphitheatre full of colour and movement.

There was a vast shuffling of thousands of feet and a subdued roar of conversation like the noise of a great mill; mingled with these were the purring of distant machinery, the splashing of a temporary fountain and the rhythmic clamour of a brass band, while in the piano exhibit the hired performer was playing a concert-grand with a great flourish. Nearer at hand one could catch ends of conversation and notes of laughter, the creaking of boots, and the rustle of moving dresses and stiff skirts. Here and there groups of school children elbowed their way through the crowd, crying shrilly, their hands full of advertisement pamphlets, fans, picture cards, and toy whips with pewter whistles on the butts, while the air itself was full of the smell of fresh popcorn.

Ellis and Bessie were in the Art Gallery upstairs. Mrs. Wade, Ida's mother, who gave lessons in hand painting, had

65

an exhibit there which they were interested to find; a bunch of yellow poppies painted on velvet and framed in gilt. They stood before it some little time hazarding their opinions and then moved on from one picture to another; Ellis bought a catalogue and made it a duty to find the title of every picture. Bessie professed to be very fond of painting; she had 'taken it up' at one time and had abandoned it, only because the oil or turpentine or something was unhealthy for her. "Of course," she said, "I'm no critic, I only know what I like. Now that one over there, I like *that*. I think those ideal heads like that are lovely, don't you, Bandy? Oh, there's Van!"

"Hello!" said Vandover, coming up. "Where's Ida?"

"Hello, Van!" answered Bessie. "Ida wouldn't come. Isn't it too mean? She said she couldn't come because she had a cold, but she was just talking through her face, I know. She's just got kind of a streak on and you can't get anything out of her. You two haven't had a row, have you? Well, I didn't *think* you had. But she's worried about something or other. I don't believe she's been out of the house this week. But isn't it mean of her to throw cold water on the procession like this? She's been giving me a lecture, too, and says she's going to reform."

"Well," said Vandover, greatly relieved, "that's too bad. We could have had a lot of fun to-night. I'm awfully sorry. Well, what are you two going to do?"

"Oh, I guess we'll follow out our part of the programme," said Ellis. "You are kind of left out, though."

"I don't know," answered Vandover. "Maybe I'll go downtown, and see if I can find some of the boys."

"Oh, Dolly Haight is around here somewheres," said Ellis. "We saw him just now over by the chess machine."

"I guess I'll try and find him, then," responded Vandover. "Well, I hope you two enjoy yourselves." As he was turning away Bessie Laguna came running back, and taking him a little to one side said:

"You'd better go round and see Ida pretty soon if you can. She's all broke up about something, I'm sure. I think she'd like to see you pretty well. Honestly," she said, suddenly very grave, "I never saw Ida so cut up in my life. She's been taking on over something in a dreadful way, and I think she'd like to see you. She won't tell *me* anything. You go around and see her."

"All right," answered Vandover smiling, "I'll go."

As he was going down the stairs on his way to find young Haight it occurred to him what Ida's trouble might be. He was all at once struck with a great fear, so that for an instant he turned cold and weak, and reached out his hand to steady himself against the railing of the stairs. Ah, what a calamity that would be! What a calamity! What a dreadful responsibility! What a crime! He could not keep the thought out of his mind. He tried to tell himself that Ida had practically given her consent by going into such a place; that he was not the only one, after all; that there was nothing certain as yet. He stood on the stairway, empty for that moment, biting the end of his thumb, saying to himself in a low voice:

"What a calamity, what a horrible calamity that would be! Ah, you scoundrel! You damned fool, not to have thought!" A couple of girls, the counter girls at one of the candy booths, came down the stairs behind him with a great babble of talk. Vandover gave an irritated shrug of his shoulders as if freeing himself from the disagreeable subject and went on.

He could not find young Haight down stairs and so went up into the gallery again. After a long time he came upon him sitting on an empty bench nursing his cane and watching the crowd go past.

"Hello, old man!" he exclaimed. "Ellis told me I would find you around somewhere. I was just going to give you up." He sat down beside his chum, and the two began to talk about the people as they passed. "Ah, get on to the red hat!" exclaimed Vandover on a sudden. "That's the third time she's passed."

"Has Ellis gone off with Bessie Laguna?" asked young Haight.

"Yes," answered Vandover. "They're going to have a time at the Cliff House."

"That's too bad," young Haight replied. "Ellis has just thrown himself away with that girl. He might have known some very nice people when he first came here. Between that girl and his whisky he has managed to spoil every chance he might have had."

"There's Charlie Geary," Vandover exclaimed suddenly, whistling and beckoning. "Hey, there, Charlie! where you going? Oh," he cried on a sudden as Geary came up, "oh, get on to his new store clothes, will you?" They both pretended to be overwhelmed by the elegance of Geary's new suit.

"O-oh!" cried young Haight. "The bloody, bloomin', bloated swell. Just let me *touch* them!"

Vandover shaded his eyes and turned away as though dazzled. "This is *too* much," he gasped. "Such magnificence, such purple and fine linen." Then suddenly he shouted, "Oh, *oh! look* at the crease in those trousers. No; it's too much, I can't stand it."

"Oh, shut up," said Geary, irritated, as they had intended he should be. "Yes," he went on, "I thought I'd blow myself. I've been working like a dog the whole month. I'm trying to get in Beale's office. Beale and Storey, you know. I got the promise of a berth last week, so I thought I'd blow myself for some rags. I've been over to San Rafael all day visiting my cousins; had a great time; went out to row. Oh, and had a great feed: lettuce sandwiches with mayonnaise. Simply out of sight. I came back on the four o'clock boat and held down the 'line' on Kearney Street for an hour or two."

"Yes?" young Haight said perfunctorily, adding after a moment, "Isn't this a gay crowd, a typical San Francisco crowd and——"

"I had a cocktail in the Imperial at about quarter of five," said Geary, "and got a cigar at the Elite; then I went around to get my clothes. Oh, you ought to have heard the blowing up I gave my tailor! I let him have it right straight."

Geary paused a moment, and Vandover said: "Come on, let's walk around a little; don't you want to? We might run on to the red hat again."

"I told him," continued Geary without moving, "that if he wanted to do any more work for me, he'd have to get in front of himself in a hurry, and that *I* wasn't full of bubbles, if *he* was. 'Why,' says he, ' why, Mr. Geary, I've never had a customer talk like this to me before since I've been in the business!' 'Well, Mr. Allen,' says I, 'it's time you *had*!' Oh, sure, I gave it to him straight."

"Vandover has gone daft over a girl in a red hat," said

young Haight, as they got up and began to walk. "Have you noticed her up here?"

"I went to the Grillroom after I left the tailor's," continued Geary, "and had supper downtown. Ah, you ought to have seen the steak they gave me! Just about as thick as it was wide. I gave the slavey a four-bit tip. Oh, it's just as well, you know, to keep in with them, if you go there often. I lunch there four or five times a week."

They descended to the ground floor and promenaded the central aisle watching for pretty girls. In front of a candy-counter, where there was a soda fountain, they saw the red hat again. Vandover looked her squarely in the face and laughed a little. When he had passed he looked back; the girl caught his eye and turned away with a droll smile. Vandover paused, grinning, and raising his hat; "I guess that's mine," he said.

"You are not going, are you?" exclaimed young Haight, as Vandover stopped. "Oh, for goodness' sake, Van, do leave the girls alone for one hour in the day. Come on! Come on downtown with us."

"No, no," answered Vandover. "I'm going to chase it up. Good-bye. I may see you fellows later," and he turned back and went up to the girl.

"Look at that!" said young Haight, exasperated. "He knows he's liable to meet his acquaintances here, and yet there he goes, almost arm in arm with a girl like that. It's too bad; why *can't* a fellow keep straight when there are such a lot of *nice* girls?"

Geary never liked to see anything done better than he could do it himself. Just now he was vexed because Vandover had got in ahead of him. He looked after the girl a moment and muttered scornfully:

"Cheap meat!" adding, "Ah, you bet *I* wouldn't do that. I flatter myself that I'm a little too clever to cut my own throat in that fashion. I look out after my interests better than that. Well, Dolly," he concluded, "*I've* got a thirst on. Van and Ellis have gone off with their girls; let's you and I go somewhere and have something wet."

"All right. What's the matter with the Luxembourg?" answered young Haight.

"Luxembourg goes, then," assented Geary, and they turned about and started for the door. As they were passing out some one came running up behind them and took an arm of each: it was Vandover.

"Hello," cried Geary, delighted, "your girl shook you, didn't she?"

"Not a bit of it," answered Vandover. "Oh, but say, she is out of sight! Says her name is Grace Irving. No, she didn't shake me. I made a date with her for next Wednesday night. I didn't want to be seen around here with her, you know."

"Of *course* she will keep that date!" said Geary.

"Well, now, I think she will," protested Vandover.

"Well, come along," interrupted young Haight. "We'll all go down to the Luxembourg and have something cold and wet."

"Ah, make it the Imperial instead," objected Vandover. "We may find Flossie."

"Say," cried Geary, "can't you *live* without trailing around after some kind of petticoats?"

"You're right," admitted Vandover, "I can't," but he persuaded them to go to the Imperial for all that.

At the Imperial, Toby, the red-eyed waiter, came to take their order.

"Good evening, gentlemen," he said. "Haven't seen you around here for some time."

"No, no," said Geary. "I've been too busy. I've been working like a dog lately to get into a certain office. You bet I'll make it all right—all right. Bring me a stringy rabbit and a pint of dog's-head."

"You bet I've been working," he continued after they had settled down to their beer and rabbits, "working like a dog. A man's got to rustle if he's going to make a success at law. *I'm* going to make it go, by George, or I'll know the reason why. I'll make my way in this town and my pile. There's money to be made here and *I* might just as well make it as the next man. Every man for himself, that's what *I* say; that's the way to get along. It may be selfish, but you've got to do it. By God! it's human nature. Isn't that right, hey? Isn't that right?"

"Oh, that's right," admitted young Haight, trying to be

polite. After this the conversation lagged a little. Young Haight drank his Apollinaris lemonade through a straw, Geary sipped his ale, and Vandover fed himself Welsh rabbit and Spanish olives with the silent enjoyment of a glutton. By and by, when they had finished and had lighted their cigars and cigarettes, they began to talk about the last Cotillon, to which Vandover and Haight belonged.

"Say, Van," said young Haight, tilting his head to one side and shutting one eye to avoid the smoke from his cigar, "say, didn't I see you dancing with Mrs. Doane after supper?"

"Yes," said Vandover laughing; "all the men were trying to get a dance with her. She had an edge on."

"No?" exclaimed Geary, incredulously.

"That's a fact," admitted young Haight. "Van is right."

"She was opposite to me at table," said Vandover, "and *I* saw her empty a whole bottle of champagne."

"Why, I didn't know they got drunk like that at the Cotillons," said Geary. "I thought they were very swell."

"Well, of course, they don't as a rule," returned Vandover. "Of course there are girls like—like Henrietta Vance who belong to the Cotillon and make it what it is, and what it ought to be. But there are other girls like Mrs. Doane and Lilly Stannard and the Trafford girls that like their champagne pretty well now, and don't you forget it! Oh, you know, I wouldn't call it getting drunk, though."

"Well, why not?" exclaimed young Haight impatiently. "Why not call it 'getting drunk?' Why not call things by their right name? You can see just how bad they are then; and I think it's shameful that such things can go on in an organization that is supposed to contain the very best people in the city. Now, I just want to tell you what I saw at one of these same Cotillons in the first part of the season. Lilly Stannard disappeared after supper and people said she was sick and was going home, but I knew exactly what was the matter, because I had seen her at the supper table. Well, I had gone outside on the steps to get a mouthful of smoke, and my little cousin, Hetty, who has just come out and who is only nineteen, was out there with me because it was so warm inside, and *she* had seen Lilly Stannard filling up with champagne at supper, and didn't know what to make of it. Well, we were just talking about it, and I was trying to make her believe too that Lilly Stannard was sick, when here comes Lilly herself out to her carriage. Her maid was supporting her, just about half-carrying her. Lilly's face was so pale that the powder on it looked like ashes, her hair was all coming down, and she was hiccoughing. Now," continued young Haight, his eyes snapping, and his voice raised so as to make itself heard above the exclamations of his two friends, "now, that's a *fact*; I give you my word of honour that it actually happened. It's not hearsay; I saw it myself. It's fine, isn't it?" he went on, wrathfully. "It sounds well, don't it, when it's told *just as it happened*? The girl was dead drunk. Oh, she may have made a mistake; it may have been the first time; but the fact remains that she always drinks a lot of champagne at the Cotillons, and other girls have been drunk there, too. Mrs. Doane, that Van tells about, was *drunk*; that's the word for it. She was dead drunk that night, and there was my little cousin, Hetty, who had never seen even a man the worse for his liquor, standing there and taking it all in. Of course, every one hushed the thing up or else said the poor girl was sick; but Hetty knew, and what effect do you suppose it had upon a little girl like that, who had always been told what nice, irreproachable people went to the Cotillons? Hetty will never be the same little girl now that she was before. Oh, it makes me damned tired."

"Well, I don't see," said Geary, " why the girls should make such a fuss about the men keeping straight. I daresay now that this Stannard girl would cut us all dead if she knew how drunk we were that night about four months ago—that night that you fellows got thrown out of the Luxembourg."

"No, I don't believe she would at all," said young Haight.

"She'd think better of you for it," put in Vandover. "Look here," he went on, "all this talk of women demanding the same moral standard for men as men do for women is fine on paper, but how does it work in real life? The women don't demand it at all. Take the average society girl in a big city like this. The girls that we meet at teas and receptions and functions—don't you suppose they know the life we men lead? Of course they do. They may not know it in detail, but they know in a general way that we get drunk a good deal and go to disreputable houses and that sort of thing, and do they ever cut us for that? No, sir; not much. Why, I tell you, they even have a little more respect for us. They like a man to know things, to be experienced. A man that keeps himself straight and clean and never goes around with fast women, they think is ridiculous. Of course, a girl don't want to know the particulars of a man's vice; what they want is that a man should have the knowledge of good and evil, yes, and lots of evil. To a large extent I really believe it's the women's fault that the men are what they are. If they demanded a higher moral standard the men would come up to it; they encourage a man to go to the devil and then—and then when he's rotten with disease and ruins his wife and has children—what is it—'spotted toads'—then there's a great cry raised against the men, and women write books and all, when half the time the woman has only encouraged him to be what he is."

"Oh, well now," retorted young Haight, "you know that all the girls are not like that."

"Most of them that you meet in society are."

"But they are the best people, aren't they?" demanded Geary.

"No," answered Vandover and young Haight in a breath, and young Haight continued:

"No; I believe that very few of what you would call the 'best people' go out in society—people like the Ravises, who have good principles, and keep up old-fashioned virtues and all that. You know," he added, "they have family prayers down there every morning after breakfast."

Geary began to smile.

"Well, now, I don't care," retorted young Haight, "I like that sort of thing."

"So do I," said Vandover. "Up home, now, the governor asks a blessing at each meal, and somehow I wouldn't like to see him leave it off. But you can't tell me," he went on, going back to the original subject of their discussion, "you can't tell me that American society girls, city-bred, and living at the end of the nineteenth century, don't know about things. Why, man alive, how can they help but know? Look at those that have brothers—don't you suppose they know, and if they know, why don't they use their influence to stop it? I tell you if any one were to write up the lives that we

young men of the city lead after dark, people wouldn't believe it. At that party that Henrietta Vance gave last month
there were about twenty fellows there and I knew every one,
and I was looking around the supper-table and wondering
how many of those young fellows had never been inside of a
disreputable house, and there was only *one* beside Dolly
Haight!"

Young Haight exclaimed at this, laughing good-naturedly,
twirling his thumbs, and casting down his eyes with mock-
modesty.

"Well, that's the truth just the same," Vandover went on.
"We young men of the cities are a fine lot. I'm not doing the
baby act. I'm not laying the blame on the girls altogether, but
I say that in a measure the girls are responsible. They want a
man to be a *man*, to be up to date, to be a man of the world
and to go in for that sort of vice, but they don't know, they
don't dream, how rotten and disgusting it is. Oh, I'm not
preaching. I know I'm just as bad as the rest, and I'm going
to have a good time while I can, but sometimes when you
stop and think, and as Dolly says 'call things by their right
names,' why you feel, don't you know— *queer*."

"I don't believe, Van," responded young Haight, "that it's
quite as bad as you say. But it's even wrong, I think, that a
good girl should know anything about vice at all."

"Oh, that's nonsense," broke in Geary; "you can't expect
nowadays that a girl, an American girl, can live twenty years
in a city and not know things. Do you think the average modern girl is going to be the absolutely pure and innocent girl
of, say, fifty years ago? Not much; they are right on to things
to-day. You can't tell them much. And it's all right, too; they
know how to look out for themselves, then. It's part of their
education; and I think if they haven't the knowledge of evil,
and don't know what sort of life the average young man
leads, that their mothers ought to tell them."

"Well, I don't agree with you," retorted young Haight.
"There's something revolting in the idea that it's necessary a
young girl should be instructed in that sort of nastiness."

"Why, not at all," answered Geary. "Without it she might
be ruined by the first man that came along. It's a protection
to her virtue."

"Oh, pshaw! I don't believe it at all," cried young Haight, impatiently. "I believe that a girl is born with a natural intuitive purity that will lead her to protect her virtue just as instinctively as she would dodge a blow; if she wants to go wrong she will have to make an effort herself to overcome that instinct."

"And if she don't," cried Vandover eagerly, "if she don't— if she don't protect her virtue, I say a man has a right to go as far with her as he can."

"If *he* don't, some one else will," said Geary.

"Ah, you can't get around it that way," answered young Haight, smiling. "It's a man's duty to protect a girl, even if he has to protect her against herself."

When he got home that night Vandover thought over this remark of young Haight's and in its light reviewed what had occurred in the room at the Imperial. He felt aroused, nervous, miserably anxious. At length he tried to dismiss the subject from his mind; he woke up his drowsing grate fire, punching it with the poker, talking to it, saying, "Wake up there, you!" When he was undressed, he sat down before it in his bathrobe, absorbing its heat luxuriously, musing into the coals, scratching himself as was his custom. But for all that he fretted nervously and did not sleep well that night.

Next morning he took his bath. Vandover enjoyed his bath and usually spent two or three hours over it. When the water was very warm he got into it with his novel on a rack in front of him and a box of chocolates conveniently near. Here he stayed, for over an hour, eating and reading, and occasionally smoking a cigarette, until at length the enervating heat of the steam gradually overcame him and he dropped off to sleep.

On this particular morning between nine and ten Geary called, and as was his custom came right up to Vandover's room. Mr. Corkle, lying on the wolfskin in the bay window, jumped up with a gruff bark, but, recognizing him, came up wiggling his short tail. Geary saw Vandover's clothes thrown about the floor and the closed door of the bathroom.

"Hey, Van!" he called. "It's Charlie Geary. Are you taking a bath?"

"Hello! What? Who is it?" came from behind the door. "Oh, is that you, Charlie? Hello! how are you? Yes, I'm taking a bath. I must have been asleep. Wait a minute; I'll be out."

"No, I can't stop," answered Geary. "I've an appointment downtown; overslept myself, and had to go without my breakfast; makes me feel all broke up. I'll get something at the Grillroom about eleven; a steak, I guess. But that isn't what I came to say. Ida Wade has killed herself! Isn't it fearful? I thought I'd drop in on my way downtown and speak to you about it. It's dreadful! It's all in the morning papers. She must have been out of her head."

"What is it—what has she done?" came back Vandover's voice. "Papers—I haven't seen—what has she done? Tell me—what has she done?"

"Why, she committed suicide last night by taking laudanum," answered Geary, "and nobody knows why. She didn't leave any message or letter or anything of the kind. It's a fearful thing to happen so suddenly, but it seems she has been very despondent and broke up about something or other for a week or two. They found her in her room last night about ten o'clock lying across her table with only her wrapper on. She was unconscious then, and between one and two she died. She was unconscious all the time. Well, I can't stop any longer, Van; I've an appointment downtown. I was just going past the house and I thought I would run up and speak to you about Ida. I'll see you again pretty soon and we'll talk this over."

Mr. Corkle politely attended Geary to the head of the stairs, then went back to Vandover's room, and after blowing under the crack of the bathroom door to see if his master was still there returned to the wolfskin and sat down on his short tail and yawned. He was impatient to see Vandover and thought he stayed in his bath an unnecessarily long time. He went up to the door again and listened. It was very still inside; he could not hear the slightest sound, and he wondered again what could keep Vandover in there so long. He had too much self-respect to whine, so he went back to the wolfskin and curled up in the sun, but did not go to sleep.

By and by, after a very long time, the bathroom door swung open, and Vandover came out. He had not dried himself and was naked and wet. He went directly to the table in the centre of the room and picked up the morning paper, looking for the article of which Geary had spoken. At first he could not find it, and then it suddenly jumped into prominence from out the gray blur of the print on an inside page beside an advertisement of a charity concert for the benefit of a home for incurable children. There was a picture of Ida taken from a photograph like one that she had given him, and which even then was thrust between the frame and glass of his mirror. He read the article through; it sketched her life and character and the circumstances of her death with the relentless terseness of the writer cramped for space. According to this view, the causes of her death were unknown. It had been remarked that she had of late been despondent and in ill health.

Vandover threw the paper down and straightened up, naked and dripping, putting both hands to his head. In a low voice under his breath he said:

"What have I done? What have I done now?"

Like the sudden unrolling of a great scroll he saw his responsibility for her death and for the ruin of that something in her which was more than life. What would become of her now? And what would become of him? For a single brief instant he tried to persuade himself that Ida had consented after all. But he knew that this was not so. She had consented, but he had forced her consent; he was none the less guilty. And then in that dreadful moment when he saw things in their true light, all the screens of conventionality and sophistry torn away, the words that young Haight had spoken came back to him. No matter if she had consented, it was his duty to have protected her, even against herself.

He walked the floor with great strides, steaming with the warm water, striking his head with his hands and crying out, "Oh, this is fearful, fearful! What have I done now? I have killed her; yes, and worse!"

He could think of nothing worse that could have happened to him. What a weight of responsibility to carry—he who hated responsibility of any kind, who had always tried to

escape from anything that was even irksome, who loved his
ease, his comfort, his peace of mind!

At every moment now he saw the different consequences
of what he had done. Now, it was that his life was ruined,
and that all through its course this crime would hang like a
millstone about his neck. There could be no more enjoyment
of anything for him; all the little pleasures and little self-in-
dulgences which till now had delighted him were spoiled and
rendered impossible. The rest of his life would have to be one
long penitence; any pleasure he might take would only make
his crime seem more abominable.

Now, it was a furious revolt against his mistake that had
led him to such a fearful misunderstanding of Ida; a silent
impotent rage against himself and against the brute in him
that he had permitted to drag him to this thing.

Now, it was a wave of an immense pity for the dead girl
that overcame him, and he saw himself as another person,
destroying what she most cherished for the sake of gratifying
an unclean passion.

Now, it was a terror for himself. What would they do to
him? His part in the affair was sure to be found out. He tried
to think what the punishment for such crime would be; but
would he not be considered a murderer as well? Could he not
hang for this? His imagination was never more active; his fear
never more keen. At once a thousand plans of concealment or
escape were tossed up in his mind.

But worse than all was the thought of that punishment
from which there was absolutely no escape, and of that
strange other place where his crime would assume right proportions and receive right judgment, no matter how it was
palliated or evaded here. Then for an instant it was as if a gulf
without bottom had opened under him, and he had to fight
himself back from its edge for sheer self-preservation. To look
too long in that direction was simple insanity beyond any
doubt.

And all this time he threw himself to and fro in his room,
his long white arms agitated and shaking, his wet and shining
hair streaming far over his face, and the sparse long fell upon
his legs and ankles, all straight and trickling with moisture.
At times an immense unreasoning terror would come upon

him all of a sudden, horrible, crushing, so that he rolled upon the bed groaning and sobbing, digging his nails into his scalp, shutting his teeth against a desire to scream out, writhing in the throes of terrible mental agony.

That day and the next were fearful. To Vandover everything in his world was changed. All that had happened before the morning of Geary's visit appeared to him to have occurred in another phase of his life, years and years ago. He lay awake all night long, listening to the creaking of the house and the drip of the water faucets. He turned from his food with repugnance, told his father that he was sick, and kept indoors as much as he could, reading all the papers to see if he had been found out. To his great surprise and relief, a theory gained ground that Ida was subject to spells of ill-health, to long fits of despondency, and that her suicide had occurred during one of these. If Ida's family knew anything of the truth, it was apparent that they were doing their best to cover up their disgrace. Vandover was too thoroughly terrified for his own safety to feel humiliated at this possible explanation of his security. There was as yet not even a guess that implicated him.

He thought that he was bearing up under the strain well enough, but on the evening of the second day, as he was pretending to eat his supper, his father sent the servant out and turning to him, said kindly:

"What is it, Van? Aren't you well nowadays?"

"Not very, sir," answered Vandover. "My throat is troubling me again."

"You look deathly pale," returned his father. "Your eyes are sunken and you don't eat."

"Yes, I know," said Vandover. "I'm not feeling well at all. I think I'll go to bed early to-night. I don't know"—he continued, after a pause, feeling a desire to escape from his father's observation—"I don't know but what I'll go up now. Will you tell the cook to feed Mr. Corkle for me?"

His father looked at him as he pushed back from the table.

"What's the matter, Van?" he said. "Is there anything wrong?"

"Oh, I'll be all right in the morning," he replied nervously. "I feel a little under the weather just now."

"Don't you think you had better tell me what the trouble is?" said his father, kindly.

"There *isn't* any trouble, sir," insisted Vandover. "I just feel a little under the weather."

But as he was starting to undress in his room a sudden impulse took possession of him, an overwhelming childish desire to tell his father all about it. It was beginning to be more than he was able to bear alone. He did not allow himself to stop and reason with this impulse, but slipped on his vest again and went downstairs. He found his father in the smoking-room, sitting unoccupied in the huge leather chair before the fireplace.

As Vandover came in the Old Gentleman rose and without a word, as if he had been expecting him, went to the door and shut and locked it. He came back and stood before the fireplace watching Vandover as he approached and took the chair he had just vacated. Vandover told him of the affair in two or three phrases, without choosing his words, repeating the same expressions over and over again, moved only with the desire to have it over and done with.

It was like a burst of thunder. The worst his father had feared was not as bad as this. He had expected some rather serious boyish trouble, but this was the crime of a man. Still watching his son, he put out his hand, groping for the edge of the mantelpiece, and took hold of it with a firm grasp. For a moment he said nothing; then:

"And—and you say you seduced her."

Without looking up, Vandover answered, "Yes, sir," and then he added, "It is horrible; when I think of it I sometimes feel as though I should go off my head. I——"

But the Old Gentleman interrupted him, putting out his hand:

"Don't," he said quickly, "don't say anything now—please."

They were both silent for a long time, Vandover gazing stupidly at a little blue and red vase on the table, wondering how his father would take the news, what next he would say; the Old Gentleman drawing his breath short, occasionally clearing his throat, his eyes wandering vaguely about the walls of the room, his fingers dancing upon the edge of the mantelpiece. Then at last he put his hand to his neck as though loosening his collar and said, looking away from Vandover:

"Won't you—won't you please go out—go away for a little while—leave me alone for a little while."

When Vandover closed the door, he shut the edge of a rug between it and the sill; as he reopened it to push the rug out of the way he saw his father sink into the chair and, resting his arm upon the table, bow his head upon it.

He did not see his father again that night, and at breakfast next morning not a word was exchanged between them, but his father did not go downtown to his office that forenoon, as was his custom. Vandover went up to his room immediately after breakfast and sat down before the window that overlooked the little garden in the rear of the house.

He was utterly miserable, his nerves were gone, and at times he would feel again a touch of that hysterical, unreasoning terror that had come upon him so suddenly the other morning.

Now there was a new trouble: the blow he had given his father. He could see that the Old Gentleman was crushed under it, and that he had never imagined that his son could have been so base as this. Vandover wondered what he was going to do. It would seem as if he had destroyed all of his father's affection for him, and he trembled lest the Old Gentleman should cast him off, everything. Even if his father did not disown him, he did not see how they could ever be the same. They might go on living together in the same house, but as far apart from each other as strangers. This, however, did not seem natural; it was much more likely that his father would send him away, anywhere out of his sight, forwarding, perhaps through his lawyer or agents, enough money to keep him alive. The more Vandover thought of this, the more he became convinced that such would be his father's decision. The Old Gentleman had spent the night over it, time enough to make up his mind, and the fact that he had neither spoken to him nor looked at him that morning was only an indication of what Vandover was to expect. He fancied he knew his father well enough to foresee how this decision would be carried out, not with any imprecations or bursts of rage, but calmly, sadly, inevitably.

Toward noon his father came into the room, and Vandover turned to face him and to hear what he had to say as best he could. He knew he should not break down under it, for he felt as though his misery had reached its limit, and that nothing could touch or affect him much now.

His father had a decanter of port in one hand and a glass in the other; he filled the glass and held it toward Vandover, saying gently:

"I think you had better take some of this: you've hardly eaten anything in three days. Do you feel pretty bad, Van?"

Vandover put the glass down and got upon his feet. All at once a great sob shook him.

"Oh, governor!" he cried.

It was as if it had been a mother or a dear sister. The prodigal son put his arms about his father's neck for the first time since he had been a little boy, and clung to him and wept as though his heart were breaking.

Chapter Eight

WE WILL BEGIN all over again, Van," his father said later that same day. "We will start in again and try to forget all this, not as much as we *can*, but as much as we *ought*, and live it down, and from now on we'll try to do the thing that is right and brave and good."

"Just try me, sir!" cried Vandover.

That was it, begin all over again. He had never seen more clearly than now that other life which it was possible for him to live, a life that was above the level of self-indulgence and animal pleasures, a life that was not made up of the society of lost women or fast girls, but yet a life of keen enjoyment.

Whenever he had been deeply moved about anything, the power and desire of art had grown big within him, and he turned to it now, instinctively and ardently.

It was all the better half of him that was aroused—the better half that he had kept in check ever since his college days, the better half that could respond to the influences of his father and of Turner Ravis, that other Vandover whom he felt was his real self, Vandover the true man, Vandover the artist, not Vandover the easy-going, the self-indulgent, not Vandover the lover of women.

From this time forward he was resolved to give up the world that he had hitherto known, and devote himself with all his strength to his art. In the first glow of that resolution he thought that he had never been happier; he wondered how he could have been blind so long; what was all that life worth compared with the life of a great artist, compared even with a life of sturdy, virile effort and patient labour even though barren of achievement?

And then something very curious happened: The little picture of Turner Ravis that hung over his mantelpiece caught his glance, looking out at him with her honest eyes and sweet smile. In an instant he seemed to love her as he had never imagined he could love any one. All that was best in him went out toward her in a wave of immense tenderness; the tears came to his eyes, he could not tell why. Ah, he was not good enough for her now, but he would love her so well that he would grow better, and between her and his good father and his art, the better Vandover, the real Vandover, would grow so large and strong within him that there should be no room for the other Vandover, the Vandover of Flossie and of the Imperial, the Vandover of the brute.

During the course of talk that day between himself and his father, it was decided that Vandover should go away for a little while. He was in a fair way to be sick from worry and nervous exhaustion, and a sea trip to San Diego and back seemed to be what he stood most in need of. Besides this, his father told him, it was inevitable that his share in Ida's death would soon be known; in any case it would be better for him to be away from the city.

"You take whatever steamer sails next," said his father, "and go down to Coronado and stay there as long as you like, three weeks anyway; stay there until you get well, and when you get back, Van, we'll have a talk about Paris again. Perhaps you would like to get away this winter, maybe as soon as next month. You think it over while you are away, and when you want to go, why, we'll go over together, Van. What do you think? Would you like to have your old governor along for a little while?"

The *Santa Rosa* cast off the company's docks the next day about noon in the midst of a thick, cold mist that was half rain. The Old Gentleman came to see Vandover off.

The steamer, which seemed gigantic, was roped and cabled to the piers, feeling the water occasionally with her screw to keep the hawsers taut. About the forward gangway a band of overworked stevedores were stowing in the last of the cargo, aided by a donkey engine, which every now and then broke out into a spasm of sputtering coughs. At the passenger gangway a great crowd was gathered, laughing and exchanging remarks with the other crowd that leaned over the railings of the decks.

There was a smell of pitch and bilge in the air mingled with the reek of hot oil from the engines. About twelve o'clock an odour of cooking arose, and the steward went about the decks drumming upon a snoring gong for dinner.

Half an hour later the great whistle roared interminably,

drowning out the chorus of "good-byes" that rose on all sides. Long before it had ceased, the huge bulk had stirred, almost imperceptibly at first, then, gathering headway, swung out into the stream and headed for the Golden Gate.

Vandover was in the stern upon the hurricane deck, shaking his hat toward his father, who had tied his handkerchief to his cane and was waving it at him as he stood upon an empty packing-case. As the throng of those who were left behind dwindled away, one by one, Vandover could see him standing there, almost the last of all, and long after the figure itself was lost in the blur of the background he still saw the tiny white dot of the handkerchief moving back and forth, as if spelling out a signal to him across the water.

The fog drew a little higher as they passed down the bay. To the left was the city swarming upon its hills, a dull gray mass, cut in parallel furrows by the streets; straggling and uneven where it approached the sand-dunes in the direction of the Presidio. To the right the long slope of Tamalpais climbed up and was lost in the fog, while directly in front of them was the Golden Gate, a bleak prospect of fog-drenched headlands on either side of a narrow strip of yellow, frothy water. Beyond that, the open Pacific.

A brisk cannonade was going on from the Presidio and from Black Point, and both forts were hidden behind a great curtain of tumbling white smoke that rolled up to mingle with the fog. Everybody was on that side of the deck watching and making guesses as to the reason of it. It was perhaps target practice. Ah, it was a good thing that the steamer was not in line with the target. Perhaps, though, that was the safest place to be. Some one told about a derelict that was anchored as a target off the heads, and shot at for fifteen hours without being touched once. Oh, they were great gunners at the Presidio! But just the same the sound of cannon was a fine thing to hear; it excited one. A noisy party of gentlemen already installed in the smoking-room came out on deck for a moment with their cards in their hands, and declared laughingly that the whole thing was only a salute in the *Santa Rosa's* honour.

By the middle of the afternoon, Vandover began to see that for him the trip was going to be tedious. He knew no one on board and had come away so hurriedly that he had neglected to get himself any interesting books. He spent an hour or two promenading the upper deck until the cold wind that was blowing drove him to the smoking-room, where he tried to interest himself in watching some of the whist games that were in progress.

It surprised him that he could find occasion to be bored so soon after what had happened; but he no longer wished to occupy his mind by brooding over anything so disagreeable and wanted some sort of amusement to divert and entertain him. Vandover had so accustomed himself to that kind of self-indulgence that he could not go long without it. It had become a simple necessity for him to be amused, and just now he thought himself justified in seeking it in order to forget about Ida's death. He had dwelt upon this now for nearly four days, until it had come to be some sort of a formless horror that it was necessary to avoid. He could get little present enjoyment by looking forward to the new life that he was going to begin and in which his father, his art, and Turner Ravis were to be the chief influences. The thought of this prospect did give him pleasure, but he had for so long a time fed his mind upon the more tangible and concrete enjoyments of the hour and minute that it demanded them now continually.

He sat for a long time upon the slippery leather cushions of the smoking-room trying desperately to become interested in the whist game, or gazing awestruck at the man at his elbow who was smoking black Perrique in a pipe, inhaling the smoke and blowing it out through his nose. After a while he returned to the deck.

There it was cold and wet and a strong wind was blowing from the ocean. Four miles to the east an endless procession of brown, bare hills filed slowly past under the fog. The sky was a dreary brown and the leagues of shifting water a melancholy desert of gray. Besides these there was nothing but the bleached hills and the drifting fog; the wind blew continually, passing between the immense reaches of sea and sky with prolonged sighs of infinite sadness.

Three seagulls followed the vessel, now in a long line, now abreast, and now in a triangle. They sailed slowly about, dipping and rising in the vast hollows between the waves, turning their heads constantly from side to side.

Vandover went to the stern and for a time found amusement in watching the indicator of the patent log, and listening for its bell. But his interest in this was soon exhausted, and he returned to the smoking-room again, reflecting that this was only the first afternoon and that there still remained two days that somehow had to be gone through with.

About five o'clock, as he was on his way to get a glass of seltzer, he saw Grace Irving, the girl of the red hat whom he had met at the Mechanics' Fair, sitting on a camp-stool just inside of her stateroom eating a banana. The sight of her startled him out of all composure for the minute. His first impulse was to speak to her, but he reflected that he was done with all that now and that it was better for him to pass on as though he had not seen her, but as he came in front of her she looked up quickly and nodded to him very pleasantly in such a way that it was evident she had already known he was on board. It was impossible for Vandover to ignore her, and though he did not stop, he looked back at her and smiled as he took off his hat.

He went down to supper in considerable agitation, marvelling at the coincidence that had brought them together again. He wondered, too, how she could be so pleasant to him now, for as a matter of course he had not kept the engagement he had made with her at the Fair. At the same time, he felt that she must think him a great fool not to have stopped and spoken to her; either he should have done that or else have ignored her little bow entirely. He was firmly resolved to have nothing to do with her, yet it chafed him to feel that she thought him diffident. It seemed now as though he owed it to himself to speak to her if only for a minute and make some sort of an excuse. By the time he had finished his supper, he had made up his mind to do this, and then to avoid her for the rest of the trip.

As he was leaving the dining saloon he met her coming down the stairs alone, dressed very prettily in a checked travelling ulster with a gray velvet collar, and a little fore and aft cap to match. He stopped her and made his excuses; she did not say much in reply and seemed a little offended, so that

Vandover could not refrain from adding that he was very glad to see her on board.

"Ah, you don't seem as if you were, very," she said, putting out her chin at him prettily and passing on. It was an awkward and embarrassing little scene and Vandover was glad that it was over. But the thing had been done now, he had managed to show the girl that he did not wish to keep up the acquaintance begun at the Fair, and from now on she would keep out of his way.

He took a few turns on the upper deck, smoking his pipe, walking about fast, while his dinner digested. The sun went down behind the black horizon in an immense blood-red nebula of mist, the sea turned from gray to dull green and then to a lifeless brown, and the *Santa Rosa's* lights began to glow at her quarters and at her masthead; in her stern the screw drummed and threshed monotonously, a puff of warm air reeking with the smell of hot oil came from the engine hatch, and in an instant Vandover saw again the curved roof of the immense iron-vaulted depot, the passengers on the platform staring curiously at the group around the invalid's chair, the repair gang in spotted blue overalls, and the huge white cat dozing on an empty baggage truck.

The wind freshened and he returned to the smoking-room to get warm. The same game of whist was going on, and the man with the Perrique tobacco had filled another pipe and continued to blow the smoke through his nose.

After a while Vandover went back to the main deck and wandered aft, where he stood a long time looking over the stern, interested in watching the receding water. It was dark by this time, the wind had increased and had blown the fog to landward, and the ocean had changed to a deep blue, the blue of the sky at night; here and there a wave broke, leaving a line of white on the sea like the trail of a falling star across the heavens, while the white haze of the steamer's wake wandered vaguely across the intense blue like the milky way across the zenith.

Vandover was horribly bored. There seemed to be absolutely nothing to amuse him, unless, indeed, he should decide to renew his acquaintance with Grace Irving. But this was out of the question now, for he knew what it would lead to. Even if he should yield to the temptation, he did not see how he could take any great pleasure in that sort of thing again, after what had happened.

Of all the consequences of what he had done, the one which had come to afflict him the most poignantly was that his enjoyment of life was spoiled. At first he had thought that he never could take pleasure in anything again so long as he should live, that his good times were gone. But as his pliable character rearranged itself to suit the new environment, he began to see that there would come a time when he would grow accustomed to Ida's death and when his grief would lose its sharpness. He had even commenced to look forward to this time and to long for it as a sort of respite and relief. He believed at first that it would not be for a great many years; but even so soon after the suicide as this, he saw with a little thrill of comfort that it would be but a matter of months. At the same time Vandover was surprised and even troubled at the ease with which he was recovering from the first shock. He wondered at himself, because he knew he had been sincere in his talk with his father. Vandover was not given to self-analysis, but now for a minute he was wondering if this reaction were due to his youth, his good health and his good spirits, or whether there was something wrong with him. However, he dismissed these thoughts with a shrug of his shoulders as though freeing himself from some disagreeable burden. Ah, he was no worse than the average; one could get accustomed to almost anything; it was only in the books that people had their lives ruined; and to brood over such things was unnatural and morbid. Ah! what a dreadful thing to become morbid! He could not bring Ida back, or mitigate what he had done, or be any more sorry for it by making himself miserable. Well, then! Only he would let that sort of thing alone after this, the lesson had been too terrible; he would try and enjoy himself again, only it should be in other ways.

Later in the evening, about nine o'clock, when nearly all the passengers were in bed, and Vandover was leaning over the side of the boat finishing his pipe before turning in himself, Grace Irving came out of her stateroom and sat down at a little distance from him, looking out over the water, humming a little song. She and Vandover were the only people to be seen on the deserted promenade.

Vandover saw her without moving, only closing his teeth tighter on his pipe. It was evident that Grace expected him to speak to her and had given him a chance for an admirable little tête-à-tête. For a moment Vandover's heart knocked at his throat; he drew his breath once or twice sharply through his nose. In an instant all the old evil instincts were back again, urging and clamouring never so strong, never so insistent. But Vandover set his face against them, honestly, recalling his resolution, telling himself that he was done with that life. As he had said, the lesson had been too terrible.

He turned about resolutely, and walked slowly away from her. The girl looked after him a moment, surprised, and then called out:

"Oh, Mr. Vandover!"

Vandover paused a moment, looking back.

"Where are you going?" she went on. "Didn't you see me here? Don't you want to come and talk to me?"

"No," answered Vandover, smiling good-humouredly, trying to be as polite as was possible. "No, I don't." Then he took a sudden resolution, and added gravely, "I don't want to have anything to do with you."

In his stateroom, as he sat on the edge of his berth winding his watch before going to bed, he thought over what he had said. "That was a mean way to talk to a girl," he told himself, "but," he added, "it's the only thing to do. I simply couldn't start in again after all that's happened. Oh, yes, that was the right thing to do!"

He felt a glow of self-respect for his firmness and his decision, a pride in the unexpected strength, the fine moral rigour that he had developed at the critical moment. He *could* turn sharp around when he wanted to, after all. Ah, yes, that was the only thing to do if one was to begin all over again and live down what had happened. He wished that the governor might know how well he had acted.

Chapter Nine

VANDOVER STAYED for two weeks at Coronado Beach and managed to pass the time very pleasantly. He was fortunate enough to find a party at the hotel whom he knew very well. In the morning they bathed or sailed on the bay, and in the afternoon rode out with a pack of greyhounds and coursed jack-rabbits on the lower end of the island. Vandover's good spirits began to come back to him, his appetite returned, his nerves steadied themselves, he slept eight hours every night. But for all that he did not think that things were the same with him. He said to himself that he was a changed man; that he was older, more serious.

During this time he received several letters from his father which he answered very promptly. In the course of their correspondence it was arranged that they should both leave for Europe on the twenty-fifth of that month, and that consequently, Vandover should return to the city not later than the fifteenth. Vandover was having such a good time, however, that he stayed over the regular steamer in order to go upon a moonlight picnic down on the beach. The next afternoon he took passage for San Francisco on a second-class boat.

This homeward passage turned out to be one long misery for Vandover. He had never been upon a second-class boat before and had never imagined that anything could be so horribly uncomfortable or disagreeable. The *Mazatlan* was overcrowded, improperly ballasted, and rolled continually. The table was bad, the accommodations inadequate, the passengers hopelessly uncongenial. Cold and foggy weather accompanied the boat continually. The same endless procession of bleached hills still filed past under the mist, going now in the opposite direction, and the same interminable game of whist was played in the smoking-room, only with greasier, second-class cards, amidst the acrid smoke of second-class tobacco. At supper, the first day out, a little Jew who sat next to Vandover, and who invariably wore a plush skull-cap with ear-laps, tried to sell him two flawed and yellow diamonds.

The evening after leaving Port Hartford the *Mazatlan* ran

into dirty weather. It was not stormy—simply rough, disagreeable, the wind and sea directly ahead. Half an hour after supper Vandover began to be sick. For a long time he sat on the slippery leather cushions in the nasty smoking-room, sucking limes, drinking seltzer, and trying to be interested in the card games. He dozed a little and awoke, feeling wretched, covered with a cold sweat, racked by a pain in the back of his head, and tortured by an abominable nausea. He groped his way out upon the swaying, gusty deck, descended to his cabin, and went to bed.

The *Mazatlan* had booked more passengers than could be accommodated, the steward being obliged to make up beds on the floor of the dining saloon and even upon some of the tables. Vandover had not been able to get a stateroom, and so had put up with a bunk in the common cabin at the stern of the vessel.

About two o'clock in the morning he woke up in this place frightfully sick at the stomach and wretched in body and mind. He had an upper bunk, and for a long time he lay on his back rolling about with the rolling of the steamer, vaguely staring straight above him at the roof of the cabin, hardly a hand's-breadth above his face. The roof was iron, painted with a white paint very thick and shiny, and was studded with innumerable bolt-heads and enormous nuts. By and by, for no particular reason, he rose on his elbow and, leaning over the side of his berth, looked about him.

The light streaming from two strong-smelling ship's lanterns showed the cabin, long and narrow. There were two cramped passageways, on either side of which the tiers of bunks, mere open racks filled with bedding, rose to the roof, those occupied by women hung with spotted turkey-red calico.

The cabin was two decks below the open air and every berth was occupied, the only ventilation being through the door. The air was foul with the stench of bilge, the reek of the untrimmed lamps, the exhalation of so many breaths, and the close, stale smell of warm bedding.

A vague murmur rose in the air, the sound of deep breathing, the moving of restless bodies between the coarse sheets, the momentary noise of the scratching of blunt finger-tips, a subdued cough, the moan of a sleeping child. All the while the shaft of the screw, seemingly close beneath the floor, pounded and rumbled without a moment's stop.

Immediately underneath Vandover two men, saloon-keepers, awoke and lit their cigars and began a long discussion on the question of license. Two or three bunks distant, a woman, a Salvation Army lassie, one of a large party of Salvationists who were on board, began to cough violently, choking for breath. Across the aisle the little Jew of the plush skull-cap with ear-laps snored monotonously in alternate keys, one a guttural bass, the other a rasping treble. The *Mazatlan* was rolling worse than ever, now up and down, now from side to side, and now with long forward lurches that combined the other two motions. During one of these latter the little Jew was half awakened. He stopped snoring, leaving an abrupt silence in the air. Then Vandover could hear him threshing about uneasily; still half asleep he began to mutter and swear: "Dat's it, r-roll; I woult if I were you; r-roll, dat's righd—dhere, soh—ah, geep it oop—r-roll, you damnt ole tub, yust *r-r-roll.*"

The continued pitching, the foul air, and the bitter smoke from the saloonkeepers' cigars became more than Vandover could stand. His stomach turned, at every instant he gagged and choked. He suddenly made up his mind that he could stand it no longer, and determined to go on deck, preferring to walk the night out rather than spend it in the cabin. He drew on his shoes without lacing them, and dressed himself hurriedly, omitting his collar and scarf; he put his hat on his tumbled hair, swung into his overcoat, and, wrapping his travelling-rug around him, started up toward the deck. On the stairs he was seized with such a nausea that he could hardly keep from vomiting where he stood, but he rushed out upon the lower deck, gaining the rail with a swimming head.

He sank back upon an iron capstan with a groan, weak and trembling, his eyes full of tears, a bursting feeling in his head. He was utterly miserable.

It was about half-past two in the morning, and a cold raw wind was whistling through the cordage and flinging the steamer's smoke down upon the decks and upon the water like a great veil of crêpe. A sickly half-light was spread out between the sea and the heavens. By its means he could barely distinguish great, livid blotches of fog or cloud whirling across the black sky, and the unnumbered multitude of white-topped waves rushing past, plunging and rising like a vast herd of black horses galloping on with shaking white manes. Low in the northeast horizon lay a long pale blur of light against which the bow of the steamer, inky black, rose and fell and heaved and sank incessantly. To the landward side and very near at hand, so near that he could hear the surf at their feet, the long procession of hills continually defiled, vague and formless masses between the sea and sky. The wind, the noise of the waves rushing past, the roll of the breakers and the groaning of the cordage all blended together and filled the air with a prolonged minor note, lamentable beyond words. The atmosphere was cold and damp, the spray flying like icy bullets. The sombre light that hung over the sea re-flected itself in long blurred streaks upon the wet decks and slippery iron rods. Here and there about the rigging a trem-ulous ball of orange haze showed where the ship's lanterns were swung. Directly under him in the stern the screw snarled incessantly in a vortex of boiling water that forever swirled away and was lost in the darkness. From time to time the indicator of the patent log, just beside him, rang its tiny bell.

Vandover drew his rug about him and went up to the main deck, dragging his shoelaces after him. The wind was stronger here, but he bent his head against it and went on toward the smoking-room, for the idea had occurred to him that he could shut himself in there and pass the rest of the night upon the cushions; anything was better than returning to the cabin downstairs.

The deck was jerked away from beneath his feet, and he was hurled forward, many times his own length, against a companionway, breaking his thumb as he fell. A second shock threw him down again as he rose; everything about him shook and danced like glassware upon a jarred table. Then the whole ship rose under his feet as no wave had ever lifted it, and fell again, not into yielding water, but upon something that drove through its sides as if they had been paper. A deaf-ening, crashing noise split the mournful howl of the wind, and far underneath him Vandover heard a rapid series of blows, a dreadful rumbling and pounding that thrilled and quivered through all the vessel's framework up to her very mast-tips. On all fours upon the deck, holding to a cleat with one hand, he braced himself, watching and listening, his senses all alive, his muscles tense. In the direction of the engine-room he heard the furious ringing of a bell. The screw stopped. The *Mazatlan* wallowed helplessly in the trough of the sea.

Vandover's very first impulse was a wild desire of saving himself; he had not the least thought for any one else. Every soul on board might drown, so only he should be saved. It was the primitive animal instinct, the blind adherence to the first great law, an impulse that in this first moment of excitement could not be resisted. He ran forward and snatched a life-preserver from the pile that was stored beneath the bridge.

As he was fastening it about him, the passengers began to pour out upon the deck, from their staterooms, from the companionways, and from the dining saloon. In an instant the deck was crowded. Men and women ran about in all directions, pushing and elbowing each other, calling shrilly over one another's heads. Near to Vandover a woman, clothed only in her night-dress, clung to the arm of a half-dressed man, crying again and again for a certain "August." She wrung her hands in her excitement; at times the man shouted "August!" in a quavering bass voice. "August, here we are over *here!*" "Oh, where *is* Gussie?" wailed the woman. "Here, here I am," another voice answered at length; "here I am, I'm all right." "Oh," exclaimed the woman with a sob of relief, "here's Gussie; now let's all keep together whatever happens."

All about the decks just such scenes were going on; most of the women wore only their night-gowns or dressing-gowns, their hair tumbling down and blowing about their cheeks, their bare feet slipping and sliding on the heaving wet decks. The men were in shirt and drawers, standing in the centre of their family groups, silent, excited, very watchful; others of them ran about searching for life-preservers, shouting hoarsely, talking to themselves, speaking all their thoughts aloud.

But there was no panic; there was excitement, confusion,

bewilderment, but no excess of fear, no unreasoning terror, deaf, blind, utterly reckless.

All at once a man parted the crowd with shoulders and elbows, passing along the deck with great strides. It was the captain. The next instant Vandover saw him on the bridge, hatless, without his vest or his coat, just as he had sprung from his berth. From time to time he shouted his orders, leaning over the rail, gesturing with his arm. The crew ran about, carrying out his directions, jostling the men out of the way, knocking over women and children, speaking to no one, intent only upon their work.

In a few moments the deck steward and one of the officers appeared amid the crowd of passengers. They were very calm, and at every instant shouted, "There is no danger; every one go back to his berth; clear the deck, please; no danger, gentlemen; everybody be quiet; go back to your berths!" The steward even came up to Vandover and pulled at the straps of his life-preserver, exclaiming, "Take this off! there is no danger; you're only exciting the other passengers. Come on, take it off and go back to your berth."

Vandover obeyed him, slowly loosening the buckles, looking around him, bewildered, but still holding the preserver in his hands.

Best of all, however, was the example of a huge old fellow wearing the cap and clothes of a boatswain's mate of a United States battleship; he seemed to dominate the excited throng in a moment, going about from group to group, quieting them all, spreading a feeling of confidence and courage throughout the whole ship. He was an inspiration to Vandover, who began to be ashamed of having yielded to the first selfish instinct of preservation.

Just as the boatswain's mate was offering his flask to the woman whom Vandover had heard calling for "August," the *Mazatlan* lurched heavily once or twice, and then slowly listed to the port side, going over farther and farther every instant. Vandover heard a renewed rumbling and smashing noise far beneath him, and in some way knew that the cargo was shifting. Instead of righting herself, the ship began to heave over more and more. The whole sea on the port side seemed to rise up to meet the rail; under Vandover's feet the incline of the deck grew steeper and steeper. All at once his excitement came back upon him with the sharpness of a blow, and he caught at the brass grating of a skylight exclaiming: "By God! we're going *over*." The women screamed with terror; one heard the men shouting, "Look out! hold on! catch hold there!" An old man, wearing only a gray flannel shirt, lost his footing; he fell, and rolled over and over down the deck stupidly, inertly, without making the slightest effort to save himself, without uttering the least cry; he brought up suddenly against the rail, with a great jar, the shock of his soft, withered body against the hard wood sounding like the sodden impact of a bundle of damp clothes. There was a cry; they thought him killed—Vandover had seen his head gashed against a sharp angle of iron—but he jumped up with sudden agility, clambering up the slope of the deck with the strength and rapidity of an acrobat.

There had been a great rush to the other side of the ship, a wild scrambling up the steep deck, over skylights and between masts and ventilators. People clung to anything, to cleats, to steamer chairs, to the brass railings, to the person who stood next to them. They no longer listened to the protestations of the brave boatswain's mate; that last long roll had terrified them. The sense of a great catastrophe began to spread and widen all about like the rising of some fearful invisible mist. "*What* had happened? What was to become of them?"

While Vandover clung to the starboard rail, rolling his eyes wildly, trying to control himself again, a young man, a waiter in the dining saloon, rushed up to him from out of the crowd, holding out his hand. "It's all up!" he shouted.

Vandover grasped his extended palm, shaking hands with him fervently, without knowing why. The two looked straight into each other's eyes, their hands gripped close; then the waiter turned away, and dropping on his knees began to pray silently to himself.

Vandover saw a great many others praying; there was even a large group gathered about the band of Salvationists trying to raise a hymn. Every now and then their voices could be heard, singing all out of tune, a medley of discords.

At one time Vandover caught sight of the little Jew of the

plush cap with the ear-laps; he was grovelling upon the deck, huddling a small black satchel to his breast; without a moment's pause he screamed, "God 'a' mercy! God 'a' mercy!"

The sight revolted Vandover and in a great measure helped to calm him. In a few moments he had himself in hand again, cool and self-collected, resolved not to act like a fool before the others, but to help them if he could.

Near to him a Salvation Army lassie was down upon her knees trying to cord up a huge bundle wrapped in sail-cloth. "Here," exclaimed Vandover coming up to her, "let me help. I'll tie this for you—you put *this* on." He took the wet, stiff ropes from between her fingers and held the life-preserver toward her; but she refused it.

"No," she cried enthusiastically, "I'm going to be saved anyhow; I ain't going to drown; Jesus is watching over me. Oh!" she suddenly exclaimed with a burst of fervor, "Jesus is going to save me. I *know* I'm going to be saved. I feel it, I feel it *here*," and she struck her palm on the breast of the man's red jersey she was wearing.

"Well, I wish *I* could have such a confidence," answered Vandover, sincerely envying the plain little woman under the ugly blue bonnet.

She seemed as if inspired, her face glowing. "Only *believe*; that's all," she told him. "It isn't too late for you now. Ah," she went on, smiling, "ah, you don't know what it is in a time like this! What a comfort! What a support! Oh, *look, look!*" she cried, breaking off and starting to her feet. "That man is going to jump!"

It was the boatswain's mate, the hero who had filled all the passengers with his own coolness and courage, who had been Vandover's inspiration. Some strange reaction seemed to have seized upon him. Of a sudden he rushed to the rail, the starboard rail that was heaved so high out of the water, stood upon it for a moment, and then with a great shout jumped over the side. His folly was as infectious as his courage. Four more men followed him, three going over all at the same time, and a fourth a little later, hanging an instant upon the outside of the rail, then dropping down feet first, disappearing with a great splash that made itself heard in the great silence that had suddenly fallen upon the throng.

Every one had seen what had happened; a thrill of fear and apprehension passed over them all like a cold breath. They were silent, struck dumb, feeling the presence of death close by.

Suddenly a long flash of yellow upon the bridge made a momentary streak on the darkness, and there was the report of a gun. A minute later it was fired again, and alternating with it the *Mazatlan's* whistle began to roar, like a hoarse shout for help. Between these sounds could be heard the renewed clamour upon the decks, the shouting, the screaming, and the rush of many feet; the little children clung about the knees of their mothers, shrieking and wailing monotonously, "Oh, ma*ma*—oh, ma*ma*!" rolling their eyes fearfully behind them.

But many of the children, even some of the older passengers, were absolutely silent, dazed, stupefied with terror and excitement, their eyes vague and distended, looking slowly about them, scarcely daring to move a limb.

Meanwhile the *Mazatlan* was settling forward, and already the spray was beginning to fly over the decks. Little by little the terror increased; people threw themselves down upon the deck, rising up again, their arms raised to heaven, praying aloud, screaming the same things over and over again. The Salvationists tried to raise another hymn, but the sound of their voices was drowned out by the tumult, the roaring of the whistle, the barking of the minute guns, the straining and snapping of the cordage, and the sound of waves drawing closer and closer. Prone upon the deck, his arms still clasped about his black satchel, the little Jew of the plush cap went into some kind of fit, his eyes rolled back, his teeth grinding upon each other. Vandover turned from him in disgust. Then he looked around and above him, drawing a long breath, saying aloud to himself:

"It looks as though it were the end—well!"

All at once Vandover knew that the water had reached the boilers; there came a noise of hissing: deafening, stunning; white billows of steam poured up over the deck.

It was no longer the *Mazatlan*, no longer a thing of wood and iron, but some strange huge living creature that was dying there under his feet, some enormous brute that was plunging and writhing in its last agony, its belly ripped open by a hidden enemy that struck from beneath, its entrails torn out, its life-breath going from it in great gasps of steam. Suddenly its bellow collapsed; the great bulk was sinking lower; the enemy was in its very vitals. The great hoarse roar dwindled to a long death rattle, then to a guttural rasp; all at once it ceased; the brute was dead—the *Mazatlan* was a wreck.

Almost at the moment, he heard an order shouted twice from the bridge, where he could see the shadowy figures of the captain and officers moving about through the clouds of steam and smoke and mist. Immediately there followed the shrill piping of the boatswain's whistle; one of the officers, the first engineer, and some half dozen of the crew came dashing through the crowd, and there was a great shout of "The boats! The boats!"

The crowd broke up, rushing here and there about the ship, reforming again in smaller bands by the boats and liferafts. Vandover followed the first engineer, running forward toward one of the boats in the bow.

"Come on!" he shouted to the little Salvationist lassie, pausing a moment to help her with her heavy canvas-covered bundle. "Come on! they're going to lower the boats."

She started up to follow him and the boom of the foremast, which the accident had in some way loosened, swung across the deck at the same moment. Vandover was already out of its path but it struck the young woman squarely across the back. She dropped in a heap upon the deck, then her body slowly straightened out, stiff and rigid, her eyes rapidly opened and shut, and a great puff of white froth slowly started from her mouth. Vandover ran forward and lifted her up, but her back was broken; she was already dead. He rose to his feet exclaiming to himself, "But she was so sure—she *knew* she was going to be saved," then suddenly fell silent again, gazing wonderingly at the body, disturbed, very thoughtful.

When Vandover finally reached the lifeboat, he found a great crowd gathered there; three people were already in the boat itself. The first engineer, who commanded that boat, and three of the crew stood by the falls preparing to cast off. Just below on the deck of the *Mazatlan* stood two sailors keeping the crowd in order, continually shouting, "Women and children first!" As the women passed their children forward, the sailors lifted them into the boats, some shrieking, others silent and stupid as if stunned. Then the women were helped up; the men, Vandover among them, climbing in afterward. The davits were turned out and the boat was swung clear of the ship's side.

Vandover looked out and below him and then made an involuntary movement to regain the ship's deck. Far below him, or so at least it seemed, were mountains of tumbling green water, huge, relentless, irresistible, rushing on by thousands, to shatter themselves with dreadful force against the ship's side. It seemed simple madness to attempt to launch the boat; even the sinking wreck would be safer than this chance. Vandover was terrified, again deserted by all his calmness and self-restraint.

The sailors standing in the bow and the stern let out the ropes little by little, the vast black hulk of the ship began to loom up above them all, higher and higher, and to their eyes the lifeboat began to grow smaller and smaller, more and more frail, more and more pitiful.

All at once it struck the water with a crash, in an instant it was tossed up again in the air, heaving on the crest of a wave, was carried in and dashed up against the ship, all the oars on that side snapping in an instant. It was a fearful moment; the little boat was unmanageable in an instant, leaping and plunging among the waves like a terrified horse, banged and battered between the heaving water and the hull of the steamer itself. Vandover believed that all was over; he partially rose from his seat preparing to jump before the boat should swamp.

There was an interval of shouting and confusion, the first engineer and the crew leaning over the sides fending off the boat with the stumps of the oars and with long boathooks. Some oars were shipped to the other side to take the place of the broken ones, and a score of hands tugging at them, the boat was at length pulled away out of danger.

The lifeboat had been built to hold thirty-five people; more than forty had crowded into it, and it needed all prudence and care to keep it afloat in the heavy seas that were running. The sailors and two of the passengers were at the oars, while the first engineer took command, standing in the stern at the steering-oar. He was dressed in a suit of oilskins, a life-preserver strapped under his arms; he wore no hat, and at every gust his drenched hair and beard whipped across his face.

Just as the boat was pulling away from the wreck, Vandover and the others saw the little Jew of the plush cap with the ear-laps standing upon the rail of the steamer, holding to a stanchion. He believed that he had been abandoned, and screamed after them, stretching out his hands. The engineer turned and saw him, but shook his head. "Give way there!" he commanded the men; "there's no more room."

The Jew flung his satchel from him and jumped; for a moment he disappeared, then suddenly came up on the crest of a wave, quite close to them, gasping and beating his hands, the water running out of his mouth, and his plush cap, glossy with wet, all awry and twisted so that one ear-lap hung over his eye like a shade. In another moment he had grasped one of the oar-blades. Every one was watching and there was a cry, "Draw him in!" But the engineer refused.

"It's too late!" he shouted, partly to the Jew and partly to the boat. "One more and we are swamped. Let go there!"

"But you can't let him drown," cried Vandover and the others who sat near. "Oh, take him in anyhow; we must risk it."

"Risk hell!" thundered the engineer. "Look here, you!" he cried to Vandover and the rest. "I'm in command here and am responsible for the lives of all of you. It's a matter of his life or ours; one life or forty. One more and we are swamped. Let go there!"

"Yes, yes," cried some. "It's too late! there's no more room!"

But others still protested. "It's too horrible; don't let him drown; take him in." They threw him their life-preservers and the stumps of the broken oars. But the Jew saw nothing, heard nothing, clinging to the oar-blade, panting and stupid, his eyes wide and staring.

"Shake him off!" commanded the engineer. The sailor at the oar jerked and twisted it, but the Jew still held on, silent and breathing hard. Vandover glanced at the fearfully overloaded boat and saw the necessity of it and held his peace, watching the thing that was being done. The sailor still attempted to tear the oar from the Jew's grip, but the Jew held on, panting, almost exhausted; they could hear his breathing in the boat. "Oh, don't!" he gasped, rolling his eyes.

"Unship that oar and throw it overboard," shouted the engineer.

"Better not, sir," answered the sailor. "Extra oars all broken." The Jew was hindering the progress of the boat and at every moment it threatened to turn broad on to the seas.

"God damn you, let go there!" shouted the engineer, himself wrenching and twisting at the oar. "Let go or I'll shoot!"

But the Jew, deaf and stupid, drew himself along the oar, hand over hand, and in a moment had caught hold of the gunwale of the boat. It careened on the instant. There was a great cry. "Push him off! We're swamping! Push him off!" And one of the women cried to the mate, "Don't let my little girls drown, sir! Push him away! Save my little girls! Let him drown!"

It was the animal in them all that had come to the surface in an instant, the primal instinct of the brute striving for its life and for the life of its young.

The engineer, exasperated, caught up the stump of one of the broken oars and beat on the Jew's hands where they were gripped whitely upon the boat's rim, shouting, "Let go! let go!" But as soon as the Jew relaxed one hand he caught again with the other. He uttered no cry, but his face as it came and went over the gunwale of the boat was white and writhing. When he was at length beaten from the boat he caught again at the oar; it was drawn in, and the engineer clubbed his head and arms and hands till the water near by grew red. The little Jew clung to the end of the oar like a cat, writhing and grunting, his mouth open, and his eyes fixed and staring. When his hands were gone, he tried to embrace the oar with his arms. He slid off in the hollow of a wave, his body turned over twice, and then he sank, his head thrown back, his eyes still open and staring, and a silver chain of bubbles escaping from his mouth.

"Give way, men!" said the engineer.

"Oh, God!" exclaimed Vandover, turning away and vomiting over the side.

A little while later some one on the bow of the boat called to the engineer asking why it was they were not heading for the shore. The engineer did not answer, but Vandover in some way understood that it was too dangerous to attempt to run the breakers in such heavy weather, and that they must keep in the open, holding the boat head on to the seas until either the wind fell or they were picked up by some other vessel.

It was still very dark, and seen under the night from the little boat, the ocean and the sky seemed immense and terrible; the great waves grew out of the obscurity ahead of them, rushing down upon the boat, big, swelling, silent, their crests occasionally hissing and breaking into irruptions of cold white froth. As one of them would draw near, the boat would rise upon it as though it would never stop, would hang a moment upon its summit and then topple into the black gulf that followed, sending the bitter icy spray high into the air. The wind blew steadily. Suddenly toward three o'clock it began to rain.

Vandover, the engineer, all the five sailors, and two of the passengers were clothed. The rest of the passengers were little better than naked. Here and there a man had snatched a blanket from his berth, and one or two of them were wearing their trousers, but the rest were clothed for the most part only with their shirts and drawers. There were eighteen women and five little girls in the boat. The little girls were well looked after. Two were wrapped in Vandover's travelling-rug and a couple of men had put their coats around the third. But there were not wraps enough to go around among the women, by far the larger part of them were covered only by their night-dresses or their bed-gowns.

It was abominably cold; the rain fell continually, and the wind blew in long gusts, piercing, cutting. Every plunge of the boat threw icy bullets of spray into the air, which the wind caught up and flung down broad upon the boat. Sometimes even a huge wave would break just upon their quarter, and then great torrents of bitter, freezing water would fall over them in a deluge, leaving a sediment of salt that cracked the skin. The women were huddled upon the bottom of the boat near the waist, where they had been placed for greater safety. They were fouled with the muddy water that gathered there, their long hair dishevelled, dripping with sleet, clinging to their wet cheeks and throats, their bodies showing pink with cold, through their thin, soaked coverings, their limbs racked with long incessant shudderings, a wretched group, miserable beyond words. One of them close by Vandover's feet, he noticed particularly, had but a single garment to cover her. She was drenched through and through, her bare feet were blue with the cold, her head was thrown back, her eyes closed. She was silent except when an unusual gust of wind whipped the rain and spray across her body like the long, fine lash of a whip. Then with every breath she moaned, drawing in her breath between her teeth with a little whistling gasp, too weak, too exhausted, too nearly unconscious to attempt to shield herself in any way.

Vandover could do nothing; he had almost stripped himself to help clothe the others. Nothing more could be done. The suffering had to go on, and he began to wonder how human beings could endure such stress and yet live.

But Vandover himself suffered too keenly to take much thought for the sufferings of the others, while besides that anguish which he shared with the whole boat, the pain in his broken thumb gnawed incessantly like a rat. From time to time he stared listlessly about him, looking at the dark sky, the tumbling ocean, and the crowded groups in the plunging, rolling lifeboat.

There was nothing picturesque about it all, nothing heroic. It was unlike any pictures he had seen of lifeboat rescues, unlike anything he had ever imagined. It was all sordid, miserable, and the sight of the half-clad women, dirty, sodden, unkempt, stirred him rather to disgust than to pity.

At last the dawn came and grew white over a world of tumbling green billows and scudding wrack. Some three miles distant, seen only when the boat topped a higher wave, the same procession of bleached hills moved gradually to the south under the fog, their feet covered by the white line of the surf. Not far behind in the wake of the boat the stern of the *Mazatlan* rose out of a ring of white foam, the waves breaking over her as if she had been there for ages, the screw writhing its flanges into the air like some enormous starfish already fastened upon the hulk.

One of the other boats could be seen now and then between them and the shore, a momentary dot of black on the vast blur of green and gray.

There was no conversation; the men relieved each other at the oars or bailed out the water with their caps and hands, scarcely interchanging a word. The only utterance was an occasional moaning from among the women and children. There was nothing to eat; long since the two whisky flasks had been exhausted. The rain fell steadily into the sea with a prolonged rippling noise.

Vandover was leaning upon the gunwale of the boat, his head buried in his arms, when suddenly he raised himself and asked of the man who sat next to him:

"What was the matter last night? What caused the accident?"

The other shook his head, wearily, turning away again. However, the engineer answered:

"We couldn't carry coal enough to keep up the right pressure of steam and drifted in upon a reef. I said once before that it would happen some time."

About an hour later Vandover dropped off to sleep, in spite of the cold, the wet, and the torment in his thumb. He dozed and woke, and dozed again all through the morning. About noon he was awakened by a more violent rolling of the boat, the sound of voices, and a stir among the other passengers.

It was still raining; the boat was no longer cutting the waves with her nose, but was being rowed seaward flank on; a sailor stood in the bow holding a coil of rope. Close in and seen over the tops of the waves were the shaking and slatting sails of a pilot-boat, lying to. One of the sails bore an enormous number six.

Vandover slept all that day and the night following, rolled in hot blankets. The next morning he awoke with a strange sense of unreality and of having dropped a day somewhere. As he lay in his stuffy little bunk between decks, and felt the rolling of the pilot-boat under him, he still fancied himself upon the *Mazatlan*; he felt the pain in his bandaged thumb and wondered how it came there. Then his fall on the deck came back to him, the wreck of the steamer, the excitement on board, the reports of the rifle fired as a minute gun, the clouds of steam that smelt of a great laundry, and the drowning of the little Jew of the plush cap with the ear-laps. He shuddered and grew sick again for a minute, telling himself that he would never forget that scene.

Such of the passengers as could get about breakfasted as best they could in the cabin with the boatkeeper and four of the pilots. Here they were informed as to what was to be done with them. The schooner would not go in for two weeks, and it was out of the question to keep the castaways on board for that length of time. However, at that moment the pilots were cruising in the neighbourhood on the lookout for two Cape Horners that were expected to be up at any moment. It was decided that when the first of these should be met with the party should be transferred.

An hour after they had been picked up, the wind had begun to freshen. By noon of the second day it had come on to blow half a gale. One could hope only for the best as regarded the rest of the *Mazatlan's* boats and rafts. Not another sign of the wreck was seen by the schooner.

The castaways filled the little schooner to overflowing, hindering her management, and getting in the way at every step. The pilot crew hustled them about without ceremony, and after dinner one had to intervene to prevent a fight between one of them and a sailor from the *Mazatlan* over the question of a broken pipe. The women of the *Mazatlan* kept in their berths continually, rolled in hot blankets, dosed with steaming whisky punches. In the afternoon, however, Vandover saw two of them in the lee of the house attempting to dry their hair; one of them was the woman he had particularly noticed in the lifeboat clad in a night-dress, and he wondered vaguely where the dress had come from she now was wearing.

About three o'clock of the afternoon of the following day Vandover was sitting on the deck near the stern, fastening on his shoes with a length of tarred rope, the laces which he had left trailing having long before broken and pulled out. By that time the wind was blowing squally out of the northeast. The schooner was put under try sails, "a three-reefed mitten with the thumb brailed up," as he heard the boatkeeper call it. This latter was at the wheel for a moment, but in a little while he called up a young man dressed in a suit of oilskins and a pea jacket and gave him the charge. For a long time Vandover watched the boy turning the spokes back and forth, his eyes alternating between the binocle and the horizon.

In the evening about half-past ten, the lookout in the crow's nest sang out: "Smoke—oh!" sounding upon his fish horn. The boatkeeper ran aft and lit a huge calcium flare, holding it so as to illuminate the big number on the mainsail. Suddenly, about a quarter of a mile off their weather-bow, a couple of rockets left a long trail of yellow against the night. It was the Cape Horner, and presently Vandover made out her lights, two glowing spots moving upon the darkness, like the eyes of some nocturnal sea-monster. In a few minutes she showed a blue light on the bridge; she wanted a pilot.

The schooner approached and was laid to, and the towering mass of the great deep-sea tramp began to be dimly seen through the darkness. There was little confusion in making the transfer of the castaways. Most of them seemed still benumbed with their recent terrible exposure. They docilely allowed themselves to be pushed into the pilot tender and again endured the experience of being lowered to the shifting waves below. Silently, like frightened sheep, they stood up in turn in the rocking tender and allowed the life preserver to be fitted about their shoulders to protect them from the bite of the rope's noose beneath their arms. There followed a sickening upward whirl between sea and sky, and then the comforting grasp of many welcoming hands from the deck above. By three o'clock in the morning the transfer had been made.

Vandover boarded the Cape Horner in company with the pilot and the rest and reached San Francisco late on the next day, which happened to be a Sunday.

Chapter Ten

ABOUT TEN O'CLOCK Vandover went ashore in the ship's yawl and landed in the city on a literally perfect day in early November. It seemed many years since he had been there. The drizzly morning upon which the *Santa Rosa* had cast off was already too long ago to be remembered. The city itself as he walked up Market Street toward Kearney seemed to have taken on a strange appearance.

It was Sunday, the downtown streets were deserted except for the cable-cars and an occasional newsboy. The stores were closed and in their vestibules one saw the peddlers who were never there on week-days, venders of canes and peddlers of glue with heavy weights attached to mended china plates.

Vandover had had no breakfast and was conscious of feeling desperately hungry. He determined to breakfast downtown, as he would arrive home too late for one meal and too early for the other.

Almost all of his money had been lost with the *Mazatlan*; he found he had but a dollar left. He would have preferred breakfasting at the Grillroom, but concluded he was too shabby in appearance, and he knew he would get more for his money at the Imperial.

It was absolutely quiet in the Imperial at the hour when he arrived. The single bartender was reading a paper, and in the passage between the private rooms a Chinese with a clean napkin wound around his head was polishing the brass and woodwork. In the passage he met Toby, the red-eyed waiter, just going off night duty, without his usual apron or white coat, dressed very carefully, wearing a brown felt hat.

"Why, how do you do, Mr. Vandover?" exclaimed Toby. "Haven't seen you round here for some time." Vandover was about to answer when the other interrupted:

"Well, what's happened to *you*? Look as though you'd been drawn through hell backward and beaten with a cat!"

In fact Vandover's appearance was extraordinary. His hat was torn and broken, and his clothes, stained with tar and dirt, shrunken and wrinkled by sea-water. His shoes were fastened with bits of tarred rope; he was wearing a red flannel

shirt with bone buttons which the boatkeeper on the pilot
boat had given him, tied at the neck with a purple handkerchief of pongee silk; his hair was long, and a week's growth
of beard was upon his lip and cheeks.

"That's a fact," he answered grimly. "I do look queer. I was
in a wreck down the coast," he added hastily.

"The *Mazatlan!*" exclaimed Toby. "That's a fact; the
papers have been full of it. That's so, you were one of the
survivors."

"The survivors!" echoed Vandover with wondering curiosity. "Tell me—you know I haven't heard a word yet—were
there many lives lost?" He marvelled at the strangeness of the
situation, that this bar waiter should know more of the wreck
than he himself who had been upon it.

"You bet there were!" answered Toby. "Twenty-three altogether; one boat capsized; Kelly, 'Bug' Kelly, son of that fellow that runs the Crystal Grotto, *he* was drowned, and one
of Hocheimer's—Hocheimer, the jeweller, you know—one
of his travelling salesmen was drowned; a little Jew named
Brann, a diamond expert; he jumped overboard and——"

"Don't!" said Vandover with a sharp gesture. "I saw him
drown—it was sickening."

"Were *you* in that boat?" exclaimed Toby. "Well, wait till I
tell you; the authorities here are right after that first engineer
with a sharp stick, and some of the passengers, too, for not
taking him in. A woman in one of the other boats saw it all
and gave the whole thing away. A thing like that is regular
murder, you know." Vandover shut his teeth against answering, and after a little Toby went on, willing to talk. "You
know, we've got a new man for the day-work down here now
—George isn't here any more. No, he's going to start a roadhouse out on the almshouse drive in a few months; swell place,
you know. I'll have him send you cards for the opening."

Vandover ordered oysters, an omelette, and a pint of claret
from the new waiter who did the day-work, and ate and
drank the meal—the like of which he had not tasted since
leaving Coronado—with delicious enjoyment.

He delayed over it long, taking a great pleasure in satisfy-
ing the demands of the animal in him. The wine made him
heavy, warm, stupid; he felt calm, soothed, and perfectly

contented, and had to struggle against a desire to go to sleep where he was. The atmosphere of the Imperial was warm and there was a tepid languor in the air as of the traces of many past debauches, a stale odour of sweetened whisky and of musk. After the roughness and hardships of the last week he felt a pleasant sense of quiet, of relaxation, of enervation. He even began to wish that Flossie would come in. This, however, made him rouse himself; he shook himself, and started home, paying his carfare with his last nickel.

He sat on the outside of the car, wondering if any one he knew would see him, half hoping that such a thing might happen, realizing the dramatic interest that would centre about him now in his present condition as a survivor of a wreck. The idea soon attracted him immensely and he began to look out for any possible acquaintance as the car began to climb over Nob Hill.

At the crossing of Polk Street he saw Ida Wade's mother in deep mourning, standing near a grocery store holding a little pink parcel.

It was like a blow between the eyes. Vandover caught his breath and started violently, feeling again for an instant the cold grip of the hysterical terror that had so nearly overcome him on the morning after Ida's death. It slowly relaxed, however, and by the time he had reached the house on California Street he was almost himself again.

It was about church time when Vandover arrived at home once more. There was a Sunday quiet in the air. The bells were ringing, and here and there family groups on their way to church, the children walking in front, very sedate in their best clothes, carrying the prayer-books carefully, by special privilege.

The butler was working in the garden, as he sometimes did of a Sunday morning, pottering about a certain bed of sweet-peas, and it was the housekeeper who answered his ring. She recognized him with a prolonged exclamation, raising her hands to heaven.

"O-oh, and is it you, Mr. Vandover, sir? Ah, how we've been upset about you and all, and it's glad to see you back again your father will be! Oh, such times as we had when we heard about the wreck and knowing you were on it! Yes, sir,

your father's *pretty* well, though he was main poorly yesterday morning. But he's better now. You'll find him in the
smoking-room now, sir."

Vandover pushed open the door of the smoking-room quietly. His father was sitting unoccupied in the huge leather
chair before the fireplace. He was dead, and must have died
some considerable time before, as he was already cold. He
could have suffered no pain, hardly a muscle had moved, and
his attitude was quite natural, the legs crossed, the right hand
holding the morning's paper. However, as soon as Vandover
touched the body it collapsed and slid down into a heap in
the depth of the chair, the jaw dropping open, the head rolling sidewise upon his shoulder.

Vandover ran out into the hall, waving his arms, shouting
for the servants. "Oh, why didn't you tell me?" he cried to
the housekeeper "Why did you let me find him so? When did
he die?" The housekeeper was distraught. She couldn't believe
it. Only a little while ago he had called her to say there were
no more matches in the little brass matchsafe. She began to
utter long cries and lamentations like a hen in distress, raising
her hands to heaven. All at once they heard some one rushing
up the stairs. It was the butler, in his shirt-sleeves and his
enormous apron of ticking, still carrying his trowel in his
hand. He was bewildered, his eyes protruding, while all about
him he spread the smell of fresh earth. At every instant he
exclaimed:

"What? What? What's the matter?"

"Oh, my dear old governor—and all alone!" cried Vandover through shut teeth.

"Oh, oh, the good God!" exclaimed the housekeeper, crossing herself and rolling her eyes. "And him asking for matches
in the little brass box only a minute since. Oh, the good, kind
master!"

Suddenly Vandover rushed down the stairs and through the
front hall, snatching his hat from the hatrack as he passed. He
ran to call the family doctor, who lived some two blocks below on the same street. He caught him just as he was getting
into the carry-all with his family, bound for church.

Vandover and the physician rode back together in the carry-
all, the two gray horses going up the steep hill at a trot. The

doctor was dressed for church; he wore red gloves with thick white seams, a spray of lilies-of-the-valley in his lapel.

"I'm afraid we can do nothing," he said warningly. "It's your father's old enemy, I suppose. This was—it was sure to happen sooner or later. Any sudden shock, you know."

Vandover scarcely listened, holding the door of the carry-all open with one hand, ready to jump out, beating the other hand upon his knee.

"Go back and take the rest of them to church now," said the doctor to his coachman when the carry-all stopped in front of Vandover's house.

The whole house was in the greatest agitation all the rest of the day. The curtains were drawn, the door bell rang incessantly, strange faces passed the windows, and the noise of strange footsteps continually mounted and descended the staircase. The hours for meals were all deranged, the table stood ready all day long, and one ate when there was a chance. The telephone was in constant use, and at every moment messenger boys came and went, people spoke in low tones, walking on tiptoe; the florist's wagon drove to the door again and again, and the house began to smell of tuberoses. Reporters came, waiting patiently for interviews, sitting on the leather chairs in the dining-room, or writing rapidly on a corner of the dining-table, the cloth pushed back. The undertaker's assistants went about in their shirt-sleeves, working very hard, and toward the middle of the afternoon the undertaker himself tied the crêpe to the bell handle.

Little by little a subdued excitement spread throughout the vicinity. The neighbours appeared at their windows, looking down into the street, watching everything that went on. It was a veritable event, a matter of comment and interest for the whole block. Women found excuses to call on each other, talking over what had happened, as they sat near their parlour windows, shaking their heads at each other, peering out between the lace curtains. The people on the cable-cars and the pedestrians looked again and again at the crêpe on the bell handle, and the curtained windows, craning their necks backward when they had passed. The neighbours' children collected in little groups on the sidewalk near the house, looking and pointing, drawn close together, talking in low tones. At last even a policeman appeared, walking deliberately, casting the shadow of his huge stomach upon the fence that was about the vacant lot. He frowned upon the children, ordering them away. But suddenly he discovered an acquaintance, the driver of an express-wagon that had just driven up with an enormous anchor of violets. He paused, exclaiming:

"Why, hello, Connors!"

"Why, hello, Mister Brodhead!"

Then a long conversation was begun, the policeman standing on the curbstone, one foot resting upon the hub of a wheel, the expressman leaning forward, his elbows on his knees, twirling his whip between his hands. The expressman told some sort of story, pointing with his elbow toward the house, but the other was incredulous, gravely shaking his head, putting his chin in the air, and closing his eyes.

Inside the house itself there was a hushed and subdued bustling that centred about a particular room. The undertaker's assistants and the barber called in low voices through the halls for basins of water and towels. There was a search for the Old Gentleman's best clothes and his clean linen; bureau drawers were opened and shut, closet doors softly closed. Relatives and friends called and departed or stayed to help. A vague murmur arose, a mingled sound of whispers and light footsteps, the rustle of silks, and the noise of stifled weeping, and then at last silence, night, solitude, a single gas-jet burning, and Vandover was left alone.

The suddenness of the thing had stunned and dizzied him, and he had gone through with all the various affairs of the day wondering at his calmness and fortitude. Toward eleven o'clock, however, after the suppressed excitement of the last hours, as he was going to bed, the sense of his grief and loss came upon him all of a sudden, with their real force for the first time, and he threw himself upon the bed face downward, weeping and groaning. During the rest of the night pictures of his father returned to him as he had seen him upon different occasions, particularly three such pictures came and went through his mind.

In one the Old Gentleman stood in that very room, with the decanter in his hand, asking him kindly if he felt very bad; in another he was on the pier with his handkerchief tied to his cane, waving it after Vandover as though spelling out a signal to him across the water. But in a third, he was in the smoking-room, fallen into the leather chair, his arm resting on the table and his head bowed upon it.

After the funeral, which took place from the house, Vandover drove back alone in the hired carriage to his home. He would have paid the driver, but the other told him that the undertaker looked out for that. Vandover watched him a moment as he started his horses downhill, the brake as it scraped against the tire making a noise like the yelping of a dog. Then he turned and faced the house. It was near four o'clock in the afternoon, and everything about the house was very quiet. All the curtains were down except in one of the rooms upstairs. The butler had already opened these windows and was airing the room. Vandover could hear him moving about, sweeping up, rearranging the furniture, making up the bed again. In front of him, between the horse-block and the front door, one or two smilax leaves were still fallen, and a tuberose, already yellow. Behind him in the street he had already noticed the marks of the wheels of the hearse where it had backed up to the curb.

The crêpe was still on the bell handle. Vandover did not know whether it had been forgotten, or whether it was proper to leave it there longer. At any rate he took it off and carried it into the house with him.

His father's hat, a stiff brown derby hat, flat on the top, hung on the hatrack. This had always been a sign to Vandover that his father was at home. The sight was so familiar, so natural, that the same idea occurred to him now involuntarily, and for an instant it was as though he had dreamed of his father's death; he even wondered what was this terrible grief that had overwhelmed him, and thought that he must go and tell his father about it. He took the hat in his hands, turning it about tenderly, catching the faint odour of the Old Gentleman's hair oil that hung about it. It all brought back his father to him as no picture ever could; he could almost *see* the kind old face underneath the broad curl of the brim. His grief came over him again keener than ever and he put his arms clumsily about the old hat, weeping and whispering to himself:

"Oh, my poor, dear old dad—I'm never going to see you again, never, never! Oh, my dear, kind old governor!"

He took the hat up to his room with him, putting it carefully away. Then he sat down before the window that overlooked the little garden in the rear of the house, looking out with eyes that saw nothing.

Chapter Eleven

THE FOLLOWING DAYS as they began to pass were miserable. Vandover had never known until now how much he loved his father, how large a place he had filled in his life. He felt horribly alone now, and a veritable feminine weakness overcame him, a crying need to be loved as his father had loved him, and also to love some one as he himself had loved his father. Worst of all, however, was his loneliness. He could think of no one who cared in the least for him; the very thought of Turner Ravis or young Haight wrought in him an expression of scorn. He was sure that he was nothing to them, though they were the ones whom he considered his best friends.

Another cause of misery was the fact that his father's death in leaving him alone had also thrown him upon his own resources. Now he would have to shoulder responsibilities which hitherto his father had assumed, and decide questions which until now his father had answered.

However, he felt that his father's death had sobered him as nothing else, not even Ida's suicide, had done. The time was come at length for him to take life seriously. He would settle down now to work at his art. He would go to Paris as his father had wished, and devote himself earnestly to painting. Yes, the time was come for him to steady himself, and give over the vicious life into which he had been drifting.

But it was not long before Vandover had become accustomed to his father's death, and had again rearranged himself to suit the new environment which it had occasioned. He wondered at himself because of the quickness with which he had recovered from this grief, just as before he had marvelled at the ease with which he had forgotten Ida's death. Could it be true, then, that nothing affected him very deeply? Was his nature shallow?

However, he was wrong in this respect; his nature was not shallow. It had merely become deteriorated.

Two days after his father's death Vandover went into the Old Gentleman's room to get a certain high-backed chair which had been moved there from his own room during the confusion of the funeral, and which, pending the arrival of the trestles, had been used to support the coffin.

As he was carrying it back his eye fell upon a little heap of objects carefully set down upon the bureau. They were the contents of the Old Gentleman's pockets that the undertaker had removed when the body was dressed for burial.

Vandover turned them over, sadly interested in them. There was the watch, some old business letters and envelopes covered with memoranda, his fountain-pen, a couple of cigars, a bank-book, a small amount of change, his pen-knife, and one or two tablets of chewing-gum.

Vandover thrust the pen and the knife into his own pocket. The bank-book, letters, and change he laid away in his father's desk, but the cigars and the tablets of gum, together with the crumpled pocket-handkerchief that he found on another part of the dressing-case, he put into the Old Gentleman's hat, which he had hidden on the top shelf of his clothes closet. The watch he hung upon a little brass thermometer that always stood on his centre table. He even wound up the watch with the resolve never to let it run down so long as he should live.

The keys, however, disturbed him, and he kept changing them from one hand to the other, looking at them very thoughtfully. They suggested to him the inquiry as to whether or no his father had made a will, and how much money he, Vandover, could now command. One of the keys was a long brass key. Vandover knew that this unlocked a little iron box that from time out of mind had been screwed upon the lower shelf of the clothes closet in his father's room. It was in this box that the Old Gentleman kept his ready money and a few important papers.

For a long time Vandover stood undecided, changing the keys about from one hand to the other, hesitating before opening this iron box; he could not tell why. By and by, however, he went softly into his father's room, and into the clothes closet near the head of the bed. Holding the key toward the lock, he paused listening; it was impossible to rid his mind of the idea that he was doing something criminal. He shook himself, smiling at the fancy, assuring himself of the honesty of the thing, yet opening the box stealthily, holding the key firmly in order that it might not spring back with a loud click, looking over his shoulder the while and breathing short through his nose.

The first thing that he saw inside was a loaded revolver, the sudden view of which sent a little qualm through the pit of his stomach. He took it out gingerly, holding it at arm's length, throwing open the cylinder and spilling out the cartridges on the bed, very careful to let none of them fall on the floor lest they should explode.

Next he drew out the familiar little canvas sack. In it were twenty-dollar gold-pieces, the coin that used to be "Good for the Masses." Behind that was about thirty dollars in two rolls, and last of all in an old, oblong tin cracker-box a great bundle of papers. A list of these papers was pasted on one end of the box. They comprised deeds, titles, insurance policies, tax receipts, mortgages, and all the papers relating to the property. Besides these there was the will.

He took out this box, laying it on the shelf beside him. He was closing the small iron safe again very quietly when all at once, before he could think of what he was doing, he ran his hand into the mouth of the canvas sack, furtively, slyly, snatched one of the heavy round coins, and thrust it into his vest pocket, looking all about him, listening intently, saying to himself with a nervous laugh, "Well, isn't it mine anyway?"

In spite of himself he could not help feeling a joy in the possession of this money as if of some treasure-trove dug up on an abandoned shore. He even began to plan vaguely how he should spend it.

However, he could not bring himself to open any of the papers, but sent them instead to a lawyer, whom he knew his father had often consulted. A few days later he received a typewritten letter asking him to call at his earliest convenience.

It was at his residence and not at his office that Vandover saw the lawyer, as the latter was not well at the time and kept to his bed. However, he was not so sick but that his doctor allowed him to transact at least some of his business. Vandover found him in his room, a huge apartment, one side entirely taken up by book-shelves filled with works of fiction. The walls were covered with rough stone-blue paper, forming an admirable background to small plaster casts of Assyrian *bas-reliefs* and large photogravures of Renaissance portraits. Underneath an enormous baize-covered table in the centre of the room were green cloth bags filled apparently with books, padlocked tin chests, and green pasteboard deed-boxes. The lawyer was sitting up in bed, wearing his dressing-gown and occasionally drinking hot water from a glass. He was a thin, small man, middle-aged, with a very round head and a small pointed beard.

"How do you do, Mr. Vandover?" he said, very pleasantly as Vandover passed by the servant holding open the door and came in.

"How do you do, Mr. Field?" answered Vandover, shaking his hand. "Well, I'm sorry to see you like this."

"Yes," answered the lawyer, "I'm—I have trouble with my digestion sometimes, more annoying than dangerous, I suppose. Take a chair, won't you? You can find a place for your hat and coat right on the table there. Well," he added, settling back on the pillows and looking at Vandover pleasantly, "I think you've grown thinner since the last time I saw you, haven't you?"

"Yes," answered Vandover grimly, "I guess I have."

"Yes, yes, I suppose so, of course," responded the lawyer with a vague air of apology and sympathy. "You have had a trying time of it lately, taking it by and large. I was *very* painfully shocked to hear of your father's death. I had met him at lunch hardly a week before; he was a far heartier man than I was. Eat? You should have seen—splendid appetite. He spoke at length of you, I remember; told me you expected to go abroad soon to study painting; in fact, I believe he was to go to Paris with you. It was very sad and very sudden. But you know we've all been expecting—been fearing—that for some time."

They both were silent for a moment, the lawyer looking absently at the foot-board of the bed, nodding his head slowly from time to time, repeating, "Yes, sir—yes, sir." Suddenly he exclaimed, "Well—now, let's see." He cleared his throat, coming back to himself again, and continued in a very businesslike and systematic tone:

"I have looked over your father's papers, Mr. Vandover, as

you requested me to, and I have taken the liberty of sending for you to let you know exactly how you stand."

"That's the idea, sir," said Vandover, very attentive, drawing up his chair.

Mr. Field took a great package of oblong papers from the small table that stood at the head of his bed, and looked them over, adjusting his eyeglasses. "Well, now, suppose we take up the real property first," he continued, drawing out three or four of these papers and unfolding them. "All of your father's money was invested in what we call 'improved realty.'"

He talked for something over an hour, occasionally stopping to answer a question of Vandover's, or interrupting himself to ask him if he understood. At the end it amounted to this:

The bulk of the estate was residence property in distant quarters of the city. Some twenty-six houses, very cheaply built, each, on an average, renting for twenty-eight dollars. When all of these were rented, the gross monthly income was seven hundred and twenty-eight dollars. At this time, however, six were vacant, bringing down the gross receipts per month to five hundred and sixty dollars. The expenses, which included water, commissions for collecting, repairs, taxes, interest on insurance, etc., when expressed in the terms of a monthly average, amounted to one hundred and eighty-six dollars.

"Well, now, let's see," said Vandover, figuring on his cuff, "one hundred and eighty-six from five hundred and sixty leaves me a net monthly income of three hundred and eighty-four—no, seventy-four. Three hundred and seventy-four dollars."

The lawyer shook his head while he drank another glass of hot water:

"You see," he said, wiping his moustache in the hollow of his palm, "you see, we haven't figured on the mortgages yet."

"Mortgages?" echoed Vandover.

"Yes," answered Mr. Field, "when I spoke of expenses I was basing them upon the monthly statements of Adams & Brunt, your father's agents. But they never looked after the mortgages. Your father acted directly with the banks in that matter. I find that there are mortgages that cover the entire property, even the homestead. They are for 6½ and 7 per cent. In some cases there are two mortgages on the same piece of property."

"Well," said Vandover.

"Well," answered the lawyer, "the interest on these foots up to about two hundred and ninety dollars a month."

Vandover made another hasty calculation on his cuff, and leaned back in his chair staring at the lawyer, saying:

"Why, that leaves eighty-four dollars a month, net."

"Yes," assented Field. "I made it that, too."

"Why, the governor used to allow *me* fifty a month," returned Vandover, "just for pocket money."

"I'm afraid you mustn't expect anything like that, now, Mr. Vandover," replied Field, smiling. "You see, when your father was alive and pursuing his profession, he made a comfortable income besides that which he derived from his realty. His law business I consider to have been excellent when you take everything into consideration. He often made five hundred dollars a month at it. Such are the figures his papers show. He could make you a handsome allowance while he was alive, but all that is stopped now!"

"Well, but didn't he—didn't he leave any money, any—any—any lump sum?" inquired Vandover incredulously.

"There was his bank account," answered the other. "You see, he invested most of his savings in this same realty, and since he stopped building he seems to have lived right up to his income."

"But eighty-four dollars!" repeated Vandover; "why, look at the house on California Street where we live. It costs that much to run it, the servants and all."

"Here's your father's domestic-account book," answered Field, taking it up and turning the leaves. "One hundred and seventy-five dollars a month were the average running expenses."

"One hundred and seventy-five!" shouted Vandover, feeling suddenly as if the ground were opening under him. "Why, great heavens! Mr. Field, where am I going to get—what am I going to *do*?"

Mr. Field smiled a little. "Well," he said, "you must make up your mind to live more modestly."

"Modestly?" exclaimed Vandover, scornfully.

"You'll have to rent the house and take rooms."

Vandover gave a gasp of relief.

"I hadn't thought of that," he answered, subsiding at once. "How much would it bring—the house?"

The lawyer hesitated as to this. "That I could hardly tell you definitely," he answered, shaking his head. "Adams & Brunt could give you more exact figures. In fact, I would suggest that you put it into their hands. California near Franklin, isn't it? Yes; the neighbourhood isn't what it used to be, you know. Every one wants to live out on Pacific Heights now. Double house? Yes, well—with the furniture, I suppose—oh, I don't know—say, a hundred and fifty. But, you know, my estimate is only guesswork. Brunt is the man you want to see."

"Well," answered Vandover, solaced, "that makes—two thirty-four; that's more like it. But," he added, hastily, "you say the homestead is mortgaged as well; how about the interest on that?"

"You needn't be bothered about that," answered Mr. Field. "The interest on *that* mortgage is included in the two hundred and ninety that I spoke of, and the insurance interest on the homestead is included in Adams & Brunt's statement. That was on the whole estate *with* the homestead, you understand? But there is another thing you must look out for. Most of the mortgages are for one year, and every time they are renewed there is an expense of between forty and fifty dollars."

"Yes, I see," assented Vandover.

"Now," resumed the lawyer, "here is your father's bank account. He had in the First National to his credit between nine and ten thousand dollars; nine thousand seven hundred and ninety, to be exact. His professional account book shows that there is now due him in bills and notes eight hundred and thirty dollars; on the debit side he owes in all nine hundred; the difference, you see, is seventy. Nine thousand seven hundred and ninety less seventy leaves a balance of nine thousand six hundred and twenty. All clear?" he asked, interrupting himself. Vandover nodded and the other continued:

"Now, your father left a will; here it is. I drew it for him a year ago last September. He has given fifteen hundred dollars to some cousin in the southern part of the state, and six hundred to a few charities here in the city. The remainder, seven thousand five hundred and twenty, and all the rest of the estate is left to you with the wish that you pursue your art studies abroad. Brunt, of Adams & Brunt, and myself are appointed executors. So now, that is just how you stand as far as I can see: seventy-five hundred dollars in ready money and, if we suppose you rent the California Street house, income property that nets you two hundred and thirty-four a month. The will will have to be probated some time next month and you will have to appear; however, I shall let you know about that in time."

During the next two weeks Vandover was plunged into the affairs of business for the first time in his life. It interested and amused him, and he felt a certain self-importance in handling large sums of money, and in figuring interest, rents, and percentages. Three days after his interview with Mr. Field the sale of his father's office effects took place, and the consequent five hundred dollars Vandover turned over into the hands of the lawyer, who was already looking for an investment for the eighty-nine hundred. This matter had given Vandover considerable anxiety.

"I don't want anything fancy," he said to Field. "No big per cents. and bigger risks. If I've got to live economically I want something that's secure. A good solid investment, don't you know, with a fair interest; that's what I'm looking for."

"Yes," answered the lawyer grimly; "I've been looking for that myself ever since I was your age."

They both laughed, and the lawyer added: "Has Brunt found a tenant for the California Street house yet? No? Well, perhaps you had better keep that five hundred for your running expenses until he does. It will probably take some time."

"All right," answered Vandover. "There were a couple of women up to look at the place yesterday, but they wanted to use it for a boarding-house. I won't hear to that. Brunt says they would ruin it, dead sure."

"I suppose you are looking around, yourself, for rooms?" inquired Mr. Field. "Have you found anything to suit you?"

"No," answered Vandover, "I have not. I don't like the idea

of living in one of the downtown hotels, and as far as I have looked, the uptown flats are rather steep. However, I haven't gone around very much as yet. I've been so busy. Oh, how about the paving of the street in front of those Bush Street houses of mine? Brunt says that the supervisors have passed a resolution of intention to that effect. Now shall I let the city contractor have the job or give it to Brunt's man?"

"Better let the city people do it," advised Field. "They may charge more, but you needn't pay *them* for a long time."

By the end of three weeks Vandover had sickened of the whole thing. The novelty was gone, and business affairs no longer amused him. Besides this, he was anxious to settle down in some comfortable rooms. It was now the middle of winter and he had determined that it was not the season for a European trip. He would wait until the summer before going to Paris.

Little by little Vandover turned over the supervision and management of his affairs and his property to Adams & Brunt, declaring that he could not afford to be bothered with them any longer. This course was much more expensive and by no means so satisfactory from a business point of view, but Vandover felt as though the loss in money was more than offset by his freedom from annoyance and responsibility.

He was eager to get settled. The idea of taking rooms that should be all his own and that he could fit up to suit his taste attracted him immensely. Already he saw himself installed in charming bachelor's apartments, the walls covered with rough stone-blue paper forming an admirable background for small plaster casts of Assyrian *bas-reliefs* and photogravures of Velasquez portraits. There would be a pipe-rack over the mantelpiece, and a window-seat with a corduroy cushion such as he had had in his room in Matthew's.

Very slowly his father's affairs were settled, and by degrees the estate began to adjust itself to the new grooves in which it was to run. By the middle of December everything was beginning to go smoothly, and the day before Christmas Mr. Field announced to Vandover that he had invested his eighty-nine hundred in registered U. S. 4 per cents. They had had several long talks concerning this sum of money, and in the end had concluded that it would be better to invest it in some

such fashion rather than to take up any of the mortgages that
were on the houses.

During the first weeks of the new year the house on California Street was rented for one hundred and twenty-five dollars to an English gentleman, the president of a fruit syndicate
in the southern part of the state. There were but three in the
family, and though the rent was below that which Vandover
had desired, Brunt advised him to close the transaction at
once, as they were desirable tenants and would probably stay
in the house a long time.

On the last evening which he was to spend in his home,
Vandover cast up his accounts and made out a schedule as to
his monthly income.

Rent from realty, net average	.$ 84.00
Rent from homestead property on California Street . . .	125.00
Interest on U. S. bonds, 4 per cent.	23.00
Total	. $232.00
In small iron safe	. $170.00
Received from sale of office effects	.$500.00
	$670.00
Expenses, outstanding bills, lawyer's fees, undertaker's	
bill, expenses for collecting, etc	. 587.00
Balance, January 16th	. $83.00

Then with a shrug of the shoulders he dismissed the whole
burdensome business from his mind. Brunt would manage his
property, sending him regularly the monthly statement in order to keep him informed. The English gentleman of the fruit
syndicate would add his hundred and twenty-five, and the 4
per cents., faithfully brooding over his eighty-nine hundred
in the dark of the safety deposit drawer, would bring forth
their little quota of twenty-three with absolute certainty. Two
thirty-two a month. Yes, he was comfortably fixed and was
free now to do exactly as he pleased.

His first object now was to settle down for the winter in
some pleasant rooms. He had decided that he would look for
a suite of three—a bedroom, studio, and sitting-room. The
bedroom he was not particular about, the studio he hoped
would have plenty of light from the north, but the sitting-
room *must* be sunny and overlook the street, else what would
be the use of a window-seat? As to the neighbourhood, he

thought he would prefer Sutter Street anywhere between Leavenworth and Powell.

In the downtown part this street was entirely given over to business houses; in the far, uptown quarter it was lined with residences; but between these two undesirable extremes was an intermediate district where the residences had given place to flats, and the business blocks to occasional stores. It was a neighbourhood affected by doctors, dentists, and reputable music-teachers; drug stores occupied many of the corners, here and there a fine residence still withstood the advance of business, there were a number of great apartment houses, and even one or two club buildings.

It was a gay locality, not too noisy, not too quiet. The street was one of the great arteries of travel between the business and the residence portions of the city, and its cable-cars were frequented by ladies going to their shopping or downtown marketing or to and from the matinées. Acquaintances of Vandover were almost sure to pass at every hour.

He took rooms temporarily at the Palace and at once set about locating on Sutter Street. He had recourse again to Brunt, who furnished him with a long list of vacancies in that neighbourhood. Apartment-hunting was an agreeable pastime to Vandover, though in the end it began to bore him. Altogether, he visited some fifteen or twenty suites, in each case trying to fit himself into the rooms, imagining how the window-seat would look in such a window, how the pipe-rack would show over such a mantel, just where on such walls the Assyrian *bas-reliefs* could be placed to the best advantage, and if his easel could receive enough steady light from such windows. Then he considered the conveniences, the baths, the electric light, and the heat.

After a two weeks' search, he had decided upon one of two suites; both of these were in the desired neighbourhood but differed widely in other respects.

The first was reasonable enough in the matter of rent, and had even been occupied by an artist for some three or four years previous. However, the room that Vandover proposed to use as a sitting-room was small and had no double windows, thus making the window-seat an impossibility. There did not seem to be any suitable place for the Assyrian *bas-reliefs*, and the mantelpiece was of old-fashioned white marble like the mantelpiece in Mrs. Wade's front parlour, a veritable horror. It revolted Vandover even to think of putting a pipe-rack over it. These defects were offset by the studio, a large and splendid room with hardwood floors and an enormous north light, the legendary studio, the dream of an artist, precisely such a studio as Vandover had hoped he would occupy in the Quarter.

The other suite was in a great apartment house, a hotel in fact, but very expensive, with electric bulbs and bells, and with a tiled bathroom connecting with the bedroom. The room which he would be obliged to use as his studio was small, dark, the light coming from the west. But the sitting-room was perfect. It had the sun all day long through a huge bay window that seemed to have been made for a window-seat; there were admirable, well-lighted spaces on the walls for casts and pictures, and the mantelpiece was charming, extremely high, and made of oak; in a word, the exact sitting-room that Vandover had in mind. Already he saw himself settled there as comfortably and snugly as a kernel in a nutshell. It was true that upon investigation he found that the grate had been plastered up and the flue arranged for a stove. But for that matter there were open-grate stoves to be had that would permit the fire to be seen and that would look just as cheerful as a grate. He had even seen such a stove in the window of a hardware store downtown, a tiled stove with a brass fender and with curious flamboyant ornaments of cast-iron— a jewel of a stove.

For two days Vandover hesitated between these two suites, undecided whether he should sacrifice his studio for his sitting-room, or his sitting-room for his studio. At length he came to the conclusion that as he was now to be an artist a good studio ought to be the first consideration, and that since he was to settle down to hard, serious work at last he owed it to himself to have a fitting place in which to paint; yes, decidedly he would take the suite with the studio. He went to the agent, told him of his decision, and put up a deposit to secure the rooms.

The same day upon which he took this decided step he had occasion to pass by both places in question. As he approached the apartment house in which the rejected suite was situated it occurred to him to tell the clerk in the office that he had decided against the rooms; he could take a last look at them at the same time.

He was shown up to the rooms again, and walked about in the sitting-room, asking the same questions about the heat, the plumbing, and the baths. He even went to the window and looked out into the street. It *was* a first-rate berth just the same, and how jolly it would be to lounge in the window-seat of a morning, with a paper, a cigarette, and a cup of coffee, watching the people on their way downtown; the women going to their shopping and morning's marketing. Then all at once he remembered that at most he would only have these rooms for five months, and reflected that if his whole life was to be devoted to painting he might easily put up with an inconvenient studio for a few months. Once at Paris all would be different.

At that the rooms took on a more charming aspect than ever; never had they appeared cheerier, sunnier, more comfortable; never had the oak mantel and the tiled stove with the flamboyant ornaments been more desirable; never had a window-seat seemed more luxurious, never a pipe-rack more delectable, while at the same time, the other rooms, the rooms of the big studio, presented themselves to his imagination more sombre, uncomfortable, and forbidding than ever. It was out of the question to think of living there; he was angry with himself for having hesitated so long. But suddenly he remembered the deposit he had already made; it was ten dollars; for a moment he paused, then dismissed the matter with an impatient shrug of the shoulders. "So much the worse," he said. "What's ten dollars?" He made up his mind then and there and went downstairs, walking on his heels, to tell the clerk that after all he would engage the rooms from that date.

Chapter Twelve

VANDOVER TOOK formal possession of his rooms on Sutter Street during the first few days of February. For a week previous they had been in the greatest confusion: the studio filled with a great number of trunks, crates, packing cases, and furniture still in its sacking. In the bedroom was stored the furniture that had been moved out of the sitting-room, while the sitting-room itself was given over to the paperhangers and carpenters. Vandover himself appeared from time to time, inquiring anxiously as to the arrival of his "stuff," or sitting on a packing-case, his hands in his pockets, his hat pushed back, and a cigarette between his lips.

He had passed a delightful week selecting the wall paper and the pattern for the frieze, buying rugs, screens, Assyrian *bas-reliefs*, photogravures of Renaissance portraits, and the famous tiled stove with its flamboyant ornaments. Just after renting his home he had had a talk with the English gentleman of the fruit syndicate and had spoken about certain ornaments and bits of furniture, valuable chiefly to himself, which he wished to keep. The president of the fruit syndicate had been very gracious in the matter, and as soon as Vandover had taken his rooms he had removed two great cases of such articles from the California Street house and had stored them in the studio.

After the workmen were gone away Vandover began the labour of arrangement, aided by one of the paperhangers he had retained for that purpose. It was a work of three days, but at last everything was in its place, and one evening toward the middle of the month Vandover stood in the middle of the sitting-room in his shirt-sleeves, holding the tweezers and a length of picture-wire in his hand, and looked around him in his new home.

The walls were hung with dull blue paper of a very rough texture set off by a narrow picture moulding of ivory white. A dark red carpet covered with rugs and skins lay on the floor. Upon the left-hand wall, reaching to the floor, hung a huge rug of sombre colours against which were fixed a fencing trophy, a pair of antlers, a little water colour sketch of a

Norwegian fjord, and Vandover's banjo; underneath it was a low but very broad divan covered with corduroy. To the right and left of this divan stood breast-high bookcases with olive green curtains, their tops serving as shelves for a multitude of small ornaments, casts of animals by Fremiet and Barye, Donatello's lovely *femme inconnue*, beer steins, a little bronze clock, a calendar, and a yellow satin slipper of Flossie's in which Vandover kept Turkish cigarettes. The writing-desk with the huge blue blotter in a silver frame, the paper-cutter, and the enormous brass inkstand filled the corner to the right of the divan, while drawn up to it was the huge leather chair, the chair in which the Old Gentleman had died. In the drawer of the desk Vandover kept his father's revolver; he never thought of loading it; of late he had only used it to drive tacks with, when he could not find the hammer. Opposite the divan, on the other side of the room, was the famous tiled stove with the flamboyant ornaments; back of this the mantel, and over the mantel a row of twelve grotesque heads in plaster, with a space between each for a pipe. To the left in the angle of the room stood the Japanese screen in black and gold, and close to this a tea-table of bamboo and a piano-lamp with a great shade of crinkly red paper that Turner Ravis had given to Vandover one Christmas. The bay window was filled by the window-seat, covered with corduroy like the divan and heaped with cushions, one of them of flaming yellow, the one spot of vivid colour amidst the dull browns and sombre blues of the room. A great sideboard with decanters and glasses and chafing-dishes faced the window from the end wall. The entrance to the studio opened to the left of it, which entrance Vandover had hung with curtains of dust-brown plush.

The casts of the Assyrian *bas-reliefs* were against the wall upon either side of the window. There were three of them, two representing scenes from the life of the king, the third the wounded lioness which Vandover never wearied of admiring.

Upon the wall over the mantel hung two very large photogravures, one of Rembrandt's "Night Watch," the other a portrait of Velasquez representing a young man with a hunting spear. Above one of the bookcases was an admirable reproduction of the "Mona Lisa"; above the other, a carbon print of a Vandyke, a Dutch lady in a silk gown and very high ruff.

By the side of the "Mona Lisa," however, was a cheap brass rack stuffed with photographs: actresses in tights, French quadrille dancers, high kickers, and chorus girls.

In the studio, Vandover had tacked great squares and stripes of turkey-red cloth against the walls to serve as a background for his sketches. Some dozen or more portfolios and stretchers were leaned against the baseboard, and a few ornaments and pieces of furniture, such things as Vandover set but little store by, were carelessly arranged about the room. The throne and huge easel were disposed so as to receive as much light as was possible.

Beyond the studio was the bedroom, but here there was only the regulation furniture. Some scores of photographs of Vandover's friends were tacked upon the walls, or thrust between the wood and glass of the mirror.

A new life now began for Vandover, a life of luxury and aimlessness which he found charming. He had no duties, no cares, no responsibilities. But there could be no doubt that he was in a manner changed; the old life of dissipation seemed to have lost its charm. For nearly twenty-six years nothing extraordinary had happened to break in upon the uneventful and ordinary course of his existence, and then, suddenly, three great catastrophes had befallen, like the springing of three successive mines beneath his feet: Ida's suicide, the wreck, and his father's death, all within a month. The whole fabric of his character had been shaken, jostled out of its old shape. His desire of vice was numbed, his evil habits all deranged; here, if ever, was the chance to begin anew, to commence all over again. It seemed an easy matter: he would merely have to remain inactive, impassive, and his character would of itself re-form upon the new conditions.

But Vandover made another fatal mistake: the brute in him had only been stunned; the snake was only soothed. His better self was as sluggish as the brute, and his desire of art as numb as his desire of vice. It was not a continued state of inaction and idleness that could help him, but rather an active and energetic arousing and spurring up of those better

qualities in him still dormant and inert. The fabric of his nature was shaken and broken up, it was true, but if he left it
to itself there was danger that it would re-form upon the old
lines.

And this was precisely what Vandover did. As rapidly as
ever his pliable character adapted itself to the new environment; he had nothing to do; there was lacking both the desire
and necessity to keep him at his easel; he neglected his painting utterly. He never thought of attending the life-class at the
art school; long since he had given up his downtown studio.
He was content to be idle, listless, apathetic, letting the days
bring whatever they chose, making no effort toward any fixed
routine, allowing his habits to be formed by the exigencies of
the hour.

He rose late and took his breakfast in his room; after breakfast he sat in his window-seat, reading his paper, smoking his
pipe, drinking his coffee, and watching the women on their
way downtown to their morning's shopping or marketing.
Then, as the fancy moved him, he read a novel, wrote a few
letters, or passed an hour in the studio dabbling with some
sketches for the "Last Enemy." Very often he put in the whole
morning doing pen and inks of pretty, smartly dressed girls,
after Gibson's manner, which he gave away afterward to his
friends. In the afternoon he read or picked the banjo or, sitting down to the little piano he had rented, played over his
three pieces, the two polkas and the air of the topical song.
At three o'clock, especially of Wednesday and Saturday afternoons, he bestirred himself, dressed very carefully, and went
downtown to promenade Kearney and Market streets, stopping occasionally at the Imperial, where he sometimes found
Ellis and Geary and where he took cocktails in their company.

He rarely went out in the evenings; his father's death had
changed all that, at least for a while. He had not seen Turner
Ravis nor Henrietta Vance for nearly two months.

Vandover took his greatest pleasure while in his new quarters, delighted to be pottering about his sitting-room by the
hour, setting it to rights, rearranging the smaller ornaments,
adjusting the calendar, winding the clock and, above all, tending the famous tiled stove.

In his idleness he grew to have small and petty ways. The entire day went in doing little things. He passed one whole afternoon delightfully, whittling out a new banjo bridge from the cover of a cigar-box, scraping it smooth afterward with a bit of glass. The winding of his clock was quite an occurrence in the course of the day, something to be looked forward to. The mixing of his tobacco was a positive event and undertaken with all gravity, while the task of keeping it moist and ripe in the blue china jar, with the sponge attachment, that always stood on the bamboo tea-table by the Japanese screen, was a wearing anxiety that was yet a pleasure.

It became a fad with him to do without matches, using as a substitute "lights," tapers of twisted paper to be ignited at the famous stove. He found amusement for two days in twisting and rolling these "lights," cutting frills in the larger ends with a pair of scissors, and stacking them afterward in a Chinese flower jar he had bought for the purpose and stood on top of the bookcases. The lights were admirably made and looked very pretty. When he had done he counted them. He had made two hundred exactly. What a coincidence!

But the stove, the famous tiled stove with flamboyant ornaments, was the chiefest joy of Vandover's new life. He was delighted with it; it was so artistic, so curious, it kept the fire so well, it looked so cheerful and inviting; a stove that was the life and soul of the whole room, a stove to draw up to and talk to; no, never was there such a stove! There was hardly a minute of the day he was not fussing with it, raking it down, turning the damper off and on, opening and shutting the door, filling it with coal, putting the blower on and then taking it off again, sweeping away the ashes with a little brass-handled broom, or studying the pictures upon the tiles: the "Punishment of Caliban and His Associates," "Romeo and Juliet," the "Fall of Phaeton." He even pretended to the chambermaid that he alone understood how to manage the stove, forbidding her to touch it, assuring her that it had to be coaxed and humoured. Often late in the evening as he was going to bed he would find the fire in it drowsing; then he would hustle it sharply to arouse it, punching it with the poker, talking to it, saying: "Wake up there, you!" And then when the fire was snapping he would sit before it in his bathrobe, absorbing its heat luxuriously and scratching himself, as was his custom, for over an hour.

But very often in the evening he would have the boys, Ellis, Geary, and young Haight, up to a little improvised supper. They would bring home *tamales* with them, and Vandover would try to make Welsh rabbits, which did not always come out well and which they oftentimes drank instead of ate. Ellis, always very silent, would mix and drink cocktails continually. Vandover would pick his banjo, and together with young Haight would listen to Geary.

"Ah, you bet," this one would say, "I'm going to make my pile in this town. I can do it. Beale sent me to court the other morning to get the judge's signature. He had a grouch on, and wanted to put me off. You ought to have heard me jolly him. I talked right up to him! Yes, sir; you bet! Didn't I have the gall? That's the way you want to do to get along—get right in and not be afraid. I got his signature, you bet. Ah, I'm right in it with Beale; he thinks I'm hot stuff."

Now that there was nothing to worry him, and little to occupy his mind, Vandover gave himself over considerably to those animal pleasures which he enjoyed so much. He lay abed late in the morning, dozing between the warm sheets; he overfed himself at table, and drank too much wine; he ate between meals, having filled his sideboard with canned patés, potted birds, and devilled meats; while upon the bamboo table stood a tin box of chocolates out of which he ate whole handfuls at a time. He would take this box into the bathroom with him and eat while he lay in the hot water until he was overcome by the enervating warmth and by the steam and would then drop off to sleep.

It was during these days that Vandover took up his banjo-playing seriously, if it could be said that he did anything seriously at this time. He took occasional lessons of a Mexican in a room above a wigmaker's store on Market Street, and learned to play by note. For a little time he really applied himself; after he had mastered the customary style of play he began to affect the more brilliant and fancy performances, playing two banjos at once, or putting nickels under the bridge and picking the strings with a calling-card to imitate a mandolin. He even made up some comical pieces that had a great success among the boys. One of these he called the "Pleasing Pan-Hellenic Production"; another was the imitation of the "Midway Plaisance Music," and a third had for title "A Sailor Robbing a Ship," in which he managed to imitate the sounds of the lapping of the water, the creaking of the oarlocks, the tramp of the sailor's feet upon the deck, the pistol shot that destroyed him, and—by running up the frets on the bass-string—his dying groans, a finale that never failed to produce a tremendous effect.

Chapter Thirteen

JUST BEFORE Lent, and about three months after the death
of Vandover's father, Henrietta Vance gave a reception and
dance at her house. The affair was one of a series that the
girls of the Cotillon had been giving to the men of the same
club. Vandover had gone to all but the last, which had occurred while he was at Coronado. He was sure of meeting
Geary, young Haight, Turner Ravis, and all the people of his
set at these functions, and had always managed to have a very
jolly time. He had been very quiet since his father's death and
had hardly gone out at all; in fact, since Ida Wade's death and
his trip down the coast he had seen none of his acquaintances
except the boys. But he determined now that he would go to
this dance and in so doing return once more to the world
that he knew. By this time he had become pretty well accustomed to his father's death and saw no reason why he should
not have a good time.

At first he thought he would ask Turner to go with him,
but in the end made up his mind to go alone, instead; one
always had a better time when one went alone. Young Haight
would have liked to have asked Turner, but did not because
he supposed, of course, that Vandover would take her. In the
end Turner had Delphine act as her escort.

Vandover arrived at Henrietta Vance's house at about half-
past eight. A couple of workmen were stretching the last guy
ropes of the awning that reached over the sidewalk; every
window of the house was lighted. The front door was opened
for the guest before he could ring, and he passed up the stairs,
catching a glimpse of the parlours through the portières of
the doors. As yet they were empty of guests, the floors were
covered with canvas, and the walls decorated with fern leaves.
In a window recess one of the caterer's men was setting out
two punch bowls and a multitude of glass cups; three or four
musicians were gathered about the piano, tuning up, and one
heard the subdued note of a cornet; the air was heavy with
the smell of pinks and of La France roses.

At the turn of the stairs the Vances' second girl in a white
lawn cap directed him to the gentlemen's dressing-room,

which was the room of Henrietta Vance's older brother. About a dozen men were here before him, some rolling up their overcoats into balls and stowing them with their canes in the corners of the room; others laughing and smoking together, and still others who were either brushing their hair before the mirrors or sitting on the bed in their stocking feet, breathing upon their patent leathers, warming them before putting them on. There were one or two who knew no one and who stood about unhappily, twisting the tissue paper from the buttons of their new gloves, and looking stupidly at the pictures on the walls of the room. Occasionally one of the gentlemen would step to the door and look out into the hall to see if the ladies whom they were escorting were yet come out of their dressing-room, ready to go down.

On the centre table stood three boxes of cigars and a great many packages of cigarettes, while extra hairbrushes, whisk-brooms, and papers of pins had been placed about the bureau.

As Vandover came in, he nodded pleasantly to such of the men as he knew, and, after hiding his hat and coat under the bed, shook himself into his clothes again and rearranged his dress tie.

The house was filling up rapidly; one heard the deadened roll of wheels in the street outside, the banging of carriage doors, and an incessant rustle of stiff skirts ascending the stairs. From the ladies' dressing-room came an increasing soprano chatter, while downstairs the orchestra around the piano in the back parlour began to snarl and whine louder and louder. About the halls and stairs one caught brief glimpses of white and blue opera cloaks edged with swan's-down alternating with the gleam of a starched shirt bosom and the glint of a highly polished silk hat. Odours of sachet and violets came and went elusively or mingled with those of the roses and pinks. An air of gayety and excitement began to spread throughout the house.

"Hello, old man!" "Hello, Van!" Charlie Geary, young Haight, and Ellis came in together. "Hello, boys!" answered Vandover, hairbrush in hand, turning about from the mirror, where he had been trying to make his hair lie very flat and smooth.

"Look here," said Geary, showing him a dance-card already

full, "I've got every dance promised. I looked out for that at the last one of these affairs; made all my arrangements and engagements then. Ah, you bet, I don't get left on any dance. That's the way you want to rustle. Ah," he went on, "had a bully sleep last night. I knew I was going to be out late to-night, so I went to bed at nine; didn't wake up till seven. Had a fine cutlet for breakfast."

It was precisely at this moment that Geary got his first advancement in life. Mr. Beale, Jr., head clerk in the great firm of Beale & Story, came up to him as he was drawing off his overcoat:

"How is Fischer?" asked Geary.

Beale, Jr., pulled him over into a corner, talking in a low voice. "He's even worse than yesterday," he answered. "I think we shall have to give him a vacation, and that's what I want to speak to you about. If you can, Geary, I should like to have you take his place for a while, at least until we get through with this contract case. I don't know about Fischer. He's sick so often, I'm afraid we may have to let him go altogether."

Suddenly the orchestra downstairs broke out into a clash of harmony and then swung off with the beat and cadence of a waltz. The dance was beginning; a great bustle and hurrying commenced about the dressing-rooms and at the head of the stairs; everybody went down. In the front parlour by the mantel Henrietta Vance and Turner stood on either side of Mrs. Vance, receiving, shaking hands, and laughing and talking with the different guests who came up singly, in couples, or in noisy groups.

No one was dancing yet. The orchestra stopped with a flourish of the cornet, and at once a great crowding and pushing began amidst a vast hum of talk. The cards were being filled up, a swarm of men gathered about each of the more popular girls, passing her card from hand to hand while she smiled upon them all helplessly and good-naturedly. The dance-cards had run short and some of the men were obliged to use their visiting cards; with these in one hand and the stump of a pencil in the other, they ran about from group to group, pushing, elbowing, and calling over one another's heads like brokers in a stock exchange.

Geary, however, walked about calmly, smiling contentedly, very good-humoured. From time to time he stopped such a one of the hurrying, excited men as he knew and showed him his card made out weeks before, saying, "Ah, how's that? *I* am all fixed; made all my engagements at the last one of these affairs, even up to six extras. That's the way you want to rustle."

Young Haight was very popular; everywhere the girls nodded and smiled at him, many even saving a place on their cards for him before he had asked.

Ellis took advantage of the confusion to disappear. He went up into the deserted dressing-room, chose a cigar, unbuttoned his vest and sat down in one chair, putting his feet upon another. The hum of the dance came to him in a prolonged and soothing murmur and he enjoyed it in some strange way of his own, listening and smoking, stretched out at ease in the deserted dressing-room.

Vandover went up to Turner Ravis smiling and holding out his hand. She seemed to be curiously embarrassed when she saw him, and did not smile back at him. He asked to see her card, but she drew her hand quickly from his, telling him that she was going home early and was not dancing at all, that in fact she had to "receive" instead of dance. It was evident to Vandover that he had done something to displease her, and he quickly concluded that it was because he had not asked her to go with him that evening.

He turned from her to Henrietta Vance as though nothing unusual had happened, resolving to see her later in the evening and in the meanwhile invent some suitable excuse. Henrietta Vance did not even see his hand; she was a very jolly girl, ordinarily, and laughed all the time. Now she looked him squarely in the face without so much as a smile, at once angry and surprised; never had anything seemed so hateful and disagreeable. Vandover put his hand back into his pocket, trying to carry it all off with a laugh, saying in order to make her laugh with him as he used to do, "Hello! how do you do this evening? It's a pleasant morning this afternoon." "How do you do?" she answered nervously, refusing to laugh. Then she turned from him abruptly to talk to young Haight's little cousin Hetty.

Mrs. Vance was neither embarrassed nor nervous as the girls had been. She stared calmly at Vandover and said with a peculiar smile, "I am surprised to see you here, Mr. Vandover."

An hour later the dance was in full swing. Almost every number was a waltz or a two-step, the music being the topical songs and popular airs of the day set to dance music.

About half-past ten o'clock, between two dances, the cornet sounded a trumpet call; the conversation ceased in a moment, and Henrietta Vance's brother, standing by the piano, called out, "The next dance will be the *first extra*," adding immediately, "a *waltz*." The dance recommenced; in the pauses of the music one heard the rhythmic movement of the feet shuffling regularly in one-two-three time.

Some of the couples waltzed fast, whirling about the rooms, bearing around corners with a swirl and swing of silk skirts, the girls' faces flushed and perspiring, their eyes half-closed, their bare, white throats warm, moist, and alternately swelling and contracting with their quick breathing. On certain of these girls the dancing produced a peculiar effect. The continued motion, the whirl of the lights, the heat of the room, the heavy perfume of the flowers, the cadence of the music, even the physical fatigue, reacted in some strange way upon their oversensitive feminine nerves, the monotony of repeated sensation producing some sort of mildly hypnotic effect, a morbid hysterical pleasure the more exquisite because mixed with pain. These were the girls whom one heard declaring that they could dance all night, the girls who could dance until they dropped.

Other of the couples danced with the greatest languor and gravity, their arms held out rigid and at right angles with their bodies.

About the doors and hallways stood the unhappy gentlemen who knew no one, watching the others dance, feigning to be amused. Some of them, however, had ascended to the dressing-room and began to strike up an acquaintance with each other and with Ellis, smoking incessantly, discussing business, politics, and even religion.

In the ladies' dressing-room two of the maids were holding a long conversation in low tones, their heads together;

evidently it was concerning something dreadful. They continually exclaimed "Oh!" and "Ah!" suddenly sitting back from each other, shaking their heads, and biting their nether lips. On the top floor in the hall the servants in their best clothes leaned over the balustrade, nudging each other, talking in hoarse whispers or pointing with thick fingers swollen with dish-water. All up and down the stairs were the couples who were sitting out the dance, some of them even upon the circular sofa in the hall over the first landing.

The music stopped, leaving a babel of talk in the air, the couples fell apart for an instant, but a great clapping of hands broke out and the tired musicians heroically recommenced.

As soon as the short *encore* was done there was a rush for the lemonade and punch bowls. The guests thronged around them joking each other. "Hello! are you here *again*?" "Oh, this is dreadful!" "This makes *six* times I've seen you here."

A smell of coffee rose into the air from the basement. It was about half-past eleven; the next dance was the supper dance and the gentlemen hurried about anxiously searching the stairs, the parlours, and the conservatory for the girls who had promised them this dance weeks before. The musicians were playing a march, and the couples crowded down the narrow stairs in single file, the ladies drawing off their gloves. The tired musicians stretched themselves, rubbed their eyes, and began to talk aloud in the deserted parlours.

Supper was served in the huge billiard-room in the basement and was eaten in a storm of gayety. The same parties and "sets" tried to get together at the same table; Henrietta Vance's party was particularly noisy: at her table there was an incessant clamour of screams and shouts of laughter. One ate oysters *à la poulette*, terrapin-salads, and croquettes; the wines were Sauternes and champagnes. With the nuts and dessert the caps came on, and in a few minutes were cracking and snapping all over the room.

Six of the unfortunates who knew no one, but who had managed through a common affliction to become acquainted with each other, gathered at a separate table. Ellis was one of their number; he levied a twenty-five assessment, and tipped the waiter a dollar and a half. This one accordingly brought

them extra bottles of champagne in which they found consolation for all the *ennui* of the evening.

After supper the dancing began again. The little stiffness
and constraint of the earlier part of the evening was gone; by
this time nearly everybody, except the unfortunates, knew everybody else. The good dinner and the champagne had put
them all into an excellent humour, and they all commenced
to be very jolly. They began a Virginia Reel still wearing the
magician's caps and Phrygian bonnets of tissue paper.

Young Haight was with Turner Ravis as much as possible
during the evening, very happy and excited. Something had
happened; it was impossible for him to say precisely what, for
on the face of things Turner was the same as ever. Nothing
in her speech or actions was different, but there was in her
manner, in the very air that surrounded her, something elusive and subtle that set him all in a tremor. There was a
change in his favour; he felt that she liked to have him with
her and that she was trying to have him feel as much in some
mysterious way of her own. He could see, however, that she
was hardly conscious of doing this and that the change was
more apparent to his eyes than it was to hers.

"Must you really go home now?" he said, as Turner began
to talk of leaving, soon after supper. They had been sitting
out the dance under a palm at the angle of the stairs.

"Yes," answered Turner; "Howard has the measles and I
promised to be home early. Delphine was to come for me and
she ought to be here now."

"Delphine?" exclaimed young Haight. "Didn't you come
with Van?"

"No," answered Turner quietly. Only by her manner, and
by something in the way she said the word, Haight knew at
once that she had broken definitely with Vandover. The talk
he had had with her at her house came back to him on the
instant. He hesitated a moment and then asked:

"There is something wrong? Has Van done anything—
never mind, I don't mean that; it's no business of mine, I
suppose. But I know you care for him. I'm sorry if——"

But he was not sorry. Try as he would, his heart was leaping in him for joy. With Vandover out of the way, he knew
that all would be different; Turner herself had said so.

"Oh, everything is wrong," said Turner, with tears in her eyes. "I have been so disappointed in Van; oh, terribly disappointed."

"I know; yes, I think I know what you mean," answered young Haight in a low voice.

"Oh, please don't let's talk about it at all," cried Turner. But young Haight could not stop now.

"Is Van really out of the question, then?" he asked.

"Oh, yes," she exclaimed, not seeing what he was coming to. "Oh, yes; how could I—how *could* I care for him after—after what has happened?"

Very much embarrassed, young Haight went on: "I know it's unfair to take advantage of you now, but do you remember what you said once? That if Vandover were out of the question, that '*perhaps*' you might—that it would be—that there might be a chance for me?"

Turner was silent for a long time, and then she said: "Yes, I remember."

"Well, how about that *now*?" asked young Haight with a nervous laugh.

"Ah," answered Turner, "how do I know—so soon!"

"But what do you *think*, Turner?" he persisted.

"But I haven't thought at all," she returned.

"Well, think now!" he went on. "Tell me—how about that?"

"About *what*?"

"Ah, you know what I mean," young Haight replied, feeling like a little boy, "about what you said at your house that Sunday night. Please tell me; you don't know how much it means to me."

"Oh, there's Delphine at the door!" suddenly exclaimed Turner. "Now, really, I *must* go down. She doesn't know where to go; she's so stupid!"

"No," he answered, "not until you tell me!" He caught her hand, refusing to let it go.

"Ah, how mean you are to corner me so!" she cried laughing and embarrassed. "Must I—well—I know I shouldn't. *O-oh*, I just *detest* you!" Young Haight turned her hand palm upward and kissed the little circle of crumpled flesh that showed where her glove buttoned. Then she tore her hand away and ran downstairs, while he followed more slowly.

On her way back to the dressing-room she met him again, crossing the hall.

"Don't you want to see me home?" she said.

"Do I *want* to?" shouted young Haight.

"Oh, but I forgot," she cried. "You can't. I won't let you. You have your other dances engaged!"

"Oh, damn the other dances!" he exclaimed, but instead of being offended, Turner only smiled.

Toward one o'clock there was a general movement to go. Henrietta Vance and Mrs. Vance were inquired for, and the blue and white opera cloaks reappeared, descending the stairs, disturbing the couples who were seated there. The banging of carriage doors and the rumble of wheels recommenced in the street. The musicians played a little longer. As the party thinned out, there was greater dance room and a consequent greater pleasure in dancing. These last dances at the end of the evening were enjoyed more than all the others. But the party was breaking up fast: Turner had already gone home; Mrs. Vance and Henrietta were back at their places in front of the mantel, surrounded by a group of gentlemen in cape-coats and ladies in opera wraps. Every one was crying "Good-bye" or "Good night!" and assuring Mrs. Vance and Henrietta of the enjoyableness of the occasion. Suddenly the musicians played "Home Sweet Home." Those still dancing uttered an exclamation of regret, but continued waltzing to this air the same as ever. Some began to dance again in their overcoats and opera wraps. Then at last the tired musicians stopped and reached for the cases of their instruments, and the remaining guests, seized with a sudden panic lest they should be the last to leave, fled to the dressing-rooms. These were in the greatest confusion, every one was in a hurry; in the gentlemen's dressing-room there was a great putting on of coats and mufflers and a searching for misplaced gloves, hats and canes. A base hum of talk rose in the air, bits and ends of conversation being tossed back and forth across the room. "*You* haven't seen my hat, have you, Jimmy?" "Did you meet that girl I was telling you about?" "Hello, old man! have a good time to-night?" "Lost your hat? No, I haven't seen it." "Yes, about half-past ten!" "Well, I told him that myself!" "Ah, you bet it's the man that rustles that gets there." "Come round about four, then." "What's the matter with coming home in *our* carriage?"

At the doors of the dressing-rooms the ladies joined their escorts, and a great crowd formed in the halls, worming down the stairs and out upon the front steps. As the first groups reached the open air there was a great cry: "Why, it's pouring rain!" This was taken up and repeated and carried all the way back into the house. There were exclamations of dismay and annoyance: "Why, it's raining right *down!*" "What *shall* we do!" Tempers were lost, brothers and sisters quarrelling with each other over the question of umbrellas. "Ah," said Geary, delighted, peeling the cover from his umbrella in the vestibule, "I *thought* it was going to rain before I left and brought mine along with me. Ah, you bet I always look out for rain!" On the horse-block stood the caller, chanting up the carriages at the top of his voice. The street was full of coupés, carriages, and hacks, the raindrops showing in a golden blur as they fell across the streaming light of their lamps. The horses were smoking and restless, and the drivers in oilskins and rubber blankets were wrangling and shouting. At every instant there was a long roll of wheels interrupted by the banging of the doors. Near the caller stood a useless policeman, his shield pinned on the outside of his wet rubber coat, on which the carriage lamps were momentarily reflected in long vertical streaks.

In a short time all the guests were gone except the one young lady whose maid and carriage had somehow not been sent. Henrietta Vance's brother took this one home in a hired hack. Mrs. Vance and Henrietta sat down to rest for a moment in the empty parlours. The canvas-covered floors were littered with leaves of smilax and La France roses, with bits of ribbon, ends of lace, and discarded Phrygian bonnets of tissue paper. The butler and the second girl were already turning down the gas in the other rooms.

Long before the party broke up Vandover had gone home, stunned and dazed, as yet hardly able to realize the meaning of what had happened. Some strange and dreadful change had taken place; things were different, people were different to him; not every one had been so outspoken as Turner,

Henrietta Vance and her mother, but even amongst others who had talked to him politely and courteously enough, the change was no less apparent. It was in the air, a certain vague shrinking and turning of the shoulder, a general atmosphere of aversion and repulsion, an unseen frown, an unexpressed rebuff, intangible, illusive, but as unmistakable as his own existence. The world he had known knew him now no longer. It was ostracism at last.

But why? Why? Sitting over his tiled flamboyant stove, brooding into the winking coals, Vandover asked himself the question in vain. He knew what latitude young men were allowed by society; he was sure nothing short of discovered crime could affect them. True enough he had at one time allowed himself to drift into considerable dissipation, but he was done with that now, he had reformed, he had turned over a new leaf. Even at his worst he had only lived the life of the other young men around him, the other young men who were received as much as ever, even though people, the girls themselves, practically knew of what they did, knew that they were often drunk, and that they frequented the society of abandoned women. What had he done to merit this casting off? What *could* he have done? He even went so far as to wonder if there was anything wrong about his father or his sudden death.

A little after one o'clock he heard Geary's whistle in the street outside. "Hello, old man!" he cried as Vandover opened the window. "I was just on my way home from the hoe-down; saw a light in your window and thought I'd call you up. Say, have you got anything wet up there? I'm extra dry."

"Yes," said Vandover, "come on up!"

"Did you hear what Beale said to me this evening?" said Geary, as he mixed himself a cocktail at the sideboard. "Oh, I tell you, I'm getting right in, down at that office. Beale wants me to take the place of one of the assistants in the firm, a fellow who's got the consumption, coughing up his lungs all the time. It's an important place, hundred a month; that's right. Yes, sir; you bet, I'm going to get in and rustle now and make myself so indispensable in that fellow's place that they can't get along without me. I'll crowd him right out; I know it may be selfish, but, damn it! that's what you have to do to get along. It's human nature. I'll tell you right here to-night," he exclaimed with sudden energy, clenching his fist and slowly rapping the knuckles on the table to emphasize each word, "that I'll be the head of that firm some day, or I'll know the reason why."

When Geary finally became silent, the two looked into the fire for some time without speaking. At last Geary said:

"You came home early to-night, didn't you?"

"Yes," answered Vandover, stirring uneasily. "Yes, I did."

There was another silence. Then Geary said abruptly: "It's too bad. They are kind of stinky-pinky to you."

"Yes," said Vandover with a grin. "*I* don't know what's the matter. Everybody seems nasty!"

"It's that business with Ida Wade, you know," replied Geary. "It got around somehow that she killed herself on your account. Everybody seems to be on to it. I heard it—oh, nearly a month ago."

"Oh," said Vandover with a short laugh, "that's it, is it? I was wondering."

"Yes, that's it," answered Geary. "You see they don't know for sure; no one *knows*, but all at once every one seemed to be talking about it, and they suspect an awful lot. I guess they are pretty near right, aren't they?" He did not wait for an answer, but laughed clumsily and went on: "You see, you always have to be awfully careful in those things, or you'll get into a box. Ah, you bet I don't let any girl *I* go with know *my* last name or *my* address if I can help it. I'm clever enough for that; you have to manage very carefully; ah, you bet! You ought to have looked out for that, old man!" He paused a moment and then went on: "Oh, I guess it will be all right, all right, in a little while. They will forget about it, you know. I wouldn't worry. I guess it will be all right."

"Yes," answered Vandover absently, "I guess so—perhaps."

A few days later Vandover was in the reading-room of the Mechanics Library, listlessly turning over the pages of a volume of *l'Art*. It was Saturday morning and the place was full of ladies who were downtown for their shopping and marketing, and who had come in either to change their books or to keep appointments with each other. On a sudden Vandover saw Turner just passing into the Biography alcove. He got up and followed her. She was standing at the end of the dim book-lined tunnel, searching the upper shelves, her head and throat bent back, and her gloved finger on her lip. The faint odour of the perfume she always affected came to him mingled with the fragrance of the jonquils at her belt and the smell of leather and of books that exhaled from the shelves on either side. He did not offer to take her hand, but came up slowly, speaking in a low voice.

It was the last time that Vandover ever met Turner Ravis. They talked for upward of an hour, leaning against the opposite book-shelves, Vandover with his fists in his pockets, his head bent down, and the point of his shoe tracing the pattern in the linoleum carpet; Turner, her hands clasped in front of her, looking him squarely in the face, speaking calmly and frankly.

"Now, I hope you see just how it is, Van," she said at length. "What has happened hasn't made me cease to care for you, because if I had really cared for you the way I thought I did, the way a girl ought to care for the man she wants to marry, I would have stood by you through everything, no matter what you did. I don't do so now, because I find I don't care for you as much as I thought I did. What has happened has only shown me that. I'm sorry, oh, so sorry to be disappointed in you, but it's because I only think of you as being once a very good friend of mine, not because I love you as you think I did. Once—a long time ago—when we first knew each other, then, perhaps—things were different then. But somehow we seem to have grown away from that. Since then we have both been mistaken; you thought I cared for you in that way, and I thought so, too, and I thought you cared for me; but it was only that we were keeping up appearances, pretending to ourselves just for the sake of old times. We don't love each other now; you know it. But I have never intentionally deceived you or tried to lead you on; when I told you I cared for you I really thought I did. I meant to be sincere; I always thought so until this happened, and then when I saw how easily I could let you go, it only proved to me that I did not care for you as I thought I did. It was wrong of me, I know, and I should have known my own mind before, but I didn't, I didn't. You talk about Dolly

Haight; but it is not Dolly Haight at all who has changed my
affection for you. I will be just as frank as I can with you,
Van. I may learn really to love Dolly Haight; I don't know, I
think perhaps I will, but it isn't that I care for him *just* because I don't care for you. Can't you see, it's just as if I had
never met you. You know it's very hard for me to say this to
you, Van, and I suppose it's all mixed up, but I can't help it.
You don't know how sorry I am, because we have been such
old friends—because I really did care for you as a friend; it's
a proof of it, that there is no other man in the world I could
talk to like this. I think, too, Van, that was the only way you
cared for me, just as a good friend—except perhaps at first,
when we first knew each other. You know yourself that is so.
We really haven't loved each other at all for a long time, and
now we have found it out before it was too late. And even if
everything were different, Van, don't you know how it is with
girls? They really love the man who loves them the most. Half
the time they're just in love with being loved. That's the way
most girls love nowadays, and you know yourself, Van, that
Dolly Haight really loves me more than you do." She gathered up her books and went on after a pause, straightening
up, ready to go: "If I should let myself think of what you
have done, I feel—as if—as if—why, dreadful—I—that I
should hate you, loathe you; but I try not to do that. I have
been thinking it all over since the other night. I shall always
try to think of you at your best; I have tried to forget everything else, and in forgetting it I forgive you. I can honestly
say that," she said, holding out her hand, "I forgive you, and
you must forgive me because once, by deceiving myself, I deceived you, and made you think that I cared for you in that
way when I didn't." As their hands fell apart Turner faced
him and added, with tears in her eyes: "You know this must
be good-bye for good. You don't know how it hurts me to
tell you. I know it looks as if I were deserting you when you
were alone in the world and had most need of some one to
influence you for the good. But, Van, won't you be better
now? Won't you break from it all and be your own self again?
I have faith in you. I believe it's in you to become a great
man and a good man. It isn't too late to begin all over again.
Just be your better self; live up to the best that's in you; if

not for your own sake, then for the sake of that other girl that's coming into your life some time; that other girl who is good and sweet and pure, whom you will really, really love and who will really, really love you."

All the rest of that month Vandover was wretched. So great was his shame and humiliation over this fresh disaster that he hardly dared to show himself out of doors. His grief was genuine and it was profound. Yet he took his punishment in the right spirit. He did not blame any one but himself; it was only a just retribution for the thing he had done. Only what made it hard to bear was the fact that the chastisement had fallen upon him long after he had repented of the crime, long after he had resolved to lead a new and upright life; but with shut teeth he determined still to carry out that resolve; he would devote all his future life to living down the past. It might be hard; it might be one long struggle through many, many years, but he would do it. Ah, yes, he would show them; they had cast him off, but he would go away to Paris now as he had always intended. As invariably happened when he was deeply moved, he turned to his art, blindly and instinctively. He would go to Paris now and study his paintings, five, ten years, and come back at last a great artist, when these same people who had cast him off would be proud to receive him. Turner was right in saying that he had in him the making of a great man. He *knew* that she was right; knew that if he only gave the better part of him, the other Vandover, the chance, that he would become a great artist. Well, he would do so, and then when he came back again, when all the world was at his feet, and there were long articles in the paper announcing his arrival, these people would throng around him; he would show them what a great and noble nature he really had; he would forgive them; he would ignore what they had done. He even dramatized a little scene between himself and Turner, then Mrs. Haight. They would both be pretty old then and he would take her children on his lap and look at her over their heads—he could almost see those heads, white, silky and very soft—and he would nod at her thoughtfully, and say, "Well, I have taken your advice, do you remember?" and she was to answer, "Yes, I remember." There were actually tears in his eyes as he saw the scene.

At the very first he thought that he could not live without Turner; that he loved her too much to be able to give her up. But in a little while he saw that this was not so. She was right, too, in saying that he had long since outlived his first sincere affection for her. He had felt for a long time that he did not love her well enough to marry her; that he did not love her as young Haight did, and he acknowledged to himself that this affair at least had ended rightly. The two loved each other, he could see that; at last he even told himself that he would be glad to see Turner married to Dolly Haight, who was his best friend. But for all that, it came very hard at first to give up Turner altogether; never to see her or speak to her again.

As the first impressions of the whole affair grew dull and blunt by the lapse of time, this humble penitential mood of Vandover's passed away and was succeeded by a feeling of gloomy revolt, a sullen rage at the world that had cast him off *only* because he had been found out. He thought it a matter of self-respect to resent the insult they had put upon him. But little by little he ceased to regret his exile; the new life was not so bad as he had at first anticipated, and his relations with the men whom he knew best, Ellis, Geary, and young Haight, were in nowise changed. He was no longer invited anywhere, and the girls he had known never saw him when he passed them on the street. It was humiliating enough at first, but he got used to it after a while, and by dint of thrusting the disagreeable subject from his thoughts, by refusing to let the disgrace sink deep in his mind, by forgetting the whole business as much as he could, he arrived after a time to be passably contented. His pliable character had again rearranged itself to suit the new environment.

Along with this, however, came a sense of freedom. Now he no longer had anything to fear from society; it had shot its bolt, it had done its worst, there was no longer anything to restrain him, now he could do anything.

He was in precisely this state of mind when he received the cards for the opening of the roadhouse, the "resort" out on the Almshouse drive, about which Toby, the waiter at the Imperial, had spoken to him.

Vandover attended it. It was a debauch of forty-eight hours, the longest and the worst he had ever indulged in. For a long time the brute had been numb and dormant; now at last when he woke he was raging, more insatiable, more irresistible than ever.

The affair at the roadhouse was but the beginning. All at once Vandover rushed into a career of dissipation, consumed with the desire of vice, the perverse, blind, and reckless desire of the male. Drunkenness, sensuality, gambling, debauchery, he knew them all. He rubbed elbows with street walkers, with bookmakers, with saloonkeepers, with the exploiters of lost women. The bartenders of the city called him by his first name, the policemen, the night detail, were familiar with his face, the drivers of the nighthawks recognized his figure by the street lamps, paling in the light of many an early dawn. At one time and another he was associated with all the different types of people in the low "sporting set," acquaintances of an evening, whose names grew faint to his recollection amidst the jingle of glasses and the popping of corks, whose faces faded from his memory in the haze of tobacco smoke and the fumes of whisky; young men of the city, rich without apparent means of livelihood, women and girls "recently from the East" with rooms over the fast restaurants; owners of trotting horses, actresses without engagements, billiard-markers, pool-sellers and the sons of the proprietors of halfway houses and "resorts." With all these Vandover kept the pace at the Imperial, at the race-track, at the gambling tables in the saloons and bars along Kearney and Market streets, and in the disreputable houses amid the strong odours of musk and the rustle of heavy silk dresses. It lasted for a year; by the end of that time he had about forgotten his determination to go to Paris and had grown out of touch with his three old friends, Ellis, Geary, and Haight. He seldom saw them now; occasionally he met them in one of the little rooms of the Imperial over their beer and Welsh rabbits, but now he always went on to the larger rooms where one had champagne and terrapin. He felt that he no longer was one of them.

That year the opera came to San Francisco, and Vandover hired a messenger boy to stand in line all night at the door of the music store where the tickets were to be sold. Vandover could still love music. In the wreckage of all that was good that had been going on in him his love for all art was yet intact. It was the strongest side of his nature and it would be the last to go.

Chapter Fourteen

THE HOUSE was crowded to the doors; there was no longer any standing room and many were even sitting on the steps of the aisles. In the boxes the gentlemen were standing up behind the chairs of large plain ladies in showy toilets and diamonds. The atmosphere was heavy with the smell of gas, of plush upholstery, of wilting bouquets and of sachet. A fine vapour as of the visible exhalation of many breaths pervaded the house, blurring the lowered lights and dimming the splendour of the great glass chandelier.

It was warm to suffocation, a dry, irritating warmth that perspiration did not relieve, while the air itself was stale and close as though fouled by being breathed over and over again. In the topmost galleries, banked with tiers of watching faces, the heat must have been unbearable.

The only movement perceptible throughout the audience was the little swaying of gay-coloured fans like the balancing of butterflies about to light. Occasionally there would be a vast rustling like the sound of wind in a forest, as the holders of librettos turned the leaves simultaneously.

The orchestra thundered; the French horns snarling, the first violins wailing in unison, while all the bows went up and down together like parts of a well-regulated machine; the kettle-drums rolled sonorously at exact intervals, and now and then one heard the tinkling of the harp like the pattering of raindrops between peals of thunder. The leader swayed from side to side in his place, beating time with his baton, his hand, and his head.

On the stage itself the act was drawing to a close. There had just been a duel. The baritone lay stretched upon the floor at left centre, his sword fallen at some paces from him. On the left of the scene, front, stood the tenor who had killed him, singing in his highest register, very red in the face, continually striking his hand upon his breast and pointing with his sword toward his fallen enemy. Next him on the extreme left was his friend the basso, in high leather boots, growling from time to time during a sustained chord, *"Mon honneur et ma foi."* In the centre of the stage, the soprano, the star, the prima donna chanted a fervid but ineffectual appeal to the tenor who cried, *"Jamais, jamais!"* striking his breast and pointing with his sword. The prima donna cried, *"Ah, mon Dieu, ayez pitié de moi."* Her confidante, the mezzo-soprano, came to her support, repeating her words with an impersonal meaning, *"Ayez pitié d'elle."* *"Mon honneur et ma foi,"* growled the basso. The contralto, dressed as a man, turned toward the audience on the extreme right, bringing out her notes with a wrench and a twist of her body and neck, and intoning, *"Ah, malheureuse! Mon Dieu, ayez pitié d'elle."*

The leader of the chorus, costumed as the captain of the watch, leaned over the dead baritone and sang, *"Il est mort, il est mort. Mon Dieu, ayez pitié de lui."* The soldiers of the watch were huddled together immediately back of him. They wore tin helmets, much too large, and green peplums, and repeated his words continually.

The chorus itself was made up of citizens of the town; it was in a semicircle at the back of the stage—the men on one side, the women on the other. They made all their gestures together and chanted without ceasing: *"O horreur, O mystére! Il est mort. Mon Dieu, ayez pitié de nous!"*

"De Grace!" cried the prima donna.

"Jamais, jamais!" echoed the tenor, striking his breast and pointing with his sword.

"O mystére!" chanted the chorus, while the basso struck his hand upon his sword hilt, growling *"Mon honneur et ma foi."*

The orchestra redoubled. The finale began; all the pieces of the orchestra, all the voices on the stage, commenced over again very loud. They all took a step forward, and the rhythm became more rapid, till it reached a climax where the prima donna's voice jumped to a C in alt, holding it long enough for the basso to thunder, *"Mon honneur et ma foi"* twice. Then they all struck the attitudes for the closing tableau and in one last burst of music sang all together, *"Mon Dieu, ayez pitié de moi"* and *"de lui"* and *"d'elle"* and *"de nous."* Then the orchestra closed with a long roll of the kettle-drums, and the prima donna fainted into the arms of her confidante. The curtain fell.

There was a roar of applause. The gallery whistled and stamped. Every one relaxed his or her position, drawing a long breath, looking about. There was a general stir; the lights in the great glass chandelier clicked and blazed up, and a murmur of conversation arose. The footlights were lowered and the orchestra left their places and disappeared underneath the stage, leaving the audience with the conviction that they had gone out after beer. All over the house one heard the shrill voices of boys crying out, "Op'ra books—books for the op'ra—words and music for the op'ra."

Throughout the boxes a great coming and going took place and an interchange of visits. The gentlemen out in the foyer stood about conversing in groups or walked up and down smoking cigarettes, often pausing in front of the big floral piece that was to be given to the prima donna at the end of the great scene in the fourth act.

There was a little titter of an electric bell. The curtain was about to go up, and a great rush for seats began. The orchestra were coming back and tuning up. They sent up a prolonged medley of sounds, little minor chirps and cries from the violins, liquid runs and mellow gurgles from the oboes, flutes, and wood-wind instruments, and an occasional deeptoned purring from the bass viols. A bell rang faintly from behind the wings, the house lights sank, and the footlights blazed up. The leader tapped with his baton; a great silence fell upon the house, while here and there one heard an energetic "Ssh! ssh!" The fourth act was about to begin.

When the curtain rose on the fourth act one saw the prima donna standing in a very dejected pose in the midst of a vast apartment that might have been a bedchamber, a council hall, or a hall of audience. She was alone. She wore a loose creamcoloured gown knotted about the waist; her arms were bare, and her hair unbound and flowing loose over her shoulders to her girdle. She was to die in this act; it promised to be harrowing; and the first few notes she uttered recurred again later on as the motif for the famous quartet in the "great scene."

But for all this, the music had little by little taken possession of Vandover, and little by little he had forgotten his surroundings, the stifling air of the house, the blinding glitter of the stage and the discomfort of his limbs cramped into the narrow orchestra chair. All music was music to him; he loved

it with an unreasoned, uncritical love, enjoying even the barrel organs and hand pianos of the streets. For the present the
slow beat and cadence of the melodies of the opera had cradled all his senses, carrying him away into a kind of exalted
dream. The quartet began; for him it was wonderfully sweet,
the long-sustained chords breathing over the subdued orches-
tral accompaniment, like some sweet south wind passing in
long sighs over the pulse of a great ocean. It seemed to him
infinitely beautiful, infinitely sad, subdued minor plaints re-
curring persistently again and again like sighs of parting, but
could not be restrained, like voices of regret for the things
that were never to be again. Or it was a pathos, a joy in all
things good, a vast tenderness, so sweet, so divinely pure that
it could not be framed in words, so great and so deep that it
found its only expression in tears. There came over him a
vague sense of those things which are too beautiful to be
comprehended, of a nobility, a self-oblivion, an immortal
eternal love and kindness, all goodness, all benignity, all pity
for sin, all sorrow for grief, all joy for the true, the right, and
the pure.

To be better, to be true and right and pure, these were the
only things that were worth while, these were the things that
he seemed to feel in the music. It was as if for the moment
he had become a little child again, not ashamed to be innocent, ignorant of vice, still believing in all his illusions, still
near to the great white gates of life.

The appeal had been made directly to what was best and
strongest in Vandover, and the answer was quick and overpowering. All the good that still survived in him leaped to life
again in an instant, clamouring for recognition, pleading for
existence. The other Vandover, the better Vandover, wrestled
with the brute in him once more, never before so strong,
never so persistent. He had not yet destroyed all that was
good in him; now it had turned in one more revolt, crying
out against him, protesting for the last time against its own
perversion and destruction. Vandover felt that he was at the
great crisis of his life.

After all was over he walked home through the silent
streets, proceeding slowly, his hands in his pockets, his head
bent down, his mind very busy. Once in his rooms he threw

off his things and, having stirred up the drowsing fire in the tiled stove, sat down before it in his shirt-sleeves, the bosom of his full dress shirt bulging from his vest and faintly creaking as from time to time he drew a long breath. He had been lured into a mood where he was himself at his very best, where the other Vandover, the better Vandover, drew apart with eyes turned askance, looking inward and downward into the depths of his own character, shuddering, terrified. Far down there in the darkest, lowest places he had seen the brute, squat, deformed, hideous; he had seen it crawling to and fro dimly, through a dark shadow he had heard it growling, chafing at the least restraint, restless to be free. For now at last it was huge, strong, insatiable, swollen and distorted out of all size, grown to be a monster, glutted yet still ravenous, some fearful bestial satyr, grovelling, perverse, horrible beyond words.

And with the eyes of this better self he saw again, little by little, the course of his whole life, and witnessed again the eternal struggle between good and evil that had been going on within him since his very earliest years. He was sure that at the first the good had been the strongest. Little by little the brute had grown, and he, pleasure-loving, adapting himself to every change of environment, luxurious, self-indulgent, shrinking with the shrinking of a sensuous artist-nature from all that was irksome and disagreeable, had shut his ears to the voices that shouted warnings of the danger, and had allowed the brute to thrive and to grow, its abominable famine gorged from the store of that in him which he felt to be the purest, the cleanest, and the best, its bulk fattened upon the rot and the decay of all that was good, growing larger day by day, noisome, swollen, poddy, a filthy inordinate ghoul, gorged and bloated by feeding on the good things that were dead.

Besides this he saw how one by one he had wrenched himself free from all those influences that had tended to foster and to cultivate all the better part of him.

First of all, long ago it seemed now, he had allowed to be destroyed that first instinctive purity, that fragile, delicate innocence which dies young in almost every human being, and that one sees evaporating under the earliest taint of vice with a smile partly of contempt, partly of pity, partly of genuine regret.

Next it had been his father. The Old Gentleman had exerted a great influence over Vandover; he had never forgotten that scene the morning after he had told him of his measure of responsibility in Ida Wade's suicide, the recovery from the first shock of dazed bewilderment and then the forgiveness, the solicitude and the encouragement to begin over again, to live it down and to do that which was right and good and true. Not only had he stopped his ears to this voice, but also, something told him, he had done much to silence it forever. Despite the Old Gentleman's apparent fortitude the blow must have carried home. What must he not have suffered during those long weeks while Vandover was away, what lonely broodings in the empty house; and then the news of the wreck, the days of suspense!

It all must have told; the Old Gentleman was not strong; Vandover could not but feel that he had hastened his death, and that in so doing he had destroyed another influence which would have cultivated and fostered his better self, would have made it strong against the attacks of the brute.

The other person who had helped to bring out all that was best in Vandover had been Turner Ravis. There was no denying that when he had first known her he had loved her sincerely. Things were vastly different with him when Turner had been his companion; things that were unworthy, that were low, that were impure and vicious, did not seem worth while then; not only did they have no attraction for him, but he even shunned and avoided them. He knew he was a better man for loving her; invariably she made him wish to be better. But little by little as he frequented the society of such girls as Ida Wade, Grace Irving, and Flossie, his affection for Turner faded. As the habits of passionate and unhealthy excitement grew upon him he lost first the taste and then the very capacity for a calm, pure feeling. His affection for her he frittered away with fast girls and abandoned women, strangled it in the foul musk-laden air of disreputable houses, dragged and defiled it in the wine-lees of the Imperial. In the end he had quite destroyed it, wilfully, wantonly killed it. As Turner herself had said, she could only be in love with being loved; her affection for him had dwindled as well; at last they had come to be indifferent to each other, she no longer inspired him to be better, and thus he had shaken off this good influence as well.

Public opinion had been a great check upon him, the fear of scandal, the desire to stand well with the world he knew. Trivial though he felt it to be, the dread of what people would say had to a great extent held Vandover back. He had a position to maintain, a reputation to keep up in the parlours and at the dinner tables where he was received. It could not be denied that society had influenced Vandover for good. But this, too, like all the others, he had cast from him. Now he was ostracized, society cared no longer what he did, his position was gone, his reputation was destroyed. There was no one now to stand in his way.

Vandover could not fall back on any religious influence. Religion had never affected him very deeply. It was true that he had been baptized, confirmed, and had gone to church with considerable regularity. If he had been asked if he was a Christian and believed in God he would have answered "Certainly, certainly." Until the time of his father's death he had even said his prayers every night, the last thing before turning out the gas, sitting upon the edge of his bed in his nightgown, his head in both his hands. He added to the Lord's Prayer certain other petitions as to those who were in trouble, sorrow, poverty, or any other privations; he asked for blessings upon his father and upon himself, praying for the former's health and prosperity, and for himself, that he might become a great artist, that the "Last Enemy" might be admitted to the Salon when he had painted it, and that it might make him famous. But, as a rule, Vandover thought very little about religious matters and when he did, told himself that he was too intelligent to believe in a literal heaven, a literal hell, and a personal God personally interfering in human affairs like any Jove or Odin. But the moment he rejected a concrete religion Vandover was almost helpless. He was not mystic enough to find any meaning in signs or symbols, nor philosophic enough to grasp vague and immense abstractions. Infinities, Presences, Forces, could not help him withstand temptation, could not strengthen him against the brute. He felt that somewhere, some time, there was punishment for evildoing, but, as happened in the case of Ida Wade's death, to dwell on such thoughts disturbed and terrified him. He did not dare to look long in that direction. Conscience, remorse, repentance, all these had been keen enough at first, but he had so persistently kicked against the pricks that little by little he had ceased to feel them at all.

Then an immense and overwhelming terror seized upon him. Was there nothing, then—nothing left which he could lay hold of to save him? He knew that he could not deliver himself by his own exertions. Religion could not help him, he had killed his father, estranged the girl he might have loved, outraged the world, and at a single breath blighted the fine innate purity of his early years. It was as if he had entered into his life in the world as into some vast labyrinth, wandering on aimlessly, flinging from him one by one the threads, the clues, that might have led him again to a safe exit, going down deeper and deeper until, when near the centre, he had suddenly felt the presence of the brute, had heard its loathsome muttering growl, had at last seen it far down at the end of a passage, dimly and in a dark shadow; terrified, he had started back, looking wildly about for any avenue of escape, searching with frantic haste and eagerness for any one of those clues he had so carelessly cast from him, realizing that without such guidance he would inevitably tend down again to that fatal central place where the brute had its lair.

There was nothing, nothing. He clearly saw the fate toward which he was hurrying; it was not too late to save himself if he only could find help, but he could find *no* help. His terror increased almost to hysteria. It was one of those dreadful moments that men sometimes undergo that must be met alone, and that when past, remain in the memory for all time; a glimpse far down into the springs and wheels of life; a glimpse that does not come often lest the reason brought to the edge of the fearful gulf should grow dizzy at the sight, and reeling, topple headlong.

But suddenly Vandover rose to his feet, the tears came to his eyes, and with a long breath he exclaimed: "Thank God for it!" He grew calmer in a moment, the crisis had passed, he had found a clue beneath his groping fingers.

He had remembered his art, turning to it instinctively as he always did when greatly moved. This was the one good thing that yet survived. It was the strongest side of him; it would be the last to go; he felt it there yet. It was the one thing that could save him.

The thought had come to him so suddenly and with such marvellous clearness that in his present exalted state of mind it filled him with a vague sense of awe, it seemed like a manifestation, a writing on the wall. Might it not be some sort of miracle? He had heard of men reforming their lives, transformed almost in an instant, and had scoffed at the idea. But might it not be true, after all? What was this wonderful thing that had happened to him? Was this less strange than a miracle? Less divine?

The following day Vandover rented a studio. It was the lofty room with hardwood floors and the immense north light in that suite which he had rejected when looking for rooms on the former occasion. He gave notice to the clerk in the apartment house where his quarters were situated that he intended to vacate after the first of the month. Charming as he had found these rooms, he gave up, with scarcely a regret, the idea of living in them any longer. In a month it would be summer and he would be on his way to Paris.

But so great was his desire for work now, so eager was he to start the "Last Enemy," so strong was the new energy that shook him, that Vandover could not wait until summer to begin work again. He grudged everything now that kept him away from his easel.

He disappeared from the sight of his ordinary companions; he did not even seek the society of Geary or of young Haight. All the sketches he had made for the "Last Enemy," together with his easel and his disused palette, his colour-box, tubes, brushes and all the other materials and tools for his work, he caused to be transferred to the new studio. Besides this he had the stretcher made, best twill canvas on a frame four feet long, two and a half feet high. This was for the large sketch of the picture. But the finished work he calculated would demand an eight by five stretcher.

He did not think of decorating the room, of putting any ornaments about the wall. He was too serious, too much in earnest now to think of that. The studio was not to be his lounging place, but his workshop. His art was work with him now, hard, serious work. It was above all *work* that he needed to set him right again, regular work, steady, earnest work, not the dilettante fancy of an amateur content with making pretty things.

Never in his life had Vandover been so happy. He came and went continually between his rooms, his studio, and his art dealers, tramping grandly about the city, whistling to himself, strong, elated, filled with energy, vigour, ambition. At times his mind was full of thankfulness at this deliverance at the eleventh hour; at times it was busy with the details of the picture, its composition, its colour scheme. The main effects he wanted to produce were isolation and intense heat, the shadows on the sand would be blue, the horizon line high on the canvas, the sky would be light in tone, almost white near the earth.

The morning when he first began to work was charming. His new studio was in the top floor of a five-story building, and on arriving there, breathless from his long climb up the stairs, Vandover threw open the window and gazed out and down upon the city spread out below him, enjoying the view a moment before settling to his work.

A little later the trades would be blowing strong and brisk from the ocean, driving steadily through the Golden Gate, filling the city with a taint of salt; but at present the air was calm, touched with a certain nimbleness, a sparkling effervescence, invigourating, exhilarating.

It was early in the forenoon, not yet past nine o'clock, and the mist that gathers over the city just before dawn was steaming off under the sun, very thin and delicate, turning all distant objects a flat tone of pale blue. Over the roofs of the houses he could catch a glimpse of the distant mountains, faint purple masses against the pale edge of the sky, rimming the horizon round with a fillet of delicate colour. But any larger view was barred by a huge frame house with a slated mansard roof, directly opposite him across the street, a residence house, one of the few in the neighbourhood. It had been newly painted white and showed brave and gay against the dark blue of the sky and the ruddy greens of the great garden in which it stood. Vandover from his window could from time to time catch the smell of eucalyptus trees coming to him in long aromatic breaths mingled with the odour of wet grass and fresh paint. Somewhere he heard a humming-bird singing, a tiny tweedling thread of song, while farther off two roosters were crowing back and forth at each other with strained and raucous trumpet calls.

Vandover turned back to his work. Under the huge north light was the easel, and clamped upon it the stretcher, blank, and untouched. The very sight of the heavy cream-white twill was an inspiration. Already Vandover saw a great picture upon it; a great wave of emotion suddenly welled up within him and he cried with enthusiasm:

"By God! it is in moods like this that *chef d'oeuvres* are made."

Around the baseboard of the room were a row of *esquisses* for the picture, on small landscape-stretchers, mere blotches of colour laid on with the palette knife and large brushes, almost unintelligible to any one but Vandover. He selected two or three of these and fastened them to the easel above the big stretcher where he could have them continually in his eye. He lit his pipe, rolled up his shirt-sleeves, and standing before the easel, began to sharpen a stick of charcoal with an old razor, drawing the blade toward him so as to keep the point of the stick from breaking. Then at last with a deep breath of satisfaction he began blocking in the first large construction lines of his picture.

It was one o'clock before he knew it. He went downtown and had a hasty lunch, jealous of every moment that was not spent on his picture. The sight of it as he re-entered the room sent a thrill all over him; he was succeeding better than he could have expected, doing better than he thought he would. He felt sure that now he should do good work; every stage of the picture's progress was an inspiration for the next one. At this time the figures had only been "placed," broadly sketched in large lines, "blocked in" as he called it. The next step was the second drawing, much more finished.

He rapped the stretcher sharply with his knuckles; it responded sonorously like a drumhead, the vibration shaking the charcoal from the tracings, filling the air with a fine dust.

The outlines grew faint, just perceptible enough to guide him in the second more detailed drawing.

He brought his stick of charcoal to a very fine edge and set to work carefully. In a moment he stopped and, with his chamois cloth, dusted out what he had drawn. He had made a false start, he began but could not recall how the lines should run, his fingers were willing enough; in his imagination he saw just how the outlines should be, but somehow he could not make his hand interpret what was in his head. Some third medium through which the one used to act upon the other was sluggish, dull; worse than that, it seemed to be absent. *"Well,"* he muttered, "can't I make this come out right?" Then he tried more carefully. His imagination saw the picture clearer, his hand moved with more assurance, but the two seemed to act independently of each other. The forms he made on the canvas were no adequate reflection of those in his brain; some third delicate and subtle faculty that coördinated the other two and that called forth a sure and instant response to the dictates of his mind, was lacking. The lines on his canvas were those of a child just learning to draw; one saw for what they were intended, but they were crude, they had no life, no meaning. The very thing that would have made them intelligible, interpretive, that would have made them art, was absent. A third, a fourth, and a fifth time Vandover made the attempt. It was useless. He knew that it was not because his hand lacked cunning on account of long disuse; such a thing, in spite of popular belief, never happened to artists—a good artist might abandon his work for five years, ten years—and take it up again precisely where he had laid it down with no loss of technical skill. No, this thing seemed more subtle, so subtle that at first he could hardly grasp it. But suddenly a great fear came upon him, a momentary return of that wild hysterical terror from which he believed he had forever escaped.

"Is it gone?" he cried out. "Is it gone from me? My art? Steady," he went on, passing his hand over his face with a reassuring smile; "steady, old man, this won't do, again—and so soon! It won't do for you to get scared twice like that. This is just nervousness, you are overexcited. Pshaw! What's the matter with me? Let's get to work."

Still another time he dusted out what he had done and recommenced, concentrating all his attention with a tremendous effort of the will. Grotesque and meaningless shapes, the mocking caricatures of those he saw in his fancy, grew under his charcoal, while slowly, slowly, a queer, numb feeling came in his head, like a rising fog, and the touch of that unreasoning terror returned, this time stronger, more persistent, more tenacious than before.

Vandover nerved himself against it, not daring to give in, fearing to allow himself to see what this really meant. He passed one hand over his cheek and along the side of his head, the fingers dancing. "Hum!" he muttered, looking vaguely about him, "this is bad. I mustn't let this get the better of me now. I'll knock off for to-day, take a little rest, begin again to-morrow."

In ten minutes he was back at his easel again. His charcoal wandered, tracing empty lines on his canvas, the strange numbness grew again in his head. All the objects in the range of his eyes seemed to move back and stand on the same plane. He became a little dizzy.

"It's the *tobacco*," he exclaimed. "That pipe always was too strong." He turned away to the open window, feeling an irresistible need of distraction, of amusement, and he remained there resting on his elbows, listening and looking, trying to be interested.

It was toward the middle of the afternoon. The morning mist was long since evaporated and the first faint puffs of the inevitable trade wind were just stirring the leaves of the eucalyptus across the street. In the music-room of the white house the young lady of the family had opened the piano and was practising finger-exercises. The scales and arpeggios following one another without interruption, came to his ears in a pleasant monotone. A Chinese "boy" in a stiff blouse of white linen, made a great splashing as he washed down the front steps with a bucket of water and the garden hose. Grocery and delivery wagons came and went, rattling over the cobbles and car-tracks, while occasionally a whistle blew very far off. At the corner of the street by a livery-stable a little boy in a flat-topped leather cap was calling incessantly for some unseen dog, whistling and slapping his knees. An express-wagon stopped a few doors below the white house and the driver pulled down the back-board with a strident rattle of chains; the cable in its slot kept up an unceasing burr and clack while the cars themselves trundled up and down the street, starting and stopping with a jangling of bells, the jostled glass windows whirring in a prolonged vibrant note. All these sounds played lightly over the steady muffled roar that seemed to come from all quarters at once; it was that deep murmur, that great minor diapason that always disengages itself from vast bodies, from mountains, from oceans, from forests, from sleeping armies.

The desire for movement, for diversion, for anything that would keep him from thinking was not to be resisted. Vandover caught up his hat and fled from the room, not daring to look again at the easel. Once outside, he began to walk, anywhere, straight before him, going on with great strides, his head in the air.

He found Charlie Geary and took him to supper. Vandover talked continually on all sorts of subjects, speaking very rapidly. In the evening he insisted on Geary going to the theatre with him. He paid the closest attention to the play, letting it occupy his mind entirely. When the play was over and the two were about to say good night, Vandover began to urge Geary to sleep up at his rooms that night. He overrode his objections, interrupting him, taking hold of his arm, and starting off. But Geary, a little surprised at his manner, refused. There were certain law papers he had taken home with him from the office that afternoon and that it was necessary he should return in the morning. Ah, you bet, he would get it right in the neck if old Beale didn't have those depositions the first thing when the office was open. Ah, he was getting to be indispensable down there. He had had Fischer's place now for a year. Fischer had never come back, and he had the promise of being taken on as head clerk as soon as Beale Jr. went into the partnership with old Beale. "I'll make my way in this town yet," he declared. "I'll be in that partnership myself some day. You see; yes, sir; ah, you bet!"

The idea of passing the night alone terrified Vandover. He started toward home, walking up Sutter Street, proceeding slowly, his hands in his pockets. All at once he stopped, without knowing why; he roused himself and looked about him. There was a smell of eucalyptus in the air. Across the street was the huge white house, and he found that he had stopped just before the door of the building on the top floor of which his studio was situated. All day Vandover's mind had been in the greatest agitation, his ideas leaping and darting hither and thither like terrified birds in a cage. Just now he underwent a sudden reaction. It had all been a matter of fancy, nothing but nervousness; he had not drawn for some time, his hand lacked cunning from long disuse. The desire for work came upon him again overpoweringly. He wanted to see again if he could not draw just as truly and freely as in the old days. No, he could not wait till morning; he must put himself to the test again at once, at the very instant. It was a sudden feminine caprice, induced, no doubt, by the exalted, strained, and unnatural condition of his nerves, a caprice that could not be reasoned with, that could not be withstood. He had his keys with him, he opened the outside door and groped his way up the four long flights of stairs to his studio.

The studio was full of a sombre half-light, like a fog, spreading downward from the great north light in the sloping roof. The window was still wide open, the stretcher showed a pale gray blur. Vandover was about to light the gas when he checked himself, his arm still raised above his head. Ah, no; he did not dare to look at the result of his day's work. It would be better to start in afresh from the beginning. He found the chamois skin on the tray of the easel and rubbed out all the drawing on the canvas. Then he lit the gas.

As he turned to his work once more a little thrill of joy and of relief passed over him. This time his hand was sure, steady, his head was clear. It had been nervousness after all. As he picked up his charcoal he even exclaimed to himself, "Just the same, that *was* a curious experience this afternoon."

But the curious experience repeated itself again that night as soon as he tried to work. Once more certain shapes and figures were born upon his canvas, but they were no longer the true children of his imagination, they were no longer his own; they were changelings, grotesque abortions. It was as if the brute in him, like some malicious witch, had stolen away the true offspring of his mind, putting in their place these deformed dwarfs, its own hideous spawn.

Through the numbness and giddiness that gradually came into his head like a poisonous murk he saw one thing clearly: It was gone—his art was gone, the one thing that could save him. That, too, like all the other good things of his life, he had destroyed. At some time during those years of debauchery it had died, that subtle, elusive something, delicate as a flower; he had ruined it. Little by little it had exhaled away, wilting in the air of unrestrained debauches, perishing in the warm musk-laden atmosphere of disreputable houses, defiled by the breath of abandoned women, trampled into the spilt wine-lees of the Imperial, dragged all fouled and polluted through the lowest mire of the great city's vice.

For a moment Vandover felt as though he was losing his hold upon his reason; the return of the hysteria shook him like a dry, light leaf. He suddenly had a sensation that the room was too small to hold him; he ran, almost reeled, to the open window, drawing his breath deep and fast, inhaling the cool night air, rolling his eyes wildly.

It was night. He looked out into a vast blue-gray space sown with points of light, winking lamps, and steady slow-burning stars. Below him was the sleeping city. All the lesser staccato noises of the day had long since died to silence; there only remained that prolonged and sullen diapason, coming from all quarters at once. It was like the breathing of some infinitely great monster, alive and palpitating, the systole and diastole of some gigantic heart. The whole existence of the great slumbering city passed upward there before him through the still night air in one long wave of sound.

It was Life, the murmur of the great, mysterious force that spun the wheels of Nature and that sent it onward like some enormous engine, resistless, relentless; an engine that sped straight forward, driving before it the infinite herd of humanity, driving it on at breathless speed through all eternity, driving it no one knew whither, crushing out inexorably all those who lagged behind the herd and who fell from exhaustion, grinding them to dust beneath its myriad iron wheels, riding over them, still driving on the herd that yet remained, driving it recklessly, blindly on and on toward some far-distant goal, some vague unknown end, some mysterious, fearful bourne forever hidden in thick darkness.

Chapter Fifteen

ABOUT A WEEK later Hiram Wade, Ida's father, brought suit against Vandover to recover twenty-five thousand dollars, claiming that his daughter had killed herself because she had been ruined by him and that he alone was responsible for her suicide.

Vandover had passed this week in an agony of grief over the loss of his art, a grief that seemed even sharper than that which he had felt over the death of his father. For this last calamity was like the death of a child of his, some dear, sweet child, that might have been his companion throughout all his life. At times it seemed to him impossible that his art should fail him in this manner, and again and again he would put himself at his easel, only to experience afresh the return of the numbness in his brain, the impotency of his fingers.

He had begun little by little to pick up the course of his life once more, and on a certain Wednesday morning was looking listlessly through the morning paper as he sat in his window-seat. The room was delightful, flooded with the morning sun, the Assyrian *bas-reliefs* just touched with a ruddy light, the Renaissance portraits looking down at him through a fine golden haze; a little fire, just enough to blunt the keenness of the early morning air, snapping in the famous tiled and flamboyant stove. All about the room was a pleasant fragrance of coffee and good tobacco.

Vandover caught sight of the announcement of the suit with a sudden sharp intake of breath that was half gasp, half cry, starting up from the window-seat, reading it over again and again with staring eyes.

It was a very short paragraph, not more than a dozen lines, lost at the bottom of a column, among the cheap advertisements. It made no allusion to any former stage of the affair; from its tone Ida might have killed herself only the day before. It seemed hardly more than a notice that some enterprising reporter, burrowing in the records at the City Hall, had unearthed and brought to light with the idea that it might be of possible interest to a few readers of the paper. But there was his name staring back at him from out the gray

blur of the type, like some reflection of himself seen in a mirror. Insignificant as the paragraph was, it seemed to Vandover
as though it was the only item in the whole paper. One might
as well have trumpeted his crime through the streets.

"But twenty-five thousand dollars!" exclaimed Vandover,
terrified. "Where will *I* find twenty-five thousand dollars?"
And at once he fell to wondering as to whether or no in
default of payment he could be sent to the penitentiary. The
idea of winning the suit did not enter his mind an instant; he
did not even dream of fighting it.

For the moment it was like fire driving out fire. He forgot
the loss of his art, his mind filled only with the sense of the
last disaster. What could he do? Twenty-five thousand dollars!
It would ruin him. A cry of exasperation, of rage at his own
folly, escaped him. "Ah, what a fool I've been!"

For an hour he raged to and fro in the delightful sunlit
room, pacing back and forth in its longest dimension between
the bamboo tea-table and the low bookcase, a thousand different plans and projects coming and going in his head. As
his wits steadied themselves he began to see that he must consult at once with some lawyer—Field, of course—perhaps
something could be done; a clever lawyer might make out a
case for him after all. But all at once he became convinced
that Field would not undertake his defence; he knew he had
no case; so what could Field do for him? He would have to
tell him the truth, and he saw with absolute clearness that the
lawyer would refuse to try to defend him. The thing could
not honourably be done. But, then, what *should* he do? He
must have legal advice from some quarter.

He was still in this state of perplexity when Charlie Geary
arrived, pounding on the door and opening it immediately
afterward as was his custom.

"Hello!" said Vandover, surprised. "Hello, Charlie! is that
you?"

"Say," exclaimed Geary without returning his greeting,
holding up his hand as if to interrupt him; "say, have you
seen your lawyer yet—seen *any* lawyer?"

"No," answered Vandover, shaking his head gravely; "no,
I've only this minute read about it in the paper." He was glad
that Geary had come; at once he felt a desire to throw this

burden upon his chum's shoulders, to let him assume the management of the affair, just as in the old college days he had willingly, weakly, submitted to the dictatorship of the shrewder, stronger man who smoothed out his difficulties for him, and extricated him from all his scrapes. He knew Geary to be full of energy and resource, and he had confidence in his ability as a lawyer, even though he was so young in years and experience. Besides this, he was his friend, his college chum; for all Geary's disagreeable qualities he knew he would do the right thing by him now.

"You're the one man of all others I wanted to see," he exclaimed as he gripped his hand. "By George! I'm glad you have come. Here, sit down and let's talk this over." Geary took the big leather chair behind the desk, and Vandover flung himself again upon the window-seat. It was as if the two were back in the room in Matthew's; hundreds of times in those days they had occupied precisely these positions, Geary bending over at the study table, intent, nervous, very keen, Vandover lounging idly upon the window-seat, resting easily on his elbow listening to the other man's advice.

"Now, what must I do, Charlie?" Vandover began. "See my lawyer, I suppose? But do you think a lawyer like Field would take my case? You know I haven't a leg to stand on."

"But you haven't seen him?" inquired Geary sharply. "Haven't seen anybody about it?" Vandover shook his head. "Sure?" insisted Geary anxiously.

"Why, I have only just heard about it twenty minutes ago," protested Vandover. "Why are you so particular about that?" he added. Then Geary exploded his mine.

"Because," he said, with a smile of triumph that he could not restrain, "because we are the counsel for the other side. I am on the case."

Vandover bounded from the window-seat speechless with astonishment, bitterly disappointed. "*You?*" he shouted. Geary slowly nodded his head, enjoying Vandover's bewilderment. Vandover dropped back upon the cushions again, staring at him wildly with growing suspicion and anger. He would not have thought it possible that Geary could so sacrifice their old friendship to his own personal interest. The two continued staring at each other across the table for a moment. In the silence they heard the long rumble of a cable-car passing the house, and the persistent jangling of its bell as it approached the street crossing. A grocery wagon went up the side street, the horses' hoofs making a cadenced clapping sound upon the asphalt.

"Well," exclaimed Vandover scornfully, "I suppose that's business, but *I* would call it damned unkind!"

"Now, look here, old man," returned Geary consolingly. "Don't you take the monkey-wrench off the safety valve like that. What am I here for if it isn't to help you? Maybe you don't know that this is a mighty unprofessional thing to do. Ah, you bet, if old Beale knew this I would get it right in the neck. Don't you suppose I can help you more as Wade's lawyer than I could as yours? And now that's the very first thing I've got to tell you—to keep this dark, that I have seen you. I can't do anything for you if you don't promise that."

"Oh, that's all right," returned Vandover, reassured. "That's all right, you can——"

"It's not considered the right thing to do," Geary continued, not heeding Vandover's answer, "but I just do it because"—he began to make awkward gestures with both his hands—"because we're old friends, like that. That was the very first thing I thought of when Beale Jr. told me that we two had the case—that I could get you out of this hole better as Wade's lawyer than as your own. Ah, you bet, I was clever enough to see that the first thing."

"I'm sure it was awfully good of you, old man," said Vandover sincerely. "I'm in a lot of trouble nowadays!"

"Well, now don't you bother, Van," answered Geary consolingly. "I guess we can pull you out of this all right." He drew up to the table, looking about from side to side. "Got any writing paper concealed about the premises?" he asked. Vandover pushed him over his writing pad, and Geary, taking the cap from his fountain pen, began asking a series of questions, taking down his answers in shorthand. After he had asked him as to his age, length of residence in the city, his property, and some few other technical matters, he leaned back in his chair and said:

"Now, let's hear your side of the story, Van. I don't suppose you like to go over the thing again, but you see I ought to know." Vandover told of the affair, Geary making notes as he went along. It was nearly noon before their interview was at an end. Then Geary gathered up the papers and reached for his hat and stick, saying:

"Well, now, that's all we can do to-day. I think I'll be up to see you again day after to-morrow, in the afternoon. Beale Jr. and I have a date with Mr. Wade again to-morrow, I think, and I can talk to you more definitely after that. You know this is the devil of a thing to do," he suddenly exclaimed apprehensively, "this playing back and forth between the two parties like this; regularly dishonourable, don't you know?"

"If you think it's dishonourable," said Vandover as he accompanied Geary to the door, "if you think it's dishonourable, Charlie, why, don't do it! I don't want to ask you to do anything dishonourable for me."

"Oh, that's all right," replied Geary uneasily; "I had just as soon do it for you, only listen to this: don't you say a word about the case to anybody, not to your lawyer, nor to anybody. If Field should write to you, you tell him you have counsel already. And, look here! you may have the reporters up here pretty soon, and don't you open your face to them; you mind that; don't you let them get a thing out of you. And there's another thing you must understand: I'm not your lawyer, of course; you see that. I could be disbarred if I was lawyer for both sides. It's like this, you see: I'm Wade's lawyer—at least the firm I am with are his lawyers—and of course I'm acting in Wade's interest. But you're an old chum of mine, and if I can I'm going to try and make it easier for you. You understand, don't you?"

"Yes, I understand, Charlie," answered Vandover, "and you are just a brick."

Vandover passed the rest of the day in his sitting-room, the suspense of the situation slowly screwing his nerves tenser and tenser. He walked for hours back and forth, his hands clasped behind his back, his head bent down, his forehead drawn into a frown of anxiety and exasperation, or he stood for a long time at the window looking out into the street with eyes that saw nothing. At supper that night he found that his appetite had left him; the very thought of food revolted him.

He returned to his room between seven and eight o'clock, his body and mind completely fagged, feeling a crying need of some diversion, some escape from the thoughts that had been hounding him all day.

He made up his mind to read a little before going to bed, and all at once remembered a book that he had once begun a long time ago but had never finished: the story of two men who had bought a wrecked opium ship for fifty thousand dollars and had afterward discovered that she contained only a few tins of the drug. He had never read on to find how that story turned out. Suddenly he found himself repeating, "Twenty-five thousand dollars, twenty-five thousand dollars—where will *I* find twenty-five thousand dollars?" He wondered if he would go to jail if he failed to pay. His interest in the book was gone in a moment, and he took up another of his favourite novels, the story of a boy at the time of Christ, a Jewish boy unjustly condemned to the galleys, liberated afterward, and devoting his life to the overthrow of his enemy, whom at last he overcame and humbled, fouling him in a chariot race, all but killing him.

He sat down in the huge leather chair, and, drawing it up to the piano lamp and cocking his feet upon the table, began to read. In a few moments the same numbness stole into his head like a rising fog, a queer, tense feeling, growing at the back of his forehead and at the base of his skull, a dulness, a strange stupefying sensation as of some torpid, murky atmosphere. He looked about him quickly; all the objects in the range of his vision—the corner of the desk, the corduroy couch, the low bookcase with Flossie's yellow slipper and Barye's lioness upon it—seemed to move back and stand upon the same plane; the objects themselves appeared immovable enough, but the sensation of them in his brain somewhere behind his eyes began to move about in a slow, dizzy whirl. The old touch of unreasoning terror came back, together with a sudden terror of the spirit, a sickening sinking of the heart, a loathing of life, terrible beyond words.

Vandover started up, striving to keep himself in hand, fighting against a wild desire to rush about from wall to wall, shrieking and waving his arms. Over and over again he exclaimed, "Oh, *what* is the matter with me?" The strangeness of the thing was what unsettled and unnerved him. He had all the sensations of terror, but without any assignable reason, and this groundless fear became in the end the cause of a new fear: he was afraid of this fear that was afraid of nothing.

Very gradually, however, the crisis passed away. He became a little calmer, and as he was mixing himself a glass of whisky and water at the sideboard he decided that he would go to bed. He was sure that he would be better for a good night's rest; evidently his nerves were out of order; it would not do for him to read late at night. He realized all at once that his mind and body alike were exhausted.

He passed a miserable night, dozing and waking at alternate hours until three o'clock, when he found it impossible to get to sleep; hour after hour he lay flat on his back staring open-eyed into the darkness, listening to the ticking of the clock, the mysterious footsteps that creaked the floors overhead, and the persistent drip of a water faucet. Outside in the street he heard at long intervals the rattling of wheels as the early milk wagons came and went; a dog began to bark, three gruff notes repeated monotonously at exact intervals; all at once there was a long muffled roll and an abrupt clacking noise; it ceased, then broke out again sharply, paused once more, then recommenced, settling to a prolonged minor hum; the cable was starting up; it was almost morning, the window of his room began to show a brighter blur in the darkness, while very far off he could hear the steady puffing of a locomotive. As the first cable-car trundled by the house he dropped off to sleep for the last time, being waked again toward nine o'clock by the sound of some one shovelling coal outside under his window, the shovel clinking and rasping upon the stone sidewalk.

He felt a little refreshed, but as he entered the dining-room for his late breakfast the smell of food repulsed him; his appetite was gone; it was impossible for him to eat. Toward eleven o'clock that same morning he was pottering idly about his sitting-room, winding his clock and shaking down the ashes in the tiled flamboyant stove; his mind was still busy going over for the hundredth time all the possibilities of Hiram Wade's suit, and he was just wondering whether something in the way of a compromise might not be arranged, when with the suddenness of a blow between the eyes the numbness in his head returned, together with the same unreasoning fear, the same depression of spirits, the same fearful sinking of the heart. What! it was coming back again, this strange attack, coming back even when his attention was not concentrated, even when there was no unusual exertion of his brain!

Then the torment began. This time the crisis did not pass off; from now on it persisted continually. Vandover began to feel strange. At first the room looked unfamiliar to him, then his own daily life no longer seemed recognizable, and, finally, all of a sudden, it was the whole world, all the existing order of things, that appeared to draw off like a refluent tide, leaving him alone, abandoned, cast upon some fearful, mysterious shore.

Nothing seemed worth while; all the thousand little trivial things that made up the course of his life and in which he found diversion and amusement palled upon him. A fearful melancholia settled over him, a despair, an abhorrence of living that could not be uttered. This only was during the day. It was that night that Vandover went down into the pit.

He went to bed early, his brain in a whirl, his frame worn out as if from long physical exertion. He was just dropping into a grateful sleep when his whole body twitched suddenly with a shock and a recoil of all his nerves; in an instant he was broad awake, panting and exhausted as if from a long run. Once more he settled himself upon the pillow, and once more the same leap, the same sharp spasm of his nerves caught him back to consciousness with the suddenness of a relaxed spring. At last sleep was out of the question; his drowsiness of the early part of the evening passed away, and he lay back, his hands clasped behind his head, staring up into the darkness, his thoughts galloping incessantly through his brain, suffering without pain as he had never imagined a human being could suffer though racked with torture from head to heel.

From time to time a slow torsion and crisping of all his nerves, beginning at his ankles, spread to every corner of his body till he had to shut his fists and teeth against the blind impulse to leap from his bed screaming. His hands felt light and, as he told himself, "jumpy." All at once he felt a peculiar sensation in them: they seemed to swell, the fingers puffing to an enormous size, the palms bulging, the whole member from the wrist to the nails distended like a glove when one has blown into it to straighten it out. Then he had a feeling that his head was swelling in the same way. He had to rub his hands together, to pass them again and again over his face to rid himself of the fancy.

But the strange numb feeling at the base of the skull did not keep him from thinking—he would have been glad if it had—and now at last when the terror overcame him it was no longer causeless; he knew now what he feared—he feared that he was going mad.

It was the punishment that he had brought upon himself, some fearful nervous disease, the result of his long indulgence of vice, his vile submission to the brute that was to destroy his reason; some collapse of all his faculties, beginning first with that which was highest, most sensitive—his art— spreading onward and downward till he should have reached the last stages of idiocy. It was Nature inexorably exacting. It was the vast fearful engine riding him down beneath its myriad spinning wheels, remorselessly, irresistibly.

The dreadful calamities that he had brought upon himself recoiled upon his head, crushing him to the dust with their weight of anguish and remorse: Ida Wade's suicide, his father's death, his social banishment, the loss of his art, Hiram Wade's lawsuit menacing him with beggary, and now this last, this approaching insanity. It was no longer fire driving out fire; the sense of all these disasters seemed to come back upon him at once, as keen, as bitter as when they had first befallen. He had told himself that he did not believe in a hell. Could there be a worse hell than this?

But all at once, without knowing why, moved by an impulse, a blind, resistless instinct, Vandover started up in bed, raising his clasped hands above him, crying out, "Oh, help me! Why don't you *help* me! You can if you only will!" Who was it to whom he had cried with such unerring intuition? He gave no name to this mysterious "You," this strange supernatural being, this mighty superhuman power. It was the cry of a soul in torment that does not stop to reason, the wild last hope that feels its own helplessness, that responds to an intuition of a force outside of itself—the force that can save it in its time of peril.

Trembling, his hands still clasped above him, Vandover waited for an answer, waited for the miracle. In the tortured exalted state of his nerves he seemed suddenly possessed of a sixth sense; he fancied that he would know, there in that room, in a few seconds, while yet his hands remained clasped above his head. It was his last hope: if this failed him there was nothing left. Still he waited; he felt that he should know when the miracle came, that he would suddenly be filled with a sense of peace, of quiet joy. Still he waited—there was nothing, nothing but the vast silence, the unbroken blackness of the night, a night that was to last forever. There was no answer, nothing but the deaf silence, the blind darkness. But in a moment he felt that the very silence, the very lack of answer, was answer in itself; there was nothing for him. Even that vast mysterious power to which he had cried could not help him now, *could* not help him, could not stay the inexorable law of nature, could not reverse that vast terrible engine with its myriad spinning wheels that was riding him down relentlessly, grinding him into the dust. And afterward? After the engine had done its work, when that strange other time should come, that other life, what then? No, not even then, nothing but outer darkness then and the gnashing of teeth, nothing but the deaf silence, nothing but the blind darkness, nothing but the unbroken blackness of an eternal night.

It was the end of everything! With a muffled cry, "Oh, I can't stand this!" Vandover threw himself from his bed, groping his way out into the sitting-room. By this time he was only conscious of a suffering too great to be borne, everything else was blurred as in a thick mist. For nearly an hour he stumbled about in the darkened room, bruising himself against the furniture, dazed, numb, trying in vain to find the drawer of the desk where he kept his father's revolver. At last his hand closed upon it, gripping it so tightly that the hundreds of little nicks and scratches made by the contact of the tacks and nails which he had hammered with it nipped and bit into his palm like the teeth of tiny mice. A vague feeling of shame overcame him at the last moment: he had no wish to be found sprawling upon the floor, dressed only in his night-gown. He lit the gas and put on his bathrobe, drawing the cords securely about his waist and neck.

When he turned about to pick up the revolver again he found that his determination had weakened considerably, and he was obliged to reflect again upon the wreck of his life and soul before he was back once more to the proper pitch of resolution. It was five minutes to two, and he made up his mind to kill himself when the clock struck the hour. He spent the intervening moments in arranging the details of the matter. At first he thought he would do it standing, but he abandoned that idea, fearing to strike his head against the furniture as he fell. He was about to decide upon the huge leather chair, when the remembrance of his father's death made that impossible. He finally concluded to sit upon the edge of his bed, leaning a little backward so as not to fall upon the floor, and he dragged the bed out into the sitting-room, preferring somehow to die there. For a moment the idea of lying at length upon the bed occurred to him, but in an instant he recoiled from it, horrified at the thought of the death that struck from above; no, it would be best to sit upon the edge of the bed, falling backward with the shot. Then he wondered as to which it should be, his heart or his head; evidently the head was the better; there upon the right side in the little hollow of the temple, and the next moment he found himself curiously touching and pressing the spot with his fingers. All at once he heard the little clicking noise that the clock makes a minute or so before the hour. It was almost two; he sat down upon the edge of the bed, cocking the revolver, waiting for the clock to strike. An idea came to him, and he looked at the calendar that stood at the right of the clock upon the top of the low bookcase. It was the twelfth of April, Thursday; that, then, was to be the date of his death— Thursday, April twelfth, at two in the morning, so it would read upon his gravestone. For an instant the awfulness of the thing he was to do came upon him, and the next instant he found himself wondering if they still coursed jack-rabbits with greyhounds down at Coronado the way they used to do when he was there. All at once the clock struck two, and at the very last instant a strange impulse to seat himself before the mirror came upon him. He drew up a chair before it, watching his reflection intently, but even as he raised the revolver he suddenly changed his purpose without knowing why, and all at once crammed the muzzle into his mouth. He drew the trigger.

He heard no sound of a report; he felt no shock, but a great feebleness ran throughout his limbs, a relaxing and weakening of all his muscles; his eyes were open and he saw everything small and seemingly very far off as through the reversed end of an opera-glass. Suddenly he fainted.

When Vandover came to himself again it was early morning. The room was full of daylight, but the gas was still burning. Little by little the fearful things of the night came back to him; he realized that he had shot himself, and he waited for the end, not daring to move, his eyes closed, his hand still gripping the scratched butt of the revolver in his lap. For a long time he lay back in the chair, motionless, his consciousness slowly returning like an incoming tide. At length he started to his feet with an expression of scorn and incredulity; he was as sound as ever, there was neither scratch nor scar upon him; he had not shot himself after all.

Curiously, he looked at the revolver, throwing open the breech—the cylinder was empty; he had forgotten to load it. "What a fool!" he exclaimed, laughing scornfully, and still laughing he walked to the centre of the room under the chandelier and turned out the gas.

But when he turned about, facing the day once more, facing that day and the next and the next throughout all the course of his life, the sense of his misery returned upon him in its full strength and he raised his clenched fist to his eyes, shutting out the light. Ah, no, he could not endure it—the horror of life overpassed the horror of death; he could not go on living. A new thought had come to him. Wretched as he was, he saw that in time his anguish of conscience, even his dread of losing his reason, would pass from him; he would become used to them; yes, even become used to the dread of insanity, and then he would return once more to vice, return once more into the power of the brute, the perverse and evil monster that was knitted to him now irrevocably, part for part, fibre for fibre. He saw clearly that nothing could save him, he had had his answer that night, there was to be no miracle. Was it not right, then, that he should destroy himself? Was it not even his duty? The better part of him seemed to demand the act; should he not comply while there yet was any better part left? In a little while the brute was to take all.

On the shelves above his washstand Vandover found the cartridges in a green pasteboard box, and loaded all the chambers of the revolver, carefully. He closed the breech; but as he was about to draw back the hammer all his courage, all his resolution, crumbled in an instant like a tower of sand. He did not dare to shoot himself—he was afraid. The night before he had been brave enough; how was it now that he could not call up the same courage, the same determination? When he thought over the wreck, the wretched failure of his life, the dreadful prospect of the future years, his anguish and his terror were as keen as ever. But now there was a shrinking of his every nerve from the thought of suicide, the instinctive animal fear of death, stronger than himself. His suffering had to go on, had to run its course, even death would not help him. Let it go on, it was only the better part of him that was suffering; in a little while this better part would be dead, leaving only the brute. It would die a natural death without any intervention from him. Was there any need of suicide? Suicide! Great God! his whole life had been one long suicide.

That same morning Charlie Geary had eaten a very thick underdone steak for breakfast after enjoying a fine long sleep of eight hours. Toward eight o'clock he went downtown. He did not take a car; he preferred to walk; it helped his digestion and it gave him exercise. At night he walked home as well; that gave him an appetite; besides, with the ten cents that he saved in this way, he bought himself a nice cigar that he smoked in the evening to help digest his supper. He was very careful of his health. Ah, you bet, one had to look out for one's health.

At the office that morning he had a long talk with Beale, Jr., as to Hiram Wade's suit. The great firm of Beale & Storey, into whose office Geary had been received, made a specialty of damage suits, and especially those suits that were brought against a certain great monopoly which it was claimed was ruining the city and the state; such a case involving nearly a quarter of a million of dollars was now occupying the attention of the heads of the firm and, indeed, of the whole office. Hiram Wade's suit was assigned to the assistants. Beale, Jr., was one of these, and Charlie Geary had managed to push himself into the position of his confidential clerk. But Beale, Jr., himself took little interest in the Wade suit; the suit against the great monopoly was coming to a head; it was a battle of giants; the whole office found itself embroiled, and little by little Beale, Jr., allowed himself to be drawn into the struggle. The management of the Wade case was given over to Geary's hands.

When he had first heard of his assignment to the case Geary had been unwilling to act against his old chum, but it was the first legal affair of any great importance with which he had been connected, and he was soon devoured with an inordinate ambition to distinguish himself in the eyes of the firm, to get a "lift," to take a long step forward toward the end of his desires, which was to become one of the firm itself. He knew he could make a brilliant success of the case. Geary was at this time nearly twenty-eight, keen, energetic, immensely clever; and the case against Vandover was strong. No one knew better than he himself how intimate Vandover had been with Ida Wade; Vandover had told him much of the details of their acquaintance. Besides this, a letter which Ida had written to Vandover the day before her suicide had been found, torn in three pieces, thrust between the leaves of one of the books that she used to study at the normal school. It directly implicated Vandover—it was evidence that could not be gainsaid. Geary had resolved to push the case against his old chum. Vandover ought to see that with Geary it was a matter of business; he, Geary, was only an instrument of the law; if Geary did not take the case some other lawyer would. At any rate, whether Van would see it in this light or not, Geary was determined to take the case; it was too good an opportunity to let slip; he was going to make his way in the law or he would know the reason why. Every man for himself, that was what he said. It might be damned selfish, but it was human nature; if he had to sacrifice Van, so much the worse. It was evident that his old college chum was going to the dogs anyway, but come whatever would, *he*, Geary, was going to be a *success*. Ah, you bet, he would make his way and he would make his money.

Ever since he had come into his little patrimony Geary had been making offers to Vandover for his block in the Mission. Geary would offer only eight thousand dollars, but Brunt steadily advised Vandover against listening to such a figure, assuring him that the property was valued at twelve thousand six hundred. Vandover had often wondered at Geary's persistence in the matter, and had often asked him what he could possibly want of the block. But Geary was very vague in his replies, generally telling Vandover that there was money in the investment if one could and would give the proper attention to pushing it. He told Vandover that he—Vandover—was no business man, which was the lamentable truth, and would much prefer to live upon the interest of his bonds rather than to be continually annoyed by defective plumbing, complaints, and repairs. The truth of the matter was that Geary knew that a certain immense boot and shoe concern was after the same piece of property. The houses themselves were nothing to the boot and shoe people; they wanted the land in order to build their manufactory upon it. A siding of the railroad ran down the alley just back of the property, a fact that hurt the lot for residence purposes, but that was indispensable for the boot and shoe people. Geary knew that the heads of the manufactory were determined to buy the lot, and he was sure that if properly handled by clever brokers they could be induced to offer at least one third more than its appraised valuation. It was a chance for a fine speculation, and it was torture to Geary to think that Vandover, or in fact any one besides himself, was going to profit by it.

The afternoon of the day upon which Hiram Wade had brought suit for twenty-five thousand dollars, while Geary was pottering about his swivel office chair with an oil can trying to find out where it creaked, a brilliant idea had suddenly occurred to him, a stroke of genius, a veritable inspiration. Why could he not make the Wade suit a machine with which to force Vandover into the sale of the property?

His first idea had been to push the case so vigorously that Vandover would surely lose it. But on second thought this course did not seem to promise any satisfactory results. Geary knew very well that though Hiram Wade had sued for twenty-five thousand dollars he could not recover more than five thousand, if as much as that. Geary did not know the exact state of Vandover's affairs, but he did not think that his chum would sell any property in order to make the payment of damages. It was much more likely that he would raise the five thousand, or whatever it might be, by placing a second mortgage on some of his property. This, however, was presuming that Wade would get judgment for about five thousand dollars. But suppose that Vandover thought that Wade could actually recover twenty-five thousand! Suppose that Geary himself should see Vandover and induce him to believe such a story, and to settle the affair out of court! Vandover was as ignorant of law as he was of business. Geary might frighten him into a sale. Yet this plan seemed very impracticable. In the first place, it would be unprofessional for Geary to have an interview with Vandover under such circumstances, the story was almost too monstrous even for Vandover's credibility, and besides, Geary would not pay, could not pay twenty-five thousand for the property. This last was a serious tangle. In order to get Vandover to sell, Geary would have to represent the damage suit as involving a larger sum of money than Geary was willing to give for the block, even a far larger sum than that which the boot and shoe manufacturers could be induced to pay for it. It seemed to be a deadlock. Geary began to see that the whole idea was out of the question. Yet the desire of it came back upon him again and again. He dwelt upon it constantly, smelling out the chance for a "deal" somewhere in the tangle with the instinct of the keen man of business. At last he seemed to have straightened it out. The idea of a compromise came into his mind. What if Vandover and Hiram Wade could be made to compromise upon eight thousand dollars! Geary would be willing to pay Vandover eight thousand for the block. That was his original offer. Wade, though he had sued for twenty-five thousand, could easily be made to see that eight thousand was as much as he could reasonably expect, and Geary knew the boot and shoe manufacturers would pay fifteen thousand for the lot, perhaps more.

But in order to carry out the delicate and complicated affair it was absolutely necessary to keep Vandover from seeing a lawyer. Geary knew that any lawyer would fight the proposition of a compromise at eight thousand dollars: five thousand was as much as Wade could possibly get in court, and if judgment for such amount was rendered, Vandover's counsel would advise him to raise the sum by mortgaging some property instead of selling the block.

Yet as soon as Geary arrived at a solution of the problem, as soon as the "deal" began to seem feasible, he commenced to hesitate. It was not so much that the affair was crooked, that his rôle in it was, to say the least, unprofessional, as it was the fact that Vandover was his old college chum and that, to put the matter into plain words, Geary was swindling his best friend out of a piece of property valued at twelve thousand six hundred dollars, and preventing him from reselling the same piece at a very advanced figure. Again and again he wished that it was some other than Vandover; he told himself that in such case he would put the screw on without the least compunction. All through one night Geary was on the rack torn between his friendship for his chum and his devouring, inordinate ambition to make his way and to make his pile. In the end Vandover was sacrificed—the opportunity was too good—Geary could not resist the chance for a "deal." Ah, you bet, just think of it, after all, not only would Vandover believe that Geary was doing him a great service, but the office would be delighted with him for winning his first case, they would get a heavy fee from Wade, and he would nearly double his money invested in the block in the Mission. As soon as he had made up his mind to put the "deal" through, he had seen Vandover at his rooms early in the morning and had induced him to promise not to engage any other counsel and in general keep very quiet about the whole business.

The day after, he and Beale, Jr., had an appointment with Hiram Wade, but toward noon Beale, Jr., disappeared, leaving word for Geary that he had gone to court with his father to hear the closing arguments in the great suit against the monopoly, the last struggle in the tremendous legal battle that had embroiled the whole office; Geary was to use his own judgment in the Wade case. Geary laboured with Hiram Wade all that afternoon. The old fellow mistrusted him on account of his youth and his inexperience, was unwilling to arrive at any definite conclusion without the sanction of Geary's older associate, and for a long time would listen to nothing less than ten thousand dollars, crying out that his gray hairs had been dishonoured, and striking his palm upon his forehead. Nothing could move him. He, also, had his ambitions; it was his dream to own the carpet-cleaning establishment in which he now had but a three-fourths interest. Summer was coming, the time of year when people were going into the country, leaving their carpets to be cleaned in their absence. If he could obtain complete ownership of his business within the month he fancied that he saw an opportunity to make more money than he had done before at any previous season.

"Why, I tell you, Mister Geary," he exclaimed indignantly, wagging his head, "it would seem like selling my daughter's honour if we should compromise at any less figure. I am a father. I—I have my feelings, haven't I?"

"Well, now, it isn't like that at all, Mr. Wade," answered Geary, making awkward gestures with both his hands. "It isn't what we *ought* to get out of him. Could any sum of money, could millions compensate you for Miss Ida's death? I guess not. It's what we *can* get. If this thing comes into court we won't get but five thousand out of him; I'll tell you that right now. He could raise that by a mortgage, easy; but if we compromise we can squeeze him for eight thousand. You see, the fact that we can act directly with him instead of through counsel makes it easier for us. Of course, as I tell you, it isn't just the legal thing to do, but I'm willing to do it for you because I think you've been wronged and outraged."

Wade struck his hand to his head. "I tell you, he's brought dishonour upon my gray hairs," he exclaimed.

"Exactly, of course, I understand how you feel," replied Geary, "but now about this eight thousand? I tell you what I'll do." He had resolved to stake everything upon one last hazard. "See here, Mr. Wade, there's a difference, of course, between eight thousand dollars and ten thousand, but the use of money is worth something, isn't it? And money down, cold hard cash, is worth something, isn't it? Well, now, suppose you got that eight thousand dollars money down within three days?"

Hiram Wade still demurred a little longer for the sake of his own self-respect and his dishonoured hairs, but in the end it was agreed that if the money was paid over to him in full before the end of the following week he would be content and would agree to the compromise. Eight thousand dollars would still be enough to buy out his partner's interest, and even then he would have a little left over with which to improve a certain steaming apparatus. If the amount was paid in full within a week he could get control of the cleaning-works in time to catch all of the summer trade.

Geary had calculated that this last argument would have its weight; the great difficulty now was to get Vandover to sell at such a low figure and upon such short notice. He almost despaired of his success in this quarter; however, it all depended upon Vandover now.

Early in the forenoon of the next day Geary pounded on the door of Vandover's sitting-room, pushing it open without waiting for an answer. Vandover was lying in his shirt-sleeves on the corduroy divan under the huge rug of sombre colours that hung against the wall, and he did not get up as Geary came in; in fact, he hardly stirred.

"Hello!" cried Geary, closing the door with his heel. "Didn't expect to find *you* up so early. *I've* been up since half-past six; had breakfast at seven, fine cutlet, and then got down to the office at twenty minutes of eight. How's that for rustling, hey?"

"Yes?" said Vandover, dully.

"But, say," exclaimed Geary, " what's all the matter with *you*? You look all frazzled out, all pale around the wattles. Ah, you've been hitting up a pace again. You're a bird, Van, there's no use talking! All night racket this trip?"

"I suppose so," answered Vandover, never moving.

"But you *do* look gone-in this morning, sure," continued Geary, seating himself on the edge of the table and pushing back his hat. "Never saw you looking so bad; you ought to be more careful, Van; there'll be a smash some time. Ah, you bet a man ought to look out for his health. I walk downtown every morning, and three times a week I take a cold shower as soon as I get up. Ah, I tell you, that braces a fellow up; you ought to try it; it's better than a dozen cocktails. You keep on getting thin like you have for the past few days and I'll have to be calling you Skinny Seldom-fed again, like we used to. Now, tell the truth, what time did you get to bed last night? Did you go to bed at all?"

"No," replied Vandover with a long breath, looking vaguely at the pipe-rack on the opposite wall.

"I thought as much," answered Geary. "Well, that's like you." He paused a moment, and then went on, nervously gesturing with both his hands simultaneously. "Well, I've had a long talk with Wade. I tell you, Van, that old boy is as stubborn as a mule. You see, he knows he's got a case. I couldn't talk him out of that. I'll tell you how it is," continued Geary, preparing to spring another mine; "he's found a letter Ida wrote you the day before she killed herself." He paused to watch the effect upon Vandover. Vandover waited for him to go on, but seeing that he did not and that he expected him to say something, nodded his head once and answered:

"I see."

"Don't you know, that letter that she wrote to you telling you how it was, how she was fixed?" repeated Geary, puzzled and irritated at Vandover's indifference.

"I know."

"Well, he's got it, anyhow," pursued Geary, "and of course that tells against you. Well, I had a long talk with him yesterday afternoon and I got him to compromise. Of course, you know in suits like this one a party sues for a great deal more than he expects to get. At first you know he said twenty-five thousand; that figure was decided upon at the first interview he had with us. Of course, he could never get judgment for that much. But he hung out at ten thousand; said it would be selling his daughter if he took any less. Now I knew you couldn't raise that much on any property you have, especially in these hard times——" Geary paused for the fraction of an instant; he had thrown out the last remark as a feeler, to see what Vandover would say; but his chum said nothing, staring vaguely at the opposite wall, merely making a faint sign to show that he understood, closing his eyes and bending his head. "And so," continued the other, "I jewed him down, and what do you suppose? Well, sir, from twenty-five thousand I brought him right down to, say, eight thousand. I could see that he had some scheme that he wants to go into right away, and that he wants ready money, right on the nail, you know, to carry it through. Ah, you bet, I was clever enough to see that. I waltzed him right over when I began to speak of ready money, cash down. As soon as he'd squeal I'd spring cold cash on him, money down, and he's hit gravel like an ostrich. Well," he went on deliberately after a pause, getting up from the table and standing before Vandover, his hands in his pockets, " well, I think that's the best I can do for you, Van. It's a good deal better than I expected, but I've done the best I could for you, and I would advise you to see him on the proposition."

"All right," said Vandover. "Go ahead."

Geary was perplexed. "Well, you think that's a good thing, don't you? You think I've done my best for you? You see it as I do, don't you?"

Vandover withdrew his eyes from the other wall, glancing under heavy eyelids at Geary, and with a slight movement of his head and shoulders replied:

"Of course."

"Have you got the money?" asked Geary eagerly; then, irritated at his indiscretion, hastened to interrupt himself. "You see, he hasn't put his proposition into writing yet, but it's like this: if you can pay him eight thousand dollars in cash before the end of next week he'll sign a document to the effect that he is satisfied."

"I've got no money," said Vandover quietly.

"I was afraid you wouldn't have," said Geary, "but you can raise it somewhere. You had better close with the old man as soon as you can, Van, while he's in the mood for it; you'll make a clear two thousand by it. You can see that as well as I can. Now, where can you—how is your property fixed? Let's see! Here's the statement you made to me the other day," continued Geary, drawing his shorthand notes from his portfolio. "How about this piece on California Street, the one that you have rented, the homestead, you know?"

"Yes, there's that," answered Vandover, changing the position of his head upon his clasped hands.

"But that's pretty well papered up already," returned Geary, consulting his notes. "You couldn't very well raise another mortgage on *that*."

"I'd forgotten," answered Vandover. "There's the block in the Mission. He can have that."

Geary began to tremble with excitement. It looked as though he might be able to make the deal after all. But the next instant he grew suspicious. Vandover's indifference puzzled him. Might he not have some game of his own? The idea of playing off his cleverness against that of an opponent strung his nerves in an instant; the notion of an impending struggle was almost an inspiration, and his innate desire of getting the better of a competitor, even though it was his closest friend, aroused his wits and sharpened his faculties like a stimulant. He had no hesitancy in sacrificing his chum. It was business now; friendship ceased to be a factor in the affair. Ah, Van was going to be foxy; he'd show him that *he* could be foxy, too.

"He can have it?" echoed Geary. "You don't mean to sign it over to him bodily?"

"Oh, I suppose it could be mortgaged," answered Vandover.

"Yes, that's the idea," returned Geary. "You want me to figure that out for you? I can just as well as not. Well, now, let's see," he went on, settling himself at the desk, and figuring upon a sheet of Vandover's stamped letter-paper. "The banks will never give you more than two thirds of the appraised value; that's as much as we can expect; that would come to—well, let's see—that would come to six thousand on that piece; then you could mortgage something else to make up the difference."

"Wouldn't it be more than six thousand?" asked Vandover with a little show of interest. "I think that block has been appraised at something over twelve thousand."

"Ah, yes," returned Geary, putting his chin in the air, "that was your agent's valuation five years ago; but you know property out there, in fact, property all over the city, what they call inside property, has been going right down for the last ten years. That's what I've always been telling you. You couldn't possibly get more than nine thousand for that block to-day. You see the railroad there hurts it."

"I suppose so," replied Vandover. "I've heard the governor say as much in his time."

"Of course," exclaimed Geary, delighted at this unexpected turn.

"Well, then, he can have my bonds," said Vandover. "I've got eighty-nine hundred in bonds; he can have those. Let him have anything he wants."

"Oh, don't touch your bonds," answered Geary. "Hang on to those. Bonds are always good—U. S. bonds. You don't want to sell those, Van. You see, the homestead is already mortgaged. And, besides, you know, too, that the banks are asking an awful big per cent. for mortgages on real estate; it's seven and a half nowadays. Don't sell your bonds. I'll tell you why: U. S. bonds are always good; they never depreciate, but it's different with realty, especially in this city just now. It's been depreciating ever since your father's time, and it's going to go right on depreciating. If you want to sell anything, sell your realty before it gets any lower. Now you don't want to sell your home, do you? You don't like that idea. You've lived there so long, and then what would you do with the furniture; besides, the rent of that," he glanced again at his notes, "is bringing you in a good hundred and twenty-five a month. If you've got to sell at all, why not sell your Mission block?"

"All right," said Vandover, as if wearied by Geary's clamour, "I'll sign it over to him."

"No, that's not the idea at all," Geary insisted. "He wants the ready money; he don't want depreciated real estate. You'll have to find a purchaser in the next week if you possibly can in such a short time, and make over the money to Wade. But if you can't sell in that time you will have to dig up ten thousand instead of eight. It's a hard position for you, Van; it's just a chance, you know, but I thought I would give you the benefit of that chance. If you want to give me a power of attorney I'll try and sell it for you."

"I guess Brunt would do that," replied Vandover.

"Yes," retorted Geary, watchful as a lynx, "but they would charge you a big commission. Of course *I* wouldn't think of asking you anything more than the actual costs. I am afraid that they would try to sell it at auction, too, if they knew you had to realize on it in so short a time, and it would go for a mere song then; you know how it is."

"I thought," inquired Vandover, "that you wanted that property."

"Yes," replied Geary, hesitating, "I—I did want to buy it of you once; well, for that matter I do now. But you know how it is with me."

"I might as well sell it to you as to any one else," returned Vandover.

"Well, now, it's like this, Van," said Geary. "I know that block is worth nine thousand dollars; I won't deceive you. But I can only give you eight thousand for it. That's all the money I've got. But I'm not going to take advantage of your position to jew you down. I want the block, I'll admit that, but I'm not going to have you sacrifice it for me, or for any one else. I think you can get nine thousand for it. I know you could if we had a little more time, and I'm not sure but what I could find a purchaser for you within the next week that would give you nine thousand."

"Oh, I don't care, Charlie; I'm sick of everything; eight thousand, nine thousand, anything you like; take it at your own figure."

Geary began to tremble once more, and this time his excitement was so great that he hardly dared to trust himself to speak; his breath grew short, his hands in his pockets twitched nervously, and curled themselves into fists, his heart seemed to him to beat high in his throat; he hesitated long, pretending to deliberate as he steadied himself.

Vandover remained silent, his hands still clasped back of his head, staring at the opposite wall with eyes that saw nothing. The little clock began to strike ten.

"I don't know, Van," said Geary; "I don't like to do this, and yet I would like to help you out of this muss. You see, if I should ever benefit by the property you would feel as though I had taken advantage of you at this time and worked a flim-flam on you!"

"Oh, I'll look out for that," returned Vandover.

"No, no, I don't feel quite right about it," answered Geary, wagging his head and shutting his eyes. "Better see what we can do at a forced sale."

"Why, don't you see you would be doing me a favour?" said Vandover wearily. "I *ask* you to buy the block. I don't care what your figure is!"

Once more Geary hesitated, for the last time going over the whole deal in his mind from beginning to end, testing it, looking for weak points. It was almost perfect. Suppose the boot and shoe people did not buy the lot? He could resell it elsewhere, even below its appraised value and yet make money by the transaction; the lot was cheap at ten thousand; it might bring twelve; even as an ordinary, legitimate speculation it was to be desired at such a figure. Suppose the boot and shoe people backed out entirely, suppose even he could not find another purchaser for the property, why, then, he could hold on to it; the income from the rents was fully 10 per cent. of the price he would have paid for it.

"Well, Van," he said at last, making a slow, awkward gesture with his left hand, all the fingers extended, " well, I'll take you up—but I don't feel as though I should——" He suddenly interrupted himself with a burst of sincerity, exclaiming: "Sure, old man, if I had nine thousand I'd give it to you for the block, that's straight goods." He felt that he was conscientious in saying this. It was true he would have given nine thousand if he had had it. For that matter he might have given ten or twelve.

"Can't we settle the whole matter to-day?" said Vandover. "Right here—now. I'm sick of it, sick of everything. Let's get it done with."

Geary nearly bounded from his seat. He had been wondering how he might accomplish this very thing. "All right," he said briskly, "no reason in waiting." He had seen to it that he should be prepared to close the sale the moment that Vandover was willing. Long ago, when he had first had the idea of buying the block, he had spent a day in the offices of the county recorder, the tax collector, and the assessor, assuring himself of the validity of the title, and only two days ago he had gone over the matter again in order to be sure that no encumbrances had been added to the block in the meanwhile. He found nothing; the title was clear.

"Isn't this rather rushing the thing through?" he asked. "Maybe you might regret it afterward. Don't you want to take two or three days to think it over?"

"No."

"Sure now?" persisted Geary.

"But I've *got* to sell before three days," answered Vandover. "Otherwise he'll want ten thousand."

"That's a fact," admitted the other. "Well," he went on, "if your mind's made up, why—we can go right ahead. As I say, there's no reason for waiting; better take up Wade while he's in the mood for it. You see, he hasn't signed any proposition as yet, and he might go back on us." Vandover drew a long breath and got up slowly, heavily, from the couch, saying:

"What's the odds to me what I sell for? *I* don't get the money."

"Well, what do you say if we go right down to a notary's office and put this thing right through," Geary suggested.

"Come on, then."

"Have you got your abstract here, the abstract of the block?" Vandover nodded. "Better bring it along, then," said Geary.

The office of the notary adjoined those of the firm of Beale & Storey; in fact, he was in a sense an attaché of the great firm and transacted a great deal of legal business for them. Vandover and Geary fell upon him in an idle moment. A man had come to regulate the water filter, which took the place of an ice cooler in a corner of one of the anterooms, and while he was engaged at his work the notary stood at his back, abusing him and exclaiming at the ineffectiveness of the contrivance. The notary was a middle-aged man with a swollen, purple face; he had a toothpick behind each ear and wore an office coat of gray linen, ripped at the shoulders.

Then the transfer was made. It was all settled in less than half an hour, unceremoniously, almost hastily. For the sake of form Geary signed a check for eight thousand dollars which Vandover in his turn made over to Hiram Wade. The notary filled out a deed of grant, bargain, and sale, pasting on his certificate of acknowledgment as soon as Vandover and Geary had signed. Geary took the abstract, thrusting it into his breast-pocket. As far as Vandover was concerned, the sale was complete, but he had neither his property nor its equivalent in money.

"Well," declared Geary at length, "I guess that's all there is to be done. I'll get a release from old man Wade and send it to you to-morrow or next day. Now, let's go down to the Imperial and have a drink on it." They went out, but the notary returned to the anteroom, turning the spigot of the filter to right and left, frowning at it suspiciously, refusing to be satisfied.

Chapter Sixteen

THAT PARTICULAR room in the Lick House was well toward the rear of the building, on one of the upper floors, and from its window, one looked out upon a vast reach of roofs that rose little by little to meet the abrupt rise of Telegraph Hill. It was a sordid and grimy wilderness, topped with a gray maze of wires and pierced with thousands of chimney stacks. Many of the roofs were covered with tin long since blackened by rust and soot. Here and there could be seen clothes hung out to dry. Occasionally upon the flanking walls of some of the larger buildings was displayed an enormous painted sign, a violent contrast of intense black and staring white amidst the sooty brown and gray, advertising some tobacco, some newspaper, or some department store. Not far in the distance two tall smokestacks of blackened tin rose high in the air, above the roof of a steam laundry, one very large like the stack of a Cunarder, the other slender, graceful, with a funnel-shaped top. All day and all night these stacks were smoking; from the first, the larger one, rolled a heavy black smoke, very gloomy, waving with a slow and continued movement like the plume of some sullen warrior. But the other one, the tall and slender pipe, threw off a series of little white puffs, three at a time, that rose buoyant and joyous into the air like so many white doves, vanishing at last, melting away in the higher sunshine, only to be followed by another flight. They came three at a time, the pipe tossing them out with a sharp gay sound like a note of laughter interrupted by a cough.

But the interior of the room presented the usual dreary aspect of the hotel bedroom—cheerless, lamentable.

The walls were whitewashed and bare of pictures or ornaments, and the floor was covered with a dull red carpet. The furniture was a "set," all the pieces having a family resemblance. On entering, one saw the bed standing against the right-hand wall, a huge double bed with the name of the hotel in the corners of its spread and pillowcases. In the exact middle of the room underneath the gas fixture was the centre-table, and upon it a pitcher of ice-water. The blank, white monotony of one side of the room was jarred upon by the grate and mantelpiece, iron, painted black, while on the mantelpiece itself stood a little porcelain matchsafe with ribbed sides in the form of a truncated cone. Precisely opposite the chimney was the bureau, flanked on one side by the door of the closet, and on the other in the corner of the room by the stationary washstand with its new cake of soap and its three clean, glossy towels. On the wall to the left of the door was the electric bell and the directions for using it, and tacked upon the door itself a card as to the hours for meals, the rules of the hotel, and the extract of the code defining the liabilities of innkeepers, all printed in bright red. Everything was clean, defiantly, aggressively clean, and there was a clean smell of new soap in the air.

But the room was bare of any personality. Of the hundreds who had lived there, perhaps suffered and died there, not a trace, not a suggestion remained; their different characters had not left the least impress upon its air or appearance. Only a few hairpins were scattered on the bottom of one of the bureau drawers, and two forgotten medicine bottles still remained upon the top shelf of the closet.

This had been the appearance of Vandover's new home when he had first come to it, after leaving his suite of rooms in the huge apartment house on Sutter Street. He had lived here now for something over a year.

It had all commenced with the seizure of his furniture by the proprietors of the apartment house. Almost before he knew it he owed for six months' room and board; when the extras were added to this bill it swelled to nearly a thousand dollars. At first he would not believe it; it was not possible that so large a bill could accumulate without his knowledge. He declared there was a mistake, tossing back the bill to the clerk who had presented it, and shaking his head incredulously. This other became angry, offered to show the books of the house. The manager was called in and attempted to prove the clerk's statement by figures, dates, and extracts from the entries. Vandover was confused by their noise, and grew angry in his turn; vociferating that he did not propose to be cheated, the others retorted in a rage, the interview ended in a scene.

But in the end they gained their point; they were right, and at length Vandover was brought around to see that he was in the wrong, but he had no ready money, and while he hesitated, unwilling to part with any of his bonds or to put an additional mortgage upon the homestead, the hotel, after two warnings, suddenly seized upon his furniture. What a misery!

In a moment of time it was all taken from him, all the lovely bric-à-brac, all the heavy pieces, all the little articles of *vertu* which he had bought with such intense delight and amongst which he had lived with such happiness, such contentment, such never-failing pleasure. Everything went—the Renaissance portraits, the pipe-rack, the chair in which the Old Gentleman had died, the Assyrian *bas-reliefs* and, worst of all, the stove, the famous tiled stove, the delightful cheery iron stove with the beautified flamboyant ornaments. For the first few months after the seizure Vandover was furious with rage and disappointment, persuaded that he could never live anywhere but in just such a room; it was as if he had been uprooted and cast away upon some barren, uncongenial soil. His new room in the hotel filled him with horror, and for a long time he used it only as a place where he could sleep and wash. For a long time even his pliable character refused to fit itself to such surroundings, refused to be content between four enormous white walls, a stuccoed ceiling, and a dark red carpet. He passed most of his time elsewhere, reading the papers at the Mechanics Library in the morning, and in the afternoon sitting about the hotel office and parlours until it was time to take his usual little four o'clock stroll on Kearney and Market streets. He had long since become a familiar figure on this promenade. Even the women and girls of Flossie's type had ceased to be interested in this tall, thin young man with the tired, heavy eyes and blue-white face. One day, however, a curious incident did for a moment invest Vandover with a sudden dramatic interest. It was just after he had moved down to the Lick House, about a month after he had sold the block in the Mission. Vandover was standing at Lotta's fountain at the corner of Kearney and Market streets, interested in watching a policeman and two boys reharnessing a horse after its tumble. All at once he fell over flat into the street, jostling one of the flower venders and nearly upsetting him. He struck the ground with a sodden shock, his arms doubled under him, his hat rolling away into the mud. Bewildered, he picked himself up; very few had seen him fall, but a little crowd gathered for all that. One asked if the man was drunk, and Vandover, terrified lest the policeman should call the patrol wagon, hurried off to a basement barber shop near by, where he brushed his clothes, still bewildered, confused, wondering how it had happened.

The fearful nervous crisis which Vandover had undergone had passed off slowly. Little by little, bit by bit, he had got himself in hand again. However, the queer numbness in his head remained, and as soon as he concentrated his attention on any certain line of thought, as soon as he had read for any length of time, especially if late at night, the numbness increased. Somewhere back of his eyes a strange blurring mist would seem to rise; he would find it impossible to keep his mind fixed upon any subject; the words of a printed page would little by little lose their meaning. At first this had been a source of infinite terror to him. He fancied it to be the symptoms of some approaching mental collapse, but, as the weeks went by and nothing unusual occurred, he became used to it, and refused to let it worry him. If it made his head feel queer to read, the remedy was easy enough—he simply would not read; and though he had been a great reader, and at one time had been used to spend many delightful afternoons lost in the pages of a novel, he now gave it all up with an easy indifference.

But, besides all this, the attack had left him with nerves all unstrung; even his little afternoon walk on Kearney and Market streets exhausted him; any trifling and sudden noise, the closing of a door, the striking of a clock, would cause him to start from his place with a gasp and a quick catch at the heart. Toward evening this little spasm of nerves would sometimes come upon him even when there was nothing to cause it, and now he could no longer drop off to sleep without first undergoing a whole series of these recoils and starts, that would sometimes bring him violently up to a sitting posture, his breath coming short and quick, his heart galloping, startled at he knew not what.

At first he had intended to see a doctor, but he had put off carrying his intention into effect until he had grown accustomed to the whole matter; otherwise, he was well enough, his appetite was good, and when he finally did get to sleep he would not wake up for a good eight hours.

One evening, however, about three months after the first crisis and just as Vandover was becoming well accustomed to the condition of body and mind in which it had left him, the second attack came on. It was fearful, much worse than on the first occasion, and this time there was no room for doubt. Vandover knew that for the moment he was actually insane.

Ellis had been with Vandover most of that afternoon, the two had been playing cards in Vandover's room until nearly six o'clock. All the afternoon they had been drinking whisky while they played, and by supper-time neither of them had any appetite. Ellis refused to go down, declaring that if he should eat now it would make him sick. Vandover went down alone, but once in the dining-room he found that *he* could not eat either. However, he knew that it was not the whisky. For two days his appetite had been failing him. The smell of food revolted him, and he left the supper-table, going up to his bare and lamentable room with the feeling that he was about to undergo a long spell of sickness. In the deserted hall, between the elevator and the door of his room, the second crisis came upon him all at once. It was so sudden that it was as if some enemy had leaped upon his back, springing out of the shadow, gripping him from behind, holding him close. Once more the hysteria shook him like a dry leaf. The little nervous starts came so fast that they ran together, mingling to form one long thrill of terror, the blind, unreasoning terror of something unknown; the numbness weighed down upon his brain until consciousness dwindled to a mere point and mercifully dulled the torture of his crisping nerves. It seemed to him that his hands and head were rapidly swelling to enormous size.

All this he had felt before; it was his old enemy, but now with this second attack began a new and even stranger sensation. In his distorted wits he fancied that he was in some manner changing, that he was becoming another man; worse than that, it seemed to him that he was no longer human, that he was sinking, all in a moment, to the level of some dreadful beast.

Later on in that same evening Ellis met young Haight coming out of one of the theatres, and told him a story that Haight did not believe. Ellis was very pale, and he seemed to young Haight to be trying to keep down some tremendous excitement.

"If he was drunk," said Ellis, "it was the strangest drunk I ever saw. He came back into the room on all fours—not on his hands and knees, you understand, but running along the floor upon the palms of his hands and his toes—and he pushed the door of the room open with his head, nuzzling at the crack like any dog. Oh, it was horrible. *I* don't know what's the matter with Van. You should have seen him; his head was hanging way down, and swinging from side to side as he came along; it shook all his hair over his eyes. He kept rattling his teeth together, and every now and then he would say, way down in his throat so it sounded like growls, 'Wolf—wolf—wolf.' I got hold of him and pulled him up to his feet. It was just as though he was asleep, and when I shook him he came to all at once and began to laugh. 'What's the matter, Van?' says I. 'What are you crawling on the floor that way for?' 'I'm damned if I know,' says he, rubbing his eyes. 'I guess I must have been out of my head. Too much whisky!' Then he says: 'Put me to bed, will you, Bandy? I feel all gone in.' Well, I put him to bed and went out to get some bromide of potassium; he said that made him sleep and kept his nerves steady. Coming back, I met a bell-boy just outside of Van's door, and told him to ask the hotel doctor to come up. You see, I had not opened the door of the room yet, and while I was talking to the bell-boy I could hear the sound of something four-footed going back and forth inside the room. When I got inside there was Van, perfectly naked, going back and forth along the wall, swinging his head very low, grumbling to himself. But he came to again as soon as I shook him, and seemed dreadfully ashamed, and went to bed all right. He got to sleep finally, and I left the doctor with him, to come out and get something for my own nerves."

"What did the doctor say was the matter?" asked young Haight, in horror.

"*Lycanthropy-Pathesis*. I never heard the name before—some kind of nervous disease. I guess Van had been hitting up a pretty rapid gait, and then I suppose he's had a good deal to worry him, too."

Once more the attack passed off, leaving Vandover exhausted, his nerves all jangling, his health impaired. Every day he seemed to grow thinner, great brown hollows grew under his eyes, and the skin of his forehead looked blue and tightly drawn. By degrees a deep gloom overcame him permanently, nothing could interest him, nothing seemed worth while. Not only were his nerves out of tune, but they were jaded, deadened, slack; they were like harpstrings that had been played upon so long and so violently that now they could no longer vibrate unless swept with a very whirlwind.

As he had foreseen, Vandover had returned again to vice, to the vice that was knitted into him now, fibre for fibre, to the ways of the brute that by degrees was taking entire possession of him. But he no longer found pleasure even in vice; once it had been his amusement, now it was his occupation. It was the only thing that seemed to ease the horrible nervousness that of late had begun to prey upon him constantly.

But though nothing could amuse him, on the other hand nothing could worry him; in the end the very riot of his nerves ceased even to annoy him. He had arrived at a state of absolute indifference. He had so often rearranged his pliable nature to suit his changing environment that at last he found that he could be content in almost any circumstances. He had no pleasures, no cares, no ambitions, no regrets, no hopes. It was mere passive existence, an inert, plantlike vegetation, the moment's pause before the final decay, the last inevitable rot.

One day after he had been living nearly a year at the Lick House, Adams & Brunt, the real estate agents, sent him word that they had an offer for his property on California Street. It was the homestead. The English gentleman, the president of the fruit syndicate who had rented the house of Vandover, was now willing to buy it. His business was by this time on a firm and paying basis and he had decided to make his home in San Francisco. He offered twenty-five thousand dollars for the house, including the furniture.

Brunt had several talks with Vandover and easily induced him to sell. "You can figure it out for yourself, Mr. Vandover," he said, as he pointed out his own calculations to him; "property has been going down in the city for the last ten years, and it will continue to do so until we can get a competing railroad through. Better sell when you can, and twenty-five thousand is a fair price. Of course, you will have to pay off the mortgage; you won't get but about fifteen thousand out of it, but at the same time you won't have to pay the interest on that mortgage to the banks; that will be so much saved a month; add that to what you could get for your fifteen thousand at, say, 6 per cent., and you would have a monthly income nearly equal to the present rent of the house, and much more certain, too. Suppose your tenant should go out, then where would you be?"

"All right, all right," answered Vandover, nodding his head vaguely. "Go ahead, *I* don't care." He parted from his old home with as much indifference as he had parted from his block in the Mission.

Vandover signed the deed that made him homeless, and at about the same time the first payment was made. Ten thousand dollars was deposited in one of the banks to his credit, and a check sent to him for the amount. The very next day Vandover drew against it for five hundred dollars.

At one time he had had an ambition to buy back his furniture from the huge apartment house in which he had formerly lived, and with it to make his cheerless bedroom in the Lick House seem more like a home. He felt it almost as a dishonour to have strangers using this furniture, sitting in the great leather chair in which the Old Gentleman had died, staring stupidly at his Renaissance portraits and copies of Assyrian *bas-reliefs*. Above all, it was torture to think that other hands than his own would tend the famous tiled and flamboyant stove, a stove that had its moods, its caprices, like any living person, a stove that had to be coaxed and humoured, a stove that he alone could understand. He had told himself that if ever again he should have money enough he would bring back this furniture to him. At first its absence had been a matter for the keenest regret and grief. He had been so used to pleasant surroundings that he languished in his new quarters as in a prison. His indulgent, luxurious character continually hungered after subdued, harmonious colours, pictures, ornaments, and soft rugs. His imagination was forever covering the white walls with rough stone-blue paper, and placing screens, divans, and window-seats in different parts of the cold bare room. One morning he had even gone so far as to pin about the walls little placards which he had painted with a twisted roll of the hotel letter-paper dipped into the inkstand. "Pipe-rack Here." "Mona Lisa Here." "Stove Here." "Window-seat Here." He had left them up there ever since, in spite of the chambermaid's protests and Ellis' clumsy satire.

Now, however, he had plenty of money. He would have his furniture back within the week. He came back from the bank, the money in his pocket, and went up to the room directly, with some vague intention of writing to the proprietors of the apartment house at once. But as he shut the door behind him, leaning his back against it and looking about, he suddenly realized that his old-time desire was passed; he had become so used to these surroundings that it now no longer made any difference to him whether or not they were cheerless, lamentable, barren. It was like all his other little ambitions—he had lost the taste for them, nothing made much difference after all. His money had come too late.

Why should he spend his five hundred dollars on something that could no longer amuse him? It would be much wiser to spend it all in having a good time somewhere— champagne dinners with Flossie, or betting on the races—he did not know exactly what. It was true that even these alternatives would not amuse him very much—he would fall back upon them as things of habit. For that matter everything was an *ennui*, and Vandover began to long for some new pleasure, some violent untried excitement.

Since the sale of the block in the Mission he had seen but little of Geary; young Haight had not been his companion since the time when Turner Ravis had broken with him, but little by little he had begun to associate with Ellis and his friend the Dummy. Almost every evening the three were together, sometimes at the theatre, sometimes in the back rooms of the Imperial, sometimes even in the parlours of certain houses, amid the murmur of heavy silks and the rustle of stiffly starched skirts. At times they would be drunk four nights of the week, and on these occasions it was tacitly understood between Ellis and Vandover that they should try to get the Dummy so full that he could talk.

However, Ellis' vice was gambling; he and the Dummy often passed the whole night over their cards, and as Vandover came more and more under Ellis' influence—succumbing to it as weakly as he had succumbed to the influence of Charlie Geary—he began to join these parties. They played Van John at five dollars a corner. Vandover won as often as he lost, but the habit of cards grew upon him steadily.

Toward eleven o'clock the evening of the day upon which he had drawn his five hundred, Vandover went around to the Imperial looking for his two friends. He found Ellis drinking whisky all alone in one of the little rooms, as was his custom; fifteen minutes later the Dummy and Flossie joined them. Flossie had grown stouter since Vandover had first known her, nearly ten years ago. She had a double chin, and puffy, discoloured pockets had come under her eyes. Now her hair was dyed, her cheeks and lips rouged, and her former air of health and good spirits gone. She never laughed. She had smoked so many cigarettes that now her voice hardly rose above a whisper. At one time she had been accustomed to boast that she never drank, and it had been one of her peculiarities for which she was well known. But on this occasion she joined Ellis in his whisky. She had long since departed from her old-time rule of temperance, and nowadays drank nothing else but whisky. She had even become well known for the quantity of whisky she could drink.

For half an hour the four sat around the little table, talking about the new, enormous Sutro Baths that were building at that time. After a while Flossie left them, and the Dummy began to imitate the motions of some one dealing cards, looking at the same time inquiringly into their faces.

"How about that, Bandy?" asked Vandover. "Shall we have a game to-night?"

The man of few words merely nodded his head and drank off the rest of his whisky at a swallow. They all went up to Vandover's room. Vandover got out the cards, the celluloid chips, and a fresh box of cigars. The Dummy held up two fingers of his left hand, shutting them together afterward with his right and making a hissing noise between his teeth. He raised his eyebrows at Vandover. Vandover understood, and, ringing for a bell-boy, ordered up three bottles of soda in siphon bottles.

The game was *vingt et un*, or, as they called it, Van John. They cut for banker. Ellis turned the first ace, and Vandover bought the bank from him. For the first hour they were very jolly, laughing and talking back and forth at each other; the Dummy especially communicative, continually scribbling upon his writing-pad, holding it toward the others. But it was not necessary for them to put their replies in writing— he understood from watching the movement of their lips. The luck had not declared itself as yet; none of them had lost or won very much. The bell-boy brought up the siphons. The Dummy took off his coat, and the other two followed his example. They were all smoking, and an acrid blue haze filled the room, making a golden blur about each gas globe.

But little by little the passion of the gambling seized upon them. The luck had begun to declare itself, alternating between Ellis and the Dummy. Vandover lost steadily; twice already his bank had been broken, and he had been forced to buy in. The play resolved itself into two parts, Vandover struggling to keep up with the game on one side, and on the other a great battle going on between Ellis and the Dummy. Long since they had ceased to laugh, and not a word was spoken; each one was absorbed in the game, intently watching the cards as they were turned. The four gas-jets of the chandelier flared steadily, filling the room with a crude raw light that was reflected with a blinding glare from the four staring white walls, the room grew hot, the layer of foul warm air just beneath the ceiling, slowly descending. The acrid tobacco smoke no longer rose, but hung in long, slow-waving threads just above their heads. They played on steadily; a great stillness grew in the room, a stillness broken only by the little rattle of chips and subdued rustle of the shuffled cards. Once Vandover stopped, just time enough to throw off his vest, his collar, and his scarf. For a moment the luck seemed about to settle on him. He was still banking, and twice in succession he drew Van John, both times winning heavily from the Dummy, and a little later tied Ellis at twenty when the latter had staked on nearly a third of his chips. But in the next half-dozen hands Ellis got back the lead again, winning from both the others. From this time on it was settled. The luck suddenly declared openly for Ellis, the Dummy and Vandover merely fighting for second place. Ellis held his lead; at one o'clock he was nearly fifty dollars ahead of the game. The profound silence of the room seemed to widen about them. After midnight the noises in the hotel, the ringing of distant call bells, the rattle of dishes from the kitchens, the clash of closing elevator doors, gradually ceased; only at long intervals one heard the hurried step of a bell-boy in the hall outside and the clink of the ice in the water pitcher that he was carrying. Outside a great quiet seemed in a sense to rise from the sleeping city, the noises in the streets died away. The last electric car went down Kearney Street, getting under way with a long minor wail. Occasionally a belated coupé, a nighthawk, rattled over the cobbles, while close by, from over the roofs, the tall slender stack upon the steam laundry puffed incessantly, three puffs at a time, like some kind of halting clock. The room became more and more close, none of them would take the time to open the window, from ceiling to floor the air was fouled by their breathing, by the tobacco smoke and by the four flaring gas-jets. By this time a sombre excitement burnt in their eyes and quivered in their fingers. Never for an instant did their glances leave the cards. Ellis was drinking whisky again, mixed with soda, his hand continually groping for the glass with a mechanical gesture; the Dummy was so excited he could not keep his cigar alight, and contented himself with chewing the end with an hysterical motion of his jaws. The perspiration stood in beads on the back of Vandover's hands, running down in tiny rivulets between his fingers, his teeth were shut close together and he was breathing short through his nose, a fine trembling had seized upon his hands so that the chips in his palm rattled like castanets. In the stale and murky atmosphere of the over-heated room in the midst of the vast silence of the sleeping city they played on steadily.

Then they began to "plunge," agreeing to play a no limit

game and raising the value of a red chip to ten dollars; at times they even played with the coins themselves when their chips were exhausted. Vandover had lost all his ready money, and now for a long time had been gambling with the five hundred dollars he had that day drawn from the bank. Ellis had practically put the Dummy out of the play, and now the game was between him and Vandover. Ellis was banking, and at length offered to sell the bank to either one of them. For the first time since the real gambling began they commenced to talk a little, but in short, brief sentences, answering by monosyllables and by signs.

"How much for the bank?" inquired Ellis, holding up the deck and looking from one to the other. Instantly the Dummy wrote ten dollars, in figures, on his pad, and showed it to him. Vandover looked at what the Dummy had written, and said:

"Fifteen."

"Twenty," scribbled the Dummy, as he watched Vandover's lips form the word.

"Twenty-five," returned Vandover. The Dummy hesitated a moment and then wrote "thirty." Ellis shook his head saying, "I'll keep the bank myself at that."

"Forty dollars!" cried Vandover. The Dummy shook his head, leaning back in his chair. Ellis shoved the pack across the table to Vandover, and Vandover gave him a twenty-dollar bill and two red chips.

On Vandover's very first deal around, the Dummy "stood" on the second card, for twelve chips; Ellis bet twenty-five on his first card, and, as he got the second, turned both of them face up. He had two jacks. "Twenty-five on each of these," he said. "I'll draw to each one." Vandover looked at his own card; it was a ten-spot. All at once he grew reckless, and seized with a sudden folly, resolved to attempt a great *coup*. "Double up!" he ordered. The Dummy set out twelve more chips, and Ellis another fifty, making his bet an even hundred. Vandover began to deal to Ellis. On the first jack Ellis drew eighteen and stood at that; the first card that fell to the second jack was an ace. "Van John," he remarked quietly. The Dummy drew three cards and stood on nineteen. Vandover turned up his own card and began to deal for himself. He already had a ten; now he drew a seven-spot and king in succession.

"The bank pays," he exclaimed. He paid the Dummy twenty-four chips. He gave Ellis fifty for the eighteen he had drawn on his first jack, and one hundred for the Van John upon the second, since the latter combination called for double the amount wagered; besides this, the bank was lost to him. Including the forty that he had paid for the bank, he had lost in all two hundred and fourteen dollars.

Never in his life had Vandover played so high a game, never before had he won or lost more than fifty dollars at a sitting. But he was content to have it thus. Here at last was the new pleasure for which he had longed, the fresh violent excitement that alone could rouse his jaded nerves, the one thing that could amuse him. However, the failure of his *coup* had left him without chips; he was out of the game. He decided that he would stop; more than half of his five hundred dollars was gone already. He drank off a glass of soda, the dregs of one of the siphon bottles, and got up yawning, shivering a little and stretching his arms high above. The other two played on steadily. The Dummy began to gain slowly upon Ellis, playing very cautiously, betting only upon face cards, aces, and ten-spots. Twice Ellis offered to sell him the bank, but he refused, fearful lest it should change his luck.

Vandover sat behind the Dummy's chair, watching his game, but at length, worn out, he began to drop off to sleep, waking every now and then with a sudden leap and recoil of all his nerves. An hour later the persistent scratching of a match awoke him. Ellis and the Dummy were still playing, and the Dummy was once more relighting the stump of his cigar. Ellis continued to deal, winning at almost every play; a great pile of chips and money lay at his elbow. For a few minutes Vandover watched the Dummy's game, leaning forward in his chair, his elbows on his knees. But it was evident that the Dummy had lost his nerve. Ellis' continued winnings had at length demoralized him. At one time he would bet heavily on worthless cards, and at another would throw back nines and tens for no apparent reason. Finally Ellis dealt him a queen, which he kept, betting ten chips. His next card was a seven-spot. He signed to Ellis that he would stand. Ellis drew twenty in three cards. Vandover could not restrain an exclamation of impatience at the Dummy's stupidity. What a fool a man must be to stand on seventeen with only two in the game. All at once he tossed twenty dollars across the table to Ellis, saying, "Give me that in chips. I'm coming in again." Once more he resumed his seat at the table, and Ellis dealt him a hand.

But Vandover's interruption had for an instant taken Ellis' mind from the game. He stirred in his chair and looked about the room, puffing out his cheeks and blowing between his lips.

"Say, this room is close enough to strangle you. Open the window behind you, Van, you're nearest to it." As Vandover raised the curtain he uttered a cry: "Look here! will you?"

It was morning; the city was flooded by the light of the sun already an hour high. The sky was without a cloud. Over the roofs and amongst the gray maze of telegraph wires swarms of sparrows were chittering hoarsely, and as Vandover raised the window he could hear the newsboys far below in the streets chanting the morning's papers.

"Come on, Van!" exclaimed Ellis impatiently; " we're waiting for you."

That night decided it. From that time on, Vandover's only pleasure was gambling. Night and day he sat over the cards, the passion growing upon him as he continued to lose, for his ill luck was extraordinary. It was a veritable mania, a wild blind frenzy that knew no limit. At first he had contented himself with a game in which twenty or thirty dollars was as much as he could win or lose at a sitting, but soon this palled upon him; he was obliged to raise the stakes continually in order to arouse in him the interest, the keen tense excitement, that his jaded nerves craved.

The five hundred dollars that he had drawn from the ten thousand, the first payment on his old home, melted away within a week. Only a few years ago Vandover would have stopped to reflect upon the meaning of this, would have resisted the temptation that drew him constantly to the gambling-table, but the idea of resistance never so much as occurred to him. He did not invest his fifteen thousand, but drew upon it continually to satisfy his last new craze. It was not with any hope of winning that he gambled—the desire of money was never strong in him—it was only the love of the excitement of the moment.

Little by little the fifteen thousand in the bank dwindled. It did not all go in cards. Certain habits of extravagance grew upon Vandover, the natural outcome of his persistent gambling, the desire of winning easily being balanced by the impulses to spend quickly. He took a certain hysterical delight in flinging away money with both hands. Now it was the chartering of a yacht for a ten-days' cruise about the bay, or it was a bicycle bought one week and thrown away the next, a fresh suit of clothes each month, gloves worn but once, gold-pieces thrust into Flossie's pockets, suppers given to bouffe actresses—twenty-four-hour acquaintances—a race-horse bought for eight hundred dollars, resold for two hundred and fifty—rings and scarf-pins given away to the women and girls of the Imperial, and a whole world of follies that his poor distorted wits conceived from hour to hour. His judgment was gone, his mind unbalanced. All his life Vandover had been sinking slowly lower and lower; this, however, was the beginning of the last plunge. The process of degeneration, though inevitable, had been gradual as long as he indulged generally in all forms of evil; it was only now when a passion for one particular vice absorbed him that he commenced to rush headlong to his ruin.

The fifteen thousand dollars—the price of his old home—he gambled or flung away in a little less than a year. He never invested it, but ate into it day after day, sometimes to pay his gambling debts, sometimes to indulge an absurd and extravagant whim, sometimes to pay his bill at the Lick House, and sometimes for no reason at all, moved simply by a reckless desire for spending.

On the evening of a certain Thanksgiving day, nine months after he had sold the house, Vandover came in through the ladies' entrance of the Imperial, going slowly down the passageway, looking into the little rooms on his right for Ellis or the Dummy. There had been a great intercollegiate football game that day, and Vandover, remembering that he had once found an interest in such things, had at first determined to see it. But toward eleven o'clock in the morning the rain had begun to fall, and Ellis, who was to have gone with him, declared that he did not care enough about the game to go out to it in the rain. Vandover was disappointed; he fancied that he could have enjoyed the game—as much as he could enjoy anything of late—but he hated to go to places alone. In the end, however, he resolved to go whether Ellis went or not. It was a holiday. Vandover had Ellis and the Dummy to lunch with him at the hotel, where they arranged the menu of a famous Thanksgiving dinner for that evening: they would meet in one of the little rooms of the Imperial and go from there to the restaurant. As they were finishing their lunch Vandover said:

"I got a new kind of liqueur yesterday—has a colour like violets and smells like cologne. You fellows better come up to my room and try it. I've got to go up and change anyway, if I go out to that game." They all went up to Vandover's cheerless room, and Ellis began to argue with Vandover against the folly of going anywhere in the rain.

"*You* don't want to go to that game, Van. Just look how it's raining. I'll bet there won't be a thousand people there. They'll probably postpone the game anyway. Say, this *is* queer looking stuff. What do you call it?"

"*Crème violette.*"

The Dummy set down his emptied liqueur glass on the mantelshelf, and nodded approvingly at Vandover; then he scribbled, "Out of sight," on his tablet.

"Tastes like cough syrup and alcohol," growled Ellis, scowling and sipping. "I think a pint of this would make the Dummy talk Dutch. Keep it up, Dummy," he continued, articulating distinctly so that the other could catch the movement of his lips. "Drink some more—make you talk." Vandover was cutting the string around a pasteboard box that had just come from his tailor's; it was a new suit of clothes, rough cheviot, brown with small checks. He dressed slowly and tipped forward the swinging mirror of the bureau to see how the trousers set. Meanwhile Ellis and the Dummy had got out the cards and chips from the drawer of the centre-table and had begun a game.

"Better change your mind, Van," said Ellis without raising his eyes from the cards.

"No, sir," answered Van. "You don't know how it is—you never were a college man. Why, I wouldn't miss a football game for anything. Talk about your horse-racing, talk about your baseball—I tell you there's nothing in the world so exciting as a hot football game." He swung into his long high-coloured waterproof and stood behind Ellis, watching his game for a moment while he tied a couple of long silk streamers to his umbrella handle.

"It's one of the college colours," he explained. "Seems like old times back at Harvard." Ellis snorted with contempt.

"Such kids!" he growled.

"I saw one of the coaches go down the street a little while ago," continued Vandover, still watching Ellis shuffle and deal. "There were about twenty college men on top, and they had a big bulldog all harnessed out in their colours, and they were blowing fish-horns, and I tell you it made me wish I was one of them again." Ellis did not answer; it was probable he did not hear. Both he and the Dummy were settling down for a game that no doubt would last all the afternoon. Vandover made them free of his room, and they often gambled there when he was away. But it invariably made Ellis nervous to have any one stand behind his chair while he was playing; he began to move about uneasily. By and by he looked at his watch. "Better get a move on," he said, "you'll be late."

"Just a minute," answered Vandover, more and more interested in the game. "Go on playing; don't bother about me. Oh, I saw Charlie Geary, too," he continued, "on another coach; there was a party of them. Charlie was with Turner Ravis on the box seat. You remember Turner Ravis, don't you, Bandy? The girl I used to go with."

"There's a girl I never liked," observed Ellis. "She always struck me as being one of these regular snobs."

"Ah, snob is no name for it," assented Vandover. "She thought she was too damned high-toned for me. As soon as I got into that mess about Ida Wade, she threw me over. No, she didn't want to be associated with me any longer. Well, she can go to the devil. Geary's welcome to her."

"I thought Dolly Haight was going to marry her," said Ellis. "What was the matter *there?*"

"*I* don't know," returned Vandover; "probably Dolly

Haight didn't have enough money to suit her. Guess she wants a man that will make his pile in this town and make his way, too. Ah, you bet!"

Half an hour later he was still behind Ellis' chair. Ellis had become so fidgety that he was losing steadily. Once more he turned to Vandover, speaking over his shoulder, "Come on, come on, Van, go along to your football; you make me nervous standing there." Vandover pushed a ten-dollar gold-piece across the table to the Dummy, who was banking, and said:

"Give me that in chips. I'm coming in."

"I thought you were going to the game?" inquired Ellis.

"Ah, the devil!" answered Vandover. "Too much rain."

They had played without interruption all that afternoon, and for once Vandover had all the luck. When they broke up about five o'clock with the understanding to meet again in the Imperial at seven, he had won nearly a hundred dollars.

When Vandover went out to keep this appointment he found the streets—especially Kearney and Market streets—crowded. It was about half-past six. The football game was over and the college men had returned. They were everywhere, marching about in long files, chain-gang fashion, each file headed by a man beating upon a gong, or parading the sidewalks ten abreast, singing college songs or shouting their slogan. At every moment one heard the college yells answering each other from street corner to street corner, "Rah, rah, rah—Rah, rah, rah!" Vandover found the Imperial crowded with students. The barroom was packed to the doors, every one of the little rooms in the front hall was full, while Flossie and Nannie had a great party of the young fellows in one of the larger rooms in the rear. Among the crowd in the barroom, three members of the winning team—heroes, with bandages about their heads—were breaking training, smoking and drinking for the first time in many long weeks.

Vandover found Ellis and the Dummy leaning against the wall in the crowded front passage. They were both in bad humour, the Dummy sulking because Flossie had left him for one of the football men, the full-back, a young blond giant with two dislocated fingers; Ellis in a rage because he could get no cocktails at the bar, only straight drinks that night—

too much of a crowd. These damn college sports thought they owned the town. "Ah, let's get out of here, Van!" he called over the heads of the throng as soon as Vandover came in sight.

They went out into the street and started in the direction of the restaurant where they had decided to eat their Thanksgiving dinner. After leaving Vandover that afternoon Ellis had seen the head waiter of this restaurant and had explained to him the bill of fare that Vandover, the Dummy, and himself had arranged during their lunch at the Lick House. The streets had relapsed into a momentary quiet—it was between half-past six and seven—and most of the college men were gathered into the hotels and cafés eating dinner. About an hour later they would reappear again for a moment on their way to the theatre, which they were to attend in a body.

But Vandover suddenly discovered that he could not eat a mouthful, the smell of food revolted him, and little by little an irregular twitching had overcome his hands and forearms.

He had received a great shock. That same evening, as he was leaving the hotel, the clerk at the office had handed him some letters that had accumulated in his box. Vandover could never think to ask for his mail in the morning as he went in to breakfast. Something was surely wrong with his head of late. Every day he found it harder and harder to remember things. There were three letters altogether: one was the tailor's bill mailed the same day that his last suit had been finished; a second was an advertisement announcing the near opening of the Sutro Baths that were building at that time; and the third a notice from the bank calling his attention to the fact that his account was overdrawn by some sixty dollars.

At first Vandover did not see the meaning of this notice, and thrust it back in his pocket together with the tailor's bill; then slowly an idea struggled into his mind. Was it possible that he no longer had any money at the bank? Was his fifteen thousand gone? From time to time his bank-book had been balanced, and invariably during the first days of each month his checks had come back to him, used and crumpled, covered with strange signatures and stamped in blue ink; but after the first few months he had never paid the least attention to these; he never kept accounts, having a veritable feminine horror of figures. But it was absurd to think that his money was gone. Pshaw! one could not spend fifteen thousand in nine months! It was preposterous! This notice was some technicality that he could not understand. He would look into it the next day. And so he dismissed the wearisome matter from his mind with a shrug of his shoulders as though ridding himself of some troublesome burden. However, the idea persisted. Somehow, between the lines of the printed form he smelt out a fresh disaster. He read it over again and again. All at once as he stood in the doorway of the hotel, turning up the collar of his waterproof and watching the little pools in the hollows of the asphalt pavement to see if it were still raining, the conviction came upon him. In a second he knew that he was ruined. The true meaning of the notice became apparent with the swiftness of a great flash of light. He had spent his fifteen thousand dollars!

The blow was strong enough, sudden enough to penetrate even Vandover's clouded and distorted wits. His nerves were gone in a minute, a sudden stupefying numbness fell upon his brain, and the fear of something unknown, the immense unreasoning terror that had gripped him for the first time the morning after Ida Wade's suicide came back upon him, horrible, crushing, so that he had to shut his teeth against a wild hysterical desire to rush through the streets screaming and waving his arms.

By the time the three friends had reached the restaurant where they were to eat their Thanksgiving dinner, Vandover's appetite had given place to a loathing of the very smell of food, his nervousness was fast approaching hysteria, the little nerve clusters all over his body seemed to be crisping and writhing like balls of tiny serpents, at intervals he would twitch sharply as though startled at some sudden noise, his breath coming short, his heart beating quick.

They had their dinner in one of the private rooms of the restaurant on the second floor. All through the meal Vandover struggled to keep himself in hand, fighting with all his strength against this reappearance of his old enemy, this sudden return of the dreadful crisis, determined not to make an exhibition of himself before the others. He pretended to eat, and forced himself to talk, joining in with Ellis, who was badgering the Dummy about Flossie. The proper thing to do was to fill the Dummy's glass while his attention was otherwise absorbed, and in the end to get him so drunk that he could talk. Toward the end of the dinner Ellis was successful. All at once the Dummy got upon his feet, his eyes were glazed with drunkenness, he swayed about in an irregular circle, holding up, now by the table, now by the chair-back, and now by the wall behind him. He was very angry, exasperated beyond control by Ellis' raillery and abuse. He forgot himself and uttered a series of peculiar cries very faint and shrill, like the sounds of a voice heard through a telephone when some imperfection of transmission prevents one from distinguishing the words. His mouth was wide open and his tongue rolled about in an absurd way between his teeth. Now and then one could catch a word or two. Ellis went into spasms of laughter, holding his sides, gasping for breath. Vandover could not help being amused, and the two laughed at the Dummy's stammering rage until their breath was spent. Throughout the rest of the evening the Dummy recommenced from time to time, rising unsteadily to his feet, shaking his fists, pouring out a stream of little ineffectual birdlike twitterings, trying to give Ellis abuse for abuse, trying to talk long after it had ceased to amuse the other two. Ellis had been drinking for nearly six hours, without the liquor producing the slightest effect upon him; long since, the Dummy was hopelessly drunk; and now Vandover, who had been drinking upon an empty stomach, began to grow very noisy and boisterous. Little by little Ellis himself commenced to lose his self-control. By and by he and Vandover began to sing, each independent of the other, very hoarse and loud. The Dummy joined them, making a hideous and lamentable noise which so affected Ellis that he pretended to howl at it like a little dog overcome by mournful music. But suddenly Ellis had an idea, crying out thickly, between two hiccoughs:

"Hey, there, Van, do your dog-act for us! Go on! Bark for us!"

By this time Vandover was very nearly out of his head, his drunkenness finishing what his nervousness had begun. The attack was fast approaching culmination; strange and unnatural fancies began to come and go in his brain.

"Go on, Van!" urged Ellis, his eyes heavy with alcohol. "Go on, do your dog-act!"

All at once it was as though an angry dog were snarling and barking over a bone there under the table about their feet. Ellis roared with laughter, but suddenly he himself was drunk. All the afternoon he had kept himself in hand; now his intoxication came upon him in a moment. The skin around his eyes was purple and swollen, the pupils themselves were contracted; they grew darker, taking on the colour of bitumen. Suddenly he swept glasses, plates, castor, knives, forks, and all from off the table with a single movement of his arm. Then the alcohol overcame him all in an instant like a poisonous gas. He swayed forward in his chair and fell across the stripped table, his head rolling inertly between his outstretched arms. He did not move again.

In a neighbouring room young Haight had been dining with some college fellows, fraternity men, all friends of his, upon whose coach he had ridden to and from the game. He had heard Vandover and Ellis in the room across the hall and had recognized their voices. Haight had never been a friend of Ellis, but no one, not even Turner, had grieved more over Vandover's ruin than had his old-time college chum.

Young Haight heard the noise of the falling crockery as Ellis swept the table clear, and turned his head sharply, listening. There was a moment's silence after this, and Haight, fearing some accident had happened, stepped out into the hall and stood there a moment listening again; his head inclined toward the closed door. He heard no groaning, no exclamations of pain, not even any noise of conversation; only through the closed door came a steady sound of barking.

Puzzled, he tried the door and, finding it locked, as he had expected, put one foot upon the knob and, catching hold of the top jamb, raised himself up and looked down through the open space that answered for a transom.

The room was very warm, the air thick with the smell of cooked food, the fumes of whisky, and the acrid odour of cigar smoke. Ellis had rolled from his chair and lay upon the floor sprawling on his face in the wreck of the table. Near to him, likewise upon the floor, but sitting up, his back against the wall, was the Dummy. He was muttering incessantly to himself, as if delighted at having found his tongue, his head swaying on his shoulders, and a strange murmur, soft, bird-like, meaningless, like sounds heard from a vast distance, coming from his wide-open mouth.

Vandover was sitting bolt upright in his chair, his hands gripping the table, his eyes staring straight before him. He was barking incessantly. It was evident that now he could not stop himself; it was like hysterical laughter, a thing beyond his control. Twice young Haight called him by name, kicking the door as his leg hung against it. At last Vandover heard him. Then as he caught sight of his face over the door he raised his upper lip above his teeth and snarled at him, long and viciously.

As Haight dropped down into the hall a waiter came running up; he, too, had heard the noise of the breaking dishes. As he thrust his key into the lock he paused a moment, listening and looking in a puzzled way at young Haight. "They have a dog in here, then? They had no dog when they came. That's funny!"

"Open the door," said young Haight quietly. Once inside Haight went directly to Vandover, crying out: "Come! come on, Van! come home with me." Vandover started suddenly, looking about him bewildered, drawing his hand across his face.

"Home," he repeated vaguely; "yes, that's the idea. Let's go home. I want to go to bed. Hello, Dolly! where did *you* come from? Say, Dolly, let me tell you—listen here—come down here close; you mustn't mind me; you know I'm a wolf mostly!"

They went down toward the Lick House. Vandover grew steadier after a few minutes in the open air. Young Haight locked arms with him; they went on together in silence. By this time the streets were crowded again, the theatres were over, and the college men were once more at large. Now they were all gathered together into one immense procession, headed by a brass band in a brewer's wagon, and they tramped aimlessly to and fro about Kearney and Market streets, making a hideous noise. At the head the band was playing a popular quick-step with a great banging of a bass drum. The college men in the front ranks were singing one song, those in the rear another, while the middle of the column was given over to an abominable medley of fish-horns, policemen's rattles and great Chinese gongs. At stated intervals the throng would halt and give the college yell.

"Dolly, you and I used to do that," said Vandover, looking after the procession. He had himself well in hand by this time. "What was the matter with me back there at the restaurant, Dolly?" he asked after a while.

"Oh, you'd been drinking a good deal, I guess," answered young Haight. "You—you had some queer idea about yourself!"

"Yes, I know," answered Vandover quickly. "Fancied I was some kind of a beast, didn't I—some kind of wolf? I have that notion sometimes and I can't get it out of my head. It's curious just the same."

They went up to Vandover's room. Vandover lit the gas, but he could hardly keep back an exclamation as the glare suddenly struck young Haight's face. What in heaven's name was the matter with his old-time chum? He seemed to be blighted, shattered, struck down by some terrible, overwhelming calamity. A dreadful anguish looked through his eyes. The sense of a hopeless misery had drawn and twisted his face. There could be no doubt that something had made shipwreck of his life. Vandover was looking at a ruined man.

"My God, Dolly!" exclaimed Vandover, "what's happened to you? You look like a death's-head, man! What's gone wrong? Aren't you well?"

Haight caught his friend's searching gaze, and for a moment they looked at each other without speaking. There was no mistaking the fearful grief that smouldered behind Haight's dull, listless eyes. For a moment Vandover thought of Turner Ravis. But even if she had turned him off, that alone would not account for his friend's fearful condition of mind and body.

"What is it, Dolly?" persisted Vandover. "We used to be pretty good chums, not so long ago."

They sat down on the edge of the bed, and for a moment their positions seemed reversed: Haight the one to be protected and consoled, Vandover the shielding and self-reliant one.

Young Haight passed his hand over his face before he answered, and Vandover noticed that his fingers trembled like an old man's.

"Do you remember that night, Van, when you and Charlie and I all went out to Turner's house, and we had *tamales* and beer, and a glass broke in that peculiar way, and I cut my lip?"

Vandover nodded, forcing his attention against the alcoholic fumes, to follow his friend's words.

"We went down to the Imperial afterward," Haight continued, "and ran into Ellis, and we had something more to eat. Do you remember that as we sat there, Toby, the waiter, brought Flossie in, and she sat there with us a while?"

He paused, choosing his words. Vandover listened closely, trying to recall the incident.

"She kissed me," said young Haight slowly, "and the court-plaster came off. You know I never had anything to do with women, Van. I always tried to keep away from them. But that's where my life practically came to an end."

"You mean—" began Vandover. "You mean—that you—that Flossie——?"

Haight nodded.

"Good God! I can't believe it. It's not possible! I *know* Flossie!"

Haight shook his head, smiling grimly.

"I can't help that, Van," said he. "There's no denying facts, there's no other possible explanation! As soon as I knew, I went to the doctors here, and then I went to New York for treatment, but there's no hope. I didn't know, you see. I didn't believe it possible. Turner Ravis and I were engaged. I waited too long! There's only one escape for me now." His voice dropped, he stared for a moment at the floor. Then he straightened up, and said in a different tone, "But, damn it, Van, let's not talk about it! I'm haunted with the thing day and night. I want to talk to you! I want to talk to you seriously. You know you are ruining yourself, old man!"

But Vandover interrupted him with a gesture, saying, "Don't go on, Dolly; it isn't the least use. There *was* a time for that, but that was long ago. I used to care, I used to be sorry and all that, but I'm not now. Ruining myself? Why, I *have* ruined myself long ago. We're both ruined—only in your case it wasn't your fault. It's too late for me now, and I'm even not sorry that it *is* too late. Dolly, I don't *want* to pull up. You can't imagine a man fallen as low as that, can you? I couldn't imagine it myself a few years ago. I'm going right straight to the devil now, and you might as well stand aside and give me a free course, for I'm bound to get there sooner or later. I suppose you would think that a man who could see this as plainly as I do would be afraid, would have remorse and all that sort of thing. Well, I did at first. I'll never forget the night when I first saw it; came near shooting myself, but I got over it, and now I'm used to the idea. Dolly, *I can get used to almost anything*. Nothing makes much difference to me nowadays—only I like to play cards. Look here!" he went on, laying out the notice from the bank upon the table, "this came to-day. You see what it is! I sold the old house on California Street. Well, I've gambled away that money in less than a year. It seems that I'm a financial ruin now, but"—and he began to laugh—"I live through it somehow. The news didn't prevent me from getting drunk to-night."

After young Haight was gone, Vandover went to bed, turning out the gas and drawing down the window half-way from the top. The wine had made him sleepy; he was dropping away into a very grateful doze when a sudden shock, a violent leap of every nerve in his body, brought him up to a sitting posture, gasping for breath, his heart fluttering, his hands beating at the empty air. He settled down again, turning upon his pillow, closing his eyes, very weary, longing for a good night's sleep. Dolly Haight's terrible story, his unjustified fate, and the hopeless tragedy of it, came back to him. Vandover would gladly have changed places with him. Young Haight had the affection and respect of even those that knew. He, Vandover, had thrown away his friends' love and their esteem with the rest of the things he had once valued. His thoughts, released from all control of his will, began to come and go through his head with incredible rapidity, confused ideas, half-remembered scenes, incidents of the past few days, bits and ends of conversation recalled for no especial reason, all galloping across his brain like a long herd of terrified horses; an excitement grew upon him, a strange thrill of exhilaration. He was broad awake now, but suddenly his left leg, his left arm and wrist, all his left side jerked with the suddenness of a sprung trap; so violent was the shock that the entire bed shook and creaked with it. Then the inevitable reaction followed, the slow crisping and torsion of his nerves, twisting upon each other like a vast swarm of tiny serpents; it seemed to begin with his ankles, spreading slowly to every part of his body; it was a veritable torture, so poignant that Vandover groaned under it, shutting his eyes. He could not keep quiet a second—to lie in bed was an impossibility; he threw the bed-clothes from him and sprang up. He did not light the gas, but threw on his bathrobe and began to walk the floor. Even as he walked, his eyelids drooped lower and lower. The need of sleep overcame him like a narcotic, but as soon as he was about to lose himself he would be suddenly and violently awakened by the same shock, the same jangling recoil of his nerves. Then his hands and head seemed to swell; next, it was as though the whole room was too small for him. He threw open the window and, leaning upon his elbows, looked out.

The clouds had begun to break, the rain was gradually ceasing, leaving in the air a damp, fresh smell, the smell of wet asphalt and the odour of dripping woodwork. It was warm; the atmosphere was dank, heavy, tepid. One or two stars were out, and a faint gray light showed him the vast reach of roofs below stretching away to meet the abrupt rise of Telegraph Hill. Not far off the slender, graceful smokestack puffed steadily, throwing off continually the little flock of white jets that rose into the air very brave and gay, but in the end dwindled irresolutely, discouraged, disheartened, fading sadly away, vanishing under the night, like illusions disappearing at the first touch of the outside world. As Vandover leaned from his window, looking out into the night with eyes that saw nothing, the college slogan rose again from the great crowd of students who still continued to hold the streets.

"Rah, rah, rah! Rah, rah, rah!"

He turned back into the room, groping among the bottles on his washstand for his bromide of potassium. As he poured out the required dose into the teaspoon his hand twitched again sharply, flirting the medicine over his bared neck and chest, exposed by the bathrobe which he had left open at the throat. It was cold, and he shivered a bit as he wiped it dry with the back of his hand.

He knew very well that his nervous attack was coming on again. As he set down the bottle upon the washstand he muttered to himself, "Now I'm going to have a night of it." He began to walk the floor again with great strides, fighting with all his pitiful, shattered mind against the increasing hysteria, trying to keep out of his brain the strange hallucination that assailed it from time to time, the hallucination of a thing four-footed, a thing that sulked and snarled. The hotel grew quiet; a watchman went down the hall turning out each alternate gas jet. Just outside of the door was a burner in a red globe, fixed at a stair landing to show the exit in case of fire. This burned all night and it streamed through the transom of Vandover's room, splotching the ceiling with a great square of red light. Vandover was in a torment, overcome now by that same fear with which he had at last become so familiar, the unreasoning terror of something unknown. He uttered an exclamation, a suppressed cry of despair, of misery, and then suddenly checked himself, astonished, seized with the fancy that his cry was not human, was not of himself, but of something four-footed, the snarl of some exasperated brute. He paused abruptly in his walk, listening, for what he did not know. The silence of the great city spread itself around him, like the still waters of some vast lagoon. Through the silence he heard the noise of the throng of college youths. They were returning, doubling upon their line of march. A long puff of tepid air breathing through the open window brought to his ears the distant joyous sound of their slogan:

"Rah, rah, rah! Rah, rah, rah!"

They passed by along the adjacent street, their sounds growing faint. Vandover took up his restless pacing again. Little by little the hallucination gained upon him; little by little his mind slipped from his grasp. The wolf—the beast— whatever the creature was, seemed in his diseased fancy to grow stronger in him from moment to moment. But with all his strength he fought against it, fought against this strange mania, that overcame him at these periodical intervals—

fought with his hands so tightly clenched that the knuckles
grew white, that the nails bit into the palm. It seemed to him
that in some way his personality divided itself into three.
There was himself, the real Vandover of every day, the same
familiar Vandover that looked back at him from his mirror;
then there was the wolf, the beast, whatever the creature was
that lived in his flesh, and that struggled with him now, striving to gain the ascendency, to absorb the real Vandover into
its own hideous identity; and last of all, there was a third self,
formless, very vague, elusive, that stood aside and watched
the strife of the other two. But as he fought against his madness, concentrating all his attention with a tremendous effort
of the will, the queer numbness that came upon his mind
whenever he exerted it enwrapped his brain like a fog, and
this third self grew vaguer than ever, dwindled and disappeared. Somehow it seemed to be associated with consciousness, for after this the sense of the reality of things grew dim
and blurred to him. He ceased to know exactly what he was
doing. His intellectual parts dropped away one by one, leaving only the instincts, the blind, unreasoning impulses of the
animal.

Still he continued his restless, lurching walk back and forth
in his room, his head hanging low and swinging from side to
side with the movement of his gait. He had become so nervous that the restraint imposed upon his freedom of movement by his bathrobe and his loose night-clothes chafed and
irritated him. At length he had stripped off everything.

Suddenly and without the slightest warning Vandover's
hands came slowly above his head and he dropped forward,
landing upon his palms. All in an instant he had given way,
yielding in a second to the strange hallucination of that four-
footed thing that sulked and snarled. Now without a moment's stop he ran back and forth along the wall of the room,
upon the palms of his hands and his toes, a ludicrous figure,
like that of certain clowns one sees at the circus, contortion-
ists walking about the sawdust, imitating some kind of enormous dog. Still he swung his head from side to side with the
motion of his shuffling gait, his eyes dull and fixed. At long
intervals he uttered a sound, half word, half cry, "Wolf—
wolf!" but it was muffled, indistinct, raucous, coming more

from his throat than from his lips. It might easily have been the growl of an animal. A long time passed. Naked, four-footed, Vandover ran back and forth the length of the room.

By an hour after midnight the sky was clear, all the stars were out, the moon a thin, low-swinging scimitar, set behind the black mass of the roofs of the city, leaving a pale bluish light that seemed to come from all quarters of the horizon. As the great stillness grew more and more complete, the persistent puffing of the slender tin stack, the three gay and joyous little noises, each sounding like a note of discreet laughter interrupted by a cough, became clear and distinct. Inside the room there was no sound except the persistent patter of something four-footed going up and down. At length even this sound ceased abruptly. Worn out, Vandover had just fallen, dropping forward upon his face with a long breath. He lay still, sleeping at last. The remnant of the great band of college men went down an adjacent street, raising their cadenced slogan for the last time. It came through the open window, softened as it were by the warm air, thick with damp, through which it travelled:

"Rah, rah, rah! Rah, rah, rah!"

Naked, exhausted, Vandover slept profoundly, stretched at full length at the foot of the bare, white wall of the room beneath two of the little placards, scrawled with ink, that read, "Stove Here"; "Mona Lisa Here."

Chapter Seventeen

O**N A CERTAIN** Saturday morning two years later Vandover awoke in his room at the Reno House, the room he had now occupied for fifteen months.

One might almost say that he had been expelled from the Lick House. For a time he had tried to retain his room there with the idea of paying his bills by the money he should win at gambling. But his bad luck was now become a settled thing—almost invariably he lost. At last Ellis and the Dummy had refused to play with him, since he was never able to pay them when they won. They had had a great quarrel. Ellis broke with him sullenly, growling wrathfully under his heavy moustache, and the Dummy had written upon his pad—so hastily and angrily that the words could hardly be read—that he would not play with professional gamblers, men who supported themselves by their winnings. Damn it! one had to be a gentleman.

Next, Vandover had tried to borrow some money of Charlie Geary. Geary had told him that he could not afford as much as Vandover needed. Then Vandover became enraged. He had long since seen that Geary had practically swindled him out of his block in the Mission, and at that very moment the huge boot and shoe "concern" was completing the factory built upon the ground that Vandover had once owned. Geary had cleared seven thousand dollars on his "deal." His refusal to loan his old-time friend fifty dollars upon this occasion had exasperated Vandover out of all bounds. There was a scene. Vandover told Geary what he thought of his "deal" in very plain words. They shouted "swindler" and "gambler" into each other's faces; the whole office was aroused; Vandover was ejected by force. On a stair landing half-way to the street he sat down and cried into his arms folded upon his knees. When he returned to his room he had a sudden return of his dreadful nervous malady and barked and whined under the bed.

Then Vandover wrote a fifty-dollar check on the bank—the same bank that had just notified him that he was overdrawn—and passed it upon young Haight. How he came to do the thing he could not tell; it might have been the influence of Geary's successful robbery, or it might have been that he had at last lost all principle, all sense of honour and integrity. At any rate, he could not bring himself to feel very sorry. He knew that young Haight would not prosecute him for the dishonesty; he traded upon Haight's magnanimity; he only felt glad that he had the fifty dollars. But by this time Vandover did not even wonder at his own baseness and degradation. A few years ago this would have been the case; now his character was so changed that the theft seemed somehow consistent. He had destroyed young Haight's friendship for him. He had cast from him his college chum, his best friend, but neither did this affect him. Nothing made much difference to him now.

Nevertheless, Vandover was evicted from the Lick House three days after he had stolen young Haight's money. Instead of paying his bills with the amount, he gambled it away in a back room of a new café on Market Street with Toby, the red-eyed waiter from the Imperial, and a certain German "professor," a billiard marker, who wore a waistcoat figured with little designs of the Eiffel Tower, and who was a third owner in a trotting mare named Tomato Ketchup.

Vandover was now left with only his bonds, his U. S. 4 per cents. These brought him in but sixty-nine dollars a quarter, or as he had had it arranged, twenty-three dollars a month. Just at this time, as if by a miracle, a veritable God from the Machine, Vandover's lawyer, Mr. Field, found him an opportunity to earn some money. For the first and only time in his life Vandover knew what it was to work for a living. The work that Field secured for him was the work of painting those little pictures on the lacquered surface of iron safes, those little oval landscapes between the lines of red and gold lettering—landscapes, rugged gorges, ocean steamships under all sail, mountain lakes with sailboats careening upon their surfaces, the boat indicated by two little triangular dabs of Chinese white, one for the sail itself and the other for its reflection in the water. Sometimes even he was called upon to paint other little pictures upon the sides of big express wagons—two horses, one white and the other bay, galloping very free in an open field, their manes and tails flying, or a bulldog, very savage, sitting upon a green and black safe, or the head of a mastiff with a spiked collar about his neck.

What with the pay for this sort of work and the interest of his bonds, Vandover managed to lead a haphazard sort of life, living about in cheap lodging-houses and cheap restaurants. But he was never more than a second-class workman, and he was so irregular that he could never be depended upon.

The moment he began to paint again—even to paint such pitiful little pictures as these—the same familiar experience repeated itself, the unwillingness of his fingers, their failure to rightly interpret his ideas, the resulting crudity of his work, the sudden numbness in his brain, the queer, tense sensation behind his eyes. But Vandover had long since become accustomed to these symptoms and would not have minded them at this time had it not been that they were occasionally followed by a nervous twitching and jerking of his whole arm, so that sometimes he could not hold the brush steady a minute at a time.

For two years he had drifted about the city, living now here and now there, a real hand-to-mouth existence, sinking a little lower each day. Now, no one knew him. He had completely passed out of the lives of Haight, Geary, and Ellis, just as before he had passed out of the life of Turner Ravis. At the end of the first year they had ceased even to think about him. For a long time they thought that he was dead, until one day Ellis declared that he had seen him far down on Kearney Street, near the Barbary Coast, looking at the pictures in the illustrated weeklies that were tacked upon the show-board on the sidewalk in front of a stationer's. Ellis had told the others that on this occasion Vandover seemed to be more sickly than ever; he described his appearance in detail, wagging his head at his own story, pursing his lips, putting his chin in the air. Vandover had worn an old paint-stained pair of blue trousers, fastened with a strap, so that his shirt showed below his vest; he had no collar, and he had allowed his beard to grow, a straggling thin beard, through which one could see the buttons of his shirt, a dirty beard full of the cracker crumbs from the free lunch-counters of cheap saloons; he had on a hat which he had worn when they had known him; but one should see that hat now!

It was all true: little by little Vandover had abandoned all interest in his personal appearance. Of course it was impossible for him to dress well at this time, but he had even lost regard for decency and cleanliness. He washed himself but rarely. He had even acquired the habit of sleeping with all his clothes on during the colder nights of the year.

Nothing made any difference. Gradually his mind grew more and more clouded; he became stupid, sluggish. He went about the city from dawn to dark, his feet dragging, his head hanging low and swinging from side to side with the motion of his gait. He rarely spoke; his eyes took on a dull, glazed appearance, filmy, like the eyes of a dead fish. At certain intervals his mania came upon him, the strange hallucination of something four-footed, the persistent fancy that the brute in him had now grown so large, so insatiable, that it had taken everything, even to his very self, his own identity—that he had literally *become the brute*. The attack passed off and left him wondering, perplexed.

The Reno House, where Vandover had lived for some fifteen months, was a sort of hotel on Sacramento Street below Kearney. The neighbourhood was low—just on the edge of the Barbary Coast, abounding in stores for second-hand clothing, saloons, pawnshops, gun-stores, bird-stores, and the shops of Chinese cobblers. Around the corner on Kearney Street was a concert hall, a dive, to which the admission was free. Near by was the old Plaza.

Underneath the hotel on the ground floor were two saloons, a barber shop, and a broom manufactory. The lodgers themselves were for the most part "transients," sailors lounging about shore between two voyages, Swedes and Danes, farmhands, grape-pickers, and cow-punchers from distant parts of the state, a few lost women, and Japanese cooks and second-boys remaining there while they advertised for positions.

Vandover sank to the grade of these people at once with that fatal adaptability to environment which he had permitted himself to foster throughout his entire life, and which had led him to be contented in almost any circumstances. It was as if the brute in him were forever seeking a lower level, wallowing itself lower and lower into the filth and into the mire, content to be foul, content to be prone, to be inert and supine.

It was Saturday morning about a quarter of nine. The wet season had begun early that year. Though this was but the middle of September, the rain had fallen steadily since the previous Wednesday. Its steady murmur, prolonged and soothing like the purring of a great cat, filled Vandover's room with a pleasant sound. The air of the room was thick and foul, heavy with the odour of cooking, onions, and stale bedding. It was very warm; there was no ventilation. Vandover lay upon the bed half awake, dozing under the thick coarse blankets and soiled counterpane. With the exception of his shoes and coat he wore all his clothes. He was glad to be warm, to be stupefied by the heat of the bedding and the bad air of the room.

In the next room a Portuguese fruit vender, very drunk, was fighting with the tin pitcher and pasteboard bowl on his wash-stand, trying to wet his head, swearing and making a hideous clatter. At length he tipped them over upon the floor and gave the pitcher a great kick. The noise roused Vandover; he sat up in bed, stretching, rubbing his hands over his face. About the same moment the clock in the office downstairs struck nine. Vandover let his feet drop to the floor and sat on the edge of the bed, looking vaguely about him. His face, ordinarily very pale, was oily from sleep and red upon one side from long contact with the pillow, the marks of the creases still showing upon his cheek. His long straight hair fell about his eyes and ears like a tangled mane. A thin straggling beard and moustache, of a brown much lighter than his hair, covered the lower part of his face. His nose was long and pinched, while brown and puffed pockets hung beneath his eyes.

He wore a white shirt very crumpled and dirty, a low standing collar and a black four-in-hand necktie, very greasy. His trousers were striped and of a slate blue colour—the "blue pants" of the ready-made clothing stores. Still sitting on the bed, Vandover continued his stupid gaze about the room.

The room was small, and at some long-forgotten, almost prehistoric period had been covered with a yellowish paper, stamped with a huge pattern of flowers that looked like the flora of a carboniferous strata, a pattern repeated to infinity wherever the eye turned. Newspapers were pasted upon the ceiling and a great square of very dirty matting covered the floor. There were a few pieces of furniture, very old-fashioned, made of pine, with a black walnut veneer, two chairs, a washstand and the bed. A great pile of old newspapers tied up with bale rope was kicked into one corner. Two gas brackets without globes stretched forth their long arms over the empty space where the bureau should have been. Under the single window was Vandover's trunk, and upon it his colour box and pots of paint. His hat hung upon a hook screwed to the door. The hat had once been black, but it had long since turned to a greenish hue, and sweat stains were showing about the band.

Vandover dressed slowly. He straightened his hair a bit before the cheap mirror that hung over the washstand, putting on his hat immediately after to keep it in place. He washed his hands in the dirty water that had stood in his pasteboard bowl since the previous afternoon, but left his face as it was. He put on his coat, an old cutaway which had been his best years ago, but which was now absurdly small for him, the breast all spotted and streaked with old stains of soup and gravy. Last of all he drew on his shoes. They were new. Vandover had bought them two days before for a dollar and ninety cents. They were lined so as to make socks superfluous.

It had been a bad week with Vandover. The paint-shop had given him no work to do for ten days, and he had been forced to get along in some way upon the interest of his bonds—that is to say, upon five dollars and seventy-five cents a week. Two dollars and seventy-five cents of this went for his room rent, one dollar and ninety for his shoes, and Tuesday afternoon he had bought a package of cigarettes for ten cents. By Saturday morning he had spent seventy-five cents for food.

When the paint-shop gave him enough work it was Vandover's custom to buy a week's commutation ticket at a certain restaurant. He never ate at the hotel; it was too expensive. By the commutation system he could buy two dollars and twenty-five cents' worth of meals for two dollars, paying in tickets at each meal.

But such a thing had been impossible this week. He had

been forced to fall back upon the free-lunch system. In two years Vandover had learned a great deal; even his dulled wits had been sharpened when it had come to a question of food. The brute in him might destroy all his finer qualities, but even the brute had to feed. When work failed him at the beginning of the week Vandover was not unprepared for the contingency; the thing had happened before and he knew how to meet it.

On Monday he beat up and down the Barbary Coast, picking out fifteen or twenty saloons which supported a free-lunch counter in connection with the bar. He took his breakfast Monday morning at the first of these. He paid five cents for a glass of beer and ate his morning's meal at the lunch counter: stew, bread, and cheese. At noon he made his dinner at the second saloon on his route. Here he had another glass of beer, a great plate of soup, potato salad, and pretzels. Thus he managed to feed himself throughout the week.

It was always his great desire to feed well at Sunday's dinner, to spend at least a quarter on that meal. It was something to be looked forward to throughout the entire week. But to get twenty-five cents ahead when he was out of work was bitter hard. That week he had started out with the determination to eat but two meals a day. He would thus save five cents daily and by Sunday morning would be thirty cents to the good. But each day his resolution broke down. At breakfast he would resolve to go without his lunch, at lunch he would make up his mind to go without supper, and at supper he would tell himself that now at least his determination was irrevocable—he would eat no breakfast the next morning. But on each and every occasion his hunger proved too strong, his feet carried him irresistibly to the saloon lunch counters, whether he would or no. At no time in his life had Vandover accustomed himself to self-denial; he could hardly begin now.

At length Saturday morning had come, and while he was dressing he realized that he could not look forward to any unusual dinner the next day at noon. The disappointment had all the force of an unexpected disaster and he began keenly to regret his weakness of the past week. Suddenly Vandover resolved that he would go without food all that day; it would be a saving of fifteen cents, which, added to the five cents that he would spend anyway for his dinner, would almost make a quarter. He knew where he could dine excellently well for twenty cents. However, he could not make up his mind to go without his Sunday morning's breakfast. That, he told himself, he must eat.

Once dressed, Vandover went out. Fortunately, the rain had stopped. He went on down through the reeking, steaming streets to one of the big fruit markets not far from the water front. The Portuguese fruit vender who roomed next to him at the Reno House was employed at a stall here. Vandover knew him a little, and it was not hard for him to get a thin slice of cocoanut out from the inside rind of one of those that were lying cracked open among his other wares.

All the morning Vandover chewed this slice of cocoanut, at the same time drinking a great deal of water; for hours he deadened the pang of hunger by this means. He passed the time for the most part sitting on the benches in the Plaza reading an old newspaper that he had found under a seat. The sun came out a little; Vandover found the warmth very grateful. He told himself that he could easily hold out until the next morning.

He had forgotten about the time and was surprised when the whistles all over the town began to blow for noon. In an instant Vandover was hungry again. It was all one that he chewed the little pulp of cocoanut rind more vigorously than ever, swallowed great draughts of water at the public fountains; the little gnawing just between his chest and his stomach began to persist. He got up and began to walk. He left the Plaza behind him, crossed Kearney Street and went on down Clay Street till he reached the water front. For a time he found a certain diversion among the shipping and especially in watching a gang of caulkers knocking away at the seams of an immense coal steamer. He sat upon a great iron clamped pile, spitting into the yellow water below. The air was full of the smell of bilge and oakum and fish; the thousands of masts made a gray maze against the sky; occasionally an empty truck trundled over the hollow docks with a sound of distant cannon. A weakness, a little trembling that seemed to come from the pit of his stomach, began upon Vandover. He was very hungry. Evidently the slice of cocoanut was no

longer effective. He swallowed it and lit a cigarette, one of
the half-dozen still left of the pack he had bought the Tuesday
before.

He smoked the cigarette slowly, inhaling as much of the
smoke as he could. This quieted him for an hour, but he had
the folly to smoke again at the end of that time, and at
once—as he might have known—was hungry again. Until
dark he struggled along, drinking water continually, chewing
chips of wood, toothpicks, bits of straw, anything so that the
action of his jaws might cheat the demands of his stomach.
Toward half-past seven in the evening he returned to his
room in the Reno House. If he could get to sleep that would
be best of all. On the stairs of the hotel, while going up to
his room, the strong smell of cooking onions came suddenly
to his nostrils. It was delicious. Vandover breathed in the
warm savour with long sighs, closing his eyes; a great feebleness overcame him. He asked himself how he could get
through the next twelve hours.

An hour later he went to bed, hiccoughing from the water
he had been drinking all day. By this time he had torn the
paper from one of his cigarettes and was chewing the tobacco. This was his last resort, an expedient which he fell back
upon only in great extremity, as it invariably made him sick
to his stomach. He slept a little, but in half an hour was broad
awake again, gagging and retching dreadfully. There was
nothing on his stomach to throw up, and now at length the
hunger in him raged like a wolf. Vandover was in veritable
torment.

He could not keep his thoughts away from the money in
his pocket, a nickel and two dimes. He could eat if he wanted
to, could satisfy this incessant craving. At every moment the
temptation grew stronger. Why should he wait until morning? He had the money; it was only a matter of a few minutes' walk to the nearest saloon. But he set his face against
this desire; he had held out so long that it would be a pity to
give in now; he was not so very hungry after all. No, no; he
would not give in, he was strong enough; as long as he used
his will he need not succumb. It was just a question of assert-
ing his strength of mind, of calling up the better part of him.
Even better than eating would be the satisfaction of knowing

that he had shown himself stronger than his lower animal appetite. No; he would not give in.

Hardly a minute after he had arrived at this resolution Vandover found himself drawing on his coat and shoes making ready to go out—to go out and eat.

The gas in the room was lit, his money, the nickel and the two dimes, was shut in one of his fists. He was dressing himself with one hand, dressing with feverish, precipitate haste. What had happened? He marvelled at himself, but did not check his preparations an instant. He could not stop, whether he would or no; there was something in him stronger than himself, something that urged him on his feet, that drove him out into the street, something that clamoured for food and that would not be gainsaid. It was the animal in him, the brute, that would be fed, the evil, hideous brute grown now so strong that Vandover could not longer resist it—the brute that had long since destroyed all his finer qualities but that still demanded to be fed, still demanded to live. All the little money that Vandover had saved during the day he spent that night among the coffee houses, the restaurants, and the saloons of the Barbary Coast, continuing to eat even after his hunger was satisfied. Toward daylight he returned to his room, and all dressed as he was flung himself face downward among the coarse blankets and greasy counterpane. For nearly eight hours he slept profoundly, with long snores, prone, inert, crammed and gorged with food.

It was the middle of Sunday afternoon when he awoke. He roused himself and going over to the Plaza sat for a long while upon one of the benches. It was a very bright afternoon and Vandover sat motionless for a long time in the sun while his heavy meal digested, very happy, content merely to be warm, to be well fed, to be comfortable.

Chapter Eighteen

THAT WINTER passed, then the summer; September and October came and went, and by the middle of November the rains set in. One very wet afternoon toward the end of the month Charlie Geary sat at his desk in his own private office. He was unoccupied for the moment, leaning back in his swivel chair, his feet on the table, smoking a cigar. Geary had broken from his old-time habit of smoking only so many cigars as he could pay for by saving carfare. He was doing so well now that he could afford to smoke whenever he chose. He was still with the great firm of Beale & Storey, and while not in the partnership as yet, had worked up to the position of an assistant. He had cases of his own now, a great many of them, for the most part damage suits against that certain enormous corporation whom it was said was ruining the city and entire state. Geary posed as one of its bitterest enemies, pushing each suit brought against it with a tireless energy, with a zeal that was almost vindictive. He began to fit into his own niche, in the eyes of the public, and just in proportion as the corporation was hated, Geary was admired. Money came to him very fast. He was hardly thirty at this time, but could already be called a rich man.

His "deal" with Vandover had given him a taste for real estate, and now and then, with the greatest caution, he made a few discreet investments. At present he had just completed a row of small cottages across the street from the boot and shoe factory. The cottages held two rooms and a large kitchen. Geary had calculated that the boot and shoe concern would employ nearly a thousand operatives, and he had built his row with the view of accommodating a few of them who had families and who desired to live near the factory. His agents were Adams & Brunt.

It was toward half-past five, there was nothing more that Geary could do that day, and for a moment he leaned back in his swivel chair, before going home, smiling a little, very well pleased with himself. He was still as clever and shrewd as ever, still devoured with an incarnate ambition, still delighted when he could get the better of any one. He was yet a young man; with the start he had secured for himself, and with the exceptional faculties, the faculties of self-confidence and "push" that he knew himself to possess, there was no telling to what position he might attain. He knew that it was only a question of time—of a short time even—when he would be the practical head of the great firm. Everything he turned his hand to was a success. His row of houses in the Mission might be enlarged to a veritable settlement for every workman in the neighbourhood. His youth, his cleverness, and his ambition, supported by his money on the one hand, and on the other by the vast machinery of the great law firm, could raise him to a great place in the world of men. Gazing through the little blue haze of his cigar smoke, he began to have vague ideas, ideas of advancement, of political successes. Politics fascinated him—such a field of action seemed to be the domain for which he was precisely suited—not the politics of the city or of the state; not the nasty little squabbling of boodlers, lobbyists, and supervisors, but something large, something inspiring, something on a tremendous scale, something to which one could give up one's whole life and energy, something to which one could sacrifice everything—friendships, fortunes, scruples, principles, life itself, no matter what, anything to be a "success," to "arrive," to "get there," to attain the desired object in spite of the whole world, to ride on at it, trampling down or smashing through everything that stood in the way, blind, deaf, fists and teeth shut tight. Not the little squabbling politics of the city or state, but national politics, the sway and government of a whole people, the House, the Senate, the cabinet and the next—why not?—the highest, the best of all, the Executive. Yes, Geary aspired even to the Presidency.

For a moment he allowed himself the indulgence of the delightful dream, then laughed a bit at his own absurdity. But even the entertainment of so vast an idea had made his mind, as it were, big; it was hard to come down to the level again. In spite of himself he went on reasoning in stupendous thoughts, in enormous ideas, figuring with immense abstractions. And then after all, why not? Other men had striven and attained; other men were even now striving, other men would "arrive"; why should not he? As well he as another. Every man for himself—that was his maxim. It might be damned selfish, but it was human nature: the weakest to the wall, the strongest to the front. Why should not he be in the front? Why not in the very front rank? Why not be even before the front rank itself—the leader? Vast, vague ideas passed slowly across the vision of his mind, ideas that could hardly be formulated into thought, ideas of the infinite herd of humanity, driven on as if by some enormous, relentless engine, driven on toward some fearful distant bourne, driven on recklessly at headlong speed. All life was but a struggle to keep from under those myriad spinning wheels that dashed so close behind. Those were happiest who were farthest to the front. To lag behind was peril; to fall was to perish, to be ridden down, to be beaten to the dust, to be inexorably crushed and blotted out beneath that myriad of spinning iron wheels. Geary looked up quickly and saw Vandover standing in the doorway.

For the moment Geary did not recognize the gaunt, shambling figure with the long hair and dirty beard, the greenish hat, and the streaked and spotted coat, but when he did it was with a feeling of anger and exasperation.

"Look here!" he cried, "don't you think you'd better knock before you come in?"

Vandover raised a hand slowly as if in deprecation, and answered slowly and with a feeble, tremulous voice, the voice of an old man: "I did knock, Mister Geary; I didn't mean no offence." He sat down on the edge of the nearest chair, looking vaguely and stupidly about on the floor, moving his head instead of his eyes, repeating under his breath from time to time, "No offence—no, sir—no offence!"

"Shut that door!" commanded Geary. Vandover obeyed. He wore no vest, and the old cutaway coat, fastened by the single remaining button, exposed his shirt to view, abominably filthy, bulging at the waist like a blouse. The "blue pants," held up by a strap, were all foul with mud and grease and paint, and there hung about him a certain odour, that peculiar smell of poverty and of degradation, the smell of stale clothes and of unwashed bodies.

"Well?" said Geary abruptly.

Vandover put the tips of his fingers to his lips and rolled

his eyes about the room, avoiding Geary's glance; then he dropped them to the floor again, looking at the pattern in the carpet.

"Well," repeated Geary, irritated, "you know I haven't got all the time in the world." All at once Vandover began to cry, very softly, snuffling with his nose, his chin twitching, the tears running through his thin, sparse beard.

"Ah, get on to yourself!" shouted Geary, now thoroughly disgusted. "Quit that! Be a man, will you? Stop that! do you hear?" Vandover obeyed, catching his breath and slowly wiping his eyes with the side of his hand.

"I'm no good!" he said at length, wagging his head and blinking through his tears. "I'm—I'm done for and I ain't got no money; yet, of course, you see I don't mean no offence. What I want, you see, is to be a man and not give in and not let the wolf get me, and then I'll go back to Paris. Everything goes round here, very slow, and seems far off; that's why I can't get along, and I'm that hungry that sometimes I twitch all over. I'm down. I ain't got another cent of money and I lost my job at the paint-shop. There's where I drew down twenty dollars a week painting landscapes on safes, you know, and then——"

Geary interrupted him, crying out, "You haven't a cent? Why, what have you done with your bonds?"

"Bonds?" repeated Vandover, dazed and bewildered. "I ain't never had any bonds. What bonds? Oh, yes," he exclaimed, suddenly remembering, "yes, I know, *my* bonds, of course; yes, yes—well, I—those—those, I had to sell those bonds—had some debts, you see, my board and my tailor's bill. They got out some sort of paper after me. Yes, I had forgotten about my bonds. I lost every damned one of them playing cards—gambled 'em all away. Ain't I no good? But I was winner once—just in two nights I won ten thousand dollars. Then I must have lost it again. You see, I get so hungry sometimes that I twitch all over—so, just like that. Lend me a dollar."

For a few moments Geary was silent, watching Vandover curiously, as he sat in a heap on the edge of the chair, fumbling his greenish hat, looking about the floor. Presently he asked:

"When did you lose your job at the paint-shop?"

"Day before yesterday."

"And you are out of work now?"

"Yes," answered Vandover. "I'm broke; I haven't a cent. I'm blest if *I* know how I'm to get along. Lately I've been working for a paint-shop, painting landscapes on safes. I drew down fifty dollars a week there, but I've lost my job."

"Good Lord, Van!" Geary suddenly exclaimed, nodding his head toward him reflectively, "I'm sorry for you!"

The other laughed. "Yes; I suppose I'm a pitiable looking object, but I'm used to it. I don't mind much now as long as I can have a place to sleep and enough to eat. If you can put me in the way of some work, Charlie, I'd be much obliged. You see, that's what I want—work. I don't want to run any bunco game. I'm an honest man—I'm too honest. I gave away all my money to help another poor duck; gave him thousands, he was good to me when I was on my uppers and I meant to repay him. I was grateful. I signed a paper that gave him everything I had. It was in Paris. There's where my bonds went to. He was a struggling artist."

"Look here!" said Geary, willing to be interested, "you might as well be truthful with me. You can't lie to me. Have you gambled away all those bonds, or have you been victimized, or have you still got them? Come, now, spit it out."

"Charlie, I haven't a cent!" answered Vandover, looking him squarely in the face. "Would I be around here and trying to get work from you if I had? No; I gambled it all away. You know I had eighty-nine hundred in U. S. 4 per cents. Well, first I began to pawn things when my money got short—the Old Gentleman's watch that I said I never would part with, then my clothes. I couldn't keep away from the cards. Of course, you can't understand that; gambling was the only thing that could amuse me. Then I began to mortgage my bonds, very little at first. Oh, I went slow! Then I got to selling them. Well, somehow, they all went. For a time I got along by the work at the paint-shop. But they have let me out now; said I was so irregular. I owe for nearly a month at my lodging-place." His eyes sought the floor again, rolling about stupidly. "Nearly a month, and that's what makes me jump and tremble so. You ought to see me sometimes— *b-r-r-r-h!*

—and I get to barking! I'm a wolf mostly, you know, or some kind of an animal, some kind of a brute. But I'd be all right if everything didn't go round very slowly, and seem far off. But I'm a wolf. You look out for me; best take care I don't bite you! Wolf—wolf! Ah! It's up four flights at the end of the hall, very dark, eight thousand dollars in a green cloth sack, and lots of lights a-burning. See how long my finger nails are—regular claws; that's the wolf, the brute! Why can't I talk in my mouth instead of in my throat? That's the devil of it. When you paint on steel and iron your colours don't dry out true; all the yellows turn green. But it would 'a' been all straight if they hadn't fired me! I never talked to anybody—that was *my* business, wasn't it? And when all those eight thousand little lights begin to burn red, why, of course that makes you nervous! So I have to drink a great deal of water and chew butcher's paper. That fools him and he thinks he's eating. Just so as I can lay quiet in the Plaza when the sun is out. There's a hack-stand there, you know, and every time that horse tosses his head so's to get the oats in the bottom of the nose-bag he jingles the chains on the poles and, by God! that's funny; makes me laugh every time; sounds gay, and the chain sparkles mighty pretty! Oh, I don't complain. Give me a dollar and I'll bark for you!"

Geary leaned back in his chair listening to Vandover, struck with wonder, marvelling at that which his old chum had come to be. He was sorry for him, too, yet, nevertheless, he felt a certain indefinite satisfaction, a faint exultation over his misfortunes, glad that their positions were not reversed, pleased that he had been clever enough to keep free from those habits, those modes of life that ended in such fashion. He rapped sharply on the table. Vandover straightened up, raising his eyes:

"You want some work?" he demanded.

"Yes; that's what I'm after," answered Vandover, adding, "I must have it!"

"Well," said Geary, hesitatingly, "I can give you something to do, but it will be pretty dirty."

Vandover smiled a little, saying, "I guess you can't give me any work that would be too dirty for me!" With the words he suddenly began to cry again. "I want to be honest, Mister

Geary," he exclaimed, drawing the backs of his fingers across his lips; "I want to be honest; I'm down and I don't mean no offence. Charlie, you and I were old chums once at Harvard. My God! to think I was a Harvard man once! Oh, I'm a goner now and I ain't got a friend. When I was in the paint-shop they paid me well. I've been in a paint-shop lately paint-ing the little pictures on the safes, little landscapes, you know, and lakes with mountains around them. I pulled down my twenty dollars and findings!"

"Oh, don't be a fool!" cried Geary, ashamed even to see such an exhibition. "If you can't be a man, you can get out. Now, see here, you came up here once and insulted me in my office, and called me a swindler. Ah, you bet you had the swelled head then and insulted me, attacked my honesty and charged me with shoving the queer. Now I never forget those things generally, but I am willing to let that pass this time. I could be nasty now and tell you to rustle for yourself. If you want half a dollar now to get something to eat, why, I'll give it to you. But I don't propose to support you. Ah, no; I guess not! If you want to work I'll give you a chance, but I shall expect you to do good work if I give you my good money for it. You may be drunk now or—*I* don't know what's the matter with you. But you come up here to-morrow at noon, and if you come up here sober or straight or"—Geary began to make awkward gestures in the air with both hands—"come up here to talk *business*, I may have something for you, but I can't stop any longer this evening."

Vandover got upon his feet slowly, turning his greenish hat about by the brim, nodding his head. "All right, all right," he answered. "Thank you very much, Mister Geary. It's very good of you, I'm sure. I'll be around at noon sure."

When Geary was left alone, he walked slowly to his win-dow, and stood there a moment looking aimlessly down into the street, shaking his head repeatedly, astonished at the deg-radation of his old-time chum. While he stood there he saw Vandover come out upon the sidewalk from the door of the great office building. Geary watched him, very interested.

Vandover paused a moment upon the sidewalk, turning up the collar of his old cutaway coat against the cold trade wind that was tearing through the streets; he thrust both his hands

deep into his trousers pockets, gripping his sides with his elbows and drawing his shoulders together, shrinking into a
small compass in order to be warm. The wind blew the tails
of his cutaway about him like flapping wings. He went up
the street, walking fast, keeping to the outside of the sidewalk, his shoulders bent, his head inclined against the wind,
his feet dragging after him as he walked. For a moment Geary
lost sight of him amid a group of men who were hoisting a
piano upon a dray. The street was rather crowded with office
boys, clerks, and typewriters going home to supper, and
Geary did not catch sight of him again immediately; then all
at once he saw him hesitating on a corner of Kearney Street,
waiting for an electric car to pass; he crossed the street, running, his hands still in his pockets, and went on hurriedly,
dodging in and out of the throng, his high shoulders, long
neck, and greenish hat coming into sight at intervals. For a
moment he paused to glance into the show window of a to-
bacconist and pipe-seller's store. A Chinese woman passed
him, pattering along lamely, her green jade ear-rings twinkling in the light of a street lamp, newly lighted. Vandover
looked after her a moment, gazing stupidly, then suddenly
took up his walk again, zigzagging amid the groups on the
asphalt, striding along at a great pace, his head low and
swinging from side to side as he walked. He was already far
down the street; it was dusk; Geary could only catch glimpses
of his head and shoulders at long intervals. He disappeared.

About ten minutes before one the next day as Geary came
back from lunch he was surprised to see Vandover peeping
through the half-open door of his office. He had not thought
that Vandover would come back.

Of the many different stories that Vandover had told about
the disappearance of his bonds, the one that was probably
truest was the one that accounted for the thing by his passion
for gambling. For a long time after his advent at the Reno
House this passion had been dormant; he knew no one with
whom he could play, and every cent of his income now went
for food and lodging. But one day, about six months before
his visit to Geary's office, Vandover saw that the proprietor
of the Reno House had set up a great bagatelle board in a

corner of the reading-room. A group of men, sailors, ranch-men, and fruit venders were already playing. Vandover ap-proached and watched the game, very interested in watching the uncertain course of the marble jog-jogging among the pins. The clear little note of the bell or the dry rattle as the marble settled quickly into one of the lucky pockets thrilled him from head to foot; his hands trembled, all at once his whole left side twitched sharply.

From that day the fate of the rest of Vandover's little money was decided. In two weeks he had lost twenty dollars at bagatelle, obtaining the money by selling a portion of his bonds at a certain broker's on Montgomery Street. As soon as he had begun to gamble again the old habits of extrava-gance had come back upon him. From the moment he knew that he could get all the money he wanted by the mere sign-ing of a paper, he ceased to be economical, scorning the for-mer niggardliness that had led him to starve on one day that he might feast the next; now, he feasted every day. He still kept his room at the Reno House, but instead of taking his meals by any ticket system, he began to affect the restaurants of the Spanish quarter, gorging himself with the hot spiced meals three and four times a day. He quickly abandoned the bagatelle board for the card-table, gambling furiously with two of the ranchmen. Almost invariably Vandover lost, and the more he lost the more eager and reckless he became.

In a little time he had sold every one of his bonds and had gambled away all but twenty dollars of the money received from the last one sold. This sum, this twenty dollars, Van-dover decided to husband carefully. It was all that was left between him and starvation. He made up his mind that he must stop gambling and find something to do. He had long since abandoned his work at the paint-shop, but at this time he returned there and asked for his old occupation. They laughed in his face. Was that the way he thought they did business? Not much; another man had his job, a much better man and one who was regular, who could be depended on. That same evening Vandover broke his twenty dollars and be-came very drunk. A game of poker was started in a back room of one of the saloons on the Barbary Coast. One of the play-ers was a rancher named Toedt, a fellow-boarder at the Reno

House, but the two other players were strangers; and there in that narrow, dirty room, sawdust on the floor, festoons of fly-specked red and blue tissue paper adorning the single swinging lamp, figures cut from bill-posters of the Black Crook pasted on the walls, there in the still hours after midnight, long after the barroom outside had been closed for the night, the last penny of Vandover's estate was gambled away.

The game ended in a quarrel, Vandover, very drunk, and exasperated at his ill luck, accusing his friend Toedt, the rancher, of cheating. Toedt kicked him in the stomach and made him abominably sick. Then they went away and left Vandover alone in the little dirty room, racked with nausea, very drunk, fallen forward upon the table and crying into his folded arms. After a little he went to sleep, but the nausea continued, nevertheless, and in a few moments he gagged and vomited. He never moved. He was too drunk to wake. His hands and his coat-sleeves, the table all about him, were foul beyond words, but he slept on in the midst of it all, inert, stupefied, a great swarm of flies buzzing about his head and face. It was the day after this that he had come to see Geary.

"Ah," said Geary, as he came up, "it's you, is it? Well, I didn't expect to see you again. Sit down outside there in the hall and wait a few minutes. I'm not ready to go yet—or, wait; here, I tell you what to do." Geary wrote off a list of articles on a slip of paper and pushed it across the table toward Vandover, together with a little money. "You get those at the nearest grocery and by the time you are back I'll be ready to go."

That day Geary took Vandover out to the Mission. They went out in the cable-car, Geary sitting inside reading the morning's paper, Vandover standing on the front platform, carrying the things that Geary had told him to buy: a bar of soap, a scrubbing brush, some wiping cloths, a broom, and a pail.

Almost at the end of the car-line they got off and crossed over to where Geary's property stood. Vandover looked about him. The ground on which his own block had once stood was now occupied by an immense red brick building with white stone trimmings; in front on either side of the main entrance were white stone medallions upon which were

chiselled the head of a workman wearing the square paper cap
that the workman never wears, and a bent-up forearm, the
biceps enormous, the fist gripping the short hammer that the
workman never uses. An enormous round chimney sprouted
from one corner; through the open windows came the vast
purring of machinery. It was a boot and shoe factory, built
by the great concern who had bought the piece of property
from Geary for fifteen thousand dollars, the same property
Geary had bought from Vandover for eight.

Across the street from the factory was a long row of little
cottages, very neat, each having a tiny garden in front where
nasturtiums grew. There were fifteen of these cottages; three
of them only were vacant.

"That was *my* idea," observed Geary, as they approached
the row, willing to explain even though he thought Vandover
would not comprehend, "and it pays like a nitrate bed. I was
clever enough to see that cottages like these were just what's
wanted by the workmen in the factory that have families. I
made some money when I sold out my block to the boot and
shoe people, and I invested it again in these cottages. They
are cheap and serviceable and they meet the demand." Vandover nodded his head in assent, looking vaguely about him,
now at the cottages, now at the great building across the
street. Geary got the keys to one of the vacant cottages and
the two went inside.

"Now here's what I want you to do," began Geary, pointing about with his stick. "You see, when some of these people
go out they leave the rooms nasty, and that tells against the
house when parties come to look at it. I want you to go all
over it, top and bottom, end to end, and give it a good cleaning, sweep the floor, and wash the paint, you know. And now
these windows, you see how dirty they are; wash those inside
and out, but don't disturb the agents' signs; you understand?"

"Yes, I understand."

"Now come out here into the kitchen. Look at these laundry tubs and that sink. See all that grease! Clean that all out,
and underneath the sink here. See that rubbish! Take that out,
too. Now in here—look at that bathtub and toilet. You see
how nasty they have left them. You want to make 'em look
like new!"

"Yes."

"Now come downstairs. You see I give 'em a little floored basement, here; kind of a storeroom and coalroom. Here's where most of the dirt and rubbish is. Just look at it! See all that pile over there?"

"I see."

"Take it all out and pile it in the back yard. I'll have an ash-man come and remove it. Whew! there is a dead hen under here; sling that out the first thing."

They went back through the house again, and Geary pointed out the tiny garden to Vandover. "Straighten that up a bit, pick up those old newspapers and the tin cans. Make it look neat. Now you understand just what I want? You make a good job of it, and when you are through with this house, you begin on the next vacant one farther down the row. You can get the keys at the same place. You get to work right away. I should think you ought to finish this house this afternoon."

"All right," answered Vandover.

"I'm going to look around a little. I'll drop in again in about an hour and see how you're getting on."

With that Geary went away. It was Saturday afternoon, and as the law office closed at noon that day, Geary very often spent the time until evening looking about his property. He left Vandover and went slowly down the street, noting each particular house with immense satisfaction, even entering some of them, talking with the womenfolk, all the men being at the factory.

Vandover took off his coat, his old and greasy cutaway, and began work. He drew a pail of water from the garden faucet in a neighbour's yard, and commenced washing the windows. First he washed the panes from the inside, very careful not to disturb Adams & Brunt's signs, and then cleaned the outside, sitting upon the window ledge, his body half in and half out of the house.

Geary enjoyed himself immensely. The news of the land-lord's visit had spread from cottage to cottage, awakening a mild excitement throughout the length of the row. The women showed themselves on the steps or on the sidewalks, very slatternly, without corsets, their hair coming down,

dressed in faded calico wrappers just as they had come from
the laundry tubs or the cook-stove. They bethought them of
their various grievances, a leak here, a broken door-bell there,
a certain bad smell that was supposed to have some connection with a rash upon the children's faces. They waited for
Geary's appearance by ones and twos, timid, very respectful, but querulous for all that, filling the air with their lamentations.

Vandover had finished with the windows. Now he was
cleaning out the sink and the laundry tubs. They smelt very
badly and were all foul with a greasy mixture of old lard,
soap, soot, and dust; a little mould was even beginning to
form about the faucets of the tubs. The escape pipe of the
sink was clogged, and he had to run his finger into it again
and again to get it free. The kitchen was very dirty; old bottles of sweet oil, mouldy vinegar and flat beer cluttered the
dusty shelves of the pantry.

Meanwhile Geary continued his rounds. He went about
among the groups of his tenants, very pleased and contented,
smiling affably upon them. He enlarged himself, giving himself the airs of an English lord in the midst of his tenantry,
listening to their complaints with a good-humoured smile of
toleration. A few men were about, some of whom were out
of work for the moment; others who were sick. To these
Geary was particularly condescending. He sat in their parlours, little, crowded rooms, smelling of stale upholstery and
of the last meal, where knitted worsted tidies, very gaudy,
covered the backs of the larger chairs and where one inevitably discovered the whatnot standing in one corner, its shelves
filled with shell-boxes, broken thermometers and little alabas-
ter jars, shaped like funeral urns, where one kept the matches.
The wife brought the children in, very dirty, looking solemnly
at Geary, their eyes enlarged in the direct unwinking gaze of
cows.

By this time Vandover had finished with the sinks and tubs
and was down upon his hands and knees scrubbing the stains
of grease upon the floor of the kitchen. It was very hard
work, as his water was cold. He was still working about
this spot when Geary returned. By this time Vandover was
so tired that he trembled all over, his spine seemed to be

breaking in two, and every now and then he paused and passed his hand over the small of his back, closing his eyes and drawing a long breath.

"Well, how are you getting on?" asked Geary, as he came into the kitchen, drawing on his gloves, about ready to go home.

"Oh, I'm getting along," replied Vandover, rising up to his knees.

"You want to hurry up," answered Geary. "You must be done with this house by this evening. You see, I want to advertise it in to-morrow's papers."

"All right; I'll have it done."

"Pretty dirty, wasn't it?"

"Yes, pretty dirty."

"You may have to work here a little later than usual this afternoon, but be sure you have everything cleaned up before you leave," Geary said.

"All right," answered Vandover, bending to his work again.

Just as Geary was leaving he had the admirable good fortune to meet on the steps of the cottage a little group who were house-hunting; two young women and a little boy. The mother of the little boy, so she explained to him, was married to one of the burnishers in the factory; the other woman was her sister.

Geary showed them about the little house, very eager to secure them as tenants then and there. He began to sing its praises, its nearness to the factory, its excellent plumbing, its bathroom and its one stationary washstand; its little garden and its location on the sunny side of the street. "I'm a good landlord," he said to them, as he ushered them into the kitchen. "Any one in the row will tell you that. I make it a point to keep my houses in good repair and to keep them clean. You see, I have a man here now cleaning out." Vandover glanced up at the women an instant. The two of them and the little boy looked down at him on all fours upon the floor. Then he went on with his work.

"This is the kitchen, you see," pursued Geary. "Notice how large it is; you see, here are your laundry tubs, your iron sink, your boiler, everything you need. Of course, it's a little grimy now, but by the time the man gets through, it will be as clean as your face. Now come downstairs here and I'll show the basement."

In a moment their voices sounded through the floor of the kitchen, an indistinct, continuous murmur. Then the party returned and passed by Vandover again and stood for a long time in the front room haggling. The cottage rented for fifteen dollars. The young woman was willing to take it at that, but with the understanding that Geary should pay the water rent. Geary refused, unwilling even to listen to such a thing. Every other tenant in the row paid for his own water. The young women went away shaking their heads sadly. Geary let them get half-way down the front steps and then called them back. He offered a compromise, the young women should pay for the water, but half of their first month's rent should be remitted. The burnisher's wife still hesitated, saying, "You know yourself this house is awfully dirty."

"Well, you see I'm having it cleaned!"

"It'll have to be cleaned pretty thoroughly. I can't stand *dirt*."

"It *will* be cleaned thoroughly," persisted Geary. "The man will work at it until it is. You can keep an eye on him and see that the work is done to suit you."

"You see," objected the burnisher's wife, "I would want to move in right away. I don't want to wait all week for the man to get through."

"But he is going to be through with this house to-night," exclaimed Geary delighted. "Come now, I know you want this cottage and I would like to have such nice-looking people have it. I know you would make good tenants. I can find lots of other tenants for this house, only you know how it is, a nasty, slovenly woman about the house and a raft of dirty children. And you don't like dirt, I can see that. Better call it a bargain, and let it go at that."

In the end the burnisher's wife took the house. Geary even induced her to deposit five dollars with him in order to secure it.

Vandover was down in the basement filling a barrel with the odds and ends of rubbish left by the previous tenants: broken bottles, old corsets, bones, rusty bedsprings. The dead hen he had taken out first of all, carrying it by one leg. It was a gruesome horror, partly eaten by rats, swollen, abnormally heavy, one side flattened from lying so long upon the floor. He could hardly stand; each time he bent over it seemed as though his backbone was disjointing. After cleaning out the débris he began to sweep. The dust was fearful, choking, blinding, so thick that he could hardly see what he was about. By and by he dimly made out Geary's figure in the doorway.

"Those people have taken the house," he called out, "and I promised them you would be through with it by this evening. So you want to stay with it now till you're finished. I guess there's not much more to do. Don't forget the little garden in front."

"No; I won't forget!"

Geary went away, and for another hour Vandover kept at his work, stolidly, his mind empty of all thought, knowing only that he was very tired, that his back pained him. He finished with the basement, but as he was pottering about the little garden, picking up the discoloured newspapers with which it was littered, the burnisher's wife returned, together with her sister and the little boy; the little boy eating a slice of bread and butter. They re-entered the house; Vandover heard their voices, now in one room, now in another. They were looking over their future home again; evidently they lived close by.

Suddenly the burnisher's wife came out upon the front steps, looking down into the little garden, calling for Vandover. She was not pretty; she had a nose like a man and her chin was broad.

"Say, there," she called to Vandover, "do you mean to say that you've finished inside here?"

"Yes," answered Vandover, straightening up, nodding his head. "Yes, I've finished."

"Well, just come in here and look at this."

Vandover followed her into the little parlour. Her sister was there, very fat, smelling somehow of tallow candles and cooked cabbage; nearby stood the little boy still eating his bread and butter.

"Look at that baseboard," exclaimed the burnisher's wife. "You never touched that, I'll bet a hat." Vandover did not answer; he brought in the pail of water, and soaping his scrubbing brush, went down again on his hands and knees,

washing the paint on the baseboard where the burnisher's
wife indicated. The two women stood by, looking on and
directing his movements. The little boy watched everything,
never speaking a word, slowly eating his bread and butter.
Streaks of butter and bread clung to his cheeks, stretching
from the corners of his mouth to his ears.

"I don't see how you come to overlook that," said the burnisher's wife to Vandover. "That's the dirtiest baseboard I
ever saw. Oh, my! I just can't naturally stand *dirt*! There, you
didn't get that stain off. That's tobacco juice, I guess. Go
back and wash that over again." Vandover obeyed, holding
the brush in one hand, crawling back along the floor upon
one palm and his two knees, a pool of soapy, dirty water very
cold gathered about him, soaking in through the old "blue
pants" and wetting him to the skin, but he slovened through
it indifferently. "Put a little more elbow grease to it," continued the burnisher's wife. "You have to rub them spots pretty
hard to get 'em out. Now scrub all along here near the floor.
You see that streak there—that's all gormed up with something or other. Bugs get in there mighty quick. There, that'll
do, I guess. Now, is everything else all clean? Mister Geary
said it was to be done to my satisfaction, and that you were
to stay here until everything was all right."

All at once her voice was interrupted by the prolonged roar
of the factory's whistle, blowing as though it would never
stop. It was half-past five. In an instant the faint purring of
the machinery dwindled and ceased, leaving an abrupt silence
in the air. A moment later the army of operatives began to
pour out of the main entrance; men and girls and young
boys, all in a great hurry, the men settling their coat collars
as they ran down the steps. The usually quiet street was
crowded in an instant.

The burnisher's wife stood on the steps of the vacant house
with her sister, watching the throng debouch into the street.
All at once the sister exclaimed, "There he is!" and the other
began to call, "Oscar, Oscar!" waving her hand to one of the
workmen on the other side of the street. It was her husband,
the burnisher, and he came across the street, crowding his
lunch basket into the pocket of his coat. He was a thin little
man with a timid air, his face white and fat and covered with

a sparse unshaven stubble of a pale straw colour. An odour as of a harness shop hung about him. Vandover gathered up his broom and pail and soap preparing to go home.

"Well, Oscar, I've taken the house!" said his wife to the burnisher as he came up the steps. "But I couldn't get him to say that he'd let me have it for fifteen, water *included*. The landlord himself, Mr. Geary, was here to-day and I made the dicker with him. He's had a man here all day cleaning up." She explained the bargain, the burnisher approving of every-thing, nodding his head continually. His wife showed him about the house, her sister and the little boy following in si-lence. "He's a good landlord, I guess," continued the young woman; "anybody in the row will tell you that, and he means to keep his houses in good repair. Now you see, here's the kitchen. You see how big it is. Here's our laundry tubs, our iron sink, our boiler, and everything we want. It's all as clean as a whistle; and get on to this big cubby under the sink where I can stow away things." She opened its door to show her husband, but all at once straightened up, exclaiming, "Well, dear me *suz*—did you *ever* see anything like that?" The cubby under the sink was abominably dirty. Vandover had altogether forgotten it.

The little burnisher himself bent down and peered in.

"Oh, that'll never do!" he cried. "Has that man gone home yet? He mustn't; he's got to clean this out first!" He had a weak, faint voice, small and timid like his figure. He hurried out to the front door and called Vandover back just as he was going down the steps. The two went back into the kitchen and stood in front of the sink. "Look under there!" piped the burnisher. "You can't leave that, that way."

"You know," protested his wife, "that this all was to be done to our satisfaction. Mr. Geary said so. That's the only way I came to take the house."

"It's about six o'clock, though," observed her fat sister, who smelt of cooked cabbage. "Perhaps he'd want to go home to his dinner." But at this both the others cried out in one voice, the burnisher exclaiming: "I can't help *that*, this has got to be done first," while his wife protested that she couldn't naturally stand dirt, adding, "This all was to be done to our satisfaction, and we ain't satisfied yet by a long shot."

Delighted at this excitement, the little boy forgot to eat into his bread and butter, rolling his eyes wildly from one to the other, still silent.

Meanwhile, without replying, Vandover had gone down upon the floor again, poking about amid the filth under the sink. The four others, the burnisher, his wife, his sister-in-law and his little boy, stood about in a half-circle behind him, seeing to it that he did the work properly, giving orders as to how he should proceed.

"Now, be sure you get everything out that's under there," said the burnisher. "Ouf! how it smells! They made a regular dump heap of it."

"What's that over in the corner there?" cried the wife, bending down. "I can't see, it's so dark under there—something gray; can't you see, in under there? You'll have to crawl way in to get at it—go way in!" Vandover obeyed. The sink pipes were so close above him that he was obliged to crouch lower and lower; at length he lay flat upon his stomach. Prone in the filth under the sink, in the sour water, the grease, the refuse, he groped about with his hand searching for the something gray that the burnisher's wife had seen. He found it and drew it out. It was an old hambone covered with a greenish fuzz.

"Oh, did you *ever!*" cried the burnisher, holding up his hands. "Here, don't drop that on my clean floor; put it in your pail. Now get out the rest of the dirt, and hurry up, it's late." Vandover crawled back, half the way under the sink again, this time bringing out a rusty pan half full of some kind of congealed gravy that exhaled a choking, acrid odour; next it was an old stocking, and then an ink bottle, a broken rat-trap, a battered teapot lacking a nozzle, a piece of rubber hose, an old comb choked with a great handful of hair, a torn overshoe, newspapers, and a great quantity of other débris that had accumulated there during the occupancy of the previous tenant.

"Now go over the floor with a rag," ordered the little burnisher, when the last of these articles had been brought out. "Wipe up all that nasty muck! Look there by your knee to your left! Scrub that big spot there with your brush—looks like grease. That's the style—scrub it hard!" His wife joined her directions to his. Then it was over here, and over there, now in that corner, now in this, and now with his brush and soap, and now with his dry rag, and hurry up all the time because it was growing late. But the little boy, carried away by the interest of the occasion, suddenly broke silence for the first time, crying out shrilly, his mouth full of bread and butter, "Hey there! Get up, you old lazee-bones!"

The others shouted with laughter. *There* was a smart little boy for you. Ah, he'd be a man before his mother. It was wonderful how that boy saw everything that went on. He took an *interest*, that was it. You ought to see, he watched everything, and sometimes he'd plump out with things that were astonishing for a boy of his years. Only four and a half, too, and they reminded each other of the first day he put on knickerbockers; stood in front of the house on the sidewalk all day long with his hands in his pockets. The interest was directed from Vandover, they turned their backs, grouping themselves about the little boy. The burnisher's sister-in-law felt called upon to tell about her little girl, a matter of family pride. *She* was going on twelve, and would you suppose that little thing was in next to the last grade in the grammar school? Her teacher had said that she was a real wonder; never had had such a bright pupil. Ah, but one should see how she studied over her books all the time. Next year they were to try to get her into the high school. Of course she was not ready for the high school yet, and it was against the rule to let children in that way, she was too young, but they had a pull, you understand. Oh, yes, for sure they had a pull. *They'd* work her in all right. The burnisher's wife was not listening. She wanted to draw the interest back to her own little boy. She bent down and straightened out his little jacket, saying, "Does he like his bread 'n butter? Well, he could have all he wanted!" But the little boy paid no attention to her. He had made a *bon-mot*, ambition stirred in him, he had tasted the delights of an appreciative audience. Bread and butter had fallen in his esteem. He wished to repeat his former success, and cried out shriller than ever:

"Hey, there! Get up, you old lazee-bones!"

But his father corrected him—his mother ought not to encourage him to be rude. "That's not right, Oscar," he observed, shaking his head. "You must be kind to the poor man."

Vandover was sitting back on his heels to rest his back, waiting till the others should finish.

"Well, all through?" inquired the burnisher in his thin voice. Vandover nodded. But his wife was not satisfied until she had herself carefully peered into the cubby, while her husband held a lighted match for her. "Ah, that's something like," she said finally.

It was nearly seven. Vandover prepared to go home a second time. The little boy stood in front of him, looking down at him as he made his brush and rags and broom into a bundle; the boy slowly eating his bread and butter the while. In one corner of the room an excited whispered conference was going on between the burnisher, his wife, and his fat sister-in-law. From time to time one heard such expressions as "Overtime, you know—not afraid of work—ah! think I'd better, looks as though he needed it." In a moment the two women went out, calling in vain for the little boy to follow, and the burnisher crossed the room toward Vandover. Vandover was on his knees tying up his bundle with a bit of bale rope.

"I'm sorry," began the burnisher awkwardly. "We didn't mean to keep you from your supper—here," he went on, holding out a quarter to Vandover, "here, you take this, that's all right—you worked overtime for us, that's all right. Come along, Oscar; come along, m' son."

Vandover put the quarter in his vest pocket.

"Thank you, sir," he said.

The burnisher hurried away, calling back, "Come along, m' son; don't keep your mama waiting for supper." But the little boy remained very interested in watching Vandover, still on the floor, tying the last knots. As he finished, he glanced up. For an instant the two remained there motionless, looking into each other's eyes, Vandover on the floor, one hand twisted into the bale rope about his bundle, the little boy standing before him eating the last mouthful of his bread and butter.

McTEAGUE

A Story of San Francisco

I

I<small>T WAS SUNDAY</small>, and, according to his custom on that day, McTeague took his dinner at two in the afternoon at the car conductors' coffee-joint on Polk Street. He had a thick gray soup; heavy, underdone meat, very hot, on a cold plate; two kinds of vegetables; and a sort of suet pudding, full of strong butter and sugar. On his way back to his office, one block above, he stopped at Joe Frenna's saloon and bought a pitcher of steam beer. It was his habit to leave the pitcher there on his way to dinner.

Once in his office, or, as he called it on his signboard, "Dental Parlors," he took off his coat and shoes, unbuttoned his vest, and, having crammed his little stove full of coke, lay back in his operating chair at the bay window, reading the paper, drinking his beer, and smoking his huge porcelain pipe while his food digested; crop-full, stupid, and warm. By and by, gorged with steam beer, and overcome by the heat of the room, the cheap tobacco, and the effects of his heavy meal, he dropped off to sleep. Late in the afternoon his canary bird, in its gilt cage just over his head, began to sing. He woke slowly, finished the rest of his beer—very flat and stale by this time—and taking down his concertina from the bookcase, where in week days it kept the company of seven volumes of "Allen's Practical Dentist," played upon it some half-dozen very mournful airs.

McTeague looked forward to these Sunday afternoons as a period of relaxation and enjoyment. He invariably spent them in the same fashion. These were his only pleasures—to eat, to smoke, to sleep, and to play upon his concertina.

The six lugubrious airs that he knew, always carried him back to the time when he was a car-boy at the Big Dipper Mine in Placer County, ten years before. He remembered the years he had spent there trundling the heavy cars of ore in and out of the tunnel under the direction of his father. For thirteen days of each fortnight his father was a steady, hard-working shift-boss of the mine. Every other Sunday he became an irresponsible animal, a beast, a brute, crazy with alcohol.

McTeague remembered his mother, too, who, with the
help of the Chinaman, cooked for forty miners. She was an
overworked drudge, fiery and energetic for all that, filled with
the one idea of having her son rise in life and enter a profession. The chance had come at last when the father died, cor-
roded with alcohol, collapsing in a few hours. Two or three
years later a travelling dentist visited the mine and put up his
tent near the bunk-house. He was more or less of a charlatan,
but he fired Mrs. McTeague's ambition, and young McTeague
went away with him to learn his profession. He had learnt it
after a fashion, mostly by watching the charlatan operate. He
had read many of the necessary books, but he was too hopelessly stupid to get much benefit from them.

Then one day at San Francisco had come the news of his
mother's death; she had left him some money—not much,
but enough to set him up in business; so he had cut loose
from the charlatan and had opened his "Dental Parlors" on
Polk Street, an "accommodation street" of small shops in the
residence quarter of the town. Here he had slowly collected a
clientele of butcher boys, shop girls, drug clerks, and car conductors. He made but few acquaintances. Polk Street called
him the "Doctor" and spoke of his enormous strength. For
McTeague was a young giant, carrying his huge shock of
blond hair six feet three inches from the ground; moving his
immense limbs, heavy with ropes of muscle, slowly, ponderously. His hands were enormous, red, and covered with a fell
of stiff yellow hair; they were hard as wooden mallets, strong
as vises, the hands of the old-time car-boy. Often he dispensed with forceps and extracted a refractory tooth with his
thumb and finger. His head was square-cut, angular; the jaw
salient, like that of the carnivora.

McTeague's mind was as his body, heavy, slow to act, sluggish. Yet there was nothing vicious about the man. Altogether
he suggested the draught horse, immensely strong, stupid,
docile, obedient.

When he opened his "Dental Parlors," he felt that his life
was a success, that he could hope for nothing better. In spite
of the name, there was but one room. It was a corner room
on the second floor over the branch post-office, and faced the
street. McTeague made it do for a bedroom as well, sleeping

on the big bed-lounge against the wall opposite the window. There was a washstand behind the screen in the corner where he manufactured his moulds. In the round bay window were his operating chair, his dental engine, and the movable rack on which he laid out his instruments. Three chairs, a bargain at the second-hand store, ranged themselves against the wall with military precision underneath a steel engraving of the court of Lorenzo de' Medici, which he had bought because there were a great many figures in it for the money. Over the bed-lounge hung a rifle manufacturer's advertisement calendar which he never used. The other ornaments were a small marble-topped centre table covered with back numbers of "The American System of Dentistry," a stone pug dog sitting before the little stove, and a thermometer. A stand of shelves occupied one corner, filled with the seven volumes of "Allen's Practical Dentist." On the top shelf McTeague kept his concertina and a bag of bird seed for the canary. The whole place exhaled a mingled odor of bedding, creosote, and ether.

But for one thing, McTeague would have been perfectly contented. Just outside his window was his signboard—a modest affair—that read: "Doctor McTeague. Dental Parlors. Gas Given"; but that was all. It was his ambition, his dream, to have projecting from that corner window a huge gilded tooth, a molar with enormous prongs, something gorgeous and attractive. He would have it some day, on that he was resolved; but as yet such a thing was far beyond his means.

When he had finished the last of his beer, McTeague slowly wiped his lips and huge yellow mustache with the side of his hand. Bull-like, he heaved himself laboriously up, and, going to the window, stood looking down into the street.

The street never failed to interest him. It was one of those cross streets peculiar to Western cities, situated in the heart of the residence quarter, but occupied by small tradespeople who lived in the rooms above their shops. There were corner drug stores with huge jars of red, yellow, and green liquids in their windows, very brave and gay; stationers' stores, where illustrated weeklies were tacked upon bulletin boards; barber shops with cigar stands in their vestibules; sad-looking plumbers' offices; cheap restaurants, in whose windows one saw piles of unopened oysters weighted down by cubes of ice, and china pigs and cows knee deep in layers of white beans. At one end of the street McTeague could see the huge power-house of the cable line. Immediately opposite him was a great market; while farther on, over the chimney stacks of the intervening houses, the glass roof of some huge public baths glittered like crystal in the afternoon sun. Underneath him the branch post-office was opening its doors, as was its custom between two and three o'clock on Sunday afternoons. An acrid odor of ink rose upward to him. Occasionally a cable car passed, trundling heavily, with a strident whirring of jostled glass windows.

On week days the street was very lively. It woke to its work about seven o'clock, at the time when the newsboys made their appearance together with the day laborers. The laborers went trudging past in a straggling file—plumbers' apprentices, their pockets stuffed with sections of lead pipe, tweezers, and pliers; carpenters, carrying nothing but their little pasteboard lunch baskets painted to imitate leather; gangs of street workers, their overalls soiled with yellow clay, their picks and long-handled shovels over their shoulders; plasterers, spotted with lime from head to foot. This little army of workers, tramping steadily in one direction, met and mingled with other toilers of a different description—conductors and "swing men" of the cable company going on duty; heavy-eyed night clerks from the drug stores on their way home to sleep; roundsmen returning to the precinct police station to make their night report, and Chinese market gardeners teetering past under their heavy baskets. The cable cars began to fill up; all along the street could be seen the shop keepers taking down their shutters.

Between seven and eight the street breakfasted. Now and then a waiter from one of the cheap restaurants crossed from one sidewalk to the other, balancing on one palm a tray covered with a napkin. Everywhere was the smell of coffee and of frying steaks. A little later, following in the path of the day laborers, came the clerks and shop girls, dressed with a certain cheap smartness, always in a hurry, glancing apprehensively at the power-house clock. Their employers followed an hour or so later—on the cable cars for the most part—whiskered gentlemen with huge stomachs, reading the morning papers with great gravity; bank cashiers and insurance clerks with flowers in their buttonholes.

At the same time the school children invaded the street, filling the air with a clamor of shrill voices, stopping at the stationers' shops, or idling a moment in the doorways of the candy stores. For over half an hour they held possession of the sidewalks, then suddenly disappeared, leaving behind one or two stragglers who hurried along with great strides of their little thin legs, very anxious and preoccupied.

Towards eleven o'clock the ladies from the great avenue a block above Polk Street made their appearance, promenading the sidewalks leisurely, deliberately. They were at their morning's marketing. They were handsome women, beautifully dressed. They knew by name their butchers and grocers and vegetable men. From his window McTeague saw them in front of the stalls, gloved and veiled and daintily shod, the subservient provision-men at their elbows, scribbling hastily in the order books. They all seemed to know one another, these grand ladies from the fashionable avenue. Meetings took place here and there; a conversation was begun; others arrived; groups were formed; little impromptu receptions were held before the chopping blocks of butchers' stalls, or on the sidewalk, around boxes of berries and fruit.

From noon to evening the population of the street was of a mixed character. The street was busiest at that time; a vast and prolonged murmur arose—the mingled shuffling of feet, the rattle of wheels, the heavy trundling of cable cars. At four o'clock the school children once more swarmed the sidewalks, again disappearing with surprising suddenness. At six the great homeward march commenced; the cars were crowded, the laborers thronged the sidewalks, the newsboys chanted the evening papers. Then all at once the street fell quiet; hardly a soul was in sight; the sidewalks were deserted. It was supper hour. Evening began; and one by one a multitude of lights, from the demoniac glare of the druggists' windows to the dazzling blue whiteness of the electric globes, grew thick from street corner to street corner. Once more the street was crowded. Now there was no thought but for amusement. The cable cars were loaded with theatre-goers—men in high hats and young girls in furred opera cloaks. On the sidewalks were groups and couples—the plumbers' apprentices, the girls of the ribbon counters, the little families that lived on the second stories over their shops, the dressmakers, the small doctors, the harness makers—all the various inhabitants of the street were abroad, strolling idly from shop window to shop window, taking the air after the day's work. Groups of girls collected on the corners, talking and laughing very loud, making remarks upon the young men that passed them. The *tamale* men appeared. A band of Salvationists began to sing before a saloon.

Then, little by little, Polk Street dropped back to solitude. Eleven o'clock struck from the power-house clock. Lights were extinguished. At one o'clock the cable stopped, leaving an abrupt silence in the air. All at once it seemed very still. The only noises were the occasional footfalls of a policeman and the persistent calling of ducks and geese in the closed market. The street was asleep.

Day after day, McTeague saw the same panorama unroll itself. The bay window of his "Dental Parlors" was for him a point of vantage from which he watched the world go past.

On Sundays, however, all was changed. As he stood in the bay window, after finishing his beer, wiping his lips, and looking out into the street, McTeague was conscious of the difference. Nearly all the stores were closed. No wagons passed. A few people hurried up and down the sidewalks, dressed in cheap Sunday finery. A cable car went by; on the outside seats were a party of returning picnickers. The mother, the father, a young man, and a young girl, and three children. The two older people held empty lunch baskets in their laps, while the bands of the children's hats were stuck full of oak leaves. The girl carried a huge bunch of wilting poppies and wild flowers.

As the car approached McTeague's window the young man got up and swung himself off the platform, waving good-by to the party. Suddenly McTeague recognized him.

"There's Marcus Schouler," he muttered behind his mustache.

Marcus Schouler was the dentist's one intimate friend. The acquaintance had begun at the car conductors' coffee-joint, where the two occupied the same table and met at every meal.

Then they made the discovery that they both lived in the same flat, Marcus occupying a room on the floor above McTeague. On different occasions McTeague had treated Marcus for an ulcerated tooth and had refused to accept payment. Soon it came to be an understood thing between them. They were "pals."

McTeague, listening, heard Marcus go up-stairs to his room above. In a few minutes his door opened again. McTeague knew that he had come out into the hall and was leaning over the banisters.

"Oh, Mac!" he called. McTeague came to his door.

"Hullo! 'sthat you, Mark?"

"Sure," answered Marcus. "Come on up."

"You come on down."

"No, come on up."

"Oh, you come on down."

"Oh, you lazy duck!" retorted Marcus, coming down the stairs.

"Been out to the Cliff House on a picnic," he explained as he sat down on the bed-lounge, " with my uncle and his people—the Sieppes, you know. By damn! it was hot," he suddenly vociferated. "Just look at that! Just look at that!" he cried, dragging at his limp collar. "That's the third one since morning; it is—it is, for a fact—and you got your stove going." He began to tell about the picnic, talking very loud and fast, gesturing furiously, very excited over trivial details. Marcus could not talk without getting excited.

"You ought t'have seen, y'ought t'have seen. I tell you, it was outa sight. It was; it was, for a fact."

"Yes, yes," answered McTeague, bewildered, trying to follow. "Yes, that's so."

In recounting a certain dispute with an awkward bicyclist, in which it appeared he had become involved, Marcus quivered with rage. " 'Say that again,' says I to um. 'Just say that once more, and' "—here a rolling explosion of oaths— " 'you'll go back to the city in the Morgue wagon. Ain't I got a right to cross a street even, I'd like to know, without being run down—what?' I say it's outrageous. I'd a knifed him in another minute. It was an outrage. I say it was an *outrage*."

"Sure it was," McTeague hastened to reply. "Sure, sure."

"Oh, and we had an accident," shouted the other, suddenly off on another tack. "It was awful. Trina was in the swing there—that's my cousin Trina, you know who I mean—and she fell out. By damn! I thought she'd killed herself; struck her face on a rock and knocked out a front tooth. It's a wonder she didn't kill herself. It *is* a wonder; it is, for a fact. Ain't it, now? Huh? Ain't it? Y'ought t'have seen."

McTeague had a vague idea that Marcus Schouler was stuck on his cousin Trina. They "kept company" a good deal; Marcus took dinner with the Sieppes every Saturday evening at their home at B Street station, across the bay, and Sunday afternoons he and the family usually made little excursions into the suburbs. McTeague began to wonder dimly how it was that on this occasion Marcus had not gone home with his cousin. As sometimes happens, Marcus furnished the explanation upon the instant.

"I promised a duck up here on the avenue I'd call for his dog at four this afternoon."

Marcus was Old Grannis's assistant in a little dog hospital that the latter had opened in a sort of alley just off Polk Street, some four blocks above. Old Grannis lived in one of the back rooms of McTeague's flat. He was an Englishman and an expert dog surgeon, but Marcus Schouler was a bungler in the profession. His father had been a veterinary surgeon who had kept a livery stable near by, on California Street, and Marcus's knowledge of the diseases of domestic animals had been picked up in a haphazard way, much after the manner of McTeague's education. Somehow he managed to impress Old Grannis, a gentle, simple-minded old man, with a sense of his fitness, bewildering him with a torrent of empty phrases that he delivered with fierce gestures and with a manner of the greatest conviction.

"You'd better come along with me, Mac," observed Marcus. "We'll get the duck's dog, and then we'll take a little walk, huh? You got nothun to do. Come along."

McTeague went out with him, and the two friends proceeded up to the avenue to the house where the dog was to be found. It was a huge mansion-like place, set in an enormous garden that occupied a whole third of the block; and while Marcus tramped up the front steps and rang the door-bell boldly, to show his independence, McTeague remained below on the sidewalk, gazing stupidly at the curtained windows, the marble steps, and the bronze griffins, troubled and a little confused by all this massive luxury.

After they had taken the dog to the hospital and had left him to whimper behind the wire netting, they returned to Polk Street and had a glass of beer in the back room of Joe Frenna's corner grocery.

Ever since they had left the huge mansion on the avenue, Marcus had been attacking the capitalists, a class which he pretended to execrate. It was a pose which he often assumed, certain of impressing the dentist. Marcus had picked up a few half-truths of political economy—it was impossible to say where—and as soon as the two had settled themselves to their beer in Frenna's back room he took up the theme of the labor question. He discussed it at the top of his voice, vociferating, shaking his fists, exciting himself with his own noise. He was continually making use of the stock phrases of the professional politician—phrases he had caught at some of the ward "rallies" and "ratification meetings." These rolled off his tongue with incredible emphasis, appearing at every turn of his conversation—"Outraged constituencies," "cause of labor," " wage earners," "opinions biased by personal interests," "eyes blinded by party prejudice." McTeague listened to him, awe-struck.

"There's where the evil lies," Marcus would cry. "The masses must learn self-control; it stands to reason. Look at the figures, look at the figures. Decrease the number of wage earners and you increase wages, don't you? don't you?"

Absolutely stupid, and understanding never a word, McTeague would answer:

"Yes, yes, that's it—self-control—that's the word."

"It's the capitalists that's ruining the cause of labor," shouted Marcus, banging the table with his fist till the beer glasses danced; " white-livered drones, traitors, with their livers white as snow, eatun the bread of widows and orphuns; there's where the evil lies."

Stupefied with his clamor, McTeague answered, wagging his head:

"Yes, that's it; I think it's their livers."

Suddenly Marcus fell calm again, forgetting his pose all in an instant.

"Say, Mac, I told my cousin Trina to come round and see you about that tooth of her's. She'll be in to-morrow, I guess."

II

AFTER HIS BREAKFAST the following Monday morning, McTeague looked over the appointments he had written down in the book-slate that hung against the screen. His writing was immense, very clumsy, and very round, with huge, full-bellied l's and h's. He saw that he had made an appointment at one o'clock for Miss Baker, the retired dressmaker, a little old maid who had a tiny room a few doors down the hall. It adjoined that of Old Grannis.

Quite an affair had arisen from this circumstance. Miss Baker and Old Grannis were both over sixty, and yet it was current talk amongst the lodgers of the flat that the two were in love with each other. Singularly enough, they were not even acquaintances; never a word had passed between them. At intervals they met on the stairway; he on his way to his little dog hospital, she returning from a bit of marketing in the street. At such times they passed each other with averted eyes, pretending a certain preoccupation, suddenly seized with a great embarrassment, the timidity of a second childhood. He went on about his business, disturbed and thoughtful. She hurried up to her tiny room, her curious little false curls shaking with her agitation, the faintest suggestion of a flush coming and going in her withered cheeks. The emotion of one of these chance meetings remained with them during all the rest of the day.

Was it the first romance in the lives of each? Did Old Grannis ever remember a certain face amongst those that he had known when he was young Grannis—the face of some pale-haired girl, such as one sees in the old cathedral towns of England? Did Miss Baker still treasure up in a seldom opened drawer or box some faded daguerreotype, some strange old-fashioned likeness, with its curling hair and high stock? It was impossible to say.

Maria Macapa, the Mexican woman who took care of the lodgers' rooms, had been the first to call the flat's attention to the affair, spreading the news of it from room to room, from floor to floor. Of late she had made a great discovery; all the women folk of the flat were yet vibrant with it. Old

Grannis came home from his work at four o'clock, and between that time and six Miss Baker would sit in her room, her hands idle in her lap, doing nothing, listening, waiting. Old Grannis did the same, drawing his armchair near to the wall, knowing that Miss Baker was upon the other side, conscious, perhaps, that she was thinking of him; and there the two would sit through the hours of the afternoon, listening and waiting, they did not know exactly for what, but near to each other, separated only by the thin partition of their rooms. They had come to know each other's habits. Old Grannis knew that at quarter of five precisely Miss Baker made a cup of tea over the oil stove on the stand between the bureau and the window. Miss Baker felt instinctively the exact moment when Old Grannis took down his little binding apparatus from the second shelf of his clothes closet and began his favorite occupation of binding pamphlets—pamphlets that he never read, for all that.

In his "Parlors" McTeague began his week's work. He glanced in the glass saucer in which he kept his sponge-gold, and noticing that he had used up all his pellets, set about making some more. In examining Miss Baker's teeth at the preliminary sitting he had found a cavity in one of the incisors. Miss Baker had decided to have it filled with gold. McTeague remembered now that it was what is called a "proximate case," where there is not sufficient room to fill with large pieces of gold. He told himself that he should have to use "mats" in the filling. He made some dozen of these "mats" from his tape of non-cohesive gold, cutting it transversely into small pieces that could be inserted edgewise between the teeth and consolidated by packing. After he had made his "mats" he continued with the other kind of gold fillings, such as he would have occasion to use during the week; "blocks" to be used in large proximal cavities, made by folding the tape on itself a number of times and then shaping it with the soldering pliers; "cylinders" for commencing fillings, which he formed by rolling the tape around a needle called a "broach," cutting it afterwards into different lengths. He worked slowly, mechanically, turning the foil between his fingers with the manual dexterity that one sometimes sees in stupid persons. His head was quite empty of all thought, and he did not whistle over his work as another man might have done. The canary made up for his silence, trilling and chittering continually, splashing about in its morning bath, keeping up an incessant noise and movement that would have been maddening to any one but McTeague, who seemed to have no nerves at all.

After he had finished his fillings, he made a hook broach from a bit of piano wire to replace an old one that he had lost. It was time for his dinner then, and when he returned from the car conductors' coffee-joint, he found Miss Baker waiting for him.

The ancient little dressmaker was at all times willing to talk of Old Grannis to anybody that would listen, quite unconscious of the gossip of the flat. McTeague found her all a-flutter with excitement. Something extraordinary had happened. She had found out that the wall-paper in Old Grannis's room was the same as that in hers.

"It has led me to thinking, Doctor McTeague," she exclaimed, shaking her little false curls at him. "You know my room is so small, anyhow, and the wall-paper being the same—the pattern from my room continues right into his—I declare, I believe at one time that was all one room. Think of it, do you suppose it was? It almost amounts to our occupying the same room. I don't know—why, really—do you think I should speak to the landlady about it? He bound pamphlets last night until half-past nine. They say that he's the younger son of a baronet; that there are reasons for his not coming to the title; his stepfather wronged him cruelly."

No one had ever said such a thing. It was preposterous to imagine any mystery connected with Old Grannis. Miss Baker had chosen to invent the little fiction, had created the title and the unjust stepfather from some dim memories of the novels of her girlhood.

She took her place in the operating chair. McTeague began the filling. There was a long silence. It was impossible for McTeague to work and talk at the same time.

He was just burnishing the last "mat" in Miss Baker's tooth, when the door of the "Parlors" opened, jangling the bell which he had hung over it, and which was absolutely unnecessary. McTeague turned, one foot on the pedal of his dental engine, the corundum disk whirling between his fingers.

It was Marcus Schouler who came in, ushering a young girl of about twenty.

"Hello, Mac," exclaimed Marcus; "busy? Brought my cousin round about that broken tooth."

McTeague nodded his head gravely.

"In a minute," he answered.

Marcus and his cousin Trina sat down in the rigid chairs underneath the steel engraving of the Court of Lorenzo de' Medici. They began talking in low tones. The girl looked about the room, noticing the stone pug dog, the rifle manufacturer's calendar, the canary in its little gilt prison, and the tumbled blankets on the unmade bed-lounge against the wall. Marcus began telling her about McTeague. "We're pals," he explained, just above a whisper. "Ah, Mac's all right, you bet. Say, Trina, he's the strongest duck you ever saw. What do you suppose? He can pull out your teeth with his fingers; yes, he can. What do you think of that? With his fingers, mind you; he can, for a fact. Get on to the size of him, anyhow. Ah, Mac's all right!"

Maria Macapa had come into the room while he had been speaking. She was making up McTeague's bed. Suddenly Marcus exclaimed under his breath: "Now we'll have some fun. It's the girl that takes care of the rooms. She's a greaser, and she's queer in the head. She ain't regularly crazy, but *I* don't know, she's queer. Y'ought to hear her go on about a gold dinner service she says her folks used to own. Ask her what her name is and see what she'll say." Trina shrank back, a little frightened.

"No, you ask," she whispered.

"Ah, go on; what you 'fraid of?" urged Marcus. Trina shook her head energetically, shutting her lips together.

"Well, listen here," answered Marcus, nudging her; then raising his voice, he said:

"How do, Maria?" Maria nodded to him over her shoulder as she bent over the lounge.

"Workun hard nowadays, Maria?"

"Pretty hard."

"Didunt always have to work for your living, though, did

you, when you ate offa gold dishes?" Maria didn't answer, except by putting her chin in the air and shutting her eyes, as though to say she knew a long story about that if she had a mind to talk. All Marcus's efforts to draw her out on the subject were unavailing. She only responded by movements of her head.

"Can't always start her going," Marcus told his cousin.

"What does she do, though, when you ask her about her name?"

"Oh, sure," said Marcus, who had forgotten. "Say, Maria, what's your name?"

"Huh?" asked Maria, straightening up, her hands on her hips.

"Tell us your name," repeated Marcus.

"Name is Maria—Miranda—Macapa." Then, after a pause, she added, as though she had but that moment thought of it, "Had a flying squirrel an' let him go."

Invariably Maria Macapa made this answer. It was not always she would talk about the famous service of gold plate, but a question as to her name never failed to elicit the same strange answer, delivered in a rapid undertone: "Name is Maria—Miranda—Macapa." Then, as if struck with an after thought, "Had a flying squirrel an' let him go."

Why Maria should associate the release of the mythical squirrel with her name could not be said. About Maria the flat knew absolutely nothing further than that she was Spanish-American. Miss Baker was the oldest lodger in the flat, and Maria was a fixture there as maid of all work when she had come. There was a legend to the effect that Maria's people had been at one time immensely wealthy in Central America.

Maria turned again to her work. Trina and Marcus watched her curiously. There was a silence. The corundum burr in McTeague's engine hummed in a prolonged monotone. The canary bird chittered occasionally. The room was warm, and the breathing of the five people in the narrow space made the air close and thick. At long intervals an acrid odor of ink floated up from the branch post-office immediately below.

Maria Macapa finished her work and started to leave. As she passed near Marcus and his cousin she stopped, and drew a bunch of blue tickets furtively from her pocket. "Buy a ticket in the lottery?" she inquired, looking at the girl. "Just a dollar."

"Go along with you, Maria," said Marcus, who had but thirty cents in his pocket. "Go along; it's against the law."

"Buy a ticket," urged Maria, thrusting the bundle toward Trina. "Try your luck. The butcher on the next block won twenty dollars the last drawing."

Very uneasy, Trina bought a ticket for the sake of being rid of her. Maria disappeared.

"Ain't she a queer bird?" muttered Marcus. He was much embarrassed and disturbed because he had not bought the ticket for Trina.

But there was a sudden movement. McTeague had just finished with Miss Baker.

"You should notice," the dressmaker said to the dentist, in a low voice, "he always leaves the door a little ajar in the afternoon." When she had gone out, Marcus Schouler brought Trina forward.

"Say, Mac, this is my cousin, Trina Sieppe." The two shook hands dumbly, McTeague slowly nodding his huge head with its great shock of yellow hair. Trina was very small and prettily made. Her face was round and rather pale; her eyes long and narrow and blue, like the half-open eyes of a little baby; her lips and the lobes of her tiny ears were pale, a little suggestive of anæmia; while across the bridge of her nose ran an adorable little line of freckles. But it was to her hair that one's attention was most attracted. Heaps and heaps of blue-black coils and braids, a royal crown of swarthy bands, a veritable sable tiara, heavy, abundant, odorous. All the vitality that should have given color to her face seemed to have been absorbed by this marvellous hair. It was the coiffure of a queen that shadowed the pale temples of this little bourgeoise. So heavy was it that it tipped her head backward, and the position thrust her chin out a little. It was a charming poise, innocent, confiding, almost infantile.

She was dressed all in black, very modest and plain. The effect of her pale face in all this contrasting black was almost monastic.

"Well," exclaimed Marcus suddenly, "I got to go. Must get back to work. Don't hurt her too much, Mac. S'long, Trina."

McTeague and Trina were left alone. He was embarrassed, troubled. These young girls disturbed and perplexed him. He did not like them, obstinately cherishing that intuitive suspicion of all things feminine—the perverse dislike of an overgrown boy. On the other hand, she was perfectly at her ease; doubtless the woman in her was not yet awakened; she was yet, as one might say, without sex. She was almost like a boy, frank, candid, unreserved.

She took her place in the operating chair and told him what was the matter, looking squarely into his face. She had fallen out of a swing the afternoon of the preceding day; one of her teeth had been knocked loose and the other altogether broken out.

McTeague listened to her with apparent stolidity, nodding his head from time to time as she spoke. The keenness of his dislike of her as a woman began to be blunted. He thought she was rather pretty, that he even liked her because she was so small, so prettily made, so good natured and straightforward.

"Let's have a look at your teeth," he said, picking up his mirror. "You better take your hat off." She leaned back in her chair and opened her mouth, showing the rows of little round teeth, as white and even as the kernels on an ear of green corn, except where an ugly gap came at the side.

McTeague put the mirror into her mouth, touching one and another of her teeth with the handle of an excavator. By and by he straightened up, wiping the moisture from the mirror on his coat-sleeve.

"Well, Doctor," said the girl, anxiously, "it's a dreadful disfigurement, isn't it?" adding, "What can you do about it?"

"Well," answered McTeague, slowly, looking vaguely about on the floor of the room, "the roots of the broken tooth are still in the gum; they'll have to come out, and I guess I'll have to pull that other bicuspid. Let me look again. Yes," he went on in a moment, peering into her mouth with the mirror, "I guess that'll have to come out, too." The tooth was loose, discolored, and evidently dead. "It's a curious case," Mc-

Teague went on. "I don't know as I ever had a tooth like that before. It's what's called necrosis. It don't often happen. It'll have to come out sure."

Then a discussion was opened on the subject, Trina sitting up in the chair, holding her hat in her lap; McTeague leaning against the window frame, his hands in his pockets, his eyes wandering about on the floor. Trina did not want the other tooth removed; one hole like that was bad enough; but two—ah, no, it was not to be thought of.

But McTeague reasoned with her, tried in vain to make her understand that there was no vascular connection between the root and the gum. Trina was blindly persistent, with the persistency of a girl who has made up her mind.

McTeague began to like her better and better, and after a while commenced himself to feel that it would be a pity to disfigure such a pretty mouth. He became interested; perhaps he could do something, something in the way of a crown or bridge. "Let's look at that again," he said, picking up his mirror. He began to study the situation very carefully, really desiring to remedy the blemish.

It was the first bicuspid that was missing, and though part of the root of the second (the loose one) would remain after its extraction, he was sure it would not be strong enough to sustain a crown. All at once he grew obstinate, resolving, with all the strength of a crude and primitive man, to conquer the difficulty in spite of everything. He turned over in his mind the technicalities of the case. No, evidently the root was not strong enough to sustain a crown; besides that, it was placed a little irregularly in the arch. But, fortunately, there were cavities in the two teeth on either side of the gap—one in the first molar and one in the palatine surface of the cuspid; might he not drill a socket in the remaining root and sockets in the molar and cuspid, and, partly by bridging, partly by crowning, fill in the gap? He made up his mind to do it.

Why he should pledge himself to this hazardous case McTeague was puzzled to know. With most of his clients he would have contented himself with the extraction of the loose tooth and the roots of the broken one. Why should he risk his reputation in this case? He could not say why.

It was the most difficult operation he had ever performed.

He bungled it considerably, but in the end he succeeded pass-ably well. He extracted the loose tooth with his bayonet for-ceps and prepared the roots of the broken one as if for filling, fitting into them a flattened piece of platinum wire to serve as a dowel. But this was only the beginning; altogether it was a fortnight's work. Trina came nearly every other day, and passed two, and even three, hours in the chair.

By degrees McTeague's first awkwardness and suspicion vanished entirely. The two became good friends. McTeague even arrived at that point where he could work and talk to her at the same time—a thing that had never before been possible for him.

Never until then had McTeague become so well acquainted with a girl of Trina's age. The younger women of Polk Street—the shop girls, the young women of the soda foun-tains, the waitresses in the cheap restaurants—preferred an-other dentist, a young fellow just graduated from the college, a poser, a rider of bicycles, a man about town, who wore astonishing waistcoats and bet money on greyhound cours-ing. Trina was McTeague's first experience. With her the fem-inine element suddenly entered his little world. It was not only her that he saw and felt, it was the woman, the whole sex, an entire new humanity, strange and alluring, that he seemed to have discovered. How had he ignored it so long? It was dazzling, delicious, charming beyond all words. His narrow point of view was at once enlarged and confused, and all at once he saw that there was something else in life besides concertinas and steam beer. Everything had to be made over again. His whole rude idea of life had to be changed. The male virile desire in him tardily awakened, aroused itself, strong and brutal. It was resistless, untrained, a thing not to be held in leash an instant.

Little by little, by gradual, almost imperceptible degrees, the thought of Trina Sieppe occupied his mind from day to day, from hour to hour. He found himself thinking of her constantly; at every instant he saw her round, pale face; her narrow, milk-blue eyes; her little out-thrust chin; her heavy, huge tiara of black hair. At night he lay awake for hours un-der the thick blankets of the bed-lounge, staring upward into the darkness, tormented with the idea of her, exasperated at the delicate, subtle mesh in which he found himself entangled. During the forenoons, while he went about his work, he thought of her. As he made his plaster-of-paris moulds at the washstand in the corner behind the screen he turned over in his mind all that had happened, all that had been said at the previous sitting. Her little tooth that he had extracted he kept wrapped in a bit of newspaper in his vest pocket. Often he took it out and held it in the palm of his immense, horny hand, seized with some strange elephantine sentiment, wagging his head at it, heaving tremendous sighs. What a folly!

At two o'clock on Tuesdays, Thursdays, and Saturdays Trina arrived and took her place in the operating chair. While at his work McTeague was every minute obliged to bend closely over her; his hands touched her face, her cheeks, her adorable little chin; her lips pressed against his fingers. She breathed warmly on his forehead and on his eyelids, while the odor of her hair, a charming feminine perfume, sweet, heavy, enervating, came to his nostrils, so penetrating, so delicious, that his flesh pricked and tingled with it; a veritable sensation of faintness passed over this huge, callous fellow, with his enormous bones and corded muscles. He drew a short breath through his nose; his jaws suddenly gripped together vise-like.

But this was only at times—a strange, vexing spasm, that subsided almost immediately. For the most part, McTeague enjoyed the pleasure of these sittings with Trina with a certain strong calmness, blindly happy that she was there. This poor crude dentist of Polk Street, stupid, ignorant, vulgar, with his sham education and plebeian tastes, whose only relaxations were to eat, to drink steam beer, and to play upon his concertina, was living through his first romance, his first idyl. It was delightful. The long hours he passed alone with Trina in the "Dental Parlors," silent, only for the scraping of the instruments and the purring of bud-burrs in the engine, in the foul atmosphere, overheated by the little stove and heavy with the smell of ether, creosote, and stale bedding, had all the charm of secret appointments and stolen meetings under the moon.

By degrees the operation progressed. One day, just after McTeague had put in the temporary gutta-percha fillings and nothing more could be done at that sitting, Trina asked him to examine the rest of her teeth. They were perfect, with one exception—a spot of white caries on the lateral surface of an incisor. McTeague filled it with gold, enlarging the cavity with hard-bits and hoe-excavators, and burring in afterward with half-cone burrs. The cavity was deep, and Trina began to wince and moan. To hurt Trina was a positive anguish for McTeague, yet an anguish which he was obliged to endure at every hour of the sitting. It was harrowing—he sweated under it—to be forced to torture her, of all women in the world; could anything be worse than that?

"Hurt?" he inquired, anxiously.

She answered by frowning, with a sharp intake of breath, putting her fingers over her closed lips and nodding her head. McTeague sprayed the tooth with glycerite of tannin, but without effect. Rather than hurt her he found himself forced to the use of anæsthesia, which he hated. He had a notion that the nitrous oxide gas was dangerous, so on this occasion, as on all others, used ether.

He put the sponge a half dozen times to Trina's face, more nervous than he had ever been before, watching the symptoms closely. Her breathing became short and irregular; there was a slight twitching of the muscles. When her thumbs turned inward toward the palms, he took the sponge away. She passed off very quickly, and, with a long sigh, sank back into the chair.

McTeague straightened up, putting the sponge upon the rack behind him, his eyes fixed upon Trina's face. For some time he stood watching her as she lay there, unconscious and helpless, and very pretty. He was alone with her, and she was absolutely without defense.

Suddenly the animal in the man stirred and woke; the evil instincts that in him were so close to the surface leaped to life, shouting and clamoring.

It was a crisis—a crisis that had arisen all in an instant; a crisis for which he was totally unprepared. Blindly, and without knowing why, McTeague fought against it, moved by an unreasoned instinct of resistance. Within him, a certain second self, another better McTeague rose with the brute; both were strong, with the huge crude strength of the man himself.

The two were at grapples. There in that cheap and shabby "Dental Parlor" a dreaded struggle began. It was the old battle, old as the world, wide as the world—the sudden panther leap of the animal, lips drawn, fangs aflash, hideous, monstrous, not to be resisted, and the simultaneous arousing of the other man, the better self that cries, "Down, down," without knowing why; that grips the monster; that fights to strangle it, to thrust it down and back.

Dizzied and bewildered with the shock, the like of which he had never known before, McTeague turned from Trina, gazing bewilderedly about the room. The struggle was bitter; his teeth ground themselves together with a little rasping sound; the blood sang in his ears; his face flushed scarlet; his hands twisted themselves together like the knotting of cables. The fury in him was as the fury of a young bull in the heat of high summer. But for all that he shook his huge head from time to time, muttering:

"No, by God! No, by God!"

Dimly he seemed to realize that should he yield now he would never be able to care for Trina again. She would never be the same to him, never so radiant, so sweet, so adorable; her charm for him would vanish in an instant. Across her forehead, her little pale forehead, under the shadow of her royal hair, he would surely see the smudge of a foul ordure, the footprint of the monster. It would be a sacrilege, an abomination. He recoiled from it, banding all his strength to the issue.

"No, by God! No, by God!"

He turned to his work, as if seeking a refuge in it. But as he drew near to her again, the charm of her innocence and helplessness came over him afresh. It was a final protest against his resolution. Suddenly he leaned over and kissed her, grossly, full on the mouth. The thing was done before he knew it. Terrified at his weakness at the very moment he believed himself strong, he threw himself once more into his work with desperate energy. By the time he was fastening the sheet of rubber upon the tooth, he had himself once more in hand. He was disturbed, still trembling, still vibrating with the throes of the crisis, but he was the master; the animal was downed, was cowed for this time, at least.

But for all that, the brute was there. Long dormant, it was now at last alive, awake. From now on he would feel its presence continually; would feel it tugging at its chain, watching its opportunity. Ah, the pity of it! Why could he not always love her purely, cleanly? What was this perverse, vicious thing that lived within him, knitted to his flesh?

Below the fine fabric of all that was good in him ran the foul stream of hereditary evil, like a sewer. The vices and sins of his father and of his father's father, to the third and fourth and five hundredth generation, tainted him. The evil of an entire race flowed in his veins. Why should it be? He did not desire it. Was he to blame?

But McTeague could not understand this thing. It had faced him, as sooner or later it faces every child of man; but its significance was not for him. To reason with it was beyond him. He could only oppose to it an instinctive stubborn resistance, blind, inert.

McTeague went on with his work. As he was rapping in the little blocks and cylinders with the mallet, Trina slowly came back to herself with a long sigh. She still felt a little confused, and lay quiet in the chair. There was a long silence, broken only by the uneven tapping of the hardwood mallet. By and by she said, "I never felt a thing," and then she smiled at him very prettily beneath the rubber dam. McTeague turned to her suddenly, his mallet in one hand, his pliers holding a pellet of sponge-gold in the other. All at once he said, with the unreasoned simplicity and directness of a child: "Listen here, Miss Trina, I like you better than any one else; what's the matter with us getting married?"

Trina sat up in the chair quickly, and then drew back from him, frightened and bewildered.

"Will you? Will you?" said McTeague. "Say, Miss Trina, will you?"

"What is it? What do you mean?" she cried, confusedly, her words muffled beneath the rubber.

"Will you?" repeated McTeague.

"No, no," she exclaimed, refusing without knowing why, suddenly seized with a fear of him, the intuitive feminine fear of the male. McTeague could only repeat the same thing over and over again. Trina, more and more frightened at his huge hands—the hands of the old-time car-boy—his immense square-cut head and his enormous brute strength, cried out: "No, no," behind the rubber dam, shaking her head violently, holding out her hands, and shrinking down before him in the operating chair. McTeague came nearer to her, repeating the same question. "No, no," she cried, terrified. Then, as she exclaimed, "Oh, I am sick," was suddenly taken with a fit of vomiting. It was the not unusual after effect of the ether, aided now by her excitement and nervousness. McTeague was checked. He poured some bromide of potassium into a graduated glass and held it to her lips.

"Here, swallow this," he said.

III

O NCE EVERY TWO MONTHS Maria Macapa set the entire
flat in commotion. She roamed the building from garret
to cellar, searching each corner, ferreting through every old
box and trunk and barrel, groping about on the top shelves
of closets, peering into ragbags, exasperating the lodgers with
her persistence and importunity. She was collecting junk,
bits of iron, stone jugs, glass bottles, old sacks, and cast-off
garments. It was one of her perquisites. She sold the junk to
Zerkow, the rags-bottles-sacks man, who lived in a filthy den
in the alley just back of the flat, and who sometimes paid her
as much as three cents a pound. The stone jugs, however,
were worth a nickel. The money that Zerkow paid her, Maria
spent on shirt waists and dotted blue neckties, trying to dress
like the girls who tended the soda-water fountain in the candy
store on the corner. She was sick with envy of these young
women. They were in the world, they were elegant, they were
debonair, they had their "young men."

On this occasion she presented herself at the door of Old
Grannis's room late in the afternoon. His door stood a little
open. That of Miss Baker was ajar a few inches. The two old
people were "keeping company" after their fashion.

"Got any junk, Mister Grannis?" inquired Maria, standing
in the door, a very dirty, half-filled pillow-case over one
arm.

"No, nothing—nothing that I can think of, Maria," replied
Old Grannis, terribly vexed at the interruption, yet not wishing to be unkind. "Nothing I think of. Yet, however—perhaps—if you wish to look."

He sat in the middle of the room before a small pine table.
His little binding apparatus was before him. In his fingers was
a huge upholsterer's needle threaded with twine, a brad-awl
lay at his elbow, on the floor beside him was a great pile of
pamphlets, the pages uncut. Old Grannis bought the "Nation" and the "Breeder and Sportsman." In the latter he occasionally found articles on dogs which interested him. The
former he seldom read. He could not afford to subscribe regularly to either of the publications, but purchased their back

numbers by the score, almost solely for the pleasure he took in binding them.

"What you alus sewing up them books for, Mister Grannis?" asked Maria, as she began rummaging about in Old Grannis's closet shelves. "There's just hundreds of 'em in here on yer shelves; they ain't no good to you."

"Well, well," answered Old Grannis, timidly, rubbing his chin, "I—I'm sure I can't quite say; a little habit, you know; a diversion, a—a—it occupies one, you know. I don't smoke; it takes the place of a pipe, perhaps."

"Here's this old yellow pitcher," said Maria, coming out of the closet with it in her hand. "The handle's cracked; you don't want it; better give me it."

Old Grannis did want the pitcher; true, he never used it now, but he had kept it a long time, and somehow he held to it as old people hold to trivial, worthless things that they have had for many years.

"Oh, that pitcher—well, Maria, I—I don't know. I'm afraid—you see, that pitcher——"

"Ah, go 'long," interrupted Maria Macapa, "what's the good of it?"

"If you insist, Maria, but I would much rather—" he rubbed his chin, perplexed and annoyed, hating to refuse, and wishing that Maria were gone.

"Why, what's the good of it?" persisted Maria. He could give no sufficient answer. "That's all right," she asserted, carrying the pitcher out.

"Ah—Maria—I say, you—you might leave the door—ah, don't quite shut it—it's a bit close in here at times." Maria grinned, and swung the door wide. Old Grannis was horribly embarrassed; positively, Maria was becoming unbearable.

"Got any junk?" cried Maria at Miss Baker's door. The little old lady was sitting close to the wall in her rocking-chair; her hands resting idly in her lap.

"Now, Maria," she said plaintively, "you are always after junk; you know I never have anything laying 'round like that."

It was true. The retired dressmaker's tiny room was a marvel of neatness, from the little red table, with its three Gorham spoons laid in exact parallels, to the decorous geraniums and mignonettes growing in the starch box at the window, underneath the fish globe with its one venerable gold fish. That day Miss Baker had been doing a bit of washing; two pocket handkerchiefs, still moist, adhered to the window panes, drying in the sun.

"Oh, I guess you got something you don't want," Maria went on, peering into the corners of the room. "Look-a-here what Mister Grannis gi' me," and she held out the yellow pitcher. Instantly Miss Baker was in a quiver of confusion. Every word spoken aloud could be perfectly heard in the next room. What a stupid drab was this Maria! Could anything be more trying than this position?

"Ain't that right, Mister Grannis?" called Maria; "didn't you gi' me this pitcher?" Old Grannis affected not to hear; perspiration stood on his forehead; his timidity overcame him as if he were a ten-year-old schoolboy. He half rose from his chair, his fingers dancing nervously upon his chin.

Maria opened Miss Baker's closet unconcernedly. "What's the matter with these old shoes?" she exclaimed, turning about with a pair of half-worn silk gaiters in her hand. They were by no means old enough to throw away, but Miss Baker was almost beside herself. There was no telling what might happen next. Her only thought was to be rid of Maria.

"Yes, yes, anything. You can have them; but go, go. There's nothing else, not a thing."

Maria went out into the hall, leaving Miss Baker's door wide open, as if maliciously. She had left the dirty pillow-case on the floor in the hall, and she stood outside, between the two open doors, stowing away the old pitcher and the half-worn silk shoes. She made remarks at the top of her voice, calling now to Miss Baker, now to Old Grannis. In a way she brought the two old people face to face. Each time they were forced to answer her questions it was as if they were talking directly to each other.

"These here are first-rate shoes, Miss Baker. Look here, Mister Grannis, get on to the shoes Miss Baker gi' me. You ain't got a pair you don't want, have you? You two people have less junk than any one else in the flat. How do you manage, Mister Grannis? You old bachelors are just like old maids, just as neat as pins. You two are just alike—you and Mister Grannis—ain't you, Miss Baker?"

Nothing could have been more horribly constrained, more awkward. The two old people suffered veritable torture. When Maria had gone, each heaved a sigh of unspeakable relief. Softly they pushed to their doors, leaving open a space of half a dozen inches. Old Grannis went back to his binding. Miss Baker brewed a cup of tea to quiet her nerves. Each tried to regain their composure, but in vain. Old Grannis's fingers trembled so that he pricked them with his needle. Miss Baker dropped her spoon twice. Their nervousness would not wear off. They were perturbed, upset. In a word, the afternoon was spoiled.

Maria went on about the flat from room to room. She had already paid Marcus Schouler a visit early that morning before he had gone out. Marcus had sworn at her, excitedly vociferating; "No, by damn! No, he hadn't a thing for her; he hadn't, for a fact. It was a positive persecution. Every day his privacy was invaded. He would complain to the landlady, he would. He'd move out of the place." In the end he had given Maria seven empty whiskey flasks, an iron grate, and ten cents—the latter because he said she wore her hair like a girl he used to know.

After coming from Miss Baker's room Maria knocked at McTeague's door. The dentist was lying on the bed-lounge in his stocking feet, doing nothing apparently, gazing up at the ceiling, lost in thought.

Since he had spoken to Trina Sieppe, asking her so abruptly to marry him, McTeague had passed a week of torment. For him there was no going back. It was Trina now, and none other. It was all one with him that his best friend, Marcus, might be in love with the same girl. He must have Trina in spite of everything; he would have her even in spite of herself. He did not stop to reflect about the matter; he followed his desire blindly, recklessly, furious and raging at every obstacle. And she had cried "No, no!" back at him; he could not forget that. She, so small and pale and delicate, had held him at bay, who was so huge, so immensely strong.

Besides that, all the charm of their intimacy was gone. After that unhappy sitting, Trina was no longer frank and straightforward. Now she was circumspect, reserved, distant. He could no longer open his mouth; words failed him. At one sitting in particular they had said but good-day and good-by to each other. He felt that he was clumsy and ungainly. He told himself that she despised him.

But the memory of her was with him constantly. Night after night he lay broad awake thinking of Trina, wondering about her, racked with the infinite desire of her. His head burnt and throbbed. The palms of his hands were dry. He dozed and woke, and walked aimlessly about the dark room, bruising himself against the three chairs drawn up "at attention" under the steel engraving, and stumbling over the stone pug dog that sat in front of the little stove.

Besides this, the jealousy of Marcus Schouler harassed him. Maria Macapa, coming into his "Parlor" to ask for junk, found him flung at length upon the bed-lounge, gnawing at his fingers in an excess of silent fury. At lunch that day Marcus had told him of an excursion that was planned for the next Sunday afternoon. Mr. Sieppe, Trina's father, belonged to a rifle club that was to hold a meet at Schuetzen Park across the bay. All the Sieppes were going; there was to be a basket picnic. Marcus, as usual, was invited to be one of the party. McTeague was in agony. It was his first experience, and he suffered all the worse for it because he was totally unprepared. What miserable complication was this in which he found himself involved? It seemed so simple to him since he loved Trina to take her straight to himself, stopping at nothing, asking no questions, to have her, and by main strength to carry her far away somewhere, he did not know exactly where, to some vague country, some undiscovered place where every day was Sunday.

"Got any junk?"

"Huh? What? What is it?" exclaimed McTeague, suddenly rousing up from the lounge. Often Maria did very well in the "Dental Parlors." McTeague was continually breaking things which he was too stupid to have mended; for him anything that was broken was lost. Now it was a cuspidor, now a fire-shovel for the little stove, now a China shaving mug.

"Got any junk?"

"I don't know—I don't remember," muttered McTeague. Maria roamed about the room, McTeague following her in his huge stockinged feet. All at once she pounced upon a sheaf of old hand instruments in a coverless cigar-box, pluggers, hard bits, and excavators. Maria had long coveted such a find in McTeague's "Parlor," knowing it should be somewhere about. The instruments were of the finest tempered steel and really valuable.

"Say, Doctor, I can have these, can't I?" exclaimed Maria. "You got no more use for them." McTeague was not at all sure of this. There were many in the sheaf that might be repaired, reshaped.

"No, no," he said, wagging his head. But Maria Macapa, knowing with whom she had to deal, at once let loose a torrent of words. She made the dentist believe that he had no right to withhold them, that he had promised to save them for her. She affected a great indignation, pursing her lips and putting her chin in the air as though wounded in some finer sense, changing so rapidly from one mood to another, filling the room with such shrill clamor, that McTeague was dazed and benumbed.

"Yes, all right, all right," he said, trying to make himself heard. "It *would* be mean. I don't want 'em." As he turned from her to pick up the box, Maria took advantage of the moment to steal three "mats" of sponge-gold out of the glass saucer. Often she stole McTeague's gold, almost under his very eyes; indeed, it was so easy to do so that there was but little pleasure in the theft. Then Maria took herself off. McTeague returned to the sofa and flung himself upon it face downward.

A little before supper time Maria completed her search. The flat was cleaned of its junk from top to bottom. The dirty pillow-case was full to bursting. She took advantage of the supper hour to carry her bundle around the corner and up into the alley where Zerkow lived.

When Maria entered his shop, Zerkow had just come in from his daily rounds. His decrepit wagon stood in front of his door like a stranded wreck; the miserable horse, with its lamentable swollen joints, fed greedily upon an armful of spoiled hay in a shed at the back.

The interior of the junk shop was dark and damp, and foul with all manner of choking odors. On the walls, on the floor, and hanging from the rafters was a world of debris, dust-blackened, rust-corroded. Everything was there, every trade was represented, every class of society; things of iron and cloth and wood; all the detritus that a great city sloughs off in its daily life. Zerkow's junk shop was the last abiding-place, the almshouse, of such articles as had outlived their usefulness.

Maria found Zerkow himself in the back room, cooking some sort of a meal over an alcohol stove. Zerkow was a Polish Jew—curiously enough his hair was fiery red. He was a dry, shrivelled old man of sixty odd. He had the thin, eager, cat-like lips of the covetous; eyes that had grown keen as those of a lynx from long searching amidst muck and debris; and claw-like, prehensile fingers—the fingers of a man who accumulates, but never disburses. It was impossible to look at Zerkow and not know instantly that greed—inordinate, insatiable greed—was the dominant passion of the man. He was the Man with the Rake, groping hourly in the muck-heap of the city for gold, for gold, for gold. It was his dream, his passion; at every instant he seemed to feel the generous solid weight of the crude fat metal in his palms. The glint of it was constantly in his eyes; the jangle of it sang forever in his ears as the jangling of cymbals.

"Who is it? Who is it?" exclaimed Zerkow, as he heard Maria's footsteps in the outer room. His voice was faint, husky, reduced almost to a whisper by his prolonged habit of street crying.

"Oh, it's you again, is it?" he added, peering through the gloom of the shop. "Let's see; you've been here before, ain't you? You're the Mexican woman from Polk Street. Macapa's your name, hey?"

Maria nodded. "Had a flying squirrel an' let him go," she muttered, absently. Zerkow was puzzled; he looked at her sharply for a moment, then dismissed the matter with a movement of his head.

"Well, what you got for me?" he said. He left his supper to grow cold, absorbed at once in the affair.

Then a long wrangle began. Every bit of junk in Maria's

pillow-case was discussed and weighed and disputed. They clamored into each other's faces over Old Grannis's cracked pitcher, over Miss Baker's silk gaiters, over Marcus Schouler's whiskey flasks, reaching the climax of disagreement when it came to McTeague's instruments.

"Ah, no, no!" shouted Maria. "Fifteen cents for the lot! I might as well make you a Christmas present! Besides, I got some gold fillings off him; look at um."

Zerkow drew a quick breath as the three pellets suddenly flashed in Maria's palm. There it was, the virgin metal, the pure, unalloyed ore, his dream, his consuming desire. His fingers twitched and hooked themselves into his palms, his thin lips drew tight across his teeth.

"Ah, you got some gold," he muttered, reaching for it.

Maria shut her fist over the pellets. "The gold goes with the others," she declared. "You'll gi' me a fair price for the lot, or I'll take um back."

In the end a bargain was struck that satisfied Maria. Zerkow was not one who would let gold go out of his house. He counted out to her the price of all her junk, grudging each piece of money as if it had been the blood of his veins. The affair was concluded.

But Zerkow still had something to say. As Maria folded up the pillow-case and rose to go, the old Jew said:

"Well, see here a minute, we'll—you'll have a drink before you go, won't you? Just to show that it's all right between us." Maria sat down again.

"Yes, I guess I'll have a drink," she answered.

Zerkow took down a whiskey bottle and a red glass tumbler with a broken base from a cupboard on the wall. The two drank together, Zerkow from the bottle, Maria from the broken tumbler. They wiped their lips slowly, drawing breath again. There was a moment's silence.

"Say," said Zerkow at last, "how about those gold dishes you told me about the last time you were here?"

"What gold dishes?" inquired Maria, puzzled.

"Ah, you know," returned the other. "The plate your father owned in Central America a long time ago. Don't you know, it rang like so many bells? Red gold, you know, like oranges?"

"Ah," said Maria, putting her chin in the air as if she knew a long story about that if she had a mind to tell it. "Ah, yes, that gold service."

"Tell us about it again," said Zerkow, his bloodless lower lip moving against the upper, his claw-like fingers feeling about his mouth and chin. "Tell us about it; go on."

He was breathing short, his limbs trembled a little. It was as if some hungry beast of prey had scented a quarry. Maria still refused, putting up her head, insisting that she had to be going.

"Let's have it," insisted the Jew. "Take another drink." Maria took another swallow of the whiskey. "Now, go on," repeated Zerkow; "let's have the story." Maria squared her elbows on the deal table, looking straight in front of her with eyes that saw nothing.

"Well, it was this way," she began. "It was when I was little. My folks must have been rich, oh, rich into the millions—coffee, I guess—and there was a large house, but I can only remember the plate. Oh, that service of plate! It was wonderful. There were more than a hundred pieces, and every one of them gold. You should have seen the sight when the leather trunk was opened. It fair dazzled your eyes. It was a yellow blaze like a fire, like a sunset; such a glory, all piled up together, one piece over the other. Why, if the room was dark you'd think you could see just the same with all that glitter there. There wa'n't a piece that was so much as scratched; every one was like a mirror, smooth and bright, just like a little pool when the sun shines into it. There was dinner dishes and soup tureens and pitchers; and great, big platters as long as that, and wide too; and cream-jugs and bowls with carved handles, all vines and things; and drinking mugs, every one a different shape; and dishes for gravy and sauces; and then a great, big punch-bowl with a ladle, and the bowl was all carved out with figures and bunches of grapes. Why, just only that punch-bowl was worth a fortune, I guess. When all that plate was set out on a table, it was a sight for a king to look at. Such a service as that was! Each piece was heavy, oh, so heavy! and thick, you know; thick, fat gold, nothing but gold—red, shining, pure gold, orange red—and when you struck it with your knuckle, ah, you should have heard! No church bell ever rang sweeter or clearer. It was soft gold, too;

you could bite into it, and leave the dent of your teeth. Oh, that gold plate! I can see it just as plain—solid, solid, heavy, rich, pure gold; nothing but gold, gold, heaps and heaps of it. What a service that was!"

Maria paused, shaking her head, thinking over the vanished splendor. Illiterate enough, unimaginative enough on all other subjects, her distorted wits called up this picture with marvellous distinctness. It was plain she saw the plate clearly. Her description was accurate, was almost eloquent.

Did that wonderful service of gold plate ever exist outside of her diseased imagination? Was Maria actually remembering some reality of a childhood of barbaric luxury? Were her parents at one time possessed of an incalculable fortune derived from some Central American coffee plantation, a fortune long since confiscated by armies of insurrectionists, or squandered in the support of revolutionary governments?

It was not impossible. Of Maria Macapa's past prior to the time of her appearance at the "flat" absolutely nothing could be learned. She suddenly appeared from the unknown, a strange woman of a mixed race, sane on all subjects but that of the famous service of gold plate; but unusual, complex, mysterious, even at her best.

But what misery Zerkow endured as he listened to her tale! For he chose to believe it, forced himself to believe it, lashed and harassed by a pitiless greed that checked at no tale of treasure, however preposterous. The story ravished him with delight. He was near someone who had possessed this wealth. He saw someone who had seen this pile of gold. He seemed near it; it was there, somewhere close by, under his eyes, under his fingers; it was red, gleaming, ponderous. He gazed about him wildly; nothing, nothing but the sordid junk shop and the rust-corroded tins. What exasperation, what positive misery, to be so near to it and yet to know that it was irrevocably, irretrievably lost! A spasm of anguish passed through him. He gnawed at his bloodless lips, at the hopelessness of it, the rage, the fury of it.

"Go on, go on," he whispered; "let's have it all over again. Polished like a mirror, hey, and heavy? Yes, I know, I know. A punch-bowl worth a fortune. Ah! and you saw it, you had it all!"

Maria rose to go. Zerkow accompanied her to the door, urging another drink upon her.

"Come again, come again," he croaked. "Don't wait till you've got junk; come any time you feel like it, and tell me more about the plate."

He followed her a step down the alley.

"How much do you think it was worth?" he inquired, anxiously.

"Oh, a million dollars," answered Maria, vaguely.

When Maria had gone, Zerkow returned to the back room of the shop, and stood in front of the alcohol stove, looking down into his cold dinner, preoccupied, thoughtful.

"A million dollars," he muttered in his rasping, guttural whisper, his finger-tips wandering over his thin, cat-like lips. "A golden service worth a million dollars; a punch-bowl worth a fortune; red gold plates, heaps and piles. God!"

IV

THE DAYS PASSED. McTeague had finished the operation on Trina's teeth. She did not come any more to the "Parlors." Matters had readjusted themselves a little between the two during the last sittings. Trina yet stood upon her reserve, and McTeague still felt himself shambling and ungainly in her presence; but that constraint and embarrassment that had followed upon McTeague's blundering declaration broke up little by little. In spite of themselves they were gradually resuming the same relative positions they had occupied when they had first met.

But McTeague suffered miserably for all that. He never would have Trina, he saw that clearly. She was too good for him; too delicate, too refined, too prettily made for him, who was so coarse, so enormous, so stupid. She was for someone else—Marcus, no doubt—or at least for some finer-grained man. She should have gone to some other dentist; the young fellow on the corner, for instance, the poser, the rider of bicycles, the courser of greyhounds. McTeague began to loathe and to envy this fellow. He spied upon him going in and out of his office, and noted his salmon-pink neckties and his astonishing waistcoats.

One Sunday, a few days after Trina's last sitting, McTeague met Marcus Schouler at his table in the car conductors' coffee-joint, next to the harness shop.

"What you got to do this afternoon, Mac?" inquired the other, as they ate their suet pudding.

"Nothing, nothing," replied McTeague, shaking his head. His mouth was full of pudding. It made him warm to eat, and little beads of perspiration stood across the bridge of his nose. He looked forward to an afternoon passed in his operating chair as usual. On leaving his "Parlors" he had put ten cents into his pitcher and had left it at Frenna's to be filled.

"What do you say we take a walk, huh?" said Marcus. "Ah, that's the thing—a walk, a long walk, by damn! It'll be outa sight. I got to take three or four of the dogs out for exercise, anyhow. Old Grannis thinks they need ut. We'll walk out to the Presidio."

Of late it had become the custom of the two friends to take long walks from time to time. On holidays and on those Sunday afternoons when Marcus was not absent with the Sieppes they went out together, sometimes to the park, sometimes to the Presidio, sometimes even across the bay. They took a great pleasure in each other's company, but silently and with reservation, having the masculine horror of any demonstration of friendship.

They walked for upwards of five hours that afternoon, out the length of California Street, and across the Presidio Reservation to the Golden Gate. Then they turned, and, following the line of the shore, brought up at the Cliff House. Here they halted for beer, Marcus swearing that his mouth was as dry as a hay-bin. Before starting on their walk they had gone around to the little dog hospital, and Marcus had let out four of the convalescents, crazed with joy at the release.

"Look at that dog," he cried to McTeague, showing him a finely-bred Irish setter. "That's the dog that belonged to the duck on the avenue, the dog we called for that day. I've bought 'um. The duck thought he had the distemper, and just threw 'um away. Nothun wrong with 'um but a little catarrh. Ain't he a bird? Say, ain't he a bird? Look at his flag; it's perfect; and see how he carries his tail on a line with his back. See how stiff and white his whiskers are. Oh, by damn! you can't fool me on a dog. That dog's a winner."

At the Cliff House the two sat down to their beer in a quiet corner of the billiard-room. There were but two players. Somewhere in another part of the building a mammoth music-box was jangling out a quickstep. From outside came the long, rhythmical rush of the surf and the sonorous barking of the seals upon the seal rocks. The four dogs curled themselves down upon the sanded floor.

"Here's how," said Marcus, half emptying his glass. "Ah-h!" he added, with a long breath, "that's good; it is, for a fact."

For the last hour of their walk Marcus had done nearly all the talking, McTeague merely answering him by uncertain movements of the head. For that matter, the dentist had been silent and preoccupied throughout the whole afternoon. At length Marcus noticed it. As he set down his glass with a bang he suddenly exclaimed:

"What's the matter with you these days, Mac? You got a bean about somethun, hey? Spit ut out."

"No, no," replied McTeague, looking about on the floor, rolling his eyes; "nothing, no, no."

"Ah, rats!" returned the other. McTeague kept silence. The two billiard players departed. The huge music-box struck into a fresh tune.

"Huh!" exclaimed Marcus, with a short laugh, "guess you're in love."

McTeague gasped, and shuffled his enormous feet under the table.

"Well, somethun's bitun you, anyhow," pursued Marcus. "Maybe I can help you. We're pals, you know. Better tell me what's up; guess we can straighten ut out. Ah, go on; spit ut out."

The situation was abominable. McTeague could not rise to it. Marcus was his best friend, his only friend. They were "pals" and McTeague was very fond of him. Yet they were both in love, presumably, with the same girl, and now Marcus would try and force the secret out of him; would rush blindly at the rock upon which the two must split, stirred by the very best of motives, wishing only to be of service. Besides this, there was nobody to whom McTeague would have better preferred to tell his troubles than to Marcus, and yet about this trouble, the greatest trouble of his life, he must keep silent; must refrain from speaking of it to Marcus above everybody.

McTeague began dimly to feel that life was too much for him. How had it all come about? A month ago he was perfectly content; he was calm and peaceful, taking his little pleasures as he found them. His life had shaped itself; was, no doubt, to continue always along these same lines. A woman had entered his small world and instantly there was discord. The disturbing element had appeared. Wherever the woman had put her foot a score of distressing complications had sprung up, like the sudden growth of strange and puzzling flowers.

"Say, Mac, go on; let's have ut straight," urged Marcus, leaning towards him. "Has any duck been doing you dirt?" he cried, his face crimson on the instant.

"No," said McTeague, helplessly.

"Come along, old man," persisted Marcus; "let's have ut. What is the row? I'll do all I can to help you."

It was more than McTeague could bear. The situation had got beyond him. Stupidly he spoke, his hands deep in his pockets, his head rolled forward.

"It's—it's Miss Sieppe," he said.

"Trina, my cousin? How do you mean?" inquired Marcus sharply.

"I—I—I don' know," stammered McTeague, hopelessly confounded.

"You mean," cried Marcus, suddenly enlightened, "that you are—that you, too."

McTeague stirred in his chair, looking at the walls of the room, avoiding the other's glance. He nodded his head, then suddenly broke out:

"I can't help it. It ain't my fault, is it?"

Marcus was struck dumb; he dropped back in his chair breathless. Suddenly McTeague found his tongue.

"I tell you, Mark, I can't help it. I don't know how it happened. It came on so slow that I was, that—that—that it was done before I knew it, before I could help myself. I know we're pals, us two, and I knew how—how you and Miss Sieppe were. I know now, I knew then; but that wouldn't have made any difference. Before I knew it—it—it—there I was. I can't help it. I wouldn't 'a' had ut happen for anything, if I could 'a' stopped it, but I don' know, it's something that's just stronger than you are, that's all. She came there—Miss Sieppe came to the parlors there three or four times a week, and she was the first girl I had ever known,—and you don' know! Why, I was so close to her I touched her face every minute, and her mouth, and smelt her hair and her breath— oh, you don't know anything about it. I can't give you any idea. I don' know exactly myself; I only know how I'm fixed. I—I—it's been done; it's too late, there's no going back. Why, I can't think of anything else night and day. It's every-thing. It's—it's—oh, it's everything! I—I—why, Mark, it's everything—I can't explain." He made a helpless movement with both hands.

Never had McTeague been so excited; never had he made

so long a speech. His arms moved in fierce, uncertain gestures, his face flushed, his enormous jaws shut together with
a sharp click at every pause. It was like some colossal brute
trapped in a delicate, invisible mesh, raging, exasperated,
powerless to extricate himself.

Marcus Schouler said nothing. There was a long silence.
Marcus got up and walked to the window and stood looking
out, but seeing nothing. "Well, who would have thought of
this?" he muttered under his breath. Here was a fix. Marcus
cared for Trina. There was no doubt in his mind about that.
He looked forward eagerly to the Sunday afternoon excursions. He liked to be with Trina. He, too, felt the charm of
the little girl—the charm of the small, pale forehead; the little
chin thrust out as if in confidence and innocence; the heavy,
odorous crown of black hair. He liked her immensely. Some
day he would speak; he would ask her to marry him. Marcus
put off this matter of marriage to some future period; it
would be some time—a year, perhaps, or two. The thing did
not take definite shape in his mind. Marcus "kept company"
with his cousin Trina, but he knew plenty of other girls. For
the matter of that, he liked all girls pretty well. Just now the
singleness and strength of McTeague's passion startled him.
McTeague would marry Trina that very afternoon if she
would have him; but would he—Marcus? No, he would not;
if it came to that, no, he would not. Yet he knew he liked
Trina. He could say—yes, he could say—he loved her. She
was his "girl." The Sieppes acknowledged him as Trina's
"young man." Marcus came back to the table and sat down
sideways upon it.

"Well, what are we going to do about it, Mac?" he said.

"I don' know," answered McTeague, in great distress. "I
don' want anything to—to come between us, Mark."

"Well, nothun will, you bet!" vociferated the other. "No,
sir; you bet not, Mac."

Marcus was thinking hard. He could see very clearly that
McTeague loved Trina more than he did; that in some strange
way this huge, brutal fellow was capable of a greater passion
than himself, who was twice as clever. Suddenly Marcus
jumped impetuously to a resolution.

"Well, say, Mac," he cried, striking the table with his fist, "go ahead. I guess you—you want her pretty bad. I'll pull out; yes, I will. I'll give her up to you, old man."

The sense of his own magnanimity all at once overcame Marcus. He saw himself as another man, very noble, self-sacrificing; he stood apart and watched this second self with boundless admiration and with infinite pity. He was so good, so magnificent, so heroic, that he almost sobbed. Marcus made a sweeping gesture of resignation, throwing out both his arms, crying:

"Mac, I'll give her up to you. I won't stand between you." There were actually tears in Marcus's eyes as he spoke. There was no doubt he thought himself sincere. At that moment he almost believed he loved Trina conscientiously, that he was sacrificing himself for the sake of his friend. The two stood up and faced each other, gripping hands. It was a great moment; even McTeague felt the drama of it. What a fine thing was this friendship between men! The dentist treats his friend for an ulcerated tooth and refuses payment; the friend reciprocates by giving up his girl. This was nobility. Their mutual affection and esteem suddenly increased enormously. It was Damon and Pythias; it was David and Jonathan; nothing could ever estrange them. Now it was for life or death.

"I'm much obliged," murmured McTeague. He could think of nothing better to say. "I'm much obliged," he repeated; "much obliged, Mark."

"That's all right, that's all right," returned Marcus Schouler, bravely, and it occurred to him to add, "You'll be happy together. Tell her for me—tell her—tell her——" Marcus could not go on. He wrung the dentist's hand silently.

It had not appeared to either of them that Trina might refuse McTeague. McTeague's spirits rose at once. In Marcus's withdrawal he fancied he saw an end to all his difficulties. Everything would come right, after all. The strained, exalted state of Marcus's nerves ended by putting him into fine humor as well. His grief suddenly changed to an excess of gaiety. The afternoon was a success. They slapped each other on the back with great blows of the open palms, and they drank each other's health in a third round of beer.

Ten minutes after his renunciation of Trina Sieppe, Marcus astounded McTeague with a tremendous feat.

"Looka here, Mac. I know somethun you can't do. I'll bet you two bits I'll stump you." They each put a quarter on the table. "Now watch me," cried Marcus. He caught up a billiard ball from the rack, poised it a moment in front of his face, then with a sudden, horrifying distension of his jaws crammed it into his mouth, and shut his lips over it.

For an instant McTeague was stupefied, his eyes bulging. Then an enormous laugh shook him. He roared and shouted, swaying in his chair, slapping his knee. What a josher was this Marcus! Sure, you never could tell what he would do next. Marcus slipped the ball out, wiped it on the table-cloth, and passed it to McTeague.

"Now let's see you do it."

McTeague fell suddenly grave. The matter was serious. He parted his thick mustaches and opened his enormous jaws like an anaconda. The ball disappeared inside his mouth. Marcus applauded vociferously, shouting, "Good work!" McTeague reached for the money and put it in his vest pocket, nodding his head with a knowing air.

Then suddenly his face grew purple, his jaws moved convulsively, he pawed at his cheeks with both hands. The billiard ball had slipped into his mouth easily enough; now, however, he could not get it out again.

It was terrible. The dentist rose to his feet, stumbling about among the dogs, his face working, his eyes starting. Try as he would, he could not stretch his jaws wide enough to slip the ball out. Marcus lost his wits, swearing at the top of his voice. McTeague sweated with terror; inarticulate sounds came from his crammed mouth; he waved his arms wildly; all the four dogs caught the excitement and began to bark. A waiter rushed in, the two billiard players returned, a little crowd formed. There was a veritable scene.

All at once the ball slipped out of McTeague's jaws as easily as it had gone in. What a relief! He dropped into a chair, wiping his forehead, gasping for breath.

On the strength of the occasion Marcus Schouler invited the entire group to drink with him.

By the time the affair was over and the group dispersed it was after five. Marcus and McTeague decided they would ride home on the cars. But they soon found this impossible. The dogs would not follow. Only Alexander, Marcus's new setter, kept his place at the rear of the car. The other three lost their senses immediately, running wildly about the streets with their heads in the air, or suddenly starting off at a furious gallop directly away from the car. Marcus whistled and shouted and lathered with rage in vain. The two friends were obliged to walk. When they finally reached Polk Street, Marcus shut up the three dogs in the hospital. Alexander he brought back to the flat with him.

There was a minute back yard in the rear, where Marcus had made a kennel for Alexander out of an old water barrel. Before he thought of his own supper Marcus put Alexander to bed and fed him a couple of dog biscuits. McTeague had followed him to the yard to keep him company. Alexander settled to his supper at once, chewing vigorously at the biscuit, his head on one side.

"What you going to do about this—about that—about—about my cousin now, Mac?" inquired Marcus.

McTeague shook his head helplessly. It was dark by now and cold. The little back yard was grimy and full of odors. McTeague was tired with their long walk. All his uneasiness about his affair with Trina had returned. No, surely she was not for him. Marcus or some other man would win her in the end. What could she ever see to desire in him—in him, a clumsy giant, with hands like wooden mallets? She had told him once that she would not marry him. Was that not final?

"I don' know what to do, Mark," he said.

"Well, you must make up to her now," answered Marcus. "Go and call on her."

McTeague started. He had not thought of calling on her. The idea frightened him a little.

"Of course," persisted Marcus, "that's the proper caper. What did you expect? Did you think you was never going to see her again?"

"I don' know, I don' know," responded the dentist, looking stupidly at the dog.

"You know where they live," continued Marcus Schouler. "Over at B Street station, across the bay. I'll take you over there whenever you want to go. I tell you what, we'll go over there Washington's Birthday. That's this next Wednesday;

sure, they'll be glad to see you." It was good of Marcus. All at once McTeague rose to an appreciation of what his friend was doing for him. He stammered:

"Say, Mark—you're—you're all right, anyhow."

"Why, pshaw!" said Marcus. "That's all right, old man. I'd like to see you two fixed, that's all. We'll go over Wednesday, sure."

They turned back to the house. Alexander left off eating and watched them go away, first with one eye, then with the other. But he was too self-respecting to whimper. However, by the time the two friends had reached the second landing on the back stairs a terrible commotion was under way in the little yard. They rushed to an open window at the end of the hall and looked down.

A thin board fence separated the flat's back yard from that used by the branch post-office. In the latter place lived a collie dog. He and Alexander had smelt each other out, blowing through the cracks of the fence at each other. Suddenly the quarrel had exploded on either side of the fence. The dogs raged at each other, snarling and barking, frantic with hate. Their teeth gleamed. They tore at the fence with their front paws. They filled the whole night with their clamor.

"By damn!" cried Marcus, "they don't love each other. Just listen; wouldn't that make a fight if the two got together? Have to try it some day."

V

WEDNESDAY MORNING, Washington's Birthday, Mc-
Teague rose very early and shaved himself. Besides the
six mournful concertina airs, the dentist knew one song.
Whenever he shaved, he sung this song; never at any other
time. His voice was a bellowing roar, enough to make the
window sashes rattle. Just now he woke up all the lodgers in
his hall with it. It was a lamentable wail:

> "No one to love, none to caress,
> Left all alone in this world's wilderness."

As he paused to strop his razor, Marcus came into his
room, half-dressed, a startling phantom in red flannels.

Marcus often ran back and forth between his room and the
dentist's "Parlors" in all sorts of undress. Old Miss Baker had
seen him thus several times through her half-open door, as
she sat in her room listening and waiting. The old dressmaker
was shocked out of all expression. She was outraged, offended, pursing her lips, putting up her head. She talked of
complaining to the landlady. "And Mr. Grannis right next
door, too. You can understand how trying it is for both of
us." She would come out in the hall after one of these appa-
ritions, her little false curls shaking, talking loud and shrill to
any one in reach of her voice.

"Well," Marcus would shout, "shut your door, then, if you
don't want to see. Look out, now, here I come again. Not
even a porous plaster on me this time."

On this Wednesday morning Marcus called McTeague out
into the hall, to the head of the stairs that led down to the
street door.

"Come and listen to Maria, Mac," said he.

Maria sat on the next to the lowest step, her chin propped
by her two fists. The red-headed Polish Jew, the ragman Zerkow, stood in the doorway. He was talking eagerly.

"Now, just once more, Maria," he was saying. "Tell it to
us just once more." Maria's voice came up the stairway in a

monotone. Marcus and McTeague caught a phrase from time to time.

"There were more than a hundred pieces, and every one of them gold—just that punch-bowl was worth a fortune—thick, fat, red gold."

"Get onto to that, will you?" observed Marcus. "The old skin has got her started on the plate. Ain't they a pair for you?"

"And it rang like bells, didn't it?" prompted Zerkow.

"Sweeter'n church bells, and clearer."

"Ah, sweeter'n bells. Wasn't that punch-bowl awful heavy?"

"All you could do to lift it."

"I know. Oh, I know," answered Zerkow, clawing at his lips. "Where did it all go to? Where did it go?"

Maria shook her head.

"It's gone, anyhow."

"Ah, gone, gone! Think of it! The punch-bowl gone, and the engraved ladle, and the plates and goblets. What a sight it must have been all heaped together!"

"It was a wonderful sight."

"Yes, wonderful; it must have been."

On the lower steps of that cheap flat, the Mexican woman and the red-haired Polish Jew mused long over that vanished, half-mythical gold plate.

Marcus and the dentist spent Washington's Birthday across the bay. The journey over was one long agony to McTeague. He shook with a formless, uncertain dread; a dozen times he would have turned back had not Marcus been with him. The stolid giant was as nervous as a schoolboy. He fancied that his call upon Miss Sieppe was an outrageous affront. She would freeze him with a stare; he would be shown the door, would be ejected, disgraced.

As they got off the local train at B Street station they suddenly collided with the whole tribe of Sieppes—the mother, father, three children, and Trina—equipped for one of their eternal picnics. They were to go to Schuetzen Park, within walking distance of the station. They were grouped about four lunch baskets. One of the children, a little boy, held a black greyhound by a rope around its neck. Trina wore a blue cloth skirt, a striped shirt waist, and a white sailor; about her round waist was a belt of imitation alligator skin.

At once Mrs. Sieppe began to talk to Marcus. He had written of their coming, but the picnic had been decided upon after the arrival of his letter. Mrs. Sieppe explained this to him. She was an immense old lady with a pink face and wonderful hair, absolutely white. The Sieppes were a German-Swiss family.

"We go to der park, Schuetzen Park, mit alle dem childern, a little eggs-kursion, eh not soh? We breathe der freshes air, a celubration, a pignic bei der seashore on. Ach, dot wull be soh gay, ah?"

"You bet it will. It'll be outa sight," cried Marcus, enthusiastic in an instant. "This is m' friend Doctor McTeague I wrote you about, Mrs. Sieppe."

"Ach, der doktor," cried Mrs. Sieppe.

McTeague was presented, shaking hands gravely as Marcus shouldered him from one to the other.

Mr. Sieppe was a little man of a military aspect, full of importance, taking himself very seriously. He was a member of a rifle team. Over his shoulder was slung a Springfield rifle, while his breast was decorated by five bronze medals.

Trina was delighted. McTeague was dumfounded. She appeared positively glad to see him.

"How do you do, Doctor McTeague," she said, smiling at him and shaking his hand. "It's nice to see you again. Look, see how fine my filling is." She lifted a corner of her lip and showed him the clumsy gold bridge.

Meanwhile, Mr. Sieppe toiled and perspired. Upon him devolved the responsibility of the excursion. He seemed to consider it a matter of vast importance, a veritable expedition.

"Owgooste!" he shouted to the little boy with the black greyhound, "you will der hound und basket number three carry. Der tervins," he added, calling to the two smallest boys, who were dressed exactly alike, "will releef one unudder mit der camp-stuhl und basket number four. Dat is comprehend, hay? When we make der start, you childern will in der advance march. Dat is your orders. But we do not start," he exclaimed, excitedly; "we re-main. Ach Gott, Selina, who does not arrive."

Selina, it appeared, was a niece of Mrs. Sieppe's. They were

on the point of starting without her, when she suddenly arrived, very much out of breath. She was a slender, unhealthy
looking girl, who overworked herself giving lessons in hand-
painting at twenty-five cents an hour. McTeague was presented. They all began to talk at once, filling the little station-
house with a confusion of tongues.

"Attention!" cried Mr. Sieppe, his gold-headed cane in one
hand, his Springfield in the other. "Attention! We depart."
The four little boys moved off ahead; the greyhound suddenly
began to bark, and tug at his leash. The others picked up their
bundles.

"Vorwarts!" shouted Mr. Sieppe, waving his rifle and assuming the attitude of a lieutenant of infantry leading a
charge. The party set off down the railroad track.

Mrs. Sieppe walked with her husband, who constantly left
her side to shout an order up and down the line. Marcus
followed with Selina. McTeague found himself with Trina at
the end of the procession.

"We go off on these picnics almost every week," said Trina,
by way of a beginning, "and almost every holiday, too. It is a
custom."

"Yes, yes, a custom," answered McTeague, nodding; "a custom—that's the word."

"Don't you think picnics are fine fun, Doctor McTeague?"
she continued. "You take your lunch; you leave the dirty city
all day; you race about in the open air, and when lunchtime
comes, oh, aren't you hungry? And the woods and the grass
smell so fine!"

"I don't know, Miss Sieppe," he answered, keeping his eyes
fixed on the ground between the rails. "I never went on a
picnic."

"Never went on a picnic?" she cried, astonished. "Oh,
you'll see what fun we'll have. In the morning father and the
children dig clams in the mud by the shore, an' we bake them,
and—oh, there's thousands of things to do."

"Once I went sailing on the bay," said McTeague. "It was
in a tugboat; we fished off the heads. I caught three cod-
fishes."

"I'm afraid to go out on the bay," answered Trina, shaking her head, "sailboats tip over so easy. A cousin of mine,

Selina's brother, was drowned one Decoration Day. They never found his body. Can you swim, Doctor McTeague?"

"I used to at the mine."

"At the mine? Oh, yes, I remember, Marcus told me you were a miner once."

"I was a car-boy; all the car-boys used to swim in the reservoir by the ditch every Thursday evening. One of them was bit by a rattlesnake once while he was dressing. He was a Frenchman, named Andrew. He swelled up and began to twitch."

"Oh, how I hate snakes! They're so crawly and graceful—but, just the same, I like to watch them. You know that drug store over in town that has a showcase full of live ones?"

"We killed the rattler with a cart whip."

"How far do you think you could swim? Did you ever try? D'you think you could swim a mile?"

"A mile? I don't know. I never tried. I guess I could."

"I can swim a little. Sometimes we all go out to the Crystal Baths."

"The Crystal Baths, huh? Can you swim across the tank?"

"Oh, I can swim all right as long as papa holds my chin up. Soon as he takes his hand away, down I go. Don't you hate to get water in your ears?"

"Bathing's good for you."

"If the water's too warm, it isn't. It weakens you."

Mr. Sieppe came running down the tracks, waving his cane.

"To one side," he shouted, motioning them off the track; "der drain gomes." A local passenger train was just passing B Street station, some quarter of a mile behind them. The party stood to one side to let it pass. Marcus put a nickel and two crossed pins upon the rail, and waved his hat to the passengers as the train roared past. The children shouted shrilly. When the train was gone, they all rushed to see the nickel and the crossed pins. The nickel had been jolted off, but the pins had been flattened out so that they bore a faint resemblance to opened scissors. A great contention arose among the children for the possession of these "scissors." Mr. Sieppe was obliged to intervene. He reflected gravely. It was a matter of tremendous moment. The whole party halted, awaiting his decision.

"Attend now," he suddenly exclaimed. "It will not be soh soon. At der end of der day, ven we shall have home gecommen, den wull it pe adjudge, eh? A *re*ward of merit to him who der bes' pehaves. It is an order. Vorwarts!"

"That was a Sacramento train," said Marcus to Selina as they started off; "it was, for a fact."

"I know a girl in Sacramento," Trina told McTeague. "She's forewoman in a glove store, and she's got consumption."

"I was in Sacramento once," observed McTeague, "nearly eight years ago."

"Is it a nice place—as nice as San Francisco?"

"It's hot. I practised there for a while."

"I like San Francisco," said Trina, looking across the bay to where the city piled itself upon its hills.

"So do I," answered McTeague. "Do you like it better than living over here?"

"Oh, sure, I wish we lived in the city. If you want to go across for anything it takes up the whole day."

"Yes, yes, the whole day—almost."

"Do you know many people in the city? Do you know anybody named Oelbermann? That's my uncle. He has a wholesale toy store in the Mission. They say he's awful rich."

"No, I don' know him."

"His stepdaughter wants to be a nun. Just fancy! And Mr. Oelbermann won't have it. He says it would be just like burying his child. Yes, she wants to enter the convent of the Sacred Heart. Are you a Catholic, Doctor McTeague?"

"No. No, I——"

"Papa is a Catholic. He goes to Mass on the feast days once in a while. But mamma's Lutheran."

"The Catholics are trying to get control of the schools," observed McTeague, suddenly remembering one of Marcus's political tirades.

"That's what cousin Mark says. We are going to send the twins to the kindergarten next month."

"What's the kindergarten?"

"Oh, they teach them to make things out of straw and toothpicks—kind of a play place to keep them off the street."

"There's one up on Sacramento Street, not far from Polk Street. I saw the sign."

"I know where. Why, Selina used to play the piano there."

"Does she play the piano?"

"Oh, you ought to hear her. She plays fine. Selina's very accomplished. She paints, too."

"I can play on the concertina."

"Oh, can you? I wish you'd brought it along. Next time you will. I hope you'll come often on our picnics. You'll see what fun we'll have."

"Fine day for a picnic, ain't it? There ain't a cloud."

"That's so," exclaimed Trina, looking up, "not a single cloud. Oh, yes; there is one, just over Telegraph Hill."

"That's smoke."

"No, it's a cloud. Smoke isn't white that way."

" 'Tis a cloud."

"I knew I was right. I never say a thing unless I'm pretty sure."

"It looks like a dog's head."

"Don't it? Isn't Marcus fond of dogs?"

"He got a new dog last week—a setter."

"Did he?"

"Yes. He and I took a lot of dogs from his hospital out for a walk to the Cliff House last Sunday, but we had to walk all the way home, because they wouldn't follow. You've been out to the Cliff House?"

"Not for a long time. We had a picnic there one Fourth of July, but it rained. Don't you love the ocean?"

"Yes—yes, I like it pretty well."

"Oh, I'd like to go off in one of those big sailing ships. Just away, and away, and away, anywhere. They're different from a little yacht. I'd love to travel."

"Sure; so would I."

"Papa and mamma came over in a sailing ship. They were twenty-one days. Mamma's uncle used to be a sailor. He was captain of a steamer on Lake Geneva, in Switzerland."

"Halt!" shouted Mr. Sieppe, brandishing his rifle. They had arrived at the gates of the park. All at once McTeague turned cold. He had only a quarter in his pocket. What was he expected to do—pay for the whole party, or for Trina and himself, or merely buy his own ticket? And even in this latter case would a quarter be enough? He lost his wits, rolling his eyes helplessly. Then it occurred to him to feign a great abstraction, pretending not to know that the time was come to pay. He looked intently up and down the tracks; perhaps a train was coming. "Here we are," cried Trina, as they came up to the rest of the party, crowded about the entrance. "Yes, yes," observed McTeague, his head in the air.

"Gi' me four bits, Mac," said Marcus, coming up. "Here's where we shell out."

"I—I—I only got a quarter," mumbled the dentist, miserably. He felt that he had ruined himself forever with Trina. What was the use of trying to win her? Destiny was against him. "I only got a quarter," he stammered. He was on the point of adding that he would not go in the park. That seemed to be the only alternative.

"Oh, all right!" said Marcus, easily. "I'll pay for you, and you can square with me when we go home."

They filed into the park, Mr. Sieppe counting them off as they entered.

"Ah," said Trina, with a long breath, as she and McTeague pushed through the wicket, "here we are once more, Doctor." She had not appeared to notice McTeague's embarrassment. The difficulty had been tided over somehow. Once more McTeague felt himself saved.

"To der beach!" shouted Mr. Sieppe. They had checked their baskets at the peanut stand. The whole party trooped down to the seashore. The greyhound was turned loose. The children raced on ahead.

From one of the larger parcels Mr. Sieppe had drawn forth a small tin steamboat—August's birthday present—a gaudy little toy which could be steamed up and navigated by means of an alcohol lamp. Her trial trip was to be made this morning.

"Gi' me it, gi' me it," shouted August, dancing around his father.

"Not soh, not soh," cried Mr. Sieppe, bearing it aloft. "I must first der eggsperimunt make."

"No, no!" wailed August. "I want to play with ut."

"Obey!" thundered Mr. Sieppe. August subsided. A little jetty ran part of the way into the water. Here, after a careful study of the directions printed on the cover of the box, Mr. Sieppe began to fire the little boat.

"I want to put ut in the wa-ater," cried August.

"Stand back!" shouted his parent. "You do not know so well as me; dere is dandger. Mitout attention he will eggs-plode."

"I want to play with ut," protested August, beginning to cry.

"Ach, soh; you cry, bube!" vociferated Mr. Sieppe. "Mom-mer," addressing Mrs. Sieppe, "he will soh soon be ge-whipt, eh?"

"I want my boa-wut," screamed August, dancing.

"Silence!" roared Mr. Sieppe. The little boat began to hiss and smoke.

"Soh," observed the father, "he gommence. Attention! I put him in der water." He was very excited. The perspiration dripped from the back of his neck. The little boat was launched. It hissed more furiously than ever. Clouds of steam rolled from it, but it refused to move.

"You don't know how she wo-rks," sobbed August.

"I know more soh mudge as der grossest liddle fool as you," cried Mr. Sieppe, fiercely, his face purple.

"You must give it sh—shove!" exclaimed the boy.

"Den he eggsplode, idiot!" shouted his father. All at once the boiler of the steamer blew up with a sharp crack. The little tin toy turned over and sank out of sight before any one could interfere.

"Ah—h! Yah! Yah!" yelled August. "It's go-one!"

Instantly Mr. Sieppe boxed his ears. There was a lamentable scene. August rent the air with his outcries; his father shook him till his boots danced on the jetty, shouting into his face:

"Ach, idiot! Ach, imbecile! Ach, miserable! I tol' you he eggsplode. Stop your cry. Stop! It is an order. Do you wish I drow you in der water, eh? Speak. Silence, bube! Mommer, where ist mein stick? He will der grossest whippun ever of his life receive."

Little by little the boy subsided, swallowing his sobs, knuckling his eyes, gazing ruefully at the spot where the boat had sunk. "Dot is better soh," commented Mr. Sieppe, finally releasing him. "Next dime berhaps you will your fat'er better pelief. Now, no more. We will der glams ge-dig. Mommer, a fire. Ach, himmel! we have der pfeffer forgotten."

The work of clam digging began at once, the little boys taking off their shoes and stockings. At first August refused to be comforted, and it was not until his father drove him into the water with his gold-headed cane that he consented to join the others.

What a day that was for McTeague! What a never-to-be-forgotten day! He was with Trina constantly. They laughed together—she demurely, her lips closed tight, her little chin thrust out, her small pale nose, with its adorable little freckles, wrinkling; he roared with all the force of his lungs, his enormous mouth distended, striking sledge-hammer blows upon his knee with his clenched fist.

The lunch was delicious. Trina and her mother made a clam chowder that melted in one's mouth. The lunch baskets were emptied. The party were fully two hours eating. There were huge loaves of rye bread full of grains of chickweed. There were wienerwurst and frankfurter sausages. There was unsalted butter. There were pretzels. There was cold underdone chicken, which one ate in slices, plastered with a wonderful kind of mustard that did not sting. There were dried apples, that gave Mr. Sieppe the hiccoughs. There were a dozen bottles of beer, and, last of all, a crowning achievement, a marvellous Gotha truffle. After lunch came tobacco. Stuffed to the eyes, McTeague drowsed over his pipe, prone on his back in the sun, while Trina, Mrs. Sieppe, and Selina washed the dishes. In the afternoon Mr. Sieppe disappeared. They heard the reports of his rifle on the range. The others swarmed over the park, now around the swings, now in the Casino, now in the museum, now invading the merry-go-round.

At half-past five o'clock Mr. Sieppe marshalled the party together. It was time to return home.

The family insisted that Marcus and McTeague should take supper with them at their home and should stay over night. Mrs. Sieppe argued they could get no decent supper if they went back to the city at that hour; that they could catch an early morning boat and reach their business in good time. The two friends accepted.

The Sieppes lived in a little box of a house at the foot of B Street, the first house to the right as one went up from the station. It was two stories high, with a funny red mansard roof of oval slates. The interior was cut up into innumerable tiny rooms, some of them so small as to be hardly better than sleeping closets. In the back yard was a contrivance for pumping water from the cistern that interested McTeague at once. It was a dog-wheel, a huge revolving box in which the unhappy black greyhound spent most of his waking hours. It was his kennel; he slept in it. From time to time during the day Mrs. Sieppe appeared on the back doorstep, crying shrilly, "Hoop, hoop!" She threw lumps of coal at him, waking him to his work.

They were all very tired, and went to bed early. After great discussion it was decided that Marcus would sleep upon the lounge in the front parlor. Trina would sleep with August, giving up her room to McTeague. Selina went to her home, a block or so above the Sieppes's. At nine o'clock Mr. Sieppe showed McTeague to his room and left him to himself with a newly lighted candle.

For a long time after Mr. Sieppe had gone McTeague stood motionless in the middle of the room, his elbows pressed close to his sides, looking obliquely from the corners of his eyes. He hardly dared to move. He was in Trina's room.

It was an ordinary little room. A clean white matting was on the floor; gray paper, spotted with pink and green flowers, covered the walls. In one corner, under a white netting, was a little bed, the woodwork gayly painted with knots of bright flowers. Near it, against the wall, was a black walnut bureau. A work-table with spiral legs stood by the window, which was hung with a green and gold window curtain. Opposite the window the closet door stood ajar, while in the corner across from the bed was a tiny washstand with two clean towels.

And that was all. But it was Trina's room. McTeague was in his lady's bower; it seemed to him a little nest, intimate, discreet. He felt hideously out of place. He was an intruder; he, with his enormous feet, his colossal bones, his crude, brutal gestures. The mere weight of his limbs, he was sure, would crush the little bedstead like an eggshell.

Then, as this first sensation wore off, he began to feel the charm of the little chamber. It was as though Trina were close by, but invisible. McTeague felt all the delight of her presence without the embarrassment that usually accompanied it. He was near to her—nearer than he had ever been before. He saw into her daily life, her little ways and manners, her habits, her very thoughts. And was there not in the air of that room a certain faint perfume that he knew, that recalled her to his mind with marvellous vividness?

As he put the candle down upon the bureau he saw her hairbrush lying there. Instantly he picked it up, and, without knowing why, held it to his face. With what a delicious odor was it redolent! That heavy, enervating odor of her hair—her wonderful, royal hair! The smell of that little hairbrush was talismanic. He had but to close his eyes to see her as distinctly as in a mirror. He saw her tiny, round figure, dressed all in black—for, curiously enough, it was his very first impression of Trina that came back to him now—not the Trina of the later occasions, not the Trina of the blue cloth skirt and white sailor. He saw her as he had seen her the day that Marcus had introduced them: saw her pale, round face; her narrow, half-open eyes, blue like the eyes of a baby; her tiny, pale ears, suggestive of anæmia; the freckles across the bridge of her nose; her pale lips; the tiara of royal black hair; and, above all, the delicious poise of the head, tipped back as though by the weight of all that hair—the poise that thrust out her chin a little, with the movement that was so confiding, so innocent, so nearly infantile.

McTeague went softly about the room from one object to another, beholding Trina in everything he touched or looked at. He came at last to the closet door. It was ajar. He opened it wide, and paused upon the threshold.

Trina's clothes were hanging there—skirts and waists, jackets, and stiff white petticoats. What a vision! For an instant McTeague caught his breath, spellbound. If he had suddenly discovered Trina herself there, smiling at him, holding out her hands, he could hardly have been more overcome. Instantly he recognized the black dress she had worn on that famous first day. There it was, the little jacket she had carried over her arm the day he had terrified her with his blundering declaration, and still others, and others—a whole group of Trinas faced him there. He went farther into the closet, touching the clothes gingerly, stroking them softly with his huge leathern palms. As he stirred them a delicate perfume disengaged itself from the folds. Ah, that exquisite feminine odor! It was not only her hair now, it was Trina herself—her mouth, her hands, her neck; the indescribably sweet, fleshly aroma that was a part of her, pure and clean, and redolent of youth and freshness. All at once, seized with an unreasoned impulse, McTeague opened his huge arms and gathered the little garments close to him, plunging his face deep amongst them, savoring their delicious odor with long breaths of luxury and supreme content.

The picnic at Schuetzen Park decided matters. McTeague began to call on Trina regularly Sunday and Wednesday afternoons. He took Marcus Schouler's place. Sometimes Marcus accompanied him, but it was generally to meet Selina by appointment at the Sieppes's house.

But Marcus made the most of his renunciation of his cousin. He remembered his pose from time to time. He made McTeague unhappy and bewildered by wringing his hand, by venting sighs that seemed to tear his heart out, or by giving evidences of an infinite melancholy. "What is my life!" he would exclaim. "What is left for me? Nothing, by damn!" And when McTeague would attempt remonstrance, he would cry: "Never mind, old man. Never mind me. Go, be happy. I forgive you."

Forgive what? McTeague was all at sea, was harassed with the thought of some shadowy, irreparable injury he had done his friend.

"Oh, don't think of me!" Marcus would exclaim at other times, even when Trina was by. "Don't think of me; I don't count any more. I ain't in it." Marcus seemed to take great pleasure in contemplating the wreck of his life. There is no doubt he enjoyed himself hugely during these days.

The Sieppes were at first puzzled as well over this change of front.

"Trina has den a new younge man," cried Mr. Sieppe. "First Schouler, now der doktor, eh? What die tevil, I say!"

Weeks passed, February went, March came in very rainy, putting a stop to all their picnics and Sunday excursions.

One Wednesday afternoon in the second week in March

McTeague came over to call on Trina, bringing his concertina with him, as was his custom nowadays. As he got off the train at the station he was surprised to find Trina waiting for him.

"This is the first day it hasn't rained in weeks," she explained, "an' I thought it would be nice to walk."

"Sure, sure," assented McTeague.

B Street station was nothing more than a little shed. There was no ticket office, nothing but a couple of whittled and carven benches. It was built close to the railroad tracks, just across which was the dirty, muddy shore of San Francisco Bay. About a quarter of a mile back from the station was the edge of the town of Oakland. Between the station and the first houses of the town lay immense salt flats, here and there broken by winding streams of black water. They were covered with a growth of wiry grass, strangely discolored in places by enormous stains of orange yellow.

Near the station a bit of fence painted with a cigar advertisement reeled over into the mud, while under its lee lay an abandoned gravel wagon with dished wheels. The station was connected with the town by the extension of B Street, which struck across the flats geometrically straight, a file of tall poles with intervening wires marching along with it. At the station these were headed by an iron electric-light pole that, with its supports and outriggers, looked for all the world like an immense grasshopper on its hind legs.

Across the flats, at the fringe of the town, were the dump heaps, the figures of a few Chinese rag-pickers moving over them. Far to the left the view was shut off by the immense red-brown drum of the gas-works; to the right it was bounded by the chimneys and workshops of an iron foundry.

Across the railroad tracks, to seaward, one saw the long stretch of black mud bank left bare by the tide, which was far out, nearly half a mile. Clouds of sea-gulls were forever rising and settling upon this mud bank; a wrecked and abandoned wharf crawled over it on tottering legs; close in an old sail-boat lay canted on her bilge.

But farther on, across the yellow waters of the bay, beyond Goat Island, lay San Francisco, a blue line of hills, rugged with roofs and spires. Far to the westward opened the Golden

Gate, a bleak cutting in the sand-hills, through which one caught a glimpse of the open Pacific.

The station at B Street was solitary; no trains passed at this hour; except the distant rag-pickers, not a soul was in sight. The wind blew strong, carrying with it the mingled smell of salt, of tar, of dead seaweed, and of bilge. The sky hung low and brown; at long intervals a few drops of rain fell.

Near the station Trina and McTeague sat on the roadbed of the tracks, at the edge of the mud bank, making the most out of the landscape, enjoying the open air, the salt marshes, and the sight of the distant water. From time to time McTeague played his six mournful airs upon his concertina.

After a while they began walking up and down the tracks, McTeague talking about his profession, Trina listening, very interested and absorbed, trying to understand.

"For pulling the roots of the upper molars we use the cow-horn forceps," continued the dentist, monotonously. "We get the inside beak over the palatal roots and the cow-horn beak over the buccal roots—that's the roots on the outside, you see. Then we close the forceps, and that breaks right through the alveolus—that's the part of the socket in the jaw, you understand."

At another moment he told her of his one unsatisfied desire. "Some day I'm going to have a big gilded tooth outside my window for a sign. Those big gold teeth are beautiful, beautiful—only they cost so much, I can't afford one just now."

"Oh, it's raining," suddenly exclaimed Trina, holding out her palm. They turned back and reached the station in a drizzle. The afternoon was closing in dark and rainy. The tide was coming back, talking and lapping for miles along the mud bank. Far off across the flats, at the edge of the town, an electric car went by, stringing out a long row of diamond sparks on the overhead wires.

"Say, Miss Trina," said McTeague, after a while, " what's the good of waiting any longer? Why can't us two get married?"

Trina still shook her head, saying "No" instinctively, in spite of herself.

"Why not?" persisted McTeague. "Don't you like me well enough?"

"Yes."

"Then why not?"

"Because."

"Ah, come on," he said, but Trina still shook her head.

"Ah, come on," urged McTeague. He could think of nothing else to say, repeating the same phrase over and over again to all her refusals.

"Ah, come on! Ah, come on!"

Suddenly he took her in his enormous arms, crushing down her struggle with his immense strength. Then Trina gave up, all in an instant, turning her head to his. They kissed each other, grossly, full in the mouth.

A roar and a jarring of the earth suddenly grew near and passed them in a reek of steam and hot air. It was the Overland, with its flaming headlight, on its way across the continent.

The passage of the train startled them both. Trina struggled to free herself from McTeague. "Oh, please! please!" she pleaded, on the point of tears. McTeague released her, but in that moment a slight, a barely perceptible, revulsion of feeling had taken place in him. The instant that Trina gave up, the instant she allowed him to kiss her, he thought less of her. She was not so desirable, after all. But this reaction was so faint, so subtle, so intangible, that in another moment he had doubted its occurrence. Yet afterward it returned. Was there not something gone from Trina now? Was he not disappointed in her for doing that very thing for which he had longed? Was Trina the submissive, the compliant, the attainable just the same, just as delicate and adorable as Trina the inaccessible? Perhaps he dimly saw that this must be so, that it belonged to the changeless order of things—the man desiring the woman only for what she withholds; the woman worshipping the man for that which she yields up to him. With each concession gained the man's desire cools; with every surrender made the woman's adoration increases. But why should it be so?

Trina wrenched herself free and drew back from McTeague, her little chin quivering; her face, even to the lobes of her pale ears, flushed scarlet; her narrow blue eyes brimming. Suddenly she put her head between her hands and began to sob.

"Say, say, Miss Trina, listen—listen here, Miss Trina," cried McTeague, coming forward a step.

"Oh, don't!" she gasped, shrinking. "I must go home," she cried, springing to her feet. "It's late. I must. I must. Don't come with me, please. Oh, I'm so—so,"—she could not find any words. "Let me go alone," she went on. "You may—you come Sunday. Good-by."

"Good-by," said McTeague, his head in a whirl at this sudden, unaccountable change. "Can't I kiss you again?" But Trina was firm now. When it came to his pleading—a mere matter of words—she was strong enough.

"No, no, you must not!" she exclaimed, with energy. She was gone in another instant. The dentist, stunned, bewildered, gazed stupidly after her as she ran up the extension of B Street through the rain.

But suddenly a great joy took possession of him. He had won her. Trina was to be for him, after all. An enormous smile distended his thick lips; his eyes grew wide, and flashed; and he drew his breath quickly, striking his mallet-like fist upon his knee, and exclaiming under his breath:

"I got her, by God! I got her, by God!" At the same time he thought better of himself; his self-respect increased enormously. The man that could win Trina Sieppe was a man of extraordinary ability.

Trina burst in upon her mother while the latter was setting a mousetrap in the kitchen.

"Oh, mamma!"

"Eh, Trina? Ach, what has happun?"

Trina told her in a breath.

"Soh soon?" was Mrs. Sieppe's first comment. "Eh, well, what you cry for, then?"

"I don't know," wailed Trina, plucking at the end of her handkerchief.

"You loaf der younge doktor?"

"I don't know."

"Well, what for you kiss him?"

"I don't know."

"You don' know, you don' know? Where haf your sensus gone, Trina? You kiss der doktor. You cry, and you don' know. Is ut Marcus den?"

"No, it's not Cousin Mark."

"Den ut must be der doktor."

Trina made no answer.

"Eh?"

"I—I guess so."

"You loaf him?"

"I don't know."

Mrs. Sieppe set down the mousetrap with such violence that it sprung with a sharp snap.

VI

No, TRINA did not know. "Do I love him? Do I love him?" A thousand times she put the question to herself during the next two or three days. At night she hardly slept, but lay broad awake for hours in her little, gayly painted bed, with its white netting, torturing herself with doubts and questions. At times she remembered the scene in the station with a veritable agony of shame, and at other times she was ashamed to recall it with a thrill of joy. Nothing could have been more sudden, more unexpected, than that surrender of herself. For over a year she had thought that Marcus would some day be her husband. They would be married, she supposed, some time in the future, she did not know exactly when; the matter did not take definite shape in her mind. She liked Cousin Mark very well. And then suddenly this cross-current had set in; this blond giant had appeared, this huge, stolid fellow, with his immense, crude strength. She had not loved him at first, that was certain. The day he had spoken to her in his "Parlors" she had only been terrified. If he had confined himself to merely speaking, as did Marcus, to pleading with her, to wooing her at a distance, forestalling her wishes, showing her little attentions, sending her boxes of candy, she could have easily withstood him. But he had only to take her in his arms, to crush down her struggle with his enormous strength, to subdue her, conquer her by sheer brute force, and she gave up in an instant.

But why—why had she done so? Why did she feel the desire, the necessity of being conquered by a superior strength? Why did it please her? Why had it suddenly thrilled her from head to foot with a quick, terrifying gust of passion, the like of which she had never known? Never at his best had Marcus made her feel like that, and yet she had always thought she cared for Cousin Mark more than for any one else.

When McTeague had all at once caught her in his huge arms, something had leaped to life in her—something that had hitherto lain dormant, something strong and overpowering. It frightened her now as she thought of it, this second self that had wakened within her, and that shouted and clamored for recognition. And yet, was it to be feared? Was it something to be ashamed of? Was it not, after all, natural, clean, spontaneous? Trina knew that she was a pure girl; knew that this sudden commotion within her carried with it no suggestion of vice.

Dimly, as figures seen in a waking dream, these ideas floated through Trina's mind. It was quite beyond her to realize them clearly; she could not know what they meant. Until that rainy day by the shore of the bay Trina had lived her life with as little self-consciousness as a tree. She was frank, straightforward, a healthy, natural human being, without sex as yet. She was almost like a boy. At once there had been a mysterious disturbance. The woman within her suddenly awoke.

Did she love McTeague? Difficult question. Did she choose him for better or for worse, deliberately, of her own free will, or was Trina herself allowed even a choice in the taking of that step that was to make or mar her life? The Woman is awakened, and, starting from her sleep, catches blindly at what first her newly opened eyes light upon. It is a spell, a witchery, ruled by chance alone, inexplicable—a fairy queen enamored of a clown with ass's ears.

McTeague had awakened the Woman, and, whether she would or no, she was his now irrevocably; struggle against it as she would, she belonged to him, body and soul, for life or for death. She had not sought it, she had not desired it. The spell was laid upon her. Was it a blessing? Was it a curse? It was all one; she was his, indissolubly, for evil or for good.

And he? The very act of submission that bound the woman to him forever had made her seem less desirable in his eyes. Their undoing had already begun. Yet neither of them was to blame. From the first they had not sought each other. Chance had brought them face to face, and mysterious instincts as ungovernable as the winds of heaven were at work knitting their lives together. Neither of them had asked that this thing should be—that their destinies, their very souls, should be the sport of chance. If they could have known, they would have shunned the fearful risk. But they were allowed no voice in the matter. Why should it all be?

It had been on a Wednesday that the scene in the B Street station had taken place. Throughout the rest of the week, at every hour of the day, Trina asked herself the same question: "Do I love him? Do I really love him? Is this what love is like?" As she recalled McTeague—recalled his huge, square-cut head, his salient jaw, his shock of yellow hair, his heavy, lumbering body, his slow wits—she found little to admire in him beyond his physical strength, and at such moments she shook her head decisively. "No, surely she did not love him." Sunday afternoon, however, McTeague called. Trina had prepared a little speech for him. She was to tell him that she did not know what had been the matter with her that Wednesday afternoon; that she had acted like a bad girl; that she did not love him well enough to marry him; that she had told him as much once before.

McTeague saw her alone in the little front parlor. The instant she appeared he came straight towards her. She saw what he was bent upon doing. "Wait a minute," she cried, putting out her hands. "Wait. You don't understand. I have got something to say to you." She might as well have talked to the wind. McTeague put aside her hands with a single gesture, and gripped her to him in a bearlike embrace that all but smothered her. Trina was but a reed before that giant strength. McTeague turned her face to his and kissed her again upon the mouth. Where was all Trina's resolve then? Where was her carefully prepared little speech? Where was all her hesitation and torturing doubts of the last few days? She clasped McTeague's huge red neck with both her slender arms; she raised her adorable little chin and kissed him in return, exclaiming: "Oh, I do love you! I do love you!" Never afterward were the two so happy as at that moment.

A little later in that same week, when Marcus and McTeague were taking lunch at the car conductors' coffee-joint, the former suddenly exclaimed:

"Say, Mac, now that you've got Trina, you ought to do more for her. By damn! you ought to, for a fact. Why don't you take her out somewhere—to the theatre, or somewhere? You ain't on to your job."

Naturally, McTeague had told Marcus of his success with Trina. Marcus had taken on a grand air.

"You've got her, have you? Well, I'm glad of it, old man. I am, for a fact. I know you'll be happy with her. I know how I would have been. I forgive you; yes, I forgive you, freely."

McTeague had not thought of taking Trina to the theatre.

"You think I ought to, Mark?" he inquired, hesitating. Marcus answered, with his mouth full of suet pudding:

"Why, of course. That's the proper caper."

"Well—well, that's so. The theatre—that's the word."

"Take her to the variety show at the Orpheum. There's a good show there this week; you'll have to take Mrs. Sieppe, too, of course," he added. Marcus was not sure of himself as regarded certain proprieties, nor, for that matter, were any of the people of the little world of Polk Street. The shop girls, the plumbers' apprentices, the small tradespeople, and their like, whose social position was not clearly defined, could never be sure how far they could go and yet preserve their "respectability." When they wished to be "proper," they invariably overdid the thing. It was not as if they belonged to the "tough" element, who had no appearances to keep up. Polk Street rubbed elbows with the "avenue" one block above. There were certain limits which its dwellers could not overstep; but unfortunately for them, these limits were poorly defined. They could never be sure of themselves. At an unguarded moment they might be taken for "toughs," so they generally erred in the other direction, and were absurdly formal. No people have a keener eye for the amenities than those whose social position is not assured.

"Oh, sure, you'll have to take her mother," insisted Marcus. "It wouldn't be the proper racket if you didn't."

McTeague undertook the affair. It was an ordeal. Never in his life had he been so perturbed, so horribly anxious. He called upon Trina the following Wednesday and made arrangements. Mrs. Sieppe asked if little August might be included. It would console him for the loss of his steamboat.

"Sure, sure," said McTeague. "August too—everybody," he added, vaguely.

"We always have to leave so early," complained Trina, "in order to catch the last boat. Just when it's becoming interesting."

At this McTeague, acting upon a suggestion of Marcus Schouler's, insisted they should stay at the flat over night.

Marcus and the dentist would give up their rooms to them and sleep at the dog hospital. There was a bed there in the sick ward that Old Grannis sometimes occupied when a bad case needed watching. All at once McTeague had an idea, a veritable inspiration.

"And we'll—we'll—we'll have—what's the matter with having something to eat afterward in my 'Parlors'?"

"Vairy goot," commented Mrs. Sieppe. "Bier, eh? And some *damales*."

"Oh, I love *tamales*!" exclaimed Trina, clasping her hands.

McTeague returned to the city, rehearsing his instructions over and over. The theatre party began to assume tremendous proportions. First of all, he was to get the seats, the third or fourth row from the front, on the left-hand side, so as to be out of the hearing of the drums in the orchestra; he must make arrangements about the rooms with Marcus, must get in the beer, but not the tamales; must buy for himself a white lawn tie—so Marcus directed; must look to it that Maria Macapa put his room in perfect order; and, finally, must meet the Sieppes at the ferry slip at half-past seven the following Monday night.

The real labor of the affair began with the buying of the tickets. At the theatre McTeague got into wrong entrances; was sent from one wicket to another; was bewildered, confused; misunderstood directions; was at one moment suddenly convinced that he had not enough money with him, and started to return home. Finally he found himself at the box-office wicket.

"Is it here you buy your seats?"

"How many?"

"Is it here——"

"What night do you want 'em? Yes, sir, here's the place."

McTeague gravely delivered himself of the formula he had been reciting for the last dozen hours.

"I want four seats for Monday night in the fourth row from the front, and on the right-hand side."

"Right hand as you face the house or as you face the stage?" McTeague was dumfounded.

"I want to be on the right-hand side," he insisted, stolidly; adding, "in order to be away from the drums."

"Well, the drums are on the right of the orchestra as you face the stage," shouted the other impatiently; "you want to the left, then, as you face the house."

"I want to be on the right-hand side," persisted the dentist.

Without a word the seller threw out four tickets with a magnificent, supercilious gesture.

"There's four seats on the right-hand side, then, and you're right up against the drums."

"But I don't want to be near the drums," protested Mc-Teague, beginning to perspire.

"Do you know what you want at all?" said the ticket seller with calmness, thrusting his head at McTeague. The dentist knew that he had hurt this young man's feelings.

"I want—I want," he stammered. The seller slammed down a plan of the house in front of him and began to explain excitedly. It was the one thing lacking to complete McTeague's confusion.

"There are your seats," finished the seller, shoving the tickets into McTeague's hands. "They are the fourth row from the front, and away from the drums. Now are you satisfied?"

"Are they on the right-hand side? I want on the right—no, I want on the left. I want—I don' know, I don' know."

The seller roared. McTeague moved slowly away, gazing stupidly at the blue slips of pasteboard. Two girls took his place at the wicket. In another moment McTeague came back, peering over the girls' shoulders and calling to the seller:

"Are these for Monday night?"

The other disdained reply. McTeague retreated again timidly, thrusting the tickets into his immense wallet. For a moment he stood thoughtful on the steps of the entrance. Then all at once he became enraged, he did not know exactly why; somehow he felt himself slighted. Once more he came back to the wicket.

"You can't make small of me," he shouted over the girls' shoulders; "you—you can't make small of me. I'll thump you in the head, you little—you little—you little—little—little pup." The ticket seller shrugged his shoulders wearily. "A dollar and a half," he said to the two girls.

McTeague glared at him and breathed loudly. Finally he decided to let the matter drop. He moved away, but on the

steps was once more seized with a sense of injury and outraged dignity.

"You can't make small of me," he called back a last time,
wagging his head and shaking his fist. "I will—I will—I
will—yes, I will." He went off muttering.

At last Monday night came. McTeague met the Sieppes at
the ferry, dressed in a black Prince Albert coat and his best
slate-blue trousers, and wearing the made-up lawn necktie
that Marcus had selected for him. Trina was very pretty in the
black dress that McTeague knew so well. She wore a pair of
new gloves. Mrs. Sieppe had on lisle-thread mits, and carried
two bananas and an orange in a net reticule. "For Owgooste," she confided to him. Owgooste was in a Fauntleroy
"costume" very much too small for him. Already he had been
crying.

"Woult you pelief, Doktor, dot bube has torn his stockun
alreatty? Walk in der front, you; stop cryun. Where is dot
berliceman?"

At the door of the theatre McTeague was suddenly seized
with a panic terror. He had lost the tickets. He tore through
his pockets, ransacked his wallet. They were nowhere to be
found. All at once he remembered, and with a gasp of relief
removed his hat and took them out from beneath the sweat-
band.

The party entered and took their places. It was absurdly
early. The lights were all darkened, the ushers stood under
the galleries in groups, the empty auditorium echoing with
their noisy talk. Occasionally a waiter with his tray and clean
white apron sauntered up and down the aisle. Directly in
front of them was the great iron curtain of the stage, painted
with all manner of advertisements. From behind this came a
noise of hammering and of occasional loud voices.

While waiting they studied their programmes. First was an
overture by the orchestra, after which came "The Gleasons,
in their mirth-moving musical farce, entitled 'McMonnigal's
Courtship.'" This was to be followed by "The Lamont Sisters, Winnie and Violet, serio-comiques and skirt dancers."
And after this came a great array of other "artists" and "specialty performers," musical wonders, acrobats, lightning artists, ventriloquists, and last of all, "The feature of the evening,

the crowning scientific achievement of the nineteenth century, the kinetoscope." McTeague was excited, dazzled. In five years he had not been twice to the theatre. Now he beheld himself inviting his "girl" and her mother to accompany him. He began to feel that he was a man of the world. He ordered a cigar.

Meanwhile the house was filling up. A few side brackets were turned on. The ushers ran up and down the aisles, stubs of tickets between their thumb and finger, and from every part of the auditorium could be heard the sharp clap-clapping of the seats as the ushers flipped them down. A buzz of talk arose. In the gallery a street gamin whistled shrilly, and called to some friends on the other side of the house.

"Are they go-wun to begin pretty soon, ma?" whined Owgooste for the fifth or sixth time; adding, "Say, ma, can't I have some candy?" A cadaverous little boy had appeared in their aisle, chanting, "Candies, French mixed candies, popcorn, peanuts and candy." The orchestra entered, each man crawling out from an opening under the stage, hardly larger than the gate of a rabbit hutch. At every instant now the crowd increased; there were but few seats that were not taken. The waiters hurried up and down the aisles, their trays laden with beer glasses. A smell of cigar-smoke filled the air, and soon a faint blue haze rose from all corners of the house.

"Ma, when are they go-wun to begin?" cried Owgooste. As he spoke the iron advertisement curtain rose, disclosing the curtain proper underneath. This latter curtain was quite an affair. Upon it was painted a wonderful picture. A flight of marble steps led down to a stream of water; two white swans, their necks arched like the capital letter S, floated about. At the head of the marble steps were two vases filled with red and yellow flowers, while at the foot was moored a gondola. This gondola was full of red velvet rugs that hung over the side and trailed in the water. In the prow of the gondola a young man in vermilion tights held a mandolin in his left hand, and gave his right to a girl in white satin. A King Charles spaniel, dragging a leading-string in the shape of a huge pink sash, followed the girl. Seven scarlet roses were scattered upon the two lowest steps, and eight floated in the water.

"Ain't that pretty, Mac?" exclaimed Trina, turning to the dentist.

"Ma, ain't they go-wun to begin now-wow?" whined Owgooste. Suddenly the lights all over the house blazed up. "Ah!" said everybody all at once.

"Ain't ut crowdut?" murmured Mrs. Sieppe. Every seat was taken; many were even standing up.

"I always like it better when there is a crowd," said Trina. She was in great spirits that evening. Her round, pale face was positively pink.

The orchestra banged away at the overture, suddenly finishing with a great flourish of violins. A short pause followed. Then the orchestra played a quick-step strain, and the curtain rose on an interior furnished with two red chairs and a green sofa. A girl in a short blue dress and black stockings entered in a hurry and began to dust the two chairs. She was in a great temper, talking very fast, disclaiming against the "new lodger." It appeared that this latter never paid his rent; that he was given to late hours. Then she came down to the foot-lights and began to sing in a tremendous voice, hoarse and flat, almost like a man's. The chorus, of a feeble originality, ran:

> "Oh, how happy I will be,
> When my darling's face I'll see;
> Oh, tell him for to meet me in the moonlight,
> Down where the golden lilies bloom."

The orchestra played the tune of this chorus a second time, with certain variations, while the girl danced to it. She sidled to one side of the stage and kicked, then sidled to the other and kicked again. As she finished with the song, a man, evidently the lodger in question, came in. Instantly McTeague exploded in a roar of laughter. The man was intoxicated, his hat was knocked in, one end of his collar was unfastened and stuck up into his face, his watch-chain dangled from his pocket, and a yellow satin slipper was tied to a button-hole of his vest; his nose was vermilion, one eye was black and blue. After a short dialogue with the girl, a third actor appeared. He was dressed like a little boy, the girl's younger brother. He wore an immense turned-down collar, and was

continually doing hand-springs and wonderful back somersaults. The "act" devolved upon these three people; the
lodger making love to the girl in the short blue dress, the boy
playing all manner of tricks upon him, giving him tremendous digs in the ribs or slaps upon the back that made him
cough, pulling chairs from under him, running on all fours
between his legs and upsetting him, knocking him over at
inopportune moments. Every one of his falls was accentuated
by a bang upon the bass drum. The whole humor of the
"act" seemed to consist in the tripping up of the intoxicated
lodger.

This horse-play delighted McTeague beyond measure. He
roared and shouted every time the lodger went down, slapping his knee, wagging his head. Owgooste crowed shrilly,
clapping his hands and continually asking, "What did he say,
ma? What did he say?" Mrs. Sieppe laughed immoderately,
her huge fat body shaking like a mountain of jelly. She exclaimed from time to time, "Ach, Gott, dot fool!" Even Trina
was moved, laughing demurely, her lips closed, putting one
hand with its new glove to her mouth.

The performance went on. Now it was the "musical mar-
vels," two men extravagantly made up as negro minstrels,
with immense shoes and plaid vests. They seemed to be able
to wrestle a tune out of almost anything—glass bottles, cigar-
box fiddles, strings of sleigh-bells, even graduated brass tubes,
which they rubbed with resined fingers. McTeague was stupefied with admiration.

"That's what you call musicians," he announced gravely.
"Home, Sweet Home," played upon a trombone. Think of
that! Art could go no farther.

The acrobats left him breathless. They were dazzling young
men with beautifully parted hair, continually making graceful
gestures to the audience. In one of them the dentist fancied
he saw a strong resemblance to the boy who had tormented
the intoxicated lodger and who had turned such marvellous
somersaults. Trina could not bear to watch their antics. She
turned away her head with a little shudder. "It always makes
me sick," she explained.

The beautiful young lady, "The Society Contralto," in evening dress, who sang the sentimental songs, and carried the

sheets of music at which she never looked, pleased McTeague less. Trina, however, was captivated. She grew pensive over

> "You do not love me—no;
> Bid me good-by and go;"

and split her new gloves in her enthusiasm when it was finished.

"Don't you love sad music, Mac?" she murmured.

Then came the two comedians. They talked with fearful rapidity; their wit and repartee seemed inexhaustible.

"As *I* was going down the street yesterday——"

"Ah! as *you* were going down the street—all right."

"*I* saw a girl at a window——"

"*You* saw a girl at a window."

"And this girl she was a corker——"

"Ah! as *you* were going down the street yesterday *you* saw a girl at a window, and this girl she was a corker. All right, go on."

The other comedian went on. The joke was suddenly evolved. A certain phrase led to a song, which was sung with lightning rapidity, each performer making precisely the same gestures at precisely the same instant. They were irresistible. McTeague, though he caught but a third of the jokes, could have listened all night.

After the comedians had gone out, the iron advertisement curtain was let down.

"What comes now?" said McTeague, bewildered.

"It's the intermission of fifteen minutes now."

The musicians disappeared through the rabbit hutch, and the audience stirred and stretched itself. Most of the young men left their seats.

During this intermission McTeague and his party had "refreshments." Mrs. Sieppe and Trina had Queen Charlottes, McTeague drank a glass of beer, Owgooste ate the orange and one of the bananas. He begged for a glass of lemonade, which was finally given him.

"Joost to geep um quiet," observed Mrs. Sieppe.

But almost immediately after drinking his lemonade Owgooste was seized with a sudden restlessness. He twisted and wriggled in his seat, swinging his legs violently, looking about him with eyes full of a vague distress. At length, just as the musicians were returning, he stood up and whispered energetically in his mother's ear. Mrs. Sieppe was exasperated at once.

"No, no," she cried, reseating him brusquely.

The performance was resumed. A lightning artist appeared, drawing caricatures and portraits with incredible swiftness. He even went so far as to ask for subjects from the audience, and the names of prominent men were shouted to him from the gallery. He drew portraits of the President, of Grant, of Washington, of Napoleon Bonaparte, of Bismarck, of Garibaldi, of P. T. Barnum.

And so the evening passed. The hall grew very hot, and the smoke of innumerable cigars made the eyes smart. A thick blue mist hung low over the heads of the audience. The air was full of varied smells—the smell of stale cigars, of flat beer, of orange peel, of gas, of sachet powders, and of cheap perfumery.

One "artist" after another came upon the stage. McTeague's attention never wandered for a minute. Trina and her mother enjoyed themselves hugely. At every moment they made comments to one another, their eyes never leaving the stage.

"Ain't dot fool joost too funny?"

"That's a pretty song. Don't you like that kind of a song?"

"Wonderful! It's wonderful! Yes, yes, wonderful! That's the word."

Owgooste, however, lost interest. He stood up in his place, his back to the stage, chewing a piece of orange peel and watching a little girl in her father's lap across the aisle, his eyes fixed in a glassy, ox-like stare. But he was uneasy. He danced from one foot to the other, and at intervals appealed in hoarse whispers to his mother, who disdained an answer.

"Ma, say, ma-ah," he whined, abstractedly chewing his orange peel, staring at the little girl.

"Ma-ah, say, ma." At times his monotonous plaint reached his mother's consciousness. She suddenly realized what this was that was annoying her.

"Owgooste, will you sit down?" She caught him up all at

once, and jammed him down into his place. "Be quiet, den; loog; listun at der yunge girls."

Three young women and a young man who played a zither occupied the stage. They were dressed in Tyrolese costume; they were yodlers, and sang in German about "mountain tops" and "bold hunters" and the like. The yodling chorus was a marvel of flute-like modulations. The girls were really pretty, and were not made up in the least. Their "turn" had a great success. Mrs. Sieppe was entranced. Instantly she remembered her girlhood and her native Swiss village.

"Ach, dot is heavunly; joost like der old country. Mein gran'mutter used to be one of der mos' famous yodlers. When I was leedle, I haf seen dem joost like dat."

"Ma-ah," began Owgooste fretfully, as soon as the yodlers had departed. He could not keep still an instant; he twisted from side to side, swinging his legs with incredible swiftness.

"Ma-ah, I want to go ho-ome."

"Pehave!" exclaimed his mother, shaking him by the arm; "loog, der leedle girl is watchun you. Dis is der last dime I take you to der blay, you see."

"I don't ca-are; I'm sleepy." At length, to their great relief, he went to sleep, his head against his mother's arm.

The kinetoscope fairly took their breaths away.

"What will they do next?" observed Trina, in amazement. "Ain't that wonderful, Mac?"

McTeague was awe-struck.

"Look at that horse move his head," he cried excitedly, quite carried away. "Look at that cable-car coming—and the man going across the street. See, here comes a truck. Well, I never in all my life! What would Marcus say to this?"

"It's all a drick!" exclaimed Mrs. Sieppe, with sudden conviction. "I ain't no fool; dot's nothun but a drick."

"Well, of course, mamma," exclaimed Trina, "it's——"

But Mrs. Sieppe put her head in the air.

"I'm too old to be fooled," she persisted. "It's a drick." Nothing more could be got out of her than this.

The party stayed to the very end of the show, though the kinetoscope was the last number but one on the programme, and fully half the audience left immediately afterward. How-

ever, while the unfortunate Irish comedian went through his
"act" to the backs of the departing people, Mrs. Sieppe woke
Owgooste, very cross and sleepy, and began getting her
"things together." As soon as he was awake Owgooste began
fidgeting again.

"Save der brogramme, Trina," whispered Mrs. Sieppe.
"Take ut home to popper. Where is der hat of Owgooste?
Haf you got mein handkerchief, Trina?"

But at this moment a dreadful accident happened to
Owgooste; his distress reached its climax; his fortitude collapsed. What a misery! It was a veritable catastrophe, deplorable, lamentable, a thing beyond words! For a moment he
gazed wildly about him, helpless and petrified with astonishment and terror. Then his grief found utterance, and the closing strains of the orchestra were mingled with a prolonged
wail of infinite sadness.

"Owgooste, what is ut?" cried his mother, eyeing him with
dawning suspicion; then suddenly, "What haf you done? You
haf ruin your new Vauntleroy gostume!" Her face blazed;
without more ado she smacked him soundly. Then it was that
Owgooste touched the limit of his misery, his unhappiness,
his horrible discomfort; his utter wretchedness was complete.
He filled the air with his doleful outcries. The more he was
smacked and shaken, the louder he wept.

"What—what is the matter?" inquired McTeague.

Trina's face was scarlet. "Nothing, nothing," she exclaimed
hastily, looking away. "Come, we must be going. It's about
over." The end of the show and the breaking up of the audience tided over the embarrassment of the moment.

The party filed out at the tail end of the audience. Already
the lights were being extinguished and the ushers spreading
druggeting over the upholstered seats.

McTeague and the Sieppes took an uptown car that would
bring them near Polk Street. The car was crowded; McTeague
and Owgooste were obliged to stand. The little boy fretted to
be taken in his mother's lap, but Mrs. Sieppe emphatically
refused.

On their way home they discussed the performance.

"I—I like best der yodlers."

"Ah, the soloist was the best—the lady who sang those sad songs."

"Wasn't—wasn't that magic lantern wonderful, where the figures moved? Wonderful—ah, wonderful! And wasn't that first act funny, where the fellow fell down all the time? And that musical act, and the fellow with the burnt-cork face who played 'Nearer, My God to Thee' on the beer bottles."

They got off at Polk Street and walked up a block to the flat. The street was dark and empty; opposite the flat, in the back of the deserted market, the ducks and geese were calling persistently.

As they were buying their *tamales* from the half-breed Mexican at the street corner, McTeague observed:

"Marcus ain't gone to bed yet. See, there's a light in his window. There!" he exclaimed at once, "I forgot the door-key. Well, Marcus can let us in."

Hardly had he rung the bell at the street door of the flat when the bolt was shot back. In the hall at the top of the long, narrow staircase there was the sound of a great scurrying. Maria Macapa stood there, her hand upon the rope that drew the bolt; Marcus was at her side; Old Grannis was in the background, looking over their shoulders; while little Miss Baker leant over the banisters, a strange man in a drab overcoat at her side. As McTeague's party stepped into the doorway a half-dozen voices cried:

"Yes, it's them."

"Is that you, Mac?"

"Is that you, Miss Sieppe?"

"Is your name Trina Sieppe?"

Then, shriller than all the rest, Maria Macapa screamed:

"Oh, Miss Sieppe, come up here quick. Your lottery ticket has won five thousand dollars!"

VII

"HAT NONSENSE!" answered Trina.

"Ach Gott! What *is* ut?" cried Mrs. Sieppe, misunderstanding, supposing a calamity.

"What—what—what," stammered the dentist, confused by the lights, the crowded stairway, the medley of voices. The party reached the landing. The others surrounded them. Marcus alone seemed to rise to the occasion.

"Le' me be the first to congratulate you," he cried, catching Trina's hand. Every one was talking at once.

"Miss Sieppe, Miss Sieppe, your ticket has won five thousand dollars," cried Maria. "Don't you remember the lottery ticket I sold you in Doctor McTeague's office?"

"Trina!" almost screamed her mother. "Five tausend thalers! five tausend thalers! If popper were only here!"

"What is it—what is it?" exclaimed McTeague, rolling his eyes.

"What are you going to do with it, Trina?" inquired Marcus.

"You're a rich woman, my dear," said Miss Baker, her little false curls quivering with excitement, "and I'm glad for your sake. Let me kiss you. To think I was in the room when you bought the ticket!"

"Oh, oh!" interrupted Trina, shaking her head, "there is a mistake. There must be. Why—why should I win five thousand dollars? It's nonsense!"

"No mistake, no mistake," screamed Maria. "Your number was 400,012. Here it is in the paper this evening. I remember it well, because I keep an account."

"But I know you're wrong," answered Trina, beginning to tremble in spite of herself. "Why should I win?"

"Eh? Why shouldn't you?" cried her mother.

In fact, why shouldn't she? The idea suddenly occurred to Trina. After all, it was not a question of effort or merit on her part. Why should she suppose a mistake? What if it were true, this wonderful fillip of fortune striking in there like some chance-driven bolt?

"Oh, do you think so?" she gasped.

The stranger in the drab overcoat came forward.

"It's the agent," cried two or three voices, simultaneously.

"I guess you're one of the lucky ones, Miss Sieppe," he said. "I suppose you have kept your ticket."

"Yes, yes; four three oughts twelve—I remember."

"That's right," admitted the other. "Present your ticket at the local branch office as soon as possible—the address is printed on the back of the ticket—and you'll receive a check on our bank for five thousand dollars. Your number will have to be verified on our official list, but there's hardly a chance of a mistake. I congratulate you."

All at once a great thrill of gladness surged up in Trina. She was to possess five thousand dollars. She was carried away with the joy of her good fortune, a natural, spontaneous joy—the gaiety of a child with a new and wonderful toy.

"Oh, I've won, I've won, I've won!" she cried, clapping her hands. "Mamma, think of it. I've won five thousand dollars, just by buying a ticket. Mac, what do you say to that? I've got five thousand dollars. August, do you hear what's happened to sister?"

"Kiss your mommer, Trina," suddenly commanded Mrs. Sieppe. "What efer will you do mit all dose money, eh, Trina?"

"Huh!" exclaimed Marcus. "Get married on it for one thing." Thereat they all shouted with laughter. McTeague grinned, and looked about sheepishly. "Talk about luck," muttered Marcus, shaking his head at the dentist; then suddenly he added:

"Well, are we going to stay talking out here in the hall all night? Can't we all come into your 'Parlors,' Mac?"

"Sure, sure," exclaimed McTeague, hastily unlocking his door.

"Efery botty gome," cried Mrs. Sieppe, genially. "Ain't ut so, Doktor?"

"Everybody," repeated the dentist. "There's—there's some beer."

"We'll celebrate, by damn!" exclaimed Marcus. "It ain't every day you win five thousand dollars. It's only Sundays and legal holidays." Again he set the company off into a gale of laughter. Anything was funny at a time like this. In some way every one of them felt elated. The wheel of fortune had come spinning close to them. They were near to this great sum of money. It was as though they too had won.

"Here's right where I sat when I bought that ticket," cried Trina, after they had come into the "Parlors," and Marcus had lit the gas. "Right here in this chair." She sat down in one of the rigid chairs under the steel engraving. "And, Marcus, you sat here——"

"And I was just getting out of the operating chair," interposed Miss Baker.

"Yes, yes. That's so; and you," continued Trina, pointing to Maria, "came up and said, 'Buy a ticket in the lottery; just a dollar.' Oh, I remember it just as plain as though it was yesterday, and I wasn't going to at first——"

"And don't you know I told Maria it was against the law?"

"Yes, I remember, and then I gave her a dollar and put the ticket in my pocketbook. It's in my pocketbook now at home in the top drawer of my bureau—oh, suppose it should be stolen now," she suddenly exclaimed.

"It's worth big money now," asserted Marcus.

"Five thousand dollars. Who would have thought it? It's wonderful." Everybody started and turned. It was McTeague. He stood in the middle of the floor, wagging his huge head. He seemed to have just realized what had happened.

"Yes, sir, five thousand dollars!" exclaimed Marcus, with a sudden unaccountable mirthlessness. "Five thousand dollars! Do you get on to that? Cousin Trina and you will be rich people."

"At six per cent, that's twenty-five dollars a month," hazarded the agent.

"Think of it. Think of it," muttered McTeague. He went aimlessly about the room, his eyes wide, his enormous hands dangling.

"A cousin of mine won forty dollars once," observed Miss Baker. "But he spent every cent of it buying more tickets, and never won anything."

Then the reminiscences began. Maria told about the butcher on the next block who had won twenty dollars the last drawing. Mrs. Sieppe knew a gas-fitter in Oakland who had won several times; once a hundred dollars. Little Miss

Baker announced that she had always believed that lotteries were wrong; but, just the same, five thousand was five thousand.

"It's all right when you win, ain't it, Miss Baker?" observed Marcus, with a certain sarcasm. What was the matter with Marcus? At moments he seemed singularly out of temper.

But the agent was full of stories. He told his experiences, the legends and myths that had grown up around the history of the lottery; he told of the poor newsboy with a dying mother to support who had drawn a prize of fifteen thousand; of the man who was driven to suicide through want, but who held (had he but known it) the number that two days after his death drew the capital prize of thirty thousand dollars; of the little milliner who for ten years had played the lottery without success, and who had one day declared that she would buy but one more ticket and then give up trying, and of how this last ticket had brought her a fortune upon which she could retire; of tickets that had been lost or destroyed, and whose numbers had won fabulous sums at the drawing; of criminals, driven to vice by poverty, and who had reformed after winning competencies; of gamblers who played the lottery as they would play a faro bank, turning in their winnings again as soon as made, buying thousands of tickets all over the country; of superstitions as to terminal and initial numbers, and as to lucky days of purchase; of marvellous coincidences—three capital prizes drawn consecutively by the same town; a ticket bought by a millionaire and given to his bootblack, who won a thousand dollars upon it; the same number winning the same amount an indefinite number of times; and so on to infinity. Invariably it was the needy who won, the destitute and starving woke to wealth and plenty, the virtuous toiler suddenly found his reward in a ticket bought at a hazard; the lottery was a great charity, the friend of the people, a vast beneficent machine that recognized neither rank nor wealth nor station.

The company began to be very gay. Chairs and tables were brought in from the adjoining rooms, and Maria was sent out for more beer and tamales, and also commissioned to buy a bottle of wine and some cake for Miss Baker, who abhorred beer.

The "Dental Parlors" were in great confusion. Empty beer bottles stood on the movable rack where the instruments were kept; plates and napkins were upon the seat of the operating chair and upon the stand of shelves in the corner, side by side with the concertina and the volumes of "Allen's Practical Dentist." The canary woke and chittered crossly, his feathers puffed out; the husks of tamales littered the floor; the stone pug dog sitting before the little stove stared at the unusual scene, his glass eyes starting from their sockets.

They drank and feasted in impromptu fashion. Marcus Schouler assumed the office of master of ceremonies; he was in a lather of excitement, rushing about here and there, opening beer bottles, serving the tamales, slapping McTeague upon the back, laughing and joking continually. He made McTeague sit at the head of the table, with Trina at his right and the agent at his left; he—when he sat down at all— occupied the foot, Maria Macapa at his left, while next to her was Mrs. Sieppe, opposite Miss Baker. Owgooste had been put to bed upon the bed-lounge.

"Where's Old Grannis?" suddenly exclaimed Marcus. Sure enough, where had the old Englishman gone? He had been there at first.

"I called him down with everybody else," cried Maria Macapa, "as soon as I saw in the paper that Miss Sieppe had won. We all came down to Mr. Schouler's room and waited for you to come home. I think he must have gone back to his room. I'll bet you'll find him sewing up his books."

"No, no," observed Miss Baker, "not at this hour."

Evidently the timid old gentleman had taken advantage of the confusion to slip unobtrusively away.

"I'll go bring him down," shouted Marcus; "he's got to join us."

Miss Baker was in great agitation.

"I—I hardly think you'd better," she murmured; "he— he—I don't think he drinks beer."

"He takes his amusement in sewin' up books," cried Maria.

Marcus brought him down, nevertheless, having found him just preparing for bed.

"I—I must apologize," stammered Old Grannis, as he stood in the doorway. "I had not quite expected—I—find—

find myself a little unprepared." He was without collar and cravat, owing to Marcus Schouler's precipitate haste. He was annoyed beyond words that Miss Baker saw him thus. Could anything be more embarrassing?

Old Grannis was introduced to Mrs. Sieppe and to Trina as Marcus's employer. They shook hands solemnly.

"I don't believe that he an' Miss Baker have ever been introduced," cried Maria Macapa, shrilly, "an' they've been livin' side by side for years."

The two old people were speechless, avoiding each other's gaze. It had come at last; they were to know each other, to talk together, to touch each other's hands.

Marcus brought Old Grannis around the table to little Miss Baker, dragging him by the coat sleeve, exclaiming: "Well, I thought you two people knew each other long ago. Miss Baker, this is Mr. Grannis; Mr. Grannis, this is Miss Baker." Neither spoke. Like two little children they faced each other, awkward, constrained, tongue-tied with embarrassment. Then Miss Baker put out her hand shyly. Old Grannis touched it for an instant and let it fall.

"Now you know each other," cried Marcus, "and it's about time." For the first time their eyes met; Old Grannis trembled a little, putting his hand uncertainly to his chin. Miss Baker flushed ever so slightly, but Maria Macapa passed suddenly between them, carrying a half empty beer bottle. The two old people fell back from one another, Miss Baker resuming her seat.

"Here's a place for you over here, Mr. Grannis," cried Marcus, making room for him at his side. Old Grannis slipped into the chair, withdrawing at once from the company's notice. He stared fixedly at his plate and did not speak again. Old Miss Baker began to talk volubly across the table to Mrs. Sieppe about hot-house flowers and medicated flannels.

It was in the midst of this little impromptu supper that the engagement of Trina and the dentist was announced. In a pause in the chatter of conversation Mrs. Sieppe leaned forward and, speaking to the agent, said:

"Vell, you know also my daughter Trina get married bretty soon. She and der dentist, Doktor McTeague, eh, yes?"

There was a general exclamation.

"I thought so all along," cried Miss Baker, excitedly. "The first time I saw them together I said, 'What a pair!'"

"Delightful!" exclaimed the agent, "to be married and win a snug little fortune at the same time."

"So—So," murmured Old Grannis, nodding at his plate.

"Good luck to you," cried Maria.

"He's lucky enough already," growled Marcus under his breath, relapsing for a moment into one of those strange moods of sullenness which had marked him throughout the evening.

Trina flushed crimson, drawing shyly nearer her mother. McTeague grinned from ear to ear, looking around from one to another, exclaiming "Huh! Huh!"

But the agent rose to his feet, a newly filled beer glass in his hand. He was a man of the world, this agent. He knew life. He was suave and easy. A diamond was on his little finger.

"Ladies and gentlemen," he began. There was an instant silence. "This is indeed a happy occasion. I—I am glad to be here to-night; to be a witness to such good fortune; to partake in these—in this celebration. Why, I feel almost as glad as if I had held four three oughts twelve myself; as if the five thousand were mine instead of belonging to our charming hostess. The good wishes of my humble self go out to Miss Sieppe in this moment of her good fortune, and I think—in fact, I am sure I can speak for the great institution, the great company I represent. The company congratulates Miss Sieppe. We—they—ah— They wish her every happiness her new fortune can procure her. It has been my duty, my—ah— cheerful duty to call upon the winners of large prizes and to offer the felicitation of the company. I have, in my experience, called upon many such; but never have I seen fortune so happily bestowed as in this case. The company have dowered the prospective bride. I am sure I but echo the sentiments of this assembly when I wish all joy and happiness to this happy pair, happy in the possession of a snug little fortune, and happy— happy in—" he finished with a sudden inspiration—"in the possession of each other; I drink to the health, wealth, and happiness of the future bride and groom. Let us drink standing up." They drank with enthusiasm. Marcus was carried away with the excitement of the moment.

"Outa sight, outa sight," he vociferated, clapping his hands. "Very well said. To the health of the bride. McTeague, McTeague, speech, speech!"

In an instant the whole table was clamoring for the dentist to speak. McTeague was terrified; he gripped the table with both hands, looking wildly about him.

"Speech, speech!" shouted Marcus, running around the table and endeavoring to drag McTeague up.

"No—no—no," muttered the other. "No speech." The company rattled upon the table with their beer glasses, insisting upon a speech. McTeague settled obstinately into his chair, very red in the face, shaking his head energetically.

"Ah, go on!" he exclaimed; "no speech."

"Ah, get up and say somethun, anyhow," persisted Marcus; "you ought to do it. It's the proper caper."

McTeague heaved himself up; there was a burst of applause; he looked slowly about him, then suddenly sat down again, shaking his head hopelessly.

"Oh, go on, Mac," cried Trina.

"Get up, say somethun, anyhow," cried Marcus, tugging at his arm; "you *got* to."

Once more McTeague rose to his feet.

"Huh!" he exclaimed, looking steadily at the table. Then he began:

"I don' know what to say—I—I—I ain't never made a speech before; I—I ain't never made a speech before. But I'm glad Trina's won the prize——"

"Yes, I'll bet you are," muttered Marcus.

"I—I—I'm glad Trina's won, and I—I want to—I want to—I want to—want to say that—you're—all—welcome, an' drink hearty, an' I'm much obliged to the agent. Trina and I are goin' to be married, an' I'm glad everybody's here to-night, an' you're—all—welcome, an' drink hearty, an' I hope you'll come again, an' you're always welcome—an'—I—an'—an'— That's—about—all—I—gotta say." He sat down, wiping his forehead, amidst tremendous applause.

Soon after that the company pushed back from the table and relaxed into couples and groups. The men, with the exception of Old Grannis, began to smoke, the smell of their tobacco mingling with the odors of ether, creosote, and stale bedding, which pervaded the "Parlors." Soon the windows had to be lowered from the top. Mrs. Sieppe and old Miss Baker sat together in the bay window exchanging confidences. Miss Baker had turned back the overskirt of her dress; a plate of cake was in her lap; from time to time she sipped her wine with the delicacy of a white cat. The two women were much interested in each other. Miss Baker told Mrs. Sieppe all about Old Grannis, not forgetting the fiction of the title and the unjust stepfather.

"He's quite a personage really," said Miss Baker.

Mrs. Sieppe led the conversation around to her children. "Ach, Trina is sudge a goote girl," she said; "always gay, yes, und sing from morgen to night. Und Owgooste, he is soh smart also, yes, eh? He has der genius for machines, always making somethun mit wheels and sbrings."

"Ah, if—if—I had children," murmured the little old maid a trifle wistfully, "one would have been a sailor; he would have begun as a midshipman on my brother's ship; in time he would have been an officer. The other would have been a landscape gardener."

"Oh, Mac!" exclaimed Trina, looking up into the dentist's face, "think of all this money coming to us just at this very moment. Isn't it wonderful? Don't it kind of scare you?"

"Wonderful, wonderful!" muttered McTeague, shaking his head. "Let's buy a lot of tickets," he added, struck with an idea.

"Now, that's how you can always tell a good cigar," observed the agent to Marcus as the two sat smoking at the end of the table. "The light end should be rolled to a point."

"Ah, the Chinese cigar-makers," cried Marcus, in a passion, brandishing his fist. "It's them as is ruining the cause of white labor. They are, they are for a *fact*. Ah, the rat-eaters! Ah, the white-livered curs!"

Over in the corner, by the stand of shelves, Old Grannis was listening to Maria Macapa. The Mexican woman had been violently stirred over Trina's sudden wealth; Maria's mind had gone back to her younger days. She leaned forward, her elbows on her knees, her chin in her hands, her eyes wide and fixed. Old Grannis listened to her attentively.

"There wa'n't a piece that was so much as scratched," Maria

was saying. "Every piece was just like a mirror, smooth and bright; oh, bright as a little sun. Such a service as that was— platters and soup tureens and an immense big punch-bowl. Five thousand dollars, what does that amount to? Why, that punch-bowl alone was worth a fortune."

"What a wonderful story!" exclaimed Old Grannis, never for an instant doubting its truth. "And it's all lost now, you say?"

"Lost, lost," repeated Maria.

"Tut, tut! What a pity! What a pity!"

Suddenly the agent rose and broke out with:

"Well, *I* must be going, if I'm to get any car."

He shook hands with everybody, offered a parting cigar to Marcus, congratulated McTeague and Trina a last time, and bowed himself out.

"What an elegant gentleman," commented Miss Baker.

"Ah," said Marcus, nodding his head, "there's a man of the world for you. Right on to himself, by damn!"

The company broke up.

"Come along, Mac," cried Marcus; " we're to sleep with the dogs to-night, you know."

The two friends said "Good-night" all around and departed for the little dog hospital.

Old Grannis hurried to his room furtively, terrified lest he should again be brought face to face with Miss Baker. He bolted himself in and listened until he heard her foot in the hall and the soft closing of her door. She was there close beside him; as one might say, in the same room; for he, too, had made the discovery as to the similarity of the wall-paper. At long intervals he could hear a faint rustling as she moved about. What an evening that had been for him! He had met her, had spoken to her, had touched her hand; he was in a tremor of excitement. In a like manner the little old dress-maker listened and quivered. *He* was there in that same room which they shared in common, separated only by the thinnest board partition. He was thinking of her, she was almost sure of it. They were strangers no longer; they were acquaintances, friends. What an event that evening had been in their lives!

Late as it was, Miss Baker brewed a cup of tea and sat

down in her rocking chair close to the partition; she rocked gently, sipping her tea, calming herself after the emotions of that wonderful evening.

Old Grannis heard the clinking of the tea things and smelt the faint odor of the tea. It seemed to him a signal, an invitation. He drew his chair close to his side of the partition, before his work-table. A pile of half-bound "Nations" was in the little binding apparatus; he threaded his huge upholsterer's needle with stout twine and set to work.

It was their *tête-à-tête*. Instinctively they felt each other's presence, felt each other's thought coming to them through the thin partition. It was charming; they were perfectly happy. There in the stillness that settled over the flat in the half hour after midnight the two old people "kept company," enjoying after their fashion their little romance that had come so late into the lives of each.

On the way to her room in the garret Maria Macapa paused under the single gas-jet that burned at the top of the well of the staircase; she assured herself that she was alone, and then drew from her pocket one of McTeague's "tapes" of non-cohesive gold. It was the most valuable steal she had ever yet made in the dentist's "Parlors." She told herself that it was worth at least a couple of dollars. Suddenly an idea occurred to her, and she went hastily to a window at the end of the hall, and, shading her face with both hands, looked down into the little alley just back of the flat. On some nights Zerkow, the red-headed Polish Jew, sat up late, taking account of the week's rag-picking. There was a dim light in his window now.

Maria went to her room, threw a shawl around her head, and descended into the little back yard of the flat by the back stairs. As she let herself out of the back gate into the alley, Alexander, Marcus's Irish setter, woke suddenly with a gruff bark. The collie who lived on the other side of the fence, in the back yard of the branch post-office, answered with a snarl. Then in an instant the endless feud between the two dogs was resumed. They dragged their respective kennels to the fence, and through the cracks raged at each other in a frenzy of hate; their teeth snapped and gleamed; the hackles on their backs rose and stiffened. Their hideous clamor could have been heard for blocks around. What a massacre should the two ever meet!

Meanwhile, Maria was knocking at Zerkow's miserable hovel.

"Who is it? Who is it?" cried the rag-picker from within, in his hoarse voice, that was half whisper, starting nervously, and sweeping a handful of silver into his drawer.

"It's me, Maria Macapa;" then in a lower voice, and as if speaking to herself, "had a flying squirrel an' let him go."

"Ah, Maria," cried Zerkow, obsequiously opening the door. "Come in, come in, my girl; you're always welcome, even as late as this. No junk, hey? But you're welcome for all that. You'll have a drink, won't you?" He led her into his back room and got down the whiskey bottle and the broken red tumbler.

After the two had drunk together Maria produced the gold "tape." Zerkow's eyes glittered on the instant. The sight of gold invariably sent a qualm all through him; try as he would, he could not repress it. His fingers trembled and clawed at his mouth; his breath grew short.

"Ah, ah, ah!" he exclaimed, "give it here, give it here; give it to me, Maria. That's a good girl, come give it to me."

They haggled as usual over the price, but to-night Maria was too excited over other matters to spend much time in bickering over a few cents.

"Look here, Zerkow," she said as soon as the transfer was made, "I got something to tell you. A little while ago I sold a lottery ticket to a girl at the flat; the drawing was in this evening's papers. How much do you suppose that girl has won?"

"I don't know. How much? How much?"

"Five thousand dollars."

It was as though a knife had been run through the Jew; a spasm of an almost physical pain twisted his face—his entire body. He raised his clenched fists into the air, his eyes shut, his teeth gnawing his lip.

"Five thousand dollars," he whispered; "five thousand dollars. For what? For nothing, for simply buying a ticket; and I have worked so hard for it, so hard, so hard. Five thousand dollars, five thousand dollars. Oh, why couldn't it have come to me?" he cried, his voice choking, the tears starting to his eyes; "why couldn't it have come to me? To come so close, so close, and yet to miss me—me who have worked for it, fought for it, starved for it, am dying for it every day. Think of it, Maria, five thousand dollars, all bright, heavy pieces——"

"Bright as a sunset," interrupted Maria, her chin propped on her hands. "Such a glory, and heavy. Yes, every piece was heavy, and it was all you could do to lift the punch-bowl. Why, that punch-bowl was worth a fortune alone——"

"And it rang when you hit it with your knuckles, didn't it?" prompted Zerkow, eagerly, his lips trembling, his fingers hooking themselves into claws.

"Sweeter'n any church bell," continued Maria.

"Go on, go on, go on," cried Zerkow, drawing his chair closer, and shutting his eyes in ecstasy.

"There were more than a hundred pieces, and every one of them gold——"

"Ah, every one of them gold."

"You should have seen the sight when the leather trunk was opened. There wa'n't a piece that was so much as scratched; every one was like a mirror, smooth and bright, polished so that it looked black—you know how I mean."

"Oh, I know, I know," cried Zerkow, moistening his lips.

Then he plied her with questions—questions that covered every detail of that service of plate. It was soft, wasn't it? You could bite into a plate and leave a dent? The handles of the knives, now, were they gold too? All the knife was made from one piece of gold, was it? And the forks the same? The interior of the trunk was quilted, of course? Did Maria ever polish the plates herself? When the company ate off this service, it must have made a fine noise—these gold knives and forks clinking together upon these gold plates.

"Now, let's have it all over again, Maria," pleaded Zerkow. "Begin now with 'There were more than a hundred pieces, and every one of them gold.' Go on, begin, begin, begin!"

The red-headed Pole was in a fever of excitement. Maria's recital had become a veritable mania with him. As he listened, with closed eyes and trembling lips, he fancied he could see that wonderful plate before him, there on the table, under his eyes, under his hand, ponderous, massive, gleaming. He tormented Maria into a second repetition of the story—into a third. The more his mind dwelt upon it, the sharper grew his desire. Then, with Maria's refusal to continue the tale, came the reaction. Zerkow awoke as from some ravishing dream. The plate was gone, was irretrievably lost. There was nothing in that miserable room but grimy rags and rust-corroded iron. What torment! what agony! to be so near—so near, to see it in one's distorted fancy as plain as in a mirror. To know every individual piece as an old friend; to feel its weight; to be dazzled by its glitter; to call it one's own, own; to have it to oneself, hugged to the breast; and then to start, to wake, to come down to the horrible reality.

"And you, *you* had it once," gasped Zerkow, clawing at her arm; "you had it once, all your own. Think of it, and now it's gone."

"Gone for good and all."

"Perhaps it's buried near your old place somewhere."

"It's gone—gone—gone," chanted Maria in a monotone.

Zerkow dug his nails into his scalp, tearing at his red hair. "Yes, yes, it's gone, it's gone—lost forever! Lost forever!"

Marcus and the dentist walked up the silent street and reached the little dog hospital. They had hardly spoken on the way. McTeague's brain was in a whirl; speech failed him. He was busy thinking of the great thing that had happened that night, and was trying to realize what its effect would be upon his life—his life and Trina's. As soon as they had found themselves in the street, Marcus had relapsed at once to a sullen silence, which McTeague was too abstracted to notice.

They entered the tiny office of the hospital with its red carpet, its gas stove, and its colored prints of famous dogs hanging against the walls. In one corner stood the iron bed which they were to occupy.

"You go on an' get to bed, Mac," observed Marcus. "I'll take a look at the dogs before I turn in."

He went outside and passed along into the yard, that was bounded on three sides by pens where the dogs were kept. A bull terrier dying of gastritis recognized him and began to whimper feebly.

Marcus paid no attention to the dogs. For the first time that evening he was alone and could give vent to his thoughts. He took a couple of turns up and down the yard, then suddenly in a low voice exclaimed:

"You fool, you fool, Marcus Schouler! If you'd kept Trina you'd have had that money. You might have had it yourself. You've thrown away your chance in life—to give up the girl, yes—but *this*," he stamped his foot with rage—"to throw five thousand dollars out of the window—to stuff it into the pockets of someone else, when it might have been yours, when you might have had Trina *and* the money—and all for what? Because we were pals. Oh, 'pals' is all right—but five thousand dollars—to have played it right into his hands— God *damn* the luck!"

VIII

THE NEXT two months were delightful. Trina and McTeague saw each other regularly, three times a week. The dentist went over to B Street Sunday and Wednesday afternoons as usual; but on Fridays it was Trina who came to the city. She spent the morning between nine and twelve o'clock down town, for the most part in the cheap department stores, doing the weekly shopping for herself and the family. At noon she took an uptown car and met McTeague at the corner of Polk Street. The two lunched together at a small uptown hotel just around the corner on Sutter Street. They were given a little room to themselves. Nothing could have been more delicious. They had but to close the sliding door to shut themselves off from the whole world.

Trina would arrive breathless from her raids upon the bargain counters, her pale cheeks flushed, her hair blown about her face and into the corners of her lips, her mother's net reticule stuffed to bursting. Once in their tiny private room, she would drop into her chair with a little groan.

"Oh, *Mac*, I am so tired; I've just been all *over* town. Oh, it's good to sit down. Just think, I had to stand up in the car all the way, after being on my feet the whole blessed morning. Look here what I've bought. Just things and things. Look, there's some dotted veiling I got for myself; see now, do you think it looks pretty?"—she spread it over her face— "and I got a box of writing paper, and a roll of crépe paper to make a lamp shade for the front parlor; and—what do you suppose—I saw a pair of Nottingham lace curtains for *forty-nine cents*; isn't that cheap? and some chenille portieres for two and a half. Now what have *you* been doing since I last saw you? Did Mr. Heise finally get up enough courage to have his tooth pulled yet?" Trina took off her hat and veil and rearranged her hair before the looking-glass.

"No, no—not yet. I went down to the sign painter's yesterday afternoon to see about that big gold tooth for a sign. It costs too much; I can't get it yet a while. There's two kinds, one German gilt and the other French gilt; but the German gilt is no good."

McTeague sighed, and wagged his head. Even Trina and the five thousand dollars could not make him forget this one unsatisfied longing.

At other times they would talk at length over their plans, while Trina sipped her chocolate and McTeague devoured huge chunks of butterless bread. They were to be married at the end of May, and the dentist already had his eye on a couple of rooms, part of the suite of a bankrupt photographer. They were situated in the flat, just back of his "Parlors," and he believed the photographer would sublet them furnished.

McTeague and Trina had no apprehensions as to their finances. They could be sure, in fact, of a tidy little income. The dentist's practice was fairly good, and they could count upon the interest of Trina's five thousand dollars. To McTeague's mind this interest seemed wofully small. He had had uncertain ideas about that five thousand dollars; had imagined that they would spend it in some lavish fashion; would buy a house, perhaps, or would furnish their new rooms with overwhelming luxury—luxury that implied red velvet carpets and continued feasting. The old-time miner's idea of wealth easily gained and quickly spent persisted in his mind. But when Trina had begun to talk of investments and interests and per cents, he was troubled and not a little disappointed. The lump sum of five thousand dollars was one thing, a miserable little twenty or twenty-five a month was quite another; and then someone else had the money.

"But don't you see, Mac," explained Trina, "it's ours just the same. We could get it back whenever we wanted it; and then it's the reasonable way to do. We mustn't let it turn our heads, Mac, dear, like that man that spent all he won in buying more tickets. How foolish we'd feel after we'd spent it all! We ought to go on just the same as before; as if we hadn't won. We must be sensible about it, mustn't we?"

"Well, well, I guess perhaps that's right," the dentist would answer, looking slowly about on the floor.

Just what should ultimately be done with the money was the subject of endless discussion in the Sieppe family. The savings bank would allow only three per cent., but Trina's parents believed that something better could be got.

"There's Uncle Oelbermann," Trina had suggested, remembering the rich relative who had the wholesale toy store in the Mission.

Mr. Sieppe struck his hand to his forehead. "Ah, an idea," he cried. In the end an agreement was made. The money was invested in Mr. Oelbermann's business. He gave Trina six per cent.

Invested in this fashion, Trina's winning would bring in twenty-five dollars a month. But, besides this, Trina had her own little trade. She made Noah's ark animals for Uncle Oelbermann's store. Trina's ancestors on both sides were German-Swiss, and some long-forgotten forefather of the sixteenth century, some worsted-leggined wood-carver of the Tyrol, had handed down the talent of the national industry, to reappear in this strangely distorted guise.

She made Noah's ark animals, whittling them out of a block of soft wood with a sharp jack-knife, the only instrument she used. Trina was very proud to explain her work to McTeague as he had already explained his own to her.

"You see, I take a block of straight-grained pine and cut out the shape, roughly at first, with the big blade; then I go over it a second time with the little blade, more carefully; then I put in the ears and tail with a drop of glue, and paint it with a 'non-poisonous' paint—Vandyke brown for the horses, foxes, and cows; slate gray for the elephants and camels; burnt umber for the chickens, zebras, and so on; then, last, a dot of Chinese white for the eyes, and there you are, all finished. They sell for nine cents a dozen. Only I can't make the manikins."

"The manikins?"

"The little figures, you know—Noah and his wife, and Shem, and all the others."

It was true. Trina could not whittle them fast enough and cheap enough to compete with the turning lathe, that could throw off whole tribes and peoples of manikins while she was fashioning one family. Everything else, however, she made— the ark itself, all windows and no door; the box in which the whole was packed; even down to pasting on the label, which read, "Made in France." She earned from three to four dollars a week.

The income from these three sources, McTeague's profession, the interest of the five thousand dollars, and Trina's whittling, made a respectable little sum taken altogether. Trina declared they could even lay by something, adding to the five thousand dollars little by little.

It soon became apparent that Trina would be an extraordinarily good housekeeper. Economy was her strong point. A good deal of peasant blood still ran undiluted in her veins, and she had all the instinct of a hardy and penurious mountain race—the instinct which saves without any thought, without idea of consequence—saving for the sake of saving, hoarding without knowing why. Even McTeague did not know how closely Trina held to her new-found wealth.

But they did not always pass their luncheon hour in this discussion of incomes and economies. As the dentist came to know his little woman better she grew to be more and more of a puzzle and a joy to him. She would suddenly interrupt a grave discourse upon the rents of rooms and the cost of light and fuel with a brusque outburst of affection that set him all a-tremble with delight. All at once she would set down her chocolate, and, leaning across the narrow table, would exclaim:

"Never mind all that! Oh, Mac, do you truly, really love me—love me *big*?"

McTeague would stammer something, gasping, and wagging his head, beside himself for the lack of words.

"Old bear," Trina would answer, grasping him by both huge ears and swaying his head from side to side. "Kiss me, then. Tell me, Mac, did you think any less of me that first time I let you kiss me there in the station? Oh, Mac, dear, what a funny nose you've got, all full of hairs inside; and, Mac, do you know you've got a bald spot—" she dragged his head down towards her—"right on the top of your head." Then she would seriously kiss the bald spot in question, declaring:

"That'll make the hair grow."

Trina took an infinite enjoyment in playing with McTeague's great square-cut head, rumpling his hair till it stood on end, putting her fingers in his eyes, or stretching his ears out straight, and watching the effect with her head on one side. It was like a little child playing with some gigantic, good-natured Saint Bernard.

One particular amusement they never wearied of. The two would lean across the table toward each other, McTeague folding his arms under his breast. Then Trina, resting on her elbows, would part his mustache—the great blond mustache of a viking—with her two hands, pushing it up from his lips, causing his face to assume the appearance of a Greek mask. She would curl it around either forefinger, drawing it to a fine end. Then all at once McTeague would make a fearful snorting noise through his nose. Invariably—though she was expecting this, though it was part of the game—Trina would jump with a stifled shriek. McTeague would bellow with laughter till his eyes watered. Then they would recommence upon the instant, Trina protesting with a nervous tremulousness:

"Now—now—now, Mac, *don't*; you *scare* me so."

But these delicious *tête-à-têtes* with Trina were offset by a certain coolness that Marcus Schouler began to affect towards the dentist. At first McTeague was unaware of it; but by this time even his slow wits began to perceive that his best friend—his "pal"—was not the same to him as formerly. They continued to meet at lunch nearly every day but Friday at the car conductors' coffee-joint. But Marcus was sulky; there could be no doubt about that. He avoided talking to McTeague, read the paper continually, answering the dentist's timid efforts at conversation in gruff monosyllables. Sometimes, even, he turned sideways to the table and talked at great length to Heise the harness-maker, whose table was next to theirs. They took no more long walks together when Marcus went out to exercise the dogs. Nor did Marcus ever again recur to his generosity in renouncing Trina.

One Tuesday, as McTeague took his place at the table in the coffee-joint, he found Marcus already there.

"Hello, Mark," said the dentist, "you here already?"

"Hello," returned the other, indifferently, helping himself to tomato catsup. There was a silence. After a long while Marcus suddenly looked up.

"Say, Mac," he exclaimed, "when you going to pay me that money you owe me?"

McTeague was astonished.

"Huh? What? I don't—do I owe you any money, Mark?"

"Well, you owe me four bits," returned Marcus, doggedly. "I paid for you and Trina that day at the picnic, and you never gave it back."

"Oh—oh!" answered McTeague, in distress. "That's so, that's so. I—you ought to have told me before. Here's your money, and I'm obliged to you."

"It ain't much," observed Marcus, sullenly. "But I need all I can get now-a-days."

"Are you—are you broke?" inquired McTeague.

"And I ain't saying anything about your sleeping at the hospital that night, either," muttered Marcus, as he pocketed the coin.

"Well—well—do you mean—should I have paid for that?"

"Well, you'd 'a' had to sleep *somewheres*, wouldn't you?" flashed out Marcus. "You 'a' had to pay half a dollar for a bed at the flat."

"All right, all right," cried the dentist, hastily, feeling in his pockets. "I don't want you should be out anything on my account, old man. Here, will four bits do?"

"I don't *want* your damn money," shouted Marcus in a sudden rage, throwing back the coin. "I ain't no beggar."

McTeague was miserable. How had he offended his pal?

"Well, I want you should take it, Mark," he said, pushing it towards him.

"I tell you I won't touch your money," exclaimed the other through his clenched teeth, white with passion. "I've been played for a sucker long enough."

"What's the matter with you lately, Mark?" remonstrated McTeague. "You've got a grouch about something. Is there anything I've done?"

"Well, that's all right, that's all right," returned Marcus as he rose from the table. "That's all right. I've been played for a sucker long enough, that's all. I've been played for a sucker long enough." He went away with a parting malevolent glance.

At the corner of Polk Street, between the flat and the car conductors' coffee-joint, was Frenna's. It was a corner grocery; advertisements for cheap butter and eggs, painted in green marking-ink upon wrapping paper, stood about on the sidewalk outside. The doorway was decorated with a huge Milwaukee beer sign. Back of the store proper was a bar where white sand covered the floor. A few tables and chairs were scattered here and there. The walls were hung with gorgeously-colored tobacco advertisements and colored lithographs of trotting horses. On the wall behind the bar was a model of a full-rigged ship enclosed in a bottle.

It was at this place that the dentist used to leave his pitcher to be filled on Sunday afternoons. Since his engagement to Trina he had discontinued this habit. However, he still dropped into Frenna's one or two nights in the week. He spent a pleasant hour there, smoking his huge porcelain pipe and drinking his beer. He never joined any of the groups of piquet players around the tables. In fact, he hardly spoke to anyone but the bartender and Marcus.

For Frenna's was one of Marcus Schouler's haunts; a great deal of his time was spent there. He involved himself in fearful political and social discussions with Heise the harnessmaker, and with one or two old Germans, *habitués* of the place. These discussions Marcus carried on, as was his custom, at the top of his voice, gesticulating fiercely, banging the table with his fists, brandishing the plates and glasses, exciting himself with his own clamor.

On a certain Saturday evening, a few days after the scene at the coffee-joint, the dentist bethought him to spend a quiet evening at Frenna's. He had not been there for some time, and, besides that, it occurred to him that the day was his birthday. He would permit himself an extra pipe and a few glasses of beer. When McTeague entered Frenna's back room by the street door, he found Marcus and Heise already installed at one of the tables. Two or three of the old Germans sat opposite them, gulping their beer from time to time. Heise was smoking a cigar, but Marcus had before him his fourth whiskey cocktail. At the moment of McTeague's entrance Marcus had the floor.

"It can't be proven," he was yelling. "I defy any sane politician whose eyes are not blinded by party prejudices, whose opinions are not warped by a personal bias, to substantiate such a statement. Look at your facts, look at your figures. I am a free American citizen, ain't I? I pay my taxes to support a good government, don't I? It's a contract between me and the government, ain't it? Well, then, by damn! if the authorities do not or *will* not afford me protection for life, liberty, and the pursuit of happiness, then my obligations are at an end; I withhold my taxes. I do—I do—I say I do. What?" He glared about him, seeking opposition.

"That's nonsense," observed Heise, quietly. "Try it once; you'll get jugged." But this observation of the harness-maker's roused Marcus to the last pitch of frenzy.

"Yes, ah, yes!" he shouted, rising to his feet, shaking his finger in the other's face. "Yes, I'd go to jail; but because I—I am crushed by a tyranny, does that make the tyranny right? Does might make right?"

"You must make less noise in here, Mister Schouler," said Frenna, from behind the bar.

"Well, it makes me mad," answered Marcus, subsiding into a growl and resuming his chair. "Hullo, Mac."

"Hullo, Mark."

But McTeague's presence made Marcus uneasy, rousing in him at once a sense of wrong. He twisted to and fro in his chair, shrugging first one shoulder and then another. Quarrelsome at all times, the heat of the previous discussion had awakened within him all his natural combativeness. Besides this, he was drinking his fourth cocktail.

McTeague began filling his big porcelain pipe. He lit it, blew a great cloud of smoke into the room, and settled himself comfortably in his chair. The smoke of his cheap tobacco drifted into the faces of the group at the adjoining table, and Marcus strangled and coughed. Instantly his eyes flamed.

"Say, for God's sake," he vociferated, "choke off on that pipe! If you've got to smoke rope like that, smoke it in a crowd of muckers; don't come here amongst gentlemen."

"Shut up, Schouler!" observed Heise in a low voice.

McTeague was stunned by the suddenness of the attack. He took his pipe from his mouth, and stared blankly at Marcus; his lips moved, but he said no word. Marcus turned his back on him, and the dentist resumed his pipe.

But Marcus was far from being appeased. McTeague could not hear the talk that followed between him and the harness-maker, but it seemed to him that Marcus was telling Heise of some injury, some grievance, and that the latter was trying to pacify him. All at once their talk grew louder. Heise laid a retaining hand upon his companion's coat sleeve, but Marcus swung himself around in his chair, and, fixing his eyes on McTeague, cried as if in answer to some protestation on the part of Heise:

"All I know is that I've been soldiered out of five thousand dollars."

McTeague gaped at him, bewildered. He removed his pipe from his mouth a second time, and stared at Marcus with eyes full of trouble and perplexity.

"If I had my rights," cried Marcus, bitterly, "I'd have part of that money. It's my due—it's only justice." The dentist still kept silence.

"If it hadn't been for me," Marcus continued, addressing himself directly to McTeague, "you wouldn't have had a cent of it—no, not a cent. Where's my share, I'd like to know? Where do I come in? No, I ain't in it any more. I've been played for a sucker, an' now that you've got all you can out of me, now that you've done me out of my girl and out of my money, you give me the go-by. Why, where would you have been *to-day* if it hadn't been for me?" Marcus shouted in a sudden exasperation, "You'd a been plugging teeth at two bits an hour. Ain't you got any gratitude? Ain't you got any sense of decency?"

"Ah, hold up, Schouler," grumbled Heise. "You don't want to get into a row."

"No, I don't, Heise," returned Marcus, with a plaintive, aggrieved air. "But it's too much sometimes when you think of it. He stole away my girl's affections, and now that he's rich and prosperous, and has got five thousand dollars that I might have had, he gives me the go-by; he's played me for a sucker. Look here," he cried, turning again to McTeague, "do I get any of that money?"

"It ain't mine to give," answered McTeague. "You're drunk, that's what you are."

"Do I get any of that money?" cried Marcus, persistently.

The dentist shook his head. "No, you don't get any of it."

"Now—*now*," clamored the other, turning to the harness-maker, as though this explained everything. "Look at that, look at that. Well, I've done with you from now on." Marcus had risen to his feet by this time and made as if to leave, but at every instant he came back, shouting his phrases into McTeague's face, moving off again as he spoke the last words, in order to give them better effect.

"This settles it right here. I've done with you. Don't you ever dare speak to me again"—his voice was shaking with fury—"and don't you sit at my table in the restaurant again. I'm sorry I ever lowered myself to keep company with such dirt. Ah, one-horse dentist! Ah, ten-cent zinc-plugger— hoodlum—*mucker!* Get your damn smoke outa my face."

Then matters reached a sudden climax. In his agitation the dentist had been pulling hard on his pipe, and as Marcus for the last time thrust his face close to his own, McTeague, in opening his lips to reply, blew a stifling, acrid cloud directly in Marcus Schouler's eyes. Marcus knocked the pipe from his fingers with a sudden flash of his hand; it spun across the room and broke into a dozen fragments in a far corner.

McTeague rose to his feet, his eyes wide. But as yet he was not angry, only surprised, taken all aback by the suddenness of Marcus Schouler's outbreak as well as by its unreasonableness. Why had Marcus broken his pipe? What did it all mean, anyway? As he rose the dentist made a vague motion with his right hand. Did Marcus misinterpret it as a gesture of menace? He sprang back as though avoiding a blow. All at once there was a cry. Marcus had made a quick, peculiar motion, swinging his arm upward with a wide and sweeping gesture; his jack-knife lay open in his palm; it shot forward as he flung it, glinted sharply by McTeague's head, and struck quivering into the wall behind.

A sudden chill ran through the room; the others stood transfixed, as at the swift passage of some cold and deadly wind. Death had stooped there for an instant, had stooped and passed, leaving a trail of terror and confusion. Then the door leading to the street slammed; Marcus had disappeared.

Thereon a great babel of exclamation arose. The tension of that all but fatal instant snapped, and speech became once more possible.

"He would have knifed you."

"Narrow escape."

"What kind of a man do you call *that*?"

" 'Tain't his fault he ain't a murderer."

"I'd have him up for it."

"And they two have been the greatest kind of friends."

"He didn't touch you, did he?"

"No—no—no."

"What a—what a devil! What treachery! A regular greaser trick!"

"Look out he don't stab you in the back. If that's the kind of man he is, you never can tell."

Frenna drew the knife from the wall.

"Guess I'll keep this toad-stabber," he observed. "That fellow won't come round for it in a hurry; good-sized blade, too." The group examined it with intense interest.

"Big enough to let the life out of any man," observed Heise.

"What—what—what did he do it for?" stammered McTeague. "I got no quarrel with him."

He was puzzled and harassed by the strangeness of it all. Marcus would have killed him; had thrown his knife at him in the true, uncanny "greaser" style. It was inexplicable. McTeague sat down again, looking stupidly about on the floor. In a corner of the room his eye encountered his broken pipe, a dozen little fragments of painted porcelain and the stem of cherry wood and amber.

At that sight his tardy wrath, ever lagging behind the original affront, suddenly blazed up. Instantly his huge jaws clicked together.

"He can't make small of *me*," he exclaimed, suddenly. "I'll show Marcus Schouler—I'll show him—I'll——"

He got up and clapped on his hat.

"Now, Doctor," remonstrated Heise, standing between him and the door, "don't go make a fool of yourself."

"Let 'um alone," joined in Frenna, catching the dentist by the arm; "he's full, anyhow."

"He broke my pipe," answered McTeague.

It was this that had roused him. The thrown knife, the attempt on his life, was beyond his solution; but the breaking of his pipe he understood clearly enough.

"I'll show him," he exclaimed.

As though they had been little children, McTeague set Frenna and the harness-maker aside, and strode out at the door like a raging elephant. Heise stood rubbing his shoulder.

"Might as well try to stop a locomotive," he muttered. "The man's made of iron."

Meanwhile, McTeague went storming up the street toward the flat, wagging his head and grumbling to himself. Ah, Marcus would break his pipe, would he? Ah, he was a zinc-plugger, was he? He'd show Marcus Schouler. No one should make small of him. He tramped up the stairs to Marcus's room. The door was locked. The dentist put one enormous hand on the knob and pushed the door in, snapping the wood-work, tearing off the lock. Nobody—the room was dark and empty. Never mind, Marcus would have to come home some time that night. McTeague would go down and wait for him in his "Parlors." He was bound to hear him as he came up the stairs.

As McTeague reached his room he stumbled over, in the darkness, a big packing-box that stood in the hallway just outside his door. Puzzled, he stepped over it, and lighting the gas in his room, dragged it inside and examined it.

It was addressed to him. What could it mean? He was expecting nothing. Never since he had first furnished his room had packing-cases been left for him in this fashion. No mistake was possible. There were his name and address unmistakably. "Dr. McTeague, dentist,—Polk Street, San Francisco, Cal.," and the red Wells-Fargo tag.

Seized with the joyful curiosity of an overgrown boy, he pried off the boards with the corner of his fire-shovel. The case was stuffed full of excelsior. On the top lay an envelope addressed to him in Trina's handwriting. He opened it and read, "For my dear Mac's birthday, from Trina;" and below, in a kind of postscript, "The man will be round to-morrow to put it in place." McTeague tore away the excelsior. Suddenly he uttered an exclamation.

It was the Tooth—the famous golden molar with its huge prongs—his sign, his ambition, the one unrealized dream of his life; and it was French gilt, too, not the cheap German gilt that was no good. Ah, what a dear little woman was this Trina, to keep so quiet, to remember his birthday!

"Ain't she—ain't she just a—just a *jewel*," exclaimed McTeague under his breath, "a *jewel*—yes, just a *jewel*; that's the word."

Very carefully he removed the rest of the excelsior, and lifting the ponderous Tooth from its box, set it upon the marble-top centre table. How immense it looked in that little room! The thing was tremendous, overpowering—the tooth of a gigantic fossil, golden and dazzling. Beside it everything seemed dwarfed. Even McTeague himself, big boned and enormous as he was, shrank and dwindled in the presence of the monster. As for an instant he bore it in his hands, it was like a puny Gulliver struggling with the molar of some vast Brobdingnag.

The dentist circled about that golden wonder, gasping with delight and stupefaction, touching it gingerly with his hands as if it were something sacred. At every moment his thought returned to Trina. No, never was there such a little woman as his—the very thing he wanted—how had she remembered? And the money, where had that come from? No one knew better than he how expensive were these signs; not another dentist on Polk Street could afford one. Where, then, had Trina found the money? It came out of her five thousand dollars, no doubt.

But what a wonderful, beautiful tooth it was, to be sure, bright as a mirror, shining there in its coat of French gilt, as if with a light of its own! No danger of that tooth turning black with the weather, as did the cheap German gilt impostures. What would that other dentist, that poser, that rider of bicycles, that courser of greyhounds, say when he should see this marvellous molar run out from McTeague's bay window like a flag of defiance? No doubt he would suffer veritable convulsions of envy; would be positively sick with jealousy. If McTeague could only see his face at the moment!

For a whole hour the dentist sat there in his little "Parlor," gazing ecstatically at his treasure, dazzled, supremely content. The whole room took on a different aspect because of it. The stone pug dog before the little stove reflected it in his protruding eyes; the canary woke and chittered feebly at this new gilt, so much brighter than the bars of its little prison. Lorenzo de' Medici, in the steel engraving, sitting in the heart of his court, seemed to ogle the thing out of the corner of one eye, while the brilliant colors of the unused rifle manufacturer's calendar seemed to fade and pale in the brilliance of this greater glory.

At length, long after midnight, the dentist started to go to bed, undressing himself with his eyes still fixed on the great tooth. All at once he heard Marcus Schouler's foot on the stairs; he started up with his fists clenched, but immediately dropped back upon the bed-lounge with a gesture of indifference.

He was in no truculent state of mind now. He could not reinstate himself in that mood of wrath wherein he had left the corner grocery. The tooth had changed all that. What was Marcus Schouler's hatred to him, who had Trina's affection? What did he care about a broken pipe now that he had the tooth? Let him go. As Frenna said, he was not worth it. He heard Marcus come out into the hall, shouting aggrievedly to anyone within sound of his voice:

"An' now he breaks into my room—into my room, by damn! How do I know how many things he's stolen? It's come to stealing from me, now, has it?" He went into his room, banging his splintered door.

McTeague looked upward at the ceiling, in the direction of the voice, muttering:

"Ah, go to bed, you."

He went to bed himself, turning out the gas, but leaving the window-curtains up so that he could see the tooth the last thing before he went to sleep and the first thing as he arose in the morning.

But he was restless during the night. Every now and then he was awakened by noises to which he had long since become accustomed. Now it was the cackling of the geese in the deserted market across the street; now it was the stoppage of the cable, the sudden silence coming almost like a shock; and now it was the infuriated barking of the dogs in the back yard—Alec, the Irish setter, and the collie that belonged to the branch post-office raging at each other through the fence, snarling their endless hatred into each other's faces. As often as he woke, McTeague turned and looked for the tooth, with a sudden suspicion that he had only that moment dreamed the whole business. But he always found it—Trina's gift, his birthday present from his little woman—a huge, vague bulk, looming there through the half darkness in the centre of the room, shining dimly out as if with some mysterious light of its own.

IX

Trina and McTeague were married on the first day of June, in the photographer's rooms that the dentist had rented. All through May the Sieppe household had been turned upside down. The little box of a house vibrated with excitement and confusion, for not only were the preparations for Trina's marriage to be made, but also the preliminaries were to be arranged for the hegira of the entire Sieppe family.

They were to move to the southern part of the State the day after Trina's marriage, Mr. Sieppe having bought a third interest in an upholstering business in the suburbs of Los Angeles. It was possible that Marcus Schouler would go with them.

Not Stanley penetrating for the first time into the Dark Continent, not Napoleon leading his army across the Alps, was more weighted with responsibility, more burdened with care, more overcome with the sense of the importance of his undertaking, than was Mr. Sieppe during this period of preparation. From dawn to dark, from dark to early dawn, he toiled and planned and fretted, organizing and reorganizing, projecting and devising. The trunks were lettered, A, B, and C, the packages and smaller bundles numbered. Each member of the family had his especial duty to perform, his particular bundles to oversee. Not a detail was forgotten—fares, prices, and tips were calculated to two places of decimals. Even the amount of food that it would be necessary to carry for the black greyhound was determined. Mrs. Sieppe was to look after the lunch, "der gomisariat." Mr. Sieppe would assume charge of the checks, the money, the tickets, and, of course, general supervision. The twins would be under the command of Owgooste, who, in turn, would report for orders to his father.

Day in and day out these minutiæ were rehearsed. The children were drilled in their parts with a military exactitude; obedience and punctuality became cardinal virtues. The vast importance of the undertaking was insisted upon with scrupulous iteration. It was a manœuvre, an army changing its base of operations, a veritable tribal migration.

On the other hand, Trina's little room was the centre around which revolved another and different order of things. The dressmaker came and went, congratulatory visitors invaded the little front parlor, the chatter of unfamiliar voices resounded from the front steps; bonnet-boxes and yards of dress-goods littered the beds and chairs; wrapping paper, tissue paper, and bits of string strewed the floor; a pair of white satin slippers stood on a corner of the toilet table; lengths of white veiling, like a snow-flurry, buried the little work-table; and a mislaid box of artificial orange blossoms was finally discovered behind the bureau.

The two systems of operation often clashed and tangled. Mrs. Sieppe was found by her harassed husband helping Trina with the waist of her gown when she should have been slicing cold chicken in the kitchen. Mr. Sieppe packed his frock coat, which he would have to wear at the wedding, at the very bottom of "Trunk C." The minister, who called to offer his congratulations and to make arrangements, was mistaken for the expressman.

McTeague came and went furtively, dizzied and made uneasy by all this bustle. He got in the way; he trod upon and tore breadths of silk; he tried to help carry the packing-boxes, and broke the hall gas fixture; he came in upon Trina and the dressmaker at an ill-timed moment, and retiring precipitately, overturned the piles of pictures stacked in the hall.

There was an incessant going and coming at every moment of the day, a great calling up and down stairs, a shouting from room to room, an opening and shutting of doors, and an intermittent sound of hammering from the laundry, where Mr. Sieppe in his shirt sleeves labored among the packing-boxes. The twins clattered about on the carpetless floors of the denuded rooms. Owgooste was smacked from hour to hour, and wept upon the front stairs; the dressmaker called over the banisters for a hot flatiron; expressmen tramped up and down the stairway. Mrs. Sieppe stopped in the preparation of the lunches to call "Hoop, Hoop" to the greyhound, throwing lumps of coal. The dog-wheel creaked, the front door bell rang, delivery wagons rumbled away, windows rattled—the little house was in a positive uproar.

Almost every day of the week now Trina was obliged to

run over to town and meet McTeague. No more philandering over their lunch now-a-days. It was business now. They haunted the house-furnishing floors of the great department houses, inspecting and pricing ranges, hardware, china, and the like. They rented the photographer's rooms furnished, and fortunately only the kitchen and dining-room utensils had to be bought.

The money for this as well as for her trousseau came out of Trina's five thousand dollars. For it had been finally decided that two hundred dollars of this amount should be devoted to the establishment of the new household. Now that Trina had made her great winning, Mr. Sieppe no longer saw the necessity of dowering her further, especially when he considered the enormous expense to which he would be put by the voyage of his own family.

It had been a dreadful wrench for Trina to break in upon her precious five thousand. She clung to this sum with a tenacity that was surprising; it had become for her a thing miraculous, a god-from-the-machine, suddenly descending upon the stage of her humble little life; she regarded it as something almost sacred and inviolable. Never, never should a penny of it be spent. Before she could be induced to part with two hundred dollars of it, more than one scene had been enacted between her and her parents.

Did Trina pay for the golden tooth out of this two hundred? Later on, the dentist often asked her about it, but Trina invariably laughed in his face, declaring that it was her secret. McTeague never found out.

One day during this period McTeague told Trina about his affair with Marcus. Instantly she was aroused.

"He threw his knife at you! The coward! He wouldn't of dared stand up to you like a man. Oh, Mac, suppose he *had* hit you?"

"Came within an inch of my head," put in McTeague, proudly.

"Think of it!" she gasped; "and he wanted part of my money. Well, I do like his cheek; part of my five thousand! Why, it's *mine*, every single penny of it. Marcus hasn't the least bit of right to it. It's mine, mine—I mean, it's ours, Mac, dear."

The elder Sieppes, however, made excuses for Marcus. He had probably been drinking a good deal and didn't know what he was about. He had a dreadful temper, anyhow. Maybe he only wanted to scare McTeague.

The week before the marriage the two men were reconciled. Mrs. Sieppe brought them together in the front parlor of the B Street house.

"Now, you two fellers, don't be dot foolish. Schake hands und maig ut oop, soh."

Marcus muttered an apology. McTeague, miserably embarrassed, rolled his eyes about the room, murmuring, "That's all right—that's all right—that's all right."

However, when it was proposed that Marcus should be McTeague's best man, he flashed out again with renewed violence. Ah, no! ah, *no!* He'd make up with the dentist now that he was going away, but he'd be damned—yes, he would—before he'd be his best man. That *was* rubbing it in. Let him get Old Grannis.

"I'm friends with um all right," vociferated Marcus, "but I'll not stand up with um. I'll not be *anybody's* best man, I won't."

The wedding was to be very quiet; Trina preferred it that way. McTeague would invite only Miss Baker and Heise the harness-maker. The Sieppes sent cards to Selina, who was counted on to furnish the music; to Marcus, of course; and to Uncle Oelbermann.

At last the great day, the first of June, arrived. The Sieppes had packed their last box and had strapped the last trunk. Trina's two trunks had already been sent to her new home—the remodelled photographer's rooms. The B Street house was deserted; the whole family came over to the city on the last day of May and stopped over night at one of the cheap downtown hotels. Trina would be married the following evening, and immediately after the wedding supper the Sieppes would leave for the South.

McTeague spent the day in a fever of agitation, frightened out of his wits each time that Old Grannis left his elbow.

Old Grannis was delighted beyond measure at the prospect of acting the part of best man in the ceremony. This wedding in which he was to figure filled his mind with vague ideas and

half-formed thoughts. He found himself continually wondering what Miss Baker would think of it. During all that day he
was in a reflective mood.

"Marriage is a—a noble institution, is it not, Doctor?" he
observed to McTeague. "The—the foundation of society. It
is not good that man should be alone. No, no," he added,
pensively, "it is not good."

"Huh? Yes, yes," McTeague answered, his eyes in the air,
hardly hearing him. "Do you think the rooms are all right?
Let's go in and look at them again."

They went down the hall to where the new rooms were
situated, and the dentist inspected them for the twentieth
time.

The rooms were three in number—first, the sitting-room,
which was also the dining-room; then the bedroom, and back
of this the tiny kitchen.

The sitting-room was particularly charming. Clean matting
covered the floor, and two or three bright-colored rugs were
scattered here and there. The backs of the chairs were hung
with knitted worsted tidies, very gay. The bay window should
have been occupied by Trina's sewing machine, but this had
been moved to the other side of the room to give place to a
little black walnut table with spiral legs, before which the pair
were to be married. In one corner stood the parlor melodeon,
a family possession of the Sieppes, but given now to Trina as
one of her parents' wedding presents. Three pictures hung
upon the walls. Two were companion pieces. One of these
represented a little boy wearing huge spectacles and trying
to smoke an enormous pipe. This was called "I'm Grandpa,"
the title being printed in large black letters; the companion
picture was entitled "I'm Grandma," a little girl in cap and
"specs," wearing mitts, and knitting. These pictures were
hung on either side of the mantelpiece. The other picture was
quite an affair, very large and striking. It was a colored lithograph of two little golden-haired girls in their nightgowns.
They were kneeling down and saying their prayers; their
eyes—very large and very blue—rolled upward. This picture
had for name, "Faith," and was bordered with a red plush
mat and a frame of imitation beaten brass.

A door hung with chenille portières—a bargain at two

dollars and a half—admitted one to the bedroom. The bed-room could boast a carpet, three-ply ingrain, the design being bunches of red and green flowers in yellow baskets on a white ground. The wall-paper was admirable—hundreds and hundreds of tiny Japanese mandarins, all identically alike, helping hundreds of almond-eyed ladies into hundreds of impossible junks, while hundreds of bamboo palms over-shadowed the pair, and hundreds of long-legged storks trailed contemptuously away from the scene. This room was prolific in pictures. Most of them were framed colored prints from Christmas editions of the London "Graphic" and "Il-lustrated News," the subject of each picture inevitably in-volving very alert fox terriers and very pretty moon-faced little girls.

Back of the bedroom was the kitchen, a creation of Trina's, a dream of a kitchen, with its range, its porcelain-lined sink, its copper boiler, and its overpowering array of flashing tin-ware. Everything was new; everything was complete.

Maria Macapa and a waiter from one of the restaurants in the street were to prepare the wedding supper here. Maria had already put in an appearance. The fire was crackling in the new stove, that smoked badly; a smell of cooking was in the air. She drove McTeague and Old Grannis from the room with great gestures of her bare arms.

This kitchen was the only one of the three rooms they had been obliged to furnish throughout. Most of the sitting-room and bedroom furniture went with the suite; a few pieces they had bought; the remainder Trina had brought over from the B Street house.

The presents had been set out on the extension table in the sitting-room. Besides the parlor melodeon, Trina's parents had given her an ice-water set, and a carving knife and fork with elk-horn handles. Selina had painted a view of the Golden Gate upon a polished slice of redwood that answered the purposes of a paper weight. Marcus Schouler—after im-pressing upon Trina that his gift was to *her*, and not to McTeague—had sent a chatelaine watch of German silver; Uncle Oelbermann's present, however, had been awaited with a good deal of curiosity. What would *he* send? He was very rich; in a sense Trina was his *protegé*. A couple of days before that upon which the wedding was to take place, two boxes arrived with his card. Trina and McTeague, assisted by Old Grannis, had opened them. The first was a box of all sorts of toys.

"But what—what—I don't make it out," McTeague had exclaimed. "Why should he send us toys? We have no need of toys." Scarlet to her hair, Trina dropped into a chair and laughed till she cried behind her handkerchief.

"We've no use of toys," muttered McTeague, looking at her in perplexity. Old Grannis smiled discreetly, raising a tremulous hand to his chin.

The other box was heavy, bound with withes at the edges, the letters and stamps burnt in.

"I think—I really think it's champagne," said Old Grannis in a whisper. So it was. A full case of Monopole. What a wonder! None of them had seen the like before. Ah, this Uncle Oelbermann! That's what it was to be rich. Not one of the other presents produced so deep an impression as this.

After Old Grannis and the dentist had gone through the rooms, giving a last look around to see that everything was ready, they returned to McTeague's "Parlors." At the door Old Grannis excused himself.

At four o'clock McTeague began to dress, shaving himself first before the hand-glass that was hung against the woodwork of the bay window. While he shaved he sang with strange inappropriateness:

> "No one to love, none to caress,
> Left all alone in this world's wilderness."

But as he stood before the mirror, intent upon his shaving, there came a roll of wheels over the cobbles in front of the house. He rushed to the window. Trina had arrived with her father and mother. He saw her get out, and as she glanced upward at his window, their eyes met.

Ah, there she was. There she was, his little woman, looking up at him, her adorable little chin thrust upward with that familiar movement of innocence and confidence. The dentist saw again, as if for the first time, her small, pale face looking out from beneath her royal tiara of black hair; he saw again her long, narrow blue eyes; her lips, nose, and tiny ears, pale and bloodless, and suggestive of anæmia, as if all the vitality that should have lent them color had been sucked up into the strands and coils of that wonderful hair.

As their eyes met they waved their hands gayly to each other; then McTeague heard Trina and her mother come up the stairs and go into the bedroom of the photographer's suite, where Trina was to dress.

No, no; surely there could be no longer any hesitation. He knew that he loved her. What was the matter with him, that he should have doubted it for an instant? The great difficulty was that she was too good, too adorable, too sweet, too delicate for him, who was so huge, so clumsy, so brutal.

There was a knock at the door. It was Old Grannis. He was dressed in his one black suit of broadcloth, much wrinkled; his hair was carefully brushed over his bald forehead.

"Miss Trina has come," he announced, "and the minister. You have an hour yet."

The dentist finished dressing. He wore a suit bought for the occasion—a ready made "Prince Albert" coat too short in the sleeves, striped "blue" trousers, and new patent leather shoes—veritable instruments of torture. Around his collar was a wonderful necktie that Trina had given him; it was of salmon-pink satin; in its centre Selina had painted a knot of blue forget-me-nots.

At length, after an interminable period of waiting, Mr. Sieppe appeared at the door.

"Are you reatty?" he asked in a sepulchral whisper. "Gome, den." It was like King Charles summoned to execution. Mr. Sieppe preceded them into the hall, moving at a funereal pace. He paused. Suddenly, in the direction of the sitting-room, came the strains of the parlor melodeon. Mr. Sieppe flung his arm into the air.

"Vowaarts!" he cried.

He left them at the door of the sitting-room, he himself going into the bedroom where Trina was waiting, entering by the hall door. He was in a tremendous state of nervous tension, fearful lest something should go wrong. He had employed the period of waiting in going through his part for the fiftieth time, repeating what he had to say in a low voice.

He had even made chalk marks on the matting in the places where he was to take positions.

The dentist and Old Grannis entered the sitting-room; the minister stood behind the little table in the bay window, holding a book, one finger marking the place; he was rigid, erect, impassive. On either side of him, in a semi-circle, stood the invited guests. A little pock-marked gentleman in glasses, no doubt the famous Uncle Oelbermann; Miss Baker, in her black grenadine, false curls, and coral brooch; Marcus Schouler, his arms folded, his brows bent, grand and gloomy; Heise the harness-maker, in yellow gloves, intently studying the pattern of the matting; and Owgooste, in his Fauntleroy "costume," stupefied and a little frightened, rolling his eyes from face to face. Selina sat at the parlor melodeon, fingering the keys, her glance wandering to the chenille portières. She stopped playing as McTeague and Old Grannis entered and took their places. A profound silence ensued. Uncle Oelbermann's shirt front could be heard creaking as he breathed. The most solemn expression pervaded every face.

All at once the portières were shaken violently. It was a signal. Selina pulled open the stops and swung into the wedding march.

Trina entered. She was dressed in white silk, a crown of orange blossoms was around her swarthy hair—dressed high for the first time—her veil reached to the floor. Her face was pink, but otherwise she was calm. She looked quietly around the room as she crossed it, until her glance rested on McTeague, smiling at him then very prettily and with perfect self-possession.

She was on her father's arm. The twins, dressed exactly alike, walked in front, each carrying an enormous bouquet of cut flowers in a "lace-paper" holder. Mrs. Sieppe followed in the rear. She was crying; her handkerchief was rolled into a wad. From time to time she looked at the train of Trina's dress through her tears. Mr. Sieppe marched his daughter to the exact middle of the floor, wheeled at right angles, and brought her up to the minister. He stepped back three paces, and stood planted upon one of his chalk marks, his face glistening with perspiration.

Then Trina and the dentist were married. The guests stood

in constrained attitudes, looking furtively out of the corners of their eyes. Mr. Sieppe never moved a muscle; Mrs. Sieppe cried into her handkerchief all the time. At the melodeon Selina played "Call Me Thine Own," very softly, the tremulo stop pulled out. She looked over her shoulder from time to time. Between the pauses of the music one could hear the low tones of the minister, the responses of the participants, and the suppressed sounds of Mrs. Sieppe's weeping. Outside the noises of the street rose to the windows in muffled undertones, a cable car rumbled past, a newsboy went by chanting the evening papers; from somewhere in the building itself came a persistent noise of sawing.

Trina and McTeague knelt. The dentist's knees thudded on the floor and he presented to view the soles of his shoes, painfully new and unworn, the leather still yellow, the brass nail heads still glittering. Trina sank at his side very gracefully, settling her dress and train with a little gesture of her free hand. The company bowed their heads, Mr. Sieppe shutting his eyes tight. But Mrs. Sieppe took advantage of the moment to stop crying and make furtive gestures towards Owgooste, signing him to pull down his coat. But Owgooste gave no heed; his eyes were starting from their sockets, his chin had dropped upon his lace collar, and his head turned vaguely from side to side with a continued and maniacal motion.

All at once the ceremony was over before any one expected it. The guests kept their positions for a moment, eying one another, each fearing to make the first move, not quite certain as to whether or not everything were finished. But the couple faced the room, Trina throwing back her veil. She—perhaps McTeague as well—felt that there was a certain inadequateness about the ceremony. Was that all there was to it? Did just those few muttered phrases make them man and wife? It had been over in a few moments, but it had bound them for life. Had not something been left out? Was not the whole affair cursory, superficial? It was disappointing.

But Trina had no time to dwell upon this. Marcus Schouler, in the manner of a man of the world, who knew how to act in every situation, stepped forward and, even before Mr. or Mrs. Sieppe, took Trina's hand.

"Let me be the first to congratulate Mrs. McTeague," he

said, feeling very noble and heroic. The strain of the previous moments was relaxed immediately, the guests crowded around the pair, shaking hands—a babel of talk arose.

"Owgooste, *will* you pull down your goat, den?"

"Well, my dear, now you're married and happy. When I first saw you two together, I said, 'What a pair!' We're to be neighbors now; you must come up and see me very often and we'll have tea together."

"Did you hear that sawing going on all the time? I declare it regularly got on my nerves."

Trina kissed her father and mother, crying a little herself as she saw the tears in Mrs. Sieppe's eyes.

Marcus came forward a second time, and, with an air of great gravity, kissed his cousin upon the forehead. Heise was introduced to Trina and Uncle Oelbermann to the dentist.

For upwards of half an hour the guests stood about in groups, filling the little sitting-room with a great chatter of talk. Then it was time to make ready for supper.

This was a tremendous task, in which nearly all the guests were obliged to assist. The sitting-room was transformed into a dining-room. The presents were removed from the extension table and the table drawn out to its full length. The cloth was laid, the chairs—rented from the dancing academy hard by—drawn up, the dishes set out, and the two bouquets of cut flowers taken from the twins under their shrill protests, and "arranged" in vases at either end of the table.

There was a great coming and going between the kitchen and the sitting-room. Trina, who was allowed to do nothing, sat in the bay window and fretted, calling to her mother from time to time:

"The napkins are in the right-hand drawer of the pantry."

"Yes, yes, I got um. Where do you geep der zoup blates?"

"The soup plates are here already."

"Say, Cousin Trina, is there a corkscrew? What is home without a corkscrew?"

"In the kitchen-table drawer, in the left-hand corner."

"Are these the forks you want to use, Mrs. McTeague?"

"No, no, there's some silver forks. Mamma knows where."

They were all very gay, laughing over their mistakes, getting in one another's way, rushing into the sitting-room, their hands full of plates or knives or glasses, and darting out again after more. Marcus and Mr. Sieppe took their coats off. Old Grannis and Miss Baker passed each other in the hall in a constrained silence, her grenadine brushing against the elbow of his wrinkled frock coat. Uncle Oelbermann superintended Heise opening the case of champagne with the gravity of a magistrate. Owgooste was assigned the task of filling the new salt and pepper canisters of red and blue glass.

In a wonderfully short time everything was ready. Marcus Schouler resumed his coat, wiping his forehead, and remarking:

"I tell you, I've been doing *chores* for *my* board."

"To der table!" commanded Mr. Sieppe.

The company sat down with a great clatter, Trina at the foot, the dentist at the head, the others arranged themselves in haphazard fashion. But it happened that Marcus Schouler crowded into the seat beside Selina, towards which Old Grannis was directing himself. There was but one other chair vacant, and that at the side of Miss Baker. Old Grannis hesitated, putting his hand to his chin. However, there was no escape. In great trepidation he sat down beside the retired dressmaker. Neither of them spoke. Old Grannis dared not move, but sat rigid, his eyes riveted on his empty soup plate.

All at once there was a report like a pistol. The men started in their places. Mrs. Sieppe uttered a muffled shriek. The waiter from the cheap restaurant, hired as Maria's assistant, rose from a bending posture, a champagne bottle frothing in his hand; he was grinning from ear to ear.

"Don't get scairt," he said, reassuringly, "it ain't loaded."

When all their glasses had been filled, Marcus proposed the health of the bride, "standing up." The guests rose and drank. Hardly one of them had ever tasted champagne before. The moment's silence after the toast was broken by McTeague exclaiming with a long breath of satisfaction: "That's the best beer *I* ever drank."

There was a roar of laughter. Especially was Marcus tickled over the dentist's blunder; he went off in a very spasm of mirth, banging the table with his fist, laughing until his eyes watered. All through the meal he kept breaking out into cackling imitations of McTeague's words: "That's the best *beer* I ever drank. Oh, Lord, ain't that a break!"

What a wonderful supper that was! There was oyster soup; there were sea bass and barracuda; there was a gigantic roast goose stuffed with chestnuts; there were egg-plant and sweet potatoes—Miss Baker called them "yams." There was calf's head in oil, over which Mr. Sieppe went into ecstasies; there was lobster salad; there were rice pudding, and strawberry ice cream, and wine jelly, and stewed prunes, and cocoanuts, and mixed nuts, and raisins, and fruit, and tea, and coffee, and mineral waters, and lemonade.

For two hours the guests ate; their faces red, their elbows wide, the perspiration beading their foreheads. All around the table one saw the same incessant movement of jaws and heard the same uninterrupted sound of chewing. Three times Heise passed his plate for more roast goose. Mr. Sieppe devoured the calf's head with long breaths of contentment; McTeague ate for the sake of eating, without choice; everything within reach of his hands found its way into his enormous mouth.

There was but little conversation, and that only of the food; one exchanged opinions with one's neighbor as to the soup, the egg-plant, or the stewed prunes. Soon the room became very warm, a faint moisture appeared upon the windows, the air was heavy with the smell of cooked food. At every moment Trina or Mrs. Sieppe urged some one of the company to have his or her plate refilled. They were constantly employed in dishing potatoes or carving the goose or ladling gravy. The hired waiter circled around the room, his limp napkin over his arm, his hands full of plates and dishes. He was a great joker; he had names of his own for different articles of food, that sent gales of laughter around the table. When he spoke of a bunch of parsley as "scenery," Heise all but strangled himself over a mouthful of potato. Out in the kitchen Maria Macapa did the work of three, her face scarlet, her sleeves rolled up; every now and then she uttered shrill but unintelligible outcries, supposedly addressed to the waiter.

"Uncle Oelbermann," said Trina, "let me give you another helping of prunes."

The Sieppes paid great deference to Uncle Oelbermann, as indeed did the whole company. Even Marcus Schouler lowered his voice when he addressed him. At the beginning of the meal he had nudged the harness-maker and had whispered behind his hand, nodding his head toward the wholesale toy dealer, "Got thirty thousand dollars in the bank; has, for a fact."

"Don't have much to say," observed Heise.

"No, no. That's his way; never opens his face."

As the evening wore on, the gas and two lamps were lit. The company were still eating. The men, gorged with food, had unbuttoned their vests. McTeague's cheeks were distended, his eyes wide, his huge, salient jaw moved with a machine-like regularity; at intervals he drew a series of short breaths through his nose. Mrs. Sieppe wiped her forehead with her napkin.

"Hey, dere, poy, gif me some more oaf dat—what you call—'bubble-water.' "

That was how the waiter had spoken of the champagne— "bubble-water." The guests had shouted applause, "Outa sight." He was a heavy josher was that waiter.

Bottle after bottle was opened, the women stopping their ears as the corks were drawn. All of a sudden the dentist uttered an exclamation, clapping his hand to his nose, his face twisting sharply.

"Mac, what is it?" cried Trina in alarm.

"That champagne came to my nose," he cried, his eyes watering. "It stings like everything."

"Great *beer*, ain't ut?" shouted Marcus.

"Now, Mark," remonstrated Trina in a low voice. "Now, Mark, you just shut up; that isn't funny any more. I don't want you should make fun of Mac. He called it beer on purpose. I guess *he* knows."

Throughout the meal old Miss Baker had occupied herself largely with Owgooste and the twins, who had been given a table by themselves—the black walnut table before which the ceremony had taken place. The little dressmaker was continually turning about in her place, inquiring of the children if they wanted for anything; inquiries they rarely answered other than by stare, fixed, ox-like, expressionless.

Suddenly the little dressmaker turned to Old Grannis and exclaimed:

"I'm so very fond of little children."

"Yes, yes, they're very interesting. I'm very fond of them, too."

The next instant both of the old people were overwhelmed with confusion. What! They had spoken to each other after all these years of silence; they had for the first time addressed remarks to each other.

The old dressmaker was in a torment of embarrassment. How was it she had come to speak? She had neither planned nor wished it. Suddenly the words had escaped her, he had answered, and it was all over—over before they knew it.

Old Grannis's fingers trembled on the table ledge, his heart beat heavily, his breath fell short. He had actually talked to the little dressmaker. That possibility to which he had looked forward, it seemed to him for years—that companionship, that intimacy with his fellow-lodger, that delightful acquaintance which was only to ripen at some far distant time, he could not exactly say when—behold, it had suddenly come to a head, here in this over-crowded, over-heated room, in the midst of all this feeding, surrounded by odors of hot dishes, accompanied by the sounds of incessant mastication. How different he had imagined it would be! They were to be alone—he and Miss Baker—in the evening somewhere, with-drawn from the world, very quiet, very calm and peaceful. Their talk was to be of their lives, their lost illusions, not of other people's children.

The two old people did not speak again. They sat there side by side, nearer than they had ever been before, motion-less, abstracted; their thoughts far away from that scene of feasting. They were thinking of each other and they were conscious of it. Timid, with the timidity of their second childhood, constrained and embarrassed by each other's pres-ence, they were, nevertheless, in a little Elysium of their own creating. They walked hand in hand in a delicious garden where it was always autumn; together and alone they entered upon the long retarded romance of their commonplace and uneventful lives.

At last that great supper was over, everything had been

eaten; the enormous roast goose had dwindled to a very skeleton. Mr. Sieppe had reduced the calf's head to a mere skull; a row of empty champagne bottles—"dead soldiers," as the facetious waiter had called them—lined the mantelpiece. Nothing of the stewed prunes remained but the juice, which was given to Owgooste and the twins. The platters were as clean as if they had been washed; crumbs of bread, potato parings, nutshells, and bits of cake littered the table; coffee and ice-cream stains and spots of congealed gravy marked the position of each plate. It was a devastation, a pillage; the table presented the appearance of an abandoned battlefield.

"Ouf," cried Mrs. Sieppe, pushing back, "I haf eatun und eatun, ach, Gott, how I haf eatun!"

"Ah, dot kaf's het," murmured her husband, passing his tongue over his lips.

The facetious waiter had disappeared. He and Maria Macapa foregathered in the kitchen. They drew up to the washboard of the sink, feasting off the remnants of the supper, slices of goose, the remains of the lobster salad, and half a bottle of champagne. They were obliged to drink the latter from teacups.

"Here's how," said the waiter gallantly, as he raised his teacup, bowing to Maria across the sink. "Hark," he added, "they're singing inside."

The company had left the table and had assembled about the melodeon, where Selina was seated. At first they attempted some of the popular songs of the day, but were obliged to give over as none of them knew any of the words beyond the first line of the chorus. Finally they pitched upon "Nearer, My God, to Thee," as the only song which they all knew. Selina sang the "alto," very much off the key; Marcus intoned the bass, scowling fiercely, his chin drawn into his collar. They sang in very slow time. The song became a dirge, a lamentable, prolonged wail of distress:

> "Nee-rah, my Gahd, to Thee,
> Nee-rah to Thee-ah."

At the end of the song, Uncle Oelbermann put on his hat without a word of warning. Instantly there was a hush. The guests rose.

"Not going so soon, Uncle Oelbermann?" protested Trina, politely. He only nodded. Marcus sprang forward to help him with his overcoat. Mr. Sieppe came up and the two men shook hands.

Then Uncle Oelbermann delivered himself of an oracular phrase. No doubt he had been meditating it during the supper. Addressing Mr. Sieppe, he said:

"You have not lost a daughter, but have gained a son."

These were the only words he had spoken the entire evening. He departed; the company was profoundly impressed.

About twenty minutes later, when Marcus Schouler was entertaining the guests by eating almonds, shells and all, Mr. Sieppe started to his feet, watch in hand.

"Haf-bast elevun," he shouted. "Attention! Der dime haf arrive, shtop eferyting. We depart."

This was a signal for tremendous confusion. Mr. Sieppe immediately threw off his previous air of relaxation, the calf's head was forgotten, he was once again the leader of vast enterprises.

"To me, to me," he cried. "Mommer, der tervins, Owgooste." He marshalled his tribe together, with tremendous commanding gestures. The sleeping twins were suddenly shaken into a dazed consciousness; Owgooste, whom the almond-eating of Marcus Schouler had petrified with admiration, was smacked to a realization of his surroundings.

Old Grannis, with a certain delicacy that was one of his characteristics, felt instinctively that the guests—the mere outsiders—should depart before the family began its leavetaking of Trina. He withdrew unobtrusively, after a hasty good-night to the bride and groom. The rest followed almost immediately.

"Well, Mr. Sieppe," exclaimed Marcus, "we won't see each other for some time." Marcus had given up his first intention of joining in the Sieppe migration. He spoke in a large way of certain affairs that would keep him in San Francisco till the fall. Of late he had entertained ambitions of a ranch life, he would breed cattle, he had a little money and was only looking for some one "to go in with." He dreamed of a cowboy's life and saw himself in an entrancing vision involving silver spurs and untamed bronchos. He told himself that Trina had cast him off, that his best friend had "played him for a sucker," that the "proper caper" was to withdraw from the world entirely.

"If you hear of anybody down there," he went on, speaking to Mr. Sieppe, "that wants to go in for ranching, why just let me know."

"Soh, soh," answered Mr. Sieppe abstractedly, peering about for Owgooste's cap.

Marcus bade the Sieppes farewell. He and Heise went out together. One heard them, as they descended the stairs, discussing the possibility of Frenna's place being still open.

Then Miss Baker departed after kissing Trina on both cheeks. Selina went with her. There was only the family left.

Trina watched them go, one by one, with an increasing feeling of uneasiness and vague apprehension. Soon they would all be gone.

"Well, Trina," exclaimed Mr. Sieppe, "goot-py; perhaps you gome visit us somedime."

Mrs. Sieppe began crying again.

"Ach, Trina, ven shall I efer see you again?"

Tears came to Trina's eyes in spite of herself. She put her arms around her mother.

"Oh, sometime, sometime," she cried. The twins and Owgooste clung to Trina's skirts, fretting and whimpering.

McTeague was miserable. He stood apart from the group, in a corner. None of them seemed to think of him; he was not one of them.

"Write to me very often, mamma, and tell me about everything—about August and the twins."

"It is dime," cried Mr. Sieppe, nervously. "Goot-py, Trina. Mommer, Owgooste, say goot-py, den we must go. Goot-py, Trina." He kissed her. Owgooste and the twins were lifted up. "Gome, gome," insisted Mr. Sieppe, moving toward the door.

"Goot-py, Trina," exclaimed Mrs. Sieppe, crying harder than ever. "Doktor—where is der doktor—Doktor, pe goot to her, eh? pe vairy goot, eh, won't you? Zum day, Doktor, you vill haf a daughter, den you know berhaps how I feel, yes."

They were standing at the door by this time. Mr. Sieppe, half way down the stairs, kept calling "Gome, gome, we miss der drain."

Mrs. Sieppe released Trina and started down the hall, the twins and Owgooste following. Trina stood in the doorway, looking after them through her tears. They were going, going. When would she ever see them again? She was to be left alone with this man to whom she had just been married. A sudden vague terror seized her; she left McTeague and ran down the hall and caught her mother around the neck.

"I don't *want* you to go," she whispered in her mother's ear, sobbing. "Oh, mamma, I—I'm 'fraid."

"Ach, Trina, you preak my heart. Don't gry, poor leetle girl." She rocked Trina in her arms as though she were a child again. "Poor leetle scairt girl, don' gry—soh—soh—soh, dere's nuttun to pe 'fraid oaf. Dere, go to your hoasban'. Listen, popper's galling again; go den; goot-by."

She loosened Trina's arms and started down the stairs. Trina leaned over the banisters, straining her eyes after her mother.

"What is ut, Trina?"

"Oh, good-by, good-by."

"Gome, gome, we miss der drain."

"Mamma, oh, mamma!"

"What is ut, Trina?"

"Good-by."

"Goot-py, leetle daughter."

"Good-by, good-by, good-by."

The street door closed. The silence was profound.

For another moment Trina stood leaning over the banisters, looking down into the empty stairway. It was dark. There was nobody. They—her father, her mother, the children—had left her, left her alone. She faced about toward the rooms—faced her husband, faced her new home, the new life that was to begin now.

The hall was empty and deserted. The great flat around her seemed new and huge and strange; she felt horribly alone. Even Maria and the hired waiter were gone. On one of the floors above she heard a baby crying. She stood there an instant in the dark hall, in her wedding finery, looking about her, listening. From the open door of the sitting-room streamed a gold bar of light.

She went down the hall, by the open door of the sitting-room, going on toward the hall door of the bedroom.

As she softly passed the sitting-room she glanced hastily in. The lamps and the gas were burning brightly, the chairs were pushed back from the table just as the guests had left them, and the table itself, abandoned, deserted, presented to view the vague confusion of its dishes, its knives and forks, its empty platters and crumpled napkins. The dentist sat there leaning on his elbows, his back toward her; against the white blur of the table he looked colossal. Above his giant shoulders rose his thick, red neck and mane of yellow hair. The light shone pink through the gristle of his enormous ears.

Trina entered the bedroom, closing the door after her. At the sound, she heard McTeague start and rise.

"Is that you, Trina?"

She did not answer, but paused in the middle of the room, holding her breath, trembling.

The dentist crossed the outside room, parted the chenille portières, and came in. He came toward her quickly, making as if to take her in his arms. His eyes were alight.

"No, no," cried Trina, shrinking from him. Suddenly seized with the fear of him—the intuitive feminine fear of the male—her whole being quailed before him. She was terrified at his huge, square-cut head; his powerful, salient jaw; his huge, red hands; his enormous, resistless strength.

"No, no—I'm afraid," she cried, drawing back from him to the other side of the room.

"Afraid?" answered the dentist in perplexity. "What are you afraid of, Trina? I'm not going to hurt you. What are you afraid of?"

What, indeed, was Trina afraid of? She could not tell. But what did she know of McTeague, after all? Who was this man that had come into her life, who had taken her from her home and from her parents, and with whom she was now left alone here in this strange, vast flat?

"Oh, I'm afraid. I'm afraid," she cried.

McTeague came nearer, sat down beside her and put one arm around her.

"What are you afraid of, Trina?" he said, reassuringly. "I don't want to frighten you."

She looked at him wildly, her adorable little chin quivering, the tears brimming in her narrow blue eyes. Then her glance took on a certain intentness, and she peered curiously into his face, saying almost in a whisper:

"I'm afraid of *you*."

But the dentist did not heed her. An immense joy seized upon him—the joy of possession. Trina was his very own now. She lay there in the hollow of his arm, helpless and very pretty.

Those instincts that in him were so close to the surface suddenly leaped to life, shouting and clamoring, not to be resisted. He loved her. Ah, did he not love her? The smell of her hair, of her neck, rose to him.

Suddenly he caught her in both his huge arms, crushing down her struggle with his immense strength, kissing her full upon the mouth. Then her great love for McTeague suddenly flashed up in Trina's breast; she gave up to him as she had done before, yielding all at once to that strange desire of being conquered and subdued. She clung to him, her hands clasped behind his neck, whispering in his ear:

"Oh, you must be good to me—very, very good to me, dear—for you're all that I have in the world now."

X

THAT SUMMER PASSED, then the winter. The wet season began in the last days of September and continued all through October, November, and December. At long intervals would come a week of perfect days, the sky without a cloud, the air motionless, but touched with a certain nimbleness, a faint effervescence that was exhilarating. Then, without warning, during a night when a south wind blew, a gray scroll of cloud would unroll and hang high over the city, and the rain would come pattering down again, at first in scattered showers, then in an uninterrupted drizzle.

All day long Trina sat in the bay window of the sitting-room that commanded a view of a small section of Polk Street. As often as she raised her head she could see the big market, a confectionery store, a bell-hanger's shop, and, farther on, above the roofs, the glass skylights and water tanks of the big public baths. In the nearer foreground ran the street itself; the cable cars trundled up and down, thumping heavily over the joints of the rails; market carts by the score came and went, driven at a great rate by preoccupied young men in their shirt sleeves, with pencils behind their ears, or by reckless boys in blood-stained butcher's aprons. Upon the sidewalks the little world of Polk Street swarmed and jostled through its daily round of life. On fine days the great ladies from the avenue, one block above, invaded the street, appearing before the butcher stalls, intent upon their day's marketing. On rainy days their servants—the Chinese cooks or the second girls—took their places. These servants gave themselves great airs, carrying their big cotton umbrellas as they had seen their mistresses carry their parasols, and haggling in supercilious fashion with the market men, their chins in the air.

The rain persisted. Everything in the range of Trina's vision, from the tarpaulins on the market-cart horses to the panes of glass in the roof of the public baths, looked glazed and varnished. The asphalt of the sidewalks shone like the surface of a patent leather boot; every hollow in the street

held its little puddle, that winked like an eye each time a drop
of rain struck into it.

Trina still continued to work for Uncle Oelbermann. In the
mornings she busied herself about the kitchen, the bedroom,
and the sitting-room; but in the afternoon, for two or three
hours after lunch, she was occupied with the Noah's ark animals. She took her work to the bay window, spreading out a
great square of canvas underneath her chair, to catch the chips
and shavings, which she used afterwards for lighting fires.
One after another she caught up the little blocks of straight-
grained pine, the knife flashed between her fingers, the little
figure grew rapidly under her touch, was finished and ready
for painting in a wonderfully short time, and was tossed into
the basket that stood at her elbow.

But very often during that rainy winter after her marriage
Trina would pause in her work, her hands falling idly into her
lap, her eyes—her narrow, pale blue eyes—growing wide
and thoughtful as she gazed, unseeing, out into the rain-
washed street.

She loved McTeague now with a blind, unreasoning love
that admitted of no doubt or hesitancy. Indeed, it seemed to
her that it was only *after* her marriage with the dentist that
she had really begun to love him. With the absolute final surrender of herself, the irrevocable, ultimate submission, had
come an affection the like of which she had never dreamed in
the old B Street days. But Trina loved her husband, not because she fancied she saw in him any of those noble and generous qualities that inspire affection. The dentist might or
might not possess them, it was all one with Trina. She loved
him because she had given herself to him freely, unreservedly;
had merged her individuality into his; she was his, she belonged to him forever and forever. Nothing that he could do
(so she told herself), nothing that she herself could do, could
change her in this respect. McTeague might cease to love her,
might leave her, might even die; it would be all the same, *she
was his.*

But it had not been so at first. During those long, rainy
days of the fall, days when Trina was left alone for hours, at
that time when the excitement and novelty of the honeymoon
were dying down, when the new household was settling into

its grooves, she passed through many an hour of misgiving, of doubt, and even of actual regret.

Never would she forget one Sunday afternoon in particular. She had been married but three weeks. After dinner she and little Miss Baker had gone for a bit of a walk to take advantage of an hour's sunshine and to look at some wonderful geraniums in a florist's window on Sutter Street. They had been caught in a shower, and on returning to the flat the little dressmaker had insisted on fetching Trina up to her tiny room and brewing her a cup of strong tea, "to take the chill off." The two women had chatted over their teacups the better part of the afternoon, then Trina had returned to her rooms. For nearly three hours McTeague had been out of her thoughts, and as she came through their little suite, singing softly to herself, she suddenly came upon him quite unexpectedly. Her husband was in the "Dental Parlors," lying back in his operating chair, fast asleep. The little stove was crammed with coke, the room was overheated, the air thick and foul with the odors of ether, of coke gas, of stale beer and cheap tobacco. The dentist sprawled his gigantic limbs over the worn velvet of the operating chair; his coat and vest and shoes were off, and his huge feet, in their thick gray socks, dangled over the edge of the foot-rest; his pipe, fallen from his half-open mouth, had spilled the ashes into his lap; while on the floor, at his side, stood the half-empty pitcher of steam beer. His head had rolled limply upon one shoulder, his face was red with sleep, and from his open mouth came a terrific sound of snoring.

For a moment Trina stood looking at him as he lay thus, prone, inert, half-dressed, and stupefied with the heat of the room, the steam beer, and the fumes of the cheap tobacco. Then her little chin quivered and a sob rose to her throat; she fled from the "Parlors," and locking herself in her bedroom, flung herself on the bed and burst into an agony of weeping. Ah, no, ah, no, she could not love him. It had all been a dreadful mistake, and now it was irrevocable; she was bound to this man for life. If it was as bad as this now, only three weeks after her marriage, how would it be in the years to come? Year after year, month after month, hour after hour, she was to see this same face, with its salient jaw, was to feel

the touch of those enormous red hands, was to hear the
heavy, elephantine tread of those huge feet—in thick gray
socks. Year after year, day after day, there would be no
change, and it would last all her life. Either it would be one
long continued revulsion, or else—worse than all—she
would come to be content with him, would come to be like
him, would sink to the level of steam beer and cheap tobacco,
and all her pretty ways, her clean, trim little habits, would be
forgotten, since they would be thrown away upon her stupid,
brutish husband. "Her husband!" *That*, was her husband in
there—she could yet hear his snores—for life, for life. A
great despair seized upon her. She buried her face in the pillow and thought of her mother with an infinite longing.

Aroused at length by the chittering of the canary, Mc-
Teague had awakened slowly. After a while he had taken
down his concertina and played upon it the six very mournful
airs that he knew.

Face downward upon the bed, Trina still wept. Throughout that little suite could be heard but two sounds, the lugubrious strains of the concertina and the noise of stifled
weeping.

That her husband should be ignorant of her distress seemed
to Trina an additional grievance. With perverse inconsistency
she began to wish him to come to her, to comfort her. He
ought to know that she was in trouble, that she was lonely
and unhappy.

"Oh, Mac," she called in a trembling voice. But the concertina still continued to wail and lament. Then Trina wished she
were dead, and on the instant jumped up and ran into the
"Dental Parlors," and threw herself into her husband's arms,
crying: "Oh, Mac, dear, love me, love me *big*! I'm *so* unhappy."

"What—what—what—" the dentist exclaimed, starting
up bewildered, a little frightened.

"Nothing, nothing, only *love* me, love me always and
always."

But this first crisis, this momentary revolt, as much a matter
of high-strung feminine nerves as of anything else, passed,
and in the end Trina's affection for her "old bear" grew in
spite of herself. She began to love him more and more, not

for what he was, but for what she had given up to him. Only once again did Trina undergo a reaction against her husband, and then it was but the matter of an instant, brought on, curiously enough, by the sight of a bit of egg on McTeague's heavy mustache one morning just after breakfast.

Then, too, the pair had learned to make concessions, little by little, and all unconsciously they adapted their modes of life to suit each other. Instead of sinking to McTeague's level as she had feared, Trina found that she could make McTeague rise to hers, and in this saw a solution of many a difficult and gloomy complication.

For one thing, the dentist began to dress a little better, Trina even succeeding in inducing him to wear a high silk hat and a frock coat of a Sunday. Next he relinquished his Sunday afternoon's nap and beer in favor of three or four hours spent in the park with her—the weather permitting. So that gradually Trina's misgivings ceased, or when they did assail her, she could at last meet them with a shrug of the shoulders, saying to herself meanwhile, "Well, it's done now and it can't be helped; one must make the best of it."

During the first months of their married life these nervous relapses of hers had alternated with brusque outbursts of affection when her only fear was that her husband's love did not equal her own. Without an instant's warning, she would clasp him about the neck, rubbing her cheek against his, murmuring:

"Dear old Mac, I love you so, I love you so. Oh, aren't we happy together, Mac, just us two and no one else? You love me as much as I love you, don't you, Mac? Oh, if you shouldn't—if you *shouldn't*."

But by the middle of the winter Trina's emotions, oscillating at first from one extreme to another, commenced to settle themselves to an equilibrium of calmness and placid quietude. Her household duties began more and more to absorb her attention, for she was an admirable housekeeper, keeping the little suite in marvellous good order and regulating the schedule of expenditure with an economy that often bordered on positive niggardliness. It was a passion with her to save money. In the bottom of her trunk, in the bedroom, she hid a brass match-safe that answered the purposes of a savings bank. Each time she added a quarter or a half dollar to the little store she laughed and sang with a veritable childish delight; whereas, if the butcher or milkman compelled her to pay an overcharge she was unhappy for the rest of the day. She did not save this money for any ulterior purpose, she hoarded instinctively, without knowing why, responding to the dentist's remonstrances with:

"Yes, yes, I know I'm a little miser, I know it."

Trina had always been an economical little body, but it was only since her great winning in the lottery that she had become especially penurious. No doubt, in her fear lest their great good luck should demoralize them and lead to habits of extravagance, she had recoiled too far in the other direction. Never, never, never should a penny of that miraculous fortune be spent; rather should it be added to. It was a nest egg, a monstrous, roc-like nest egg, not so large, however, but that it could be made larger. Already by the end of that winter Trina had begun to make up the deficit of two hundred dollars that she had been forced to expend on the preparations for her marriage.

McTeague, on his part, never asked himself now-a-days whether he loved Trina the wife as much as he had loved Trina the young girl. There had been a time when to kiss Trina, to take her in his arms, had thrilled him from head to heel with a happiness that was beyond words; even the smell of her wonderful odorous hair had sent a sensation of faintness all through him. That time was long past now. Those sudden outbursts of affection on the part of his little woman, outbursts that only increased in vehemence the longer they lived together, puzzled rather than pleased him. He had come to submit to them good-naturedly, answering her passionate inquiries with a "Sure, sure, Trina, sure I love you. What— what's the matter with you?"

There was no passion in the dentist's regard for his wife. He dearly liked to have her near him, he took an enormous pleasure in watching her as she moved about their rooms, very much at home, gay and singing from morning till night; and it was his great delight to call her into the "Dental Parlors" when a patient was in the chair and, while he held the plugger, to have her rap in the gold fillings with the little boxwood mallet as he had taught her. But that tempest of passion, that overpowering desire that had suddenly taken possession of him that day when he had given her ether, again when he had caught her in his arms in the B Street station, and again and again during the early days of their married life, rarely stirred him now. On the other hand, he was never assailed with doubts as to the wisdom of his marriage.

McTeague had relapsed to his wonted stolidity. He never questioned himself, never looked for motives, never went to the bottom of things. The year following upon the summer of his marriage was a time of great contentment for him; after the novelty of the honeymoon had passed he slipped easily into the new order of things without a question. Thus his life would be for years to come. Trina was there; he was married and settled. He accepted the situation. The little animal comforts which for him constituted the enjoyment of life were ministered to at every turn, or when they were interfered with—as in the case of his Sunday afternoon's nap and beer—some agreeable substitute was found. In her attempts to improve McTeague—to raise him from the stupid animal life to which he had been accustomed in his bachelor days— Trina was tactful enough to move so cautiously and with such slowness that the dentist was unconscious of any process of change. In the matter of the high silk hat, it seemed to him that the initiative had come from himself.

Gradually the dentist improved under the influence of his little wife. He no longer went abroad with frayed cuffs about his huge red wrists—or worse, without any cuffs at all. Trina kept his linen clean and mended, doing most of his washing herself, and insisting that he should change his flannels— thick red flannels they were, with enormous bone buttons— once a week, his linen shirts twice a week, and his collars and cuffs every second day. She broke him of the habit of eating with his knife, she caused him to substitute bottled beer in the place of steam beer, and she induced him to take off his hat to Miss Baker, to Heise's wife, and to the other women of his acquaintance. McTeague no longer spent an evening at Frenna's. Instead of this he brought a couple of bottles of beer up to the rooms and shared it with Trina. In his "Parlors" he was no longer gruff and indifferent to his female

patients; he arrived at that stage where he could work and
talk to them at the same time; he even accompanied them to
the door, and held it open for them when the operation was
finished, bowing them out with great nods of his huge
square-cut head.

Besides all this, he began to observe the broader, larger interests of life, interests that affected him not as an individual,
but as a member of a class, a profession, or a political party.
He read the papers, he subscribed to a dental magazine; on
Easter, Christmas, and New Year's he went to church with
Trina. He commenced to have opinions, convictions—it was
not fair to deprive tax-paying women of the privilege to vote;
a university education should not be a prerequisite for admission to a dental college; the Catholic priests were to be restrained in their efforts to gain control of the public schools.

But most wonderful of all, McTeague began to have ambitions—very vague, very confused ideas of something better—
ideas for the most part borrowed from Trina. Some day, perhaps, he and his wife would have a house of their own. What
a dream! A little home all to themselves, with six rooms and
a bath, with a grass plat in front and calla-lilies. Then there
would be children. He would have a son, whose name would
be Daniel, who would go to High School, and perhaps turn
out to be a prosperous plumber or house painter. Then this
son Daniel would marry a wife, and they would all live together in that six-room-and-bath house; Daniel would have
little children. McTeague would grow old among them all.
The dentist saw himself as a venerable patriarch surrounded
by children and grandchildren.

So the winter passed. It was a season of great happiness for
the McTeagues; the new life jostled itself into its grooves. A
routine began.

On week-days they rose at half-past six, being awakened by
the boy who brought the bottled milk, and who had instructions to pound upon the bedroom door in passing. Trina
made breakfast—coffee, bacon and eggs, and a roll of Vienna
bread from the bakery. The breakfast was eaten in the
kitchen, on the round deal table covered with the shiny oilcloth table-spread tacked on. After breakfast the dentist immediately betook himself to his "Parlors" to meet his early

morning appointments—those made with the clerks and shop girls who stopped in for half an hour on their way to their work.

Trina, meanwhile, busied herself about the suite, clearing away the breakfast, sponging off the oilcloth table-spread, making the bed, pottering about with a broom or duster or cleaning rag. Towards ten o'clock she opened the windows to air the rooms, then put on her drab jacket, her little round turban with its red wing, took the butcher's and grocer's books from the knife basket in the drawer of the kitchen table, and descended to the street, where she spent a delicious hour—now in the huge market across the way, now in the grocer's store with its fragrant aroma of coffee and spices, and now before the counters of the haberdasher's, intent on a bit of shopping, turning over ends of veiling, strips of elastic, or slivers of whalebone. On the street she rubbed elbows with the great ladies of the avenue in their beautiful dresses, or at intervals she met an acquaintance or two—Miss Baker, or Heise's lame wife, or Mrs. Ryer. At times she passed the flat and looked up at the windows of her home, marked by the huge golden molar that projected, flashing, from the bay window of the "Parlors." She saw the open windows of the sitting-room, the Nottingham lace curtains stirring and billowing in the draft, and she caught sight of Maria Macapa's towelled head as the Mexican maid-of-all-work went to and fro in the suite, sweeping or carrying away the ashes. Occasionally in the windows of the "Parlors" she beheld McTeague's rounded back as he bent to his work. Sometimes, even, they saw each other and waved their hands gayly in recognition.

By eleven o'clock Trina returned to the flat, her brown net reticule—once her mother's—full of parcels. At once she set about getting lunch—sausages, perhaps, with mashed potatoes; or last evening's joint warmed over or made into a stew; chocolate, which Trina adored, and a side dish or two—a salted herring or a couple of artichokes or a salad. At half-past twelve the dentist came in from the "Parlors," bringing with him the smell of creosote and of ether. They sat down to lunch in the sitting-room. They told each other of their doings throughout the forenoon; Trina showed her purchases, McTeague recounted the progress of an operation. At one o'clock they separated, the dentist returning to the "Parlors," Trina settling to her work on the Noah's ark animals. At about three o'clock she put this work away, and for the rest of the afternoon was variously occupied—sometimes it was the mending, sometimes the wash, sometimes new curtains to be put up, or a bit of carpet to be tacked down, or a letter to be written, or a visit—generally to Miss Baker—to be returned. Towards five o'clock the old woman whom they had hired for that purpose came to cook supper, for even Trina was not equal to the task of preparing three meals a day.

This woman was French, and was known to the flat as Augustine, no one taking enough interest in her to inquire for her last name; all that was known of her was that she was a decayed French laundress, miserably poor, her trade long since ruined by Chinese competition. Augustine cooked well, but she was otherwise undesirable, and Trina lost patience with her at every moment. The old French woman's most marked characteristic was her timidity. Trina could scarcely address her a simple direction without Augustine quailing and shrinking; a reproof, however gentle, threw her into an agony of confusion; while Trina's anger promptly reduced her to a state of nervous collapse, wherein she lost all power of speech, while her head began to bob and nod with an incontrollable twitching of the muscles, much like the oscillations of the head of a toy donkey. Her timidity was exasperating, her very presence in the room unstrung the nerves, while her morbid eagerness to avoid offence only served to develop in her a clumsiness that was at times beyond belief. More than once Trina had decided that she could no longer put up with Augustine, but each time she had retained her as she reflected upon her admirably cooked cabbage soups and tapioca puddings, and—which in Trina's eyes was her chiefest recommendation—the pittance for which she was contented to work.

Augustine had a husband. He was a spirit-medium—a "professor." At times he held seances in the larger rooms of the flat, playing vigorously upon a mouth-organ and invoking a familiar whom he called "Edna," and whom he asserted was an Indian maiden.

The evening was a period of relaxation for Trina and McTeague. They had supper at six, after which McTeague smoked his pipe and read the papers for half an hour, while Trina and Augustine cleared away the table and washed the dishes. Then, as often as not, they went out together. One of their amusements was to go "down town" after dark and promenade Market and Kearney Streets. It was very gay; a great many others were promenading there also. All of the stores were brilliantly lighted and many of them still open. They walked about aimlessly, looking into the shop windows. Trina would take McTeague's arm, and he, very much embarrassed at that, would thrust both hands into his pockets and pretend not to notice. They stopped before the jewellers' and milliners' windows, finding a great delight in picking out things for each other, saying how they would choose this and that if they were rich. Trina did most of the talking, McTeague merely approving by a growl or a movement of the head or shoulders; she was interested in the displays of some of the cheaper stores, but he found an irresistible charm in an enormous golden molar with four prongs that hung at a corner of Kearney Street. Sometimes they would look at Mars or at the moon through the street telescopes or sit for a time in the rotunda of a vast department store where a band played every evening.

Occasionally they met Heise the harness-maker and his wife, with whom they had become acquainted. Then the evening was concluded by a four-cornered party in the Luxembourg, a quiet German restaurant under a theatre. Trina had a *tamale* and a glass of beer, Mrs. Heise (who was a decayed writing teacher) ate salads, with glasses of grenadine and currant syrups. Heise drank cocktails and whiskey straight, and urged the dentist to join him. But McTeague was obstinate, shaking his head. "I can't drink that stuff," he said. "It don't agree with me, somehow; I go kinda crazy after two glasses." So he gorged himself with beer and frankfurter sausages plastered with German mustard.

When the annual Mechanics' Fair opened, McTeague and Trina often spent their evenings there, studying the exhibits carefully (since in Trina's estimation education meant knowing things and being able to talk about them). Wearying of this they would go up into the gallery, and, leaning over, look down into the huge amphitheatre full of light and color and movement.

There rose to them the vast shuffling noise of thousands of feet and a subdued roar of conversation like the sound of a great mill. Mingled with this was the purring of distant machinery, the splashing of a temporary fountain, and the rhythmic jangling of a brass band, while in the piano exhibit a hired performer was playing upon a concert grand with a great flourish. Nearer at hand they could catch ends of conversation and notes of laughter, the noise of moving dresses, and the rustle of stiffly starched skirts. Here and there school children elbowed their way through the crowd, crying shrilly, their hands full of advertisement pamphlets, fans, picture cards, and toy whips, while the air itself was full of the smell of fresh popcorn.

They even spent some time in the art gallery. Trina's cousin Selina, who gave lessons in hand painting at two bits an hour, generally had an exhibit on the walls, which they were interested to find. It usually was a bunch of yellow poppies painted on black velvet and framed in gilt. They stood before it some little time, hazarding their opinions, and then moved on slowly from one picture to another. Trina had McTeague buy a catalogue and made a duty of finding the title of every picture. This, too, she told McTeague, was a kind of education one ought to cultivate. Trina professed to be fond of art, having perhaps acquired a taste for painting and sculpture from her experience with the Noah's ark animals.

"Of course," she told the dentist, "I'm no critic, I only know what I like." She knew that she liked the "Ideal Heads," lovely girls with flowing straw-colored hair and immense, upturned eyes. These always had for title, "Reverie," or "An Idyll," or "Dreams of Love."

"I think those are lovely, don't you, Mac?" she said.

"Yes, yes," answered McTeague, nodding his head, bewildered, trying to understand. "Yes, yes, lovely, that's the word. Are you dead sure now, Trina, that all that's hand-painted just like the poppies?"

Thus the winter passed, a year went by, then two. The little life of Polk Street, the life of small traders, drug clerks,

grocers, stationers, plumbers, dentists, doctors, spirit-medi-
ums, and the like, ran on monotonously in its accustomed
grooves. The first three years of their married life wrought
little change in the fortunes of the McTeagues. In the third
summer the branch post-office was moved from the ground
floor of the flat to a corner farther up the street in order to
be near the cable line that ran mail cars. Its place was taken
by a German saloon, called a "Wein Stube," in the face of the
protests of every female lodger. A few months later quite a
little flurry of excitement ran through the street on the occasion of "The Polk Street Open Air Festival," organized to
celebrate the introduction there of electric lights. The festival
lasted three days and was quite an affair. The street was gar-
landed with yellow and white bunting; there were processions
and "floats" and brass bands. Marcus Schouler was in his element during the whole time of the celebration. He was one
of the marshals of the parade, and was to be seen at every
hour of the day, wearing a borrowed high hat and cotton
gloves, and galloping a broken-down cab-horse over the cobbles. He carried a baton covered with yellow and white calico,
with which he made furious passes and gestures. His voice
was soon reduced to a whisper by continued shouting, and
he raged and fretted over trifles till he wore himself thin.
McTeague was disgusted with him. As often as Marcus passed
the window of the flat the dentist would mutter:

"Ah, you think you're smart, don't you?"

The result of the festival was the organizing of a body
known as the "Polk Street Improvement Club," of which
Marcus was elected secretary. McTeague and Trina often
heard of him in this capacity through Heise the harness-
maker. Marcus had evidently come to have political aspira-
tions. It appeared that he was gaining a reputation as a maker
of speeches, delivered with fiery emphasis, and occasionally
reprinted in the "Progress," the organ of the club—"outraged
constituencies," "opinions warped by personal bias," "eyes
blinded by party prejudice," etc.

Of her family, Trina heard every fortnight in letters from
her mother. The upholstery business which Mr. Sieppe had
bought was doing poorly, and Mrs. Sieppe bewailed the day
she had ever left B Street. Mr. Sieppe was losing money every

month. Owgooste, who was to have gone to school, had been
forced to go to work in "the store," picking waste. Mrs.
Sieppe was obliged to take a lodger or two. Affairs were in a
very bad way. Occasionally she spoke of Marcus. Mr. Sieppe
had not forgotten him despite his own troubles, but still had
an eye out for some one whom Marcus could "go in with"
on a ranch.

It was toward the end of this period of three years that
Trina and McTeague had their first serious quarrel. Trina had
talked so much about having a little house of their own at
some future day, that McTeague had at length come to regard
the affair as the end and object of all their labors. For a long
time they had had their eyes upon one house in particular. It
was situated on a cross street close by, between Polk Street
and the great avenue one block above, and hardly a Sunday
afternoon passed that Trina and McTeague did not go and
look at it. They stood for fully half an hour upon the other
side of the street, examining every detail of its exterior, hazarding guesses as to the arrangement of the rooms, commenting upon its immediate neighborhood—which was rather
sordid. The house was a wooden two-story arrangement,
built by a misguided contractor in a sort of hideous Queen
Anne style, all scrolls and meaningless mill-work, with a cheap
imitation of stained glass in the light over the door. There
was a microscopic front yard full of dusty calla-lilies. The
front door boasted an electric bell. But for the McTeagues it
was an ideal home. Their idea was to live in this little house,
the dentist retaining merely his office in the flat. The two
places were but around the corner from each other, so that
McTeague could lunch with his wife, as usual, and could even
keep his early morning appointments and return to breakfast
if he so desired.

However, the house was occupied. A Hungarian family
lived in it. The father kept a stationery and notion "bazaar"
next to Heise's harness-shop on Polk Street, while the oldest
son played a third violin in the orchestra of a theatre. The
family rented the house unfurnished for thirty-five dollars,
paying extra for the water.

But one Sunday as Trina and McTeague on their way home
from their usual walk turned into the cross street on which

the little house was situated, they became promptly aware of an unwonted bustle going on upon the sidewalk in front of it. A dray was back against the curb, an express wagon drove away loaded with furniture; bedsteads, looking-glasses, and washbowls littered the sidewalks. The Hungarian family were moving out.

"Oh, Mac, look!" gasped Trina.

"Sure, sure," muttered the dentist.

After that they spoke but little. For upwards of an hour the two stood upon the sidewalk opposite, watching intently all that went forward, absorbed, excited.

On the evening of the next day they returned and visited the house, finding a great delight in going from room to room and imagining themselves installed therein. Here would be the bedroom, here the dining-room, here a charming little parlor. As they came out upon the front steps once more they met the owner, an enormous, red-faced fellow, so fat that his walking seemed merely a certain movement of his feet by which he pushed his stomach along in front of him. Trina talked with him a few moments, but arrived at no understanding, and the two went away after giving him their address. At supper that night McTeague said:

"Huh—what do you think, Trina?"

Trina put her chin in the air, tilting back her heavy tiara of swarthy hair.

"I'm not so sure yet. Thirty-five dollars and the water extra. I don't think we can afford it, Mac."

"Ah, pshaw!" growled the dentist, "sure we can."

"It isn't only that," said Trina, "but it'll cost so much to make the change."

"Ah, you talk's though we were paupers. Ain't we got five thousand dollars?"

Trina flushed on the instant, even to the lobes of her tiny pale ears, and put her lips together.

"Now, Mac, you know I don't want you should talk like that. That money's never, never to be touched."

"And you've been savun up a good deal, besides," went on McTeague, exasperated at Trina's persistent economies. "How much money have you got in that little brass match-safe in the bottom of your trunk? Pretty near a hundred dollars, I guess—ah, sure." He shut his eyes and nodded his great head in a knowing way.

Trina had more than that in the brass match-safe in question, but her instinct of hoarding had led her to keep it a secret from her husband. Now she lied to him with prompt fluency.

"A hundred dollars! What are you talking of, Mac? I've not got fifty. I've not got *thirty*."

"Oh, let's take that little house," broke in McTeague. "We got the chance now, and it may never come again. Come on, Trina, shall we? Say, come on, shall we, huh?"

"We'd have to be awful saving if we did, Mac."

"Well, sure, *I* say let's take it."

"I don't know," said Trina, hesitating. "Wouldn't it be lovely to have a house all to ourselves? But let's not decide until to-morrow."

The next day the owner of the house called. Trina was out at her morning's marketing and the dentist, who had no one in the chair at the time, received him in the "Parlors." Before he was well aware of it, McTeague had concluded the bargain. The owner bewildered him with a world of phrases, made him believe that it would be a great saving to move into the little house, and finally offered it to him "water free."

"All right, all right," said McTeague, "I'll take it."

The other immediately produced a paper.

"Well, then, suppose you sign for the first month's rent, and we'll call it a bargain. That's business, you know," and McTeague, hesitating, signed.

"I'd like to have talked more with my wife about it first," he said, dubiously.

"Oh, that's all right," answered the owner, easily. "I guess if the head of the family wants a thing, that's enough."

McTeague could not wait until lunch time to tell the news to Trina. As soon as he heard her come in, he laid down the plaster-of-paris mould he was making and went out into the kitchen and found her chopping up onions.

"Well, Trina," he said, " we got that house. I've taken it."

"What do you mean?" she answered, quickly. The dentist told her.

"And you signed a paper for the first month's rent?"

"Sure, sure. That's business, you know."

"Well, why did you *do* it?" cried Trina. "You might have asked *me* something about it. Now, what have you done? I was talking with Mrs. Ryer about that house while I was out this morning, and she said the Hungarians moved out because it was absolutely unhealthy; there's water been standing in the basement for months. And she told me, too," Trina went on indignantly, "that she knew the owner, and she was sure we could get the house for thirty if we'd bargain for it. Now what have you gone and done? I hadn't made up my mind about taking the house at all. And now I *won't* take it, with the water in the basement and all."

"Well—well," stammered McTeague, helplessly, "we needn't go in if it's unhealthy."

"But you've signed a *paper*," cried Trina, exasperated. "You've got to pay that first month's rent, anyhow—to forfeit it. Oh, you are so stupid! There's thirty-five dollars just thrown away. I *shan't* go into that house; we won't move a *foot* out of here. I've changed my mind about it, and there's water in the basement besides."

"Well, I guess we can stand thirty-five dollars," mumbled the dentist, "if we've got to."

"Thirty-five dollars just thrown out of the window," cried Trina, her teeth clicking, every instinct of her parsimony aroused. "Oh, you are the thick-wittedest man that I ever knew. Do you think we're millionaires? Oh, to think of losing thirty-five dollars like that." Tears were in her eyes, tears of grief as well as of anger. Never had McTeague seen his little woman so aroused. Suddenly she rose to her feet and slammed the chopping-bowl down upon the table. "Well, *I* won't pay a nickel of it," she exclaimed.

"Huh? What, what?" stammered the dentist, taken all aback by her outburst.

"I say that you will find that money, that thirty-five dollars, yourself."

"Why—why——"

"It's your stupidity got us into this fix, and you'll be the one that'll suffer by it."

"I can't do it, I *won't* do it. We'll—we'll share and share alike. Why, you said—you told me you'd take the house if the water was free."

"I *never* did. I *never* did. How can you stand there and say such a thing?"

"You did tell me that," vociferated McTeague, beginning to get angry in his turn.

"Mac, I didn't, and you know it. And what's more, I won't pay a nickel. Mr. Heise pays his bill next week, it's forty-three dollars, and you can just pay the thirty-five out of that."

"Why, you got a whole hundred dollars saved up in your match-safe," shouted the dentist, throwing out an arm with an awkward gesture. "You pay half and I'll pay half, that's only fair."

"No, no, *no*," exclaimed Trina. "It's not a hundred dollars. You won't touch it; you won't touch my money, I tell you."

"Ah, how does it happen to be yours, I'd like to know?"

"It's mine! It's mine! It's mine!" cried Trina, her face scarlet, her teeth clicking like the snap of a closing purse.

"It ain't any more yours than it is mine."

"Every penny of it is mine."

"Ah, what a fine fix you'd get me into," growled the dentist. "I've signed the paper with the owner; that's business, you know, that's business, you know; and now you go back on me. Suppose we'd taken the house, we'd 'a' shared the rent, wouldn't we, just as we do here?"

Trina shrugged her shoulders with a great affectation of indifference and began chopping the onions again.

"You settle it with the owner," she said. "It's your affair; you've got the money." She pretended to assume a certain calmness as though the matter was something that no longer affected her. Her manner exasperated McTeague all the more.

"No, I won't; no, I won't; I won't either," he shouted. "I'll pay my half and he can come to you for the other half." Trina put a hand over her ear to shut out his clamor.

"Ah, don't try and be smart," cried McTeague. "Come, now, yes or no, will you pay your half?"

"You heard what I said."

"Will you pay it?"

"No."

"Miser!" shouted McTeague. "Miser! you're worse than old

Zerkow. All right, all right, keep your money. I'll pay the whole thirty-five. I'd rather lose it than be such a miser as you."

"Haven't you got anything to do," returned Trina, "instead of staying here and abusing me?"

"Well, then, for the last time, will you help me out?" Trina cut the heads of a fresh bunch of onions and gave no answer.

"Huh? will you?"

"I'd like to have my kitchen to myself, please," she said in a mincing way, irritating to a last degree. The dentist stamped out of the room, banging the door behind him.

For nearly a week the breach between them remained unhealed. Trina only spoke to the dentist in monosyllables, while he, exasperated at her calmness and frigid reserve, sulked in his "Dental Parlors," muttering terrible things beneath his mustache, or finding solace in his concertina, playing his six lugubrious airs over and over again, or swearing frightful oaths at his canary. When Heise paid his bill, McTeague, in a fury, sent the amount to the owner of the little house.

There was no formal reconciliation between the dentist and his little woman. Their relations readjusted themselves inevitably. By the end of the week they were as amicable as ever, but it was long before they spoke of the little house again. Nor did they ever revisit it of a Sunday afternoon. A month or so later the Ryers told them that the owner himself had moved in. The McTeagues never occupied that little house.

But Trina suffered a reaction after the quarrel. She began to be sorry she had refused to help her husband, sorry she had brought matters to such an issue. One afternoon as she was at work on the Noah's ark animals, she surprised herself crying over the affair. She loved her "old bear" too much to do him an injustice, and perhaps, after all, she had been in the wrong. Then it occurred to her how pretty it would be to come up behind him unexpectedly, and slip the money, thirty-five dollars, into his hand, and pull his huge head down to her and kiss his bald spot as she used to do in the days before they were married.

Then she hesitated, pausing in her work, her knife dropping into her lap, a half-whittled figure between her fingers.

If not thirty-five dollars, then at least fifteen or sixteen, her share of it. But a feeling of reluctance, a sudden revolt against this intended generosity, arose in her.

"No, no," she said to herself. "I'll give him ten dollars. I'll tell him it's all I can afford. It *is* all I can afford."

She hastened to finish the figure of the animal she was then at work upon, putting in the ears and tail with a drop of glue, and tossing it into the basket at her side. Then she rose and went into the bedroom and opened her trunk, taking the key from under a corner of the carpet where she kept it hid.

At the very bottom of her trunk, under her bridal dress, she kept her savings. It was all in change—half dollars and dollars for the most part, with here and there a gold piece. Long since the little brass match-box had overflowed. Trina kept the surplus in a chamois-skin sack she had made from an old chest protector. Just now, yielding to an impulse which often seized her, she drew out the match-box and the chamois sack, and emptying the contents on the bed, counted them carefully. It came to one hundred and sixty-five dollars, all told. She counted it and recounted it and made little piles of it, and rubbed the gold pieces between the folds of her apron until they shone.

"Ah, yes, ten dollars is all I can afford to give Mac," said Trina, "and even then, think of it, ten dollars—it will be four or five months before I can save that again. But, dear old Mac, I know it would make him feel glad, and perhaps," she added, suddenly taken with an idea, "perhaps Mac will refuse to take it."

She took a ten-dollar piece from the heap and put the rest away. Then she paused:

"No, not the gold piece," she said to herself. "It's too pretty. He can have the silver." She made the change and counted out ten silver dollars into her palm. But what a difference it made in the appearance and weight of the little chamois bag! The bag was shrunken and withered, long wrinkles appeared running downward from the draw-string. It was a lamentable sight. Trina looked longingly at the ten broad pieces in her hand. Then suddenly all her intuitive desire of saving, her instinct of hoarding, her love of money for the money's sake, rose strong within her.

"No, no, no," she said. "I can't do it. It may be mean, but I can't help it. It's stronger than I." She returned the money to the bag and locked it and the brass match-box in her trunk, turning the key with a long breath of satisfaction.

She was a little troubled, however, as she went back into the sitting-room and took up her work.

"I didn't use to be so stingy," she told herself. "Since I won in the lottery I've become a regular little miser. It's growing on me, but never mind, it's a good fault, and, anyhow, I can't help it."

XI

O N THAT particular morning the McTeagues had risen a
half hour earlier than usual and taken a hurried breakfast in the kitchen on the deal table with its oilcloth cover.
Trina was house-cleaning that week and had a presentiment
of a hard day's work ahead of her, while McTeague remembered a seven o'clock appointment with a little German shoemaker.

At about eight o'clock, when the dentist had been in his
office for over an hour, Trina descended upon the bedroom,
a towel about her head and the roller-sweeper in her hand.
She covered the bureau and sewing machine with sheets, and
unhooked the chenille portières between the bedroom and
the sitting-room. As she was tying the Nottingham lace curtains at the window into great knots, she saw old Miss Baker
on the opposite sidewalk in the street below, and raising the
sash called down to her.

"Oh, it's you, Mrs. McTeague," cried the retired dressmaker, facing about, her head in the air. Then a long conversation was begun, Trina, her arms folded under her breast,
her elbows resting on the window ledge, willing to be idle
for a moment; old Miss Baker, her market-basket on her arm,
her hands wrapped in the ends of her worsted shawl against
the cold of the early morning. They exchanged phrases, calling to each other from window to curb, their breath coming
from their lips in faint puffs of vapor, their voices shrill, and
raised to dominate the clamor of the waking street. The newsboys had made their appearance on the street, together with
the day laborers. The cable cars had begun to fill up; all along
the street could be seen the shopkeepers taking down their
shutters; some were still breakfasting. Now and then a waiter
from one of the cheap restaurants crossed from one sidewalk
to another, balancing on one palm a tray covered with a
napkin.

"Aren't you out pretty early this morning, Miss Baker?"
called Trina.

"No, no," answered the other. "I'm always up at half-past
six, but I don't always get out so soon. I wanted to get a nice

head of cabbage and some lentils for a soup, and if you don't go to market early, the restaurants get all the best."

"And you've been to market already, Miss Baker?"

"Oh, my, yes; and I got a fish—a sole—see." She drew the sole in question from her basket.

"Oh, the lovely sole!" exclaimed Trina.

"I got this one at Spadella's; he always has good fish on Friday. How is the doctor, Mrs. McTeague?"

"Ah, Mac is always well, thank you, Miss Baker."

"You know, Mrs. Ryer told me," cried the little dressmaker, moving forward a step out of the way of a "glass-put-in" man, "that Doctor McTeague pulled a tooth of that Catholic priest, Father—oh, I forget his name—anyhow, he pulled his tooth with his fingers. Was that true, Mrs. McTeague?"

"Oh, of course. Mac does that almost all the time now, 'specially with front teeth. He's got a regular reputation for it. He says it's brought him more patients than even the sign I gave him," she added, pointing to the big golden molar projecting from the office window.

"With his fingers! Now, think of that," exclaimed Miss Baker, wagging her head. "Isn't he that strong! It's just won-derful. Cleaning house to-day?" she inquired, glancing at Trina's towelled head.

"Um hum," answered Trina. "Maria Macapa's coming in to help pretty soon."

At the mention of Maria's name the little old dressmaker suddenly uttered an exclamation.

"Well, if I'm not here talking to you and forgetting some-thing I was just dying to tell you. Mrs. McTeague, what ever in the world do you suppose? Maria and old Zerkow, that red-headed Polish Jew, the rag-bottles-sacks man, you know, they're going to be married."

"No!" cried Trina, in blank amazement. "You don't mean it."

"Of course I do. Isn't it the funniest thing you ever heard of?"

"Oh, tell me all about it," said Trina, leaning eagerly from the window. Miss Baker crossed the street and stood just be-neath her.

"Well, Maria came to me last night and wanted me to make

her a new gown, said she wanted something gay, like what the girls at the candy store wear when they go out with their young men. I couldn't tell what had got into the girl, until finally she told me she wanted something to get married in, and that Zerkow had asked her to marry him, and that she was going to do it. Poor Maria! I guess it's the first and only offer she ever received, and it's just turned her head."

"But what *do* those two see in each other?" cried Trina. "Zerkow is a horror, he's an old man, and his hair is red and his voice is gone, and then he's a Jew, isn't he?"

"I know, I know; but it's Maria's only chance for a husband, and she don't mean to let it pass. You know she isn't quite right in her head, anyhow. I'm awfully sorry for poor Maria. But *I* can't see what Zerkow wants to marry her for. It's not possible that he's in love with Maria, it's out of the question. Maria hasn't a sou, either, and I'm just positive that Zerkow has lots of money."

"I'll bet I know why," exclaimed Trina, with sudden conviction; "yes, I know just why. See here, Miss Baker, you know how crazy old Zerkow is after money and gold and those sort of things."

"Yes, I know; but you know Maria hasn't——"

"Now, just listen. You've heard Maria tell about that wonderful service of gold dishes she says her folks used to own in Central America; she's crazy on that subject, don't you know. She's all right on everything else, but just start her on that service of gold plate and she'll talk you deaf. She can describe it just as though she saw it, and she can make you see it, too, almost. Now, you see, Maria and Zerkow have known each other pretty well. Maria goes to him every two weeks or so to sell him junk; they got acquainted that way, and I know Maria's been dropping in to see him pretty often this last year, and sometimes he comes here to see her. He's made Maria tell him the story of that plate over and over and over again, and Maria does it and is glad to, because he's the only one that believes it. Now he's going to marry her just so's he can hear that story every day, every hour. He's pretty near as crazy on the subject as Maria is. They're a pair for you, aren't they? Both crazy over a lot of gold dishes that never existed. Perhaps Maria'll marry him because it's her only chance to get a husband, but I'm sure it's more for the reason that she's got some one to talk to now who believes her story. Don't you think I'm right?"

"Yes, yes, I guess you're right," admitted Miss Baker.

"But it's a queer match anyway you put it," said Trina, musingly.

"Ah, you may well say that," returned the other, nodding her head. There was a silence. For a long moment the dentist's wife and the retired dressmaker, the one at the window, the other on the sidewalk, remained lost in thought, wondering over the strangeness of the affair.

But suddenly there was a diversion. Alexander, Marcus Schouler's Irish setter, whom his master had long since allowed the liberty of running untrammelled about the neighborhood, turned the corner briskly and came trotting along the sidewalk where Miss Baker stood. At the same moment the Scotch collie who had at one time belonged to the branch post-office issued from the side door of a house not fifty feet away. In an instant the two enemies had recognized each other. They halted abruptly, their fore feet planted rigidly. Trina uttered a little cry.

"Oh, look out, Miss Baker. Those two dogs hate each other just like humans. You best look out. They'll fight sure." Miss Baker sought safety in a nearby vestibule, whence she peered forth at the scene, very interested and curious. Maria Macapa's head thrust itself from one of the top-story windows of the flat, with a shrill cry. Even McTeague's huge form appeared above the half curtains of the "Parlor" windows, while over his shoulder could be seen the face of the "patient," a napkin tucked in his collar, the rubber dam depending from his mouth. All the flat knew of the feud between the dogs, but never before had the pair been brought face to face.

Meanwhile, the collie and the setter had drawn near to each other; five feet apart they paused as if by mutual consent. The collie turned sidewise to the setter; the setter instantly wheeled himself flank on to the collie. Their tails rose and stiffened, they raised their lips over their long white fangs, the napes of their necks bristled, and they showed each other the vicious whites of their eyes, while they drew in their breaths with prolonged and rasping snarls. Each dog seemed

to be the personification of fury and unsatisfied hate. They
began to circle about each other with infinite slowness, walking stiffed-legged and upon the very points of their feet. Then
they wheeled about and began to circle in the opposite direction. Twice they repeated this motion, their snarls growing
louder. But still they did not come together, and the distance
of five feet between them was maintained with an almost
mathematical precision. It was magnificent, but it was not
war. Then the setter, pausing in his walk, turned his head
slowly from his enemy. The collie sniffed the air and pretended an interest in an old shoe lying in the gutter. Gradually and with all the dignity of monarchs they moved away
from each other. Alexander stalked back to the corner of the
street. The collie paced toward the side gate whence he had
issued, affecting to remember something of great importance.
They disappeared. Once out of sight of one another they began to bark furiously.

"Well, I *never*!" exclaimed Trina in great disgust. "The way
those two dogs have been carrying on you'd 'a' thought they
would 'a' just torn each other to pieces when they had the
chance, and here I'm wasting the whole morning——" she
closed her window with a bang.

"Sick 'im, sick 'im," called Maria Macapa, in a vain attempt
to promote a fight.

Old Miss Baker came out of the vestibule, pursing her lips,
quite put out at the fiasco. "And after all that fuss," she said
to herself aggrievedly.

The little dressmaker bought an envelope of nasturtium
seeds at the florist's, and returned to her tiny room in the flat.
But as she slowly mounted the first flight of steps she suddenly came face to face with Old Grannis, who was coming
down. It was between eight and nine, and he was on his way
to his little dog hospital, no doubt. Instantly Miss Baker was
seized with trepidation, her curious little false curls shook, a
faint—a very faint—flush came into her withered cheeks, and
her heart beat so violently under the worsted shawl that she
felt obliged to shift the market-basket to her other arm and
put out her free hand to steady herself against the rail.

On his part, Old Grannis was instantly overwhelmed with
confusion. His awkwardness seemed to paralyze his limbs, his

lips twitched and turned dry, his hand went tremblingly to his chin. But what added to Miss Baker's miserable embarrassment on this occasion was the fact that the old Englishman should meet her thus, carrying a sordid market-basket full of sordid fish and cabbage. It seemed as if a malicious fate persisted in bringing the two old people face to face at the most inopportune moments.

Just now, however, a veritable catastrophe occurred. The little old dressmaker changed her basket to her other arm at precisely the wrong moment, and Old Grannis, hastening to pass, removing his hat in a hurried salutation, struck it with his forearm, knocking it from her grasp, and sending it rolling and bumping down the stairs. The sole fell flat upon the first landing; the lentils scattered themselves over the entire flight; while the cabbage, leaping from step to step, thundered down the incline and brought up against the street door with a shock that reverberated through the entire building.

The little retired dressmaker, horribly vexed, nervous and embarrassed, was hard put to it to keep back the tears. Old Grannis stood for a moment with averted eyes, murmuring: "Oh, I'm so sorry, I'm so sorry. I—I really—I beg your pardon, really—really."

Marcus Schouler, coming down stairs from his room, saved the situation.

"Hello, people," he cried. "By damn! you've upset your basket—you have, for a fact. Here, let's pick um up." He and Old Grannis went up and down the flight, gathering up the fish, the lentils, and the sadly battered cabbage. Marcus was raging over the pusillanimity of Alexander, of which Maria had just told him.

"I'll cut him in two with the whip," he shouted. "I will, I will, I say I will, for a fact. He wouldn't fight, hey? I'll give um all the fight he wants, nasty, mangy cur. If he won't fight he won't eat. I'm going to get the butcher's bull pup and I'll put um both in a bag and shake um up. I will, for a fact, and I guess Alec will fight. Come along, Mister Grannis," and he took the old Englishman away.

Little Miss Baker hastened to her room and locked herself in. She was excited and upset during all the rest of the day, and listened eagerly for Old Grannis's return that evening. He

went instantly to work binding up "The Breeder and Sportsman," and back numbers of the "Nation." She heard him
softly draw his chair and the table on which he had placed his
little binding apparatus close to the wall. At once she did the
same, brewing herself a cup of tea. All through that evening
the two old people "kept company" with each other, after
their own peculiar fashion. "Setting out with each other"
Miss Baker had begun to call it. That they had been presented, that they had even been forced to talk together, had
made no change in their relative positions. Almost immediately they had fallen back into their old ways again, quite
unable to master their timidity, to overcome the stifling
embarrassment that seized upon them when in each other's
presence. It was a sort of hypnotism, a thing stronger than
themselves. But they were not altogether dissatisfied with the
way things had come to be. It was their little romance, their
last, and they were living through it with supreme enjoyment
and calm contentment.

Marcus Schouler still occupied his old room on the floor
above the McTeagues. They saw but little of him, however.
At long intervals the dentist or his wife met him on the stairs
of the flat. Sometimes he would stop and talk with Trina,
inquiring after the Sieppes, asking her if Mr. Sieppe had yet
heard of any one with whom he, Marcus, could "go in with
on a ranch." McTeague, Marcus merely nodded to. Never had
the quarrel between the two men been completely patched
up. It did not seem possible to the dentist now that Marcus
had ever been his "pal," that they had ever taken long walks
together. He was sorry that he had treated Marcus gratis for
an ulcerated tooth, while Marcus daily recalled the fact that
he had given up his "girl" to his friend—the girl who had
won a fortune—as the great mistake of his life. Only once
since the wedding had he called upon Trina, at a time when
he knew McTeague would be out. Trina had shown him
through the rooms and had told him, innocently enough,
how gay was their life there. Marcus had come away fairly
sick with envy; his rancor against the dentist—and against
himself, for that matter—knew no bounds. "And you might
'a' had it all yourself, Marcus Schouler," he muttered to himself on the stairs. "You mushhead, you damn fool!"

Meanwhile, Marcus was becoming involved in the politics of his ward. As secretary of the Polk Street Improvement Club—which soon developed into quite an affair and began to assume the proportions of a Republican political machine—he found he could make a little, a very little more than enough to live on. At once he had given up his position as Old Grannis's assistant in the dog hospital. Marcus felt that he needed a wider sphere. He had his eye upon a place connected with the city pound. When the great railroad strike occurred, he promptly got himself engaged as deputy-sheriff, and spent a memorable week in Sacramento, where he involved himself in more than one terrible melée with the strikers. Marcus had that quickness of temper and passionate readiness to take offence which passes among his class for bravery. But whatever were his motives, his promptness to face danger could not for a moment be doubted. After the strike he returned to Polk Street, and throwing himself into the Improvement Club, heart, soul, and body, soon became one of its ruling spirits. In a certain local election, where a huge paving contract was at stake, the club made itself felt in the ward, and Marcus so managed his cards and pulled his wires that, at the end of the matter, he found himself some four hundred dollars to the good.

When McTeague came out of his "Parlors" at noon of the day upon which Trina had heard the news of Maria Macapa's intended marriage, he found Trina burning coffee on a shovel in the sitting-room. Try as she would, Trina could never quite eradicate from their rooms a certain faint and indefinable odor, particularly offensive to her. The smell of the photographer's chemicals persisted in spite of all Trina could do to combat it. She burnt pastilles and Chinese punk, and even, as now, coffee on a shovel, all to no purpose. Indeed, the only drawback to their delightful home was the general unpleasant smell that pervaded it—a smell that arose partly from the photographer's chemicals, partly from the cooking in the little kitchen, and partly from the ether and creosote of the dentist's "Parlors."

As McTeague came in to lunch on this occasion, he found the table already laid, a red cloth figured with white flowers was spread, and as he took his seat his wife put down the shovel on a chair and brought in the stewed codfish and the pot of chocolate. As he tucked his napkin into his enormous collar, McTeague looked vaguely about the room, rolling his eyes.

During the three years of their married life the McTeagues had made but few additions to their furniture, Trina declaring that they could not afford it. The sitting-room could boast of but three new ornaments. Over the melodeon hung their marriage certificate in a black frame. It was balanced upon one side by Trina's wedding bouquet under a glass case, preserved by some fearful unknown process, and upon the other by the photograph of Trina and the dentist in their wedding finery. This latter picture was quite an affair, and had been taken immediately after the wedding, while McTeague's broadcloth was still new, and before Trina's silks and veil had lost their stiffness. It represented Trina, her veil thrown back, sitting very straight in a rep armchair, her elbows well in at her sides, holding her bouquet of cut flowers directly before her. The dentist stood at her side, one hand on her shoulder, the other thrust into the breast of his "Prince Albert," his chin in the air, his eyes to one side, his left foot forward in the attitude of a statue of a Secretary of State.

"Say, Trina," said McTeague, his mouth full of codfish, "Heise looked in on me this morning. He says 'What's the matter with a basket picnic over at Schuetzen Park next Tuesday?' You know the paper-hangers are going to be in the 'Parlors' all that day, so I'll have a holiday. That's what made Heise think of it. Heise says he'll get the Ryers to go too. It's the anniversary of their wedding day. We'll ask Selina to go; she can meet us on the other side. Come on, let's go, huh, will you?"

Trina still had her mania for family picnics, which had been one of the Sieppes most cherished customs; but now there were other considerations.

"I don't know as we can afford it this month, Mac," she said, pouring the chocolate. "I got to pay the gas bill next week, and there's the papering of your office to be paid for some time."

"I know, I know," answered her husband. "But I got a new patient this week, had two molars and an upper incisor filled at the very first sitting, and he's going to bring his children round. He's a barber on the next block."

"Well, you pay half, then," said Trina. "It'll cost three or four dollars at the very least; and mind, the Heises pay their *own* fare both ways, Mac, and everybody gets their own lunch. Yes," she added, after a pause, "I'll write and have Selina join us. I haven't seen Selina in months. I guess I'll have to put up a lunch for her, though," admitted Trina, "the way we did last time, because she lives in a boarding-house now, and they make a fuss about putting up a lunch."

They could count on pleasant weather at this time of the year—it was May—and that particular Tuesday was all that could be desired. The party assembled at the ferry slip at nine o'clock, laden with baskets. The McTeagues came last of all; Ryer and his wife had already boarded the boat. They met the Heises in the waiting-room.

"Hello, Doctor," cried the harness-maker as the McTeagues came up. "This is what you'd call an old folks' picnic, all married people this time."

The party foregathered on the upper deck as the boat started, and sat down to listen to the band of Italian musicians who were playing outside this morning because of the fineness of the weather.

"Oh, we're going to have lots of fun," cried Trina. "If it's anything I do love it's a picnic. Do you remember our first picnic, Mac?"

"Sure, sure," replied the dentist; " we had a Gotha truffle."

"And August lost his steamboat," put in Trina, "and papa smacked him. I remember it just as well."

"Why, look there," said Mrs. Heise, nodding at a figure coming up the companion-way. "Ain't that Mr. Schouler?"

It was Marcus, sure enough. As he caught sight of the party he gaped at them a moment in blank astonishment, and then ran up, his eyes wide.

"Well, by damn!" he exclaimed, excitedly. "What's up? Where you all going, anyhow? Say, ain't ut queer we should all run up against each other like this?" He made great sweeping bows to the three women, and shook hands with "Cousin Trina," adding, as he turned to the men of the party, "Glad to see you, Mister Heise. How do, Mister Ryer?" The dentist,

who had formulated some sort of reserved greeting, he
ignored completely. McTeague settled himself in his seat,
growling inarticulately behind his mustache.

"Say, say, what's all up, anyhow?" cried Marcus again.

"It's a picnic," exclaimed the three women, all speaking at
once; and Trina added, "We're going over to the same old
Schuetzen Park again. But you're all fixed up yourself, Cousin
Mark; you look as though you were going somewhere yourself."

In fact, Marcus was dressed with great care. He wore a new
pair of slate-blue trousers, a black "cutaway," and a white
lawn "tie" (for him the symbol of the height of elegance). He
carried also his cane, a thin wand of ebony with a gold head,
presented to him by the Improvement Club in "recognition
of services."

"That's right, that's right," said Marcus, with a grin. "I'm
takun a holiday myself to-day. I had a bit of business to do
over at Oakland, an' I thought I'd go up to B Street afterward
and see Selina. I haven't called on——"

But the party uttered an exclamation.

"Why, Selina is going with us."

"She's going to meet us at the Schuetzen Park station," explained Trina.

Marcus's business in Oakland was a fiction. He was crossing the bay that morning solely to see Selina. Marcus had
"taken up with" Selina a little after Trina had married, and
had been "rushing" her ever since, dazzled and attracted by
her accomplishments, for which he pretended a great respect. At the prospect of missing Selina on this occasion, he
was genuinely disappointed. His vexation at once assumed
the form of exasperation against McTeague. It was all the
dentist's fault. Ah, McTeague was coming between him and
Selina now as he had come between him and Trina. Best
look out, by damn! how he monkeyed with him now. Instantly his face flamed and he glanced over furiously at the
dentist, who, catching his eye, began again to mutter behind
his mustache.

"Well, say," began Mrs. Ryer, with some hesitation, looking to Ryer for approval, "why can't Marcus come along
with us?"

"Why, of course," exclaimed Mrs. Heise, disregarding her husband's vigorous nudges. "I guess we got lunch enough to go round, all right; don't you say so, Mrs. McTeague?"

Thus appealed to, Trina could only concur.

"Why, of course, Cousin Mark," she said; "of course, come along with us if you want to."

"Why, you bet I will," cried Marcus, enthusiastic in an instant. "Say, this is outa sight; it is, for a fact; a picnic—ah, sure—and we'll meet Selina at the station."

Just as the boat was passing Goat Island, the harness-maker proposed that the men of the party should go down to the bar on the lower deck and shake for the drinks. The idea had an immediate success.

"Have to see you on that," said Ryer.

"By damn, we'll have a drink! Yes, sir, we will, for a fact."

"Sure, sure, drinks, that's the word."

At the bar Heise and Ryer ordered cocktails, Marcus called for a "crème Yvette" in order to astonish the others. The dentist spoke for a glass of beer.

"Say, look here," suddenly exclaimed Heise as they took their glasses. "Look here, you fellahs," he had turned to Marcus and the dentist. "You two fellahs have had a grouch at each other for the last year or so; now what's the matter with your shaking hands and calling quits?"

McTeague was at once overcome with a great feeling of magnanimity. He put out his great hand.

"I got nothing against Marcus," he growled.

"Well, I don't care if I shake," admitted Marcus, a little shamefacedly, as their palms touched. "I guess that's all right."

"That's the idea," exclaimed Heise, delighted at his success. "Come on, boys, now let's drink." Their elbows crooked and they drank silently.

Their picnic that day was very jolly. Nothing had changed at Schuetzen Park since the day of that other memorable Sieppe picnic four years previous. After lunch the men took themselves off to the rifle range, while Selina, Trina, and the other two women put away the dishes. An hour later the men joined them in great spirits. Ryer had won the impromptu match which they had arranged, making quite a wonderful

score, which included three clean bulls' eyes, while McTeague
had not been able even to hit the target itself.

Their shooting match had awakened a spirit of rivalry in
the men, and the rest of the afternoon was passed in athletic
exercises between them. The women sat on the slope of the
grass, their hats and gloves laid aside, watching the men as
they strove together. Aroused by the little feminine cries of
wonder and the clapping of their ungloved palms, these latter
began to show off at once. They took off their coats and
vests, even their neckties and collars, and worked themselves
into a lather of perspiration for the sake of making an impression on their wives. They ran hundred-yard sprints on the
cinder path and executed clumsy feats on the rings and on
the parallel bars. They even found a huge round stone on the
beach and "put the shot" for a while. As long as it was a
question of agility, Marcus was easily the best of the four; but
the dentist's enormous strength, his crude, untutored brute
force, was a matter of wonder for the entire party. McTeague
cracked English walnuts—taken from the lunch baskets—in
the hollow of his arm, and tossed the round stone a full five
feet beyond their best mark. Heise believed himself to be particularly strong in the wrists, but the dentist, using but one
hand, twisted a cane out of Heise's two with a wrench that
all but sprained the harness-maker's arm. Then the dentist
raised weights and chinned himself on the rings till they
thought he would never tire.

His great success quite turned his head; he strutted back
and forth in front of the women, his chest thrown out, and
his great mouth perpetually expanded in a triumphant grin.
As he felt his strength more and more, he began to abuse it;
he domineered over the others, gripping suddenly at their
arms till they squirmed with pain, and slapping Marcus on
the back so that he gasped and gagged for breath. The childish vanity of the great fellow was as undisguised as that of a
schoolboy. He began to tell of wonderful feats of strength he
had accomplished when he was a young man. Why, at one
time he had knocked down a half-grown heifer with a blow
of his fist between the eyes, sure, and the heifer had just stiffened out and trembled all over and died without getting up.

McTeague told this story again, and yet again. All through

the afternoon he could be overheard relating the wonder to any one who would listen, exaggerating the effect of his blow, inventing terrific details. Why, the heifer had just frothed at the mouth, and his eyes had rolled up—ah, sure, his eyes rolled up just like that—and the butcher had said his skull was all mashed in—just all mashed in, sure, that's the word —just as if from a sledge-hammer.

Notwithstanding his reconciliation with the dentist on the boat, Marcus's gorge rose within him at McTeague's boasting swagger. When McTeague had slapped him on the back, Marcus had retired to some little distance while he recovered his breath, and glared at the dentist fiercely as he strode up and down, glorying in the admiring glances of the women.

"Ah, one-horse dentist," he muttered between his teeth. "Ah, zinc-plugger, cow-killer, I'd like to show you once, you overgrown mucker, you—you— *cow-killer!* "

When he rejoined the group, he found them preparing for a wrestling bout.

"I tell you what," said Heise, " we'll have a tournament. Marcus and I will rastle, and Doc and Ryer, and then the winners will rastle each other."

The women clapped their hands excitedly. This would be exciting. Trina cried:

"Better let me hold your money, Mac, and your keys, so as you won't lose them out of your pockets." The men gave their valuables into the keeping of their wives and promptly set to work.

The dentist thrust Ryer down without even changing his grip; Marcus and the harness-maker struggled together for a few moments till Heise all at once slipped on a bit of turf and fell backwards. As they toppled over together, Marcus writhed himself from under his opponent, and, as they reached the ground, forced down first one shoulder and then the other.

"All right, all right," panted the harness-maker, good-naturedly, "I'm down. It's up to you and Doc now," he added, as he got to his feet.

The match between McTeague and Marcus promised to be interesting. The dentist, of course, had an enormous advantage in point of strength, but Marcus prided himself on his wrestling, and knew something about strangle-holds and half-Nelsons. The men drew back to allow them a free space as they faced each other, while Trina and the other women rose to their feet in their excitement.

"I bet Mac will throw him, all the same," said Trina.

"All ready!" cried Ryer.

The dentist and Marcus stepped forward, eying each other cautiously. They circled around the impromptu ring, Marcus watching eagerly for an opening. He ground his teeth, telling himself he would throw McTeague if it killed him. Ah, he'd show him now. Suddenly the two men caught at each other; Marcus went to his knees. The dentist threw his vast bulk on his adversary's shoulders and, thrusting a huge palm against his face, pushed him backwards and downwards. It was out of the question to resist that enormous strength. Marcus wrenched himself over and fell face downward on the ground.

McTeague rose on the instant with a great laugh of exultation.

"You're down!" he exclaimed.

Marcus leaped to his feet.

"Down nothing," he vociferated, with clenched fists. "Down nothing, by damn! You got to throw me so's my shoulders touch."

McTeague was stalking about, swelling with pride.

"Hoh, you're down. I threw you. Didn't I throw him, Trina? Hoh, you can't rastle *me*."

Marcus capered with rage.

"You didn't! you didn't! you didn't! and you can't! You got to give me another try."

The other men came crowding up. Everybody was talking at once.

"He's right."

"You didn't throw him."

"Both his shoulders at the same time."

Trina clapped and waved her hand at McTeague from where she stood on the little slope of lawn above the wrestlers. Marcus broke through the group, shaking all over with excitement and rage.

"I tell you that ain't the *way* to rastle. You've got to throw a man so's his shoulders touch. You got to give me another bout."

"That's straight," put in Heise, "both his shoulders down at the same time. Try it again. You and Schouler have another try."

McTeague was bewildered by so much simultaneous talk. He could not make out what it was all about. Could he have offended Marcus again?

"What? What? Huh? What is it?" he exclaimed in perplexity, looking from one to the other.

"Come on, you must rastle me again," shouted Marcus.

"Sure, sure," cried the dentist. "I'll rastle you again. I'll rastle everybody," he cried, suddenly struck with an idea. Trina looked on in some apprehension.

"Mark gets so mad," she said, half aloud.

"Yes," admitted Selina. "Mister Schouler's got an awful quick temper, but he ain't afraid of anything."

"All ready!" shouted Ryer.

This time Marcus was more careful. Twice, as McTeague rushed at him, he slipped cleverly away. But as the dentist came in a third time, with his head bowed, Marcus, raising himself to his full height, caught him with both arms around the neck. The dentist gripped at him and rent away the sleeve of his shirt. There was a great laugh.

"Keep your shirt on," cried Mrs. Ryer.

The two men were grappling at each other wildly. The party could hear them panting and grunting as they labored and struggled. Their boots tore up great clods of turf. Suddenly they came to the ground with a tremendous shock. But even as they were in the act of falling, Marcus, like a very eel, writhed in the dentist's clasp and fell upon his side. McTeague crashed down upon him like the collapse of a felled ox.

"Now, you gotta turn him on his back," shouted Heise to the dentist. "He ain't down if you don't."

With his huge salient chin digging into Marcus's shoulder, the dentist heaved and tugged. His face was flaming, his huge shock of yellow hair fell over his forehead, matted with sweat. Marcus began to yield despite his frantic efforts. One shoulder was down, now the other began to go; gradually,

gradually it was forced over. The little audience held its breath in the suspense of the moment. Selina broke the silence, calling out shrilly:

"Ain't Doctor McTeague just that strong!"

Marcus heard it, and his fury came instantly to a head. Rage at his defeat at the hands of the dentist and before Selina's eyes, the hate he still bore his old-time "pal" and the impotent wrath of his own powerlessness were suddenly unleashed.

"God damn you! get off of me," he cried under his breath, spitting the words as a snake spits its venom. The little audience uttered a cry. With the oath Marcus had twisted his head and had bitten through the lobe of the dentist's ear. There was a sudden flash of bright-red blood.

Then followed a terrible scene. The brute that in McTeague lay so close to the surface leaped instantly to life, monstrous, not to be resisted. He sprang to his feet with a shrill and meaningless clamor, totally unlike the ordinary bass of his speaking tones. It was the hideous yelling of a hurt beast, the squealing of a wounded elephant. He framed no words; in the rush of high-pitched sound that issued from his wide-open mouth there was nothing articulate. It was something no longer human; it was rather an echo from the jungle.

Sluggish enough and slow to anger on ordinary occasions, McTeague when finally aroused became another man. His rage was a kind of obsession, an evil mania, the drunkenness of passion, the exalted and perverted fury of the Berserker, blind and deaf, a thing insensate.

As he rose he caught Marcus's wrist in both his hands. He did not strike, he did not know what he was doing. His only idea was to batter the life out of the man before him, to crush and annihilate him upon the instant. Gripping his enemy in his enormous hands, hard and knotted, and covered with a stiff fell of yellow hair—the hands of the old-time car-boy— he swung him wide, as a hammer-thrower swings his hammer. Marcus's feet flipped from the ground, he spun through the air about McTeague as helpless as a bundle of clothes. All at once there was a sharp snap, almost like the report of a small pistol. Then Marcus rolled over and over upon the ground as McTeague released his grip; his arm, the one the dentist had seized, bending suddenly, as though a third joint had formed between wrist and elbow. The arm was broken.

But by this time every one was crying out at once. Heise and Ryer ran in between the two men. Selina turned her head away. Trina was wringing her hands and crying in an agony of dread:

"Oh, stop them, stop them! Don't let them fight. Oh, it's too awful."

"Here, here, Doc, quit. Don't make a fool of yourself," cried Heise, clinging to the dentist. "That's enough now. *Listen* to me, will you?"

"Oh, Mac, Mac," cried Trina, running to her husband. "Mac, dear, listen; it's me, it's Trina, look at me, you——"

"Get hold of his other arm, will you, Ryer?" panted Heise. "Quick!"

"Mac, Mac," cried Trina, her arms about his neck.

"For God's sake, hold up, Doc, will you?" shouted the harness-maker. "You don't want to kill him, do you?"

Mrs. Ryer and Heise's lame wife were filling the air with their outcries. Selina was giggling with hysteria. Marcus, terrified, but too brave to run, had picked up a jagged stone with his left hand and stood on the defensive. His swollen right arm, from which the shirt sleeve had been torn, dangled at his side, the back of the hand twisted where the palm should have been. The shirt itself was a mass of grass stains and was spotted with the dentist's blood.

But McTeague, in the centre of the group that struggled to hold him, was nigh to madness. The side of his face, his neck, and all the shoulder and breast of his shirt were covered with blood. He had ceased to cry out, but kept muttering between his gripped jaws, as he labored to tear himself free of the retaining hands:

"Ah, I'll kill him! Ah, I'll kill him! I'll kill him! Damn you, Heise," he exclaimed suddenly, trying to strike the harness-maker, "let go of me, will you!"

Little by little they pacified him, or rather (for he paid but little attention to what was said to him) his bestial fury lapsed by degrees. He turned away and let fall his arms, drawing long breaths, and looking stupidly about him, now searching helplessly upon the ground, now gazing vaguely into the circle of faces about him. His ear bled as though it would never stop.

"Say, Doctor," asked Heise, " what's the best thing to do?"

"Huh?" answered McTeague. "What—what do you mean? What is it?"

"What'll we do to stop this bleeding here?"

McTeague did not answer, but looked intently at the blood-stained bosom of his shirt.

"Mac," cried Trina, her face close to his, "tell us something—the best thing we can do to stop your ear bleeding."

"Collodium," said the dentist.

"But we can't get to that right away; we——"

"There's some ice in our lunch basket," broke in Heise. "We brought it for the beer; and take the napkins and make a bandage."

"Ice," muttered the dentist, "sure, ice, that's the word."

Mrs. Heise and the Ryers were looking after Marcus's broken arm. Selina sat on the slope of the grass, gasping and sobbing. Trina tore the napkins into strips, and, crushing some of the ice, made a bandage for her husband's head.

The party resolved itself into two groups; the Ryers and Mrs. Heise bending over Marcus, while the harness-maker and Trina came and went about McTeague, sitting on the ground, his shirt, a mere blur of red and white, detaching itself violently from the background of pale-green grass. Between the two groups was the torn and trampled bit of turf, the wrestling ring; the picnic baskets, together with empty beer bottles, broken egg-shells, and discarded sardine tins, were scattered here and there. In the middle of the improvised wrestling ring the sleeve of Marcus's shirt fluttered occasionally in the sea breeze.

Nobody was paying any attention to Selina. All at once she began to giggle hysterically again, then cried out with a peal of laughter:

"Oh, what a way for our picnic to end!"

XII

"Now, then, Maria," said Zerkow, his cracked, strained voice just rising above a whisper, hitching his chair closer to the table, "now, then, my girl, let's have it all over again. Tell us about the gold plate—the service. Begin with, 'There were over a hundred pieces and every one of them gold.'"

"I don't know what you're talking about, Zerkow," answered Maria. "There never was no gold plate, no gold service. I guess you must have dreamed it."

Maria and the red-headed Polish Jew had been married about a month after the McTeague's picnic which had ended in such lamentable fashion. Zerkow had taken Maria home to his wretched hovel in the alley back of the flat, and the flat had been obliged to get another maid of all work. Time passed, a month, six months, a whole year went by. At length Maria gave birth to a child, a wretched, sickly child, with not even strength enough nor wits enough to cry. At the time of its birth Maria was out of her mind, and continued in a state of dementia for nearly ten days. She recovered just in time to make the arrangements for the baby's burial. Neither Zerkow nor Maria was much affected by either the birth or the death of this little child. Zerkow had welcomed it with pronounced disfavor, since it had a mouth to be fed and wants to be provided for. Maria was out of her head so much of the time that she could scarcely remember how it looked when alive. The child was a mere incident in their lives, a thing that had come undesired and had gone unregretted. It had not even a name; a strange, hybrid little being, come and gone within a fortnight's time, yet combining in its puny little body the blood of the Hebrew, the Pole, and the Spaniard.

But the birth of this child had peculiar consequences. Maria came out of her dementia, and in a few days the household settled itself again to its sordid régime and Maria went about her duties as usual. Then one evening, about a week after the child's burial, Zerkow had asked Maria to tell him the story of the famous service of gold plate for the hundredth time.

Zerkow had come to believe in this story infallibly. He was

immovably persuaded that at one time Maria or Maria's people had possessed these hundred golden dishes. In his perverted mind the hallucination had developed still further. Not
only had that service of gold plate once existed, but it existed
now, entire, intact; not a single burnished golden piece of it
was missing. It was somewhere, somebody had it, locked
away in that leather trunk with its quilted lining and round
brass locks. It was to be searched for and secured, to be
fought for, to be gained at all hazards. Maria must know
where it was; by dint of questioning, Zerkow would surely
get the information from her. Some day, if only he was persistent, he would hit upon the right combination of questions, the right suggestion that would disentangle Maria's
confused recollections. Maria would tell him where the thing
was kept, was concealed, was buried, and he would go to that
place and secure it, and all that wonderful gold would be his
forever and forever. This service of plate had come to be
Zerkow's mania.

On this particular evening, about a week after the child's
burial, in the wretched back room of the junk shop, Zerkow
had made Maria sit down to the table opposite him—the
whiskey bottle and the red glass tumbler with its broken base
between them—and had said:

"Now, then, Maria, tell us that story of the gold dishes
again."

Maria stared at him, an expression of perplexity coming
into her face.

"What gold dishes?" said she.

"The ones your people used to own in Central America.
Come on, Maria, begin, begin." The Jew craned himself forward, his lean fingers clawing eagerly at his lips.

"What gold plate?" said Maria, frowning at him as she
drank her whiskey. "What gold plate? *I* don' know what
you're talking about, Zerkow."

Zerkow sat back in his chair, staring at her.

"Why, your people's gold dishes, what they used to eat off
of. You've told me about it a hundred times."

"You're crazy, Zerkow," said Maria. "Push the bottle here,
will you?"

"Come, now," insisted Zerkow, sweating with desire,

"come, now, my girl, don't be a fool; let's have it, let's have it. Begin now, 'There were more'n a hundred pieces, and every one of 'em gold.' Oh, *you* know; come on, come on."

"I don't remember nothing of the kind," protested Maria, reaching for the bottle. Zerkow snatched it from her.

"You fool!" he wheezed, trying to raise his broken voice to a shout. "You fool! Don't you dare try an' cheat *me*, or I'll *do* for you. You know about the gold plate, and you know where it is." Suddenly he pitched his voice at the prolonged rasping shout with which he made his street cry. He rose to his feet, his long, prehensile fingers curled into fists. He was menacing, terrible in his rage. He leaned over Maria, his fists in her face.

"I believe you've got it!" he yelled. "I believe you've got it, an' are hiding it from me. Where is it, where is it? Is it here?" he rolled his eyes wildly about the room. "Hey? hey?" he went on, shaking Maria by the shoulders. "Where is it? Is it here? Tell me where it is. Tell me, or I'll do for you!"

"It ain't here," cried Maria, wrenching from him. "It ain't anywhere. What gold plate? What are you talking about? I don't remember nothing about no gold plate at all."

No, Maria did not remember. The trouble and turmoil of her mind consequent upon the birth of her child seemed to have readjusted her disordered ideas upon this point. Her mania had come to a crisis, which in subsiding had cleared her brain of its one illusion. She did not remember. Or it was possible that the gold plate she had once remembered had had some foundation in fact, that her recital of its splendors had been truth, sound and sane. It was possible that now her *forgetfulness* of it was some form of brain trouble, a relic of the dementia of childbirth. At all events Maria did not remember; the idea of the gold plate had passed entirely out of her mind, and it was now Zerkow who labored under its hallucination. It was now Zerkow, the raker of the city's muck heap, the searcher after gold, that saw that wonderful service in the eye of his perverted mind. It was he who could now describe it in a language almost eloquent. Maria had been content merely to remember it; but Zerkow's avarice goaded him to a belief that it was still in existence, hid somewhere, perhaps in that very house, stowed away there by Maria. For it stood to reason, didn't it, that Maria could not have described it with such wonderful accuracy and such careful detail unless she had seen it recently—the day before, perhaps, or that very day, or that very hour, that *very hour*?

"Look out for yourself," he whispered, hoarsely, to his wife. "Look out for yourself, my girl. I'll hunt for it, and hunt for it, and hunt for it, and some day I'll find it—*I* will, you'll see—I'll find it, I'll find it; and if I don't, I'll find a way that'll make you tell me where it is. I'll make you speak—believe me, I will, I will, my girl—trust me for that."

And at night Maria would sometimes wake to find Zerkow gone from the bed, and would see him burrowing into some corner by the light of his dark-lantern and would hear him mumbling to himself: "There were more'n a hundred pieces, and every one of 'em gold—when the leather trunk was opened it fair dazzled your eyes—why, just that punch-bowl was worth a fortune, I guess; solid, solid, heavy, rich, pure gold, nothun but gold, gold, heaps and heaps of it—what a glory! I'll find it yet, I'll find it. It's here somewheres, hid somewheres in this house."

At length his continued ill success began to exasperate him. One day he took his whip from his junk wagon and thrashed Maria with it, gasping the while, "Where is it, you beast? Where is it? Tell me where it is; I'll make you speak."

"I don' know, I don' know," cried Maria, dodging his blows. "I'd tell you, Zerkow, if I knew; but I don' know nothing about it. How can I tell you if I don' know?"

Then one evening matters reached a crisis. Marcus Schouler was in his room, the room in the flat just over McTeague's "Parlors" which he had always occupied. It was between eleven and twelve o'clock. The vast house was quiet; Polk Street outside was very still, except for the occasional whirr and trundle of a passing cable car and the persistent calling of ducks and geese in the deserted market directly opposite. Marcus was in his shirt sleeves, perspiring and swearing with exertion as he tried to get all his belongings into an absurdly inadequate trunk. The room was in great confusion. It looked as though Marcus was about to move. He stood in front of his trunk, his precious silk hat in its hat-box in his hand. He was raging at the perverseness of a pair of boots that refused to fit in his trunk, no matter how he arranged them.

"I've tried you *so*, and I've tried you *so*," he exclaimed fiercely, between his teeth, "and you won't go." He began to swear horribly, grabbing at the boots with his free hand. "Pretty soon I won't take you at all; I won't, for a fact."

He was interrupted by a rush of feet upon the back stairs and a clamorous pounding upon the door. He opened it to let in Maria Macapa, her hair dishevelled and her eyes starting with terror.

"Oh, *Mister* Schouler," she gasped, "lock the door quick. Don't let him get me. He's got a knife, and he says sure he's going to do for me, if I don't tell him where it is."

"Who has? What has? Where is what?" shouted Marcus, flaming with excitement upon the instant. He opened the door and peered down the dark hall, both fists clenched, ready to fight—he did not know whom, and he did not know why.

"It's Zerkow," wailed Maria, pulling him back into the room and bolting the door, "and he's got a knife as long as *that*. Oh, my Lord, here he comes now! Ain't that him? Listen."

Zerkow was coming up the stairs, calling for Maria.

"Don't you let him get me, will you, Mister Schouler?" gasped Maria.

"I'll break him in two," shouted Marcus, livid with rage. "Think I'm afraid of his knife?"

"I know where you are," cried Zerkow, on the landing outside. "You're in Schouler's room. What are you doing in Schouler's room at this time of night? Come outa there; you oughta be ashamed. I'll do for you yet, my girl. Come outa there once, an' see if I don't."

"I'll do for you myself, you dirty Jew," shouted Marcus, unbolting the door and running out into the hall.

"I want my wife," exclaimed the Jew, backing down the stairs. "What's she mean by running away from me and going into your room?"

"Look out, he's got a knife!" cried Maria through the crack of the door.

"Ah, there you are. Come outa that, and come back home," exclaimed Zerkow.

"Get outa here yourself," cried Marcus, advancing on him angrily. "Get outa here."

"Maria's gota come too."

"Get outa here," vociferated Marcus, "an' put up that knife. *I* see it; you needn't try an' hide it behind your leg. Give it to me, anyhow," he shouted suddenly, and before Zerkow was aware, Marcus had wrenched it away. "Now, get outa here."

Zerkow backed away, peering and peeping over Marcus's shoulder.

"I want Maria."

"Get outa here. Get along out, or I'll *put* you out." The street door closed. The Jew was gone.

"Huh!" snorted Marcus, swelling with arrogance. "Huh! Think I'm afraid of his knife? I ain't afraid of *anybody*," he shouted pointedly, for McTeague and his wife, roused by the clamor, were peering over the banisters from the landing above. "Not of anybody," repeated Marcus.

Maria came out into the hall.

"Is he gone? Is he sure gone?"

"What was the trouble?" inquired Marcus, suddenly.

"I woke up about an hour ago," Maria explained, "and Zerkow wasn't in bed; maybe he hadn't come to bed at all. He was down on his knees by the sink, and he'd pried up some boards off the floor and was digging there. He had his dark-lantern. He was digging with that knife, I guess, and all the time he kept mumbling to himself, 'More'n a hundred pieces, an' every one of 'em gold; more'n a hundred pieces, an' every one of 'em gold.' Then, all of a sudden, he caught sight of me. I was sitting up in bed, and he jumped up and came at me with his knife, an' he says, 'Where is it? Where is it? I know you got it hid somewheres. Where is it? Tell me or I'll knife you.' I kind of fooled him and kept him off till I got my wrapper on, an' then I run out. I didn't dare stay."

"Well, what did you tell him about your gold dishes for in the first place?" cried Marcus.

"I never told him," protested Maria, with the greatest energy. "I never told him; I never heard of any gold dishes. I don' know where he got the idea; he must be crazy."

By this time Trina and McTeague, Old Grannis, and little

Miss Baker—all the lodgers on the upper floors of the flat—had gathered about Maria. Trina and the dentist, who had gone to bed, were partially dressed, and Trina's enormous mane of black hair was hanging in two thick braids far down her back. But, late as it was, Old Grannis and the retired dressmaker had still been up and about when Maria had aroused them.

"Why, Maria," said Trina, "you always used to tell us about your gold dishes. You said your folks used to have them."

"Never, never, never!" exclaimed Maria, vehemently. "You folks must all be crazy. I never *heard* of any gold dishes."

"Well," spoke up Miss Baker, "you're a queer girl, Maria; that's all I can say." She left the group and returned to her room. Old Grannis watched her go from the corner of his eye, and in a few moments followed her, leaving the group as unnoticed as he had joined it. By degrees the flat quieted down again. Trina and McTeague returned to their rooms.

"I guess I'll go back now," said Maria. "He's all right now. I ain't afraid of him so long as he ain't got his knife."

"Well, say," Marcus called to her as she went down stairs, "if he gets funny again, you just yell out; *I'll* hear you. *I* won't let him hurt you."

Marcus went into his room again and resumed his wrangle with the refractory boots. His eye fell on Zerkow's knife, a long, keen-bladed hunting-knife, with a buckhorn handle. "I'll take you along with me," he exclaimed, suddenly. "I'll just need you where I'm going."

Meanwhile, old Miss Baker was making tea to calm her nerves after the excitement of Maria's incursion. This evening she went so far as to make tea for two, laying an extra place on the other side of her little tea-table, setting out a cup and saucer and one of the Gorham silver spoons. Close upon the other side of the partition Old Grannis bound uncut numbers of the "Nation."

"Do you know what I think, Mac?" said Trina, when the couple had returned to their rooms. "I think Marcus is going away."

"What? What?" muttered the dentist, very sleepy and stupid, " what you saying? What's that about Marcus?"

"I believe Marcus has been packing up, the last two or three days. I wonder if he's going away."

"Who's going away?" said McTeague, blinking at her.

"Oh, go to bed," said Trina, pushing him good-naturedly. "Mac, you're the stupidest man I ever knew."

But it was true. Marcus was going away. Trina received a letter the next morning from her mother. The carpet-cleaning and upholstery business in which Mr. Sieppe had involved himself was going from bad to worse. Mr. Sieppe had even been obliged to put a mortgage upon their house. Mrs. Sieppe didn't know what was to become of them all. Her husband had even begun to talk of emigrating to New Zealand. Meanwhile, she informed Trina that Mr. Sieppe had finally come across a man with whom Marcus could "go in with on a ranch," a cattle ranch in the southeastern portion of the State. Her ideas were vague upon the subject, but she knew that Marcus was wildly enthusiastic at the prospect, and was expected down before the end of the month. In the meantime, could Trina send them fifty dollars?

"Marcus *is* going away, after all, Mac," said Trina to her husband that day as he came out of his "Parlors" and sat down to the lunch of sausages, mashed potatoes, and chocolate in the sitting-room.

"Huh?" said the dentist, a little confused. "Who's going away? Schouler going away? Why's Schouler going away?"

Trina explained. "Oh!" growled McTeague, behind his thick mustache, "he can go far before *I'll* stop him."

"And, say, Mac," continued Trina, pouring the chocolate, " what do you think? Mamma wants me—wants us to send her fifty dollars. She says they're hard up."

"Well," said the dentist, after a moment, " well, I guess we can send it, can't we?"

"Oh, that's easy to say," complained Trina, her little chin in the air, her small pale lips pursed. "I wonder if mamma thinks we're millionaires?"

"Trina, you're getting to be regular stingy," muttered McTeague. "You're getting worse and worse every day."

"But fifty dollars is fifty dollars, Mac. Just think how long it takes you to earn fifty dollars. Fifty dollars! That's two months of our interest."

"Well," said McTeague, easily, his mouth full of mashed potato, "you got a lot saved up."

Upon every reference to that little hoard in the brass match-safe and chamois-skin bag at the bottom of her trunk, Trina bridled on the instant.

"Don't *talk* that way, Mac. 'A lot of money.' What do you call a lot of money? I don't believe I've got fifty dollars saved."

"Hoh!" exclaimed McTeague. "Hoh! I guess you got nearer a hundred *an'* fifty. That's what I guess *you* got."

"I've *not*, I've *not*," declared Trina, "and you know I've not. I wish mamma hadn't asked me for any money. Why can't she be a little more economical? *I* manage all right. No, no, I can't possibly afford to send her fifty."

"Oh, pshaw! What *will* you do, then?" grumbled her husband.

"I'll send her twenty-five this month, and tell her I'll send the rest as soon as I can afford it."

"Trina, you're a regular little miser," said McTeague.

"I don't care," answered Trina, beginning to laugh. "I guess I am, but I can't help it, and it's a good fault."

Trina put off sending this money for a couple of weeks, and her mother made no mention of it in her next letter. "Oh, I guess if she wants it so bad," said Trina, "she'll speak about it again." So she again postponed the sending of it. Day by day she put it off. When her mother asked her for it a second time, it seemed harder than ever for Trina to part with even half the sum requested. She answered her mother, telling her that they were very hard up themselves for that month, but that she would send down the amount in a few weeks.

"I'll tell you what we'll do, Mac," she said to her husband, "you send half and I'll send half; we'll send twenty-five dollars altogether. Twelve and a half apiece. That's an idea. How will that do?"

"Sure, sure," McTeague had answered, giving her the money. Trina sent McTeague's twelve dollars, but never sent the twelve that was to be her share. One day the dentist happened to ask her about it.

"You sent that twenty-five to your mother, didn't you?" said he.

"Oh, long ago," answered Trina, without thinking.

In fact, Trina never allowed herself to think very much of this affair. And, in fact, another matter soon came to engross her attention.

One Sunday evening Trina and her husband were in their sitting-room together. It was dark, but the lamp had not been lit. McTeague had brought up some bottles of beer from the "Wein Stube" on the ground floor, where the branch post-office used to be. But they had not opened the beer. It was a warm evening in summer. Trina was sitting on McTeague's lap in the bay window, and had looped back the Nottingham curtains so the two could look out into the darkened street and watch the moon coming up over the glass roof of the huge public baths. On occasions they sat like this for an hour or so, "philandering," Trina cuddling herself down upon McTeague's enormous body, rubbing her cheek against the grain of his unshaven chin, kissing the bald spot on the top of his head, or putting her fingers into his ears and eyes. At times, a brusque access of passion would seize upon her, and, with a nervous little sigh, she would clasp his thick red neck in both her small arms and whisper in his ear:

"Do you love me, Mac, dear? love me *big*, *big*? Sure, do you love me as much as you did when we were married?"

Puzzled, McTeague would answer: "Well, you know it, don't you, Trina?"

"But I want you to *say* so; say so always and always."

"Well, I do, of course I do."

"Say it, then."

"Well, then, I love you."

"But you don't say it of your own accord."

"Well, what—what—what—I don't understand," stammered the dentist, bewildered.

There was a knock on the door. Confused and embarrassed, as if they were not married, Trina scrambled off McTeague's lap, hastening to light the lamp, whispering, "Put on your coat, Mac, and smooth your hair," and making gestures for him to put the beer bottles out of sight. She opened the door and uttered an exclamation.

"Why, Cousin Mark!" she said. McTeague glared at him, struck speechless, confused beyond expression. Marcus

Schouler, perfectly at his ease, stood in the doorway, smiling with great affability.

"Say," he remarked, "can I come in?"

Taken all aback, Trina could only answer:

"Why—I suppose so. Yes, of course—come in."

"Yes, yes, come in," exclaimed the dentist, suddenly, speaking without thought. "Have some beer?" he added, struck with an idea.

"No, thanks, Doctor," said Marcus, pleasantly.

McTeague and Trina were puzzled. What could it all mean? Did Marcus want to become reconciled to his enemy? "*I* know." Trina said to herself. "He's going away, and he wants to borrow some money. He won't get a penny, not a penny." She set her teeth together hard.

"Well," said Marcus, "how's business, Doctor?"

"Oh," said McTeague, uneasily, "oh, I don' know. I guess —I guess," he broke off in helpless embarrassment. They had all sat down by now. Marcus continued, holding his hat and his cane—the black wand of ebony with the gold top presented to him by the "Improvement Club."

"Ah!" said he, wagging his head and looking about the sitting-room, "you people have got the best fixed rooms in the whole flat. Yes, sir; you have, for a fact." He glanced from the lithograph framed in gilt and red plush—the two little girls at their prayers—to the "I'm Grandpa" and "I'm Grandma" pictures, noted the clean white matting and the gay worsted tidies over the chair backs, and appeared to contemplate in ecstasy the framed photograph of McTeague and Trina in their wedding finery.

"Well, you two are pretty happy together, ain't you?" said he, smiling good-humoredly.

"Oh, we don't complain," answered Trina.

"Plenty of money, lots to do, everything fine, hey?"

"We've got lots to do," returned Trina, thinking to head him off, "but we've not got lots of money."

But evidently Marcus wanted no money.

"Well, Cousin Trina," he said, rubbing his knee, "I'm going away."

"Yes, mamma wrote me; you're going on a ranch."

"I'm going in ranching with an English duck," corrected

Marcus. "Mr. Sieppe has fixed things. We'll see if we can't raise some cattle. I know a lot about horses, and he's ranched some before—this English duck. And then I'm going to keep my eye open for a political chance down there. I got some introductions from the President of the Improvement Club. I'll work things somehow, oh, sure."

"How long you going to be gone?" asked Trina.

Marcus stared.

"Why, I ain't *ever* coming back," he vociferated. "I'm going to-morrow, and I'm going for good. I come to say good-by."

Marcus stayed for upwards of an hour that evening. He talked on easily and agreeably, addressing himself as much to McTeague as to Trina. At last he rose.

"Well, good-by, Doc."

"Good-by, Marcus," returned McTeague. The two shook hands.

"Guess we won't ever see each other again," continued Marcus. "But good luck to you, Doc. Hope some day you'll have the patients standing in line on the stairs."

"Huh! I guess so, I guess so," said the dentist.

"Good-by, Cousin Trina."

"Good-by, Marcus," answered Trina. "You be sure to remember me to mamma, and papa, and everybody. I'm going to make two great big sets of Noah's ark animals for the twins on their next birthday; August is too old for toys. But you tell the twins that I'll make them some great big animals. Good-by, success to you, Marcus."

"Good-by, good-by. Good luck to you both."

"Good-by, Cousin Mark."

"Good-by, Marcus."

He was gone.

XIII

ONE MORNING about a week after Marcus had left for the southern part of the State, McTeague found an oblong letter thrust through the letter-drop of the door of his "Parlors." The address was type-written. He opened it. The letter had been sent from the City Hall and was stamped in one corner with the seal of the State of California, very official; the form and file numbers superscribed.

McTeague had been making fillings when this letter arrived. He was in his "Parlors," pottering over his movable rack underneath the bird cage in the bay window. He was making "blocks" to be used in large proximal cavities and "cylinders" for commencing fillings. He heard the postman's step in the hall and saw the envelopes begin to shuttle themselves through the slit of his letter-drop. Then came the fat oblong envelope, with its official seal, that dropped flat-wise to the floor with a sodden, dull impact.

The dentist put down the broach and scissors and gathered up his mail. There were four letters altogether. One was for Trina, in Selina's "elegant" handwriting; another was an advertisement of a new kind of operating chair for dentists; the third was a card from a milliner on the next block, announcing an opening; and the fourth, contained in the fat oblong envelope, was a printed form with blanks left for names and dates, and addressed to McTeague, from an office in the City Hall. McTeague read it through laboriously. "I don' know, I don' know," he muttered, looking stupidly at the rifle manufacturer's calendar. Then he heard Trina, from the kitchen, singing as she made a clattering noise with the breakfast dishes. "I guess I'll ask Trina about it," he muttered.

He went through the suite, by the sitting-room, where the sun was pouring in through the looped backed Nottingham curtains upon the clean white matting and the varnished surface of the melodeon, passed on through the bedroom, with its framed lithographs of round-cheeked English babies and alert fox terriers, and came out into the brick-paved kitchen. The kitchen was clean as a new whistle; the freshly blackened cook stove glowed like a negro's hide; the tins and porcelain-lined stewpans might have been of silver and of ivory. Trina was in the centre of the room, wiping off, with a damp sponge, the oilcloth table-cover, on which they had breakfasted. Never had she looked so pretty. Early though it was, her enormous tiara of swarthy hair was neatly combed and coiled, not a pin was so much as loose. She wore a blue calico skirt with a white figure, and a belt of imitation alligator skin clasped around her small, firmly-corseted waist; her shirt waist was of pink linen, so new and crisp that it crackled with every movement, while around the collar, tied in a neat knot, was one of McTeague's lawn ties which she had appropriated. Her sleeves were carefully rolled up almost to her shoulders, and nothing could have been more delicious than the sight of her small round arms, white as milk, moving back and forth as she sponged the table-cover, a faint touch of pink coming and going at the elbows as they bent and straightened. She looked up quickly as her husband entered, her narrow eyes alight, her adorable little chin in the air; her lips rounded and opened with the last words of her song, so that one could catch a glint of gold in the fillings of her upper teeth.

The whole scene—the clean kitchen and its clean brick floor; the smell of coffee that lingered in the air; Trina herself, fresh as if from a bath, and singing at her work; the morning sun, striking obliquely through the white muslin half-curtain of the window and spanning the little kitchen with a bridge of golden mist—gave off, as it were, a note of gayety that was not to be resisted. Through the opened top of the window came the noises of Polk Street, already long awake. One heard the chanting of street cries, the shrill calling of children on their way to school, the merry rattle of a butcher's cart, the brisk noise of hammering, or the occasional prolonged roll of a cable car trundling heavily past, with a vibrant whirring of its jostled glass and the joyous clanging of its bells.

"What is it, Mac, dear?" said Trina.

McTeague shut the door behind him with his heel and handed her the letter. Trina read it through. Then suddenly her small hand gripped tightly upon the sponge, so that the water started from it and dripped in a little pattering deluge upon the bricks.

The letter—or rather printed notice—informed McTeague that he had never received a diploma from a dental college, and that in consequence he was forbidden to practise his profession any longer. A legal extract bearing upon the case was attached in small type.

"Why, what's all this?" said Trina, calmly, without thought as yet.

"I don' know, *I* don' know," answered her husband.

"You can't practise any longer," continued Trina,—" 'is herewith prohibited and enjoined from further continuing——' " She re-read the extract, her forehead lifting and puckering. She put the sponge carefully away in its wire rack over the sink, and drew up a chair to the table, spreading out the notice before her. "Sit down," she said to McTeague. "Draw up to the table here, Mac, and let's see what this is."

"I got it this morning," murmured the dentist. "It just now came. I was making some fillings—there, in the 'Parlors,' in the window—and the postman shoved it through the door. I thought it was a number of the 'American System of Dentistry' at first, and when I'd opened it and looked at it I thought I'd better——"

"Say, Mac," interrupted Trina, looking up from the notice, "*didn't* you ever go to a dental college?"

"Huh? What? What?" exclaimed McTeague.

"How did you learn to be a dentist? Did you go to a college?"

"I went along with a fellow who came to the mine once. My mother sent me. We used to go from one camp to another. I sharpened his excavators for him, and put up his notices in the towns—stuck them up in the post-offices and on the doors of the Odd Fellows' halls. He had a wagon."

"But didn't you never go to a college?"

"Huh? What? College? No, I never went; learned from the fellow."

Trina rolled down her sleeves. She was a little paler than usual. She fastened the buttons into the cuffs and said:

"But do you know you can't practise unless you're graduated from a college? You haven't the right to call yourself, 'doctor.' "

McTeague stared a moment; then:

"Why, I've been practising ten years. More—nearly twelve."

"But it's the law."

"What's the law?"

"That you can't practise, or call yourself doctor, unless you've got a diploma."

"What's that—a diploma?"

"I don't know exactly. It's a kind of paper that—that—oh, Mac, we're ruined." Trina's voice rose to a cry.

"What do you mean, Trina? Ain't I a dentist? Ain't I a doctor? Look at my sign, and the gold tooth you gave me. Why, I've been practising nearly twelve years."

Trina shut her lips tightly, cleared her throat, and pretended to resettle a hair-pin at the back of her head.

"I guess it isn't as bad as that," she said, very quietly. "Let's read this again. 'Herewith prohibited and enjoined from further continuing——' " She read to the end.

"Why, it isn't possible," she cried. "They can't mean—oh, Mac, I do believe—pshaw!" she exclaimed, her pale face flushing. "They don't know how good a dentist you are. What difference does a diploma make, if you're a first-class dentist? I guess that's all right. Mac, didn't you ever go to a dental college?"

"No," answered McTeague, doggedly. "What was the good? I learned how to operate; wa'n't that enough?"

"Hark," said Trina, suddenly. "Wasn't that the bell of your office?" They had both heard the jangling of the bell that McTeague had hung over the door of his "Parlors." The dentist looked at the kitchen clock.

"That's Vanovitch," said he. "He's a plumber round on Sutter Street. He's got an appointment with me to have a bicuspid pulled. I got to go back to work." He rose.

"But you can't," cried Trina, the back of her hand upon her lips, her eyes brimming. "Mac, don't you see? Can't you understand? You've got to stop. Oh, it's dreadful! Listen." She hurried around the table to him and caught his arm in both her hands.

"Huh?" growled McTeague, looking at her with a puzzled frown.

"They'll arrest you. You'll go to prison. You can't work—can't work any more. We're ruined."

Vanovitch was pounding on the door of the sitting-room.

"He'll be gone in a minute," exclaimed McTeague.

"Well, let him go. Tell him to go; tell him to come again."

"Why, he's got an *appointment* with me," exclaimed Mc-Teague, his hand upon the door.

Trina caught him back. "But, Mac, you ain't a dentist any longer; you ain't a doctor. You haven't the right to work. You never went to a dental college."

"Well, suppose I never went to a college, ain't I a dentist just the same? Listen, he's pounding there again. No, I'm going, sure."

"Well, of course, go," said Trina, with sudden reaction. "It ain't possible they'll make you stop. If you're a good dentist, that's all that's wanted. Go on, Mac; hurry, before he goes."

McTeague went out, closing the door. Trina stood for a moment looking intently at the bricks at her feet. Then she returned to the table, and sat down again before the notice, and, resting her head in both her fists, read it yet another time. Suddenly the conviction seized upon her that it was all true. McTeague would be obliged to stop work, no matter how good a dentist he was. But why had the authorities at the City Hall waited this long before serving the notice? All at once Trina snapped her fingers, with a quick flash of intelligence.

"It's Marcus that's done it," she cried.

It was like a clap of thunder. McTeague was stunned, stupefied. He said nothing. Never in his life had he been so taciturn. At times he did not seem to hear Trina when she spoke to him, and often she had to shake him by the shoulder to arouse his attention. He would sit apart in his "Parlors," turning the notice about in his enormous clumsy fingers, reading it stupidly over and over again. He couldn't understand. What had a clerk at the City Hall to do with him? Why couldn't they let him alone?

"Oh, what's to become of us *now*?" wailed Trina. "What's

to become of us now? We're paupers, beggars—and all so sudden." And once, in a quick, inexplicable fury, totally unlike anything that McTeague had noticed in her before, she had started up, with fists and teeth shut tight, and had cried, "Oh, if you'd only *killed* Marcus Schouler that time he fought you!"

McTeague had continued his work, acting from sheer force of habit; his sluggish, deliberate nature, methodical, obstinate, refusing to adapt itself to the new conditions.

"Maybe Marcus was only trying to scare us," Trina had said. "How are they going to know whether you're practising or not?"

"I got a mould to make to-morrow," McTeague said, "and Vanovitch, that plumber round on Sutter Street, he's coming again at three."

"Well, you go right ahead," Trina told him, decisively; "you go right ahead and make the mould, and pull every tooth in Vanovitch's head if you want to. Who's going to know? Maybe they just sent that notice as a matter of form. Maybe Marcus got that paper and filled it in himself."

The two would lie awake all night long, staring up into the dark, talking, talking, talking.

"Haven't you got any right to practise if you've not been to a dental college, Mac? Didn't you ever go?" Trina would ask again and again.

"No, no," answered the dentist, "I never went. I learnt from the fellow I was apprenticed to. I don' know anything about a dental college. Ain't I got a right to do as I like?" he suddenly exclaimed.

"If you know your profession, isn't that enough?" cried Trina.

"Sure, sure," growled McTeague. "I ain't going to stop for them."

"You go right on," Trina said, "and I bet you won't hear another word about it."

"Suppose I go round to the City Hall and see them," hazarded McTeague.

"No, no, don't you do it, Mac," exclaimed Trina. "Because, if Marcus has done this just to scare you, they won't know anything about it there at the City Hall; but they'll begin to ask you questions, and find out that you never *had* graduated from a dental college, and you'd be just as bad off as ever."

"Well, I ain't going to quit for just a piece of paper," declared the dentist. The phrase stuck to him. All day long he went about their rooms or continued at his work in the "Parlors," growling behind his thick mustache: "I ain't going to quit for just a piece of paper. No, I ain't going to quit for just a piece of paper. Sure not."

The days passed, a week went by, McTeague continued his work as usual. They heard no more from the City Hall, but the suspense of the situation was harrowing. Trina was actually sick with it. The terror of the thing was ever at their elbows, going to bed with them, sitting down with them at breakfast in the kitchen, keeping them company all through the day. Trina dared not think of what would be their fate if the income derived from McTeague's practice was suddenly taken from them. Then they would have to fall back on the interest of her lottery money and the pittance she derived from the manufacture of the Noah's ark animals, a little over thirty dollars a month. No, no, it was not to be thought of. It could not be that their means of livelihood was to be thus stricken from them.

A fortnight went by. "I guess we're all right, Mac," Trina allowed herself to say. "It looks as though we were all right. How *are* they going to tell whether you're practising or not?"

That day a second and much more peremptory notice was served upon McTeague by an official in person. Then suddenly Trina was seized with a panic terror, unreasoned, instinctive. If McTeague persisted they would both be sent to a prison, she was sure of it; a place where people were chained to the wall, in the dark, and fed on bread and water.

"Oh, Mac, you've got to quit," she wailed. "You can't go on. They can make you stop. Oh, why didn't you go to a dental college? Why didn't you find out that you had to have a college degree? And now we're paupers, beggars. We've got to leave here—leave this flat where I've been—where *we've* been so happy, and sell all the pretty things; sell the pictures and the melodeon, and—Oh, it's too dreadful!"

"Huh? Huh? What? What?" exclaimed the dentist, bewildered. "I ain't going to quit for just a piece of paper. Let

them put me out. I'll show them. They—they can't make
small of me."

"Oh, that's all very fine to talk that way, but you'll have to
quit."

"Well, we ain't paupers," McTeague suddenly exclaimed, an
idea entering his mind. "We've got our money yet. You've got
your five thousand dollars and the money you've been saving
up. People ain't paupers when they've got over five thousand
dollars."

"What do you mean, Mac?" cried Trina, apprehensively.

"Well, we can live on *that* money until—until—until—"
he broke off with an uncertain movement of his shoulders,
looking about him stupidly.

"Until *when*?" cried Trina. "There ain't ever going to be
any '*until*.' We've got the *interest* of that five thousand and
we've got what Uncle Oelbermann gives me, a little over
thirty dollars a month, and that's all we've got. You'll have to
find something else to do."

"What will I find to do?"

What, indeed? McTeague was over thirty now, sluggish and
slow-witted at best. What new trade could he learn at this
age?

Little by little Trina made the dentist understand the calamity that had befallen them, and McTeague at last began can-
celling his appointments. Trina gave it out that he was sick.

"Not a soul need know what's happened to us," she said to
her husband.

But it was only by slow degrees that McTeague abandoned
his profession. Every morning after breakfast he would go
into his "Parlors" as usual and potter about his instruments,
his dental engine, and his washstand in the corner behind his
screen where he made his moulds. Now he would sharpen a
"hoe" excavator, now he would busy himself for a whole hour
making "mats" and "cylinders." Then he would look over his
slate where he kept a record of his appointments.

One day Trina softly opened the door of the "Parlors" and
came in from the sitting-room. She had not heard McTeague
moving about for some time and had begun to wonder what
he was doing. She came in, quietly shutting the door behind
her.

McTeague had tidied the room with the greatest care. The volumes of the "Practical Dentist" and the "American System of Dentistry" were piled upon the marble-top centre-table in rectangular blocks. The few chairs were drawn up against the wall under the steel engraving of "Lorenzo de' Medici" with more than usual precision. The dental engine and the nickelled trimmings of the operating chair had been furbished till they shone, while on the movable rack in the bay window McTeague had arranged his instruments with the greatest neatness and regularity. "Hoe" excavators, pluggers, forceps, pliers, corundum disks and burrs, even the boxwood mallet that Trina was never to use again, all were laid out and ready for immediate use.

McTeague himself sat in his operating chair, looking stupidly out of the windows, across the roofs opposite, with an unseeing gaze, his red hands lying idly in his lap. Trina came up to him. There was something in his eyes that made her put both arms around his neck and lay his huge head with its coarse blond hair upon her shoulder.

"I—I got everything fixed," he said. "I got everything fixed an' ready. See, everything ready an' waiting, an'—an'—an' nobody comes, an' nobody's ever going to come any more. Oh, Trina!" He put his arms about her and drew her down closer to him.

"Never mind, dear; never mind," cried Trina, through her tears. "It'll all come right in the end, and we'll be poor together if we have to. You can sure find something else to do. We'll start in again."

"Look at the slate there," said McTeague, pulling away from her and reaching down the slate on which he kept a record of his appointments. "Look at them. There's Vanovitch at two on Wednesday, and Loughhead's wife Thursday morning, and Heise's little girl Thursday afternoon at one-thirty; Mrs. Watson on Friday, and Vanovitch again Saturday morning early—at seven. That's what I was to have had, and they ain't going to come. They ain't ever going to come any more."

Trina took the little slate from him and looked at it ruefully.

"Rub them out," she said, her voice trembling; "rub it all

out;" and as she spoke her eyes brimmed again, and a great tear dropped on the slate. "That's it," she said; "that's the way to rub it out, by me crying on it." Then she passed her fingers over the tear-blurred writing and washed the slate clean. "All gone, all gone," she said.

"All gone," echoed the dentist. There was a silence. Then McTeague heaved himself up to his full six feet two, his face purpling, his enormous mallet-like fists raised over his head. His massive jaw protruded more than ever, while his teeth clicked and grated together; then he growled:

"If ever I meet Marcus Schouler—" he broke off abruptly, the white of his eyes growing suddenly pink.

"Oh, if ever you *do*," exclaimed Trina, catching her breath.

XIV

"WELL, WHAT do you think?" said Trina.

She and McTeague stood in a tiny room at the back of the flat and on its very top floor. The room was white-washed. It contained a bed, three cane-seated chairs, and a wooden washstand with its washbowl and pitcher. From its single uncurtained window one looked down into the flat's dirty back yard and upon the roofs of the hovels that bordered the alley in the rear. There was a rag carpet on the floor. In place of a closet some dozen wooden pegs were affixed to the wall over the washstand. There was a smell of cheap soap and of ancient hair-oil in the air.

"That's a single bed," said Trina, "but the landlady says she'll put in a double one for us. You see——"

"I ain't going to live here," growled McTeague.

"Well, you've got to live somewhere," said Trina, impatiently. "We've looked Polk Street over, and this is the only thing we can afford."

"Afford, afford," muttered the dentist. "You with your five thousand dollars, and the two or three hundred you got saved up, talking about 'afford.' You make me sick."

"Now, Mac," exclaimed Trina, deliberately, sitting down in one of the cane-seated chairs; "now, Mac, let's have this thing——"

"Well, I don't figure on living in one room," growled the dentist, sullenly. "Let's live decently until we can get a fresh start. We've got the money."

"Who's got the money?"

"*We've* got it."

"We!"

"Well, it's all in the family. What's yours is mine, and what's mine is yours, ain't it?"

"No, it's not; no, it's not; no, it's not," cried Trina, vehemently. "It's all mine, mine. There's not a penny of it belongs to anybody else. I don't like to have to talk this way to you, but you just make me. We're not going to touch a penny of my five thousand nor a penny of that little money I managed to save—that seventy-five."

"That *two hundred*, you mean."

"That *seventy-five*. We're just going to live on the interest of that and on what I earn from Uncle Oelbermann—on just that thirty-one or two dollars."

"Huh! Think I'm going to do that, an' live in such a room as this?"

Trina folded her arms and looked him squarely in the face.

"Well, what *are* you going to do, then?"

"Huh?"

"I say, what *are* you going to do? You can go on and find something to do and earn some more money, and *then* we'll talk."

"Well, I ain't going to live here."

"Oh, very well, suit yourself. *I'm* going to live here."

"You'll live where I *tell* you," the dentist suddenly cried, exasperated at the mincing tone she affected.

"Then *you'll* pay the rent," exclaimed Trina, quite as angry as he.

"Are you my boss, I'd like to know? Who's the boss, you or I?"

"Who's got the *money*, I'd like to know?" cried Trina, flushing to her pale lips. "Answer me that, McTeague, who's got the money?"

"You make me sick, you and your money. Why, you're a miser. I never saw anything like it. When I was practising, I never thought of my fees as my own; we lumped everything in together."

"Exactly; and *I'm* doing the working now. I'm working for Uncle Oelbermann, and you're not lumping in *anything* now. I'm doing it all. Do you know what I'm doing, McTeague? I'm supporting you."

"Ah, shut up; you make me sick."

"You got no *right* to talk to me that way. I won't let you. I—I won't have it." She caught her breath. Tears were in her eyes.

"Oh, live where you like, then," said McTeague, sullenly.

"Well, shall we take this room then?"

"All right, we'll take it. But why can't you take a little of your money an'—an'—sort of fix it up?"

"Not a penny, not a single penny."

"Oh, I don't care *what* you do." And for the rest of the day the dentist and his wife did not speak.

This was not the only quarrel they had during these days when they were occupied in moving from their suite and in looking for new quarters. Every hour the question of money came up. Trina had become more niggardly than ever since the loss of McTeague's practice. It was not mere economy with her now. It was a panic terror lest a fraction of a cent of her little savings should be touched; a passionate eagerness to continue to save in spite of all that had happened. Trina could have easily afforded better quarters than the single white-washed room at the top of the flat, but she made McTeague believe that it was impossible.

"I can still save a little," she said to herself, after the room had been engaged; "perhaps almost as much as ever. I'll have three hundred dollars pretty soon, and Mac thinks it's only two hundred. It's almost two hundred and fifty; and I'll get a good deal out of the sale."

But this sale was a long agony. It lasted a week. Everything went—everything but the few big pieces that went with the suite, and that belonged to the photographer. The melodeon, the chairs, the black walnut table before which they were married, the extension table in the sitting-room, the kitchen table with its oilcloth cover, the framed lithographs from the English illustrated papers, the very carpets on the floors. But Trina's heart nearly broke when the kitchen utensils and furnishings began to go. Every pot, every stewpan, every knife and fork, was an old friend. How she had worked over them! How clean she had kept them! What a pleasure it had been to invade that little brick-paved kitchen every morning, and to wash up and put to rights after breakfast, turning on the hot water at the sink, raking down the ashes in the cookstove, going and coming over the warm bricks, her head in the air, singing at her work, proud in the sense of her proprietorship and her independence! How happy had she been the day after her marriage when she had first entered that kitchen and knew that it was all her own! And how well she remembered her raids upon the bargain counters in the house-furnishing departments of the great down-town stores! And now it was all to go. Some one else would have it all, while she was relegated to cheap restaurants and meals cooked by hired servants. Night after night she sobbed herself to sleep at the thought of her past happiness and her present wretchedness. However, she was not alone in her unhappiness.

"Anyhow, I'm going to keep the steel engraving an' the stone pug dog," declared the dentist, his fist clenching. When it had come to the sale of his office effects McTeague had rebelled with the instinctive obstinacy of a boy, shutting his eyes and ears. Only little by little did Trina induce him to part with his office furniture. He fought over every article, over the little iron stove, the bed-lounge, the marble-topped centre table, the whatnot in the corner, the bound volumes of "Allen's Practical Dentist," the rifle manufacturer's calendar, and the prim, military chairs. A veritable scene took place between him and his wife before he could bring himself to part with the steel engraving of "Lorenzo de' Medici and His Court" and the stone pug dog with its goggle eyes.

"Why," he would cry, "I've had 'em ever since—ever since I *began*; long before I knew you, Trina. That steel engraving I bought in Sacramento one day when it was raining. I saw it in the window of a second-hand store, and a fellow *gave* me that stone pug dog. He was a druggist. It was in Sacramento too. We traded. I gave him a shaving-mug and a razor, and he gave me the pug dog."

There were, however, two of his belongings that even Trina could not induce him to part with.

"And your concertina, Mac," she prompted, as they were making out the list for the second-hand dealer. "The concertina, and—oh, yes, the canary and the bird cage."

"No."

"Mac, you *must* be reasonable. The concertina would bring quite a sum, and the bird cage is as good as new. I'll sell the canary to the bird-store man on Kearney Street."

"No."

"If you're going to make objections to every single thing, we might as well quit. Come, now, Mac, the concertina and the bird cage. We'll put them in Lot D."

"No."

"You'll have to come to it sooner or later. *I'm* giving up everything. I'm going to put them down, see."

"No."

And she could get no further than that. The dentist did not lose his temper, as in the case of the steel engraving or the stone pug dog; he simply opposed her entreaties and persuasions with a passive, inert obstinacy that nothing could move. In the end Trina was obliged to submit. McTeague kept his concertina and his canary, even going so far as to put them both away in the bedroom, attaching to them tags on which he had scrawled in immense round letters, "Not for Sale."

One evening during that same week the dentist and his wife were in the dismantled sitting-room. The room presented the appearance of a wreck. The Nottingham lace curtains were down. The extension table was heaped high with dishes, with tea and coffee pots, and with baskets of spoons and knives and forks. The melodeon was hauled out into the middle of the floor, and covered with a sheet marked "Lot A," the pictures were in a pile in a corner, the chenille portières were folded on top of the black walnut table. The room was desolate, lamentable. Trina was going over the inventory; McTeague, in his shirt sleeves, was smoking his pipe, looking stupidly out of the window. All at once there was a brisk rapping at the door.

"Come in," called Trina, apprehensively. Now-a-days at every unexpected visit she anticipated a fresh calamity. The door opened to let in a young man wearing a checked suit, a gay cravat, and a marvellously figured waistcoat. Trina and McTeague recognized him at once. It was the Other Dentist, the debonair fellow whose clients were the barbers and the young women of the candy stores and soda-water fountains, the poser, the wearer of waistcoats, who bet money on greyhound races.

"How'do?" said this one, bowing gracefully to the McTeagues as they stared at him distrustfully. "How'do? They tell me, Doctor, that you are going out of the profession."

McTeague muttered indistinctly behind his mustache and glowered at him.

"Well, say," continued the other, cheerily, "I'd like to talk business with you. That sign of yours, that big golden tooth that you got outside of your window, I don't suppose you'll have any further use for it. Maybe I'd buy it if we could agree on terms."

Trina shot a glance at her husband. McTeague began to glower again.

"What do you say?" said the Other Dentist.

"I guess not," growled McTeague.

"What do you say to ten dollars?"

"Ten dollars!" cried Trina, her chin in the air.

"Well, what figure *do* you put on it?"

Trina was about to answer when she was interrupted by McTeague.

"You go out of here."

"Hey? What?"

"You go out of here."

The other retreated toward the door.

"You can't make small of me. Go out of here."

McTeague came forward a step, his great red fist clenching. The young man fled. But half way down the stairs he paused long enough to call back:

"You don't want to trade anything for a diploma, do you?"

McTeague and his wife exchanged looks.

"How did he know?" exclaimed Trina, sharply. They had invented and spread the fiction that McTeague was merely retiring from business, without assigning any reason. But evidently every one knew the real cause. The humiliation was complete now. Old Miss Baker confirmed their suspicions on this point the next day. The little retired dressmaker came down and wept with Trina over her misfortune, and did what she could to encourage her. But she too knew that McTeague had been forbidden by the authorities from practising. Marcus had evidently left them no loophole of escape.

"It's just like cutting off your husband's hands, my dear," said Miss Baker. "And you two were so happy. When I first saw you together I said, 'What a pair!'"

Old Grannis also called during this period of the breaking up of the McTeague household.

"Dreadful, dreadful," murmured the old Englishman, his hand going tremulously to his chin. "It seems unjust; it does. But Mr. Schouler could not have set them on to do it. I can't quite believe it of him."

"Of Marcus!" cried Trina. "Hoh! Why, he threw his knife at Mac one time, and another time he bit him, actually bit him with his teeth, while they were wrestling just for fun. Marcus would do anything to injure Mac."

"Dear, dear," returned Old Grannis, genuinely pained. "I had always believed Schouler to be such a good fellow."

"That's because you're so good yourself, Mr. Grannis," responded Trina.

"I tell you what, Doc," declared Heise the harness-maker, shaking his finger impressively at the dentist, "you must fight it; you must appeal to the courts; you've been practising too long to be debarred now. The statute of limitations, you know."

"No, no," Trina had exclaimed, when the dentist had repeated this advice to her. "No, no, don't go near the law courts. *I* know them. The lawyers take all your money, and you lose your case. We're bad off as it is, without lawing about it."

Then at last came the sale. McTeague and Trina, whom Miss Baker had invited to her room for that day, sat there side by side, holding each other's hands, listening nervously to the turmoil that rose to them from the direction of their suite. From nine o'clock till dark the crowds came and went. All Polk Street seemed to have invaded the suite, lured on by the red flag that waved from the front windows. It was a *fête*, a veritable holiday, for the whole neighborhood. People with no thought of buying presented themselves. Young women— the candy-store girls and florist's apprentices—came to see the fun, walking arm in arm from room to room, making jokes about the pretty lithographs and mimicking the picture of the two little girls saying their prayers.

"Look here," they would cry, "look here what she used for curtains—*Nottingham lace*, actually! Whoever thinks of buying Nottingham lace now-a-days? Say, don't that *jar* you?"

"And a melodeon," another one would exclaim, lifting the sheet. "A melodeon, when you can rent a piano for a dollar a week; and say, I really believe they used to eat in the kitchen."

"Dollarn-half, dollarn-half, dollarn-half, give me two," intoned the auctioneer from the second-hand store. By noon the crowd became a jam. Wagons backed up to the curb outside and departed heavily laden. In all directions people could be seen going away from the house, carrying small articles of furniture—a clock, a water pitcher, a towel rack. Every now and then old Miss Baker, who had gone below to see how things were progressing, returned with reports of the foray.

"Mrs. Heise bought the chenille portières. Mister Ryer made a bid for your bed, but a man in a gray coat bid over him. It was knocked down for three dollars and a half. The German shoemaker on the next block bought the stone pug dog. I saw our postman going away with a lot of the pictures. Zerkow has come, on my word! the rags-bottles-sacks man; he's buying lots; he bought all Doctor McTeague's gold tape and some of the instruments. Maria's there too. That dentist on the corner took the dental engine, and wanted to get the sign, the big gold tooth," and so on and so on. Cruelest of all, however, at least to Trina, was when Miss Baker herself began to buy, unable to resist a bargain. The last time she came up she carried a bundle of the gay tidies that used to hang over the chair backs.

"He offered them, three for a nickel," she explained to Trina, "and I thought I'd spend just a quarter. You don't mind, now, do you, Mrs. McTeague?"

"Why, no, of course not, Miss Baker," answered Trina, bravely.

"They'll look very pretty on some of my chairs," went on the little old dressmaker, innocently. "See." She spread one of them on a chair back for inspection. Trina's chin quivered.

"Oh, *very* pretty," she answered.

At length that dreadful day was over. The crowd dispersed. Even the auctioneer went at last, and as he closed the door with a bang, the reverberation that went through the suite gave evidence of its emptiness.

"Come," said Trina to the dentist, "let's go down and look—take a last look."

They went out of Miss Baker's room and descended to the floor below. On the stairs, however, they were met by Old Grannis. In his hands he carried a little package. Was it possible that he too had taken advantage of their misfortunes to join in the raid upon the suite?

"I went in," he began, timidly, "for—for a few moments.

This"—he indicated the little package he carried—"this was put up. It was of no value but to you. I—I ventured to bid it in. I thought perhaps"—his hand went to his chin, "that you wouldn't mind; that—in fact, I bought it for you—as a present. Will you take it?" He handed the package to Trina and hurried on. Trina tore off the wrappings.

It was the framed photograph of McTeague and his wife in their wedding finery, the one that had been taken immediately after the marriage. It represented Trina sitting very erect in a rep armchair, holding her wedding bouquet straight before her, McTeague standing at her side, his left foot forward, one hand upon her shoulder, and the other thrust into the breast of his "Prince Albert" coat, in the attitude of a statue of a Secretary of State.

"Oh, it *was* good of him, it *was* good of him," cried Trina, her eyes filling again. "I had forgotten to put it away. Of course it was not for sale."

They went on down the stairs, and arriving at the door of the sitting-room, opened it and looked in. It was late in the afternoon, and there was just light enough for the dentist and his wife to see the results of that day of sale. Nothing was left, not even the carpet. It was a pillage, a devastation, the barrenness of a field after the passage of a swarm of locusts. The room had been picked and stripped till only the bare walls and floor remained. Here where they had been married, where the wedding supper had taken place, where Trina had bade farewell to her father and mother, here where she had spent those first few hard months of her married life, where afterward she had grown to be happy and contented, where she had passed the long hours of the afternoon at her work of whittling, and where she and her husband had spent so many evenings looking out of the window before the lamp was lit—here in what had been her home, nothing was left but echoes and the emptiness of complete desolation. Only one thing remained. On the wall between the windows, in its oval glass frame, preserved by some unknown and fearful process, a melancholy relic of a vanished happiness, unsold, neglected, and forgotten, a thing that nobody wanted, hung Trina's wedding bouquet.

XV

THEN THE grind began. It would have been easier for the McTeagues to have faced their misfortunes had they befallen them immediately after their marriage, when their love for each other was fresh and fine, and when they could have found a certain happiness in helping each other and sharing each other's privations. Trina, no doubt, loved her husband more than ever, in the sense that she felt she belonged to him. But McTeague's affection for his wife was dwindling a little every day—*had* been dwindling for a long time, in fact. He had become used to her by now. She was part of the order of the things with which he found himself surrounded. He saw nothing extraordinary about her; it was no longer a pleasure for him to kiss her and take her in his arms; she was merely his wife. He did not dislike her; he did not love her. She was his wife, that was all. But he sadly missed and regretted all those little animal comforts which in the old prosperous life Trina had managed to find for him. He missed the cabbage soups and steaming chocolate that Trina had taught him to like; he missed his good tobacco that Trina had educated him to prefer; he missed the Sunday afternoon walks that she had caused him to substitute in place of his nap in the operating chair; and he missed the bottled beer that she had induced him to drink in place of the steam beer from Frenna's. In the end he grew morose and sulky, and sometimes neglected to answer his wife when she spoke to him. Besides this, Trina's avarice was a perpetual annoyance to him. Oftentimes when a considerable alleviation of this unhappiness could have been obtained at the expense of a nickel or a dime, Trina refused the money with a pettishness that was exasperating.

"No, no," she would exclaim. "To ride to the park Sunday afternoon, that means ten cents, and I can't afford it."

"Let's walk there, then."

"I've got to work."

"But you've worked morning and afternoon every day this week."

"I don't care, I've got to work."

There had been a time when Trina had hated the idea of McTeague drinking steam beer as common and vulgar.

"Say, let's have a bottle of beer to-night. We haven't had a drop of beer in three weeks."

"We can't afford it. It's fifteen cents a bottle."

"But I haven't had a swallow of beer in three weeks."

"Drink *steam* beer, then. You've got a nickel. I gave you a quarter day before yesterday."

"But I don't like steam beer now."

It was so with everything. Unfortunately, Trina had culti-vated tastes in McTeague which now could not be gratified. He had come to be very proud of his silk hat and "Prince Albert" coat, and liked to wear them on Sundays. Trina had made him sell both. He preferred "Yale mixture" in his pipe; Trina had made him come down to "Mastiff," a five-cent to-bacco with which he was once contented, but now abhorred. He liked to wear clean cuffs; Trina allowed him a fresh pair on Sundays only. At first these deprivations angered Mc-Teague. Then, all of a sudden, he slipped back into the old habits (that had been his before he knew Trina) with an ease that was surprising. Sundays he dined at the car conductors' coffee-joint once more, and spent the afternoon lying full length upon the bed, crop-full, stupid, warm, smoking his huge pipe, drinking his steam beer, and playing his six mournful tunes upon his concertina, dozing off to sleep to-wards four o'clock.

The sale of their furniture had, after paying the rent and outstanding bills, netted about a hundred and thirty dollars. Trina believed that the auctioneer from the second-hand store had swindled and cheated them and had made a great outcry to no effect. But she had arranged the affair with the auction-eer herself, and offset her disappointment in the matter of the sale by deceiving her husband as to the real amount of the returns. It was easy to lie to McTeague, who took everything for granted; and since the occasion of her trickery with the money that was to have been sent to her mother, Trina had found falsehood easier than ever.

"Seventy dollars is all the auctioneer gave me," she told her husband; "and after paying the balance due on the rent, and the grocer's bill, there's only fifty left."

"Only fifty?" murmured McTeague, wagging his head, "only fifty? Think of that."

"Only fifty," declared Trina. Afterwards she said to herself with a certain admiration for her cleverness:

"Couldn't save sixty dollars much easier than that," and she had added the hundred and thirty to the little hoard in the chamois-skin bag and brass match-box in the bottom of her trunk.

In these first months of their misfortunes the routine of the McTeagues was as follows: They rose at seven and breakfasted in their room, Trina cooking the very meagre meal on an oil stove. Immediately after breakfast Trina sat down to her work of whittling the Noah's ark animals, and McTeague took himself off to walk down town. He had by the greatest good luck secured a position with a manufacturer of surgical instruments, where his manual dexterity in the making of excavators, pluggers, and other dental contrivances stood him in fairly good stead. He lunched at a sailor's boarding-house near the water front, and in the afternoon worked till six. He was home at six-thirty, and he and Trina had supper together in the "ladies' dining parlor," an adjunct of the car conductors' coffee-joint. Trina, meanwhile, had worked at her whittling all day long, with but half an hour's interval for lunch, which she herself prepared upon the oil stove. In the evening they were both so tired that they were in no mood for conversation, and went to bed early, worn out, harried, nervous, and cross.

Trina was not quite so scrupulously tidy now as in the old days. At one time while whittling the Noah's ark animals she had worn gloves. She never wore them now. She still took pride in neatly combing and coiling her wonderful black hair, but as the days passed she found it more and more comfortable to work in her blue flannel wrapper. Whittlings and chips accumulated under the window where she did her work, and she was at no great pains to clear the air of the room vitiated by the fumes of the oil stove and heavy with the smell of cooking. It was not gay, that life. The room itself was not gay. The huge double bed sprawled over nearly a fourth of the available space; the angles of Trina's trunk and the washstand projected into the room from the walls, and barked shins and scraped elbows. Streaks and spots of the "non-poisonous" paint that Trina used were upon the walls and woodwork. However, in one corner of the room, next the window, monstrous, distorted, brilliant, shining with a light of its own, stood the dentist's sign, the enormous golden tooth, the tooth of a Brobdingnag.

One afternoon in September, about four months after the McTeagues had left their suite, Trina was at her work by the window. She had whittled some half-dozen sets of animals, and was now busy painting them and making the arks. Little pots of "non-poisonous" paint stood at her elbow on the table, together with a box of labels that read, "Made in France." Her huge clasp-knife was stuck into the under side of the table. She was now occupied solely with the brushes and the glue pot. She turned the little figures in her fingers with a wonderful lightness and deftness, painting the chickens Naples yellow, the elephants blue gray, the horses Vandyke brown, adding a dot of Chinese white for the eyes and sticking in the ears and tail with a drop of glue. The animals once done, she put together and painted the arks, some dozen of them, all windows and no doors, each one opening only by a lid which was half the roof. She had all the work she could handle these days, for, from this time till a week before Christmas, Uncle Oelbermann could take as many "Noah's ark sets" as she could make.

Suddenly Trina paused in her work, looking expectantly toward the door. McTeague came in.

"Why, Mac," exclaimed Trina. "It's only three o'clock. What are you home so early for? Have they discharged you?"

"They've fired me," said McTeague, sitting down on the bed.

"Fired you! What for?"

"I don' know. Said the times were getting hard an' they had to let me go."

Trina let her paint-stained hands fall into her lap.

"*Oh!*" she cried. "If we don't have the *hardest* luck of any two people I ever heard of. What can you do now? Is there another place like that where they make surgical instruments?"

"Huh? No, I don' know. There's three more."

"Well, you must try them right away. Go down there right now."

"Huh? Right now? No, I'm tired. I'll go down in the morning."

"Mac," cried Trina, in alarm, "what are you thinking of? You talk as though we were millionaires. You must go down this minute. You're losing money every second you sit there." She goaded the huge fellow to his feet again, thrust his hat into his hands, and pushed him out of the door, he obeying the while, docile and obedient as a big cart horse. He was on the stairs when she came running after him.

"Mac, they paid you off, didn't they, when they discharged you?"

"Yes."

"Then you must have some money. Give it to me."

The dentist heaved a shoulder uneasily.

"No, I don' want to."

"I've got to have that money. There's no more oil for the stove, and I must buy some more meal tickets to-night."

"Always after me about money," muttered the dentist; but he emptied his pockets for her, nevertheless.

"I—you've taken it all," he grumbled. "Better leave me something for car fare. It's going to rain."

"Pshaw! You can walk just as well as not. A big fellow like you 'fraid of a little walk; and it ain't going to rain."

Trina had lied again both as to the want of oil for the stove and the commutation ticket for the restaurant. But she knew by instinct that McTeague had money about him, and she did not intend to let it go out of the house. She listened intently until she was sure McTeague was gone. Then she hurriedly opened her trunk and hid the money in the chamois bag at the bottom.

The dentist presented himself at every one of the makers of surgical instruments that afternoon and was promptly turned away in each case. Then it came on to rain, a fine, cold drizzle, that chilled him and wet him to the bone. He had no umbrella, and Trina had not left him even five cents for car fare. He started to walk home through the rain. It was a long way to Polk Street, as the last manufactory he had visited was beyond even Folsom Street, and not far from the city front.

By the time McTeague reached Polk Street his teeth were chattering with the cold. He was wet from head to foot. As he was passing Heise's harness shop a sudden deluge of rain overtook him and he was obliged to dodge into the vestibule for shelter. He, who loved to be warm, to sleep and to be well fed, was icy cold, was exhausted and footsore from tramping the city. He could look forward to nothing better than a badly-cooked supper at the coffee-joint—hot meat on a cold plate, half done suet pudding, muddy coffee, and bad bread, and he was cold, miserably cold, and wet to the bone. All at once a sudden rage against Trina took possession of him. It was her fault. She knew it was going to rain, and she had not let him have a nickel for car fare—she who had five thousand dollars. She let him walk the streets in the cold and in the rain. "Miser," he growled behind his mustache. "Miser, nasty little old miser. You're worse than old Zerkow, always nagging about money, money, and you got five thousand dollars. You got more, an' you live in that stinking hole of a room, and you won't drink any decent beer. I ain't going to stand it much longer. She knew it was going to rain. She *knew* it. Didn't I *tell* her? And she drives me out of my own home in the rain, for me to get money for her; more money, and she takes it. She took that money from me that I earned. 'Twasn't hers; it was mine, I earned it—and not a nickel for car fare. She don't care if I get wet and get a cold and *die*. No, she don't, as long as she's warm and's got her money." He became more and more indignant at the picture he made of himself. "I ain't going to stand it much longer," he repeated.

"Why, hello, Doc. Is that you?" exclaimed Heise, opening the door of the harness shop behind him. "Come in out of the wet. Why, you're soaked through," he added as he and McTeague came back into the shop, that reeked of oiled leather. "Didn't you have any umbrella? Ought to have taken a car."

"I guess so—I guess so," murmured the dentist, confused. His teeth were chattering.

"*You're* going to catch your death-a-cold," exclaimed Heise. "Tell you what," he said, reaching for his hat, "come in next door to Frenna's and have something to warm you up. I'll get

the old lady to mind the shop." He called Mrs. Heise down
from the floor above and took McTeague into Joe Frenna's
saloon, which was two doors above his harness shop.

"Whiskey and gum twice, Joe," said he to the barkeeper as
he and the dentist approached the bar.

"Huh? What?" said McTeague. "Whiskey? No, I can't drink
whiskey. It kind of disagrees with me."

"Oh, the hell!" returned Heise, easily. "Take it as medicine.
You'll get your death-a-cold if you stand round soaked like
that. Two whiskey and gum, Joe."

McTeague emptied the pony glass at a single enormous
gulp.

"That's the way," said Heise, approvingly. "Do you good."
He drank his off slowly.

"I'd—I'd ask you to have a drink with me, Heise," said the
dentist, who had an indistinct idea of the amenities of the
barroom, "only," he added shamefacedly, "only—you see, I
don't believe I got any change." His anger against Trina,
heated by the whiskey he had drank, flamed up afresh. What
a humiliating position for Trina to place him in, not to leave
him the price of a drink with a friend, she who had five thousand dollars!

"Sha! That's all right, Doc," returned Heise, nibbling on a
grain of coffee. "Want another? Hey? This my treat. Two
more of the same, Joe."

McTeague hesitated. It was lamentably true that whiskey
did not agree with him; he knew it well enough. However,
by this time he felt very comfortably warm at the pit of his
stomach. The blood was beginning to circulate in his chilled
finger-tips and in his soggy, wet feet. He had had a hard day
of it; in fact, the last week, the last month, the last three or
four months, had been hard. He deserved a little consolation.
Nor could Trina object to this. It wasn't costing a cent. He
drank again with Heise.

"Get up here to the stove and warm yourself," urged Heise,
drawing up a couple of chairs and cocking his feet upon the
guard. The two fell to talking while McTeague's draggled coat
and trousers smoked.

"What a dirty turn that was that Marcus Schouler did
you!" said Heise, wagging his head. "You ought to have

fought that, Doc, sure. You'd been practising too long." They discussed this question some ten or fifteen minutes and then Heise rose.

"Well, this ain't earning any money. I got to get back to the shop." McTeague got up as well, and the pair started for the door. Just as they were going out Ryer met them.

"Hello, hello," he cried. "Lord, what a wet day! You two are going the wrong way. You're going to have a drink with me. Three whiskey punches, Joe."

"No, no," answered McTeague, shaking his head. "I'm going back home. I've had two glasses of whiskey already."

"Sha!" cried Heise, catching his arm. "A strapping big chap like you ain't afraid of a little whiskey."

"Well, I—I—I got to go right afterwards," protested McTeague.

About half an hour after the dentist had left to go down town, Maria Macapa had come in to see Trina. Occasionally Maria dropped in on Trina in this fashion and spent an hour or so chatting with her while she worked. At first Trina had been inclined to resent these intrusions of the Mexican woman, but of late she had begun to tolerate them. Her day was long and cheerless at the best, and there was no one to talk to. Trina even fancied that old Miss Baker had come to be less cordial since their misfortune. Maria retailed to her all the gossip of the flat and the neighborhood, and, which was much more interesting, told her of her troubles with Zerkow.

Trina said to herself that Maria was common and vulgar, but one had to have some diversion, and Trina could talk and listen without interrupting her work. On this particular occasion Maria was much excited over Zerkow's demeanor of late.

"He's gettun worse an' worse," she informed Trina as she sat on the edge of the bed, her chin in her hand. "He says he knows I got the dishes and am hidun them from him. The other day I thought he'd gone off with his wagon, and I was doin' a bit of ir'ning, an' by an' by all of a sudden I saw him peeping at me through the crack of the door. I never let on that I saw him, and, honest, he stayed there over two hours, watchun everything I did. I could just feel his eyes on the back of my neck all the time. Last Sunday he took down part of the wall, 'cause he said he'd seen me making figures on it. Well, I was, but it was just the wash list. All the time he says he'll kill me if I don't tell!"

"Why, what do you stay with him for?" exclaimed Trina. "I'd be deathly 'fraid of a man like that; and he did take a knife to you once."

"Hoh! *he* won't kill me, never fear. If he'd kill me he'd never know where the dishes were; that's what *he* thinks."

"But I can't understand, Maria; you told him about those gold dishes yourself."

"Never, never! I never saw such a lot of crazy folks as you are."

"But you say he hits you sometimes."

"Ah!" said Maria, tossing her head scornfully, "I ain't afraid of him. He takes his horsewhip to me now and then, but I can always manage. I say, 'If you touch me with that, then I'll *never* tell you.' Just pretending, you know, and he drops it as though it was red hot. Say, Mrs. McTeague, have you got any tea? Let's make a cup of tea over the stove."

"No, no," cried Trina, with niggardly apprehension; "no, I haven't got a bit of tea." Trina's stinginess had increased to such an extent that it had gone beyond the mere hoarding of money. She grudged even the food that she and McTeague ate, and even brought away half loaves of bread, lumps of sugar, and fruit from the car conductors' coffee-joint. She hid these pilferings away on the shelf by the window, and often managed to make a very creditable lunch from them, enjoying the meal with the greater relish because it cost her nothing.

"No, Maria, I haven't got a bit of tea," she said, shaking her head decisively. "Hark, ain't that Mac?" she added, her chin in the air. "That's his step, sure."

"Well, I'm going to skip," said Maria. She left hurriedly, passing the dentist in the hall just outside the door.

"Well?" said Trina interrogatively as her husband entered. McTeague did not answer. He hung his hat on the hook behind the door and dropped heavily into a chair.

"Well," asked Trina, anxiously, "how did you make out, Mac?"

Still the dentist pretended not to hear, scowling fiercely at his muddy boots.

"Tell me, Mac, I want to know. Did you get a place? Did you get caught in the rain?"

"Did I? Did I?" cried the dentist, sharply, an alacrity in his manner and voice that Trina had never observed before.

"Look at me. Look at me," he went on, speaking with an unwonted rapidity, his wits sharp, his ideas succeeding each other quickly. "Look at me, drenched through, shivering cold. I've walked the city over. Caught in the rain! Yes, I guess I did get caught in the rain, and it ain't your fault I didn't catch my death-a-cold; wouldn't even let me have a nickel for car fare."

"But, Mac," protested Trina, "I didn't know it was going to rain."

The dentist put back his head and laughed scornfully. His face was very red, and his small eyes twinkled. "Hoh! no, you didn't know it was going to rain. Didn't I *tell* you it was?" he exclaimed, suddenly angry again. "Oh, you're a *daisy*, you are. Think I'm going to put up with your foolishness *all* the time? Who's the boss, you or I?"

"Why, Mac, I never saw you this way before. You talk like a different man."

"Well, I *am* a different man," retorted the dentist, savagely. "You can't make small of me *always*."

"Well, never mind that. You know I'm not trying to make small of you. But never mind that. Did you get a place?"

"Give me my money," exclaimed McTeague, jumping up briskly. There was an activity, a positive nimbleness about the huge blond giant that had never been his before; also his stupidity, the sluggishness of his brain, seemed to be unusually stimulated.

"Give me my money, the money I gave you as I was going away."

"I can't," exclaimed Trina. "I paid the grocer's bill with it while you were gone."

"Don't believe you."

"Truly, truly, Mac. Do you think I'd lie to you? Do you think I'd lower myself to do that?"

"Well, the next time I earn any money I'll keep it myself."

"But tell me, Mac, *did* you get a place?"

McTeague turned his back on her.

"Tell me, Mac, please, did you?"

The dentist jumped up and thrust his face close to hers, his heavy jaw protruding, his little eyes twinkling meanly.

"No," he shouted. "No, no, *no*. Do you hear? *No*."

Trina cowered before him. Then suddenly she began to sob aloud, weeping partly at his strange brutality, partly at the disappointment of his failure to find employment.

McTeague cast a contemptuous glance about him, a glance that embraced the dingy, cheerless room, the rain streaming down the panes of the one window, and the figure of his weeping wife.

"Oh, ain't this all *fine*?" he exclaimed. "Ain't it lovely?"

"It's not my fault," sobbed Trina.

"It is too," vociferated McTeague. "It is too. We could live like Christians and decent people if you wanted to. You got more'n five thousand dollars, and you're so damned stingy that you'd rather live in a rat hole—and make me live there too—before you'd part with a nickel of it. I tell you I'm sick and tired of the whole business."

An allusion to her lottery money never failed to rouse Trina.

"And I'll tell you this much too," she cried, winking back the tears. "Now that you're out of a job, we can't afford even to live in your rat hole, as you call it. We've got to find a cheaper place than *this* even."

"What!" exclaimed the dentist, purple with rage. "What, get into a worse hole in the wall than this? Well, we'll *see* if we will. We'll just see about that. You're going to do just as I tell you after this, Trina McTeague," and once more he thrust his face close to hers.

"*I* know what's the matter," cried Trina, with a half sob; "*I* know, I can smell it on your breath. You've been drinking whiskey."

"Yes, I've been drinking whiskey," retorted her husband. "I've been drinking whiskey. Have you got anything to say about it? Ah, yes, you're *right*, I've been drinking whiskey. What have *you* got to say about my drinking whiskey? Let's hear it."

"Oh! Oh! Oh!" sobbed Trina, covering her face with her hands. McTeague caught her wrists in one palm and pulled them down. Trina's pale face was streaming with tears; her long, narrow blue eyes were swimming; her adorable little chin upraised and quivering.

"Let's hear what you got to say," exclaimed McTeague.

"Nothing, nothing," said Trina, between her sobs.

"Then stop that noise. Stop it, do you hear me? Stop it." He threw up his open hand threateningly. *"Stop!"* he exclaimed.

Trina looked at him fearfully, half blinded with weeping. Her husband's thick mane of yellow hair was disordered and rumpled upon his great square-cut head; his big red ears were redder than ever; his face was purple; the thick eyebrows were knotted over the small, twinkling eyes; the heavy yellow mustache, that smelt of alcohol, drooped over the massive, protruding chin, salient, like that of the carnivora; the veins were swollen and throbbing on his thick red neck; while over her head Trina saw his upraised palm, calloused, enormous.

"Stop!" he exclaimed. And Trina, watching fearfully, saw the palm suddenly contract into a fist, a fist that was hard as a wooden mallet, the fist of the old-time car-boy. And then her ancient terror of him, the intuitive fear of the male, leaped to life again. She was afraid of him. Every nerve of her quailed and shrank from him. She choked back her sobs, catching her breath.

"There," growled the dentist, releasing her, "that's more like. Now," he went on, fixing her with his little eyes, "now listen to me. I'm beat out. I've walked the city over—ten miles, I guess—an' I'm going to bed, an' I don't want to be bothered. You understand? I want to be let alone." Trina was silent.

"Do you *hear?*" he snarled.

"Yes, Mac."

The dentist took off his coat, his collar and necktie, unbuttoned his vest, and slipped his heavy-soled boots from his big feet. Then he stretched himself upon the bed and rolled over towards the wall. In a few minutes the sound of his snoring filled the room.

Trina craned her neck and looked at her husband over the footboard of the bed. She saw his red, congested face; the huge mouth wide open; his unclean shirt, with its frayed wristbands; and his huge feet encased in thick woollen socks. Then her grief and the sense of her unhappiness returned more poignant than ever. She stretched her arms out in front of her on her work-table, and, burying her face in them, cried and sobbed as though her heart would break.

The rain continued. The panes of the single window ran with sheets of water; the eaves dripped incessantly. It grew darker. The tiny, grimy room, full of the smells of cooking and of "non-poisonous" paint, took on an aspect of desolation and cheerlessness lamentable beyond words. The canary in its little gilt prison chittered feebly from time to time. Sprawled at full length upon the bed, the dentist snored and snored, stupefied, inert, his legs wide apart, his hands lying palm upward at his sides.

At last Trina raised her head, with a long, trembling breath. She rose, and going over to the washstand, poured some water from the pitcher into the basin, and washed her face and swollen eyelids, and rearranged her hair. Suddenly, as she was about to return to her work, she was struck with an idea.

"I wonder," she said to herself, "I wonder where he got the money to buy his whiskey." She searched the pockets of his coat, which he had flung into a corner of the room, and even came up to him as he lay upon the bed and went through the pockets of his vest and trousers. She found nothing.

"I wonder," she murmured, "I wonder if he's got any money he don't tell me about. I'll have to look out for that."

XVI

A WEEK PASSED, then a fortnight, then a month. It was a month of the greatest anxiety and unquietude for Trina. McTeague was out of a job, could find nothing to do; and Trina, who saw the impossibility of saving as much money as usual out of her earnings under the present conditions, was on the lookout for cheaper quarters. In spite of his outcries and sulky resistance Trina had induced her husband to consent to such a move, bewildering him with a torrent of phrases and marvellous columns of figures by which she proved conclusively that they were in a condition but one remove from downright destitution.

The dentist continued idle. Since his ill success with the manufacturers of surgical instruments he had made but two attempts to secure a job. Trina had gone to see Uncle Oelbermann and had obtained for McTeague a position in the shipping department of the wholesale toy store. However, it was a position that involved a certain amount of ciphering, and McTeague had been obliged to throw it up in two days.

Then for a time they had entertained a wild idea that a place on the police force could be secured for McTeague. He could pass the physical examination with flying colors, and Ryer, who had become the secretary of the Polk Street Improvement Club, promised the requisite political "pull." If McTeague had shown a certain energy in the matter the attempt might have been successful; but he was too stupid, or of late had become too listless to exert himself greatly, and the affair resulted only in a violent quarrel with Ryer.

McTeague had lost his ambition. He did not care to better his situation. All he wanted was a warm place to sleep and three good meals a day. At the first—at the very first—he had chafed at his idleness and had spent the days with his wife in their one narrow room, walking back and forth with the restlessness of a caged brute, or sitting motionless for hours, watching Trina at her work, feeling a dull glow of shame at the idea that she was supporting him. This feeling had worn off quickly, however. Trina's work was only hard when she chose to make it so, and as a rule she supported their misfortunes with a silent fortitude.

Then, wearied at his inaction and feeling the need of movement and exercise, McTeague would light his pipe and take a turn upon the great avenue one block above Polk Street. A gang of laborers were digging the foundations for a large brownstone house, and McTeague found interest and amusement in leaning over the barrier that surrounded the excavations and watching the progress of the work. He came to see it every afternoon; by and by he even got to know the foreman who superintended the job, and the two had long talks together. Then McTeague would return to Polk Street and find Heise in the back room of the harness shop, and occasionally the day ended with some half dozen drinks of whiskey at Joe Frenna's saloon.

It was curious to note the effect of the alcohol upon the dentist. It did not make him drunk, it made him vicious. So far from being stupefied, he became, after the fourth glass, active, alert, quick-witted, even talkative; a certain wickedness stirred in him then; he was intractable, mean; and when he had drunk a little more heavily than usual, he found a certain pleasure in annoying and exasperating Trina, even in abusing and hurting her.

It had begun on the evening of Thanksgiving Day, when Heise had taken McTeague out to dinner with him. The dentist on this occasion had drunk very freely. He and Heise had returned to Polk Street towards ten o'clock, and Heise at once suggested a couple of drinks at Frenna's.

"All right, all right," said McTeague. "Drinks, that's the word. I'll go home and get some money and meet you at Joe's."

Trina was awakened by her husband pinching her arm.

"Oh, Mac," she cried, jumping up in bed with a little scream, "how you hurt! Oh, that hurt me dreadfully."

"Give me a little money," answered the dentist, grinning, and pinching her again.

"I haven't a cent. There's not a—oh, *Mac*, will you stop? I won't have you pinch me that way."

"Hurry up," answered her husband, calmly, nipping the flesh of her shoulder between his thumb and finger. "Heise's waiting for me." Trina wrenched from him with a sharp intake of breath, frowning with pain, and caressing her shoulder.

"Mac, you've no idea how that hurts. Mac, *stop!*"

"Give me some money, then."

In the end Trina had to comply. She gave him half a dollar from her dress pocket, protesting that it was the only piece of money she had.

"One more, just for luck," said McTeague, pinching her again; "and another."

"How can you—how *can* you hurt a woman so!" exclaimed Trina, beginning to cry with the pain.

"Ah, now, *cry*," retorted the dentist. "That's right, *cry*. I never saw such a little fool." He went out, slamming the door in disgust.

But McTeague never became a drunkard in the generally received sense of the term. He did not drink to excess more than two or three times in a month, and never upon any occasion did he become maudlin or staggering. Perhaps his nerves were naturally too dull to admit of any excitation; perhaps he did not really care for the whiskey, and only drank because Heise and the other men at Frenna's did. Trina could often reproach him with drinking too much; she never could say that he was drunk. The alcohol had its effect for all that. It roused the man, or rather the brute in the man, and now not only roused it, but goaded it to evil. McTeague's nature changed. It was not only the alcohol, it was idleness and a general throwing off of the good influence his wife had had over him in the days of their prosperity. McTeague disliked Trina. She was a perpetual irritation to him. She annoyed him because she was so small, so prettily made, so invariably correct and precise. Her avarice incessantly harassed him. Her industry was a constant reproach to him. She seemed to flaunt her work defiantly in his face. It was the red flag in the eyes of the bull. One time when he had just come back from Frenna's and had been sitting in the chair near her, silently watching her at her work, he exclaimed all of a sudden:

"Stop working. Stop it, I tell you. Put 'em away. Put 'em all away, or I'll pinch you."

"But why—why?" Trina protested.

The dentist cuffed her ears. "I won't have you work." He took her knife and her paint-pots away, and made her sit idly in the window the rest of the afternoon.

It was, however, only when his wits had been stirred with alcohol that the dentist was brutal to his wife. At other times, say three weeks of every month, she was merely an incumbrance to him. They often quarrelled about Trina's money, her savings. The dentist was bent upon having at least a part of them. What he would do with the money once he had it, he did not precisely know. He would spend it in royal fashion, no doubt, feasting continually, buying himself wonderful clothes. The miner's idea of money quickly gained and lavishly squandered, persisted in his mind. As for Trina, the more her husband stormed, the tighter she drew the strings of the little chamois-skin bag that she hid at the bottom of her trunk underneath her bridal dress. Her five thousand dollars invested in Uncle Oelbermann's business was a glittering, splendid dream which came to her almost every hour of the day as a solace and a compensation for all her unhappiness.

At times, when she knew that McTeague was far from home, she would lock her door, open her trunk, and pile all her little hoard on her table. By now it was four hundred and seven dollars and fifty cents. Trina would play with this money by the hour, piling it, and repiling it, or gathering it all into one heap, and drawing back to the farthest corner of the room to note the effect, her head on one side. She polished the gold pieces with a mixture of soap and ashes until they shone, wiping them carefully on her apron. Or, again, she would draw the heap lovingly toward her and bury her face in it, delighted at the smell of it and the feel of the smooth, cool metal on her cheeks. She even put the smaller gold pieces in her mouth, and jingled them there. She loved her money with an intensity that she could hardly express. She would plunge her small fingers into the pile with little murmurs of affection, her long, narrow eyes half closed and shining, her breath coming in long sighs.

"Ah, the dear money, the dear money," she would whisper. "I love you so! All mine, every penny of it. No one shall ever, ever get you. How I've worked for you! How I've slaved and saved for you! And I'm going to get more; I'm going to get more, more, more; a little every day."

She was still looking for cheaper quarters. Whenever she could spare a moment from her work, she would put on her hat and range up and down the entire neighborhood from Sutter to Sacramento Streets, going into all the alleys and by-streets, her head in the air, looking for the "Rooms-to-let" sign. But she was in despair. All the cheaper tenements were occupied. She could find no room more reasonable than the one she and the dentist now occupied.

As time went on, McTeague's idleness became habitual. He drank no more whiskey than at first, but his dislike for Trina increased with every day of their poverty, with every day of Trina's persistent stinginess. At times—fortunately rare—he was more than ever brutal to her. He would box her ears or hit her a great blow with the back of a hair-brush, or even with his closed fist. His old-time affection for his "little woman," unable to stand the test of privation, had lapsed by degrees, and what little of it was left was changed, distorted, and made monstrous by the alcohol.

The people about the house and the clerks at the provision stores often remarked that Trina's finger-tips were swollen and the nails purple as though they had been shut in a door. Indeed, this was the explanation she gave. The fact of the matter was that McTeague, when he had been drinking, used to bite them, crunching and grinding them with his immense teeth, always ingenious enough to remember which were the sorest. Sometimes he extorted money from her by this means, but as often as not he did it for his own satisfaction.

And in some strange, inexplicable way this brutality made Trina all the more affectionate; aroused in her a morbid, un-wholesome love of submission, a strange, unnatural pleasure in yielding, in surrendering herself to the will of an irresist-ible, virile power.

Trina's emotions had narrowed with the narrowing of her daily life. They reduced themselves at last to but two, her passion for her money and her perverted love for her husband when he was brutal. She was a strange woman during these days.

Trina had come to be on very intimate terms with Maria

Macapa, and in the end the dentist's wife and the maid of all work became great friends. Maria was constantly in and out of Trina's room, and, whenever she could, Trina threw a shawl over her head and returned Maria's calls. Trina could reach Zerkow's dirty house without going into the street. The back yard of the flat had a gate that opened into a little inclosure where Zerkow kept his decrepit horse and ram-shackle wagon, and from thence Trina could enter directly into Maria's kitchen. Trina made long visits to Maria during the morning in her dressing-gown and curl papers, and the two talked at great length over a cup of tea served on the edge of the sink or a corner of the laundry table. The talk was all of their husbands and of what to do when they came home in aggressive moods.

"You never ought to fight um," advised Maria. "It only makes um worse. Just hump your back, and it's soonest over."

They told each other of their husbands' brutalities, taking a strange sort of pride in recounting some particularly savage blow, each trying to make out that her own husband was the most cruel. They critically compared each other's bruises, each one glad when she could exhibit the worst. They exag-gerated, they invented details, and, as if proud of their beat-ings, as if glorying in their husbands' mishandling, lied to each other, magnifying their own maltreatment. They had long and excited arguments as to which were the most effec-tive means of punishment, the rope's ends and cart whips such as Zerkow used, or the fists and backs of hair-brushes affected by McTeague. Maria contended that the lash of the whip hurt the most; Trina, that the butt did the most injury.

Maria showed Trina the holes in the walls and the loosened boards in the flooring where Zerkow had been searching for the gold plate. Of late he had been digging in the back yard and had ransacked the hay in his horse-shed for the concealed leather chest he imagined he would find. But he was becom-ing impatient, evidently.

"The way he goes on," Maria told Trina, "is somethun dreadful. He's gettun regularly sick with it—got a fever every night—don't sleep, and when he does, talks to himself. Says 'More'n a hundred pieces, an' every one of 'em gold. More'n a hundred pieces, an' every one of 'em gold.' Then he'll whale me with his whip, and shout, '*You* know where it is. Tell me, tell me, you swine, or I'll do for you.' An' then he'll get down on his knees and whimper, and beg me to tell um where I've hid it. He's just gone plum crazy. Sometimes he has regular fits, he gets so mad, and rolls on the floor and scratches himself."

One morning in November, about ten o'clock, Trina pasted a "Made in France" label on the bottom of a Noah's ark, and leaned back in her chair with a long sigh of relief. She had just finished a large Christmas order for Uncle Oelbermann, and there was nothing else she could do that morning. The bed had not yet been made, nor had the breakfast things been washed. Trina hesitated for a moment, then put her chin in the air indifferently.

"Bah!" she said, "let them go till this afternoon. I don't care *when* the room is put to rights, and I know Mac don't." She determined that instead of making the bed or washing the dishes she would go and call on Miss Baker on the floor below. The little dressmaker might ask her to stay to lunch, and that would be something saved, as the dentist had announced his intention that morning of taking a long walk out to the Presidio to be gone all day.

But Trina rapped on Miss Baker's door in vain that morning. She was out. Perhaps she was gone to the florist's to buy some geranium seeds. However, Old Grannis's door stood a little ajar, and on hearing Trina at Miss Baker's room, the old Englishman came out into the hall.

"She's gone out," he said, uncertainly, and in a half whisper, " went out about half an hour ago. I—I think she went to the drug store to get some wafers for the goldfish."

"Don't you go to your dog hospital any more, Mister Grannis?" said Trina, leaning against the balustrade in the hall, willing to talk a moment.

Old Grannis stood in the doorway of his room, in his carpet slippers and faded corduroy jacket that he wore when at home.

"Why—why," he said, hesitating, tapping his chin thoughtfully. "You see I'm thinking of giving up the little hospital."

"Giving it up?"

"You see, the people at the book store where I buy my pamphlets have found out—I told them of my contrivance for binding books, and one of the members of the firm came up to look at it. He offered me quite a sum if I would sell him the right of it—the—the patent of it—quite a sum. In fact—in fact—yes, quite a sum, quite." He rubbed his chin tremulously and looked about him on the floor.

"Why, isn't that fine?" said Trina, good-naturedly. "I'm very glad, Mister Grannis. Is it a good price?"

"Quite a sum—quite. In fact, I never dreamed of having so much money."

"Now, see here, Mister Grannis," said Trina, decisively, "I want to give you a good piece of advice. Here are you and Miss Baker——" The old Englishman started nervously— "You and Miss Baker, that have been in love with each other for——"

"Oh, Mrs. McTeague, that subject—if you would please— Miss Baker is such an estimable lady."

"Fiddlesticks!" said Trina. "You're in love with each other, and the whole flat knows it; and you two have been living here side by side year in and year out, and you've never said a word to each other. It's all nonsense. Now, I want you should go right in and speak to her just as soon as she comes home, and say you've come into money and you want her to marry you."

"Impossible—impossible!" exclaimed the old Englishman, alarmed and perturbed. "It's quite out of the question. I wouldn't presume."

"Well, do you love her, or not?"

"Really, Mrs. McTeague, I—I—you must excuse me. It's a matter so personal—so—I—Oh, yes, I love her. Oh, yes, indeed," he exclaimed, suddenly.

"Well, then, she loves you. She told me so."

"Oh!"

"She did. She said those very words."

Miss Baker had said nothing of the kind—would have died sooner than have made such a confession; but Trina had drawn her own conclusions, like every other lodger of the flat, and thought the time was come for decided action.

"Now you do just as I tell you, and when she comes home, go right in and see her, and have it over with. Now, don't say another word. I'm going; but you do just as I tell you."

Trina turned about and went down-stairs. She had decided, since Miss Baker was not at home, that she would run over and see Maria; possibly she could have lunch there. At any rate, Maria would offer her a cup of tea.

Old Grannis stood for a long time just as Trina had left him, his hands trembling, the blood coming and going in his withered cheeks.

"She said, she—she—she told her—she said that—that——" he could get no farther.

Then he faced about and entered his room, closing the door behind him. For a long time he sat in his armchair, drawn close to the wall in front of the table on which stood his piles of pamphlets and his little binding apparatus.

"I wonder," said Trina, as she crossed the yard back of Zerkow's house, "I wonder what rent Zerkow and Maria pay for this place. I'll bet it's cheaper than where Mac and I are."

Trina found Maria sitting in front of the kitchen stove, her chin upon her breast. Trina went up to her. She was dead. And as Trina touched her shoulder, her head rolled sideways and showed a fearful gash in her throat under her ear. All the front of her dress was soaked through and through.

Trina backed sharply away from the body, drawing her hands up to her very shoulders, her eyes staring and wide, an expression of unutterable horror twisting her face.

"Oh-h-h!" she exclaimed in a long breath, her voice hardly rising above a whisper. "Oh-h, isn't that horrible!" Suddenly she turned and fled through the front part of the house to the street door, that opened upon the little alley. She looked wildly about her. Directly across the way a butcher's boy was getting into his two-wheeled cart drawn up in front of the opposite house, while near by a peddler of wild game was coming down the street, a brace of ducks in his hand.

"Oh, say—say," gasped Trina, trying to get her voice, "say, come over here quick."

The butcher's boy paused, one foot on the wheel, and stared. Trina beckoned frantically.

"Come over here, come over here quick."

The young fellow swung himself into his seat.

"What's the matter with that woman?" he said, half aloud.

"There's a murder been done," cried Trina, swaying in the doorway.

The young fellow drove away, his head over his shoulder, staring at Trina with eyes that were fixed and absolutely devoid of expression.

"What's the matter with that woman?" he said again to himself as he turned the corner.

Trina wondered why she didn't scream, how she could keep from it—how, at such a moment as this, she could remember that it was improper to make a disturbance and create a scene in the street. The peddler of wild game was looking at her suspiciously. It would not do to tell him. He would go away like the butcher's boy.

"Now, wait a minute," Trina said to herself, speaking aloud. She put her hands to her head. "Now, wait a minute. It won't do for me to lose my wits now. What must I do?" She looked about her. There was the same familiar aspect of Polk Street. She could see it at the end of the alley. The big market opposite the flat, the delivery carts rattling up and down, the great ladies from the avenue at their morning shopping, the cable cars trundling past, loaded with passengers. She saw a little boy in a flat leather cap whistling and calling for an unseen dog, slapping his small knee from time to time. Two men came out of Frenna's saloon, laughing heartily. Heise the harness-maker stood in the vestibule of his shop, a bundle of whittlings in his apron of greasy ticking. And all this was going on, people were laughing and living, buying and selling, walking about out there on the sunny sidewalks, while behind her in there—in there—in there——

Heise started back from the sudden apparition of a white-lipped woman in a blue dressing-gown that seemed to rise up before him from his very doorstep.

"Well, Mrs. McTeague, you did scare me, for——"

"Oh, come over here quick." Trina put her hand to her neck, swallowing something that seemed to be choking her. "Maria's killed—Zerkow's wife—I found her."

"Get out!" exclaimed Heise, "you're joking."

"Come over here—over into the house—I found her—she's dead."

Heise dashed across the street on the run, with Trina at his heels, a trail of spilled whittlings marking his course. The two ran down the alley. The wild-game peddler, a woman who had been washing down the steps in a neighboring house, and a man in a broad-brimmed hat stood at Zerkow's doorway, looking in from time to time, and talking together. They seemed puzzled.

"Anything wrong in here?" asked the wild-game peddler as Heise and Trina came up. Two more men stopped on the corner of the alley and Polk Street and looked at the group. A woman with a towel round her head raised a window opposite Zerkow's house and called to the woman who had been washing the steps, "What is it, Mrs. Flint?"

Heise was already inside the house. He turned to Trina, panting from his run.

"Where did you say—where was it—where?"

"In there," said Trina, "farther in—the next room." They burst into the kitchen.

"*Lord!*" ejaculated Heise, stopping a yard or so from the body, and bending down to peer into the gray face with its brown lips.

"By God! he's killed her."

"Who?"

"Zerkow, by God! he's killed her. Cut her throat. He always said he would."

"Zerkow?"

"He's killed her. Her throat's cut. Good Lord, how she did bleed! By God! he's done for her in *good* shape this time."

"Oh, I told her—I *told* her," cried Trina.

"He's done for her *sure* this time."

"She said she could always manage—Oh-h! It's horrible."

"He's done for her sure this trip. Cut her throat. *Lord*, how she has *bled*! Did you ever *see* so much—that's murder—that's cold-blooded murder. He's killed her. Say, we must get a policeman. Come on."

They turned back through the house. Half a dozen people—the wild-game peddler, the man with the broad-

brimmed hat, the washwoman, and three other men—were
in the front room of the junk shop, a bank of excited faces
surged at the door. Beyond this, outside, the crowd was
packed solid from one end of the alley to the other. Out in
Polk Street the cable cars were nearly blocked and were bunting a way slowly through the throng with clanging bells.
Every window had its group. And as Trina and the harness-
maker tried to force the way from the door of the junk shop
the throng suddenly parted right and left before the passage
of two blue-coated policemen who clove a passage through
the press, working their elbows energetically. They were accompanied by a third man in citizen's clothes.

Heise and Trina went back into the kitchen with the two
policemen, the third man in citizen's clothes cleared the in-
truders from the front room of the junk shop and kept the
crowd back, his arm across the open door.

"Whew!" whistled one of the officers as they came out into
the kitchen, "cutting scrape? By George! *somebody's* been using his knife all right." He turned to the other officer. "Better
get the wagon. There's a box on the second corner south.
Now, then," he continued, turning to Trina and the harness-
maker and taking out his note-book and pencil, "I want your
names and addresses."

It was a day of tremendous excitement for the entire street.
Long after the patrol wagon had driven away, the crowd remained. In fact, until seven o'clock that evening groups collected about the door of the junk shop, where a policeman
stood guard, asking all manner of questions, advancing all
manner of opinions.

"Do you think they'll get him?" asked Ryer of the policeman. A dozen necks craned forward eagerly.

"Hoh, we'll get him all right, easy enough," answered the
other, with a grand air.

"What? What's that? What did he say?" asked the people
on the outskirts of the group. Those in front passed the answer back.

"He says they'll get him all right, easy enough."

The group looked at the policeman admiringly.

"He's skipped to San José."

Where the rumor started, and how, no one knew. But

every one seemed persuaded that Zerkow had gone to San José.

"But what did he kill her for? Was he drunk?"

"No, he was crazy, I tell you—crazy in the head. Thought she was hiding some money from him."

Frenna did a big business all day long. The murder was the one subject of conversation. Little parties were made up in his saloon—parties of twos and threes—to go over and have a look at the outside of the junk shop. Heise was the most important man the length and breadth of Polk Street; almost invariably he accompanied these parties, telling again and again of the part he had played in the affair.

"It was about eleven o'clock. I was standing in front of the shop, when Mrs. McTeague—you know, the dentist's wife—came running across the street," and so on and so on.

The next day came a fresh sensation. Polk Street read of it in the morning papers. Towards midnight on the day of the murder Zerkow's body had been found floating in the bay near Black Point. No one knew whether he had drowned himself or fallen from one of the wharves. Clutched in both his hands was a sack full of old and rusty pans, tin dishes—fully a hundred of them—tin cans, and iron knives and forks, collected from some dump heap.

"And all this," exclaimed Trina, "on account of a set of gold dishes that never existed."

XVII

O NE DAY, about a fortnight after the coroner's inquest had been held, and when the excitement of the terrible affair was calming down and Polk Street beginning to resume its monotonous routine, Old Grannis sat in his clean, well-kept little room, in his cushioned armchair, his hands lying idly upon his knees. It was evening; not quite time to light the lamps. Old Grannis had drawn his chair close to the wall—so close, in fact, that he could hear Miss Baker's grenadine brushing against the other side of the thin partition, at his very elbow, while she rocked gently back and forth, a cup of tea in her hands.

Old Grannis's occupation was gone. That morning the book-selling firm where he had bought his pamphlets had taken his little binding apparatus from him to use as a model. The transaction had been concluded. Old Grannis had received his check. It was large enough, to be sure, but when all was over, he returned to his room and sat there sad and unoccupied, looking at the pattern in the carpet and counting the heads of the tacks in the zinc guard that was fastened to the wall behind his little stove. By and by he heard Miss Baker moving about. It was five o'clock, the time when she was accustomed to make her cup of tea and "keep company" with him on her side of the partition. Old Grannis drew up his chair to the wall near where he knew she was sitting. The minutes passed; side by side, and separated by only a couple of inches of board, the two old people sat there together, while the afternoon grew darker.

But for Old Grannis all was different that evening. There was nothing for him to do. His hands lay idly in his lap. His table, with its pile of pamphlets, was in a far corner of the room, and, from time to time, stirred with an uncertain trouble, he turned his head and looked at it sadly, reflecting that he would never use it again. The absence of his accustomed work seemed to leave something out of his life. It did not appear to him that he could be the same to Miss Baker now; their little habits were disarranged, their customs broken up. He could no longer fancy himself so near to her. They would

drift apart now, and she would no longer make herself a cup
of tea and "keep company" with him when she knew that he
would never again sit before his table binding uncut pamphlets. He had sold his happiness for money; he had bartered
all his tardy romance for some miserable bank-notes. He had
not foreseen that it would be like this. A vast regret welled
up within him. What was that on the back of his hand? He
wiped it dry with his ancient silk handkerchief.

Old Grannis leant his face in his hands. Not only did an
inexplicable regret stir within him, but a certain great tenderness came upon him. The tears that swam in his faded blue
eyes were not altogether those of unhappiness. No, this long-
delayed affection that had come upon him in his later years
filled him with a joy for which tears seemed to be the natural
expression. For thirty years his eyes had not been wet, but to-
night he felt as if he were young again. He had never loved
before, and there was still a part of him that was only twenty
years of age. He could not tell whether he was profoundly
sad or deeply happy; but he was not ashamed of the tears that
brought the smart to his eyes and the ache to his throat. He
did not hear the timid rapping on his door, and it was not until the door itself opened that he looked up quickly and saw the
little retired dressmaker standing on the threshold, carrying
a cup of tea on a tiny Japanese tray. She held it toward him.

"I was making some tea," she said, "and I thought you
would like to have a cup."

Never after could the little dressmaker understand how she
had brought herself to do this thing. One moment she had
been sitting quietly on her side of the partition, stirring her
cup of tea with one of her Gorham spoons. She was quiet,
she was peaceful. The evening was closing down tranquilly.
Her room was the picture of calmness and order. The geraniums blooming in the starch boxes in the window, the aged
goldfish occasionally turning his iridescent flank to catch a
sudden glow of the setting sun. The next moment she had
been all trepidation. It seemed to her the most natural thing
in the world to make a steaming cup of tea and carry it in to
Old Grannis next door. It seemed to her that he was wanting
her, that she ought to go to him. With the brusque resolve
and intrepidity that sometimes seizes upon very timid people

—the courage of the coward greater than all others—she had presented herself at the old Englishman's half-open door, and, when he had not heeded her knock, had pushed it open, and at last, after all these years, stood upon the threshold of his room. She had found courage enough to explain her intrusion.

"I was making some tea, and I thought you would like to have a cup."

Old Grannis dropped his hands upon either arm of his chair, and, leaning forward a little, looked at her blankly. He did not speak.

The retired dressmaker's courage had carried her thus far; now it deserted her as abruptly as it had come. Her cheeks became scarlet; her funny little false curls trembled with her agitation. What she had done seemed to her indecorous beyond expression. It was an enormity. Fancy, she had gone into his room, *into his room*—Mister Grannis's room. She had done this—she who could not pass him on the stairs without a qualm. What to do she did not know. She stood, a fixture, on the threshold of his room, without even resolution enough to beat a retreat. Helplessly, and with a little quaver in her voice, she repeated obstinately:

"I was making some tea, and I thought you would like to have a cup of tea." Her agitation betrayed itself in the repetition of the word. She felt that she could not hold the tray out another instant. Already she was trembling so that half the tea was spilled.

Old Grannis still kept silence, still bending forward, with wide eyes, his hands gripping the arms of his chair.

Then with the tea-tray still held straight before her, the little dressmaker exclaimed tearfully:

"Oh, I didn't mean—I didn't mean—I didn't know it would seem like this. I only meant to be kind and bring you some tea; and now it seems *so* improper. I—I—I'm *so* ashamed! I don't know what you will think of me. I—" she caught her breath—"improper—" she managed to exclaim, "unlady-like—you can never think well of me—I'll go. I'll go." She turned about.

"Stop," cried Old Grannis, finding his voice at last. Miss Baker paused, looking at him over her shoulder, her eyes very wide open, blinking through her tears, for all the world like a frightened child.

"Stop," exclaimed the old Englishman, rising to his feet. "I didn't know it was you at first. I hadn't dreamed—I couldn't believe you would be so good, so kind to me. Oh," he cried, with a sudden sharp breath, "oh, you *are* kind. I—I—you have—have made me very happy."

"No, no," exclaimed Miss Baker, ready to sob. "It was unlady-like. You will—you must think ill of me." She stood in the hall. The tears were running down her cheeks, and she had no free hand to dry them.

"Let me—I'll take the tray from you," cried Old Grannis, coming forward. A tremulous joy came upon him. Never in his life had he been so happy. At last it had come—come when he had least expected it. That which he had longed for and hoped for through so many years, behold, it was come to-night. He felt his awkwardness leaving him. He was almost certain that the little dressmaker loved him, and the thought gave him boldness. He came toward her and took the tray from her hands, and, turning back into the room with it, made as if to set it upon his table. But the piles of his pamphlets were in the way. Both of his hands were occupied with the tray; he could not make a place for it on the table. He stood for a moment uncertain, his embarrassment returning.

"Oh, won't you—won't you please—" He turned his head, looking appealingly at the little old dressmaker.

"Wait, I'll help you," she said. She came into the room, up to the table, and moved the pamphlets to one side.

"Thanks, thanks," murmured Old Grannis, setting down the tray.

"Now—now—now I will go back," she exclaimed, hurriedly.

"No—no," returned the old Englishman. "Don't go, don't go. I've been so lonely to-night—and last night too—all this year—all my life," he suddenly cried.

"I—I—I've forgotten the sugar."

"But I never take sugar in my tea."

"But it's rather cold, and I've spilled it—almost all of it."

"I'll drink it from the saucer." Old Grannis had drawn up his armchair for her.

"Oh, I shouldn't. This is—this is *so*—You must think ill of me." Suddenly she sat down, and resting her elbows on the table, hid her face in her hands.

"Think *ill* of you?" cried Old Grannis, "think *ill* of you? Why, you don't know—you have no idea—all these years—living so close to you, I—I—" he paused suddenly. It seemed to him as if the beating of his heart was choking him.

"I thought you were binding your books to-night," said Miss Baker, suddenly, "and you looked tired. I thought you looked tired when I last saw you, and a cup of tea, you know, it—that—that does you so much good when you're tired. But you weren't binding books."

"No, no," returned Old Grannis, drawing up a chair and sitting down. "No, I—the fact is, I've sold my apparatus; a firm of booksellers has bought the rights of it."

"And aren't you going to bind books any more?" exclaimed the little dressmaker, a shade of disappointment in her manner. "I thought you always did about four o'clock. I used to hear you when I was making tea."

It hardly seemed possible to Miss Baker that she was actually talking to Old Grannis, that the two were really chatting together, face to face, and without the dreadful embarrassment that used to overwhelm them both when they met on the stairs. She had often dreamed of this, but had always put it off to some far-distant day. It was to come gradually, little by little, instead of, as now, abruptly and with no preparation. That she should permit herself the indiscretion of actually intruding herself into his room had never so much as occurred to her. Yet here she was, *in his room*, and they were talking together, and little by little her embarrassment was wearing away.

"Yes, yes, I always heard you when you were making tea," returned the old Englishman; "I heard the tea things. Then I used to draw my chair and my work-table close to the wall on my side, and sit there and work while you drank your tea just on the other side; and I used to feel very near to you then. I used to pass the whole evening that way."

"And, yes—yes—I did too," she answered. "I used to make tea just at that time and sit there for a whole hour."

"And didn't you sit close to the partition on your side?

Sometimes I was sure of it. I could even fancy that I could hear your dress brushing against the wall-paper close beside me. Didn't you sit close to the partition?"

"I—I don't know where I sat."

Old Grannis shyly put out his hand and took hers as it lay upon her lap.

"Didn't you sit close to the partition on your side?" he insisted.

"No—I don't know—perhaps—sometimes. Oh, yes," she exclaimed, with a little gasp, "Oh, yes, I often did."

Then Old Grannis put his arm about her, and kissed her faded cheek, that flushed to pink upon the instant.

After that they spoke but little. The day lapsed slowly into twilight, and the two old people sat there in the gray evening, quietly, quietly, their hands in each other's hands, "keeping company," but now with nothing to separate them. It had come at last. After all these years they were together; they understood each other. They stood at length in a little Elysium of their own creating. They walked hand in hand in a delicious garden where it was always autumn. Far from the world and together they entered upon the long retarded romance of their commonplace and uneventful lives.

XVIII

THAT SAME NIGHT McTeague was awakened by a shrill scream, and woke to find Trina's arms around his neck. She was trembling so that the bed-springs creaked.

"Huh?" cried the dentist, sitting up in bed, raising his clinched fists. "Huh? What? What? What is it? What is it?"

"Oh, Mac," gasped his wife, "I had such an awful dream. I dreamed about Maria. I thought she was chasing me, and I couldn't run, and her throat was—Oh, she was all covered with blood. Oh-h, I am so frightened!"

Trina had borne up very well for the first day or so after the affair, and had given her testimony to the coroner with far greater calmness than Heise. It was only a week later that the horror of the thing came upon her again. She was so nervous that she hardly dared to be alone in the daytime, and almost every night woke with a cry of terror, trembling with the recollection of some dreadful nightmare. The dentist was irritated beyond all expression by her nervousness, and especially was he exasperated when her cries woke him suddenly in the middle of the night. He would sit up in bed, rolling his eyes wildly, throwing out his huge fists—at what, he did not know—exclaiming, "What—what—" bewildered and hopelessly confused. Then when he realized that it was only Trina, his anger kindled abruptly.

"Oh, you and your dreams! You go to sleep, or I'll give you a dressing down." Sometimes he would hit her a great thwack with his open palm, or catch her hand and bite the tips of her fingers. Trina would lie awake for hours afterward, crying softly to herself. Then, by and by, "Mac," she would say timidly.

"Huh?"

"Mac, do you love me?"

"Huh? What? Go to sleep."

"Don't you love me any more, Mac?"

"Oh, go to sleep. Don't bother me."

"Well, do you *love* me, Mac?"

"*I* guess so."

"Oh, Mac, I've only you now, and if *you* don't love me, what is going to become of me?"

"Shut up, an' let me go to sleep."

"Well, just tell me that you love me."

The dentist would turn abruptly away from her, burying his big blond head in the pillow, and covering up his ears with the blankets. Then Trina would sob herself to sleep.

The dentist had long since given up looking for a job. Between breakfast and supper time Trina saw but little of him. Once the morning meal over, McTeague bestirred himself, put on his cap—he had given up wearing even a hat since his wife had made him sell his silk hat—and went out. He had fallen into the habit of taking long and solitary walks beyond the suburbs of the city. Sometimes it was to the Cliff House, occasionally to the Park (where he would sit on the sun-warmed benches, smoking his pipe and reading ragged ends of old newspapers), but more often it was to the Presidio Reservation. McTeague would walk out to the end of the Union Street car line, entering the Reservation at the terminus, then he would work down to the shore of the bay, follow the shore line to the Old Fort at the Golden Gate, and, turning the Point here, come out suddenly upon the full sweep of the Pacific. Then he would follow the beach down to a certain point of rocks that he knew. Here he would turn inland, climbing the bluffs to a rolling grassy down sown with blue iris and a yellow flower that he did not know the name of. On the far side of this down was a broad, well-kept road. McTeague would keep to this road until he reached the city again by the way of the Sacramento Street car line. The dentist loved these walks. He liked to be alone. He liked the solitude of the tremendous, tumbling ocean; the fresh, windy downs; he liked to feel the gusty Trades flogging his face, and he would remain for hours watching the roll and plunge of the breakers with the silent, unreasoned enjoyment of a child. All at once he developed a passion for fishing. He would sit all day nearly motionless upon a point of rocks, his fish-line between his fingers, happy if he caught three perch in twelve hours. At noon he would retire to a bit of level turf around an angle of the shore and cook his fish, eating them without salt or knife or fork. He thrust a pointed stick down the mouth of the perch, and turned it slowly over the blaze. When the grease stopped dripping, he knew that it was done, and would devour it slowly and with tremendous relish, picking the bones clean, eating even the head. He remembered how often he used to do this sort of thing when he was a boy in the mountains of Placer County, before he became a carboy at the mine. The dentist enjoyed himself hugely during these days. The instincts of the old-time miner were returning. In the stress of his misfortune McTeague was lapsing back to his early estate.

One evening as he reached home after such a tramp, he was surprised to find Trina standing in front of what had been Zerkow's house, looking at it thoughtfully, her finger on her lips.

"What you doing here?" growled the dentist as he came up. There was a "Rooms-to-let" sign on the street door of the house.

"Now we've found a place to move to," exclaimed Trina.

"What?" cried McTeague. "There, in that dirty house, where you found Maria?"

"I can't afford that room in the flat any more, now that you can't get any work to do."

"But there's where Zerkow killed Maria—the very house— an' you wake up an' squeal in the night just thinking of it."

"I know. I know it will be bad at first, but I'll get used to it, an' it's just half again as cheap as where we are now. I was looking at a room; we can have it dirt cheap. It's a back room over the kitchen. A German family are going to take the front part of the house and sublet the rest. I'm going to take it. It'll be money in my pocket."

"But it won't be any in mine," vociferated the dentist, angrily. "I'll have to live in that dirty rat hole just so's you can save money. *I* ain't any the better off for it."

"Find work to do, and then we'll talk," declared Trina. "*I'm* going to save up some money against a rainy day; and if I can save more by living here I'm going to do it, even if it is the house Maria was killed in. I don't care."

"All right," said McTeague, and did not make any further protest. His wife looked at him surprised. She could not understand this sudden acquiescence. Perhaps McTeague was so much away from home of late that he had ceased to care where or how he lived. But this sudden change troubled her a little for all that.

The next day the McTeagues moved for a second time. It did not take them long. They were obliged to buy the bed from the landlady, a circumstance which nearly broke Trina's heart; and this bed, a couple of chairs, Trina's trunk, an ornament or two, the oil stove, and some plates and kitchen ware were all that they could call their own now; and this back room in that wretched house with its grisly memories, the one window looking out into a grimy maze of back yards and broken sheds, was what they now knew as their home.

The McTeagues now began to sink rapidly lower and lower. They became accustomed to their surroundings. Worst of all, Trina lost her pretty ways and her good looks. The combined effects of hard work, avarice, poor food, and her husband's brutalities told on her swiftly. Her charming little figure grew coarse, stunted, and dumpy. She who had once been of a cat-like neatness, now slovened all day about the room in a dirty flannel wrapper, her slippers clap-clapping after her as she walked. At last she even neglected her hair, the wonderful swarthy tiara, the coiffure of a queen, that shaded her little pale forehead. In the morning she braided it before it was half combed, and piled and coiled it about her head in haphazard fashion. It came down half a dozen times a day; by evening it was an unkempt, tangled mass, a veritable rat's nest.

Ah, no, it was not very gay, that life of hers, when one had to rustle for two, cook and work and wash, to say nothing of paying the rent. What odds was it if she was slatternly, dirty, coarse? Was there time to make herself look otherwise, and who was there to be pleased when she was all prinked out? Surely not a great brute of a husband who bit you like a dog, and kicked and pounded you as though you were made of iron. Ah, no, better let things go, and take it as easy as you could. Hump your back, and it was soonest over.

The one room grew abominably dirty, reeking with the odors of cooking and of "non-poisonous" paint. The bed was not made until late in the afternoon, sometimes not at all. Dirty, unwashed crockery, greasy knives, sodden fragments of yesterday's meals cluttered the table, while in one corner was the heap of evil-smelling, dirty linen. Cockroaches appeared in the crevices of the woodwork, the wall-paper bulged from the damp walls and began to peel. Trina had long ago ceased to dust or to wipe the furniture with a bit of rag. The grime grew thick upon the window panes and in the corners of the room. All the filth of the alley invaded their quarters like a rising muddy tide.

Between the windows, however, the faded photograph of the couple in their wedding finery looked down upon the wretchedness, Trina still holding her set bouquet straight before her, McTeague standing at her side, his left foot forward, in the attitude of a Secretary of State; while near by hung the canary, the one thing the dentist clung to obstinately, piping and chittering all day in its little gilt prison.

And the tooth, the gigantic golden molar of French gilt, enormous and ungainly, sprawled its branching prongs in one corner of the room, by the footboard of the bed. The Mc-Teagues had come to use it as a sort of substitute for a table. After breakfast and supper Trina piled the plates and greasy dishes upon it to have them out of the way.

One afternoon the Other Dentist, McTeague's old-time rival, the wearer of marvellous waistcoats, was surprised out of all countenance to receive a visit from McTeague. The Other Dentist was in his operating room at the time, at work upon a plaster-of-paris mould. To his call of "Come right in. Don't you see the sign, 'Enter without knocking'?" McTeague came in. He noted at once how airy and cheerful was the room. A little fire coughed and tittered on the hearth, a brindled greyhound sat on his haunches watching it intently, a great mirror over the mantle offered to view an array of actresses' pictures thrust between the glass and the frame, and a big bunch of freshly-cut violets stood in a glass bowl on the polished cherry-wood table. The Other Dentist came forward briskly, exclaiming cheerfully:

"Oh, Doctor—Mister McTeague, how do? how do?"

The fellow was actually wearing a velvet smoking jacket. A cigarette was between his lips; his patent leather boots reflected the firelight. McTeague wore a black surah negligé shirt without a cravat; huge buckled brogans, hob-nailed, gross, encased his feet; the hems of his trousers were spotted with mud; his coat was frayed at the sleeves and a button was gone. In three days he had not shaved; his shock of heavy blond hair escaped from beneath the visor of his woollen cap and hung low over his forehead. He stood with awkward, shifting feet and uncertain eyes before this dapper young fellow who reeked of the barber shop, and whom he had once ordered from his rooms.

"What can I do for you this morning, Mister McTeague? Something wrong with the teeth, eh?"

"No, no." McTeague, floundering in the difficulties of his speech, forgot the carefully rehearsed words with which he had intended to begin this interview.

"I want to sell you my sign," he said, stupidly. "That big tooth of French gilt—*you* know—that you made an offer for once."

"Oh, *I* don't want that now," said the other loftily. "I prefer a little quiet signboard, nothing pretentious—just the name, and 'Dentist' after it. These big signs are vulgar. No, I don't want it."

McTeague remained, looking about on the floor, horribly embarrassed, not knowing whether to go or to stay.

"But I don't know," said the Other Dentist, reflectively. "If it will help you out any—I guess you're pretty hard up—I'll—well, I tell you what—I'll give you five dollars for it."

"All right, all right."

On the following Thursday morning McTeague woke to hear the eaves dripping and the prolonged rattle of the rain upon the roof.

"Raining," he growled, in deep disgust, sitting up in bed, and winking at the blurred window.

"It's been raining all night," said Trina. She was already up and dressed, and was cooking breakfast on the oil stove.

McTeague dressed himself, grumbling, "Well, I'll go, *anyhow*. The fish will bite all the better for the rain."

"Look here, Mac," said Trina, slicing a bit of bacon as thinly as she could. "Look here, why don't you bring some of your fish home sometime?"

"Huh!" snorted the dentist, "so's we could have 'em for breakfast. Might save you a nickel, mightn't it?"

"Well, and if it did? Or you might fish for the market. The fishman across the street would buy 'em of you."

"Shut up!" exclaimed the dentist, and Trina obediently subsided.

"Look here," continued her husband, fumbling in his trousers pocket and bringing out a dollar, "I'm sick and tired of coffee and bacon and mashed potatoes. Go over to the market and get some kind of meat for breakfast. Get a steak, or chops, or something."

"Why, Mac, that's a whole dollar, and he only gave you five for your sign. We can't afford it. Sure, Mac. Let me put that money away against a rainy day. You're just as well off without meat for breakfast."

"You do as I tell you. Get some steak, or chops, or something."

"Please, Mac, dear."

"Go on, now. I'll bite your fingers again pretty soon."

"But——"

The dentist took a step towards her, snatching at her hand.

"All right, I'll go," cried Trina, wincing and shrinking. "I'll go."

She did not get the chops at the big market, however. Instead, she hurried to a cheaper butcher shop on a side street two blocks away, and bought fifteen cents' worth of chops from a side of mutton some two or three days old. She was gone some little time.

"Give me the change," exclaimed the dentist as soon as she returned. Trina handed him a quarter; and when McTeague was about to protest, broke in upon him with a rapid stream of talk that confused him upon the instant. But for that matter, it was never difficult for Trina to deceive the dentist. He never went to the bottom of things. He would have believed her if she had told him the chops had cost a dollar.

"There's sixty cents saved, anyhow," thought Trina, as she clutched the money in her pocket to keep it from rattling.

Trina cooked the chops, and they breakfasted in silence.

"Now," said McTeague as he rose, wiping the coffee from his thick mustache with the hollow of his palm, "now I'm going fishing, rain or no rain. I'm going to be gone all day."

He stood for a moment at the door, his fish-line in his hand, swinging the heavy sinker back and forth. He looked at Trina as she cleared away the breakfast things.

"So long," said he, nodding his huge square-cut head. This amiability in the matter of leave taking was unusual. Trina put the dishes down and came up to him, her little chin, once so adorable, in the air:

"Kiss me good-by, Mac," she said, putting her arms around his neck. "You *do* love me a little yet, don't you, Mac? We'll be happy again some day. This is hard times now, but we'll pull out. You'll find something to do pretty soon."

"*I* guess so," growled McTeague, allowing her to kiss him.

The canary was stirring nimbly in its cage, and just now broke out into a shrill trilling, its little throat bulging and quivering. The dentist stared at it. "Say," he remarked slowly, "I think I'll take that bird of mine along."

"Sell it?" inquired Trina.

"Yes, yes, sell it."

"Well, you *are* coming to your senses at last," answered Trina, approvingly. "But don't you let the bird-store man cheat you. That's a good songster; and with the cage, you ought to make him give you five dollars. You stick out for that at first, anyhow."

McTeague unhooked the cage and carefully wrapped it in an old newspaper, remarking, "He might get cold. Well, so long," he repeated, "so long."

"Good-by, Mac."

When he was gone, Trina took the sixty cents she had stolen from him out of her pocket and recounted it. "It's sixty cents, all right," she said proudly. "But I *do* believe that dime is too smooth." She looked at it critically. The clock on the power-house of the Sutter Street cable struck eight. "Eight o'clock already," she exclaimed. "I must get to work." She cleared the breakfast things from the table, and drawing up her chair and her workbox began painting the sets of Noah's ark animals she had whittled the day before. She worked steadily all the morning. At noon she lunched, warming over the coffee left from breakfast, and frying a couple of sausages. By one she was bending over her table again. Her fingers—some of them lacerated by McTeague's teeth—flew, and the little pile of cheap toys in the basket at her elbow grew steadily.

"Where *do* all the toys go to?" she murmured. "The thousands and thousands of these Noah's arks that I have made— horses and chickens and elephants—and always there never seems to be enough. It's a good thing for me that children break their things, and that they all have to have birthdays and Christmases." She dipped her brush into a pot of Vandyke brown and painted one of the whittled toy horses in two strokes. Then a touch of ivory black with a small flat brush created the tail and mane, and dots of Chinese white made the eyes. The turpentine in the paint dried it almost immediately, and she tossed the completed little horse into the basket.

At six o'clock the dentist had not returned. Trina waited until seven, and then put her work away, and ate her supper alone.

"I wonder what's keeping Mac," she exclaimed as the clock from the power-house on Sutter Street struck half-past seven. "I *know* he's drinking somewhere," she cried, apprehensively. "He had the money from his sign with him."

At eight o'clock she threw a shawl over her head and went over to the harness shop. If anybody would know where McTeague was it would be Heise. But the harness-maker had seen nothing of him since the day before.

"He was in here yesterday afternoon, and we had a drink or two at Frenna's. Maybe he's been in there to-day."

"Oh, won't you go in and see?" said Trina. "Mac always came home to his supper—he never likes to miss his meals— and I'm getting frightened about him."

Heise went into the barroom next door, and returned with no definite news. Frenna had not seen the dentist since he had come in with the harness-maker the previous afternoon. Trina even humbled herself to ask of the Ryers—with whom they had quarrelled—if they knew anything of the dentist's whereabouts, but received a contemptuous negative.

"Maybe he's come in while I've been out," said Trina to herself. She went down Polk Street again, going towards the flat. The rain had stopped, but the sidewalks were still glistening. The cable cars trundled by, loaded with theatregoers. The barbers were just closing their shops. The candy store on the corner was brilliantly lighted and was filling up, while the green and yellow lamps from the drug store directly opposite threw kaleidoscopic reflections deep down into the shining surface of the asphalt. A band of Salvationists began to play and pray in front of Frenna's saloon. Trina hurried on down the gay street, with its evening's brilliancy and small activities, her shawl over her head, one hand lifting her faded skirt from off the wet pavements. She turned into the alley, entered Zerkow's old home by the ever-open door, and ran up-stairs to the room. Nobody.

"Why, isn't this *funny*," she exclaimed, half aloud, standing on the threshold, her little milk-white forehead curdling to a frown, one sore finger on her lips. Then a great fear seized upon her. Inevitably she associated the house with a scene of violent death.

"No, no," she said to the darkness, "Mac is all right. *He* can take care of himself." But for all that she had a clear-cut vision of her husband's body, bloated with sea-water, his blond hair streaming like kelp, rolling inertly in shifting waters.

"He couldn't have fallen off the rocks," she declared firmly. "There—*there* he is now." She heaved a great sigh of relief as a heavy tread sounded in the hallway below. She ran to the banisters, looking over, and calling, "Oh, Mac! Is that you, Mac?" It was the German whose family occupied the lower floor. The power-house clock struck nine.

"My God, where *is* Mac?" cried Trina, stamping her foot.

She put the shawl over her head again, and went out and stood on the corner of the alley and Polk Street, watching and waiting, craning her neck to see down the street. Once, even, she went out upon the sidewalk in front of the flat and sat down for a moment upon the horse-block there. She could not help remembering the day when she had been driven up to that horse-block in a hack. Her mother and father and Owgooste and the twins were with her. It was her wedding day. Her wedding dress was in a huge tin trunk on the driver's seat. She had never been happier before in all her life. She remembered how she got out of the hack and stood for a moment upon the horse-block, looking up at McTeague's windows. She had caught a glimpse of him at his shaving, the lather still on his cheek, and they had waved their hands at each other. Instinctively Trina looked up at the flat behind her; looked up at the bay window where her husband's "Dental Parlors" had been. It was all dark; the windows had the blind, sightless appearance imparted by vacant, untenanted rooms. A rusty iron rod projected mournfully from one of the window ledges.

"There's where our sign hung once," said Trina. She turned her head and looked down Polk Street towards where the Other Dentist had his rooms, and there, overhanging the street from his window, newly furbished and brightened, hung the huge tooth, her birthday present to her husband, flashing and glowing in the white glare of the electric lights like a beacon of defiance and triumph.

"Ah, no; ah, no," whispered Trina, choking back a sob. "Life isn't so gay. But I wouldn't mind, no I wouldn't mind anything, if only Mac was home all right." She got up from the horse-block and stood again on the corner of the alley, watching and listening.

It grew later. The hours passed. Trina kept at her post. The noise of approaching footfalls grew less and less frequent. Little by little Polk Street dropped back into solitude. Eleven o'clock struck from the power-house clock; lights were extinguished; at one o'clock the cable stopped, leaving an abrupt and numbing silence in the air. All at once it seemed very still. The only noises were the occasional footfalls of a policeman and the persistent calling of ducks and geese in the closed market across the way. The street was asleep.

When it is night and dark, and one is awake and alone, one's thoughts take the color of the surroundings; become gloomy, sombre, and very dismal. All at once an idea came to Trina, a dark, terrible idea; worse, even, than the idea of McTeague's death.

"Oh, no," she cried. "Oh, no. It isn't true. But suppose—suppose."

She left her post and hurried back to the house.

"No, no," she was saying under her breath, "it isn't possible. Maybe he's even come home already by another way. But suppose—suppose—suppose."

She ran up the stairs, opened the door of the room, and paused, out of breath. The room was dark and empty. With cold, trembling fingers she lighted the lamp, and, turning about, looked at her trunk. The lock was burst.

"No, no, no," cried Trina, "it's not true; it's not true." She dropped on her knees before the trunk, and tossed back the lid, and plunged her hands down into the corner underneath her wedding dress, where she always kept the savings. The brass match-safe and the chamois-skin bag were there. They were empty.

Trina flung herself full length upon the floor, burying her face in her arms, rolling her head from side to side. Her voice rose to a wail.

"No, no, no, it's not true; it's not true; it's not true. Oh, he couldn't have done it. Oh, how could he have done it? All my money, all my little savings—and deserted me. He's gone, my money's gone, my dear money—my dear, dear gold pieces that I've worked so hard for. Oh, to have deserted me—gone for good—gone and never coming back—gone with my gold pieces. Gone—gone—gone. I'll never see them again, and I've worked so hard, so *so* hard for him—for them. No, no, *no*, it's not true. It *is* true. What will become of me now? Oh, if you'll only come back you can have all the money—half of it. Oh, give me back my money. Give me back my money, and I'll forgive you. You can leave me then if you want to. Oh, my money. Mac, Mac, you've gone for good. You don't love me any more, and now I'm a beggar. My money's gone, my husband's gone, gone, gone, gone!"

Her grief was terrible. She dug her nails into her scalp, and clutching the heavy coils of her thick black hair tore it again and again. She struck her forehead with her clenched fists. Her little body shook from head to foot with the violence of her sobbing. She ground her small teeth together and beat her head upon the floor with all her strength.

Her hair was uncoiled and hanging a tangled, dishevelled mass far below her waist; her dress was torn; a spot of blood was upon her forehead; her eyes were swollen; her cheeks flamed vermilion from the fever that raged in her veins. Old Miss Baker found her thus towards five o'clock the next morning.

What had happened between one o'clock and dawn of that fearful night Trina never remembered. She could only recall herself, as in a picture, kneeling before her broken and rifled trunk, and then—weeks later, so it seemed to her—she woke to find herself in her own bed with an iced bandage about her forehead and the little old dressmaker at her side, stroking her hot, dry palm.

The facts of the matter were that the German woman who lived below had been awakened some hours after midnight by the sounds of Trina's weeping. She had come up-stairs and into the room to find Trina stretched face downward upon the floor, half conscious and sobbing, in the throes of an hysteria for which there was no relief. The woman, terrified, had called her husband, and between them they had got Trina upon the bed. Then the German woman happened to remember that Trina had friends in the big flat near by, and had sent her husband to fetch the retired dressmaker, while she herself remained behind to undress Trina and put her to bed. Miss Baker had come over at once, and began to cry herself at the sight of the dentist's poor little wife. She did not stop to ask what the trouble was, and indeed it would have been useless to attempt to get any coherent explanation from Trina at that time. Miss Baker had sent the German woman's husband to get some ice at one of the "all-night" restaurants of the street; had kept cold, wet towels on Trina's head; had combed and recombed her wonderful thick hair; and had sat down by the side of the bed, holding her hot hand, with its poor maimed fingers, waiting patiently until Trina should be able to speak.

Towards morning Trina awoke—or perhaps it was a mere regaining of consciousness—looked a moment at Miss Baker, then about the room until her eyes fell upon her trunk with its broken lock. Then she turned over upon the pillow and began to sob again. She refused to answer any of the little dressmaker's questions, shaking her head violently, her face hidden in the pillow.

By breakfast time her fever had increased to such a point that Miss Baker took matters into her own hands and had the German woman call a doctor. He arrived some twenty minutes later. He was a big, kindly fellow who lived over the drug store on the corner. He had a deep voice and a tremendous striding gait less suggestive of a physician than of a sergeant of a cavalry troop.

By the time of his arrival little Miss Baker had divined intuitively the entire trouble. She heard the doctor's swinging tramp in the entry below, and heard the German woman saying:

"Righd oop der stairs, at der back of der halle. Der room mit der door oppen."

Miss Baker met the doctor at the landing, she told him in a whisper of the trouble.

"Her husband's deserted her, I'm afraid, doctor, and took all of her money—a good deal of it. It's about killed the poor child. She was out of her head a good deal of the night, and now she's got a raging fever."

The doctor and Miss Baker returned to the room and entered, closing the door. The big doctor stood for a moment looking down at Trina rolling her head from side to side upon the pillow, her face scarlet, her enormous mane of hair spread out on either side of her. The little dressmaker remained at his elbow, looking from him to Trina.

"Poor little woman!" said the doctor; "poor little woman!"

Miss Baker pointed to the trunk, whispering:

"See, there's where she kept her savings. See, he broke the lock."

"Well, Mrs. McTeague," said the doctor, sitting down by the bed, and taking Trina's wrist, "a little fever, eh?"

Trina opened her eyes and looked at him, and then at Miss Baker. She did not seem in the least surprised at the unfamiliar faces. She appeared to consider it all as a matter of course.

"Yes," she said, with a long, tremulous breath, "I have a fever, and my head—my head aches and aches."

The doctor prescribed rest and mild opiates. Then his eye fell upon the fingers of Trina's right hand. He looked at them sharply. A deep red glow, unmistakable to a physician's eyes, was upon some of them, extending from the finger tips up to the second knuckle.

"Hello," he exclaimed, "what's the matter here?" In fact something was very wrong indeed. For days Trina had noticed it. The fingers of her right hand had swollen as never before, aching and discolored. Cruelly lacerated by Mc-

Teague's brutality as they were, she had nevertheless gone on about her work on the Noah's ark animals, constantly in contact with the "non-poisonous" paint. She told as much to the doctor in answer to his questions. He shook his head with an exclamation.

"Why, this is blood-poisoning, you know," he told her; "the worst kind. You'll have to have those fingers amputated, beyond a doubt, or lose the entire hand—or even worse."

"And my work!" exclaimed Trina.

XIX

ONE CAN HOLD a scrubbing-brush with two good fingers and the stumps of two others even if both joints of the thumb are gone, but it takes considerable practice to get used to it.

Trina became a scrub-woman. She had taken counsel of Selina, and through her had obtained the position of care-taker in a little memorial kindergarten over on Pacific Street. Like Polk Street, it was an accommodation street, but running through a much poorer and more sordid quarter. Trina had a little room over the kindergarten schoolroom. It was not an unpleasant room. It looked out upon a sunny little court floored with boards and used as the children's playground. Two great cherry trees grew here, the leaves almost brushing against the window of Trina's room and filtering the sunlight so that it fell in round golden spots upon the floor of the room. "Like gold pieces," Trina said to herself.

Trina's work consisted in taking care of the kindergarten rooms, scrubbing the floors, washing the windows, dusting and airing, and carrying out the ashes. Besides this she earned some five dollars a month by washing down the front steps of some big flats on Washington Street, and by cleaning out vacant houses after the tenants had left. She saw no one. Nobody knew her. She went about her work from dawn to dark, and often entire days passed when she did not hear the sound of her own voice. She was alone, a solitary, abandoned woman, lost in the lowest eddies of the great city's tide—the tide that always ebbs.

When Trina had been discharged from the hospital after the operation on her fingers, she found herself alone in the world, alone with her five thousand dollars. The interest of this would support her, and yet allow her to save a little.

But for a time Trina had thought of giving up the fight altogether and of joining her family in the southern part of the State. But even while she hesitated about this she received a long letter from her mother, an answer to one she herself had written just before the amputation of her right-hand fingers—the last letter she would ever be able to write. Mrs.

Sieppe's letter was one long lamentation; she had her own misfortunes to bewail as well as those of her daughter. The carpet-cleaning and upholstery business had failed. Mr. Sieppe and Owgooste had left for New Zealand with a colonization company, whither Mrs. Sieppe and the twins were to follow them as soon as the colony established itself. So far from helping Trina in her ill fortune, it was she, her mother, who might some day in the near future be obliged to turn to Trina for aid. So Trina had given up the idea of any help from her family. For that matter she needed none. She still had her five thousand, and Uncle Oelbermann paid her the interest with a machine-like regularity. Now that McTeague had left her, there was one less mouth to feed; and with this saving, together with the little she could earn as scrub-woman, Trina could almost manage to make good the amount she lost by being obliged to cease work upon the Noah's ark animals.

Little by little her sorrow over the loss of her precious savings overcame the grief of McTeague's desertion of her. Her avarice had grown to be her one dominant passion; her love of money for the money's sake brooded in her heart, driving out by degrees every other natural affection. She grew thin and meagre; her flesh clove tight to her small skeleton; her small pale mouth and little uplifted chin grew to have a certain feline eagerness of expression; her long, narrow eyes glistened continually, as if they caught and held the glint of metal. One day as she sat in her room, the empty brass matchbox and the limp chamois bag in her hands, she suddenly exclaimed:

"I could have forgiven him if he had only gone away and left me my money. I could have—yes, I could have forgiven him even *this*"—she looked at the stumps of her fingers. "But now," her teeth closed tight and her eyes flashed, "now— I'll—never—forgive—him—as—long—as—I—live."

The empty bag and the hollow, light match-box troubled her. Day after day she took them from her trunk and wept over them as other women weep over a dead baby's shoe. Her four hundred dollars were gone, were gone, were gone. She would never see them again. She could plainly see her husband spending her savings by handfuls; squandering her beautiful gold pieces that she had been at such pains to polish with soap and ashes. The thought filled her with an unspeakable anguish. She would wake at night from a dream of McTeague revelling down her money, and ask of the darkness, "How much did he spend to-day? How many of the gold pieces are left? Has he broken either of the two twenty-dollar pieces yet? What did he spend it for?"

The instant she was out of the hospital Trina had begun to save again, but now it was with an eagerness that amounted at times to a veritable frenzy. She even denied herself lights and fuel in order to put by a quarter or so, grudging every penny she was obliged to spend. She did her own washing and cooking. Finally she sold her wedding dress, that had hitherto lain in the bottom of her trunk.

The day she moved from Zerkow's old house, she came suddenly upon the dentist's concertina under a heap of old clothes in the closet. Within twenty minutes she had sold it to the dealer in second-hand furniture, returning to her room with seven dollars in her pocket, happy for the first time since McTeague had left her.

But for all that the match-box and the bag refused to fill up; after three weeks of the most rigid economy they contained but eighteen dollars and some small change. What was that compared with four hundred? Trina told herself that she must have her money in hand. She longed to see again the heap of it upon her work-table, where she could plunge her hands into it, her face into it, feeling the cool, smooth metal upon her cheeks. At such moments she would see in her imagination her wonderful five thousand dollars piled in columns, shining and gleaming somewhere at the bottom of Uncle Oelbermann's vault. She would look at the paper that Uncle Oelbermann had given her, and tell herself that it represented five thousand dollars. But in the end this ceased to satisfy her, she must have the money itself. She must have her four hundred dollars back again, there in her trunk, in her bag and her match-box, where she could touch it and see it whenever she desired.

At length she could stand it no longer, and one day presented herself before Uncle Oelbermann as he sat in his office in the wholesale toy store, and told him she wanted to have four hundred dollars of her money.

"But this is very irregular, you know, Mrs. McTeague," said the great man. "Not business-like at all."

But his niece's misfortunes and the sight of her poor maimed hand appealed to him. He opened his check-book. "You understand, of course," he said, "that this will reduce the amount of your interest by just so much."

"I know, I know. I've thought of that," said Trina.

"Four hundred, did you say?" remarked Uncle Oelbermann, taking the cap from his fountain pen.

"Yes, four hundred," exclaimed Trina, quickly, her eyes glistening.

Trina cashed the check and returned home with the money—all in twenty-dollar pieces as she had desired—in an ecstasy of delight. For half of that night she sat up playing with her money, counting it and recounting it, polishing the duller pieces until they shone. Altogether there were twenty twenty-dollar gold pieces.

"Oh-h, you beauties!" murmured Trina, running her palms over them, fairly quivering with pleasure. "You beauties! *Is* there anything prettier than a twenty-dollar gold piece? You dear, dear money! Oh, don't I *love* you! Mine, mine, mine— all of you mine."

She laid them out in a row on the ledge of the table, or arranged them in patterns—triangles, circles, and squares— or built them all up into a pyramid which she afterward overthrew for the sake of hearing the delicious clink of the pieces tumbling against each other. Then at last she put them away in the brass match-box and chamois bag, delighted beyond words that they were once more full and heavy.

Then, a few days after, the thought of the money still remaining in Uncle Oelbermann's keeping returned to her. It was hers, all hers—all that four thousand six hundred. She could have as much of it or as little of it as she chose. She only had to ask. For a week Trina resisted, knowing very well that taking from her capital was proportionately reducing her monthly income. Then at last she yielded.

"Just to make it an even five hundred, anyhow," she told herself. That day she drew a hundred dollars more, in twenty-dollar gold pieces as before. From that time Trina began to draw steadily upon her capital, a little at a time. It was a

passion with her, a mania, a veritable mental disease; a temptation such as drunkards only know.

It would come upon her all of a sudden. While she was
about her work, scrubbing the floor of some vacant house; or
in her room, in the morning, as she made her coffee on the
oil stove, or when she woke in the night, a brusque access of
cupidity would seize upon her. Her cheeks flushed, her eyes
glistened, her breath came short. At times she would leave her
work just as it was, put on her old bonnet of black straw,
throw her shawl about her, and go straight to Uncle Oelbermann's store and draw against her money. Now it would be
a hundred dollars, now sixty; now she would content herself
with only twenty; and once, after a fortnight's abstinence, she
permitted herself a positive debauch of five hundred. Little by
little she drew her capital from Uncle Oelbermann, and little
by little her original interest of twenty-five dollars a month
dwindled.

One day she presented herself again in the office of the
wholesale toy store.

"Will you let me have a check for two hundred dollars,
Uncle Oelbermann?" she said.

The great man laid down his fountain pen and leaned back
in his swivel chair with great deliberation.

"I don't understand, Mrs. McTeague," he said. "Every week
you come here and draw out a little of your money. I've told
you that it is not at all regular or business-like for me to let
you have it this way. And more than this, it's a great inconvenience to me to give you these checks at unstated times. If
you wish to draw out the whole amount let's have some understanding. Draw it in monthly installments of, say, five
hundred dollars, or else," he added, abruptly, "draw it all at
once, now, to-day. I would even prefer it that way. Otherwise
it's—it's annoying. Come, shall I draw you a check for
thirty-seven hundred, and have it over and done with?"

"No, no," cried Trina, with instinctive apprehension, refusing, she did not know why. "No, I'll leave it with you. I
won't draw out any more."

She took her departure, but paused on the pavement outside the store, and stood for a moment lost in thought, her
eyes beginning to glisten and her breath coming short. Slowly

she turned about and reëntered the store; she came back into the office, and stood trembling at the corner of Uncle Oelbermann's desk. He looked up sharply. Twice Trina tried to get her voice, and when it did come to her, she could hardly recognize it. Between breaths she said:

"Yes, all right—I'll—you can give me—will you give me a check for thirty-seven hundred? Give me *all* of my money."

A few hours later she entered her little room over the kindergarten, bolted the door with shaking fingers, and emptied a heavy canvas sack upon the middle of her bed. Then she opened her trunk, and taking thence the brass match-box and the chamois-skin bag added their contents to the pile. Next she laid herself upon the bed and gathered the gleaming heaps of gold pieces to her with both arms, burying her face in them with long sighs of unspeakable delight.

It was a little past noon, and the day was fine and warm. The leaves of the huge cherry trees threw off a certain pungent aroma that entered through the open window, together with long thin shafts of golden sunlight. Below, in the kindergarten, the children were singing gayly and marching to the jangling of the piano. Trina heard nothing, saw nothing. She lay on her bed, her eyes closed, her face buried in a pile of gold that she encircled with both her arms.

Trina even told herself at last that she was happy once more. McTeague became a memory—a memory that faded a little every day—dim and indistinct in the golden splendor of five thousand dollars.

"And yet," Trina would say, "I did love Mac, loved him dearly, only a little while ago. Even when he hurt me, it only made me love him more. How is it I've changed so sudden? How *could* I forget him so soon? It must be because he stole my money. That is it. I couldn't forgive anyone that—no, not even my *mother*. And I never—never—will forgive him."

What had become of her husband Trina did not know. She never saw any of the old Polk Street people. There was no way she could have news of him, even if she had cared to have it. She had her money, that was the main thing. Her passion for it excluded every other sentiment. There it was in the bottom of her trunk, in the canvas sack, the chamois-skin bag, and the little brass match-safe. Not a day passed that

Trina did not have it out where she could see and touch it. One evening she had even spread all the gold pieces between the sheets, and had then gone to bed, stripping herself, and had slept all night upon the money, taking a strange and ecstatic pleasure in the touch of the smooth flat pieces the length of her entire body.

One night, some three months after she had come to live at the kindergarten, Trina was awakened by a sharp tap on the pane of the window. She sat up quickly in bed, her heart beating thickly, her eyes rolling wildly in the direction of her trunk. The tap was repeated. Trina rose and went fearfully to the window. The little court below was bright with moon-light, and standing just on the edge of the shadow thrown by one of the cherry trees was McTeague. A bunch of half-ripe cherries was in his hand. He was eating them and throwing the pits at the window. As he caught sight of her, he made an eager sign for her to raise the sash. Reluctant and wonder-ing, Trina obeyed, and the dentist came quickly forward. He was wearing a pair of blue overalls; a navy-blue flannel shirt without a cravat; an old coat, faded, rain-washed, and ripped at the seams; and his woollen cap.

"Say, Trina," he exclaimed, his heavy bass voice pitched just above a whisper, "let me in, will you, huh? Say, will you? I'm regularly starving, and I haven't slept in a Christian bed for two weeks."

At sight at him standing there in the moonlight, Trina could only think of him as the man who had beaten and bit-ten her, had deserted her and stolen her money, had made her suffer as she had never suffered before in all her life. Now that he had spent the money that he had stolen from her, he was whining to come back—so that he might steal more, no doubt. Once in her room he could not help but smell out her five thousand dollars. Her indignation rose.

"No," she whispered back at him. "No, I will not let you in."

"But listen here, Trina, I tell you I am starving, regu-larly——"

"Hoh!" interrupted Trina scornfully. "A man can't starve with four hundred dollars, I guess."

"Well—well—I—well—" faltered the dentist. "Never mind now. Give me something to eat, an' let me in an' sleep.

I've been sleeping in the Plaza for the last ten nights, and say,
I—Damn it, Trina, I ain't had anything to eat since——"

"Where's the four hundred dollars you robbed me of when
you deserted me?" returned Trina, coldly.

"Well, I've spent it," growled the dentist. "But you *can't*
see me starve, Trina, no matter what's happened. Give me a
little money, then."

"I'll see you starve before you get any more of *my* money."

The dentist stepped back a pace and stared up at her,
wonder-stricken. His face was lean and pinched. Never had
the jaw bone looked so enormous, nor the square-cut head
so huge. The moonlight made deep black shadows in the
shrunken cheeks.

"Huh?" asked the dentist, puzzled. "What did you say?"

"I won't give you any money—never again—not a cent."

"But do you know that I'm hungry?"

"Well, I've been hungry myself. Besides, I *don't* believe
you."

"Trina, I ain't had a thing to eat since yesterday morning;
that's God's truth. Even if I did get off with your money, you
can't see me starve, can you? You can't see me walk the streets
all night because I ain't got a place to sleep. Will you let me
in? Say, will you? Huh?"

"No."

"Well, will you give me some money then—just a little?
Give me a dollar. Give me half a dol—— Say, give me a *dime*,
an' I can get a cup of coffee."

"No."

The dentist paused and looked at her with curious intentness, bewildered, nonplussed.

"Say, you—you must be crazy, Trina. I—I—wouldn't let
a *dog* go hungry."

"Not even if he'd bitten you, perhaps."

The dentist stared again.

There was another pause. McTeague looked up at her in
silence, a mean and vicious twinkle coming into his small
eyes. He uttered a low exclamation, and then checked himself.

"Well, look here, for the last time. I'm starving. I've got
nowhere to sleep. Will you give me some money, or something to eat? Will you let me in?"

"No—no—no."

Trina could fancy she almost saw the brassy glint in her husband's eyes. He raised one enormous lean fist. Then he growled:

"If I had hold of you for a minute, by God, I'd make you dance. An' I will yet, I will yet. Don't you be afraid of that."

He turned about, the moonlight showing like a layer of snow upon his massive shoulders. Trina watched him as he passed under the shadow of the cherry trees and crossed the little court. She heard his great feet grinding on the board flooring. He disappeared.

Miser though she was, Trina was only human, and the echo of the dentist's heavy feet had not died away before she began to be sorry for what she had done. She stood by the open window in her nightgown, her finger upon her lips.

"He did look pinched," she said half aloud. "Maybe he *was* hungry. I ought to have given him something. I wish I had, I *wish* I had. Oh," she cried, suddenly, with a frightened gesture of both hands, " what have I come to be that I would see Mac—my husband—that I would see him starve rather than give him money? No, no. It's too dreadful. I *will* give him some. I'll send it to him to-morrow. Where?—well, he'll come back." She leaned from the window and called as loudly as she dared, "Mac, oh, Mac." There was no answer.

When McTeague had told Trina he had been without food for nearly two days he was speaking the truth. The week before he had spent the last of the four hundred dollars in the bar of a sailor's lodging-house near the water front, and since that time had lived a veritable hand-to-mouth existence.

He had spent her money here and there about the city in royal fashion, absolutely reckless of the morrow, feasting and drinking for the most part with companions he picked up heaven knows where, acquaintances of twenty-four hours, whose names he forgot in two days. Then suddenly he found himself at the end of his money. He no longer had any friends. Hunger rode him and rowelled him. He was no longer well fed, comfortable. There was no longer a warm place for him to sleep. He went back to Polk Street in the evening, walking on the dark side of the street, lurking in the shadows, ashamed to have any of his old-time friends see him.

He entered Zerkow's old house and knocked at the door of the room Trina and he had occupied. It was empty.

Next day he went to Uncle Oelbermann's store and asked news of Trina. Trina had not told Uncle Oelbermann of McTeague's brutalities, giving him other reasons to explain the loss of her fingers; neither had she told him of her husband's robbery. So when the dentist had asked where Trina could be found, Uncle Oelbermann, believing that McTeague was seeking a reconciliation, had told him without hesitation, and, he added:

"She was in here only yesterday and drew out the balance of her money. She's been drawing against her money for the last month or so. She's got it all now, I guess."

"Ah, she's got it all."

The dentist went away from his bootless visit to his wife shaking with rage, hating her with all the strength of a crude and primitive nature. He clenched his fists till his knuckles whitened, his teeth ground furiously upon one another.

"Ah, if I had hold of you once, I'd make you dance. She had five thousand dollars in that room, while I stood there, not twenty feet away, and told her I was starving, and she wouldn't give me a dime to get a cup of coffee with; not a dime to get a cup of coffee. Oh, if I once get my hands on you!" His wrath strangled him. He clutched at the darkness in front of him, his breath fairly whistling between his teeth.

That night he walked the streets until the morning, wondering what now he was to do to fight the wolf away. The morning of the next day towards ten o'clock he was on Kearney Street, still walking, still tramping the streets, since there was nothing else for him to do. By and by he paused on a corner near a music store, finding a momentary amusement in watching two or three men loading a piano upon a dray. Already half its weight was supported by the dray's backboard. One of the men, a big mulatto, almost hidden under the mass of glistening rosewood, was guiding its course, while the other two heaved and tugged in the rear. Something in the street frightened the horses and they shied abruptly. The end of the piano was twitched sharply from the backboard. There was a cry, the mulatto staggered and fell with the falling piano, and its weight dropped squarely upon his thigh, which broke with a resounding crack.

An hour later McTeague had found his job. The music store engaged him as handler at six dollars a week. McTeague's enormous strength, useless all his life, stood him in good stead at last.

He slept in a tiny back room opening from the storeroom of the music store. He was in some sense a watchman as well as handler, and went the rounds of the store twice every night. His room was a box of a place that reeked with odors of stale tobacco smoke. The former occupant had papered the walls with newspapers and had pasted up figures cut out from the posters of some Kiralfy ballet, very gaudy. By the one window, chittering all day in its little gilt prison, hung the canary bird, a tiny atom of life that McTeague still clung to with a strange obstinacy.

McTeague drank a good deal of whiskey in these days, but the only effect it had upon him was to increase the viciousness and bad temper that had developed in him since the beginning of his misfortunes. He terrorized his fellow-handlers, powerful men though they were. For a gruff word, for an awkward movement in lading the pianos, for a surly look or a muttered oath, the dentist's elbow would crook and his hand contract to a mallet-like fist. As often as not the blow followed, colossal in its force, swift as the leap of the piston from its cylinder.

His hatred of Trina increased from day to day. He'd make her dance yet. Wait only till he got his hands upon her. She'd let him starve, would she? She'd turn him out of doors while she hid her five thousand dollars in the bottom of her trunk. Aha, he would see about that some day. She couldn't make small of him. Ah, no. She'd dance all right—all right. McTeague was not an imaginative man by nature, but he would lie awake nights, his clumsy wits galloping and frisking under the lash of the alcohol, and fancy himself thrashing his wife, till a sudden frenzy of rage would overcome him, and he would shake all over, rolling upon the bed and biting the mattress.

On a certain day, about a week after Christmas of that year, McTeague was on one of the top floors of the music store, where the second-hand instruments were kept, helping to move about and re-arrange some old pianos. As he passed by one of the counters he paused abruptly, his eye caught by an object that was strangely familiar.

"Say," he inquired, addressing the clerk in charge, "say, where'd this come from?"

"Why, let's see. We got that from a second-hand store up on Polk Street, I guess. It's a fairly good machine; a little tinkering with the stops and a bit of shellac, and we'll make it about's good as new. Good tone. See." And the clerk drew a long, sonorous wail from the depths of McTeague's old concertina.

"Well, it's mine," growled the dentist.

The other laughed. "It's yours for eleven dollars."

"It's mine," persisted McTeague. "I want it."

"Go 'long with you, Mac. What do you mean?"

"I mean that it's mine, that's what I mean. You got no right to it. It was *stolen* from me, that's what I mean," he added, a sullen anger flaming up in his little eyes.

The clerk raised a shoulder and put the concertina on an upper shelf.

"You talk to the boss about that; t'ain't none of *my* affair. If you want to buy it, it's eleven dollars."

The dentist had been paid off the day before and had four dollars in his wallet at the moment. He gave the money to the clerk.

"Here, there's part of the money. You—you put that concertina aside for me, an' I'll give you the rest in a week or so—I'll give it to you to-morrow," he exclaimed, struck with a sudden idea.

McTeague had sadly missed his concertina. Sunday afternoons when there was no work to be done, he was accustomed to lie flat on his back on his springless bed in the little room in the rear of the music store, his coat and shoes off, reading the paper, drinking steam beer from a pitcher, and smoking his pipe. But he could no longer play his six lugubrious airs upon his concertina, and it was a deprivation. He often wondered where it was gone. It had been lost, no doubt, in the general wreck of his fortunes. Once, even, the dentist had taken a concertina from the lot kept by the music store. It was a Sunday and no one was about. But he found he could not play upon it. The stops were arranged upon a system he did not understand.

Now his own concertina was come back to him. He would buy it back. He had given the clerk four dollars. He knew where he would get the remaining seven.

The clerk had told him the concertina had been sold on Polk Street to the second-hand store there. Trina had sold it. McTeague knew it. Trina had sold his concertina—had stolen it and sold it—his concertina, his beloved concertina, that he had had all his life. Why, barring the canary, there was not one of all his belongings that McTeague had cherished more dearly. His steel engraving of "Lorenzo de' Medici and his Court" might be lost, his stone pug dog might go, but his concertina!

"And she sold it—stole it from me and sold it. Just because I happened to forget to take it along with me. Well, we'll just see about that. You'll give me the money to buy it back, or——"

His rage loomed big within him. His hatred of Trina came back upon him like a returning surge. He saw her small, prim mouth, her narrow blue eyes, her black mane of hair, and uptilted chin, and hated her the more because of them. Aha, he'd show her; he'd make her dance. He'd get that seven dollars from her, or he'd know the reason why. He went through his work that day, heaving and hauling at the ponderous pianos, handling them with the ease of a lifting crane, impatient for the coming of evening, when he could be left to his own devices. As often as he had a moment to spare he went down the street to the nearest saloon and drank a pony of whiskey. Now and then as he fought and struggled with the vast masses of ebony, rosewood, and mahogany on the upper floor of the music store, raging and chafing at their inertness and unwillingness, while the whiskey pirouetted in his brain, he would mutter to himself:

"An' I got to do this. I got to work like a dray horse while she sits at home by her stove and counts her money—and sells my concertina."

Six o'clock came. Instead of supper, McTeague drank some more whiskey, five ponies in rapid succession. After supper he

was obliged to go out with the dray to deliver a concert grand
at the Odd Fellows' Hall, where a piano "recital" was to take
place.

"Ain't you coming back with us?" asked one of the handlers
as he climbed upon the driver's seat after the piano had been
put in place.

"No, no," returned the dentist; "I got something else to
do." The brilliant lights of a saloon near the City Hall caught
his eye. He decided he would have another drink of whiskey.
It was about eight o'clock.

The following day was to be a *fête* day at the kindergarten,
the Christmas and New Year festivals combined. All that afternoon the little two-story building on Pacific Street had
been filled with a number of grand ladies of the Kindergarten
Board, who were hanging up ropes of evergreen and sprays
of holly, and arranging a great Christmas tree that stood in
the centre of the ring in the schoolroom. The whole place was
pervaded with a pungent, piney odor. Trina had been very
busy since the early morning, coming and going at everybody's call, now running down the street after another tack-
hammer or a fresh supply of cranberries, now tying together
the ropes of evergreen and passing them up to one of the
grand ladies as she carefully balanced herself on a step-ladder.
By evening everything was in place. As the last grand lady left
the school, she gave Trina an extra dollar for her work, and
said:

"Now, if you'll just tidy up here, Mrs. McTeague, I think
that will be all. Sweep up the pine needles here—you see they
are all over the floor—and look through all the rooms, and
tidy up generally. Good night—and a Happy New Year," she
cried pleasantly as she went out.

Trina put the dollar away in her trunk before she did anything else and cooked herself a bit of supper. Then she came
down-stairs again.

The kindergarten was not large. On the lower floor were
but two rooms, the main schoolroom and another room, a
cloakroom, very small, where the children hung their hats and
coats. This cloakroom opened off the back of the main
schoolroom. Trina cast a critical glance into both of these
rooms. There had been a great deal of going and coming in

them during the day, and she decided that the first thing to do would be to scrub the floors. She went up again to her room overhead and heated some water over her oil stove; then, re-descending, set to work vigorously.

By nine o'clock she had almost finished with the school-room. She was down on her hands and knees in the midst of a steaming muck of soapy water. On her feet were a pair of man's shoes fastened with buckles; a dirty cotton gown, damp with the water, clung about her shapeless, stunted figure. From time to time she sat back on her heels to ease the strain of her position, and with one smoking hand, white and par-boiled with the hot water, brushed her hair, already streaked with gray, out of her weazened, pale face and the corners of her mouth.

It was very quiet. A gas-jet without a globe lit up the place with a crude, raw light. The cat who lived on the premises, preferring to be dirty rather than to be wet, had got into the coal scuttle, and over its rim watched her sleepily with a long, complacent purr.

All at once he stopped purring, leaving an abrupt silence in the air like the sudden shutting off of a stream of water, while his eyes grew wide, two lambent disks of yellow in the heap of black fur.

"Who is there?" cried Trina, sitting back on her heels. In the stillness that succeeded, the water dripped from her hands with the steady tick of a clock. Then a brutal fist swung open the street door of the schoolroom and McTeague came in. He was drunk; not with that drunkenness which is stupid, maud-lin, wavering on its feet, but with that which is alert, un-naturally intelligent, vicious, perfectly steady, deadly wicked. Trina only had to look once at him, and in an instant, with some strange sixth sense, born of the occasion, knew what she had to expect.

She jumped up and ran from him into the little cloakroom. She locked and bolted the door after her, and leaned her weight against it, panting and trembling, every nerve shrink-ing and quivering with the fear of him.

McTeague put his hand on the knob of the door outside and opened it, tearing off the lock and bolt guard, and send-ing her staggering across the room.

"Mac," she cried to him, as he came in, speaking with horrid rapidity, cringing and holding out her hands, "Mac, listen. Wait a minute—look here—listen here. It wasn't my fault. I'll give you some money. You can come back. I'll do *anything* you want. Won't you just *listen* to me? Oh, don't! I'll scream. I can't help it, you know. The people will hear."

McTeague came towards her slowly, his immense feet dragging and grinding on the floor; his enormous fists, hard as wooden mallets, swinging at his sides. Trina backed from him to the corner of the room, cowering before him, holding her elbow crooked in front of her face, watching him with fearful intentness, ready to dodge.

"I want that money," he said, pausing in front of her.

"What money?" cried Trina.

"I want that money. You got it—that five thousand dollars. I want every nickel of it! You understand?"

"I haven't it. It isn't here. Uncle Oelbermann's got it."

"That's a lie. He told me that you came and got it. You've had it long enough; now *I* want it. Do you hear?"

"Mac, I can't give you that money. I—I *won't* give it to you," Trina cried, with sudden resolution.

"Yes, you will. You'll give me every nickel of it."

"No, *no*."

"You ain't going to make small of me this time. Give me that money."

"*No*."

"For the last time, will you give me that money?"

"No."

"You won't, huh? You won't give me it? For the last time."

"No, *no*."

Usually the dentist was slow in his movements, but now the alcohol had awakened in him an ape-like agility. He kept his small dull eyes upon her, and all at once sent his fist into the middle of her face with the suddenness of a relaxed spring.

Beside herself with terror, Trina turned and fought him back; fought for her miserable life with the exasperation and strength of a harassed cat; and with such energy and such wild, unnatural force, that even McTeague for the moment drew back from her. But her resistance was the one thing to drive him to the top of his fury. He came back at her again, his eyes drawn to two fine twinkling points, and his enormous fists, clenched till the knuckles whitened, raised in the air.

Then it became abominable.

In the schoolroom outside, behind the coal scuttle, the cat listened to the sounds of stamping and struggling and the muffled noise of blows, wildly terrified, his eyes bulging like brass knobs. At last the sounds stopped on a sudden; he heard nothing more. Then McTeague came out, closing the door. The cat followed him with distended eyes as he crossed the room and disappeared through the street door.

The dentist paused for a moment on the sidewalk, looking carefully up and down the street. It was deserted and quiet. He turned sharply to the right and went down a narrow passage that led into the little court yard behind the school. A candle was burning in Trina's room. He went up by the outside stairway and entered.

The trunk stood locked in one corner of the room. The dentist took the lid-lifter from the little oil stove, put it underneath the lock-clasp and wrenched it open. Groping beneath a pile of dresses he found the chamois-skin bag, the little brass match-box, and, at the very bottom, carefully thrust into one corner, the canvas sack crammed to the mouth with twenty-dollar gold pieces. He emptied the chamois-skin bag and the match-box into the pockets of his trousers. But the canvas sack was too bulky to hide about his clothes.

"I guess I'll just naturally have to carry *you*," he muttered. He blew out the candle, closed the door, and gained the street again.

The dentist crossed the city, going back to the music store. It was a little after eleven o'clock. The night was moonless, filled with a gray blur of faint light that seemed to come from all quarters of the horizon at once. From time to time there were sudden explosions of a southeast wind at the street corners. McTeague went on, slanting his head against the gusts, to keep his cap from blowing off, carrying the sack close to his side. Once he looked critically at the sky.

"I bet it'll rain to-morrow," he muttered, "if this wind works round to the south."

Once in his little den behind the music store, he washed his hands and forearms, and put on his working clothes, blue overalls and a jumper, over cheap trousers and vest. Then he got together his small belongings—an old campaign hat, a pair of boots, a tin of tobacco, and a pinchbeck bracelet which he had found one Sunday in the Park, and which he believed to be valuable. He stripped his blanket from his bed and rolled up in it all these objects, together with the canvas sack, fastening the roll with a half hitch such as miners use, the instincts of the old-time car-boy coming back to him in his present confusion of mind. He changed his pipe and his knife—a huge jackknife with a yellowed bone handle—to the pockets of his overalls.

Then at last he stood with his hand on the door, holding up the lamp before blowing it out, looking about to make sure he was ready to go. The wavering light woke his canary. It stirred and began to chitter feebly, very sleepy and cross at being awakened. McTeague started, staring at it, and reflecting. He believed that it would be a long time before anyone came into that room again. The canary would be days without food; it was likely it would starve, would die there, hour by hour, in its little gilt prison. McTeague resolved to take it with him. He took down the cage, touching it gently with his enormous hands, and tied a couple of sacks about it to shelter the little bird from the sharp night wind.

Then he went out, locking all the doors behind him, and turned toward the ferry slips. The boats had ceased running hours ago, but he told himself that by waiting till four o'clock he could get across the bay on the tug that took over the morning papers.

Trina lay unconscious, just as she had fallen under the last of McTeague's blows, her body twitching with an occasional hiccough that stirred the pool of blood in which she lay face downward. Towards morning she died with a rapid series of hiccoughs that sounded like a piece of clockwork running down.

The thing had been done in the cloakroom where the kindergarten children hung their hats and coats. There was no other entrance except by going through the main schoolroom. McTeague going out had shut the door of the cloak-room, but had left the street door open; so when the children arrived in the morning, they entered as usual.

About half-past eight, two or three five-year-olds, one a lit-tle colored girl, came into the schoolroom of the kindergarten with a great chatter of voices, going across to the cloakroom to hang up their hats and coats as they had been taught.

Half way across the room one of them stopped and put her small nose in the air, crying, "Um-o-o, what a funnee smell!" The others began to sniff the air as well, and one, the daugh-ter of a butcher, exclaimed, "'Tsmells like my pa's shop," adding in the next breath, "Look, what's the matter with the kittee?"

In fact, the cat was acting strangely. He lay quite flat on the floor, his nose pressed close to the crevice under the door of the little cloakroom, winding his tail slowly back and forth, excited, very eager. At times he would draw back and make a strange little clacking noise down in his throat.

"Ain't he funnee?" said the little girl again. The cat slunk swiftly away as the children came up. Then the tallest of the little girls swung the door of the little cloakroom wide open and they all ran in.

XX

THE DAY was very hot, and the silence of high noon lay close and thick between the steep slopes of the cañons like an invisible, muffling fluid. At intervals the drone of an insect bored the air and trailed slowly to silence again. Everywhere were pungent, aromatic smells. The vast, moveless heat seemed to distil countless odors from the brush—odors of warm sap, of pine needles, and of tar-weed, and above all the medicinal odor of witch hazel. As far as one could look, uncounted multitudes of trees and manzanita bushes were quietly and motionlessly growing, growing, growing. A tremendous, immeasurable Life pushed steadily heavenward without a sound, without a motion. At turns of the road, on the higher points, cañons disclosed themselves far away, gigantic grooves in the landscape, deep blue in the distance, opening one into another, ocean-deep, silent, huge, and suggestive of colossal primeval forces held in reserve. At their bottoms they were solid, massive; on their crests they broke delicately into fine serrated edges where the pines and redwoods outlined their million of tops against the high white horizon. Here and there the mountains lifted themselves out of the narrow river beds in groups like giant lions rearing their heads after drinking. The entire region was untamed. In some places east of the Mississippi nature is cosey, intimate, small, and homelike, like a good-natured housewife. In Placer County, California, she is a vast, unconquered brute of the Pliocene epoch, savage, sullen, and magnificently indifferent to man.

But there were men in these mountains, like lice on mammoths' hides, fighting them stubbornly, now with hydraulic "monitors," now with drill and dynamite, boring into the vitals of them, or tearing away great yellow gravelly scars in the flanks of them, sucking their blood, extracting gold.

Here and there at long distances upon the cañon sides rose the headgear of a mine, surrounded with its few unpainted houses, and topped by its never-failing feather of black smoke. On near approach one heard the prolonged thunder of the stamp-mill, the crusher, the insatiable monster, gnashing the rocks to powder with its long iron teeth, vomiting them out again in a thin stream of wet gray mud. Its enormous maw, fed night and day with the car-boys' loads, gorged itself with gravel, and spat out the gold, grinding the rocks between its jaws, glutted, as it were, with the very entrails of the earth, and growling over its endless meal, like some savage animal, some legendary dragon, some fabulous beast, symbol of inordinate and monstrous gluttony.

McTeague had left the Overland train at Colfax, and the same afternoon had ridden some eight miles across the mountains in the stage that connects Colfax with Iowa Hill. Iowa Hill was a small one-street town, the headquarters of the mines of the district. Originally it had been built upon the summit of a mountain, but the sides of this mountain have long since been "hydraulicked" away, so that the town now clings to a mere back bone, and the rear windows of the houses on both sides of the street look down over sheer precipices, into vast pits hundreds of feet deep.

The dentist stayed over night at the Hill, and the next morning started off on foot farther into the mountains. He still wore his blue overalls and jumper; his woollen cap was pulled down over his eyes; on his feet were hob-nailed boots he had bought at the store in Colfax; his blanket roll was over his back; in his left hand swung the bird cage wrapped in sacks.

Just outside the town he paused, as if suddenly remembering something.

"There ought to be a trail just off the road here," he muttered. "There used to be a trail—a short cut."

The next instant, without moving from his position, he saw where it opened just before him. His instinct had halted him at the exact spot. The trail zigzagged down the abrupt descent of the cañon, debouching into a gravelly river bed.

"Indian River," muttered the dentist. "I remember—I remember. I ought to hear the Morning Star's stamps from here." He cocked his head. A low, sustained roar, like a distant cataract, came to his ears from across the river. "That's right," he said, contentedly. He crossed the river and regained the road beyond. The slope rose under his feet; a little farther on he passed the Morning Star mine, smoking and thun-

dering. McTeague pushed steadily on. The road rose with the
rise of the mountain, turned at a sharp angle where a great
live-oak grew, and held level for nearly a quarter of a mile.
Twice again the dentist left the road and took to the trail that
cut through deserted hydraulic pits. He knew exactly where
to look for these trails; not once did his instinct deceive him.
He recognized familiar points at once. Here was Cold Cañon,
where invariably, winter and summer, a chilly wind was blowing; here was where the road to Spencer's branched off; here
was Bussy's old place, where at one time there were so many
dogs; here was Delmue's cabin, where unlicensed whiskey
used to be sold; here was the plank bridge with its one rotten
board; and here the flat overgrown with manzanita, where he
once had shot three quail.

At noon, after he had been tramping for some two hours,
he halted at a point where the road dipped suddenly. A little
to the right of him, and flanking the road, an enormous yellow gravel-pit like an emptied lake gaped to heaven. Farther
on, in the distance, a cañon zigzagged toward the horizon,
rugged with pine-clad mountain crests. Nearer at hand, and
directly in the line of the road, was an irregular cluster of
unpainted cabins. A dull, prolonged roar vibrated in the air.
McTeague nodded his head as if satisfied.

"That's the place," he muttered.

He reshouldered his blanket roll and descended the road.
At last he halted again. He stood before a low one-story
building, differing from the others in that it was painted. A
verandah, shut in with mosquito netting, surrounded it.
McTeague dropped his blanket roll on a lumber pile outside,
and came up and knocked at the open door. Some one called
to him to come in.

McTeague entered, rolling his eyes about him, noting the
changes that had been made since he had last seen this place.
A partition had been knocked down, making one big room
out of the two former small ones. A counter and railing stood
inside the door. There was a telephone on the wall. In one
corner he also observed a stack of surveyor's instruments; a
big drawing-board straddled on spindle legs across one end
of the room, a mechanical drawing of some kind, no doubt
the plan of the mine, unrolled upon it; a chromo representing

a couple of peasants in a ploughed field (Millet's "Angelus") was nailed unframed upon the wall, and hanging from the same wire nail that secured one of its corners in place was a bullion bag and a cartridge belt with a loaded revolver in the pouch.

The dentist approached the counter and leaned his elbows upon it. Three men were in the room—a tall, lean young man, with a thick head of hair surprisingly gray, who was playing with a half-grown great Dane puppy; another fellow about as young, but with a jaw almost as salient as McTeague's, stood at the letter-press taking a copy of a letter; a third man, a little older than the other two, was pottering over a transit. This latter was massively built, and wore overalls and low boots streaked and stained and spotted in every direction with gray mud. The dentist looked slowly from one to the other; then at length, "Is the foreman about?" he asked.

The man in the muddy overalls came forward.

"What you want?"

He spoke with a strong German accent.

The old invariable formula came back to McTeague on the instant.

"What's the show for a job?"

At once the German foreman became preoccupied, looking aimlessly out of the window. There was a silence.

"You hev been miner alretty?"

"Yes, yes."

"Know how to hendle pick'n shov'le?"

"Yes, I know."

The other seemed unsatisfied. "Are you a 'cousin Jack'?"

The dentist grinned. This prejudice against Cornishmen he remembered too.

"No. American."

"How long sence you mine?"

"Oh, year or two."

"Show your hends." McTeague exhibited his hard, calloused palms.

"When ken you go to work? I want a chuck-tender on der night-shift."

"I can tend a chuck. I'll go on to-night."

"What's your name?"

The dentist started. He had forgotten to be prepared for this.

"Huh? What?"

"What's the name?"

McTeague's eye was caught by a railroad calendar hanging over the desk. There was no time to think.

"Burlington," he said, loudly.

The German took a card from a file and wrote it down.

"Give dis card to der boarding-boss, down at der boarding-haus, den gome find me bei der mill at sex o'clock, und I set you to work."

Straight as a homing pigeon, and following a blind and unreasoned instinct, McTeague had returned to the Big Dipper mine. Within a week's time it seemed to him as though he had never been away. He picked up his life again exactly where he had left it the day when his mother had sent him away with the travelling dentist, the charlatan who had set up his tent by the bunk house. The house McTeague had once lived in was still there, occupied by one of the shift bosses and his family. The dentist passed it on his way to and from the mine.

He himself slept in the bunk house with some thirty others of his shift. At half-past five in the evening the cook at the boarding-house sounded a prolonged alarm upon a crowbar bent in the form of a triangle, that hung upon the porch of the boarding-house. McTeague rose and dressed, and with his shift had supper. Their lunch-pails were distributed to them. Then he made his way to the tunnel mouth, climbed into a car in the waiting ore train, and was hauled into the mine.

Once inside, the hot evening air turned to a cool dampness, and the forest odors gave place to the smell of stale dynamite smoke, suggestive of burning rubber. A cloud of steam came from McTeague's mouth; underneath, the water swashed and rippled around the car-wheels, while the light from the miner's candlesticks threw wavering blurs of pale yellow over the gray rotting quartz of the roof and walls. Occasionally McTeague bent down his head to avoid the lagging of the roof or the projections of an overhanging shute. From car to car

all along the line the miners called to one another as the train
trundled along, joshing and laughing.

A mile from the entrance the train reached the breast where
McTeague's gang worked. The men clambered from the cars
and took up the labor where the day shift had left it, burrowing their way steadily through a primeval river bed.

The candlesticks thrust into the crevices of the gravel strata
lit up faintly the half dozen moving figures befouled with
sweat and with wet gray mould. The picks struck into the
loose gravel with a yielding shock. The long-handled shovels
clinked amidst the piles of bowlders and scraped dully in the
heaps of rotten quartz. The Burly drill boring for blasts broke
out from time to time in an irregular chug-chug, chug-chug,
while the engine that pumped the water from the mine
coughed and strangled at short intervals.

McTeague tended the chuck. In a way he was the assistant
of the man who worked the Burly. It was his duty to replace
the drills in the Burly, putting in longer ones as the hole got
deeper and deeper. From time to time he rapped the drill
with a pole-pick when it stuck fast or fitchered.

Once it even occurred to him that there was a resemblance
between his present work and the profession he had been
forced to abandon. In the Burly drill he saw a queer counterpart of his old-time dental engine; and what were the drills
and chucks but enormous hoe excavators, hard bits, and
burrs? It was the same work he had so often performed in his
"Parlors," only magnified, made monstrous, distorted, and
grotesqued, the caricature of dentistry.

He passed his nights thus in the midst of the play of crude
and simple forces—the powerful attacks of the Burly drills;
the great exertions of bared, bent backs overlaid with muscle;
the brusque, resistless expansion of dynamite; and the silent,
vast, Titanic force, mysterious and slow, that cracked the tim-
bers supporting the roof of the tunnel, and that gradually flattened the lagging till it was thin as paper.

The life pleased the dentist beyond words. The still, colossal mountains took him back again like a returning prodigal,
and vaguely, without knowing why, he yielded to their influence—their immensity, their enormous power, crude and
blind, reflecting themselves in his own nature, huge, strong,

brutal in its simplicity. And this, though he only saw the
mountains at night. They appeared far different then than in
the daytime. At twelve o'clock he came out of the mine and
lunched on the contents of his dinner-pail, sitting upon the
embankment of the track, eating with both hands, and looking around him with a steady ox-like gaze. The mountains
rose sheer from every side, heaving their gigantic crests far up
into the night, the black peaks crowding together, and looking now less like beasts than like a company of cowled giants.
In the daytime they were silent; but at night they seemed to
stir and rouse themselves. Occasionally the stamp-mill
stopped, its thunder ceasing abruptly. Then one could hear
the noises that the mountains made in their living. From the
cañon, from the crowding crests, from the whole immense
landscape, there rose a steady and prolonged sound, coming
from all sides at once. It was that incessant and muffled roar
which disengages itself from all vast bodies, from oceans,
from cities, from forests, from sleeping armies, and which
is like the breathing of an infinitely great monster, alive, palpitating.

McTeague returned to his work. At six in the morning his
shift was taken off, and he went out of the mine and back to
the bunk house. All day long he slept, flung at length upon
the strong-smelling blankets—slept the dreamless sleep of exhaustion, crushed and overpowered with the work, flat and
prone upon his belly, till again in the evening the cook
sounded the alarm upon the crowbar bent into a triangle.

Every alternate week the shifts were changed. The second
week McTeague's shift worked in the daytime and slept at
night. Wednesday night of this second week the dentist woke
suddenly. He sat up in his bed in the bunk house, looking
about him from side to side; an alarm clock hanging on the
wall, over a lantern, marked half-past three.

"What was it?" muttered the dentist. "I wonder what it
was." The rest of the shift were sleeping soundly, filling the
room with the rasping sound of snoring. Everything was in
its accustomed place; nothing stirred. But for all that Mc-
Teague got up and lit his miner's candlestick and went carefully about the room, throwing the light into the dark
corners, peering under all the beds, including his own. Then

he went to the door and stepped outside. The night was warm and still; the moon, very low, and canted on her side like a galleon foundering. The camp was very quiet; nobody was in sight. "I wonder what it was," muttered the dentist. "There was something—why did I wake up? Huh?" He made a circuit about the bunk house, unusually alert, his small eyes twinkling rapidly, seeing everything. All was quiet. An old dog who invariably slept on the steps of the bunk house had not even wakened. McTeague went back to bed, but did not sleep.

"There was *something*," he muttered, looking in a puzzled way at his canary in the cage that hung from the wall at his bedside; "something. What was it? There is something *now*. There it is again—the same thing." He sat up in bed with eyes and ears strained. "What is it? I don' know what it is. I don' hear anything, an' I don' see anything. I feel something—right now; feel it now. I wonder—I don' know—I don' know."

Once more he got up, and this time dressed himself. He made a complete tour of the camp, looking and listening, for what he did not know. He even went to the outskirts of the camp and for nearly half an hour watched the road that led into the camp from the direction of Iowa Hill. He saw nothing; not even a rabbit stirred. He went to bed.

But from this time on there was a change. The dentist grew restless, uneasy. Suspicion of something, he could not say what, annoyed him incessantly. He went wide around sharp corners. At every moment he looked sharply over his shoulder. He even went to bed with his clothes and cap on, and at every hour during the night would get up and prowl about the bunk house, one ear turned down the wind, his eyes gimleting the darkness. From time to time he would murmur:

"There's something. What is it? I wonder what it is."

What strange sixth sense stirred in McTeague at this time? What animal cunning, what brute instinct clamored for recognition and obedience? What lower faculty was it that roused his suspicion, that drove him out into the night a score of times between dark and dawn, his head in the air, his eyes and ears keenly alert?

One night as he stood on the steps of the bunk house,

peering into the shadows of the camp, he uttered an exclamation as of a man suddenly enlightened. He turned back into the house, drew from under his bed the blanket roll in which he kept his money hid, and took the canary down from the wall. He strode to the door and disappeared into the night. When the sheriff of Placer County and the two deputies from San Francisco reached the Big Dipper mine, McTeague had been gone two days.

XXI

WELL," said one of the deputies, as he backed the horse into the shafts of the buggy in which the pursuers had driven over from the Hill, " we've about as good as got him. It isn't hard to follow a man who carries a bird cage with him wherever he goes."

McTeague crossed the mountains on foot the Friday and Saturday of that week, going over through Emigrant Gap, following the line of the Overland railroad. He reached Reno Monday night. By degrees a vague plan of action outlined itself in the dentist's mind.

"Mexico," he muttered to himself. "Mexico, that's the place. They'll watch the coast and they'll watch the Eastern trains, but they won't think of Mexico."

The sense of pursuit which had harassed him during the last week of his stay at the Big Dipper mine had worn off, and he believed himself to be very cunning.

"I'm pretty far ahead now, I guess," he said. At Reno he boarded a south-bound freight on the line of the Carson and Colorado railroad, paying for a passage in the caboose. "Freights don' run on schedule time," he muttered, "and a conductor on a passenger train makes it his business to study faces. I'll stay with this train as far as it goes."

The freight worked slowly southward, through western Nevada, the country becoming hourly more and more desolate and abandoned. After leaving Walker Lake the sage-brush country began, and the freight rolled heavily over tracks that threw off visible layers of heat. At times it stopped whole half days on sidings or by water tanks, and the engineer and fireman came back to the caboose and played poker with the conductor and train crew. The dentist sat apart, behind the stove, smoking pipe after pipe of cheap tobacco. Sometimes he joined in the poker games. He had learned poker when a boy at the mine, and after a few deals his knowledge returned to him; but for the most part he was taciturn and unsociable, and rarely spoke to the others unless spoken to first. The crew recognized the type, and the impression gained ground among them that he had "done for" a livery-stable keeper at Truckee and was trying to get down into Arizona.

McTeague heard two brakemen discussing him one night as they stood outside by the halted train. "The livery-stable keeper called him a bastard; that's what Picachos told me," one of them remarked, "and started to draw his gun; an' this fellar did for him with a hayfork. He's a horse doctor, this chap is, and the livery-stable keeper had got the law on him so's he couldn't practise any more, an' he was sore about it."

Near a place called Queen's the train reëntered California, and McTeague observed with relief that the line of track which had hitherto held westward curved sharply to the south again. The train was unmolested; occasionally the crew fought with a gang of tramps who attempted to ride the brake beams, and once in the northern part of Inyo County, while they were halted at a water tank, an immense Indian buck, blanketed to the ground, approached McTeague as he stood on the roadbed stretching his legs, and without a word presented to him a filthy, crumpled letter. The letter was to the effect that the buck Big Jim was a good Indian and deserving of charity; the signature was illegible. The dentist stared at the letter, returned it to the buck, and regained the train just as it started. Neither had spoken; the buck did not move from his position, and fully five minutes afterward, when the slow-moving freight was miles away, the dentist looked back and saw him still standing motionless between the rails, a forlorn and solitary point of red, lost in the immensity of the surrounding white blur of the desert.

At length the mountains began again, rising up on either side of the track; vast, naked hills of white sand and red rock, spotted with blue shadows. Here and there a patch of green was spread like a gay table-cloth over the sand. All at once Mount Whitney leaped over the horizon. Independence was reached and passed; the freight, nearly emptied by now, and much shortened, rolled along the shores of Owen Lake. At a place called Keeler it stopped definitely. It was the terminus of the road.

The town of Keeler was a one-street town, not unlike Iowa Hill—the post-office, the bar and hotel, the Odd Fellows' Hall, and the livery stable being the principal buildings.

"Where to now?" muttered McTeague to himself as he sat on the edge of the bed in his room in the hotel. He hung the canary in the window, filled its little bathtub, and watched it take its bath with enormous satisfaction. "Where to now?" he muttered again. "This is as far as the railroad goes, an' it won' do for me to stay in a town yet a while; no, it won' do. I got to clear out. Where to? That's the word, where to? I'll go down to supper now"—He went on whispering his thoughts aloud, so that they would take more concrete shape in his mind—"I'll go down to supper now, an' then I'll hang aroun' the bar this evening till I get the lay of this land. Maybe this is fruit country, though it looks more like a cattle country. Maybe it's a mining country. If it's a mining country," he continued, puckering his heavy eyebrows, "if it's a mining country, an' the mines are far enough off the roads, maybe I'd better get to the mines an' lay quiet for a month before I try to get any farther south."

He washed the cinders and dust of a week's railroading from his face and hair, put on a fresh pair of boots, and went down to supper. The dining-room was of the invariable type of the smaller interior towns of California. There was but one table, covered with oilcloth; rows of benches answered for chairs; a railroad map, a chromo with a gilt frame protected by mosquito netting, hung on the walls, together with a yellowed photograph of the proprietor in Masonic regalia. Two waitresses whom the guests—all men—called by their first names, came and went with large trays.

Through the windows outside McTeague observed a great number of saddle horses tied to trees and fences. Each one of these horses had a riata on the pommel of the saddle. He sat down to the table, eating his thick hot soup, watching his neighbors covertly, listening to everything that was said. It did not take him long to gather that the country to the east and south of Keeler was a cattle country.

Not far off, across a range of hills, was the Panamint Valley, where the big cattle ranges were. Every now and then this name was tossed to and fro across the table in the flow of conversation—"Over in the Panamint." "Just going down for a rodeo in the Panamint." "Panamint brands." "Has a range down in the Panamint." Then by and by the remark, "Hoh, yes, Gold Gulch, they're down to good pay there. That's on the other side the Panamint Range. Peters came in yesterday and told me."

McTeague turned to the speaker.

"Is that a gravel mine?" he asked.

"No, no, quartz."

"I'm a miner; that's why I asked."

"Well I've mined some too. I had a hole in the ground meself, but she was silver; and when the skunks at Washington lowered the price of silver, where was I? Fitchered, b'God!"

"I was looking for a job."

"Well, it's mostly cattle down here in the Panamint, but since the strike over at Gold Gulch some of the boys have gone prospecting. There's gold in them damn Panamint Mountains. If you can find a good long 'contact' of country rocks you ain't far from it. There's a couple of fellars from Redlands has located four claims around Gold Gulch. They got a vein eighteen inches wide, an' Peters says you can trace it for more'n a thousand feet. Were you thinking of prospecting over there?"

"Well, well, I don' know, I don' know."

"Well, I'm going over to the other side of the range day after t'morrow after some ponies of mine, an' I'm going to have a look around. You say you've been a miner?"

"Yes, yes."

"If you're going over that way, you might come along and see if we can't find a contact, or copper sulphurets, or something. Even if we don't find color we may find silver-bearing galena." Then, after a pause, "Let's see, I didn't catch your name."

"Huh? My name's Carter," answered McTeague, promptly. Why he should change his name again the dentist could not say. "Carter" came to his mind at once, and he answered without reflecting that he had registered as "Burlington" when he had arrived at the hotel.

"Well, my name's Cribbens," answered the other. The two shook hands solemnly.

"You're about finished?" continued Cribbens, pushing back. "Le's go out in the bar an' have a drink on it."

"Sure, sure," said the dentist.

The two sat up late that night in a corner of the barroom discussing the probability of finding gold in the Panamint hills. It soon became evident that they held differing theories. McTeague clung to the old prospector's idea that there was no way of telling where gold was until you actually saw it. Cribbens had evidently read a good many books upon the subject, and had already prospected in something of a scientific manner.

"Shucks!" he exclaimed. "Gi' me a long distinct contact between sedimentary and igneous rocks, an' I'll sink a shaft without ever *seeing* 'color.'"

The dentist put his huge chin in the air. "Gold is where you find it," he returned, doggedly.

"Well, it's my idea as how pardners ought to work along different lines," said Cribbens. He tucked the corners of his mustache into his mouth and sucked the tobacco juice from them. For a moment he was thoughtful, then he blew out his mustache abruptly, and exclaimed:

"Say, Carter, le's make a go of this. You got a little cash I suppose—fifty dollars or so?"

"Huh? Yes—I—I——"

"Well, *I* got about fifty. We'll go pardners on the proposition, an' we'll dally 'round the range yonder an' see what we can see. What do you say?"

"Sure, sure," answered the dentist.

"Well, it's a go then, hey?"

"That's the word."

"Well, le's have a drink on it."

They drank with profound gravity.

They fitted out the next day at the general merchandise store of Keeler—picks, shovels, prospectors' hammers, a couple of cradles, pans, bacon, flour, coffee, and the like, and they bought a burro on which to pack their kit.

"Say, by jingo, you ain't got a horse," suddenly exclaimed Cribbens as they came out of the store. "You can't get around this country without a pony of some kind."

Cribbens already owned and rode a buckskin cayuse that had to be knocked in the head and stunned before it could be saddled. "I got an extry saddle an' a headstall at the hotel that you can use," he said, "but you'll have to get a horse."

In the end the dentist bought a mule at the livery stable for forty dollars. It turned out to be a good bargain, however, for the mule was a good traveller and seemed actually to fatten on sage-brush and potato parings. When the actual transaction took place, McTeague had been obliged to get the money to pay for the mule out of the canvas sack. Cribbens was with him at the time, and as the dentist unrolled his blankets and disclosed the sack, whistled in amazement.

"An' me asking you if you had fifty dollars!" he exclaimed. "You carry your mine right around with you, don't you?"

"Huh, I guess so," muttered the dentist. "I—I just sold a claim I had up in El Dorado County," he added.

At five o'clock on a magnificent May morning the "pardners" jogged out of Keeler, driving the burro before them. Cribbens rode his cayuse, McTeague following in his rear on the mule.

"Say," remarked Cribbens, "why in thunder don't you leave that fool canary behind at the hotel? It's going to be in your way all the time, an' it will sure die. Better break its neck an' chuck it."

"No, no," insisted the dentist. "I've had it too long. I'll take it with me."

"Well, that's the craziest idea I ever heard of," remarked Cribbens, "to take a canary along prospecting. Why not kid gloves, and be done with it?"

They travelled leisurely to the southeast during the day, following a well-beaten cattle road, and that evening camped on a spur of some hills at the head of the Panamint Valley where there was a spring. The next day they crossed the Panamint itself.

"That's a smart looking valley," observed the dentist.

"*Now* you're talking straight talk," returned Cribbens, sucking his mustache. The valley was beautiful, wide, level, and very green. Everywhere were herds of cattle, scarcely less wild than deer. Once or twice cowboys passed them on the road, big-boned fellows, picturesque in their broad hats, hairy trousers, jingling spurs, and revolver belts, surprisingly like the pictures McTeague remembered to have seen. Everyone of them knew Cribbens, and almost invariably joshed him on his venture.

"Say, Crib, ye'd best take a wagon train with ye to bring your dust back."

Cribbens resented their humor, and after they had passed, chewed fiercely on his mustache.

"I'd like to make a strike, b'God! if it was only to get the laugh on them joshers."

By noon they were climbing the eastern slope of the Panamint Range. Long since they had abandoned the road; vegetation ceased; not a tree was in sight. They followed faint cattle trails that led from one water hole to another. By degrees these water holes grew dryer and dryer, and at three o'clock Cribbens halted and filled their canteens.

"There ain't any *too* much water on the other side," he observed grimly.

"It's pretty hot," muttered the dentist, wiping his streaming forehead with the back of his hand.

"Huh!" snorted the other more grimly than ever. The motionless air was like the mouth of a furnace. Cribbens's pony lathered and panted. McTeague's mule began to droop his long ears. Only the little burro plodded resolutely on, picking the trail where McTeague could see but trackless sand and stunted sage. Towards evening Cribbens, who was in the lead, drew rein on the summit of the hills.

Behind them was the beautiful green Panamint Valley, but before and below them for miles and miles, as far as the eye could reach, a flat, white desert, empty even of sage-brush, unrolled toward the horizon. In the immediate foreground a broken system of arroyos, and little cañons tumbled down to meet it. To the north faint blue hills shouldered themselves above the horizon.

"Well," observed Cribbens, " we're on the top of the Panamint Range now. It's along this eastern slope, right below us here, that we're going to prospect. Gold Gulch"—he pointed with the butt of his quirt—"is about eighteen or nineteen miles along here to the north of us. Those hills way over yonder to the northeast are the Telescope hills."

"What do you call the desert out yonder?" McTeague's eyes wandered over the illimitable stretch of alkali that stretched out forever and forever to the east, to the north, and to the south.

"That," said Cribbens, "that's Death Valley."

There was a long pause. The horses panted irregularly, the sweat dripping from their heaving bellies. Cribbens and the dentist sat motionless in their saddles, looking out over that abominable desolation, silent, troubled.

"God!" ejaculated Cribbens at length, under his breath, with a shake of his head. Then he seemed to rouse himself. "Well," he remarked, "first thing we got to do now is to find water."

This was a long and difficult task. They descended into one little cañon after another, followed the course of numberless arroyos, and even dug where there seemed indications of moisture, all to no purpose. But at length McTeague's mule put his nose in the air and blew once or twice through his nostrils.

"Smells it, the son of a gun!" exclaimed Cribbens. The dentist let the animal have his head, and in a few minutes he had brought them to the bed of a tiny cañon where a thin stream of brackish water filtered over a ledge of rocks.

"We'll camp here," observed Cribbens, "but we can't turn the horses loose. We'll have to picket 'em with the lariats. I saw some loco-weed back here a piece, and if they get to eating that, they'll sure go plum crazy. The burro won't eat it, but I wouldn't trust the others."

A new life began for McTeague. After breakfast the "pardners" separated, going in opposite directions along the slope of the range, examining rocks, picking and chipping at ledges and bowlders, looking for signs, prospecting. McTeague went up into the little cañons where the streams had cut through the bed rock, searching for veins of quartz, breaking out this quartz when he had found it, pulverizing and panning it. Cribbens hunted for "contacts," closely examining country rocks and out-crops, continually on the lookout for spots where sedimentary and igneous rock came together.

One day, after a week of prospecting, they met unexpectedly on the slope of an arroyo. It was late in the afternoon. "Hello, pardner," exclaimed Cribbens as he came down to where McTeague was bending over his pan. "What luck?"

The dentist emptied his pan and straightened up. "Nothing, nothing. You struck anything?"

"Not a trace. Guess we might as well be moving towards camp." They returned together, Cribbens telling the dentist of a group of antelope he had seen.

"We might lay off to-morrow, an' see if we can plug a couple of them fellers. Antelope steak would go pretty well after beans an' bacon an' coffee week in an' week out."

McTeague was answering, when Cribbens interrupted him with an exclamation of profound disgust. "I thought we were the first to prospect along in here, an' now look at that. Don't it make you sick?"

He pointed out evidences of an abandoned prospector's camp just before them—charred ashes, empty tin cans, one or two gold-miner's pans, and a broken pick. "Don't that make you sick?" muttered Cribbens, sucking his mustache furiously. "To think of us mushheads going over ground that's been covered already! Say, pardner, we'll dig out of here to-morrow. I've been thinking, anyhow, we'd better move to the south; that water of ours is pretty low."

"Yes, yes, I guess so," assented the dentist. "There ain't any gold here."

"Yes, there is," protested Cribbens doggedly; "there's gold all through these hills, if we could only strike it. I tell you what, pardner, I got a place in mind where I'll bet no one ain't prospected—least not very many. There don't very many care to try an' get to it. It's over on the other side of Death Valley. It's called Gold Mountain, an' there's only one mine been located there, an' it's paying like a nitrate bed. There ain't many people in that country, because it's all hell to get into. First place, you got to cross Death Valley and strike the Armagosa Range fur off to the south. Well, no one ain't stuck on crossing the Valley, not if they can help it. But we could work down the Panamint some hundred or so miles, maybe two hundred, an' fetch around by the Armagosa River, way to the south'erd. We could prospect on the way. But I guess the Armagosa'd be dried up at this season. Anyhow," he concluded, " we'll move camp to the south to-morrow. We got to get new feed an' water for the horses. We'll see if we can knock over a couple of antelope to-morrow, and then we'll scoot."

"I ain't got a gun," said the dentist; "not even a revolver. I——"

"Wait a second," said Cribbens, pausing in his scramble down the side of one of the smaller gulches. "Here's some slate here; I ain't seen no slate around here yet. Let's see where it goes to."

McTeague followed him along the side of the gulch. Cribbens went on ahead, muttering to himself from time to time:

"Runs right along here, even enough, and here's water too. Didn't know this stream was here; pretty near dry, though. Here's the slate again. See where it runs, pardner?"

"Look at it up there ahead," said McTeague. "It runs right up over the back of this hill."

"That's right," assented Cribbens. "Hi!" he shouted suddenly, "here's a 'contact,' and here it is again, and there, and yonder. Oh, look at it, will you? That's grano-diorite on slate. Couldn't want it any more distinct than that. God! if we could only find the quartz between the two now."

"Well, there it is," exclaimed McTeague. "Look on ahead there; ain't that quartz?"

"You're shouting right out loud," vociferated Cribbens, looking where McTeague was pointing. His face went suddenly pale. He turned to the dentist, his eyes wide.

"By God, pardner," he exclaimed, breathlessly, "By God—" he broke off abruptly.

"That's what you been looking for, ain't it?" asked the dentist.

"Looking for! Looking for!" Cribbens checked himself. "That's slate all right, and that's grano-diorite, I know"—he bent down and examined the rock—"and here's the quartz between 'em; there can't be no mistake about that. Gi' me that hammer," he cried, excitedly. "Come on, git to work. Jab into the quartz with your pick; git out some chunks of it." Cribbens went down on his hands and knees, attacking the quartz vein furiously. The dentist followed his example, swinging his pick with enormous force, splintering the rocks at every stroke. Cribbens was talking to himself in his excitement.

"Got you this time, you son of a gun! By God! I guess we got you this time, at last. Looks like it, anyhow. Get a move on, pardner. There ain't anybody 'round, is there? Hey?" Without looking, he drew his revolver and threw it to the dentist. "Take the gun an' look around, pardner. If you see any son of a gun *anywhere*, *plug* him. This yere's *our* claim. I guess we got it *this* tide, pardner. Come on." He gathered up the chunks of quartz he had broken out, and put them in his hat and started towards their camp. The two went along with great strides, hurrying as fast as they could over the uneven ground.

"I don' know," exclaimed Cribbens, breathlessly, "I don' want to say too much. Maybe we're fooled. Lord, that damn camp's a long ways off. Oh, I ain't goin' to fool along this way. Come on, pardner." He broke into a run. McTeague followed at a lumbering gallop. Over the scorched, parched ground, stumbling and tripping over sage-brush and sharp-pointed rocks, under the palpitating heat of the desert sun, they ran and scrambled, carrying the quartz lumps in their hats.

"See any '*color*' in it, pardner?" gasped Cribbens. "I can't, can you? 'Twouldn't be visible nohow, I guess. Hurry up. Lord, we ain't ever going to get to that camp."

Finally they arrived. Cribbens dumped the quartz fragments into a pan.

"You pestle her, pardner, an' I'll fix the scales." McTeague ground the lumps to fine dust in the iron mortar while Cribbens set up the tiny scales and got out the "spoons" from their outfit.

"That's fine enough," Cribbens exclaimed, impatiently. "Now we'll spoon her. Gi' me the water."

Cribbens scooped up a spoonful of the fine white powder and began to spoon it carefully. The two were on their hands and knees upon the ground, their heads close together, still panting with excitement and the exertion of their run.

"Can't do it," exclaimed Cribbens, sitting back on his heels, "hand shakes so. *You* take it, pardner. Careful, now."

McTeague took the horn spoon and began rocking it gently in his huge fingers, sluicing the water over the edge a little at a time, each movement washing away a little more of the powdered quartz. The two watched it with the intensest eagerness.

"Don't see it yet; don't see it yet," whispered Cribbens,

chewing his mustache. "*Leetle* faster, pardner. That's the ticket. Careful, steady, now; leetle more, leetle more. Don't see color yet, do you?"

The quartz sediment dwindled by degrees as McTeague spooned it steadily. Then at last a thin streak of a foreign substance began to show just along the edge. It was yellow.

Neither spoke. Cribbens dug his nails into the sand, and ground his mustache between his teeth. The yellow streak broadened as the quartz sediment washed away. Cribbens whispered:

"We got it, pardner. That's gold."

McTeague washed the last of the white quartz dust away, and let the water trickle after it. A pinch of gold, fine as flour, was left in the bottom of the spoon.

"There you are," he said. The two looked at each other. Then Cribbens rose into the air with a great leap and a yell that could have been heard for half a mile.

"Yee-e-ow! We *got* it, we struck it. Pardner, we got it. Out of sight. We're millionaires." He snatched up his revolver and fired it with inconceivable rapidity. "*Put* it there, old man," he shouted, gripping McTeague's palm.

"That's gold, all right," muttered McTeague, studying the contents of the spoon.

"You bet your great-grandma's Cochin-China Chessy cat it's gold," shouted Cribbens. "Here, now, we got a lot to do. We got to stake her out an' put up the location notice. We'll take our full acreage, you bet. You—we haven't weighed this yet. Where's the scales?" He weighed the pinch of gold with shaking hands. "Two grains," he cried. "That'll run five dollars to the ton. Rich, it's rich; it's the richest kind of pay, pardner. We're millionaires. Why don't you say something? Why don't you get excited? Why don't you run around an' *do* something?"

"Huh!" said McTeague, rolling his eyes. "Huh! *I* know, I know, we've struck it pretty rich."

"Come on," exclaimed Cribbens, jumping up again. "We'll stake her out an' put up the location notice. Lord, suppose anyone should have come on her while we've been away." He reloaded his revolver deliberately. "We'll drop *him* all right, if there's anyone fooling round there; I'll tell you those right now. Bring the rifle, pardner, an' if you see anyone, *plug* him, an' ask him what he wants afterward."

They hurried back to where they had made their discovery.

"To think," exclaimed Cribbens, as he drove the first stake, "to think those other mushheads had their camp within gunshot of her and never located her. Guess they didn't know the meaning of a 'contact.' Oh, I knew I was solid on 'contacts.' "

They staked out their claim, and Cribbens put up the notice of location. It was dark before they were through. Cribbens broke off some more chunks of quartz in the vein.

"I'll spoon this too, just for the fun of it, when I get home," he explained, as they tramped back to the camp.

"Well," said the dentist, " we got the laugh on those cowboys."

"Have we?" shouted Cribbens. "*Have* we? Just wait and see the rush for this place when we tell 'em about it down in Keeler. Say, what'll we call her?"

"I don' know, I don' know."

"We might call her the 'Last Chance.' 'Twas our last chance, wasn't it? We'd 'a' gone antelope shooting tomorrow, and the next day we'd 'a'—say, what you stopping for?" he added, interrupting himself. "What's up?"

The dentist had paused abruptly on the crest of a cañon. Cribbens, looking back, saw him standing motionless in his tracks.

"What's up?" asked Cribbens a second time.

McTeague slowly turned his head and looked over one shoulder, then over the other. Suddenly he wheeled sharply about, cocking the Winchester and tossing it to his shoulder.

Cribbens ran back to his side, whipping out his revolver.

"What is it?" he cried. "See anybody?" He peered on ahead through the gathering twilight.

"No, no."

"Hear anything?"

"No, didn't hear anything."

"What is it then? What's up?"

"I don' know, I don' know," muttered the dentist, lowering the rifle. "There was something."

"What?"

"Something—didn't you notice?"

"Notice what?"

"I don' know. Something—something or other."

"Who? What? Notice what? What did you see?"

The dentist let down the hammer of the rifle.

"I guess it wasn't anything," he said rather foolishly.

"What d'you think you saw—anybody on the claim?"

"I didn't see anything. I didn't hear anything either. I had an idea, that's all; came all of a sudden, like that. Something, I don' know what."

"I guess you just imagined something. There ain't anybody within twenty miles of us, I guess."

"Yes, I guess so, just imagined it, that's the word."

Half an hour later they had the fire going. McTeague was frying strips of bacon over the coals, and Cribbens was still chattering and exclaiming over their great strike. All at once McTeague put down the frying-pan.

"What's that?" he growled.

"Hey? What's what?" exclaimed Cribbens, getting up.

"Didn't you notice something?"

"Where?"

"Off there." The dentist made a vague gesture toward the eastern horizon. "Didn't you hear something—I mean see something—I mean——"

"What's the matter with you, pardner?"

"Nothing. I guess I just imagined it."

But it was not imagination. Until midnight the partners lay broad awake, rolled in their blankets under the open sky, talking and discussing and making plans. At last Cribbens rolled over on his side and slept. The dentist could not sleep.

What! It was warning him again, that strange sixth sense, that obscure brute instinct. It was aroused again and clamoring to be obeyed. Here, in these desolate barren hills, twenty miles from the nearest human being, it stirred and woke and rowelled him to be moving on. It had goaded him to flight from the Big Dipper mine, and he had obeyed. But now it was different; now he had suddenly become rich; he had lighted on a treasure—a treasure far more valuable than the Big Dipper mine itself. How was he to leave that? He could not move on now. He turned about in his blankets. No, he would not move on. Perhaps it was his fancy, after all. He

saw nothing, heard nothing. The emptiness of primeval desolation stretched from him leagues and leagues upon either
hand. The gigantic silence of the night lay close over everything, like a muffling Titanic palm. Of what was he suspicious? In that treeless waste an object could be seen at half a
day's journey distant. In that vast silence the click of a pebble
was as audible as a pistol-shot. And yet there was nothing,
nothing.

The dentist settled himself in his blankets and tried to sleep.
In five minutes he was sitting up, staring into the blue-gray
shimmer of the moonlight, straining his ears, watching and
listening intently. Nothing was in sight. The browned and
broken flanks of the Panamint hills lay quiet and familiar under the moon. The burro moved its head with a clinking of
its bell; and McTeague's mule, dozing on three legs, changed
its weight to another foot, with a long breath. Everything fell
silent again.

"What is it?" muttered the dentist. "If I could only see
something, hear something."

He threw off the blankets, and, rising, climbed to the summit of the nearest hill and looked back in the direction in
which he and Cribbens had travelled a fortnight before. For
half an hour he waited, watching and listening in vain. But as
he returned to camp, and prepared to roll his blankets about
him, the strange impulse rose in him again abruptly, never so
strong, never so insistent. It seemed as though he were bitted
and ridden; as if some unseen hand were turning him toward
the east; some unseen heel spurring him to precipitate and
instant flight.

Flight from what? "No," he muttered under his breath.
"Go now and leave the claim, and leave a fortune! What a
fool I'd be, when I can't see anything or hear anything. To
leave a fortune! No, I won't. No, by God!" He drew Cribbens's Winchester toward him and slipped a cartridge into the
magazine.

"No," he growled. "Whatever happens, I'm going to stay.
If anybody comes—" He depressed the lever of the rifle, and
sent the cartridge clashing into the breech.

"I ain't going to sleep," he muttered under his mustache.
"I can't sleep; I'll watch." He rose a second time, clambered

to the nearest hilltop and sat down, drawing the blanket around him, and laying the Winchester across his knees. The hours passed. The dentist sat on the hilltop a motionless, crouching figure, inky black against the pale blur of the sky. By and by the edge of the eastern horizon began to grow blacker and more distinct in outline. The dawn was coming. Once more McTeague felt the mysterious intuition of approaching danger; an unseen hand seemed reining his head eastward; a spur was in his flanks that seemed to urge him to hurry, hurry, hurry. The influence grew stronger with every moment. The dentist set his great jaws together and held his ground.

"No," he growled between his set teeth. "No, I'll stay." He made a long circuit around the camp, even going as far as the first stake of the new claim, his Winchester cocked, his ears pricked, his eyes alert. There was nothing; yet as plainly as though it were shouted at the very nape of his neck he felt an enemy. It was not fear. McTeague was not afraid.

"If I could only *see* something—somebody," he muttered, as he held the cocked rifle ready, "I—I'd show him."

He returned to camp. Cribbens was snoring. The burro had come down to the stream for its morning drink. The mule was awake and browsing. McTeague stood irresolutely by the cold ashes of the camp-fire, looking from side to side with all the suspicion and wariness of a tracked stag. Stronger and stronger grew the strange impulse. It seemed to him that on the next instant he *must* perforce wheel sharply eastward and rush away headlong in a clumsy, lumbering gallop. He fought against it with all the ferocious obstinacy of his simple brute nature.

"Go, and leave the mine? Go and leave a million dollars? No, *no*, I won't go. No, I'll stay. Ah," he exclaimed, under his breath, with a shake of his huge head, like an exasperated and harassed brute, "ah, show yourself, will you?" He brought the rifle to his shoulder and covered point after point along the range of hills to the west. "Come on, show yourself. Come on a little, all of you. I ain't afraid of you; but don't skulk this way. You ain't going to drive me away from my mine. I'm going to *stay*."

An hour passed. Then two. The stars winked out, and the

dawn whitened. The air became warmer. The whole east, clean of clouds, flamed opalescent from horizon to zenith, crimson at the base, where the earth blackened against it; at the top fading from pink to pale yellow, to green, to light blue, to the turquoise iridescence of the desert sky. The long, thin shadows of the early hours drew backward like receding serpents, then suddenly the sun looked over the shoulder of the world, and it was day.

At that moment McTeague was already eight miles away from the camp, going steadily eastward. He was descending the lowest spurs of the Panamint hills, following an old and faint cattle trail. Before him he drove his mule, laden with blankets, provisions for six days, Cribbens's rifle, and a canteen full of water. Securely bound to the pommel of the saddle was the canvas sack with its precious five thousand dollars, all in twenty-dollar gold pieces. But strange enough in that horrid waste of sand and sage was the object that McTeague himself persistently carried—the canary in its cage, about which he had carefully wrapped a couple of old flour-bags.

At about five o'clock that morning McTeague had crossed several trails which seemed to be converging, and, guessing that they led to a water hole, had followed one of them and had brought up at a sort of small sun-dried sink which nevertheless contained a little water at the bottom. He had watered the mule here, refilled the canteen, and drank deep himself. He had also dampened the old flour-sacks around the bird cage to protect the little canary as far as possible from the heat that he knew would increase now with every hour. He had made ready to go forward again, but had paused irresolute again, hesitating for the last time.

"I'm a fool," he growled, scowling back at the range behind him. "I'm a fool. What's the matter with me? I'm just walking right away from a million dollars. I know it's there. No, by God!" he exclaimed, savagely, "I ain't going to do it. I'm going back. I can't leave a mine like that." He had wheeled the mule about, and had started to return on his tracks, grinding his teeth fiercely, inclining his head forward as though butting against a wind that would beat him back. "Go on, go on," he cried, sometimes addressing the mule, sometimes himself. "Go on, go back, go back. I *will* go back." It was as though he were climbing a hill that grew steeper with every stride. The strange impelling instinct fought his advance yard by yard. By degrees the dentist's steps grew slower; he stopped, went forward again cautiously, almost feeling his way, like someone approaching a pit in the darkness. He stopped again, hesitating, gnashing his teeth, clinching his fists with blind fury. Suddenly he turned the mule about, and once more set his face to the eastward.

"I can't," he cried aloud to the desert; "I can't, I can't. It's stronger than I am. I *can't* go back. Hurry now, hurry, hurry, hurry."

He hastened on furtively, his head and shoulders bent. At times one could almost say he crouched as he pushed forward with long strides; now and then he even looked over his shoulder. Sweat rolled from him, he lost his hat, and the matted mane of thick yellow hair swept over his forehead and shaded his small, twinkling eyes. At times, with a vague, nearly automatic gesture, he reached his hand forward, the fingers prehensile, and directed towards the horizon, as if he would clutch it and draw it nearer; and at intervals he muttered, "Hurry, hurry, hurry on, hurry on." For now at last McTeague was afraid.

His plans were uncertain. He remembered what Cribbens had said about the Armagosa Mountains in the country on the other side of Death Valley. It was all hell to get into that country, Cribbens had said, and not many men went there, because of the terrible valley of alkali that barred the way, a horrible vast sink of white sand and salt below even the sea level, the dry bed, no doubt, of some prehistoric lake. But McTeague resolved to make a circuit of the valley, keeping to the south, until he should strike the Armagosa River. He would make a circuit of the valley and come up on the other side. He would get into that country around Gold Mountain in the Armagosa hills, barred off from the world by the leagues of the red-hot alkali of Death Valley. "They" would hardly reach him there. He would stay at Gold Mountain two or three months, and then work his way down into Mexico.

McTeague tramped steadily forward, still descending the lower irregularities of the Panamint Range. By nine o'clock the slope flattened out abruptly; the hills were behind him; before him, to the east, all was level. He had reached the region where even the sand and sage-brush begin to dwindle, giving place to white, powdered alkali. The trails were numerous, but old and faint; and they had been made by cattle, not by men. They led in all directions but one—north, south, and west; but not one, however faint, struck out towards the valley.

"If I keep along the edge of the hills where these trails are," muttered the dentist, "I ought to find water up in the arroyos from time to time."

At once he uttered an exclamation. The mule had begun to squeal and lash out with alternate hoofs, his eyes rolling, his ears flattened. He ran a few steps, halted, and squealed again. Then, suddenly wheeling at right angles, set off on a jog trot to the north, squealing and kicking from time to time. McTeague ran after him shouting and swearing, but for a long time the mule would not allow himself to be caught. He seemed more bewildered than frightened.

"He's eatun some of that loco-weed that Cribbens spoke about," panted McTeague. "Whoa, there; steady, you." At length the mule stopped of his own accord, and seemed to come to his senses again. McTeague came up and took the bridle rein, speaking to him and rubbing his nose.

"There, there, what's the matter with you?" The mule was docile again. McTeague washed his mouth and set forward once more.

The day was magnificent. From horizon to horizon was one vast span of blue, whitening as it dipped earthward. Miles upon miles to the east and southeast the desert unrolled itself, white, naked, inhospitable, palpitating and shimmering under the sun, unbroken by so much as a rock or cactus stump. In the distance it assumed all manner of faint colors, pink, purple, and pale orange. To the west rose the Panamint Range, sparsely sprinkled with gray sage-brush; here the earths and sands were yellow, ochre, and rich, deep red, the hollows and cañons picked out with intense blue shadows. It seemed strange that such barrenness could exhibit this radiance of color, but nothing could have been more beautiful than the deep red of the higher bluffs and ridges, seamed with purple shadows, standing sharply out against the pale-blue whiteness of the horizon.

By nine o'clock the sun stood high in the sky. The heat was intense; the atmosphere was thick and heavy with it. McTeague gasped for breath and wiped the beads of perspiration from his forehead, his cheeks, and his neck. Every inch and pore of his skin was tingling and pricking under the merciless lash of the sun's rays.

"If it gets much hotter," he muttered, with a long breath, "If it gets much hotter, I—I don' know—" he wagged his head and wiped the sweat from his eyelids, where it was running like tears.

The sun rose higher; hour by hour, as the dentist tramped steadily on, the heat increased. The baked dry sand crackled into innumerable tiny flakes under his feet. The twigs of the sage-brush snapped like brittle pipestems as he pushed through them. It grew hotter. At eleven the earth was like the surface of a furnace; the air, as McTeague breathed it in, was hot to his lips and the roof of his mouth. The sun was a disk of molten brass swimming in the burnt-out blue of the sky. McTeague stripped off his woollen shirt, and even unbuttoned his flannel undershirt, tying a handkerchief loosely about his neck.

"Lord!" he exclaimed. "I never knew it *could* get as hot as this."

The heat grew steadily fiercer; all distant objects were visibly shimmering and palpitating under it. At noon a mirage appeared on the hills to the northwest. McTeague halted the mule, and drank from the tepid water in the canteen, dampening the sack around the canary's cage. As soon as he ceased his tramp and the noise of his crunching, grinding footsteps died away, the silence, vast, illimitable, enfolded him like an immeasurable tide. From all that gigantic landscape, that colossal reach of baking sand, there arose not a single sound. Not a twig rattled, not an insect hummed, not a bird or beast invaded that huge solitude with call or cry. Everything as far as the eye could reach, to north, to south, to east, and west, lay inert, absolutely quiet and moveless under the remorseless scourge of the noon sun. The very shadows shrank away, hiding under sage-bushes, retreating to the farthest nooks and crevices in the cañons of the hills. All the world was one gigantic blinding glare, silent, motionless. "If it gets much hotter," murmured the dentist again, moving his head from side to side, "If it gets much hotter, I don' know what I'll do."

Steadily the heat increased. At three o'clock it was even more terrible than it had been at noon.

"Ain't it *ever* going to let up?" groaned the dentist, rolling his eyes at the sky of hot blue brass. Then, as he spoke, the stillness was abruptly stabbed through and through by a shrill sound that seemed to come from all sides at once. It ceased; then, as McTeague took another forward step, began again with the suddenness of a blow, shriller, nearer at hand, a hideous, prolonged note that brought both man and mule to an instant halt.

"I know what *that* is," exclaimed the dentist. His eyes searched the ground swiftly until he saw what he expected he should see—the round thick coil, the slowly waving clover-shaped head and erect whirring tail with its vibrant rattles.

For fully thirty seconds the man and snake remained looking into each other's eyes. Then the snake uncoiled and swiftly wound from sight amidst the sage-brush. McTeague drew breath again, and his eyes once more beheld the illimitable leagues of quivering sand and alkali.

"Good Lord! What a country!" he exclaimed. But his voice was trembling as he urged forward the mule once more.

Fiercer and fiercer grew the heat as the afternoon advanced. At four McTeague stopped again. He was dripping at every pore, but there was no relief in perspiration. The very touch of his clothes upon his body was unendurable. The mule's ears were drooping and his tongue lolled from his mouth. The cattle trails seemed to be drawing together toward a common point; perhaps a water hole was near by.

"I'll have to lay up, sure," muttered the dentist. "I ain't made to travel in such heat as this."

He drove the mule up into one of the larger cañons and halted in the shadow of a pile of red rock. After a long search he found water, a few quarts, warm and brackish, at the bottom of a hollow of sun-cracked mud; it was little more than enough to water the mule and refill his canteen. Here he camped, easing the mule of the saddle, and turning him loose to find what nourishment he might. A few hours later the sun set in a cloudless glory of red and gold, and the heat became by degrees less intolerable. McTeague cooked his supper, chiefly coffee and bacon, and watched the twilight come on, revelling in the delicious coolness of the evening. As he spread his blankets on the ground he resolved that hereafter he would travel only at night, laying up in the daytime in the shade of the cañons. He was exhausted with his terrible day's march. Never in his life had sleep seemed so sweet to him.

But suddenly he was broad awake, his jaded senses all alert.

"What was that?" he muttered. "I thought I heard something—saw something."

He rose to his feet, reaching for the Winchester. Desolation lay still around him. There was not a sound but his own breathing; on the face of the desert not a grain of sand was in motion. McTeague looked furtively and quickly from side to side, his teeth set, his eyes rolling. Once more the rowel was in his flanks, once more an unseen hand reined him toward the east. After all the miles of that dreadful day's flight he was no better off than when he started. If anything, he was worse, for never had that mysterious instinct in him been more insistent than now; never had the impulse toward precipitate flight been stronger; never had the spur bit deeper. Every nerve of his body cried aloud for rest; yet every instinct seemed aroused and alive, goading him to hurry on, to hurry on.

"What *is* it, then? What *is* it?" he cried, between his teeth. "Can't I ever get rid of you? Ain't I *ever* going to shake you off? Don' keep it up this way. Show yourselves. Let's have it out right away. Come on. I ain't afraid if you'll only come on; but don't skulk this way." Suddenly he cried aloud in a frenzy of exasperation, "Damn you, come on, will you? Come on and have it out." His rifle was at his shoulder, he was covering bush after bush, rock after rock, aiming at every denser shadow. All at once, and quite involuntarily, his forefinger crooked, and the rifle spoke and flamed. The cañons roared back the echo, tossing it out far over the desert in a rippling, widening wave of sound.

McTeague lowered the rifle hastily, with an exclamation of dismay.

"You fool," he said to himself, "you fool. You've done it now. They could hear that miles away. You've done it now."

He stood listening intently, the rifle smoking in his hands. The last echo died away. The smoke vanished, the vast silence closed upon the passing echoes of the rifle as the ocean closes upon a ship's wake. Nothing moved; yet McTeague bestirred himself sharply, rolling up his blankets, resaddling the mule, getting his outfit together again. From time to time he muttered:

"Hurry now; hurry on. You fool, you've done it now. They could hear that miles away. Hurry now. They ain't far off now."

As he depressed the lever of the rifle to reload it, he found that the magazine was empty. He clapped his hands to his sides, feeling rapidly first in one pocket, then in another. He had forgotten to take extra cartridges with him. McTeague swore under his breath as he flung the rifle away. Henceforth he must travel unarmed.

A little more water had gathered in the mud hole near which he had camped. He watered the mule for the last time and wet the sacks around the canary's cage. Then once more he set forward.

But there was a change in the direction of McTeague's flight. Hitherto he had held to the south, keeping upon the very edge of the hills; now he turned sharply at right angles. The slope fell away beneath his hurrying feet; the sage-brush dwindled, and at length ceased; the sand gave place to a fine powder, white as snow; and an hour after he had fired the rifle his mule's hoofs were crisping and cracking the sun-baked flakes of alkali on the surface of Death Valley.

Tracked and harried, as he felt himself to be, from one camping place to another, McTeague had suddenly resolved to make one last effort to rid himself of the enemy that seemed to hang upon his heels. He would strike straight out into that horrible wilderness where even the beasts were afraid. He would cross Death Valley at once and put its arid wastes between him and his pursuer.

"You don't dare follow me now," he muttered, as he hurried on. "Let's see you come out *here* after me."

He hurried on swiftly, urging the mule to a rapid racking

walk. Towards four o'clock the sky in front of him began to
flush pink and golden. McTeague halted and breakfasted,
pushing on again immediately afterward. The dawn flamed
and glowed like a brazier, and the sun rose a vast red-hot coal
floating in fire. An hour passed, then another, and another. It
was about nine o'clock. Once more the dentist paused, and
stood panting and blowing, his arms dangling, his eyes
screwed up and blinking as he looked about him.

Far behind him the Panamint hills were already but blue
hummocks on the horizon. Before him and upon either side,
to the north and to the east and to the south, stretched primordial desolation. League upon league the infinite reaches
of dazzling white alkali laid themselves out like an immeasurable scroll unrolled from horizon to horizon; not a bush, not
a twig relieved that horrible monotony. Even the sand of the
desert would have been a welcome sight; a single clump of
sage-brush would have fascinated the eye; but this was worse
than the desert. It was abominable, this hideous sink of alkali,
this bed of some primeval lake lying so far below the level of
the ocean. The great mountains of Placer County had been
merely indifferent to man; but this awful sink of alkali was
openly and unreservedly iniquitous and malignant.

McTeague had told himself that the heat upon the lower
slopes of the Panamint had been dreadful; here in Death Valley it became a thing of terror. There was no longer any
shadow but his own. He was scorched and parched from
head to heel. It seemed to him that the smart of his tortured
body could not have been keener if he had been flayed.

"If it gets much hotter," he muttered, wringing the sweat
from his thick fell of hair and mustache, "If it gets much hotter, I don' know what I'll do." He was thirsty, and drank a
little from his canteen. "I ain't got any too much water," he
murmured, shaking the canteen. "I got to get out of this place
in a hurry, sure."

By eleven o'clock the heat had increased to such an extent
that McTeague could feel the burning of the ground come
pringling and stinging through the soles of his boots. Every
step he took threw up clouds of impalpable alkali dust, salty
and choking, so that he strangled and coughed and sneezed
with it.

"*Lord!* what a country!" exclaimed the dentist.

An hour later, the mule stopped and lay down, his jaws wide open, his ears dangling. McTeague washed his mouth with a handful of water and for a second time since sunrise wetted the flour-sacks around the bird cage. The air was quivering and palpitating like that in the stoke-hold of a steamship. The sun, small and contracted, swam molten overhead.

"I can't stand it," said McTeague at length. "I'll have to stop and make some kinda shade."

The mule was crouched upon the ground, panting rapidly, with half-closed eyes. The dentist removed the saddle, and unrolling his blanket, propped it up as best he could between him and the sun. As he stooped down to crawl beneath it, his palm touched the ground. He snatched it away with a cry of pain. The surface alkali was oven-hot; he was obliged to scoop out a trench in it before he dared to lie down.

By degrees the dentist began to doze. He had had little or no sleep the night before, and the hurry of his flight under the blazing sun had exhausted him. But his rest was broken; between waking and sleeping, all manner of troublous images galloped through his brain. He thought he was back in the Panamint hills again with Cribbens. They had just discovered the mine and were returning toward camp. McTeague saw himself as another man, striding along over the sand and sage-brush. At once he saw himself stop and wheel sharply about, peering back suspiciously. There was something behind him; something was following him. He looked, as it were, over the shoulder of this other McTeague, and saw down there, in the half light of the cañon, something dark crawling upon the ground, an indistinct gray figure, man or brute, he did not know. Then he saw another, and another; then another. A score of black, crawling objects were following him, crawling from bush to bush, converging upon him. "*They*" were after him, were closing in upon him, were within touch of his hand, were at his feet— *were at his throat*.

McTeague jumped up with a shout, oversetting the blanket. There was nothing in sight. For miles around, the alkali was empty, solitary, quivering and shimmering under the pelting fire of the afternoon's sun.

But once more the spur bit into his body, goading him on. There was to be no rest, no going back, no pause, no stop. Hurry, hurry, hurry on. The brute that in him slept so close to the surface was alive and alert, and tugging to be gone. There was no resisting that instinct. The brute felt an enemy, scented the trackers, clamored and struggled and fought, and would not be gainsaid.

"I *can't* go on," groaned McTeague, his eyes sweeping the horizon behind him, "I'm beat out. I'm dog tired. I ain't slept any for two nights." But for all that he roused himself again, saddled the mule, scarcely less exhausted than himself, and pushed on once more over the scorching alkali and under the blazing sun.

From that time on the fear never left him, the spur never ceased to bite, the instinct that goaded him to flight never was dumb; hurry or halt, it was all the same. On he went, straight on, chasing the receding horizon; flagellated with heat; tortured with thirst; crouching over; looking furtively behind, and at times reaching his hand forward, the fingers prehensile, grasping, as it were, toward the horizon, that always fled before him.

The sun set upon the third day of McTeague's flight, night came on, the stars burned slowly into the cool dark purple of the sky. The gigantic sink of white alkali glowed like snow. McTeague, now far into the desert, held steadily on, swinging forward with great strides. His enormous strength held him doggedly to his work. Sullenly, with his huge jaws gripping stolidly together, he pushed on. At midnight he stopped.

"Now," he growled, with a certain desperate defiance, as though he expected to be heard, "Now, I'm going to lay up and get some sleep. You can come or not."

He cleared away the hot surface alkali, spread out his blanket, and slept until the next day's heat aroused him. His water was so low that he dared not make coffee now, and so breakfasted without it. Until ten o'clock he tramped forward, then camped again in the shade of one of the rare rock ledges, and "lay up" during the heat of the day. By five o'clock he was once more on the march.

He travelled on for the greater part of that night, stopping only once towards three in the morning to water the mule from the canteen. Again the red-hot day burned up over the horizon. Even at six o'clock it was hot.

"It's going to be worse than ever to-day," he groaned. "I wish I could find another rock to camp by. Ain't I *ever* going to get out of this place?"

There was no change in the character of the desert. Always the same measureless leagues of white-hot alkali stretched away toward the horizon on every hand. Here and there the flat, dazzling surface of the desert broke and raised into long low mounds, from the summit of which McTeague could look for miles and miles over its horrible desolation. No shade was in sight. Not a rock, not a stone broke the monotony of the ground. Again and again he ascended the low unevennesses, looking and searching for a camping place, shading his eyes from the glitter of sand and sky.

He tramped forward a little farther, then paused at length in a hollow between two breaks, resolving to make camp there.

Suddenly there was a shout.

"Hands up. By damn, I got the drop on you!"

McTeague looked up.

It was Marcus.

XXII

WITHIN A MONTH after his departure from San Francisco, Marcus had "gone in on a cattle ranch" in the Panamint Valley with an Englishman, an acquaintance of Mr. Sieppe's. His headquarters were at a place called Modoc, at the lower extremity of the valley, about fifty miles by trail to the south of Keeler.

His life was the life of a cowboy. He realized his former vision of himself, booted, sombreroed, and revolvered, passing his days in the saddle and the better part of his nights around the poker tables in Modoc's one saloon. To his intense satisfaction he even involved himself in a gun fight that arose over a disputed brand, with the result that two fingers of his left hand were shot away.

News from the outside world filtered slowly into the Panamint Valley, and the telegraph had never been built beyond Keeler. At intervals one of the local papers of Independence, the nearest large town, found its way into the cattle camps on the ranges, and occasionally one of the Sunday editions of a Sacramento journal, weeks old, was passed from hand to hand. Marcus ceased to hear from the Sieppes. As for San Francisco, it was as far from him as was London or Vienna.

One day, a fortnight after McTeague's flight from San Francisco, Marcus rode into Modoc, to find a group of men gathered about a notice affixed to the outside of the Wells-Fargo office. It was an offer of reward for the arrest and apprehension of a murderer. The crime had been committed in San Francisco, but the man wanted had been traced as far as the western portion of Inyo County, and was believed at that time to be in hiding in either the Pinto or Panamint hills, in the vicinity of Keeler.

Marcus reached Keeler on the afternoon of that same day. Half a mile from the town his pony fell and died from exhaustion. Marcus did not stop even to remove the saddle. He arrived in the barroom of the hotel in Keeler just after the posse had been made up. The sheriff, who had come down from Independence that morning, at first refused his offer of assistance. He had enough men already—too many, in fact.

The country travelled through would be hard, and it would be difficult to find water for so many men and horses.

"But none of you fellers have ever seen um," vociferated Marcus, quivering with excitement and wrath. "I know um well. I could pick um out in a million. I can identify um, and you fellers can't. And I knew—I knew—good *God*! I knew that girl—his wife—in Frisco. She's a cousin of mine, she is—she was—I thought once of— This thing's a personal matter of mine—an' that money he got away with, that five thousand, belongs to me by rights. Oh, never mind, I'm going along. Do you hear?" he shouted, his fists raised, "I'm going along, I tell you. There ain't a man of you big enough to stop me. Let's see you try and stop me going. Let's see you once, any two of you." He filled the barroom with his clamor.

"Lord love you, come along, then," said the sheriff.

The posse rode out of Keeler that same night. The keeper of the general merchandise store, from whom Marcus had borrowed a second pony, had informed them that Cribbens and his partner, whose description tallied exactly with that given in the notice of reward, had outfitted at his place with a view to prospecting in the Panamint hills. The posse trailed them at once to their first camp at the head of the valley. It was an easy matter. It was only necessary to inquire of the cowboys and range riders of the valley if they had seen and noted the passage of two men, one of whom carried a bird cage.

Beyond this first camp the trail was lost, and a week was wasted in a bootless search around the mine at Gold Gulch, whither it seemed probable the partners had gone. Then a travelling peddler, who included Gold Gulch in his route, brought in the news of a wonderful strike of gold-bearing quartz some ten miles to the south on the western slope of the range. Two men from Keeler had made a strike, the peddler had said, and added the curious detail that one of the men had a canary bird in a cage with him.

The posse made Cribbens's camp three days after the unaccountable disappearance of his partner. Their man was gone, but the narrow hoof prints of a mule, mixed with those of huge hob-nailed boots, could be plainly followed in the sand. Here they picked up the trail and held to it steadily till the point was reached where, instead of tending southward it swerved abruptly to the east. The men could hardly believe their eyes.

"It ain't reason," exclaimed the sheriff. "What in thunder is he up to? This beats me. Cutting out into Death Valley at this time of year."

"He's heading for Gold Mountain over in the Armagosa, sure."

The men decided that this conjecture was true. It was the only inhabited locality in that direction. A discussion began as to the further movements of the posse.

"I don't figure on going into that alkali sink with no eight men and horses," declared the sheriff. "One man can't carry enough water to take him and his mount across, let alone *eight*. No, sir. Four couldn't do it. No, *three* couldn't. We've got to make a circuit round the valley and come up on the other side and head him off at Gold Mountain. That's what we got to do, and ride like hell to do it, too."

But Marcus protested with all the strength of his lungs against abandoning the trail now that they had found it. He argued that they were but a day and a half behind their man now. There was no possibility of their missing the trail—as distinct in the white alkali as in snow. They could make a dash into the valley, secure their man, and return long before their water failed them. He, for one, would not give up the pursuit, now that they were so close. In the haste of the departure from Keeler the sheriff had neglected to swear him in. He was under no orders. He would do as he pleased.

"Go on, then, you darn fool," answered the sheriff. "We'll cut on round the valley, for all that. It's a gamble he'll be at Gold Mountain before you're half way across. But if you catch him, here"—he tossed Marcus a pair of handcuffs— "put 'em on him and bring him back to Keeler."

Two days after he had left the posse, and when he was already far out in the desert, Marcus's horse gave out. In the fury of his impatience he had spurred mercilessly forward on the trail, and on the morning of the third day found that his horse was unable to move. The joints of his legs seemed locked rigidly. He would go his own length, stumbling and interfering, then collapse helplessly upon the ground with a pitiful groan. He was used up.

Marcus believed himself to be close upon McTeague now. The ashes at his last camp had still been smoldering. Marcus took what supplies of food and water he could carry, and hurried on. But McTeague was farther ahead than he had guessed, and by evening of his third day upon the desert Marcus, raging with thirst, had drunk his last mouthful of water and had flung away the empty canteen.

"If he ain't got water with um," he said to himself as he pushed on, "If he ain't got water with um, by damn! I'll be in a bad way. I will, for a fact."

At Marcus's shout McTeague looked up and around him. For the instant he saw no one. The white glare of alkali was still unbroken. Then his swiftly rolling eyes lighted upon a head and shoulder that protruded above the low crest of the break directly in front of him. A man was there, lying at full length upon the ground, covering him with a revolver. For a few seconds McTeague looked at the man stupidly, bewildered, confused, as yet without definite thought. Then he noticed that the man was singularly like Marcus Schouler. It *was* Marcus Schouler. How in the world did Marcus Schouler come to be in that desert? What did he mean by pointing a pistol at him that way? He'd best look out or the pistol would go off. Then his thoughts readjusted themselves with a swiftness born of a vivid sense of danger. Here was the enemy at last, the tracker he had felt upon his footsteps. Now at length he had "come on" and shown himself, after all those days of skulking. McTeague was glad of it. He'd show him now. They two would have it out right then and there. His rifle! He had thrown it away long since. He was helpless. Marcus had ordered him to put up his hands. If he did not, Marcus would kill him. He had the drop on him. McTeague stared, scowling fiercely at the levelled pistol. He did not move.

"Hands up!" shouted Marcus a second time. "I'll give you three to do it in. One, two——"

Instinctively McTeague put his hands above his head.

Marcus rose and came towards him over the break.

"Keep 'em up," he cried. "If you move 'em once I'll kill you, sure."

He came up to McTeague and searched him, going through his pockets; but McTeague had no revolver; not even a hunting knife.

"What did you do with that money, with that five thousand dollars?"

"It's on the mule," answered McTeague, sullenly.

Marcus grunted, and cast a glance at the mule, who was standing some distance away, snorting nervously, and from time to time flattening his long ears.

"Is that it there on the horn of the saddle, there in that canvas sack?" Marcus demanded.

"Yes, that's it."

A gleam of satisfaction came into Marcus's eyes, and under his breath he muttered:

"Got it at last."

He was singularly puzzled to know what next to do. He had got McTeague. There he stood at length, with his big hands over his head, scowling at him sullenly. Marcus had caught his enemy, had run down the man for whom every officer in the State had been looking. What should he do with him now? He couldn't keep him standing there forever with his hands over his head.

"Got any water?" he demanded.

"There's a canteen of water on the mule."

Marcus moved toward the mule and made as if to reach the bridle-rein. The mule squealed, threw up his head, and galloped to a little distance, rolling his eyes and flattening his ears.

Marcus swore wrathfully.

"He acted that way once before," explained McTeague, his hands still in the air. "He ate some loco-weed back in the hills before I started."

For a moment Marcus hesitated. While he was catching the mule McTeague might get away. But where to, in heaven's name? A rat could not hide on the surface of that glistening alkali, and besides, all McTeague's store of provisions and his priceless supply of water were on the mule. Marcus ran after the mule, revolver in hand, shouting and cursing. But the

mule would not be caught. He acted as if possessed, squealing, lashing out, and galloping in wide circles, his head high
in the air.

"Come on," shouted Marcus, furious, turning back to
McTeague. "Come on, help me catch him. We got to catch
him. All the water we got is on the saddle."

McTeague came up.

"He's eatun some loco-weed," he repeated. "He went kinda
crazy once before."

"If he should take it into his head to bolt and keep on
running——"

Marcus did not finish. A sudden great fear seemed to widen
around and inclose the two men. Once their water gone, the
end would not be long.

"We can catch him all right," said the dentist. "I caught
him once before."

"Oh, I guess we can catch him," answered Marcus, reassuringly.

Already the sense of enmity between the two had weakened
in the face of a common peril. Marcus let down the hammer
of his revolver and slid it back into the holster.

The mule was trotting on ahead, snorting and throwing up
great clouds of alkali dust. At every step the canvas sack jingled, and McTeague's bird cage, still wrapped in the flour-
bags, bumped against the saddle-pads. By and by the mule
stopped, blowing out his nostrils excitedly.

"He's clean crazy," fumed Marcus, panting and swearing.

"We ought to come up on him quiet," observed McTeague.

"I'll try and sneak up," said Marcus; "two of us would scare
him again. You stay here."

Marcus went forward a step at a time. He was almost
within arm's length of the bridle when the mule shied from
him abruptly and galloped away.

Marcus danced with rage, shaking his fists, and swearing
horribly. Some hundred yards away the mule paused and began blowing and snuffing in the alkali as though in search of
feed. Then, for no reason, he shied again, and started off on
a jog trot toward the east.

"We've *got* to follow him," exclaimed Marcus as McTeague
came up. "There's no water within seventy miles of here."

Then began an interminable pursuit. Mile after mile, under
the terrible heat of the desert sun, the two men followed the
mule, racked with a thirst that grew fiercer every hour. A
dozen times they could almost touch the canteen of water,
and as often the distraught animal shied away and fled before
them. At length Marcus cried:

"It's no use, we can't catch him, and we're killing ourselves
with thirst. We got to take our chances." He drew his revolver
from its holster, cocked it, and crept forward.

"Steady, now," said McTeague; "it won' do to shoot
through the canteen."

Within twenty yards Marcus paused, made a rest of his left
forearm and fired.

"You *got* him," cried McTeague. "No, he's up again. Shoot
him again. He's going to bolt."

Marcus ran on, firing as he ran. The mule, one foreleg trailing, scrambled along, squealing and snorting. Marcus fired his
last shot. The mule pitched forward upon his head, then, rolling sideways, fell upon the canteen, bursting it open and spilling its entire contents into the sand.

Marcus and McTeague ran up, and Marcus snatched the
battered canteen from under the reeking, bloody hide. There
was no water left. Marcus flung the canteen from him and
stood up, facing McTeague. There was a pause.

"We're dead men," said Marcus.

McTeague looked from him out over the desert. Chaotic
desolation stretched from them on either hand, flaming and
glaring with the afternoon heat. There was the brazen sky and
the leagues upon leagues of alkali, leper white. There was
nothing more. They were in the heart of Death Valley.

"Not a drop of water," muttered McTeague; "not a drop of
water."

"We can drink the mule's blood," said Marcus. "It's been
done before. But—but—" he looked down at the quivering,
gory body—"but I ain't thirsty enough for that yet."

"Where's the nearest water?"

"Well, it's about a hundred miles or more back of us in the
Panamint hills," returned Marcus, doggedly. "We'd be crazy
long before we reached it. I tell you, we're done for, by damn,
we're *done* for. We ain't ever going to get outa here."

"Done for?" murmured the other, looking about stupidly. "Done for, that's the word. Done for? Yes, I guess we're done for."

"What are we going to do *now*?" exclaimed Marcus, sharply, after a while.

"Well, let's—let's be moving along—somewhere."

"*Where*, I'd like to know? What's the good of moving on?"

"What's the good of stopping here?"

There was a silence.

"Lord, it's hot," said the dentist, finally, wiping his forehead with the back of his hand. Marcus ground his teeth.

"Done for," he muttered; "done for."

"I never *was* so thirsty," continued McTeague. "I'm that dry I can hear my tongue rubbing against the roof of my mouth."

"Well, we can't stop here," said Marcus, finally; "we got to go somewhere. We'll try and get back, but it ain't no manner of use. Anything we want to take along with us from the mule? We can——"

Suddenly he paused. In an instant the eyes of the two doomed men had met as the same thought simultaneously rose in their minds. The canvas sack with its five thousand dollars was still tied to the horn of the saddle.

Marcus had emptied his revolver at the mule, and though he still wore his cartridge belt, he was for the moment as unarmed as McTeague.

"I guess," began McTeague coming forward a step, "I guess, even if we are done for, I'll take—some of my truck along."

"Hold on," exclaimed Marcus, with rising aggressiveness. "Let's talk about that. I ain't so sure about who that—who that money belongs to."

"Well, I *am*, you see," growled the dentist.

The old enmity between the two men, their ancient hate, was flaming up again.

"Don't try an' load that gun either," cried McTeague, fixing Marcus with his little eyes.

"Then don't lay your finger on that sack," shouted the other. "You're my prisoner, do you understand? You'll do as I say." Marcus had drawn the handcuffs from his pocket, and

stood ready with his revolver held as a club. "You soldiered
me out of that money once, and played me for a sucker, an'
it's *my* turn now. Don't you lay your finger on that sack."

Marcus barred McTeague's way, white with passion. Mc-
Teague did not answer. His eyes drew to two fine, twinkling
points, and his enormous hands knotted themselves into fists,
hard as wooden mallets. He moved a step nearer to Marcus,
then another.

Suddenly the men grappled, and in another instant were
rolling and struggling upon the hot white ground. McTeague
thrust Marcus backward until he tripped and fell over the
body of the dead mule. The little bird cage broke from the
saddle with the violence of their fall, and rolled out upon
the ground, the flour-bags slipping from it. McTeague tore
the revolver from Marcus's grip and struck out with it blindly.
Clouds of alkali dust, fine and pungent, enveloped the two
fighting men, all but strangling them.

McTeague did not know how he killed his enemy, but all
at once Marcus grew still beneath his blows. Then there was
a sudden last return of energy. McTeague's right wrist was
caught, something clicked upon it, then the struggling body
fell limp and motionless with a long breath.

As McTeague rose to his feet, he felt a pull at his right
wrist; something held it fast. Looking down, he saw that
Marcus in that last struggle had found strength to handcuff
their wrists together. Marcus was dead now; McTeague was
locked to the body. All about him, vast, interminable,
stretched the measureless leagues of Death Valley.

McTeague remained stupidly looking around him, now at
the distant horizon, now at the ground, now at the half-dead
canary chittering feebly in its little gilt prison.

THE OCTOPUS

A Story of California

DEDICATED
TO
MY WIFE

PRINCIPAL CHARACTERS IN THE NOVEL.

MAGNUS DERRICK (the "Governor"), *proprietor of the Los Muertos Rancho.*

ANNIE DERRICK, *wife of Magnus Derrick.*

LYMAN DERRICK,
HARRAN DERRICK, } *sons of Magnus Derrick.*

BRODERSON,
OSTERMAN, } *friends and neighbors of Magnus Derrick.*

ANNIXTER, *proprietor of the Quien Sabe Rancho.*

HILMA TREE, *a dairy girl on Annixter's ranch.*

GENSLINGER, *editor of the Bonneville "Mercury," the railroad organ.*

S. BEHRMAN, *representative of the Pacific and Southwestern Railroad.*

PRESLEY, *a* protégé *of Magnus Derrick.*

VANAMEE, *a sheep herder and range rider.*

ANGÉLE VARIAN.

FATHER SARRIA, *a Mission priest.*

DYKE, *a black-listed railroad engineer.*

MRS. DYKE, *Dyke's mother.*

SIDNEY DYKE, *Dyke's daughter.*

CARAHER, *a saloon keeper.*

HOOVEN, *a tenant of Derrick.*

MRS. HOOVEN, *his wife.*

MINNA HOOVEN, *his daughter.*

CEDARQUIST, *a manufacturer and shipbuilder.*

Mrs. Cedarquist, *his wife.*

Garnett,
Dabney,
Keast,
Chattern,

ranchers of the San Joaquin Valley.

The Trilogy of The Epic of the Wheat will include the following novels:

> THE OCTOPUS, *a Story of California.*
> THE PIT, *a Story of Chicago.*
> THE WOLF, *a Story of Europe.*

These novels, while forming a series, will be in no way connected with each other save only in their relation to (1) the production, (2) the distribution, (3) the consumption of American wheat. When complete, they will form the story of a crop of wheat from the time of its sowing as seed in California to the time of its consumption as bread in a village of Western Europe.

The first novel, "The Octopus," deals with the war between the wheat grower and the Railroad Trust; the second, "The Pit," will be the fictitious narrative of a "deal" in the Chicago wheat pit; while the third, "The Wolf," will probably have for its pivotal episode the relieving of a famine in an Old World community.

F. N.

ROSELLE, NEW JERSEY,
December 15, 1900.

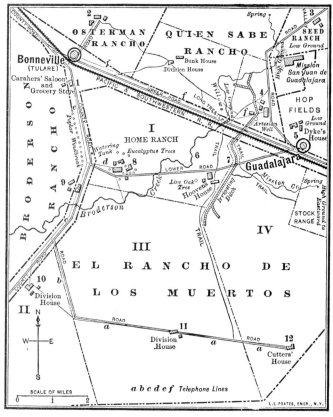

2. Osterman's Ranch House.   8. Derrick's Ranch House.
4. Annixter's Ranch House.   9. Broderson's Ranch House.

MAP OF THE COUNTRY DESCRIBED IN "THE OCTOPUS."

I

J UST AFTER passing Caraher's saloon, on the County Road that ran south from Bonneville, and that divided the Broderson ranch from that of Los Muertos, Presley was suddenly aware of the faint and prolonged blowing of a steam whistle that he knew must come from the railroad shops near the depot at Bonneville. In starting out from the ranch house that morning, he had forgotten his watch, and was now perplexed to know whether the whistle was blowing for twelve or for one o'clock. He hoped the former. Early that morning he had decided to make a long excursion through the neighbouring country, partly on foot and partly on his bicycle, and now noon was come already, and as yet he had hardly started. As he was leaving the house after breakfast, Mrs. Derrick had asked him to go for the mail at Bonneville, and he had not been able to refuse.

He took a firmer hold of the cork grips of his handle-bars— the road being in a wretched condition after the recent hauling of the crop—and quickened his pace. He told himself that, no matter what the time was, he would not stop for luncheon at the ranch house, but would push on to Guadalajara and have a Spanish dinner at Solotari's, as he had originally planned.

There had not been much of a crop to haul that year. Half of the wheat on the Broderson ranch had failed entirely, and Derrick himself had hardly raised more than enough to supply seed for the winter's sowing. But such little hauling as there had been had reduced the roads thereabouts to a lamentable condition, and, during the dry season of the past few months, the layer of dust had deepened and thickened to such an extent that more than once Presley was obliged to dismount and trudge along on foot, pushing his bicycle in front of him.

It was the last half of September, the very end of the dry season, and all Tulare County, all the vast reaches of the San Joaquin Valley—in fact all South Central California, was bone dry, parched, and baked and crisped after four months of cloudless weather, when the day seemed always at noon, and the sun blazed white hot over the valley from the Coast Range in the west to the foothills of the Sierras in the east.

As Presley drew near to the point where what was known as the Lower Road struck off through the Rancho de Los Muertos, leading on to Guadalajara, he came upon one of the county watering-tanks, a great, iron-hooped tower of wood, straddling clumsily on its four uprights by the roadside. Since the day of its completion, the storekeepers and retailers of Bonneville had painted their advertisements upon it. It was a landmark. In that reach of level fields, the white letters upon it could be read for miles. A watering-trough stood near by, and, as he was very thirsty, Presley resolved to stop for a moment to get a drink.

He drew abreast of the tank and halted there, leaning his bicycle against the fence. A couple of men in white overalls were repainting the surface of the tank, seated on swinging platforms that hung by hooks from the roof. They were painting a sign—an advertisement. It was all but finished and read, "S. Behrman, Real Estate, Mortgages, Main Street, Bonneville, Opposite the Post Office." On the horse-trough that stood in the shadow of the tank was another freshly painted inscription: "S. Behrman Has Something To Say To *You*."

As Presley straightened up after drinking from the faucet at one end of the horse-trough, the watering-cart itself laboured into view around the turn of the Lower Road. Two mules and two horses, white with dust, strained leisurely in the traces, moving at a snail's pace, their limp ears marking the time; while perched high upon the seat, under a yellow cotton wagon umbrella, Presley recognised Hooven, one of Derrick's tenants, a German, whom every one called "Bismarck," an excitable little man with a perpetual grievance and an endless flow of broken English.

"Hello, Bismarck," said Presley, as Hooven brought his team to a standstill by the tank, preparatory to refilling.

"Yoost der men I look for, Mist'r Praicely," cried the other, twisting the reins around the brake. "Yoost one minute, you wait, hey? I wanta talk mit you."

Presley was impatient to be on his way again. A little more time wasted, and the day would be lost. He had nothing to do with the management of the ranch, and if Hooven wanted any advice from him, it was so much breath wasted. These uncouth brutes of farm-hands and petty ranchers, grimed with the soil they worked upon, were odious to him beyond words. Never could he feel in sympathy with them, nor with their lives, their ways, their marriages, deaths, bickerings, and all the monotonous round of their sordid existence.

"Well, you must be quick about it, Bismarck," he answered sharply. "I'm late for dinner, as it is."

"Soh, now. Two minuten, und I be mit you." He drew down the overhanging spout of the tank to the vent in the circumference of the cart and pulled the chain that let out the water. Then he climbed down from the seat, jumping from the tire of the wheel, and taking Presley by the arm led him a few steps down the road.

"Say," he began. "Say, I want to hef some converzations mit you. Yoost der men I want to see. Say, Caraher, he tole me dis morgen—say, he tole me Mist'r Derrick gowun to farm der whole demn rench hisseluf der next yahr. No more tenants. Say, Caraher, he tole me all der tenants get der sach; Mist'r Derrick gowun to work der whole demn rench hisseluf, hey? *Me*, I get der sach alzoh, hey? You hef hear about dose ting? Say, me, I hef on der ranch been sieben yahr— seven yahr. Do I alzoh——"

"You'll have to see Derrick himself or Harran about that, Bismarck," interrupted Presley, trying to draw away. "That's something outside of me entirely."

But Hooven was not to be put off. No doubt he had been meditating his speech all the morning, formulating his words, preparing his phrases.

"Say, no, no," he continued. "Me, I wanta stay bei der place; seven yahr I hef stay. Mist'r Derrick, he doand want dot I should be ge-sacked. Who, den, will der ditch ge-tend? Say, you tell 'um Bismarck hef gotta sure stay bei der place. Say, you hef der pull mit der Governor. You speak der gut word for me."

"Harran is the man that has the pull with his father,

Bismarck," answered Presley. "You get Harran to speak for you, and you're all right."

"Sieben yahr I hef stay," protested Hooven, "and who will der ditch ge-tend, und alle dem cettles drive?"

"Well, Harran's your man," answered Presley, preparing to mount his bicycle.

"Say, you hef hear about dose ting?"

"I don't hear about anything, Bismarck. I don't know the first thing about how the ranch is run."

"*Und der pipe-line ge-mend,*" Hooven burst out, suddenly remembering a forgotten argument. He waved an arm. "Ach, der pipe-line bei der Mission Greek, und der waäter-hole for dose cettles. Say, he doand doo ut *himselluf,* berhaps, I doand tink."

"Well, talk to Harran about it."

"Say, he doand farm der whole demn rench bei hisseluf. Me, I gotta stay."

But on a sudden the water in the cart gushed over the sides from the vent in the top with a smart sound of splashing. Hooven was forced to turn his attention to it. Presley got his wheel under way.

"I hef some converzations mit Herran," Hooven called after him. "He doand doo ut bei hisseluf, den, Mist'r Derrick; ach, no. I stay bei der rench to drive dose cettles."

He climbed back to his seat under the wagon umbrella, and, as he started his team again with great cracks of his long whip, turned to the painters still at work upon the sign and declared with some defiance:

"Sieben yahr; yais, sir, seiben yahr I hef been on dis rench. Git oop, you mule you, hoop!"

Meanwhile Presley had turned into the Lower Road. He was now on Derrick's land, division No. 1, or, as it was called, the Home ranch, of the great Los Muertos Rancho. The road was better here, the dust laid after the passage of Hooven's watering-cart, and, in a few minutes, he had come to the ranch house itself, with its white picket fence, its few flower beds, and grove of eucalyptus trees. On the lawn at the side of the house, he saw Harran in the act of setting out the automatic sprinkler. In the shade of the house, by the porch, were two or three of the greyhounds, part of the pack that were used to hunt down jack-rabbits, and Godfrey, Harran's prize deerhound.

Presley wheeled up the driveway and met Harran by the horse-block. Harran was Magnus Derrick's youngest son, a very well-looking young fellow of twenty-three or twenty-five. He had the fine carriage that marked his father, and still further resembled him in that he had the Derrick nose—hawk-like and prominent, such as one sees in the later portraits of the Duke of Wellington. He was blond, and incessant exposure to the sun had, instead of tanning him brown, merely heightened the colour of his cheeks. His yellow hair had a tendency to curl in a forward direction, just in front of the ears.

Beside him, Presley made the sharpest of contrasts. Presley seemed to have come of a mixed origin; appeared to have a nature more composite, a temperament more complex. Unlike Harran Derrick, he seemed more of a character than a type. The sun had browned his face till it was almost swarthy. His eyes were a dark brown, and his forehead was the forehead of the intellectual, wide and high, with a certain unmistakable lift about it that argued education, not only of himself, but of his people before him. The impression conveyed by his mouth and chin was that of a delicate and highly sensitive nature, the lips thin and loosely shut together, the chin small and rather receding. One guessed that Presley's refinement had been gained only by a certain loss of strength. One expected to find him nervous, introspective, to discover that his mental life was not at all the result of impressions and sensations that came to him from without, but rather of thoughts and reflections germinating from within. Though morbidly sensitive to changes in his physical surroundings, he would be slow to act upon such sensations, would not prove impulsive, not because he was sluggish, but because he was merely irresolute. It could be foreseen that morally he was of that sort who avoid evil through good taste, lack of decision, and want of opportunity. His temperament was that of the poet; when he told himself he had been thinking, he deceived himself. He had, on such occasions, been only brooding.

Some eighteen months before this time, he had been threatened with consumption, and, taking advantage of a standing invitation on the part of Magnus Derrick, had come to stay in the dry, even climate of the San Joaquin for an indefinite length of time. He was thirty years old, and had graduated and post-graduated with high honours from an Eastern college, where he had devoted himself to a passionate study of literature, and, more especially, of poetry.

It was his insatiable ambition to write verse. But up to this time, his work had been fugitive, ephemeral, a note here and there, heard, appreciated, and forgotten. He was in search of a subject; something magnificent, he did not know exactly what; some vast, tremendous theme, heroic, terrible, to be unrolled in all the thundering progression of hexameters.

But whatever he wrote, and in whatever fashion, Presley was determined that his poem should be of the West, that world's frontier of Romance, where a new race, a new people—hardy, brave, and passionate—were building an empire; where the tumultuous life ran like fire from dawn to dark, and from dark to dawn again, primitive, brutal, honest, and without fear. Something (to his idea not much) had been done to catch at that life in passing, but its poet had not yet arisen. The few sporadic attempts, thus he told himself, had only touched the keynote. He strove for the diapason, the great song that should embrace in itself a whole epoch, a complete era, the voice of an entire people, wherein all people should be included—they and their legends, their folk lore, their fightings, their loves and their lusts, their blunt, grim humour, their stoicism under stress, their adventures, their treasures found in a day and gambled in a night, their direct, crude speech, their generosity and cruelty, their heroism and bestiality, their religion and profanity, their self-sacrifice and obscenity—a true and fearless setting forth of a passing phase of history, uncompromising, sincere; each group in its proper environment; the valley, the plain, and the mountain; the ranch, the range, and the mine—all this, all the traits and types of every community from the Dakotas to the Mexicos, from Winnipeg to Guadalupe, gathered together, swept together, welded and riven together in one single, mighty song, the Song of the West. That was what he dreamed, while things without names—thoughts for which no man had yet invented words, terrible formless shapes, vague figures, colossal, monstrous, distorted—whirled at a gallop through his imagination.

As Harran came up, Presley reached down into the pouches of the sun-bleached shooting coat he wore and drew out and handed him the packet of letters and papers.

"Here's the mail. I think I shall go on."

"But dinner is ready," said Harran; "we are just sitting down."

Presley shook his head. "No, I'm in a hurry. Perhaps I shall have something to eat at Guadalajara. I shall be gone all day."

He delayed a few moments longer, tightening a loose nut on his forward wheel, while Harran, recognising his father's handwriting on one of the envelopes, slit it open and cast his eye rapidly over its pages.

"The Governor is coming home," he exclaimed, "to-morrow morning on the early train; wants me to meet him with the team at Guadalajara; *and*," he cried between his clenched teeth, as he continued to read, "we've lost the case."

"What case? Oh, in the matter of rates?"

Harran nodded, his eyes flashing, his face growing suddenly scarlet.

"Ulsteen gave his decision yesterday," he continued, reading from his father's letter. "He holds, Ulsteen does, that 'grain rates as low as the new figure would amount to confiscation of property, and that, on such a basis, the railroad could not be operated at a legitimate profit. As he is powerless to legislate in the matter, he can only put the rates back at what they originally were before the commissioners made the cut, and it is so ordered.' That's our friend S. Behrman again," added Harran, grinding his teeth. "He was up in the city the whole of the time the new schedule was being drawn, and he and Ulsteen and the Railroad Commission were as thick as thieves. He has been up there all this last week, too, doing the railroad's dirty work, and backing Ulsteen up. 'Legitimate profit, legitimate profit,'" he broke out. "Can we raise wheat at a legitimate profit with a tariff of four dollars a ton for moving it two hundred miles to tide-water, with wheat at eighty-seven cents? Why not hold us up with a gun in our faces, and say, 'hands up,' and be done with it?"

He dug his boot-heel into the ground and turned away to the house abruptly, cursing beneath his breath.

"By the way," Presley called after him, "Hooven wants to see you. He asked me about this idea of the Governor's of getting along without the tenants this year. Hooven wants to stay to tend the ditch and look after the stock. I told him to see you."

Harran, his mind full of other things, nodded to say he understood. Presley only waited till he had disappeared indoors, so that he might not seem too indifferent to his trouble; then, remounting, struck at once into a brisk pace, and, turning out from the carriage gate, held on swiftly down the Lower Road, going in the direction of Guadalajara. These matters, these eternal fierce bickerings between the farmers of the San Joaquin and the Pacific and Southwestern Railroad irritated him and wearied him. He cared for none of these things. They did not belong to his world. In the picture of that huge romantic West that he saw in his imagination, these dissensions made the one note of harsh colour that refused to enter into the great scheme of harmony. It was material, sordid, deadly commonplace. But, however he strove to shut his eyes to it or his ears to it, the thing persisted and persisted. The romance seemed complete up to that point. There it broke, there it failed, there it became realism, grim, unlovely, unyielding. To be true—and it was the first article of his creed to be unflinchingly true—he could not ignore it. All the noble poetry of the ranch—the valley—seemed in his mind to be marred and disfigured by the presence of certain immovable facts. Just what he wanted, Presley hardly knew. On one hand, it was his ambition to portray life as he saw it—directly, frankly, and through no medium of personality or temperament. But, on the other hand, as well, he wished to see everything through a rose-coloured mist—a mist that dulled all harsh outlines, all crude and violent colours. He told himself that, as a part of the people, he loved the people and sympathised with their hopes and fears, and joys and griefs; and yet Hooven, grimy and perspiring, with his perpetual grievance and his contracted horizon, only revolted him. He had set himself the task of giving true, absolutely true, poetical expression to the life of the ranch, and yet, again and again, he brought up against the railroad, that stubborn iron barrier against which his romance shattered itself to froth and disintegrated, flying spume. His heart went out to the people, and his groping hand met that of a slovenly little Dutchman, whom it was impossible to consider seriously. He searched for the True Romance, and, in the end, found grain rates and unjust freight tariffs.

"But the stuff is *here*," he muttered, as he sent his wheel rumbling across the bridge over Broderson Creek. "The romance, the real romance, is here somewhere. I'll get hold of it yet."

He shot a glance about him as if in search of the inspiration. By now he was not quite half way across the northern and narrowest corner of Los Muertos, at this point some eight miles wide. He was still on the Home ranch. A few miles to the south he could just make out the line of wire fence that separated it from the third division; and to the north, seen faint and blue through the haze and shimmer of the noon sun, a long file of telegraph poles showed the line of the railroad and marked Derrick's northeast boundary. The road over which Presley was travelling ran almost diametrically straight. In front of him, but at a great distance, he could make out the giant live-oak and the red roof of Hooven's barn that stood near it.

All about him the country was flat. In all directions he could see for miles. The harvest was just over. Nothing but stubble remained on the ground. With the one exception of the live-oak by Hooven's place, there was nothing green in sight. The wheat stubble was of a dirty yellow; the ground, parched, cracked, and dry, of a cheerless brown. By the roadside the dust lay thick and grey, and, on either hand, stretching on toward the horizon, losing itself in a mere smudge in the distance, ran the illimitable parallels of the wire fence. And that was all; that and the burnt-out blue of the sky and the steady shimmer of the heat.

The silence was infinite. After the harvest, small though that harvest had been, the ranches seemed asleep. It was as though the earth, after its period of reproduction, its pains of labour, had been delivered of the fruit of its loins, and now slept the sleep of exhaustion.

It was the period between seasons, when nothing was being done, when the natural forces seemed to hang suspended. There was no rain, there was no wind, there was no growth, no life; the very stubble had no force even to rot. The sun alone moved.

Toward two o'clock, Presley reached Hooven's place, two or three grimy frame buildings, infested with a swarm of dogs. A hog or two wandered aimlessly about. Under a shed by the barn, a broken-down seeder lay rusting to its ruin. But overhead, a mammoth live-oak, the largest tree in all the country-side, towered superb and magnificent. Grey bunches of mistletoe and festoons of trailing moss hung from its bark. From its lowest branch hung Hooven's meat-safe, a square box, faced with wire screens.

What gave a special interest to Hooven's was the fact that here was the intersection of the Lower Road and Derrick's main irrigating ditch, a vast trench not yet completed, which he and Annixter, who worked the Quien Sabe ranch, were jointly constructing. It ran directly across the road and at right angles to it, and lay a deep groove in the field between Hooven's and the town of Guadalajara, some three miles farther on. Besides this, the ditch was a natural boundary between two divisions of the Los Muertos ranch, the first and fourth.

Presley now had the choice of two routes. His objective point was the spring at the headwaters of Broderson Creek, in the hills on the eastern side of the Quien Sabe ranch. The trail afforded him a short cut thitherward. As he passed the house, Mrs. Hooven came to the door, her little daughter Hilda, dressed in a boy's overalls and clumsy boots, at her skirts. Minna, her oldest daughter, a very pretty girl, whose love affairs were continually the talk of all Los Muertos, was visible through a window of the house, busy at the week's washing. Mrs. Hooven was a faded, colourless woman, middle-aged and commonplace, and offering not the least characteristic that would distinguish her from a thousand other women of her class and kind. She nodded to Presley, watching him with a stolid gaze from under her arm, which she held across her forehead to shade her eyes.

But now Presley exerted himself in good earnest. His

bicycle flew. He resolved that after all he would go to Guadalajara. He crossed the bridge over the irrigating ditch with a brusque spurt of hollow sound, and shot forward down the last stretch of the Lower Road that yet intervened between Hooven's and the town. He was on the fourth division of the ranch now, the only one whereon the wheat had been successful, no doubt because of the Little Mission Creek that ran through it. But he no longer occupied himself with the landscape. His only concern was to get on as fast as possible. He had looked forward to spending nearly the whole day on the crest of the wooded hills in the northern corner of the Quien Sabe ranch, reading, idling, smoking his pipe. But now he would do well if he arrived there by the middle of the afternoon. In a few moments he had reached the line fence that marked the limits of the ranch. Here were the railroad tracks, and just beyond—a huddled mass of roofs, with here and there an adobe house on its outskirts—the little town of Guadalajara. Nearer at hand, and directly in front of Presley, were the freight and passenger depots of the P. and S. W., painted in the grey and white, which seemed to be the official colours of all the buildings owned by the corporation. The station was deserted. No trains passed at this hour. From the direction of the ticket window, Presley heard the unsteady chittering of the telegraph key. In the shadow of one of the baggage trucks upon the platform, the great yellow cat that belonged to the agent dozed complacently, her paws tucked under her body. Three flat cars, loaded with bright-painted farming machines, were on the siding above the station, while, on the switch below, a huge freight engine that lacked its cowcatcher sat back upon its monstrous driving-wheels, motionless, solid, drawing long breaths that were punctuated by the subdued sound of its steam-pump clicking at exact intervals.

But evidently it had been decreed that Presley should be stopped at every point of his ride that day, for, as he was pushing his bicycle across the tracks, he was surprised to hear his name called. "Hello, there, Mr. Presley. What's the good word?"

Presley looked up quickly, and saw Dyke, the engineer, leaning on his folded arms from the cab window of the freight engine. But at the prospect of this further delay,

Presley was less troubled. Dyke and he were well acquainted and the best of friends. The picturesqueness of the engineer's life was always attractive to Presley, and more than once he had ridden on Dyke's engine between Guadalajara and Bonneville. Once, even, he had made the entire run between the latter town and San Francisco in the cab.

Dyke's home was in Guadalajara. He lived in one of the remodelled 'dobe cottages, where his mother kept house for him. His wife had died some five years before this time, leaving him a little daughter, Sidney, to bring up as best he could. Dyke himself was a heavy built, well-looking fellow, nearly twice the weight of Presley, with great shoulders and massive, hairy arms, and a tremendous, rumbling voice.

"Hello, old man," answered Presley, coming up to the engine. "What are you doing about here at this time of day? I thought you were on the night service this month."

"We've changed about a bit," answered the other. "Come up here and sit down, and get out of the sun. They've held us here to wait orders," he explained, as Presley, after leaning his bicycle against the tender, climbed to the fireman's seat of worn green leather. "They are changing the run of one of the crack passenger engines down below, and are sending her up to Fresno. There was a smash of some kind on the Bakersfield division, and she's to hell and gone behind her time. I suppose when she comes, she'll come a-humming. It will be stand clear and an open track all the way to Fresno. They have held me here to let her go by."

He took his pipe, an old T. D. clay, but coloured to a beautiful shiny black, from the pocket of his jumper and filled and lit it.

"Well, I don't suppose you object to being held here," observed Presley. "Gives you a chance to visit your mother and the little girl."

"And precisely they choose this day to go up to Sacramento," answered Dyke. "Just my luck. Went up to visit my brother's people. By the way, my brother may come down here—locate here, I mean—and go into the hop-raising business. He's got an option on five hundred acres just back of the town here. He says there's going to be money in hops. I don't know; maybe I'll go in with him."

"Why, what's the matter with railroading?"

Dyke drew a couple of puffs on his pipe, and fixed Presley with a glance.

"There's this the matter with it," he said; "I'm fired."

"Fired! You!" exclaimed Presley, turning abruptly toward him.

"That's what I'm telling you," returned Dyke grimly.

"You don't mean it. Why, what for, Dyke?"

"Now, *you* tell me what for," growled the other savagely. "Boy and man, I've worked for the P. and S. W. for over ten years, and never one yelp of a complaint did I ever hear from them. They know damn well they've not got a steadier man on the road. And more than that, more than that, I don't belong to the Brotherhood. And when the strike came along, I stood by them—stood by the company. *You* know that. And you know, and they know, that at Sacramento that time, I ran my train according to schedule, with a gun in each hand, never knowing when I was going over a mined culvert, and there was talk of giving me a gold watch at the time. To hell with their gold watches! I want ordinary justice and fair treatment. And now, when hard times come along, and they are cutting wages, what do they do? Do they make any discrimination in my case? Do they remember the man that stood by them and risked his life in their service? No. They cut my pay down just as off-hand as they do the pay of any dirty little wiper in the yard. Cut me along with—listen to this—cut me along with men that they had *black-listed*; strikers that they took back because they were short of hands." He drew fiercely on his pipe. "I went to them, yes, I did; I went to the General Office, and ate dirt. I told them I was a family man, and that I didn't see how I was going to get along on the new scale, and I reminded them of my service during the strike. The swine told me that it wouldn't be fair to discriminate in favour of one man, and that the cut must apply to all their employees alike. Fair!" he shouted with laughter. "Fair! Hear the P. and S. W. talking about fairness and discrimination. That's good, that is. Well, I got furious. I was a fool, I suppose. I told them that, in justice to myself, I wouldn't do first-class work for third-class pay. And they said, 'Well, Mr. Dyke, you know what you can do.' Well, I did know. I said, 'I'll ask for my time, if you please,' and they gave it to me just as if they were glad to be shut of me. So there you are, Presley. That's the P. & S. W. Railroad Company of California. I am on my last run now."

"Shameful," declared Presley, his sympathies all aroused, now that the trouble concerned a friend of his. "It's shameful, Dyke. But," he added, an idea occurring to him, "that don't shut you out from work. There are other railroads in the State that are not controlled by the P. and S. W."

Dyke smote his knee with his clenched fist.

"Name one."

Presley was silent. Dyke's challenge was unanswerable. There was a lapse in their talk, Presley drumming on the arm of the seat, meditating on this injustice; Dyke looking off over the fields beyond the town, his frown lowering, his teeth rasping upon his pipestem. The station agent came to the door of the depot, stretching and yawning. On ahead of the engine, the empty rails of the track, reaching out toward the horizon, threw off visible layers of heat. The telegraph key clicked incessantly.

"So I'm going to quit," Dyke remarked after a while, his anger somewhat subsided. "My brother and I will take up this hop ranch. I've saved a good deal in the last ten years, and there ought to be money in hops."

Presley went on, remounting his bicycle, wheeling silently through the deserted streets of the decayed and dying Mexican town. It was the hour of the siesta. Nobody was about. There was no business in the town. It was too close to Bonneville for that. Before the railroad came, and in the days when the raising of cattle was the great industry of the country, it had enjoyed a fierce and brilliant life. Now it was moribund. The drug store, the two bar-rooms, the hotel at the corner of the old Plaza, and the shops where Mexican "curios" were sold to those occasional Eastern tourists who came to visit the Mission of San Juan, sufficed for the town's activity.

At Solotari's, the restaurant on the Plaza, diagonally across from the hotel, Presley ate his long-deferred Mexican dinner—an omelette in Spanish-Mexican style, frijoles and tortillas, a salad, and a glass of white wine. In a corner of the room, during the whole course of his dinner, two young Mexicans (one of whom was astonishingly handsome, after the melodramatic fashion of his race) and an old fellow, the centenarian of the town, decrepit beyond belief, sang an interminable love-song to the accompaniment of a guitar and an accordion.

These Spanish-Mexicans, decayed, picturesque, vicious, and romantic, never failed to interest Presley. A few of them still remained in Guadalajara, drifting from the saloon to the restaurant, and from the restaurant to the Plaza, relics of a former generation, standing for a different order of things, absolutely idle, living God knew how, happy with their cigarette, their guitar, their glass of mescal, and their siesta. The centenarian remembered Fremont and Governor Alvarado, and the bandit Jésus Tejéda, and the days when Los Muertos was a Spanish grant, a veritable principality, leagues in extent, and when there was never a fence from Visalia to Fresno. Upon this occasion, Presley offered the old man a drink of mescal, and excited him to talk of the things he remembered. Their talk was in Spanish, a language with which Presley was familiar.

"De La Cuesta held the grant of Los Muertos in those days," the centenarian said; "a grand man. He had the power of life and death over his people, and there was no law but his word. There was no thought of wheat then, you may believe. It was all cattle in those days, sheep, horses—steers, not so many—and if money was scarce, there was always plenty to eat, and clothes enough for all, and wine, ah, yes, by the vat, and oil too; the Mission Fathers had that. Yes, and there was wheat as well, now that I come to think; but a very little—in the field north of the Mission where now it is the Seed ranch; wheat fields were there, and also a vineyard, all on Mission grounds. Wheat, olives, and the vine; the Fathers planted those, to provide the elements of the Holy Sacrament—bread, oil, and wine, you understand. It was like that, those industries began in California—from the Church; and now," he put his chin in the air, " what would Father Ullivari have said to such a crop as Señor Derrick plants these days? Ten thousand acres of wheat! Nothing but wheat from the Sierra to the Coast Range. I remember when De La Cuesta was married. He had never seen the young lady, only her miniature portrait, painted"—he raised a shoulder—"I do not know by whom, small, a little thing to be held in the palm. But he fell in love with that, and marry her he would. The affair was arranged between him and the girl's parents. But when the time came that De La Cuesta was to go to Monterey to meet and marry the girl, behold, Jésus Tejéda broke in upon the small rancheros near Terrabella. It was no time for De La Cuesta to be away, so he sent his brother Esteban to Monterey to marry the girl by proxy for him. I went with Esteban. We were a company, nearly a hundred men. And De La Cuesta sent a horse for the girl to ride, white, pure white; and the saddle was of red leather; the head-stall, the bit, and buckles, all the metal work, of virgin silver. Well, there was a ceremony in the Monterey Mission, and Esteban, in the name of his brother, was married to the girl. On our way back, De La Cuesta rode out to meet us. His company met ours at Agatha dos Palos. Never will I forget De La Cuesta's face as his eyes fell upon the girl. It was a look, a glance, come and gone like *that*," he snapped his fingers. "No one but I saw it, but I was close by. There was no mistaking that look. De La Cuesta was disappointed."

"And the girl?" demanded Presley.

"She never knew. Ah, he was a grand gentleman, De La Cuesta. Always he treated her as a queen. Never was husband more devoted, more respectful, more chivalrous. But love?" The old fellow put his chin in the air, shutting his eyes in a knowing fashion. "It was not there. I could tell. They were married over again at the Mission San Juan de Guadalajara— *our* Mission—and for a week all the town of Guadalajara was in *fête*. There were bull-fights in the Plaza—this very one— for five days, and to each of his tenants-in-chief, De La Cuesta gave a horse, a barrel of tallow, an ounce of silver, and half an ounce of gold dust. Ah, those were days. That was a gay life. This"—he made a comprehensive gesture with his left hand—"this is stupid."

"You may well say that," observed Presley moodily, discouraged by the other's talk. All his doubts and uncertainty had returned to him. Never would he grasp the subject of his great poem. To-day, the life was colourless. Romance was dead. He had lived too late. To write of the past was not what he desired. Reality was what he longed for, things that he had seen. Yet how to make this compatible with romance. He rose, putting on his hat, offering the old man a cigarette. The centenarian accepted with the air of a grandee, and extended his horn snuff-box. Presley shook his head.

"I was born too late for that," he declared, "for that, and for many other things. *Adios.*"

"You are travelling to-day, señor?"

"A little turn through the country, to get the kinks out of the muscles," Presley answered. "I go up into the Quien Sabe, into the high country beyond the Mission."

"Ah, the Quien Sabe rancho. The sheep are grazing there this week."

Solotari, the keeper of the restaurant, explained:

"Young Annixter sold his wheat stubble on the ground to the sheep raisers off yonder;" he motioned eastward toward the Sierra foothills. "Since Sunday the herd has been down. Very clever, that young Annixter. He gets a price for his stubble, which else he would have to burn, and also manures his land as the sheep move from place to place. A true Yankee, that Annixter, a good gringo."

After his meal, Presley once more mounted his bicycle, and leaving the restaurant and the Plaza behind him, held on through the main street of the drowsing town—the street that farther on developed into the road which turned abruptly northward and led onward through the hop-fields and the Quien Sabe ranch toward the Mission of San Juan.

The Home ranch of the Quien Sabe was in the little triangle bounded on the south by the railroad, on the northwest by Broderson Creek, and on the east by the hop fields and the Mission lands. It was traversed in all directions, now by the trail from Hooven's, now by the irrigating ditch—the same which Presley had crossed earlier in the day—and again by the road upon which Presley then found himself. In its centre were Annixter's ranch house and barns, topped by the skeleton-like tower of the artesian well that was to feed the irrigating ditch. Farther on, the course of Broderson Creek was marked by a curved line of grey-green willows, while on the low hills to the north, as Presley advanced, the ancient

Mission of San Juan de Guadalajara, with its belfry tower and red-tiled roof, began to show itself over the crests of the venerable pear trees that clustered in its garden.

When Presley reached Annixter's ranch house, he found young Annixter himself stretched in his hammock behind the mosquito-bar on the front porch, reading "David Copperfield," and gorging himself with dried prunes.

Annixter—after the two had exchanged greetings—complained of terrific colics all the preceding night. His stomach was out of whack, but you bet he knew how to take care of himself; the last spell, he had consulted a doctor at Bonneville, a gibbering busy-face who had filled him up to the neck with a dose of some hog-wash stuff that had made him worse—a healthy lot the doctors knew, anyhow. *His* case was peculiar. *He* knew; prunes were what he needed, and by the pound.

Annixter, who worked the Quien Sabe ranch—some four thousand acres of rich clay and heavy loams—was a very young man, younger even than Presley, like him a college graduate. He looked never a year older than he was. He was smooth-shaven and lean built. But his youthful appearance was offset by a certain male cast of countenance, the lower lip thrust out, the chin large and deeply cleft. His university course had hardened rather than polished him. He still remained one of the people, rough almost to insolence, direct in speech, intolerant in his opinions, relying upon absolutely no one but himself; yet, with all this, of an astonishing degree of intelligence, and possessed of an executive ability little short of positive genius. He was a ferocious worker, allowing himself no pleasures, and exacting the same degree of energy from all his subordinates. He was widely hated, and as widely trusted. Every one spoke of his crusty temper and bullying disposition, invariably qualifying the statement with a commendation of his resources and capabilities. The devil of a driver, a hard man to get along with, obstinate, contrary, cantankerous; but brains! No doubt of that; brains to his boots. One would like to see the man who could get ahead of him on a deal. Twice he had been shot at, once from ambush on Osterman's ranch, and once by one of his own men whom he had kicked from the sacking platform of his harvester for gross negligence. At college, he had specialised on finance, political economy, and scientific agriculture. After his graduation (he stood almost at the very top of his class) he had returned and obtained the degree of civil engineer. Then suddenly he had taken a notion that a practical knowledge of law was indispensable to a modern farmer. In eight months he did the work of three years, studying for his bar examinations. His method of study was characteristic. He reduced all the material of his text-books to notes. Tearing out the leaves of these note-books, he pasted them upon the walls of his room; then, in his shirt-sleeves, a cheap cigar in his teeth, his hands in his pockets, he walked around and around the room, scowling fiercely at his notes, memorising, devouring, digesting. At intervals, he drank great cupfuls of unsweetened, black coffee. When the bar examinations were held, he was admitted at the very head of all the applicants, and was complimented by the judge. Immediately afterwards, he collapsed with nervous prostration; his stomach "got out of whack," and he all but died in a Sacramento boarding-house, obstinately refusing to have anything to do with doctors, whom he vituperated as a rabble of quacks, dosing himself with a patent medicine and stuffing himself almost to bursting with liver pills and dried prunes.

He had taken a trip to Europe after this sickness to put himself completely to rights. He intended to be gone a year, but returned at the end of six weeks, fulminating abuse of European cooking. Nearly his entire time had been spent in Paris; but of this sojourn he had brought back but two souvenirs, an electro-plated bill-hook and an empty bird cage which had tickled his fancy immensely.

He was wealthy. Only a year previous to this his father—a widower, who had amassed a fortune in land speculation— had died, and Annixter, the only son, had come into the inheritance.

For Presley, Annixter professed a great admiration, holding in deep respect the man who could rhyme words, deferring to him whenever there was question of literature or works of fiction. No doubt, there was not much use in poetry, and as for novels, to his mind, there were only Dickens's works. Everything else was a lot of lies. But just the same, it took brains to grind out a poem. It wasn't every one who could rhyme "brave" and "glaive," and make sense out of it. Sure not.

But Presley's case was a notable exception. On no occasion was Annixter prepared to accept another man's opinion without reserve. In conversation with him, it was almost impossible to make any direct statement, however trivial, that he would accept without either modification or open contradiction. He had a passion for violent discussion. He would argue upon every subject in the range of human knowledge, from astronomy to the tariff, from the doctrine of predestination to the height of a horse. Never would he admit himself to be mistaken; when cornered, he would intrench himself behind the remark, "Yes, that's all very well. In some ways, it is, and then, again, in some ways, it *isn't*."

Singularly enough, he and Presley were the best of friends. More than once, Presley marvelled at this state of affairs, telling himself that he and Annixter had nothing in common. In all his circle of acquaintances, Presley was the one man with whom Annixter had never quarrelled. The two men were diametrically opposed in temperament. Presley was easy-going; Annixter, alert. Presley was a confirmed dreamer, irresolute, inactive, with a strong tendency to melancholy; the young farmer was a man of affairs, decisive, combative, whose only reflection upon his interior economy was a morbid concern in the vagaries of his stomach. Yet the two never met without a mutual pleasure, taking a genuine interest in each other's affairs, and often putting themselves to great inconvenience to be of trifling service to help one another.

As a last characteristic, Annixter pretended to be a woman-hater, for no other reason than that he was a very bull-calf of awkwardness in feminine surroundings. Feemales! Rot! There was a fine way for a man to waste his time and his good money, lally gagging with a lot of feemales. No, thank you; none of it in *his*, if you please. Once only he had an affair— a timid, little creature in a glove-cleaning establishment in Sacramento, whom he had picked up, Heaven knew how. After his return to his ranch, a correspondence had been maintained between the two, Annixter taking the precaution to typewrite his letters, and never affixing his signature, in an excess of prudence. He furthermore made carbon copies of all his letters, filing them away in a compartment of his safe. Ah, it would be a clever feemale who would get him into a mess. Then, suddenly smitten with a panic terror that he had committed himself, that he was involving himself too deeply, he had abruptly sent the little woman about her business. It was his only love affair. After that, he kept himself free. No petticoats should ever have a hold on him. Sure not.

As Presley came up to the edge of the porch, pushing his bicycle in front of him, Annixter excused himself for not getting up, alleging that the cramps returned the moment he was off his back.

"What are you doing up this way?" he demanded.

"Oh, just having a look around," answered Presley. "How's the ranch?"

"Say," observed the other, ignoring his question, "what's this I hear about Derrick giving his tenants the bounce, and working Los Muertos himself—working *all* his land?"

Presley made a sharp movement of impatience with his free hand. "I've heard nothing else myself since morning. I suppose it must be so."

"Huh!" grunted Annixter, spitting out a prune stone. "You give Magnus Derrick my compliments and tell him he's a fool."

"What do you mean?"

"I suppose Derrick thinks he's still running his mine, and that the same principles will apply to getting grain out of the earth as to getting gold. Oh, let him go on and see where he brings up. That's right, there's your Western farmer," he exclaimed contemptuously. "Get the guts out of your land; work it to death; never give it a rest. Never alternate your crop, and then when your soil is exhausted, sit down and roar about hard times."

"I suppose Magnus thinks the land has had rest enough these last two dry seasons," observed Presley. "He has raised no crop to speak of for two years. The land has had a good rest."

"Ah, yes, that sounds well," Annixter contradicted, unwilling to be convinced. "In a way, the land's been rested, and then, again, in a way, it hasn't."

But Presley, scenting an argument, refrained from answering, and bethought himself of moving on.

"I'm going to leave my wheel here for a while, Buck," he said, "if you don't mind. I'm going up to the spring, and the road is rough between here and there."

"Stop in for dinner on your way back," said Annixter. "There'll be a venison steak. One of the boys got a deer over in the foothills last week. Out of season, but never mind that. I can't eat it. This stomach of mine wouldn't digest sweet oil to-day. Get here about six."

"Well, maybe I will, thank you," said Presley, moving off. "By the way," he added, "I see your barn is about done."

"You bet," answered Annixter. "In about a fortnight now she'll be all ready."

"It's a big barn," murmured Presley, glancing around the angle of the house toward where the great structure stood.

"Guess we'll have to have a dance there before we move the stock in," observed Annixter. "That's the custom all around here."

Presley took himself off, but at the gate Annixter called after him, his mouth full of prunes, "Say, take a look at that herd of sheep as you go up. They are right off here to the east of the road, about half a mile from here. I guess that's the biggest lot of sheep *you* ever saw. You might write a poem about 'em. Lamb—ram; sheep graze—sunny days. Catch on?"

Beyond Broderson Creek, as Presley advanced, tramping along on foot now, the land opened out again into the same vast spaces of dull brown earth, sprinkled with stubble, such as had been characteristic of Derrick's ranch. To the east the reach seemed infinite, flat, cheerless, heat-ridden, unrolling like a gigantic scroll toward the faint shimmer of the distant horizons, with here and there an isolated live-oak to break the sombre monotony. But bordering the road to the westward, the surface roughened and raised, clambering up to the higher ground, on the crest of which the old Mission and its surrounding pear trees were now plainly visible.

Just beyond the Mission, the road bent abruptly eastward, striking off across the Seed ranch. But Presley left the road at this point, going on across the open fields. There was no longer any trail. It was toward three o'clock. The sun still spun, a silent, blazing disc, high in the heavens, and tramping through the clods of uneven, broken plough was fatiguing work. The slope of the lowest foothills begun, the surface of the country became rolling, and, suddenly, as he topped a higher ridge, Presley came upon the sheep.

Already he had passed the larger part of the herd—an intervening rise of ground having hidden it from sight. Now, as he turned half way about, looking down into the shallow hollow between him and the curve of the creek, he saw them very plainly. The fringe of the herd was some two hundred yards distant, but its farther side, in that illusive shimmer of hot surface air, seemed miles away. The sheep were spread out roughly in the shape of a figure eight, two larger herds connected by a smaller, and were headed to the southward, moving slowly, grazing on the wheat stubble as they proceeded. But the number seemed incalculable. Hundreds upon hundreds upon hundreds of grey, rounded backs, all exactly alike, huddled, close-packed, alive, hid the earth from sight. It was no longer an aggregate of individuals. It was a mass— a compact, solid, slowly moving mass, huge, without form, like a thick-pressed growth of mushrooms, spreading out in all directions over the earth. From it there arose a vague murmur, confused, inarticulate, like the sound of very distant surf, while all the air in the vicinity was heavy with the warm, ammoniacal odour of the thousands of crowding bodies.

All the colours of the scene were sombre—the brown of the earth, the faded yellow of the dead stubble, the grey of the myriad of undulating backs. Only on the far side of the herd, erect, motionless—a single note of black, a speck, a dot—the shepherd stood, leaning upon an empty water-trough, solitary, grave, impressive.

For a few moments, Presley stood, watching. Then, as he started to move on, a curious thing occurred. At first, he thought he had heard some one call his name. He paused, listening; there was no sound but the vague noise of the moving sheep. Then, as this first impression passed, it seemed to him that he had been beckoned to. Yet nothing stirred; except for the lonely figure beyond the herd there was no one in sight. He started on again, and in half a dozen steps found himself looking over his shoulder. Without knowing why, he looked toward the shepherd; then halted and looked a second time and a third. Had the shepherd called to him? Presley knew that he had heard no voice. Brusquely, all his attention seemed riveted upon this distant figure. He put one forearm over his eyes, to keep off the sun, gazing across the intervening herd. Surely, the shepherd had called him. But at the next instant he started, uttering an exclamation under his breath. The far-away speck of black became animated. Presley remarked a sweeping gesture. Though the man had not beckoned to him before, there was no doubt that he was beckoning now. Without any hesitation, and singularly interested in the incident, Presley turned sharply aside and hurried on toward the shepherd, skirting the herd, wondering all the time that he should answer the call with so little question, so little hesitation.

But the shepherd came forward to meet Presley, followed by one of his dogs. As the two men approached each other, Presley, closely studying the other, began to wonder where he had seen him before. It must have been a very long time ago, upon one of his previous visits to the ranch. Certainly, however, there was something familiar in the shepherd's face and figure. When they came closer to each other, and Presley could see him more distinctly, this sense of a previous acquaintance was increased and sharpened.

The shepherd was a man of about thirty-five. He was very lean and spare. His brown canvas overalls were thrust into laced boots. A cartridge belt without any cartridges encircled his waist. A grey flannel shirt, open at the throat, showed his breast, tanned and ruddy. He wore no hat. His hair was very black and rather long. A pointed beard covered his chin, growing straight and fine from the hollow cheeks. The absence of any covering for his head was, no doubt, habitual with him, for his face was as brown as an Indian's—a ruddy brown—quite different from Presley's dark olive. To Presley's morbidly keen observation, the general impression of the shepherd's face was intensely interesting. It was uncommon to an astonishing degree. Presley's vivid imagination chose to see in it the face of an ascetic, of a recluse, almost that of a young seer. So must have appeared the half-inspired shepherds of the Hebraic legends, the younger prophets of Israel, dwellers in the wilderness, beholders of visions, having their existence in a continual dream, talkers with God, gifted with strange powers.

Suddenly, at some twenty paces distant from the approaching shepherd, Presley stopped short, his eyes riveted upon the other.

"Vanamee!" he exclaimed.

The shepherd smiled and came forward, holding out his hands, saying, "I thought it was you. When I saw you come over the hill, I called you."

"But not with your voice," returned Presley. "I knew that some one wanted me. I felt it. I should have remembered that you could do that kind of thing."

"I have never known it to fail. It helps with the sheep."

"With the sheep?"

"In a way. I can't tell exactly how. We don't understand these things yet. There are times when, if I close my eyes and dig my fists into my temples, I can hold the entire herd for perhaps a minute. Perhaps, though, it's imagination, who knows? But it's good to see you again. How long has it been since the last time? Two, three, nearly five years."

It was more than that. It was six years since Presley and Vanamee had met, and then it had been for a short time only, during one of the shepherd's periodical brief returns to that part of the country. During a week he and Presley had been much together, for the two were devoted friends. Then, as abruptly, as mysteriously as he had come, Vanamee disappeared. Presley awoke one morning to find him gone. Thus, it had been with Vanamee for a period of sixteen years. He lived his life in the unknown, one could not tell where—in the desert, in the mountains, throughout all the vast and vague Southwest, solitary, strange. Three, four, five years passed. The shepherd would be almost forgotten. Never the most trivial scrap of information as to his whereabouts reached Los Muertos. He had melted off into the surface-shimmer of the desert, into the mirage; he sank below the horizons; he was swallowed up in the waste of sand and sage. Then, without warning, he would reappear, coming in from the wilderness, emerging from the unknown. No one knew him well. In all that countryside he had but three friends, Presley, Magnus Derrick, and the priest at the Mission of San Juan de Guadalajara, Father Sarria. He remained always a mystery, living a life half-real, half-legendary. In all those years he did not seem to have grown older by a single day. At this time, Presley knew him to be thirty-six years of age. But since the first day the two had met, the shepherd's face and bearing had, to his eyes, remained the same. At this moment, Presley was looking into the same face he had first seen many, many years ago. It was a face stamped with an unspeakable sadness, a deathless grief, the permanent imprint of a tragedy long past, but yet a living issue. Presley told himself that it was impossible to look long into Vanamee's eyes without knowing that here was a man whose whole being had been at one time shattered and riven to its lowest depths, whose life had suddenly stopped at a certain moment of its development.

The two friends sat down upon the ledge of the watering-trough, their eyes wandering incessantly toward the slow moving herd, grazing on the wheat stubble, moving southward as they grazed.

"Where have you come from this time?" Presley had asked. "Where have you kept yourself?"

The other swept the horizon to the south and east with a vague gesture.

"Off there, down to the south, very far off. So many places that I can't remember. I went the Long Trail this time; a long, long ways. Arizona, The Mexicos, and, then, afterwards, Utah and Nevada, following the horizon, travelling at hazard. Into Arizona first, going in by Monument Pass, and then on to the south, through the country of the Navajos, down by the Aga Thia Needle—a great blade of red rock jutting from out the desert, like a knife thrust. Then on and on through The Mexicos, all through the Southwest, then back again in a great circle by Chihuahua and Aldama to Laredo, to Torreon, and Albuquerque. From there across the Uncompahgre plateau into the Uintah country; then at last due west through Nevada to California and to the valley of the San Joaquin."

His voice lapsed to a monotone, his eyes becoming fixed;

he continued to speak as though half awake, his thoughts elsewhere, seeing again in the eye of his mind the reach of desert and red hill, the purple mountain, the level stretch of alkali, leper white, all the savage, gorgeous desolation of the Long Trail.

He ignored Presley for the moment, but, on the other hand, Presley himself gave him but half his attention. The return of Vanamee had stimulated the poet's memory. He recalled the incidents of Vanamee's life, reviewing again that terrible drama which had uprooted his soul, which had driven him forth a wanderer, a shunner of men, a sojourner in waste places. He was, strangely enough, a college graduate and a man of wide reading and great intelligence, but he had chosen to lead his own life, which was that of a recluse.

Of a temperament similar in many ways to Presley's, there were capabilities in Vanamee that were not ordinarily to be found in the rank and file of men. Living close to nature, a poet by instinct, where Presley was but a poet by training, there developed in him a great sensitiveness to beauty and an almost abnormal capacity for great happiness and great sorrow; he felt things intensely, deeply. He never forgot. It was when he was eighteen or nineteen, at the formative and most impressionable period of his life, that he had met Angéle Varian. Presley barely remembered her as a girl of sixteen, beautiful almost beyond expression, who lived with an aged aunt on the Seed ranch back of the Mission. At this moment he was trying to recall how she looked, with her hair of gold hanging in two straight plaits on either side of her face, making three-cornered her round, white forehead; her wonderful eyes, violet blue, heavy lidded, with their astonishing upward slant toward the temples, the slant that gave a strange, oriental cast to her face, perplexing, enchanting. He remembered the Egyptian fulness of the lips, the strange balancing movement of her head upon her slender neck, the same movement that one sees in a snake at poise. Never had he seen a girl more radiantly beautiful, never a beauty so strange, so troublous, so out of all accepted standards. It was small wonder that Vanamee had loved her, and less wonder, still, that his love had been so intense, so passionate, so part of himself. Angéle had loved him with a love no less than his own.

It was one of those legendary passions that sometimes occur, idyllic, untouched by civilisation, spontaneous as the
growth of trees, natural as dew-fall, strong as the firm-seated
mountains.

At the time of his meeting with Angéle, Vanamee was living on the Los Muertos ranch. It was there he had chosen to
spend one of his college vacations. But he preferred to pass it
in out-of-door work, sometimes herding cattle, sometimes
pitching hay, sometimes working with pick and dynamite-
stick on the ditches in the fourth division of the ranch, riding
the range, mending breaks in the wire fences, making himself
generally useful. College bred though he was, the life pleased
him. He was, as he desired, close to nature, living the full
measure of life, a worker among workers, taking enjoyment
in simple pleasures, healthy in mind and body. He believed
in an existence passed in this fashion in the country, working
hard, eating full, drinking deep, sleeping dreamlessly.

But every night, after supper, he saddled his pony and rode
over to the garden of the old Mission. The 'dobe dividing
wall on that side, which once had separated the Mission garden and the Seed ranch, had long since crumbled away, and
the boundary between the two pieces of ground was marked
only by a line of venerable pear trees. Here, under these trees,
he found Angéle awaiting him, and there the two would sit
through the hot, still evening, their arms about each other,
watching the moon rise over the foothills, listening to the
trickle of the water in the moss-encrusted fountain in the garden, and the steady croak of the great frogs that lived in the
damp north corner of the enclosure. Through all one summer
the enchantment of that new-found, wonderful love, pure and
untainted, filled the lives of each of them with its sweetness.
The summer passed, the harvest moon came and went. The
nights were very dark. In the deep shade of the pear trees they
could no longer see each other. When they met at the rendezvous, Vanamee found her only with his groping hands. They
did not speak, mere words were useless between them. Silently as his reaching hands touched her warm body, he took
her in his arms, searching for her lips with his. Then one
night the tragedy had suddenly leaped from out the shadow
with the abruptness of an explosion.

It was impossible afterwards to reconstruct the manner of its occurrence. To Angéle's mind—what there was left of it— the matter always remained a hideous blur, a blot, a vague, terrible confusion. No doubt they two had been watched; the plan succeeded too well for any other supposition. One moonless night, Angéle, arriving under the black shadow of the pear trees a little earlier than usual, found the apparently familiar figure waiting for her. All unsuspecting she gave herself to the embrace of a strange pair of arms, and Vanamee arriving but a score of moments later, stumbled over her prostrate body, inert and unconscious, in the shadow of the overspiring trees.

Who was the Other? Angéle was carried to her home on the Seed ranch, delirious, all but raving, and Vanamee, with knife and revolver ready, ranged the countryside like a wolf. He was not alone. The whole county rose, raging, horror-struck. Posse after posse was formed, sent out, and returned, without so much as a clue. Upon no one could even the shadow of suspicion be thrown. The Other had withdrawn into an impenetrable mystery. There he remained. He never was found; he never was so much as heard of. A legend arose about him, this prowler of the night, this strange, fearful figure, with an unseen face, swooping in there from out the darkness, come and gone in an instant, but leaving behind him a track of terror and death and rage and undying grief. Within the year, in giving birth to the child, Angéle had died.

The little babe was taken by Angéle's parents, and Angéle was buried in the Mission garden near to the aged, grey sun dial. Vanamee stood by during the ceremony, but half conscious of what was going forward. At the last moment he had stepped forward, looked long into the dead face framed in its plaits of gold hair, the hair that made three-cornered the round, white forehead; looked again at the closed eyes, with their perplexing upward slant toward the temples, oriental, bizarre; at the lips with their Egyptian fulness; at the sweet, slender neck; the long, slim hands; then abruptly turned about. The last clods were filling the grave at a time when he was already far away, his horse's head turned toward the desert.

For two years no syllable was heard of him. It was believed

that he had killed himself. But Vanamee had no thought of that. For two years he wandered through Arizona, living in the desert, in the wilderness, a recluse, a nomad, an ascetic. But, doubtless, all his heart was in the little coffin in the Mission garden. Once in so often he must come back thither. One day he was seen again in the San Joaquin. The priest, Father Sarria, returning from a visit to the sick at Bonneville, met him on the Upper Road.

Eighteen years had passed since Angéle had died, but the thread of Vanamee's life had been snapped. Nothing remained now but the tangled ends. He had never forgotten. The long, dull ache, the poignant grief had now become a part of him. Presley knew this to be so.

While Presley had been reflecting upon all this, Vanamee had continued to speak. Presley, however, had not been wholly inattentive. While his memory was busy reconstructing the details of the drama of the shepherd's life, another part of his brain had been swiftly registering picture after picture that Vanamee's monotonous flow of words struck off, as it were, upon a steadily moving scroll. The music of the unfamiliar names that occurred in his recital was a stimulant to the poet's imagination. Presley had the poet's passion for expressive, sonorous names. As these came and went in Vanamee's monotonous undertones, like little notes of harmony in a musical progression, he listened, delighted with their resonance. Navajo, Quijotoa, Uintah, Sonora, Laredo, Uncompahgre—to him they were so many symbols. It was his West that passed, unrolling there before the eye of his mind: the open, heat-scourged round of desert; the mesa, like a vast altar, shimmering purple in the royal sunset; the still, gigantic mountains, heaving into the sky from out the cañons; the strenuous, fierce life of isolated towns, lost and forgotten, down there, far off, below the horizon. Abruptly his great poem, his Song of the West, leaped up again in his imagination. For the moment, he all but held it. It was there, close at hand. In another instant he would grasp it.

"Yes, yes," he exclaimed, "I can see it all. The desert, the mountains, all wild, primordial, untamed. How I should have loved to have been with you. Then, perhaps, I should have got hold of my idea."

"Your idea?"

"The great poem of the West. It's that which I want to write. Oh, to put it all into hexameters; strike the great iron note; sing the vast, terrible song; the song of the People; the forerunners of empire!"

Vanamee understood him perfectly. He nodded gravely.

"Yes, it is there. It is Life, the primitive, simple, direct Life, passionate, tumultuous. Yes, there is an epic there."

Presley caught at the word. It had never before occurred to him.

"Epic, yes, that's it. It is the epic I'm searching for. And *how* I search for it. You don't know. It is sometimes almost an agony. Often and often I can feel it right there, there, at my finger-tips, but I never quite catch it. It always eludes me. I was born too late. Ah, to get back to that first clear-eyed view of things, to see as Homer saw, as Beowulf saw, as the Nibelungen poets saw. The life is here, the same as then; the Poem is here; my West is here; the primeval, epic life is here, here under our hands, in the desert, in the mountain, on the ranch, all over here, from Winnipeg to Guadalupe. It is the man who is lacking, the poet; we have been educated away from it all. We are out of touch. We are out of tune."

Vanamee heard him to the end, his grave, sad face thoughtful and attentive. Then he rose.

"I am going over to the Mission," he said, "to see Father Sarria. I have not seen him yet."

"How about the sheep?"

"The dogs will keep them in hand, and I shall not be gone long. Besides that, I have a boy here to help. He is over yonder on the other side of the herd. We can't see him from here."

Presley wondered at the heedlessness of leaving the sheep so slightly guarded, but made no comment, and the two started off across the field in the direction of the Mission church.

"Well, yes, it is there—your epic," observed Vanamee, as they went along. "But why write? Why not *live* in it? Steep oneself in the heat of the desert, the glory of the sunset, the blue haze of the mesa and the cañon."

"As you have done, for instance?"

Vanamee nodded.

"No, I could not do that," declared Presley; "I want to go back, but not so far as you. I feel that I must compromise. I must find expression. I could not lose myself like that in your desert. When its vastness overwhelmed me, or its beauty dazzled me, or its loneliness weighed down upon me, I should have to record my impressions. Otherwise, I should suffocate."

"Each to his own life," observed Vanamee.

The Mission of San Juan, built of brown 'dobe blocks, covered with yellow plaster, that at many points had dropped away from the walls, stood on the crest of a low rise of the ground, facing to the south. A covered colonnade, paved with round, worn bricks, from whence opened the doors of the abandoned cells, once used by the monks, adjoined it on the left. The roof was of tiled half-cylinders, split longitudinally, and laid in alternate rows, now concave, now convex. The main body of the church itself was at right angles to the colonnade, and at the point of intersection rose the belfry tower, an ancient campanile, where swung the three cracked bells, the gift of the King of Spain. Beyond the church was the Mission garden and the graveyard that overlooked the Seed ranch in a little hollow beyond.

Presley and Vanamee went down the long colonnade to the last door next the belfry tower, and Vanamee pulled the leather thong that hung from a hole in the door, setting a little bell jangling somewhere in the interior. The place, but for this noise, was shrouded in a Sunday stillness, an absolute repose. Only at intervals, one heard the trickle of the unseen fountain, and the liquid cooing of doves in the garden.

Father Sarria opened the door. He was a small man, somewhat stout, with a smooth and shiny face. He wore a frock coat that was rather dirty, slippers, and an old yachting cap of blue cloth, with a broken leather vizor. He was smoking a cheap cigar, very fat and black.

But instantly he recognised Vanamee. His face went all alight with pleasure and astonishment. It seemed as if he would never have finished shaking both his hands; and, as it was, he released but one of them, patting him affectionately

on the shoulder with the other. He was voluble in his welcome, talking partly in Spanish, partly in English.

So he had come back again, this great fellow, tanned as an
Indian, lean as an Indian, with an Indian's long, black hair.
But he had not changed, not in the very least. His beard had
not grown an inch. Aha! The rascal, never to give warning,
to drop down, as it were, from out the sky. Such a hermit!
To live in the desert! A veritable Saint Jerome. Did a lion feed
him down there in Arizona, or was it a raven, like Elijah? The
good God had not fattened him, at any rate, and, apropos, he
was just about to dine himself. He had made a salad from his
own lettuce. The two would dine with him, eh? For this, my
son, that was lost is found again.

But Presley excused himself. Instinctively, he felt that Sarria
and Vanamee wanted to talk of things concerning which he
was an outsider. It was not at all unlikely that Vanamee would
spend half the night before the high altar in the church.

He took himself away, his mind still busy with Vanamee's
extraordinary life and character. But, as he descended the hill,
he was startled by a prolonged and raucous cry, discordant,
very harsh, thrice repeated at exact intervals, and, looking up,
he saw one of Father Sarria's peacocks balancing himself upon
the topmost wire of the fence, his long tail trailing, his neck
outstretched, filling the air with his stupid outcry, for no reason than the desire to make a noise.

About an hour later, toward four in the afternoon, Presley
reached the spring at the head of the little cañon in the northeast corner of the Quien Sabe ranch, the point toward which
he had been travelling since early in the forenoon. The place
was not without its charm. Innumerable live-oaks overhung
the cañon, and Broderson Creek—there a mere rivulet, running down from the spring—gave a certain coolness to the
air. It was one of the few spots thereabouts that had survived
the dry season of the last year. Nearly all the other springs
had dried completely, while Mission Creek on Derrick's ranch
was nothing better than a dusty cutting in the ground, filled
with brittle, concave flakes of dried and sun-cracked mud.

Presley climbed to the summit of one of the hills—the
highest—that rose out of the cañon, from the crest of which
he could see for thirty, fifty, sixty miles down the valley, and,

filling his pipe, smoked lazily for upwards of an hour, his head empty of thought, allowing himself to succumb to a pleasant, gentle inanition, a little drowsy, comfortable in his place, prone upon the ground, warmed just enough by such sunlight as filtered through the live-oaks, soothed by the good tobacco and the prolonged murmur of the spring and creek. By degrees, the sense of his own personality became blunted, the little wheels and cogs of thought moved slower and slower; consciousness dwindled to a point, the animal in him stretched itself, purring. A delightful numbness invaded his mind and his body. He was not asleep, he was not awake, stupefied merely, lapsing back to the state of the faun, the satyr.

After a while, rousing himself a little, he shifted his position and, drawing from the pocket of his shooting coat his little tree-calf edition of the Odyssey, read far into the twenty-first book, where, after the failure of all the suitors to bend Ulysses's bow, it is finally put, with mockery, into his own hands. Abruptly the drama of the story roused him from all his languor. In an instant, he was the poet again, his nerves tingling, alive to every sensation, responsive to every impression. The desire of creation, of composition, grew big within him. Hexameters of his own clamoured, tumultuous, in his brain. Not for a long time had he "felt his poem," as he called this sensation, so poignantly. For an instant he told himself that he actually held it.

It was, no doubt, Vanamee's talk that had stimulated him to this point. The story of the Long Trail, with its desert and mountain, its cliff-dwellers, its Aztec ruins, its colour, movement, and romance, filled his mind with picture after picture. The epic defiled before his vision like a pageant. Once more, he shot a glance about him, as if in search of the inspiration, and this time he all but found it. He rose to his feet, looking out and off below him.

As from a pinnacle, Presley, from where he now stood, dominated the entire country. The sun had begun to set, everything in the range of his vision was overlaid with a sheen of gold.

First, close at hand, it was the Seed ranch, carpeting the little hollow behind the Mission with a spread of greens, some dark, some vivid, some pale almost to yellowness. Beyond that was the Mission itself, its venerable campanile, in whose arches hung the Spanish King's bells, already glowing ruddy in the sunset. Farther on, he could make out Annixter's ranch house, marked by the skeleton-like tower of the artesian well, and, a little farther to the east, the huddled, tiled roofs of Guadalajara. Far to the west and north, he saw Bonneville very plain, and the dome of the courthouse, a purple silhouette against the glare of the sky. Other points detached themselves, swimming in a golden mist, projecting blue shadows far before them; the mammoth live-oak by Hooven's, towering superb and magnificent; the line of eucalyptus trees, behind which he knew was the Los Muertos ranch house—his home; the watering-tank, the great iron-hooped tower of wood that stood at the joining of the Lower Road and the County Road; the long wind-break of poplar trees and the white walls of Caraher's saloon on the County Road.

But all this seemed to be only foreground, a mere array of accessories—a mass of irrelevant details. Beyond Annixter's, beyond Guadalajara, beyond the Lower Road, beyond Broderson Creek, on to the south and west, infinite, illimitable, stretching out there under the sheen of the sunset forever and forever, flat, vast, unbroken, a huge scroll, unrolling between the horizons, spread the great stretches of the ranch of Los Muertos, bare of crops, shaved close in the recent harvest. Near at hand were hills, but on that far southern horizon only the curve of the great earth itself checked the view. Adjoining Los Muertos, and widening to the west, opened the Broderson ranch. The Osterman ranch to the northwest carried on the great sweep of landscape; ranch after ranch. Then, as the imagination itself expanded under the stimulus of that measureless range of vision, even those great ranches resolved themselves into mere foreground, mere accessories, irrelevant details. Beyond the fine line of the horizons, over the curve of the globe, the shoulder of the earth, were other ranches, equally vast, and beyond these, others, and beyond these, still others, the immensities multiplying, lengthening out vaster and vaster. The whole gigantic sweep of the San Joaquin expanded, Titanic, before the eye of the mind, flagellated with heat, quivering and shimmering under the sun's red eye. At long intervals, a faint breath of wind out of the south passed slowly over the levels of the baked and empty earth, accentuating the silence, marking off the stillness. It seemed to exhale from the land itself, a prolonged sigh as of deep fatigue. It was the season after the harvest, and the great earth, the mother, after its period of reproduction, its pains of labour, delivered of the fruit of its loins, slept the sleep of exhaustion, the infinite repose of the colossus, benignant, eternal, strong, the nourisher of nations, the feeder of an entire world.

Ha! there it was, his epic, his inspiration, his West, his thundering progression of hexameters. A sudden uplift, a sense of exhilaration, of physical exaltation appeared abruptly to sweep Presley from his feet. As from a point high above the world, he seemed to dominate a universe, a whole order of things. He was dizzied, stunned, stupefied, his morbid supersensitive mind reeling, drunk with the intoxication of mere immensity. Stupendous ideas for which there were no names drove headlong through his brain. Terrible, formless shapes, vague figures, gigantic, monstrous, distorted, whirled at a gallop through his imagination.

He started homeward, still in his dream, descending from the hill, emerging from the cañon, and took the short cut straight across the Quien Sabe ranch, leaving Guadalajara far to his left. He tramped steadily on through the wheat stubble, walking fast, his head in a whirl.

Never had he so nearly grasped his inspiration as at that moment on the hill-top. Even now, though the sunset was fading, though the wide reach of valley was shut from sight, it still kept him company. Now the details came thronging back—the component parts of his poem, the signs and symbols of the West. It was there, close at hand, he had been in touch with it all day. It was in the centenarian's vividly coloured reminiscences—De La Cuesta, holding his grant from the Spanish crown, with his power of life and death; the romance of his marriage; the white horse with its pillion of red leather and silver bridle mountings; the bull-fights in the Plaza; the gifts of gold dust, and horses and tallow. It was in Vanamee's strange history, the tragedy of his love; Angéle Varian, with her marvellous loveliness; the Egyptian fulness of her lips, the perplexing upward slant of her violet eyes, bizarre, oriental; her white forehead made three cornered by her plaits of gold hair; the mystery of the Other; her death at the moment of her child's birth. It was in Vanamee's flight into the wilderness; the story of the Long Trail; the sunsets behind the altar-like mesas, the baking desolation of the deserts; the strenuous, fierce life of forgotten towns, down there, far off, lost below the horizons of the southwest; the sonorous music of unfamiliar names—Quijotoa, Uintah, Sonora, Laredo, Uncompahgre. It was in the Mission, with its cracked bells, its decaying walls, its venerable sun dial, its fountain and old garden, and in the Mission Fathers themselves, the priests, the padres, planting the first wheat and oil and wine to produce the elements of the Sacrament—a trinity of great industries, taking their rise in a religious rite.

Abruptly, as if in confirmation, Presley heard the sound of a bell from the direction of the Mission itself. It was the *de Profundis*, a note of the Old World; of the ancient régime, an echo from the hillsides of mediæval Europe, sounding there in this new land, unfamiliar and strange at this end-of-the-century time.

By now, however, it was dark. Presley hurried forward. He came to the line fence of the Quien Sabe ranch. Everything was very still. The stars were all out. There was not a sound other than the *de Profundis*, still sounding from very far away. At long intervals the great earth sighed dreamily in its sleep. All about, the feeling of absolute peace and quiet and security and untroubled happiness and content seemed descending from the stars like a benediction. The beauty of his poem, its idyl, came to him like a caress; that alone had been lacking. It was that, perhaps, which had left it hitherto incomplete. At last he was to grasp his song in all its entity.

But suddenly there was an interruption. Presley had climbed the fence at the limit of the Quien Sabe ranch. Beyond was Los Muertos, but between the two ran the railroad. He had only time to jump back upon the embankment when, with a quivering of all the earth, a locomotive, single, unattached, shot by him with a roar, filling the air with the reek of hot oil, vomiting smoke and sparks; its enormous eye, cyclopean, red, throwing a glare far in advance, shooting by in a sudden crash of confused thunder; filling the night with the terrific clamour of its iron hoofs.

Abruptly Presley remembered. This must be the crack passenger engine of which Dyke had told him, the one delayed by the accident on the Bakersfield division and for whose passage the track had been opened all the way to Fresno.

Before Presley could recover from the shock of the irruption, while the earth was still vibrating, the rails still humming, the engine was far away, flinging the echo of its frantic gallop over all the valley. For a brief instant it roared with a hollow diapason on the Long Trestle over Broderson Creek, then plunged into a cutting farther on, the quivering glare of its fires losing itself in the night, its thunder abruptly diminishing to a subdued and distant humming. All at once this ceased. The engine was gone.

But the moment the noise of the engine lapsed, Presley—about to start forward again—was conscious of a confusion of lamentable sounds that rose into the night from out the engine's wake. Prolonged cries of agony, sobbing wails of infinite pain, heart-rending, pitiful.

The noises came from a little distance. He ran down the track, crossing the culvert, over the irrigating ditch, and at the head of the long reach of track—between the culvert and the Long Trestle—paused abruptly, held immovable at the sight of the ground and rails all about him.

In some way, the herd of sheep—Vanamee's herd—had found a breach in the wire fence by the right of way and had wandered out upon the tracks. A band had been crossing just at the moment of the engine's passage. The pathos of it was beyond expression. It was a slaughter, a massacre of innocents. The iron monster had charged full into the midst, merciless, inexorable. To the right and left, all the width of the right of way, the little bodies had been flung; backs were snapped against the fence posts; brains knocked out. Caught in the barbs of the wire, wedged in, the bodies hung suspended. Under foot it was terrible. The black blood, winking in the starlight, seeped down into the clinkers between the ties with a prolonged sucking murmur.

Presley turned away, horror-struck, sick at heart, overwhelmed with a quick burst of irresistible compassion for this brute agony he could not relieve. The sweetness was gone from the evening, the sense of peace, of security, and placid contentment was stricken from the landscape. The hideous ruin in the engine's path drove all thought of his poem from his mind. The inspiration vanished like a mist. The *de Profundis* had ceased to ring.

He hurried on across the Los Muertos ranch, almost running, even putting his hands over his ears till he was out of hearing distance of that all but human distress. Not until he was beyond ear-shot did he pause, looking back, listening. The night had shut down again. For a moment the silence was profound, unbroken.

Then, faint and prolonged, across the levels of the ranch, he heard the engine whistling for Bonneville. Again and again, at rapid intervals in its flying course, it whistled for road crossings, for sharp curves, for trestles; ominous notes, hoarse, bellowing, ringing with the accents of menace and defiance; and abruptly Presley saw again, in his imagination, the galloping monster, the terror of steel and steam, with its single eye, cyclopean, red, shooting from horizon to horizon; but saw it now as the symbol of a vast power, huge, terrible, flinging the echo of its thunder over all the reaches of the valley, leaving blood and destruction in its path; the leviathan, with tentacles of steel clutching into the soil, the soulless Force, the iron-hearted Power, the monster, the Colossus, the Octopus.

II

ON THE FOLLOWING morning, Harran Derrick was up and about by a little after six o'clock, and a quarter of an hour later had breakfast in the kitchen of the ranch house, preferring not to wait until the Chinese cook laid the table in the regular dining-room. He scented a hard day's work ahead of him, and was anxious to be at it betimes. He was practically the manager of Los Muertos, and, with the aid of his foreman and three division superintendents, carried forward nearly the entire direction of the ranch, occupying himself with the details of his father's plans, executing his orders, signing contracts, paying bills, and keeping the books.

For the last three weeks little had been done. The crop—such as it was—had been harvested and sold, and there had been a general relaxation of activity for upwards of a month. Now, however, the fall was coming on, the dry season was about at its end; any time after the twentieth of the month the first rains might be expected, softening the ground, putting it into condition for the plough. Two days before this, Harran had notified his superintendents on Three and Four to send in such grain as they had reserved for seed. On Two the wheat had not even shown itself above the ground, while on One, the Home ranch, which was under his own immediate supervision, the seed had already been graded and selected.

It was Harran's intention to commence blue-stoning his seed that day, a delicate and important process which prevented rust and smut appearing in the crop when the wheat should come up. But, furthermore, he wanted to find time to go to Guadalajara to meet the Governor on the morning train. His day promised to be busy.

But as Harran was finishing his last cup of coffee, Phelps, the foreman on the Home ranch, who also looked after the storage barns where the seed was kept, presented himself, cap in hand, on the back porch by the kitchen door.

"I thought I'd speak to you about the seed from Four, sir," he said. "That hasn't been brought in yet."

Harran nodded.

"I'll see about it. You've got all the blue-stone you want, have you, Phelps?" and without waiting for an answer he added, "Tell the stableman I shall want the team about nine o'clock to go to Guadalajara. Put them in the buggy. The bays, you understand."

When the other had gone, Harran drank off the rest of his coffee, and, rising, passed through the dining-room and across a stone-paved hallway with a glass roof into the office just beyond.

The office was the nerve-centre of the entire ten thousand acres of Los Muertos, but its appearance and furnishings were not in the least suggestive of a farm. It was divided at about its middle by a wire railing, painted green and gold, and behind this railing were the high desks where the books were kept, the safe, the letter-press and letter-files, and Harran's typewriting machine. A great map of Los Muertos with every water-course, depression, and elevation, together with indications of the varying depths of the clays and loams in the soil, accurately plotted, hung against the wall between the windows, while near at hand by the safe was the telephone.

But, no doubt, the most significant object in the office was the ticker. This was an innovation in the San Joaquin, an idea of shrewd, quick-witted young Annixter, which Harran and Magnus Derrick had been quick to adopt, and after them Broderson and Osterman, and many others of the wheat growers of the county. The offices of the ranches were thus connected by wire with San Francisco, and through that city with Minneapolis, Duluth, Chicago, New York, and at last, and most important of all, with Liverpool. Fluctuations in the price of the world's crop during and after the harvest thrilled straight to the office of Los Muertos, to that of the Quien Sabe, to Osterman's, and to Broderson's. During a flurry in the Chicago wheat pits in the August of that year, which had affected even the San Francisco market, Harran and Magnus had sat up nearly half of one night watching the strip of white tape jerking unsteadily from the reel. At such moments they no longer felt their individuality. The ranch became merely the part of an enormous whole, a unit in the vast agglomeration of wheat land the whole world round, feeling the effects of causes thousands of miles distant—a drought on the prairies of Dakota, a rain on the plains of India, a frost on the Russian steppes, a hot wind on the llanos of the Argentine.

Harran crossed over to the telephone and rang six bells, the call for the division house on Four. It was the most distant, the most isolated point on all the ranch, situated at its far southeastern extremity, where few people ever went, close to the line fence, a dot, a speck, lost in the immensity of the open country. By the road it was eleven miles distant from the office, and by the trail to Hooven's and the Lower Road all of nine.

"How about that seed?" demanded Harran when he had got Cutter on the line.

The other made excuses for an unavoidable delay, and was adding that he was on the point of starting out, when Harran cut in with:

"You had better go the trail. It will save a little time and I am in a hurry. Put your sacks on the horses' backs. And, Cutter, if you see Hooven when you go by his place, tell him I want him, and, by the way, take a look at the end of the irrigating ditch when you get to it. See how they are getting along there and if Billy wants anything. Tell him we are expecting those new scoops down to-morrow or next day and to get along with what he has until then. . . . How's everything on Four? . . . All right, then. Give your seed to Phelps when you get here if I am not about. I am going to Guadalajara to meet the Governor. He's coming down to-day. And that makes me think; we lost the case, you know. I had a letter from the Governor yesterday. . . . Yes, hard luck. S. Behrman did us up. Well, good-bye, and don't lose any time with that seed. I want to blue-stone to-day."

After telephoning Cutter, Harran put on his hat, went over to the barns, and found Phelps. Phelps had already cleaned out the vat which was to contain the solution of blue-stone, and was now at work regrading the seed. Against the wall behind him ranged the row of sacks. Harran cut the fastenings of these and examined the contents carefully, taking handfuls of wheat from each and allowing it to run through his fingers, or nipping the grains between his nails, testing their hardness.

The seed was all of the white varieties of wheat and of a very high grade, the berries hard and heavy, rigid and swollen with starch.

"If it was all like that, sir, hey?" observed Phelps.

Harran put his chin in the air.

"Bread would be as good as cake, then," he answered, going from sack to sack, inspecting the contents and consulting the tags affixed to the mouths.

"Hello," he remarked, "here's a red wheat. Where did this come from?"

"That's that red Clawson we sowed to the piece on Four, north the Mission Creek, just to see how it would do here. We didn't get a very good catch."

"We can't do better than to stay by White Sonora and Propo," remarked Harran. "We've got our best results with that, and European millers like it to mix with the Eastern wheats that have more gluten than ours. That is, if we have any wheat at all next year."

A feeling of discouragement for the moment bore down heavily upon him. At intervals this came to him and for the moment it was overpowering. The idea of "what's-the-use" was upon occasion a veritable oppression. Everything seemed to combine to lower the price of wheat. The extension of wheat areas always exceeded increase of population; competition was growing fiercer every year. The farmer's profits were the object of attack from a score of different quarters. It was a flock of vultures descending upon a common prey—the commission merchant, the elevator combine, the mixing-house ring, the banks, the warehouse men, the labouring man, and, above all, the railroad. Steadily the Liverpool buyers cut and cut and cut. Everything, every element of the world's markets, tended to force down the price to the lowest possible figure at which it could be profitably farmed. Now it was down to eighty-seven. It was at that figure the crop had sold that year; and to think that the Governor had seen wheat at two dollars and five cents in the year of the Turko-Russian War!

He turned back to the house after giving Phelps final directions, gloomy, disheartened, his hands deep in his pockets, wondering what was to be the outcome. So narrow had the margin of profit shrunk that a dry season meant bankruptcy to the smaller farmers throughout all the valley. He knew very well how widespread had been the distress the last two years. With their own tenants on Los Muertos, affairs had reached the stage of desperation. Derrick had practically been obliged to "carry" Hooven and some of the others. The Governor himself had made almost nothing during the last season; a third year like the last, with the price steadily sagging, meant nothing else but ruin.

But here he checked himself. Two consecutive dry seasons in California were almost unprecedented; a third would be beyond belief, and the complete rest for nearly all the land was a compensation. They had made no money, that was true; but they had lost none. Thank God, the homestead was free of mortgage; one good season would more than make up the difference.

He was in a better mood by the time he reached the drive-way that led up to the ranch house, and as he raised his eyes toward the house itself, he could not but feel that the sight of his home was cheering. The ranch house was set in a great grove of eucalyptus, oak, and cypress, enormous trees growing from out a lawn that was as green, as fresh, and as well-groomed as any in a garden in the city. This lawn flanked all one side of the house, and it was on this side that the family elected to spend most of its time. The other side, looking out upon the Home ranch toward Bonneville and the railroad, was but little used. A deep porch ran the whole length of the house here, and in the lower branches of a live-oak near the steps Harran had built a little summer house for his mother. To the left of the ranch house itself, toward the County Road, was the bunk-house and kitchen for some of the hands. From the steps of the porch the view to the southward expanded to infinity. There was not so much as a twig to obstruct the view. In one leap the eye reached the fine, delicate line where earth and sky met, miles away. The flat monotony of the land, clean of fencing, was broken by one spot only, the roof of the Division Superintendent's house on Three—a mere speck, just darker than the ground. Cutter's house on Four was not even in sight. That was below the horizon.

As Harran came up he saw his mother at breakfast. The

table had been set on the porch and Mrs. Derrick, stirring her coffee with one hand, held open with the other the pages of Walter Pater's "Marius." At her feet, Princess Nathalie, the white Angora cat, sleek, over-fed, self-centred, sat on her haunches, industriously licking at the white fur of her breast, while near at hand, by the railing of the porch, Presley pottered with a new bicycle lamp, filling it with oil, adjusting the wicks.

Harran kissed his mother and sat down in a wicker chair on the porch, removing his hat, running his fingers through his yellow hair.

Magnus Derrick's wife looked hardly old enough to be the mother of two such big fellows as Harran and Lyman Derrick. She was not far into the fifties, and her brown hair still retained much of its brightness. She could yet be called pretty. Her eyes were large and easily assumed a look of inquiry and innocence, such as one might expect to see in a young girl. By disposition she was retiring; she easily obliterated herself. She was not made for the harshness of the world, and yet she had known these harshnesses in her younger days. Magnus had married her when she was twenty-one years old, at a time when she was a graduate of some years' standing from the State Normal School and was teaching literature, music, and penmanship in a seminary in the town of Marysville. She overworked herself here continually, loathing the strain of teaching, yet clinging to it with a tenacity born of the knowledge that it was her only means of support. Both her parents were dead; she was dependent upon herself. Her one ambition was to see Italy and the Bay of Naples. The "Marble Faun," Raphael's "Madonnas" and "Il Trovatore" were her beau ideals of literature and art. She dreamed of Italy, Rome, Naples, and the world's great "art-centres." There was no doubt that her affair with Magnus had been a love-match, but Annie Payne would have loved any man who would have taken her out of the droning, heart-breaking routine of the class and music room. She had followed his fortunes unquestioningly. First at Sacramento, during the turmoil of his political career, later on at Placerville in El Dorado County, after Derrick had interested himself in the Corpus Christi group of mines, and finally at Los Muertos, where, after selling out his fourth interest in Corpus Christi, he had turned rancher and had "come in" on the new tracts of wheat land just thrown open by the railroad. She had lived here now for nearly ten years. But never for one moment since the time her glance first lost itself in the unbroken immensity of the ranches had she known a moment's content. Continually there came into her pretty, wide-open eyes—the eyes of a young doe—a look of uneasiness, of distrust, and aversion. Los Muertos frightened her. She remembered the days of her young girlhood passed on a farm in eastern Ohio—five hundred acres, neatly partitioned into the water lot, the cow pasture, the corn lot, the barley field, and wheat farm; cosey, comfortable, home-like; where the farmers loved their land, caressing it, coaxing it, nourishing it as though it were a thing almost conscious; where the seed was sown by hand, and a single two-horse plough was sufficient for the entire farm; where the scythe sufficed to cut the harvest and the grain was thrashed with flails.

But this new order of things—a ranch bounded only by the horizons, where, as far as one could see, to the north, to the east, to the south and to the west, was all one holding, a principality ruled with iron and steam, bullied into a yield of three hundred and fifty thousand bushels, where even when the land was resting, unploughed, unharrowed, and unsown, the wheat came up—troubled her, and even at times filled her with an undefinable terror. To her mind there was something inordinate about it all; something almost unnatural. The direct brutality of ten thousand acres of wheat, nothing but wheat as far as the eye could see, stunned her a little. The one-time writing-teacher of a young ladies' seminary, with her pretty deer-like eyes and delicate fingers, shrank from it. She did not want to look at so much wheat. There was something vaguely indecent in the sight, this food of the people, this elemental force, this basic energy, weltering here under the sun in all the unconscious nakedness of a sprawling, primordial Titan.

The monotony of the ranch ate into her heart hour by hour, year by year. And with it all, when was she to see Rome, Italy, and the Bay of Naples? It was a different prospect truly. Magnus had given her his promise that once the ranch was well established, they two should travel. But continually he had been obliged to put her off, now for one reason, now for another; the machine would not as yet run of itself, he must still feel his hand upon the lever; next year, perhaps, when wheat should go to ninety, or the rains were good. She did not insist. She obliterated herself, only allowing, from time to time, her pretty, questioning eyes to meet his. In the meantime she retired within herself. She surrounded herself with books. Her taste was of the delicacy of point lace. She knew her Austin Dobson by heart. She read poems, essays, the ideas of the seminary at Marysville persisting in her mind. "Marius the Epicurean," "The Essays of Elia," "Sesame and Lilies," "The Stones of Venice," and the little toy magazines, full of the flaccid banalities of the "Minor Poets," were continually in her hands.

When Presley had appeared on Los Muertos, she had welcomed his arrival with delight. Here at last was a congenial spirit. She looked forward to long conversations with the young man on literature, art, and ethics. But Presley had disappointed her. That he—outside of his few chosen deities— should care little for literature, shocked her beyond words. His indifference to "style," to elegant English, was a positive affront. His savage abuse and open ridicule of the neatly phrased rondeaux and sestinas and chansonettes of the little magazines was to her mind a wanton and uncalled-for cruelty. She found his Homer, with its slaughters and hecatombs and barbaric feastings and headstrong passions, violent and coarse. She could not see with him any romance, any poetry in the life around her; she looked to Italy for that. His "Song of the West," which only once, incoherent and fierce, he had tried to explain to her, its swift, tumultuous life, its truth, its nobility and savagery, its heroism and obscenity, had revolted her.

"But, Presley," she had murmured, "that is not literature."

"No," he had cried between his teeth, "no, thank God, it is not."

A little later, one of the stablemen brought the buggy with the team of bays up to the steps of the porch, and Harran, putting on a different coat and a black hat, took himself off to Guadalajara.

The morning was fine; there was no cloud in the sky, but as Harran's buggy drew away from the grove of trees about the ranch house, emerging into the open country on either side of the Lower Road, he caught himself looking sharply at the sky and the faint line of hills beyond the Quien Sabe ranch. There was a certain indefinite cast to the landscape that to Harran's eye was not to be mistaken. Rain, the first of the season, was not far off.

"That's good," he muttered, touching the bays with the whip, "we can't get our ploughs to hand any too soon."

These ploughs Magnus Derrick had ordered from an Eastern manufacturer some months before, since he was dissatisfied with the results obtained from the ones he had used hitherto, which were of local make. However, there had been exasperating and unexpected delays in their shipment. Magnus and Harran both had counted upon having the ploughs in their implement barns that very week, but a tracer sent after them had only resulted in locating them, still *en route*, somewhere between The Needles and Bakersfield. Now there was likelihood of rain within the week. Ploughing could be undertaken immediately afterward, so soon as the ground was softened, but there was a fair chance that the ranch would lie idle for want of proper machinery.

It was ten minutes before train time when Harran reached the depot at Guadalajara. The San Francisco papers of the preceding day had arrived on an earlier train. He bought a couple from the station agent and looked them over till a distant and prolonged whistle announced the approach of the down train.

In one of the four passengers that alighted from the train, he recognised his father. He half rose in his seat, whistling shrilly between his teeth, waving his hand, and Magnus Derrick, catching sight of him, came forward quickly.

Magnus—the Governor—was all of six feet tall, and though now well toward his sixtieth year, was as erect as an officer of cavalry. He was broad in proportion, a fine commanding figure, imposing an immediate respect, impressing one with a sense of gravity, of dignity and a certain pride of race. He was smooth-shaven, thin-lipped, with a broad chin, and a prominent hawk-like nose—the characteristic of the family—thin, with a high bridge, such as one sees in the later portraits of the Duke of Wellington. His hair was thick and iron-grey, and had a tendency to curl in a forward direction just in front of his ears. He wore a top-hat of grey, with a wide brim, and a frock coat, and carried a cane with a yellowed ivory head.

As a young man it had been his ambition to represent his native State—North Carolina—in the United States Senate. Calhoun was his "great man," but in two successive campaigns he had been defeated. His career checked in this direction, he had come to California in the fifties. He had known and had been the intimate friend of such men as Terry, Broderick, General Baker, Lick, Alvarado, Emerich, Larkin, and, above all, of the unfortunate and misunderstood Ralston. Once he had been put forward as the Democratic candidate for governor, but failed of election. After this Magnus had definitely abandoned politics and had invested all his money in the Corpus Christi mines. Then he had sold out his interest at a small profit—just in time to miss his chance of becoming a multi-millionaire in the Comstock boom—and was looking for reinvestments in other lines when the news that "wheat had been discovered in California" was passed from mouth to mouth. Practically it amounted to a discovery. Dr. Glenn's first harvest of wheat in Colusa County, quietly undertaken but suddenly realised with dramatic abruptness, gave a new matter for reflection to the thinking men of the New West. California suddenly leaped unheralded into the world's market as a competitor in wheat production. In a few years her output of wheat exceeded the value of her output of gold, and when, later on, the Pacific and Southwestern Railroad threw open to settlers the rich lands of Tulare County—conceded to the corporation by the government as a bonus for the construction of the road—Magnus had been quick to seize the opportunity and had taken up the ten thousand acres of Los Muertos. Wherever he had gone, Magnus had taken his family with him. Lyman had been born at Sacramento during the turmoil and excitement of Derrick's campaign for governor, and Harran at Shingle Springs, in El Dorado County, six years later.

But Magnus was in every sense the "prominent man." In

whatever circle he moved he was the chief figure. Instinctively other men looked to him as the leader. He himself was proud of this distinction; he assumed the grand manner very easily and carried it well. As a public speaker he was one of the last of the followers of the old school of orators. He even carried the diction and manner of the rostrum into private life. It was said of him that his most colloquial conversation could be taken down in shorthand and read off as an admirable specimen of pure, well-chosen English. He loved to do things upon a grand scale, to preside, to dominate. In his good humour there was something Jovian. When angry, everybody around him trembled. But he had not the genius for detail, was not patient. The certain grandiose lavishness of his disposition occupied itself more with results than with means. He was always ready to take chances, to hazard everything on the hopes of colossal returns. In the mining days at Placerville there was no more redoubtable poker player in the county. He had been as lucky in his mines as in his gambling, sinking shafts and tunnelling in violation of expert theory and finding "pay" in every case. Without knowing it, he allowed himself to work his ranch much as if he was still working his mine. The old-time spirit of '49, hap-hazard, unscientific, persisted in his mind. Everything was a gamble—who took the greatest chances was most apt to be the greatest winner. The idea of manuring Los Muertos, of husbanding his great resources, he would have scouted as niggardly, Hebraic, ungenerous.

Magnus climbed into the buggy, helping himself with Harran's outstretched hand which he still held. The two were immensely fond of each other, proud of each other. They were constantly together and Magnus kept no secrets from his favourite son.

"Well, boy."

"Well, Governor."

"I am very pleased you came yourself, Harran. I feared that you might be too busy and send Phelps. It was thoughtful."

Harran was about to reply, but at that moment Magnus caught sight of the three flat cars loaded with bright-painted farming machines which still remained on the siding above the station. He laid his hands on the reins and Harran checked the team.

"Harran," observed Magnus, fixing the machinery with a judicial frown, "Harran, those look singularly like our ploughs. Drive over, boy."

The train had by this time gone on its way and Harran brought the team up to the siding.

"Ah, I was right," said the Governor. " 'Magnus Derrick, Los Muertos, Bonneville, from Ditson & Co., Rochester.' These are ours, boy."

Harran breathed a sigh of relief.

"At last," he answered, "and just in time, too. We'll have rain before the week is out. I think, now that I am here, I will telephone Phelps to send the wagon right down for these. I started blue-stoning to-day."

Magnus nodded a grave approval.

"That was shrewd, boy. As to the rain, I think you are well informed; we will have an early season. The ploughs have arrived at a happy moment."

"It means money to us, Governor," remarked Harran.

But as he turned the horses to allow his father to get into the buggy again, the two were surprised to hear a thick, throaty voice wishing them good-morning, and turning about were aware of S. Behrman, who had come up while they were examining the ploughs. Harran's eyes flashed on the instant and through his nostrils he drew a sharp, quick breath, while a certain rigour of carriage stiffened the set of Magnus Derrick's shoulders and back. Magnus had not yet got into the buggy, but stood with the team between him and S. Behrman, eyeing him calmly across the horses' backs. S. Behrman came around to the other side of the buggy and faced Magnus.

He was a large, fat man, with a great stomach; his cheek and the upper part of his thick neck ran together to form a great tremulous jowl, shaven and blue-grey in colour; a roll of fat, sprinkled with sparse hair, moist with perspiration, protruded over the back of his collar. He wore a heavy black moustache. On his head was a round-topped hat of stiff brown straw, highly varnished. A light-brown linen vest, stamped with innumerable interlocked horseshoes, covered his protuberant stomach, upon which a heavy watch chain of hollow links rose and fell with his difficult breathing, clinking against the vest buttons of imitation mother-of-pearl.

S. Behrman was the banker of Bonneville. But besides this he was many other things. He was a real estate agent. He bought grain; he dealt in mortgages. He was one of the local political bosses, but more important than all this, he was the representative of the Pacific and Southwestern Railroad in that section of Tulare County. The railroad did little business in that part of the country that S. Behrman did not supervise, from the consignment of a shipment of wheat to the management of a damage suit, or even to the repair and maintenance of the right of way. During the time when the ranchers of the county were fighting the grain-rate case, S. Behrman had been much in evidence in and about the San Francisco court rooms and the lobby of the legislature in Sacramento. He had returned to Bonneville only recently, a decision adverse to the ranchers being foreseen. The position he occupied on the salary list of the Pacific and Southwestern could not readily be defined, for he was neither freight agent, passenger agent, attorney, real-estate broker, nor political servant, though his influence in all these offices was undoubted and enormous. But for all that, the ranchers about Bonneville knew whom to look to as a source of trouble. There was no denying the fact that for Osterman, Broderson, Annixter and Derrick, S. Behrman was the railroad.

"Mr. Derrick, good-morning," he cried as he came up. "Good-morning, Harran. Glad to see you back, Mr. Derrick." He held out a thick hand.

Magnus, head and shoulders above the other, tall, thin, erect, looked down upon S. Behrman, inclining his head, failing to see his extended hand.

"Good-morning, sir," he observed, and waited for S. Behrman's further speech.

"Well, Mr. Derrick," continued S. Behrman, wiping the back of his neck with his handkerchief, "I saw in the city papers yesterday that our case had gone against you."

"I guess it wasn't any great news to *you*," commented Harran, his face scarlet. "I guess you knew which way Ulsteen was going to jump after your very first interview with him. You don't like to be surprised in this sort of thing, S. Behrman."

"Now, you know better than that, Harran," remonstrated S. Behrman blandly. "I know what you mean to imply, but I ain't going to let it make me get mad. I wanted to say to your Governor—I wanted to say to you, Mr. Derrick—as one man to another—letting alone for the minute that we were on opposite sides of the case—that I'm sorry you didn't win. Your side made a good fight, but it was in a mistaken cause. That's the whole trouble. Why, you could have figured out before you ever went into the case that such rates are confiscation of property. You must allow us—must allow the railroad—a fair interest on the investment. You don't want us to go into the receiver's hands, do you now, Mr. Derrick?"

"The Board of Railroad Commissioners was bought," remarked Magnus sharply, a keen, brisk flash glinting in his eye.

"It was part of the game," put in Harran, "for the Railroad Commission to cut rates to a ridiculous figure, far below a *reasonable* figure, just so that it *would* be confiscation. Whether Ulsteen is a tool of yours or not, he had to put the rates back to what they were originally."

"If you enforced those rates, Mr. Harran," returned S. Behrman calmly, "we wouldn't be able to earn sufficient money to meet operating expenses or fixed charges, to say nothing of a surplus left over to pay dividends——"

"Tell me when the P. and S. W. ever paid dividends."

"The lowest rates," continued S. Behrman, "that the legislature can establish must be such as will secure us a fair interest on our investment."

"Well, what's your standard? Come, let's hear it. Who is to say what's a fair rate? The railroad has its own notions of fairness sometimes."

"The laws of the State," returned S. Behrman, "fix the rate of interest at seven per cent. That's a good enough standard for us. There is no reason, Mr. Harran, why a dollar invested in a railroad should not earn as much as a dollar represented by a promissory note—seven per cent. By applying your schedule of rates we would not earn a cent; we would be bankrupt."

"Interest on your investment!" cried Harran, furious. "It's fine to talk about fair interest. *I* know and *you* know that the total earnings of the P. and S. W.—their main, branch and leased lines for last year—was between nineteen and twenty millions of dollars. Do you mean to say that twenty million dollars is seven per cent. of the original cost of the road?"

S. Behrman spread out his hands, smiling.

"That was the gross, not the net figure—and how can you tell what was the original cost of the road?"

"Ah, that's just it," shouted Harran, emphasising each word with a blow of his fist upon his knee, his eyes sparkling, "you take cursed good care that we don't know anything about the original cost of the road. But we know you are bonded for treble your value; and we know this: that the road *could* have been built for fifty-four thousand dollars per mile and that you *say* it cost you eighty-seven thousand. It makes a difference, S. Behrman, on which of these two figures you are basing your seven per cent."

"That all may show obstinacy, Harran," observed S. Behrman vaguely, "but it don't show common sense."

"We are threshing out old straw, I believe, gentlemen," remarked Magnus. "The question was thoroughly sifted in the courts."

"Quite right," assented S. Behrman. "The best way is that the railroad and the farmer understand each other and get along peaceably. We are both dependent on each other. Your ploughs, I believe, Mr. Derrick." S. Behrman nodded toward the flat cars.

"They are consigned to me," admitted Magnus.

"It looks a trifle like rain," observed S. Behrman, easing his neck and jowl in his limp collar. "I suppose you will want to begin ploughing next week."

"Possibly," said Magnus.

"I'll see that your ploughs are hurried through for you then, Mr. Derrick. We will route them by fast freight for you and it won't cost you anything extra."

"What do you mean?" demanded Harran. "The ploughs are here. We have nothing more to do with the railroad. I am going to have my wagons down here this afternoon."

"I am sorry," answered S. Behrman, "but the cars are going north, not, as you thought, coming *from* the north. They have not been to San Francisco yet."

Magnus made a slight movement of the head as one who

remembers a fact hitherto forgotten. But Harran was as yet unenlightened.

"To San Francisco!" he answered, "we want them here—what are you talking about?"

"Well, you know, of course, the regulations," answered S. Behrman. "Freight of this kind coming from the Eastern points into the State must go first to one of our common points and be reshipped from there."

Harran did remember now, but never before had the matter so struck home. He leaned back in his seat in dumb amazement for the instant. Even Magnus had turned a little pale. Then, abruptly, Harran broke out violent and raging.

"What next? My God, why don't you break into our houses at night? Why don't you steal the watch out of my pocket, steal the horses out of the harness, hold us up with a shotgun; yes, 'stand and deliver; your money or your life.' Here we bring our ploughs from the East over your lines, but you're not content with your long-haul rate between Eastern points and Bonneville. You want to get us under your ruinous short-haul rate between Bonneville and San Francisco, *and return*. Think of it! Here's a load of stuff for Bonneville that can't stop at Bonneville, where it is consigned, but has got to go up to San Francisco first *by way of* Bonneville, at forty cents per ton and then be reshipped from San Francisco back to Bonneville again at *fifty-one* cents per ton, the short-haul rate. And we have to pay it all or go without. Here are the ploughs right here, in sight of the land they have got to be used on, the season just ready for them, and we can't touch them. Oh," he exclaimed in deep disgust, "isn't it a pretty mess! Isn't it a farce! the whole dirty business!"

S. Behrman listened to him unmoved, his little eyes blinking under his fat forehead, the gold chain of hollow links clicking against the pearl buttons of his waistcoat as he breathed.

"It don't do any good to let loose like that, Harran," he said at length. "I am willing to do what I can for you. I'll hurry the ploughs through, but I can't change the freight regulation of the road."

"What's your blackmail for this?" vociferated Harran. "How much do you want to let us go? How much have we got to pay you to be *allowed* to use our own ploughs—what's your figure? Come, spit it out."

"I see you are trying to make me angry, Harran," returned S. Behrman, "but you won't succeed. Better give up trying, my boy. As I said, the best way is to have the railroad and the farmer get along amicably. It is the only way we can do business. Well, s'long, Governor, I must trot along. S'long, Harran." He took himself off.

But before leaving Guadalajara Magnus dropped into the town's small grocery store to purchase a box of cigars of a certain Mexican brand, unprocurable elsewhere. Harran remained in the buggy.

While he waited, Dyke appeared at the end of the street, and, seeing Derrick's younger son, came over to shake hands with him. He explained his affair with the P. and S. W., and asked the young man what he thought of the expected rise in the price of hops.

"Hops ought to be a good thing," Harran told him. "The crop in Germany and in New York has been a dead failure for the last three years, and so many people have gone out of the business that there's likely to be a shortage and a stiff advance in the price. They ought to go to a dollar next year. Sure, hops ought to be a good thing. How's the old lady and Sidney, Dyke?"

"Why, fairly well, thank you, Harran. They're up to Sacramento just now to see my brother. I was thinking of going in with my brother into this hop business. But I had a letter from him this morning. He may not be able to meet me on this proposition. He's got other business on hand. If he pulls out—and he probably will—I'll have to go it alone, but I'll have to borrow. I had thought with his money and mine we would have enough to pull off the affair without mortgaging anything. As it is, I guess I'll have to see S. Behrman."

"I'll be cursed if I would!" exclaimed Harran.

"Well, S. Behrman is a screw," admitted the engineer, "and he is 'railroad' to his boots; but business is business, and he would have to stand by a contract in black and white, and this chance in hops is too good to let slide. I guess we'll try it on, Harran. I can get a good foreman that knows all about hops just now, and if the deal pays—well, I want to send Sid to a seminary up in San Francisco."

"Well, mortgage the crops, but don't mortgage the homestead, Dyke," said Harran. "And, by the way, have you looked up the freight rates on hops?"

"No, I haven't yet," answered Dyke, "and I had better be sure of *that*, hadn't I? I hear that the rate is reasonable, though."

"You be sure to have a clear understanding with the railroad first about the rate," Harran warned him.

When Magnus came out of the grocery store and once more seated himself in the buggy, he said to Harran, "Boy, drive over here to Annixter's before we start home. I want to ask him to dine with us to-night. Osterman and Broderson are to drop in, I believe, and I should like to have Annixter as well."

Magnus was lavishly hospitable. Los Muertos's doors invariably stood open to all the Derricks' neighbours, and once in so often Magnus had a few of his intimates to dinner.

As Harran and his father drove along the road toward Annixter's ranch house, Magnus asked about what had happened during his absence.

He inquired after his wife and the ranch, commenting upon the work on the irrigating ditch. Harran gave him the news of the past week, Dyke's discharge, his resolve to raise a crop of hops; Vanamee's return, the killing of the sheep, and Hooven's petition to remain upon the ranch as Magnus's tenant. It needed only Harran's recommendation that the German should remain to have Magnus consent upon the instant.

"You know more about it than I, boy," he said, "and whatever you think is wise shall be done."

Harran touched the bays with the whip, urging them to their briskest pace. They were not yet at Annixter's and he was anxious to get back to the ranch house to supervise the blue-stoning of his seed.

"By the way, Governor," he demanded suddenly, "how is Lyman getting on?"

Lyman, Magnus's eldest son, had never taken kindly toward ranch life. He resembled his mother more than he did

Magnus, and had inherited from her a distaste for agriculture and a tendency toward a profession. At a time when Harran was learning the rudiments of farming, Lyman was entering the State University, and, graduating thence, had spent three years in the study of law. But later on, traits that were particularly his father's developed. Politics interested him. He told himself he was a born politician, was diplomatic, approachable, had a talent for intrigue, a gift of making friends easily and, most indispensable of all, a veritable genius for putting influential men under obligations to himself. Already he had succeeded in gaining for himself two important offices in the municipal administration of San Francisco—where he had his home—sheriff's attorney, and, later on, assistant district attorney. But with these small achievements he was by no means satisfied. The largeness of his father's character, modified in Lyman by a counter-influence of selfishness, had produced in him an inordinate ambition. Where his father during his political career had considered himself only as an exponent of principles he strove to apply, Lyman saw but the office, his own personal aggrandisement. He belonged to the new school, wherein objects were attained not by orations before senates and assemblies, but by sessions of committees, caucuses, compromises and expedients. His goal was to be in fact what Magnus was only in name—governor. Lyman, with shut teeth, had resolved that some day he would sit in the gubernatorial chair in Sacramento.

"Lyman is doing well," answered Magnus. "I could wish he was more pronounced in his convictions, less willing to compromise, but I believe him to be earnest and to have a talent for government and civics. His ambition does him credit, and if he occupied himself a little more with means and a little less with ends, he would, I am sure, be the ideal servant of the people. But I am not afraid. The time will come when the State will be proud of him."

As Harran turned the team into the driveway that led up to Annixter's house, Magnus remarked:

"Harran, isn't that young Annixter himself on the porch?"

Harran nodded and remarked:

"By the way, Governor, I wouldn't seem too cordial in your invitation to Annixter. He will be glad to come, I know, but if you seem to want him too much, it is just like his confounded obstinacy to make objections."

"There is something in that," observed Magnus, as Harran drew up at the porch of the house. "He is a queer, cross-grained fellow, but in many ways sterling."

Annixter was lying in the hammock on the porch, precisely as Presley had found him the day before, reading "David Copperfield" and stuffing himself with dried prunes. When he recognised Magnus, however, he got up, though careful to give evidence of the most poignant discomfort. He explained his difficulty at great length, protesting that his stomach was no better than a sponge-bag. Would Magnus and Harran get down and have a drink? There was whiskey somewhere about.

Magnus, however, declined. He stated his errand, asking Annixter to come over to Los Muertos that evening for seven o'clock dinner. Osterman and Broderson would be there.

At once Annixter, even to Harran's surprise, put his chin in the air, making excuses, fearing to compromise himself if he accepted too readily. No, he did not think he could get around—was sure of it, in fact. There were certain businesses he had on hand that evening. He had practically made an appointment with a man at Bonneville; then, too, he was thinking of going up to San Francisco to-morrow and needed his sleep; would go to bed early; and besides all that, he was a very sick man; his stomach was out of whack; if he moved about it brought the gripes back. No, they must get along without him.

Magnus, knowing with whom he had to deal, did not urge the point, being convinced that Annixter would argue over the affair the rest of the morning. He resettled himself in the buggy and Harran gathered up the reins.

"Well," he observed, "you know your business best. Come if you can. We dine at seven."

"I hear you are going to farm the whole of Los Muertos this season," remarked Annixter, with a certain note of challenge in his voice.

"We are thinking of it," replied Magnus.

Annixter grunted scornfully.

"Did you get the message I sent you by Presley?" he began.

Tactless, blunt, and direct, Annixter was quite capable of calling even Magnus a fool to his face. But before he could proceed, S. Behrman in his single buggy turned into the gate, and driving leisurely up to the porch halted on the other side of Magnus's team.

"Good-morning, gentlemen," he remarked, nodding to the two Derricks as though he had not seen them earlier in the day. "Mr. Annixter, how do you do?"

"What in hell do *you* want?" demanded Annixter with a stare.

S. Behrman hiccoughed slightly and passed a fat hand over his waistcoat.

"Why, not very much, Mr. Annixter," he replied, ignoring the belligerency in the young ranchman's voice, "but I will have to lodge a protest against you, Mr. Annixter, in the matter of keeping your line fence in repair. The sheep were all over the track last night, this side the Long Trestle, and I am afraid they have seriously disturbed our ballast along there. We—the railroad—can't fence along our right of way. The farmers have the prescriptive right of that, so we have to look to you to keep your fence in repair. I am sorry, but I shall have to protest——"

Annixter returned to the hammock and stretched himself out in it to his full length, remarking tranquilly:

"Go to the devil!"

"It is as much to your interest as to ours that the safety of the public——"

"You heard what I said. Go to the devil!"

"That all may show obstinacy, Mr. Annixter, but——"

Suddenly Annixter jumped up again and came to the edge of the porch; his face flamed scarlet to the roots of his stiff yellow hair. He thrust out his jaw aggressively, clenching his teeth.

"*You,*" he vociferated, "I'll tell you what you are. You're a—a—a *pip*!"

To his mind it was the last insult, the most outrageous calumny. He had no worse epithet at his command.

"——may show obstinacy," pursued S. Behrman, bent upon finishing the phrase, "but it don't show common sense."

"I'll mend my fence, and then, again, maybe I won't mend

my fence," shouted Annixter. "I know what you mean—that wild engine last night. Well, you've no right to run at that speed in the town limits."

"How the town limits? The sheep were this side the Long Trestle."

"Well, that's in the town limits of Guadalajara."

"Why, Mr. Annixter, the Long Trestle is a good two miles out of Guadalajara.

Annixter squared himself, leaping to the chance of an argument.

"Two miles! It's not a mile and a quarter. No, it's not a mile. I'll leave it to Magnus here."

"Oh, I know nothing about it," declared Magnus, refusing to be involved.

"Yes, you do. Yes, you do, too. Any fool knows how far it is from Guadalajara to the Long Trestle. It's about five-eighths of a mile."

"From the depot of the town," remarked S. Behrman placidly, "to the head of the Long Trestle is about two miles."

"That's a lie and you know it's a lie," shouted the other, furious at S. Behrman's calmness, "and I can prove it's a lie. I've walked that distance on the Upper Road, and I know just how fast I walk, and if I can walk four miles in one hour——"

Magnus and Harran drove on, leaving Annixter trying to draw S. Behrman into a wrangle.

When at length S. Behrman as well took himself away, Annixter returned to his hammock, finished the rest of his prunes and read another chapter of "Copperfield." Then he put the book, open, over his face and went to sleep.

An hour later, toward noon, his own terrific snoring woke him up suddenly, and he sat up, rubbing his face and blinking at the sunlight. There was a bad taste in his mouth from sleeping with it wide open, and going into the dining-room of the house, he mixed himself a drink of whiskey and soda and swallowed it in three great gulps. He told himself that he felt not only better but hungry, and pressed an electric button in the wall near the sideboard three times to let the kitchen— situated in a separate building near the ranch house—know that he was ready for his dinner. As he did so, an idea occurred to him. He wondered if Hilma Tree would bring up his dinner and wait on the table while he ate it.

In connection with his ranch, Annixter ran a dairy farm on a very small scale, making just enough butter and cheese for the consumption of the ranch's *personnel*. Old man Tree, his wife, and his daughter Hilma looked after the dairy. But there was not always work enough to keep the three of them occupied and Hilma at times made herself useful in other ways. As often as not she lent a hand in the kitchen, and two or three times a week she took her mother's place in looking after Annixter's house, making the beds, putting his room to rights, bringing his meals up from the kitchen. For the last summer she had been away visiting with relatives in one of the towns on the coast. But the week previous to this she had returned and Annixter had come upon her suddenly one day in the dairy, making cheese, the sleeves of her crisp blue shirt waist rolled back to her very shoulders. Annixter had carried away with him a clear-cut recollection of these smooth white arms of hers, bare to the shoulder, very round and cool and fresh. He would not have believed that a girl so young should have had arms so big and perfect. To his surprise he found himself thinking of her after he had gone to bed that night, and in the morning when he woke he was bothered to know whether he had dreamed about Hilma's fine white arms over night. Then abruptly he had lost patience with himself for being so occupied with the subject, raging and furious with all the breed of feemales—a fine way for a man to waste his time. He had had his experience with the timid little creature in the glove-cleaning establishment in Sacramento. That was enough. Feemales! Rot! None of them in *his*, thank you. *He* had seen Hilma Tree give him a look in the dairy. Aha, he saw through her! She was trying to get a hold on him, was she? He would show her. Wait till he saw her again. He would send her about her business in a hurry. He resolved upon a terrible demeanour in the presence of the dairy girl— a great show of indifference, a fierce masculine nonchalance; and when, the next morning, she brought him his breakfast, he had been smitten dumb as soon as she entered the room, glueing his eyes upon his plate, his elbows close to his side, awkward, clumsy, overwhelmed with constraint.

While true to his convictions as a woman-hater and genuinely despising Hilma both as a girl and as an inferior, the
idea of her worried him. Most of all, he was angry with himself because of his inane sheepishness when she was about.
He at first had told himself that he was a fool not to be able
to ignore her existence as hitherto, and then that he was a
greater fool not to take advantage of his position. Certainly
he had not the remotest idea of any affection, but Hilma was
a fine looking girl. He imagined an affair with her.

As he reflected upon the matter now, scowling abstractedly
at the button of the electric bell, turning the whole business
over in his mind, he remembered that to-day was butter-
making day and that Mrs. Tree would be occupied in the
dairy. That meant that Hilma would take her place. He
turned to the mirror of the sideboard, scrutinising his reflection with grim disfavour. After a moment, rubbing the
roughened surface of his chin the wrong way, he muttered to
his image in the glass:

"What a mug! Good Lord! what a looking mug!" Then,
after a moment's silence. "Wonder if that fool feemale will be
up here to-day."

He crossed over into his bedroom and peeped around the
edge of the lowered curtain. The window looked out upon
the skeleton-like tower of the artesian well and the cook-
house and dairy-house close beside it. As he watched, he saw
Hilma come out from the cook-house and hurry across toward the kitchen. Evidently, she was going to see about his
dinner. But as she passed by the artesian well, she met
young Delaney, one of Annixter's hands, coming up the trail
by the irrigating ditch, leading his horse toward the stables,
a great coil of barbed wire in his gloved hands and a pair of
nippers thrust into his belt. No doubt, he had been mending
the break in the line fence by the Long Trestle. Annixter saw
him take off his wide-brimmed hat as he met Hilma, and the
two stood there for some moments talking together. Annixter even heard Hilma laughing very gayly at something Delaney was saying. She patted his horse's neck affectionately,
and Delaney, drawing the nippers from his belt, made as if
to pinch her arm with them. She caught at his wrist and
pushed him away, laughing again. To Annixter's mind the

pair seemed astonishingly intimate. Brusquely his anger flamed up.

Ah, that was it, was it? Delaney and Hilma had an understanding between themselves. They carried on their affair right out there in the open, under his very eyes. It was absolutely disgusting. Had they no sense of decency, those two? Well, this ended it. He would stop that sort of thing short off; none of that on *his* ranch if he knew it. No, sir. He would pack that girl off before he was a day older. He wouldn't have that kind about the place. Not much! She'd have to get out. He would talk to old man Tree about it this afternoon. Whatever happened, *he* insisted upon morality.

"And my dinner!" he suddenly exclaimed. "I've got to wait and go hungry—and maybe get sick again—while they carry on their disgusting love-making."

He turned about on the instant, and striding over to the electric bell, rang it again with all his might.

"When that feemale gets up here," he declared, "I'll just find out why I've got to wait like this. I'll take her down, to the Queen's taste. I'm lenient enough, Lord knows, but I don't propose to be imposed upon *all* the time."

A few moments later, while Annixter was pretending to read the county newspaper by the window in the dining-room, Hilma came in to set the table. At the time Annixter had his feet cocked on the window ledge and was smoking a cigar, but as soon as she entered the room he—without premeditation—brought his feet down to the floor and crushed out the lighted tip of his cigar under the window ledge. Over the top of the paper he glanced at her covertly from time to time.

Though Hilma was only nineteen years old, she was a large girl with all the development of a much older woman. There was a certain generous amplitude to the full, round curves of her hips and shoulders that suggested the precocious maturity of a healthy, vigorous animal life passed under the hot southern sun of a half-tropical country. She was, one knew at a glance, warm-blooded, full-blooded, with an even, comfortable balance of temperament. Her neck was thick, and sloped to her shoulders, with full, beautiful curves, and under her chin and under her ears the flesh was as white and smooth as floss satin, shading exquisitely to a faint delicate brown on her nape at the roots of her hair. Her throat rounded to meet her chin and cheek, with a soft swell of the skin, tinted pale amber in the shadows, but blending by barely perceptible gradations to the sweet, warm flush of her cheek. This colour on her temples was just touched with a certain blueness where the flesh was thin over the fine veining underneath. Her eyes were light brown, and so wide open that on the slightest provocation the full disc of the pupil was disclosed; the lids— just a fraction of a shade darker than the hue of her face— were edged with lashes that were almost black. While these lashes were not long, they were thick and rimmed her eyes with a fine, thin line. Her mouth was rather large, the lips shut tight, and nothing could have been more graceful, more charming than the outline of these full lips of hers, and her round white chin, modulating downward with a certain delicious roundness to her neck, her throat and the sweet feminine amplitude of her breast. The slightest movement of her head and shoulders sent a gentle undulation through all this beauty of soft outlines and smooth surfaces, the delicate amber shadows deepening or fading or losing themselves imperceptibly in the pretty rose-colour of her cheeks, or the dark, warm-tinted shadow of her thick brown hair.

Her hair seemed almost to have a life of its own, almost Medusa-like, thick, glossy and moist, lying in heavy, sweet-smelling masses over her forehead, over her small ears with their pink lobes, and far down upon her nape. Deep in between the coils and braids it was of a bitumen brownness, but in the sunlight it vibrated with a sheen like tarnished gold.

Like most large girls, her movements were not hurried, and this indefinite deliberateness of gesture, this slow grace, this certain ease of attitude, was a charm that was all her own.

But Hilma's greatest charm of all was her simplicity—a simplicity that was not only in the calm regularity of her face, with its statuesque evenness of contour, its broad surface of cheek and forehead and the masses of her straight smooth hair, but was apparent as well in the long line of her carriage, from her foot to her waist and the single deep swell from her waist to her shoulder. Almost unconsciously she dressed in harmony with this note of simplicity, and on this occasion wore a skirt of plain dark blue calico and a white shirt waist crisp from the laundry.

And yet, for all the dignity of this rigourous simplicity, there were about Hilma small contradictory suggestions of feminine daintiness, charming beyond words. Even Annixter could not help noticing that her feet were narrow and slender, and that the little steel buckles of her low shoes were polished bright, and that her finger-tips and nails were of a fine rosy pink.

He found himself wondering how it was that a girl in Hilma's position should be able to keep herself so pretty, so trim, so clean and feminine, but he reflected that her work was chiefly in the dairy, and even there of the lightest order. She was on the ranch more for the sake of being with her parents than from any necessity of employment. Vaguely he seemed to understand that, in that great new land of the West, in the open-air, healthy life of the ranches, where the conditions of earning a livelihood were of the easiest, refinement among the younger women was easily to be found—not the refinement of education, nor culture, but the natural, intuitive refinement of the woman, not as yet defiled and crushed out by the sordid, strenuous life-struggle of over-populated districts. It was the original, intended and natural delicacy of an elemental existence, close to nature, close to life, close to the great, kindly earth.

As Hilma laid the table-spread, her arms opened to their widest reach, the white cloth setting a little glisten of reflected light underneath the chin, Annixter stirred in his place uneasily.

"Oh, it's you, is it, Miss Hilma?" he remarked, for the sake of saying something. "Good-morning. How do you do?"

"*Good*-morning, sir," she answered, looking up, resting for a moment on her outspread palms. "I hope you are better."

Her voice was low in pitch and of a velvety huskiness, seeming to come more from her chest than from her throat.

"Well, I'm some better," growled Annixter. Then suddenly he demanded, "Where's that dog?"

A decrepit Irish setter sometimes made his appearance in and about the ranch house, sleeping under the bed and eating when anyone about the place thought to give him a plate of bread.

Annixter had no particular interest in the dog. For weeks at a time he ignored its existence. It was not his dog. But to-day it seemed as if he could not let the subject rest. For no reason that he could explain even to himself, he recurred to it continually. He questioned Hilma minutely all about the dog. Who owned him? How old did she think he was? Did she imagine the dog was sick? Where had he got to? Maybe he had crawled off to die somewhere. He recurred to the subject all through the meal; apparently, he could talk of nothing else, and as she finally went away after clearing off the table, he went onto the porch and called after her:

"Say, Miss Hilma."

"Yes, sir."

"If that dog turns up again you let me know."

"Very well, sir."

Annixter returned to the dining-room and sat down in the chair he had just vacated.

"To hell with the dog!" he muttered, enraged, he could not tell why.

When at length he allowed his attention to wander from Hilma Tree, he found that he had been staring fixedly at a thermometer upon the wall opposite, and this made him think that it had long been his intention to buy a fine barom-eter, an instrument that could be accurately depended on. But the barometer suggested the present condition of the weather and the likelihood of rain. In such case, much was to be done in the way of getting the seed ready and overhauling his ploughs and drills. He had not been away from the house in two days. It was time to be up and doing. He determined to put in the afternoon "taking a look around," and have a late supper. He would not go to Los Muertos; he would ignore Magnus Derrick's invitation. Possibly, though, it might be well to run over and see what was up.

"If I do," he said to himself, "I'll ride the buckskin."

The buckskin was a half-broken broncho that fought like a fiend under the saddle until the quirt and spur brought her to her senses. But Annixter remembered that the Trees' cottage, next the dairy-house, looked out upon the stables, and per-haps Hilma would see him while he was mounting the horse and be impressed with his courage.

"Huh!" grunted Annixter under his breath, "I should like to see that fool Delaney try to bust that bronch. That's what *I'd* like to see."

However, as Annixter stepped from the porch of the ranch house, he was surprised to notice a grey haze over all the sky; the sunlight was gone; there was a sense of coolness in the air; the weather-vane on the barn—a fine golden trotting horse with flamboyant mane and tail—was veering in a southwest wind. Evidently the expected rain was close at hand.

Annixter crossed over to the stables reflecting that he could ride the buckskin to the Trees' cottage and tell Hilma that he would not be home to supper. The conference at Los Muertos would be an admirable excuse for this, and upon the spot he resolved to go over to the Derrick ranch house, after all.

As he passed the Trees' cottage, he observed with satisfaction that Hilma was going to and fro in the front room. If he busted the buckskin in the yard before the stable she could not help but see. Annixter found the stableman in the back of the barn greasing the axles of the buggy, and ordered him to put the saddle on the buckskin.

"Why, I don't think she's here, sir," answered the stableman, glancing into the stalls. "No, I remember now. Delaney took her out just after dinner. His other horse went lame and he wanted to go down by the Long Trestle to mend the fence. He started out, but had to come back."

"Oh, Delaney got her, did he?"

"Yes, sir. He had a circus with her, but he busted her right enough. When it comes to horse, Delaney can wipe the eye of any cow-puncher in the county, I guess."

"He can, can he?" observed Annixter. Then after a silence, "Well, all right, Billy; put my saddle on whatever you've got here. I'm going over to Los Muertos this afternoon."

"Want to look out for the rain, Mr. Annixter," remarked Billy. "Guess we'll have rain before night."

"I'll take a rubber coat," answered Annixter. "Bring the horse up to the ranch house when you're ready."

Annixter returned to the house to look for his rubber coat in deep disgust, not permitting himself to glance toward the dairy-house and the Trees' cottage. But as he reached the porch he heard the telephone ringing his call. It was Presley, who rang up from Los Muertos. He had heard from Harran that Annixter was, perhaps, coming over that evening. If he came, would he mind bringing over his—Presley's—bicycle. He had left it at the Quien Sabe ranch the day before and had forgotten to come back that way for it.

"Well," objected Annixter, a surly note in his voice, "I *was* going to *ride* over."

"Oh, never mind, then," returned Presley easily. "I was to blame for forgetting it. Don't bother about it. I'll come over some of these days and get it myself."

Annixter hung up the transmitter with a vehement wrench and stamped out of the room, banging the door. He found his rubber coat hanging in the hallway and swung into it with a fierce movement of the shoulders that all but started the seams. Everything seemed to conspire to thwart him. It was just like that absent-minded, crazy poet, Presley, to forget his wheel. Well, he could come after it himself. He, Annixter, would ride *some* horse, anyhow. When he came out upon the porch he saw the wheel leaning against the fence where Presley had left it. If it stayed there much longer the rain would catch it. Annixter ripped out an oath. At every moment his ill-humour was increasing. Yet, for all that, he went back to the stable, pushing the bicycle before him, and counter-manded his order, directing the stableman to get the buggy ready. He himself carefully stowed Presley's bicycle under the seat, covering it with a couple of empty sacks and a tarpaulin carriage cover.

While he was doing this, the stableman uttered an exclamation and paused in the act of backing the horse into the shafts, holding up a hand, listening.

From the hollow roof of the barn and from the thick vel-vet-like padding of dust over the ground outside, and from among the leaves of the few nearby trees and plants there came a vast, monotonous murmur that seemed to issue from all quarters of the horizon at once, a prolonged and subdued rustling sound, steady, even, persistent.

"There's your rain," announced the stableman. "The first of the season."

"And I got to be out in it," fumed Annixter, "and I sup-pose those swine will quit work on the big barn now."

When the buggy was finally ready, he put on his rubber coat, climbed in, and without waiting for the stableman to raise the top, drove out into the rain, a new-lit cigar in his teeth. As he passed the dairy-house, he saw Hilma standing in the doorway, holding out her hand to the rain, her face turned upward toward the grey sky, amused and interested at this first shower of the wet season. She was so absorbed that she did not see Annixter, and his clumsy nod in her direction passed unnoticed.

"She did it on purpose," Annixter told himself, chewing fiercely on his cigar. "Cuts me now, hey? Well, this *does* settle it. She leaves this ranch before I'm a day older."

He decided that he would put off his tour of inspection till the next day. Travelling in the buggy as he did, he must keep to the road which led to Derrick's, in very roundabout fashion, by way of Guadalajara. This rain would reduce the thick dust of the road to two feet of viscid mud. It would take him quite three hours to reach the ranch house on Los Muertos. He thought of Delaney and the buckskin and ground his teeth. And all this trouble, if you please, because of a fool feemale girl. A fine way for him to waste his time. Well, now he was done with it. His decision was taken now. She should pack.

Steadily the rain increased. There was no wind. The thick veil of wet descended straight from sky to earth, blurring distant outlines, spreading a vast sheen of grey over all the landscape. Its volume became greater, the prolonged murmuring note took on a deeper tone. At the gate to the road which led across Dyke's hop-fields toward Guadalajara, Annixter was obliged to descend and raise the top of the buggy. In doing so he caught the flesh of his hand in the joint of the iron elbow that supported the top and pinched it cruelly. It was the last misery, the culmination of a long train of wretchedness. On the instant he hated Hilma Tree so fiercely that his sharply set teeth all but bit his cigar in two.

While he was grabbing and wrenching at the buggy-top, the water from his hat brim dripping down upon his nose, the horse, restive under the drench of the rain, moved uneasily.

"Yah-h-h you!" he shouted, inarticulate with exasperation.

"You—you—Gor-r-r, wait till I get hold of you. *Whoa,* you!"

But there was an interruption. Delaney, riding the buckskin, came around a bend in the road at a slow trot and Annixter, getting into the buggy again, found himself face to face with him.

"Why, hello, Mr. Annixter," said he, pulling up. "Kind of sort of wet, isn't it?"

Annixter, his face suddenly scarlet, sat back in his place abruptly, exclaiming:

"Oh—oh, there you are, are you?"

"I've been down there," explained Delaney, with a motion of his head toward the railroad, "to mend that break in the fence by the Long Trestle and I thought while I was about it I'd follow down along the fence toward Guadalajara to see if there were any more breaks. But I guess it's all right."

"Oh, you guess it's all right, do you?" observed Annixter through his teeth.

"Why—why—yes," returned the other, bewildered at the truculent ring in Annixter's voice. "I mended that break by the Long Trestle just now and——"

"Well, why didn't you mend it a week ago?" shouted Annixter wrathfully. "I've been looking for you all the morning, I have, and who told you you could take that buckskin? And the sheep were all over the right of way last night because of that break, and here that filthy pip, S. Behrman, comes down here this morning and wants to make trouble for me." Suddenly he cried out, "What do I *feed* you for? What do I keep you around here for? Think it's just to fatten up your carcass, hey?"

"Why, Mr. Annixter——" began Delaney.

"And don't *talk* to me," vociferated the other, exciting himself with his own noise. "Don't you say a word to me even to apologise. If I've spoken to you once about that break, I've spoken fifty times."

"Why, sir," declared Delaney, beginning to get indignant, "the sheep did it themselves last night."

"I told you not to *talk* to me," clamoured Annixter.

"But, say, look here——"

"Get off the ranch. You get off the ranch. And taking that

buckskin against my express orders. I won't have your kind about the place, not much. I'm easy-going enough, Lord knows, but I don't propose to be imposed on *all* the time. Pack off, you understand, and do it lively. Go to the foreman and tell him I told him to pay you off and then clear out. And, you hear *me*," he concluded, with a menacing outthrust of his lower jaw, "you hear me, if I catch you hanging around the ranch house after this, or if I so much as see you on Quien Sabe, I'll show you the way off of it, my friend, at the toe of my boot. Now, then, get out of the way and let me pass."

Angry beyond the power of retort, Delaney drove the spurs into the buckskin and passed the buggy in a single bound. Annixter gathered up the reins and drove on, muttering to himself, and occasionally looking back to observe the buckskin flying toward the ranch house in a spattering shower of mud, Delaney urging her on, his head bent down against the falling rain.

"Huh," grunted Annixter with grim satisfaction, a certain sense of good humour at length returning to him, "that just about takes the saleratus out of *your* dough, my friend."

A little farther on, Annixter got out of the buggy a second time to open another gate that let him out upon the Upper Road, not far distant from Guadalajara. It was the road that connected that town with Bonneville, and that ran parallel with the railroad tracks. On the other side of the track he could see the infinite extension of the brown, bare land of Los Muertos, turning now to a soft, moist welter of fertility under the insistent caressing of the rain. The hard, sun-baked clods were decomposing, the crevices between drinking the wet with an eager, sucking noise. But the prospect was dreary; the distant horizons were blotted under drifting mists of rain; the eternal monotony of the earth lay open to the sombre low sky without a single adornment, without a single variation from its melancholy flatness. Near at hand the wires between the telegraph poles vibrated with a faint humming under the multitudinous fingering of the myriad of falling drops, striking among them and dripping off steadily from one to another. The poles themselves were dark and swollen and glistening with wet, while the little cones of glass on the transverse bars reflected the dull grey light of the end of the afternoon.

As Annixter was about to drive on, a freight train passed, coming from Guadalajara, going northward toward Bonneville, Fresno and San Francisco. It was a long train, moving slowly, methodically, with a measured coughing of its locomotive and a rhythmic cadence of its trucks over the interstices of the rails. On two or three of the flat cars near its end, Annixter plainly saw Magnus Derrick's ploughs, their bright coating of red and green paint setting a single brilliant note in all this array of grey and brown.

Annixter halted, watching the train file past, carrying Derrick's ploughs away from his ranch, at this very time of the first rain, when they would be most needed. He watched it, silent, thoughtful, and without articulate comment. Even after it passed he sat in his place a long time, watching it lose itself slowly in the distance, its prolonged rumble diminishing to a faint murmur. Soon he heard the engine sounding its whistle for the Long Trestle.

But the moving train no longer carried with it that impression of terror and destruction that had so thrilled Presley's imagination the night before. It passed slowly on its way with a mournful roll of wheels, like the passing of a cortege, like a file of artillery-caissons charioting dead bodies; the engine's smoke enveloping it in a mournful veil, leaving a sense of melancholy in its wake, moving past there, lugubrious, lamentable, infinitely sad, under the grey sky and under the grey mist of rain which continued to fall with a subdued, rustling sound, steady, persistent, a vast monotonous murmur that seemed to come from all quarters of the horizon at once.

III

WHEN ANNIXTER arrived at the Los Muertos ranch house that same evening, he found a little group already assembled in the dining-room. Magnus Derrick, wearing the frock coat of broadcloth that he had put on for the occasion, stood with his back to the fireplace. Harran sat close at hand, one leg thrown over the arm of his chair. Presley lounged on the sofa, in corduroys and high laced boots, smoking cigarettes. Broderson leaned on his folded arms at one corner of the dining table, and Genslinger, editor and proprietor of the principal newspaper of the county, the "Bonneville Mercury," stood with his hat and driving gloves under his arm, opposite Derrick, a half-emptied glass of whiskey and water in his hand.

As Annixter entered he heard Genslinger observe: "I'll have a leader in the 'Mercury' to-morrow that will interest you people. There's some talk of your ranch lands being graded in value this winter. I suppose you will all buy?"

In an instant the editor's words had riveted upon him the attention of every man in the room. Annixter broke the moment's silence that followed with the remark:

"Well, it's about time they graded these lands of theirs."

The question in issue in Genslinger's remark was of the most vital interest to the ranchers around Bonneville and Guadalajara. Neither Magnus Derrick, Broderson, Annixter, nor Osterman actually owned all the ranches which they worked. As yet, the vast majority of these wheat lands were the property of the P. and S. W. The explanation of this condition of affairs went back to the early history of the Pacific and Southwestern, when, as a bonus for the construction of the road, the national government had granted to the company the odd numbered sections of land on either side of the proposed line of route for a distance of twenty miles. Indisputably, these sections belonged to the P. and S. W. The even-numbered sections being government property could be and had been taken up by the ranchers, but the railroad sections, or, as they were called, the "alternate sections," would have to be purchased direct from the railroad itself.

But this had not prevented the farmers from "coming in" upon that part of the San Joaquin. Long before this the railroad had thrown open these lands, and, by means of circulars, distributed broadcast throughout the State, had expressly invited settlement thereon. At that time patents had not been issued to the railroad for their odd-numbered sections, but as soon as the land was patented the railroad would grade it in value and offer it for sale, the first occupants having the first chance of purchase. The price of these lands was to be fixed by the price the government put upon its own adjoining lands—about two dollars and a half per acre.

With cultivation and improvement the ranches must inevitably appreciate in value. There was every chance to make fortunes. When the railroad lands about Bonneville had been thrown open, there had been almost a rush in the matter of settlement, and Broderson, Annixter, Derrick, and Osterman, being foremost with their claims, had secured the pick of the country. But the land once settled upon, the P. and S. W. seemed to be in no hurry as to fixing exactly the value of its sections included in the various ranches and offering them for sale. The matter dragged along from year to year, was forgotten for months together, being only brought to mind on such occasions as this, when the rumour spread that the General Office was about to take definite action in the affair.

"As soon as the railroad wants to talk business with me," observed Annixter, "about selling me their interest in Quien Sabe, I'm ready. The land has more than quadrupled in value. I'll bet I could sell it to-morrow for fifteen dollars an acre, and if I buy of the railroad for two and a half an acre, there's boodle in the game."

"For two and a half!" exclaimed Genslinger. "You don't suppose the railroad will let their land go for any such figure as that, do you? Wherever did you get that idea?"

"From the circulars and pamphlets," answered Harran, "that the railroad issued to us when they opened these lands. They are pledged to that. Even the P. and S. W. couldn't break such a pledge as that. You are new in the country, Mr. Genslinger. You don't remember the conditions upon which we took up this land."

"And our improvements," exclaimed Annixter. "Why, Magnus and I have put about five thousand dollars between us into that irrigating ditch already. I guess we are not improving the land just to make it valuable for the railroad people. No matter how much we improve the land, or how much it increases in value, they have got to stick by their agreement on the basis of two-fifty per acre. Here's one case where the P. and S. W. *don't* get everything in sight."

Genslinger frowned, perplexed.

"I *am* new in the country, as Harran says," he answered, "but it seems to me that there's no fairness in that proposition. The presence of the railroad has helped increase the value of your ranches quite as much as your improvements. Why should you get all the benefit of the rise in value and the railroad nothing? The fair way would be to share it between you."

"I don't care anything about that," declared Annixter. "They agreed to charge but two-fifty, and they've got to stick to it."

"Well," murmured Genslinger, "from what I know of the affair, I don't believe the P. and S. W. intends to sell for two-fifty an acre, at all. The managers of the road want the best price they can get for everything in these hard times."

"Times aren't ever very hard for the railroad," hazards old Broderson.

Broderson was the oldest man in the room. He was about sixty-five years of age, venerable, with a white beard, his figure bent earthwards with hard work.

He was a narrow-minded man, painfully conscientious in his statements lest he should be unjust to somebody; a slow thinker, unable to let a subject drop when once he had started upon it. He had no sooner uttered his remark about hard times than he was moved to qualify it.

"Hard times," he repeated, a troubled, perplexed note in his voice; " well, yes—yes. I suppose the road *does* have hard times, maybe. Everybody does—of course. I didn't mean that exactly. I believe in being just and fair to everybody. I mean that we've got to use their lines and pay their charges good years *and* bad years, the P. and S. W. being the only road in the State. That is—well, when I say the only road—no, I won't say the *only* road. Of course there are other roads. There's the D. P. and M. and the San Francisco and North Pacific, that runs up to Ukiah. I got a brother-in-law in Ukiah. That's not much of a wheat country round Ukiah, though they *do* grow *some* wheat there, come to think. But I guess it's too far north. Well, of course there isn't *much*. Perhaps sixty thousand acres in the whole county—if you include barley and oats. I don't know; maybe it's nearer forty thousand. I don't remember very well. That's a good many years ago. I——"

But Annixter, at the end of all patience, turned to Genslinger, cutting short the old man:

"Oh, rot! Of course the railroad will sell at two-fifty," he cried. "We've got the contracts."

"Look to them, then, Mr. Annixter," retorted Genslinger significantly, "look to them. Be sure that you are protected."

Soon after this Genslinger took himself away, and Derrick's Chinaman came in to set the table.

"What do you suppose he meant?" asked Broderson, when Genslinger was gone.

"About this land business?" said Annixter. "Oh, I don't know. Some tom fool idea. Haven't we got their terms printed in black and white in their circulars? There's their pledge."

"Oh, as to pledges," murmured Broderson, "the railroad is not always *too* much hindered by those."

"Where's Osterman?" demanded Annixter, abruptly changing the subject as if it were not worth discussion. "Isn't that goat Osterman coming down here to-night?"

"You telephoned him, didn't you, Presley?" inquired Magnus.

Presley had taken Princess Nathalie upon his knee, stroking her long, sleek hair, and the cat, stupefied with beatitude, had closed her eyes to two fine lines, clawing softly at the corduroy of Presley's trousers with alternate paws.

"Yes, sir," returned Presley. "He said he would be here."

And as he spoke, young Osterman arrived.

He was a young fellow, but singularly inclined to baldness. His ears, very red and large, stuck out at right angles from either side of his head, and his mouth, too, was large—a great horizontal slit beneath his nose. His cheeks were of a brownish red, the cheek bones a little salient. His face was that of a comic actor, a singer of songs, a man never at a loss for an answer, continually striving to make a laugh. But he took no great interest in ranching and left the management of his land to his superintendents and foremen, he, himself, living in Bonneville. He was a poser, a wearer of clothes, forever acting a part, striving to create an impression, to draw attention to himself. He was not without a certain energy, but he devoted it to small ends, to perfecting himself in little accomplishments, continually running after some new thing, incapable of persisting long in any one course. At one moment his mania would be fencing; the next, sleight-of-hand tricks; the next, archery. For upwards of one month he had devoted himself to learning how to play two banjos simultaneously, then abandoning this had developed a sudden passion for stamped leather work and had made a quantity of purses, tennis belts, and hat bands, which he presented to young ladies of his acquaintance. It was his policy never to make an enemy. He was liked far better than he was respected. People spoke of him as "that goat Osterman," or "that fool Osterman kid," and invited him to dinner. He was of the sort who somehow cannot be ignored. If only because of his clamour he made himself important. If he had one abiding trait, it was his desire of astonishing people, and in some way, best known to himself, managed to cause the circulation of the most extraordinary stories wherein he, himself, was the chief actor. He was glib, voluble, dexterous, ubiquitous, a teller of funny stories, a cracker of jokes.

Naturally enough, he was heavily in debt, but carried the burden of it with perfect nonchalance. The year before S. Behrman had held mortgages for fully a third of his crop and had squeezed him viciously for interest. But for all that, Osterman and S. Behrman were continually seen arm-in-arm on the main street of Bonneville. Osterman was accustomed to slap S. Behrman on his fat back, declaring:

"You're a good fellow, old jelly-belly, after all, hey?"

As Osterman entered from the porch, after hanging his cavalry poncho and dripping hat on the rack outside, Mrs. Derrick appeared in the door that opened from the dining-room into the glass-roofed hallway just beyond. Osterman saluted her with effusive cordiality and with ingratiating blandness.

"I am not going to stay," she explained, smiling pleasantly at the group of men, her pretty, wide-open brown eyes, with their look of inquiry and innocence, glancing from face to face, "I only came to see if you wanted anything and to say how do you do."

She began talking to old Broderson, making inquiries as to his wife, who had been sick the last week, and Osterman turned to the company, shaking hands all around, keeping up an incessant stream of conversation.

"Hello, boys and girls. Hello, Governor. Sort of a gathering of the clans to-night. Well, if here isn't that man Annixter. Hello, Buck. What do you know? Kind of dusty out to-night."

At once Annixter began to get red in the face, retiring towards a corner of the room, standing in an awkward position by the case of stuffed birds, shambling and confused, while Mrs. Derrick was present, standing rigidly on both feet, his elbows close to his sides. But he was angry with Osterman, muttering imprecations to himself, horribly vexed that the young fellow should call him "Buck" before Magnus's wife. This goat Osterman! Hadn't he any sense, that fool? Couldn't he ever learn how to behave before a feemale? Calling him "Buck" like that while Mrs. Derrick was there. Why a stable-boy would know better; a hired man would have better manners.

All through the dinner that followed Annixter was out of sorts, sulking in his place, refusing to eat by way of vindicating his self-respect, resolving to bring Osterman up with a sharp turn if he called him "Buck" again.

The Chinaman had made a certain kind of plum pudding for dessert, and Annixter, who remembered other dinners at the Derricks', had been saving himself for this, and had meditated upon it all through the meal. No doubt, it would restore all his good humour, and he believed his stomach was so far recovered as to be able to stand it.

But, unfortunately, the pudding was served with a sauce that he abhorred—a thick, gruel-like, colourless mixture, made from plain water and sugar. Before he could interfere, the Chinaman had poured a quantity of it upon his plate.

"Faugh!" exclaimed Annixter. "It makes me sick. Such—such *sloop*. Take it away. I'll have mine straight, if you don't mind."

"That's good for your stomach, Buck," observed young Osterman; "makes it go down kind of sort of slick; don't you see? Sloop, hey? That's a good name."

"Look here, don't you call me Buck. You don't seem to have any sense, and, besides, it *isn't* good for my stomach. I know better. What do *you* know about my stomach, anyhow? Just looking at sloop like that makes me sick."

A little while after this the Chinaman cleared away the dessert and brought in coffee and cigars. The whiskey bottle and the syphon of soda-water reappeared. The men eased themselves in their places, pushing back from the table, lighting their cigars, talking of the beginning of the rains and the prospects of a rise in wheat. Broderson began an elaborate mental calculation, trying to settle in his mind the exact date of his visit to Ukiah, and Osterman did sleight-of-hand tricks with bread pills. But Princess Nathalie, the cat, was uneasy. Annixter was occupying her own particular chair in which she slept every night. She could not go to sleep, but spied upon him continually, watching his every movement with her lambent, yellow eyes, clear as amber.

Then, at length, Magnus, who was at the head of the table, moved in his place, assuming a certain magisterial attitude. "Well, gentlemen," he observed, "I have lost my case against the railroad, the grain-rate case. Ulsteen decided against me, and now I hear rumours to the effect that rates for the hauling of grain are to be advanced."

When Magnus had finished, there was a moment's silence, each member of the group maintaining his attitude of attention and interest. It was Harran who first spoke.

"S. Behrman manipulated the whole affair. There's a big deal of some kind in the air, and if there is, we all know who is back of it; S. Behrman, of course, but who's back of him? It's Shelgrim."

Shelgrim! The name fell squarely in the midst of the conversation, abrupt, grave, sombre, big with suggestion, pregnant with huge associations. No one in the group who was not familiar with it; no one, for that matter, in the county, the State, the whole reach of the West, the entire Union, that did not entertain convictions as to the man who carried it; a giant figure in the end-of-the-century finance, a product of circumstance, an inevitable result of conditions, characteristic, typical, symbolic of ungovernable forces. In the New Movement, the New Finance, the reorganisation of capital, the amalgamation of powers, the consolidation of enormous enterprises—no one individual was more constantly in the eye of the world; no one was more hated, more dreaded, no one more compelling of unwilling tribute to his commanding genius, to the colossal intellect operating the width of an entire continent than the president and owner of the Pacific and Southwestern.

"I don't think, however, he has moved yet," said Magnus.

"The thing for us, then," exclaimed Osterman, "is to stand from under before he does."

"Moved yet!" snorted Annixter. "He's probably moved so long ago that we've never noticed it."

"In any case," hazarded Magnus, "it is scarcely probable that the deal—whatever it is to be—has been consummated. If we act quickly, there may be a chance."

"Act quickly! How?" demanded Annixter. "Good Lord! what can you do? We're cinched already. It all amounts to just this: *You can't buck against the railroad.* We've tried it and tried it, and we are stuck every time. You, yourself, Derrick, have just lost your grain-rate case. S. Behrman did you up. Shelgrim owns the courts. He's got men like Ulsteen in his pocket. He's got the Railroad Commission in his pocket. He's got the Governor of the State in his pocket. He keeps a million-dollar lobby at Sacramento every minute of the time the legislature is in session; he's got his own men on the floor of the United States Senate. He has the whole thing organised like an army corps. What *are* you going to do? He sits in his office in San Francisco and pulls the strings and we've got to dance."

"But—well—but," hazarded Broderson, "but there's the Interstate Commerce Commission. At least on long-haul rates they——"

"Hoh, yes, the Interstate Commerce Commission," shouted Annixter, scornfully, "that's great, ain't it? The greatest Punch

and Judy show on earth. It's almost as good as the Railroad
Commission. There never was and there never will be a California Railroad Commission not in the pay of the P. and S. W."

"It is to the Railroad Commission, nevertheless," remarked
Magnus, "that the people of the State must look for relief.
That is our only hope. Once elect Commissioners who would
be loyal to the people, and the whole system of excessive rates
falls to the ground."

"Well, why not *have* a Railroad Commission of our own,
then?" suddenly declared young Osterman.

"Because it can't be done," retorted Annixter. "*You can't
buck against the railroad* and if you could you can't organise
the farmers in the San Joaquin. We tried it once, and it was
enough to turn your stomach. The railroad quietly bought
delegates through S. Behrman and did us up."

"Well, that's the game to play," said Osterman decisively,
"buy delegates."

"It's the only game that seems to win," admitted Harran
gloomily.

"Or ever will win," exclaimed Osterman, a sudden excitement seeming to take possession of him. His face—the face
of a comic actor, with its great slit of mouth and stiff, red
ears—went abruptly pink.

"Look here," he cried, "this thing is getting desperate.
We've fought and fought in the courts and out and we've
tried agitation and—and all the rest of it and S. Behrman
sacks us every time. Now comes the time when there's a prospect of a big crop; we've had no rain for two years and the
land has had a long rest. If there is any rain at all this winter,
we'll have a bonanza year, and just at this very moment when
we've got our chance—a chance to pay off our mortgages
and get clear of debt and make a strike—here is Shelgrim
making a deal to cinch us and put up rates. And now here's
the primaries coming off and a new Railroad Commission
going in. That's why Shelgrim chose this time to make his
deal. If we wait till Shelgrim pulls it off, we're done for, that's
flat. I tell you we're in a fix if we don't keep an eye open.
Things are getting desperate. Magnus has just said that the
key to the whole thing is the Railroad Commission. Well,
why not have a Commission of our own? Never mind how

we get it, let's get it. If it's got to be bought, let's buy it and put our own men on it and dictate what the rates will be. Suppose it costs a hundred thousand dollars. Well, we'll get back more than that in cheap rates."

"Mr. Osterman," said Magnus, fixing the young man with a swift glance, "Mr. Osterman, you are proposing a scheme of bribery, sir."

"I am proposing," repeated Osterman, "a scheme of bribery. Exactly so."

"And a crazy, wild-eyed scheme at that," said Annixter gruffly. "Even supposing you bought a Railroad Commission and got your schedule of low rates, what happens? The P. and S. W. crowd get out an injunction and tie you up."

"They would tie themselves up, too. Hauling at low rates is better than no hauling at all. The wheat has got to be moved."

"Oh, rot!" cried Annixter. "Aren't you ever going to learn any sense? Don't you know that cheap transportation would benefit the Liverpool buyers and not us? Can't it be *fed* into you that you can't buck against the railroad? When you try to buy a Board of Commissioners don't you see that you'll have to bid against the railroad, bid against a corporation that can chuck out millions to our thousands? Do you think you can bid against the P. and S. W.?"

"The railroad don't need to know we are in the game against them till we've got our men seated."

"And when you've got them seated, what's to prevent the corporation buying them right over your head?"

"If we've got the right kind of men in they could not be bought that way," interposed Harran. "I don't know but what there's something in what Osterman says. We'd have the naming of the Commission and we'd name honest men."

Annixter struck the table with his fist in exasperation.

"Honest men!" he shouted; "the kind of men you could get to go into such a scheme would have to be *dis*honest to begin with."

Broderson, shifting uneasily in his place, fingering his beard with a vague, uncertain gesture, spoke again:

"It would be the *chance* of them—our Commissioners—selling out against the certainty of Shelgrim doing us up. That is," he hastened to add, "*almost* a certainty; pretty near a certainty."

"Of course, it would be a chance," exclaimed Osterman. "But it's come to the point where we've got to take chances, risk a big stake to make a big strike, and risk is better than sure failure."

"I can be no party to a scheme of avowed bribery and corruption, Mr. Osterman," declared Magnus, a ring of severity in his voice. "I am surprised, sir, that you should even broach the subject in my hearing."

"And," cried Annixter, "it can't be done."

"I don't know," muttered Harran, "maybe it just wants a little spark like this to fire the whole train."

Magnus glanced at his son in considerable surprise. He had not expected this of Harran. But so great was his affection for his son, so accustomed had he become to listening to his advice, to respecting his opinions, that, for the moment, after the first shock of surprise and disappointment, he was influenced to give a certain degree of attention to this new proposition. He in no way countenanced it. At any moment he was prepared to rise in his place and denounce it and Osterman both. It was trickery of the most contemptible order, a thing he believed to be unknown to the old school of politics and statesmanship to which he was proud to belong; but since Harran, even for one moment, considered it, he, Magnus, who trusted Harran implicitly, would do likewise—if it was only to oppose and defeat it in its very beginnings.

And abruptly the discussion began. Gradually Osterman, by dint of his clamour, his strident reiteration, the plausibility of his glib, ready assertions, the ease with which he extricated himself when apparently driven to a corner, completely won over old Broderson to his way of thinking. Osterman bewildered him with his volubility, the lightning rapidity with which he leaped from one subject to another, garrulous, witty, flamboyant, terrifying the old man with pictures of the swift approach of ruin, the imminence of danger.

Annixter, who led the argument against him—loving argument though he did—appeared to poor advantage, unable to present his side effectively. He called Osterman a fool, a goat, a senseless, crazy-headed jackass, but was unable to refute his assertions. His debate was the clumsy heaving of brickbats, brutal, direct. He contradicted everything Osterman said as a matter of principle, made conflicting assertions, declarations that were absolutely inconsistent, and when Osterman or Harran used these against him, could only exclaim:

"Well, in a way it's so, and then again in a way it isn't."

But suddenly Osterman discovered a new argument. "If we swing this deal," he cried, " we've got old jelly-belly Behrman right where we want him."

"He's the man that does us every time," cried Harran. "If there is dirty work to be done in which the railroad doesn't wish to appear, it is S. Behrman who does it. If the freight rates are to be 'adjusted' to squeeze us a little harder, it is S. Behrman who regulates what we can stand. If there's a judge to be bought, it is S. Behrman who does the bargaining. If there is a jury to be bribed, it is S. Behrman who handles the money. If there is an election to be jobbed, it is S. Behrman who manipulates it. It's Behrman here and Behrman there. It is Behrman we come against every time we make a move. It is Behrman who has the grip of us and will never let go till he has squeezed us bone dry. Why, when I think of it all sometimes I wonder I keep my hands off the man."

Osterman got on his feet; leaning across the table, gesturing wildly with his right hand, his serio-comic face, with its bald forehead and stiff, red ears, was inflamed with excitement. He took the floor, creating an impression, attracting all attention to himself, playing to the gallery, gesticulating, clamourous, full of noise.

"Well, now is your chance to get even," he vociferated. "It is now or never. You can take it and save the situation for yourselves and all California or you can leave it and rot on your own ranches. Buck, I know you. I know you're not afraid of anything that wears skin. I know you've got sand all through you, and I know if I showed you how we could put our deal through and seat a Commission of our own, you wouldn't hang back. Governor, you're a brave man. You know the advantage of prompt and fearless action. You are not the sort to shrink from taking chances. To play for big stakes is just your game—to stake a fortune on the turn of a card. You didn't get the reputation of being the strongest poker player in El Dorado County for nothing. Now, here's the biggest gamble that ever came your way. If we stand up to it like men with guts in us, we'll win out. If we hesitate, we're lost."

"I don't suppose you can help playing the goat, Osterman," remarked Annixter, "but what's your idea? What do you think we can do? I'm not saying," he hastened to interpose, "that you've anyways convinced me by all this cackling. I know as well as you that we are in a hole. But I knew that before I came here to-night. *You've* not done anything to make me change my mind. But just what do you propose? Let's hear it."

"Well, I say the first thing to do is to see Disbrow. He's the political boss of the Denver, Pueblo, and Mojave road. We will have to get in with the machine some way and that's particularly why I want Magnus with us. He knows politics better than any of us and if we don't want to get sold again we will have to have some one that's in the know to steer us."

"The only politics I understand, Mr. Osterman," answered Magnus sternly, "are honest politics. You must look elsewhere for your political manager. I refuse to have any part in this matter. If the Railroad Commission can be nominated legitimately, if your arrangements can be made without bribery, I am with you to the last iota of my ability."

"Well, you can't get what you want without paying for it," contradicted Annixter.

Broderson was about to speak when Osterman kicked his foot under the table. He, himself, held his peace. He was quick to see that if he could involve Magnus and Annixter in an argument, Annixter, for the mere love of contention, would oppose the Governor and, without knowing it, would commit himself to his—Osterman's—scheme.

This was precisely what happened. In a few moments Annixter was declaring at top voice his readiness to mortgage the crop of Quien Sabe, if necessary, for the sake of "busting S. Behrman." He could see no great obstacle in the way of controlling the nominating convention so far as securing the naming of two Railroad Commissioners was concerned. Two was all they needed. Probably it *would* cost money. You didn't get something for nothing. It would cost them all a good deal more if they sat like lumps on a log and played tiddledy-winks while Shelgrim sold out from under them. Then there was this, too: the P. and S. W. were hard up just then. The shortage on the State's wheat crop for the last two years had affected them, too. They were retrenching in expenditures all along the line. Hadn't they just cut wages in all departments? There was this affair of Dyke's to prove it. The railroad didn't always act as a unit, either. There was always a party in it that opposed spending too much money. He would bet that party was strong just now. He was kind of sick himself of being kicked by S. Behrman. Hadn't that pip turned up on his ranch that very day to bully him about his own line fence? Next he would be telling him what kind of clothes he ought to wear. Harran had the right idea. Somebody had got to be busted mighty soon now and he didn't propose that it should be he.

"Now you are talking something like sense," observed Osterman. "I thought you would see it like that when you got my idea."

"Your idea, *your* idea!" cried Annixter. "Why, I've had this idea myself for over three years."

"What about Disbrow?" asked Harran, hastening to interrupt. "Why do we want to see Disbrow?"

"Disbrow is the political man for the Denver, Pueblo, and Mojave," answered Osterman, "and you see it's like this: the Mojave road don't run up into the valley at all. Their terminus is way to the south of us, and they don't care anything about grain rates through the San Joaquin. They don't care how anti-railroad the Commission is, because the Commission's rulings can't affect them. But they divide traffic with the P. and S. W. in the southern part of the State and they have a good deal of influence with that road. I want to get the Mojave road, through Disbrow, to recommend a Commissioner of our choosing to the P. and S. W. and have the P. and S. W. adopt him as their own."

"Who, for instance?"

"Darrell, that Los Angeles man—remember?"

"Well, Darrell is no particular friend of Disbrow," said Annixter. "Why should Disbrow take him up?"

"*Pree*-cisely," cried Osterman. "We make it worth Disbrow's while to do it. We go to him and say, 'Mr. Disbrow, you manage the politics for the Mojave railroad, and what you say goes with your Board of Directors. We want you to adopt our candidate for Railroad Commissioner for the third district. How much do you want for doing it?' I *know* we can buy Disbrow. That gives us one Commissioner. We need not bother about that any more. In the first district we don't make any move at all. We let the political managers of the P. and S. W. nominate whoever they like. Then we concentrate all our efforts to putting in our man in the second district. There is where the big fight will come."

"I see perfectly well what you mean, Mr. Osterman," observed Magnus, "but make no mistake, sir, as to my attitude in this business. You may count me as out of it entirely."

"Well, suppose we win," put in Annixter truculently, already acknowledging himself as involved in the proposed undertaking; "suppose we win and get low rates for hauling grain. How about you, then? You count yourself *in* then, don't you? You get all the benefit of lower rates without sharing any of the risks *we* take to secure them. No, nor any of the expense, either. No, you won't dirty your fingers with helping us put this deal through, but you won't be so cursed particular when it comes to sharing the profits, will you?"

Magnus rose abruptly to his full height, the nostrils of his thin, hawk-like nose vibrating, his smooth-shaven face paler than ever.

"Stop right where you are, sir," he exclaimed. "You forget yourself, Mr. Annixter. Please understand that I tolerate such words as you have permitted yourself to make use of from no man, not even from my guest. I shall ask you to apologise."

In an instant he dominated the entire group, imposing a respect that was as much fear as admiration. No one made response. For the moment he was the Master again, the Leader. Like so many delinquent schoolboys, the others cowered before him, ashamed, put to confusion, unable to find their tongues. In that brief instant of silence following upon Magnus's outburst, and while he held them subdued and over-mastered, the fabric of their scheme of corruption and dishonesty trembled to its base. It was the last protest of the Old School, rising up there in denunciation of the new order of things, the statesman opposed to the politician; honesty, rectitude, uncompromising integrity, prevailing for the last time against the devious manœuvring, the evil communications, the rotten expediency of a corrupted institution.

For a few seconds no one answered. Then, Annixter, moving abruptly and uneasily in his place, muttered:

"I spoke upon provocation. If you like, we'll consider it unsaid. *I* don't know what's going to become of us—go out of business, I presume."

"I understand Magnus all right," put in Osterman. "He don't have to go into this thing, if it's against his conscience. That's all right. Magnus can stay out if he wants to, but that won't prevent us going ahead and seeing what we can do. Only there's this about it." He turned again to Magnus, speaking with every degree of earnestness, every appearance of conviction. "I did not deny, Governor, from the very start that this would mean bribery. But you don't suppose that *I* like the idea either. If there was one legitimate hope that was yet left untried, no matter how forlorn it was, I would try it. But there's not. It is literally and soberly true that every means of help—every honest means—has been attempted. Shelgrim is going to cinch us. Grain rates are increasing, while, on the other hand, the price of wheat is sagging lower and lower all the time. If we don't do something we are ruined."

Osterman paused for a moment, allowing precisely the right number of seconds to elapse, then altering and lowering his voice, added:

"I respect the Governor's principles. I admire them. They do him every degree of credit." Then, turning directly to Magnus, he concluded with, "But I only want you to ask yourself, sir, if, at such a crisis, one ought to think of oneself, to consider purely personal motives in such a desperate situation as this? Now, we want you with us, Governor; perhaps not openly, if you don't wish it, but tacitly, at least. I won't ask you for an answer to-night, but what I do ask of you is to consider this matter seriously and think over the whole business. Will you do it?"

Osterman ceased definitely to speak, leaning forward

across the table, his eyes fixed on Magnus's face. There was a silence. Outside, the rain fell continually with an even, monotonous murmur. In the group of men around the table no one stirred nor spoke. They looked steadily at Magnus, who, for the moment, kept his glance fixed thoughtfully upon the table before him. In another moment he raised his head and looked from face to face around the group. After all, these were his neighbours, his friends, men with whom he had been upon the closest terms of association. In a way they represented what now had come to be his world. His single swift glance took in the men, one after another. Annixter, rugged, crude, sitting awkwardly and uncomfortably in his chair, his unhandsome face, with its outthrust lower lip and deeply cleft masculine chin, flushed and eager, his yellow hair disordered, the one tuft on the crown standing stiffly forth like the feather in an Indian's scalp lock; Broderson, vaguely combing at his long beard with a persistent maniacal gesture, distressed, troubled and uneasy; Osterman, with his comedy face, the face of a music-hall singer, his head bald and set off by his great red ears, leaning back in his place, softly cracking the knuckle of a forefinger, and, last of all and close to his elbow, his son, his support, his confidant and companion, Harran, so like himself, with his own erect, fine carriage, his thin, beak-like nose and his blond hair, with its tendency to curl in a forward direction in front of the ears, young, strong, courageous, full of the promise of the future years. His blue eyes looked straight into his father's with what Magnus could fancy a glance of appeal. Magnus could see that expression in the faces of the others very plainly. They looked to him as their natural leader, their chief who was to bring them out from this abominable trouble which was closing in upon them, and in them all he saw many types. They—these men around his table on that night of the first rain of a coming season—seemed to stand in his imagination for many others—all the farmers, ranchers, and wheat growers of the great San Joaquin. Their words were the words of a whole community; their distress, the distress of an entire State, harried beyond the bounds of endurance, driven to the wall, coerced, exploited, harassed to the limits of exasperation.

"I will think of it," he said, then hastened to add, "but I can tell you beforehand that you may expect only a refusal."

After Magnus had spoken, there was a prolonged silence. The conference seemed of itself to have come to an end for that evening. Presley lighted another cigarette from the butt of the one he had been smoking, and the cat, Princess Nathalie, disturbed by his movement and by a whiff of drifting smoke, jumped from his knee to the floor and picking her way across the room to Annixter, rubbed gently against his legs, her tail in the air, her back delicately arched. No doubt she thought it time to settle herself for the night, and as Annixter gave no indication of vacating his chair, she chose this way of cajoling him into ceding his place to her. But Annixter was irritated at the Princess's attentions, misunderstanding their motive.

"Get out!" he exclaimed, lifting his feet to the rung of the chair. "Lord love me, but I sure do hate a cat."

"By the way," observed Osterman, "I passed Genslinger by the gate as I came in to-night. Had he been here?"

"Yes, he was here," said Harran, "and—" but Annixter took the words out of his mouth.

"He says there's some talk of the railroad selling us their sections this winter."

"Oh, he did, did he?" exclaimed Osterman, interested at once. "Where did he hear that?"

"Where does a railroad paper get its news? From the General Office, I suppose."

"I hope he didn't get it straight from headquarters that the land was to be graded at twenty dollars an acre," murmured Broderson.

"What's that?" demanded Osterman. "Twenty dollars! Here, put me on, somebody. What's all up? What did Genslinger say?"

"Oh, you needn't get scared," said Annixter. "Genslinger don't know, that's all. He thinks there was no understanding that the price of the land should not be advanced when the P. and S. W. came to sell to us."

"Oh," muttered Osterman relieved. Magnus, who had gone out into the office on the other side of the glass-roofed hallway, returned with a long, yellow envelope in his hand, stuffed with newspaper clippings and thin, closely printed pamphlets.

"Here is the circular," he remarked, drawing out one of the pamphlets. "The conditions of settlement to which the railroad obligated itself are very explicit."

He ran over the pages of the circular, then read aloud:

" '*The Company invites settlers to go upon its lands before patents are issued or the road is completed, and intends in such cases to sell to them in preference to any other applicants and at a price based upon the value of the land without improvements,*' and on the other page here," he remarked, "they refer to this again. '*In ascertaining the value of the lands, any improvements that a settler or any other person may have on the lands will not be taken into consideration, neither will the price be increased in consequence thereof. . . . Settlers are thus insured that in addition to being accorded the first privilege of purchase, at the graded price, they will also be protected in their improvements.*' And here," he commented, "in Section IX. it reads, '*The lands are not uniform in price, but are offered at various figures from $2.50 upward per acre. Usually land covered with tall timber is held at $5.00 per acre, and that with pine at $10.00. Most is for sale at $2.50 and $5.00.*' "

"When you come to read that carefully," hazarded old Broderson, "it—it's not so *very* reassuring. '*Most* is for sale at two-fifty an acre,' it says. That don't mean '*all,*' that only means *some*. I wish now that I had secured a more iron-clad agreement from the P. and S. W. when I took up its sections on my ranch, and—and Genslinger is in a position to know the intentions of the railroad. At least, he—he—he is in *touch* with them. All newspaper men are. Those, I mean, who are subsidised by the General Office. But, perhaps, Genslinger isn't subsidised, I don't know. I—I am not sure. Maybe—perhaps——"

"Oh, you don't know and you do know, and maybe and perhaps, and you're not so sure," vociferated Annixter. "How about ignoring the value of our improvements? Nothing hazy about *that* statement, I guess. It says in so many words that any improvements we make will not be considered when the land is appraised and that's the same thing, isn't it? The unimproved land is worth two-fifty an acre;

only timber land is worth more and there's none too much timber about here."

"Well, one thing at a time," said Harran. "The thing for us now is to get into this primary election and the convention and see if we can push our men for Railroad Commissioners."

"Right," declared Annixter. He rose, stretching his arms above his head. "I've about talked all the wind out of me," he said. "Think I'll be moving along. It's pretty near midnight."

But when Magnus's guests turned their attention to the matter of returning to their different ranches, they abruptly realised that the downpour had doubled and trebled in its volume since earlier in the evening. The fields and roads were veritable seas of viscid mud, the night absolutely black-dark; assuredly not a night in which to venture out. Magnus insisted that the three ranchers should put up at Los Muertos. Osterman accepted at once, Annixter, after an interminable discussion, allowed himself to be persuaded, in the end accepting as though granting a favour. Broderson protested that his wife, who was not well, would expect him to return that night and would, no doubt, fret if he did not appear. Furthermore, he lived close by, at the junction of the County and Lower Road. He put a sack over his head and shoulders, persistently declining Magnus's offered umbrella and rubber coat, and hurried away, remarking that he had no foreman on his ranch and had to be up and about at five the next morning to put his men to work.

"Fool!" muttered Annixter when the old man had gone. "Imagine farming a ranch the size of his without a foreman."

Harran showed Osterman and Annixter where they were to sleep, in adjoining rooms. Magnus soon afterward retired.

Osterman found an excuse for going to bed, but Annixter and Harran remained in the latter's room, in a haze of blue tobacco smoke, talking, talking. But at length, at the end of all argument, Annixter got up, remarking:

"Well, *I'm* going to turn in. It's nearly two o'clock."

He went to his room, closing the door, and Harran, opening his window to clear out the tobacco smoke, looked out for a moment across the country toward the south.

The darkness was profound, impenetrable; the rain fell with an uninterrupted roar. Near at hand one could hear the

sound of dripping eaves and foliage and the eager, sucking
sound of the drinking earth, and abruptly while Harran
stood looking out, one hand upon the upraised sash, a great
puff of the outside air invaded the room, odourous with the
reek of the soaking earth, redolent with fertility, pungent,
heavy, tepid. He closed the window again and sat for a few
moments on the edge of the bed, one shoe in his hand,
thoughtful and absorbed, wondering if his father would involve himself in this new scheme, wondering if, after all, he
wanted him to.

But suddenly he was aware of a commotion, issuing from
the direction of Annixter's room, and the voice of Annixter
himself upraised in expostulation and exasperation. The door
of the room to which Annixter had been assigned opened
with a violent wrench and an angry voice exclaimed to anybody who would listen:

"Oh, yes, funny, isn't it? In a way, it's funny, and then,
again, in a way it isn't."

The door banged to so that all the windows of the house
rattled in their frames.

Harran hurried out into the dining-room and there met
Presley and his father, who had been aroused as well by Annixter's clamour. Osterman was there, too, his bald head
gleaming like a bulb of ivory in the light of the lamp that
Magnus carried.

"What's all up?" demanded Osterman. "Whatever in the
world is the matter with Buck?"

Confused and terrible sounds came from behind the door
of Annixter's room. A prolonged monologue of grievance,
broken by explosions of wrath and the vague noise of some
one in a furious hurry. All at once and before Harran had a
chance to knock on the door, Annixter flung it open. His face
was blazing with anger, his outthrust lip more prominent
than ever, his wiry, yellow hair in disarray, the tuft on the
crown sticking straight into the air like the upraised hackles
of an angry hound. Evidently he had been dressing himself
with the most headlong rapidity; he had not yet put on his
coat and vest, but carried them over his arm, while with
his disengaged hand he kept hitching his suspenders over his
shoulders with a persistent and hypnotic gesture. Without a

moment's pause he gave vent to his indignation in a torrent
of words.

"Ah, yes, in my bed, sloop, aha! I know the man who put
it there," he went on, glaring at Osterman, "and that man is
a *pip*. Sloop! Slimy, disgusting stuff; you heard me say I
didn't like it when the Chink passed it to me at dinner—and
just for that reason you put it in my bed, and I stick my feet
into it when I turn in. Funny, isn't it? Oh, yes, too funny for
any use. I'd laugh a little louder if I was you."

"Well, Buck," protested Harran, as he noticed the hat in
Annixter's hand, "you're not going home just for——"

Annixter turned on him with a shout.

"I'll get plumb out of here," he trumpeted. "I won't stay
here another minute."

He swung into his waistcoat and coat, scrabbling at the
buttons in the violence of his emotions. "And I don't know
but what it will make me sick again to go out in a night like
this. *No*, I won't stay. Some things are funny, and then,
again, there are some things that are not. Ah, yes, sloop! Well,
that's all right. I can be funny, too, when you come to that.
You don't get a cent of money out of me. You can do your
dirty bribery in your own dirty way. I won't come into this
scheme at all. I wash my hands of the whole business. It's
rotten and it's wild-eyed; it's dirt from start to finish; and
you'll all land in State's prison. You can count *me* out."

"But, Buck, look here, you crazy fool," cried Harran, "I
don't know who put that stuff in your bed, but I'm not going
to let you go back to Quien Sabe in a rain like this."

"*I* know who put it in," clamoured the other, shaking his
fists, "and don't call me Buck and I'll do as I please. I *will* go
back home. I'll get plumb out of here. Sorry I came. Sorry I
ever lent myself to such a disgusting, dishonest, dirty bribery
game as this all to-night. I won't put a dime into it, no, not
a penny."

He stormed to the door leading out upon the porch, deaf
to all reason. Harran and Presley followed him, trying to dis-
suade him from going home at that time of night and in such
a storm, but Annixter was not to be placated. He stamped
across to the barn where his horse and buggy had been sta-
bled, splashing through the puddles under foot, going out of

his way to drench himself, refusing even to allow Presley and Harran to help him harness the horse.

"What's the use of making a fool of yourself, Annixter?" remonstrated Presley, as Annixter backed the horse from the stall. "You act just like a ten-year-old boy. If Osterman wants to play the goat, why should you help him out?"

"He's a *pip*," vociferated Annixter. "You don't understand, Presley. It runs in my family to hate anything sticky. It's— it's—it's heredity. How would you like to get into bed at two in the morning and jam your feet down into a slimy mess like that? Oh, no. It's not so funny then. And you mark my words, Mr. Harran Derrick," he continued, as he climbed into the buggy, shaking the whip toward Harran, "this business we talked over to-night—I'm *out* of it. It's yellow. It's too *cursed* dishonest."

He cut the horse across the back with the whip and drove out into the pelting rain. In a few seconds the sound of his buggy wheels was lost in the muffled roar of the downpour.

Harran and Presley closed the barn and returned to the house, sheltering themselves under a tarpaulin carriage cover. Once inside, Harran went to remonstrate with Osterman, who was still up. Magnus had again retired. The house had fallen quiet again.

As Presley crossed the dining-room on the way to his own apartment in the second story of the house, he paused for a moment, looking about him. In the dull light of the lowered lamps, the redwood panelling of the room showed a dark crimson as though stained with blood. On the massive slab of the dining table the half-emptied glasses and bottles stood about in the confusion in which they had been left, reflecting themselves deep into the polished wood; the glass doors of the case of stuffed birds was a subdued shimmer; the many-coloured Navajo blanket over the couch seemed a mere patch of brown.

Around the table the chairs in which the men had sat throughout the evening still ranged themselves in a semi-circle, vaguely suggestive of the conference of the past few hours, with all its possibilities of good and evil, its significance of a future big with portent. The room was still. Only on the cushions of the chair that Annixter had occupied, the cat, Princess Nathalie, at last comfortably settled in her accustomed place, dozed complacently, her paws tucked under her breast, filling the deserted room with the subdued murmur of her contented purr.

IV

O N THE QUIEN SABE ranch, in one of its western divisions, near the line fence that divided it from the Osterman holding, Vanamee was harnessing the horses to the plough to which he had been assigned two days before, a stable-boy from the division barn helping him.

Promptly discharged from the employ of the sheep-raisers after the lamentable accident near the Long Trestle, Vanamee had presented himself to Harran, asking for employment. The season was beginning; on all the ranches work was being resumed. The rain had put the ground into admirable condition for ploughing, and Annixter, Broderson, and Osterman all had their gangs at work. Thus, Vanamee was vastly surprised to find Los Muertos idle, the horses still in the barns, the men gathering in the shade of the bunk-house and eating-house, smoking, dozing, or going aimlessly about, their arms dangling. The ploughs for which Magnus and Harran were waiting in a fury of impatience had not yet arrived, and since the management of Los Muertos had counted upon having these in hand long before this time, no provision had been made for keeping the old stock in repair; many of these old ploughs were useless, broken, and out of order; some had been sold. It could not be said definitely when the new ploughs would arrive. Harran had decided to wait one week longer, and then, in case of their non-appearance, to buy a consignment of the old style of plough from the dealers in Bonneville. He could afford to lose the money better than he could afford to lose the season.

Failing of work on Los Muertos, Vanamee had gone to Quien Sabe. Annixter, whom he had spoken to first, had sent him across the ranch to one of his division superintendents, and this latter, after assuring himself of Vanamee's familiarity with horses and his previous experience—even though somewhat remote—on Los Muertos, had taken him on as a driver of one of the gang ploughs, then at work on his division.

The evening before, when the foreman had blown his whistle at six o'clock, the long line of ploughs had halted upon the instant, and the drivers, unharnessing their teams, had taken them back to the division barns—leaving the ploughs as they were in the furrows. But an hour after daylight the next morning the work was resumed. After breakfast, Vanamee, riding one horse and leading the others, had returned to the line of ploughs together with the other drivers. Now he was busy harnessing the team. At the division blacksmith shop—temporarily put up—he had been obliged to wait while one of his lead horses was shod, and he had thus been delayed quite five minutes. Nearly all the other teams were harnessed, the drivers on their seats, waiting for the foreman's signal.

"All ready here?" inquired the foreman, driving up to Vanamee's team in his buggy.

"All ready, sir," answered Vanamee, buckling the last strap.

He climbed to his seat, shaking out the reins, and turning about, looked back along the line, then all around him at the landscape inundated with the brilliant glow of the early morning.

The day was fine. Since the first rain of the season, there had been no other. Now the sky was without a cloud, pale blue, delicate, luminous, scintillating with morning. The great brown earth turned a huge flank to it, exhaling the moisture of the early dew. The atmosphere, washed clean of dust and mist, was translucent as crystal. Far off to the east, the hills on the other side of Broderson Creek stood out against the pallid saffron of the horizon as flat and as sharply outlined as if pasted on the sky. The campanile of the ancient Mission of San Juan seemed as fine as frost work. All about between the horizons, the carpet of the land unrolled itself to infinity. But now it was no longer parched with heat, cracked and warped by a merciless sun, powdered with dust. The rain had done its work; not a clod that was not swollen with fertility, not a fissure that did not exhale the sense of fecundity. One could not take a dozen steps upon the ranches without the brusque sensation that underfoot the land was alive; roused at last from its sleep, palpitating with the desire of reproduction. Deep down there in the recesses of the soil, the great heart throbbed once more, thrilling with passion, vibrating with desire, offering itself to the caress of the plough, insistent, eager, imperious. Dimly one felt the deep-seated trouble of the earth, the uneasy agitation of its members, the hidden tumult of its womb, demanding to be made fruitful, to reproduce, to disengage the eternal renascent germ of Life that stirred and struggled in its loins.

The ploughs, thirty-five in number, each drawn by its team of ten, stretched in an interminable line, nearly a quarter of a mile in length, behind and ahead of Vanamee. They were arranged, as it were, *en echelon*, not in file—not one directly behind the other, but each succeeding plough its own width farther in the field than the one in front of it. Each of these ploughs held five shears, so that when the entire company was in motion, one hundred and seventy-five furrows were made at the same instant. At a distance, the ploughs resembled a great column of field artillery. Each driver was in his place, his glance alternating between his horses and the foreman nearest at hand. Other foremen, in their buggies or buckboards, were at intervals along the line, like battery lieutenants. Annixter himself, on horseback, in boots and campaign hat, a cigar in his teeth, overlooked the scene.

The division superintendent, on the opposite side of the line, galloped past to a position at the head. For a long moment there was a silence. A sense of preparedness ran from end to end of the column. All things were ready, each man in his place. The day's work was about to begin.

Suddenly, from a distance at the head of the line came the shrill trilling of a whistle. At once the foreman nearest Vanamee repeated it, at the same time turning down the line, and waving one arm. The signal was repeated, whistle answering whistle, till the sounds lost themselves in the distance. At once the line of ploughs lost its immobility, moving forward, getting slowly under way, the horses straining in the traces. A prolonged movement rippled from team to team, disengaging in its passage a multitude of sounds—the click of buckles, the creak of straining leather, the subdued clash of machinery, the cracking of whips, the deep breathing of nearly four hundred horses, the abrupt commands and cries of the drivers, and, last of all, the prolonged, soothing murmur of the thick brown earth turning steadily from the multitude of advancing shears.

The ploughing thus commenced, continued. The sun rose

higher. Steadily the hundred iron hands kneaded and furrowed and stroked the brown, humid earth, the hundred iron teeth bit deep into the Titan's flesh. Perched on his seat, the moist living reins slipping and tugging in his hands, Vanamee, in the midst of this steady confusion of constantly varying sensation, sight interrupted by sound, sound mingling with sight, on this swaying, vibrating seat, quivering with the prolonged thrill of the earth, lapsed to a sort of pleasing numbness, in a sense, hypnotised by the weaving maze of things in which he found himself involved. To keep his team at an even, regular gait, maintaining the precise interval, to run his furrows as closely as possible to those already made by the plough in front—this for the moment was the entire sum of his duties. But while one part of his brain, alert and watchful, took cognisance of these matters, all the greater part was lulled and stupefied with the long monotony of the affair.

The ploughing, now in full swing, enveloped him in a vague, slow-moving whirl of things. Underneath him was the jarring, jolting, trembling machine; not a clod was turned, not an obstacle encountered, that he did not receive the swift impression of it through all his body, the very friction of the damp soil, sliding incessantly from the shiny surface of the shears, seemed to reproduce itself in his finger-tips and along the back of his head. He heard the horse-hoofs by the myriads crushing down easily, deeply, into the loam, the prolonged clinking of trace-chains, the working of the smooth brown flanks in the harness, the clatter of wooden hames, the champing of bits, the click of iron shoes against pebbles, the brittle stubble of the surface ground crackling and snapping as the furrows turned, the sonorous, steady breaths wrenched from the deep, labouring chests, strap-bound, shining with sweat, and all along the line the voices of the men talking to the horses. Everywhere there were visions of glossy brown backs, straining, heaving, swollen with muscle; harness streaked with specks of froth, broad, cup-shaped hoofs, heavy with brown loam, men's faces red with tan, blue overalls spotted with axle-grease; muscled hands, the knuckles whitened in their grip on the reins, and through it all the ammoniacal smell of the horses, the bitter reek of perspiration of beasts and men, the aroma of warm leather, the scent of dead stubble—and stronger and more penetrating than everything else, the heavy, enervating odour of the upturned, living earth.

At intervals, from the tops of one of the rare, low swells of the land, Vanamee overlooked a wider horizon. On the other divisions of Quien Sabe the same work was in progress. Occasionally he could see another column of ploughs in the adjoining division—sometimes so close at hand that the subdued murmur of its movements reached his ear; sometimes so distant that it resolved itself into a long, brown streak upon the grey of the ground. Farther off to the west on the Osterman ranch other columns came and went, and, once, from the crest of the highest swell on his division, Vanamee caught a distant glimpse of the Broderson ranch. There, too, moving specks indicated that the ploughing was under way. And farther away still, far off there beyond the fine line of the horizons, over the curve of the globe, the shoulder of the earth, he knew were other ranches, and beyond these others, and beyond these still others, the immensities multiplying to infinity.

Everywhere throughout the great San Joaquin, unseen and unheard, a thousand ploughs up-stirred the land, tens of thousands of shears clutched deep into the warm, moist soil.

It was the long stroking caress, vigorous, male, powerful, for which the Earth seemed panting. The heroic embrace of a multitude of iron hands, gripping deep into the brown, warm flesh of the land that quivered responsive and passionate under this rude advance, so robust as to be almost an assault, so violent as to be veritably brutal. There, under the sun and under the speckless sheen of the sky, the wooing of the Titan began, the vast primal passion, the two world-forces, the elemental Male and Female, locked in a colossal embrace, at grapples in the throes of an infinite desire, at once terrible and divine, knowing no law, untamed, savage, natural, sublime.

From time to time the gang in which Vanamee worked halted on the signal from foreman or overseer. The horses came to a standstill, the vague clamour of the work lapsed away. Then the minutes passed. The whole work hung suspended. All up and down the line one demanded what had happened. The division superintendent galloped past, perplexed and anxious. For the moment, one of the ploughs was out of order, a bolt had slipped, a lever refused to work, or a machine had become immobilised in heavy ground, or a horse had lamed himself. Once, even, toward noon, an entire plough was taken out of the line, so out of gear that a messenger had to be sent to the division forge to summon the machinist.

Annixter had disappeared. He had ridden farther on to the other divisions of his ranch, to watch the work in progress there. At twelve o'clock, according to his orders, all the division superintendents put themselves in communication with him by means of the telephone wires that connected each of the division houses, reporting the condition of the work, the number of acres covered, the prospects of each plough traversing its daily average of twenty miles.

At half-past twelve, Vanamee and the rest of the drivers ate their lunch in the field, the tin buckets having been distributed to them that morning after breakfast. But in the evening, the routine of the previous day was repeated, and Vanamee, unharnessing his team, riding one horse and leading the others, returned to the division barns and bunk-house.

It was between six and seven o'clock. The half hundred men of the gang threw themselves upon the supper the Chinese cooks had set out in the shed of the eating-house, long as a bowling alley, unpainted, crude, the seats benches, the table covered with oil cloth. Overhead a half-dozen kerosene lamps flared and smoked.

The table was taken as if by assault; the clatter of iron knives upon the tin plates was as the reverberation of hail upon a metal roof. The ploughmen rinsed their throats with great draughts of wine, and, their elbows wide, their foreheads flushed, resumed the attack upon the beef and bread, eating as though they would never have enough. All up and down the long table, where the kerosene lamps reflected themselves deep in the oil-cloth cover, one heard the incessant sounds of mastication, and saw the uninterrupted movement of great jaws. At every moment one or another of the men demanded a fresh portion of beef, another pint of wine, another half-loaf of bread. For upwards of an hour the gang ate.

It was no longer a supper. It was a veritable barbecue, a crude and primitive feasting, barbaric, homeric.

But in all this scene Vanamee saw nothing repulsive. Presley would have abhorred it—this feeding of the People, this gorging of the human animal, eager for its meat. Vanamee, simple, uncomplicated, living so close to nature and the rudimentary life, understood its significance. He knew very well that within a short half-hour after this meal the men would throw themselves down in their bunks to sleep without moving, inert and stupefied with fatigue, till the morning. Work, food, and sleep, all life reduced to its bare essentials, uncomplex, honest, healthy. They were strong, these men, with the strength of the soil they worked, in touch with the essential things, back again to the starting point of civilisation, coarse, vital, real, and sane.

For a brief moment immediately after the meal, pipes were lit, and the air grew thick with fragrant tobacco smoke. On a corner of the dining-room table, a game of poker was begun. One of the drivers, a Swede, produced an accordion; a group on the steps of the bunk-house listened, with alternate gravity and shouts of laughter, to the acknowledged story-teller of the gang. But soon the men began to turn in, stretching themselves at full length on the horse blankets in the racklike bunks. The sounds of heavy breathing increased steadily, lights were put out, and before the afterglow had faded from the sky, the gang was asleep.

Vanamee, however, remained awake. The night was fine, warm; the sky silver-grey with starlight. By and by there would be a moon. In the first watch after the twilight, a faint puff of breeze came up out of the south. From all around, the heavy penetrating smell of the new-turned earth exhaled steadily into the darkness. After a while, when the moon came up, he could see the vast brown breast of the earth turn toward it. Far off, distant objects came into view: The giant oak tree at Hooven's ranch house near the irrigating ditch on Los Muertos, the skeleton-like tower of the windmill on Annixter's Home ranch, the clump of willows along Broderson Creek close to the Long Trestle, and, last of all, the venerable tower of the Mission of San Juan on the high ground beyond the creek.

Thitherward, like homing pigeons, Vanamee's thoughts turned irresistibly. Near to that tower, just beyond, in the little hollow, hidden now from his sight, was the Seed ranch where Angéle Varian had lived. Straining his eyes, peering across the intervening levels, Vanamee fancied he could almost see the line of venerable pear trees in whose shadow she had been accustomed to wait for him. On many such a night as this he had crossed the ranches to find her there. His mind went back to that wonderful time of his life sixteen years before this, when Angéle was alive, when they two were involved in the sweet intricacies of a love so fine, so pure, so marvellous that it seemed to them a miracle, a manifestation, a thing veritably divine, put into the life of them and the hearts of them by God Himself. To that they had been born. For this love's sake they had come into the world, and the mingling of their lives was to be the Perfect Life, the intended, ordained union of the soul of man with the soul of woman, indissoluble, harmonious as music, beautiful beyond all thought, a foretaste of Heaven, a hostage of immortality.

No, he, Vanamee, could never, never forget; never was the edge of his grief to lose its sharpness; never would the lapse of time blunt the tooth of his pain. Once more, as he sat there, looking off across the ranches, his eyes fixed on the ancient campanile of the Mission church, the anguish that would not die leaped at his throat, tearing at his heart, shaking him and rending him with a violence as fierce and as profound as if it all had been but yesterday. The ache returned to his heart, a physical keen pain; his hands gripped tight together, twisting, interlocked, his eyes filled with tears, his whole body shaken and riven from head to heel.

He had lost her. God had not meant it, after all. The whole matter had been a mistake. That vast, wonderful love that had come upon them had been only the flimsiest mockery. Abruptly Vanamee rose. He knew the night that was before him. At intervals throughout the course of his prolonged wanderings, in the desert, on the mesa, deep in the cañon, lost and forgotten on the flanks of unnamed mountains, alone under the stars and under the moon's white eye, these hours came to him, his grief recoiling upon him like the recoil of a vast and terrible engine. Then he must fight out the night, wrestling with his sorrow, praying sometimes, incoherent, hardly conscious, asking "Why" of the night and of the stars.

Such another night had come to him now. Until dawn he knew he must struggle with his grief, torn with memories, his imagination assaulted with visions of a vanished happiness. If this paroxysm of sorrow was to assail him again that night, there was but one place for him to be. He would go to the Mission—he would see Father Sarria; he would pass the night in the deep shadow of the aged pear trees in the Mission garden.

He struck out across Quien Sabe, his face, the face of an ascetic, lean, brown, infinitely sad, set toward the Mission church. In about an hour he reached and crossed the road that led northward from Guadalajara toward the Seed ranch, and, a little farther on, forded Broderson Creek where it ran through one corner of the Mission land. He climbed the hill and halted, out of breath from his brisk walk, at the end of the colonnade of the Mission itself.

Until this moment Vanamee had not trusted himself to see the Mission at night. On the occasion of his first daytime visit with Presley, he had hurried away even before the twilight had set in, not daring for the moment to face the crowding phantoms that in his imagination filled the Mission garden after dark. In the daylight, the place had seemed strange to him. None of his associations with the old building and its surroundings were those of sunlight and brightness. Whenever, during his long sojourns in the wilderness of the Southwest, he had called up the picture in the eye of his mind, it had always appeared to him in the dim mystery of moonless nights, the venerable pear trees black with shadow, the fountain a thing to be heard rather than seen.

But as yet he had not entered the garden. That lay on the other side of the Mission. Vanamee passed down the colonnade, with its uneven pavement of worn red bricks, to the last door by the belfry tower, and rang the little bell by pulling the leather thong that hung from a hole in the door above the knob.

But the maid-servant, who, after a long interval, opened the door, blinking and confused at being roused from her

sleep, told Vanamee that Sarria was not in his room. Vanamee, however, was known to her as the priest's *protégé* and
great friend, and she allowed him to enter, telling him that,
no doubt, he would find Sarria in the church itself. The servant led the way down the cool adobe passage to a larger
room that occupied the entire width of the bottom of the
belfry tower, and whence a flight of aged steps led upward
into the dark. At the foot of the stairs was a door opening
into the church. The servant admitted Vanamee, closing the
door behind her.

The interior of the Mission, a great oblong of white-
washed adobe with a flat ceiling, was lighted dimly by the
sanctuary lamp that hung from three long chains just over the
chancel rail at the far end of the church, and by two or three
cheap kerosene lamps in brackets of imitation bronze. All
around the walls was the inevitable series of pictures representing the Stations of the Cross. They were of a hideous
crudity of design and composition, yet were wrought out
with an innocent, unquestioning sincerity that was not
without its charm. Each picture framed alike in gilt, bore its
suitable inscription in staring black letters. "Simon, The
Cyrenean, Helps Jesus to Carry His Cross." "Saint Veronica
Wipes the Face of Jesus." "Jesus Falls for the Fourth Time,"
and so on. Half-way up the length of the church the pews
began, coffin-like boxes of blackened oak, shining from years
of friction, each with its door; while over them, and built out
from the wall, was the pulpit, with its tarnished gilt sound-
ing-board above it, like the raised cover of a great hat-box.
Between the pews, in the aisle, the violent vermilion of a strip
of ingrain carpet assaulted the eye. Farther on were the steps
to the altar, the chancel rail of worm-riddled oak, the high
altar, with its napery from the bargain counters of a San Francisco store, the massive silver candlesticks, each as much as
one man could lift, the gift of a dead Spanish queen, and,
last, the pictures of the chancel, the Virgin in a glory, a Christ
in agony on the cross, and St. John the Baptist, the patron
saint of the Mission, the San Juan Bautista, of the early days,
a gaunt grey figure, in skins, two fingers upraised in the gesture of benediction.

The air of the place was cool and damp, and heavy with

the flat, sweet scent of stale incense smoke. It was of a vault-like stillness, and the closing of the door behind Vanamee re-échoed from corner to corner with a prolonged reverberation of thunder.

However, Father Sarria was not in the church. Vanamee took a couple of turns the length of the aisle, looking about into the chapels on either side of the chancel. But the building was deserted. The priest had been there recently, nevertheless, for the altar furniture was in disarray, as though he had been rearranging it but a moment before. On both sides of the church and halfway up their length, the walls were pierced by low archways, in which were massive wooden doors, clamped with iron bolts. One of these doors, on the pulpit side of the church, stood ajar, and stepping to it and pushing it wide open, Vanamee looked diagonally across a little patch of vegetables—beets, radishes, and lettuce—to the rear of the building that had once contained the cloisters, and through an open window saw Father Sarria diligently polishing the silver crucifix that usually stood on the high altar. Vanamee did not call to the priest. Putting a finger to either temple, he fixed his eyes steadily upon him for a moment as he moved about at his work. In a few seconds he closed his eyes, but only part way. The pupils contracted; his forehead lowered to an expression of poignant intensity. Soon afterward he saw the priest pause abruptly in the act of drawing the cover over the crucifix, looking about him from side to side. He turned again to his work, and again came to a stop, perplexed, curious. With uncertain steps, and evidently wondering why he did so, he came to the door of the room and opened it, looking out into the night. Vanamee, hidden in the deep shadow of the archway, did not move, but his eyes closed, and the intense expression deepened on his face. The priest hesitated, moved forward a step, turned back, paused again, then came straight across the garden patch, brusquely colliding with Vanamee, still motionless in the recess of the archway.

Sarria gave a great start, catching his breath.

"Oh—oh, it's you. Was it you I heard calling? No, I could not have heard—I remember now. What a strange power! I am not sure that it is right to do this thing, Vanamee. I—I *had* to come. I do not know why. It is a great force—a power—I don't like it. Vanamee, sometimes it frightens me."

Vanamee put his chin in the air.

"If I had wanted to, sir, I could have made you come to me from back there in the Quien Sabe ranch."

The priest shook his head.

"It troubles me," he said, "to think that my own will can count for so little. Just now I could not resist. If a deep river had been between us, I must have crossed it. Suppose I had been asleep now?"

"It would have been all the easier," answered Vanamee. "I understand as little of these things as you. But I think if you had been asleep, your power of resistance would have been so much the more weakened."

"Perhaps I should not have waked. Perhaps I should have come to you in my sleep."

"Perhaps."

Sarria crossed himself. "It is occult," he hazarded. "No; I do not like it. Dear fellow," he put his hand on Vanamee's shoulder, "don't—call me that way again; promise. See," he held out his hand, "I am all of a tremble. There, we won't speak of it further. Wait for me a moment. I have only to put the cross in its place, and a fresh altar cloth, and then I am done. To-morrow is the feast of The Holy Cross, and I am preparing against it. The night is fine. We will smoke a cigar in the cloister garden."

A few moments later the two passed out of the door on the other side of the church, opposite the pulpit, Sarria adjusting a silk skull cap on his tonsured head. He wore his cassock now, and was far more the churchman in appearance than when Vanamee and Presley had seen him on a former occasion.

They were now in the cloister garden. The place was charming. Everywhere grew clumps of palms and magnolia trees. A grapevine, over a century old, occupied a trellis in one angle of the walls which surrounded the garden on two sides. Along the third side was the church itself, while the fourth was open, the wall having crumbled away, its site marked only by a line of eight great pear trees, older even than the grapevine, gnarled, twisted, bearing no fruit.

Directly opposite the pear trees, in the south wall of the garden, was a round, arched portal, whose gate giving upon the esplanade in front of the Mission was always closed. Small gravelled walks, well kept, bordered with mignonette, twisted about among the flower beds, and underneath the magnolia trees. In the centre was a little fountain in a stone basin green with moss, while just beyond, between the fountain and the pear trees, stood what was left of a sun dial, the bronze gnomon, green with the beatings of the weather, the figures on the half-circle of the dial worn away, illegible.

But on the other side of the fountain, and directly opposite the door of the Mission, ranged against the wall, were nine graves—three with headstones, the rest with slabs. Two of Sarria's predecessors were buried here; three of the graves were those of Mission Indians. One was thought to contain a former alcalde of Guadalajara; two more held the bodies of De La Cuesta and his young wife (taking with her to the grave the illusion of her husband's love), and the last one, the ninth, at the end of the line, nearest the pear trees, was marked by a little headstone, the smallest of any, on which, together with the proper dates—only sixteen years apart—was cut the name "Angéle Varian."

But the quiet, the repose, the isolation of the little cloister garden was infinitely delicious. It was a tiny corner of the great valley that stretched in all directions around it—shut off, discreet, romantic, a garden of dreams, of enchantments, of illusions. Outside there, far off, the great grim world went clashing through its grooves, but in here never an echo of the grinding of its wheels entered to jar upon the subdued modulation of the fountain's uninterrupted murmur.

Sarria and Vanamee found their way to a stone bench against the side wall of the Mission, near the door from which they had just issued, and sat down, Sarria lighting a cigar, Vanamee rolling and smoking cigarettes in Mexican fashion.

All about them widened the vast calm night. All the stars were out. The moon was coming up. There was no wind, no sound. The insistent flowing of the fountain seemed only as the symbol of the passing of time, a thing that was understood rather than heard, inevitable, prolonged. At long in-

tervals, a faint breeze, hardly more than a breath, found its
way into the garden over the enclosing walls, and passed
overhead, spreading everywhere the delicious, mingled perfume of magnolia blossoms, of mignonette, of moss, of grass,
and all the calm green life silently teeming within the enclosure of the walls.

From where he sat, Vanamee, turning his head, could look
out underneath the pear trees to the north. Close at hand, a
little valley lay between the high ground on which the Mission was built, and the line of low hills just beyond Broderson
Creek on the Quien Sabe. In here was the Seed ranch, which
Angéle's people had cultivated, a unique and beautiful stretch
of five hundred acres, planted thick with roses, violets, lilies,
tulips, iris, carnations, tube-roses, poppies, heliotrope—all
manner and description of flowers, five hundred acres of
them, solid, thick, exuberant; blooming and fading, and leaving their seed or slips to be marketed broadcast all over the
United States. This had been the vocation of Angéle's parents—raising flowers for their seeds. All over the country the
Seed ranch was known. Now it was arid, almost dry, but
when in full flower, toward the middle of summer, the sight
of these half-thousand acres royal with colour—vermilion,
azure, flaming yellow—was a marvel. When an east wind
blew, men on the streets of Bonneville, nearly twelve miles
away, could catch the scent of this valley of flowers, this chaos
of perfume.

And into this life of flowers, this world of colour, this atmosphere oppressive and clogged and cloyed and thickened
with sweet odour, Angéle had been born. There she had lived
her sixteen years. There she had died. It was not surprising
that Vanamee, with his intense, delicate sensitiveness to
beauty, his almost abnormal capacity for great happiness, had
been drawn to her, had loved her so deeply.

She came to him from out of the flowers, the smell of the
roses in her hair of gold, that hung in two straight plaits on
either side of her face; the reflection of the violets in the profound dark blue of her eyes, perplexing, heavy-lidded, almond-
shaped, oriental; the aroma and the imperial red of the carnations in her lips, with their almost Egyptian fulness; the
whiteness of the lilies, the perfume of the lilies, and the lilies'

slender balancing grace in her neck. Her hands disengaged the odour of the heliotropes. The folds of her dress gave off the enervating scent of poppies. Her feet were redolent of hyacinths.

For a long time after sitting down upon the bench, neither the priest nor Vanamee spoke. But after a while Sarria took his cigar from his lips, saying:

"How still it is! This is a beautiful old garden, peaceful, very quiet. Some day I shall be buried here. I like to remember that; and you, too, Vanamee."

"Quien sabe?"

"Yes, you, too. Where else? No, it is better here, yonder, by the side of the little girl."

"I am not able to look forward yet, sir. The things that are to be are somehow nothing to me at all. For me they amount to nothing."

"They amount to everything, my boy."

"Yes, to one part of me, but not to the part of me that belonged to Angéle—the best part. Oh, you don't know," he exclaimed with a sudden movement, "no one can understand. What is it to me when you tell me that sometime after I shall die too, somewhere, in a vague place you call Heaven, I shall see her again? Do you think that the idea of that ever made any one's sorrow easier to bear? Ever took the edge from any one's grief?"

"But you believe that——"

"Oh, believe, believe!" echoed the other. "What do I believe? I don't know. I believe, or I don't believe. I can remember what she *was*, but I cannot hope what she will be. Hope, after all, is only memory seen reversed. When I try to see her in another life—whatever you call it—in Heaven—beyond the grave—this vague place of yours; when I try to see her there, she comes to my imagination only as what she was, material, earthly, as I loved her. Imperfect, you say; but that is as I saw her, and as I saw her, I loved her; and as she *was*, material, earthly, imperfect, she loved me. It's that, that I want," he exclaimed. "I don't want her changed. I don't want her spiritualised, exalted, glorified, celestial. I want *her*. I think it is only this feeling that has kept me from killing myself. I would rather be unhappy in the memory of what she

actually was, than be happy in the realisation of her transformed, changed, made celestial. I am only human. Her soul!
That was beautiful, no doubt. But, again, it was something
very vague, intangible, hardly more than a phrase. But the
touch of her hand was real, the sound of her voice was real,
the clasp of her arms about my neck was real. Oh," he cried,
shaken with a sudden wrench of passion, "give those back to
me. Tell your God to give those back to me—the sound of
her voice, the touch of her hand, the clasp of her dear arms,
real, *real*, and then you may talk to me of Heaven."

Sarria shook his head. "But when you meet her again," he
observed, "in Heaven, you, too, will be changed. You will see
her spiritualised, with spiritual eyes. As she is now, she does
not appeal to you. I understand that. It is because, as you say,
you are only human, while she is divine. But when you come
to be like her, as she is now, you will know her as she really
is, not as she seemed to be, because her voice was sweet, because her hair was pretty, because her hand was warm in
yours. Vanamee, your talk is that of a foolish child. You are
like one of the Corinthians to whom Paul wrote. Do you remember? Listen now. I can recall the words, and such words,
beautiful and terrible at the same time, such a majesty. They
march like soldiers with trumpets. 'But some man will say'—
as you have said just now—'How are the dead raised up?
And with what body do they come? Thou fool! That which
thou sowest is not quickened except it die, and that which
thou sowest, thou sowest not that body that shall be, but bare
grain. It may chance of wheat, or of some other grain. But
God giveth it a body as it hath pleased him, and to every seed
his own body. . . . It is sown a natural body; it is raised a
spiritual body.' It is because you are a natural body that you
cannot understand her, nor wish for her as a spiritual body,
but when you are both spiritual, then you shall know each
other as you are—know as you never knew before. Your
grain of wheat is your symbol of immortality. You bury it in
the earth. It dies, and rises again a thousand times more beautiful. Vanamee, your dear girl was only a grain of humanity
that we have buried here, and the end is not yet. But all this
is so old, so old. The world learned it a thousand years ago,
and yet each man that has ever stood by the open grave of

any one he loved must learn it all over again from the beginning."

Vanamee was silent for a moment, looking off with unseeing eyes between the trunks of the pear trees, over the little
valley.

"That may all be as you say," he answered after a while. "I
have not learned it yet, in any case. Now, I only know that I
love her—oh, as if it all were yesterday—and that I am suffering, suffering, always."

He leaned forward, his head supported on his clenched
fists, the infinite sadness of his face deepening like a shadow,
the tears brimming in his deep-set eyes. A question that he
must ask, which involved the thing that was scarcely to be
thought of, occurred to him at this moment. After hesitating
for a long moment, he said:

"I have been away a long time, and I have had no news of
this place since I left. Is there anything to tell, Father? Has
any discovery been made, any suspicion developed, as to—
the Other?"

The priest shook his head.

"Not a word, not a whisper. It is a mystery. It always will
be."

Vanamee clasped his head between his clenched fists, rocking himself to and fro.

"Oh, the terror of it," he murmured. "The horror of it.
And she—think of it, Sarria, only sixteen, a little girl; so innocent, that she never knew what wrong meant, pure as a
little child is pure, who believed that all things were good;
mature only in her love. And to be struck down like that,
while your God looked down from Heaven and would not
take her part." All at once he seemed to lose control of himself. One of those furies of impotent grief and wrath that assailed him from time to time, blind, insensate, incoherent,
suddenly took possession of him. A torrent of words issued
from his lips, and he flung out an arm, the fist clenched, in a
fierce, quick gesture, partly of despair, partly of defiance,
partly of supplication.

"No, your God would not take her part. Where was God's
mercy in that? Where was Heaven's protection in that? Where
was the loving kindness you preach about? Why did God give

her life if it was to be stamped out? Why did God give her the power of love if it was to come to nothing? Sarria, listen to me. Why did God make her so divinely pure if He permitted that abomination? Ha!" he exclaimed bitterly, "your God! Why, an Apache buck would have been more merciful. Your God! There is no God. There is only the Devil. The Heaven you pray to is only a joke, a wretched trick, a delusion. It is only Hell that is real."

Sarria caught him by the arm.

"You are a fool and a child," he exclaimed, "and it is blasphemy that you are saying. I forbid it. You understand? I forbid it."

Vanamee turned on him with a sudden cry.

"Then, tell your God to give her back to me!"

Sarria started away from him, his eyes widening in astonishment, surprised out of all composure by the other's outburst. Vanamee's swarthy face was pale, the sunken cheeks and deep-set eyes were marked with great black shadows. The priest no longer recognised him. The face, that face of the ascetic, lean, framed in its long black hair and pointed beard, was quivering with the excitement of hallucination. It was the face of the inspired shepherds of the Hebraic legends, living close to nature, the younger prophets of Israel, dwellers in the wilderness, solitary, imaginative, believing in the Vision, having strange delusions, gifted with strange powers. In a brief second of thought, Sarria understood. Out into the wilderness, the vast arid desert of the Southwest, Vanamee had carried his grief. For days, for weeks, months even, he had been alone, a solitary speck lost in the immensity of the horizons; continually he was brooding, haunted with his sorrow, thinking, thinking, often hard put to it for food. The body was ill-nourished, and the mind, concentrated forever upon one subject, had recoiled upon itself, had preyed upon the naturally nervous temperament, till the imagination had become exalted, morbidly active, diseased, beset with hallucinations, forever in search of the manifestation, of the miracle. It was small wonder that, bringing a fancy so distorted back to the scene of a vanished happiness, Vanamee should be racked with the most violent illusions, beset in the throes of a veritable hysteria.

"Tell your God to give her back to me," he repeated with fierce insistence.

It was the pitch of mysticism, the imagination harassed and goaded beyond the normal round, suddenly flipping from the circumference, spinning off at a tangent, out into the void, where all things seemed possible, hurtling through the dark there, groping for the supernatural, clamouring for the miracle. And it was also the human, natural protest against the inevitable, the irrevocable; the spasm of revolt under the sting of death, the rebellion of the soul at the victory of the grave.

"He can give her back to me if He only will," Vanamee cried. "Sarria, you must help me. I tell you—I warn you, sir, I can't last much longer under it. My head is all wrong with it—I've no more hold on my mind. Something must happen or I shall lose my senses. I am breaking down under it all, my body and my mind alike. Bring her to me; make God show her to me. If all tales are true, it would not be the first time. If I cannot have her, at least let me see her as she was, real, earthly, not her spirit, her ghost. I want her real self, undefiled again. If this is dementia, then let me be demented. But help me, you and your God; create the delusion, do the miracle."

"Stop!" cried the priest again, shaking him roughly by the shoulder. "Stop. Be yourself. This *is* dementia; but I shall *not* let you be demented. Think of what you are saying. Bring her back to you! Is that the way of God? I thought you were a man; this is the talk of a weak-minded girl."

Vanamee stirred abruptly in his place, drawing a long breath and looking about him vaguely, as if he came to himself.

"You are right," he muttered. "I hardly know what I am saying at times. But there are moments when my whole mind and soul seem to rise up in rebellion against what has happened; when it seems to me that I am stronger than death, and that if I only knew how to use the strength of my will, concentrate my power of thought—volition—that I could— I don't know—not call her back—but—something——"

"A diseased and distorted mind is capable of hallucinations, if that is what you mean," observed Sarria.

"Perhaps that is what I mean. Perhaps I want only the delusion, after all."

Sarria did not reply, and there was a long silence. In the damp south corners of the walls a frog began to croak at exact intervals. The little fountain rippled monotonously, and a magnolia flower dropped from one of the trees, falling straight as a plummet through the motionless air, and settling upon the gravelled walk with a faint rustling sound. Otherwise the stillness was profound.

A little later, the priest's cigar, long since out, slipped from his fingers to the ground. He began to nod gently. Vanamee touched his arm.

"Asleep, sir?"

The other started, rubbing his eyes.

"Upon my word, I believe I was."

"Better go to bed, sir. I am not tired. I think I shall sit out here a little longer."

"Well, perhaps I would be better off in bed. *Your* bed is always ready for you here whenever you want to use it."

"No—I shall go back to Quien Sabe—later. Good-night, sir."

"Good-night, my boy."

Vanamee was left alone. For a long time he sat motionless in his place, his elbows on his knees, his chin propped in his hands. The minutes passed—then the hours. The moon climbed steadily higher among the stars. Vanamee rolled and smoked cigarette after cigarette, the blue haze of smoke hanging motionless above his head, or drifting in slowly weaving filaments across the open spaces of the garden.

But the influence of the old enclosure, this corner of romance and mystery, this isolated garden of dreams, savouring of the past, with its legends, its graves, its crumbling sun dial, its fountain with its rime of moss, was not to be resisted. Now that the priest had left him, the same exaltation of spirit that had seized upon Vanamee earlier in the evening, by degrees grew big again in his mind and imagination. His sorrow assaulted him like the flagellations of a fine whiplash, and his love for Angéle rose again in his heart, it seemed to him never so deep, so tender, so infinitely strong. No doubt, it was his familiarity with the Mission garden, his clear-cut remembrance of it, as it was in the days when he had met Angéle there, tallying now so exactly with the reality there under his eyes, that brought her to his imagination so vividly. As yet he dared not trust himself near her grave, but, for the moment, he rose and, his hands clasped behind him, walked slowly from point to point amid the tiny gravelled walks, recalling the incidents of eighteen years ago. On the bench he had quitted he and Angéle had often sat. Here by the crumbling sun dial, he recalled the night when he had kissed her for the first time. Here, again, by the rim of the fountain, with its fringe of green, she once had paused, and, baring her arm to the shoulder, had thrust it deep into the water, and then withdrawing it, had given it to him to kiss, all wet and cool; and here, at last, under the shadow of the pear trees they had sat, evening after evening, looking off over the little valley below them, watching the night build itself, dome-like, from horizon to zenith.

Brusquely Vanamee turned away from the prospect. The Seed ranch was dark at this time of the year, and flowerless. Far off toward its centre, he had caught a brief glimpse of the house where Angéle had lived, and a faint light burning in its window. But he turned from it sharply. The deep-seated travail of his grief abruptly reached the paroxysm. With long strides he crossed the garden and reëntered the Mission church itself, plunging into the coolness of its atmosphere as into a bath. What he searched for he did not know, or, rather, did not define. He knew only that he was suffering, that a longing for Angéle, for some object around which his great love could enfold itself, was tearing at his heart with iron teeth. He was ready to be deluded; craved the hallucination; begged pitifully for the illusion; anything rather than the empty, tenantless night, the voiceless silence, the vast loneliness of the overspanning arc of the heavens.

Before the chancel rail of the altar, under the sanctuary lamp, Vanamee sank upon his knees, his arms folded upon the rail, his head bowed down upon them. He prayed, with what words he could not say, for what he did not understand—for help, merely, for relief, for an Answer to his cry.

It was upon that, at length, that his disordered mind concentrated itself, an Answer—he demanded, he implored an Answer. Not a vague visitation of Grace, not a formless sense of Peace; but an Answer, something real, even if the reality were fancied, a voice out of the night, responding to his, a hand in the dark clasping his groping fingers, a breath, human, warm, fragrant, familiar, like a soft, sweet caress on his shrunken cheeks. Alone there in the dim half-light of the decaying Mission, with its crumbling plaster, its naïve crudity of ornament and picture, he wrestled fiercely with his desires—words, fragments of sentences, inarticulate, incoherent, wrenched from his tight-shut teeth.

But the Answer was not in the church. Above him, over the high altar, the Virgin in a glory, with downcast eyes and folded hands, grew vague and indistinct in the shadow, the colours fading, tarnished by centuries of incense smoke. The Christ in agony on the Cross was but a lamentable vision of tormented anatomy, grey flesh, spotted with crimson. The St. John, the San Juan Bautista, patron saint of the Mission, the gaunt figure in skins, two fingers upraised in the gesture of benediction, gazed stolidly out into the half-gloom under the ceiling, ignoring the human distress that beat itself in vain against the altar rail below, and Angéle remained as before— only a memory, far distant, intangible, lost.

Vanamee rose, turning his back upon the altar with a vague gesture of despair. He crossed the church, and issuing from the low-arched door opposite the pulpit, once more stepped out into the garden. Here, at least, was reality. The warm, still air descended upon him like a cloak, grateful, comforting, dispelling the chill that lurked in the damp mould of plaster and crumbling adobe.

But now he found his way across the garden on the other side of the fountain, where, ranged against the eastern wall, were nine graves. Here Angéle was buried, in the smallest grave of them all, marked by the little headstone, with its two dates, only sixteen years apart. To this spot, at last, he had returned, after the years spent in the desert, the wilderness— after all the wanderings of the Long Trail. Here, if ever, he must have a sense of her nearness. Close at hand, a short four feet under that mound of grass, was the form he had so often held in the embrace of his arms; the face, the very face he had kissed, that face with the hair of gold making three-cornered the round white forehead, the violet-blue eyes, heavy-lidded, with their strange oriental slant upward toward the temples;

the sweet full lips, almost Egyptian in their fulness—all that strange, perplexing, wonderful beauty, so troublous, so enchanting, so out of all accepted standards.

He bent down, dropping upon one knee, a hand upon the headstone, and read again the inscription. Then instinctively his hand left the stone and rested upon the low mound of turf, touching it with the softness of a caress; and then, before he was aware of it, he was stretched at full length upon the earth, beside the grave, his arms about the low mound, his lips pressed against the grass with which it was covered. The pent-up grief of nearly twenty years rose again within his heart, and overflowed, irresistible, violent, passionate. There was no one to see, no one to hear. Vanamee had no thought of restraint. He no longer wrestled with his pain—strove against it. There was even a sense of relief in permitting himself to be overcome. But the reaction from this outburst was equally violent. His revolt against the inevitable, his protest against the grave, shook him from head to foot, goaded him beyond all bounds of reason, hounded him on and into the domain of hysteria, dementia. Vanamee was no longer master of himself—no longer knew what he was doing.

At first, he had been content with merely a wild, unreasoned cry to Heaven that Angéle should be restored to him, but the vast egotism that seems to run through all forms of disordered intelligence gave his fancy another turn. He forgot God. He no longer reckoned with Heaven. He arrogated their powers to himself—struggled to be, of his own unaided might, stronger than death, more powerful than the grave. He had demanded of Sarria that God should restore Angéle to him, but now he appealed directly to Angéle herself. As he lay there, his arms clasped about her grave, she seemed so near to him that he fancied she *must* hear. And suddenly, at this moment, his recollection of his strange compelling power—the same power by which he had called Presley to him half-way across the Quien Sabe ranch, the same power which had brought Sarria to his side that very evening—recurred to him. Concentrating his mind upon the one object with which it had so long been filled, Vanamee, his eyes closed, his face buried in his arms, exclaimed:

"Come to me—Angéle—don't you hear? Come to me."

But the Answer was not in the Grave. Below him the voiceless Earth lay silent, moveless, withholding the secret, jealous
of that which it held so close in its grip, refusing to give up
that which had been confided to its keeping, untouched by
the human anguish that above there, on its surface, clutched
with despairing hands at a grave long made. The Earth that
only that morning had been so eager, so responsive to the
lightest summons, so vibrant with Life, now at night, holding
death within its embrace, guarding inviolate the secret of the
Grave, was deaf to all entreaty, refused the Answer, and Angéle remained as before, only a memory, far distant, intangible, lost.

Vanamee lifted his head, looking about him with unseeing
eyes, trembling with the exertion of his vain effort. But he
could not as yet allow himself to despair. Never before had
that curious power of attraction failed him. He felt himself to
be so strong in this respect that he was persuaded if he exerted himself to the limit of his capacity, something—he
could not say what—*must* come of it. If it was only a self-
delusion, an hallucination, he told himself that he would be
content.

Almost of its own accord, his distorted mind concentrated
itself again, every thought, all the power of his will riveting
themselves upon Angéle. As if she were alive, he summoned
her to him. His eyes, fixed upon the name cut into the headstone, contracted, the pupils growing small, his fists shut
tight, his nerves braced rigid.

For a few seconds he stood thus, breathless, expectant,
awaiting the manifestation, the Miracle. Then, without knowing why, hardly conscious of what was transpiring, he found
that his glance was leaving the headstone, was turning from
the grave. Not only this, but his whole body was following
the direction of his eyes. Before he knew it, he was standing
with his back to Angéle's grave, was facing the north, facing
the line of pear trees and the little valley where the Seed ranch
lay. At first, he thought this was because he had allowed his
will to weaken, the concentrated power of his mind to grow
slack. And once more turning toward the grave, he banded
all his thoughts together in a consummate effort, his teeth
grinding together, his hands pressed to his forehead. He

forced himself to the notion that Angéle was alive, and to this creature of his imagination he addressed himself:

"Angéle!" he cried in a low voice; "Angéle, I am calling you—do you hear? Come to me—come to me now, now."

Instead of the Answer he demanded, that inexplicable counter-influence cut across the current of his thought. Strive as he would against it, he must veer to the north, toward the pear trees. Obeying it, he turned, and, still wondering, took a step in that direction, then another and another. The next moment he came abruptly to himself, in the black shadow of the pear trees themselves, and, opening his eyes, found himself looking off over the Seed ranch, toward the little house in the centre where Angéle had once lived.

Perplexed, he returned to the grave, once more calling upon the resources of his will, and abruptly, so soon as these reached a certain point, the same cross-current set in. He could no longer keep his eyes upon the headstone, could no longer think of the grave and what it held. He must face the north; he must be drawn toward the pear trees, and there left standing in their shadow, looking out aimlessly over the Seed ranch, wondering, bewildered. Farther than this the influence never drew him, but up to this point—the line of pear trees—it was not to be resisted.

For a time the peculiarity of the affair was of more interest to Vanamee than even his own distress of spirit, and once or twice he repeated the attempt, almost experimentally, and invariably with the same result: so soon as he seemed to hold Angéle in the grip of his mind, he was moved to turn about toward the north, and hurry toward the pear trees on the crest of the hill that overlooked the little valley.

But Vanamee's unhappiness was too keen this night for him to dwell long upon the vagaries of his mind. Submitting at length, and abandoning the grave, he flung himself down in the black shade of the pear trees, his chin in his hands, and resigned himself finally and definitely to the inrush of recollection and the exquisite grief of an infinite regret.

To his fancy, she came to him again. He put himself back many years. He remembered the warm nights of July and August, profoundly still, the sky encrusted with stars, the little Mission garden exhaling the mingled perfumes that all through the scorching day had been distilled under the steady blaze of a summer's sun. He saw himself as another person, arriving at this, their rendezvous. All day long she had been in his mind. All day long he had looked forward to this quiet hour that belonged to her. It was dark. He could see nothing, but, by and by, he heard a step, a gentle rustle of the grass on the slope of the hill pressed under an advancing foot. Then he saw the faint gleam of pallid gold of her hair, a barely visible glow in the starlight, and heard the murmur of her breath in the lapse of the over-passing breeze. And then, in the midst of the gentle perfumes of the garden, the perfumes of the magnolia flowers, of the mignonette borders, of the crumbling walls, there expanded a new odour, or the faint mingling of many odours, the smell of the roses that lingered in her hair, of the lilies that exhaled from her neck, of the heliotrope that disengaged itself from her hands and arms, and of the hyacinths with which her little feet were redolent. And then, suddenly, it was herself—her eyes, heavy-lidded, violet blue, full of the love of him; her sweet full lips speaking his name; her hands clasping his hands, his shoulders, his neck—her whole dear body giving itself into his embrace; her lips against his; her hands holding his head, drawing his face down to hers.

Vanamee, as he remembered all this, flung out an arm with a cry of pain, his eyes searching the gloom, all his mind in strenuous mutiny against the triumph of Death. His glance shot swiftly out across the night, unconsciously following the direction from which Angéle used to come to him.

"Come to me now," he exclaimed under his breath, tense and rigid with the vast futile effort of his will. "Come to me now, now. Don't you hear me, Angéle? You must, you must come."

Suddenly Vanamee returned to himself with the abruptness of a blow. His eyes opened. He half raised himself from the ground. Swiftly his scattered wits readjusted themselves. Never more sane, never more himself, he rose to his feet and stood looking off into the night across the Seed ranch.

"What was it?" he murmured, bewildered.

He looked around him from side to side, as if to get in touch with reality once more. He looked at his hands, at the rough bark of the pear tree next which he stood, at the streaked and rain-eroded walls of the Mission and garden. The exaltation of his mind calmed itself; the unnatural strain under which he laboured slackened. He became thoroughly master of himself again, matter-of-fact, practical, keen.

But just so sure as his hands were his own, just so sure as the bark of the pear tree was rough, the mouldering adobe of the Mission walls damp—just so sure had Something occurred. It was vague, intangible, appealing only to some strange, nameless sixth sense, but none the less perceptible. His mind, his imagination, sent out from him across the night, across the little valley below him, speeding hither and thither through the dark, lost, confused, had suddenly paused, hovering, had found Something. It had not returned to him empty-handed. It had come back, but now there was a change—mysterious, illusive. There were no words for this that had transpired. But for the moment, one thing only was certain. The night was no longer voiceless, the dark was no longer empty. Far off there, beyond the reach of vision, un-localised, strange, a ripple had formed on the still black pool of the night, had formed, flashed one instant to the stars, then swiftly faded again. The night shut down once more. There was no sound—nothing stirred.

For the moment, Vanamee stood transfixed, struck rigid in his place, stupefied, his eyes staring, breathless with utter amazement. Then, step by step, he shrank back into the deeper shadow, treading with the infinite precaution of a prowling leopard. A qualm of something very much like fear seized upon him. But immediately on the heels of this first impression came the doubt of his own senses. Whatever had happened had been so ephemeral, so faint, so intangible, that now he wondered if he had not deceived himself, after all. But the reaction followed. Surely, there had been Something. And from that moment began for him the most poignant un-certainty of mind. Gradually he drew back into the garden, holding his breath, listening to every faintest sound, walking upon tiptoe. He reached the fountain, and wetting his hands, passed them across his forehead and eyes. Once more he stood listening. The silence was profound.

Troubled, disturbed, Vanamee went away, passing out of

the garden, descending the hill. He forded Broderson Creek where it intersected the road to Guadalajara, and went on across Quien Sabe, walking slowly, his head bent down, his hands clasped behind his back, thoughtful, perplexed.

V

A<small>T</small> <small>SEVEN O'CLOCK</small>, in the bedroom of his ranch house, in the white-painted iron bedstead with its blue-grey army blankets and red counterpane, Annixter was still asleep, his face red, his mouth open, his stiff yellow hair in wild disorder. On the wooden chair at the bed-head, stood the kerosene lamp, by the light of which he had been reading the previous evening. Beside it was a paper bag of dried prunes, and the limp volume of "Copperfield," the place marked by a slip of paper torn from the edge of the bag.

Annixter slept soundly, making great work of the business, unable to take even his rest gracefully. His eyes were shut so tight that the skin at their angles was drawn into puckers. Under his pillow, his two hands were doubled up into fists. At intervals, he gritted his teeth ferociously, while, from time to time, the abrupt sound of his snoring dominated the brisk ticking of the alarm clock that hung from the brass knob of the bed-post, within six inches of his ear.

But immediately after seven, this clock sprung its alarm with the abruptness of an explosion, and within the second, Annixter had hurled the bed-clothes from him and flung himself up to a sitting posture on the edge of the bed, panting and gasping, blinking at the light, rubbing his head, dazed and bewildered, stupefied at the hideous suddenness with which he had been wrenched from his sleep.

His first act was to take down the alarm clock and stifle its prolonged whirring under the pillows and blankets. But when this had been done, he continued to sit stupidly on the edge of the bed, curling his toes away from the cold of the floor; his half-shut eyes, heavy with sleep, fixed and vacant, closing and opening by turns. For upwards of three minutes he alternately dozed and woke, his head and the whole upper half of his body sagging abruptly sideways from moment to moment. But at length, coming more to himself, he straightened up, ran his fingers through his hair, and with a prodigious yawn, murmured vaguely:

"Oh, Lord! Oh-h, *Lord!*"

He stretched three or four times, twisting about in his

place, curling and uncurling his toes, muttering from time to time between two yawns:

"Oh, Lord! Oh, Lord!"

He stared about the room, collecting his thoughts, re-adjusting himself for the day's work.

The room was barren, the walls of tongue-and-groove sheathing—alternate brown and yellow boards—like the walls of a stable, were adorned with two or three unframed lithographs, the Christmas "souvenirs" of weekly periodicals, fastened with great wire nails; a bunch of herbs or flowers, lamentably withered and grey with dust, was affixed to the mirror over the black walnut washstand by the window, and a yellowed photograph of Annixter's combined harvester—himself and his men in a group before it—hung close at hand. On the floor, at the bedside and before the bureau, were two oval rag-carpet rugs. In the corners of the room were muddy boots, a McClellan saddle, a surveyor's transit, an empty coal-hod and a box of iron bolts and nuts. On the wall over the bed, in a gilt frame, was Annixter's college diploma, while on the bureau, amid a litter of hair-brushes, dirty collars, driving gloves, cigars and the like, stood a broken machine for loading shells.

It was essentially a man's room, rugged, uncouth, virile, full of the odours of tobacco, of leather, of rusty iron; the bare floor hollowed by the grind of hob-nailed boots, the walls marred by the friction of heavy things of metal. Strangely enough, Annixter's clothes were disposed of on the single chair with the precision of an old maid. Thus he had placed them the night before; the boots set carefully side by side, the trousers, with the overalls still upon them, neatly folded upon the seat of the chair, the coat hanging from its back.

The Quien Sabe ranch house was a six-room affair, all on one floor. By no excess of charity could it have been called a home. Annixter was a wealthy man; he could have furnished his dwelling with quite as much elegance as that of Magnus Derrick. As it was, however, he considered his house merely as a place to eat, to sleep, to change his clothes in; as a shelter from the rain, an office where business was transacted—nothing more.

When he was sufficiently awake, Annixter thrust his feet

into a pair of wicker slippers, and shuffled across the office adjoining his bedroom, to the bathroom just beyond, and stood under the icy shower a few minutes, his teeth chattering, fulminating oaths at the coldness of the water. Still shivering, he hurried into his clothes, and, having pushed the button of the electric bell to announce that he was ready for breakfast, immediately plunged into the business of the day. While he was thus occupied, the butcher's cart from Bonneville drove into the yard with the day's supply of meat. This cart also brought the Bonneville paper and the mail of the previous night. In the bundle of correspondence that the butcher handed to Annixter that morning, was a telegram from Osterman, at that time on his second trip to Los Angeles. It read:

> "Flotation of company in this district assured. Have secured services of desirable party. Am now in position to sell you your share stock, as per original plan."

Annixter grunted as he tore the despatch into strips.

"Well," he muttered, "that part is settled, then."

He made a little pile of the torn strips on the top of the unlighted stove, and burned them carefully, scowling down into the flicker of fire, thoughtful and preoccupied.

He knew very well what Osterman referred to by "Flotation of company," and also who was the "desirable party" he spoke of.

Under protest, as he was particular to declare, and after interminable argument, Annixter had allowed himself to be reconciled with Osterman, and to be persuaded to reënter the proposed political "deal." A committee had been formed to finance the affair—Osterman, old Broderson, Annixter himself, and, with reservations, hardly more than a looker-on, Harran Derrick. Of this committee, Osterman was considered chairman. Magnus Derrick had formally and definitely refused his adherence to the scheme. He was trying to steer a middle course. His position was difficult, anomalous. If freight rates were cut through the efforts of the members of the committee, he could not very well avoid taking advantage of the new schedule. He would be the gainer, though sharing neither the risk nor the expense. But, meanwhile, the days were passing;

the primary elections were drawing nearer. The committee could not afford to wait, and by way of a beginning, Osterman had gone to Los Angeles, fortified by a large sum of money—a purse to which Annixter, Broderson and himself had contributed. He had put himself in touch with Disbrow, the political man of the Denver, Pueblo and Mojave road, and had had two interviews with him. The telegram that Annixter received that morning was to say that Disbrow had been bought over, and would adopt Darrell as the D., P. and M. candidate for Railroad Commissioner from the third district.

One of the cooks brought up Annixter's breakfast that morning, and he went through it hastily, reading his mail at the same time and glancing over the pages of the "Mercury," Genslinger's paper. The "Mercury," Annixter was persuaded, received a subsidy from the Pacific and Southwestern Railroad, and was hardly better than the mouthpiece by which Shelgrim and the General Office spoke to ranchers about Bonneville.

An editorial in that morning's issue said:

"It would not be surprising to the well-informed, if the long-deferred re-grade of the value of the railroad sections included in the Los Muertos, Quien Sabe, Osterman and Broderson properties was made before the first of the year. Naturally, the tenants of these lands feel an interest in the price which the railroad will put upon its holdings, and it is rumoured they expect the land will be offered to them for two dollars and fifty cents per acre. It needs no seventh daughter of a seventh daughter to foresee that these gentlemen will be disappointed."

"Rot!" vociferated Annixter to himself as he finished. He rolled the paper into a wad and hurled it from him.

"Rot! rot! What does Genslinger know about it? I stand on my agreement with the P. and S. W.—from two fifty to five dollars an acre—there it is in black and white. The road *is* obligated. And my improvements! I made the land valuable by improving it, irrigating it, draining it, and cultivating it. Talk to *me*. I know better."

The most abiding impression that Genslinger's editorial made upon him was, that possibly the "Mercury" was not subsidised by the corporation after all. If it was, Genslinger

would not have been led into making his mistake as to the
value of the land. He would have known that the railroad was
under contract to sell at two dollars and a half an acre, and
not only this, but that when the land was put upon the market, it was to be offered to the present holders first of all.
Annixter called to mind the explicit terms of the agreement
between himself and the railroad, and dismissed the matter
from his mind. He lit a cigar, put on his hat and went out.

The morning was fine, the air nimble, brisk. On the summit of the skeleton-like tower of the artesian well, the windmill was turning steadily in a breeze from the southwest. The
water in the irrigating ditch was well up. There was no cloud
in the sky. Far off to the east and west, the bulwarks of the
valley, the Coast Range and the foothills of the Sierras stood
out, pale amethyst against the delicate pink and white sheen
of the horizon. The sunlight was a veritable flood, crystal,
limpid, sparkling, setting a feeling of gayety in the air, stirring
up an effervescence in the blood, a tumult of exuberance in
the veins.

But on his way to the barns, Annixter was obliged to pass
by the open door of the dairy-house. Hilma Tree was inside,
singing at her work; her voice of a velvety huskiness, more of
the chest than of the throat, mingling with the liquid dashing
of the milk in the vats and churns, and the clear, sonorous
clinking of the cans and pans. Annixter turned into the dairy-
house, pausing on the threshold, looking about him. Hilma
stood bathed from head to foot in the torrent of sunlight that
poured in upon her from the three wide-open windows. She
was charming, delicious, radiant of youth, of health, of well-
being. Into her eyes, wide open, brown, rimmed with their
fine, thin line of intense black lashes, the sun set a diamond
flash; the same golden light glowed all around her thick,
moist hair, lambent, beautiful, a sheen of almost metallic
lustre, and reflected itself upon her wet lips, moving with the
words of her singing. The whiteness of her skin under the
caress of this hale, vigorous morning light was dazzling, pure,
of a fineness beyond words. Beneath the sweet modulation of
her chin, the reflected light from the burnished copper vessel
she was carrying set a vibration of pale gold. Overlaying the
flush of rose in her cheeks, seen only when she stood against

the sunlight, was a faint sheen of down, a lustrous floss, delicate as the pollen of a flower, or the impalpable powder of a moth's wing. She was moving to and fro about her work, alert, joyous, robust; and from all the fine, full amplitude of her figure, from her thick white neck, sloping downward to her shoulders, from the deep, feminine swell of her breast, the vigorous maturity of her hips, there was disengaged a vibrant note of gayety, of exuberant animal life, sane, honest, strong. She wore a skirt of plain blue calico and a shirtwaist of pink linen, clean, trim; while her sleeves turned back to her shoulders, showed her large, white arms, wet with milk, redolent and fragrant with milk, glowing and resplendent in the early morning light.

On the threshold, Annixter took off his hat.

"Good morning, Miss Hilma."

Hilma, who had set down the copper can on top of the vat, turned about quickly.

"Oh, *good* morning, sir;" and, unconsciously, she made a little gesture of salutation with her hand, raising it part way toward her head, as a man would have done.

"Well," began Annixter vaguely, "how are you getting along down here?"

"Oh, very fine. To-day, there is not so much to do. We drew the whey hours ago, and now we are just done putting the curd to press. I have been cleaning. See my pans. Wouldn't they do for mirrors, sir? And the copper things. I have scrubbed and scrubbed. Oh, you can look into the tiniest corners, everywhere, you won't find so much as the littlest speck of dirt or grease. I love *clean* things, and this room is my own particular place. Here I can do just as I please, and that is, to keep the cement floor, and the vats, and the churns and the separators, and especially the cans and coppers, clean; clean, and to see that the milk is pure, oh, so that a little baby could drink it; and to have the air always sweet, and the sun—oh, lots and lots of sun, morning, noon and afternoon, so that everything shines. You know, I never see the sun set that it don't make me a little sad; yes, always, just a little. Isn't it funny? I should want it to be day all the time. And when the day is gloomy and dark, I am just as sad as if a very good friend of mine had left me. Would you believe it? Just until within a few years, when I was a big girl, sixteen and over, mamma had to sit by my bed every night before I could go to sleep. I was afraid in the dark. Sometimes I am now. Just imagine, and now I am nineteen—a young lady."

"You were, hey?" observed Annixter, for the sake of saying something. "Afraid in the dark? What of—ghosts?"

"N-no; I don't know what. I wanted the light, I wanted——" She drew a deep breath, turning towards the window and spreading her pink finger-tips to the light. "Oh, the *sun*. I love the sun. See, put your hand there—here on the top of the vat—like that. Isn't it warm? Isn't it fine? And don't you love to see it coming in like that through the windows, floods of it; and all the little dust in it shining? Where there is lots of sunlight, I think the people must be very good. It's only wicked people that love the dark. And the wicked things are always done and planned in the dark, I think. Perhaps, too, that's why I hate things that are mysterious—things that I can't see, that happen in the dark." She wrinkled her nose with a little expression of aversion. "I hate a mystery. Maybe that's why I am afraid in the dark—or was. I shouldn't like to think that anything could happen around me that I couldn't see or understand or explain."

She ran on from subject to subject, positively garrulous, talking in her low-pitched voice of velvety huskiness for the mere enjoyment of putting her ideas into speech, innocently assuming that they were quite as interesting to others as to herself. She was yet a great child, ignoring the fact that she had ever grown up, taking a child's interest in her immediate surroundings, direct, straightforward, plain. While speaking, she continued about her work, rinsing out the cans with a mixture of hot water and soda, scouring them bright, and piling them in the sunlight on top of the vat.

Obliquely, and from between his narrowed lids, Annixter scrutinised her from time to time, more and more won over by her adorable freshness, her clean, fine youth. The clumsiness that he usually experienced in the presence of women was wearing off. Hilma Tree's direct simplicity put him at his ease. He began to wonder if he dared to kiss Hilma, and if he did dare, how she would take it. A spark of suspicion flickered up in his mind. Did not her manner imply, vaguely, an invitation? One never could tell with feemales. That was why she was talking so much, no doubt, holding him there, affording the opportunity. Aha! She had best look out, or he would take her at her word.

"Oh, I had forgotten," suddenly exclaimed Hilma, "the very thing I wanted to show you—the new press. You remember I asked for one last month? This is it. See, this is how it works. Here is where the curds go; look. And this cover is screwed down like this, and then you work the lever this way." She grasped the lever in both hands, throwing her weight upon it, her smooth, bare arm swelling round and firm with the effort, one slim foot, in its low shoe set off with the bright, steel buckle, braced against the wall.

"My, but that takes strength," she panted, looking up at him and smiling. "But isn't it a fine press? Just what we needed."

"And," Annixter cleared his throat, "and where do you keep the cheeses and the butter?" He thought it very likely that these were in the cellar of the dairy.

"In the cellar," answered Hilma. "Down here, see?" She raised the flap of the cellar door at the end of the room. "Would you like to see? Come down; I'll show you."

She went before him down into the cool obscurity underneath, redolent of new cheese and fresh butter. Annixter followed, a certain excitement beginning to gain upon him. He was almost sure now that Hilma wanted him to kiss her. At all events, one could but try. But, as yet, he was not absolutely sure. Suppose he had been mistaken in her; suppose she should consider herself insulted and freeze him with an icy stare. Annixter winced at the very thought of it. Better let the whole business go, and get to work. He was wasting half the morning. Yet, if she *did* want to give him the opportunity of kissing her, and he failed to take advantage of it, what a ninny she would think him; she would despise him for being afraid. He afraid! He, Annixter, afraid of a fool, feemale girl. Why, he owed it to himself as a man to go as far as he could. He told himself that that goat Osterman would have kissed Hilma Tree weeks ago. To test his state of mind, he imagined himself as having decided to kiss her, after all, and at once was surprised to experience a poignant qualm of excitement, his heart beating heavily, his breath coming short. At the same time, his courage remained with him. He was not afraid to try. He felt a greater respect for himself because of this. His self-assurance hardened within him, and as Hilma turned to him, asking him to taste a cut from one of the ripe cheeses, he suddenly stepped close to her, throwing an arm about her shoulders, advancing his head.

But at the last second, he bungled, hesitated; Hilma shrank from him, supple as a young reed; Annixter clutched harshly at her arm, and trod his full weight upon one of her slender feet, his cheek and chin barely touching the delicate pink lobe of one of her ears, his lips brushing merely a fold of her shirt waist between neck and shoulder. The thing was a failure, and at once he realised that nothing had been further from Hilma's mind than the idea of his kissing her.

She started back from him abruptly, her hands nervously clasped against her breast, drawing in her breath sharply and holding it with a little, tremulous catch of the throat that sent a quivering vibration the length of her smooth, white neck. Her eyes opened wide with a childlike look, more of astonishment than anger. She was surprised, out of all measure, discountenanced, taken all aback, and when she found her breath, gave voice to a great "Oh" of dismay and distress.

For an instant, Annixter stood awkwardly in his place, ridiculous, clumsy, murmuring over and over again:

"Well—well—that's all right—who's going to hurt you? You needn't be afraid—who's going to hurt you—that's all right."

Then, suddenly, with a quick, indefinite gesture of one arm, he exclaimed:

"Good-bye, I—I'm sorry."

He turned away, striding up the stairs, crossing the dairy-room, and regained the open air, raging and furious. He turned toward the barns, clapping his hat upon his head, muttering the while under his breath:

"Oh, you goat! You beastly fool *pip*. Good *Lord*, what an ass you've made of yourself now!"

Suddenly he resolved to put Hilma Tree out of his thoughts. The matter was interfering with his work. This kind of thing was sure not earning any money. He shook himself as though freeing his shoulders of an irksome burden, and turned his entire attention to the work nearest at hand.

The prolonged rattle of the shinglers' hammers upon the roof of the big barn attracted him, and, crossing over between the ranch house and the artesian well, he stood for some time absorbed in the contemplation of the vast building, amused and interested with the confusion of sounds—the clatter of hammers, the cadenced scrape of saws, and the rhythmic shuffle of planes—that issued from the gang of carpenters who were at that moment putting the finishing touches upon the roof and rows of stalls. A boy and two men were busy hanging the great sliding door at the south end, while the painters—come down from Bonneville early that morning—were engaged in adjusting the spray and force engine, by means of which Annixter had insisted upon painting the vast surfaces of the barn, condemning the use of brushes and pots for such work as old-fashioned and out-of-date.

He called to one of the foremen, to ask when the barn would be entirely finished, and was told that at the end of the week the hay and stock could be installed.

"And a precious long time you've been at it, too," Annixter declared.

"Well, you know the rain——"

"Oh, rot the rain! *I* work in the rain. You and your unions make me sick."

"But, Mr. Annixter, we couldn't have begun painting in the rain. The job would have been spoiled."

"Hoh, yes, spoiled. That's all very well. Maybe it would, and then, again, maybe it wouldn't."

But when the foreman had left him, Annixter could not forbear a growl of satisfaction. It could not be denied that the barn was superb, monumental even. Almost any one of the other barns in the county could be swung, bird-cage fashion, inside of it, with room to spare. In every sense, the barn was precisely what Annixter had hoped of it. In his pleasure over the success of his idea, even Hilma for the moment was forgotten.

"And, now," murmured Annixter, "I'll give that dance in it. I'll make 'em sit up."

It occurred to him that he had better set about sending out

the invitations for the affair. He was puzzled to decide just how the thing should be managed, and resolved that it might be as well to consult Magnus and Mrs. Derrick.

"I want to talk of this telegram of the goat's with Magnus, anyhow," he said to himself reflectively, "and there's things I got to do in Bonneville before the first of the month."

He turned about on his heel with a last look at the barn, and set off toward the stable. He had decided to have his horse saddled and ride over to Bonneville by way of Los Muertos. He would make a day of it, would see Magnus, Harran, old Broderson and some of the business men of Bonneville.

A few moments later, he rode out of the barn and the stable-yard, a fresh cigar between his teeth, his hat slanted over his face against the rays of the sun, as yet low in the east. He crossed the irrigating ditch and gained the trail—the short cut over into Los Muertos, by way of Hooven's. It led south and west into the low ground overgrown by grey-green willows by Broderson Creek, at this time of the rainy season a stream of considerable volume, farther on dipping sharply to pass underneath the Long Trestle of the railroad. On the other side of the right of way, Annixter was obliged to open the gate in Derrick's line fence. He managed this without dismounting, swearing at the horse the while, and spurring him continually. But once inside the gate he cantered forward briskly.

This part of Los Muertos was Hooven's holding, some five hundred acres enclosed between the irrigating ditch and Broderson Creek, and half the way across, Annixter came up with Hooven himself, busily at work replacing a broken washer in his seeder. Upon one of the horses hitched to the machine, her hands gripped tightly upon the harness of the collar, Hilda, his little daughter, with her small, hob-nailed boots and boy's canvas overalls, sat, exalted and petrified with ecstasy and excitement, her eyes wide opened, her hair in a tangle.

"Hello, Bismarck," said Annixter, drawing up beside him. "What are *you* doing here? I thought the Governor was going to manage without his tenants this year."

"Ach, Meest'r Ennixter," cried the other, straightening up.

"Ach, dat's you, eh? Ach, you bedt he doand menege mitout me. Me, I gotta stay. I talk der straighd talk mit der Governor. I fix 'em. Ach, you bedt. Sieben yahr I hef bei der rench ge-stopped; yais, sir. Efery oder sohn-of-a-guhn bei der plaice ged der sach bud me. Eh? Wat you tink von dose ting?"

"I think that's a crazy-looking monkey-wrench you've got there," observed Annixter, glancing at the instrument in Hooven's hand.

"Ach, dot wrainch," returned Hooven. "Soh! Wail, I tell you dose ting now whair I got 'em. Say, you see dot wrainch. Dat's not Emericen wrainch at alle. I got 'em at Gravelotte der day we licked der stuffun oudt der Frainch, ach, you bedt. Me, I pelong to der Würtemberg redgimend, dot dey use to suppord der batterie von der Brince von Hohenlohe. Alle der day we lay down bei der stomach in der feildt behindt der batterie, und der schells von der Frainch cennon hef eggs-blode—*ach, donnerwetter!*—I tink efery schell eggsblode bei der beckside my neck. Und dat go on der whole day, noddun else, noddun aber der Frainch schell, b-r-r, b-r-r, b-r-r, b-r-*am*, und der smoag, und unzer batterie, dat go off slow, steady, yoost like der glock, eins, zwei, boom! eins, zwei, boom! yoost like der glock, ofer und ofer again, alle der day. Den vhen der night come dey say we hev der great victorie made. I doand know. Vhat do I see von der bettle? Noddun. Den we gedt oop und maerch und maerch alle night, und in der morgen we hear dose cennon egain, hell oaf der way, far-off, I doand know vhair. Budt, nef'r mindt. Bretty quick, ach, Gott—" his face flamed scarlet, "*Ach, du lieber Gott!* Bretty zoon, dere wass der Kaiser, glose bei, und Fritz, Unzer Fritz. Bei Gott, den I go grazy, und yell, ach, you bedt, der whole redgimend: *'Hoch der Kaiser! Hoch der Vaterland!'* Und der dears come to der eyes, I doand know because vhy, und der mens gry und shaike der hend, und der whole redgimend maerch off like dat, fairy broudt, bei Gott, der head oop high, und sing 'Die Wacht am Rhein.' Dot wass Gravelotte."

"And the monkey-wrench?"

"Ach, I pick 'um oop vhen der batterie go. Der cennoniers hef forgedt und leaf 'um. I carry 'um in der sack. I tink I use 'um vhen I gedt home in der business. I was maker von vagons in Carlsruhe, und I nef'r gedt home again. Vhen der war hef godt over, I go beck to Ulm und gedt marriet, und den I gedt demn sick von der armie. Vhen I gedt der release, I clair oudt, you bedt. I come to Emerica. First, New Yorruk; den Milwaukee; den Sbringfieldt-Illinoy; den Galifornie, und heir I stay."

"And the Fatherland? Ever want to go back?"

"Wail, I tell you dose ting, Meest'r Ennixter. Alleways, I tink a lot oaf Shairmany, und der Kaiser, und nef'r I forgedt Gravelotte. Budt, say, I tell you dose ting. Vhair der wife is, und der kinder—der leedle girl Hilda—*dere is der Vaterland.* Eh? Emerica, dat's my gountry now, und dere," he pointed behind him to the house under the mammoth oak tree on the Lower Road, "dat's my home. Dat's goot enough Vaterland for me."

Annixter gathered up the reins, about to go on.

"So you like America, do you, Bismarck?" he said. "Who do you vote for?"

"Emerica? I doand know," returned the other, insistently. "Dat's my home yonder. Dat's my Vaterland. Alle von we Shairmens yoost like dot. Shairmany, dot's hell oaf some fine plaice, sure. Budt der Vaterland iss vhair der home und der wife und kinder iss. Eh? Yes? Voad? Ach, no. Me, I nef'r voad. I doand bodder der haid mit dose ting. I maig der wheat grow, und ged der braid fur der wife und Hilda, dot's all. Dot's me; dot's Bismarck."

"Good-bye," commented Annixter, moving off.

Hooven, the washer replaced, turned to his work again, starting up the horses. The seeder advanced, whirring.

"Ach, Hilda, leedle girl," he cried, "hold tight bei der shdrap on. Hey *mule!* Hoop! Gedt oop, you."

Annixter cantered on. In a few moments, he had crossed Broderson Creek and had entered upon the Home ranch of Los Muertos. Ahead of him, but so far off that the greater portion of its bulk was below the horizon, he could see the Derricks' home, a roof or two between the dull green of cypress and eucalyptus. Nothing else was in sight. The brown earth, smooth, unbroken, was as a limitless, mud-coloured ocean. The silence was profound.

Then, at length, Annixter's searching eye made out a blur on the horizon to the northward; the blur concentrated itself to a speck; the speck grew by steady degrees to a spot, slowly moving, a note of dull colour, barely darker than the land, but an inky black silhouette as it topped a low rise of ground and stood for a moment outlined against the pale blue of the sky. Annixter turned his horse from the road and rode across the ranch land to meet this new object of interest. As the spot grew larger, it resolved itself into constituents, a collection of units; its shape grew irregular, fragmentary. A disintegrated, nebulous confusion advanced toward Annixter, preceded, as he discovered on nearer approach, by a medley of faint sounds. Now it was no longer a spot, but a column, a column that moved, accompanied by spots. As Annixter lessened the distance, these spots resolved themselves into buggies or men on horseback that kept pace with the advancing column. There were horses in the column itself. At first glance, it appeared as if there were nothing else, a riderless squadron tramping steadily over the upturned plough land of the ranch. But it drew nearer. The horses were in lines, six abreast, harnessed to machines. The noise increased, defined itself. There was a shout or two; occasionally a horse blew through his nostrils with a prolonged, vibrating snort. The click and clink of metal work was incessant, the machines throwing off a continual rattle of wheels and cogs and clashing springs. The column approached nearer; was close at hand. The noises mingled to a subdued uproar, a bewildering confusion; the impact of innumerable hoofs was a veritable rumble. Machine after machine appeared; and Annixter, drawing to one side, remained for nearly ten minutes watching and interested, while, like an array of chariots—clattering, jostling, creaking, clashing, an interminable procession, machine succeeding machine, six-horse team succeeding six-horse team—bustling, hurried—Magnus Derrick's thirty-three grain drills, each with its eight hoes, went clamouring past, like an advance of military, seeding the ten thousand acres of the great ranch; fecundating the living soil; implanting deep in the dark womb of the Earth the germ of life, the sustenance of a whole world, the food of an entire People.

When the drills had passed, Annixter turned and rode back to the Lower Road, over the land now thick with seed. He did not wonder that the seeding on Los Muertos seemed to be hastily conducted. Magnus and Harran Derrick had not yet been able to make up the time lost at the beginning of the season, when they had waited so long for the ploughs to arrive. They had been behindhand all the time. On Annixter's ranch, the land had not only been harrowed, as well as seeded, but in some cases, cross-harrowed as well. The labour of putting in the vast crop was over. Now there was nothing to do but wait, while the seed silently germinated; nothing to do but watch for the wheat to come up.

When Annixter reached the ranch house of Los Muertos, under the shade of the cypress and eucalyptus trees, he found Mrs. Derrick on the porch, seated in a long wicker chair. She had been washing her hair, and the light brown locks that yet retained so much of their brightness, were carefully spread in the sun over the back of her chair. Annixter could not but remark that, spite of her more than fifty years, Annie Derrick was yet rather pretty. Her eyes were still those of a young girl, just touched with an uncertain expression of innocence and inquiry, but as her glance fell upon him, he found that that expression changed to one of uneasiness, of distrust, almost of aversion.

The night before this, after Magnus and his wife had gone to bed, they had lain awake for hours, staring up into the dark, talking, talking. Magnus had not long been able to keep from his wife the news of the coalition that was forming against the railroad, nor the fact that this coalition was determined to gain its ends by any means at its command. He had told her of Osterman's scheme of a fraudulent election to seat a Board of Railroad Commissioners, who should be nominees of the farming interests. Magnus and his wife had talked this matter over and over again; and the same discussion, begun immediately after supper the evening before, had lasted till far into the night.

At once, Annie Derrick had been seized with a sudden terror lest Magnus, after all, should allow himself to be persuaded; should yield to the pressure that was every day growing stronger. None better than she knew the iron integrity of her husband's character. None better than she remembered how his dearest ambition, that of political preferment, had been thwarted by his refusal to truckle, to connive, to

compromise with his ideas of right. Now, at last, there
seemed to be a change. Long continued oppression, petty tyranny, injustice and extortion had driven him to exasperation.
S. Behrman's insults still rankled. He seemed nearly ready to
countenance Osterman's scheme. The very fact that he was
willing to talk of it to her so often and at such great length,
was proof positive that it occupied his mind. The pity of it,
the tragedy of it! He, Magnus, the "Governor," who had
been so staunch, so rigidly upright, so loyal to his convictions, so bitter in his denunciation of the New Politics, so
scathing in his attacks on bribery and corruption in high
places; was it possible that now, at last, he could be brought
to withhold his condemnation of the devious intrigues of the
unscrupulous, going on there under his very eyes? That Magnus should not command Harran to refrain from all inter-
course with the conspirators, had been a matter of vast
surprise to Mrs. Derrick. Time was when Magnus would have
forbidden his son to so much as recognise a dishonourable
man.

But besides all this, Derrick's wife trembled at the thought
of her husband and son engaging in so desperate a grapple
with the railroad—that great monster, iron-hearted, relentless, infinitely powerful. Always it had issued triumphant
from the fight; always S. Behrman, the Corporation's champion, remained upon the field as victor, placid, unperturbed,
unassailable. But now a more terrible struggle than any hitherto loomed menacing over the rim of the future; money
was to be spent like water; personal reputations were to be
hazarded in the issue; failure meant ruin in all directions, financial ruin, moral ruin, ruin of prestige, ruin of character.
Success, to her mind, was almost impossible. Annie Derrick
feared the railroad. At night, when everything else was still,
the distant roar of passing trains echoed across Los Muertos,
from Guadalajara, from Bonneville, or from the Long Trestle, straight into her heart. At such moments she saw very
plainly the galloping terror of steam and steel, with its single
eye, cyclopean, red, shooting from horizon to horizon, symbol of a vast power, huge and terrible; the leviathan with
tentacles of steel, to oppose which meant to be ground to
instant destruction beneath the clashing wheels. No, it was

better to submit, to resign oneself to the inevitable. She obliterated herself, shrinking from the harshness of the world,
striving, with vain hands, to draw her husband back with
her.

Just before Annixter's arrival, she had been sitting,
thoughtful, in her long chair, an open volume of poems
turned down upon her lap, her glance losing itself in the immensity of Los Muertos that, from the edge of the lawn
close by, unrolled itself, gigantic, toward the far, southern
horizon, wrinkled and serrated after the season's ploughing.
The earth, hitherto grey with dust, was now upturned and
brown. As far as the eye could reach, it was empty of all life,
bare, mournful, absolutely still; and, as she looked, there
seemed to her morbid imagination—diseased and disturbed
with long brooding, sick with the monotony of repeated
sensation—to be disengaged from all this immensity, a sense
of a vast oppression, formless, disquieting. The terror of
sheer bigness grew slowly in her mind; loneliness beyond
words gradually enveloped her. She was lost in all these limitless reaches of space. Had she been abandoned in mid-
ocean, in an open boat, her terror could hardly have been
greater. She felt vividly that certain uncongeniality which,
when all is said, forever remains between humanity and the
earth which supports it. She recognised the colossal indifference of nature, not hostile, even kindly and friendly, so long
as the human ant-swarm was submissive, working with it,
hurrying along at its side in the mysterious march of the
centuries. Let, however, the insect rebel, strive to make head
against the power of this nature, and at once it became relentless, a gigantic engine, a vast power, huge, terrible; a leviathan with a heart of steel, knowing no compunction, no
forgiveness, no tolerance; crushing out the human atom
with soundless calm, the agony of destruction sending never
a jar, never the faintest tremour through all that prodigious
mechanism of wheels and cogs.

Such thoughts as these did not take shape distinctly in her
mind. She could not have told herself exactly what it was that
disquieted her. She only received the vague sensation of these
things, as it were a breath of wind upon her face, confused,
troublous, an indefinite sense of hostility in the air.

The sound of hoofs grinding upon the gravel of the drive-way brought her to herself again, and, withdrawing her gaze from the empty plain of Los Muertos, she saw young Annixter stopping his horse by the carriage steps. But the sight of him only diverted her mind to the other trouble. She could not but regard him with aversion. He was one of the conspirators, was one of the leaders in the battle that impended; no doubt, he had come to make a fresh attempt to win over Magnus to the unholy alliance.

However, there was little trace of enmity in her greeting. Her hair was still spread, like a broad patch of brown sea-weed, upon the white towel over the chair-back, and she made that her excuse for not getting up. In answer to Annixter's embarrassed inquiry after Magnus, she sent the Chinese cook to call him from the office; and Annixter, after tying his horse to the ring driven into the trunk of one of the eucalyptus trees, came up to the porch, and, taking off his hat, sat down upon the steps.

"Is Harran anywhere about?" he asked. "I'd like to see Harran, too."

"No," said Mrs. Derrick, "Harran went to Bonneville early this morning."

She glanced toward Annixter nervously, without turning her head, lest she should disturb her outspread hair.

"What is it you want to see Mr. Derrick about?" she inquired hastily. "Is it about this plan to elect a Railroad Commission? Magnus does not approve of it," she declared with energy. "He told me so last night."

Annixter moved about awkwardly where he sat, smoothing down with his hand the one stiff lock of yellow hair that persistently stood up from his crown like an Indian's scalp-lock. At once his suspicions were all aroused. Ah! this feemale woman was trying to get a hold on him, trying to involve him in a petticoat mess, trying to cajole him. Upon the instant, he became very crafty; an excess of prudence promptly congealed his natural impulses. In an actual spasm of caution, he scarcely trusted himself to speak, terrified lest he should commit himself to something. He glanced about apprehensively, praying that Magnus might join them speedily, relieving the tension.

"I came to see about giving a dance in my new barn," he answered, scowling into the depths of his hat, as though reading from notes he had concealed there. "I wanted to ask how I should send out the *in*vites. I thought of just putting an ad. in the 'Mercury.' "

But as he spoke, Presley had come up behind Annixter in time to get the drift of the conversation, and now observed:

"That's nonsense, Buck. You're not giving a public ball. You *must* send out invitations."

"Hello, Presley, you there?" exclaimed Annixter, turning round. The two shook hands.

"Send out invitations?" repeated Annixter uneasily. "Why must I?"

"Because that's the only way to do."

"It is, is it?" answered Annixter, perplexed and troubled. No other man of his acquaintance could have so contradicted Annixter without provoking a quarrel upon the instant. Why the young rancher, irascible, obstinate, belligerent, should invariably defer to the poet, was an inconsistency never to be explained. It was with great surprise that Mrs. Derrick heard him continue:

"Well, I suppose you know what you're talking about, Pres. Must have written *in*vites, hey?"

"Of course."

"Typewritten?"

"Why, what an ass you are, Buck," observed Presley calmly. "Before you get through with it, you will probably insult three-fourths of the people you intend to invite, and have about a hundred quarrels on your hands, and a lawsuit or two."

However, before Annixter could reply, Magnus came out on the porch, erect, grave, freshly shaven. Without realising what he was doing, Annixter instinctively rose to his feet. It was as though Magnus was a commander-in-chief of an unseen army, and he a subaltern. There was some little conversation as to the proposed dance, and then Annixter found an excuse for drawing the Governor aside. Mrs. Derrick watched the two with eyes full of poignant anxiety, as they slowly paced the length of the gravel driveway to the road gate, and stood there, leaning upon it, talking earnestly; Magnus tall, thin-lipped, impassive, one hand in the breast of his frock coat, his head bare, his keen, blue eyes fixed upon Annixter's face. Annixter came at once to the main point.

"I got a wire from Osterman this morning, Governor, and, well—we've got Disbrow. That means that the Denver, Pueblo and Mojave is back of us. There's half the fight won, first off."

"Osterman bribed him, I suppose," observed Magnus.

Annixter raised a shoulder vexatiously.

"You've got to pay for what you get," he returned. "You don't get something for nothing, I guess. Governor," he went on, "I don't see how you can stay out of this business much longer. You see how it will be. We're going to win, and I don't see how you can feel that it's right of you to let us do all the work and stand all the expense. There's never been a movement of any importance that went on around you that you weren't the leader in it. All Tulare County, all the San Joaquin, for that matter, knows you. They want a leader, and they are looking to you. I know how you feel about politics nowadays. But, Governor, standards have changed since your time; everybody plays the game now as we are playing it— the most honourable men. You can't play it any other way, and, pshaw! if the right wins out in the end, that's the main thing. We want you in this thing, and we want you bad. You've been chewing on this affair now a long time. Have you made up your mind? Do you come in? I tell you what, you've got to look at these things in a large way. You've got to judge by results. Well, now, what do you think? Do you come in?"

Magnus's glance left Annixter's face, and for an instant sought the ground. His frown lowered, but now it was in perplexity, rather than in anger. His mind was troubled, harassed with a thousand dissensions.

But one of Magnus's strongest instincts, one of his keenest desires, was to be, if only for a short time, the master. To control men had ever been his ambition; submission of any kind, his greatest horror. His energy stirred within him, goaded by the lash of his anger, his sense of indignity, of insult. Oh for one moment to be able to strike back, to crush his enemy, to defeat the railroad, hold the Corporation in the grip of his fist, put down S. Behrman, rehabilitate himself, regain his self-respect. To be once more powerful, to command, to dominate. His thin lips pressed themselves together, the nostrils of his prominent hawk-like nose dilated, his erect, commanding figure stiffened unconsciously. For a moment, he saw himself controlling the situation, the foremost figure in his State, feared, respected, thousands of men beneath him, his ambition at length gratified; his career, once apparently brought to naught, completed; success a palpable achievement. What if this were his chance, after all, come at last after all these years. His chance! The instincts of the old-time gambler, the most redoubtable poker player of El Dorado County, stirred at the word. Chance! To know it when it came, to recognise it as it passed fleet as a wind-flurry, grip at it, catch at it, blind, reckless, staking all upon the hazard of the issue, that was genius. Was this his Chance? All of a sudden, it seemed to him that it was. But his honour! His cherished, lifelong integrity, the unstained purity of his principles? At this late date, were they to be sacrificed? Could he now go counter to all the firm built fabric of his character? How, afterward, could he bear to look Harran and Lyman in the face? And, yet—and, yet—back swung the pendulum—to neglect his Chance meant failure; a life begun in promise, and ended in obscurity, perhaps in financial ruin, poverty even. To seize it meant achievement, fame, influence, prestige, possibly great wealth.

"I am so sorry to interrupt," said Mrs. Derrick, as she came up. "I hope Mr. Annixter will excuse me, but I want Magnus to open the safe for me. I have lost the combination, and I must have some money. Phelps is going into town, and I want him to pay some bills for me. Can't you come right away, Magnus? Phelps is ready and waiting."

Annixter struck his heel into the ground with a suppressed oath. Always these fool feemale women came between him and his plans, mixing themselves up in his affairs. Magnus had been on the very point of saying something, perhaps committing himself to some course of action, and, at precisely the wrong moment, his wife had cut in. The opportunity was lost. The three returned toward the ranch house; but before saying good-bye, Annixter had secured from Magnus a promise to the effect that, before coming to a definite decision in the matter under discussion, he would talk further with him.

Presley met him at the porch. He was going into town with Phelps, and proposed to Annixter that he should accompany them.

"I want to go over and see old Broderson," Annixter objected.

But Presley informed him that Broderson had gone to Bonneville earlier in the morning. He had seen him go past in his buckboard. The three men set off, Phelps and Annixter on horseback, Presley on his bicycle.

When they had gone, Mrs. Derrick sought out her husband in the office of the ranch house. She was at her prettiest that morning, her cheeks flushed with excitement, her innocent, wide-open eyes almost girlish. She had fastened her hair, still moist, with a black ribbon tied at the back of her head, and the soft mass of light brown reached to below her waist, making her look very young.

"What was it he was saying to you just now," she exclaimed, as she came through the gate in the green-painted wire railing of the office. "What was Mr. Annixter saying? I know. He was trying to get you to join him, trying to persuade you to be dishonest, wasn't that it? Tell me, Magnus, wasn't that it?"

Magnus nodded.

His wife drew close to him, putting a hand on his shoulder.

"But you won't, will you? You won't listen to him again; you won't so much as allow him— *anybody*—to even suppose you would lend yourself to bribery? Oh, Magnus, I don't know what has come over you these last few weeks. Why, before this, you would have been insulted if any one thought you would even consider anything like dishonesty. Magnus, it would break my heart if you joined Mr. Annixter and Mr. Osterman. Why, you couldn't be the same man to me afterward; you, who have kept yourself so clean till now. And the boys; what would Lyman say, and Harran, and every one who knows you and respects you, if you lowered yourself to be just a political adventurer!"

For a moment, Derrick leaned his head upon his hand, avoiding her gaze. At length, he said, drawing a deep breath:

"I am troubled, Annie. These are the evil days. I have much upon my mind."

"Evil days or not," she insisted, "promise me this one thing, that you will not join Mr. Annixter's scheme."

She had taken his hand in both of hers and was looking into his face, her pretty eyes full of pleading.

"Promise me," she repeated; "give me your word. Whatever happens, let me always be able to be proud of you, as I always have been. Give me your word. I know you never seriously thought of joining Mr. Annixter, but I am so nervous and frightened sometimes. Just to relieve my mind, Magnus, give me your word."

"Why—you are right," he answered. "No, I never thought seriously of it. Only for a moment, I was ambitious to be—I don't know what—what I had hoped to be once—well, that is over now. Annie, your husband is a disappointed man."

"Give me your word," she insisted. "We can talk about other things afterward."

Again Magnus wavered, about to yield to his better instincts and to the entreaties of his wife. He began to see how perilously far he had gone in this business. He was drifting closer to it every hour. Already he was entangled, already his foot was caught in the mesh that was being spun. Sharply he recoiled. Again all his instincts of honesty revolted. No, whatever happened, he would preserve his integrity. His wife was right. Always she had influenced his better side. At that moment, Magnus's repugnance of the proposed political campaign was at its pitch of intensity. He wondered how he had ever allowed himself to so much as entertain the idea of joining with the others. Now, he would wrench free, would, in a single instant of power, clear himself of all compromising relations. He turned to his wife. Upon his lips trembled the promise she implored. But suddenly there came to his mind the recollection of his new-made pledge to Annixter. He had given his word that before arriving at a decision he would have a last interview with him. To Magnus, his given word was sacred. Though now he wanted to, he could not as yet draw back, could not promise his wife that he would decide to do right. The matter must be delayed a few days longer.

Lamely, he explained this to her. Annie Derrick made but

little response when he had done. She kissed his forehead and went out of the room, uneasy, depressed, her mind thronging with vague fears, leaving Magnus before his office desk, his head in his hands, thoughtful, gloomy, assaulted by forebodings.

Meanwhile, Annixter, Phelps, and Presley continued on their way toward Bonneville. In a short time they had turned into the County Road by the great watering-tank, and proceeded onward in the shade of the interminable line of poplar trees, the wind-break that stretched along the roadside bordering the Broderson ranch. But as they drew near to Caraher's saloon and grocery, about half a mile outside of Bonneville, they recognised Harran's horse tied to the railing in front of it. Annixter left the others and went in to see Harran.

"Harran," he said, when the two had sat down on either side of one of the small tables, "you've got to make up your mind one way or another pretty soon. What are you going to do? Are you going to stand by and see the rest of the Committee spending money by the bucketful in this thing and keep your hands in your pockets? If we win, you'll benefit just as much as the rest of us. I suppose you've got some money of your own—you have, haven't you? You are your father's manager, aren't you?"

Disconcerted at Annixter's directness, Harran stammered an affirmative, adding:

"It's hard to know just what to do. It's a mean position for me, Buck. I want to help you others, but I do want to play fair. I don't know how to play any other way. I should like to have a line from the Governor as to how to act, but there's no getting a word out of him these days. He seems to want to let me decide for myself."

"Well, look here," put in Annixter. "Suppose you keep out of the thing till it's all over, and then share and share alike with the Committee on campaign expenses."

Harran fell thoughtful, his hands in his pockets, frowning moodily at the toe of his boot. There was a silence. Then:

"I don't like to go it blind," he hazarded. "I'm sort of sharing the responsibility of what you do, then. I'm a silent partner. And, then—I don't want to have any difficulties with the

Governor. We've always got along well together. He wouldn't like it, *you* know, if I did anything like that."

"Say," exclaimed Annixter abruptly, "if the Governor says he will keep his hands off, and that you can do as you please, will you come in? For God's sake, let us ranchers act together for once. Let's stand in with each other in *one* fight."

Without knowing it, Annixter had touched the right spring.

"I don't know but what you're right," Harran murmured vaguely. His sense of discouragement, that feeling of what's-the-use, was never more oppressive. All fair means had been tried. The wheat grower was at last with his back to the wall. If he chose his own means of fighting, the responsibility must rest upon his enemies, not on himself.

"It's the only way to accomplish anything," he continued, "standing in with each other . . . well, . . . go ahead and see what you can do. If the Governor is willing, I'll come in for my share of the campaign fund."

"That's some sense," exclaimed Annixter, shaking him by the hand. "Half the fight is over already. We've got Disbrow you know; and the next thing is to get hold of some of those rotten San Francisco bosses. Osterman will——" But Harran interrupted him, making a quick gesture with his hand.

"Don't tell me about it," he said. "I don't want to know what you and Osterman are going to do. If I did, I shouldn't come in."

Yet, for all this, before they said good-bye Annixter had obtained Harran's promise that he would attend the next meeting of the Committee, when Osterman should return from Los Angeles and make his report. Harran went on toward Los Muertos. Annixter mounted and rode into Bonneville.

Bonneville was very lively at all times. It was a little city of some twenty or thirty thousand inhabitants, where, as yet, the city hall, the high school building, and the opera house were objects of civic pride. It was well governed, beautifully clean, full of the energy and strenuous young life of a new city. An air of the briskest activity pervaded its streets and sidewalks. The business portion of the town, centring about Main Street, was always crowded. Annixter, arriving at the Post

Office, found himself involved in a scene of swiftly shifting sights and sounds. Saddle horses, farm wagons—the inevitable Studebakers—buggies grey with the dust of country roads, buckboards with squashes and grocery packages stowed under the seat, two-wheeled sulkies and training carts, were hitched to the gnawed railings and zinc-sheathed telegraph poles along the curb. Here and there, on the edge of the sidewalk, were bicycles, wedged into bicycle racks painted with cigar advertisements. Upon the asphalt sidewalk itself, soft and sticky with the morning's heat, was a continuous movement. Men with large stomachs, wearing linen coats but no vests, laboured ponderously up and down. Girls in lawn skirts, shirt waists, and garden hats, went to and fro, invariably in couples, coming in and out of the drug store, the grocery store, and haberdasher's, or lingering in front of the Post Office, which was on a corner under the I.O.O.F. hall. Young men, in shirt sleeves, with brown, wicker cuff-protectors over their forearms, and pencils behind their ears, bustled in front of the grocery store, anxious and preoccupied. A very old man, a Mexican, in ragged white trousers and bare feet, sat on a horse-block in front of the barber shop, holding a horse by a rope around its neck. A Chinaman went by, teetering under the weight of his market baskets slung on a pole across his shoulders. In the neighbourhood of the hotel, the Yosemite House, travelling salesmen, drummers for jewelry firms of San Francisco, commercial agents, insurance men, well-dressed, metropolitan, debonair, stood about cracking jokes, or hurried in and out of the flapping white doors of the Yosemite bar-room. The Yosemite 'bus and City 'bus passed up the street, on the way from the morning train, each with its two or three passengers. A very narrow wagon, belonging to the Cole & Colemore Harvester Works, went by, loaded with long strips of iron that made a horrible din as they jarred over the unevenness of the pavement. The electric car line, the city's boast, did a brisk business, its cars whirring from end to end of the street, with a jangling of bells and a moaning plaint of gearing. On the stone bulkheads of the grass plat around the new City Hall, the usual loafers sat, chewing tobacco, swapping stories. In the park were the inevitable array of nursemaids, skylarking couples, and ragged little boys. A single policeman, in grey coat and helmet, friend and acquaintance of every man and woman in the town, stood by the park entrance, leaning an elbow on the fence post, twirling his club.

But in the centre of the best business block of the street was a three-story building of rough brown stone, set off with plate glass windows and gold-lettered signs. One of these latter read, "Pacific and Southwestern Railroad, Freight and Passenger Office," while another, much smaller, beneath the windows of the second story, bore the inscription, "P. and S. W. Land Office."

Annixter hitched his horse to the iron post in front of this building, and tramped up to the second floor, letting himself into an office where a couple of clerks and bookkeepers sat at work behind a high wire screen. One of these latter recognised him and came forward.

"Hello," said Annixter abruptly, scowling the while. "Is your boss in? Is Ruggles in?"

The bookkeeper led Annixter to the private office in an adjoining room, ushering him through a door, on the frosted glass of which was painted the name, "Cyrus Blakelee Ruggles." Inside, a man in a frock coat, shoe-string necktie, and Stetson hat, sat writing at a roller-top desk. Over this desk was a vast map of the railroad holdings in the country about Bonneville and Guadalajara, the alternate sections belonging to the Corporation accurately plotted.

Ruggles was cordial in his welcome of Annixter. He had a way of fiddling with his pencil continually while he talked, scribbling vague lines and fragments of words and names on stray bits of paper, and no sooner had Annixter sat down than he had begun to write, in full-bellied script, *Ann Ann* all over his blotting pad.

"I want to see about those lands of mine—I mean of yours—of the railroad's," Annixter commenced at once. "I want to know when I can buy. I'm sick of fooling along like this."

"Well, Mr. Annixter," observed Ruggles, writing a great *L* before the *Ann*, and finishing it off with a flourishing *d*. "The lands"—he crossed out one of the *n*'s and noted the effect with a hasty glance—"the lands are practically yours. You have an option on them indefinitely, and, as it is, you don't have to pay the taxes."

"Rot your option! I want to own them," Annixter declared. "What have you people got to gain by putting off selling them to us. Here this thing has dragged along for over eight years. When I came in on Quien Sabe, the understanding was that the lands—your alternate sections—were to be conveyed to me within a few months."

"The land had not been patented to us then," answered Ruggles.

"Well, it has been now, I guess," retorted Annixter.

"I'm sure I couldn't tell you, Mr. Annixter."

Annixter crossed his legs weariedly.

"Oh, what's the good of lying, Ruggles? You know better than to talk that way to me."

Ruggles's face flushed on the instant, but he checked his answer and laughed instead.

"Oh, if you know so much about it—" he observed.

"Well, when are you going to sell to me?"

"I'm only acting for the General Office, Mr. Annixter," returned Ruggles. "Whenever the Directors are ready to take that matter up, I'll be only too glad to put it through for you."

"As if you didn't know. Look here, you're not talking to old Broderson. Wake up, Ruggles. What's all this talk in Genslinger's rag about the grading of the value of our lands this winter and an advance in the price?"

Ruggles spread out his hands with a deprecatory gesture.

"I don't own the 'Mercury,' " he said.

"Well, your company does."

"If it does, I don't know anything about it."

"Oh, rot! As if you and Genslinger and S. Behrman didn't run the whole show down here. Come on, let's have it, Ruggles. What does S. Behrman pay Genslinger for inserting that three-inch ad. of the P. and S. W. in his paper? Ten thousand a year, hey?"

"Oh, why not a hundred thousand and be done with it?" returned the other, willing to take it as a joke.

Instead of replying, Annixter drew his check-book from his inside pocket.

"Let me take that fountain pen of yours," he said. Holding the book on his knee he wrote out a check, tore it carefully from the stub, and laid it on the desk in front of Ruggles.

"What's this?" asked Ruggles.

"Three-fourths payment for the sections of railroad land included in my ranch, based on a valuation of two dollars and a half per acre. You can have the balance in sixty-day notes."

Ruggles shook his head, drawing hastily back from the check as though it carried contamination.

"I can't touch it," he declared. "I've no authority to sell to you yet."

"I don't understand you people," exclaimed Annixter. "I offered to buy of you the same way four years ago and you sang the same song. Why, it isn't business. You lose the interest on your money. Seven per cent. of that capital for four years—you can figure it out. It's big money."

"Well, then, I don't see why you're so keen on parting with it. You can get seven per cent. the same as us."

"I want to own my own land," returned Annixter. "I want to feel that every lump of dirt inside my fence is my personal property. Why, the very house I live in now—the ranch house—stands on railroad ground."

"But, you've an option——"

"I tell you I don't want your cursed option. I want ownership; and it's the same with Magnus Derrick and old Broderson and Osterman and all the ranchers of the county. We want to own our land, want to feel we can do as we blame please with it. Suppose I should want to sell Quien Sabe. I can't sell it as a whole till I've bought of you. I can't give anybody a clear title. The land has doubled in value ten times over again since I came in on it and improved it. It's worth easily twenty an acre now. But I can't take advantage of that rise in value so long as you won't sell, so long as I don't own it. You're blocking me."

"But, according to you, the railroad can't take advantage of the rise in any case. According to you, you can sell for twenty dollars, but *we* can only get two and a half."

"Who made it worth twenty?" cried Annixter. "I've improved it up to that figure. Genslinger seems to have that idea in his nut, too. Do you people think you can hold that land, untaxed, for speculative purposes until it goes up to thirty dollars and then sell out to some one else—sell it over our heads? You and Genslinger weren't in office when those contracts were drawn. You ask your boss, you ask S. Behrman, *he* knows. The General Office is pledged to sell to us in preference to any one else, for two and a half."

"Well," observed Ruggles decidedly, tapping the end of his pencil on his desk and leaning forward to emphasise his words, " we're not selling *now*. That's said and signed, Mr. Annixter."

"Why not? Come, spit it out. What's the bunco game this time?"

"Because we're not ready. Here's your check."

"You won't take it?"

"No."

"I'll make it a cash payment, money down—the whole of it—payable to Cyrus Blakelee Ruggles, for the P. and S. W."

"No."

"Third and last time."

"No."

"Oh, go to the devil!"

"I don't like your tone, Mr. Annixter," returned Ruggles, flushing angrily.

"I don't give a curse whether you like it or not," retorted Annixter, rising and thrusting the check into his pocket, "but never you mind, Mr. Ruggles, you and S. Behrman and Genslinger and Shelgrim and the whole gang of thieves of you— you'll wake this State of California up some of these days by going just one little bit *too* far, and there'll be an election of Railroad Commissioners of, by, and for the people, that'll get a twist of you, my bunco-steering friend—you and your backers and cappers and swindlers and thimble-riggers, and *smash* you, lock, stock, and barrel. That's my tip to you and be damned to you, Mr. Cyrus Blackleg Ruggles."

Annixter stormed out of the room, slamming the door behind him, and Ruggles, trembling with anger, turned to his desk and to the blotting pad written all over with the words *Lands, Twenty dollars, Two and a half, Option,* and, over and over again, with great swelling curves and flourishes, *Railroad, Railroad, Railroad.*

But as Annixter passed into the outside office, on the other side of the wire partition he noted the figure of a man at the counter in conversation with one of the clerks. There was something familiar to Annixter's eye about the man's heavy built frame, his great shoulders and massive back, and as he spoke to the clerk in a tremendous, rumbling voice, Annixter promptly recognised Dyke.

There was a meeting. Annixter liked Dyke, as did every one else in and about Bonneville. He paused now to shake hands with the discharged engineer and to ask about his little daughter, Sidney, to whom he knew Dyke was devotedly attached.

"Smartest little tad in Tulare County," asserted Dyke. "She's getting prettier every day, Mr. Annixter. *There's* a little tad that was just born to be a lady. Can recite the whole of 'Snow Bound' without ever stopping. You don't believe that, maybe, hey? Well, it's true. She'll be just old enough to enter the Seminary up at Marysville next winter, and if my hop business pays two per cent. on the investment, there's where she's going to go."

"How's it coming on?" inquired Annixter.

"The hop ranch? Prime. I've about got the land in shape, and I've engaged a foreman who knows all about hops. I've been in luck. Everybody will go into the business next year when they see hops go to a dollar, and they'll overstock the market and bust the price. But I'm going to get the cream of it now. I say two per cent. Why, Lord love you, it will pay a good deal more than that. It's got to. It's cost more than I figured to start the thing, so, perhaps, I may have to borrow somewheres; but then on such a sure game as this—and I do want to make something out of that little tad of mine."

"Through here?" inquired Annixter, making ready to move off.

"In just a minute," answered Dyke. "Wait for me and I'll walk down the street with you."

Annixter grumbled that he was in a hurry, but waited, nevertheless, while Dyke again approached the clerk.

"I shall want some empty cars of you people this fall," he explained. "I'm a hop-raiser now, and I just want to make sure what your rates on hops are. I've been told, but I want to make sure. Savvy?"

There was a long delay while the clerk consulted the tariff schedules, and Annixter fretted impatiently. Dyke, growing uneasy, leaned heavily on his elbows, watching the clerk anxiously. If the tariff was exorbitant, he saw his plans brought to naught, his money jeopardised, the little tad, Sidney, deprived of her education. He began to blame himself that he had not long before determined definitely what the railroad would charge for moving his hops. He told himself he was not much of a business man; that he managed carelessly.

"Two cents," suddenly announced the clerk with a certain surly indifference.

"Two cents a pound?"

"Yes, two cents a pound—that's in car-load lots, of course. I won't give you that rate on smaller consignments."

"Yes, car-load lots, of course . . . two cents. Well, all right."

He turned away with a great sigh of relief.

"He sure did have me scared for a minute," he said to Annixter, as the two went down to the street, "fiddling and fussing so long. Two cents is all right, though. Seems fair to me. That fiddling of his was all put on. I know 'em, these railroad heelers. He knew I was a discharged employee first off, and he played the game just to make me seem small because I had to ask favours of him. I don't suppose the General Office tips its slavees off to act like swine, but there's the feeling through the whole herd of them. 'Ye got to come to us. We let ye live only so long as we choose, and what are ye going to do about it? If ye don't like it, git out.'"

Annixter and the engineer descended to the street and had a drink at the Yosemite bar, and Annixter went into the General Store while Dyke bought a little pair of red slippers for Sidney. Before the salesman had wrapped them up, Dyke slipped a dime into the toe of each with a wink at Annixter.

"Let the little tad find 'em there," he said behind his hand in a hoarse whisper. "That'll be one on Sid."

"Where to now?" demanded Annixter as they regained the street. "I'm going down to the Post Office and then pull out for the ranch. Going my way?"

Dyke hesitated in some confusion, tugging at the ends of his fine blonde beard.

"No, no. I guess I'll leave you here. I've got—got other things to do up the street. So long."

The two separated, and Annixter hurried through the crowd to the Post Office, but the mail that had come in on that morning's train was unusually heavy. It was nearly half an hour before it was distributed. Naturally enough, Annixter placed all the blame of the delay upon the railroad, and delivered himself of some pointed remarks in the midst of the waiting crowd. He was irritated to the last degree when he finally emerged upon the sidewalk again, cramming his mail into his pockets. One cause of his bad temper was the fact that in the bundle of Quien Sabe letters was one to Hilma Tree in a man's handwriting.

"Huh!" Annixter had growled to himself, "that pip Delaney. Seems now that I'm to act as go-between for 'em. Well, maybe that feemale girl gets this letter, and then, again, maybe she don't."

But suddenly his attention was diverted. Directly opposite the Post Office, upon the corner of the street, stood quite the best business building of which Bonneville could boast. It was built of Colusa granite, very solid, ornate, imposing. Upon the heavy plate of the window of its main floor, in gold and red letters, one read the words: "Loan and Savings Bank of Tulare County." It was of this bank that S. Behrman was president. At the street entrance of the building was a curved sign of polished brass, fixed upon the angle of the masonry; this sign bore the name, "S. Behrman," and under it in smaller letters were the words, "Real Estate, Mortgages."

As Annixter's glance fell upon this building, he was surprised to see Dyke standing upon the curb in front of it, apparently reading from a newspaper that he held in his hand. But Annixter promptly discovered that he was not reading at all. From time to time the former engineer shot a swift glance out of the corner of his eye up and down the street. Annixter jumped at a conclusion. An idea suddenly occurred to him. Dyke was watching to see if he was observed—was waiting an opportunity when no one who knew him should be in sight. Annixter stepped back a little, getting a telegraph pole somewhat between him and the other. Very interested, he watched what was going on. Pretty soon Dyke thrust the paper into his pocket and sauntered slowly to the windows of a stationery store, next the street entrance of S. Behrman's offices. For a few seconds he stood there, his back turned, seemingly absorbed in the display, but eyeing the street narrowly nevertheless; then he turned around, gave a last look about and stepped swiftly into the doorway by the great brass sign. He disappeared. Annixter came from behind the telegraph pole with a flush of actual shame upon his face. There had been something so slinking, so mean, in the movements and manner of this great, burly honest fellow of an engineer, that he could not help but feel ashamed for him. Circumstances were such that a simple business transaction was to Dyke almost culpable, a degradation, a thing to be concealed.

"Borrowing money of S. Behrman," commented Annixter, "mortgaging your little homestead to the railroad, putting your neck in the halter. Poor fool! The pity of it. Good Lord, your hops must pay you big, now, old man."

Annixter lunched at the Yosemite Hotel, and then later on, toward the middle of the afternoon, rode out of the town at a canter by the way of the Upper Road that paralleled the railroad tracks and that ran diametrically straight between Bonneville and Guadalajara. About half-way between the two places he overtook Father Sarria trudging back to San Juan, his long cassock powdered with dust. He had a wicker crate in one hand, and in the other, in a small square valise, the materials for the Holy Sacrament. Since early morning the priest had covered nearly fifteen miles on foot, in order to administer Extreme Unction to a moribund good-for-nothing, a greaser, half Indian, half Portuguese, who lived in a remote corner of Osterman's stock range, at the head of a cañon there. But he had returned by way of Bonneville to get a crate that had come for him from San Diego. He had been notified of its arrival the day before.

Annixter pulled up and passed the time of day with the priest.

"I don't often get up your way," he said, slowing down his horse to accommodate Sarria's deliberate plodding. Sarria wiped the perspiration from his smooth, shiny face.

"You? Well, with you it is different," he answered. "But there are a great many Catholics in the county—some on your ranch. And so few come to the Mission. At High Mass on Sundays, there are a few—Mexicans and Spaniards from Guadalajara mostly; but weekdays, for matins, vespers, and the like, I often say the offices to an empty church—'the voice of one crying in the wilderness.' You Americans are not good churchmen. Sundays you sleep—you read the newspapers."

"Well, there's Vanamee," observed Annixter. "I suppose he's there early and late."

Sarria made a sharp movement of interest.

"Ah, Vanamee—a strange lad; a wonderful character, for all that. If there were only more like him. I am troubled about him. You know I am a very owl at night. I come and go about the Mission at all hours. Within the week, three times I have seen Vanamee in the little garden by the Mission, and at the dead of night. He had come without asking for me. He did not see me. It was strange. Once, when I had got up at dawn to ring for early matins, I saw him stealing away out of the garden. He must have been there all the night. He is acting queerly. He is pale; his cheeks are more sunken than ever. There is something wrong with him. I can't make it out. It is a mystery. Suppose you ask him?"

"Not I. I've enough to bother myself about. Vanamee is crazy in the head. Some morning he will turn up missing again, and drop out of sight for another three years. Best let him alone, Sarria. He's a crank. How is that greaser of yours up on Osterman's stock range?"

"Ah, the poor fellow—the poor fellow," returned the other, the tears coming to his eyes. "He died this morning— as you might say, in my arms, painfully, but in the faith, in the faith. A good fellow."

"A lazy, cattle-stealing, knife-in-his-boot Dago."

"You misjudge him. A really good fellow on better acquaintance."

Annixter grunted scornfully. Sarria's kindness and goodwill toward the most outrageous reprobates of the ranches was proverbial. He practically supported some half-dozen families that lived in forgotten cabins, lost and all but inacces-

sible, in the far corners of stock range and cañon. This particular greaser was the laziest, the dirtiest, the most worthless of
the lot. But in Sarria's mind, the lout was an object of affection, sincere, unquestioning. Thrice a week the priest, with a
basket of provisions—cold ham, a bottle of wine, olives,
loaves of bread, even a chicken or two—toiled over the interminable stretch of country between the Mission and his cabin.
Of late, during the rascal's sickness, these visits had been almost daily. Hardly once did the priest leave the bedside that
he did not slip a half-dollar into the palm of his wife or oldest
daughter. And this was but one case out of many.

His kindliness toward animals was the same. A horde of
mange-corroded curs lived off his bounty, wolfish, ungrateful,
often marking him with their teeth, yet never knowing the
meaning of a harsh word. A burro, over-fed, lazy, incorrigible,
browsed on the hill back of the Mission, obstinately refusing
to be harnessed to Sarria's little cart, squealing and biting
whenever the attempt was made; and the priest suffered him,
submitting to his humour, inventing excuses for him, alleging
that the burro was foundered, or was in need of shoes, or was
feeble from extreme age. The two peacocks, magnificent,
proud, cold-hearted, resenting all familiarity, he served with
the timorous, apologetic affection of a queen's lady-in-wait-
ing, resigned to their disdain, happy if only they condescended to enjoy the grain he spread for them.

At the Long Trestle, Annixter and the priest left the road
and took the trail that crossed Broderson Creek by the clumps
of grey-green willows and led across Quien Sabe to the ranch
house, and to the Mission farther on. They were obliged to
proceed in single file here, and Annixter, who had allowed
the priest to go in front, promptly took notice of the wicker
basket he carried. Upon his inquiry, Sarria became confused.
"It was a basket that he had had sent down to him from the
city."

"Well, I know—but what's in it?"

"Why—I'm sure—ah, poultry—a chicken or two."

"Fancy breed?"

"Yes, yes, that's it, a fancy breed."

At the ranch house, where they arrived toward five o'clock,
Annixter insisted that the priest should stop long enough for

a glass of sherry. Sarria left the basket and his small black valise at the foot of the porch steps, and sat down in a rocker on the porch itself, fanning himself with his broad-brimmed hat, and shaking the dust from his cassock. Annixter brought out the decanter of sherry and glasses, and the two drank to each other's health.

But as the priest set down his glass, wiping his lips with a murmur of satisfaction, the decrepit Irish setter that had attached himself to Annixter's house came out from underneath the porch, and nosed vigorously about the wicker basket. He upset it. The little peg holding down the cover slipped, the basket fell sideways, opening as it fell, and a cock, his head enclosed in a little chamois bag such as are used for gold watches, struggled blindly out into the open air. A second, similarly hooded, followed. The pair, stupefied in their headgear, stood rigid and bewildered in their tracks, clucking uneasily. Their tails were closely sheared. Their legs, thickly muscled, and extraordinarily long, were furnished with enormous cruel-looking spurs. The breed was unmistakable. Annixter looked once at the pair, then shouted with laughter.

"'Poultry'—'a chicken or two'—'fancy breed'—ho! yes, I should think so. Game cocks! Fighting cocks! Oh, you old rat! You'll be a dry nurse to a burro, and keep a hospital for infirm puppies, but you will fight game cocks. Oh, Lord! Why, Sarria, this is as good a grind as I ever heard. There's the Spanish cropping out, after all."

Speechless with chagrin, the priest bundled the cocks into the basket and catching up the valise, took himself abruptly away, almost running till he had put himself out of hearing of Annixter's raillery. And even ten minutes later, when Annixter, still chuckling, stood upon the porch steps, he saw the priest, far in the distance, climbing the slope of the high ground, in the direction of the Mission, still hurrying on at a great pace, his cassock flapping behind him, his head bent; to Annixter's notion the very picture of discomfiture and confusion.

As Annixter turned about to reënter the house, he found himself almost face to face with Hilma Tree. She was just going in at the doorway, and a great flame of the sunset, shooting in under the eaves of the porch, enveloped her from her head, with its thick, moist hair that hung low over her neck, to her slim feet, setting a golden flash in the little steel buckles of her low shoes. She had come to set the table for Annixter's supper. Taken all aback by the suddenness of the encounter, Annixter ejaculated an abrupt and senseless, "Excuse me." But Hilma, without raising her eyes, passed on unmoved into the dining-room, leaving Annixter trying to find his breath, and fumbling with the brim of his hat, that he was surprised to find he had taken from his head. Resolutely, and taking a quick advantage of his opportunity, he followed her into the dining-room.

"I see that dog has turned up," he announced with brisk cheerfulness. "That Irish setter I was asking about."

Hilma, a swift, pink flush deepening the delicate rose of her cheeks, did not reply, except by nodding her head. She flung the table-cloth out from under her arms across the table, spreading it smooth, with quick little caresses of her hands. There was a moment's silence. Then Annixter said:

"Here's a letter for you." He laid it down on the table near her, and Hilma picked it up. "And see here, Miss Hilma," Annixter continued, "about that—this morning—I suppose you think I am a first-class mucker. If it will do any good to apologise, why, I will. I want to be friends with you. I made a bad mistake, and started in the wrong way. I don't know much about women people. I want you to forget about that—this morning, and not think I am a galoot and a mucker. Will you do it? Will you be friends with me?"

Hilma set the plate and coffee cup by Annixter's place before answering, and Annixter repeated his question. Then she drew a deep, quick breath, the flush in her cheeks returning.

"I think it was—it was so wrong of you," she murmured. "Oh! you don't know how it hurt me. I cried—oh, for an hour."

"Well, that's just it," returned Annixter vaguely, moving his head uneasily. "I didn't know what kind of a girl you were—I mean, I made a mistake. I thought it didn't make much difference. I thought all feemales were about alike."

"I hope you know now," murmured Hilma ruefully. "I've paid enough to have you find out. I cried—you don't know.

Why, it hurt me worse than anything I can remember. I hope you know now."

"Well, I do know now," he exclaimed.

"It wasn't so much that you tried to do—what you did," answered Hilma, the single deep swell from her waist to her throat rising and falling in her emotion. "It was that you thought that you could—that anybody could that wanted to—that I held myself so cheap. Oh!" she cried, with a sudden sobbing catch in her throat, "I never can forget it, and you don't know what it means to a girl."

"Well, that's just what I do want," he repeated. "I want you to forget it and have us be good friends."

In his embarrassment, Annixter could think of no other words. He kept reiterating again and again during the pauses of the conversation:

"I want you to forget it. Will you? Will you forget it— that—this morning, and have us be good friends?"

He could see that her trouble was keen. He was astonished that the matter should be so grave in her estimation. After all, what was it that a girl should be kissed? But he wanted to regain his lost ground.

"Will you forget it, Miss Hilma? I want you to like me."

She took a clean napkin from the sideboard drawer and laid it down by the plate.

"I—I do want you to like me," persisted Annixter. "I want you to forget all about this business and like me."

Hilma was silent. Annixter saw the tears in her eyes.

"How about that? Will you forget it? Will you—will—will you *like* me?"

She shook her head.

"No," she said.

"No what? You won't like me? Is that it?"

Hilma, blinking at the napkin through her tears, nodded to say, Yes, that was it.

Annixter hesitated a moment, frowning, harassed and perplexed.

"You don't like me at all, hey?"

At length Hilma found her speech. In her low voice, lower and more velvety than ever, she said:

"No—I don't like you at all."

Then, as the tears suddenly overpowered her, she dashed a hand across her eyes, and ran from the room and out of doors.

Annixter stood for a moment thoughtful, his protruding lower lip thrust out, his hands in his pocket.

"I suppose she'll quit now," he muttered. "Suppose she'll leave the ranch—if she hates me like that. Well, she can go—that's all—she can go. Fool feemale girl," he muttered between his teeth, "petticoat mess."

He was about to sit down to his supper when his eye fell upon the Irish setter, on his haunches in the doorway. There was an expectant, ingratiating look on the dog's face. No doubt, he suspected it was time for eating.

"Get out—*you!*" roared Annixter in a tempest of wrath.

The dog slunk back, his tail shut down close, his ears drooping, but instead of running away, he lay down and rolled supinely upon his back, the very image of submission, tame, abject, disgusting. It was the one thing to drive Annixter to a fury. He kicked the dog off the porch in a rolling explosion of oaths, and flung himself down to his seat before the table, fuming and panting.

"Damn the dog and the girl and the whole rotten business—and *now*," he exclaimed, as a sudden fancied qualm arose in his stomach, "*now*, it's all made me sick. Might have known it. Oh, it only lacked that to wind up the whole day. Let her go, I don't care, and the sooner the better."

He countermanded the supper and went to bed before it was dark, lighting his lamp, on the chair near the head of the bed, and opening his "Copperfield" at the place marked by the strip of paper torn from the bag of prunes. For upward of an hour he read the novel, methodically swallowing one prune every time he reached the bottom of a page. About nine o'clock he blew out the lamp and, punching up his pillow, settled himself for the night.

Then, as his mind relaxed in that strange, hypnotic condition that comes just before sleep, a series of pictures of the day's doings passed before his imagination like the roll of a kinetoscope.

First, it was Hilma Tree, as he had seen her in the dairy-house —charming, delicious, radiant of youth, her thick, white neck with its pale amber shadows under the chin; her wide, open eyes rimmed with fine, black lashes; the deep swell of her breast and hips, the delicate, lustrous floss on her cheek, impalpable as the pollen of a flower. He saw her standing there in the scintillating light of the morning, her smooth arms wet with milk, redolent and fragrant of milk, her whole, desirable figure moving in the golden glory of the sun, steeped in a lambent flame, saturated with it, glowing with it, joyous as the dawn itself.

Then it was Los Muertos and Hooven, the sordid little Dutchman, grimed with the soil he worked in, yet vividly remembering a period of military glory, exciting himself with recollections of Gravelotte and the Kaiser, but contented now in the country of his adoption, defining the Fatherland as the place where wife and children lived. Then came the ranch house of Los Muertos, under the grove of cypress and eucalyptus, with its smooth, gravelled driveway and well-groomed lawns; Mrs. Derrick with her wide-opened eyes, that so easily took on a look of uneasiness, of innocence, of anxious inquiry, her face still pretty, her brown hair that still retained so much of its brightness spread over her chair back, drying in the sun; Magnus, erect as an officer of cavalry, smooth-shaven, grey, thin-lipped, imposing, with his hawk-like nose and forward-curling grey hair; Presley with his dark face, delicate mouth and sensitive, loose lips, in corduroys and laced boots, smoking cigarettes—an interesting figure, suggestive of a mixed origin, morbid, excitable, melancholy, brooding upon things that had no names. Then it was Bonneville, with the gayety and confusion of Main Street, the whirring electric cars, the zinc-sheathed telegraph poles, the buckboards with squashes stowed under the seats; Ruggles in frock coat, Stetson hat and shoe-string necktie, writing abstractedly upon his blotting pad; Dyke, the engineer, big-boned, powerful, deep-voiced, good-natured, with his fine blonde beard and massive arms, rehearsing the praises of his little daughter Sidney, guided only by the one ambition that she should be educated at a seminary, slipping a dime into the toe of her diminutive slipper, then, later, overwhelmed with shame, slinking into S. Behrman's office to mortgage his homestead to the heeler of the corporation that had discharged him. By suggestion,

Annixter saw S. Behrman, too, fat, with a vast stomach, the cheek and neck meeting to form a great, tremulous jowl, the roll of fat over his collar, sprinkled with sparse, stiff hairs; saw his brown, round-topped hat of varnished straw, the linen vest stamped with innumerable interlocked horseshoes, the heavy watch chain, clinking against the pearl vest buttons; invariably placid, unruffled, never losing his temper, serene, unassailable, enthroned.

Then, at the end of all, it was the ranch again, seen in a last brief glance before he had gone to bed; the fecundated earth, calm at last, nursing the emplanted germ of life, ruddy with the sunset, the horizons purple, the small clamour of the day lapsing into quiet, the great, still twilight, building itself, dome-like, toward the zenith. The barn fowls were roosting in the trees near the stable, the horses crunching their fodder in the stalls, the day's work ceasing by slow degrees; and the priest, the Spanish churchman, Father Sarria, relic of a departed régime, kindly, benign, believing in all goodness, a lover of his fellows and of dumb animals, yet, for all that, hurrying away in confusion and discomfiture, carrying in one hand the vessels of the Holy Communion and in the other a basket of game cocks.

VI

I T WAS HIGH NOON, and the rays of the sun, that hung poised directly overhead in an intolerable white glory, fell straight as plummets upon the roofs and streets of Guadalajara. The adobe walls and sparse brick sidewalks of the drowsing town radiated the heat in an oily, quivering shimmer. The leaves of the eucalyptus trees around the Plaza drooped motionless, limp and relaxed under the scorching, searching blaze. The shadows of these trees had shrunk to their smallest circumference, contracting close about the trunks. The shade had dwindled to the breadth of a mere line. The sun was everywhere. The heat exhaling from brick and plaster and metal met the heat that steadily descended blanketwise and smothering, from the pale, scorched sky. Only the lizards— they lived in chinks of the crumbling adobe and in interstices of the sidewalk—remained without, motionless, as if stuffed, their eyes closed to mere slits, basking, stupefied with heat. At long intervals the prolonged drone of an insect developed out of the silence, vibrated a moment in a soothing, somnolent, long note, then trailed slowly into the quiet again. Somewhere in the interior of one of the 'dobe houses a guitar snored and hummed sleepily. On the roof of the hotel a group of pigeons cooed incessantly with subdued, liquid murmurs, very plaintive; a cat, perfectly white, with a pink nose and thin, pink lips, dozed complacently on a fence rail, full in the sun. In a corner of the Plaza three hens wallowed in the baking hot dust, their wings fluttering, clucking comfortably.

And this was all. A Sunday repose prevailed the whole moribund town, peaceful, profound. A certain pleasing numbness, a sense of grateful enervation exhaled from the scorching plaster. There was no movement, no sound of human business. The faint hum of the insect, the intermittent murmur of the guitar, the mellow complainings of the pigeons, the prolonged purr of the white cat, the contented clucking of the hens—all these noises mingled together to form a faint, drowsy bourdon, prolonged, stupefying, suggestive of an infinite quiet, of a calm, complacent life, centuries old, lapsing gradually to its end under the gorgeous loneliness of a cloudless, pale blue sky and the steady fire of an interminable sun.

In Solotari's Spanish-Mexican restaurant, Vanamee and Presley sat opposite each other at one of the tables near the door, a bottle of white wine, tortillas, and an earthen pot of frijoles between them. They were the sole occupants of the place. It was the day that Annixter had chosen for his barndance and, in consequence, Quien Sabe was in *fête* and work suspended. Presley and Vanamee had arranged to spend the day in each other's company, lunching at Solotari's and taking a long tramp in the afternoon. For the moment they sat back in their chairs, their meal all but finished. Solotari brought black coffee and a small carafe of mescal, and retiring to a corner of the room, went to sleep.

All through the meal Presley had been wondering over a certain change he observed in his friend. He looked at him again.

Vanamee's lean, spare face was of an olive pallor. His long, black hair, such as one sees in the saints and evangelists of the pre-Raphaelite artists, hung over his ears. Presley again remarked his pointed beard, black and fine, growing from the hollow cheeks. He looked at his face, a face like that of a young seer, like a half-inspired shepherd of the Hebraic legends, a dweller in the wilderness, gifted with strange powers. He was dressed as when Presley had first met him, herding his sheep, in brown canvas overalls, thrust into top boots; grey flannel shirt, open at the throat, showing the breast ruddy with tan; the waist encircled with a cartridge belt, empty of cartridges.

But now, as Presley took more careful note of him, he was surprised to observe a certain new look in Vanamee's deep-set eyes. He remembered now that all through the morning Vanamee had been singularly reserved. He was continually drifting into reveries, abstracted, distrait. Indubitably, something of moment had happened.

At length Vanamee spoke. Leaning back in his chair, his thumbs in his belt, his bearded chin upon his breast, his voice was the even monotone of one speaking in his sleep.

He told Presley in a few words what had happened during

the first night he had spent in the garden of the old Mission, of the Answer, half-fancied, half-real, that had come to him.

"To no other person but you would I speak of this," he said, "but you, I think, will understand—will be sympathetic, at least, and I feel the need of unburdening myself of it to some one. At first I would not trust my own senses. I was sure I had deceived myself, but on a second night it happened again. Then I was afraid—or no, not afraid, but disturbed—oh, shaken to my very heart's core. I resolved to go no further in the matter, never again to put it to test. For a long time I stayed away from the Mission, occupying myself with my work, keeping it out of my mind. But the temptation was too strong. One night I found myself there again, under the black shadow of the pear trees calling for Angéle, summoning her from out the dark, from out the night. This time the Answer was prompt, unmistakable. I cannot explain to you what it was, nor how it came to me, for there was no sound. I saw absolutely nothing but the empty night. There was no moon. But somewhere off there over the little valley, far off, the darkness was troubled; that *me* that went out upon my thought—out from the Mission garden, out over the valley, calling for her, searching for her, found, I don't know what, but found a resting place—a companion. Three times since then I have gone to the Mission garden at night. Last night was the third time."

He paused, his eyes shining with excitement. Presley leaned forward toward him, motionless with intense absorption.

"Well—and last night," he prompted.

Vanamee stirred in his seat, his glance fell, he drummed an instant upon the table.

"Last night," he answered, "there was—there was a change. The Answer was—" he drew a deep breath—"nearer."

"You are sure?"

The other smiled with absolute certainty.

"It was not that I found the Answer sooner, easier. I could not be mistaken. No, that which has troubled the darkness, that which has entered into the empty night—is coming nearer to me—physically nearer, actually nearer."

His voice sank again. His face like the face of younger

prophets, the seers, took on a half-inspired expression. He looked vaguely before him with unseeing eyes.

"Suppose," he murmured, "suppose I stand there under the pear trees at night and call her again and again, and each time the Answer comes nearer and nearer and I wait until at last one night, the supreme night of all, she—she——"

Suddenly the tension broke. With a sharp cry and a violent uncertain gesture of the hand Vanamee came to himself.

"Oh," he exclaimed, "what is it? Do I dare? What does it mean? There are times when it appals me and there are times when it thrills me with a sweetness and a happiness that I have not known since she died. The vagueness of it! How can I explain it to you, this that happens when I call to her across the night—that faint, far-off, unseen tremble in the darkness, that intangible, scarcely perceptible stir. Something neither heard nor seen, appealing to a sixth sense only. Listen, it is something like this: On Quien Sabe, all last week, we have been seeding the earth. The grain is there now under the earth buried in the dark, in the black stillness, under the clods. Can you imagine the first—the very first little quiver of life that the grain of wheat must feel after it is sown, when it answers to the call of the sun, down there in the dark of the earth, blind, deaf; the very first stir from the inert, long, long before any physical change has occurred,—long before the microscope could discover the slightest change,—when the shell first tightens with the first faint premonition of life? Well, it is something as illusive as that." He paused again, dreaming, lost in a reverie, then, just above a whisper, murmured:

" 'That which thou sowest is not quickened except it die,' . . . and she, Angéle . . . died."

"You could not have been mistaken?" said Presley. "You were sure that there was something? Imagination can do so much and the influence of the surroundings was strong. How impossible it would be that anything *should* happen. And you say you heard nothing, saw nothing."

"I believe," answered Vanamee, "in a sixth sense, or, rather, a whole system of other unnamed senses beyond the reach of our understanding. People who live much alone and close to nature experience the sensation of it. Perhaps it is something fundamental that we share with plants and animals. The same thing that sends the birds south long before the first colds, the same thing that makes the grain of wheat struggle up to meet the sun. And this sense never deceives. You may see wrong, hear wrong, but once touch this sixth sense and it acts with absolute fidelity, you are certain. No, I hear nothing in the Mission garden. I see nothing, nothing touches me, but I am *certain* for all that."

Presley hesitated for a moment, then he asked:

"Shall you go back to the garden again? Make the test again?"

"I don't know."

"Strange enough," commented Presley, wondering.

Vanamee sank back in his chair, his eyes growing vacant again:

"Strange enough," he murmured.

There was a long silence. Neither spoke nor moved. There, in that moribund, ancient town, wrapped in its siesta, flagellated with heat, deserted, ignored, baking in a noon-day silence, these two strange men, the one a poet by nature, the other by training, both out of tune with their world, dreamers, introspective, morbid, lost and unfamiliar at that end-of-the-century time, searching for a sign, groping and baffled amidst the perplexing obscurity of the Delusion, sat over empty wine glasses, silent with the pervading silence that surrounded them, hearing only the cooing of doves and the drone of bees, the quiet so profound, that at length they could plainly distinguish at intervals the puffing and coughing of a locomotive switching cars in the station yard of Bonneville.

It was, no doubt, this jarring sound that at length roused Presley from his lethargy. The two friends rose; Solotari very sleepily came forward; they paid for the luncheon, and stepping out into the heat and glare of the streets of the town, passed on through it and took the road that led northward across a corner of Dyke's hop fields. They were bound for the hills in the northeastern corner of Quien Sabe. It was the same walk which Presley had taken on the previous occasion when he had first met Vanamee herding the sheep. This encompassing detour around the whole country-side was a favorite pastime of his and he was anxious that Vanamee should share his pleasure in it.

But soon after leaving Guadalajara, they found themselves upon the land that Dyke had bought and upon which he was to raise his famous crop of hops. Dyke's house was close at hand, a very pleasant little cottage, painted white, with green blinds and deep porches, while near it and yet in process of construction, were two great storehouses and a drying and curing house, where the hops were to be stored and treated. All about were evidences that the former engineer had already been hard at work. The ground had been put in readiness to receive the crop and a bewildering, innumerable multitude of poles, connected with a maze of wire and twine, had been set out. Farther on at a turn of the road, they came upon Dyke himself, driving a farm wagon loaded with more poles. He was in his shirt sleeves, his massive, hairy arms bare to the elbow, glistening with sweat, red with heat. In his bell-like, rumbling voice, he was calling to his foreman and a boy at work in stringing the poles together. At sight of Presley and Vanamee he hailed them jovially, addressing them as "boys," and insisting that they should get into the wagon with him and drive to the house for a glass of beer. His mother had only the day before returned from Marysville, where she had been looking up a seminary for the little tad. She would be delighted to see the two boys; besides, Vanamee must see how the little tad had grown since he last set eyes on her; wouldn't know her for the same little girl; and the beer had been on ice since morning. Presley and Vanamee could not well refuse.

They climbed into the wagon and jolted over the uneven ground through the bare forest of hop-poles to the house. Inside they found Mrs. Dyke, an old lady with a very gentle face, who wore a cap and a very old-fashioned gown with hoop skirts, dusting the what-not in a corner of the parlor. The two men were presented and the beer was had from off the ice.

"Mother," said Dyke, as he wiped the froth from his great blond beard, "ain't Sid anywheres about? I want Mr. Vanamee to see how she has grown. Smartest little tad in Tulare County, boys. Can recite the whole of 'Snow Bound,' end to end, without skipping or looking at the book. Maybe you don't believe that. Mother, ain't I right—without skipping a line, hey?"

Mrs. Dyke nodded to say that it was so, but explained that Sidney was in Guadalajara. In putting on her new slippers for the first time the morning before, she had found a dime in the toe of one of them and had had the whole house by the ears ever since till she could spend it.

"Was it for licorice to make her licorice water?" inquired Dyke gravely.

"Yes," said Mrs. Dyke. "I made her tell me what she was going to get before she went, and it was licorice."

Dyke, though his mother protested that he was foolish and that Presley and Vanamee had no great interest in "young ones," insisted upon showing the visitors Sidney's copy-books. They were monuments of laborious, elaborate neatness, the trite moralities and ready-made aphorisms of the philanthropists and publicists, repeated from page to page with wearying insistence. "I, too, am an American Citizen. S. D.," "As the Twig is Bent the Tree is Inclined," "Truth Crushed to Earth Will Rise Again," "As for Me, Give Me Liberty or Give Me Death," and last of all, a strange intrusion amongst the mild, well-worn phrases, two legends. "My motto—Public Control of Public Franchises," and "The P. and S. W. is an Enemy of the State."

"I see," commented Presley, "you mean the little tad to understand 'the situation' early."

"I told him he was foolish to give that to Sid to copy," said Mrs. Dyke, with indulgent remonstrance. "What can she understand of public franchises?"

"Never mind," observed Dyke, "she'll remember it when she grows up and when the seminary people have rubbed her up a bit, and then she'll begin to ask questions and understand. And don't you make any mistake, mother," he went on, "about the little tad not knowing who her dad's enemies are. What do you think, boys? Listen, here. Precious little I've ever told her of the railroad or how I was turned off, but the other day I was working down by the fence next the railroad tracks and Sid was there. She'd brought her doll rags down and she was playing house behind a pile of hop poles. Well, along comes a through freight—mixed train from Missouri points and a string of empties from New Orleans,—and when it had passed, what do you suppose the tad did? *She* didn't know I was watching her. She goes to the fence and spits a little spit after the caboose and puts out her little head and, if you'll believe me, *hisses* at the train; and mother says she does that same every time she sees a train go by, and never crosses the tracks that she don't spit her little spit on 'em. What do you *think* of *that?*"

"But I correct her every time," protested Mrs. Dyke seriously. "Where she picked up the trick of hissing I don't know. No, it's not funny. It seems dreadful to see a little girl who's as sweet and gentle as can be in every other way, so venomous. She says the other little girls at school and the boys, too, are all the same way. Oh, dear," she sighed, "why will the General Office be so unkind and unjust? Why, I couldn't be happy, with all the money in the world, if I thought that even one little child hated me—hated me so that it would spit and hiss at me. And it's not one child, it's all of them, so Sidney says; and think of all the grown people who hate the road, women and men, the whole county, the whole State, thousands and thousands of people. Don't the managers and the directors of the road ever think of that? Don't they ever think of all the hate that surrounds them, everywhere, everywhere, and the good people that just grit their teeth when the name of the road is mentioned? Why do they want to make the people hate them? No," she murmured, the tears starting to her eyes, "No, I tell you, Mr. Presley, the men who own the railroad are wicked, bad-hearted men who don't care how much the poor people suffer, so long as the road makes its eighteen million a year. They don't care whether the people hate them or love them, just so long as they are afraid of them. It's not right and God will punish them sooner or later."

A little after this the two young men took themselves away, Dyke obligingly carrying them in the wagon as far as the gate that opened into the Quien Sabe ranch. On the way, Presley referred to what Mrs. Dyke had said and led Dyke, himself, to speak of the P. and S. W.

"Well," Dyke said, "it's like this, Mr. Presley. I, personally, haven't got the right to kick. With you wheat-growing people I guess it's different, but hops, you see, don't count for much in the State. It's such a little business that the road don't want to bother themselves to tax it. It's the wheat growers that the road cinches. The rates on hops *are fair*. I've got to admit that; I was in to Bonneville a while ago to find out. It's two cents a pound, and Lord love you, that's reasonable enough to suit any man. No," he concluded, "I'm on the way to make money now. The road sacking me as they did was, maybe, a good thing for me, after all. It came just at the right time. I had a bit of money put by and here was the chance to go into hops with the certainty that hops would quadruple and quin-tuple in price inside the year. No, it was my chance, and though they didn't mean it by a long chalk, the railroad peo-ple did me a good turn when they gave me my time—and the tad'll enter the seminary next fall."

About a quarter of an hour after they had said good-bye to the one-time engineer, Presley and Vanamee, tramping briskly along the road that led northward through Quien Sabe, ar-rived at Annixter's ranch house. At once they were aware of a vast and unwonted bustle that revolved about the place. They stopped a few moments looking on, amused and inter-ested in what was going forward.

The colossal barn was finished. Its freshly white-washed sides glared intolerably in the sun, but its interior was as yet innocent of paint and through the yawning vent of the sliding doors came a delicious odour of new, fresh wood and shavings. A crowd of men—Annixter's farm hands—were swarming all about it. Some were balanced on the topmost rounds of ladders, hanging festoons of Japanese lanterns from tree to tree, and all across the front of the barn itself. Mrs. Tree, her daughter Hilma and another woman were inside the barn cutting into long strips bolt after bolt of red, white and blue cambric and directing how these strips should be draped from the ceiling and on the walls; everywhere resounded the tapping of tack hammers. A farm wagon drove up loaded to overflowing with evergreens and with great bundles of palm leaves, and these were immediately seized upon and affixed as supplementary decorations to the tri-coloured cambric upon the inside walls of the barn. Two of the larger evergreen trees were placed on either side the barn door and their tops bent over to form an arch. In the middle of this arch it was proposed to hang a mammoth pasteboard escutcheon with gold letters, spelling the word *Welcome*. Piles of chairs, rented from I.O.O.F. hall in Bonneville, heaped themselves in an apparently hopeless entanglement on the ground; while at the far extremity of the barn a couple of carpenters clattered about the impromptu staging which was to accommodate the band.

There was a strenuous gayety in the air; everybody was in the best of spirits. Notes of laughter continually interrupted the conversation on every hand. At every moment a group of men involved themselves in uproarious horse-play. They passed oblique jokes behind their hands to each other— grossly veiled double-meanings meant for the women—and bellowed with laughter thereat, stamping on the ground. The relations between the sexes grew more intimate, the women and girls pushing the young fellows away from their sides with vigorous thrusts of their elbows. It was passed from group to group that Adela Vacca, a division superintendent's wife, had lost her garter; the daughter of the foreman of the Home ranch was kissed behind the door of the dairy-house.

Annixter, in execrable temper, appeared from time to time, hatless, his stiff yellow hair in wild disorder. He hurried between the barn and the ranch house, carrying now a wickered demijohn, now a case of wine, now a basket of lemons and pineapples. Besides general supervision, he had elected to assume the responsibility of composing the punch—something stiff, by jingo, a punch that would raise you right out of your boots; a regular hairlifter.

The harness room of the barn he had set apart for himself and intimates. He had brought a long table down from the house and upon it had set out boxes of cigars, bottles of whiskey and of beer and the great china bowls for the punch. It would be no fault of his, he declared, if half the number of his men friends were not uproarious before they left. His barn dance would be the talk of all Tulare County for years to come. For this one day he had resolved to put all thoughts of business out of his head. For the matter of that, things were going well enough. Osterman was back from Los Angeles with a favourable report as to his affair with Disbrow and

Darrell. There had been another meeting of the committee. Harran Derrick had attended. Though he had taken no part in the discussion, Annixter was satisfied. The Governor had consented to allow Harran to "come in," if he so desired, and Harran had pledged himself to share one-sixth of the campaign expenses, providing these did not exceed a certain figure.

As Annixter came to the door of the barn to shout abuse at the distraught Chinese cook who was cutting up lemons in the kitchen, he caught sight of Presley and Vanamee and hailed them.

"Hello, Pres," he called. "Come over here and see how she looks;" he indicated the barn with a movement of his head. "Well, we're getting ready for you to-night," he went on as the two friends came up. "But how we are going to get straightened out by eight o'clock I don't know. Would you believe that pip Caraher is short of lemons—at this last minute and I told him I'd want three cases o' 'em as much as a month ago, and here, just when I want a good lively saddle horse to get around on, somebody hikes the buckskin out the corral. *Stole* her, by jingo. I'll have the law on that thief if it breaks me—and a sixty-dollar saddle 'n' head-stall gone with her; and only about half the number of Jap lanterns that I ordered have shown up and not candles enough for those. It's enough to make a dog sick. There's nothing done that you don't do yourself, unless you stand over these loafers with a club. I'm sick of the whole business—and I've lost my hat; wish to God I'd never dreamed of givin' this rotten fool dance. Clutter the whole place up with a lot of feemales. I sure did lose my presence of mind when I got *that* idea."

Then, ignoring the fact that it was he, himself, who had called the young men to him, he added:

"Well, this is my busy day. Sorry I can't stop and talk to you longer."

He shouted a last imprecation at the Chinaman and turned back into the barn. Presley and Vanamee went on, but Annixter, as he crossed the floor of the barn, all but collided with Hilma Tree, who came out from one of the stalls, a box of candles in her arms.

Gasping out an apology, Annixter reëntered the harness room, closing the door behind him, and forgetting all the responsibility of the moment, lit a cigar and sat down in one of the hired chairs, his hands in his pockets, his feet on the table, frowning thoughtfully through the blue smoke.

Annixter was at last driven to confess to himself that he could not get the thought of Hilma Tree out of his mind. Finally she had "got a hold on him." The thing that of all others he most dreaded had happened. A feemale girl had got a hold on him, and now there was no longer for him any such thing as peace of mind. The idea of the young woman was with him continually. He went to bed with it; he got up with it. At every moment of the day he was pestered with it. It interfered with his work, got mixed up in his business. What a miserable confession for a man to make; a fine way to waste his time. Was it possible that only the other day he had stood in front of the music store in Bonneville and seriously considered making Hilma a present of a music-box? Even now, the very thought of it made him flush with shame, and this after she had told him plainly that she did not like him. He was running after her—he, Annixter! He ripped out a furious oath, striking the table with his boot heel. Again and again he had resolved to put the whole affair from out his mind. Once he had been able to do so, but of late it was becoming harder and harder with every successive day. He had only to close his eyes to see her as plain as if she stood before him; he saw her in a glory of sunlight that set a fine tinted lustre of pale carnation and gold on the silken sheen of her white skin, her hair sparkled with it, her thick, strong neck, sloping to her shoulders with beautiful, full curves, seemed to radiate the light; her eyes, brown, wide, innocent in expression, disclosing the full disc of the pupil upon the slightest provocation, flashed in this sunlight like diamonds.

Annixter was all bewildered. With the exception of the timid little creature in the glove-cleaning establishment in Sacramento, he had had no acquaintance with any woman. His world was harsh, crude, a world of men only—men who were to be combatted, opposed—his hand was against nearly every one of them. Women he distrusted with the instinctive distrust of the overgrown schoolboy. Now, at length, a young woman had come into his life. Promptly he was struck with discomfiture, annoyed almost beyond endurance, harassed, bedevilled, excited, made angry and exasperated. He was suspicious of the woman, yet desired her, totally ignorant of how to approach her, hating the sex, yet drawn to the individual, confusing the two emotions, sometimes even hating Hilma as a result of this confusion, but at all times disturbed, vexed, irritated beyond power of expression.

At length, Annixter cast his cigar from him and plunged again into the work of the day. The afternoon wore to evening, to the accompaniment of wearying and clamorous endeavour. In some unexplained fashion, the labour of putting the great barn in readiness for the dance was accomplished; the last bolt of cambric was hung in place from the rafters. The last evergreen tree was nailed to the joists of the walls; the last lantern hung, the last nail driven into the musicians' platform. The sun set. There was a great scurry to have supper and dress. Annixter, last of all the other workers, left the barn in the dusk of twilight. He was alone; he had a saw under one arm, a bag of tools was in his hand. He was in his shirt sleeves and carried his coat over his shoulder; a hammer was thrust into one of his hip pockets. He was in execrable temper. The day's work had fagged him out. He had not been able to find his hat.

"And the buckskin with sixty dollars' worth of saddle gone, too," he groaned. "Oh, ain't it sweet?"

At his house, Mrs. Tree had set out a cold supper for him, the inevitable dish of prunes serving as dessert. After supper Annixter bathed and dressed. He decided at the last moment to wear his usual town-going suit, a sack suit of black, made by a Bonneville tailor. But his hat was gone. There were other hats he might have worn, but because this particular one was lost he fretted about it all through his dressing and then decided to have one more look around the barn for it.

For over a quarter of an hour he pottered about the barn, going from stall to stall, rummaging the harness room and feed room, all to no purpose. At last he came out again upon the main floor, definitely giving up the search, looking about him to see if everything was in order.

The festoons of Japanese lanterns in and around the barn were not yet lighted, but some half-dozen lamps, with great, tin reflectors, that hung against the walls, were burning low.

A dull half light pervaded the vast interior, hollow, echoing, leaving the corners and roof thick with impenetrable black shadows. The barn faced the west and through the open sliding doors was streaming a single bright bar from the afterglow, incongruous and out of all harmony with the dull flare of the kerosene lamps.

As Annixter glanced about him, he saw a figure step briskly out of the shadows of one corner of the building, pause for the fraction of one instant in the bar of light, then, at sight of him, dart back again. There was a sound of hurried footsteps.

Annixter, with recollections of the stolen buckskin in his mind, cried out sharply:

"Who's there?"

There was no answer. In a second his pistol was in his hand.

"Who's there? Quick, speak up or I'll shoot."

"No, no, no, don't shoot," cried an answering voice. "Oh, be careful. It's I—Hilma Tree."

Annixter slid the pistol into his pocket with a great qualm of apprehension. He came forward and met Hilma in the doorway.

"Good Lord," he murmured, "that sure did give me a start. If I *had* shot——"

Hilma stood abashed and confused before him. She was dressed in a white organdie frock of the most rigorous simplicity and wore neither flower nor ornament. The severity of her dress made her look even larger than usual, and even as it was her eyes were on a level with Annixter's. There was a certain fascination in the contradiction of stature and character of Hilma—a great girl, half-child as yet, but tall as a man for all that.

There was a moment's awkward silence, then Hilma explained:

"I—I came back to look for my hat. I thought I left it here this afternoon."

"And I was looking for *my* hat," cried Annixter. "Funny enough, hey?"

They laughed at this as heartily as children might have done. The constraint of the situation was a little relaxed and

Annixter, with sudden directness, glanced sharply at the young woman and demanded:

"Well, Miss Hilma, hate me as much as ever?"

"Oh, no, sir," she answered, "I never said I hated you."

"Well,—dislike me, then; I know you said that."

"I—I disliked what you did—*tried* to do. It made me angry and it hurt me. I shouldn't have said what I did that time, but it was your fault."

"You mean you shouldn't have said you didn't like me?" asked Annixter. "Why?"

"Well, well,—I don't—I don't *dis*like anybody," admitted Hilma.

"Then I can take it that you don't dislike *me*? Is that it?"

"I don't dislike anybody," persisted Hilma.

"Well, I asked you more than that, didn't I?" queried Annixter uneasily. "I asked you to like me, remember, the other day. I'm asking you that again, now. I want you to like me."

Hilma lifted her eyes inquiringly to his. In her words was an unmistakable ring of absolute sincerity. Innocently she inquired:

"Why?"

Annixter was struck speechless. In the face of such candour, such perfect ingenuousness, he was at a loss for any words.

"Well—well," he stammered, "well—I don't know," he suddenly burst out. "That is," he went on, groping for his wits, "I can't quite say why." The idea of a colossal lie occurred to him, a thing actually royal.

"I like to have the people who are around me like me," he declared. "I—I like to be popular, understand? Yes, that's it," he continued, more reassured. "I don't like the idea of any one disliking me. That's the way I am. It's my nature."

"Oh, then," returned Hilma, "you needn't bother. No, I don't dislike you."

"Well, that's good," declared Annixter judicially. "That's good. But hold on," he interrupted, "I'm forgetting. It's not enough to not dislike me. I want you to like me. How about *that*?"

Hilma paused for a moment, glancing vaguely out of the doorway toward the lighted window of the dairy-house, her head tilted.

"I don't know that I ever thought about that," she said.

"Well, think about it now," insisted Annixter.

"But I never thought about liking anybody particularly," she observed. "It's because I like everybody, don't you see?"

"Well, you've got to like some people more than other people," hazarded Annixter, "and I want to be one of those 'some people,' savvy? Good Lord, I don't know how to say these fool things. I talk like a galoot when I get talking to feemale girls and I can't lay my tongue to anything that sounds right. It isn't my nature. And look here, I lied when I said I liked to have people like me—to be popular. Rot! I don't care a curse about people's opinions of me. But there's a few people that are more to me than most others—that chap Presley, for instance—and those people I *do* want to have like me. What they think counts. Pshaw! I know I've got enemies; piles of them. I could name you half a dozen men right now that are naturally itching to take a shot at me. How about this ranch? Don't I know, can't I hear the men growling oaths under their breath after I've gone by? And in business ways, too," he went on, speaking half to himself, "in Bonneville and all over the county there's not a man of them wouldn't howl for joy if they got a chance to down Buck Annixter. Think I care? Why, I *like* it. I run my ranch to suit myself and I play my game my own way. I'm a 'driver,' I know it, and a 'bully,' too. Oh, I know what they call me—'a brute beast, with a twist in my temper that would rile up a new-born lamb,' and I'm 'crusty' and 'pig-headed' and 'obstinate.' They say all that, but they've *got* to say, too, that I'm cleverer than any man-jack in the running. There's nobody can get ahead of me." His eyes snapped. "Let 'em grind their teeth. They can't 'down' me. When I shut my fist there's not one of them can open it. No, not with a *chisel*." He turned to Hilma again. "Well, when a man's hated as much as that, it stands to reason, don't it, Miss Hilma, that the few friends he has got he wants to keep? I'm not such an entire swine to the people that know me best—that jackass, Presley, for instance. I'd put my hand in the fire to do him a real service. Sometimes I get kind of lonesome; wonder if you would understand? It's my fault, but there's not a horse about the place that don't lay his ears back when I get on him; there's not a dog don't put his tail between his legs as soon as I come near him. The cayuse isn't foaled yet here on Quien Sabe that can throw me, nor the dog whelped that would dare show his teeth at me. I kick that Irish setter every time I see him—but wonder what I'd do, though, if he didn't slink so much, if he wagged his tail and was glad to see me? So it all comes to this: I'd like to have you—well, sort of feel that I was a good friend of yours and like me because of it."

The flame in the lamp on the wall in front of Hilma stretched upward tall and thin and began to smoke. She went over to where the lamp hung and, standing on tip-toe, lowered the wick. As she reached her hand up, Annixter noted how the sombre, lurid red of the lamp made a warm reflection on her smooth, round arm.

"Do you understand?" he queried.

"Yes, why, yes," she answered, turning around. "It's very good of you to want to be a friend of mine. I didn't think so, though, when you tried to kiss me. But maybe it's all right since you've explained things. You see I'm different from you. I like everybody to like me and I like to like everybody. It makes one so much happier. You wouldn't believe it, but you ought to try it, sir, just to see. It's so good to be good to people and to have people good to you. And everybody has always been so good to me. Mamma and papa, of course, and Billy, the stableman, and Montalegre, the Portugee foreman, and the Chinese cook, even, and Mr. Delaney—only he went away—and Mrs. Vacca and her little——"

"Delaney, hey?" demanded Annixter abruptly. "You and he were pretty good friends, were you?"

"Oh, yes," she answered. "He was just as *good* to me. Every day in the summer time he used to ride over to the Seed ranch back of the Mission and bring me a great armful of flowers, the prettiest things, and I used to pretend to pay him for them with dollars made of cheese that I cut out of the cheese with a biscuit cutter. It was such fun. We were the best of friends."

"There's another lamp smoking," growled Annixter. "Turn it down, will you?—and see that somebody sweeps this floor here. It's all littered up with pine needles. I've got a lot to do. Good-bye."

"Good-bye, sir."

Annixter returned to the ranch house, his teeth clenched, enraged, his face flushed.

"Ah," he muttered, "Delaney, hey? Throwing it up to me that I fired him." His teeth gripped together more fiercely than ever. "The best of friends, hey? By God, I'll have that girl yet. I'll show that cow-puncher. Ain't I her employer, her boss? I'll show her—and Delaney, too. It would be easy enough—and then Delaney can have her—if he wants her—after me."

An evil light flashing from under his scowl, spread over his face. The male instincts of possession, unreasoned, treacherous, oblique, came twisting to the surface. All the lower nature of the man, ignorant of women, racked at one and the same time with enmity and desire, roused itself like a hideous and abominable beast. And at the same moment, Hilma returned to her house, humming to herself as she walked, her white dress glowing with a shimmer of faint saffron light in the last ray of the after-glow.

A little after half-past seven, the first carry-all, bearing the druggist of Bonneville and his women-folk, arrived in front of the new barn. Immediately afterward an express wagon loaded down with a swarming family of Spanish-Mexicans, gorgeous in red and yellow colours, followed. Billy, the stableman, and his assistant took charge of the teams, unchecking the horses and hitching them to a fence back of the barn. Then Caraher, the saloon-keeper, in "derby" hat, "Prince Albert" coat, pointed yellow shoes and inevitable red necktie, drove into the yard on his buckboard, the delayed box of lemons under the seat. It looked as if the whole array of invited guests was to arrive in one unbroken procession, but for a long half-hour nobody else appeared. Annixter and Caraher withdrew to the harness room and promptly involved themselves in a wrangle as to the make-up of the famous punch. From time to time their voices could be heard uplifted in clamorous argument.

"Two quarts and a half and a cupful of chartreuse."

"Rot, rot, I know better. Champagne straight and a dash of brandy."

The druggist's wife and sister retired to the feed room,

where a bureau with a swinging mirror had been placed for the convenience of the women. The druggist stood awkwardly outside the door of the feed room, his coat collar turned up against the draughts that drifted through the barn, his face troubled, debating anxiously as to the propriety of putting on his gloves. The Spanish-Mexican family, a father, mother and five children and sister-in-law, sat rigid on the edges of the hired chairs, silent, constrained, their eyes lowered, their elbows in at their sides, glancing furtively from under their eyebrows at the decorations or watching with intense absorption young Vacca, son of one of the division superintendents, who wore a checked coat and white thread gloves and who paced up and down the length of the barn, frowning, very important, whittling a wax candle over the floor to make it slippery for dancing.

The musicians arrived, the City Band of Bonneville—Annixter having managed to offend the leader of the "Dirigo" Club orchestra, at the very last moment, to such a point that he had refused his services. These members of the City Band repaired at once to their platform in the corner. At every instant they laughed uproariously among themselves, joshing one of their number, a Frenchman, whom they called "Skee-zicks." Their hilarity reverberated in a hollow, metallic roll among the rafters overhead. The druggist observed to young Vacca as he passed by that he thought them pretty fresh, just the same.

"I'm busy, I'm very busy," returned the young man, continuing on his way, still frowning and paring the stump of candle.

"Two quarts 'n' a half. Two quarts 'n' a half."

"Ah, yes, in a way, that's so; and then, again, in a way, it *isn't. I* know better."

All along one side of the barn were a row of stalls, fourteen of them, clean as yet, redolent of new cut wood, the sawdust still in the cracks of the flooring. Deliberately the druggist went from one to the other, pausing contemplatively before each. He returned down the line and again took up his position by the door of the feed room, nodding his head judicially, as if satisfied. He decided to put on his gloves.

By now it was quite dark. Outside, between the barn and

the ranch houses one could see a group of men on step-ladders lighting the festoons of Japanese lanterns. In the darkness, only their faces appeared here and there, high above the ground, seen in a haze of red, strange, grotesque. Gradually as the multitude of lanterns were lit, the light spread. The grass underfoot looked like green excelsior. Another group of men invaded the barn itself, lighting the lamps and lanterns there. Soon the whole place was gleaming with points of light. Young Vacca, who had disappeared, returned with his pockets full of wax candles. He resumed his whittling, refusing to answer any questions, vociferating that he was busy.

Outside there was a sound of hoofs and voices. More guests had arrived. The druggist, seized with confusion, terrified lest he had put on his gloves too soon, thrust his hands into his pockets. It was Cutter, Magnus Derrick's division superintendent, who came, bringing his wife and her two girl cousins. They had come fifteen miles by the trail from the far distant division house on "Four" of Los Muertos and had ridden on horseback instead of driving. Mrs. Cutter could be heard declaring that she was nearly dead and felt more like going to bed than dancing. The two girl cousins, in dresses of dotted Swiss over blue sateen, were doing their utmost to pacify her. She could be heard protesting from moment to moment. One distinguished the phrases "straight to my bed," "back nearly broken in two," "never wanted to come in the first place." The druggist, observing Cutter take a pair of gloves from Mrs. Cutter's reticule, drew his hands from his pockets.

But abruptly there was an interruption. In the musicians' corner a scuffle broke out. A chair was overturned. There was a noise of imprecations mingled with shouts of derision. Skeezicks, the Frenchman, had turned upon the joshers.

"Ah, no," he was heard to exclaim, "at the end of the end it is too much. Kind of a bad canary—we will go to see about that. Aha, let him close up his face before I demolish it with a good stroke of the fist."

The men who were lighting the lanterns were obliged to intervene before he could be placated.

Hooven and his wife and daughters arrived. Minna was carrying little Hilda, already asleep, in her arms. Minna looked very pretty, striking even, with her black hair, pale face, very red lips and greenish-blue eyes. She was dressed in what had been Mrs. Hooven's wedding gown, a cheap affair of "farmer's satin." Mrs. Hooven had pendent earrings of imitation jet in her ears. Hooven was wearing an old frock coat of Magnus Derrick's, the sleeves too long, the shoulders absurdly too wide. He and Cutter at once entered into an excited conversation as to the ownership of a certain steer.

"Why, the brand——"

"Ach, Gott, der brendt," Hooven clasped his head, "ach, der brendt, dot maks me laugh some laughs. Dot's goot— der brendt—doand I see um—shoor der boole mit der bleck star bei der vore-head in der middle oaf. Any someones you esk tell you dot is mein boole. You esk any someones. Der brendt? To hell mit der brendt. You aindt got some memorie aboudt does ting I guess nodt."

"Please step aside, gentlemen," said young Vacca, who was still making the rounds of the floor.

Hooven whirled about. "Eh? What den," he exclaimed, still excited, willing to be angry at any one for the moment. "Doand you push soh, you. I tink berhapz you doand *own* dose barn, hey?"

"I'm busy, I'm very busy." The young man pushed by with grave preoccupation.

"Two quarts 'n' a half. Two quarts 'n' a half."

"I know better. That's all rot."

But the barn was filling up rapidly. At every moment there was a rattle of a newly arrived vehicle from outside. Guest after guest appeared in the doorway, singly or in couples, or in families, or in garrulous parties of five and six. Now it was Phelps and his mother from Los Muertos, now a foreman from Broderson's with his family, now a gayly apparelled clerk from a Bonneville store, solitary and bewildered, look- ing for a place to put his hat, now a couple of Spanish- Mexican girls from Guadalajara with coquettish effects of black and yellow about their dress, now a group of Oster- man's tenants, Portuguese, swarthy, with plastered hair and curled mustaches, redolent of cheap perfumes. Sarria arrived, his smooth, shiny face glistening with perspiration. He wore a new cassock and carried his broad-brimmed hat under his arm. His appearance made quite a stir. He passed from group to group, urbane, affable, shaking hands right and left; he assumed a set smile of amiability which never left his face the whole evening.

But abruptly there was a veritable sensation. From out the little crowd that persistently huddled about the doorway came Osterman. He wore a dress-suit with a white waistcoat and patent leather pumps—what a wonder! A little qualm of excitement spread around the barn. One exchanged nudges of the elbow with one's neighbour, whispering earnestly behind the hand. What astonishing clothes! Catch on to the coat-tails! It was a masquerade costume, maybe; that goat Osterman was such a josher, one never could tell what he would do next.

The musicians began to tune up. From their corner came a medley of mellow sounds, the subdued chirps of the violins, the dull bourdon of the bass viol, the liquid gurgling of the flageolet and the deep-toned snarl of the big horn, with now and then a rasping stridulating of the snare drum. A sense of gayety began to spread throughout the assembly. At every moment the crowd increased. The aroma of new-sawn timber and sawdust began to be mingled with the feminine odour of sachet and flowers. There was a babel of talk in the air—male baritone and soprano chatter—varied by an occasional note of laughter and the swish of stiffly starched petticoats. On the row of chairs that went around three sides of the wall groups began to settle themselves. For a long time the guests huddled close to the doorway; the lower end of the floor was crowded, the upper end deserted; but by degrees the lines of white muslin and pink and blue sateen extended, dotted with the darker figures of men in black suits. The conversation grew louder as the timidity of the early moments wore off. Groups at a distance called back and forth; conversations were carried on at top voice. Once, even a whole party hurried across the floor from one side of the barn to the other.

Annixter emerged from the harness room, his face red with wrangling. He took a position to the right of the door, shaking hands with newcomers, inviting them over and over again to cut loose and whoop it along. Into the ears of his more intimate male acquaintances he dropped a word as to punch and cigars in the harness room later on, winking with vast intelligence.

Ranchers from remoter parts of the country appeared: Garnett, from the Ruby rancho, Keast, from the ranch of the same name, Gethings, of the San Pablo, Chattern, of the Bonanza, and others and still others, a score of them—elderly men, for the most part, bearded, slow of speech, deliberate, dressed in broadcloth. Old Broderson, who entered with his wife on his arm, fell in with this type, and with them came a certain Dabney, of whom nothing but his name was known, a silent old man, who made no friends, whom nobody knew or spoke to, who was seen only upon such occasions as this, coming from no one knew where, going, no one cared to inquire whither.

Between eight and half-past, Magnus Derrick and his family were seen. Magnus's entry caused no little impression. Some said: "There's the Governor," and called their companions' attention to the thin, erect figure, commanding, imposing, dominating all in his immediate neighbourhood. Harran came with him, wearing a cutaway suit of black. He was undeniably handsome, young and fresh looking, his cheeks highly coloured, quite the finest looking of all the younger men; blond, strong, with that certain courtliness of manner that had always made him liked. He took his mother upon his arm and conducted her to a seat by the side of Mrs. Broderson.

Annie Derrick was very pretty that evening. She was dressed in a grey silk gown with a collar of pink velvet. Her light brown hair that yet retained so much of its brightness was transfixed by a high, shell comb, very Spanish. But the look of uneasiness in her large eyes—the eyes of a young girl—was deepening every day. The expression of innocence and inquiry which they so easily assumed, was disturbed by a faint suggestion of aversion, almost of terror. She settled herself in her place, in the corner of the hall, in the rear rank of chairs, a little frightened by the glare of lights, the hum of talk and the shifting crowd, glad to be out of the way, to attract no attention, willing to obliterate herself.

All at once Annixter, who had just shaken hands with Dyke, his mother and the little tad, moved abruptly in his place, drawing in his breath sharply. The crowd around the great, wide-open main door of the barn had somewhat thinned out and in the few groups that still remained there he had suddenly recognised Mr. and Mrs. Tree and Hilma, making their way towards some empty seats near the entrance of the feed room.

In the dusky light of the barn earlier in the evening, Annixter had not been able to see Hilma plainly. Now, however, as she passed before his eyes in the glittering radiance of the lamps and lanterns, he caught his breath in astonishment. Never had she appeared more beautiful in his eyes. It did not seem possible that this was the same girl whom he saw every day in and around the ranch house and dairy, the girl of simple calico frocks and plain shirt waists, who brought him his dinner, who made up his bed. Now he could not take his eyes from her. Hilma, for the first time, was wearing her hair done high upon her head. The thick, sweet-smelling masses, bitumen brown in the shadows, coruscated like golden filaments in the light. Her organdie frock was long, longer than any she had yet worn. It left a little of her neck and breast bare and all of her arm.

Annixter muttered an exclamation. Such arms! How did she manage to keep them hid on ordinary occasions. Big at the shoulder, tapering with delicious modulations to the elbow and wrist, overlaid with a delicate, gleaming lustre. As often as she turned her head the movement sent a slow undulation over her neck and shoulders, the pale amber-tinted shadows under her chin, coming and going over the creamy whiteness of the skin like the changing moire of silk. The pretty rose colour of her cheek had deepened to a pale carnation. Annixter, his hands clasped behind him, stood watching.

In a few moments Hilma was surrounded by a group of young men, clamouring for dances. They came from all corners of the barn, leaving the other girls precipitately, almost rudely. There could be little doubt as to who was to be the belle of the occasion. Hilma's little triumph was immediate, complete. Annixter could hear her voice from time to time, its usual velvety huskiness vibrating to a note of exuberant gayety.

All at once the orchestra swung off into a march—the Grand March. There was a great rush to secure "partners." Young Vacca, still going the rounds, was pushed to one side. The gayly apparelled clerk from the Bonneville store lost his head in the confusion. He could not find his "partner." He roamed wildly about the barn, bewildered, his eyes rolling. He resolved to prepare an elaborate programme card on the back of an old envelope. Rapidly the line was formed, Hilma and Harran Derrick in the lead, Annixter having obstinately refused to engage in either march, set or dance the whole evening. Soon the confused shuffling of feet settled to a measured cadence; the orchestra blared and wailed, the snare drum, rolling at exact intervals, the cornet marking the time. It was half-past eight o'clock.

Annixter drew a long breath:

"Good," he muttered, "the thing is under way at last."

Singularly enough, Osterman also refused to dance. The week before he had returned from Los Angeles, bursting with the importance of his mission. He had been successful. He had Disbrow "in his pocket." He was impatient to pose before the others of the committee as a skilful political agent, a manipulator. He forgot his attitude of the early part of the evening when he had drawn attention to himself with his wonderful clothes. Now his comic actor's face, with its brownish-red cheeks, protuberant ears and horizontal slit of a mouth, was overcast with gravity. His bald forehead was seamed with the wrinkles of responsibility. He drew Annixter into one of the empty stalls and began an elaborate explanation, glib, voluble, interminable, going over again in detail what he had reported to the committee in outline.

"I managed—I schemed—I kept dark—I lay low——"

But Annixter refused to listen.

"Oh, rot your schemes. There's a punch in the harness room that will make the hair grow on the top of your head in the place where the hair ought to grow. Come on, we'll round up some of the boys and walk into it."

They edged their way around the hall outside "The Grand March," toward the harness room, picking up on their way

Caraher, Dyke, Hooven and old Broderson. Once in the harness room, Annixter shot the bolt.

"That affair outside," he observed, "will take care of itself, but here's a little orphan child that gets lonesome without company."

Annixter began ladling the punch, filling the glasses. Osterman proposed a toast to Quien Sabe and the Biggest Barn. Their elbows crooked in silence. Old Broderson set down his glass, wiping his long beard and remarking:

"That—that certainly is very—very agreeable. I remember a punch I drank on Christmas day in '83, or no, it was '84— anyhow, that punch—it was in Ukiah—'twas '83—" He wandered on aimlessly, unable to stop his flow of speech, losing himself in details, involving his talk in a hopeless maze of trivialities to which nobody paid any attention.

"I don't drink myself," observed Dyke, "but just a taste of that with a lot of water wouldn't be bad for the little tad. She'd think it was lemonade." He was about to mix a glass for Sidney, but thought better of it at the last moment.

"It's the chartreuse that's lacking," commented Caraher, lowering at Annixter. The other flared up on the instant.

"Rot, rot. I know better. In some punches it goes; and then, again, in others it don't."

But it was left to Hooven to launch the successful phrase:

"*Gesundheit,*" he exclaimed, holding out his second glass. After drinking, he replaced it on the table with a long breath. "Ach Gott!" he cried, "dat poonsch, say I tink dot poonsch mek some demn goot vertilizer, hey?"

Fertiliser! The others roared with laughter.

"Good eye, Bismarck," commented Annixter. The name had a great success. Thereafter throughout the evening the punch was invariably spoken of as the "Fertiliser." Osterman, having spilt the bottom of a glassful on the floor, pretended that he saw shoots of grain coming up on the spot. Suddenly he turned upon old Broderson.

"I'm bald, ain't I? Want to know how I lost my hair? Promise you won't ask a single other question and I'll tell you. Promise your word of honour."

"Eh? What—wh—I—I don't understand. Your hair? Yes, I'll promise. How *did* you lose it?"

"It was bit off."

The other gazed at him stupefied; his jaw dropped. The company shouted, and old Broderson, believing he had somehow accomplished a witticism, chuckled in his beard, wagging his head. But suddenly he fell grave, struck with an idea. He demanded:

"Yes—I know—but—but what bit it off?"

"Ah," vociferated Osterman, "that's *just* what you promised not to ask."

The company doubled up with hilarity. Caraher leaned against the door, holding his sides, but Hooven, all abroad, unable to follow, gazed from face to face with a vacant grin, thinking it was still a question of his famous phrase.

"Vertilizer, hey? Dots some fine joke, hey? You bedt."

What with the noise of their talk and laughter, it was some time before Dyke, first of all, heard a persistent knocking on the bolted door. He called Annixter's attention to the sound. Cursing the intruder, Annixter unbolted and opened the door. But at once his manner changed.

"Hello. It's Presley. Come in, come in, Pres."

There was a shout of welcome from the others. A spirit of effusive cordiality had begun to dominate the gathering. Annixter caught sight of Vanamee back of Presley, and waiving for the moment the distinction of employer and employee, insisted that both the friends should come in.

"Any friend of Pres is my friend," he declared.

But when the two had entered and had exchanged greetings, Presley drew Annixter aside.

"Vanamee and I have just come from Bonneville," he explained. "We saw Delaney there. He's got the buckskin, and he's full of bad whiskey and dago-red. You should see him; he's wearing all his cow-punching outfit, hair trousers, sombrero, spurs and all the rest of it, and he has strapped himself to a big revolver. He says he wasn't invited to your barn dance but that he's coming over to shoot up the place. He says you promised to show him off Quien Sabe at the toe of your boot and that he's going to give you the chance tonight!"

"Ah," commented Annixter, nodding his head, "he is, is he?"

Presley was disappointed. Knowing Annixter's irascibility, he had expected to produce a more dramatic effect. He began to explain the danger of the business. Delaney had once knifed a greaser in the Panamint country. He was known as a "bad" man. But Annixter refused to be drawn.

"All right," he said, "that's all right. Don't tell anybody else. You might scare the girls off. Get in and drink."

Outside the dancing was by this time in full swing. The orchestra was playing a polka. Young Vacca, now at his fiftieth wax candle, had brought the floor to the slippery surface of glass. The druggist was dancing with one of the Spanish-Mexican girls with the solemnity of an automaton, turning about and about, always in the same direction, his eyes glassy, his teeth set. Hilma Tree was dancing for the second time with Harran Derrick. She danced with infinite grace. Her cheeks were bright red, her eyes half-closed, and through her parted lips she drew from time to time a long, tremulous breath of pure delight. The music, the weaving colours, the heat of the air, by now a little oppressive, the monotony of repeated sensation, even the pain of physical fatigue had exalted all her senses. She was in a dreamy lethargy of happiness. It was her "first ball." She could have danced without stopping until morning. Minna Hooven and Cutter were "promenading." Mrs. Hooven, with little Hilda already asleep on her knees, never took her eyes from her daughter's gown. As often as Minna passed near her she vented an energetic "pst! pst!" The metal tip of a white draw string was showing from underneath the waist of Minna's dress. Mrs. Hooven was on the point of tears.

The solitary gayly apparelled clerk from Bonneville was in a fever of agitation. He had lost his elaborate programme card. Bewildered, beside himself with trepidation, he hurried about the room, jostled by the dancing couples, tripping over the feet of those who were seated; he peered distressfully under the chairs and about the floor, asking anxious questions.

Magnus Derrick, the centre of a listening circle of ranchers—Garnett from the Ruby rancho, Keast from the ranch of the same name, Gethings and Chattern of the San Pablo and Bonanza—stood near the great open doorway of the barn, discussing the possibility of a shortage in the world's wheat crop for the next year.

Abruptly the orchestra ceased playing with a roll of the snare drum, a flourish of the cornet and a prolonged growl of the bass viol. The dance broke up, the couples hurrying to their seats, leaving the gayly apparelled clerk suddenly isolated in the middle of the floor, rolling his eyes. The druggist released the Spanish-Mexican girl with mechanical precision out amidst the crowd of dancers. He bowed, dropping his chin upon his cravat; throughout the dance neither had hazarded a word. The girl found her way alone to a chair, but the druggist, sick from continually revolving in the same direction, walked unsteadily toward the wall. All at once the barn reeled around him; he fell down. There was a great laugh, but he scrambled to his feet and disappeared abruptly out into the night through the doorway of the barn, deathly pale, his hand upon his stomach.

Dabney, the old man whom nobody knew, approached the group of ranchers around Magnus Derrick and stood, a little removed, listening gravely to what the governor was saying, his chin sunk in his collar, silent, offering no opinions.

But the leader of the orchestra, with a great gesture of his violin bow, cried out:

"All take partners for the lancers and promenade around the hall!"

However, there was a delay. A little crowd formed around the musicians' platform; voices were raised; there was a commotion. Skeezicks, who played the big horn, accused the cornet and the snare-drum of stealing his cold lunch. At intervals he could be heard expostulating:

"Ah, no! at the end of the end! Render me the sausages, you, or less I break your throat! Aha! I know you. You are going to play me there a bad farce. My sausages and the pork sandwich, else I go away from this place!"

He made an exaggerated show of replacing his big horn in its case, but the by-standers raised a great protest. The sandwiches and one sausage were produced; the other had disappeared. In the end Skeezicks allowed himself to be appeased. The dance was resumed.

Half an hour later the gathering in the harness room was considerably reinforced. It was the corner of the barn toward which the male guests naturally gravitated. Harran Derrick, who only cared to dance with Hilma Tree, was admitted. Garnett from the Ruby rancho and Gethings from the San Pablo, came in a little afterwards. A fourth bowl of punch was mixed, Annixter and Caraher clamouring into each other's face as to its ingredients. Cigars were lighted. Soon the air of the room became blue with an acrid haze of smoke. It was very warm. Ranged in their chairs around the side of the room, the guests emptied glass after glass.

Vanamee alone refused to drink. He sat a little to one side, disassociating himself from what was going forward, watching the others calmly, a little contemptuously, a cigarette in his fingers.

Hooven, after drinking his third glass, however, was afflicted with a great sadness; his breast heaved with immense sighs. He asserted that he was "obbressed;" Cutter had taken his steer. He retired to a corner and seated himself in a heap on his chair, his heels on the rungs, wiping the tears from his eyes, refusing to be comforted.

Old Broderson startled Annixter, who sat next to him, out of all measure by suddenly winking at him with infinite craftiness.

"When I was a lad in Ukiah," he whispered hoarsely, "I was a devil of a fellow with the girls; but Lordy!" he nudged him slyly, "I wouldn't have it known!"

Of those who were drinking, Annixter alone retained all his wits. Though keeping pace with the others, glass for glass, the punch left him solid upon his feet, clear-headed. The tough, cross-grained fibre of him seemed proof against alcohol. Never in his life had he been drunk. He prided himself upon his power of resistance. It was his nature.

"Say!" exclaimed old Broderson, gravely addressing the company, pulling at his beard uneasily—"say! I—I—listen! I'm a devil of a fellow with the girls." He wagged his head doggedly, shutting his eyes in a knowing fashion. "Yes, sir, I am. There was a young lady in Ukiah—that was when I was a lad of seventeen. We used to meet in the cemetery in the afternoons. I was to go away to school at Sacramento, and the afternoon I left we met in the cemetery and we stayed so long I almost missed the train. Her name was Celestine."

There was a pause. The others waited for the rest of the story.

"And afterwards?" prompted Annixter.

"Afterwards? Nothing afterwards. I never saw her again. Her name was Celestine."

The company raised a chorus of derision, and Osterman cried ironically:

"Say! *that's* a pretty good one! Tell us another."

The old man laughed with the rest, believing he had made another hit. He called Osterman to him, whispering in his ear:

"Sh! Look here! Some night you and I will go up to San Francisco—hey? We'll go skylarking. We'll be gay. Oh, I'm a—a—a rare old *buck*, I am! I ain't too old. You'll see."

Annixter gave over the making of the fifth bowl of punch to Osterman, who affirmed that he had a recipe for a "fertiliser" from Solotari that would take the plating off the ladle. He left him wrangling with Caraher, who still persisted in adding chartreuse, and stepped out into the dance to see how things were getting on.

It was the interval between two dances. In and around a stall at the farther end of the floor, where lemonade was being served, was a great throng of young men. Others hurried across the floor singly or by twos and threes, gingerly carrying overflowing glasses to their "partners," sitting in long rows of white and blue and pink against the opposite wall, their mothers and older sisters in a second dark-clothed rank behind them. A babel of talk was in the air, mingled with gusts of laughter. Everybody seemed having a good time. In the increasing heat the decorations of evergreen trees and festoons threw off a pungent aroma that suggested a Sunday-school Christmas festival. In the other stalls, lower down the barn, the young men had brought chairs, and in these deep recesses the most desperate love-making was in progress, the young man, his hair neatly parted, leaning with great solicitation over the girl, his "partner" for the moment, fanning her conscientiously, his arm carefully laid along the back of her chair.

By the doorway, Annixter met Sarria, who had stepped out to smoke a fat, black cigar. The set smile of amiability was still fixed on the priest's smooth, shiny face; the cigar ashes had left grey streaks on the front of his cassock. He avoided Annixter, fearing, no doubt, an allusion to his game cocks, and took up his position back of the second rank of chairs by the musicians' stand, beaming encouragingly upon every one who caught his eye.

Annixter was saluted right and left as he slowly went the round of the floor. At every moment he had to pause to shake hands and to listen to congratulations upon the size of his barn and the success of his dance. But he was distrait, his thoughts elsewhere; he did not attempt to hide his impatience when some of the young men tried to engage him in conversation, asking him to be introduced to their sisters, or their friends' sisters. He sent them about their business harshly, abominably rude, leaving a wake of angry disturbance behind him, sowing the seeds of future quarrels and renewed unpopularity. He was looking for Hilma Tree.

When at last he came unexpectedly upon her, standing near where Mrs. Tree was seated, some half-dozen young men hovering uneasily in her neighbourhood, all his audacity was suddenly stricken from him; his gruffness, his overbearing insolence vanished with an abruptness that left him cold. His old-time confusion and embarrassment returned to him. Instead of speaking to her as he intended, he affected not to see her, but passed by, his head in the air, pretending a sudden interest in a Japanese lantern that was about to catch fire.

But he had had a single distinct glimpse of her, definite, precise, and this glimpse was enough. Hilma had changed. The change was subtle, evanescent, hard to define, but not the less unmistakable. The excitement, the enchanting delight, the delicious disturbance of "the first ball," had produced its result. Perhaps there had only been this lacking. It was hard to say, but for that brief instant of time Annixter was looking at Hilma, the woman. She was no longer the young girl upon whom he might look down, to whom he might condescend, whose little, infantile graces were to be considered with amused toleration.

When Annixter returned to the harness room, he let himself into a clamour of masculine hilarity. Osterman had, indeed, made a marvellous "fertiliser," whiskey for the most
part, diluted with champagne and lemon juice. The first
round of this drink had been welcomed with a salvo of cheers.
Hooven, recovering his spirits under its violent stimulation,
spoke of "heving ut oudt mit Cudder, bei Gott," while Osterman, standing on a chair at the end of the room, shouted for
a "few moments quiet, gentlemen," so that he might tell a
certain story he knew.

But, abruptly, Annixter discovered that the liquors—the
champagne, whiskey, brandy, and the like—were running
low. This would never do. He felt that he would stand disgraced if it could be said afterward that he had not provided
sufficient drink at his entertainment. He slipped out, unobserved, and, finding two of his ranch hands near the doorway,
sent them down to the ranch house to bring up all the cases
of "stuff" they found there.

However, when this matter had been attended to, Annixter
did not immediately return to the harness room. On the floor
of the barn a square dance was under way, the leader of the
City Band calling the figures. Young Vacca indefatigably continued the rounds of the barn, paring candle after candle, possessed with this single idea of duty, pushing the dancers out
of his way, refusing to admit that the floor was yet sufficiently
slippery. The druggist had returned indoors, and leaned dejected and melancholy against the wall near the doorway, unable to dance, his evening's enjoyment spoiled. The gayly
apparelled clerk from Bonneville had just involved himself in
a deplorable incident. In a search for his handkerchief, which
he had lost while trying to find his programme card, he had
inadvertently wandered into the feed room, set apart as the
ladies' dressing room, at the moment when Mrs. Hooven,
having removed the waist of Minna's dress, was relacing her
corsets. There was a tremendous scene. The clerk was ejected
forcibly, Mrs. Hooven filling all the neighbourhood with
shrill expostulation. A young man, Minna's "partner," who
stood near the feed room door, waiting for her to come out,
had invited the clerk, with elaborate sarcasm, to step outside
for a moment; and the clerk, breathless, stupefied, hustled

from hand to hand, remained petrified, with staring eyes, turning about and about, looking wildly from face to face, speechless, witless, wondering what had happened.

But the square dance was over. The City Band was just beginning to play a waltz. Annixter assuring himself that everything was going all right, was picking his way across the floor, when he came upon Hilma Tree quite alone, and looking anxiously among the crowd of dancers.

"Having a good time, Miss Hilma?" he demanded, pausing for a moment.

"Oh, am I, *just!*" she exclaimed. "The best time—but I don't know what has become of my partner. See! I'm left all alone—the only time this whole evening," she added proudly. "Have you seen him—my partner, sir? I forget his name. I only met him this evening, and I've met *so* many I can't begin to remember half of them. He was a young man from Bonneville—a clerk, I think, because I remember seeing him in a store there, and he wore the prettiest clothes!"

"I guess he got lost in the shuffle," observed Annixter. Suddenly an idea occurred to him. He took his resolution in both hands. He clenched his teeth.

"Say! look here, Miss Hilma. What's the matter with you and I stealing this one for ourselves? I don't mean to dance. I don't propose to make a jumping-jack of myself for some galoot to give me the laugh, but we'll walk around. Will you? What do you say?"

Hilma consented.

"I'm not so *very* sorry I missed my dance with that— that—little clerk," she said guiltily. "I suppose that's very bad of me, isn't it?"

Annixter fulminated a vigorous protest.

"I *am* so warm!" murmured Hilma, fanning herself with her handkerchief; "and, oh! *such* a good time as I have had! I was so afraid that I would be a wall-flower and sit up by mamma and papa the whole evening; and as it is, I have had every single dance, and even some dances I had to split. Oh-h!" she breathed, glancing lovingly around the barn, noting again the festoons of tri-coloured cambric, the Japanese lanterns, flaring lamps, and "decorations" of evergreen; "oh-h! it's all so lovely, just like a fairy story; and to think that it can't last but for one little evening, and that to-morrow morning one must wake up to the every-day things again!"

"Well," observed Annixter doggedly, unwilling that she should forget whom she ought to thank, "I did my best, and my best is as good as another man's, I guess."

Hilma overwhelmed him with a burst of gratitude which he gruffly pretended to deprecate. Oh, that was all right. It hadn't cost him much. He liked to see people having a good time himself, and the crowd did seem to be enjoying themselves. What did *she* think? Did things look lively enough? And how about herself—was she enjoying it?

Stupidly Annixter drove the question home again, at his wits' end as to how to make conversation. Hilma protested volubly she would never forget this night, adding:

"Dance! Oh, you don't know how I love it! I didn't know myself. I could dance all night and never stop once!"

Annixter was smitten with uneasiness. No doubt this "promenading" was not at all to her taste. Wondering what kind of a spectacle he was about to make of himself, he exclaimed:

"Want to dance now?"

"Oh, yes!" she returned.

They paused in their walk, and Hilma, facing him, gave herself into his arms. Annixter shut his teeth, the perspiration starting from his forehead. For five years he had abandoned dancing. Never in his best days had it been one of his accomplishments.

They hesitated a moment, waiting to catch the time from the musicians. Another couple bore down upon them at precisely the wrong moment, jostling them out of step. Annixter swore under his breath. His arm still about the young woman, he pulled her over to one corner.

"Now," he muttered, " we'll try again."

A second time, listening to the one-two-three, one-two-three cadence of the musicians, they endeavoured to get under way. Annixter waited the fraction of a second too long and stepped on Hilma's foot. On the third attempt, having worked out of the corner, a pair of dancers bumped into them once more, and as they were recovering themselves another couple caromed violently against Annixter so that he all but lost his footing. He was in a rage. Hilma, very embarrassed, was trying not to laugh, and thus they found themselves, out in the middle of the floor, continually jostled from their position, holding clumsily to each other, stammering excuses into one another's faces, when Delaney arrived.

He came with the suddenness of an explosion. There was a commotion by the doorway, a rolling burst of oaths, a furious stamping of hoofs, a wild scramble of the dancers to either side of the room, and there he was. He had ridden the buckskin at a gallop straight through the doorway and out into the middle of the floor of the barn.

Once well inside, Delaney hauled up on the cruel spade-bit, at the same time driving home the spurs, and the buckskin, without halting in her gait, rose into the air upon her hind feet, and coming down again with a thunder of iron hoofs upon the hollow floor, lashed out with both heels simultaneously, her back arched, her head between her knees. It was the running buck, and had not Delaney been the hardest buster in the county, would have flung him headlong like a sack of sand. But he eased off the bit, gripping the mare's flanks with his knees, and the buckskin, having long since known her master, came to hand quivering, the bloody spume dripping from the bit upon the slippery floor.

Delaney had arrayed himself with painful elaboration, determined to look the part, bent upon creating the impression, resolved that his appearance at least should justify his reputation of being "bad." Nothing was lacking—neither the campaign hat with up-turned brim, nor the dotted blue handkerchief knotted behind the neck, nor the heavy gauntlets stitched with red, nor—this above all—the bear-skin "chaparejos," the hair trousers of the mountain cowboy, the pistol holster low on the thigh. But for the moment this holster was empty, and in his right hand, the hammer at full cock, the chamber loaded, the puncher flourished his teaser, an army Colt's, the lamp-light dully reflected in the dark blue steel.

In a second of time the dance was a bedlam. The musicians stopped with a discord, and the middle of the crowded floor bared itself instantly. It was like sand blown from off a rock; the throng of guests, carried by an impulse that was not to be resisted, bore back against the sides of the barn, overturning chairs, tripping upon each other, falling down, scrambling to their feet again, stepping over one another, getting behind each other, diving under chairs, flattening themselves against the wall—a wild, clamouring pell-mell, blind, deaf, panic-stricken; a confused tangle of waving arms, torn muslin, crushed flowers, pale faces, tangled legs, that swept in all directions back from the centre of the floor, leaving Annixter and Hilma, alone, deserted, their arms about each other, face to face with Delaney, mad with alcohol, bursting with remembered insult, bent on evil, reckless of results.

After the first scramble for safety, the crowd fell quiet for the fraction of an instant, glued to the walls, afraid to stir, struck dumb and motionless with surprise and terror, and in the instant's silence that followed Annixter, his eyes on Delaney, muttered rapidly to Hilma:

"Get back, get away to one side. The fool *might* shoot."

There was a second's respite afforded while Delaney occupied himself in quieting the buckskin, and in that second of time, at this moment of crisis, the wonderful thing occurred. Hilma, turning from Delaney, her hands clasped on Annixter's arm, her eyes meeting his, exclaimed:

"You, too!"

And that was all; but to Annixter it was a revelation. Never more alive to his surroundings, never more observant, he suddenly understood. For the briefest lapse of time he and Hilma looked deep into each other's eyes, and from that moment on, Annixter knew that Hilma cared.

The whole matter was brief as the snapping of a finger. Two words and a glance and all was done. But as though nothing had occurred, Annixter pushed Hilma from him, repeating harshly:

"Get back, I tell you. Don't you see he's got a gun? Haven't I enough on my hands without you?"

He loosed her clasp and his eyes once more on Delaney, moved diagonally backwards toward the side of the barn, pushing Hilma from him. In the end he thrust her away so sharply that she gave back with a long stagger; somebody caught her arm and drew her in, leaving Annixter alone once more in the middle of the floor, his hands in his coat pockets, watchful, alert, facing his enemy.

But the cow-puncher was not ready to come to grapples yet. Fearless, his wits gambolling under the lash of the alcohol, he wished to make the most of the occasion, maintaining the suspense, playing for the gallery. By touches of the hand and knee he kept the buckskin in continual, nervous movement, her hoofs clattering, snorting, tossing her head, while he, himself, addressing himself to Annixter, poured out a torrent of invective.

"Well, strike me blind if it ain't old Buck Annixter! He was going to show me off Quien Sabe at the toe of his boot, was he? Well, here's your chance,—with the ladies to see you do it. Gives a dance, does he, high-falutin' hoe-down in his barn and forgets to invite his old broncho-bustin' friend. But his friend don't forget him; no, he don't. He remembers little things, does his broncho-bustin' friend. Likes to see a dance hisself on occasion, his friend does. Comes anyhow, trustin' his welcome will be hearty; just to see old Buck Annixter dance, just to show Buck Annixter's friends how Buck can dance—dance all by hisself, a little hen-on-a-hot-plate dance when his broncho-bustin' friend asks him so polite. A little dance for the ladies, Buck. This feature of the entertainment is alone worth the price of admission. Tune up, Buck. Attention now! I'll give you the key."

He "fanned" his revolver, spinning it about his index finger by the trigger-guard with incredible swiftness, the twirling weapon a mere blur of blue steel in his hand. Suddenly and without any apparent cessation of the movement, he fired, and a little splinter of wood flipped into the air at Annixter's feet.

"Time!" he shouted, while the buckskin reared to the report. "Hold on—wait a minute. This place is too light to suit. That big light yonder is in my eyes. Look out, I'm going to throw lead."

A second shot put out the lamp over the musicians' stand. The assembled guests shrieked, a frantic, shrinking quiver ran through the crowd like the huddling of frightened rabbits in their pen.

Annixter hardly moved. He stood some thirty paces from

the buster, his hands still in his coat pockets, his eyes glistening, watchful.

Excitable and turbulent in trifling matters, when actual bodily danger threatened he was of an abnormal quiet.

"I'm watching you," cried the other. "Don't make any mistake about that. Keep your hands in your *coat* pockets, if you'd like to live a little longer, understand? And don't let me see you make a move toward your hip or your friends will be asked to identify you at the morgue to-morrow morning. When I'm bad, I'm called the Undertaker's Friend, so I am, and I'm that bad to-night that I'm scared of myself. They'll have to revise the census returns before I'm done with this place. Come on, now, I'm getting tired waiting. I come to see a dance."

"Hand over that horse, Delaney," said Annixter, without raising his voice, "and clear out."

The other affected to be overwhelmed with infinite astonishment, his eyes staring. He peered down from the saddle.

"Wh-a-a-t!" he exclaimed; "wh-a-a-t did you say? Why, I guess you must be looking for trouble; that's what I guess."

"There's where you're wrong, m'son," muttered Annixter, partly to Delaney, partly to himself. "If I was looking for trouble there wouldn't be any guess-work about it."

With the words he began firing. Delaney had hardly entered the barn before Annixter's plan had been formed. Long since his revolver was in the pocket of his coat, and he fired now through the coat itself, without withdrawing his hands.

Until that moment Annixter had not been sure of himself. There was no doubt that for the first few moments of the affair he would have welcomed with joy any reasonable excuse for getting out of the situation. But the sound of his own revolver gave him confidence. He whipped it from his pocket and fired again.

Abruptly the duel began, report following report, spurts of pale blue smoke jetting like the darts of short spears between the two men, expanding to a haze and drifting overhead in wavering strata. It was quite probable that no thought of killing each other suggested itself to either Annixter or Delaney. Both fired without aiming very deliberately. To empty their revolvers and avoid being hit was the desire common to both.

They no longer vituperated each other. The revolvers spoke for them.

Long after, Annixter could recall this moment. For years he could with but little effort reconstruct the scene—the densely packed crowd flattened against the sides of the barn, the festoons of lanterns, the mingled smell of evergreens, new wood, sachets, and powder smoke; the vague clamour of distress and terror that rose from the throng of guests, the squealing of the buckskin, the uneven explosions of the revolvers, the reverberation of trampling hoofs, a brief glimpse of Harran Derrick's excited face at the door of the harness room, and in the open space in the centre of the floor, himself and Delaney, manœuvring swiftly in a cloud of smoke.

Annixter's revolver contained but six cartridges. Already it seemed to him as if he had fired twenty times. Without doubt the next shot was his last. Then what? He peered through the blue haze that with every discharge thickened between him and the buster. For his own safety he must "place" at least one shot. Delaney's chest and shoulders rose suddenly above the smoke close upon him as the distraught buckskin reared again. Annixter, for the first time during the fight, took definite aim, but before he could draw the trigger there was a great shout and he was aware of the buckskin, the bridle trailing, the saddle empty, plunging headlong across the floor, crashing into the line of chairs. Delaney was scrambling off the floor. There was blood on the buster's wrist and he no longer carried his revolver. Suddenly he turned and ran. The crowd parted right and left before him as he made toward the doorway. He disappeared.

Twenty men promptly sprang to the buckskin's head, but she broke away, and wild with terror, bewildered, blind, insensate, charged into the corner of the barn by the musicians' stand. She brought up against the wall with cruel force and with impact of a sack of stones; her head was cut. She turned and charged again, bull-like, the blood streaming from her forehead. The crowd, shrieking, melted before her rush. An old man was thrown down and trampled. The buckskin trod upon the dragging bridle, somersaulted into a confusion of chairs in one corner, and came down with a terrific clatter in a wild disorder of kicking hoofs and splintered wood. But a crowd of men fell upon her, tugging at the bit, sitting on her head, shouting, gesticulating. For five minutes she struggled and fought; then, by degrees, she recovered herself, drawing great sobbing breaths at long intervals that all but burst the girths, rolling her eyes in bewildered, supplicating fashion, trembling in every muscle, and starting and shrinking now and then like a young girl in hysterics. At last she lay quiet. The men allowed her to struggle to her feet. The saddle was removed and she was led to one of the empty stalls, where she remained the rest of the evening, her head low, her pasterns quivering, turning her head apprehensively from time to time, showing the white of one eye and at long intervals heaving a single prolonged sigh.

And an hour later the dance was progressing as evenly as though nothing in the least extraordinary had occurred. The incident was closed—that abrupt swoop of terror and impending death dropping down there from out the darkness, cutting abruptly athwart the gayety of the moment, come and gone with the swiftness of a thunderclap. Many of the women had gone home, taking their men with them; but the great bulk of the crowd still remained, seeing no reason why the episode should interfere with the evening's enjoyment, resolved to hold the ground for mere bravado, if for nothing else. Delaney would not come back, of that everybody was persuaded, and in case he should, there was not found wanting fully half a hundred young men who would give him a dressing down, by jingo! They had been too surprised to act when Delaney had first appeared, and before they knew where they were at, the buster had cleared out. In another minute, just another second, they would have shown him— yes, sir, by jingo!—ah, you bet!

On all sides the reminiscences began to circulate. At least one man in every three had been involved in a gun fight at some time of his life. "Ah, you ought to have seen in Yuba County one time—" "Why, in Butte County in the early days—" "Pshaw! this to-night wasn't anything! Why, once in a saloon in Arizona when I was there—" and so on, over and over again. Osterman solemnly asserted that he had seen a greaser sawn in two in a Nevada sawmill. Old Broderson had witnessed a Vigilante lynching in '55 on California Street in

San Francisco. Dyke recalled how once in his engineering days he had run over a drunk at a street crossing. Gethings of the San Pablo had taken a shot at a highwayman. Hooven had bayonetted a French *Chasseur* at Sedan. An old Spanish-Mexican, a centenarian from Guadalajara, remembered Fremont's stand on a mountain top in San Benito County. The druggist had fired at a burglar trying to break into his store one New Year's eve. Young Vacca had seen a dog shot in Guadalajara. Father Sarria had more than once administered the sacraments to Portuguese desperadoes dying of gunshot wounds. Even the women recalled terrible scenes. Mrs. Cutter recounted to an interested group how she had seen a claim jumped in Placer County in 1851, when three men were shot, falling in a fusillade of rifle shots, and expiring later upon the floor of her kitchen while she looked on. Mrs. Dyke had been in a stage hold-up, when the shotgun messenger was murdered. Stories by the hundreds went the round of the company. The air was surcharged with blood, dying groans, the reek of powder smoke, the crack of rifles. All the legends of '49, the violent, wild life of the early days, were recalled to view, defiling before them there in an endless procession under the glare of paper lanterns and kerosene lamps.

But the affair had aroused a combative spirit amongst the men of the assembly. Instantly a spirit of aggression, of truculence, swelled up underneath waistcoats and starched shirt bosoms. More than one offender was promptly asked to "step outside." It was like young bucks excited by an encounter of stags, lowering their horns upon the slightest provocation, showing off before the does and fawns. Old quarrels were remembered. One sought laboriously for slights and insults, veiled in ordinary conversation. The sense of personal honour became refined to a delicate, fine point. Upon the slightest pretext there was a haughty drawing up of the figure, a twisting of the lips into a smile of scorn. Caraher spoke of shooting S. Behrman on sight before the end of the week. Twice it became necessary to separate Hooven and Cutter, renewing their quarrel as to the ownership of the steer. All at once Minna Hooven's "partner" fell upon the gayly apparelled clerk from Bonneville, pummelling him with his fists, hustling him out of the hall, vociferating that Miss Hooven had been grossly insulted. It took three men to extricate the clerk from his clutches, dazed, gasping, his collar unfastened and sticking up into his face, his eyes staring wildly into the faces of the crowd.

But Annixter, bursting with pride, his chest thrown out, his chin in the air, reigned enthroned in a circle of adulation. He was the Hero. To shake him by the hand was an honour to be struggled for. One clapped him on the back with solemn nods of approval. "There's the *boy* for you;" "There was nerve for you;" "What's the matter with Annixter?" "How about *that* for sand, and how was *that* for a *shot*?" "Why, Apache Kid couldn't have bettered that." "Cool enough." "Took a steady eye and a sure hand to make a shot like that." "There was a shot that would be told about in Tulare County fifty years to come."

Annixter had refrained from replying, all ears to this conversation, wondering just what had happened. He knew only that Delaney had run, leaving his revolver and a spatter of blood behind him. By degrees, however, he ascertained that his last shot but one had struck Delaney's pistol hand, shattering it and knocking the revolver from his grip. He was overwhelmed with astonishment. Why, after the shooting began he had not so much as seen Delaney with any degree of plainness. The whole affair was a whirl.

"Well, where did *you* learn to shoot *that* way?" some one in the crowd demanded. Annixter moved his shoulders with a gesture of vast unconcern.

"Oh," he observed carelessly, "it's not my *shooting* that ever worried *me*, m'son."

The crowd gaped with delight. There was a great wagging of heads.

"Well, I guess not."

"No, sir, not much."

"Ah, no, you bet not."

When the women pressed around him, shaking his hands, declaring that he had saved their daughters' lives, Annixter assumed a pose of superb deprecation, the modest self-obliteration of the chevalier. He delivered himself of a remembered phrase, very elegant, refined. It was Lancelot after the tournament, Bayard receiving felicitations after the battle.

"Oh, don't say anything about it," he murmured. "I only did what any man would have done in my place."

To restore completely the equanimity of the company, he announced supper. This he had calculated as a tremendous surprise. It was to have been served at midnight, but the irruption of Delaney had dislocated the order of events, and the tables were brought in an hour ahead of time. They were arranged around three sides of the barn and were loaded down with cold roasts of beef, cold chickens and cold ducks, mountains of sandwiches, pitchers of milk and lemonade, entire cheeses, bowls of olives, plates of oranges and nuts. The advent of this supper was received with a volley of applause. The musicians played a quick step. The company threw themselves upon the food with a great scraping of chairs and a vast rustle of muslins, tarletans, and organdies; soon the clatter of dishes was a veritable uproar. The tables were taken by assault. One ate whatever was nearest at hand, some even beginning with oranges and nuts and ending with beef and chicken. At the end the paper caps were brought on, together with the ice cream. All up and down the tables the pulled "crackers" snapped continually like the discharge of innumerable tiny rifles. The caps of tissue paper were put on—"Phrygian Bonnets," "Magicians' Caps," "Liberty Caps;" the young girls looked across the table at their vis-a-vis with bursts of laughter and vigorous clapping of the hands.

The harness room crowd had a table to themselves, at the head of which sat Annixter and at the foot Harran. The gun fight had sobered Presley thoroughly. He sat by the side of Vanamee, who ate but little, preferring rather to watch the scene with calm observation, a little contemptuous when the uproar around the table was too boisterous, savouring of intoxication. Osterman rolled bullets of bread and shot them with astonishing force up and down the table, but the others—Dyke, old Broderson, Caraher, Harran Derrick, Hooven, Cutter, Garnett of the Ruby rancho, Keast from the ranch of the same name, Gethings of the San Pablo, and Chattern of the Bonanza—occupied themselves with eating as much as they could before the supper gave out. At a corner of the table, speechless, unobserved, ignored, sat Dabney, of whom nothing was known but his name, the silent old man who made no friends. He ate and drank quietly, dipping his sandwich in his lemonade.

Osterman ate all the olives he could lay his hands on, a score of them, fifty of them, a hundred of them. He touched no crumb of anything else. Old Broderson stared at him, his jaw fallen. Osterman declared he had once eaten a thousand on a bet. The men called each others' attention to him. Delighted to create a sensation, Osterman persevered. The contents of an entire bowl disappeared in his huge, reptilian slit of a mouth. His cheeks of brownish red were extended, his bald forehead glistened. Colics seized upon him. His stomach revolted. It was all one with him. He was satisfied, contented. He was astonishing the people.

"Once I swallowed a tree toad," he told old Broderson, "by mistake. I was eating grapes, and the beggar lived in me three weeks. In rainy weather he would sing. You don't believe that," he vociferated. "Haven't I got the toad at home now in a bottle of alcohol."

And the old man, never doubting, his eyes starting, wagged his head in amazement.

"Oh, yes," cried Caraher, the length of the table, "that's a pretty good one. Tell us another."

"That reminds me of a story," hazarded old Broderson uncertainly; "once when I was a lad in Ukiah, fifty years——"

"Oh, yes," cried half a dozen voices, "*that's* a pretty good one. Tell us another."

"Eh—wh—what?" murmured Broderson, looking about him. "I—I don't know. It *was* Ukiah. You—you—you mix me all up."

As soon as supper was over, the floor was cleared again. The guests clamoured for a Virginia reel. The last quarter of the evening, the time of the most riotous fun, was beginning. The young men caught the girls who sat next to them. The orchestra dashed off into a rollicking movement. The two lines were formed. In a second of time the dance was under way again; the guests still wearing the Phrygian bonnets and liberty caps of pink and blue tissue paper.

But the group of men once more adjourned to the harness room. Fresh boxes of cigars were opened; the seventh bowl of fertiliser was mixed. Osterman poured the dregs of a glass of it upon his bald head, declaring that he could feel the hair beginning to grow.

But suddenly old Broderson rose to his feet.

"Aha," he cackled, "*I'm* going to have a dance, I am. Think I'm too old? I'll show you young fellows. I'm a regular old *rooster* when I get started."

He marched out into the barn, the others following, holding their sides. He found an aged Mexican woman by the door and hustled her, all confused and giggling, into the Virginia reel, then at its height. Every one crowded around to see. Old Broderson stepped off with the alacrity of a colt, snapping his fingers, slapping his thigh, his mouth widening in an excited grin. The entire company of the guests shouted. The City Band redoubled their efforts; and the old man, losing his head, breathless, gasping, dislocated his stiff joints in his efforts. He became possessed, bowing, scraping, advancing, retreating, wagging his beard, cutting pigeons' wings, distraught with the music, the clamour, the applause, the effects of the fertiliser.

Annixter shouted:

"Nice eye, Santa Claus."

But Annixter's attention wandered. He searched for Hilma Tree, having still in mind the look in her eyes at that swift moment of danger. He had not seen her since then. At last he caught sight of her. She was not dancing, but, instead, was sitting with her "partner" at the end of the barn near her father and mother, her eyes wide, a serious expression on her face, her thoughts, no doubt, elsewhere. Annixter was about to go to her when he was interrupted by a cry.

Old Broderson, in the midst of a double shuffle, had clapped his hand to his side with a gasp, which he followed by a whoop of anguish. He had got a stitch or had started a twinge somewhere. With a gesture of resignation, he drew himself laboriously out of the dance, limping abominably, one leg dragging. He was heard asking for his wife. Old Mrs. Broderson took him in charge. She jawed him for making an exhibition of himself, scolding as though he were a ten-year-old.

"Well, I want to know!" she exclaimed, as he hobbled off, dejected and melancholy, leaning upon her arm, "thought he had to dance, indeed! What next? A gay old grandpa, this. He'd better be thinking of his coffin."

It was almost midnight. The dance drew towards its close in a storm of jubilation. The perspiring musicians toiled like galley slaves; the guests singing as they danced.

The group of men reassembled in the harness room. Even Magnus Derrick condescended to enter and drink a toast. Presley and Vanamee, still holding themselves aloof, looked on, Vanamee more and more disgusted. Dabney, standing to one side, overlooked and forgotten, continued to sip steadily at his glass, solemn, reserved. Garnett of the Ruby rancho, Keast from the ranch of the same name, Gethings of the San Pablo, and Chattern of the Bonanza, leaned back in their chairs, their waistcoats unbuttoned, their legs spread wide, laughing—they could not tell why. Other ranchers, men whom Annixter had never seen, appeared in the room, wheat growers from places as far distant as Goshen and Pixley; young men and old, proprietors of veritable principalities, hundreds of thousands of acres of wheat lands, a dozen of them, a score of them; men who were strangers to each other, but who made it a point to shake hands with Magnus Derrick, the "prominent man" of the valley. Old Broderson, whom every one had believed had gone home, returned, though much sobered, and took his place, refusing, however, to drink another spoonful.

Soon the entire number of Annixter's guests found themselves in two companies, the dancers on the floor of the barn, frolicking through the last figures of the Virginia reel and the boisterous gathering of men in the harness room, downing the last quarts of fertiliser. Both assemblies had been increased. Even the older people had joined in the dance, while nearly every one of the men who did not dance had found their way into the harness room. The two groups rivalled each other in their noise. Out on the floor of the barn was a very whirlwind of gayety, a tempest of laughter, hand-clapping and cries of amusement. In the harness room the confused shouting and singing, the stamping of heavy feet, set a quivering reverberation in the oil of the kerosene lamps, the flame of the candles in the Japanese lanterns flaring and swaying in the gusts of hilarity. At intervals, between the two, one heard the music, the wailing of the violins, the vigorous snarling of the cornet, and the harsh, incessant rasping of the snare drum.

And at times all these various sounds mingled in a single vague note, huge, clamorous, that rose up into the night from the colossal, reverberating compass of the barn and sent its echoes far off across the unbroken levels of the surrounding ranches, stretching out to infinity under the clouded sky, calm, mysterious, still.

Annixter, the punch bowl clasped in his arms, was pouring out the last spoonful of liquor into Caraher's glass when he was aware that some one was pulling at the sleeve of his coat. He set down the punch bowl.

"Well, where did *you* come from?" he demanded.

It was a messenger from Bonneville, the uniformed boy that the telephone company employed to carry messages. He had just arrived from town on his bicycle, out of breath and panting.

"Message for you, sir. Will you sign?"

He held the book to Annixter, who signed the receipt, wondering.

The boy departed, leaving a thick envelope of yellow paper in Annixter's hands, the address typewritten, the word "Urgent" written in blue pencil in one corner.

Annixter tore it open. The envelope contained other sealed envelopes, some eight or ten of them, addressed to Magnus Derrick, Osterman, Broderson, Garnett, Keast, Gethings, Chattern, Dabney, and to Annixter himself.

Still puzzled, Annixter distributed the envelopes, muttering to himself:

"What's up now?"

The incident had attracted attention. A comparative quiet followed, the guests following the letters with their eyes as they were passed around the table. They fancied that Annixter had arranged a surprise.

Magnus Derrick, who sat next to Annixter, was the first to receive his letter. With a word of excuse he opened it.

"Read it, read it, Governor," shouted a half-dozen voices. "No secrets, you know. Everything above board here to-night."

Magnus cast a glance at the contents of the letter, then rose to his feet and read:

Magnus Derrick,
    Bonneville, Tulare Co., Cal.
Dear Sir:
By regrade of October 1st, the value of the railroad land you occupy, included in your ranch of Los Muertos, has been fixed at $27.00 per acre. The land is now for sale at that price to any one.

Yours, etc.,

CYRUS BLAKELEE RUGGLES,
Land Agent, P. and S. W. R. R.

S. BEHRMAN,
Local Agent, P. and S. W. R. R.

In the midst of the profound silence that followed, Osterman was heard to exclaim grimly:

"*That's* a pretty good one. Tell us another."

But for a long moment this was the only remark.

The silence widened, broken only by the sound of torn paper as Annixter, Osterman, old Broderson, Garnett, Keast, Gethings, Chattern, and Dabney opened and read their letters. They were all to the same effect, almost word for word like the Governor's. Only the figures and the proper names varied. In some cases the price per acre was twenty-two dollars. In Annixter's case it was thirty.

"And—and the company promised to sell to me, to—to all of us," gasped old Broderson, "at *two dollars and a half* an acre."

It was not alone the ranchers immediately around Bonneville who would be plundered by this move on the part of the Railroad. The "alternate section" system applied throughout all the San Joaquin. By striking at the Bonneville ranchers a terrible precedent was established. Of the crowd of guests in the harness room alone, nearly every man was affected, every man menaced with ruin. All of a million acres was suddenly involved.

Then suddenly the tempest burst. A dozen men were on their feet in an instant, their teeth set, their fists clenched, their faces purple with rage. Oaths, curses, maledictions exploded like the firing of successive mines. Voices quivered with wrath, hands flung upward, the fingers hooked, prehensile, trembled with anger. The sense of wrongs, the injustices, the oppression, extortion, and pillage of twenty years suddenly culminated and found voice in a raucous howl of execration. For a second there was nothing articulate in that cry of savage exasperation, nothing even intelligent. It was the human animal hounded to its corner, exploited, harried to its last stand, at bay, ferocious, terrible, turning at last with bared teeth and upraised claws to meet the death grapple. It was the hideous squealing of the tormented brute, its back to the wall, defending its lair, its mate and its whelps, ready to bite, to rend, to trample, to batter out the life of The Enemy in a primeval, bestial welter of blood and fury.

The roar subsided to intermittent clamour, in the pauses of which the sounds of music and dancing made themselves audible once more.

"S. Behrman again," vociferated Harran Derrick.

"Chose his moment well," muttered Annixter. "Hits his hardest when we're all rounded up having a good time."

"Gentlemen, this is ruin."

"What's to be done now?"

"*Fight!* My God! do you think we are going to stand this? Do you think we *can*?"

The uproar swelled again. The clearer the assembly of ranchers understood the significance of this move on the part of the Railroad, the more terrible it appeared, the more flagrant, the more intolerable. Was it possible, was it within the bounds of imagination that this tyranny should be contemplated? But they knew—past years had driven home the lesson—the implacable, iron monster with whom they had to deal, and again and again the sense of outrage and oppression lashed them to their feet, their mouths wide with curses, their fists clenched tight, their throats hoarse with shouting.

"Fight! How fight? What *are* you going to do?"

"If there's a law in this land——"

"If there is, it is in Shelgrim's pocket. Who owns the courts in California? Ain't it Shelgrim?"

"God damn him."

"Well, how long are you going to stand it? How long before you'll settle up accounts with six inches of plugged gas-pipe?"

"And our contracts, the solemn pledges of the corporation to sell to us first of all——"

"And now the land is for sale to anybody."

"Why, it is a question of my home. Am I to be turned out? Why, I have put eight thousand dollars into improving this land."

"And I six thousand, and now that I have, the Railroad grabs it."

"And the system of irrigating ditches that Derrick and I have been laying out. There's thousands of dollars in that!"

"I'll fight this out till I've spent every cent of my money."

"Where? In the courts that the company owns?"

"Think I am going to give in to this? Think I am to get off my land? By God, gentlemen, law or no law, railroad or no railroad, I—will—not."

"Nor I."

"Nor I."

"Nor I."

"This is the last. Legal means first; if those fail—the shotgun."

"They can kill me. They can shoot me down, but I'll die—die fighting for my home—before I'll give in to this."

At length Annixter made himself heard:

"All out of the room but the ranch owners," he shouted. "Hooven, Caraher, Dyke, you'll have to clear out. This is a family affair. Presley, you and your friend can remain."

Reluctantly the others filed through the door. There remained in the harness room—besides Vanamee and Presley— Magnus Derrick, Annixter, old Broderson, Harran, Garnett from the Ruby rancho, Keast from the ranch of the same name, Gethings of the San Pablo, Chattern of the Bonanza, about a score of others, ranchers from various parts of the county, and, last of all, Dabney, ignored, silent, to whom nobody spoke and who, as yet, had not uttered a word.

But the men who had been asked to leave the harness room spread the news throughout the barn. It was repeated from lip to lip. One by one the guests dropped out of the dance. Groups were formed. By swift degrees the gayety lapsed away. The Virginia reel broke up. The musicians ceased playing, and in the place of the noisy, effervescent revelry of the previous half hour, a subdued murmur filled all the barn, a mingling of whispers, lowered voices, the coming and going of light footsteps, the uneasy shifting of positions, while from behind the closed doors of the harness room came a prolonged, sullen hum of anger and strenuous debate. The dance came to an abrupt end. The guests, unwilling to go as yet, stunned, distressed, stood clumsily about, their eyes vague, their hands swinging at their sides, looking stupidly into each others' faces. A sense of impending calamity, oppressive, foreboding, gloomy, passed through the air overhead in the night, a long shiver of anguish and of terror, mysterious, despairing.

In the harness room, however, the excitement continued unchecked. One rancher after another delivered himself of a torrent of furious words. There was no order, merely the frenzied outcry of blind fury. One spirit alone was common to all—resistance at whatever cost and to whatever lengths.

Suddenly Osterman leaped to his feet, his bald head gleaming in the lamp-light, his red ears distended, a flood of words filling his great, horizontal slit of a mouth, his comic actor's face flaming. Like the hero of a melodrama, he took stage with a great sweeping gesture.

"*Organisation,*" he shouted, "that must be our watch-word. The curse of the ranchers is that they fritter away their strength. Now, we must stand together, now, *now*. Here's the crisis, here's the moment. Shall we meet it? *I call for the League*. Not next week, not to-morrow, not in the morning, but now, now, now, this very moment, before we go out of that door. Every one of us here to join it, to form the beginnings of a vast organisation, banded together to death, if needs be, for the protection of our rights and homes. Are you ready? Is it now or never? I call for the League."

Instantly there was a shout. With an actor's instinct, Osterman had spoken at the precise psychological moment. He carried the others off their feet, glib, dexterous, voluble. Just what was meant by the League the others did not know, but it was something, a vague engine, a machine with which to fight. Osterman had not done speaking before the room rang with outcries, the crowd of men shouting, for what they did not know.

"The League! The League!"

"Now, to-night, this moment; sign our names before we leave."

"He's right. Organisation! The League!"

"We have a committee at work already," Osterman vociferated. "I am a member, and also Mr. Broderson, Mr. Annixter, and Mr. Harran Derrick. What our aims are we will explain to you later. Let this committee be the nucleus of the League—temporarily, at least. Trust us. We are working for you and with you. Let this committee be merged into the larger committee of the League, and for President of the League"—he paused the fraction of a second—"for President there can be but one name mentioned, one man to whom we all must look as leader—Magnus Derrick."

The Governor's name was received with a storm of cheers. The harness room reëchoed with shouts of:

"Derrick! Derrick!"

"Magnus for President!"

"Derrick, our natural leader."

"Derrick, Derrick, Derrick for President."

Magnus rose to his feet. He made no gesture. Erect as a cavalry officer, tall, thin, commanding, he dominated the crowd in an instant. There was a moment's hush.

"Gentlemen," he said, "if organisation is a good word, moderation is a better one. The matter is too grave for haste. I would suggest that we each and severally return to our respective homes for the night, sleep over what has happened, and convene again to-morrow, when we are calmer and can approach this affair in a more judicious mood. As for the honour with which you would inform me, I must affirm that that, too, is a matter for grave deliberation. This League is but a name as yet. To accept control of an organisation whose principles are not yet fixed is a heavy responsibility. I shrink from it——"

But he was allowed to proceed no farther. A storm of protest developed. There were shouts of:

"No, no. The League to-night and Derrick for President."

"We have been moderate too long."

"The League first, principles afterward."

"We can't wait," declared Osterman. "Many of us cannot attend a meeting to-morrow. Our business affairs would prevent it. Now we are all together. I propose a temporary chairman and secretary be named and a ballot be taken. But first the League. Let us draw up a set of resolutions to stand together, for the defence of our homes, to death, if needs be, and each man present affix his signature thereto."

He subsided amidst vigorous applause. The next quarter of an hour was a vague confusion, every one talking at once, conversations going on in low tones in various corners of the room. Ink, pens, and a sheaf of foolscap were brought from the ranch house. A set of resolutions was draughted, having the force of a pledge, organising the League of Defence. Annixter was the first to sign. Others followed, only a few holding back, refusing to join till they had thought the matter over. The roll grew; the paper circulated about the table; each signature was welcomed by a salvo of cheers. At length, it reached Harran Derrick, who signed amid tremendous uproar. He released the pen only to shake a score of hands.

"Now, Magnus Derrick."

"Gentlemen," began the Governor, once more rising, "I beg of you to allow me further consideration. Gentlemen——"

He was interrupted by renewed shouting.

"No, no, now or never. Sign, join the League."

"Don't leave us. We look to you to help."

But presently the excited throng that turned their faces towards the Governor were aware of a new face at his elbow. The door of the harness room had been left unbolted and Mrs. Derrick, unable to endure the heart-breaking suspense of waiting outside, had gathered up all her courage and had come into the room. Trembling, she clung to Magnus's arm, her pretty light-brown hair in disarray, her large young girl's eyes wide with terror and distrust. What was about to happen she did not understand, but these men were clamouring for Magnus to pledge himself to something, to some terrible course of action, some ruthless, unscrupulous battle to the death with the iron-hearted monster of steel and steam. Nerved with a coward's intrepidity, she, who so easily obliterated herself, had found her way into the midst of this frantic crowd, into this hot, close room, reeking of alcohol and tobacco smoke, into this atmosphere surcharged with hatred and curses. She seized her husband's arm imploring, distraught with terror.

"No, no," she murmured; "no, don't sign."

She was the feather caught in the whirlwind. *En masse*, the crowd surged toward the erect figure of the Governor, the pen in one hand, his wife's fingers in the other, the roll of signatures before him. The clamour was deafening; the excitement culminated brusquely. Half a hundred hands stretched toward him; thirty voices, at top pitch, implored, expostulated, urged, almost commanded. The reverberation of the shouting was as the plunge of a cataract.

It was the uprising of The People; the thunder of the outbreak of revolt; the mob demanding to be led, aroused at last, imperious, resistless, overwhelming. It was the blind fury of insurrection, the brute, many-tongued, red-eyed, bellowing for guidance, baring its teeth, unsheathing its claws, imposing its will with the abrupt, resistless pressure of the relaxed piston, inexorable, knowing no pity.

"No, no," implored Annie Derrick. "No, Magnus, don't sign."

"He *must*," declared Harran, shouting in her ear to make himself heard, "he must. Don't you understand?"

Again the crowd surged forward, roaring. Mrs. Derrick was swept back, pushed to one side. Her husband no longer belonged to her. She paid the penalty for being the wife of a great man. The world, like a colossal iron wedge, crushed itself between. She was thrust to the wall. The throng of men, stamping, surrounded Magnus; she could no longer see him, but, terror-struck, she listened. There was a moment's lull, then a vast thunder of savage jubilation. Magnus had signed.

Harran found his mother leaning against the wall, her hands shut over her ears; her eyes, dilated with fear, brimming with tears. He led her from the harness room to the outer room, where Mrs. Tree and Hilma took charge of her, and then, impatient, refusing to answer the hundreds of anxious questions that assailed him, hurried back to the harness room.

Already the balloting was in progress, Osterman acting as temporary chairman. On the very first ballot he was made secretary of the League *pro tem.*, and Magnus unanimously chosen for its President. An executive committee was formed, which was to meet the next day at the Los Muertos ranch house.

It was half-past one o'clock. In the barn outside the greater number of the guests had departed. Long since the musicians had disappeared. There only remained the families of the ranch owners involved in the meeting in the harness room. These huddled in isolated groups in corners of the garish, echoing barn, the women in their wraps, the young men with their coat collars turned up against the draughts that once more made themselves felt.

For a long half hour the loud hum of eager conversation continued to issue from behind the door of the harness room. Then, at length, there was a prolonged scraping of chairs. The session was over. The men came out in groups, searching for their families.

At once the homeward movement began. Every one was worn out. Some of the ranchers' daughters had gone to sleep against their mothers' shoulders.

Billy, the stableman, and his assistant were awakened, and the teams were hitched up. The stable yard was full of a maze of swinging lanterns and buggy lamps. The horses fretted, champing the bits; the carry-alls creaked with the straining of leather and springs as they received their loads. At every instant one heard the rattle of wheels, as vehicle after vehicle disappeared in the night. A fine, drizzling rain was falling, and the lamps began to show dim in a vague haze of orange light.

Magnus Derrick was the last to go. At the doorway of the barn he found Annixter, the roll of names—which it had been decided he was to keep in his safe for the moment—under his arm. Silently the two shook hands. Magnus departed. The grind of the wheels of his carry-all grated sharply on the gravel of the driveway in front of the ranch house, then, with a hollow roll across a little plank bridge, gained the roadway. For a moment the beat of the horses' hoofs made itself heard on the roadway. It ceased. Suddenly there was a great silence.

Annixter, in the doorway of the great barn, stood looking about him for a moment, alone, thoughtful. The barn was empty. That astonishing evening had come to an end. The whirl of things and people, the crowd of dancers, Delaney, the gun fight, Hilma Tree, her eyes fixed on him in mute confession, the rabble in the harness room, the news of the regrade, the fierce outburst of wrath, the hasty organising of the League, all went spinning confusedly through his recollection. But he was exhausted. Time enough in the morning to think it all over. By now it was raining sharply. He put the roll of names into his inside pocket, threw a sack over his head and shoulders, and went down to the ranch house.

But in the harness room, lighted by the glittering lanterns and flaring lamps, in the midst of overturned chairs, spilled liquor, cigar stumps, and broken glasses, Vanamee and Presley still remained talking, talking. At length, they rose, and came out upon the floor of the barn and stood for a moment looking about them.

Billy, the stableman, was going the rounds of the walls, putting out light after light. By degrees, the vast interior was growing dim. Upon the roof overhead the rain drummed incessantly, the eaves dripping. The floor was littered with pine needles, bits of orange peel, ends and fragments of torn organdies and muslins and bits of tissue paper from the "Phrygian Bonnets" and "Liberty Caps." The buckskin mare in the stall, dozing on three legs, changed position with a long sigh. The sweat stiffening the hair upon her back and loins, as it dried, gave off a penetrating, ammoniacal odour that mingled with the stale perfume of sachet and wilted flowers.

Presley and Vanamee stood looking at the deserted barn. There was a long silence. Then Presley said:

"Well . . . what do you think of it all?"

"I think," answered Vanamee slowly, "I think that there was a dance in Brussels the night before Waterloo."

BOOK II

I

IN HIS OFFICE at San Francisco, seated before a massive desk of polished redwood, very ornate, Lyman Derrick sat dictating letters to his typewriter, on a certain morning early in the spring of the year. The subdued monotone of his voice proceeded evenly from sentence to sentence, regular, precise, businesslike.

"I have the honour to acknowledge herewith your favour of the 14th instant, and in reply would state——"

"Please find enclosed draft upon New Orleans to be applied as per our understanding——"

"In answer to your favour No. 1107, referring to the case of the City and County of San Francisco against Excelsior Warehouse & Storage Co., I would say——"

His voice continued, expressionless, measured, distinct. While he spoke, he swung slowly back and forth in his leather swivel chair, his elbows resting on the arms, his pop eyes fixed vaguely upon the calendar on the opposite wall, winking at intervals when he paused, searching for a word.

"That's all for the present," he said at length.

Without reply, the typewriter rose and withdrew, thrusting her pencil into the coil of her hair, closing the door behind her, softly, discreetly.

When she had gone, Lyman rose, stretching himself, putting up three fingers to hide his yawn. To further loosen his muscles, he took a couple of turns the length of the room, noting with satisfaction its fine appointments, the padded red carpet, the dull olive green tint of the walls, the few choice engravings—portraits of Marshall, Taney, Field, and a coloured lithograph—excellently done—of the Grand Cañon of the Colorado—the deep-seated leather chairs, the large and crowded bookcase (topped with a bust of James Lick, and a huge greenish globe), the waste basket of woven coloured grass, made by Navajo Indians, the massive silver inkstand on the desk, the elaborate filing cabinet, complete in every particular, and the shelves of tin boxes, padlocked, impressive, grave, bearing the names of clients, cases and estates.

He was between thirty-one and thirty-five years of age. Unlike Harran, he resembled his mother, but he was much darker than Annie Derrick and his eyes were much fuller, the eyeball protruding, giving him a pop-eyed, foreign expression, quite unusual and unexpected. His hair was black, and he wore a small, tight, pointed mustache, which he was in the habit of pushing delicately upward from the corners of his lips with the ball of his thumb, the little finger extended. As often as he made this gesture, he prefaced it with a little twisting gesture of the forearm in order to bring his cuff into view, and, in fact, this movement by itself was habitual.

He was dressed carefully, his trousers creased, a pink rose in his lapel. His shoes were of patent leather, his cutaway coat was of very rough black cheviot, his double-breasted waistcoat of tan covert cloth with buttons of smoked pearl. An Ascot scarf—a great puff of heavy black silk—was at his neck, the knot transfixed by a tiny golden pin set off with an opal and four small diamonds.

At one end of the room were two great windows of plate glass, and pausing at length before one of these, Lyman selected a cigarette from his curved box of oxydized silver, lit it and stood looking down and out, willing to be idle for a moment, amused and interested in the view.

His office was on the tenth floor of the *Exchange Building*, a beautiful, tower-like affair of white stone, that stood on the corner of Market Street near its intersection with Kearney, the most imposing office building of the city.

Below him the city swarmed tumultuous through its grooves, the cable-cars starting and stopping with a gay jangling of bells and a strident whirring of jostled glass windows. Drays and carts clattered over the cobbles, and an incessant shuffling of thousands of feet rose from the pavement. Around Lotta's fountain the baskets of the flower sellers, crammed with chrysanthemums, violets, pinks, roses, lilies, hyacinths, set a brisk note of colour in the grey of the street.

But to Lyman's notion the general impression of this centre of the city's life was not one of strenuous business activity. It was a continuous interest in small things, a people ever willing to be amused at trifles, refusing to consider serious matters—good-natured, allowing themselves to be imposed upon, taking life easily—generous, companionable, enthusiastic; living, as it were, from day to day, in a place where the luxuries of life were had without effort; in a city that offered to consideration the restlessness of a New York, without its earnestness; the serenity of a Naples, without its languor; the romance of a Seville, without its picturesqueness.

As Lyman turned from the window, about to resume his work, the office boy appeared at the door.

"The man from the lithograph company, sir," announced the boy.

"Well, what does he want?" demanded Lyman, adding, however, upon the instant: "Show him in."

A young man entered, carrying a great bundle, which he deposited on a chair, with a gasp of relief, exclaiming, all out of breath:

"From the Standard Lithograph Company."

"What is?"

"Don't know," replied the other. "Maps, I guess."

"I don't want any maps. Who sent them? I guess you're mistaken."

Lyman tore the cover from the top of the package, drawing out one of a great many huge sheets of white paper, folded eight times. Suddenly, he uttered an exclamation:

"Ah, I see. They *are* maps. But these should not have come here. They are to go to the regular office for distribution." He wrote a new direction on the label of the package: "Take them to that address," he went on. "I'll keep this one here. The others go to that address. If you see Mr. Darrell, tell him that Mr. Derrick—you get the name—Mr. Derrick may not be able to get around this afternoon, but to go ahead with any business just the same."

The young man departed with the package and Lyman, spreading out the map upon the table, remained for some time studying it thoughtfully.

It was a commissioner's official railway map of the State of California, completed to March 30th of that year. Upon it the different railways of the State were accurately plotted in various colours, blue, green, yellow. However, the blue, the yellow, and the green were but brief traceries, very short, isolated, unimportant. At a little distance these could hardly be seen. The whole map was gridironed by a vast, complicated network of red lines marked P. and S. W. R. R. These centralised at San Francisco and thence ramified and spread north, east, and south, to every quarter of the State. From Coles, in the topmost corner of the map, to Yuma in the lowest, from Reno on one side to San Francisco on the other, ran the plexus of red, a veritable system of blood circulation, complicated, dividing, and reuniting, branching, splitting, extending, throwing out feelers, off-shoots, tap roots, feeders— diminutive little blood suckers that shot out from the main jugular and went twisting up into some remote county, laying hold upon some forgotten village or town, involving it in one of a myriad branching coils, one of a hundred tentacles, drawing it, as it were, toward that centre from which all this system sprang.

The map was white, and it seemed as if all the colour which should have gone to vivify the various counties, towns, and cities marked upon it had been absorbed by that huge, sprawling organism, with its ruddy arteries converging to a central point. It was as though the State had been sucked white and colourless, and against this pallid background the red arteries of the monster stood out, swollen with life-blood, reaching out to infinity, gorged to bursting; an excrescence, a gigantic parasite fattening upon the life-blood of an entire commonwealth.

However, in an upper corner of the map appeared the names of the three new commissioners: Jones McNish for the first district, Lyman Derrick for the second, and James Darrell for the third.

Nominated in the Democratic State convention in the fall of the preceding year, Lyman, backed by the coteries of San Francisco bosses in the pay of his father's political committee of ranchers, had been elected together with Darrell, the candidate of the Pueblo and Mojave road, and McNish, the avowed candidate of the Pacific and Southwestern. Darrell was rabidly against the P. and S. W., McNish rabidly for it. Lyman was supposed to be the conservative member of the board, the ranchers' candidate, it was true, and faithful to their interests, but a calm man, deliberative, swayed by no such violent emotions as his colleagues.

Osterman's dexterity had at last succeeded in entangling Magnus inextricably in the new politics. The famous League, organised in the heat of passion the night of Annixter's barn dance, had been consolidated all through the winter months. Its executive committee, of which Magnus was chairman, had been, through Osterman's manipulation, merged into the old committee composed of Broderson, Annixter, and himself. Promptly thereat he had resigned the chairmanship of this committee, thus leaving Magnus at its head. Precisely as Osterman had planned, Magnus was now one of them. The new committee accordingly had two objects in view: to resist the attempted grabbing of their lands by the Railroad, and to push forward their own secret scheme of electing a board of railroad commissioners who should regulate wheat rates so as to favour the ranchers of the San Joaquin. The land cases were promptly taken to the courts and the new grading—fixing the price of the lands at twenty and thirty dollars an acre instead of two—bitterly and stubbornly fought. But delays occurred, the process of the law was interminable, and in the intervals the committee addressed itself to the work of seating the "Ranchers' Commission," as the projected Board of Commissioners came to be called.

It was Harran who first suggested that his brother, Lyman, be put forward as the candidate for this district. At once the proposition had a great success. Lyman seemed made for the place. While allied by every tie of blood to the ranching interests, he had never been identified with them. He was city-bred. The Railroad would not be over-suspicious of him. He was a good lawyer, a good business man, keen, clear-headed, far-sighted, had already some practical knowledge of politics, having served a term as assistant district attorney, and even at the present moment occupying the position of sheriff's attorney. More than all, he was the son of Magnus Derrick; he could be relied upon, could be trusted implicitly to remain loyal to the ranchers' cause.

The campaign for Railroad Commissioner had been very interesting. At the very outset Magnus's committee found itself involved in corrupt politics. The primaries had to be captured at all costs and by any means, and when the convention assembled it was found necessary to buy outright the votes of certain delegates. The campaign fund raised by contributions from Magnus, Annixter, Broderson, and Osterman was drawn upon to the extent of five thousand dollars.

Only the committee knew of this corruption. The League, ignoring ways and means, supposed as a matter of course that the campaign was honorably conducted.

For a whole week after the consummation of this part of the deal, Magnus had kept to his house, refusing to be seen, alleging that he was ill, which was not far from the truth. The shame of the business, the loathing of what he had done, were to him things unspeakable. He could no longer look Harran in the face. He began a course of deception with his wife. More than once, he had resolved to break with the whole affair, resigning his position, allowing the others to proceed without him. But now it was too late. He was pledged. He had joined the League. He was its chief, and his defection might mean its disintegration at the very time when it needed all its strength to fight the land cases. More than a mere deal in bad politics was involved. There was the land grab. His withdrawal from an unholy cause would mean the weakening, perhaps the collapse, of another cause that he believed to be righteous as truth itself. He was hopelessly caught in the mesh. Wrong seemed indissolubly knitted into the texture of Right. He was blinded, dizzied, overwhelmed, caught in the current of events, and hurried along he knew not where. He resigned himself.

In the end, and after much ostentatious opposition on the part of the railroad heelers, Lyman was nominated and subsequently elected.

When this consummation was reached Magnus, Osterman, Broderson, and Annixter stared at each other. Their wildest hopes had not dared to fix themselves upon so easy a victory as this. It was not believable that the corporation would allow itself to be fooled so easily, would rush open-eyed into the trap. How had it happened?

Osterman, however, threw his hat into the air with wild whoops of delight. Old Broderson permitted himself a feeble cheer. Even Magnus beamed satisfaction. The other members of the League, present at the time, shook hands all around and spoke of opening a few bottles on the strength of the occasion. Annixter alone was recalcitrant.

"It's too easy," he declared. "No, I'm not satisfied. Where's Shelgrim in all this? Why don't he show his hand, damn his soul? The thing is yellow, I tell you. There's a big fish in these waters somewheres. I don't know his name, and I don't know his game, but he's moving round off and on, just out of sight. If you think you've netted him, I *don't*, that's all I've got to say."

But he was jeered down as a croaker. There was the Commission. He couldn't get around that, could he? There was Darrell and Lyman Derrick, both pledged to the ranches. Good Lord, he was never satisfied. He'd be obstinate till the very last gun was fired. Why, if he got drowned in a river he'd float up-stream just to be contrary.

In the course of time, the new board was seated. For the first few months of its term, it was occupied in clearing up the business left over by the old board and in the completion of the railway map. But now, the decks were cleared. It was about to address itself to the consideration of a revision of the tariff for the carriage of grain between the San Joaquin Valley and tide-water.

Both Lyman and Darrell were pledged to an average ten per cent. cut of the grain rates throughout the entire State.

The typewriter returned with the letters for Lyman to sign, and he put away the map and took up his morning's routine of business, wondering, the while, what would become of his practice during the time he was involved in the business of the Ranchers' Railroad Commission.

But towards noon, at the moment when Lyman was drawing off a glass of mineral water from the siphon that stood at his elbow, there was an interruption. Some one rapped vigorously upon the door, which was immediately after opened, and Magnus and Harran came in, followed by Presley.

"Hello, hello!" cried Lyman, jumping up, extending his hands, "why, here's a surprise. I didn't expect you all till to-night. Come in, come in and sit down. Have a glass of sizz-water, Governor."

The others explained that they had come up from Bonne-ville the night before, as the Executive Committee of the

League had received a despatch from the lawyers it had retained to fight the Railroad, that the judge of the court in
San Francisco, where the test cases were being tried, might
be expected to hand down his decision the next day.

Very soon after the announcement of the new grading of
the ranchers' lands, the corporation had offered, through S.
Behrman, to lease the disputed lands to the ranchers at a
nominal figure. The offer had been angrily rejected, and the
Railroad had put up the lands for sale at Ruggles's office in
Bonneville. At the exorbitant price named, buyers promptly
appeared—dummy buyers, beyond shadow of doubt, acting
either for the Railroad or for S. Behrman—men hitherto unknown in the county, men without property, without money,
adventurers, heelers. Prominent among them, and bidding for
the railroad's holdings included on Annixter's ranch, was
Delaney.

The farce of deeding the corporation's sections to these fictitious purchasers was solemnly gone through with at Ruggles's office, the Railroad guaranteeing them possession. The
League refused to allow the supposed buyers to come upon
the land, and the Railroad, faithful to its pledge in the matter
of guaranteeing its dummies possession, at once began suits
in ejectment in the district court in Visalia, the county seat.

It was the preliminary skirmish, the reconnaissance in force,
the combatants feeling each other's strength, willing to proceed with caution, postponing the actual death-grip for a
while till each had strengthened its position and organised its
forces.

During the time the cases were on trial at Visalia, S. Behrman was much in evidence in and about the courts. The trial
itself, after tedious preliminaries, was brief. The ranchers lost.
The test cases were immediately carried up to the United
States Circuit Court in San Francisco. At the moment the
decision of this court was pending.

"Why, this is news," exclaimed Lyman, in response to the
Governor's announcement; "I did not expect them to be so
prompt. I was in court only last week and there seemed to be
no end of business ahead. I suppose you are very anxious?"

Magnus nodded. He had seated himself in one of Lyman's
deep chairs, his grey top-hat, with its wide brim, on the floor

beside him. His coat of black broadcloth that had been tightly packed in his valise, was yet wrinkled and creased; his trousers were strapped under his high boots. As he spoke, he stroked the bridge of his hawklike nose with his bent forefinger.

Leaning back in his chair, he watched his two sons with secret delight. To his eye, both were perfect specimens of their class, intelligent, well-looking, resourceful. He was intensely proud of them. He was never happier, never more nearly jovial, never more erect, more military, more alert, and buoyant than when in the company of his two sons. He honestly believed that no finer examples of young manhood existed throughout the entire nation.

"I think we should win in this court," Harran observed, watching the bubbles break in his glass. "The investigation has been much more complete than in the Visalia trial. Our case this time is too good. It has made too much talk. The court would not dare render a decision for the Railroad. Why, there's the agreement in black and white—and the circulars the Railroad issued. How *can* one get around those?"

"Well, well, we shall know in a few hours now," remarked Magnus.

"Oh," exclaimed Lyman, surprised, "it is for this morning, then. Why aren't you at the court?"

"It seemed undignified, boy," answered the Governor. "We shall know soon enough."

"Good God!" exclaimed Harran abruptly, " when I think of what is involved. Why, Lyman, it's our home, the ranch house itself, nearly all Los Muertos, practically our whole fortune, and just now when there is promise of an enormous crop of wheat. And it is not only us. There are over half a million acres of the San Joaquin involved. In some cases of the smaller ranches, it is the confiscation of the whole of the rancher's land. If this thing goes through, it will absolutely beggar nearly a hundred men. Broderson wouldn't have a thousand acres to his name. Why, it's monstrous."

"But the corporations offered to lease these lands," remarked Lyman. "Are any of the ranchers taking up that offer—or are any of them buying outright?"

"Buying! At the new figure!" exclaimed Harran, "at twenty and thirty an acre! Why, there's not one in ten that *can*. They are land-poor. And as for leasing—leasing land they virtually own—no, there's precious few are doing that, thank God! That would be acknowledging the railroad's ownership right away—forfeiting their rights for good. None of the *Leaguers* are doing it, I know. That would be the rankest treachery."

He paused for a moment, drinking the rest of the mineral water, then interrupting Lyman, who was about to speak to Presley, drawing him into the conversation through politeness, said: "Matters are just romping right along to a crisis these days. It's a make or break for the wheat growers of the State now, no mistake. Here are the land cases and the new grain tariff drawing to a head at about the same time. If we win our land cases, there's your new freight rates to be applied, and then all is beer and skittles. Won't the San Joaquin go wild if we pull it off, and I believe we will."

"How we wheat growers are exploited and trapped and deceived at every turn," observed Magnus sadly. "The courts, the capitalists, the railroads, each of them in turn hoodwinks us into some new and wonderful scheme, only to betray us in the end. Well," he added, turning to Lyman, "one thing at least we can depend on. We will cut their grain rates for them, eh, Lyman?"

Lyman crossed his legs and settled himself in his office chair.

"I have wanted to have a talk with you about that, sir," he said. "Yes, we will cut the rates—an average 10 per cent. cut throughout the State, as we are pledged. But I am going to warn you, Governor, and you, Harran; don't expect too much at first. The man who, even after twenty years' training in the operation of railroads, can draw an equitable, smoothly working schedule of freight rates between shipping point and common point, is capable of governing the United States. What with main lines, and leased lines, and points of transfer, and the laws governing common carriers, and the rulings of the Inter-State Commerce Commission, the whole matter has become so confused that Vanderbilt himself couldn't straighten it out. And how can it be expected that railroad commissions who are chosen—well, let's be frank—as ours was, for instance, from out a number of men who don't know the difference between a switching charge and a differential rate, are going to regulate the whole business in six months' time? Cut rates; yes, any fool can do that; any fool can write one dollar instead of two, but if you cut too low by a fraction of one per cent. and if the railroad can get out an injunction, tie you up and show that your new rate prevents the road being operated at a profit, how are you any better off?"

"Your conscientiousness does you credit, Lyman," said the Governor. "I respect you for it, my son. I know you will be fair to the railroad. That is all we want. Fairness to the corporation is fairness to the farmer, and we won't expect you to readjust the whole matter out of hand. Take your time. We can afford to wait."

"And suppose the next commission is a railroad board, and reverses all our figures?"

The one-time mining king, the most redoubtable poker player of Calaveras County, permitted himself a momentary twinkle of his eyes.

"By then it will be too late. We will, all of us, have made our fortunes by then."

The remark left Presley astonished out of all measure. He never could accustom himself to these strange lapses in the Governor's character. Magnus was by nature a public man, judicious, deliberate, standing firm for principle, yet upon rare occasion, by some such remark as this, he would betray the presence of a sub-nature of recklessness, inconsistent, all at variance with his creeds and tenets.

At the very bottom, when all was said and done, Magnus remained the Forty-niner. Deep down in his heart the spirit of the Adventurer yet persisted. "We will all of us have made fortunes by then." That was it precisely. "After us the deluge." For all his public spirit, for all his championship of justice and truth, his respect for law, Magnus remained the gambler, willing to play for colossal stakes, to hazard a fortune on the chance of winning a million. It was the true California spirit that found expression through him, the spirit of the West, unwilling to occupy itself with details, refusing to wait, to be patient, to achieve by legitimate plodding; the miner's instinct of wealth acquired in a single night prevailed, in spite of all. It was in this frame of mind that Magnus and the multitude of other ranchers of whom he was a type, farmed their ranches. They had no love for their land. They were not attached to the soil. They worked their ranches as a quarter of a century before they had worked their mines. To husband the resources of their marvellous San Joaquin, they considered niggardly, petty, Hebraic. To get all there was out of the land, to squeeze it dry, to exhaust it, seemed their policy. When, at last, the land worn out, would refuse to yield, they would invest their money in something else; by then, they would all have made fortunes. They did not care. "After us the deluge."

Lyman, however, was obviously uneasy, willing to change the subject. He rose to his feet, pulling down his cuffs.

"By the way," he observed, "I want you three to lunch with me to-day at my club. It is close by. You can wait there for news of the court's decision as well as anywhere else, and I should like to show you the place. I have just joined."

At the club, when the four men were seated at a small table in the round window of the main room, Lyman's popularity with all classes was very apparent. Hardly a man entered that did not call out a salutation to him, some even coming over to shake his hand. He seemed to be every man's friend, and to all he seemed equally genial. His affability, even to those whom he disliked, was unfailing.

"See that fellow yonder," he said to Magnus, indicating a certain middle-aged man, flamboyantly dressed, who wore his hair long, who was afflicted with sore eyes, and the collar of whose velvet coat was sprinkled with dandruff, "that's Hartrath, the artist, a man absolutely devoid of even the commonest decency. How he got in here is a mystery to me."

Yet, when this Hartrath came across to say "How do you do" to Lyman, Lyman was as eager in his cordiality as his warmest friend could have expected.

"Why the devil are you so chummy with him, then?" observed Harran when Hartrath had gone away.

Lyman's explanation was vague. The truth of the matter was, that Magnus's oldest son was consumed by inordinate ambition. Political preferment was his dream, and to the realisation of this dream popularity was an essential. Every man who could vote, blackguard or gentleman, was to be conciliated, if possible. He made it his study to become known throughout the entire community—to put influential men under obligations to himself. He never forgot a name or a face. With everybody he was the hail-fellow-well-met. His ambition was not trivial. In his disregard for small things, he resembled his father. Municipal office had no attraction for him. His goal was higher. He had planned his life twenty years ahead. Already Sheriff's Attorney, Assistant District Attorney and Railroad Commissioner, he could, if he desired, attain the office of District Attorney itself. Just now, it was a question with him whether or not it would be politic to fill this office. Would it advance or sidetrack him in the career he had outlined for himself? Lyman wanted to be something better than District Attorney, better than Mayor, than State Senator, or even than member of the United States Congress. He wanted to be, in fact, what his father was only in name— to succeed where Magnus had failed. He wanted to be governor of the State. He had put his teeth together, and, deaf to all other considerations, blind to all other issues, he worked with the infinite slowness, the unshakable tenacity of the coral insect to this one end.

After luncheon was over, Lyman ordered cigars and liqueurs, and with the three others returned to the main room of the club. However, their former place in the round window was occupied. A middle-aged man, with iron grey hair and moustache, who wore a frock coat and a white waistcoat, and in some indefinable manner suggested a retired naval officer, was sitting at their table smoking a long, thin cigar. At sight of him, Presley became animated. He uttered a mild exclamation:

"Why, isn't that Mr. Cedarquist?"

"Cedarquist?" repeated Lyman Derrick. "I know him well. Yes, of course, it is," he continued. "Governor, you must know him. He is one of our representative men. You would enjoy talking to him. He was the head of the big Atlas Iron Works. They have shut down recently, you know. Not failed exactly, but just ceased to be a paying investment, and Cedarquist closed them out. He has other interests, though. He's a rich man—a capitalist."

Lyman brought the group up to the gentleman in question and introduced them.

"Mr. Magnus Derrick, of course," observed Cedarquist, as he took the Governor's hand. "I've known you by repute for some time, sir. This is a great pleasure, I assure you." Then, turning to Presley, he added: "Hello, Pres, my boy. How is the great, the very great Poem getting on?"

"It's not getting on at all, sir," answered Presley, in some embarrassment, as they all sat down. "In fact, I've about given up the idea. There's so much interest in what you might call 'living issues' down at Los Muertos now, that I'm getting further and further from it every day."

"I should say as much," remarked the manufacturer, turning towards Magnus. "I'm watching your fight with Shelgrim, Mr. Derrick, with every degree of interest." He raised his drink of whiskey and soda. "Here's success to you."

As he replaced his glass, the artist Hartrath joined the group uninvited. As a pretext, he engaged Lyman in conversation. Lyman, he believed, was a man with a "pull" at the City Hall. In connection with a projected Million-Dollar Fair and Flower Festival, which at that moment was the talk of the city, certain statues were to be erected, and Hartrath bespoke Lyman's influence to further the pretensions of a sculptor friend of his, who wished to be Art Director of the affair. In the matter of this Fair and Flower Festival, Hartrath was not lacking in enthusiasm. He addressed the others with extravagant gestures, blinking his inflamed eyelids.

"A million dollars," he exclaimed. "Hey! think of that. Why, do you know that we have five hundred thousand practically pledged already? Talk about public spirit, gentlemen, this is the most public-spirited city on the continent. And the money is not thrown away. We will have Eastern visitors here by the thousands—capitalists—men with money to invest. The million we spend on our fair will be money in our pockets. Ah, you should see how the women of this city are taking hold of the matter. They are giving all kinds of little entertainments, teas, 'Olde Tyme Singing Skules,' amateur theatricals, gingerbread *fêtes*, all for the benefit of the fund, and the business men, too—pouring out their money like water. It is splendid, splendid, to see a community so patriotic."

The manufacturer, Cedarquist, fixed the artist with a glance of melancholy interest.

"And how much," he remarked, "will they contribute—your gingerbread women and public-spirited capitalists, towards the blowing up of the ruins of the Atlas Iron Works?"

"Blowing up? I don't understand," murmured the artist, surprised.

"When you get your Eastern capitalists out here with your Million-Dollar Fair," continued Cedarquist, "you don't propose, do you, to let them see a Million-Dollar Iron Foundry standing idle, because of the indifference of San Francisco business men? They might ask pertinent questions, your capitalists, and we should have to answer that our business men preferred to invest their money in corner lots and government bonds, rather than to back up a legitimate, industrial enterprise. We don't want fairs. We want active furnaces. We don't want public statues, and fountains, and park extensions and gingerbread *fêtes*. We want business enterprise. Isn't it like us? Isn't it like us?" he exclaimed sadly. "What a melancholy comment! San Francisco! It is not a city—it is a Midway Plaisance. California likes to be fooled. Do you suppose Shelgrim could convert the whole San Joaquin Valley into his back yard otherwise? Indifference to public affairs—absolute indifference, it stamps us all. Our State is the very paradise of fakirs. You and your Million-Dollar Fair!" He turned to Hartrath with a quiet smile. "It is just such men as you, Mr. Hartrath, that are the ruin of us. You organise a sham of tinsel and pasteboard, put on fool's cap and bells, beat a gong at a street corner, and the crowd cheers you and drops nickels into your hat. Your gingerbread *fête*; yes, I saw it in full blast the other night on the grounds of one of your women's places on Sutter Street. I was on my way home from the last board meeting of the Atlas Company. A *gingerbread fête*, my God! and the Atlas plant shutting down for want of financial backing. A million dollars spent to attract the Eastern investor, in order to show him an abandoned rolling mill, wherein the only activity is the sale of remnant material and scrap steel."

Lyman, however, interfered. The situation was becoming strained. He tried to conciliate the three men—the artist, the manufacturer, and the farmer, the warring elements. But Hartrath, unwilling to face the enmity that he felt accumulating against him, took himself away. A picture of his—"A Study of the Contra Costa Foothills"—was to be raffled in the club rooms for the benefit of the Fair. He, himself, was in charge of the matter. He disappeared.

Cedarquist looked after him with contemplative interest. Then, turning to Magnus, excused himself for the acridity of his words.

"He's no worse than many others, and the people of this State and city are, after all, only a little more addle-headed than other Americans." It was his favourite topic. Sure of the interest of his hearers, he unburdened himself.

"If I were to name the one crying evil of American life, Mr. Derrick," he continued, "it would be the indifference of the better people to public affairs. It is so in all our great centres. There are other great trusts, God knows, in the United States besides our own dear P. and S. W. Railroad. Every State has its own grievance. If it is not a railroad trust, it is a sugar trust, or an oil trust, or an industrial trust, that exploits the People, *because the People allow it*. The indifference of the People is the opportunity of the despot. It is as true as that the whole is greater than the part, and the maxim is so old that it is trite—it is laughable. It is neglected and disused for the sake of some new ingenious and complicated theory, some wonderful scheme of reorganisation, but the fact remains, nevertheless, simple, fundamental, everlasting. The People have but to say 'No,' and not the strongest tyranny, political, religious, or financial, that was ever organised, could survive one week."

The others, absorbed, attentive, approved, nodding their heads in silence as the manufacturer finished.

"That's one reason, Mr. Derrick," the other resumed after a moment, " why I have been so glad to meet you. You and your League are trying to say 'No' to the trust. I hope you will succeed. If your example will rally the People to your cause, you will. Otherwise—" he shook his head.

"One stage of the fight is to be passed this very day," observed Magnus. "My sons and myself are expecting hourly news from the City Hall, a decision in our case is pending."

"We are both of us fighters, it seems, Mr. Derrick," said Cedarquist. "Each with his particular enemy. We are well met, indeed, the farmer and the manufacturer, both in the same grist between the two millstones of the lethargy of the Public and the aggression of the Trust, the two great evils of modern America. Pres, my boy, there is your epic poem ready to hand."

But Cedarquist was full of another idea. Rarely did so favourable an opportunity present itself for explaining his theories, his ambitions. Addressing himself to Magnus, he continued:

"Fortunately for myself, the Atlas Company was not my only investment. I have other interests. The building of ships—steel sailing ships—has been an ambition of mine,— for this purpose, Mr. Derrick, to carry American wheat. For years, I have studied this question of American wheat, and at last, I have arrived at a theory. Let me explain. At present, all our California wheat goes to Liverpool, and from that port is distributed over the world. But a change is coming. I am sure of it. You young men," he turned to Presley, Lyman, and Harran, " will live to see it. Our century is about done. The great word of this nineteenth century has been Production. The great word of the twentieth century will be—listen to me, you youngsters—Markets. As a market for our Production—or let me take a concrete example—as a market for our *Wheat*, Europe is played out. Population in Europe is not increasing fast enough to keep up with the rapidity of our production. In some cases, as in France, the population is stationary. *We*, however, have gone on producing wheat at a tremendous rate. The result is over-production. We supply more than Europe can eat, and down go the prices. The remedy is *not* in the curtailing of our wheat areas, but in this, we *must have new markets, greater markets*. For years we have been sending our wheat from East to West, from California to Europe. But the time will come when we must send it from West to East. We must march with the course of empire, not against it. I mean, we must look to China. Rice in China is losing its nutritive quality. The Asiatics, though, must be fed; if not on rice, then on wheat. Why, Mr. Derrick, if only one-half the population of China ate a half ounce of flour per man per day all the wheat areas in California could not feed them. Ah, if I could only hammer that into the brains of every rancher of the San Joaquin, yes, and of every owner of every

bonanza farm in Dakota and Minnesota. Send your wheat to
China; handle it yourselves; do away with the middleman;
break up the Chicago wheat pits and elevator rings and mixing houses. When in feeding China you have decreased the
European shipments, the effect is instantaneous. Prices go up
in Europe without having the least effect upon the prices in
China. We hold the key, we have the wheat,—infinitely more
than we ourselves can eat. Asia and Europe must look to
America to be fed. What fatuous neglect of opportunity to
continue to deluge Europe with our surplus food when the
East trembles upon the verge of starvation!"

The two men, Cedarquist and Magnus, continued the conversation a little further. The manufacturer's idea was new to
the Governor. He was greatly interested. He withdrew from
the conversation. Thoughtful, he leaned back in his place,
stroking the bridge of his beak-like nose with a crooked forefinger.

Cedarquist turned to Harran and began asking details as to
the conditions of the wheat growers of the San Joaquin. Lyman still maintained an attitude of polite aloofness, yawning
occasionally behind three fingers, and Presley was left to the
company of his own thoughts.

There had been a day when the affairs and grievances of
the farmers of his acquaintance—Magnus, Annixter, Osterman, and old Broderson—had filled him only with disgust.
His mind full of a great, vague epic poem of the West, he had
kept himself apart, disdainful of what he chose to consider
their petty squabbles. But the scene in Annixter's harness
room had thrilled and uplifted him. He was palpitating with
excitement all through the succeeding months. He abandoned
the idea of an epic poem. In six months he had not written a
single verse. Day after day he trembled with excitement as the
relations between the Trust and League became more and
more strained. He saw the matter in its true light. It was typical. It was the world-old war between Freedom and Tyranny,
and at times his hatred of the railroad shook him like a crisp
and withered reed, while the languid indifference of the
people of the State to the quarrel filled him with a blind exasperation.

But, as he had once explained to Vanamee, he must find

expression. He felt that he would suffocate otherwise. He had begun to keep a journal. As the inclination spurred him, he wrote down his thoughts and ideas in this, sometimes every day, sometimes only three or four times a month. Also he flung aside his books of poems—Milton, Tennyson, Browning, even Homer—and addressed himself to Mill, Malthus, Young, Poushkin, Henry George, Schopenhauer. He attacked the subject of Social Inequality with unbounded enthusiasm. He devoured, rather than read, and emerged from the affair, his mind a confused jumble of conflicting notions, sick with over-effort, raging against injustice and oppression, and with not one sane suggestion as to remedy or redress.

The butt of his cigarette scorched his fingers and roused him from his brooding. In the act of lighting another, he glanced across the room and was surprised to see two very prettily dressed young women in the company of an older gentleman, in a long frock coat, standing before Hartrath's painting, examining it, their heads upon one side.

Presley uttered a murmur of surprise. He, himself, was a member of the club, and the presence of women within its doors, except on special occasions, was not tolerated. He turned to Lyman Derrick for an explanation, but this other had also seen the women and abruptly exclaimed:

"I declare, I had forgotten about it. Why, this is Ladies' Day, of course."

"Why, yes," interposed Cedarquist, glancing at the women over his shoulder. "Didn't you know? They let 'em in twice a year, you remember, and this is a double occasion. They are going to raffle Hartrath's picture,—for the benefit of the Gingerbread Fair. Why, you are not up to date, Lyman. This is a sacred and religious rite,—an important public event."

"Of course, of course," murmured Lyman. He found means to survey Harran and Magnus. Certainly, neither his father nor his brother were dressed for the function that impended. He had been stupid. Magnus invariably attracted attention, and now with his trousers strapped under his boots, his wrinkled frock coat—Lyman twisted his cuffs into sight with an impatient, nervous movement of his wrists, glancing a second time at his brother's pink face, forward curling, yellow hair and clothes of a country cut. But there was no help for it. He wondered what were the club regulations in the matter of bringing in visitors on Ladies' Day.

"Sure enough, Ladies' Day," he remarked, "I am very glad you struck it, Governor. We can sit right where we are. I guess this is as good a place as any to see the crowd. It's a good chance to see all the big guns of the city. Do you expect your people here, Mr. Cedarquist?"

"My wife may come, and my daughters," said the manufacturer.

"Ah," murmured Presley, "so much the better. I was going to give myself the pleasure of calling upon your daughters, Mr. Cedarquist, this afternoon."

"You can save your carfare, Pres," said Cedarquist, "you will see them here."

No doubt, the invitations for the occasion had appointed one o'clock as the time, for between that hour and two, the guests arrived in an almost unbroken stream. From their point of vantage in the round window of the main room, Magnus, his two sons, and Presley looked on very interested. Cedarquist had excused himself, affirming that he must look out for his women folk.

Of every ten of the arrivals, seven, at least, were ladies. They entered the room—this unfamiliar masculine haunt, where their husbands, brothers, and sons spent so much of their time—with a certain show of hesitancy and little, nervous, oblique glances, moving their heads from side to side like a file of hens venturing into a strange barn. They came in groups, ushered by a single member of the club, doing the honours with effusive bows and polite gestures, indicating the various objects of interest, pictures, busts, and the like, that decorated the room.

Fresh from his recollections of Bonneville, Guadalajara, and the dance in Annixter's barn, Presley was astonished at the beauty of these women and the elegance of their toilettes. The crowd thickened rapidly. A murmur of conversation arose, subdued, gracious, mingled with the soft rustle of silk, grenadines, velvet. The scent of delicate perfumes spread in the air, Violet de Parme, Peau d'Espagne. Colours of the most harmonious blends appeared and disappeared at intervals in the slowly moving press, touches of lavender-

tinted velvets, pale violet crêpes and cream-coloured appli-
quéd laces.

There seemed to be no need of introductions. Everybody
appeared to be acquainted. There was no awkwardness, no
constraint. The assembly disengaged an impression of refined
pleasure. On every hand, innumerable dialogues seemed to go
forward easily and naturally, without break or interruption,
witty, engaging, the couple never at a loss for repartee. A
third party was gracefully included, then a fourth. Little
groups were formed,—groups that divided themselves, or
melted into other groups, or disintegrated again into isolated
pairs, or lost themselves in the background of the mass,—all
without friction, without embarrassment,—the whole affair
going forward of itself, decorous, tactful, well-bred.

At a distance, and not too loud, a stringed orchestra sent
up a pleasing hum. Waiters, with brass buttons on their full
dress coats, went from group to group, silent, unobtrusive,
serving salads and ices.

But the focus of the assembly was the little space before
Hartrath's painting. It was called "A Study of the Contra
Costa Foothills," and was set in a frame of natural redwood,
the bark still adhering. It was conspicuously displayed on an
easel at the right of the entrance to the main room of the
club, and was very large. In the foreground, and to the left,
under the shade of a live-oak, stood a couple of reddish
cows, knee-deep in a patch of yellow poppies, while in the
right-hand corner, to balance the composition, was placed a
girl in a pink dress and white sunbonnet, in which the shadows were indicated by broad dashes of pale blue paint. The
ladies and young girls examined the production with little
murmurs of admiration, hazarding remembered phrases,
searching for the exact balance between generous praise
and critical discrimination, expressing their opinions in the
mild technicalities of the Art Books and painting classes.
They spoke of atmospheric effects, of middle distance, of
"*chiaro-oscuro*," of fore-shortening, of the decomposition of
light, of the subordination of individuality to fidelity of in-
terpretation.

One tall girl, with hair almost white in its blondness, having observed that the handling of the masses reminded her

strongly of Corot, her companion, who carried a gold lorgnette by a chain around her neck, answered:

"Ah! *Millet*, perhaps, but not Corot."

This verdict had an immediate success. It was passed from group to group. It seemed to imply a delicate distinction that carried conviction at once. It was decided formally that the reddish brown cows in the picture were reminiscent of Daubigny, and that the handling of the masses was altogether Millet, but that the general effect was *not quite* Corot.

Presley, curious to see the painting that was the subject of so much discussion, had left the group in the round window, and stood close by Hartrath, craning his head over the shoulders of the crowd, trying to catch a glimpse of the reddish cows, the milk-maid and the blue painted foothills. He was suddenly aware of Cedarquist's voice in his ear, and, turning about, found himself face to face with the manufacturer, his wife and his two daughters.

There was a meeting. Salutations were exchanged, Presley shaking hands all around, expressing his delight at seeing his old friends once more, for he had known the family from his boyhood, Mrs. Cedarquist being his aunt. Mrs. Cedarquist and her two daughters declared that the air of Los Muertos must certainly have done him a world of good. He was stouter, there could be no doubt of it. A little pale, perhaps. He was fatiguing himself with his writing, no doubt. Ah, he must take care. Health was everything, after all. Had he been writing any more verse? Every month they scanned the magazines, looking for his name.

Mrs. Cedarquist was a fashionable woman, the president or chairman of a score of clubs. She was forever running after fads, appearing continually in the society wherein she moved with new and astounding *protégés*—fakirs whom she unearthed no one knew where, discovering them long in advance of her companions. Now it was a Russian Countess, with dirty finger nails, who travelled throughout America and borrowed money; now an Æsthete who possessed a wonderful collection of topaz gems, who submitted decorative schemes for the interior arrangement of houses and who "received" in Mrs. Cedarquist's drawing-rooms dressed in a white velvet cassock; now a widow of some Mohammedan of

Bengal or Rajputana, who had a blue spot in the middle of her forehead and who solicited contributions for her sisters in affliction; now a certain bearded poet, recently back from the Klondike; now a decayed musician who had been ejected from a young ladies' musical conservatory of Europe because of certain surprising pamphlets on free love, and who had come to San Francisco to introduce the community to the music of Brahms; now a Japanese youth who wore spectacles and a grey flannel shirt and who, at intervals, delivered himself of the most astonishing poems, vague, unrhymed, unmetrical lucubrations, incoherent, bizarre; now a Christian Scientist, a lean, grey woman, whose creed was neither Christian nor scientific; now a university professor, with the bristling beard of an anarchist chief-of-section, and a roaring, guttural voice, whose intenseness left him gasping and apoplectic; now a civilised Cherokee with a mission; now a female elocutionist, whose forte was Byron's Songs of Greece; now a high caste Chinaman; now a miniature painter; now a tenor, a pianiste, a mandolin player, a missionary, a drawing master, a virtuoso, a collector, an Armenian, a botanist with a new flower, a critic with a new theory, a doctor with a new treatment.

And all these people had a veritable mania for declamation and fancy dress. The Russian Countess gave talks on the prisons of Siberia, wearing the headdress and pinchbeck ornaments of a Slav bride; the Æsthete, in his white cassock, gave readings on obscure questions of art and ethics. The widow of India, in the costume of her caste, described the social life of her people at home. The bearded poet, perspiring in furs and boots of reindeer skin, declaimed verses of his own composition about the wild life of the Alaskan mining camps. The Japanese youth, in the silk robes of the *Samurai* two-sworded nobles, read from his own works—"The flat-bordered earth, nailed down at night, rusting under the darkness," "The brave, upright rains that came down like errands from iron-bodied yore-time." The Christian Scientist, in funereal, impressive black, discussed the contra-will and pan-psychic hylozoism. The university professor put on a full dress suit and lisle thread gloves at three in the afternoon and before literary clubs and circles bellowed extracts from Goethe and Schiller in the German, shaking his fists, purple with vehemence. The Cherokee, arrayed in fringed buckskin and blue beads, rented from a costumer, intoned folk songs of his people in the vernacular. The elocutionist in cheese-cloth toga and tin bracelets, rendered "The Isles of Greece, where burning Sappho loved and sung." The Chinaman, in the robes of a mandarin, lectured on Confucius. The Armenian, in fez and baggy trousers, spoke of the Unspeakable Turk. The mandolin player, dressed like a bull fighter, held musical *conversaziones*, interpreting the peasant songs of Andalusia.

It was the Fake, the eternal, irrepressible Sham; glib, nimble, ubiquitous, tricked out in all the paraphernalia of imposture, an endless defile of charlatans that passed interminably before the gaze of the city, marshalled by "lady presidents," exploited by clubs of women, by literary societies, reading circles, and culture organisations. The attention the Fake received, the time devoted to it, the money which it absorbed, were incredible. It was all one that impostor after impostor was exposed; it was all one that the clubs, the circles, the societies were proved beyond doubt to have been swindled. The more the Philistine press of the city railed and guyed, the more the women rallied to the defence of their *protégé* of the hour. That their favourite was persecuted, was to them a veritable rapture. Promptly they invested the apostle of culture with the glamour of a martyr.

The fakirs worked the community as shell-game tricksters work a county fair, departing with bursting pocketbooks, passing on the word to the next in line, assured that the place was not worked out, knowing well that there was enough for all.

More frequently the public of the city, unable to think of more than one thing at one time, prostrated itself at the feet of a single apostle, but at other moments, such as the present, when a Flower Festival or a Million-Dollar Fair aroused enthusiasm in all quarters, the occasion was one of gala for the entire Fake. The decayed professors, virtuosi, litterateurs, and artists thronged to the place *en masse*. Their clamour filled all the air. On every hand one heard the scraping of violins, the tinkling of mandolins, the suave accents of "art talks," the incoherencies of poets, the declamation of elocutionists, the inarticulate wanderings of the Japanese, the confused mutterings of the Cherokee, the guttural bellowing of the German university professor, all in the name of the Million-Dollar Fair. Money to the extent of hundreds of thousands was set in motion.

Mrs. Cedarquist was busy from morning until night. One after another, she was introduced to newly arrived fakirs. To each poet, to each litterateur, to each professor she addressed the same question:

"How long have you known you had this power?"

She spent her days in one quiver of excitement and jubilation. She was "in the movement." The people of the city were awakening to a Realisation of the Beautiful, to a sense of the higher needs of life. This was Art, this was Literature, this was Culture and Refinement. The Renaissance had appeared in the West.

She was a short, rather stout, red-faced, very much overdressed little woman of some fifty years. She was rich in her own name, even before her marriage, being a relative of Shelgrim himself and on familiar terms with the great financier and his family. Her husband, while deploring the policy of the railroad, saw no good reason for quarrelling with Shelgrim, and on more than one occasion had dined at his house.

On this occasion, delighted that she had come upon a "minor poet," she insisted upon presenting him to Hartrath.

"You two should have so much in common," she explained.

Presley shook the flaccid hand of the artist, murmuring conventionalities, while Mrs. Cedarquist hastened to say:

"I am sure you know Mr. Presley's verse, Mr. Hartrath. You should, believe me. You two have much in common. I can see so much that is alike in your modes of interpreting nature. In Mr. Presley's sonnet, 'The Better Part,' there is the same note as in your picture, the same sincerity of tone, the same subtlety of touch, the same *nuances*,—ah."

"Oh, my dear Madame," murmured the artist, interrupting Presley's impatient retort; "I am a mere bungler. You don't mean quite that, I am sure. I am *too* sensitive. It is my cross. Beauty," he closed his sore eyes with a little expression of pain, "beauty unmans me."

But Mrs. Cedarquist was not listening. Her eyes were fixed

on the artist's luxuriant hair, a thick and glossy mane, that all but covered his coat collar.

"Leonine!" she murmured—"leonine! Like Samson of old."

However, abruptly bestirring herself, she exclaimed a second later:

"But I must run away. I am selling tickets for you this afternoon, Mr. Hartrath. I am having such success. Twenty-five already. Mr. Presley, you will take two chances, I am sure, and, oh, by the way, I have such good news. You know I am one of the lady members of the subscription committee for our Fair, and you know we approached Mr. Shelgrim for a donation to help along. Oh, such a liberal patron, a real Lorenzo di' Medici. In the name of the Pacific and Southwestern he has subscribed, think of it, five thousand dollars; and yet they will talk of the meanness of the railroad."

"Possibly it is to his interest," murmured Presley. "The fairs and festivals bring people to the city over his railroad."

But the others turned on him, expostulating.

"Ah, you Philistine," declared Mrs. Cedarquist. "And this from *you*, Presley; to attribute such base motives——"

"If the poets become materialised, Mr. Presley," declared Hartrath, " what can we say to the people?"

"And Shelgrim encourages your million-dollar fairs and *fêtes*," said a voice at Presley's elbow, "because it is throwing dust in the people's eyes."

The group turned about and saw Cedarquist, who had come up unobserved in time to catch the drift of the talk. But he spoke without bitterness; there was even a good-humoured twinkle in his eyes.

"Yes," he continued, smiling, "our dear Shelgrim promotes your fairs, not only as Pres says, because it is money in his pocket, but because it amuses the people, distracts their attention from the doings of his railroad. When Beatrice was a baby and had little colics, I used to jingle my keys in front of her nose, and it took her attention from the pain in her tummy; so Shelgrim."

The others laughed good-humouredly, protesting, nevertheless, and Mrs. Cedarquist shook her finger in warning at the artist and exclaimed:

"The Philistines be upon thee, Samson!"

"By the way," observed Hartrath, willing to change the subject, "I hear you are on the Famine Relief Committee. Does your work progress?"

"Oh, most famously, I assure you," she said. "Such a movement as we have started. Those poor creatures. The photographs of them are simply dreadful. I had the committee to luncheon the other day and we passed them around. We are getting subscriptions from all over the State, and Mr. Cedarquist is to arrange for the ship."

The Relief Committee in question was one of a great number that had been formed in California—and all over the Union, for the matter of that—to provide relief for the victims of a great famine in Central India. The whole world had been struck with horror at the reports of suffering and mortality in the affected districts, and had hastened to send aid. Certain women of San Francisco, with Mrs. Cedarquist at their head, had organised a number of committees, but the manufacturer's wife turned the meetings of these committees into social affairs—luncheons, teas, where one discussed the ways and means of assisting the starving Asiatics over teacups and plates of salad.

Shortly afterward a mild commotion spread throughout the assemblage of the club's guests. The drawing of the numbers in the raffle was about to be made. Hartrath, in a flurry of agitation, excused himself. Cedarquist took Presley by the arm.

"Pres, let's get out of this," he said. "Come into the wine room and I will shake you for a glass of sherry."

They had some difficulty in extricating themselves. The main room where the drawing was to take place suddenly became densely thronged. All the guests pressed eagerly about the table near the picture, upon which one of the hall boys had just placed a ballot box containing the numbers. The ladies, holding their tickets in their hands, pushed forward. A staccato chatter of excited murmurs arose.

"What became of Harran and Lyman and the Governor?" inquired Presley.

Lyman had disappeared, alleging a business engagement, but Magnus and his younger son had retired to the library of

the club on the floor above. It was almost deserted. They
were deep in earnest conversation.

"Harran," said the Governor, with decision, "there is a
deal, there, in what Cedarquist says. Our wheat to China,
hey, boy?"

"It is certainly worth thinking of, sir."

"It appeals to me, boy; it appeals to me. It's big and there's
a fortune in it. Big chances mean big returns; and I know—
your old father isn't a back number yet, Harran—I may not
have so wide an outlook as our friend Cedarquist, but I am
quick to see my chance. Boy, the whole East is opening, dis-
integrating before the Anglo-Saxon. It is time that bread
stuffs, as well, should make markets for themselves in the Orient. Just at this moment, too, when Lyman will scale down
freight rates so we can haul to tidewater at little cost."

Magnus paused again, his frown beetling, and in the silence
the excited murmur from the main room of the club, the soprano chatter of a multitude of women, found its way to the
deserted library.

"I believe it's worth looking into, Governor," asserted
Harran.

Magnus rose, and, his hands behind him, paced the floor
of the library a couple of times, his imagination all stimulated and vivid. The great gambler perceived his Chance, the
kaleidoscopic shifting of circumstances that made a Situation. It had come silently, unexpectedly. He had not seen its
approach. Abruptly he woke one morning to see the combination realised. But also he saw a vision. A sudden and
abrupt revolution in the Wheat. A new world of markets
discovered, the matter as important as the discovery of
America. The torrent of wheat was to be diverted, flowing
back upon itself in a sudden, colossal eddy, stranding the
middleman, the *entre-preneur*, the elevator- and mixing-
house men dry and despairing, their occupation gone. He
saw the farmer suddenly emancipated, the world's food no
longer at the mercy of the speculator, thousands upon thousands of men set free of the grip of Trust and ring and monopoly acting for themselves, selling their own wheat,
organising into one gigantic trust, themselves, sending their
agents to all the entry ports of China. Himself, Annixter,

Broderson and Osterman would pool their issues. He would convince them of the magnificence of the new movement. They would be its pioneers. Harran would be sent to Hong Kong to represent the four. They would charter—probably buy—a ship, perhaps one of Cedarquist's, American built, the nation's flag at the peak, and the sailing of that ship, gorged with the crops from Broderson's and Osterman's ranches, from Quien Sabe and Los Muertos, would be like the sailing of the caravels from Palos. It would mark a new era; it would make an epoch.

With this vision still expanding before the eye of his mind, Magnus, with Harran at his elbow, prepared to depart.

They descended to the lower floor and involved themselves for a moment in the throng of fashionables that blocked the hallway and the entrance to the main room, where the numbers of the raffle were being drawn. Near the head of the stairs they encountered Presley and Cedarquist, who had just come out of the wine room.

Magnus, still on fire with the new idea, pressed a few questions upon the manufacturer before bidding him good-bye. He wished to talk further upon the great subject, interested as to details, but Cedarquist was vague in his replies. He was no farmer, he hardly knew wheat when he saw it, only he knew the trend of the world's affairs; he felt them to be setting inevitably eastward.

However, his very vagueness was a further inspiration to the Governor. He swept details aside. He saw only the grand *coup*, the huge results, the East conquered, the march of empire rolling westward, finally arriving at its starting point, the vague, mysterious Orient. He saw his wheat, like the crest of an advancing billow, crossing the Pacific, bursting upon Asia, flooding the Orient in a golden torrent. It was the new era. He had lived to see the death of the old and the birth of the new; first the mine, now the ranch; first gold, now wheat. Once again he became the pioneer, hardy, brilliant, taking colossal chances, blazing the way, grasping a fortune—a million in a single day. All the bigness of his nature leaped up again within him. At the magnitude of the inspiration he felt young again, indomitable, the leader at last, king of his fellows, wresting from fortune at this eleventh hour, before his

old age, the place of high command which so long had been
denied him. At last he could achieve.

Abruptly Magnus was aware that some one had spoken his
name. He looked about and saw behind him, at a little distance, two gentlemen, strangers to him. They had withdrawn
from the crowd into a little recess. Evidently having no
women to look after, they had lost interest in the afternoon's
affair. Magnus realised that they had not seen him. One of
them was reading aloud to his companion from an evening
edition of that day's newspaper. It was in the course of this
reading that Magnus caught the sound of his name. He
paused, listening, and Presley, Harran and Cedarquist followed his example. Soon they all understood. They were
listening to the report of the judge's decision, for which
Magnus was waiting—the decision in the case of the League
vs. the Railroad. For the moment, the polite clamour of the
raffle hushed itself—the winning number was being drawn.
The guests held their breath, and in the ensuing silence Magnus and the others heard these words distinctly:

". . . . It follows that the title to the lands in question is
in the plaintiff—the Pacific and Southwestern Railroad, and
the defendants have no title, and their possession is wrongful.
There must be findings and judgment for the plaintiff, and it
is so ordered."

In spite of himself, Magnus paled. Harran shut his teeth
with an oath. Their exaltation of the previous moment collapsed like a pyramid of cards. The vision of the new movement of the wheat, the conquest of the East, the invasion
of the Orient, seemed only the flimsiest mockery. With a
brusque wrench, they were snatched back to reality. Between
them and the vision, between the fecund San Joaquin, reeking
with fruitfulness, and the millions of Asia crowding toward
the verge of starvation, lay the iron-hearted monster of steel
and steam, implacable, insatiable, huge—its entrails gorged
with the life blood that it sucked from an entire commonwealth, its ever hungry maw glutted with the harvests that
should have fed the famished bellies of the whole world of
the Orient.

But abruptly, while the four men stood there, gazing into
each other's faces, a vigorous hand-clapping broke out. The

raffle of Hartrath's picture was over, and as Presley turned about he saw Mrs. Cedarquist and her two daughters signalling eagerly to the manufacturer, unable to reach him because of the intervening crowd. Then Mrs. Cedarquist raised her voice and cried:

"I've won. I've won."

Unnoticed, and with but a brief word to Cedarquist, Magnus and Harran went down the marble steps leading to the street door, silent, Harran's arm tight around his father's shoulder.

At once the orchestra struck into a lively air. A renewed murmur of conversation broke out, and Cedarquist, as he said good-bye to Presley, looked first at the retreating figures of the ranchers, then at the gayly dressed throng of beautiful women and debonair young men, and indicating the whole scene with a single gesture, said, smiling sadly as he spoke:

"Not a city, Presley, not a city, but a Midway Plaisance."

II

UNDERNEATH the Long Trestle where Broderson Creek cut the line of the railroad and the Upper Road, the ground was low and covered with a second growth of grey green willows. Along the borders of the creek were occasional marshy spots, and now and then Hilma Tree came here to gather water-cresses, which she made into salads.

The place was picturesque, secluded, an oasis of green shade in all the limitless, flat monotony of the surrounding wheat lands. The creek had eroded deep into the little gully, and no matter how hot it was on the baking, shimmering levels of the ranches above, down here one always found one's self enveloped in an odorous, moist coolness. From time to time, the incessant murmur of the creek, pouring over and around the larger stones, was interrupted by the thunder of trains roaring out upon the trestle overhead, passing on with the furious gallop of their hundreds of iron wheels, leaving in the air a taint of hot oil, acrid smoke, and reek of escaping steam.

On a certain afternoon, in the spring of the year, Hilma was returning to Quien Sabe from Hooven's by the trail that led from Los Muertos to Annixter's ranch houses, under the trestle. She had spent the afternoon with Minna Hooven, who, for the time being, was kept indoors because of a wrenched ankle. As Hilma descended into the gravel flats and thickets of willows underneath the trestle, she decided that she would gather some cresses for her supper that night. She found a spot around the base of one of the supports of the trestle where the cresses grew thickest, and plucked a couple of handfuls, washing them in the creek and pinning them up in her handkerchief. It made a little, round, cold bundle, and Hilma, warm from her walk, found a delicious enjoyment in pressing the damp ball of it to her cheeks and neck.

For all the change that Annixter had noted in her upon the occasion of the barn dance, Hilma remained in many things a young child. She was never at loss for enjoyment, and could always amuse herself when left alone. Just now, she chose to drink from the creek, lying prone on the ground, her face half-buried in the water, and this, not because she was thirsty, but because it was a new way to drink. She imagined herself a belated traveller, a poor girl, an outcast, quenching her thirst at the wayside brook, her little packet of cresses doing duty for a bundle of clothes. Night was coming on. Perhaps it would storm. She had nowhere to go. She would apply at a hut for shelter.

Abruptly, the temptation to dabble her feet in the creek presented itself to her. Always she had liked to play in the water. What a delight now to take off her shoes and stockings and wade out into the shallows near the bank! She had worn low shoes that afternoon, and the dust of the trail had filtered in above the edges. At times, she felt the grit and grey sand on the soles of her feet, and the sensation had set her teeth on edge. What a delicious alternative the cold, clean water suggested, and how easy it would be to do as she pleased just then, if only she were a little girl. In the end, it was stupid to be grown up.

Sitting upon the bank, one finger tucked into the heel of her shoe, Hilma hesitated. Suppose a train should come! She fancied she could see the engineer leaning from the cab with a great grin on his face, or the brakeman shouting gibes at her from the platform. Abruptly she blushed scarlet. The blood throbbed in her temples. Her heart beat.

Since the famous evening of the barn dance, Annixter had spoken to her but twice. Hilma no longer looked after the ranch house these days. The thought of setting foot within Annixter's dining-room and bed-room terrified her, and in the end her mother had taken over that part of her work. Of the two meetings with the master of Quien Sabe, one had been a mere exchange of good mornings as the two happened to meet over by the artesian well; the other, more complicated, had occurred in the dairy-house again, Annixter, pretending to look over the new cheese press, asking about details of her work. When this had happened on that previous occasion, ending with Annixter's attempt to kiss her, Hilma had been talkative enough, chattering on from one subject to another, never at a loss for a theme. But this last time was a veritable ordeal. No sooner had Annixter appeared than her heart leaped and quivered like that of the hound-harried doe. Her speech failed her. Throughout the whole brief interview she had been miserably tongue-tied, stammering monosyllables, confused, horribly awkward, and when Annixter had gone away, she had fled to her little room, and bolting the door, had flung herself face downward on the bed and wept as though her heart were breaking, she did not know why.

That Annixter had been overwhelmed with business all through the winter was an inexpressible relief to Hilma. His affairs took him away from the ranch continually. He was absent sometimes for weeks, making trips to San Francisco, or to Sacramento, or to Bonneville. Perhaps he was forgetting her, overlooking her; and while, at first, she told herself that she asked nothing better, the idea of it began to occupy her mind. She began to wonder if it was really so.

She knew his trouble. Everybody did. The news of the sudden forward movement of the Railroad's forces, inaugurating the campaign, had flared white-hot and blazing all over the country side. To Hilma's notion, Annixter's attitude was heroic beyond all expression. His courage in facing the Railroad, as he had faced Delaney in the barn, seemed to her the pitch of sublimity. She refused to see any auxiliaries aiding him in his fight. To her imagination, the great League, which all the ranchers were joining, was a mere form. Singlehanded, Annixter fronted the monster. But for him the corporation would gobble Quien Sabe, as a whale would a minnow. He was a hero who stood between them all and destruction. He was a protector of her family. He was her champion. She began to mention him in her prayers every night, adding a further petition to the effect that he would become a *good* man, and that he should not swear so much, and that he should never meet Delaney again.

However, as Hilma still debated the idea of bathing her feet in the creek, a train did actually thunder past overhead— the regular evening Overland,—the through express, that never stopped between Bakersfield and Fresno. It stormed by with a deafening clamour, and a swirl of smoke, in a long succession of way-coaches, and chocolate coloured Pullmans, grimy with the dust of the great deserts of the Southwest. The quivering of the trestle's supports set a tremble in the ground underfoot. The thunder of wheels drowned all sound of the flowing of the creek, and also the noise of the buckskin mare's hoofs descending from the trail upon the gravel about the creek, so that Hilma, turning about after the passage of the train, saw Annixter close at hand, with the abruptness of a vision.

He was looking at her, smiling as he rarely did, the firm line of his out-thrust lower lip relaxed good-humouredly. He had taken off his campaign hat to her, and though his stiff, yellow hair was twisted into a bristling mop, the little persistent tuft on the crown, usually defiantly erect as an Apache's scalp-lock, was nowhere in sight.

"Hello, it's you, is it, Miss Hilma?" he exclaimed, getting down from the buckskin, and allowing her to drink.

Hilma nodded, scrambling to her feet, dusting her skirt with nervous pats of both hands.

Annixter sat down on a great rock close by and, the loop of the bridle over his arm, lit a cigar, and began to talk. He complained of the heat of the day, the bad condition of the Lower Road, over which he had come on his way from a committee meeting of the League at Los Muertos; of the slowness of the work on the irrigating ditch, and, as a matter of course, of the general hard times.

"Miss Hilma," he said abruptly, "never you marry a ranchman. He's never out of trouble."

Hilma gasped, her eyes widening till the full round of the pupil was disclosed. Instantly, a certain, inexplicable guiltiness overpowered her with incredible confusion. Her hands trembled as she pressed the bundle of cresses into a hard ball between her palms.

Annixter continued to talk. He was disturbed and excited himself at this unexpected meeting. Never through all the past winter months of strenuous activity, the fever of political campaigns, the harrowing delays and ultimate defeat in one law court after another, had he forgotten the look in Hilma's face as he stood with one arm around her on the floor of his barn, in peril of his life from the buster's revolver. That dumb confession of Hilma's wide-open eyes had been enough for him. Yet, somehow, he never had had a chance to act upon it. During the short period when he could be on his ranch

Hilma had always managed to avoid him. Once, even, she
had spent a month, about Christmas time, with her mother's
father, who kept a hotel in San Francisco.

Now, to-day, however, he had her all to himself. He would
put an end to the situation that troubled him, and vexed him,
day after day, month after month. Beyond question, the moment had come for something definite, he could not say precisely what. Readjusting his cigar between his teeth, he
resumed his speech. It suited his humour to take the girl into
his confidence, following an instinct which warned him that
this would bring about a certain closeness of their relations, a
certain intimacy.

"What do you think of this row, anyways, Miss Hilma,—
this railroad fuss in general? Think Shelgrim and his rushers
are going to jump Quien Sabe—are going to run us off the
ranch?"

"Oh, no, sir," protested Hilma, still breathless. "Oh, no,
indeed not."

"Well, what then?"

Hilma made a little uncertain movement of ignorance.

"I don't know what."

"Well, the League agreed to-day that if the test cases were
lost in the Supreme Court—you know we've appealed to the
Supreme Court, at Washington—we'd fight."

"Fight?"

"Yes, fight."

"Fight like—like you and Mr. Delaney that time with—
oh, dear—with guns?"

"I don't know," grumbled Annixter vaguely. "What do *you*
think?"

Hilma's low-pitched, almost husky voice trembled a little as
she replied, "Fighting—with guns—that's so terrible. Oh,
those revolvers in the barn! I can hear them yet. Every shot
seemed like the explosion of tons of powder."

"Shall we clear out, then? Shall we let Delaney have possession, and S. Behrman, and all that lot? Shall we give in to
them?"

"Never, never," she exclaimed, her great eyes flashing.

"*You* wouldn't like to be turned out of your home, would
you, Miss Hilma, because Quien Sabe *is* your home isn't it?

You've lived here ever since you were as big as a minute. You wouldn't like to have S. Behrman and the rest of 'em turn you out?"

"N-no," she murmured. "No, I shouldn't like that. There's mamma and——"

"Well, do you think for one second I'm going to *let* 'em?" cried Annixter, his teeth tightening on his cigar. "You stay right where you are. I'll take care of you, right enough. Look here," he demanded abruptly, "you've no use for that roaring lush, Delaney, have you?"

"I think he is a wicked man," she declared. "I know the Railroad has pretended to sell him part of the ranch, and he lets Mr. S. Behrman and Mr. Ruggles just use him."

"Right. I thought you wouldn't be keen on him."

There was a long pause. The buckskin began blowing among the pebbles, nosing for grass, and Annixter shifted his cigar to the other corner of his mouth.

"Pretty place," he muttered, looking around him. Then he added: "Miss Hilma, see here, I want to have a kind of talk with you, if you don't mind. I don't know just how to say these sort of things, and if I get all balled up as I go along, you just set it down to the fact that I've never had any experience in dealing with feemale girls; understand? You see, ever since the barn dance—yes, and long before then—I've been thinking a lot about you. Straight, I have, and I guess you know it. You're about the only girl that I ever knew well, and I guess," he declared deliberately, "you're about the only one I want to know. It's my nature. You didn't say anything that time when we stood there together and Delaney was playing the fool, but, somehow, I got the idea that you didn't want Delaney to do for me one little bit; that if he'd got me then you would have been sorrier than if he'd got any one else. Well, I felt just that way about you. I would rather have had him shoot any other girl in the room than you; yes, or in the whole State. Why, if anything should happen to you, Miss Hilma—well, I wouldn't care to go on with anything. S. Behrman could jump Quien Sabe, and welcome. And Delaney could shoot me full of holes whenever he got good and ready. I'd quit. I'd lay right down. I wouldn't care a whoop about anything any more. You are the only girl for me in the whole world. I didn't think so at first. I didn't want to. But seeing you around every day, and seeing how pretty you were, and how clever, and hearing your voice and all, why, it just got all inside of me somehow, and now I can't think of anything else. I hate to go to San Francisco, or Sacramento, or Visalia, or even Bonneville, for only a day, just because you aren't there, in any of those places, and I just rush what I've got to do so as I can get back here. While you were away that Christmas time, why, I was as lonesome as—oh, you don't know anything about it. I just scratched off the days on the calendar every night, one by one, till you got back. And it just comes to this, I want you with me all the time. I want you should have a home that's my home, too. I want to take care of you, and have you all for myself, you understand. What do you say?"

Hilma, standing up before him, retied a knot in her handkerchief bundle with elaborate precaution, blinking at it through her tears.

"What do you say, Miss Hilma?" Annixter repeated. "How about that? What do you say?"

Just above a whisper, Hilma murmured:

"I—I don't know."

"Don't know what? Don't you think we could hit it off together?"

"I don't know."

"I know we could, Hilma. I don't mean to scare you. What are you crying for?"

"I don't know."

Annixter got up, cast away his cigar, and dropping the buckskin's bridle, came and stood beside her, putting a hand on her shoulder. Hilma did not move, and he felt her trembling. She still plucked at the knot of the handkerchief.

"I can't do without you, little girl," Annixter continued, "and I want you. I want you bad. I don't get much fun out of life ever. It, sure, isn't my nature, I guess. I'm a hard man. Everybody is trying to down me, and now I'm up against the Railroad. I'm fighting 'em all, Hilma, night and day, lock, stock, and barrel, and I'm fighting now for my home, my land, everything I have in the world. If I win out, I want somebody to be glad with me. If I don't—I want somebody to be sorry for me, sorry with me,—and that somebody is you. I am dog-tired of going it alone. I want some one to back me up. I want to feel you alongside of me, to give me a touch of the shoulder now and then. I'm tired of fighting for *things*—land, property, money. I want to fight for some *person*—somebody beside myself. Understand? I want to feel that it isn't all selfishness—that there are other interests than mine in the game—that there's some one dependent on me, and that's thinking of me as I'm thinking of them—some one I can come home to at night and put my arm around—like this, and have her put her two arms around me—like—" He paused a second, and once again, as it had been in that moment of imminent peril, when he stood with his arm around her, their eyes met,—"put her two arms around me," prompted Annixter, half smiling, "like—like what, Hilma?"

"I don't know."

"Like what, Hilma?" he insisted.

"Like—like this?" she questioned. With a movement of infinite tenderness and affection she slid her arms around his neck, still crying a little.

The sensation of her warm body in his embrace, the feeling of her smooth, round arm, through the thinness of her sleeve, pressing against his cheek, thrilled Annixter with a delight such as he had never known. He bent his head and kissed her upon the nape of her neck, where the delicate amber tint melted into the thick, sweet smelling mass of her dark brown hair. She shivered a little, holding him closer, ashamed as yet to look up. Without speech, they stood there for a long minute, holding each other close. Then Hilma pulled away from him, mopping her tear-stained cheeks with the little moist ball of her handkerchief.

"What do you say? Is it a go?" demanded Annixter jovially.

"I thought I hated you all the time," she said, and the velvety huskiness of her voice never sounded so sweet to him.

"And I thought it was that crockery smashing goat of a lout of a cow-puncher."

"Delaney? The idea! Oh, dear! I think it must always have been you."

"Since when, Hilma?" he asked, putting his arm around her. "Ah, but it is good to have you, my girl," he exclaimed, delighted beyond words that she permitted this freedom. "Since when? Tell us all about it."

"Oh, since always. It was ever so long before I came to think of you—to, well, to think about—I mean to remember—oh, you know what I mean. But when I did, oh, *then*!"

"Then what?"

"I don't know—I haven't thought—that way long enough to know."

"But you said you thought it must have been me always."

"I know; but that was different—oh, I'm all mixed up. I'm so nervous and trembly now. Oh," she cried suddenly, her face overcast with a look of earnestness and great seriousness, both her hands catching at his wrist, "Oh, you *will* be good to me, now, won't you? I'm only a little, little child in so many ways, and I've given myself to you, all in a minute, and I can't go back of it now, and it's for always. I don't know how it happened or why. Sometimes I think I didn't wish it, but now it's done, and I am glad and happy. But *now* if you weren't good to me—oh, think of how it would be with me. You are strong, and big, and rich, and I am only a servant of yours, a little nobody, but I've given all I had to you—myself—and you must be so good to me now. Always remember that. Be good to me and be gentle and kind to me in *little* things,—in everything, or you will break my heart."

Annixter took her in his arms. He was speechless. No words that he had at his command seemed adequate. All he could say was:

"That's all right, little girl. Don't you be frightened. I'll take care of you. That's all right, that's all right."

For a long time they sat there under the shade of the great trestle, their arms about each other, speaking only at intervals. An hour passed. The buckskin, finding no feed to her taste, took the trail stablewards, the bridle dragging. Annixter let her go. Rather than to take his arm from around Hilma's waist he would have lost his whole stable. At last, however, he bestirred himself and began to talk. He thought it time to formulate some plan of action.

"Well, now, Hilma, what are we going to do?"

"Do?" she repeated. "Why, must we do anything? Oh, isn't this enough?"

"There's better ahead," he went on. "I want to fix you up somewhere where you can have a bit of a home all to yourself. Let's see; Bonneville wouldn't do. There's always a lot of yaps about there that know us, and they would begin to cackle first off. How about San Francisco. We might go up next week and have a look around. I would find rooms you could take somewheres, and we would fix 'em up as lovely as how-do-you-do."

"Oh, but why go away from Quien Sabe?" she protested. "And, then, so soon, too. Why must we have a wedding trip, now that you are so busy? Wouldn't it be better—oh, I tell you, we could go to Monterey after we were married, for a little week, where mamma's people live, and then come back here to the ranch house and settle right down where we are and let me keep house for you. I wouldn't even want a single servant."

Annixter heard and his face grew troubled.

"Hum," he said, "I see."

He gathered up a handful of pebbles and began snapping them carefully into the creek. He fell thoughtful. Here was a phase of the affair he had not planned in the least. He had supposed all the time that Hilma took his meaning. His old suspicion that she was trying to get a hold on him stirred again for a moment. There was no good of such talk as that. Always these feemale girls seemed crazy to get married, bent on complicating the situation.

"Isn't that best?" said Hilma, glancing at him.

"I don't know," he muttered gloomily.

"Well, then, let's not. Let's come right back to Quien Sabe without going to Monterey. Anything that you want I want."

"I hadn't thought of it in just that way," he observed.

"In what way, then?"

"Can't we—can't we wait about this marrying business?"

"That's just it," she said gayly. "I said it was too soon. There would be so much to do between whiles. Why not say at the end of the summer?"

"Say what?"

"Our marriage, I mean."

"Why get married, then? What's the good of all that fuss about it? I don't go anything upon a minister puddling round in my affairs. What's the difference, anyhow? We understand each other. Isn't that enough? Pshaw, Hilma, *I'm* no marrying man."

She looked at him a moment, bewildered, then slowly she took his meaning. She rose to her feet, her eyes wide, her face paling with terror. He did not look at her, but he could hear the catch in her throat.

"Oh!" she exclaimed, with a long, deep breath, and again "Oh!" the back of her hand against her lips.

It was a quick gasp of a veritable physical anguish. Her eyes brimmed over. Annixter rose, looking at her.

"Well?" he said, awkwardly, "Well?"

Hilma leaped back from him with an instinctive recoil of her whole being, throwing out her hands in a gesture of defence, fearing she knew not what. There was as yet no sense of insult in her mind, no outraged modesty. She was only terrified. It was as though searching for wild flowers she had come suddenly upon a snake.

She stood for an instant, spellbound, her eyes wide, her bosom swelling; then, all at once, turned and fled, darting across the plank that served for a foot bridge over the creek, gaining the opposite bank and disappearing with a brisk rustle of underbrush, such as might have been made by the flight of a frightened fawn.

Abruptly Annixter found himself alone. For a moment he did not move, then he picked up his campaign hat, carefully creased its limp crown and put it on his head and stood for a moment, looking vaguely at the ground on both sides of him. He went away without uttering a word, without change of countenance, his hands in his pockets, his feet taking great strides along the trail in the direction of the ranch house.

He had no sight of Hilma again that evening, and the next morning he was up early and did not breakfast at the ranch house. Business of the League called him to Bonneville to confer with Magnus and the firm of lawyers retained by the League to fight the land-grabbing cases. An appeal was to be taken to the Supreme Court at Washington, and it was to be settled that day which of the cases involved should be considered as test cases.

Instead of driving or riding into Bonneville, as he usually

did, Annixter took an early morning train, the Bakersfield-Fresno local at Guadalajara, and went to Bonneville by rail, arriving there at twenty minutes after seven and breakfasting by appointment with Magnus Derrick and Osterman at the Yosemite House, on Main Street.

The conference of the committee with the lawyers took place in a front room of the Yosemite, one of the latter bringing with him his clerk, who made a stenographic report of the proceedings and took carbon copies of all letters written. The conference was long and complicated, the business transacted of the utmost moment, and it was not until two o'clock that Annixter found himself at liberty.

However, as he and Magnus descended into the lobby of the hotel, they were aware of an excited and interested group collected about the swing doors that opened from the lobby of the Yosemite into the bar of the same name. Dyke was there—even at a distance they could hear the reverberation of his deep-toned voice, uplifted in wrath and furious expostulation. Magnus and Annixter joined the group wondering, and all at once fell full upon the first scene of a drama.

That same morning Dyke's mother had awakened him according to his instructions at daybreak. A consignment of his hop poles from the north had arrived at the freight office of the P. and S. W. in Bonneville, and he was to drive in on his farm wagon and bring them out. He would have a busy day.

"Hello, hello," he said, as his mother pulled his ear to arouse him; "morning, mamma."

"It's time," she said, "after five already. Your breakfast is on the stove."

He took her hand and kissed it with great affection. He loved his mother devotedly, quite as much as he did the little tad. In their little cottage, in the forest of green hops that surrounded them on every hand, the three led a joyous and secluded life, contented, industrious, happy, asking nothing better. Dyke, himself, was a big-hearted, jovial man who spread an atmosphere of good-humour wherever he went. In the evenings he played with Sidney like a big boy, an older brother, lying on the bed, or the sofa, taking her in his arms. Between them they had invented a great game. The ex-engineer, his boots removed, his huge legs in the air, hoisted the little tad on the soles of his stockinged feet like a circus acrobat, dandling her there, pretending he was about to let her fall. Sidney, choking with delight, held on nervously, with little screams and chirps of excitement, while he shifted her gingerly from one foot to another, and thence, the final act, the great gallery play, to the palm of one great hand. At this point Mrs. Dyke was called in, both father and daughter, children both, crying out that she was to come in and look, look. She arrived out of breath from the kitchen, the potato masher in her hand.

"Such children," she murmured, shaking her head at them, amused for all that, tucking the potato masher under her arm and clapping her hands.

In the end, it was part of the game that Sidney should tumble down upon Dyke, whereat he invariably vented a great bellow as if in pain, declaring that his ribs were broken. Gasping, his eyes shut, he pretended to be in the extreme of dissolution—perhaps he was dying. Sidney, always a little uncertain, amused but distressed, shook him nervously, tugging at his beard, pushing open his eyelid with one finger, imploring him not to frighten her, to wake up and be good.

On this occasion, while yet he was half-dressed, Dyke tiptoed into his mother's room to look at Sidney fast asleep in her little iron cot, her arm under her head, her lips parted. With infinite precaution he kissed her twice, and then finding one little stocking, hung with its mate very neatly over the back of a chair, dropped into it a dime, rolled up in a wad of paper. He winked all to himself and went out again, closing the door with exaggerated carefulness.

He breakfasted alone, Mrs. Dyke pouring his coffee and handing him his plate of ham and eggs, and half an hour later took himself off in his springless, skeleton wagon, humming a tune behind his beard and cracking the whip over the backs of his staid and solid farm horses.

The morning was fine, the sun just coming up. He left Guadalajara, sleeping and lifeless, on his left, and going across lots, over an angle of Quien Sabe, came out upon the Upper Road, a mile below the Long Trestle. He was in great spirits, looking about him over the brown fields, ruddy with the dawn. Almost directly in front of him, but far off, the gilded dome of the court-house at Bonneville was glinting radiant in the first rays of the sun, while a few miles distant, toward the north, the venerable campanile of the Mission San Juan stood silhouetted in purplish black against the flaming east. As he proceeded, the great farm horses jogging forward, placid, deliberate, the country side waked to another day. Crossing the irrigating ditch further on, he met a gang of Portuguese, with picks and shovels over their shoulders, just going to work. Hooven, already abroad, shouted him a "Goot mornun" from behind the fence of Los Muertos. Far off, toward the southwest, in the bare expanse of the open fields, where a clump of eucalyptus and cypress trees set a dark green note, a thin stream of smoke rose straight into the air from the kitchen of Derrick's ranch houses.

But a mile or so beyond the Long Trestle he was surprised to see Magnus Derrick's *protégé*, the one-time shepherd, Vanamee, coming across Quien Sabe, by a trail from one of Annixter's division houses. Without knowing exactly why, Dyke received the impression that the young man had not been in bed all of that night.

As the two approached each other, Dyke eyed the young fellow. He was distrustful of Vanamee, having the country-bred suspicion of any person he could not understand. Vanamee was, beyond doubt, no part of the life of ranch and country town. He was an alien, a vagabond, a strange fellow who came and went in mysterious fashion, making no friends, keeping to himself. Why did he never wear a hat, why indulge in a fine, black, pointed beard, when either a round beard or a mustache was the invariable custom? Why did he not cut his hair? Above all, why did he prowl about so much at night? As the two passed each other, Dyke, for all his good-nature, was a little blunt in his greeting and looked back at the ex-shepherd over his shoulder.

Dyke was right in his suspicion. Vanamee's bed had not been disturbed for three nights. On the Monday of that week he had passed the entire night in the garden of the Mission, overlooking the Seed ranch, in the little valley. Tuesday evening had found him miles away from that spot, in a deep arroyo in the Sierra foothills to the eastward, while Wednesday he had slept in an abandoned 'dobe on Osterman's stock range, twenty miles from his resting place of the night before.

The fact of the matter was that the old restlessness had once more seized upon Vanamee. Something began tugging at him; the spur of some unseen rider touched his flank. The instinct of the wanderer woke and moved. For some time now he had been a part of the Los Muertos staff. On Quien Sabe, as on the other ranches, the slack season was at hand. While waiting for the wheat to come up no one was doing much of anything. Vanamee had come over to Los Muertos and spent most of his days on horseback, riding the range, rounding up and watching the cattle in the fourth division of the ranch. But if the vagabond instinct now roused itself in the strange fellow's nature, a counter influence had also set in. More and more Vanamee frequented the Mission garden after nightfall, sometimes remaining there till the dawn began to whiten, lying prone on the ground, his chin on his folded arms, his eyes searching the darkness over the little valley of the Seed ranch, watching, watching. As the days went by, he became more reticent than ever. Presley often came to find him on the stock range, a lonely figure in the great wilderness of bare, green hillsides, but Vanamee no longer took him into his confidence. Father Sarria alone heard his strange stories.

Dyke drove on toward Bonneville, thinking over the whole matter. He knew, as every one did in that part of the country, the legend of Vanamee and Angéle, the romance of the Mission garden, the mystery of the Other, Vanamee's flight to the deserts of the southwest, his periodic returns, his strange, reticent, solitary character, but, like many another of the country people, he accounted for Vanamee by a short and easy method. No doubt, the fellow's wits were turned. That was the long and short of it.

The ex-engineer reached the Post Office in Bonneville towards eleven o'clock, but he did not at once present his notice of the arrival of his consignment at Ruggles's office. It entertained him to indulge in an hour's lounging about the streets. It was seldom he got into town, and when he did he permitted himself the luxury of enjoying his evident popularity. He met friends everywhere, in the Post Office, in the drug store, in the barber shop and around the court-house. With each

one he held a moment's conversation; almost invariably this
ended in the same way:

"Come on 'n have a drink."

"Well, I don't care if I do."

And the friends proceeded to the Yosemite bar, pledging
each other with punctilious ceremony. Dyke, however, was a
strictly temperate man. His life on the engine had trained him
well. Alcohol he never touched, drinking instead ginger ale,
sarsaparilla-and-iron—soft drinks.

At the drug store, which also kept a stock of miscellaneous
stationery, his eye was caught by a "transparent slate," a
child's toy, where upon a little pane of frosted glass one could
trace with considerable elaboration outline figures of cows,
ploughs, bunches of fruit and even rural water mills that were
printed on slips of paper underneath.

"Now, there's an idea, Jim," he observed to the boy behind
the soda-water fountain; "I know a little tad that would just
about jump out of her skin for that. Think I'll have to take it
with me."

"How's Sidney getting along?" the other asked, while
wrapping up the package.

Dyke's enthusiasm had made of his little girl a celebrity
throughout Bonneville.

The ex-engineer promptly became voluble, assertive,
doggedly emphatic.

"Smartest little tad in all Tulare County, and more fun! A
regular whole show in herself."

"And the hops?" inquired the other.

"Bully," declared Dyke, with the good-natured man's readiness to talk of his private affairs to any one who would listen.
"Bully. I'm dead sure of a bonanza crop by now. The rain
came *just* right. I actually don't know as I can store the crop
in those barns I built, it's going to be so big. That foreman
of mine was a daisy. Jim, I'm going to make money in that
deal. After I've paid off the mortgage—you know I had to
mortgage, yes, crop and homestead both, but I can pay it off
and all the interest to boot, lovely,—well, and as I was saying, after all expenses are paid off I'll clear big money, m' son.
Yes, sir. I *knew* there was boodle in hops. You know the crop
is contracted for already. Sure, the foreman managed that.

He's a daisy. Chap in San Francisco will take it all and at the advanced price. I wanted to hang on, to see if it wouldn't go to six cents, but the foreman said, 'No, that's good enough.' So I signed. Ain't it bully, hey?"

"Then what'll you do?"

"Well, I don't know. I'll have a lay-off for a month or so and take the little tad and mother up and show 'em the city—'Frisco—until it's time for the schools to open, and then we'll put Sid in the seminary at Marysville. Catch on?"

"I suppose you'll stay right by hops now?"

"Right you are, m'son. I know a good thing when I see it. There's plenty others going into hops next season. I set 'em the example. Wouldn't be surprised if it came to be a regular industry hereabouts. I'm planning ahead for next year already. I can let the foreman go, now that I've learned the game myself, and I think I'll buy a piece of land off Quien Sabe and get a bigger crop, and build a couple more barns, and, by George, in about five years time I'll have things humming. I'm going to make *money*, Jim."

He emerged once more into the street and went up the block leisurely, planting his feet squarely. He fancied that he could feel he was considered of more importance nowadays. He was no longer a subordinate, an employee. He was his own man, a proprietor, an owner of land, furthering a successful enterprise. No one had helped him; he had followed no one's lead. He had struck out unaided for himself, and his success was due solely to his own intelligence, industry, and foresight. He squared his great shoulders till the blue gingham of his jumper all but cracked. Of late, his great blond beard had grown and the work in the sun had made his face very red. Under the visor of his cap—relic of his engineering days—his blue eyes twinkled with vast good-nature. He felt that he made a fine figure as he went by a group of young girls in lawns and muslins and garden hats on their way to the Post Office. He wondered if they looked after him, wondered if they had heard that he was in a fair way to become a rich man.

But the chronometer in the window of the jewelry store warned him that time was passing. He turned about, and, crossing the street, took his way to Ruggles's office, which was the freight as well as the land office of the P. and S. W. Railroad.

As he stood for a moment at the counter in front of the wire partition, waiting for the clerk to make out the order for the freight agent at the depot, Dyke was surprised to see a familiar figure in conference with Ruggles himself, by a desk inside the railing.

The figure was that of a middle-aged man, fat, with a great stomach, which he stroked from time to time. As he turned about, addressing a remark to the clerk, Dyke recognised S. Behrman. The banker, railroad agent, and political manipulator seemed to the ex-engineer's eyes to be more gross than ever. His smooth-shaven jowl stood out big and tremulous on either side of his face; the roll of fat on the nape of his neck, sprinkled with sparse, stiff hairs, bulged out with greater prominence. His great stomach, covered with a light brown linen vest, stamped with innumerable interlocked horseshoes, protruded far in advance, enormous, aggressive. He wore his inevitable round-topped hat of stiff brown straw, varnished so bright that it reflected the light of the office windows like a helmet, and even from where he stood Dyke could hear his loud breathing and the clink of the hollow links of his watch chain upon the vest buttons of imitation pearl, as his stomach rose and fell.

Dyke looked at him with attention. There was the enemy, the representative of the Trust with which Derrick's League was locking horns. The great struggle had begun to invest the combatants with interest. Daily, almost hourly, Dyke was in touch with the ranchers, the wheat-growers. He heard their denunciations, their growls of exasperation and defiance. Here was the other side—this placid, fat man, with a stiff straw hat and linen vest, who never lost his temper, who smiled affably upon his enemies, giving them good advice, commiserating with them in one defeat after another, never ruffled, never excited, sure of his power, conscious that back of him was the Machine, the colossal force, the inexhaustible coffers of a mighty organisation, vomiting millions to the League's thousands.

The League was clamorous, ubiquitous, its objects known to every urchin on the streets, but the Trust was silent, its ways inscrutable, the public saw only results. It worked on in the dark, calm, disciplined, irresistible. Abruptly Dyke received the impression of the multitudinous ramifications of the colossus. Under his feet the ground seemed mined; down there below him in the dark the huge tentacles went silently twisting and advancing, spreading out in every direction, sapping the strength of all opposition, quiet, gradual, biding the time to reach up and out and grip with a sudden unleashing of gigantic strength.

"I'll be wanting some cars of you people before the summer is out," observed Dyke to the clerk as he folded up and put away the order that the other had handed him. He remembered perfectly well that he had arranged the matter of transporting his crop some months before, but his rôle of proprietor amused him and he liked to busy himself again and again with the details of his undertaking.

"I suppose," he added, "you'll be able to give 'em to me. There'll be a big wheat crop to move this year and I don't want to be caught in any car famine."

"Oh, you'll get your cars," murmured the other.

"I'll be the means of bringing business your way," Dyke went on; "I've done so well with my hops that there are a lot of others going into the business next season. Suppose," he continued, struck with an idea, "suppose we went into some sort of pool, a sort of shippers' organisation, could you give us special rates, cheaper rates—say a cent and a half?"

The other looked up.

"A cent and a half! Say *four* cents and a half and maybe I'll talk business with you."

"Four cents and a half," returned Dyke, "I don't see it. Why, the regular rate is only two cents."

"No, it isn't," answered the clerk, looking him gravely in the eye, "it's five cents."

"Well, there's where you are wrong, m'son," Dyke retorted, genially. "You look it up. You'll find the freight on hops from Bonneville to 'Frisco is two cents a pound for car load lots. You told me that yourself last fall."

"That was last fall," observed the clerk. There was a silence. Dyke shot a glance of suspicion at the other. Then, reassured, he remarked:

"You look it up. You'll see I'm right."

S. Behrman came forward and shook hands politely with the ex-engineer.

"Anything I can do for you, Mr. Dyke?"

Dyke explained. When he had done speaking, the clerk turned to S. Behrman and observed, respectfully:

"Our regular rate on hops is five cents."

"Yes," answered S. Behrman, pausing to reflect; "yes, Mr. Dyke, that's right—five cents."

The clerk brought forward a folder of yellow paper and handed it to Dyke. It was inscribed at the top "Tariff Schedule No. 8," and underneath these words, in brackets, was a smaller inscription, *Supersedes No. 7 of Aug. 1.*"

"See for yourself," said S. Behrman. He indicated an item under the head of "Miscellany."

"The following rates for carriage of hops in car load lots," read Dyke, "take effect June 1, and will remain in force until superseded by a later tariff. Those quoted beyond Stockton are subject to changes in traffic arrangements with carriers by water from that point."

In the list that was printed below, Dyke saw that the rate for hops between Bonneville or Guadalajara and San Francisco was five cents.

For a moment Dyke was confused. Then swiftly the matter became clear in his mind. The Railroad had raised the freight on hops from two cents to five.

All his calculations as to a profit on his little investment he had based on a freight rate of two cents a pound. He was under contract to deliver his crop. He could not draw back. The new rate ate up every cent of his gains. He stood there ruined.

"Why, what do you mean?" he burst out. "You promised me a rate of two cents and I went ahead with my business with that understanding. What do you mean?"

S. Behrman and the clerk watched him from the other side of the counter.

"The rate is five cents," declared the clerk doggedly.

"Well, that ruins me," shouted Dyke. "Do you understand? I won't make fifty cents. *Make!* Why, I will *owe*,—I'll be—be— That ruins me, do you understand?"

The other raised a shoulder.

"We don't force you to ship. You can do as you like. The rate is five cents."

"Well—but—damn you, I'm under contract to deliver. What am I going to do? Why, you told me—you promised me a two-cent rate."

"I don't remember it," said the clerk. "I don't know anything about that. But I know this; I know that hops have gone up. I know the German crop was a failure and that the crop in New York wasn't worth the hauling. Hops have gone up to nearly a dollar. You don't suppose we don't know that, do you, Mr. Dyke?"

"What's the price of hops got to do with you?"

"It's got *this* to do with us," returned the other with a sudden aggressiveness, "that the freight rate has gone up to meet the price. We're not doing business for our health. My orders are to raise your rate to five cents, and I think you are getting off easy."

Dyke stared in blank astonishment. For the moment, the audacity of the affair was what most appealed to him. He forgot its personal application.

"Good Lord," he murmured, "good Lord! What will you people do next? Look here. What's your basis of applying freight rates, anyhow?" he suddenly vociferated with furious sarcasm. "What's your rule? What are you guided by?"

But at the words, S. Behrman, who had kept silent during the heat of the discussion, leaned abruptly forward. For the only time in his knowledge, Dyke saw his face inflamed with anger and with the enmity and contempt of all this farming element with whom he was contending.

"Yes, what's your rule? What's your basis?" demanded Dyke, turning swiftly to him.

S. Behrman emphasised each word of his reply with a tap of one forefinger on the counter before him:

"All—the—traffic—will—bear."

The ex-engineer stepped back a pace, his fingers on the ledge of the counter, to steady himself. He felt himself grow pale, his heart became a mere leaden weight in his chest, inert, refusing to beat.

In a second the whole affair, in all its bearings, went speeding before the eye of his imagination like the rapid unrolling of a panorama. Every cent of his earnings was sunk in this hop business of his. More than that, he had borrowed money to carry it on, certain of success—borrowed of S. Behrman, offering his crop and his little home as security. Once he failed to meet his obligations, S. Behrman would foreclose. Not only would the Railroad devour every morsel of his profits, but also it would take from him his home; at a blow he would be left penniless and without a home. What would then become of his mother—and what would become of the little tad? She, whom he had been planning to educate like a veritable lady. For all that year he had talked of his ambition for his little daughter to every one he met. All Bonneville knew of it. What a mark for gibes he had made of himself. The workingman turned farmer! What a target for jeers—he who had fancied he could elude the Railroad! He remembered he had once said the great Trust had overlooked his little enterprise, disdaining to plunder such small fry. He should have known better than that. How had he ever imagined the Road would permit him to make any money?

Anger was not in him yet; no rousing of the blind, white-hot wrath that leaps to the attack with prehensile fingers, moved him. The blow merely crushed, staggered, confused.

He stepped aside to give place to a coatless man in a pink shirt, who entered, carrying in his hands an automatic door-closing apparatus.

"Where does this go?" inquired the man.

Dyke sat down for a moment on a seat that had been removed from a worn-out railway car to do duty in Ruggles's office. On the back of a yellow envelope he made some vague figures with a stump of blue pencil, multiplying, subtracting, perplexing himself with many errors.

S. Behrman, the clerk, and the man with the door-closing apparatus involved themselves in a long argument, gazing intently at the top panel of the door. The man who had come to fix the apparatus was unwilling to guarantee it, unless a sign was put on the outside of the door, warning incomers that the door was self-closing. This sign would cost fifteen cents extra.

"But you didn't say anything about this when the thing was

ordered," declared S. Behrman. "No, I won't pay it, my friend. It's an overcharge."

"You needn't think," observed the clerk, "that just because you are dealing with the Railroad you are going to work us."

Genslinger came in, accompanied by Delaney. S. Behrman and the clerk, abruptly dismissing the man with the door-closing machine, put themselves behind the counter and engaged in conversation with these two. Genslinger introduced Delaney. The buster had a string of horses he was shipping southward. No doubt he had come to make arrangements with the Railroad in the matter of stock cars. The conference of the four men was amicable in the extreme.

Dyke, studying the figures on the back of the envelope, came forward again. Absorbed only in his own distress, he ignored the editor and the cow-puncher.

"Say," he hazarded, "how about this? I make out——"

"We've told you what our rates are, Mr. Dyke," exclaimed the clerk angrily. "That's all the arrangement we will make. Take it or leave it." He turned again to Genslinger, giving the ex-engineer his back.

Dyke moved away and stood for a moment in the centre of the room, staring at the figures on the envelope.

"I don't see," he muttered, "just what I'm going to do. No, I don't see what I'm going to do at all."

Ruggles came in, bringing with him two other men in whom Dyke recognised dummy buyers of the Los Muertos and Osterman ranchos. They brushed by him, jostling his elbow, and as he went out of the door he heard them exchange jovial greetings with Delaney, Genslinger, and S. Behrman.

Dyke went down the stairs to the street and proceeded onward aimlessly in the direction of the Yosemite House, fingering the yellow envelope and looking vacantly at the sidewalk.

There was a stoop to his massive shoulders. His great arms dangled loosely at his sides, the palms of his hands open.

As he went along, a certain feeling of shame touched him. Surely his predicament must be apparent to every passer-by. No doubt, every one recognised the unsuccessful man in the very way he slouched along. The young girls in lawns, muslins, and garden hats, returning from the Post Office, their hands full of letters, must surely see in him the type of the failure, the bankrupt.

Then brusquely his tardy rage flamed up. By God, *no*, it was not his fault; he had made no mistake. His energy, industry, and foresight had been sound. He had been merely the object of a colossal trick, a sordid injustice, a victim of the insatiate greed of the monster, caught and choked by one of those millions of tentacles suddenly reaching up from below, from out the dark beneath his feet, coiling around his throat, throttling him, strangling him, sucking his blood. For a moment he thought of the courts, but instantly laughed at the idea. What court was immune from the power of the monster? Ah, the rage of helplessness, the fury of impotence! No help, no hope,—ruined in a brief instant—he a veritable giant, built of great sinews, powerful, in the full tide of his manhood, having all his health, all his wits. How could he now face his home? How could he tell his mother of this catastrophe? And Sidney—the little tad; how could he explain to her this wretchedness—how soften her disappointment? How keep the tears from out her eyes—how keep alive her confidence in him—her faith in his resources?

Bitter, fierce, ominous, his wrath loomed up in his heart. His fists gripped tight together, his teeth clenched. Oh, for a moment to have his hand upon the throat of S. Behrman, wringing the breath from him, wrenching out the red life of him—staining the street with the blood sucked from the veins of the People!

To the first friend that he met, Dyke told the tale of the tragedy, and to the next, and to the next. The affair went from mouth to mouth, spreading with electrical swiftness, overpassing and running ahead of Dyke himself, so that by the time he reached the lobby of the Yosemite House, he found his story awaiting him. A group formed about him. In his immediate vicinity business for the instant was suspended. The group swelled. One after another of his friends added themselves to it. Magnus Derrick joined it, and Annixter. Again and again, Dyke recounted the matter, beginning with the time when he was discharged from the same corporation's service for refusing to accept an unfair wage. His voice quivered with exasperation; his heavy frame shook with rage; his eyes were injected, blood-shot; his face flamed vermilion, while his deep bass rumbled throughout the running comments of his auditors like the thunderous reverberation of diapason.

From all points of view, the story was discussed by those who listened to him, now in the heat of excitement, now calmly, judicially. One verdict, however, prevailed. It was voiced by Annixter: "You're stuck. You can roar till you're black in the face, but you can't buck against the Railroad. There's nothing to be done."

"You can shoot the ruffian, you can shoot S. Behrman," clamoured one of the group. "Yes, sir; by the Lord, you can shoot him."

"Poor fool," commented Annixter, turning away.

Nothing to be done. No, there was nothing to be done— not one thing. Dyke, at last alone and driving his team out of the town, turned the business confusedly over in his mind from end to end. Advice, suggestion, even offers of financial aid had been showered upon him from all directions. Friends were not wanting who heatedly presented to his consideration all manner of ingenious plans, wonderful devices. They were worthless. The tentacle held fast. He was stuck.

By degrees, as his wagon carried him farther out into the country, and open empty fields, his anger lapsed, and the numbness of bewilderment returned. He could not look one hour ahead into the future; could formulate no plans even for the next day. He did not know what to do. He was stuck.

With the limpness and inertia of a sack of sand, the reins slipping loosely in his dangling fingers, his eyes fixed, staring between the horses' heads, he allowed himself to be carried aimlessly along. He resigned himself. What did he care? What was the use of going on? He was stuck.

The team he was driving had once belonged to the Los Muertos stables, and unguided as the horses were, they took the country road towards Derrick's ranch house. Dyke, all abroad, was unaware of the fact till, drawn by the smell of water, the horses halted by the trough in front of Caraher's saloon.

The ex-engineer dismounted, looking about him, realising where he was. So much the worse; it did not matter. Now that he had come so far it was as short to go home by this route as to return on his tracks. Slowly he unchecked the horses and stood at their heads, watching them drink.

"I don't see," he muttered, "just what I am going to do."

Caraher appeared at the door of his place, his red face, red beard, and flaming cravat standing sharply out from the shadow of the doorway. He called a welcome to Dyke.

"Hello, Captain."

Dyke looked up, nodding his head listlessly.

"Hello, Caraher," he answered.

"Well," continued the saloonkeeper, coming forward a step, " what's the news in town?"

Dyke told him. Caraher's red face suddenly took on a darker colour. The red glint in his eyes shot from under his eyebrows. Furious, he vented a rolling explosion of oaths.

"And now it's your turn," he vociferated. "They ain't after only the big wheat-growers, the rich men. By God, they'll even pick the poor man's pocket. Oh, they'll get their bellies full some day. It can't last forever. They'll wake up the wrong kind of man some morning, the man that's got guts in him, that will hit back when he's kicked and that will talk to 'em with a torch in one hand and a stick of dynamite in the other." He raised his clenched fists in the air. "So help me, God," he cried, " when I think it all over I go crazy, I see red. Oh, if the people only knew their strength. Oh, if I could wake 'em up. There's not only Shelgrim, but there's others. All the magnates, all the butchers, all the blood-suckers, by the thousands. Their day will come, by God, it will."

By now, the ex-engineer and the bar-keeper had retired to the saloon back of the grocery to talk over the details of this new outrage. Dyke, still a little dazed, sat down by one of the tables, preoccupied, saying but little, and Caraher as a matter of course set the whiskey bottle at his elbow.

It happened that at this same moment, Presley, returning to Los Muertos from Bonneville, his pockets full of mail, stopped in at the grocery to buy some black lead for his bi-cycle. In the saloon, on the other side of the narrow partition, he overheard the conversation between Dyke and Caraher. The door was open. He caught every word distinctly.

"Tell us all about it, Dyke," urged Caraher.

For the fiftieth time Dyke told the story. Already it had crystallised into a certain form. He used the same phrases with each repetition, the same sentences, the same words. In his mind it became set. Thus he would tell it to any one who would listen from now on, week after week, year after year, all the rest of his life—"And I based my calculations on a two-cent rate. So soon as they saw I was to make money they doubled the tariff—all the traffic would bear—and I mortgaged to S. Behrman—ruined me with a turn of the hand—stuck, cinched, and not one thing to be done."

As he talked, he drank glass after glass of whiskey, and the honest rage, the open, above-board fury of his mind coagulated, thickened, and sunk to a dull, evil hatred, a wicked, oblique malevolence. Caraher, sure now of winning a disciple, replenished his glass.

"Do you blame us now," he cried, "us others, the Reds? Ah, yes, it's all very well for your middle class to preach moderation. I could do it, too. You could do it, too, if your belly was fed, if your property was safe, if your wife had not been murdered, if your children were not starving. Easy enough then to preach law-abiding methods, legal redress, and all such rot. But how about *us*?" he vociferated. "Ah, yes, I'm a loud-mouthed rum-seller, ain't I? I'm a wild-eyed striker, ain't I? I'm a blood-thirsty anarchist, ain't I? Wait till you've seen your wife brought home to you with the face you used to kiss smashed in by a horse's hoof—killed by the Trust, as it happened to me. Then talk about moderation! And you, Dyke, black-listed engineer, discharged employee, ruined agriculturist, wait till you see your little tad and your mother turned out of doors when S. Behrman forecloses. Wait till you see 'em getting thin and white, and till you hear your little girl ask you why you all don't eat a little more and that she wants her dinner and you can't give it to her. Wait till you see—at the same time that your family is dying for lack of bread—a hundred thousand acres of wheat—millions of bushels of food—grabbed and gobbled by the Railroad Trust, and then talk of moderation. That talk is just what the Trust wants to hear. It ain't frightened of that. There's one thing only it does listen to, one thing it is frightened of—the people with dynamite in their hands,—six inches of plugged gaspipe. *That* talks."

Dyke did not reply. He filled another pony of whiskey and drank it in two gulps. His frown had lowered to a scowl, his face was a dark red, his head had sunk, bull-like, between his massive shoulders; without winking he gazed long and with troubled eyes at his knotted, muscular hands, lying open on the table before him, idle, their occupation gone.

Presley forgot his black lead. He listened to Caraher. Through the open door he caught a glimpse of Dyke's back, broad, muscled, bowed down, the great shoulders stooping.

The whole drama of the doubled freight rate leaped salient and distinct in the eye of his mind. And this was but one instance, an isolated case. Because he was near at hand he happened to see it. How many others were there, the length and breadth of the State? Constantly this sort of thing must occur—little industries choked out in their very beginnings, the air full of the death rattles of little enterprises, expiring unobserved in far-off counties, up in cañons and arroyos of the foothills, forgotten by every one but the monster who was daunted by the magnitude of no business, however great, who overlooked no opportunity of plunder, however petty, who with one tentacle grabbed a hundred thousand acres of wheat, and with another pilfered a pocketful of growing hops.

He went away without a word, his head bent, his hands clutched tightly on the cork grips of the handle bars of his bicycle. His lips were white. In his heart a blind demon of revolt raged tumultuous, shrieking blasphemies.

At Los Muertos, Presley overtook Annixter. As he guided his wheel up the driveway to Derrick's ranch house, he saw the master of Quien Sabe and Harran in conversation on the steps of the porch. Magnus stood in the doorway, talking to his wife.

Occupied with the press of business and involved in the final conference with the League's lawyers on the eve of the latter's departure for Washington, Annixter had missed the train that was to take him back to Guadalajara and Quien Sabe. Accordingly, he had accepted the Governor's invitation to return with him on his buck-board to Los Muertos, and before leaving Bonneville had telephoned to his ranch to have young Vacca bring the buckskin, by way of the Lower Road, to meet him at Los Muertos. He found her waiting there for him, but before going on, delayed a few moments to tell Harran of Dyke's affair.

"I wonder what he will do now?" observed Harran when his first outburst of indignation had subsided.

"Nothing," declared Annixter. "He's stuck."

"That eats up every cent of Dyke's earnings," Harran went on. "He has been ten years saving them. Oh, I told him to make sure of the Railroad when he first spoke to me about growing hops."

"I've just seen him," said Presley, as he joined the others. "He was at Caraher's. I only saw his back. He was drinking at a table and his back was towards me. But the man looked broken—absolutely crushed. It is terrible, terrible."

"He was at Caraher's, was he?" demanded Annixter.

"Yes."

"Drinking, hey?"

"I think so. Yes, I saw a bottle."

"Drinking at Caraher's," exclaimed Annixter, rancorously; "I can see *his* finish."

There was a silence. It seemed as if nothing more was to be said. They paused, looking thoughtfully on the ground.

In silence, grim, bitter, infinitely sad, the three men, as if at that moment actually standing in the bar-room of Caraher's roadside saloon, contemplated the slow sinking, the inevitable collapse and submerging of one of their companions, the wreck of a career, the ruin of an individual; an honest man, strong, fearless, upright, struck down by a colossal power, perverted by an evil influence, go reeling to his ruin.

"I see his finish," repeated Annixter. "Exit Dyke, and score another tally for S. Behrman, Shelgrim and Co."

He moved away impatiently, loosening the tie-rope with which the buckskin was fastened. He swung himself up.

"God for us all," he declared as he rode away, "and the devil take the hindmost. Good-bye, I'm going home. I still have one a little longer."

He galloped away along the Lower Road, in the direction of Quien Sabe, emerging from the grove of cypress and

eucalyptus about the ranch house, and coming out upon the
bare brown plain of the wheat land, stretching away from him
in apparent barrenness on either hand.

It was late in the day, already his shadow was long upon
the padded dust of the road in front of him. On ahead, a long
ways off, and a little to the north, the venerable campanile of
the Mission San Juan was glinting radiant in the last rays of
the sun, while behind him, towards the north and west, the
gilded dome of the court-house at Bonneville stood silhouetted in purplish black against the flaming west. Annixter
spurred the buckskin forward. He feared he might be late to
his supper. He wondered if it would be brought to him by
Hilma.

Hilma! The name struck across in his brain with a pleasant,
glowing tremour. All through that day of activity, of strenuous business, the minute and cautious planning of the final
campaign in the great war of the League and the Trust, the
idea of her and the recollection of her had been the undercur-
rent of his thoughts. At last he was alone. He could put all
other things behind him and occupy himself solely with her.

In that glory of the day's end, in that chaos of sunshine, he
saw her again. Unimaginative, crude, direct, his fancy, nevertheless, placed her before him, steeped in sunshine, saturated
with glorious light, brilliant, radiant, alluring. He saw the
sweet simplicity of her carriage, the statuesque evenness of the
contours of her figure, the single, deep swell of her bosom,
the solid masses of her hair. He remembered the small contradictory suggestions of feminine daintiness he had so often remarked about her, her slim, narrow feet, the little steel
buckles of her low shoes, the knot of black ribbon she had
begun to wear of late on the back of her head, and he heard
her voice, low-pitched, velvety, a sweet, murmuring huskiness
that seemed to come more from her chest than from her
throat.

The buckskin's hoofs clattered upon the gravelly flats of
Broderson's Creek underneath the Long Trestle. Annixter's
mind went back to the scene of the previous evening, when
he had come upon her at this place. He set his teeth with
anger and disappointment. Why had she not been able to understand? What was the matter with these women, always set

upon this marrying notion? Was it not enough that he wanted
her more than any other girl he knew and that she wanted
him? She had said as much. Did she think she was going to
be mistress of Quien Sabe? Ah, that was it. She was after his
property, was for marrying him because of his money. His
unconquerable suspicion of the woman, his innate distrust of
the feminine element would not be done away with. What
fathomless duplicity was hers, that she could appear so innocent. It was almost unbelievable; in fact, *was* it believable?

For the first time doubt assailed him. Suppose Hilma was
indeed all that she appeared to be. Suppose it was not with
her a question of his property, after all; it was a poor time to
think of marrying him for his property when all Quien Sabe
hung in the issue of the next few months. Suppose she had
been sincere. But he caught himself up. Was he to be fooled
by a feemale girl at this late date? He, Buck Annixter, crafty,
hard-headed, a man of affairs? Not much. Whatever transpired he would remain the master.

He reached Quien Sabe in this frame of mind. But at this
hour, Annixter, for all his resolutions, could no longer control
his thoughts. As he stripped the saddle from the buckskin and
led her to the watering trough by the stable corral, his heart
was beating thick at the very notion of being near Hilma
again. It was growing dark, but covertly he glanced here and
there out of the corners of his eyes to see if she was anywhere
about. Annixter—how, he could not tell—had become possessed of the idea that Hilma would not inform her parents
of what had passed between them the previous evening under
the Long Trestle. He had no idea that matters were at an end
between himself and the young woman. He must apologise,
he saw that clearly enough, must eat crow, as he told himself.
Well, he would eat crow. He was not afraid of her any longer,
now that she had made her confession to him. He would see
her as soon as possible and get this business straightened out,
and begin again from a new starting point. What he wanted
with Hilma, Annixter did not define clearly in his mind. At
one time he had known perfectly well what he wanted. Now,
the goal of his desires had become vague. He could not say
exactly what it was. He preferred that things should go forward without much idea of consequences; if consequences

came, they would do so naturally enough, and of themselves; all that he positively knew was that Hilma occupied his thoughts morning, noon, and night; that he was happy when he was with her, and miserable when away from her.

The Chinese cook served his supper in silence. Annixter ate and drank and lighted a cigar, and after his meal sat on the porch of his house, smoking and enjoying the twilight. The evening was beautiful, warm, the sky one powder of stars. From the direction of the stables he heard one of the Portuguese hands picking a guitar.

But he wanted to see Hilma. The idea of going to bed without at least a glimpse of her became distasteful to him. Annixter got up and descending from the porch began to walk aimlessly about between the ranch buildings, with eye and ear alert. Possibly he might meet her somewheres.

The Trees' little house, toward which inevitably Annixter directed his steps, was dark. Had they all gone to bed so soon? He made a wide circuit about it, listening, but heard no sound. The door of the dairy-house stood ajar. He pushed it open, and stepped into the odorous darkness of its interior. The pans and deep cans of polished metal glowed faintly from the corners and from the walls. The smell of new cheese was pungent in his nostrils. Everything was quiet. There was nobody there. He went out again, closing the door, and stood for a moment in the space between the dairy-house and the new barn, uncertain as to what he should do next.

As he waited there, his foreman came out of the men's bunk house, on the other side of the kitchens, and crossed over toward the barn. "Hello, Billy," muttered Annixter as he passed.

"Oh, good evening, Mr. Annixter," said the other, pausing in front of him. "I didn't know you were back. By the way," he added, speaking as though the matter was already known to Annixter, "I see old man Tree and his family have left us. Are they going to be gone long? Have they left for good?"

"What's that?" Annixter exclaimed. "When did they go? Did all of them go, all three?"

"Why, I thought you knew. Sure, they all left on the afternoon train for San Francisco. Cleared out in a hurry—took all their trunks. Yes, all three went—the young lady, too.

They gave me notice early this morning. They ain't ought to have done that. I don't know who I'm to get to run the dairy on such short notice. Do you know any one, Mr. Annixter?"

"Well, why in hell did you let them go?" vociferated Annixter. "Why didn't you keep them here till I got back? Why didn't you find out if they were going for good? I can't be everywhere. What do I feed you for if it ain't to look after things I can't attend to?"

He turned on his heel and strode away straight before him, not caring where he was going. He tramped out from the group of ranch buildings; holding on over the open reach of his ranch, his teeth set, his heels digging furiously into the ground. The minutes passed. He walked on swiftly, muttering to himself from time to time.

"Gone, by the Lord. Gone, by the Lord. By the Lord Harry, she's cleared out."

As yet his head was empty of all thought. He could not steady his wits to consider this new turn of affairs. He did not even try.

"Gone, by the Lord," he exclaimed. "By the Lord, she's cleared out."

He found the irrigating ditch, and the beaten path made by the ditch tenders that bordered it, and followed it some five minutes; then struck off at right angles over the rugged surface of the ranch land, to where a great white stone jutted from the ground. There he sat down, and leaning forward, rested his elbows on his knees, and looked out vaguely into the night, his thoughts swiftly readjusting themselves.

He was alone. The silence of the night, the infinite repose of the flat, bare earth—two immensities—widened around and above him like illimitable seas. A grey half-light, mysterious, grave, flooded downward from the stars.

Annixter was in torment. Now, there could be no longer any doubt—now it was Hilma or nothing. Once out of his reach, once lost to him, and the recollection of her assailed him with unconquerable vehemence. Much as she had occupied his mind, he had never realised till now how vast had been the place she had filled in his life. He had told her as much, but even then he did not believe it.

Suddenly, a bitter rage against himself overwhelmed him as

he thought of the hurt he had given her the previous evening. He should have managed differently. How, he did not know, but the sense of the outrage he had put upon her abruptly recoiled against him with cruel force. Now, he was sorry for it, infinitely sorry, passionately sorry. He had hurt her. He had brought the tears to her eyes. He had so flagrantly insulted her that she could no longer bear to breathe the same air with him. She had told her parents all. She had left Quien Sabe—had left him for good, at the very moment when he believed he had won her. Brute, beast that he was, he had driven her away.

An hour went by; then two, then four, then six. Annixter still sat in his place, groping and battling in a confusion of spirit, the like of which he had never felt before. He did not know what was the matter with him. He could not find his way out of the dark and out of the turmoil that wheeled around him. He had had no experience with women. There was no precedent to guide him. How was he to get out of this? What was the clew that would set everything straight again?

That he would give Hilma up, never once entered his head. Have her he would. She had given herself to him. Everything should have been easy after that, and instead, here he was alone in the night, wrestling with himself, in deeper trouble than ever, and Hilma farther than ever away from him.

It was true, he might have Hilma, even now, if he was willing to marry her. But marriage, to his mind, had been always a vague, most remote possibility, almost as vague and as remote as his death,—a thing that happened to some men, but that would surely never occur to him, or, if it did, it would be after long years had passed, when he was older, more settled, more mature—an event that belonged to the period of his middle life, distant as yet.

He had never faced the question of his marriage. He had kept it at an immense distance from him. It had never been a part of his order of things. He was not a marrying man.

But Hilma was an ever-present reality, as near to him as his right hand. Marriage was a formless, far distant abstraction. Hilma a tangible, imminent fact. Before he could think of the two as one; before he could consider the idea of marriage, side by side with the idea of Hilma, measureless distances had to be traversed, things as disassociated in his mind as fire and water, had to be fused together; and between the two he was torn as if upon a rack.

Slowly, by imperceptible degrees, the imagination, unused, unwilling machine, began to work. The brain's activity lapsed proportionately. He began to think less, and feel more. In that rugged composition, confused, dark, harsh, a furrow had been driven deep, a little seed planted, a little seed at first weak, forgotten, lost in the lower dark places of his character.

But as the intellect moved slower, its functions growing numb, the idea of self dwindled. Annixter no longer considered himself; no longer considered the notion of marriage from the point of view of his own comfort, his own wishes, his own advantage. He realised that in his new-found desire to make her happy, he was sincere. There was something in that idea, after all. To make some one happy—how about that now? It was worth thinking of.

Far away, low down in the east, a dim belt, a grey light began to whiten over the horizon. The tower of the Mission stood black against it. The dawn was coming. The baffling obscurity of the night was passing. Hidden things were coming into view.

Annixter, his eyes half-closed, his chin upon his fist, allowed his imagination full play. How would it be if he should take Hilma into his life, this beautiful young girl, pure as he now knew her to be; innocent, noble with the inborn nobility of dawning womanhood? An overwhelming sense of his own unworthiness suddenly bore down upon him with crushing force, as he thought of this. He had gone about the whole affair wrongly. He had been mistaken from the very first. She was infinitely above him. He did not want—he should not desire to be the master. It was she, his servant, poor, simple, lowly even, who should condescend to him.

Abruptly there was presented to his mind's eye a picture of the years to come, if he now should follow his best, his highest, his most unselfish impulse. He saw Hilma, his own, for better or for worse, for richer or for poorer, all barriers down between them, he giving himself to her as freely, as nobly, as she had given herself to him. By a supreme effort, not of the will, but of the emotion, he fought his way across that vast gulf that for a time had gaped between Hilma and the idea of his marriage. Instantly, like the swift blending of beautiful colours, like the harmony of beautiful chords of music, the two ideas melted into one, and in that moment into his harsh, unlovely world a new idea was born. Annixter stood suddenly upright, a mighty tenderness, a gentleness of spirit, such as he had never conceived of, in his heart strained, swelled, and in a moment seemed to burst. Out of the dark furrows of his soul, up from the deep rugged recesses of his being, something rose, expanding. He opened his arms wide. An immense happiness overpowered him. Actual tears came to his eyes. Without knowing why, he was not ashamed of it. This poor, crude fellow, harsh, hard, narrow, with his unlovely nature, his fierce truculency, his selfishness, his obstinacy, abruptly knew that all the sweetness of life, all the great vivifying eternal force of humanity had burst into life within him.

The little seed, long since planted, gathering strength quietly, had at last germinated.

Then as the realisation of this hardened into certainty, in the growing light of the new day that had just dawned for him, Annixter uttered a cry. Now at length, he knew the meaning of it all.

"Why—I—I, I *love* her," he cried. Never until then had it occurred to him. Never until then, in all his thoughts of Hilma, had that great word passed his lips.

It was a Memnonian cry, the greeting of the hard, harsh image of man, rough-hewn, flinty, granitic, uttering a note of joy, acclaiming the new risen sun.

By now it was almost day. The east glowed opalescent. All about him Annixter saw the land inundated with light. But there was a change. Overnight something had occurred. In his perturbation the change seemed to him, at first, elusive, almost fanciful, unreal. But now as the light spread, he looked again at the gigantic scroll of ranch lands unrolled before him from edge to edge of the horizon. The change was not fanciful. The change was real. The earth was no longer bare. The land was no longer barren,—no longer empty, no longer dull brown. All at once Annixter shouted aloud.

There it was, the Wheat, the Wheat! The little seed long

planted, germinating in the deep, dark furrows of the soil, straining, swelling, suddenly in one night had burst upward to the light. The wheat had come up. It was there before him, around him, everywhere, illimitable, immeasurable. The winter brownness of the ground was overlaid with a little shimmer of green. The promise of the sowing was being fulfilled. The earth, the loyal mother, who never failed, who never disappointed, was keeping her faith again. Once more the strength of nations was renewed. Once more the force of the world was revivified. Once more the Titan, benignant, calm, stirred and woke, and the morning abruptly blazed into glory upon the spectacle of a man whose heart leaped exuberant with the love of a woman, and an exulting earth gleaming transcendent with the radiant magnificence of an inviolable pledge.

III

PRESLEY'S ROOM in the ranch house of Los Muertos was in the second story of the building. It was a corner room; one of its windows facing the south, the other the east. Its appointments were of the simplest. In one angle was the small white painted iron bed, covered with a white counterpane. The walls were hung with a white paper figured with knots of pale green leaves, very gay and bright. There was a straw matting on the floor. White muslin half-curtains hung in the windows, upon the sills of which certain plants bearing pink waxen flowers of which Presley did not know the name, grew in oblong green boxes. The walls were unadorned, save by two pictures, one a reproduction of the "Reading from Homer," the other a charcoal drawing of the Mission of San Juan de Guadalajara, which Presley had made himself. By the east window stood the plainest of deal tables, innocent of any cloth or covering, such as might have been used in a kitchen. It was Presley's work table, and was invariably littered with papers, half-finished manuscripts, drafts of poems, notebooks, pens, half-smoked cigarettes, and the like. Near at hand, upon a shelf, were his books. There were but two chairs in the room—the straight backed wooden chair, that stood in front of the table, angular, upright, and in which it was impossible to take one's ease, and the long comfortable wicker steamer chair, stretching its length in front of the south window. Presley was immensely fond of this room. It amused and interested him to maintain its air of rigorous simplicity and freshness. He abhorred cluttered bric-a-brac and meaningless *objets d'art*. Once in so often he submitted his room to a vigorous inspection; setting it to rights, removing everything but the essentials, the few ornaments which, in a way, were part of his life.

His writing had by this time undergone a complete change. The notes for his great Song of the West, the epic poem he once had hoped to write he had flung aside, together with all the abortive attempts at its beginning. Also he had torn up a great quantity of "fugitive" verses, preserving only a certain half-finished poem, that he called "The Toilers." This poem was a comment upon the social fabric, and had been inspired by the sight of a painting he had seen in Cedarquist's art gallery. He had written all but the last verse.

On the day that he had overheard the conversation between Dyke and Caraher, in the latter's saloon, which had acquainted him with the monstrous injustice of the increased tariff, Presley had returned to Los Muertos, white and trembling, roused to a pitch of exaltation, the like of which he had never known in all his life. His wrath was little short of even Caraher's. He too "saw red"; a mighty spirit of revolt heaved tumultuous within him. It did not seem possible that this outrage could go on much longer. The oppression was incredible; the plain story of it set down in truthful statement of fact would not be believed by the outside world.

He went up to his little room and paced the floor with clenched fists and burning face, till at last, the repression of his contending thoughts all but suffocated him, and he flung himself before his table and began to write. For a time, his pen seemed to travel of itself; words came to him without searching, shaping themselves into phrases,—the phrases building themselves up to great, forcible sentences, full of eloquence, of fire, of passion. As his prose grew more exalted, it passed easily into the domain of poetry. Soon the cadence of his paragraphs settled to an ordered beat and rhythm, and in the end Presley had thrust aside his journal and was once more writing verse.

He picked up his incomplete poem of "The Toilers," read it hastily a couple of times to catch its swing, then the Idea of the last verse—the idea for which he so long had sought in vain—abruptly springing to his brain, wrote it off without so much as replenishing his pen with ink. He added still another verse, bringing the poem to a definite close, resuming its entire conception, and ending with a single majestic thought, simple, noble, dignified, absolutely convincing.

Presley laid down his pen and leaned back in his chair, with the certainty that for one moment he had touched untrod heights. His hands were cold, his head on fire, his heart leaping tumultuous in his breast.

Now at last, he had achieved. He saw why he had never grasped the inspiration for his vast, vague, *impersonal* Song of the West. At the time when he sought for it, his convictions had not been aroused; he had not then cared for the People. His sympathies had not been touched. Small wonder that he had missed it. Now he was of the People; he had been stirred to his lowest depths. His earnestness was almost a frenzy. He *believed*, and so to him all things were possible at once.

Then the artist in him reasserted itself. He became more interested in his poem, as such, than in the cause that had inspired it. He went over it again, retouching it carefully, changing a word here and there, and improving its rhythm. For the moment, he forgot the People, forgot his rage, his agitation of the previous hour, he remembered only that he had written a great poem.

Then doubt intruded. After all, was it so great? Did not its sublimity overpass a little the bounds of the ridiculous? Had he seen true? Had he failed again? He re-read the poem carefully; and it seemed all at once to lose force.

By now, Presley could not tell whether what he had written was true poetry or doggerel. He distrusted profoundly his own judgment. He must have the opinion of some one else, some one competent to judge. He could not wait; to-morrow would not do. He must know to a certainty before he could rest that night.

He made a careful copy of what he had written, and putting on his hat and laced boots, went down stairs and out upon the lawn, crossing over to the stables. He found Phelps there, washing down the buckboard.

"Do you know where Vanamee is to-day?" he asked the latter. Phelps put his chin in the air.

"Ask me something easy," he responded. "He might be at Guadalajara, or he might be up at Osterman's, or he might be a hundred miles away from either place. I know where he ought to be, Mr. Presley, but that ain't saying where the crazy gesabe is. He *ought* to be range-riding over east of Four, at the head waters of Mission Creek."

"I'll try for him there, at all events," answered Presley. "If you see Harran when he comes in, tell him I may not be back in time for supper."

Presley found the pony in the corral, cinched the saddle

upon him, and went off over the Lower Road, going east-ward at a brisk canter.

At Hooven's he called a "How do you do" to Minna, whom he saw lying in a slat hammock under the mammoth live oak, her foot in bandages; and then galloped on over the bridge across the irrigating ditch, wondering vaguely what would become of such a pretty girl as Minna, and if in the end she would marry the Portuguese foreman in charge of the ditching-gang. He told himself that he hoped she would, and that speedily. There was no lack of comment as to Minna Hooven about the ranches. Certainly she was a good girl, but she was seen at all hours here and there about Bonneville and Guadalajara, skylarking with the Portuguese farm hands of Quien Sabe and Los Muertos. She was very pretty; the men made fools of themselves over her. Presley hoped they would not end by making a fool of her.

Just beyond the irrigating ditch, Presley left the Lower Road, and following a trail that branched off southeasterly from this point, held on across the Fourth Division of the ranch, keeping the Mission Creek on his left. A few miles farther on, he went through a gate in a barbed wire fence, and at once engaged himself in a system of little arroyos and low rolling hills, that steadily lifted and increased in size as he proceeded. This higher ground was the advance guard of the Sierra foothills, and served as the stock range for Los Muertos. The hills were huge rolling hummocks of bare ground, covered only by wild oats. At long intervals, were isolated live oaks. In the cañons and arroyos, the chaparral and manzanita grew in dark olive-green thickets. The ground was honey-combed with gopher-holes, and the gophers themselves were everywhere. Occasionally a jack rabbit bounded across the open, from one growth of chaparral to another, taking long leaps, his ears erect. High overhead, a hawk or two swung at anchor, and once, with a startling rush of wings, a covey of quail flushed from the brush at the side of the trail.

On the hillsides, in thinly scattered groups were the cattle, grazing deliberately, working slowly toward the water-holes for their evening drink, the horses keeping to themselves, the colts nuzzling at their mothers' bellies, whisking their tails, stamping their unshod feet. But once in a remoter field, solitary, magnificent, enormous, the short hair curling tight upon his forehead, his small red eyes twinkling, his vast neck heavy with muscles, Presley came upon the monarch, the king, the great Durham bull, maintaining his lonely state, un-approachable, austere.

Presley found the one-time shepherd by a water-hole, in a far distant corner of the range. He had made his simple camp for the night. His blue-grey army blanket lay spread under a live oak, his horse grazed near at hand. He himself sat on his heels before a little fire of dead manzanita roots, cooking his coffee and bacon. Never had Presley conceived so keen an impression of loneliness as his crouching figure presented. The bald, bare landscape widened about him to infinity. Van-amee was a spot in it all, a tiny dot, a single atom of human organisation, floating endlessly on the ocean of an illimitable nature.

The two friends ate together, and Vanamee, having snared a brace of quails, dressed and then roasted them on a sharp-ened stick. After eating, they drank great refreshing draughts from the water-hole. Then, at length, Presley having lit his cigarette, and Vanamee his pipe, the former said:

"Vanamee, I have been writing again."

Vanamee turned his lean ascetic face toward him, his black eyes fixed attentively.

"I know," he said, "your journal."

"No, this is a poem. You remember, I told you about it once. 'The Toilers,' I called it."

"Oh, verse! Well, I am glad you have gone back to it. It is your natural vehicle."

"You remember the poem?" asked Presley. "It was un-finished."

"Yes, I remember it. There was better promise in it than anything you ever wrote. Now, I suppose, you have finished it."

Without reply, Presley brought it from out the breast pocket of his shooting coat. The moment seemed propitious. The stillness of the vast, bare hills was profound. The sun was setting in a cloudless brazier of red light; a golden dust per-vaded all the landscape. Presley read his poem aloud. When he had finished, his friend looked at him.

"What have you been doing lately?" he demanded. Presley, wondering, told of his various comings and goings.

"I don't mean that," returned the other. "Something has happened to you, something has aroused you. I am right, am I not? Yes, I thought so. In this poem of yours, you have not been trying to make a sounding piece of literature. You wrote it under tremendous stress. Its very imperfections show that. It is better than a mere rhyme. It is an Utterance—a Message. It is Truth. You have come back to the primal heart of things, and you have seen clearly. Yes, it is a great poem."

"Thank you," exclaimed Presley fervidly. "I had begun to mistrust myself."

"Now," observed Vanamee, "I presume you will rush it into print. To have formulated a great thought, simply to have accomplished, is not enough."

"I think I am sincere," objected Presley. "If it is good it will do good to others. You said yourself it was a Message. If it has any value, I do not think it would be right to keep it back from even a very small and most indifferent public."

"Don't publish it in the magazines at all events," Vanamee answered. "Your inspiration has come *from* the People. Then let it go straight *to* the People—not the literary readers of the monthly periodicals, the rich, who would only be indirectly interested. If you must publish it, let it be in the daily press. Don't interrupt. I know what you will say. It will be that the daily press is common, is vulgar, is undignified; and I tell you that such a poem as this of yours, called as it is, 'The Toilers,' must be read *by* the Toilers. It *must be* common; it must be vulgarised. You must not stand upon your dignity with the People, if you are to reach them."

"That is true, I suppose," Presley admitted, "but I can't get rid of the idea that it would be throwing my poem away. The great magazine gives me such—a—background; gives me such weight."

"Gives *you* such weight, gives *you* such background. Is it *yourself* you think of? You helper of the helpless. Is that your sincerity? You must sink yourself; must forget yourself and your own desire of fame, of admitted success. It is your *poem*, your *message*, that must prevail,—not *you*, who wrote it. You preach a doctrine of abnegation, of self-obliteration, and you sign your name to your words as high on the tablets as you can reach, so that all the world may see, not the poem, but the poet. Presley, there are many like you. The social reformer writes a book on the iniquity of the possession of land, and out of the proceeds, buys a corner lot. The economist who laments the hardships of the poor, allows himself to grow rich upon the sale of his book."

But Presley would hear no further.

"No," he cried, "I know I am sincere, and to prove it to you, I will publish my poem, as you say, in the daily press, and I will accept no money for it."

They talked on for about an hour, while the evening wore away. Presley very soon noticed that Vanamee was again preoccupied. More than ever of late, his silence, his brooding had increased. By and by he rose abruptly, turning his head to the north, in the direction of the Mission church of San Juan.

"I think," he said to Presley, "that I must be going."

"Going? Where to at this time of night?"

"Off there." Vanamee made an uncertain gesture toward the north. "Good-bye," and without another word he disappeared in the grey of the twilight. Presley was left alone wondering. He found his horse, and, tightening the girths, mounted and rode home under the sheen of the stars, thoughtful, his head bowed. Before he went to bed that night he sent "The Toilers" to the Sunday Editor of a daily newspaper in San Francisco.

Upon leaving Presley, Vanamee, his thumbs hooked into his empty cartridge belt, strode swiftly down from the hills of the Los Muertos stock-range and on through the silent town of Guadalajara. His lean, swarthy face, with its hollow cheeks, fine, black, pointed beard, and sad eyes, was set to the northward. As was his custom, he was bareheaded, and the rapidity of his stride made a breeze in his long, black hair. He knew where he was going. He knew what he must live through that night.

Again, the deathless grief that never slept leaped out of the shadows, and fastened upon his shoulders. It was scourging him back to that scene of a vanished happiness, a dead romance, a perished idyl,—the Mission garden in the shade of the venerable pear trees.

But, besides this, other influences tugged at his heart. There was a mystery in the garden. In that spot the night was not always empty, the darkness not always silent. Something far off stirred and listened to his cry, at times drawing nearer to him. At first this presence had been a matter for terror; but of late, as he felt it gradually drawing nearer, the terror had at long intervals given place to a feeling of an almost ineffable sweetness. But distrusting his own senses, unwilling to submit himself to such torturing, uncertain happiness, averse to the terrible confusion of spirit that followed upon a night spent in the garden, Vanamee had tried to keep away from the place. However, when the sorrow of his life reassailed him, and the thoughts and recollections of Angéle brought the ache into his heart, and the tears to his eyes, the temptation to return to the garden invariably gripped him close. There were times when he could not resist. Of themselves, his footsteps turned in that direction. It was almost as if he himself had been called.

Guadalajara was silent, dark. Not even in Solotari's was there a light. The town was asleep. Only the inevitable guitar hummed from an unseen 'dobe. Vanamee pushed on. The smell of the fields and open country, and a distant scent of flowers that he knew well, came to his nostrils, as he emerged from the town by way of the road that led on towards the Mission through Quien Sabe. On either side of him lay the brown earth, silently nurturing the implanted seed. Two days before it had rained copiously, and the soil, still moist, disengaged a pungent aroma of fecundity.

Vanamee, following the road, passed through the collection of buildings of Annixter's home ranch. Everything slept. At intervals, the aër-motor on the artesian well creaked audibly, as it turned in a languid breeze from the northeast. A cat, hunting field-mice, crept from the shadow of the gigantic barn and paused uncertainly in the open, the tip of her tail twitching. From within the barn itself came the sound of the friction of a heavy body and a stir of hoofs, as one of the dozing cows lay down with a long breath.

Vanamee left the ranch house behind him and proceeded on his way. Beyond him, to the right of the road, he could make out the higher ground in the Mission enclosure, and the watching tower of the Mission itself. The minutes passed. He went steadily forward. Then abruptly he paused, his head in the air, eye and ear alert. To that strange sixth sense of his, responsive as the leaves of the sensitive plant, had suddenly come the impression of a human being near at hand. He had neither seen nor heard, but for all that he stopped an instant in his tracks; then, the sensation confirmed, went on again with slow steps, advancing warily.

At last, his swiftly roving eyes lighted upon an object, just darker than the grey-brown of the night-ridden land. It was at some distance from the roadside. Vanamee approached it cautiously, leaving the road, treading carefully upon the moist clods of earth underfoot. Twenty paces distant, he halted.

Annixter was there, seated upon a round, white rock, his back towards him. He was leaning forward, his elbows on his knees, his chin in his hands. He did not move. Silent, motionless, he gazed out upon the flat, sombre land.

It was the night wherein the master of Quien Sabe wrought out his salvation, struggling with Self from dusk to dawn. At the moment when Vanamee came upon him, the turmoil within him had only begun. The heart of the man had not yet wakened. The night was young, the dawn far distant, and all around him the fields of upturned clods lay bare and brown, empty of all life, unbroken by a single green shoot.

For a moment, the life-circles of these two men, of so widely differing characters, touched each other, there in the silence of the night under the stars. Then silently Vanamee withdrew, going on his way, wondering at the trouble that, like himself, drove this hardheaded man of affairs, untroubled by dreams, out into the night to brood over an empty land.

Then speedily he forgot all else. The material world drew off from him. Reality dwindled to a point and vanished like the vanishing of a star at moonrise. Earthly things dissolved and disappeared, as a strange, unnamed essence flowed in upon him. A new atmosphere for him pervaded his surroundings. He entered the world of the Vision, of the Legend, of the Miracle, where all things were possible. He stood at the gate of the Mission garden.

Above him rose the ancient tower of the Mission church.

Through the arches at its summit, where swung the Spanish queen's bells, he saw the slow-burning stars. The silent bats, with flickering wings, threw their dancing shadows on the pallid surface of the venerable façade.

Not the faintest chirring of a cricket broke the silence. The bees were asleep. In the grasses, in the trees, deep in the calix of punka flower and magnolia bloom, the gnats, the caterpillars, the beetles, all the microscopic, multitudinous life of the daytime drowsed and dozed. Not even the minute scuffling of a lizard over the warm, worn pavement of the colonnade disturbed the infinite repose, the profound stillness. Only within the garden, the intermittent trickling of the fountain made itself heard, flowing steadily, marking off the lapse of seconds, the progress of hours, the cycle of years, the inevitable march of centuries.

At one time, the doorway before which Vanamee now stood had been hermetically closed. But he, himself, had long since changed that. He stood before it for a moment, steeping himself in the mystery and romance of the place, then raising the latch, pushed open the gate, entered, and closed it softly behind him. He was in the cloister garden.

The stars were out, strewn thick and close in the deep blue of the sky, the milky way glowing like a silver veil. Ursa Major wheeled gigantic in the north. The great nebula in Orion was a whorl of shimmering star dust. Venus flamed a lambent disk of pale saffron, low over the horizon. From edge to edge of the world marched the constellations, like the progress of emperors, and from the innumerable glory of their courses a mysterious sheen of diaphanous light disengaged itself, expanding over all the earth, serene, infinite, majestic.

The little garden revealed itself but dimly beneath the brooding light, only half emerging from the shadow. The polished surfaces of the leaves of the pear trees winked faintly back the reflected light as the trees just stirred in the uncertain breeze. A blurred shield of silver marked the ripples of the fountain. Under the flood of dull blue lustre, the gravelled walks lay vague amid the grasses, like webs of white satin on the bed of a lake. Against the eastern wall the headstones of the graves, an indistinct procession of grey cowls ranged themselves.

Vanamee crossed the garden, pausing to kiss the turf upon Angéle's grave. Then he approached the line of pear trees, and laid himself down in their shadow, his chin propped upon his hands, his eyes wandering over the expanse of the little valley that stretched away from the foot of the hill upon which the Mission was built.

Once again he summoned the Vision. Once again he conjured up the Illusion. Once again, tortured with doubt, racked with a deathless grief, he craved an Answer of the night. Once again, mystic that he was, he sent his mind out from him across the enchanted sea of the Supernatural. Hope, of what he did not know, roused up within him. Surely, on such a night as this, the hallucination must define itself. Surely, the Manifestation must be vouchsafed.

His eyes closed, his will girding itself to a supreme effort, his senses exalted to a state of pleasing numbness, he called upon Angéle to come to him, his voiceless cry penetrating far out into that sea of faint, ephemeral light that floated tideless over the little valley beneath him. Then motionless, prone upon the ground, he waited.

Months had passed since that first night when, at length, an Answer had come to Vanamee. At first, startled out of all composure, troubled and stirred to his lowest depths, because of the very thing for which he sought, he resolved never again to put his strange powers to the test. But for all that, he had come a second night to the garden, and a third, and a fourth. At last, his visits were habitual. Night after night he was there, surrendering himself to the influences of the place, gradually convinced that something did actually answer when he called. His faith increased as the winter grew into spring. As the spring advanced and the nights became shorter, it crystallised into certainty. Would he have her again, his love, long dead? Would she come to him once more out of the grave, out of the night? He could not tell; he could only hope. All that he knew was that his cry found an answer, that his outstretched hands, groping in the darkness, met the touch of other fingers. Patiently he waited. The nights became warmer as the spring drew on. The stars shone clearer. The nights seemed brighter. For nearly a month after the occasion of his first answer nothing new occurred. Some nights it failed him entirely; upon others it was faint, illusive.

Then, at last, the most subtle, the barest of perceptible changes began. His groping mind far-off there, wandering like a lost bird over the valley, touched upon some thing again, touched and held it, and this time drew it a single step closer to him. His heart beating, the blood surging in his temples, he watched with the eyes of his imagination, this gradual approach. What was coming to him? Who was coming to him? Shrouded in the obscurity of the night, whose was the face now turned towards his? Whose the footsteps that with such infinite slowness drew nearer to where he waited? He did not dare to say.

His mind went back many years to that time before the tragedy of Angéle's death, before the mystery of the Other. He waited then as he waited now. But then he had not waited in vain. Then, as now, he had seemed to feel her approach, seemed to feel her drawing nearer and nearer to their rendezvous. Now, what would happen? He did not know. He waited. He waited, hoping all things. He waited, believing all things. He waited, enduring all things. He trusted in the Vision.

Meanwhile, as spring advanced, the flowers in the Seed ranch began to come to life. Over the five hundred acres whereon the flowers were planted, the widening growth of vines and bushes spread like the waves of a green sea. Then, timidly, colours of the faintest tints began to appear. Under the moonlight, Vanamee saw them expanding, delicate pink, faint blue, tenderest variations of lavender and yellow, white shimmering with reflections of gold, all subdued and pallid in the moonlight.

By degrees, the night became impregnated with the perfume of the flowers. Illusive at first, evanescent as filaments of gossamer; then as the buds opened, emphasising itself, breathing deeper, stronger. An exquisite mingling of many odours passed continually over the Mission, from the garden of the Seed ranch, meeting and blending with the aroma of its magnolia buds and punka blossoms.

As the colours of the flowers of the Seed ranch deepened, and as their odours penetrated deeper and more distinctly, as the starlight of each succeeding night grew brighter and the air became warmer, the illusion defined itself. By imperceptible degrees, as Vanamee waited under the shadows of the pear trees, the Answer grew nearer and nearer. He saw nothing but the distant glimmer of the flowers. He heard nothing but the drip of the fountain. Nothing moved about him but the invisible, slow-passing breaths of perfume; yet he felt the approach of the Vision.

It came first to about the middle of the Seed ranch itself, some half a mile away, where the violets grew; shrinking, timid flowers, hiding close to the ground. Then it passed forward beyond the violets, and drew nearer and stood amid the mignonette, hardier blooms that dared look heavenward from out the leaves. A few nights later it left the mignonette behind, and advanced into the beds of white iris that pushed more boldly forth from the earth, their waxen petals claiming the attention. It advanced then a long step into the proud, challenging beauty of the carnations and roses; and at last, after many nights, Vanamee felt that it paused, as if trembling at its hardihood, full in the superb glory of the royal lilies themselves, that grew on the extreme border of the Seed ranch nearest to him. After this, there was a certain long wait. Then, upon a dark midnight, it advanced again. Vanamee could scarcely repress a cry. Now, the illusion emerged from the flowers. It stood, not distant, but unseen, almost at the base of the hill upon whose crest he waited, in a depression of the ground where the shadows lay thickest. It was nearly within earshot.

The nights passed. The spring grew warmer. In the daytime intermittent rains freshened all the earth. The flowers of the Seed ranch grew rapidly. Bud after bud burst forth, while those already opened expanded to full maturity. The colour of the Seed ranch deepened.

One night, after hours of waiting, Vanamee felt upon his cheek the touch of a prolonged puff of warm wind, breathing across the little valley from out the east. It reached the Mission garden and stirred the branches of the pear trees. It seemed veritably to be compounded of the very essence of the flowers. Never had the aroma been so sweet, so pervasive. It passed and faded, leaving in its wake an absolute silence.

Then, at length, the silence of the night, that silence to which Vanamee had so long appealed, was broken by a tiny sound. Alert, half-risen from the ground, he listened; for now, at length, he heard something. The sound repeated itself. It came from near at hand, from the thick shadow at the foot of the hill. What it was, he could not tell, but it did not belong to a single one of the infinite similar noises of the place with which he was so familiar. It was neither the rustle of a leaf, the snap of a parted twig, the drone of an insect, the dropping of a magnolia blossom. It was a vibration merely, faint, elusive, impossible of definition; a minute notch in the fine, keen edge of stillness.

Again the nights passed. The summer stars became brighter. The warmth increased. The flowers of the Seed ranch grew still more. The five hundred acres of the ranch were carpeted with them.

At length, upon a certain midnight, a new light began to spread in the sky. The thin scimitar of the moon rose, veiled and dim behind the earth-mists. The light increased. Distant objects, until now hidden, came into view, and as the radiance brightened, Vanamee, looking down upon the little valley, saw a spectacle of incomparable beauty. All the buds of the Seed ranch had opened. The faint tints of the flowers had deepened, had asserted themselves. They challenged the eye. Pink became a royal red. Blue rose into purple. Yellow flamed into orange. Orange glowed golden and brilliant. The earth disappeared under great bands and fields of resplendent colour. Then, at length, the moon abruptly soared zenithward from out the veiling mist, passing from one filmy haze to another. For a moment there was a gleam of a golden light, and Vanamee, his eyes searching the shade at the foot of the hill, felt his heart suddenly leap, and then hang poised, refusing to beat. In that instant of passing light, something had caught his eye. Something that moved, down there, half in and half out of the shadow, at the hill's foot. It had come and gone in an instant. The haze once more screened the moonlight. The shade again engulfed the vision. What was it he had seen? He did not know. So brief had been that movement, the drowsy brain had not been quick enough to interpret the cipher message of the eye. Now it was gone. But something had been there. He had seen it. Was it the lifting of a strand of hair, the wave of a white hand, the flutter of a garment's edge? He could not tell, but it did not belong to any of those sights which he had seen so often in that place. It was neither the glancing of a moth's wing, the nodding of a wind-touched blossom, nor the noiseless flitting of a bat. It was a gleam merely, faint, elusive, impossible of definition, an intangible agitation, in the vast, dim blur of the darkness.

And that was all. Until now no single real thing had occurred, nothing that Vanamee could reduce to terms of actuality, nothing he could put into words. The manifestation, when not recognisable to that strange sixth sense of his, appealed only to the most refined, the most delicate perception of eye and ear. It was all ephemeral, filmy, dreamy, the mystic forming of the Vision—the invisible developing a concrete nucleus, the starlight coagulating, the radiance of the flowers thickening to something actual; perfume, the most delicious fragrance, becoming a tangible presence.

But into that garden the serpent intruded. Though cradled in the slow rhythm of the dream, lulled by this beauty of a summer's night, heavy with the scent of flowers, the silence broken only by a rippling fountain, the darkness illuminated by a world of radiant blossoms, Vanamee could not forget the tragedy of the Other; that terror of many years ago,—that prowler of the night, that strange, fearful figure with the unseen face, swooping in there from out the darkness, gone in an instant, yet leaving behind the trail and trace of death and of pollution.

Never had Vanamee seen this more clearly than when leaving Presley on the stock range of Los Muertos, he had come across to the Mission garden by way of the Quien Sabe ranch.

It was the same night in which Annixter out-watched the stars, coming, at last, to himself.

As the hours passed, the two men, far apart, ignoring each other, waited for the Manifestation,—Annixter on the ranch, Vanamee in the garden.

Prone upon his face, under the pear trees, his forehead buried in the hollow of his arm, Vanamee lay motionless. For the last time, raising his head, he sent his voiceless cry out into the night across the multi-coloured levels of the little valley, calling upon the miracle, summoning the darkness to give Angéle back to him, resigning himself to the hallucination. He bowed his head upon his arm again and waited. The minutes passed. The fountain dripped steadily. Over the hills a haze of saffron light foretold the rising of the full moon. Nothing stirred. The silence was profound.

Then, abruptly, Vanamee's right hand shut tight upon his wrist. There—there it was. It began again, his invocation was answered. Far off there, the ripple formed again upon the still, black pool of the night. No sound, no sight; vibration merely, appreciable by some sublimated faculty of the mind as yet unnamed. Rigid, his nerves taut, motionless, prone on the ground, he waited.

It advanced with infinite slowness. Now it passed through the beds of violets, now through the mignonette. A moment later, and he knew it stood among the white iris. Then it left those behind. It was in the splendour of the red roses and carnations. It passed like a moving star into the superb abundance, the imperial opulence of the royal lilies. It was advancing slowly, but there was no pause. He held his breath, not daring to raise his head. It passed beyond the limits of the Seed ranch, and entered the shade at the foot of the hill below him. Would it come farther than this? Here it had always stopped hitherto, stopped for a moment, and then, in spite of his efforts, had slipped from his grasp and faded back into the night. But now he wondered if he had been willing to put forth his utmost strength, after all. Had there not always been an element of dread in the thought of beholding the mystery face to face? Had he not even allowed the Vision to dissolve, the Answer to recede into the obscurity whence it came?

But never a night had been so beautiful as this. It was the full period of the spring. The air was a veritable caress. The infinite repose of the little garden, sleeping under the night, was delicious beyond expression. It was a tiny corner of the world, shut off, discreet, distilling romance, a garden of dreams, of enchantments.

Below, in the little valley, the resplendent colourations of the million flowers, roses, lilies, hyacinths, carnations, violets, glowed like incandescence in the golden light of the rising moon. The air was thick with the perfume, heavy with it, clogged with it. The sweetness filled the very mouth. The throat choked with it. Overhead wheeled the illimitable procession of the constellations. Underfoot, the earth was asleep. The very flowers were dreaming. A cathedral hush overlay all the land, and a sense of benediction brooded low,—a divine kindliness manifesting itself in beauty, in peace, in absolute repose.

It was a time for visions. It was the hour when dreams come true, and lying deep in the grasses beneath the pear trees, Vanamee, dizzied with mysticism, reaching up and out toward the supernatural, felt, as it were, his mind begin to rise upward from out his body. He passed into a state of being the like of which he had not known before. He felt that his imagination was reshaping itself, preparing to receive an impression never experienced until now. His body felt light to him, then it dwindled, vanished. He saw with new eyes, heard with new ears, felt with a new heart.

"Come to me," he murmured.

Then slowly he felt the advance of the Vision. It was approaching. Every instant it drew gradually nearer. At last, he was to see. It had left the shadow at the base of the hill; it was on the hill itself. Slowly, steadily, it ascended the slope; just below him there, he heard a faint stirring. The grasses rustled under the touch of a foot. The leaves of the bushes murmured, as a hand brushed against them; a slender twig creaked. The sounds of approach were more distinct. They came nearer. They reached the top of the hill. They were within whispering distance.

Vanamee, trembling, kept his head buried in his arm. The sounds, at length, paused definitely. The Vision could come no nearer. He raised his head and looked.

The moon had risen. Its great shield of gold stood over the eastern horizon. Within six feet of Vanamee, clear and distinct, against the disk of the moon, stood the figure of a young girl. She was dressed in a gown of scarlet silk, with flowing sleeves, such as Japanese wear, embroidered with flowers and figures of birds worked in gold threads. On either side of her face, making three-cornered her round, white forehead, hung the soft masses of her hair of gold. Her hands hung limply at her sides. But from between her parted lips—

lips of almost an Egyptian fulness—her breath came slow and
regular, and her eyes, heavy lidded, slanting upwards toward
the temples, perplexing, oriental, were closed. She was asleep.

From out this life of flowers, this world of colour, this atmosphere oppressive with perfume, this darkness clogged and
cloyed, and thickened with sweet odours, she came to him.
She came to him from out of the flowers, the smell of the
roses in her hair of gold, the aroma and the imperial red of
the carnations in her lips, the whiteness of the lilies, the perfume of the lilies, and the lilies' slender, balancing grace in
her neck. Her hands disengaged the scent of the heliotrope.
The folds of her scarlet gown gave off the enervating smell of
poppies. Her feet were redolent of hyacinth. She stood before
him, a Vision realised—a dream come true. She emerged
from out the invisible. He beheld her, a figure of gold and
pale vermilion, redolent of perfume, poised motionless in the
faint saffron sheen of the new-risen moon. She, a creation of
sleep, was herself asleep. She, a dream, was herself dreaming.

Called forth from out the darkness, from the grip of the
earth, the embrace of the grave, from out the memory of corruption, she rose into light and life, divinely pure. Across that
white forehead was no smudge, no trace of an earthly pollution—no mark of a terrestrial dishonour. He saw in her the
same beauty of untainted innocence he had known in his
youth. Years had made no difference with her. She was still
young. It was the old purity that returned, the deathless
beauty, the ever-renascent life, the eternal consecrated and immortal youth. For a few seconds, she stood there before him,
and he, upon the ground at her feet, looked up at her, spellbound. Then, slowly she withdrew. Still asleep, her eyelids
closed, she turned from him, descending the slope. She was
gone.

Vanamee started up, coming, as it were, to himself, looking
wildly about him. Sarria was there.

"I saw her," said the priest. "It was Angéle, the little girl,
your Angéle's daughter. She is like her mother."

But Vanamee scarcely heard. He walked as if in a trance,
pushing by Sarria, going forth from the garden. Angéle or
Angéle's daughter, it was all one with him. It was She. Death
was overcome. The grave vanquished. Life, ever-renewed,

alone existed. Time was naught; change was naught; all things were immortal but evil; all things eternal but grief.

Suddenly, the dawn came; the east burned roseate toward the zenith. Vanamee walked on, he knew not where. The dawn grew brighter. At length, he paused upon the crest of a hill overlooking the ranchos, and cast his eye below him to the southward. Then, suddenly flinging up his arms, he uttered a great cry.

There it was. The Wheat! The Wheat! In the night it had come up. It was there, everywhere, from margin to margin of the horizon. The earth, long empty, teemed with green life. Once more the pendulum of the seasons swung in its mighty arc, from death back to life. Life out of death, eternity rising from out dissolution. There was the lesson. Angéle was not the symbol, but the *proof* of immortality. The seed dying, rotting and corrupting in the earth; rising again in life unconquerable, and in immaculate purity,—Angéle dying as she gave birth to her little daughter, life springing from her death,—the pure, unconquerable, coming forth from the defiled. Why had he not had the knowledge of God? Thou fool, that which thou sowest is not quickened except it die. So the seed had died. So died Angéle. And that which thou sowest, thou sowest not that body that shall be, but bare grain. It may chance of wheat, or of some other grain. The wheat called forth from out the darkness, from out the grip of the earth, of the grave, from out corruption, rose triumphant into light and life. So Angéle, so life, so also the resurrection of the dead. It is sown in corruption. It is raised in incorruption. It is sown in dishonour. It is raised in glory. It is sown in weakness. It is raised in power. Death was swallowed up in Victory.

The sun rose. The night was over. The glory of the terrestrial was one, and the glory of the celestial was another. Then, as the glory of sun banished the lesser glory of moon and stars, Vanamee, from his mountain top, beholding the eternal green life of the growing Wheat, bursting its bonds, and in his heart exulting in his triumph over the grave, flung out his arms with a mighty shout:

"Oh, Death, where is thy sting? Oh, Grave, where is thy victory?"

IV

PRESLEY'S SOCIALISTIC poem, "The Toilers," had an enormous success. The editor of the Sunday supplement of the San Francisco paper to which it was sent, printed it in Gothic type, with a scare-head title so decorative as to be almost illegible, and furthermore caused the poem to be illustrated by one of the paper's staff artists in a most impressive fashion. The whole affair occupied an entire page. Thus advertised, the poem attracted attention. It was promptly copied in New York, Boston, and Chicago papers. It was discussed, attacked, defended, eulogised, ridiculed. It was praised with the most fulsome adulation; assailed with the most violent condemnation. Editorials were written upon it. Special articles, in literary pamphlets, dissected its rhetoric and prosody. The phrases were quoted,—were used as texts for revolutionary sermons, reactionary speeches. It was parodied; it was distorted so as to read as an advertisement for patented cereals and infants' foods. Finally, the editor of an enterprising monthly magazine reprinted the poem, supplementing it by a photograph and biography of Presley himself.

Presley was stunned, bewildered. He began to wonder at himself. Was he actually the "greatest American poet since Bryant"? He had had no thought of fame while composing "The Toilers." He had only been moved to his heart's foundations,—thoroughly in earnest, seeing clearly,—and had addressed himself to the poem's composition in a happy moment when words came easily to him, and the elaboration of fine sentences was not difficult. Was it thus fame was achieved? For a while he was tempted to cross the continent and go to New York and there come unto his own, enjoying the triumph that awaited him. But soon he denied himself this cheap reward. Now he was too much in earnest. He wanted to help his People, the community in which he lived—the little world of the San Joaquin, at grapples with the Railroad. The struggle had found its poet. He told himself that his place was here. Only the words of the manager of a lecture bureau troubled him for a moment. To range the entire nation, telling all his countrymen of the drama that was working itself out on this fringe of the continent, this ignored and distant Pacific Coast, rousing their interest and stirring them up to action—appealed to him. It might do great good. To devote himself to "the Cause," accepting no penny of remuneration; to give his life to loosing the grip of the iron-hearted monster of steel and steam would be beyond question heroic. Other States than California had their grievances. All over the country the family of cyclops was growing. He would declare himself the champion of the People in their opposition to the Trust. He would be an apostle, a prophet, a martyr of Freedom.

But Presley was essentially a dreamer, not a man of affairs. He hesitated to act at this precise psychological moment, striking while the iron was yet hot, and while he hesitated, other affairs near at hand began to absorb his attention.

One night, about an hour after he had gone to bed, he was awakened by the sound of voices on the porch of the ranch house, and, descending, found Mrs. Dyke there with Sidney. The ex-engineer's mother was talking to Magnus and Harran, and crying as she talked. It seemed that Dyke was missing. He had gone into town early that afternoon with the wagon and team, and was to have been home for supper. By now it was ten o'clock and there was no news of him. Mrs. Dyke told how she first had gone to Quien Sabe, intending to telephone from there to Bonneville, but Annixter was in San Francisco, and in his absence the house was locked up, and the overseer, who had a duplicate key, was himself in Bonneville. She had telegraphed three times from Guadalajara to Bonneville for news of her son, but without result. Then, at last, tortured with anxiety, she had gone to Hooven's, taking Sidney with her, and had prevailed upon "Bismarck" to hitch up and drive her across Los Muertos to the Governor's, to beg him to telephone into Bonneville, to know what had become of Dyke.

While Harran rang up Central in town, Mrs. Dyke told Presley and Magnus of the lamentable change in Dyke.

"They have broken my son's spirit, Mr. Derrick," she said. "If you were only there to see. Hour after hour, he sits on the porch with his hands lying open in his lap, looking at them without a word. He won't look me in the face any more, and he don't sleep. Night after night, he has walked the floor until morning. And he will go on that way for days together, very silent, without a word, and sitting still in his chair, and then, all of a sudden, he will break out—oh, Mr. Derrick, it is terrible—into an awful rage, cursing, swearing, grinding his teeth, his hands clenched over his head, stamping so that the house shakes, and saying that if S. Behrman don't give him back his money, he will kill him with his two hands. But that isn't the worst, Mr. Derrick. He goes to Mr. Caraher's saloon now, and stays there for hours, and listens to Mr. Caraher. There is something on my son's mind; I know there is—something that he and Mr. Caraher have talked over together, and I can't find out what it is. Mr. Caraher is a bad man, and my son has fallen under his influence." The tears filled her eyes. Bravely, she turned to hide them, turning away to take Sidney in her arms, putting her head upon the little girl's shoulder.

"I—I haven't broken down before, Mr. Derrick," she said, "but after we have been so happy in our little house, just us three—and the future seemed so bright—oh, God will punish the gentlemen who own the railroad for being so hard and cruel."

Harran came out on the porch, from the telephone, and she interrupted herself, fixing her eyes eagerly upon him.

"I think it is all right, Mrs. Dyke," he said, reassuringly. "We know where he is, I believe. You and the little tad stay here, and Hooven and I will go after him."

About two hours later, Harran brought Dyke back to Los Muertos in Hooven's wagon. He had found him at Caraher's saloon, very drunk.

There was nothing maudlin about Dyke's drunkenness. In him the alcohol merely roused the spirit of evil, vengeful, reckless.

As the wagon passed out from under the eucalyptus trees about the ranch house, taking Mrs. Dyke, Sidney, and the one-time engineer back to the hop ranch, Presley leaning from his window heard the latter remark:

"Caraher is right. There is only one thing they listen to, and that's dynamite."

The following day Presley drove Magnus over to Guadala-jara to take the train for San Francisco. But after he had said good-bye to the Governor, he was moved to go on to the hop ranch to see the condition of affairs in that quarter. He returned to Los Muertos overwhelmed with sadness and trembling with anger. The hop ranch that he had last seen in the full tide of prosperity was almost a ruin. Work had evi-dently been abandoned long since. Weeds were already chok-ing the vines. Everywhere the poles sagged and drooped. Many had even fallen, dragging the vines with them, spread-ing them over the ground in an inextricable tangle of dead leaves, decaying tendrils, and snarled string. The fence was broken; the unfinished storehouse, which never was to see completion, was a lamentable spectacle of gaping doors and windows—a melancholy skeleton. Last of all, Presley had caught a glimpse of Dyke himself, seated in his rocking chair on the porch, his beard and hair unkempt, motionless, look-ing with vague eyes upon his hands that lay palm upwards and idle in his lap.

Magnus on his way to San Francisco was joined at Bonne-ville by Osterman. Upon seating himself in front of the mas-ter of Los Muertos in the smoking-car of the train, this latter, pushing back his hat and smoothing his bald head, observed:

"Governor, you look all frazeled out. Anything wrong these days?"

The other answered in the negative, but, for all that, Oster-man was right. The Governor had aged suddenly. His former erectness was gone, the broad shoulders stooped a little, the strong lines of his thin-lipped mouth were relaxed, and his hand, as it clasped over the yellowed ivory knob of his cane, had an unwonted tremulousness not hitherto noticeable. But the change in Magnus was more than physical. At last, in the full tide of power, President of the League, known and talked of in every county of the State, leader in a great struggle, consulted, deferred to as the "Prominent Man," at length at-taining that position, so long and vainly sought for, he yet found no pleasure in his triumph, and little but bitterness in life. His success had come by devious methods, had been reached by obscure means.

He was a briber. He could never forget that. To further

his ends, disinterested, public-spirited, even philanthropic as those were, he had connived with knavery, he, the politician of the old school, of such rigorous integrity, who had abandoned a "career" rather than compromise with honesty. At this eleventh hour, involved and entrapped in the fine-spun web of a new order of things, bewildered by Osterman's dexterity, by his volubility and glibness, goaded and harassed beyond the point of reason by the aggression of the Trust he fought, he had at last failed. He had fallen; he had given a bribe. He had thought that, after all, this would make but little difference with him. The affair was known only to Osterman, Broderson, and Annixter; they would not judge him, being themselves involved. He could still preserve a bold front; could still hold his head high. As time went on the affair would lose its point.

But this was not so. Some subtle element of his character had forsaken him. He felt it. He knew it. Some certain stiffness that had given him all his rigidity, that had lent force to his authority, weight to his dominance, temper to his fine, inflexible hardness, was diminishing day by day. In the decisions which he, as President of the League, was called upon to make so often, he now hesitated. He could no longer be arrogant, masterful, acting upon his own judgment, independent of opinion. He began to consult his lieutenants, asking their advice, distrusting his own opinions. He made mistakes, blunders, and when those were brought to his notice, took refuge in bluster. He knew it to be bluster—knew that sooner or later his subordinates would recognise it as such. How long could he maintain his position? So only he could keep his grip upon the lever of control till the battle was over, all would be well. If not, he would fall, and, once fallen, he knew that now, briber that he was, he would never rise again.

He was on his way at this moment to the city to consult with Lyman as to a certain issue of the contest between the Railroad and the ranchers, which, of late, had been brought to his notice.

When appeal had been taken to the Supreme Court by the League's Executive Committee, certain test cases had been chosen, which should represent all the lands in question.

Neither Magnus nor Annixter had so appealed, believing, of course, that their cases were covered by the test cases on trial at Washington. Magnus had here blundered again, and the League's agents in San Francisco had written to warn him that the Railroad might be able to take advantage of a technicality, and by pretending that neither Quien Sabe nor Los Muertos were included in the appeal, attempt to put its dummy buyers in possession of the two ranches before the Supreme Court handed down its decision. The ninety days allowed for taking this appeal were nearly at an end and after then the Railroad could act. Osterman and Magnus at once decided to go up to the city, there joining Annixter (who had been absent from Quien Sabe for the last ten days), and talk the matter over with Lyman. Lyman, because of his position as Commissioner, might be cognisant of the Railroad's plans, and, at the same time, could give sound legal advice as to what was to be done should the new rumour prove true.

"Say," remarked Osterman, as the train pulled out of the Bonneville station, and the two men settled themselves for the long journey, "say Governor, what's all up with Buck Annixter these days? He's got a bean about something, sure."

"I had not noticed," answered Magnus. "Mr. Annixter has been away some time lately. I cannot imagine what should keep him so long in San Francisco."

"That's it," said Osterman, winking. "Have three guesses. Guess right and you get a cigar. I guess g-i-r-l spells Hilma Tree. And a little while ago she quit Quien Sabe and hiked out to 'Frisco. So did Buck. Do I draw the cigar? It's up to you."

"I have noticed her," observed Magnus. "A fine figure of a woman. She would make some man a good wife."

"Hoh! Wife! Buck Annixter marry! Not much. He's gone a-girling at last, old Buck! It's as funny as twins. Have to josh him about it when I see him, sure."

But when Osterman and Magnus at last fell in with Annixter in the vestibule of the Lick House, on Montgomery Street, nothing could be got out of him. He was in an execrable humour. When Magnus had broached the subject of business, he had declared that all business could go to pot, and when Osterman, his tongue in his cheek, had permitted himself a most distant allusion to a feemale girl, Annixter had cursed him for a "busy-face" so vociferously and tersely, that even Osterman was cowed.

"Well," insinuated Osterman, "what are you dallying 'round 'Frisco so much for?"

"Cat fur, to make kitten-breeches," retorted Annixter with oracular vagueness.

Two weeks before this time, Annixter had come up to the city and had gone at once to a certain hotel on Bush Street, behind the First National Bank, that he knew was kept by a family connection of the Trees. In his conjecture that Hilma and her parents would stop here, he was right. Their names were on the register. Ignoring custom, Annixter marched straight up to their rooms, and before he was well aware of it, was "eating crow" before old man Tree.

Hilma and her mother were out at the time. Later on, Mrs. Tree returned alone, leaving Hilma to spend the day with one of her cousins who lived far out on Stanyan Street in a little house facing the park.

Between Annixter and Hilma's parents, a reconciliation had been effected, Annixter convincing them both of his sincerity in wishing to make Hilma his wife. Hilma, however, refused to see him. As soon as she knew he had followed her to San Francisco she had been unwilling to return to the hotel and had arranged with her cousin to spend an indefinite time at her house.

She was wretchedly unhappy during all this time; would not set foot out of doors, and cried herself to sleep night after night. She detested the city. Already she was miserably home-sick for the ranch. She remembered the days she had spent in the little dairy-house, happy in her work, making butter and cheese; skimming the great pans of milk, scouring the copper vessels and vats, plunging her arms, elbow deep, into the white curds; coming and going in that atmosphere of fresh-ness, cleanliness, and sunlight, gay, singing, supremely happy just because the sun shone. She remembered her long walks toward the Mission late in the afternoons, her excursions for cresses underneath the Long Trestle, the crowing of the cocks, the distant whistle of the passing trains, the faint sounding of the Angelus. She recalled with infinite longing the solitary expanse of the ranches, the level reaches between the horizons, full of light and silence; the heat at noon, the cloudless iridescence of the sunrise and sunset. She had been so happy in that life! Now, all those days were passed. This crude, raw city, with its crowding houses all of wood and tin, its blotting fogs, its uproarious trade winds, disturbed and saddened her. There was no outlook for the future.

At length, one day, about a week after Annixter's arrival in the city, she was prevailed upon to go for a walk in the park. She went alone, putting on for the first time the little hat of black straw with its puff of white silk her mother had bought for her, a pink shirtwaist, her belt of imitation alligator skin, her new skirt of brown cloth, and her low shoes, set off with their little steel buckles.

She found a tiny summer house, built in Japanese fashion, around a diminutive pond, and sat there for a while, her hands folded in her lap, amused with watching the goldfish, wishing—she knew not what.

Without any warning, Annixter sat down beside her. She was too frightened to move. She looked at him with wide eyes that began to fill with tears.

"Oh," she said, at last, "oh—I didn't know."

"Well," exclaimed Annixter, "here you are at last. I've been watching that blamed house till I was afraid the policeman would move me on. By the Lord," he suddenly cried, "you're pale. You—you, Hilma, do you feel well?"

"Yes—I am well," she faltered.

"No, you're not," he declared. "I know better. You are coming back to Quien Sabe with me. This place don't agree with you. Hilma, what's all the matter? Why haven't you let me see you all this time? Do you know—how things are with me? Your mother told you, didn't she? Do you know how sorry I am? Do you know that I see now that I made the mistake of my life there, that time, under the Long Trestle? I found it out the night after you went away. I sat all night on a stone out on the ranch somewhere and I don't know exactly what happened, but I've been a different man since then. I see things all different now. Why, I've only begun to live since then. I know what love means now, and instead of being ashamed of it, I'm proud of it. If I never was to see you again I would be glad I'd lived through that night, just the same. I just woke up that night. I'd been absolutely and completely selfish up to the moment I realised I really loved you, and now, whether you'll let me marry you or not, I mean to live—I don't know, in a different way. I've *got* to live different. I—well—oh, I can't make you understand, but just loving you has changed my life all around. It's made it easier to do the straight, clean thing. I want to do it, it's fun doing it. Remember, once I said I was proud of being a hard man, a driver, of being glad that people hated me and were afraid of me? Well, since I've loved you I'm ashamed of it all. I don't want to be hard any more, and nobody is going to hate me if I can help it. I'm happy and I want other people so. I love you," he suddenly exclaimed; "I love you, and if you will forgive me, and if you will come down to such a beast as I am, I want to be to you the best a man can be to a woman, Hilma. Do you understand, little girl? I want to be your husband."

Hilma looked at the goldfishes through her tears.

"Have you got anything to say to me, Hilma?" he asked, after a while.

"I don't know what you want me to say," she murmured.

"Yes, you do," he insisted. "I've followed you 'way up here to hear it. I've waited around in these beastly, draughty picnic grounds for over a week to hear it. You know what I want to hear, Hilma."

"Well—I forgive you," she hazarded.

"That will do for a starter," he answered. "But that's not *it*."

"Then, I don't know what."

"Shall I say it for you?"

She hesitated a long minute, then:

"You mightn't say it right," she replied.

"Trust me for that. Shall I say it for you, Hilma?"

"I don't know what you'll say."

"I'll say what you are thinking of. Shall I say it?"

There was a very long pause. A goldfish rose to the surface of the little pond, with a sharp, rippling sound. The fog drifted overhead. There was nobody about.

"No," said Hilma, at length. "I—I—I can say it for myself. I—" All at once she turned to him and put her arms around his neck. "Oh, *do* you love me?" she cried. "Is it really true? Do you mean every word of it? And you are sorry and you *will* be good to me if I will be your wife? You will be my dear, dear husband?"

The tears sprang to Annixter's eyes. He took her in his arms and held her there for a moment. Never in his life had he felt so unworthy, so undeserving of this clean, pure girl who forgave him and trusted his spoken word and believed him to be the good man he could only wish to be. She was so far above him, so exalted, so noble that he should have bowed his forehead to her feet, and instead, she took him in her arms, believing him to be good, to be her equal. He could think of no words to say. The tears overflowed his eyes and ran down upon his cheeks. She drew away from him and held him a second at arm's length, looking at him, and he saw that she, too, had been crying.

"I think," he said, " we are a couple of softies."

"No, no," she insisted. "I want to cry and want you to cry, too. Oh, dear, I haven't a handkerchief."

"Here, take mine."

They wiped each other's eyes like two children and for a long time sat in the deserted little Japanese pleasure house, their arms about each other, talking, talking, talking.

On the following Saturday they were married in an uptown Presbyterian church, and spent the week of their honeymoon at a small, family hotel on Sutter Street. As a matter of course, they saw the sights of the city together. They made the inevitable bridal trip to the Cliff House and spent an afternoon in the grewsome and made-to-order beauties of Sutro's Gardens; they went through Chinatown, the Palace Hotel, the park museum—where Hilma resolutely refused to believe in the Egyptian mummy—and they drove out in a hired hack to the Presidio and the Golden Gate.

On the sixth day of their excursions, Hilma abruptly declared they had had enough of "playing out," and must be serious and get to work.

This work was nothing less than the buying of the furniture and appointments for the rejuvenated ranch house at Quien

Sabe, where they were to live. Annixter had telegraphed to
his overseer to have the building repainted, replastered, and
reshingled and to empty the rooms of everything but the telephone and safe. He also sent instructions to have the dimensions of each room noted down and the result forwarded to
him. It was the arrival of these memoranda that had roused
Hilma to action.

Then ensued a most delicious week. Armed with formidable lists, written by Annixter on hotel envelopes, they two
descended upon the department stores of the city, the carpet
stores, the furniture stores. Right and left they bought and
bargained, sending each consignment as soon as purchased to
Quien Sabe. Nearly an entire car load of carpets, curtains,
kitchen furniture, pictures, fixtures, lamps, straw matting,
chairs, and the like were sent down to the ranch, Annixter
making a point that their new home should be entirely
equipped by San Francisco dealers.

The furnishings of the bedroom and sitting-room were left
to the very last. For the former, Hilma bought a "set" of pure
white enamel, three chairs, a washstand and bureau, a marvellous bargain of thirty dollars, discovered by a wonderful
accident at a "Friday Sale." The bed was a piece by itself,
bought elsewhere, but none the less a wonder. It was of brass,
very brave and gay, and actually boasted a canopy! They
bought it complete, just as it stood in the window of the
department store, and Hilma was in an ecstasy over its crisp,
clean, muslin curtains, spread, and shams. Never was there
such a bed, the luxury of a princess, such a bed as she had
dreamed about her whole life.

Next the appointments of the sitting-room occupied her—
since Annixter, himself, bewildered by this astonishing display, unable to offer a single suggestion himself, merely approved of all she bought. In the sitting-room was to be a
beautiful blue and white paper, cool straw matting, set off
with white wool rugs, a stand of flowers in the window, a
globe of goldfish, rocking chairs, a sewing machine, and a
great, round centre table of yellow oak whereon should stand
a lamp covered with a deep shade of crinkly red tissue paper.
On the walls were to hang several pictures—lovely affairs,
photographs from life, all properly tinted—of choir boys in

robes, with beautiful eyes; pensive young girls in pink gowns, with flowing yellow hair, drooping over golden harps; a coloured reproduction of "Rouget de Lisle, Singing the Mar-seillaise," and two "pieces" of wood carving, representing a quail and a wild duck, hung by one leg in the midst of game bags and powder horns,—quite masterpieces, both.

At last everything had been bought, all arrangements made, Hilma's trunks packed with her new dresses, and the tickets to Bonneville bought.

"We'll go by the Overland, by Jingo," declared Annixter across the table to his wife, at their last meal in the hotel where they had been stopping; "no way trains or locals for us, hey?"

"But we reach Bonneville at *such* an hour," protested Hilma. "Five in the morning!"

"Never mind," he declared, "We'll go home in *Pullman's*, Hilma. I'm not going to have any of those slobs in Bonneville say I didn't know how to do the thing in style, and we'll have Vacca meet us with the team. No, sir, it is Pullman's or noth-ing. When it comes to buying furniture, I don't shine, per-haps, but I know what's due my wife."

He was obdurate, and late one afternoon the couple boarded the Transcontinental (the crack Overland Flyer of the Pacific and Southwestern) at the Oakland mole. Only Hilma's parents were there to say good-bye. Annixter knew that Mag-nus and Osterman were in the city, but he had laid his plans to elude them. Magnus, he could trust to be dignified, but that goat Osterman, one could never tell what he would do next. He did not propose to start his journey home in a shower of rice.

Annixter marched down the line of cars, his hands encum-bered with wicker telescope baskets, satchels, and valises, his tickets in his mouth, his hat on wrong side foremost, Hilma and her parents hurrying on behind him, trying to keep up. Annixter was in a turmoil of nerves lest something should go wrong; catching a train was always for him a little crisis. He rushed ahead so furiously that when he had found his Pull-man he had lost his party. He set down his valises to mark the place and charged back along the platform, waving his arms.

"Come on," he cried, when, at length, he espied the others. "We've no more time."

He shouldered and urged them forward to where he had set his valises, only to find one of them gone. Instantly he raised an outcry. Aha, a fine way to treat passengers! There was P. and S. W. management for you. He would, by the Lord, he would—but the porter appeared in the vestibule of the car to placate him. He had already taken his valises inside.

Annixter would not permit Hilma's parents to board the car, declaring that the train might pull out any moment. So he and his wife, following the porter down the narrow passage by the stateroom, took their places and, raising the window, leaned out to say good-bye to Mr. and Mrs. Tree. These latter would not return to Quien Sabe. Old man Tree had found a business chance awaiting him in the matter of supplying his relative's hotel with dairy products. But Bonneville was not too far from San Francisco; the separation was by no means final.

The porters began taking up the steps that stood by the vestibule of each sleeping-car.

"Well, have a good time, daughter," observed her father; "and come up to see us whenever you can."

From beyond the enclosure of the depot's reverberating roof came the measured clang of a bell.

"I guess we're off," cried Annixter. "Good-bye, Mrs. Tree."

"Remember your promise, Hilma," her mother hastened to exclaim, "to write every Sunday afternoon."

There came a prolonged creaking and groan of straining wood and iron work, all along the length of the train. They all began to cry their good-byes at once. The train stirred, moved forward, and gathering slow headway, rolled slowly out into the sunlight. Hilma leaned out of the window and as long as she could keep her mother in sight waved her handkerchief. Then at length she sat back in her seat and looked at her husband.

"Well," she said.

"Well," echoed Annixter, "happy?" for the tears rose in her eyes.

She nodded energetically, smiling at him bravely.

"You look a little pale," he declared, frowning uneasily; "feel well?"

"Pretty well."

Promptly he was seized with uneasiness.

"But not *all* well, hey? Is that it?"

It was true that Hilma had felt a faint tremour of sea-sickness on the ferry-boat coming from the city to the Oakland mole. No doubt a little nausea yet remained with her. But Annixter refused to accept this explanation. He was distressed beyond expression.

"Now you're going to be sick," he cried anxiously.

"No, no," she protested, "not a bit."

"But you said you didn't feel very well. Where is it you feel sick?"

"I don't know. I'm not sick. Oh, dear me, why will you bother?"

"Headache?"

"Not the least."

"You feel tired, then. That's it. No wonder, the way I've rushed you 'round to-day."

"Dear, I'm *not* tired, and I'm *not* sick, and I'm all *right*."

"No, no; I can tell. I think we'd best have the berth made up and you lie down."

"That would be perfectly ridiculous."

"Well, where is it you feel sick? Show me; put your hand on the place. Want to eat something?"

With elaborate minuteness, he cross-questioned her, refusing to let the subject drop, protesting that she had dark circles under her eyes; that she had grown thinner.

"Wonder if there's a doctor on board," he murmured, looking uncertainly about the car. "Let me see your tongue. I know—a little whiskey is what you want, that and some pru——"

"No, no, *no*," she exclaimed. "I'm as well as I ever was in all my life. Look at me. Now, tell me, do I look like a sick lady?"

He scrutinised her face distressfully.

"Now, don't I look the picture of health?" she challenged.

"In a way you do," he began, "and then again——"

Hilma beat a tattoo with her heels upon the floor, shutting

her fists, the thumbs tucked inside. She closed her eyes, shaking her head energetically.

"I won't listen, I won't listen, I won't listen," she cried.

"But, just the same——"

"Gibble—gibble—gibble," she mocked. "I won't listen, I won't listen." She put a hand over his mouth. "Look, here's the dining-car waiter, and the first call for supper, and your wife is hungry."

They went forward and had supper in the diner, while the long train, now out upon the main line, settled itself to its pace, the prolonged, even gallop that it would hold for the better part of the week, spinning out the miles as a cotton spinner spins thread.

It was already dark when Antioch was left behind. Abruptly the sunset appeared to wheel in the sky and readjusted itself to the right of the track behind Mount Diablo, here visible almost to its base. The train had turned southward. Neroly was passed, then Brentwood, then Byron. In the gathering dusk, mountains began to build themselves up on either hand, far off, blocking the horizon. The train shot forward, roaring. Between the mountains the land lay level, cut up into farms, ranches. These continually grew larger; growing wheat began to appear, billowing in the wind of the train's passage. The mountains grew higher, the land richer, and by the time the moon rose, the train was well into the northernmost limits of the valley of the San Joaquin.

Annixter had engaged an entire section, and after he and his wife went to bed had the porter close the upper berth. Hilma sat up in bed to say her prayers, both hands over her face, and then kissing Annixter good-night, went to sleep with the directness of a little child, holding his hand in both her own.

Annixter, who never could sleep on the train, dozed and tossed and fretted for hours, consulting his watch and time-table whenever there was a stop; twice he rose to get a drink of ice water, and between whiles was forever sitting up in the narrow berth, stretching himself and yawning, murmuring with uncertain relevance:

"Oh, Lord! Oh-h-h *Lord!*"

There were some dozen other passengers in the car—a lady

with three children, a group of school-teachers, a couple of drummers, a stout gentleman with whiskers, and a well-dressed young man in a plaid travelling cap, whom Annixter had observed before supper time reading Daudet's "Tartarin" in the French.

But by nine o'clock, all these people were in their berths. Occasionally, above the rhythmic rumble of the wheels, Annixter could hear one of the lady's children fidgeting and complaining. The stout gentleman snored monotonously in two notes, one a rasping bass, the other a prolonged treble. At intervals, a brakeman or the passenger conductor pushed down the aisle, between the curtains, his red and white lamp over his arm. Looking out into the car Annixter saw in an end section where the berths had not been made up, the porter, in his white duck coat, dozing, his mouth wide open, his head on his shoulder.

The hours passed. Midnight came and went. Annixter, checking off the stations, noted their passage of Modesto, Merced, and Madeira. Then, after another broken nap, he lost count. He wondered where they were. Had they reached Fresno yet? Raising the window curtain, he made a shade with both hands on either side of his face and looked out. The night was thick, dark, clouded over. A fine rain was falling, leaving horizontal streaks on the glass of the outside window. Only the faintest grey blur indicated the sky. Everything else was impenetrable blackness.

"I think sure we must have passed Fresno," he muttered. He looked at his watch. It was about half-past three. "If we have passed Fresno," he said to himself, "I'd better wake the little girl pretty soon. She'll need about an hour to dress. Better find out for sure."

He drew on his trousers and shoes, got into his coat, and stepped out into the aisle. In the seat that had been occupied by the porter, the Pullman conductor, his cash box and car-schedules before him, was checking up his berths, a blue pencil behind his ear.

"What's the next stop, Captain?" inquired Annixter, coming up. "Have we reached Fresno yet?"

"Just passed it," the other responded, looking at Annixter over his spectacles.

"What's the next stop?"

"Goshen. We will be there in about forty-five minutes."

"Fair black night, isn't it?"

"Black as a pocket. Let's see, you're the party in upper and lower 9."

Annixter caught at the back of the nearest seat, just in time to prevent a fall, and the conductor's cash box was shunted off the surface of the plush seat and came clanking to the floor. The Pintsch lights overhead vibrated with blinding rapidity in the long, sliding jar that ran through the train from end to end, and the momentum of its speed suddenly decreasing, all but pitched the conductor from his seat. A hideous ear-splitting rasp made itself heard from the clamped-down Westinghouse gear underneath, and Annixter knew that the wheels had ceased to revolve and that the train was sliding forward upon the motionless flanges.

"Hello, hello," he exclaimed, " what's all up now?"

"Emergency brakes," declared the conductor, catching up his cash box and thrusting his papers and tickets into it. "Nothing much; probably a cow on the track."

He disappeared, carrying his lantern with him.

But the other passengers, all but the stout gentleman, were awake; heads were thrust from out the curtains, and Annixter, hurrying back to Hilma, was assailed by all manner of questions.

"What was that?"

"Anything wrong?"

"What's up, anyways?"

Hilma was just waking as Annixter pushed the curtain aside.

"Oh, I was so frightened. What's the matter, dear?" she exclaimed.

"I don't know," he answered. "Only the emergency brakes. Just a cow on the track, I guess. Don't get scared. It isn't anything."

But with a final shriek of the Westinghouse appliance, the train came to a definite halt.

At once the silence was absolute. The ears, still numb with the long-continued roar of wheels and clashing iron, at first refused to register correctly the smaller noises of the surroundings. Voices came from the other end of the car, strange and unfamiliar, as though heard at a great distance across the water. The stillness of the night outside was so profound that the rain, dripping from the car roof upon the road-bed underneath, was as distinct as the ticking of a clock.

"Well, we've sure stopped," observed one of the drummers.

"What is it?" asked Hilma again. "Are you sure there's nothing wrong?"

"Sure," said Annixter.

Outside, underneath their window, they heard the sound of hurried footsteps crushing into the clinkers by the side of the ties. They passed on, and Annixter heard some one in the distance shout:

"Yes, on the other side."

Then the door at the end of their car opened and a brakeman with a red beard ran down the aisle and out upon the platform in front. The forward door closed. Everything was quiet again. In the stillness the fat gentleman's snores made themselves heard once more.

The minutes passed; nothing stirred. There was no sound but the dripping rain. The line of cars lay immobilised and inert under the night. One of the drummers, having stepped outside on the platform for a look around, returned, saying:

"There sure isn't any station anywheres about and no siding. Bet you they have had an accident of some kind."

"Ask the porter."

"I did. He don't know."

"Maybe they stopped to take on wood or water, or something."

"Well, they wouldn't use the emergency brakes for that, would they? Why, this train stopped almost in her own length. Pretty near slung me out the berth. Those were the emergency brakes. I heard some one say so."

From far out towards the front of the train, near the locomotive, came the sharp, incisive report of a revolver; then two more almost simultaneously; then, after a long interval, a fourth.

"Say, that's *shooting*. By God, boys, they're shooting. Say, this is a hold-up."

Instantly a white-hot excitement flared from end to end of the car. Incredibly sinister, heard thus in the night, and in the rain, mysterious, fearful, those four pistol shots started confusion from out the sense of security like a frightened rabbit hunted from her burrow. Wide-eyed, the passengers of the car looked into each other's faces. It had come to them at last, this, they had so often read about. Now they were to see the real thing, now they were to face actuality, face this danger of the night, leaping in from out the blackness of the roadside, masked, armed, ready to kill. They were facing it now. They were held up.

Hilma said nothing, only catching Annixter's hand, looking squarely into his eyes.

"Steady, little girl," he said. "They can't hurt you. I won't leave you. By the Lord," he suddenly exclaimed, his excitement getting the better of him for a moment. "By the Lord, it's a hold-up."

The school-teachers were in the aisle of the car, in night gown, wrapper, and dressing sack, huddled together like sheep, holding on to each other, looking to the men, silently appealing for protection. Two of them were weeping, white to the lips.

"Oh, oh, oh, it's terrible. Oh, if they only won't hurt me."

But the lady with the children looked out from her berth, smiled reassuringly, and said:

"I'm not a bit frightened. They won't do anything to us if we keep quiet. I've my watch and jewelry all ready for them in my little black bag, see?"

She exhibited it to the passengers. Her children were all awake. They were quiet, looking about them with eager faces, interested and amused at this surprise. In his berth, the fat gentleman with whiskers snored profoundly.

"Say, I'm going out there," suddenly declared one of the drummers, flourishing a pocket revolver.

His friend caught his arm.

"Don't make a fool of yourself, Max," he said.

"They won't come near us," observed the well-dressed young man; "they are after the Wells-Fargo box and the registered mail. You won't do any good out there."

But the other loudly protested. No; he was going out. He

didn't propose to be buncoed without a fight. He wasn't any coward.

"Well, you don't go, that's all," said his friend, angrily. "There's women and children in this car. You ain't going to draw the fire here."

"Well, that's to be thought of," said the other, allowing himself to be pacified, but still holding his pistol.

"Don't let him open that window," cried Annixter sharply from his place by Hilma's side, for the drummer had made as if to open the sash in one of the sections that had not been made up.

"Sure, that's right," said the others. "Don't open any windows. Keep your head in. You'll get us all shot if you aren't careful."

However, the drummer had got the window up and had leaned out before the others could interfere and draw him away.

"Say, by jove," he shouted, as he turned back to the car, "our engine's gone. We're standing on a curve and you can see the end of the train. She's gone, I tell you. Well, look for yourself."

In spite of their precautions, one after another, his friends looked out. Sure enough, the train was without a loco-motive.

"They've done it so we can't get away," vociferated the drummer with the pistol. "Now, by jiminy-Christmas, they'll come through the cars and stand us up. They'll be in here in a minute. *Lord! What was that?*"

From far away up the track, apparently some half-mile ahead of the train, came the sound of a heavy explosion. The windows of the car vibrated with it.

"Shooting again."

"That isn't shooting," exclaimed Annixter. "They've pulled the express and mail car on ahead with the engine and now they are dynamiting her open."

"That must be it. Yes, sure, that's just what they are doing."

The forward door of the car opened and closed and the school-teachers shrieked and cowered. The drummer with the revolver faced about, his eyes bulging. However, it was only the train conductor, hatless, his lantern in his hand. He was soaked with rain. He appeared in the aisle.

"Is there a doctor in this car?" he asked.

Promptly the passengers surrounded him, voluble with questions. But he was in a bad temper.

"I don't know anything more than you," he shouted angrily. "It was a hold-up. I guess you know that, don't you? Well, what more do you want to know? I ain't got time to fool around. They cut off our express car and have cracked it open, and they shot one of our train crew, that's all, and I want a doctor."

"Did they shoot him—kill him, do you mean?"

"Is he hurt bad?"

"Did the men get away?"

"Oh, shut up, will you all?" exclaimed the conductor. "What do I know? Is there a *doctor* in this car, that's what I want to know?"

The well-dressed young man stepped forward.

"I'm a doctor," he said.

"Well, come along then," returned the conductor, in a surly voice, "and the passengers in this car," he added, turning back at the door and nodding his head menacingly, "will go back to bed and *stay* there. It's all over and there's nothing to see."

He went out, followed by the young doctor.

Then ensued an interminable period of silence. The entire train seemed deserted. Helpless, bereft of its engine, a huge, decapitated monster it lay, half-way around a curve, rained upon, abandoned.

There was more fear in this last condition of affairs, more terror in the idea of this prolonged line of sleepers, with their nickelled fittings, their plate glass, their upholstery, vestibules, and the like, loaded down with people, lost and forgotten in the night and the rain, than there had been when the actual danger threatened.

What was to become of them now? Who was there to help them? Their engine was gone; they were helpless. What next was to happen?

Nobody came near the car. Even the porter had disappeared. The wait seemed endless, and the persistent snoring of the whiskered gentleman rasped the nerves like the scrape of a file.

"Well, how long are we going to stick here now?" began one of the drummers. "Wonder if they hurt the engine with their dynamite?"

"Oh, I know they will come through the car and rob us," wailed the school-teachers.

The lady with the little children went back to bed, and Annixter, assured that the trouble was over, did likewise. But nobody slept. From berth to berth came the sound of suppressed voices talking it all over, formulating conjectures. Certain points seemed to be settled upon, no one knew how, as indisputable. The highwaymen had been four in number and had stopped the train by pulling the bell cord. A brakeman had attempted to interfere and had been shot. The robbers had been on the train all the way from San Francisco. The drummer named Max remembered to have seen four "suspicious-looking characters" in the smoking-car at Lathrop, and had intended to speak to the conductor about them. This drummer had been in a hold-up before, and told the story of it over and over again.

At last, after what seemed to have been an hour's delay, and when the dawn had already begun to show in the east, the locomotive backed on to the train again with a reverberating jar that ran from car to car. At the jolting, the school-teachers screamed in chorus, and the whiskered gentleman stopped snoring and thrust his head from his curtains, blinking at the Pintsch lights. It appeared that he was an Englishman.

"I say," he asked of the drummer named Max, "I say, my friend, what place is this?"

The others roared with derision.

"We were *held up*, sir, that's what we were. We were held up and you slept through it all. You missed the show of your life."

The gentleman fixed the group with a prolonged gaze. He said never a word, but little by little he was convinced that the drummers told the truth. All at once he grew wrathful, his face purpling. He withdrew his head angrily, buttoning his curtains together in a fury. The cause of his rage was inexplicable, but they could hear him resettling himself upon his pillows with exasperated movements of his head and shoulders. In a few moments the deep bass and shrill treble of his snoring once more sounded through the car.

At last the train got under way again, with useless warning blasts of the engine's whistle. In a few moments it was tearing away through the dawn at a wonderful speed, rocking around curves, roaring across culverts, making up time.

And all the rest of that strange night the passengers, sitting up in their unmade beds, in the swaying car, lighted by a strange mingling of pallid dawn and trembling Pintsch lights, rushing at break-neck speed through the misty rain, were oppressed by a vision of figures of terror, far behind them in the night they had left, masked, armed, galloping toward the mountains, pistol in hand, the booty bound to the saddle bow, galloping, galloping on, sending a thrill of fear through all the country side.

The young doctor returned. He sat down in the smoking-room, lighting a cigarette, and Annixter and the drummers pressed around him to know the story of the whole affair.

"The man is dead," he declared; "the brakeman. He was shot through the lungs twice. They think the fellow got away with about five thousand in gold coin."

"The fellow? Wasn't there four of them?"

"No; only one. And say, let me tell you, he had his nerve with him. It seems he was on the roof of the express car all the time, and going as fast as we were, he jumped from the roof of the car down on to the coal on the engine's tender, and crawled over that and held up the men in the cab with his gun, took their guns from 'em and made 'em stop the train. Even ordered 'em to use the emergency gear, seems he knew all about it. Then he went back and uncoupled the express car himself. While he was doing this, a brakeman—you remember that brakeman that came through here once or twice—had a red mustache."

"*That* chap?"

"Sure. Well, as soon as the train stopped, this brakeman guessed something was wrong and ran up, saw the fellow cutting off the express car and took a couple of shots at him, and the fireman says the fellow didn't even take his hand off the coupling-pin; just turned around as cool as how-do-you-do and *nailed* the brakeman right there. They weren't five feet apart when they began shooting. The brakeman had come on him unexpected, had no idea he was so close."

"And the express messenger, all this time?"

"Well, he did his best. Jumped out with his repeating shot-gun, but the fellow had him covered before he could turn round. Held him up and took his gun away from him. Say, you know I call that nerve, just the same. One man standing up a whole train-load, like that. Then, as soon as he'd cut the express car off, he made the engineer run her up the track about half a mile to a road crossing, *where he had a horse tied.* What do you think of that? Didn't he have it all figured out close? And when he got there, he dynamited the safe and got the Wells-Fargo box. He took five thousand in gold coin; the messenger says it was railroad money that the company were sending down to Bakersfield to pay off with. It was in a bag. He never touched the registered mail, nor a whole wad of greenbacks that were in the safe, but just took the coin, got on his horse, and lit out. The engineer says he went to the east'ard."

"He got away, did he?"

"Yes, but they think they'll get him. He wore a kind of mask, but the brakeman recognised him positively. We got his ante-mortem statement. The brakeman said the fellow had a grudge against the road. He was a discharged employee, and lives near Bonneville."

"Dyke, by the Lord!" exclaimed Annixter.

"That's the name," said the young doctor.

When the train arrived at Bonneville, forty minutes be-hind time, it landed Annixter and Hilma in the midst of the very thing they most wished to avoid—an enormous crowd. The news that the Overland had been held up thirty miles south of Fresno, a brakeman killed and the safe looted, and that Dyke alone was responsible for the night's work, had been wired on ahead from Fowler, the train conductor throwing the despatch to the station agent from the flying train.

Before the train had come to a standstill under the arched

roof of the Bonneville depot, it was all but taken by assault. Annixter, with Hilma on his arm, had almost to fight his way out of the car. The depot was black with people. S. Behrman was there, Delaney, Cyrus Ruggles, the town marshal, the mayor. Genslinger, his hat on the back of his head, ranged the train from cab to rear-lights, note-book in hand, interviewing, questioning, collecting facts for his extra. As Annixter descended finally to the platform, the editor, alert as a black-and-tan terrier, his thin, osseous hands quivering with eagerness, his brown, dry face working with excitement, caught his elbow.

"Can I have your version of the affair, Mr. Annixter?"

Annixter turned on him abruptly.

"Yes!" he exclaimed fiercely. "You and your gang drove Dyke from his job because he wouldn't work for starvation wages. Then you raised freight rates on him and robbed him of all he had. You ruined him and drove him to fill himself up with Caraher's whiskey. He's only taken back what you plundered him of, and now you're going to hound him over the State, hunt him down like a wild animal, and bring him to the gallows at San Quentin. That's *my* version of the affair, Mister Genslinger, but it's worth your subsidy from the P. and S. W. to print it."

There was a murmur of approval from the crowd that stood around, and Genslinger, with an angry shrug of one shoulder, took himself away.

At length, Annixter brought Hilma through the crowd to where young Vacca was waiting with the team. However, they could not at once start for the ranch, Annixter wishing to ask some questions at the freight office about a final consignment of chairs. It was nearly eleven o'clock before they could start home. But to gain the Upper Road to Quien Sabe, it was necessary to traverse all of Main Street, running through the heart of Bonneville.

The entire town seemed to be upon the sidewalks. By now the rain was over and the sun shining. The story of the hold-up—the work of a man whom every one knew and liked—was in every mouth. How had Dyke come to do it? Who would have believed it of him? Think of his poor mother and the little tad. Well, after all, he was not so much to blame; the railroad people had brought it on themselves. But he had shot a man to death. Ah, that was a serious business. Good-natured, big, broad-shouldered, jovial Dyke, the man they knew, with whom they had shaken hands only yesterday, yes, and drank with him. He had shot a man, killed him, had stood there in the dark and in the rain while they were asleep in their beds, and had killed a man. Now where was he? Instinctively eyes were turned eastward, over the tops of the houses, or down vistas of side streets to where the foot-hills of the mountains rose dim and vast over the edge of the valley. He was in amongst them; somewhere, in all that pile of blue crests and purple cañons he was hidden away. Now for weeks of searching, false alarms, clews, trailings, watchings, all the thrill and heart-bursting excitement of a man-hunt. Would he get away? Hardly a man on the sidewalks of the town that day who did not hope for it.

As Annixter's team trotted through the central portion of the town, young Vacca pointed to a denser and larger crowd around the rear entrance of the City Hall. Fully twenty saddle horses were tied to the iron rail underneath the scant, half-grown trees near by, and as Annixter and Hilma drove by, the crowd parted and a dozen men with revolvers on their hips pushed their way to the curbstone, and, mounting their horses, rode away at a gallop.

"It's the posse," said young Vacca.

Outside the town limits the ground was level. There was nothing to obstruct the view, and to the north, in the direction of Osterman's ranch, Vacca made out another party of horsemen, galloping eastward, and beyond these still another.

"There're the other posses," he announced. "That further one is Archie Moore's. He's the sheriff. He came down from Visalia on a special engine this morning."

When the team turned into the driveway to the ranch house, Hilma uttered a little cry, clasping her hands joyfully. The house was one glitter of new white paint, the driveway had been freshly gravelled, the flower-beds replenished. Mrs. Vacca and her daughter, who had been busy putting on the finishing touches, came to the door to welcome them.

"What's this case here?" asked Annixter, when, after

helping his wife from the carry-all, his eye fell upon a wooden box of some three by five feet that stood on the porch and bore the red Wells-Fargo label.

"It came here last night, addressed to you, sir," exclaimed Mrs. Vacca. "We were sure it wasn't any of your furniture, so we didn't open it."

"Oh, maybe it's a wedding present," exclaimed Hilma, her eyes sparkling.

"Well, maybe it is," returned her husband. "Here, m' son, help me in with this."

Annixter and young Vacca bore the case into the sitting-room of the house, and Annixter, hammer in hand, attacked it vigorously. Vacca discreetly withdrew on signal from his mother, closing the door after him. Annixter and his wife were left alone.

"Oh, hurry, hurry," cried Hilma, dancing around him. "I want to see what it is. Who do you suppose could have sent it to us? And so heavy, too. What *do* you think it can be?"

Annixter put the claw of the hammer underneath the edge of the board top and wrenched with all his might. The boards had been clamped together by a transverse bar and the whole top of the box came away in one piece. A layer of excelsior was disclosed, and on it a letter addressed by typewriter to Annixter. It bore the trade-mark of a business firm of Los Angeles. Annixter glanced at this and promptly caught it up before Hilma could see, with an exclamation of intelligence.

"Oh, I know what this is," he observed, carelessly trying to restrain her busy hands. "It isn't anything. Just some machinery. Let it go."

But already she had pulled away the excelsior. Underneath, in temporary racks, were two dozen Winchester repeating rifles.

"Why—what—what—" murmured Hilma blankly.

"Well, I told you not to mind," said Annixter. "It isn't anything. Let's look through the rooms."

"But you said you knew what it was," she protested, bewildered. "You wanted to make believe it was machinery. Are you keeping anything from me? Tell me what it all means. Oh, why are you getting—these?"

She caught his arm, looking with intense eagerness into his face. She half understood already. Annixter saw that.

"Well," he said, lamely, "*you* know—it may not come to anything at all, but you know—well, this League of ours—suppose the Railroad tries to jump Quien Sabe or Los Muertos or any of the other ranches—we made up our minds—the Leaguers have—that we wouldn't let it. That's all."

"And I thought," cried Hilma, drawing back fearfully from the case of rifles, "and I thought it was a wedding present."

And that was their home-coming, the end of their bridal trip. Through the terror of the night, echoing with pistol shots, through that scene of robbery and murder, into this atmosphere of alarms, a man-hunt organising, armed horsemen silhouetted against the horizons, cases of rifles where wedding presents should have been, Annixter brought his young wife to be mistress of a home he might at any moment be called upon to defend with his life.

The days passed. Soon a week had gone by. Magnus Derrick and Osterman returned from the city without any definite idea as to the Corporation's plans. Lyman had been reticent. He knew nothing as to the progress of the land cases in Washington. There was no news. The Executive Committee of the League held a perfunctory meeting at Los Muertos at which nothing but routine business was transacted. A scheme put forward by Osterman for a conference with the railroad managers fell through because of the refusal of the company to treat with the ranchers upon any other basis than that of the new grading. It was impossible to learn whether or not the company considered Los Muertos, Quien Sabe, and the ranches around Bonneville covered by the test cases then on appeal.

Meanwhile there was no decrease in the excitement that Dyke's hold-up had set loose over all the county. Day after day it was the one topic of conversation, at street corners, at cross-roads, over dinner tables, in office, bank, and store. S. Behrman placarded the town with a notice of $500.00 reward for the ex-engineer's capture, dead or alive, and the express company supplemented this by another offer of an equal amount. The country was thick with parties of horsemen, armed with rifles and revolvers, recruited from Visalia,

Goshen, and the few railroad sympathisers around Bonneville and Guadalajara. One after another of these returned, empty-handed, covered with dust and mud, their horses exhausted, to be met and passed by fresh posses starting out to continue the pursuit. The sheriff of Santa Clara County sent down his bloodhounds from San José—small, harmless-looking dogs, with a terrific bay—to help in the chase. Reporters from the San Francisco papers appeared, interviewing every one, sometimes even accompanying the searching bands. Horse hoofs clattered over the roads at night; bells were rung, the "Mercury" issued extra after extra; the bloodhounds bayed, gun butts clashed on the asphalt pavements of Bonneville; accidental discharges of revolvers brought the whole town into the street; farm hands called to each other across the fences of ranch-divisions—in a word, the country-side was in an uproar.

And all to no effect. The hoof-marks of Dyke's horse had been traced in the mud of the road to within a quarter of a mile of the foot-hills and there irretrievably lost. Three days after the hold-up, a sheep-herder was found who had seen the highwayman on a ridge in the higher mountains, to the northeast of Taurusa. And that was absolutely all. Rumours were thick, promising clews were discovered, new trails taken up, but nothing transpired to bring the pursuers and pursued any closer together. Then, after ten days of strain, public interest began to flag. It was believed that Dyke had succeeded in getting away. If this was true, he had gone to the southward, after gaining the mountains, and it would be his intention to work out of the range somewhere near the southern part of the San Joaquin, near Bakersfield. Thus, the sheriffs, marshals, and deputies decided. They had hunted too many criminals in these mountains before not to know the usual courses taken. In time, Dyke *must* come out of the mountains to get water and provisions. But this time passed, and from not one of the watched points came any word of his appearance. At last the posses began to disband. Little by little the pursuit was given up.

Only S. Behrman persisted. He had made up his mind to bring Dyke in. He succeeded in arousing the same degree of determination in Delaney—by now, a trusted aide of the

Railroad—and of his own cousin, a real estate broker, named Christian, who knew the mountains and had once been mar-shal of Visalia in the old stock-raising days. These two went into the Sierras, accompanied by two hired deputies, and car-rying with them a month's provisions and two of the blood-hounds loaned by the Santa Clara sheriff.

On a certain Sunday, a few days after the departure of Christian and Delaney, Annixter, who had been reading "David Copperfield" in his hammock on the porch of the ranch house, put down the book and went to find Hilma, who was helping Louisa Vacca set the table for dinner. He found her in the dining-room, her hands full of the gold-bordered china plates, only used on special occasions and which Louisa was forbidden to touch.

His wife was more than ordinarily pretty that day. She wore a dress of flowered organdie over pink sateen, with pink ribbons about her waist and neck, and on her slim feet the low shoes she always affected, with their smart, bright buck-les. Her thick, brown, sweet-smelling hair was heaped high upon her head and set off with a bow of black velvet, and underneath the shadow of its coils, her wide-open eyes, rimmed with the thin, black line of her lashes, shone contin-ually, reflecting the sunlight. Marriage had only accentuated the beautiful maturity of Hilma's figure—now no longer pre-cocious—defining the single, deep swell from her throat to her waist, the strong, fine amplitude of her hips, the sweet, feminine undulation of her neck and shoulders. Her cheeks were pink with health, and her large round arms carried the piled-up dishes with never a tremour. Annixter, observant enough where his wife was concerned, noted how the reflec-tion of the white china set a glow of pale light underneath her chin.

"Hilma," he said, "I've been wondering lately about things. We're so blamed happy ourselves it won't do for us to forget about other people who are down, will it? Might change our luck. And I'm just likely to forget that way, too. It's my nature."

His wife looked up at him joyfully. Here was the new An-nixter, certainly.

"In all this hullabaloo about Dyke," he went on, "there's

some one nobody ain't thought about at all. That's *Mrs.
Dyke*—and the little tad. I wouldn't be surprised if they were
in a hole over there. What do you say we drive over to the
hop ranch after dinner and see if she wants anything?"

Hilma put down the plates and came around the table and
kissed him without a word.

As soon as their dinner was over, Annixter had the carry-
all hitched up, and, dispensing with young Vacca, drove over
to the hop ranch with Hilma.

Hilma could not keep back the tears as they passed through
the lamentable desolation of the withered, brown vines, symbols of perished hopes and abandoned effort, and Annixter
swore between his teeth.

Though the wheels of the carry-all grated loudly on the
roadway in front of the house, nobody came to the door nor
looked from the windows. The place seemed tenantless, infinitely lonely, infinitely sad.

Annixter tied the team, and with Hilma approached the
wide-open door, scuffling and tramping on the porch to attract attention. Nobody stirred. A Sunday stillness pervaded
the place. Outside, the withered hop-leaves rustled like dry
paper in the breeze. The quiet was ominous. They peered into
the front room from the doorway, Hilma holding her husband's hand. Mrs. Dyke was there. She sat at the table in the
middle of the room, her head, with its white hair, down upon
her arm. A clutter of unwashed dishes were strewed over the
red and white tablecloth. The unkempt room, once a marvel
of neatness, had not been cleaned for days. Newspapers, Genslinger's extras and copies of San Francisco and Los Angeles
dailies were scattered all over the room. On the table itself
were crumpled yellow telegrams, a dozen of them, a score of
them, blowing about in the draught from the door. And in
the midst of all this disarray, surrounded by the published
accounts of her son's crime, the telegraphed answers to her
pitiful appeals for tidings fluttering about her head, the highwayman's mother, worn out, abandoned and forgotten, slept
through the stillness of the Sunday afternoon.

Neither Hilma nor Annixter ever forgot their interview
with Mrs. Dyke that day. Suddenly waking, she had caught
sight of Annixter, and at once exclaimed eagerly:

"Is there any news?"

For a long time afterwards nothing could be got from her. She was numb to all other issues than the one question of Dyke's capture. She did not answer their questions nor reply to their offers of assistance. Hilma and Annixter conferred together without lowering their voices, at her very elbow, while she looked vacantly at the floor, drawing one hand over the other in a persistent, maniacal gesture. From time to time she would start suddenly from her chair, her eyes wide, and as if all at once realising Annixter's presence, would cry out:

"Is there any news?"

"Where is Sidney, Mrs. Dyke?" asked Hilma for the fourth time. "Is she well? Is she taken care of?"

"Here's the last telegram," said Mrs. Dyke, in a loud, monotonous voice. "See, it says there is no news. He didn't do it," she moaned, rocking herself back and forth, drawing one hand over the other, "he didn't do it, he didn't do it, he didn't do it. I don't know where he is."

When at last she came to herself, it was with a flood of tears. Hilma put her arms around the poor, old woman, as she bowed herself again upon the table, sobbing and weeping.

"Oh, my son, my son," she cried, "my own boy, my only son! If I could have died for you to have prevented this. I remember him when he was little. Such a splendid little fellow, so brave, so loving, with never an unkind thought, never a mean action. So it was all his life. We were never apart. It was always 'dear little son,' and 'dear mammy' between us—never once was he unkind, and he loved me and was the gentlest son to me. And he was a *good* man. He is now, he is now. They don't understand him. They are not even sure that he did this. He never meant it. They don't know my son. Why, he wouldn't have hurt a kitten. Everybody loved him. He was driven to it. They hounded him down, they wouldn't let him alone. He was not right in his mind. They hounded him to it," she cried fiercely, "they hounded him to it. They drove him and goaded him till he couldn't stand it any longer, and now they mean to kill him for turning on them. They are hunting him with dogs; night after night I have stood on the porch and heard the dogs baying far off. They are tracking my boy with dogs like a wild animal. May God never forgive them." She rose to her feet, terrible, her white hair unbound. "May God punish them as they deserve, may they never prosper—on my knees I shall pray for it every night—may their money be a curse to them, may their sons, their first-born, only sons, be taken from them in their youth."

But Hilma interrupted, begging her to be silent, to be quiet. The tears came again then and the choking sobs. Hilma took her in her arms.

"Oh, my little boy, my little boy," she cried. "My only son, all that I had, to have come to this! He was not right in his mind or he would have known it would break my heart. Oh, my son, my son, if I could have died for you."

Sidney came in, clinging to her dress, weeping, imploring her not to cry, protesting that they never could catch her papa, that he would come back soon. Hilma took them both, the little child and the broken-down old woman, in the great embrace of her strong arms, and they all three sobbed together.

Annixter stood on the porch outside, his back turned, looking straight before him into the wilderness of dead vines, his teeth shut hard, his lower lip thrust out.

"I hope S. Behrman is satisfied with all this," he muttered. "I hope he is satisfied now, damn his soul!"

All at once an idea occurred to him. He turned about and reëntered the room.

"Mrs. Dyke," he began, "I want you and Sidney to come over and live at Quien Sabe. I know—you can't make me believe that the reporters and officers and officious busy-faces that pretend to offer help just so as they can satisfy their curiosity aren't nagging you to death. I want you to let me take care of you and the little tad till all this trouble of yours is over with. There's plenty of place for you. You can have the house my wife's people used to live in. You've got to look these things in the face. What are you going to do to get along? You must be very short of money. S. Behrman will foreclose on you and take the whole place in a little while, now. I want you to let me help you, let Hilma and me be good friends to you. It would be a privilege."

Mrs. Dyke tried bravely to assume her pride, insisting that she could manage, but her spirit was broken. The whole affair ended unexpectedly, with Annixter and Hilma bringing Dyke's mother and little girl back to Quien Sabe in the carryall.

Mrs. Dyke would not take with her a stick of furniture nor a single ornament. It would only serve to remind her of a vanished happiness. She packed a few clothes of her own and Sidney's in a little trunk, Hilma helping her, and Annixter stowed the trunk under the carry-all's back seat. Mrs. Dyke turned the key in the door of the house and Annixter helped her to her seat beside his wife. They drove through the sear, brown hop vines. At the angle of the road Mrs. Dyke turned around and looked back at the ruin of the hop ranch, the roof of the house just showing above the trees. She never saw it again.

As soon as Annixter and Hilma were alone, after their return to Quien Sabe—Mrs. Dyke and Sidney having been installed in the Trees' old house—Hilma threw her arms around her husband's neck.

"Fine," she exclaimed, "oh, it was fine of you, dear, to think of them and to be so good to them. My husband is such a *good* man. So unselfish. You wouldn't have thought of being kind to Mrs. Dyke and Sidney a little while ago. You wouldn't have thought of them at all. But you did now, and it's just because you love me true, isn't it? Isn't it? And because it's made you a better man. I'm so proud and glad to think it's so. It is so, isn't it? Just because you love me true."

"You bet it is, Hilma," he told her.

As Hilma and Annixter were sitting down to the supper which they found waiting for them, Louisa Vacca came to the door of the dining-room to say that Harran Derrick had telephoned over from Los Muertos for Annixter, and had left word for him to ring up Los Muertos as soon as he came in.

"He said it was important," added Louisa Vacca.

"Maybe they have news from Washington," suggested Hilma.

Annixter would not wait to have supper, but telephoned to

Los Muertos at once. Magnus answered the call. There was a special meeting of the Executive Committee of the League summoned for the next day, he told Annixter. It was for the purpose of considering the new grain tariff prepared by the Railroad Commissioners. Lyman had written that the schedule of this tariff had just been issued, that he had not been able to construct it precisely according to the wheat-growers' wishes, and that he, himself, would come down to Los Muertos and explain its apparent discrepancies. Magnus said Lyman would be present at the session.

Annixter, curious for details, forbore, nevertheless, to question. The connection from Los Muertos to Quien Sabe was made through Bonneville, and in those troublesome times no one could be trusted. It could not be known who would overhear conversations carried on over the lines. He assured Magnus that he would be on hand.

The time for the Committee meeting had been set for seven o'clock in the evening, in order to accommodate Lyman, who wrote that he would be down on the evening train, but would be compelled, by pressure of business, to return to the city early the next morning.

At the time appointed, the men composing the Committee gathered about the table in the dining-room of the Los Muertos ranch house. It was almost a reproduction of the scene of the famous evening when Osterman had proposed the plan of the Ranchers' Railroad Commission. Magnus Derrick sat at the head of the table, in his buttoned frock coat. Whiskey bottles and siphons of soda-water were within easy reach. Presley, who by now was considered the confidential friend of every member of the Committee, lounged as before on the sofa, smoking cigarettes, the cat Nathalie on his knee. Besides Magnus and Annixter, Osterman was present, and old Broderson and Harran; Garnet from the Ruby Rancho and Gethings of the San Pablo, who were also members of the Executive Committee, were on hand, preoccupied, bearded men, smoking black cigars, and, last of all, Dabney, the silent old man, of whom little was known but his name, and who had been made a member of the Committee, nobody could tell why.

"My son Lyman should be here, gentlemen, within at least

ten minutes. I have sent my team to meet him at Bonneville," explained Magnus, as he called the meeting to order. "The Secretary will call the roll."

Osterman called the roll, and, to fill in the time, read over the minutes of the previous meeting. The treasurer was making his report as to the funds at the disposal of the League when Lyman arrived.

Magnus and Harran went forward to meet him, and the Committee rather awkwardly rose and remained standing while the three exchanged greetings, the members, some of whom had never seen their commissioner, eyeing him out of the corners of their eyes.

Lyman was dressed with his usual correctness. His cravat was of the latest fashion, his clothes of careful design and unimpeachable fit. His shoes, of patent leather, reflected the lamplight, and he carried a drab overcoat over his arm. Before being introduced to the Committee, he excused himself a moment and ran to see his mother, who waited for him in the adjoining sitting-room. But in a few moments he returned, asking pardon for the delay.

He was all affability; his protruding eyes, that gave such an unusual, foreign appearance to his very dark face, radiated geniality. He was evidently anxious to please, to produce a good impression upon the grave, clumsy farmers before whom he stood. But at the same time, Presley, watching him from his place on the sofa, could imagine that he was rather nervous. He was too nimble in his cordiality, and the little gestures he made in bringing his cuffs into view and in touching the ends of his tight, black mustache with the ball of his thumb were repeated with unnecessary frequency.

"Mr. Broderson, my son, Lyman, my eldest son. Mr. Annixter, my son, Lyman."

The Governor introduced him to the ranchers, proud of Lyman's good looks, his correct dress, his ease of manner. Lyman shook hands all around, keeping up a flow of small talk, finding a new phrase for each member, complimenting Osterman, whom he already knew, upon his talent for organisation, recalling a mutual acquaintance to the mind of old Broderson. At length, however, he sat down at the end of the table, opposite his brother. There was a silence.

Magnus rose to recapitulate the reasons for the extra session of the Committee, stating again that the Board of Railway Commissioners which they—the ranchers—had succeeded in seating had at length issued the new schedule of reduced rates, and that Mr. Derrick had been obliging enough to offer to come down to Los Muertos in person to acquaint the wheat-growers of the San Joaquin with the new rates for the carriage of their grain.

But Lyman very politely protested, addressing his father punctiliously as "Mr. Chairman," and the other ranchers as "Gentlemen of the Executive Committee of the League." He had no wish, he said, to disarrange the regular proceedings of the Committee. Would it not be preferable to defer the reading of his report till "new business" was called for? In the meanwhile, let the Committee proceed with its usual work. He understood the necessarily delicate nature of this work, and would be pleased to withdraw till the proper time arrived for him to speak.

"Good deal of backing and filling about the reading of a column of figures," muttered Annixter to the man at his elbow.

Lyman "awaited the Committee's decision." He sat down, touching the ends of his mustache.

"Oh, play ball," growled Annixter.

Gethings rose to say that as the meeting had been called solely for the purpose of hearing and considering the new grain tariff, he was of the opinion that routine business could be dispensed with and the schedule read at once. It was so ordered.

Lyman rose and made a long speech. Voluble as Osterman himself, he, nevertheless, had at his command a vast number of ready-made phrases, the staples of a political speaker, the stock in trade of the commercial lawyer, which rolled off his tongue with the most persuasive fluency. By degrees, in the course of his speech, he began to insinuate the idea that the wheat-growers had never expected to settle their difficulties with the Railroad by the work of a single commission; that they had counted upon a long, continued campaign of many years, railway commission succeeding railway commission, before the desired low rates should be secured; that the present Board of Commissioners was only the beginning and that too great results were not expected from them. All this he contrived to mention casually, in the talk, as if it were a foregone conclusion, a matter understood by all.

As the speech continued, the eyes of the ranchers around the table were fixed with growing attention upon this well-dressed, city-bred young man, who spoke so fluently and who told them of their own intentions. A feeling of perplexity began to spread, and the first taint of distrust invaded their minds.

"But the good work has been most auspiciously inaugurated," continued Lyman. "Reforms so sweeping as the one contemplated cannot be accomplished in a single night. Great things grow slowly, benefits to be permanent must accrue gradually. Yet, in spite of all this, your commissioners have done much. Already the phalanx of the enemy is pierced, already his armour is dinted. Pledged as were your commissioners to an average ten per cent. reduction in rates for the carriage of grain by the Pacific and Southwestern Railroad, we have rigidly adhered to the demands of our constituency, we have obeyed the People. The main problem has not yet been completely solved; that is for later, when we shall have gathered sufficient strength to attack the enemy in his very stronghold; *but an average ten per cent. cut has been made all over the State*. We have made a great advance, have taken a great step forward, and if the work is carried ahead, upon the lines laid down by the present commissioners and their constituents, there is every reason to believe that within a very few years equitable and stable rates for the shipment of grain from the San Joaquin Valley to Stockton, Port Costa, and tidewater will be permanently imposed."

"Well, hold on," exclaimed Annixter, out of order and ignoring the Governor's reproof, "hasn't your commission reduced grain rates in the San Joaquin?"

"We have reduced grain rates by ten per cent. all over the State," rejoined Lyman. "Here are copies of the new schedule."

He drew them from his valise and passed them around the table.

"You see," he observed, "the rate between Mayfield and

Oakland, for instance, has been reduced by twenty-five cents a ton."

"Yes—but—but—" said old Broderson, "it is rather unusual, isn't it, for wheat in that district to be sent to Oakland?"

"Why, look here," exclaimed Annixter, looking up from the schedule, "where is there any reduction in rates in the San Joaquin—from Bonneville and Guadalajara, for instance? I don't see as you've made any reduction at all. Is this right? Did you give me the right schedule?"

"Of course, *all* the points in the State could not be covered at once," returned Lyman. "We never expected, you know, that we could cut rates in the San Joaquin the very first move; that is for later. But you will see we made very material reductions on shipments from the upper Sacramento Valley; also the rate from Ione to Marysville has been reduced eighty cents a ton."

"Why, rot," cried Annixter, "no one ever ships wheat that way."

"The Salinas rate," continued Lyman, "has been lowered seventy-five cents; the St. Helena rate fifty cents, and please notice the very drastic cut from Red Bluff, north, along the Oregon route, to the Oregon State Line."

"Where not a carload of wheat is shipped in a year," commented Gethings of the San Pablo.

"Oh, you will find yourself mistaken there, Mr. Gethings," returned Lyman courteously. "And for the matter of that, a low rate would stimulate wheat-production in that district."

The order of the meeting was broken up, neglected; Magnus did not even pretend to preside. In the growing excitement over the inexplicable schedule, routine was not thought of. Every one spoke at will.

"Why, Lyman," demanded Magnus, looking across the table to his son, "is this schedule correct? You have not cut rates in the San Joaquin at all. We—these gentlemen here and myself, we are no better off than we were before we secured your election as commissioner."

"We were pledged to make an average ten per cent. cut, sir——"

"It *is* an average ten per cent. cut," cried Osterman. "Oh, yes, that's plain. It's an average ten per cent. cut all right, but you've made it by cutting grain rates between points where practically no grain is shipped. *We*, the wheat-growers in the San Joaquin, where all the wheat is grown, are right where we were before. The Railroad won't lose a nickel. By Jingo, boys," he glanced around the table, "I'd like to know what this means."

"The Railroad, if you come to that," returned Lyman, "has already lodged a protest against the new rate."

Annixter uttered a derisive shout.

"A protest! That's good, that is. When the P. and S. W. objects to rates it don't 'protest,' m' son. The first you hear from Mr. Shelgrim is an injunction from the courts preventing the order for new rates from taking effect. By the Lord," he cried angrily, leaping to his feet, "I would like to know what all this means, too. Why didn't you reduce our grain rates? What did we elect you for?"

"Yes, what did we elect you for?" demanded Osterman and Gethings, also getting to their feet.

"Order, order, gentlemen," cried Magnus, remembering the duties of his office and rapping his knuckles on the table. "This meeting has been allowed to degenerate too far already."

"You elected us," declared Lyman doggedly, "to make an average ten per cent. cut on grain rates. We have done it. Only because you don't benefit at once, you object. It makes a difference whose ox is gored, it seems."

"Lyman!"

It was Magnus who spoke. He had drawn himself to his full six feet. His eyes were flashing direct into his son's. His voice rang with severity.

"Lyman, what does this mean?"

The other spread out his hands.

"As you see, sir. We have done our best. I warned you not to expect too much. I told you that this question of transportation was difficult. You would not wish to put rates so low that the action would amount to confiscation of property."

"Why did you not lower rates in the valley of the San Joaquin?"

"That was not a *prominent* issue in the affair," responded Lyman, carefully emphasising his words. "I understand, of course, it was to be approached *in time*. The main point was *an average ten per cent. reduction*. Rates *will* be lowered in the San Joaquin. The ranchers around Bonneville will be able to ship to Port Costa at equitable rates, but so radical a measure as that cannot be put through in a turn of the hand. We must study——"

"You *knew* the San Joaquin rate *was* an issue," shouted Annixter, shaking his finger across the table. "What do we men who backed you care about rates up in Del Norte and Siskiyou Counties? Not a whoop in hell. It was the San Joaquin rate we were fighting for, and we elected you to reduce that. You didn't do it and you don't intend to, and, by the Lord Harry, I want to know why."

"You'll know, sir——" began Lyman.

"Well, I'll tell you why," vociferated Osterman. "I'll tell you why. It's because we have been sold out. It's because the P. and S. W. have had their spoon in this boiling. It's because our commissioners have betrayed us. It's because we're a set of damn fool farmers and have been cinched again."

Lyman paled under his dark skin at the direct attack. He evidently had not expected this so soon. For the fraction of one instant he lost his poise. He strove to speak, but caught his breath, stammering.

"What have you to say, then?" cried Harran, who, until now, had not spoken.

"I have this to say," answered Lyman, making head as best he might, "that this is no proper spirit in which to discuss business. The Commission has fulfilled its obligations. It has adjusted rates to the best of its ability. We have been at work for two months on the preparation of this schedule——"

"That's a lie," shouted Annixter, his face scarlet; "that's a lie. That schedule was drawn in the offices of the Pacific and Southwestern and you know it. It's a scheme of rates made for the Railroad and by the Railroad and you were bought over to put your name to it."

There was a concerted outburst at the words. All the men in the room were on their feet, gesticulating and vociferating.

"Gentlemen, gentlemen," cried Magnus, "are we schoolboys, are we ruffians of the street?"

"We're a set of fool farmers and we've been betrayed," cried Osterman.

"Well, what have you to say? What have you to say?" persisted Harran, leaning across the table toward his brother. "For God's sake, Lyman, you've got *some* explanation."

"You've misunderstood," protested Lyman, white and trembling. "You've misunderstood. You've expected too much. Next year,—next year,—soon now, the Commission will take up the—the Commission will consider the San Joaquin rate. We've done our best, that is all."

"Have you, sir?" demanded Magnus.

The Governor's head was in a whirl; a sensation, almost of faintness, had seized upon him. Was it possible? Was it possible?

"Have you done your best?" For a second he compelled Lyman's eye. The glances of father and son met, and, in spite of his best efforts, Lyman's eyes wavered. He began to protest once more, explaining the matter over again from the beginning. But Magnus did not listen. In that brief lapse of time he was convinced that the terrible thing had happened, that the unbelievable had come to pass. It was in the air. Between father and son, in some subtle fashion, the truth that was a lie stood suddenly revealed. But even then Magnus would not receive it. Lyman do this! His son, his eldest son, descend to this! Once more and for the last time he turned to him and in his voice there was that ring that compelled silence.

"Lyman," he said, "I adjure you—I—I demand of you as you are my son and an honourable man, explain yourself. What is there behind all this? It is no longer as Chairman of the Committee I speak to you, you a member of the Railroad Commission. It is your father who speaks, and I address you as my son. Do you understand the gravity of this crisis; do you realise the responsibility of your position; do you not see the importance of this moment? Explain yourself."

"There is nothing to explain."

"You have not reduced rates in the San Joaquin? You have not reduced rates between Bonneville and tidewater?"

"I repeat, sir, what I said before. An average ten per cent. cut——"

"Lyman, answer me, yes or no. Have you reduced the Bonneville rate?"

"It could not be done so soon. Give us time. We——"

"Yes or no! By God, sir, do you dare equivocate with me? Yes or no; have you reduced the Bonneville rate?"

"No."

"And answer *me*," shouted Harran, leaning far across the table, "answer *me*. Were you paid by the Railroad to leave the San Joaquin rate untouched?"

Lyman, whiter than ever, turned furious upon his brother.

"Don't you dare put that question to me again."

"No, I won't," cried Harran, "because I'll *tell* you to your villain's face that you *were* paid to do it."

On the instant the clamour burst forth afresh. Still on their feet, the ranchers had, little by little, worked around the table, Magnus alone keeping his place. The others were in a group before Lyman, crowding him, as it were, to the wall, shouting into his face with menacing gestures. The truth that was a lie, the certainty of a trust betrayed, a pledge ruthlessly broken, was plain to every one of them.

"By the Lord! men have been shot for less than this," cried Osterman. "You've sold us out, you, and if you ever bring that dago face of yours on a level with mine again, I'll slap it."

"Keep your hands off," exclaimed Lyman quickly, the aggressiveness of the cornered rat flaming up within him. "No violence. Don't you go too far."

"How much were you paid? How much were you paid?" vociferated Harran.

"Yes, yes, what was your price?" cried the others. They were beside themselves with anger; their words came harsh from between their set teeth; their gestures were made with their fists clenched.

"You know the Commission acted in good faith," retorted Lyman. "You know that all was fair and above board."

"Liar," shouted Annixter; "liar, bribe-eater. You were bought and paid for," and with the words his arm seemed almost of itself to leap out from his shoulder. Lyman received the blow squarely in the face and the force of it sent him staggering backwards toward the wall. He tripped over his valise and fell half way, his back supported against the closed door of the room. Magnus sprang forward. His son had been struck, and the instincts of a father rose up in instant protest; rose for a moment, then forever died away in his heart. He checked the words that flashed to his mind. He lowered his upraised arm. No, he had but one son. The poor, staggering creature with the fine clothes, white face, and blood-streaked lips was no longer his. A blow could not dishonour him more than he had dishonoured himself.

But Gethings, the older man, intervened, pulling Annixter back, crying:

"Stop, this won't do. Not before his father."

"I am no father to this man, gentlemen," exclaimed Magnus. "From now on, I have but one son. You, sir," he turned to Lyman, "you, sir, leave my house."

Lyman, his handkerchief to his lips, his smart cravat in disarray, caught up his hat and coat. He was shaking with fury, his protruding eyes were blood-shot. He swung open the door.

"Ruffians," he shouted from the threshold, "ruffians, bullies. Do your own dirty business yourselves after this. I'm done with you. How is it, all of a sudden you talk about honour? How is it that all at once you're so clean and straight? You weren't so particular at Sacramento just before the nominations. How was the Board elected? I'm a bribe-eater, am I? Is it any worse than *giving* a bribe? Ask Magnus Derrick what he thinks about that. Ask him how much he paid the Democratic bosses at Sacramento to swing the convention."

He went out, slamming the door.

Presley followed. The whole affair made him sick at heart, filled him with infinite disgust, infinite weariness. He wished to get away from it all. He left the dining-room and the excited, clamouring men behind him and stepped out on the porch of the ranch house, closing the door behind him. Lyman was nowhere in sight. Presley was alone. It was late, and after the lamp-heated air of the dining-room, the coolness of the night was delicious, and its vast silence, after the noise and fury of the committee meeting, descended from the stars like a benediction. Presley stepped to the edge of the porch, looking off to southward.

And there before him, mile after mile, illimitable, covering the earth from horizon to horizon, lay the Wheat. The growth, now many days old, was already high from the ground. There it lay, a vast, silent ocean, shimmering a pallid green under the moon and under the stars; a mighty force, the strength of nations, the life of the world. There in the night, under the dome of the sky, it was growing steadily. To Presley's mind, the scene in the room he had just left dwindled to paltry insignificance before this sight. Ah, yes, the Wheat—it was over this that the Railroad, the ranchers, the traitor false to his trust, all the members of an obscure conspiracy, were wrangling. As if human agency could affect this colossal power! What were these heated, tiny squabbles, this feverish, small bustle of mankind, this minute swarming of the human insect, to the great, majestic, silent ocean of the Wheat itself! Indifferent, gigantic, resistless, it moved in its appointed grooves. Men, Liliputians, gnats in the sunshine, buzzed impudently in their tiny battles, were born, lived through their little day, died, and were forgotten; while the Wheat, wrapped in Nirvanic calm, grew steadily under the night, alone with the stars and with God.

V

J ACK-RABBITS were a pest that year and Presley occasionally
found amusement in hunting them with Harran's half-
dozen greyhounds, following the chase on horseback. One
day, between two and three months after Lyman's visit to Los
Muertos, as he was returning toward the ranch house from a
distant and lonely quarter of Los Muertos, he came unexpectedly upon a strange sight.

Some twenty men, Annixter's and Osterman's tenants, and
small ranchers from east of Guadalajara—all members of the
League—were going through the manual of arms under Harran Derrick's supervision. They were all equipped with new
Winchester rifles. Harran carried one of these himself and
with it he illustrated the various commands he gave. As soon
as one of the men under his supervision became more than
usually proficient, he was told off to instruct a file of the more
backward. After the manual of arms, Harran gave the command to take distance as skirmishers, and when the line had
opened out so that some half-dozen feet intervened between
each man, an advance was made across the field, the men
stooping low and snapping the hammers of their rifles at an
imaginary enemy.

The League had its agents in San Francisco, who watched
the movements of the Railroad as closely as was possible, and
some time before this, Annixter had received word that the
Marshal and his deputies were coming down to Bonneville to
put the dummy buyers of his ranch in possession. The report
proved to be but the first of many false alarms, but it had
stimulated the League to unusual activity, and some three or
four hundred men were furnished with arms and from time
to time were drilled in secret.

Among themselves, the ranchers said that if the Railroad
managers did not believe they were terribly in earnest in the
stand they had taken, they were making a fatal mistake.

Harran reasserted this statement to Presley on the way
home to the ranch house that same day. Harran had caught
up with him by the time he reached the Lower Road, and the
two jogged homeward through the miles of standing wheat.

935

"They may jump the ranch, Pres," he said, "if they try hard enough, but they will never do it while I am alive. By the way," he added, "you know we served notices yesterday upon S. Behrman and Cy. Ruggles to quit the country. Of course, they won't do it, but they won't be able to say they didn't have warning."

About an hour later, the two reached the ranch house, but as Harran rode up the driveway, he uttered an exclamation.

"Hello," he said, "something is up. That's Genslinger's buckboard."

In fact, the editor's team was tied underneath the shade of a giant eucalyptus tree near by. Harran, uneasy under this unexpected visit of the enemy's friend, dismounted without stabling his horse, and went at once to the dining-room, where visitors were invariably received. But the dining-room was empty, and his mother told him that Magnus and the editor were in the "office." Magnus had said they were not to be disturbed.

Earlier in the afternoon, the editor had driven up to the porch and had asked Mrs. Derrick, whom he found reading a book of poems on the porch, if he could see Magnus. At the time, the Governor had gone with Phelps to inspect the condition of the young wheat on Hooven's holding, but within half an hour he returned, and Genslinger had asked him for a "few moments' talk in private."

The two went into the "office," Magnus locking the door behind him.

"Very complete you are here, Governor," observed the editor in his alert, jerky manner, his black, bead-like eyes twinkling around the room from behind his glasses. "Telephone, safe, ticker, account-books—well, that's progress, isn't it? Only way to manage a big ranch these days. But the day of the big ranch is over. As the land appreciates in value, the temptation to sell off small holdings will be too strong. And then the small holding can be cultivated to better advantage. I shall have an editorial on that some day."

"The cost of maintaining a number of small holdings," said Magnus, indifferently, "is, of course, greater than if they were all under one management."

"That may be, that may be," rejoined the other.

There was a long pause. Genslinger leaned back in his chair and rubbed a knee. Magnus, standing erect in front of the safe, waited for him to speak.

"This is an unfortunate business, Governor," began the editor, "this misunderstanding between the ranchers and the Railroad. I wish it could be adjusted. *Here* are two industries that *must* be in harmony with one another, or we all go to pot."

"I should prefer not to be interviewed on the subject, Mr. Genslinger," said Magnus.

"Oh, no, oh, no. Lord love you, Governor, I don't want to interview you. We all know how *you* stand."

Again there was a long silence. Magnus wondered what this little man, usually so garrulous, could want of him. At length, Genslinger began again. He did not look at Magnus, except at long intervals.

"About the present Railroad Commission," he remarked. "That was an interesting campaign you conducted in Sacramento and San Francisco."

Magnus held his peace, his hands shut tight. Did Genslinger know of Lyman's disgrace? Was it for this he had come? Would the story of it be the leading article in to-morrow's *Mercury*?

"An interesting campaign," repeated Genslinger, slowly; "a very interesting campaign. I watched it with every degree of interest. I saw its every phase, Mr. Derrick."

"The campaign was not without its interest," admitted Magnus.

"Yes," said Genslinger, still more deliberately, "and some phases of it were—more interesting than others, as, for instance, let us say the way in which you—personally—secured the votes of certain chairmen of delegations—*need* I particularise further? Yes, those men—the way you got their votes. Now, *that* I should say, Mr. Derrick, was the most interesting move in the whole game—to you. Hm, curious," he murmured, musingly. "Let's see. You deposited two one-thousand dollar bills and four five-hundred dollar bills in a box—three hundred and eight was the number—in a box in the Safety Deposit Vaults in San Francisco, and then—let's see, you gave a key to this box to each of the gentlemen in question, and after the election the box was empty. Now, I call that interesting—curious, because it's a new, safe, and highly ingenious method of bribery. How did you happen to think of it, Governor?"

"Do you know what you are doing, sir?" Magnus burst forth. "Do you know what you are insinuating, here, in my own house?"

"Why, Governor," returned the editor, blandly, "I'm not *insinuating* anything. I'm talking about what I *know*."

"It's a lie."

Genslinger rubbed his chin reflectively.

"Well," he answered, "you can have a chance to prove it before the Grand Jury, if you want to."

"My character is known all over the State," blustered Magnus. "My politics are pure politics. My——"

"No one needs a better reputation for pure politics than the man who sets out to be a briber," interrupted Genslinger, "and I might as well tell you, Governor, that you can't shout me down. I can put my hand on the two chairmen you bought before it's dark to-day. I've had their depositions in my safe for the last six weeks. We could make the arrests to-morrow, if we wanted. Governor, you sure did a risky thing when you went into that Sacramento fight, an awful risky thing. Some men can afford to have bribery charges preferred against them, and it don't hurt one little bit, but *you*—Lord, it would *bust* you, Governor, bust you dead. I know all about the whole shananigan business from A to Z, and if you don't believe it—here," he drew a long strip of paper from his pocket, "here's a galley proof of the story."

Magnus took it in his hands. There, under his eyes, scare-headed, double-leaded, the more important clauses printed in bold type, was the detailed account of the "deal" Magnus had made with the two delegates. It was pitiless, remorseless, bald. Every statement was substantiated, every statistic veri-fied with Genslinger's meticulous love for exactness. Besides all that, it had the ring of truth. It was exposure, ruin, abso-lute annihilation.

"That's about correct, isn't it?" commented Genslinger, as Derrick finished reading. Magnus did not reply. "I think it is correct enough," the editor continued. "But I thought it would only be fair to you to let you see it before it was published."

The one thought uppermost in Derrick's mind, his one impulse of the moment was, at whatever cost, to preserve his dignity, not to allow this man to exult in the sight of one quiver of weakness, one trace of defeat, one suggestion of humiliation. By an effort that put all his iron rigidity to the test, he forced himself to look straight into Genslinger's eyes.

"I congratulate you," he observed, handing back the proof, "upon your journalistic enterprise. Your paper will sell to-morrow."

"Oh, I don't know as I want to publish this story," remarked the editor, indifferently, putting away the galley. "I'm just like that. The fun for me is running a good story to earth, but once I've got it, I lose interest. And, then, I wouldn't like to see you—holding the position you do, President of the League and a leading man of the county—I wouldn't like to see a story like this smash you over. It's worth more to you to keep it out of print than for me to put it in. I've got nothing much to gain but a few extra editions, but you—Lord, you would lose everything. Your committee was in the deal right enough. But your League, all the San Joaquin Valley, everybody in the State believes the commissioners were fairly elected."

"Your story," suddenly exclaimed Magnus, struck with an idea, " will be thoroughly discredited just so soon as the new grain tariff is published. I have means of knowing that the San Joaquin rate—the issue upon which the board was elected—is not to be touched. Is it likely the ranchers would secure the election of a board that plays them false?"

"Oh, we know all about that," answered Genslinger, smiling. "You thought you were electing Lyman easily. You thought you had got the Railroad to walk right into your trap. You didn't understand how you could pull off your deal so easily. Why, Governor, *Lyman was pledged to the Railroad two years ago.* He was *the one particular* man the corporation wanted for commissioner. And your people elected him— saved the Railroad all the trouble of campaigning for him. And you can't make any counter charge of bribery there. No, sir, the corporation don't use such amateurish methods

as that. Confidentially and between us two, all that the Railroad has done for Lyman, in order to attach him to their interests, is to promise to back him politically in the next
campaign for Governor. It's too bad," he continued, dropping his voice, and changing his position. "It really is too
bad to see good men trying to bunt a stone wall over with
their bare heads. You couldn't have won at any stage of the
game. I wish I could have talked to you and your friends before you went into that Sacramento fight. I could have told
you then how little chance you had. When will you people
realise that you can't buck against the Railroad? Why, Magnus, it's like me going out in a paper boat and shooting peas
at a battleship."

"Is that all you wished to see me about, Mr. Genslinger?"
remarked Magnus, bestirring himself. "I am rather occupied
to-day."

"Well," returned the other, "you know what the publication of this article would mean for you." He paused again,
took off his glasses, breathed on them, polished the lenses
with his handkerchief and readjusted them on his nose. "I've
been thinking, Governor," he began again, with renewed
alertness, and quite irrelevantly, "of enlarging the scope of the
'Mercury.' You see, I'm midway between the two big centres
of the State, San Francisco and Los Angeles, and I want to
extend the 'Mercury's' sphere of influence as far up and down
the valley as I can. I want to illustrate the paper. You see, if I
had a photo-engraving plant of my own, I could do a good
deal of outside jobbing as well, and the investment would pay
ten per cent. But it takes money to make money. I wouldn't
want to put in any dinky, one-horse affair. I want a good
plant. I've been figuring out the business. Besides the plant,
there would be the expense of a high grade paper. Can't print
half-tones on anything but coated paper, and that *costs*. Well,
what with this and with that and running expenses till the
thing began to pay, it would cost me about ten thousand
dollars, and I was wondering if, perhaps, you couldn't see
your way clear to accommodating me."

"Ten thousand?"

"Yes. Say five thousand down, and the balance within sixty
days."

Magnus, for the moment blind to what Genslinger had in mind, turned on him in astonishment.

"Why, man, what security could *you* give me for such an amount?"

"Well, to tell the truth," answered the editor, "I hadn't thought much about securities. In fact, I believed you would see how greatly it was to your advantage to talk business with me. You see, I'm not going to print this article about you, Governor, and I'm not going to let it get out so as any one else can print it, and it seems to me that one good turn deserves another. You understand?"

Magnus understood. An overwhelming desire suddenly took possession of him to grip this blackmailer by the throat, to strangle him where he stood; or, if not, at least to turn upon him with that old-time terrible anger, before which whole conventions had once cowered. But in the same moment the Governor realised this was not to be. Only its righteousness had made his wrath terrible; only the justice of his anger had made him feared. Now the foundation was gone from under his feet; he had knocked it away himself. Three times feeble was he whose quarrel was unjust. Before this country editor, this paid speaker of the Railroad, he stood, convicted. The man had him at his mercy. The detected briber could not resent an insult. Genslinger rose, smoothing his hat.

"Well," he said, "of course, you want time to think it over, and you can't raise money like that on short notice. I'll wait till Friday noon of this week. We begin to set Saturday's paper at about four, Friday afternoon, and the forms are locked about two in the morning. I hope," he added, turning back at the door of the room, "that you won't find anything disagreeable in your Saturday morning 'Mercury,' Mr. Derrick."

He went out, closing the door behind him, and in a moment, Magnus heard the wheels of his buckboard grating on the driveway.

The following morning brought a letter to Magnus from Gethings, of the San Pueblo ranch, which was situated very close to Visalia. The letter was to the effect that all around Visalia, upon the ranches affected by the regrade of the Railroad, men were arming and drilling, and that the strength of the League in that quarter was undoubted. "But to refer," continued the letter, "to a most painful recollection. You will, no doubt, remember that, at the close of our last committee meeting, specific charges were made as to fraud in the nomination and election of one of our commissioners, emanating, most unfortunately, from the commissioner himself. These charges, my dear Mr. Derrick, were directed at yourself. How the secrets of the committee have been noised about, I cannot understand. You may be, of course, assured of my own unquestioning confidence and loyalty. However, I regret exceedingly to state not only that the rumour of the charges referred to above is spreading in this district, but that also they are made use of by the enemies of the League. It is to be deplored that some of the Leaguers themselves—you know, we number in our ranks many small farmers, ignorant Portuguese and foreigners—have listened to these stories and have permitted a feeling of uneasiness to develop among them. Even though it were admitted that fraudulent means had been employed in the elections, which, of course, I personally do not admit, I do not think it would make very much difference in the confidence which the vast majority of the Leaguers repose in their chiefs. Yet we have so insisted upon the probity of our position as opposed to Railroad chicanery, that I believe it advisable to quell this distant suspicion at once; to publish a denial of these rumoured charges would only be to give them too much importance. However, can you not write me a letter, stating exactly how the campaign was conducted, and the commission nominated and elected? I could show this to some of the more disaffected, and it would serve to allay all suspicion on the instant. I think it would be well to write as though the initiative came, not from me, but from yourself, ignoring this present letter. I offer this only as a suggestion, and will confidently endorse any decision you may arrive at."

The letter closed with renewed protestations of confidence.

Magnus was alone when he read this. He put it carefully away in the filing cabinet in his office, and wiped the sweat from his forehead and face. He stood for one moment, his hands rigid at his sides, his fists clinched.

"This is piling up," he muttered, looking blankly at the opposite wall. "My God, this is piling up. What am I to do?"

Ah, the bitterness of unavailing regret, the anguish of compromise with conscience, the remorse of a bad deed done in a moment of excitement. Ah, the humiliation of detection, the degradation of being caught, caught like a schoolboy pilfering his fellows' desks, and, worse than all, worse than all, the consciousness of lost self-respect, the knowledge of a prestige vanishing, a dignity impaired, knowledge that the grip which held a multitude in check was trembling, that control was wavering, that command was being weakened. Then the little tricks to deceive the crowd, the little subterfuges, the little pretences that kept up appearances, the lies, the bluster, the pose, the strut, the gasconade, where once was iron authority; the turning of the head so as not to see that which could not be prevented; the suspicion of suspicion, the haunting fear of the Man on the Street, the uneasiness of the direct glance, the questioning as to motives—why had this been said, what was meant by that word, that gesture, that glance?

Wednesday passed, and Thursday. Magnus kept to himself, seeing no visitors, avoiding even his family. How to break through the mesh of the net, how to regain the old position, how to prevent discovery? If there were only some way, some vast, superhuman effort by which he could rise in his old strength once more, crushing Lyman with one hand, Genslinger with the other, and for one more moment, the last, to stand supreme again, indomitable, the leader; then go to his death, triumphant at the end, his memory untarnished, his fame undimmed. But the plague-spot was in himself, knitted forever into the fabric of his being. Though Genslinger should be silenced, though Lyman should be crushed, though even the League should overcome the Railroad, though he should be the acknowledged leader of a resplendent victory, yet the plague-spot would remain. There was no success for him now. However conspicuous the outward achievement, he, he himself, Magnus Derrick, had failed, miserably and irredeemably.

Petty, material complications intruded, sordid considerations. Even if Genslinger was to be paid, where was the money to come from? His legal battles with the Railroad, extending now over a period of many years, had cost him dear; his plan of sowing all of Los Muertos to wheat, discharging the tenants, had proved expensive, the campaign resulting in Lyman's election had drawn heavily upon his account. All along he had been relying upon a "bonanza crop" to reimburse him. It was not believable that the Railroad would "jump" Los Muertos, but if this should happen, he would be left without resources. Ten thousand dollars! Could he raise the amount? Possibly. But to pay it out to a blackmailer! To be held up thus in road-agent fashion, without a single means of redress! Would it not cripple him financially? Genslinger could do his worst. He, Magnus, would brave it out. Was not his character above suspicion?

Was it? This letter of Gethings's. Already the murmur of uneasiness made itself heard. Was this not the thin edge of the wedge? How the publication of Genslinger's story would drive it home! How the spark of suspicion would flare into the blaze of open accusation! There would be investigations. Investigation! There was terror in the word. He could not stand investigation. Magnus groaned aloud, covering his head with his clasped hands. Briber, corrupter of government, ballot-box stuffer, descending to the level of back-room politicians, of bar-room heelers, he, Magnus Derrick, statesman of the old school, Roman in his iron integrity, abandoning a career rather than enter the "new politics," had, in one moment of weakness, hazarding all, even honour, on a single stake, taking great chances to achieve great results, swept away the work of a lifetime.

Gambler that he was, he had at last chanced his highest stake, his personal honour, in the greatest game of his life, and had lost.

It was Presley's morbidly keen observation that first noticed the evidence of a new trouble in the Governor's face and manner. Presley was sure that Lyman's defection had not so upset him. The morning after the committee meeting, Magnus had called Harran and Annie Derrick into the office, and, after telling his wife of Lyman's betrayal, had forbidden either of them to mention his name again. His attitude towards his prodigal son was that of stern, unrelenting resentment. But now, Presley could not fail to detect traces of a more deep-seated travail. Something was in the wind. The times were troublous. What next was about to happen? What fresh calamity impended?

One morning, toward the very end of the week, Presley woke early in his small, white-painted iron bed. He hastened to get up and dress. There was much to be done that day. Until late the night before, he had been at work on a collection of some of his verses, gathered from the magazines in which they had first appeared. Presley had received a liberal offer for the publication of these verses in book form. "The Toilers" was to be included in this book, and, indeed, was to give it its name—"The Toilers and Other Poems." Thus it was that, until the previous midnight, he had been preparing the collection for publication, revising, annotating, arranging. The book was to be sent off that morning.

But also Presley had received a typewritten note from Annixter, inviting him to Quien Sabe that same day. Annixter explained that it was Hilma's birthday, and that he had planned a picnic on the high ground of his ranch, at the headwaters of Broderson Creek. They were to go in the carry-all, Hilma, Presley, Mrs. Dyke, Sidney, and himself, and were to make a day of it. They would leave Quien Sabe at ten in the morning. Presley had at once resolved to go. He was immensely fond of Annixter—more so than ever since his marriage with Hilma and the astonishing transformation of his character. Hilma, as well, was delightful as Mrs. Annixter; and Mrs. Dyke and the little tad had always been his friends. He would have a good time.

But nobody was to go into Bonneville that morning with the mail, and if he wished to send his manuscript, he would have to take it in himself. He had resolved to do this, getting an early start, and going on horseback to Quien Sabe, by way of Bonneville.

It was barely six o'clock when Presley sat down to his coffee and eggs in the dining-room of Los Muertos. The day promised to be hot, and for the first time, Presley had put on a new khaki riding suit, very English-looking, though in place of the regulation top-boots, he wore his laced knee-boots, with a great spur on the left heel. Harran joined him at breakfast, in his working clothes of blue canvas. He was bound for the irrigating ditch to see how the work was getting on there.

"How is the wheat looking?" asked Presley.

"Bully," answered the other, stirring his coffee. "The Governor has had his usual luck. Practically, every acre of the ranch was sown to wheat, and everywhere the stand is good. I was over on Two, day before yesterday, and if nothing happens, I believe it will go thirty sacks to the acre there. Cutter reports that there are spots on Four where we will get forty-two or three. Hooven, too, brought up some wonderful fine ears for me to look at. The grains were just beginning to show. Some of the ears carried twenty grains. That means nearly forty bushels of wheat to every acre. I call it a bonanza year."

"Have you got any mail?" said Presley, rising. "I'm going into town."

Harran shook his head, and took himself away, and Presley went down to the stable-corral to get his pony.

As he rode out of the stable-yard and passed by the ranch house, on the driveway, he was surprised to see Magnus on the lowest step of the porch.

"Good morning, Governor," called Presley. "Aren't you up pretty early?"

"Good morning, Pres, my boy." The Governor came forward and, putting his hand on the pony's withers, walked along by his side.

"Going to town, Pres?" he asked.

"Yes, sir. Can I do anything for you, Governor?"

Magnus drew a sealed envelope from his pocket.

"I wish you would drop in at the office of the *Mercury* for me," he said, "and see Mr. Genslinger personally, and give him this envelope. It is a package of papers, but they involve a considerable sum of money, and you must be careful of them. A few years ago, when our enmity was not so strong, Mr. Genslinger and I had some business dealings with each other. I thought it as well just now, considering that we are so openly opposed, to terminate the whole affair, and break off relations. We came to a settlement a few days ago. These are the final papers. They must be given to him in person, Presley. You understand."

Presley cantered on, turning into the county road, and holding northward by the mammoth watering tank and Broderson's poplar windbreak. As he passed Caraher's, he saw the saloon-keeper in the doorway of his place, and waved him a salutation which the other returned.

By degrees, Presley had come to consider Caraher in a more favourable light. He found, to his immense astonishment, that Caraher knew something of Mill and Bakounin, not, however, from their books, but from extracts and quotations from their writings, reprinted in the anarchistic journals to which he subscribed. More than once, the two had held long conversations, and from Caraher's own lips, Presley heard the terrible story of the death of his wife, who had been accidentally killed by Pinkertons during a "demonstration" of strikers. It invested the saloon-keeper, in Presley's imagination, with all the dignity of the tragedy. He could not blame Caraher for being a "red." He even wondered how it was the saloon-keeper had not put his theories into practice, and adjusted his ancient wrong with his "six inches of plugged gaspipe." Presley began to conceive of the man as a "character."

"You wait, Mr. Presley," the saloon-keeper had once said, when Presley had protested against his radical ideas. "You don't know the Railroad yet. Watch it and its doings long enough, and you'll come over to my way of thinking, too."

It was about half-past seven when Presley reached Bonneville. The business part of the town was as yet hardly astir; he despatched his manuscript, and then hurried to the office of the "Mercury." Genslinger, as he feared, had not yet put in appearance, but the janitor of the building gave Presley the address of the editor's residence, and it was there he found him in the act of sitting down to breakfast. Presley was hardly courteous to the little man, and abruptly refused his offer of a drink. He delivered Magnus's envelope to him and departed.

It had occurred to him that it would not do to present himself at Quien Sabe on Hilma's birthday, empty-handed, and, on leaving Genslinger's house, he turned his pony's head toward the business part of the town again, pulling up in front of the jeweller's, just as the clerk was taking down the shutters.

At the jeweller's, he purchased a little brooch for Hilma, and at the cigar stand in the lobby of the Yosemite House, a

box of superfine cigars, which, when it was too late, he realised that the master of Quien Sabe would never smoke, holding, as he did, with defiant inconsistency, to miserable weeds,
black, bitter, and flagrantly doctored, which he bought, three
for a nickel, at Guadalajara.

Presley arrived at Quien Sabe nearly half an hour behind
the appointed time; but, as he had expected, the party were
in no way ready to start. The carry-all, its horses covered with
white fly-nets, stood under a tree near the house, young Vacca
dozing on the seat. Hilma and Sidney, the latter exuberant
with a gayety that all but brought the tears to Presley's eyes,
were making sandwiches on the back porch. Mrs. Dyke was
nowhere to be seen, and Annixter was shaving himself in his
bedroom.

This latter put a half-lathered face out of the window as
Presley cantered through the gate, and waved his razor with
a beckoning motion.

"Come on in, Pres," he cried. "Nobody's ready yet. You're
hours ahead of time."

Presley came into the bedroom, his huge spur clinking on
the straw matting. Annixter was without coat, vest, or collar,
his blue silk suspenders hung in loops over either hip, his hair
was disordered, the crown lock stiffer than ever.

"Glad to see you, old boy," he announced, as Presley came
in. "No, don't shake hands, I'm all lather. Here, find a chair,
will you? I won't be long."

"I thought you said ten o'clock," observed Presley, sitting
down on the edge of the bed.

"Well, I did, but——"

"But, then again, in a way, you didn't, hey?" his friend interrupted.

Annixter grunted good-humouredly, and turned to strop
his razor. Presley looked with suspicious disfavour at his suspenders.

"Why is it," he observed, "that as soon as a man is about
to get married, he buys himself pale blue suspenders, silk
ones? Think of it. You, Buck Annixter, with sky-blue, silk suspenders. It ought to be a strap and a nail."

"Old fool," observed Annixter, whose repartee was the
heaving of brick bats. "Say," he continued, holding the razor

from his face, and jerking his head over his shoulder, while he looked at Presley's reflection in his mirror; "say, look around. Isn't this a nifty little room? We refitted the whole house, you know. Notice she's all painted?"

"I have been looking around," answered Presley, sweeping the room with a series of glances. He forbore criticism. Annixter was so boyishly proud of the effect that it would have been unkind to have undeceived him. Presley looked at the marvellous, department-store bed of brass, with its brave, gay canopy; the mill-made washstand, with its pitcher and bowl of blinding red and green china, the straw-framed lithographs of symbolic female figures against the multi-coloured, new wall-paper; the inadequate spindle chairs of white and gold; the sphere of tissue paper hanging from the gas fixture, and the plumes of pampas grass tacked to the wall at artistic angles, and overhanging two astonishing oil paintings, in dazzling golden frames.

"Say, how about those paintings, Pres?" inquired Annixter a little uneasily. "I don't know whether they're good or not. They were painted by a three-fingered Chinaman in Monterey, and I got the lot for thirty dollars, frames thrown in. Why, I think the frames alone are worth thirty dollars."

"Well, so do I," declared Presley. He hastened to change the subject.

"Buck," he said, "I hear you've brought Mrs. Dyke and Sidney to live with you. You know, I think that's rather white of you."

"Oh, rot, Pres," muttered Annixter, turning abruptly to his shaving.

"And you can't fool me, either, old man," Presley continued. "You're giving this picnic as much for Mrs. Dyke and the little tad as you are for your wife, just to cheer them up a bit."

"Oh, pshaw, you make me sick."

"Well, that's the right thing to do, Buck, and I'm as glad for your sake as I am for theirs. There was a time when you would have let them all go to grass, and never so much as thought of them. I don't want to seem to be officious, but you've changed for the better, old man, and I guess I know why. She—" Presley caught his friend's eye, and added gravely, "She's a good woman, Buck."

Annixter turned around abruptly, his face flushing under its lather.

"Pres," he exclaimed, "she's made a man of me. I was a machine before, and if another man, or woman, or child got in my way, I rode 'em down, and I never *dreamed* of anybody else but myself. But as soon as I woke up to the fact that I really loved her, why, it was glory hallelujah all in a minute, and, in a way, I kind of loved everybody then, and wanted to be everybody's friend. And I began to see that a fellow can't live *for* himself any more than he can live *by* himself. He's got to think of others. If he's got brains, he's got to think for the poor ducks that haven't 'em, and not give 'em a boot in the backsides because they happen to be stupid; and if he's got money, he's got to help those that are busted, and if he's got a house, he's got to think of those that ain't got anywhere to go. I've got a whole lot of ideas since I began to love Hilma, and just as soon as I can, I'm going to get in and *help* people, and I'm going to keep to that idea the rest of my natural life. That ain't much of a religion, but it's the best I've got, and Henry Ward Beecher couldn't do any more than that. And it's all come about because of Hilma, and because we cared for each other."

Presley jumped up, and caught Annixter about the shoulders with one arm, gripping his hand hard. This absurd figure, with dangling silk suspenders, lathered chin, and tearful eyes, seemed to be suddenly invested with true nobility. Beside this blundering struggle to do right, to help his fellows, Presley's own vague schemes, glittering systems of reconstruction, collapsed to ruin, and he himself, with all his refinement, with all his poetry, culture, and education, stood, a bungler at the world's workbench.

"You're all *right*, old man," he exclaimed, unable to think of anything adequate. "You're all right. That's the way to talk, and here, by the way, I brought you a box of cigars."

Annixter stared as Presley laid the box on the edge of the washstand.

"Old fool," he remarked, " what in hell did you do that for?"

"Oh, just for fun."

"I suppose they're rotten stinkodoras, or you wouldn't give 'em away."

"This cringing gratitude—" Presley began.

"Shut up," shouted Annixter, and the incident was closed.

Annixter resumed his shaving, and Presley lit a cigarette.

"Any news from Washington?" he queried.

"Nothing that's any good," grunted Annixter. "Hello," he added, raising his head, "there's somebody in a hurry for sure."

The noise of a horse galloping so fast that the hoof-beats sounded in one uninterrupted rattle, abruptly made itself heard. The noise was coming from the direction of the road that led from the Mission to Quien Sabe. With incredible swiftness, the hoof-beats drew nearer. There was that in their sound which brought Presley to his feet. Annixter threw open the window.

"Runaway," exclaimed Presley.

Annixter, with thoughts of the Railroad, and the "jumping" of the ranch, flung his hand to his hip pocket.

"What is it, Vacca?" he cried.

Young Vacca, turning in his seat in the carryall, was looking up the road. All at once, he jumped from his place, and dashed towards the window.

"Dyke," he shouted. "Dyke, it's Dyke."

While the words were yet in his mouth, the sound of the hoof-beats rose to a roar, and a great, bell-toned voice shouted:

"Annixter, Annixter, Annixter!"

It was Dyke's voice, and the next instant he shot into view in the open square in front of the house.

"Oh, my God!" cried Presley.

The ex-engineer threw the horse on its haunches, springing from the saddle; and, as he did so, the beast collapsed, shuddering, to the ground. Annixter sprang from the window, and ran forward, Presley following.

There was Dyke, hatless, his pistol in his hand, a gaunt, terrible figure, the beard immeasurably long, the cheeks fallen in, the eyes sunken. His clothes ripped and torn by weeks of flight and hiding in the chaparral, were ragged beyond words, the boots were shreds of leather, bloody to the ankle with furious spurring.

"Annixter," he shouted, and again, rolling his sunken eyes, "Annixter, Annixter!"

"Here, here," cried Annixter.

The other turned, levelling his pistol.

"Give me a horse, give me a horse, quick, do you hear? Give me a horse, or I'll shoot."

"Steady, steady. That won't do. You know me, Dyke. We're friends here."

The other lowered his weapon.

"I know, I know," he panted. "I'd forgotten. I'm unstrung, Mr. Annixter, and I'm running for my life. They're not ten minutes behind me."

"Come on, come on," shouted Annixter, dashing stable-wards, his suspenders flying.

"Here's a horse."

"Mine?" exclaimed Presley. "He wouldn't carry you a mile."

Annixter was already far ahead, trumpeting orders.

"The buckskin," he yelled. "Get her out, Billy. Where's the stable-man? Get out that buckskin. Get out that saddle."

Then followed minutes of furious haste, Presley, Annixter, Billy the stable-man, and Dyke himself, darting hither and thither about the yellow mare, buckling, strapping, cinching, their lips pale, their fingers trembling with excitement.

"Want anything to eat?" Annixter's head was under the saddle flap as he tore at the cinch. "Want anything to eat? Want any money? Want a gun?"

"Water," returned Dyke. "They've watched every spring. I'm killed with thirst."

"There's the hydrant. Quick now."

"I got as far as the Kern River, but they turned me back," he said between breaths as he drank.

"Don't stop to talk."

"My mother, and the little tad——"

"I'm taking care of them. They're stopping with me."

"Here?"

"You won't see 'em; by the Lord, you won't. You'll get away. Where's that back cinch strap, *Billy*? God damn it, are you going to let him be shot before he can get away? Now, Dyke, up you go. She'll kill herself running before they can catch you."

"God bless you, Annixter. Where's the little tad? Is she well, Annixter, and the mother? Tell them——"

"Yes, yes, yes. All clear, Pres? Let her have her own gait, Dyke. You're on the best horse in the county now. Let go her head, Billy. Now, Dyke,—shake hands? You bet I will. That's all right. Yes, God bless you. Let her go. You're *off*."

Answering the goad of the spur, and already quivering with the excitement of the men who surrounded her, the buckskin cleared the stable-corral in two leaps; then, gathering her legs under her, her head low, her neck stretched out, swung into the road from out the driveway, disappearing in a blur of dust.

With the agility of a monkey, young Vacca swung himself into the framework of the artesian well, clambering aloft to its very top. He swept the country with a glance.

"Well?" demanded Annixter from the ground. The others cocked their heads to listen.

"I see him; I see him!" shouted Vacca. "He's going like the devil. He's headed for Guadalajara."

"Look back, up the road, toward the Mission. Anything there?"

The answer came down in a shout of apprehension.

"There's a party of men. Three or four—on horseback. There's dogs with 'em. They're coming this way. Oh, I can hear the dogs. And, say, oh, say, there's another party coming down the Lower Road, going towards Guadalajara, too. They got guns. I can see the shine of the barrels. And, oh, Lord, say, there's three more men on horses coming down on the jump from the hills on the Los Muertos stock range. They're making towards Guadalajara. And I can hear the courthouse bell in Bonneville ringing. Say, the whole county is up."

As young Vacca slid down to the ground, two small black-and-tan hounds, with flapping ears and lolling tongues, loped into view on the road in front of the house. They were grey with dust, their noses were to the ground. At the gate where Dyke had turned into the ranch house grounds, they halted in confusion a moment. One started to follow the highway-man's trail towards the stable corral, but the other, quartering over the road with lightning swiftness, suddenly picked up the new scent leading on towards Guadalajara. He tossed his head in the air, and Presley abruptly shut his hands over his ears.

Ah, that terrible cry! deep-toned, reverberating like the bourdon of a great bell. It was the trackers exulting on the trail of the pursued, the prolonged, raucous howl, eager, ominous, vibrating with the alarm of the tocsin, sullen with the heavy muffling note of death. But close upon the bay of the hounds, came the gallop of horses. Five men, their eyes upon the hounds, their rifles across their pommels, their horses reeking and black with sweat, swept by in a storm of dust, glinting hoofs, and streaming manes.

"That was Delaney's gang," exclaimed Annixter. "I saw him."

"The other was that chap Christian," said Vacca, "S. Behrman's cousin. He had two deputies with him; and the chap in the white slouch hat was the sheriff from Visalia."

"By the Lord, they aren't far behind," declared Annixter.

As the men turned towards the house again they saw Hilma and Mrs. Dyke in the doorway of the little house where the latter lived. They were looking out, bewildered, ignorant of what had happened. But on the porch of the Ranch house itself, alone, forgotten in the excitement, Sidney—the little tad—stood, with pale face and serious, wide-open eyes. She had seen everything, and had understood. She said nothing. Her head inclined towards the roadway, she listened to the faint and distant baying of the dogs.

Dyke thundered across the railway tracks by the depot at Guadalajara not five minutes ahead of his pursuers. Luck seemed to have deserted him. The station, usually so quiet, was now occupied by the crew of a freight train that lay on the down track; while on the up line, near at hand and headed in the same direction, was a detached locomotive, whose engineer and fireman recognized him, he was sure, as the buckskin leaped across the rails.

He had had no time to formulate a plan since that morning, when, tortured with thirst, he had ventured near the spring at the headwaters of Broderson Creek, on Quien Sabe, and had all but fallen into the hands of the posse that had been watching for that very move. It was useless now to regret that he had tried to foil pursuit by turning back on his tracks to regain the mountains east of Bonneville. Now Delaney was almost on him. To distance that posse, was the only thing to be thought of now. It was no longer a question of hiding till pursuit should flag; they had driven him out from the shelter of the mountains, down into this populous countryside, where an enemy might be met with at every turn of the road. Now it was life or death. He would either escape or be killed. He knew very well that he would never allow himself to be taken alive. But he had no mind to be killed— to turn and fight—till escape was blocked. His one thought was to leave pursuit behind.

Weeks of flight had sharpened Dyke's every sense. As he turned into the Upper Road beyond Guadalajara, he saw the three men galloping down from Derrick's stock range, making for the road ahead of him. They would cut him off there. He swung the buckskin about. He must take the Lower Road across Los Muertos from Guadalajara, and he must reach it before Delaney's dogs and posse. Back he galloped, the buckskin measuring her length with every leap. Once more the station came in sight. Rising in his stirrups, he looked across the fields in the direction of the Lower Road. There was a cloud of dust there. From a wagon? No, horses on the run, and their riders were armed! He could catch the flash of gun barrels. They were all closing in on him, converging on Guadalajara by every available road. The Upper Road west of Guadalajara led straight to Bonneville. That way was impossible. Was he in a trap? Had the time for fighting come at last?

But as Dyke neared the depot at Guadalajara, his eye fell upon the detached locomotive that lay quietly steaming on the up line, and with a thrill of exultation, he remembered that he was an engineer born and bred. Delaney's dogs were already to be heard, and the roll of hoofs on the Lower Road was dinning in his ears, as he leaped from the buckskin before the depot. The train crew scattered like frightened sheep before him, but Dyke ignored them. His pistol was in his hand as, once more on foot, he sprang toward the lone engine.

"Out of the cab," he shouted. "Both of you. Quick, or I'll kill you both."

The two men tumbled from the iron apron of the tender as Dyke swung himself up, dropping his pistol on the floor of the cab and reaching with the old instinct for the familiar levers.

The great compound hissed and trembled as the steam was released, and the huge drivers stirred, turning slowly on the tracks. But there was a shout. Delaney's posse, dogs and men, swung into view at the turn of the road, their figures leaning over as they took the curve at full speed. Dyke threw everything wide open and caught up his revolver. From behind came the challenge of a Winchester. The party on the Lower Road were even closer than Delaney. They had seen his manœuvre, and the first shot of the fight shivered the cab windows above the engineer's head.

But spinning futilely at first, the drivers of the engine at last caught the rails. The engine moved, advanced, travelled past the depot and the freight train, and gathering speed, rolled out on the track beyond. Smoke, black and boiling, shot skyward from the stack; not a joint that did not shudder with the mighty strain of the steam; but the great iron brute—one of Baldwin's newest and best—came to call, obedient and docile as soon as ever the great pulsing heart of it felt a master hand upon its levers. It gathered its speed, bracing its steel muscles, its thews of iron, and roared out upon the open track, filling the air with the rasp of its tempest-breath, blotting the sunshine with the belch of its hot, thick smoke. Already it was lessening in the distance, when Delaney, Christian, and the sheriff of Visalia dashed up to the station.

The posse had seen everything.

"Stuck. Curse the luck!" vociferated the cow-puncher.

But the sheriff was already out of the saddle and into the telegraph office.

"There's a derailing switch between here and Pixley, isn't there?" he cried.

"Yes."

"Wire ahead to open it. We'll derail him there. Come on;" he turned to Delaney and the others. They sprang into the cab of the locomotive that was attached to the freight train.

"Name of the State of California," shouted the sheriff to the bewildered engineer. "Cut off from your train."

The sheriff was a man to be obeyed without hesitating.

Time was not allowed the crew of the freight train for debating as to the right or the wrong of requisitioning the engine, and before anyone thought of the safety or danger of the affair, the freight engine was already flying out upon the down line, hot in pursuit of Dyke, now far ahead upon the up track.

"I remember perfectly well there's a derailing switch between here and Pixley," shouted the sheriff above the roar of the locomotive. "They use it in case they have to derail runaway engines. It runs right off into the country. We'll pile him up there. Ready with your guns, boys."

"If we should meet another train coming up on this track——" protested the frightened engineer.

"Then we'd jump or be smashed. Hi! look! There he is." As the freight engine rounded a curve, Dyke's engine came into view, shooting on some quarter of a mile ahead of them, wreathed in whirling smoke.

"The switch ain't much further on," clamoured the engineer. "You can see Pixley now."

Dyke, his hand on the grip of the valve that controlled the steam, his head out of the cab window, thundered on. He was back in his old place again; once more he was the engineer; once more he felt the engine quiver under him; the familiar noises were in his ears; the familiar buffeting of the wind surged, roaring at his face; the familiar odours of hot steam and smoke reeked in his nostrils, and on either side of him, parallel panoramas, the two halves of the landscape sliced, as it were, in two by the clashing wheels of his engine, streamed by in green and brown blurs.

He found himself settling to the old position on the cab seat, leaning on his elbow from the window, one hand on the controller. All at once, the instinct of the pursuit that of late had become so strong within him, prompted him to shoot a glance behind. He saw the other engine on the down line, plunging after him, rocking from side to side with the fury of its gallop. Not yet had he shaken the trackers from his heels; not yet was he out of the reach of danger. He set his teeth and, throwing open the fire-door, stoked vigorously for a few moments. The indicator of the steam gauge rose; his speed increased; a glance at the telegraph poles told him he was doing his fifty miles an hour. The freight engine behind him was never built for that pace. Barring the terrible risk of accident, his chances were good.

But suddenly—the engineer dominating the highwayman—he shut off his steam and threw back his brake to the extreme notch. Directly ahead of him rose a semaphore, placed at a point where evidently a derailing switch branched from the line. The semaphore's arm was dropped over the track, setting the danger signal that showed the switch was open.

In an instant, Dyke saw the trick. They had meant to smash him here; had been clever enough, quick-witted enough to open the switch, but had forgotten the automatic semaphore that worked simultaneously with the movement of the rails. To go forward was certain destruction. Dyke reversed. There was nothing for it but to go back. With a wrench and a spasm of all its metal fibres, the great compound braced itself, sliding with rigid wheels along the rails. Then, as Dyke applied the reverse, it drew back from the greater danger, returning towards the less. Inevitably now the two engines, one on the up, the other on the down line, must meet and pass each other.

Dyke released the levers, reaching for his revolver. The engineer once more became the highwayman, in peril of his life. Now, beyond all doubt, the time for fighting was at hand.

The party in the heavy freight engine, that lumbered after in pursuit, their eyes fixed on the smudge of smoke on ahead that marked the path of the fugitive, suddenly raised a shout.

"He's stopped. He's broke down. Watch, now, and see if he jumps off."

"Broke *nothing. He's coming back.* Ready, now, he's got to pass us."

The engineer applied the brakes, but the heavy freight locomotive, far less mobile than Dyke's flyer, was slow to obey. The smudge on the rails ahead grew swiftly larger.

"He's coming. He's coming—look out, there's a shot. He's shooting already."

A bright, white sliver of wood leaped into the air from the sooty window sill of the cab.

"Fire on him! Fire on him!"

While the engines were yet two hundred yards apart, the

duel began, shot answering shot, the sharp staccato reports punctuating the thunder of wheels and the clamour of steam.

Then the ground trembled and rocked; a roar as of heavy ordnance developed with the abruptness of an explosion. The two engines passed each other, the men firing the while, emptying their revolvers, shattering wood, shivering glass, the bullets clanging against the metal work as they struck and struck and struck. The men leaned from the cabs towards each other, frantic with excitement, shouting curses, the engines rocking, the steam roaring; confusion whirling in the scene like the whirl of a witch's dance, the white clouds of steam, the black eddies from the smokestack, the blue wreaths from the hot mouths of revolvers, swirling together in a blinding maze of vapour, spinning around them, dazing them, dizzying them, while the head rang with hideous clamour and the body twitched and trembled with the leap and jar of the tumult of machinery.

Roaring, clamouring, reeking with the smell of powder and hot oil, spitting death, resistless, huge, furious, an abrupt vision of chaos, faces, rage-distorted, peering through smoke, hands gripping outward from sudden darkness, prehensile, malevolent; terrible as thunder, swift as lightning, the two engines met and passed.

"He's hit," cried Delaney. "I know I hit him. He can't go far now. After him again. He won't dare go through Bonneville."

It was true. Dyke had stood between cab and tender throughout all the duel, exposed, reckless, thinking only of attack and not of defence, and a bullet from one of the pistols had grazed his hip. How serious was the wound he did not know, but he had no thought of giving up. He tore back through the depot at Guadalajara in a storm of bullets, and, clinging to the broken window ledge of his cab, was carried towards Bonneville, on over the Long Trestle and Broderson Creek and through the open country between the two ranches of Los Muertos and Quien Sabe.

But to go on to Bonneville meant certain death. Before, as well as behind him, the roads were now blocked. Once more he thought of the mountains. He resolved to abandon the engine and make another final attempt to get into the shelter of the hills in the northernmost corner of Quien Sabe. He set his teeth. He would not give in. There was one more fight left in him yet. Now to try the final hope.

He slowed the engine down, and, reloading his revolver, jumped from the platform to the road. He looked about him, listening. All around him widened an ocean of wheat. There was no one in sight.

The released engine, alone, unattended, drew slowly away from him, jolting ponderously over the rail joints. As he watched it go, a certain indefinite sense of abandonment, even in that moment, came over Dyke. His last friend, that also had been his first, was leaving him. He remembered that day, long ago, when he had opened the throttle of his first machine. To-day, it was leaving him alone, his last friend turning against him. Slowly it was going back towards Bonneville, to the shops of the Railroad, the camp of the enemy, that enemy that had ruined him and wrecked him. For the last time in his life, he had been the engineer. Now, once more, he became the highwayman, the outlaw against whom all hands were raised, the fugitive skulking in the mountains, listening for the cry of dogs.

But he would not give in. They had not broken him yet. Never, while he could fight, would he allow S. Behrman the triumph of his capture.

He found his wound was not bad. He plunged into the wheat on Quien Sabe, making northward for a division house that rose with its surrounding trees out of the wheat like an island. He reached it, the blood squelching in his shoes. But the sight of two men, Portuguese farm-hands, staring at him from an angle of the barn, abruptly roused him to action. He sprang forward with peremptory commands, demanding a horse.

At Guadalajara, Delaney and the sheriff descended from the freight engine.

"Horses now," declared the sheriff. "He won't go into Bonneville, that's certain. He'll leave the engine between here and there, and strike off into the country. We'll follow after him now in the saddle. Soon as he leaves his engine, *he's* on foot. We've as good as got him now."

Their horses, including even the buckskin mare that Dyke

had ridden, were still at the station. The party swung themselves up, Delaney exclaiming, "Here's *my* mount," as he be-
strode the buckskin.

At Guadalajara, the two bloodhounds were picked up
again. Urging the jaded horses to a gallop, the party set off
along the Upper Road, keeping a sharp lookout to right and
left for traces of Dyke's abandonment of the engine.

Three miles beyond the Long Trestle, they found S. Behrman holding his saddle horse by the bridle, and looking attentively at a trail that had been broken through the standing
wheat on Quien Sabe. The party drew rein.

"The engine passed me on the tracks further up, and
empty," said S. Behrman. "Boys, I think he left her here."

But before anyone could answer, the bloodhounds gave
tongue again, as they picked up the scent.

"That's him," cried S. Behrman. "Get on, boys."

They dashed forward, following the hounds. S. Behrman
laboriously climbed to his saddle, panting, perspiring, mopping the roll of fat over his coat collar, and turned in after
them, trotting along far in the rear, his great stomach and
tremulous jowl shaking with the horse's gait.

"What a day," he murmured. "What a day."

Dyke's trail was fresh, and was followed as easily as if made
on new-fallen snow. In a short time, the posse swept into the
open space around the division house. The two Portuguese
were still there, wide-eyed, terribly excited.

Yes, yes, Dyke had been there not half an hour since, had
held them up, taken a horse and galloped to the northeast,
towards the foothills at the headwaters of Broderson Creek.

On again, at full gallop, through the young wheat, trampling it under the flying hoofs; the hounds hot on the scent,
baying continually; the men, on fresh mounts, secured at the
division house, bending forward in their saddles, spurring relentlessly. S. Behrman jolted along far in the rear.

And even then, harried through an open country, where
there was no place to hide, it was a matter of amazement how
long a chase the highwayman led them. Fences were passed;
fences whose barbed wire had been slashed apart by the
fugitive's knife. The ground rose under foot; the hills were
at hand; still the pursuit held on. The sun, long past the

meridian, began to turn earthward. Would night come on before they were up with him?

"Look! Look! There he is! Quick, there he goes!"

High on the bare slope of the nearest hill, all the posse,
looking in the direction of Delaney's gesture, saw the figure
of a horseman emerge from an arroyo, filled with chaparral,
and struggle at a labouring gallop straight up the slope. Suddenly, every member of the party shouted aloud. The horse
had fallen, pitching the rider from the saddle. The man rose
to his feet, caught at the bridle, missed it and the horse
dashed on alone. The man, pausing for a second, looked
around, saw the chase drawing nearer, then, turning back,
disappeared in the chaparral. Delaney raised a great
whoop.

"We've got you now."

Into the slopes and valleys of the hills dashed the band of
horsemen, the trail now so fresh that it could be easily dis-
cerned by all. On and on it led them, a furious, wild scramble
straight up the slopes. The minutes went by. The dry bed of
a rivulet was passed; then another fence; then a tangle of
manzanita; a meadow of wild oats, full of agitated cattle; then
an arroyo, thick with chaparral and scrub oaks, and then,
without warning, the pistol shots ripped out and ran from
rider to rider with the rapidity of a gatling discharge, and one
of the deputies bent forward in the saddle, both hands to his
face, the blood jetting from between his fingers.

Dyke was there, at bay at last, his back against a bank of
rock, the roots of a fallen tree serving him as a rampart, his
revolver smoking in his hand.

"You're under arrest, Dyke," cried the sheriff. "It's not the
least use to fight. The whole country is up."

Dyke fired again, the shot splintering the foreleg of the
horse the sheriff rode.

The posse, four men all told—the wounded deputy having
crawled out of the fight after Dyke's first shot—fell back after
the preliminary fusillade, dismounted, and took shelter behind rocks and trees. On that rugged ground, fighting from
the saddle was impracticable. Dyke, in the meanwhile, held
his fire, for he knew that, once his pistol was empty, he would
never be allowed time to reload.

"Dyke," called the sheriff again, "for the last time, I summon you to surrender."

Dyke did not reply. The sheriff, Delaney, and the man named Christian conferred together in a low voice. Then Delaney and Christian left the others, making a wide detour up the sides of the arroyo, to gain a position to the left and somewhat to the rear of Dyke.

But it was at this moment that S. Behrman arrived. It could not be said whether it was courage or carelessness that brought the Railroad's agent within reach of Dyke's revolver. Possibly he was really a brave man; possibly occupied with keeping an uncertain seat upon the back of his labouring, scrambling horse, he had not noticed that he was so close upon that scene of battle. He certainly did not observe the posse lying upon the ground behind sheltering rocks and trees, and before anyone could call a warning, he had ridden out into the open, within thirty paces of Dyke's intrenchment.

Dyke saw. There was the arch-enemy; the man of all men whom he most hated; the man who had ruined him, who had exasperated him and driven him to crime, and who had instigated tireless pursuit through all those past terrible weeks. Suddenly, inviting death, he leaped up and forward; he had forgotten all else, all other considerations, at the sight of this man. He would die, gladly, so only that S. Behrman died before him.

"I've got *you*, anyway," he shouted, as he ran forward.

The muzzle of the weapon was not ten feet from S. Behrman's huge stomach as Dyke drew the trigger. Had the cartridge exploded, death, certain and swift, would have followed, but at this, of all moments, the revolver missed fire.

S. Behrman, with an unexpected agility, leaped from the saddle, and, keeping his horse between him and Dyke, ran, dodging and ducking, from tree to tree. His first shot a failure, Dyke fired again and again at his enemy, emptying his revolver, reckless of consequences. His every shot went wild, and before he could draw his knife, the whole posse was upon him.

Without concerted plans, obeying no signal but the promptings of the impulse that snatched, unerring, at opportunity—the men, Delaney and Christian from one side, the sheriff and the deputy from the other, rushed in. They did not fire. It was Dyke alive they wanted. One of them had a riata snatched from a saddle-pommel, and with this they tried to bind him.

The fight was four to one—four men with law on their side, to one wounded freebooter, half-starved, exhausted by days and nights of pursuit, worn down with loss of sleep, thirst, privation, and the grinding, nerve-racking consciousness of an ever-present peril.

They swarmed upon him from all sides, gripping at his legs, at his arms, his throat, his head, striking, clutching, kicking, falling to the ground, rolling over and over, now under, now above, now staggering forward, now toppling back.

Still Dyke fought. Through that scrambling, struggling group, through that maze of twisting bodies, twining arms, straining legs, S. Behrman saw him from moment to moment, his face flaming, his eyes bloodshot, his hair matted with sweat. Now he was down, pinned under, two men across his legs, and now half-way up again, struggling to one knee. Then upright again, with half his enemies hanging on his back. His colossal strength seemed doubled; when his arms were held, he fought bull-like with his head. A score of times, it seemed as if they were about to secure him finally and irrevocably, and then he would free an arm, a leg, a shoulder, and the group that, for the fraction of an instant, had settled, locked and rigid, on its prey, would break up again as he flung a man from him, reeling and bloody, and he himself twisting, squirming, dodging, his great fists working like pistons, backed away, dragging and carrying the others with him.

More than once, he loosened almost every grip, and for an instant stood nearly free, panting, rolling his eyes, his clothes torn from his body, bleeding, dripping with sweat, a terrible figure, nearly free. The sheriff, under his breath, uttered an exclamation:

"By God, he'll get away yet."

S. Behrman watched the fight complacently.

"That all may show obstinacy," he commented, "but it don't show common sense."

Yet, however Dyke might throw off the clutches and fettering embraces that encircled him, however he might disintegrate and scatter the band of foes that heaped themselves upon him, however he might gain one instant of comparative liberty, some one of his assailants always hung, doggedly, blindly to an arm, a leg, or a foot, and the others, drawing a second's breath, closed in again, implacable, unconquerable, ferocious, like hounds upon a wolf.

At length, two of the men managed to bring Dyke's wrists close enough together to allow the sheriff to snap the handcuffs on. Even then, Dyke, clasping his hands, and using the handcuffs themselves as a weapon, knocked down Delaney by the crushing impact of the steel bracelets upon the cow-puncher's forehead. But he could no longer protect himself from attacks from behind, and the riata was finally passed around his body, pinioning his arms to his sides. After this it was useless to resist.

The wounded deputy sat with his back to a rock, holding his broken jaw in both hands. The sheriff's horse, with its splintered foreleg, would have to be shot. Delaney's head was cut from temple to cheekbone. The right wrist of the sheriff was all but dislocated. The other deputy was so exhausted he had to be helped to his horse. But Dyke was taken.

He himself had suddenly lapsed into semi-unconsciousness, unable to walk. They sat him on the buckskin, S. Behrman supporting him, the sheriff, on foot, leading the horse by the bridle. The little procession formed, and descended from the hills, turning in the direction of Bonneville. A special train, one car and an engine, would be made up there, and the highwayman would sleep in the Visalia jail that night.

Delaney and S. Behrman found themselves in the rear of the cavalcade as it moved off. The cow-puncher turned to his chief:

"Well, captain," he said, still panting, as he bound up his forehead; "well—we *got* him."

VI

OSTERMAN CUT his wheat that summer before any of the other ranchers, and as soon as his harvest was over organized a jack-rabbit drive. Like Annixter's barn-dance, it was to be an event in which all the country-side should take part. The drive was to begin on the most western division of the Osterman ranch, whence it would proceed towards the southeast, crossing into the northern part of Quien Sabe—on which Annixter had sown no wheat—and ending in the hills at the headwaters of Broderson Creek, where a barbecue was to be held.

Early on the morning of the day of the drive, as Harran and Presley were saddling their horses before the stables on Los Muertos, the foreman, Phelps, remarked:

"I was into town last night, and I hear that Christian has been after Ruggles early and late to have him put him in possession here on Los Muertos, and Delaney is doing the same for Quien Sabe."

It was this man Christian, the real estate broker, and cousin of S. Behrman, one of the main actors in the drama of Dyke's capture, who had come forward as a purchaser of Los Muertos when the Railroad had regraded its holdings on the ranches around Bonneville.

"He claims, of course," Phelps went on, "that when he bought Los Muertos of the Railroad he was guaranteed possession, and he wants the place in time for the harvest."

"That's almost as thin," muttered Harran as he thrust the bit into his horse's mouth, "as Delaney buying Annixter's Home ranch. That slice of Quien Sabe, according to the Railroad's grading, is worth about ten thousand dollars; yes, even fifteen, and I don't believe Delaney is worth the price of a good horse. Why, those people don't even *try* to preserve appearances. Where would Christian find the money to buy Los Muertos? There's no one man in all Bonneville rich enough to do it. Damned rascals! as if we didn't see that Christian and Delaney are S. Behrman's right and left hands. Well, he'll get 'em cut off," he cried with sudden fierceness, "if he comes too near the machine."

"How is it, Harran," asked Presley as the two young men rode out of the stable yard, "how is it the Railroad gang can do anything before the Supreme Court hands down a decision?"

"Well, you know how they talk," growled Harran. "They have claimed that the cases taken up to the Supreme Court were not test cases as *we* claim they *are*, and that because neither Annixter nor the Governor appealed, they've lost their cases by default. It's the rottenest kind of sharp practice, but it won't do any good. The League is too strong. They won't dare move on us yet awhile. Why, Pres, the moment they'd try to jump any of these ranches around here, they would have six hundred rifles cracking at them as quick as how-do-you-do. Why, it would take a regiment of U. S. soldiers to put any one of us off our land. No, sir; they know the League means business this time."

As Presley and Harran trotted on along the county road they continually passed or overtook other horsemen, or buggies, carry-alls, buck-boards or even farm wagons, going in the same direction. These were full of the farming people from all the country round about Bonneville, on their way to the rabbit drive—the same people seen at the barn-dance—in their Sunday finery, the girls in muslin frocks and garden hats, the men with linen dusters over their black clothes; the older women in prints and dotted calicoes. Many of these latter had already taken off their bonnets—the day was very hot—and pinning them in newspapers, stowed them under the seats. They tucked their handkerchiefs into the collars of their dresses, or knotted them about their fat necks, to keep out the dust. From the axle trees of the vehicles swung carefully covered buckets of galvanised iron, in which the lunch was packed. The younger children, the boys with great frilled collars, the girls with ill-fitting shoes cramping their feet, leaned from the sides of buggy and carry-all, eating bananas and "macaroons," staring about with ox-like stolidity. Tied to the axles, the dogs followed the horses' hoofs with lolling tongues coated with dust.

The California summer lay blanket-wise and smothering over all the land. The hills, bone-dry, were browned and parched. The grasses and wild-oats, sear and yellow, snapped like glass filaments under foot. The roads, the bordering fences, even the lower leaves and branches of the trees, were thick and grey with dust. All colour had been burned from the landscape, except in the irrigated patches, that in the waste of brown and dull yellow glowed like oases.

The wheat, now close to its maturity, had turned from pale yellow to golden yellow, and from that to brown. Like a gigantic carpet, it spread itself over all the land. There was nothing else to be seen but the limitless sea of wheat as far as the eye could reach, dry, rustling, crisp and harsh in the rare breaths of hot wind out of the southeast.

As Harran and Presley went along the county road, the number of vehicles and riders increased. They overtook and passed Hooven and his family in the former's farm wagon, a saddled horse tied to the back board. The little Dutchman, wearing the old frock coat of Magnus Derrick, and a new broad-brimmed straw hat, sat on the front seat with Mrs. Hooven. The little girl Hilda, and the older daughter Minna, were behind them on a board laid across the sides of the wagon. Presley and Harran stopped to shake hands.

"Say," cried Hooven, exhibiting an old, but extremely well kept, rifle, "say, bei Gott, me, I tek some schatz at dose rebbit, you bedt. Ven he hef shtop to run und sit oop soh, bei der hind laigs on, I oop mit der guhn und—bing! *I* cetch um."

"The marshals won't allow you to shoot, Bismarck," observed Presley, looking at Minna.

Hooven doubled up with merriment.

"Ho! dot's hell of some fine joak. Me, *I'm one oaf dose mairschell mine-selluf*," he roared with delight, beating his knee. To his notion, the joke was irresistible. All day long, he could be heard repeating it. "Und Mist'r Praicelie, he say, 'Dose mairschell woand led you schoot, Bismarck,' und *me*, ach Gott, *me*, aindt I mine-selluf one oaf dose mairschell?"

As the two friends rode on, Presley had in his mind the image of Minna Hooven, very pretty in a clean gown of pink gingham, a cheap straw sailor hat from a Bonneville store on her blue black hair. He remembered her very pale face, very red lips and eyes of greenish blue,—a pretty girl certainly, always trailing a group of men behind her. Her love affairs were the talk of all Los Muertos.

"I hope that Hooven girl won't go to the bad," Presley said to Harran.

"Oh, she's all right," the other answered. "There's nothing vicious about Minna, and I guess she'll marry that foreman on the ditch gang, right enough."

"Well, as a matter of course, she's a good girl," Presley hastened to reply, "only she's too pretty for a poor girl, and too sure of her prettiness besides. That's the kind," he continued, "who would find it pretty easy to go wrong if they lived in a city."

Around Caraher's was a veritable throng. Saddle horses and buggies by the score were clustered underneath the shed or hitched to the railings in front of the watering trough. Three of Broderson's Portuguese tenants and a couple of workmen from the Railroad shops in Bonneville were on the porch, already very drunk.

Continually, young men, singly or in groups, came from the door-way, wiping their lips with sidelong gestures of the hand. The whole place exhaled the febrile bustle of the saloon on a holiday morning.

The procession of teams streamed on through Bonneville, reënforced at every street corner. Along the Upper Road from Quien Sabe and Guadalajara came fresh auxiliaries, Spanish-Mexicans from the town itself,—swarthy young men on capering horses, dark-eyed girls and matrons, in red and black and yellow, more Portuguese in brand-new overalls, smoking long thin cigars. Even Father Sarria appeared.

"Look," said Presley, "there goes Annixter and Hilma. He's got his buckskin back." The master of Quien Sabe, in top laced boots and campaign hat, a cigar in his teeth, followed along beside the carry-all. Hilma and Mrs. Derrick were on the back seat, young Vacca driving. Harran and Presley bowed, taking off their hats.

"Hello, hello, Pres," cried Annixter, over the heads of the intervening crowd, standing up in his stirrups and waving a hand. "Great day! What a mob, hey? Say, when this thing is over and everybody starts to walk into the barbecue, come and have lunch with us. I'll look for you, you and Harran. Hello, Harran, where's the Governor?"

"He didn't come to-day," Harran shouted back, as the

crowd carried him further away from Annixter. "Left him and old Broderson at Los Muertos."

The throng emerged into the open country again, spreading out upon the Osterman ranch. From all directions could be seen horses and buggies driving across the stubble, converging upon the rendezvous. Osterman's Ranch house was left to the eastward; the army of the guests hurrying forward—for it began to be late—to where around a flag pole, flying a red flag, a vast crowd of buggies and horses was already forming. The marshals began to appear. Hooven, descending from the farm wagon, pinned his white badge to his hat brim and mounted his horse. Osterman, in marvellous riding clothes of English pattern, galloped up and down upon his best thoroughbred, cracking jokes with everybody, chaffing, joshing, his great mouth distended in a perpetual grin of amiability.

"Stop here, stop here," he vociferated, dashing along in front of Presley and Harran, waving his crop. The procession came to a halt, the horses' heads pointing eastward. The line began to be formed. The marshals perspiring, shouting, fretting, galloping about, urging this one forward, ordering this one back, ranged the thousands of conveyances and cavaliers in a long line, shaped like a wide open crescent. Its wings, under the command of lieutenants, were slightly advanced. Far out before its centre Osterman took his place, delighted beyond expression at his conspicuousness, posing for the gallery, making his horse dance.

"Wail, aindt dey gowun to gommence den bretty soohn," exclaimed Mrs. Hooven, who had taken her husband's place on the forward seat of the wagon.

"I never was so warm," murmured Minna, fanning herself with her hat. All seemed in readiness. For miles over the flat expanse of stubble, curved the interminable lines of horses and vehicles. At a guess, nearly five thousand people were present. The drive was one of the largest ever held. But no start was made; immobilized, the vast crescent stuck motionless under the blazing sun. Here and there could be heard voices uplifted in jocular remonstrance.

"Oh, I say, get a move on, somebody."

"*All* aboard."

"Say, I'll take root here pretty soon."

Some took malicious pleasure in starting false alarms.

"Ah, *here* we must go."

"Off, at last."

"We're off."

Invariably these jokes fooled some one in the line. An old man, or some old woman, nervous, hard of hearing, always gathered up the reins and started off, only to be hustled and ordered back in to the line by the nearest marshal. This manœuvre never failed to produce its effect of hilarity upon those near at hand. Everybody laughed at the blunderer, the joker jeering audibly.

"Hey, come back here."

"Oh, he's easy."

"Don't be in a hurry, Grandpa."

"Say, you want to drive all the rabbits yourself."

Later on, a certain group of these fellows started a huge "josh."

"Say, that's what we're waiting for, the 'do-funny.' "

"The do-funny?"

"Sure, you can't drive rabbits without the 'do-funny.' "

"What's the do-funny?"

"Oh, say, she don't know what the do-funny is. We can't start without it, sure. Pete went back to get it."

"Oh, you're joking me, there's no such thing."

"Well, aren't we *waiting* for it?"

"Oh, look, look," cried some women in a covered rig. "See, they are starting already 'way over there."

In fact, it did appear as if the far extremity of the line was in motion. Dust rose in the air above it.

"They *are* starting. Why don't we start?"

"No, they've stopped. False alarm."

"They've not, either. Why don't we move?"

But as one or two began to move off, the nearest marshal shouted wrathfully:

"Get back there, get back there."

"Well, they've started over there."

"Get back, I tell you."

"Where's the 'do-funny?' "

"Say, we're going to miss it all. They've all started over there."

A lieutenant came galloping along in front of the line, shouting:

"Here, what's the matter here? Why don't you start?"

There was a great shout. Everybody simultaneously uttered a prolonged "Oh-h."

"We're off."

"Here we go for sure this time."

"Remember to keep the alignment," roared the lieutenant. "Don't go too fast."

And the marshals, rushing here and there on their sweating horses to points where the line bulged forward, shouted, waving their arms: "Not too fast, not too fast. . . . Keep back here. . . . Here, keep closer together here. Do you want to let all the rabbits run back between you?"

A great confused sound rose into the air,—the creaking of axles, the jolt of iron tires over the dry clods, the click of brittle stubble under the horses' hoofs, the barking of dogs, the shouts of conversation and laughter.

The entire line, horses, buggies, wagons, gigs, dogs, men and boys on foot, and armed with clubs, moved slowly across the fields, sending up a cloud of white dust, that hung above the scene like smoke. A brisk gaiety was in the air. Everyone was in the best of humor, calling from team to team, laughing, skylarking, joshing. Garnett, of the Ruby Rancho, and Gethings, of the San Pablo, both on horseback, found themselves side by side. Ignoring the drive and the spirit of the occasion, they kept up a prolonged and serious conversation on an expected rise in the price of wheat. Dabney, also on horseback, followed them, listening attentively to every word, but hazarding no remark.

Mrs. Derrick and Hilma sat in the back seat of the carryall, behind young Vacca. Mrs. Derrick, a little disturbed by such a great concourse of people, frightened at the idea of the killing of so many rabbits, drew back in her place, her young-girl eyes troubled and filled with a vague distress. Hilma, very much excited, leaned from the carry-all, anxious to see everything, watching for rabbits, asking innumerable questions of Annixter, who rode at her side.

The change that had been progressing in Hilma, ever since the night of the famous barn-dance, now seemed to be ap-

proaching its climax; first the girl, then the woman, last of all
the Mother. Conscious dignity, a new element in her character, developed. The shrinking, the timidity of the girl just
awakening to the consciousness of sex, passed away from her.
The confusion, the troublous complexity of the woman, a
mystery even to herself, disappeared. Motherhood dawned,
the old simplicity of her maiden days came back to her. It was
no longer a simplicity of ignorance, but of supreme knowledge, the simplicity of the perfect, the simplicity of greatness.
She looked the world fearlessly in the eyes. At last, the confusion of her ideas, like frightened birds, re-settling, adjusted
itself, and she emerged from the trouble calm, serene, entering into her divine right, like a queen into the rule of a realm
of perpetual peace.

And with this, with the knowledge that the crown hung
poised above her head, there came upon Hilma a gentleness
infinitely beautiful, infinitely pathetic; a sweetness that
touched all who came near her with the softness of a caress.
She moved surrounded by an invisible atmosphere of Love.
Love was in her wide-opened brown eyes, Love—the dim
reflection of that descending crown poised over her head—
radiated in a faint lustre from her dark, thick hair. Around
her beautiful neck, sloping to her shoulders with full, graceful
curves, Love lay encircled like a necklace—Love that was beyond words, sweet, breathed from her parted lips. From her
white, large arms downward to her pink finger-tips—Love,
an invisible electric fluid, disengaged itself, subtle, alluring. In
the velvety huskiness of her voice, Love vibrated like a note
of unknown music.

Annixter, her uncouth, rugged husband, living in this influence of a wife, who was also a mother, at all hours touched
to the quick by this sense of nobility, of gentleness and of
love, the instincts of a father already clutching and tugging at
his heart, was trembling on the verge of a mighty transformation. The hardness and inhumanity of the man was fast
breaking up. One night, returning late to the Ranch house,
after a compulsory visit to the city, he had come upon Hilma
asleep. He had never forgotten that night. A realization of his
boundless happiness in this love he gave and received, the
thought that Hilma *trusted* him, a knowledge of his own un-

worthiness, a vast and humble thankfulness that his God had
chosen him of all men for this great joy, had brought him to
his knees for the first time in all his troubled, restless life of
combat and aggression. He prayed, he knew not what,—
vague words, wordless thoughts, resolving fiercely to do
right, to make some return for God's gift thus placed within
his hands.

Where once Annixter had thought only of himself, he now
thought only of Hilma. The time when this thought of another should broaden and widen into thought of *Others*, was
yet to come; but already it had expanded to include the un-
born child—already, as in the case of Mrs. Dyke, it had
broadened to enfold another child and another mother bound
to him by no ties other than those of humanity and pity. In
time, starting from this point it would reach out more and
more till it should take in all men and all women, and the
intolerant selfish man, while retaining all of his native
strength, should become tolerant and generous, kind and for-
giving.

For the moment, however, the two natures struggled
within him. A fight was to be fought, one more, the last, the
fiercest, the attack of the enemy who menaced his very home
and hearth, was to be resisted. Then, peace attained, arrested
development would once more proceed.

Hilma looked from the carry-all, scanning the open plain
in front of the advancing line of the drive.

"Where are the rabbits?" she asked of Annixter. "I don't
see any at all."

"They are way ahead of us yet," he said. "Here, take the
glasses."

He passed her his field glasses, and she adjusted them.

"Oh, yes," she cried, "I see. I can see five or six, but oh, so
far off."

"The beggars run 'way ahead, at first."

"I should say so. See them run,—little specks. Every
now and then they sit up, their ears straight up, in the
air."

"Here, look, Hilma, there goes one close by."

From out of the ground apparently, some twenty yards
distant, a great jack sprang into view, bounding away with

tremendous leaps, his black-tipped ears erect. He disappeared, his grey body losing itself against the grey of the ground.

"Oh, a big fellow."

"Hi, yonder's another."

"Yes, yes, oh, look at him run."

From off the surface of the ground, at first apparently empty of all life, and seemingly unable to afford hiding place for so much as a field-mouse, jack-rabbits started up at every moment as the line went forward. At first, they appeared singly and at long intervals; then in twos and threes, as the drive continued to advance. They leaped across the plain, and stopped in the distance, sitting up with straight ears, then ran on again, were joined by others; sank down flush to the soil—their ears flattened; started up again, ran to the side, turned back once more, darted away with incredible swiftness, and were lost to view only to be replaced by a score of others.

Gradually, the number of jacks to be seen over the expanse of stubble in front of the line of teams increased. Their antics were infinite. No two acted precisely alike. Some lay stubbornly close in a little depression between two clods, till the horses' hoofs were all but upon them, then sprang out from their hiding-place at the last second. Others ran forward but a few yards at a time, refusing to take flight, scenting a greater danger before them than behind. Still others, forced up at the last moment, doubled with lightning alacrity in their tracks, turning back to scuttle between the teams, taking desperate chances. As often as this occurred, it was the signal for a great uproar.

"Don't let him get through; don't let him get through."

"Look out for him, there he goes."

Horns were blown, bells rung, tin pans clamorously beaten. Either the jack escaped, or confused by the noise, darted back again, fleeing away as if his life depended on the issue of the instant. Once even, a bewildered rabbit jumped fair into Mrs. Derrick's lap as she sat in the carry-all, and was out again like a flash.

"Poor frightened thing," she exclaimed; and for a long time afterward, she retained upon her knees the sensation of the four little paws quivering with excitement, and the feel of the trembling furry body, with its wildly beating heart, pressed against her own.

By noon the number of rabbits discernible by Annixter's field glasses on ahead was far into the thousands. What seemed to be ground resolved itself, when seen through the glasses, into a maze of small, moving bodies, leaping, ducking, doubling, running back and forth—a wilderness of agitated ears, white tails and twinkling legs. The outside wings of the curved line of vehicles began to draw in a little; Osterman's ranch was left behind, the drive continued on over Quien Sabe.

As the day advanced, the rabbits, singularly enough, became less wild. When flushed, they no longer ran so far nor so fast, limping off instead a few feet at a time, and crouching down, their ears close upon their backs. Thus it was, that by degrees the teams began to close up on the main herd. At every instant the numbers increased. It was no longer thousands, it was tens of thousands. The earth was alive with rabbits.

Denser and denser grew the throng. In all directions nothing was to be seen but the loose mass of the moving jacks. The horns of the crescent of teams began to contract. Far off the corral came into sight. The disintegrated mass of rabbits commenced, as it were, to solidify, to coagulate. At first, each jack was some three feet distant from his nearest neighbor, but this space diminished to two feet, then to one, then to but a few inches. The rabbits began leaping over one another.

Then the strange scene defined itself. It was no longer a herd covering the earth. It was a sea, whipped into confusion, tossing incessantly, leaping, falling, agitated by unseen forces. At times the unexpected tameness of the rabbits all at once vanished. Throughout certain portions of the herd eddies of terror abruptly burst forth. A panic spread; then there would ensue a blind, wild rushing together of thousands of crowded bodies, and a furious scrambling over backs, till the scuffing thud of innumerable feet over the earth rose to a reverberating murmur as of distant thunder, here and there pierced by the strange, wild cry of the rabbit in distress.

The line of vehicles was halted. To go forward now meant to trample the rabbits under foot. The drive came to a standstill while the herd entered the corral. This took time, for the rabbits were by now too crowded to run. However, like an opened sluice-gate, the extending flanks of the entrance of the corral slowly engulfed the herd. The mass, packed tight as ever, by degrees diminished, precisely as a pool of water when a dam is opened. The last stragglers went in with a rush, and the gate was dropped.

"Come, just have a look in here," called Annixter.

Hilma, descending from the carry-all and joined by Presley and Harran, approached and looked over the high board fence.

"Oh, did you ever see anything like that?" she exclaimed.

The corral, a really large enclosure, had proved all too small for the number of rabbits collected by the drive. Inside it was a living, moving, leaping, breathing, twisting mass. The rabbits were packed two, three, and four feet deep. They were in constant movement; those beneath struggling to the top, those on top sinking and disappearing below their fellows. All wildness, all fear of man, seemed to have entirely disappeared. Men and boys reaching over the sides of the corral, picked up a jack in each hand, holding them by the ears, while two reporters from San Francisco papers took photographs of the scene. The noise made by the tens of thousands of moving bodies was as the noise of wind in a forest, while from the hot and sweating mass there rose a strange odor, penetrating, ammoniacal, savouring of wild life.

On signal, the killing began. Dogs that had been brought there for that purpose when let into the corral refused, as had been half expected, to do the work. They snuffed curiously at the pile, then backed off, disturbed, perplexed. But the men and boys—Portuguese for the most part—were more eager. Annixter drew Hilma away, and, indeed, most of the people set about the barbecue at once.

In the corral, however, the killing went forward. Armed with a club in each hand, the young fellows from Guadalajara and Bonneville, and the farm boys from the ranches, leaped over the rails of the corral. They walked unsteadily upon the myriad of crowding bodies underfoot, or, as space was cleared, sank almost waist deep into the mass that leaped and squirmed about them. Blindly, furiously, they struck and struck. The Anglo-Saxon spectators round about drew back in disgust, but the hot, degenerated blood of Portuguese, Mexican, and mixed Spaniard boiled up in excitement at this wholesale slaughter.

But only a few of the participants of the drive cared to look on. All the guests betook themselves some quarter of a mile farther on into the hills.

The picnic and barbecue were to be held around the spring where Broderson Creek took its rise. Already two entire beeves were roasting there; teams were hitched, saddles removed, and men, women, and children, a great throng, spread out under the shade of the live oaks. A vast confused clamour rose in the air, a babel of talk, a clatter of tin plates, of knives and forks. Bottles were uncorked, napkins and oilcloths spread over the ground. The men lit pipes and cigars, the women seized the occasion to nurse their babies.

Osterman, ubiquitous as ever, resplendent in his boots and English riding breeches, moved about between the groups, keeping up an endless flow of talk, cracking jokes, winking, nudging, gesturing, putting his tongue in his cheek, never at a loss for a reply, playing the goat.

"That josher, Osterman, always at his monkey-shines, but a good fellow for all that; brainy too. Nothing stuck up about him either, like Magnus Derrick."

"Everything all right, Buck?" inquired Osterman, coming up to where Annixter, Hilma and Mrs. Derrick were sitting down to their lunch.

"Yes, yes, everything right. But we've no cork-screw."

"No screw-cork—no scare-crow? Here you are," and he drew from his pocket a silver-plated jack-knife with a cork-screw attachment.

Harran and Presley came up, bearing between them a great smoking, roasted portion of beef just off the fire. Hilma hastened to put forward a huge china platter.

Osterman had a joke to crack with the two boys, a joke that was rather broad, but as he turned about, the words almost on his lips, his glance fell upon Hilma herself, whom he had not seen for more than two months. She had handed Presley the platter, and was now sitting with her back against the tree, between two boles of the roots. The position was a little elevated and the supporting roots on either side of her were like the arms of a great chair—a chair of state. She sat thus, as on a throne, raised above the rest, the radiance of the unseen crown of motherhood glowing from her forehead, the beauty of the perfect woman surrounding her like a glory.

And the josh died away on Osterman's lips, and unconsciously and swiftly he bared his head. Something was passing there in the air about him that he did not understand, something, however, that imposed reverence and profound respect. For the first time in his life, embarrassment seized upon him, upon this joker, this wearer of clothes, this teller of funny stories, with his large, red ears, bald head and comic actor's face. He stammered confusedly and took himself away, for the moment abstracted, serious, lost in thought.

By now everyone was eating. It was the feeding of the People, elemental, gross, a great appeasing of appetite, an enormous quenching of thirst. Quarters of beef, roasts, ribs, shoulders, haunches were consumed, loaves of bread by the thousands disappeared, whole barrels of wine went down the dry and dusty throats of the multitude. Conversation lagged while the People ate, while hunger was appeased. Everybody had their fill. One ate for the sake of eating, resolved that there should be nothing left, considering it a matter of pride to exhibit a clean plate.

After dinner, preparations were made for games. On a flat plateau at the top of one of the hills the contestants were to strive. There was to be a footrace of young girls under seventeen, a fat men's race, the younger fellows were to put the shot, to compete in the running broad jump, and the standing high jump, in the hop, skip, and step and in wrestling.

Presley was delighted with it all. It was Homeric, this feasting, this vast consuming of meat and bread and wine, followed now by games of strength. An epic simplicity and directness, an honest Anglo-Saxon mirth and innocence, commended it. Crude it was; coarse it was, but no taint of viciousness was here. These people were good people, kindly, benignant even, always readier to give than to receive, always more willing to help than to be helped. They were good stock. Of such was the backbone of the nation—sturdy Americans everyone of them. Where else in the world round were such strong, honest men, such strong, beautiful women?

Annixter, Harran, and Presley climbed to the level plateau where the games were to be held, to lay out the courses, and mark the distances. It was the very place where once Presley had loved to lounge entire afternoons, reading his books of poems, smoking and dozing. From this high point one dominated the entire valley to the south and west. The view was superb. The three men paused for a moment on the crest of the hill to consider it.

Young Vacca came running and panting up the hill after them, calling for Annixter.

"Well, well, what is it?"

"Mr. Osterman's looking for you, sir, you and Mr. Harran. Vanamee, that cow-boy over at Derrick's, has just come from the Governor with a message. I guess it's important."

"Hello, what's up now?" muttered Annixter, as they turned back.

They found Osterman saddling his horse in furious haste. Near-by him was Vanamee holding by the bridle an animal that was one lather of sweat. A few of the picnickers were turning their heads curiously in that direction. Evidently something of moment was in the wind.

"What's all up?" demanded Annixter, as he and Harran, followed by Presley, drew near.

"There's hell to pay," exclaimed Osterman under his breath. "Read that. Vanamee just brought it."

He handed Annixter a sheet of note paper, and turned again to the cinching of his saddle.

"We've got to be quick," he cried. "They've stolen a march on us."

Annixter read the note, Harran and Presley looking over his shoulder.

"Ah, it's them, is it," exclaimed Annixter.

Harran set his teeth. "Now for it," he exclaimed.

"They've been to your place already, Mr. Annixter," said Vanamee. "I passed by it on my way up. They have put Delaney in possession, and have set all your furniture out in the road."

Annixter turned about, his lips white. Already Presley and Harran had run to their horses.

"Vacca," cried Annixter, "where's Vacca? Put the saddle on the buckskin, *quick*. Osterman, get as many of the League as are here together at *this* spot, understand. I'll be back in a minute. I must tell Hilma this."

Hooven ran up as Annixter disappeared. His little eyes were blazing, he was dragging his horse with him.

"Say, dose fellers come, hey? Me, I'm alretty, see I hev der guhn."

"They've jumped the ranch, little girl," said Annixter, putting one arm around Hilma. "They're in our house now. I'm off. Go to Derrick's and wait for me there."

She put her arms around his neck.

"You're going?" she demanded.

"I must. Don't be frightened. It will be all right. Go to Derrick's and—good-bye."

She said never a word. She looked once long into his eyes, then kissed him on the mouth.

Meanwhile, the news had spread. The multitude rose to its feet. Women and men, with pale faces, looked at each other speechless, or broke forth into inarticulate exclamations. A strange, unfamiliar murmur took the place of the tumultuous gaiety of the previous moments. A sense of dread, of confusion, of impending terror weighed heavily in the air. What was now to happen?

When Annixter got back to Osterman, he found a number of the Leaguers already assembled. They were all mounted. Hooven was there and Harran, and besides these, Garnett of the Ruby ranch and Gethings of the San Pablo, Phelps the foreman of Los Muertos, and, last of all, Dabney, silent as ever, speaking to no one. Presley came riding up.

"Best keep out of this, Pres," cried Annixter.

"Are we ready?" exclaimed Gethings.

"Ready, ready, we're all here."

"*All*. Is this all of us?" cried Annixter. "Where are the six hundred men who were going to rise when this happened?"

They had wavered, these other Leaguers. Now, when the actual crisis impended, they were smitten with confusion. Ah, no, they were not going to stand up and be shot at just to save Derrick's land. They were not armed. What did Annixter and Osterman take them for? No, sir; the Railroad had stolen a march on them. After all his big talk Derrick had allowed them to be taken by surprise. The only thing to do was to call a meeting of the Executive Committee. That was the only thing. As for going down there with no weapons in their hands, *no*, sir. That was asking a little *too* much.

"Come on, then, boys," shouted Osterman, turning his back on the others. "The Governor says to meet him at Hooven's. We'll make for the Long Trestle and strike the trail to Hooven's there."

They set off. It was a terrible ride. Twice during the scrambling descent from the hills, Presley's pony fell beneath him. Annixter, on his buckskin, and Osterman, on his thoroughbred, good horsemen both, led the others, setting a terrific pace. The hills were left behind. Broderson Creek was crossed and on the levels of Quien Sabe, straight through the standing wheat, the nine horses, flogged and spurred, stretched out to their utmost. Their passage through the wheat sounded like the rip and tear of a gigantic web of cloth. The landscape on either hand resolved itself into a long blur. Tears came to the eyes, flying pebbles, clods of earth, grains of wheat flung up in the flight, stung the face like shot. Osterman's thoroughbred took the second crossing of Broderson's Creek in a single leap. Down under the Long Trestle tore the cavalcade in a shower of mud and gravel; up again on the further bank, the horses blowing like steam engines; on into the trail to Hooven's, single file now, Presley's pony lagging, Hooven's horse bleeding at the eyes, the buckskin, game as a fighting cock, catching her second wind, far in the lead now, distancing even the English thoroughbred that Osterman rode.

At last Hooven's unpainted house, beneath the enormous live oak tree, came in sight. Across the Lower Road, breaking through fences and into the yard around the house, thundered the Leaguers. Magnus was waiting for them.

The riders dismounted, hardly less exhausted than their horses.

"Why, where's all the men?" Annixter demanded of Magnus.

"Broderson is here and Cutter," replied the Governor, "no one else. I thought *you* would bring more men with you."

"There are only nine of us."

"And the six hundred Leaguers who were going to rise when this happened!" exclaimed Garnett, bitterly.

"Rot the League," cried Annixter. "It's gone to pot—went to pieces at the first touch."

"We have been taken by surprise, gentlemen, after all," said Magnus. "Totally off our guard. But there are eleven of us. It is enough."

"Well, what's the game? Has the marshal come? How many men are with him?"

"The United States marshal from San Francisco," explained Magnus, "came down early this morning and stopped at Guadalajara. We learned it all through our friends in Bonneville about an hour ago. They telephoned me and Mr. Broderson. S. Behrman met him and provided about a dozen deputies. Delaney, Ruggles, and Christian joined them at Guadalajara. They left Guadalajara, going towards Mr. Annixter's ranch house on Quien Sabe. They are serving the writs in ejectment and putting the dummy buyers in possession. They are armed. S. Behrman is with them."

"Where are they now?"

"Cutter is watching them from the Long Trestle. They returned to Guadalajara. They are there now."

"Well," observed Gethings, "from Guadalajara they can only go to two places. Either they will take the Upper Road and go on to Osterman's next, or they will take the Lower Road to Mr. Derrick's."

"That is as I supposed," said Magnus. "That is why I wanted you to come here. From Hooven's, here, we can watch both roads simultaneously."

"Is anybody on the lookout on the Upper Road?"

"Cutter. He is on the Long Trestle."

"Say," observed Hooven, the instincts of the old-time soldier stirring him, "say, dose feller pretty demn schmart, I tink. We got to put some picket way oudt bei der Lower Roadt alzoh, und he tek dose glassus Mist'r Ennixt'r got bei um. Say, look at dose irregation ditsch. Dot ditsch he run righd across *both* dose road, hey? Dat's some fine entrenchment, you bedt. We fighd um from dose ditsch."

In fact, the dry irrigating ditch was a natural trench, admirably suited to the purpose, crossing both roads as Hooven pointed out and barring approach from Guadalajara to all the ranches save Annixter's—which had already been seized.

Gethings departed to join Cutter on the Long Trestle, while Phelps and Harran, taking Annixter's field glasses with them, and mounting their horses, went out towards Guadalajara on the Lower Road to watch for the marshal's approach from that direction.

After the outposts had left them, the party in Hooven's cottage looked to their weapons. Long since, every member of the League had been in the habit of carrying his revolver with him. They were all armed and, in addition, Hooven had his rifle. Presley alone carried no weapon.

The main room of Hooven's house, in which the Leaguers were now assembled, was barren, poverty-stricken, but tolerably clean. An old clock ticked vociferously on a shelf. In one corner was a bed, with a patched, faded quilt. In the centre of the room, straddling over the bare floor, stood a pine table. Around this the men gathered, two or three occupying chairs, Annixter sitting sideways on the table, the rest standing.

"I believe, gentlemen," said Magnus, "that we can go through this day without bloodshed. I believe not one shot need be fired. The Railroad will not force the issue, will not bring about actual fighting. When the marshal realises that we are thoroughly in earnest, thoroughly determined, I am convinced that he will withdraw."

There were murmurs of assent.

"Look here," said Annixter, "if this thing can by any means be settled peaceably, I say let's do it, so long as we don't give in."

The others stared. Was this Annixter who spoke—the Hotspur of the League, the quarrelsome, irascible fellow who loved and sought a quarrel? Was it Annixter, who now had been the first and only one of them all to suffer, whose ranch had been seized, whose household possessions had been flung out into the road?

"When you come right down to it," he continued, "killing a man, no matter what he's done to you, is a serious business. I propose we make one more attempt to stave this thing off. Let's see if we can't get to talk with the marshal himself; at any rate, warn him of the danger of going any further. Boys, let's not fire the first shot. What do you say?"

The others agreed unanimously and promptly; and old Broderson, tugging uneasily at his long beard, added:

"No—no—no violence, no *unnecessary* violence, that is. I should hate to have innocent blood on my hands—that is, if it *is* innocent. I don't know, that S. Behrman—ah, he is a—a—surely he had innocent blood on *his* head. That Dyke affair, terrible, terrible; but then Dyke *was* in the wrong—driven to it, though; the Railroad did drive him to it. I want to be fair and just to everybody——"

"There's a team coming up the road from Los Muertos," announced Presley from the door.

"Fair and just to everybody," murmured old Broderson, wagging his head, frowning perplexedly. "I don't want to—to—to harm anybody unless they harm me."

"Is the team going towards Guadalajara?" enquired Garnett, getting up and coming to the door.

"Yes, it's a Portuguese, one of the garden truck men."

"We must turn him back," declared Osterman. "He can't go through here. We don't want him to take any news on to the marshal and S. Behrman."

"I'll turn him back," said Presley.

He rode out towards the market cart, and the others, watching from the road in front of Hooven's, saw him halt it. An excited interview followed. They could hear the Portuguese expostulating volubly, but in the end he turned back.

"Martial law on Los Muertos, isn't it?" observed Osterman. "Steady all," he exclaimed as he turned about, "here comes Harran."

Harran rode up at a gallop. The others surrounded him.

"I saw them," he cried. "They are coming this way. S. Behrman and Ruggles are in a two-horse buggy. All the others are on horseback. There are eleven of them. Christian and Delaney are with them. Those two have rifles. I left Hooven watching them."

"Better call in Gethings and Cutter right away," said Annixter. "We'll need all our men."

"I'll call them in," Presley volunteered at once. "Can I have the buckskin? My pony is about done up."

He departed at a brisk gallop, but on the way met Gethings and Cutter returning. They, too, from their elevated position, had observed the marshal's party leaving Guadalajara by the Lower Road. Presley told them of the decision of the Leaguers not to fire until fired upon.

"All right," said Gethings. "But if it comes to a gun-fight, that means it's all up with at least one of us. Delaney never misses his man."

When they reached Hooven's again, they found that the Leaguers had already taken their position in the ditch. The plank bridge across it had been torn up. Magnus, two long revolvers lying on the embankment in front of him, was in the middle, Harran at his side. On either side, some five feet intervening between each man, stood the other Leaguers, their revolvers ready. Dabney, the silent old man, had taken off his coat.

"Take your places between Mr. Osterman and Mr. Broderson," said Magnus, as the three men rode up. "Presley," he added, "I forbid you to take any part in this affair."

"Yes, keep him out of it," cried Annixter from his position at the extreme end of the line. "Go back to Hooven's house, Pres, and look after the horses," he added. "This is no business of yours. And keep the road behind us clear. Don't let *any one* come near, not *any one*, understand?"

Presley withdrew, leading the buckskin and the horses that Gethings and Cutter had ridden. He fastened them under the great live oak and then came out and stood in the road in front of the house to watch what was going on.

In the ditch, shoulder deep, the Leaguers, ready, watchful, waited in silence, their eyes fixed on the white shimmer of the road leading to Guadalajara.

"Where's Hooven?" enquired Cutter.

"I don't know," Osterman replied. "He was out watching the Lower Road with Harran Derrick. Oh, Harran," he called, "isn't Hooven coming in?"

"I don't know what he is waiting for," answered Harran.

"He was to have come in just after me. He thought maybe the marshal's party might make a feint in this direction, then go around by the Upper Road, after all. He wanted to watch them a little longer. But he ought to be here now."

"Think he'll take a shot at them on his own account?"

"Oh, no, he wouldn't do that."

"Maybe they took him prisoner."

"Well, that's to be thought of, too."

Suddenly there was a cry. Around the bend of the road in front of them came a cloud of dust. From it emerged a horse's head.

"Hello, hello, there's something."

"Remember, we are not to fire first."

"Perhaps that's Hooven; I can't see. Is it? There only seems to be one horse."

"Too much dust for one horse."

Annixter, who had taken his field glasses from Harran, adjusted them to his eyes.

"That's not them," he announced presently, "nor Hooven either. That's a cart." Then after another moment, he added, "The butcher's cart from Guadalajara."

The tension was relaxed. The men drew long breaths, settling back in their places.

"Do we let him go on, Governor?"

"The bridge is down. He can't go by and we must not let him go back. We shall have to detain him and question him. I wonder the marshal let him pass."

The cart approached at a lively trot.

"Anybody else in that cart, Mr. Annixter?" asked Magnus. "Look carefully. It may be a ruse. It is strange the marshal should have let him pass."

The Leaguers roused themselves again. Osterman laid his hand on his revolver.

"No," called Annixter, in another instant, "no, there's only one man in it."

The cart came up, and Cutter and Phelps, clambering from the ditch, stopped it as it arrived in front of the party.

"Hey—what—what?" exclaimed the young butcher, pulling up. "Is that bridge broke?"

But at the idea of being held, the boy protested at top

voice, badly frightened, bewildered, not knowing what was to happen next.

"No, no, I got my meat to deliver. Say, you let me go. Say, I ain't got nothing to do with you."

He tugged at the reins, trying to turn the cart about. Cutter, with his jack-knife, parted the reins just back of the bit.

"You'll stay where you are, m' son, for a while. We're not going to hurt you. But you are not going back to town till we say so. Did you pass anybody on the road out of town?"

In reply to the Leaguers' questions, the young butcher at last told them he had passed a two-horse buggy and a lot of men on horseback just beyond the railroad tracks. They were headed for Los Muertos.

"That's them, all right," muttered Annixter. "They're coming by this road, sure."

The butcher's horse and cart were led to one side of the road, and the horse tied to the fence with one of the severed lines. The butcher, himself, was passed over to Presley, who locked him in Hooven's barn.

"Well, what the devil," demanded Osterman, "has become of Bismarck?"

In fact, the butcher had seen nothing of Hooven. The minutes were passing, and still he failed to appear.

"What's he up to, anyways?"

"Bet you what you like, they caught him. Just like that crazy Dutchman to get excited and go too near. You can always depend on Hooven to lose his head."

Five minutes passed, then ten. The road towards Guadalajara lay empty, baking and white under the sun.

"Well, the marshal and S. Behrman don't seem to be in any hurry, either."

"Shall I go forward and reconnoitre, Governor?" asked Harran.

But Dabney, who stood next to Annixter, touched him on the shoulder and, without speaking, pointed down the road. Annixter looked, then suddenly cried out:

"Here comes Hooven."

The German galloped into sight, around the turn of the road, his rifle laid across his saddle. He came on rapidly, pulled up, and dismounted at the ditch.

"Dey're commen," he cried, trembling with excitement. "I watch um long dime bei der side oaf der roadt in der busches. Dey shtop bei der gate oder side der relroadt trecks and talk long dime mit one n'udder. Den dey gome on. Dey're gowun sure do zum monkey-doodle pizeness. Me, I see Gritschun put der kertridges in his guhn. I tink dey gowun to gome *my* blace first. Dey gowun to try put me off, tek my home, bei Gott."

"All right, get down in here and keep quiet, Hooven. Don't fire unless——"

"Here they are."

A half-dozen voices uttered the cry at once.

There could be no mistake this time. A buggy, drawn by two horses, came into view around the curve of the road. Three riders accompanied it, and behind these, seen at intervals in a cloud of dust were two—three—five—six others.

This, then, was S. Behrman with the United States marshal and his posse. The event that had been so long in preparation, the event which it had been said would never come to pass, the last trial of strength, the last fight between the Trust and the People, the direct, brutal grapple of armed men, the law defied, the Government ignored, behold, here it was close at hand.

Osterman cocked his revolver, and in the profound silence that had fallen upon the scene, the click was plainly audible from end to end of the line.

"Remember our agreement, gentlemen," cried Magnus, in a warning voice. "Mr. Osterman, I must ask you to let down the hammer of your weapon."

No one answered. In absolute quiet, standing motionless in their places, the Leaguers watched the approach of the marshal.

Five minutes passed. The riders came on steadily. They drew nearer. The grind of the buggy wheels in the grit and dust of the road, and the prolonged clatter of the horses' feet began to make itself heard. The Leaguers could distinguish the faces of their enemies.

In the buggy were S. Behrman and Cyrus Ruggles, the latter driving. A tall man in a frock coat and slouched hat—the marshal, beyond question—rode at the left of the buggy;

Delaney, carrying a Winchester, at the right. Christian, the real estate broker, S. Behrman's cousin, also with a rifle, could be made out just behind the marshal. Back of these, riding well up, was a group of horsemen, indistinguishable in the dust raised by the buggy's wheels.

Steadily the distance between the Leaguers and the posse diminished.

"Don't let them get too close, Governor," whispered Harran.

When S. Behrman's buggy was about one hundred yards distant from the irrigating ditch, Magnus sprang out upon the road, leaving his revolvers behind him. He beckoned Garnett and Gethings to follow, and the three ranchers, who, with the exception of Broderson, were the oldest men present, advanced, without arms, to meet the marshal.

Magnus cried aloud:

"Halt where you are."

From their places in the ditch, Annixter, Osterman, Dabney, Harran, Hooven, Broderson, Cutter, and Phelps, their hands laid upon their revolvers, watched silently, alert, keen, ready for anything.

At the Governor's words, they saw Ruggles pull sharply on the reins. The buggy came to a standstill, the riders doing likewise. Magnus approached the marshal, still followed by Garnett and Gethings, and began to speak. His voice was audible to the men in the ditch, but his words could not be made out. They heard the marshal reply quietly enough and the two shook hands. Delaney came around from the side of the buggy, his horse standing before the team across the road. He leaned from the saddle, listening to what was being said, but made no remark. From time to time, S. Behrman and Ruggles, from their seats in the buggy, interposed a sentence or two in to the conversation, but at first, so far as the Leaguers could discern, neither Magnus nor the marshal paid them any attention. They saw, however, that the latter repeatedly shook his head and once they heard him exclaim in a loud voice:

"I only know my duty, Mr. Derrick."

Then Gethings turned about, and seeing Delaney close at hand, addressed an unheard remark to him. The cow-puncher replied curtly and the words seemed to anger Gethings. He made a gesture, pointing back to the ditch, showing the in-trenched Leaguers to the posse. Delaney appeared to com-municate the news that the Leaguers were on hand and prepared to resist, to the other members of the party. They all looked toward the ditch and plainly saw the ranchers there, standing to their arms.

But meanwhile Ruggles had addressed himself more di-rectly to Magnus, and between the two an angry discussion was going forward. Once even Harran heard his father exclaim:

"The statement is a lie and no one knows it better than yourself."

"Here," growled Annixter to Dabney, who stood next him in the ditch, "those fellows are getting too close. Look at them edging up. Don't Magnus see that?"

The other members of the marshal's force had come for-ward from their places behind the buggy and were spread out across the road. Some of them were gathered about Magnus, Garnett, and Gethings; and some were talking to-gether, looking and pointing towards the ditch. Whether acting upon signal or not, the Leaguers in the ditch could not tell, but it was certain that one or two of the posse had moved considerably forward. Besides this, Delaney had now placed his horse between Magnus and the ditch, and two others riding up from the rear had followed his example. The posse surrounded the three ranchers, and, by now, ev-erybody was talking at once.

"Look here," Harran called to Annixter, "this won't do. I don't like the looks of this thing. They all seem to be edging up, and before we know it they may take the Governor and the other men prisoners."

"They ought to come back," declared Annixter.

"Somebody ought to tell them that those fellows are creep-ing up."

By now, the angry argument between the Governor and Ruggles had become more heated than ever. Their voices were raised; now and then they made furious gestures.

"They ought to come back," cried Osterman. "We couldn't shoot now if anything should happen, for fear of hitting them."

"Well, it sounds as though something were going to happen pretty soon."

They could hear Gethings and Delaney wrangling furiously; another deputy joined in.

"I'm going to call the Governor back," exclaimed Annixter, suddenly, clambering out of the ditch.

"No, no," cried Osterman, "keep in the ditch. They can't drive us out if we keep here."

Hooven and Harran, who had instinctively followed Annixter, hesitated at Osterman's words and the three halted irresolutely on the road before the ditch, their weapons in their hands.

"Governor," shouted Harran, "come on back. You can't do anything."

Still the wrangle continued, and one of the deputies, advancing a little from out the group, cried out:

"Keep back there! Keep back there, you!"

"Go to hell, will you?" shouted Harran on the instant. "You're on my land."

"Oh, come back here, Harran," called Osterman. "That ain't going to do any good."

"There—listen," suddenly exclaimed Harran. "The Governor is calling us. Come on; I'm going."

Osterman got out of the ditch and came forward, catching Harran by the arm and pulling him back.

"He didn't call. Don't get excited. You'll ruin everything. Get back into the ditch again."

But Cutter, Phelps, and the old man Dabney, misunderstanding what was happening, and seeing Osterman leave the ditch, had followed his example. All the Leaguers were now out of the ditch, and a little way down the road, Hooven, Osterman, Annixter, and Harran in front, Dabney, Phelps, and Cutter coming up from behind.

"Keep back, you," cried the deputy again.

In the group around S. Behrman's buggy, Gethings and Delaney were yet quarrelling, and the angry debate between Magnus, Garnett, and the marshall still continued.

Till this moment, the real estate broker, Christian, had taken no part in the argument, but had kept himself in the rear of the buggy. Now, however, he pushed forward. There was but little room for him to pass, and, as he rode by the buggy, his horse scraped his flank against the hub of the wheel. The animal recoiled sharply, and, striking against Garnett, threw him to the ground. Delaney's horse stood between the buggy and the Leaguers gathered on the road in front of the ditch; the incident, indistinctly seen by them, was misinterpreted.

Garnett had not yet risen when Hooven raised a great shout:

"Hoch, der Kaiser! Hoch, der Vaterland!"

With the words, he dropped to one knee, and sighting his rifle carefully, fired into the group of men around the buggy.

Instantly the revolvers and rifles seemed to go off of themselves. Both sides, deputies and Leaguers, opened fire simultaneously. At first, it was nothing but a confused roar of explosions; then the roar lapsed to an irregular, quick succession of reports, shot leaping after shot; then a moment's silence, and, last of all, regular as clock-ticks, three shots at exact intervals. Then stillness.

Delaney, shot through the stomach, slid down from his horse, and, on his hands and knees, crawled from the road into the standing wheat. Christian fell backward from the saddle toward the buggy, and hung suspended in that position, his head and shoulders on the wheel, one stiff leg still across his saddle. Hooven, in attempting to rise from his kneeling position, received a rifle ball squarely in the throat, and rolled forward upon his face. Old Broderson, crying out, "Oh, they've shot me, boys," staggered sideways, his head bent, his hands rigid at his sides, and fell into the ditch. Osterman, blood running from his mouth and nose, turned about and walked back. Presley helped him across the irrigating ditch and Osterman laid himself down, his head on his folded arms. Harran Derrick dropped where he stood, turning over on his face, and lay motionless, groaning terribly, a pool of blood forming under his stomach. The old man Dabney, silent as ever, received his death, speechless. He fell to his knees, got up again, fell once more, and died without a word. Annixter, instantly killed, fell his length to the ground, and lay without movement, just as he had fallen, one arm across his face.

VII

ON THEIR WAY to Derrick's ranch house, Hilma and Mrs. Derrick heard the sounds of distant firing.

"Stop!" cried Hilma, laying her hand upon young Vacca's arm. "Stop the horses. Listen, what was that?"

The carry-all came to a halt and from far away across the rustling wheat came the faint rattle of rifles and revolvers.

"Say," cried Vacca, rolling his eyes, "oh, say, they're fighting over there."

Mrs. Derrick put her hands over her face.

"Fighting," she cried, "oh, oh, it's terrible. Magnus is there—and Harran."

"Where do you think it is?" demanded Hilma.

"That's over toward Hooven's."

"I'm going. Turn back. Drive to Hooven's, quick."

"Better not, Mrs. Annixter," protested the young man. "Mr. Annixter said we were to go to Derrick's. Better keep away from Hooven's if there's trouble there. We wouldn't get there till it's all over, anyhow."

"Yes, yes, let's go home," cried Mrs. Derrick, "I'm afraid. Oh, Hilma, I'm afraid."

"Come with me to Hooven's then."

"There, where they are fighting? Oh, I couldn't. I—I can't. It would be all over before we got there as Mr. Vacca says."

"Sure," repeated young Vacca.

"Drive to Hooven's," commanded Hilma. "If you won't, I'll walk there." She threw off the lap-robes, preparing to descend. "And you," she exclaimed, turning to Mrs. Derrick, "how *can* you—when Harran and your husband may be—may—are in danger."

Grumbling, Vacca turned the carry-all about and drove across the open fields till he reached the road to Guadalajara, just below the Mission.

"Hurry!" cried Hilma.

The horses started forward under the touch of the whip. The ranch houses of Quien Sabe came in sight.

"Do you want to stop at the house?" inquired Vacca over his shoulder.

"No, no; oh, go faster—make the horses run."

They dashed through the houses of the Home ranch.

"Oh, oh," cried Hilma suddenly, "look, look there. Look what they have done."

Vacca pulled the horses up, for the road in front of Annixter's house was blocked.

A vast, confused heap of household effects was there—chairs, sofas, pictures, fixtures, lamps. Hilma's little home had been gutted; everything had been taken from it and ruthlessly flung out upon the road, everything that she and her husband had bought during that wonderful week after their marriage. Here was the white enamelled "set" of the bedroom furniture, the three chairs, washstand and bureau,—the bureau drawers falling out, spilling their contents into the dust; there were the white wool rugs of the sitting-room, the flower stand, with its pots all broken, its flowers wilting; the cracked goldfish globe, the fishes already dead; the rocking chair, the sewing machine, the great round table of yellow oak, the lamp with its deep shade of crinkly red tissue paper, the pretty tinted photographs that had hung on the wall—the choir boys with beautiful eyes, the pensive young girls in pink gowns—the pieces of wood carving that represented quails and ducks, and, last of all, its curtains of crisp, clean muslin, cruelly torn and crushed—the bed, the wonderful canopied bed so brave and gay, of which Hilma had been so proud, thrust out there into the common road, torn from its place, from the discreet intimacy of her bridal chamber, violated, profaned, flung out into the dust and garish sunshine for all men to stare at, a mockery and a shame.

To Hilma it was as though something of herself, of her person, had been thus exposed and degraded; all that she held sacred pilloried, gibbeted, and exhibited to the world's derision. Tears of anguish sprang to her eyes, a red flame of outraged modesty overspread her face.

"Oh," she cried, a sob catching her throat, "oh, how could they do it?" But other fears intruded; other greater terrors impended.

"Go on," she cried to Vacca, "go on quickly."

But Vacca would go no further. He had seen what had escaped Hilma's attention, two men, deputies, no doubt, on the porch of the ranch house. They held possession there, and the evidence of the presence of the enemy in this raid upon Quien Sabe had daunted him.

"No, *sir*," he declared, getting out of the carry-all, "I ain't going to take you anywhere where you're liable to get hurt. Besides, the road's blocked by all this stuff. You can't get the team by."

Hilma sprang from the carry-all.

"Come," she said to Mrs. Derrick.

The older woman, trembling, hesitating, faint with dread, obeyed, and Hilma, picking her way through and around the wreck of her home, set off by the trail towards the Long Trestle and Hooven's.

When she arrived, she found the road in front of the German's house, and, indeed, all the surrounding yard, crowded with people. An overturned buggy lay on the side of the road in the distance, its horses in a tangle of harness, held by two or three men. She saw Caraher's buckboard under the live oak and near it a second buggy which she recognised as belonging to a doctor in Guadalajara.

"Oh, what has happened; oh, what has happened?" moaned Mrs. Derrick.

"Come," repeated Hilma. The young girl took her by the hand and together they pushed their way through the crowd of men and women and entered the yard.

The throng gave way before the two women, parting to right and left without a word.

"Presley," cried Mrs. Derrick, as she caught sight of him in the doorway of the house, "oh, Presley, what has happened? Is Harran safe? Is Magnus safe? Where are they?"

"Don't go in, Mrs. Derrick," said Presley, coming forward, "don't go in."

"Where is my husband?" demanded Hilma.

Presley turned away and steadied himself against the jamb of the door.

Hilma, leaving Mrs. Derrick, entered the house. The front room was full of men. She was dimly conscious of Cyrus Ruggles and S. Behrman, both deadly pale, talking earnestly and in whispers to Cutter and Phelps. There was a strange, acrid odour of an unfamiliar drug in the air. On the table before her was a satchel, surgical instruments, rolls of bandages, and a blue, oblong paper box full of cotton. But above the hushed noises of voices and footsteps, one terrible sound made itself heard—the prolonged, rasping sound of breathing, half choked, laboured, agonised.

"Where is my husband?" she cried. She pushed the men aside. She saw Magnus, bareheaded, three or four men lying on the floor, one half naked, his body swathed in white bandages; the doctor in shirt sleeves, on one knee beside a figure of a man stretched out beside him.

Garnett turned a white face to her.

"Where is my husband?"

The other did not reply, but stepped aside and Hilma saw the dead body of her husband lying upon the bed. She did not cry out. She said no word. She went to the bed, and sitting upon it, took Annixter's head in her lap, holding it gently between her hands. Thereafter she did not move, but sat holding her dead husband's head in her lap, looking vaguely about from face to face of those in the room, while, without a sob, without a cry, the great tears filled her wide-opened eyes and rolled slowly down upon her cheeks.

On hearing that his wife was outside, Magnus came quickly forward. She threw herself into his arms.

"Tell me, tell me," she cried, "is Harran—is——"

"We don't know yet," he answered. "Oh, Annie——"

Then suddenly the Governor checked himself. He, the indomitable, could not break down now.

"The doctor is with him," he said; "we are doing all we can. Try and be brave, Annie. There is always hope. This is a terrible day's work. God forgive us all."

She pressed forward, but he held her back.

"No, don't see him now. Go into the next room. Garnett, take care of her."

But she would not be denied. She pushed by Magnus, and, breaking through the group that surrounded her son, sank on her knees beside him, moaning, in compassion and terror.

Harran lay straight and rigid upon the floor, his head propped by a pillow, his coat that had been taken off spread over his chest. One leg of his trousers was soaked through and through with blood. His eyes were half-closed, and with the regularity of a machine, the eyeballs twitched and twitched. His face was so white that it made his yellow hair look brown, while from his opened mouth, there issued that loud and terrible sound of guttering, rasping, laboured breathing that gagged and choked and gurgled with every inhalation.

"Oh, Harrie, Harrie," called Mrs. Derrick, catching at one of his hands.

The doctor shook his head.

"He is unconscious, Mrs. Derrick."

"Where was he—where is—the—the——"

"Through the lungs."

"Will he get well? Tell me the truth."

"I don't know, Mrs. Derrick."

She had all but fainted, and the old rancher, Garnett, half-carrying, half-leading her, took her to the one adjoining room—Minna Hooven's bedchamber. Dazed, numb with fear, she sat down on the edge of the bed, rocking herself back and forth, murmuring:

"Harrie, Harrie, oh, my son, my little boy."

In the outside room, Presley came and went, doing what he could to be of service, sick with horror, trembling from head to foot.

The surviving members of both Leaguers and deputies—the warring factions of the Railroad and the People—mingled together now with no thought of hostility. Presley helped the doctor to cover Christian's body. S. Behrman and Ruggles held bowls of water while Osterman was attended to. The horror of that dreadful business had driven all other considerations from the mind. The sworn foes of the last hour had no thought of anything but to care for those whom, in their fury, they had shot down. The marshal, abandoning for that day the attempt to serve the writs, departed for San Francisco.

The bodies had been brought in from the road where they fell. Annixter's corpse had been laid upon the bed; those of Dabney and Hooven, whose wounds had all been in the face and head, were covered with a tablecloth. Upon the floor, places were made for the others. Cutter and Ruggles rode

into Guadalajara to bring out the doctor there, and to telephone to Bonneville for others.

Osterman had not at any time since the shooting, lost
consciousness. He lay upon the floor of Hooven's house,
bare to the waist, bandages of adhesive tape reeved about his
abdomen and shoulder. His eyes were half-closed. Presley,
who looked after him, pending the arrival of a hack from
Bonneville that was to take him home, knew that he was in
agony.

But this poser, this silly fellow, this cracker of jokes, whom
no one had ever taken very seriously, at the last redeemed
himself. When at length, the doctor had arrived, he had, for
the first time, opened his eyes.

"I can wait," he said. "Take Harran first."

And when at length, his turn had come, and while the
sweat rolled from his forehead as the doctor began probing
for the bullet, he had reached out his free arm and taken
Presley's hand in his, gripping it harder and harder, as the
probe entered the wound. His breath came short through
his nostrils; his face, the face of a comic actor, with its high
cheek bones, bald forehead, and salient ears, grew paler and
paler, his great slit of a mouth shut tight, but he uttered no
groan.

When the worst anguish was over and he could find breath
to speak, his first words had been:

"Were any of the others badly hurt?"

As Presley stood by the door of the house after bringing in
a pail of water for the doctor, he was aware of a party of men
who had struck off from the road on the other side of the
irrigating ditch and were advancing cautiously into the field
of wheat. He wondered what it meant and Cutter, coming up
at that moment, Presley asked him if he knew.

"It's Delaney," said Cutter. "It seems that when he was
shot he crawled off into the wheat. They are looking for him
there."

Presley had forgotten all about the buster and had only a
vague recollection of seeing him slide from his horse at the
beginning of the fight. Anxious to know what had become of
him, he hurried up and joined the party of searchers.

"We better look out," said one of the young men, "how we

go fooling around in here. If he's alive yet he's just as liable as not to think we're after him and take a shot at us."

"I guess there ain't much fight left in him," another answered. "Look at the wheat here."

"Lord! He's bled like a stuck pig."

"Here's his hat," abruptly exclaimed the leader of the party. "He can't be far off. Let's call him."

They called repeatedly without getting any answer, then proceeded cautiously. All at once the men in advance stopped so suddenly that those following carromed against them. There was an outburst of exclamation.

"Here he is!"

"Good Lord! Sure, that's him."

"Poor fellow, poor fellow."

The cow-puncher lay on his back, deep in the wheat, his knees drawn up, his eyes wide open, his lips brown. Rigidly gripped in one hand was his empty revolver.

The men, farm hands from the neighbouring ranches, young fellows from Guadalajara, drew back in instinctive repulsion. One at length ventured near, peering down into the face.

"Is he dead?" inquired those in the rear.

"*I* don't know."

"Well, put your hand on his heart."

"No! I—I don't want to."

"What you afraid of?"

"Well, I just don't want to touch him, that's all. It's bad luck. *You* feel his heart."

"You can't always tell by that."

"How can you tell, then? Pshaw, you fellows make me sick. Here, let me get there. I'll do it."

There was a long pause, as the other bent down and laid his hand on the cow-puncher's breast.

"Well?"

"I can't tell. Sometimes I think I feel it beat and sometimes I don't. I never saw a dead man before."

"Well, you can't tell by the heart."

"What's the good of talking so blame much. Dead or not, let's carry him back to the house."

Two or three ran back to the road for planks from the

broken bridge. When they returned with these a litter was improvised, and throwing their coats over the body, the party carried it back to the road. The doctor was summoned and declared the cow-puncher to have been dead over half an hour.

"What did I tell you?" exclaimed one of the group.

"Well, I never said he wasn't dead," protested the other. "I only said you couldn't always tell by whether his heart beat or not."

But all at once there was a commotion. The wagon containing Mrs. Hooven, Minna, and little Hilda drove up.

"Eh, den, my men," cried Mrs. Hooven, wildly interrogating the faces of the crowd. "Whadt has happun? Sey, den, dose vellers, hev dey hurdt my men, eh, whadt?"

She sprang from the wagon, followed by Minna with Hilda in her arms. The crowd bore back as they advanced, staring at them in silence.

"Eh, whadt has happun, whadt has happun?" wailed Mrs. Hooven, as she hurried on, her two hands out before her, the fingers spread wide. "Eh, Hooven, eh, my men, are you alle righdt?"

She burst into the house. Hooven's body had been removed to an adjoining room, the bedroom of the house, and to this room Mrs. Hooven—Minna still at her heels—proceeded, guided by an instinct born of the occasion. Those in the outside room, saying no word, made way for them. They entered, closing the door behind them, and through all the rest of that terrible day, no sound nor sight of them was had by those who crowded into and about that house of death. Of all the main actors of the tragedy of the fight in the ditch, they remained the least noted, obtruded themselves the least upon the world's observation. They were, for the moment, forgotten.

But by now Hooven's house was the centre of an enormous crowd. A vast concourse of people from Bonneville, from Guadalajara, from the ranches, swelled by the thousands who had that morning participated in the rabbit drive, surged about the place; men and women, young boys, young girls, farm hands, villagers, townspeople, ranchers, railroad employees, Mexicans, Spaniards, Portuguese. Presley, returning from the search for Delaney's body, had to fight his way to the house again.

And from all this multitude there rose an indefinable murmur. As yet, there was no menace in it, no anger. It was confusion merely, bewilderment, the first long-drawn "oh!" that greets the news of some great tragedy. The people had taken no thought as yet. Curiosity was their dominant impulse. Every one wanted to see what had been done; failing that, to hear of it, and failing that, to be near the scene of the affair. The crowd of people packed the road in front of the house for nearly a quarter of a mile in either direction. They balanced themselves upon the lower strands of the barbed wire fence in their effort to see over each others' shoulders; they stood on the seats of their carts, buggies, and farm wagons, a few even upon the saddles of their riding horses. They crowded, pushed, struggled, surged forward and back without knowing why, converging incessantly upon Hooven's house.

When, at length, Presley got to the gate, he found a carry-all drawn up before it. Between the gate and the door of the house a lane had been formed, and as he paused there a moment, a group of Leaguers, among whom were Garnett and Gethings, came slowly from the door carrying old Broderson in their arms. The doctor, bareheaded and in his shirt sleeves, squinting in the sunlight, attended them, repeating at every step:

"Slow, slow, take it easy, gentlemen."

Old Broderson was unconscious. His face was not pale, no bandages could be seen. With infinite precautions, the men bore him to the carry-all and deposited him on the back seat; the rain flaps were let down on one side to shut off the gaze of the multitude.

But at this point a moment of confusion ensued. Presley, because of half a dozen people who stood in his way, could not see what was going on. There were exclamations, hurried movements. The doctor uttered a sharp command and a man ran back to the house, returning on the instant with the doctor's satchel. By this time, Presley was close to the wheels of the carry-all and could see the doctor inside the vehicle bending over old Broderson.

"Here it is, here it is," exclaimed the man who had been sent to the house.

"I won't need it," answered the doctor, "he's dying now."

At the words a great hush widened throughout the throng near at hand. Some men took off their hats.

"Stand back," protested the doctor quietly, "stand back, good people, please."

The crowd bore back a little. In the silence, a woman began to sob. The seconds passed, then a minute. The horses of the carry-all shifted their feet and whisked their tails, driving off the flies. At length, the doctor got down from the carry-all, letting down the rain-flaps on that side as well.

"Will somebody go home with the body?" he asked. Gethings stepped forward and took his place by the driver. The carry-all drove away.

Presley reëntered the house. During his absence it had been cleared of all but one or two of the Leaguers, who had taken part in the fight. Hilma still sat on the bed with Annixter's head in her lap. S. Behrman, Ruggles, and all the railroad party had gone. Osterman had been taken away in a hack and the tablecloth over Dabney's body replaced with a sheet. But still unabated, agonised, raucous, came the sounds of Harran's breathing. Everything possible had already been done. For the moment it was out of the question to attempt to move him. His mother and father were at his side, Magnus, with a face of stone, his look fixed on those persistently twitching eyes, Annie Derrick crouching at her son's side, one of his hands in hers, fanning his face continually with the crumbled sheet of an old newspaper.

Presley on tip-toes joined the group, looking on attentively. One of the surgeons who had been called from Bonneville stood close by, watching Harran's face, his arms folded.

"How is he?" Presley whispered.

"He won't live," the other responded.

By degrees the choke and gurgle of the breathing became more irregular and the lids closed over the twitching eyes. All at once the breath ceased. Magnus shot an inquiring glance at the surgeon.

"He is dead, Mr. Derrick," the surgeon replied.

Annie Derrick, with a cry that rang through all the house,

stretched herself over the body of her son, her head upon his breast, and the Governor's great shoulders bowed never to rise again.

"God help me and forgive me," he groaned.

Presley rushed from the house, beside himself with grief, with horror, with pity, and with mad, insensate rage. On the porch outside Caraher met him.

"Is he—is he—" began the saloon-keeper.

"Yes, he's dead," cried Presley. "They're all dead, murdered, shot down, dead, dead, all of them. Whose turn is next?"

"That's the way they killed my wife, Presley."

"Caraher," cried Presley, "give me your hand. I've been wrong all the time. The League is wrong. All the world is wrong. You are the only one of us all who is right. I'm with you from now on. *By God, I too, I'm a Red!*"

In course of time, a farm wagon from Bonneville arrived at Hooven's. The bodies of Annixter and Harran were placed in it, and it drove down the Lower Road towards the Los Muertos ranch houses.

The bodies of Delaney and Christian had already been carried to Guadalajara and thence taken by train to Bonneville.

Hilma followed the farm wagon in the Derricks' carry-all, with Magnus and his wife. During all that ride none of them spoke a word. It had been arranged that, since Quien Sabe was in the hands of the Railroad, Hilma should come to Los Muertos. To that place also Annixter's body was carried.

Later on in the day, when it was almost evening, the undertaker's black wagon passed the Derricks' Home ranch on its way from Hooven's and turned into the county road towards Bonneville. The initial excitement of the affair of the irrigating ditch had died down; the crowd long since had dispersed. By the time the wagon passed Caraher's saloon, the sun had set. Night was coming on.

And the black wagon went on through the darkness, unattended, ignored, solitary, carrying the dead body of Dabney, the silent old man of whom nothing was known but his name, who made no friends, whom nobody knew or spoke to, who had come from no one knew whence and who went no one knew whither.

Towards midnight of that same day, Mrs. Dyke was awakened by the sounds of groaning in the room next to hers. Magnus Derrick was not so occupied by Harran's death that he could not think of others who were in distress, and when he had heard that Mrs. Dyke and Sidney, like Hilma, had been turned out of Quien Sabe, he had thrown open Los Muertos to them.

"Though," he warned them, "it is precarious hospitality at the best."

Until late, Mrs. Dyke had sat up with Hilma, comforting her as best she could, rocking her to and fro in her arms, crying with her, trying to quiet her, for once having given way to her grief, Hilma wept with a terrible anguish and a violence that racked her from head to foot, and at last, worn out, a little child again, had sobbed herself to sleep in the older woman's arms, and as a little child, Mrs. Dyke had put her to bed and had retired herself.

Aroused a few hours later by the sounds of a distress that was physical, as well as mental, Mrs. Dyke hurried into Hilma's room, carrying the lamp with her.

Mrs. Dyke needed no enlightenment. She woke Presley and besought him to telephone to Bonneville at once, summoning a doctor. That night Hilma in great pain suffered a miscarriage.

Presley did not close his eyes once during the night; he did not even remove his clothes. Long after the doctor had departed and that house of tragedy had quieted down, he still remained in his place by the open window of his little room, looking off across the leagues of growing wheat, watching the slow kindling of the dawn. Horror weighed intolerably upon him. Monstrous things, huge, terrible, whose names he knew only too well, whirled at a gallop through his imagination, or rose spectral and grisly before the eyes of his mind. Harran dead, Annixter dead, Broderson dead, Osterman, perhaps, even at that moment dying. Why, these men had made up his world. Annixter had been his best friend, Harran, his almost daily companion; Broderson and Osterman were familiar to him as brothers. They were all his associates, his good friends, the group was his environment, belonging to his daily life. And he, standing there in the dust of the road by the irrigating ditch, had seen them shot. He found himself suddenly at his table, the candle burning at his elbow, his journal before him, writing swiftly, the desire for expression, the craving for outlet to the thoughts that clamoured tumultuous at his brain, never more insistent, more imperious. Thus he wrote:

"Dabney dead, Hooven dead, Harran dead, Annixter dead, Broderson dead, Osterman dying, S. Behrman alive, successful; the Railroad in possession of Quien Sabe. I saw them shot. Not twelve hours since I stood there at the irrigating ditch. Ah, that terrible moment of horror and confusion! powder smoke—flashing pistol barrels—blood stains—rearing horses—men staggering to their death—Christian in a horrible posture, one rigid leg high in the air across his saddle—Broderson falling sideways into the ditch—Osterman laying himself down, his head on his arms, as if tired, tired out. These things, I have seen them. The picture of this day's work is from henceforth part of my mind, part of *me*. They have done it, S. Behrman and the owners of the railroad have done it, while all the world looked on, while the people of these United States looked on. Oh, come now and try your theories upon us, us of the ranchos, us, who have suffered, us, who *know*. Oh, talk to *us* now of the 'rights of Capital,' talk to *us* of the Trust, talk to *us* of the 'equilibrium between the classes.' Try your ingenious ideas upon us. *We Know.* I cannot tell whether or not your theories are excellent. I do not know if your ideas are plausible. I do not know how practical is your scheme of society. I do not know if the Railroad has a right to our lands, but I *do* know that Harran is dead, that Annixter is dead, that Broderson is dead, that Hooven is dead, that Osterman is dying, and that S. Behrman is alive, successful, triumphant; that he has ridden into possession of a principality over the dead bodies of five men shot down by his hired associates.

"I can see the outcome. The Railroad will prevail. The Trust will overpower us. Here in this corner of a great nation, here, on the edge of the continent, here, in this valley of the West, far from the great centres, isolated, remote, lost, the great iron hand crushes life from us, crushes liberty and the pursuit of happiness from us, and our little struggles, our moment's convulsion of death agony causes not one jar in the vast, clashing machinery of the nation's life; a fleck of grit in the wheels, perhaps, a grain of sand in the cogs—the momentary creak of the axle is the mother's wail of bereavement, the wife's cry of anguish—and the great wheel turns, spinning smooth again, even again, and the tiny impediment of a second, scarce noticed, is forgotten. Make the people believe that the faint tremour in their great engine is a menace to its function? What a folly to think of it. Tell them of the danger and they will laugh at you. Tell them, five years from now, the story of the fight between the League of the San Joaquin and the Railroad and it will not be believed. What! a pitched battle between Farmer and Railroad, a battle that cost the lives of seven men? Impossible, it could not have happened. Your story is fiction—is exaggerated.

"Yet it is Lexington—God help us, God enlighten us, God rouse us from our lethargy—it is Lexington; farmers with guns in their hands fighting for Liberty. Is our State of California the only one that has its ancient and hereditary foe? Are there no other Trusts between the oceans than this of the Pacific and Southwestern Railroad? Ask yourselves, you of the Middle West, ask yourselves, you of the North, ask yourselves, you of the East, ask yourselves, you of the South—ask yourselves, every citizen of every State from Maine to Mexico, from the Dakotas to the Carolinas, have you not the monster in your boundaries? If it is not a Trust of transportation, it is only another head of the same Hydra. Is not our death struggle typical? Is it not one of many, is it not symbolical of the great and terrible conflict that is going on everywhere in these United States? Ah, you people, blind, bound, tricked, betrayed, can you not see it? Can you not see how the monsters have plundered your treasures and holding them in the grip of their iron claws, dole them out to you only at the price of your blood, at the price of the lives of your wives and your little children? You give your babies to Moloch for the loaf of bread you have kneaded yourselves. You offer your starved wives to Juggernaut for the iron nail you have yourselves compounded."

He spent the night over his journal, writing down such thoughts as these or walking the floor from wall to wall, or, seized at times with unreasoning horror and blind rage, flinging himself face downward upon his bed, vowing with inarticulate cries that neither S. Behrman nor Shelgrim should ever live to consummate their triumph.

Morning came and with it the daily papers and news. Presley did not even glance at the "Mercury." Bonneville published two other daily journals that professed to voice the will and reflect the temper of the people and these he read eagerly.

Osterman was yet alive and there were chances of his recovery. The League—some three hundred of its members had gathered at Bonneville over night and were patrolling the streets and, still resolved to keep the peace, were even guarding the railroad shops and buildings. Furthermore, the Leaguers had issued manifestoes, urging all citizens to preserve law and order, yet summoning an indignation meeting to be convened that afternoon at the City Opera House.

It appeared from the newspapers that those who obstructed the marshal in the discharge of his duty could be proceeded against by the District Attorney on information or by bringing the matter before the Grand Jury. But the Grand Jury was not at that time in session, and it was known that there were no funds in the marshal's office to pay expenses for the summoning of jurors or the serving of processes. S. Behrman and Ruggles in interviews stated that the Railroad withdrew entirely from the fight; the matter now, according to them, was between the Leaguers and the United States Government; they washed their hands of the whole business. The ranchers could settle with Washington. But it seemed that Congress had recently forbade the use of troops for civil purposes; the whole matter of the League-Railroad contest was evidently for the moment to be left in *statu quo*.

But to Presley's mind the most important piece of news that morning was the report of the action of the Railroad upon hearing of the battle.

Instantly Bonneville had been isolated. Not a single local train was running, not one of the through trains made any halt at the station. The mails were not moved. Further than this, by some arrangement difficult to understand, the telegraph operators at Bonneville and Guadalajara, acting under orders, refused to receive any telegrams except those emanating from railway officials. The story of the fight, the story creating the first impression, was to be told to San Francisco and the outside world by S. Behrman, Ruggles, and the local P. and S. W. agents.

An hour before breakfast, the undertakers arrived and took charge of the bodies of Harran and Annixter. Presley saw neither Hilma, Magnus, nor Mrs. Derrick. The doctor came to look after Hilma. He breakfasted with Mrs. Dyke and Presley, and from him Presley learned that Hilma would recover both from the shock of her husband's death and from her miscarriage of the previous night.

"She ought to have her mother with her," said the physician. "She does nothing but call for her or beg to be allowed to go to her. I have tried to get a wire through to Mrs. Tree, but the company will not take it, and even if I could get word to her, how could she get down here? There are no trains."

But Presley found that it was impossible for him to stay at Los Muertos that day. Gloom and the shadow of tragedy brooded heavy over the place. A great silence pervaded everything, a silence broken only by the subdued coming and going of the undertaker and his assistants. When Presley, having resolved to go into Bonneville, came out through the doorway of the house, he found the undertaker tying a long strip of crape to the bell-handle.

Presley saddled his pony and rode into town. By this time, after long hours of continued reflection upon one subject, a sombre brooding malevolence, a deep-seated desire of revenge, had grown big within his mind. The first numbness had passed off; familiarity with what had been done had blunted the edge of horror, and now the impulse of retaliation prevailed. At first, the sullen anger of defeat, the sense of outrage, had only smouldered, but the more he brooded, the fiercer flamed his rage. Sudden paroxysms of wrath gripped him by the throat; abrupt outbursts of fury injected his eyes with blood. He ground his teeth, his mouth filled with curses, his hands clenched till they grew white and bloodless. Was the Railroad to triumph then in the end? After all those months of preparation, after all those grandiloquent resolutions, after all the arrogant presumption of the League! The League! what a farce; what had it amounted to when the crisis came? Was the Trust to crush them all so easily? Was S. Behrman to swallow Los Muertos? S. Behrman! Presley saw him plainly, huge, rotund, white; saw his jowl tremulous and obese, the roll of fat over his collar sprinkled with sparse hairs, the great stomach with its brown linen vest and heavy watch chain of hollow links, clinking against the buttons of imitation pearl. And this man was to crush Magnus Derrick—had already stamped the life from such men as Harran and Annixter. This man, in the name of the Trust, was to grab Los Muertos as he had grabbed Quien Sabe, and after Los Muertos, Broderson's ranch, then Osterman's, then others, and still others, the whole valley, the whole State.

Presley beat his forehead with his clenched fist as he rode on.

"No," he cried, "no, kill him, kill him, kill him with my hands."

The idea of it put him beside himself. Oh, to sink his fingers deep into the white, fat throat of the man, to clutch like iron into the great puffed jowl of him, to wrench out the life, to batter it out, strangle it out, to pay him back for the long years of extortion and oppression, to square accounts for bribed jurors, bought judges, corrupted legislatures, to have justice for the trick of the Ranchers' Railroad Commission, the charlatanism of the "ten per cent. cut," the ruin of Dyke, the seizure of Quien Sabe, the murder of Harran, the assassination of Annixter!

It was in such mood that he reached Caraher's. The saloon-keeper had just opened his place and was standing in his doorway, smoking his pipe. Presley dismounted and went in and the two had a long talk.

When, three hours later, Presley came out of the saloon and rode on towards Bonneville, his face was very pale, his lips shut tight, resolute, determined. His manner was that of a man whose mind is made up.

The hour for the mass meeting at the Opera House had been set for one o'clock, but long before noon the street in front of the building and, in fact, all the streets in its vicinity, were packed from side to side with a shifting, struggling, surging, and excited multitude. There were few women in the

throng, but hardly a single male inhabitant of either Bonneville or Guadalajara was absent. Men had even come from
Visalia and Pixley. It was no longer the crowd of curiosity
seekers that had thronged around Hooven's place by the irrigating ditch; the People were no longer confused, bewildered.
A full realisation of just what had been done the day before
was clear now in the minds of all. Business was suspended;
nearly all the stores were closed. Since early morning the
members of the League had put in an appearance and rode
from point to point, their rifles across their saddle pommels.
Then, by ten o'clock, the streets had begun to fill up, the
groups on the corners grew and merged into one another;
pedestrians, unable to find room on the sidewalks, took to
the streets. Hourly the crowd increased till shoulders touched
and elbows, till free circulation became impeded, then congested, then impossible. The crowd, a solid mass, was wedged
tight from store front to store front. And from all this throng,
this single unit, this living, breathing organism—the People—there rose a droning, terrible note. It was not yet the
wild, fierce clamour of riot and insurrection, shrill, high
pitched; but it was a beginning, the growl of the awakened
brute, feeling the iron in its flank, heaving up its head with
bared teeth, the throat vibrating to the long, indrawn snarl of
wrath.

Thus the forenoon passed, while the people, their bulk
growing hourly vaster, kept to the streets, moving slowly
backward and forward, oscillating in the grooves of the thoroughfares, the steady, low-pitched growl rising continually
into the hot, still air.

Then, at length, about twelve o'clock, the movement of the
throng assumed definite direction. It set towards the Opera
House. Presley, who had left his pony at the City livery stable, found himself caught in the current and carried slowly
forward in its direction. His arms were pinioned to his sides
by the press, the crush against his body was all but rib-crack-
ing, he could hardly draw his breath. All around him rose and
fell wave after wave of faces, hundreds upon hundreds, thousands upon thousands, red, lowering, sullen. All were set in
one direction and slowly, slowly they advanced, crowding
closer, till they almost touched one another. For reasons that

were inexplicable, great, tumultuous heavings, like ground-swells of an incoming tide, surged over and through the multitude. At times, Presley, lifted from his feet, was swept back, back, back, with the crowd, till the entrance of the Opera House was half a block away; then, the returning billow beat back again and swung him along, gasping, staggering, clutching, till he was landed once more in the vortex of frantic action in front of the foyer. Here the waves were shorter, quicker, the crushing pressure on all sides of his body left him without strength to utter the cry that rose to his lips; then, suddenly the whole mass of struggling, stamping, fighting, writhing men about him seemed, as it were, to rise, to lift, multitudinous, swelling, gigantic. A mighty rush dashed Presley forward in its leap. There was a moment's whirl of confused sights, congested faces, opened mouths, bloodshot eyes, clutching hands; a moment's outburst of furious sound, shouts, cheers, oaths; a moment's jam wherein Presley veritably believed his ribs must snap like pipestems and he was carried, dazed, breathless, helpless, an atom on the crest of a storm-driven wave, up the steps of the Opera House, on into the vestibule, through the doors, and at last into the auditorium of the house itself.

There was a mad rush for places; men disdaining the aisle, stepped from one orchestra chair to another, striding over the backs of seats, leaving the print of dusty feet upon the red plush cushions. In a twinkling the house was filled from stage to topmost gallery. The aisles were packed solid, even on the edge of the stage itself men were sitting, a black fringe on either side of the footlights.

The curtain was up, disclosing a half-set scene,—the flats, leaning at perilous angles,—that represented some sort of terrace, the pavement, alternate squares of black and white marble, while red, white, and yellow flowers were represented as growing from urns and vases. A long, double row of chairs stretched across the scene from wing to wing, flanking a table covered with a red cloth, on which was set a pitcher of water and a speaker's gavel.

Promptly these chairs were filled up with members of the League, the audience cheering as certain well-known figures made their appearance—Garnett of the Ruby ranch, Gethings of the San Pablo, Keast of the ranch of the same name, Chattern of the Bonanza, elderly men, bearded, slow of speech, deliberate.

Garnett opened the meeting; his speech was plain, straightforward, matter-of-fact. He simply told what had happened. He announced that certain resolutions were to be drawn up. He introduced the next speaker.

This one pleaded for moderation. He was conservative. All along he had opposed the idea of armed resistance except as the very last resort. He "deplored" the terrible affair of yesterday. He begged the people to wait in patience, to attempt no more violence. He informed them that armed guards of the League were, at that moment, patrolling Los Muertos, Broderson's, and Osterman's. It was well known that the United States marshal confessed himself powerless to serve the writs. There would be no more bloodshed.

"We have had," he continued, "bloodshed enough, and I want to say right here that I am not so sure but what yesterday's terrible affair might have been avoided. A gentleman whom we all esteem, who from the first has been our recognised leader, is, at this moment, mourning the loss of a young son, killed before his eyes. God knows that I sympathise, as do we all, in the affliction of our President. I am sorry for him. My heart goes out to him in this hour of distress, but, at the same time, the position of the League must be defined. We owe it to ourselves, we owe it to the people of this county. The League armed for the very purposes of preserving the peace, not of breaking it. We believed that with six hundred armed and drilled men at our disposal, ready to muster at a moment's call, we could so overawe any attempt to expel us from our lands that such an attempt would not be made until the cases pending before the Supreme Court had been decided. If when the enemy appeared in our midst yesterday they had been met by six hundred rifles, it is not conceivable that the issue would have been forced. No fight would have ensued, and to-day we would not have to mourn the deaths of four of our fellow-citizens. A mistake has been made and we of the League must not be held responsible."

The speaker sat down amidst loud applause from the Leaguers and less pronounced demonstrations on the part of the audience.

A second Leaguer took his place, a tall, clumsy man, half-rancher, half-politician.

"I want to second what my colleague has just said," he began. "This matter of resisting the marshal when he tried to put the Railroad dummies in possession on the ranches around here, was all talked over in the committee meetings of the League long ago. It never was our intention to fire a single shot. No such absolute authority as was assumed yesterday was delegated to anybody. Our esteemed President is all right, but we all know that he is a man who loves authority and who likes to go his own gait without accounting to anybody. We—the rest of us Leaguers—never were informed as to what was going on. We supposed, of course, that watch was being kept on the Railroad so as we wouldn't be taken by surprise as we were yesterday. And it seems no watch was kept at all, or if there was, it was mighty ineffective. Our idea was to forestall any movement on the part of the Railroad and then when we knew the marshal was coming down, to call a meeting of our Executive Committee and decide as to what should be done. We ought to have had time to call out the whole League. Instead of that, what happens? While we're all off chasing rabbits, the Railroad is allowed to steal a march on us and when it is too late, a handful of Leaguers is got together and a fight is precipitated and our men killed. *I'm* sorry for our President, too. No one is more so, but I want to put myself on record as believing he did a hasty and inconsiderate thing. If he had managed right, he could have had six hundred men to oppose the Railroad and there would not have been any gun fight or any killing. He *didn't* manage right and there *was* a killing and I don't see as how the League ought to be held responsible. The idea of the League, the whole reason why it was organized, was to protect *all* the ranches of this valley from the Railroad, and it looks to me as if the lives of our fellow-citizens had been sacrificed, not in defending *all* of our ranches, but just in defence of one of them—Los Muertos—the one that Mr. Derrick owns."

The speaker had no more than regained his seat when a

man was seen pushing his way from the back of the stage towards Garnett. He handed the rancher a note, at the same time whispering in his ear. Garnett read the note, then came forward to the edge of the stage, holding up his hand. When the audience had fallen silent he said:

"I have just received sad news. Our friend and fellow-citizen, Mr. Osterman, died this morning between eleven and twelve o'clock."

Instantly there was a roar. Every man in the building rose to his feet, shouting, gesticulating. The roar increased, the Opera House trembled to it, the gas jets in the lighted chandeliers vibrated to it. It was a raucous howl of execration, a bellow of rage, inarticulate, deafening.

A tornado of confusion swept whirling from wall to wall and the madness of the moment seized irresistibly upon Presley. He forgot himself; he no longer was master of his emotions or his impulses. All at once he found himself upon the stage, facing the audience, flaming with excitement, his imagination on fire, his arms uplifted in fierce, wild gestures, words leaping to his mind in a torrent that could not be withheld.

"One more dead," he cried, "one more. Harran dead, Annixter dead, Broderson dead, Dabney dead, Osterman dead, Hooven dead; shot down, killed, killed in the defence of their homes, killed in the defence of their rights, killed for the sake of liberty. How long must it go on? How long must we suffer? Where is the end; what is the end? How long must the iron-hearted monster feed on our life's blood? How long must this terror of steam and steel ride upon our necks? Will you never be satisfied, will you never relent, you, our masters, you, our lords, you, our kings, you, our task-masters, you, our Pharaohs. Will you never listen to that command '*Let My people go*'? Oh, that cry ringing down the ages. Hear it, hear it. It is the voice of the Lord God speaking in his prophets. Hear it, hear it—'Let My people go!' Rameses heard it in his pylons at Thebes, Cæsar heard it on the Palatine, the Bourbon Louis heard it at Versailles, Charles Stuart heard it at Whitehall, the white Czar heard it in the Kremlin,—'*Let My people go.*' It is the cry of the nations, the great voice of the centuries; everywhere it is raised. The voice of God is the voice of the People. The people cry out 'Let us, the People, God's people, go.' You, our masters, you, our kings, you, our tyrants, don't you hear us? Don't you hear God speaking in us? Will you never let us go? How long at length will you abuse our patience? How long will you drive us? How long will you harass us? Will nothing daunt you? Does nothing check you? Do you not know that to ignore our cry too long is to wake the Red Terror? Rameses refused to listen to it and perished miserably. Cæsar refused to listen and was stabbed in the Senate House. The Bourbon Louis refused to listen and died on the guillotine; Charles Stuart refused to listen and died on the block; the white Czar refused to listen and was blown up in his own capital. Will you let it come to that? Will you drive us to it? We who boast of our land of freedom, we who live in the country of liberty?

"Go on as you have begun and it *will* come to that. Turn a deaf ear to that cry of 'Let My people go' too long and another cry will be raised, that you cannot choose but hear, a cry that you cannot shut out. It will be the cry of the man on the street, the *'à la Bastille'* that wakes the Red Terror and unleashes Revolution. Harassed, plundered, exasperated, desperate, the people will turn at last as they have turned so many, many times before. You, our lords, you, our task-masters, you, our kings; you have caught your Samson, you have made his strength your own. You have shorn his head; you have put out his eyes; you have set him to turn your millstones, to grind the grist for your mills; you have made him a shame and a mock. Take care, oh, as you love your lives, take care, lest some day calling upon the Lord his God he reach not out his arms for the pillars of your temples."

The audience, at first bewildered, confused by this unexpected invective, suddenly took fire at his last words. There was a roar of applause; then, more significant than mere vociferation, Presley's listeners, as he began to speak again, grew suddenly silent. His next sentences were uttered in the midst of a profound stillness.

"They own us, these task-masters of ours; they own our homes, they own our legislatures. We cannot escape from them. There is no redress. We are told we can defeat them by the ballot-box. They own the ballot-box. We are told that we must look to the courts for redress; they own the courts. We know them for what they are,—ruffians in politics, ruffians in finance, ruffians in law, ruffians in trade, bribers, swindlers, and tricksters. No outrage too great to daunt them, no petty larceny too small to shame them; despoiling a government treasury of a million dollars, yet picking the pockets of a farm hand of the price of a loaf of bread.

"They swindle a nation of a hundred million and call it Financiering; they levy a blackmail and call it Commerce; they corrupt a legislature and call it Politics; they bribe a judge and call it Law; they hire blacklegs to carry out their plans and call it Organisation; they prostitute the honour of a State and call it Competition.

"And this is America. We fought Lexington to free ourselves; we fought Gettysburg to free others. Yet the yoke remains; we have only shifted it to the other shoulder. We talk of liberty—oh, the farce of it, oh, the folly of it! We tell ourselves and teach our children that we have achieved liberty, that we no longer need fight for it. Why, the fight is just beginning and so long as our conception of liberty remains as it is to-day, it will continue.

"For we conceive of Liberty in the statues we raise to her as a beautiful woman, crowned, victorious, in bright armour and white robes, a light in her uplifted hand—a serene, calm, conquering goddess. Oh, the farce of it, oh, the folly of it! Liberty is *not* a crowned goddess, beautiful, in spotless garments, victorious, supreme. Liberty is the Man In the Street, a terrible figure, rushing through powder smoke, fouled with the mud and ordure of the gutter, bloody, rampant, brutal, yelling curses, in one hand a smoking rifle, in the other, a blazing torch.

"Freedom is *not* given free to any who ask; Liberty is not born of the gods. She is a child of the People, born in the very height and heat of battle, born from death, stained with blood, grimed with powder. And she grows to be not a goddess, but a Fury, a fearful figure, slaying friend and foe alike, raging, insatiable, merciless, the Red Terror."

Presley ceased speaking. Weak, shaking, scarcely knowing what he was about, he descended from the stage. A prolonged explosion of applause followed, the Opera House roaring to the roof, men cheering, stamping, waving their hats. But it was not intelligent applause. Instinctively as he made his way out, Presley knew that, after all, he had not once held the hearts of his audience. He had talked as he would have written; for all his scorn of literature, he had been literary. The men who listened to him, ranchers, country people, store-keepers, attentive though they were, were not once sympathetic. Vaguely they had felt that here was something which other men—more educated—would possibly consider eloquent. They applauded vociferously but perfunctorily, in order to appear to understand.

Presley, for all his love of the people, saw clearly for one moment that he was an outsider to their minds. He had not helped them nor their cause in the least; he never would.

Disappointed, bewildered, ashamed, he made his way slowly from the Opera House and stood on the steps outside, thoughtful, his head bent.

He had failed, thus he told himself. In that moment of crisis, that at the time he believed had been an inspiration, he had failed. The people would not consider him, would not believe that he could do them service. Then suddenly he seemed to remember. The resolute set of his lips returned once more. Pushing his way through the crowded streets, he went on towards the stable where he had left his pony.

Meanwhile, in the Opera House, a great commotion had occurred. Magnus Derrick had appeared.

Only a sense of enormous responsibility, of gravest duty could have prevailed upon Magnus to have left his house and the dead body of his son that day. But he was the President of the League, and never since its organisation had a meeting of such importance as this one been held. He had been in command at the irrigating ditch the day before. It was he who had gathered the handful of Leaguers together. It was he who must bear the responsibility of the fight.

When he had entered the Opera House, making his way down the central aisle towards the stage, a loud disturbance had broken out, partly applause, partly a meaningless uproar. Many had pressed forward to shake his hand, but others were not found wanting who, formerly his staunch supporters, now scenting opposition in the air, held back, hesitating, afraid to compromise themselves by adhering to the fortunes of a man whose actions might be discredited by the very organisation of which he was the head.

Declining to take the chair of presiding officer which Garnett offered him, the Governor withdrew to an angle of the stage, where he was joined by Keast.

This one, still unalterably devoted to Magnus, acquainted him briefly with the tenor of the speeches that had been made.

"I am ashamed of them, Governor," he protested indignantly, "to lose their nerve now! To fail you now! it makes my blood boil. If you had succeeded yesterday, if all had gone well, do you think we would have heard of any talk of 'assumption of authority,' or 'acting without advice and consent'? As if there was any time to call a meeting of the Executive Committee. If you hadn't acted as you did, the whole county would have been grabbed by the Railroad. Get up, Governor, and bring 'em all up standing. Just tear 'em all to pieces, show 'em that you are the head, the boss. That's what they need. That killing yesterday has shaken the nerve clean out of them."

For the instant the Governor was taken all aback. What, his lieutenants were failing him? What, he was to be questioned, interpolated upon yesterday's "irrepressible conflict"? Had disaffection appeared in the ranks of the League—at this, of all moments? He put from him his terrible grief. The cause was in danger. At the instant he was the President of the League only, the chief, the master. A royal anger surged within him, a wide, towering scorn of opposition. He would crush this disaffection in its incipiency, would vindicate himself and strengthen the cause at one and the same time. He stepped forward and stood in the speaker's place, turning partly toward the audience, partly toward the assembled Leaguers.

"Gentlemen of the League," he began, "citizens of Bonneville——"

But at once the silence in which the Governor had begun to speak was broken by a shout. It was as though his words had furnished a signal. In a certain quarter of the gallery, directly opposite, a man arose, and in a voice partly of derision, partly of defiance, cried out:

"How about the bribery of those two delegates at Sacramento? Tell us about that. That's what we want to hear about."

A great confusion broke out. The first cry was repeated not only by the original speaker, but by a whole group of which he was but a part. Others in the audience, however, seeing in the disturbance only the clamour of a few Railroad supporters, attempted to howl them down, hissing vigorously and exclaiming:

"Put 'em out, put 'em out."

"Order, order," called Garnett, pounding with his gavel. The whole Opera House was in an uproar.

But the interruption of the Governor's speech was evidently not unpremeditated. It began to look like a deliberate and planned attack. Persistently, doggedly, the group in the gallery vociferated:

"Tell us how you bribed the delegates at Sacramento. Before you throw mud at the Railroad, let's see if you are clean yourself."

"Put 'em out, put 'em out."

"Briber, briber—Magnus Derrick, unconvicted briber! Put *him* out."

Keast, beside himself with anger, pushed down the aisle underneath where the recalcitrant group had its place and, shaking his fist, called up at them:

"You were paid to break up this meeting. If you have anything to say, you will be afforded the opportunity, but if you do not let the gentleman proceed, the police will be called upon to put you out."

But at this, the man who had raised the first shout leaned over the balcony rail, and, his face flaming with wrath, shouted:

"*Yah!* talk to me of your police. Look out we don't call on them first to arrest your President for bribery. You and your howl about law and justice and corruption! Here"—he turned to the audience—"read about him, read the story of how the Sacramento convention was bought by Magnus

Derrick, President of the San Joaquin League. Here's the facts printed and proved."

With the words, he stooped down and from under his seat dragged forth a great package of extra editions of the "Bonneville Mercury," not an hour off the presses. Other equally large bundles of the paper appeared in the hands of the surrounding group. The strings were cut and in handfuls and armfuls the papers were flung out over the heads of the audience underneath. The air was full of the flutter of the newly printed sheets. They swarmed over the rim of the gallery like clouds of monstrous, winged insects, settled upon the heads and into the hands of the audience, were passed swiftly from man to man, and within five minutes of the first outbreak every one in the Opera House had read Genslinger's detailed and substantiated account of Magnus Derrick's "deal" with the political bosses of the Sacramento convention.

Genslinger, after pocketing the Governor's hush money, had, "sold him out."

Keast, one quiver of indignation, made his way back upon the stage. The Leaguers were in wild confusion. Half the assembly of them were on their feet, bewildered, shouting vaguely. From proscenium wall to foyer, the Opera House was a tumult of noise. The gleam of the thousands of the "Mercury" extras was like the flash of white caps on a troubled sea.

Keast faced the audience.

"Liars," he shouted, striving with all the power of his voice to dominate the clamour, "liars and slanderers. Your paper is the paid organ of the corporation. You have not one shadow of proof to back you up. Do you choose this, of all times, to heap your calumny upon the head of an honourable gentleman, already prostrated by your murder of his son? Proofs— we demand your proofs!"

"We've got the very assemblymen themselves," came back the answering shout. "Let Derrick speak. Where is he hiding? If this is a lie, let him deny it. Let *him disprove* the charge."

"Derrick, Derrick," thundered the Opera House.

Keast wheeled about. Where was Magnus? He was not in sight upon the stage. He had disappeared. Crowding through the throng of Leaguers, Keast got from off the stage into the wings. Here the crowd was no less dense. Nearly every one had a copy of the "Mercury." It was being read aloud to groups here and there, and once Keast overheard the words, "Say, I wonder if this is true, after all?"

"Well, and even if it was," cried Keast, turning upon the speaker, " we should be the last ones to kick. In any case, it was done for our benefit. It elected the Ranchers' Commission."

"A lot of benefit we got out of the Ranchers' Commission," retorted the other.

"And then," protested a third speaker, "that ain't the way to do—if he *did* do it—bribing legislatures. Why, we were bucking against corrupt politics. We couldn't afford to be corrupt."

Keast turned away with a gesture of impatience. He pushed his way farther on. At last, opening a small door in a hallway back of the stage, he came upon Magnus.

The room was tiny. It was a dressing-room. Only two nights before it had been used by the leading actress of a comic opera troupe which had played for three nights at Bonneville. A tattered sofa and limping toilet table occupied a third of the space. The air was heavy with the smell of stale grease paint, ointments, and sachet. Faded photographs of young women in tights and gauzes ornamented the mirror and the walls. Underneath the sofa was an old pair of corsets. The spangled skirt of a pink dress, turned inside out, hung against the wall.

And in the midst of such environment, surrounded by an excited group of men who gesticulated and shouted in his very face, pale, alert, agitated, his thin lips pressed tightly together, stood Magnus Derrick.

"Here," cried Keast, as he entered, closing the door behind him, " where's the Governor? Here, Magnus, I've been looking for you. The crowd has gone wild out there. You've got to talk 'em down. Come out there and give those blacklegs the lie. They are saying you are hiding."

But before Magnus could reply, Garnett turned to Keast.

"Well, that's what we want him to do, and he won't do it."

"Yes, yes," cried the half-dozen men who crowded around Magnus, "yes, that's what we want him to do."

Keast turned to Magnus.

"Why, what's all this, Governor?" he exclaimed. "You've *got* to answer that. Hey? why don't you give 'em the lie?"

"I—I," Magnus loosened the collar about his throat, "it is a lie. I will not stoop—I would not—would be—it would be beneath my—my—it would be beneath me."

Keast stared in amazement. Was this the Great Man, the Leader, indomitable, of Roman integrity, of Roman valour, before whose voice whole conventions had quailed? Was it possible he was *afraid* to face those hired vilifiers?

"Well, how about this?" demanded Garnett suddenly. "It *is* a lie, isn't it? That Commission was elected honestly, wasn't it?"

"How dare you, sir!" Magnus burst out. "How dare you question me—call me to account! Please understand, sir, that I tolerate——"

"Oh, quit it!" cried a voice from the group. "You can't scare us, Derrick. That sort of talk was well enough once, but it don't go any more. We want a yes or no answer."

It was gone—that old-time power of mastery, that faculty of command. The ground crumbled beneath his feet. Long since it had been, by his own hand, undermined. Authority was gone. Why keep up this miserable sham any longer? Could they not read the lie in his face, in his voice? What a folly to maintain the wretched pretence! He had failed. He was ruined. Harran was gone. His ranch would soon go; his money was gone. Lyman was worse than dead. His own honour had been prostituted. Gone, gone, everything he held dear, gone, lost, and swept away in that fierce struggle. And suddenly and all in a moment the last remaining shells of the fabric of his being, the sham that had stood already wonderfully long, cracked and collapsed.

"Was the Commission honestly elected?" insisted Garnett. "Were the delegates—did you bribe the delegates?"

"We were obliged to shut our eyes to means," faltered Magnus. "There was no other way to—" Then suddenly and with the last dregs of his resolution, he concluded with: "Yes, I gave them two thousand dollars each."

"Oh, hell! Oh, my God!" exclaimed Keast, sitting swiftly down upon the ragged sofa.

There was a long silence. A sense of poignant embarrassment descended upon those present. No one knew what to say or where to look. Garnett, with a laboured attempt at nonchalance, murmured:

"I see. Well, that's what I was trying to get at. Yes, I see."

"Well," said Gethings at length, bestirring himself, "I guess *I'll* go home."

There was a movement. The group broke up, the men making for the door. One by one they went out. The last to go was Keast. He came up to Magnus and shook the Governor's limp hand.

"Good-bye, Governor," he said. "I'll see you again pretty soon. Don't let this discourage you. They'll come around all right after a while. So long."

He went out, shutting the door.

And seated in the one chair of the room, Magnus Derrick remained a long time, looking at his face in the cracked mirror that for so many years had reflected the painted faces of soubrettes, in this atmosphere of stale perfume and mouldy rice powder.

It had come—his fall, his ruin. After so many years of integrity and honest battle, his life had ended here—in an actress's dressing-room, deserted by his friends, his son murdered, his dishonesty known, an old man, broken, discarded, discredited, and abandoned.

Before nightfall of that day, Bonneville was further excited by an astonishing bit of news. S. Behrman lived in a detached house at some distance from the town, surrounded by a grove of live oak and eucalyptus trees. At a little after half-past six, as he was sitting down to his supper, a bomb was thrown through the window of his dining-room, exploding near the doorway leading into the hall. The room was wrecked and nearly every window of the house shattered. By a miracle, S. Behrman, himself, remained untouched.

VIII

O N A CERTAIN afternoon in the early part of July, about a month after the fight at the irrigating ditch and the mass meeting at Bonneville, Cedarquist, at the moment opening his mail in his office in San Francisco, was genuinely surprised to receive a visit from Presley.

"Well, upon my word, Pres," exclaimed the manufacturer, as the young man came in through the door that the office boy held open for him, "upon my word, have you been sick? Sit down, my boy. Have a glass of sherry. I always keep a bottle here."

Presley accepted the wine and sank into the depths of a great leather chair near by.

"Sick?" he answered. "Yes, I have been sick. I'm sick now. I'm gone to pieces, sir."

His manner was the extreme of listlessness—the listlessness of great fatigue. "Well, well," observed the other. "I'm right sorry to hear that. What's the trouble, Pres?"

"Oh, nerves mostly, I suppose, and my head, and insomnia, and weakness, a general collapse all along the line, the doctor tells me. 'Over-cerebration,' he says; 'over-excitement.' I fancy I rather narrowly missed brain fever."

"Well, I can easily suppose it," answered Cedarquist gravely, "after all you have been through."

Presley closed his eyes—they were sunken in circles of dark brown flesh—and pressed a thin hand to the back of his head.

"It is a nightmare," he murmured. "A frightful nightmare, and it's not over yet. You have heard of it all only through the newspaper reports. But down there, at Bonneville, at Los Muertos—oh, you can have no idea of it, of the misery caused by the defeat of the ranchers and by this decision of the Supreme Court that dispossesses them all. We had gone on hoping to the last that we would win there. We had thought that in the Supreme Court of the United States, at least, we could find justice. And the news of its decision was the worst, last blow of all. For Magnus it was the last—positively the very last."

"Poor, poor Derrick," murmured Cedarquist. "Tell me about him, Pres. How does he take it? What is he going to do?"

"It beggars him, sir. He sunk a great deal more than any of us believed in his ranch, when he resolved to turn off most of the tenants and farm the ranch himself. Then the fight he made against the Railroad in the Courts and the political campaign he went into, to get Lyman on the Railroad Commission, took more of it. The money that Genslinger blackmailed him of, it seems, was about all he had left. He had been gambling—you know the Governor—on another bonanza crop this year to recoup him. Well, the bonanza came right enough—just in time for S. Behrman and the Railroad to grab it. Magnus is ruined."

"What a tragedy! what a tragedy!" murmured the other. "Lyman turning rascal, Harran killed, and now this; and all within so short a time—all at the *same* time, you might almost say."

"If it had only killed him," continued Presley; "but that is the worst of it."

"How the worst?"

"I'm afraid, honestly, I'm afraid it is going to turn his wits, sir. It's broken him; oh, you should see him, you should see him. A shambling, stooping, trembling old man, in his dotage already. He sits all day in the dining-room, turning over papers, sorting them, tying them up, opening them again, forgetting them—all fumbling and mumbling and confused. And at table sometimes he forgets to eat. And, listen, you know, from the house we can hear the trains whistling for the Long Trestle. As often as that happens the Governor seems to be—oh, I don't know, frightened. He will sink his head between his shoulders, as though he were dodging something, and he won't fetch a long breath again till the train is out of hearing. He seems to have conceived an abject, unreasoned terror of the Railroad."

"But he will have to leave Los Muertos now, of course?"

"Yes, they will all have to leave. They have a fortnight more. The few tenants that were still on Los Muertos are leaving. That is one thing that brings me to the city. The family of one of the men who was killed—Hooven was his

name—have come to the city to find work. I think they are
liable to be in great distress, unless they have been wonderfully lucky, and I am trying to find them in order to look after
them."

"You need looking after yourself, Pres."

"Oh, once away from Bonneville and the sight of the ruin
there, I'm better. But I intend to go away. And that makes
me think, I came to ask you if you could help me. If you
would let me take passage on one of your wheat ships. The
Doctor says an ocean voyage would set me up."

"Why, certainly, Pres," declared Cedarquist. "But I'm sorry
you'll have to go. We expected to have you down in the country with us this winter."

Presley shook his head.

"No," he answered. "I must go. Even if I had all my health,
I could not bring myself to stay in California just now. If you
can introduce me to one of your captains——"

"With pleasure. When do you want to go? You may have
to wait a few weeks. Our first ship won't clear till the end of
the month."

"That would do very well. Thank you, sir."

But Cedarquist was still interested in the land troubles of
the Bonneville farmers, and took the first occasion to ask:

"So, the Railroad are in possession on most of the
ranches?"

"On all of them," returned Presley. "The League went all
to pieces, so soon as Magnus was forced to resign. The old
story—they got quarrelling among themselves. Somebody
started a compromise party, and upon that issue a new president was elected. Then there were defections. The Railroad
offered to lease the lands in question to the ranchers—the
ranchers who owned them," he exclaimed bitterly, "and because the terms were nominal—almost nothing—plenty of
the men took the chance of saving themselves. And, of
course, once signing the lease, they acknowledged the Railroad's title. But the road would not lease to Magnus. S. Behrman takes over Los Muertos in a few weeks now."

"No doubt, the road made over their title in the property
to him," observed Cedarquist, "as a reward of his services."

"No doubt," murmured Presley wearily. He rose to go.

"By the way," said Cedarquist, "what have you on hand for, let us say, Friday evening? Won't you dine with us then? The girls are going to the country Monday of next week, and you probably won't see them again for some time if you take that ocean voyage of yours."

"I'm afraid I shall be very poor company, sir," hazarded Presley. "There's no 'go,' no life in me at all these days. I am like a clock with a broken spring."

"Not broken, Pres, my boy," urged the other, "only run down. Try and see if we can't wind you up a bit. Say that we can expect you. We dine at seven."

"Thank you, sir. Till Friday at seven, then."

Regaining the street, Presley sent his valise to his club (where he had engaged a room) by a messenger boy, and boarded a Castro Street car. Before leaving Bonneville, he had ascertained, by strenuous enquiry, Mrs. Hooven's address in the city, and thitherward he now directed his steps.

When Presley had told Cedarquist that he was ill, that he was jaded, worn out, he had only told half the truth. Exhausted he was, nerveless, weak, but this apathy was still invaded from time to time with fierce incursions of a spirit of unrest and revolt, reactions, momentary returns of the blind, undirected energy that at one time had prompted him to a vast desire to acquit himself of some terrible deed of readjustment, just what, he could not say, some terrifying martyrdom, some awe-inspiring immolation, consummate, incisive, conclusive. He fancied himself to be fired with the purblind, mistaken heroism of the anarchist, hurling his victim to destruction with full knowledge that the catastrophe shall sweep him also into the vortex it creates.

But his constitutional irresoluteness obstructed his path continually; brain-sick, weak of will, emotional, timid even, he temporised, procrastinated, brooded; came to decisions in the dark hours of the night, only to abandon them in the morning.

Once only he had *acted*. And at this moment, as he was carried through the windy, squalid streets, he trembled at the remembrance of it. The horror of "what might have been" incompatible with the vengeance whose minister he fancied he was, oppressed him. The scene perpetually reconstructed itself in his imagination. He saw himself under the shade of the encompassing trees and shrubbery, creeping on his belly toward the house, in the suburbs of Bonneville, watching his chances, seizing opportunities, spying upon the lighted windows where the raised curtains afforded a view of the interior. Then had come the appearance in the glare of the gas of the figure of the man for whom he waited. He saw himself rise and run forward. He remembered the feel and weight in his hand of Caraher's bomb—the six inches of plugged gas pipe. His upraised arm shot forward. There was a shiver of smashed window-panes, then—a void—a red whirl of confusion, the air rent, the ground rocking, himself flung headlong, flung off the spinning circumference of things out into a place of terror and vacancy and darkness. And then after a long time the return of reason, the consciousness that his feet were set upon the road to Los Muertos, and that he was fleeing terror-stricken, gasping, all but insane with hysteria. Then the never-to-be-forgotten night that ensued, when he descended into the pit, horrified at what he supposed he had done, at one moment ridden with remorse, at another raging against his own feebleness, his lack of courage, his wretched, vacillating spirit. But morning had come, and with it the knowledge that he had failed, and the baser assurance that he was not even remotely suspected. His own escape had been no less miraculous than that of his enemy, and he had fallen on his knees in inarticulate prayer, weeping, pouring out his thanks to God for the deliverance from the gulf to the very brink of which his feet had been drawn.

After this, however, there had come to Presley a deep-rooted suspicion that he was—of all human beings, the most wretched—a failure. Everything to which he had set his mind failed—his great epic, his efforts to help the people who surrounded him, even his attempted destruction of the enemy, all these had come to nothing. Girding his shattered strength together, he resolved upon one last attempt to live up to the best that was in him, and to that end had set himself to lift out of the despair into which they had been thrust, the bereaved family of the German, Hooven.

After all was over, and Hooven, together with the seven others who had fallen at the irrigating ditch, was buried in the Bonneville cemetery, Mrs. Hooven, asking no one's aid or advice, and taking with her Minna and little Hilda, had gone to San Francisco—had gone to find work, abandoning Los Muertos and her home forever. Presley only learned of the departure of the family after fifteen days had elapsed.

At once, however, the suspicion forced itself upon him that Mrs. Hooven—and Minna, too for the matter of that—country-bred, ignorant of city ways, might easily come to grief in the hard, huge struggle of city life. This suspicion had swiftly hardened to a conviction, acting at last upon which Presley had followed them to San Francisco, bent upon finding and assisting them.

The house to which Presley was led by the address in his memorandum book was a cheap but fairly decent hotel near the power house of the Castro Street cable. He inquired for Mrs. Hooven.

The landlady recollected the Hoovens perfectly.

"German woman, with a little girl-baby, and an older daughter, sure. The older daughter was main pretty. Sure I remember them, but they ain't here no more. They left a week ago. I had to ask them for their room. As it was, they owed a week's room-rent. Mister, I can't afford——"

"Well, do you know where they went? Did you hear what address they had their trunk expressed to?"

"Ah, yes, their trunk," vociferated the woman, clapping her hands to her hips, her face purpling. "Their trunk, ah, sure. I got their trunk, and what are you going to do about it? I'm holding it till I get my money. What have you got to say about it? Let's hear it."

Presley turned away with a gesture of discouragement, his heart sinking. On the street corner he stood for a long time, frowning in trouble and perplexity. His suspicions had been only too well founded. So long ago as a week, the Hoovens had exhausted all their little store of money. For seven days now they had been without resources, unless, indeed, work had been found; "and what," he asked himself, " what work in God's name could they find to do here in the city?"

Seven days! He quailed at the thought of it. Seven days without money, knowing not a soul in all that swarming city. Ignorant of city life as both Minna and her mother were, would they even realise that there were institutions built and generously endowed for just such as they? He knew them to have their share of pride, the dogged sullen pride of the peasant; even if they knew of charitable organisations, would they, could they bring themselves to apply there? A poignant anxiety thrust itself sharply into Presley's heart. Where were they now? Where had they slept last night? Where breakfasted this morning? Had there even been any breakfast this morning? Had there even been any bed last night? Lost, and forgotten in the plexus of the city's life, what had befallen them? Towards what fate was the ebb tide of the streets drifting them?

Was this to be still another theme wrought out by iron hands upon the old, the world-old, world-wide keynote? How far were the consequences of that dreadful day's work at the irrigating ditch to reach? To what length was the tentacle of the monster to extend?

Presley returned toward the central, the business quarter of the city, alternately formulating and dismissing from his mind plan after plan for the finding and aiding of Mrs. Hooven and her daughters. He reached Montgomery Street, and turned toward his club, his imagination once more reviewing all the causes and circumstances of the great battle of which for the last eighteen months he had been witness.

All at once he paused, his eye caught by a sign affixed to the wall just inside the street entrance of a huge office building, and smitten with an idea, stood for an instant motionless, upon the sidewalk, his eyes wide, his fists shut tight.

The building contained the General Office of the Pacific and Southwestern Railroad. Large though it was, it nevertheless, was not pretentious, and during his visits to the city, Presley must have passed it, unheeding, many times.

But for all that it was the stronghold of the enemy—the centre of all that vast ramifying system of arteries that drained the life-blood of the State; the nucleus of the web in which so many lives, so many fortunes, so many destinies had been enmeshed. From this place—so he told himself—had emanated that policy of extortion, oppression and injustice that little by little had shouldered the ranchers from their rights, till, their backs to the wall, exasperated and despairing they had turned and fought and died. From here had come the orders to S. Behrman, to Cyrus Ruggles and to Genslinger, the orders that had brought Dyke to a prison, that had killed Annixter, that had ruined Magnus, that had corrupted Lyman. Here was the keep of the castle, and here, behind one of those many windows, in one of those many offices, his hand upon the levers of his mighty engine, sat the master, Shelgrim himself.

Instantly, upon the realisation of this fact an ungovernable desire seized upon Presley, an inordinate curiosity. Why not see, face to face, the man whose power was so vast, whose will was so resistless, whose potency for evil so limitless, the man who for so long and so hopelessly they had all been fighting. By reputation he knew him to be approachable; why should he not then approach him? Presley took his resolution in both hands. If he failed to act upon this impulse, he knew he would never act at all. His heart beating, his breath coming short, he entered the building, and in a few moments found himself seated in an ante-room, his eyes fixed with hypnotic intensity upon the frosted pane of an adjoining door, whereon in gold letters was inscribed the word, *"President."*

In the end, Presley had been surprised to find that Shelgrim was still in. It was already very late, after six o'clock, and the other offices in the building were in the act of closing. Many of them were already deserted. At every instant, through the open door of the ante-room, he caught a glimpse of clerks, office boys, book-keepers, and other employees hurrying towards the stairs and elevators, quitting business for the day. Shelgrim, it seemed, still remained at his desk, knowing no fatigue, requiring no leisure.

"What time does Mr. Shelgrim usually go home?" inquired Presley of the young man who sat ruling forms at the table in the ante-room.

"Anywhere between half-past six and seven," the other answered, adding, "Very often he comes back in the evening."

And the man was seventy years old. Presley could not repress a murmur of astonishment. Not only mentally, then, was the President of the P. and S. W. a giant. Seventy years of age and still at his post, holding there with the energy, with a concentration of purpose that would have wrecked the health and impaired the mind of many men in the prime of their manhood.

But the next instant Presley set his teeth.

"It is an ogre's vitality," he said to himself. "Just so is the man-eating tiger strong. The man should have energy who has sucked the life-blood from an entire People."

A little electric bell on the wall near at hand trilled a warning. The young man who was ruling forms laid down his pen, and opening the door of the President's office, thrust in his head, then after a word exchanged with the unseen occupant of the room, he swung the door wide, saying to Presley:

"Mr. Shelgrim will see you, sir."

Presley entered a large, well lighted, but singularly barren office. A well-worn carpet was on the floor, two steel engravings hung against the wall, an extra chair or two stood near a large, plain, littered table. That was absolutely all, unless he excepted the corner washstand, on which was set a pitcher of ice water, covered with a clean, stiff napkin. A man, evidently some sort of manager's assistant, stood at the end of the table, leaning on the back of one of the chairs. Shelgrim himself sat at the table.

He was large, almost to massiveness. An iron-grey beard and a mustache that completely hid the mouth covered the lower part of his face. His eyes were a pale blue, and a little watery; here and there upon his face were moth spots. But the enormous breadth of the shoulders was what, at first, most vividly forced itself upon Presley's notice. Never had he seen a broader man; the neck, however, seemed in a manner to have settled into the shoulders, and furthermore they were humped and rounded, as if to bear great responsibilities, and great abuse.

At the moment he was wearing a silk skull-cap, pushed to one side and a little awry, a frock coat of broadcloth, with long sleeves, and a waistcoat from the lower buttons of which the cloth was worn and, upon the edges, rubbed away, showing the metal underneath. At the top this waistcoat was unbuttoned and in the shirt front disclosed were two pearl studs.

Presley, uninvited, unnoticed apparently, sat down. The assistant manager was in the act of making a report. His voice was not lowered, and Presley heard every word that was spoken.

The report proved interesting. It concerned a book-keeper in the office of the auditor of disbursements. It seems he was at most times thoroughly reliable, hard-working, industrious, ambitious. But at long intervals the vice of drunkenness seized upon the man and for three days rode him like a hag. Not only during the period of this intemperance, but for the few days immediately following, the man was useless, his work untrustworthy. He was a family man and earnestly strove to rid himself of his habit; he was, when sober, valuable. In consideration of these facts, he had been pardoned again and again.

"You remember, Mr. Shelgrim," observed the manager, "that you have more than once interfered in his behalf, when we were disposed to let him go. I don't think we can do anything with him, sir. He promises to reform continually, but it is the same old story. This last time we saw nothing of him for four days. Honestly, Mr. Shelgrim, I think we ought to let Tentell out. We can't afford to keep him. He is really losing us too much money. Here's the order ready now, if you care to let it go."

There was a pause. Presley all attention, listened breathlessly. The assistant manager laid before his President the typewritten order in question. The silence lengthened; in the hall outside, the wrought-iron door of the elevator cage slid to with a clash. Shelgrim did not look at the order. He turned his swivel chair about and faced the windows behind him, looking out with unseeing eyes. At last he spoke:

"Tentell has a family, wife and three children. . . . How much do we pay him?"

"One hundred and thirty."

"Let's double that, or say two hundred and fifty. Let's see how that will do."

"Why—of course—if you say so, but really, Mr. Shelgrim——"

"Well, we'll try that, anyhow."

Presley had not time to readjust his perspective to this new point of view of the President of the P. and S. W. before the assistant manager had withdrawn. Shelgrim wrote a few

memoranda on his calendar pad, and signed a couple of letters before turning his attention to Presley. At last, he looked
up and fixed the young man with a direct, grave glance. He
did not smile. It was some time before he spoke. At last, he
said:

"Well, sir."

Presley advanced and took a chair nearer at hand. Shelgrim
turned and from his desk picked up and consulted Presley's
card. Presley observed that he read without the use of glasses.

"You," he said, again facing about, "you are the young man
who wrote the poem called 'The Toilers.'"

"Yes, sir."

"It seems to have made a great deal of talk. I've read it, and
I've seen the picture in Cedarquist's house, the picture you
took the idea from."

Presley, his senses never more alive, observed that, curiously enough, Shelgrim did not move his body. His arms
moved, and his head, but the great bulk of the man remained
immobile in its place, and as the interview proceeded and this
peculiarity emphasised itself, Presley began to conceive the
odd idea that Shelgrim had, as it were, placed his body in the
chair to rest, while his head and brain and hands went on
working independently. A saucer of shelled filberts stood near
his elbow, and from time to time he picked up one of these
in a great thumb and forefinger and put it between his teeth.

"I've seen the picture called 'The Toilers,'" continued Shelgrim, "and of the two, I like the picture better than the
poem."

"The picture is by a master," Presley hastened to interpose.

"And for that reason," said Shelgrim, "it leaves nothing
more to be said. You might just as well have kept quiet.
There's only one best way to say anything. And what has
made the picture of 'The Toilers' great is that the artist said
in it the *best* that could be said on the subject."

"I had never looked at it in just that light," observed Presley. He was confused, all at sea, embarrassed. What he had
expected to find in Shelgrim, he could not have exactly said.
But he had been prepared to come upon an ogre, a brute, a
terrible man of blood and iron, and instead had discovered a
sentimentalist and an art critic. No standards of measurement

in his mental equipment would apply to the actual man, and it began to dawn upon him that possibly it was not because these standards were different in kind, but that they were lamentably deficient in size. He began to see that here was the man not only great, but large; many-sided, of vast sympathies, who understood with equal intelligence, the human nature in an habitual drunkard, the ethics of a masterpiece of painting, and the financiering and operation of ten thousand miles of railroad.

"I had never looked at it in just that light," repeated Presley. "There is a great deal in what you say."

"If I am to listen," continued Shelgrim, "to that kind of talk, I prefer to listen to it first hand. I would rather listen to what the great French painter has to say, than to what *you* have to say about what he has already said."

His speech, loud and emphatic at first, when the idea of what he had to say was fresh in his mind, lapsed and lowered itself at the end of his sentences as though he had already abandoned and lost interest in that thought, so that the concluding words were indistinct, beneath the grey beard and mustache. Also at times there was the faintest suggestion of a lisp.

"I wrote that poem," hazarded Presley, "at a time when I was terribly upset. I live," he concluded, "or did live on the Los Muertos ranch in Tulare County—Magnus Derrick's ranch."

"The Railroad's ranch *leased* to Mr. Derrick," observed Shelgrim.

Presley spread out his hands with a helpless, resigned gesture.

"And," continued the President of the P. and S. W. with grave intensity, looking at Presley keenly, "I suppose you believe I am a grand old rascal."

"I believe," answered Presley, "I am persuaded——" He hesitated, searching for his words.

"Believe this, young man," exclaimed Shelgrim, laying a thick powerful forefinger on the table to emphasise his words, "try to believe this—to begin with—*that Railroads build themselves*. Where there is a demand sooner or later there will be a supply. Mr. Derrick, does he grow his wheat? The Wheat grows itself. What does he count for? Does he supply the force? What do I count for? Do I build the Railroad? You are dealing with forces, young man, when you speak of Wheat and the Railroads, not with men. There is the Wheat, the supply. It must be carried to feed the People. There is the demand. The Wheat is one force, the Railroad, another, and there is the law that governs them—supply and demand. Men have only little to do in the whole business. Complications may arise, conditions that bear hard on the individual—crush him maybe— *but the Wheat will be carried to feed the people* as inevitably as it will grow. If you want to fasten the blame of the affair at Los Muertos on any one person, you will make a mistake. Blame conditions, not men."

"But—but," faltered Presley, "you are the head, you control the road."

"You are a very young man. Control the road! Can I stop it? I can go into bankruptcy if you like. But otherwise if I run my road, as a business proposition, I can do nothing. I can *not* control it. It is a force born out of certain conditions, and I—no man—can stop it or control it. Can your Mr. Derrick stop the Wheat growing? He can burn his crop, or he can give it away, or sell it for a cent a bushel—just as I could go into bankruptcy—but otherwise his Wheat must grow. Can any one stop the Wheat? Well, then no more can I stop the Road."

Presley regained the street stupefied, his brain in a whirl. This new idea, this new conception dumfounded him. Somehow, he could not deny it. It rang with the clear reverberation of truth. Was no one, then, to blame for the horror at the irrigating ditch? Forces, conditions, laws of supply and demand—were these then the enemies, after all? Not enemies; there was no malevolence in Nature. Colossal indifference only, a vast trend toward appointed goals. Nature was, then, a gigantic engine, a vast cyclopean power, huge, terrible, a leviathan with a heart of steel, knowing no compunction, no forgiveness, no tolerance; crushing out the human atom standing in its way, with nirvanic calm, the agony of destruction sending never a jar, never the faintest tremour through all that prodigious mechanism of wheels and cogs.

He went to his club and ate his supper alone, in gloomy agitation. He was sombre, brooding, lost in a dark maze of gloomy reflections. However, just as he was rising from the table an incident occurred that for the moment roused him and sharply diverted his mind.

His table had been placed near a window and as he was sipping his after-dinner coffee, he happened to glance across the street. His eye was at once caught by the sight of a familiar figure. Was it Minna Hooven? The figure turned the street corner and was lost to sight; but it had been strangely like. On the moment, Presley had risen from the table and, clapping on his hat, had hurried into the streets, where the lamps were already beginning to shine.

But search though he would, Presley could not again come upon the young woman, in whom he fancied he had seen the daughter of the unfortunate German. At last, he gave up the hunt, and returning to his club—at this hour almost deserted—smoked a few cigarettes, vainly attempted to read from a volume of essays in the library, and at last, nervous, distraught, exhausted, retired to his bed.

But none the less, Presley had not been mistaken. The girl whom he had tried to follow had been indeed Minna Hooven.

When Minna, a week before this time, had returned to the lodging house on Castro Street, after a day's unsuccessful effort to find employment, and was told that her mother and Hilda had gone, she was struck speechless with surprise and dismay. She had never before been in any town larger than Bonneville, and now knew not which way to turn nor how to account for the disappearance of her mother and little Hilda. That the landlady was on the point of turning them out, she understood, but it had been agreed that the family should be allowed to stay yet one more day, in the hope that Minna would find work. Of this she reminded the landlady. But this latter at once launched upon her such a torrent of vituperation, that the girl was frightened to speechless submission.

"Oh, oh," she faltered, "I know. I am sorry. I know we owe you money, but where did my mother go? I only want to find her."

"Oh, I ain't going to be bothered," shrilled the other. "How do I know?"

The truth of the matter was that Mrs. Hooven, afraid to stay in the vicinity of the house, after her eviction, and threatened with arrest by the landlady if she persisted in hanging around, had left with the woman a note scrawled on an old blotter, to be given to Minna when she returned. This the landlady had lost. To cover her confusion, she affected a vast indignation, and a turbulent, irascible demeanour.

"I ain't going to be bothered with such cattle as you," she vociferated in Minna's face. "I don't know where your folks is. Me, I only have dealings with honest people. I ain't got a word to say so long as the rent is paid. But when I'm soldiered out of a week's lodging, then I'm done. You get right along now. *I* don't know you. I ain't going to have my place get a bad name by having any South of Market Street chippies hanging around. You get along, or I'll call an officer."

Minna sought the street, her head in a whirl. It was about five o'clock. In her pocket was thirty-five cents, all she had in the world. What now?

All at once, the Terror of the City, that blind, unreasoned fear that only the outcast knows, swooped upon her, and clutched her vulture-wise, by the throat.

Her first few days' experience in the matter of finding employment, had taught her just what she might expect from this new world upon which she had been thrown. What was to become of her? What was she to do, where was she to go? Unanswerable, grim questions, and now she no longer had herself to fear for. Her mother and the baby, little Hilda, both of them equally unable to look after themselves, what was to become of them, where were they gone? Lost, lost, all of them, herself as well. But she rallied herself, as she walked along. The idea of her starving, of her mother and Hilda starving, was out of all reason. Of course, it would not come to that, of course not. It was not thus that starvation came. Something would happen, of course, it would—in time. But meanwhile, meanwhile, how to get through this approaching night, and the next few days. That was the thing to think of just now.

The suddenness of it all was what most unnerved her.

During all the nineteen years of her life, she had never known what it meant to shift for herself. Her father had always sufficed for the family; he had taken care of her, then, all of a sudden, her father had been killed, her mother snatched from her. Then all of a sudden there was no help anywhere. Then all of a sudden a terrible voice demanded of her, "Now just what can you do to keep yourself alive?" Life faced her; she looked the huge stone image squarely in the lustreless eyes.

It was nearly twilight. Minna, for the sake of avoiding observation—for it seemed to her that now a thousand prying glances followed her—assumed a matter-of-fact demeanour, and began to walk briskly toward the business quarter of the town.

She was dressed neatly enough, in a blue cloth skirt with a blue plush belt, fairly decent shoes, once her mother's, a pink shirt waist, and jacket and a straw sailor. She was, in an unusual fashion, pretty. Even her troubles had not dimmed the bright light of her pale, greenish-blue eyes, nor faded the astonishing redness of her lips, nor hollowed her strangely white face. Her blue-black hair was trim. She carried her well-shaped, well-rounded figure erectly. Even in her distress, she observed that men looked keenly at her, and sometimes after her as she went along. But this she noted with a dim subconscious faculty. The real Minna, harassed, terrified, lashed with a thousand anxieties, kept murmuring under her breath:

"What shall I do, what shall I do, oh, what shall I do, now?"

After an interminable walk, she gained Kearney Street, and held it till the well-lighted, well-kept neighbourhood of the shopping district gave place to the vice-crowded saloons and concert halls of the Barbary Coast. She turned aside in avoidance of this, only to plunge into the purlieus of Chinatown, whence only she emerged, panic-stricken and out of breath, after a half hour of never-to-be-forgotten terrors, and at a time when it had grown quite dark.

On the corner of California and Dupont streets, she stood a long moment, pondering.

"I *must* do something," she said to herself. "I must do *something*."

She was tired out by now, and the idea occurred to her to

enter the Catholic church in whose shadow she stood, and sit down and rest. This she did. The evening service was just being concluded. But long after the priests and altar boys had departed from the chancel, Minna still sat in the dim, echoing interior, confronting her desperate situation as best she might.

Two or three hours later, the sexton woke her. The church was being closed; she must leave. Once more, chilled with the sharp night air, numb with long sitting in the same attitude, still oppressed with drowsiness, confused, frightened, Minna found herself on the pavement. She began to be hungry, and, at length, yielding to the demand that every moment grew more imperious, bought and eagerly devoured a five-cent bag of fruit. Then, once more she took up the round of walking.

At length, in an obscure street that branched from Kearney Street, near the corner of the Plaza, she came upon an illuminated sign, bearing the inscription, "Beds for the Night, 15 and 25 cents."

Fifteen cents! Could she afford it? It would leave her with only that much more, that much between herself and a state of privation of which she dared not think; and, besides, the forbidding look of the building frightened her. It was dark, gloomy, dirty, a place suggestive of obscure crimes and hidden terrors. For twenty minutes or half an hour, she hesitated, walking twice and three times around the block. At last, she made up her mind. Exhaustion such as she had never known, weighed like lead upon her shoulders and dragged at her heels. She must sleep. She could not walk the streets all night. She entered the door-way under the sign, and found her way up a filthy flight of stairs. At the top, a man in a blue checked "jumper" was filling a lamp behind a high desk. To him Minna applied.

"I should like," she faltered, "to have a room—a bed for the night. One of those for fifteen cents will be good enough, I think."

"Well, this place is only for men," said the man, looking up from the lamp.

"Oh," said Minna, "oh—I—I didn't know."

She looked at him stupidly, and he, with equal stupidity,

returned the gaze. Thus, for a long moment, they held each other's eyes.

"I—I didn't know," repeated Minna.

"Yes, it's for men," repeated the other.

She slowly descended the stairs, and once more came out upon the streets.

And upon those streets that, as the hours advanced, grew more and more deserted, more and more silent, more and more oppressive with the sense of the bitter hardness of life towards those who have no means of living, Minna Hooven spent the first night of her struggle to keep her head above the ebb-tide of the city's sea, into which she had been plunged.

Morning came, and with it renewed hunger. At this time, she had found her way uptown again, and towards ten o'clock was sitting upon a bench in a little park full of nurse-maids and children. A group of the maids drew their baby-buggies to Minna's bench, and sat down, continuing a conversation they had already begun. Minna listened. A friend of one of the maids had suddenly thrown up her position, leaving her "madame" in what would appear to have been deserved embarrassment.

"Oh," said Minna, breaking in, and lying with sudden unwonted fluency, "I am a nurse-girl. I am out of a place. Do you think I could get that one?"

The group turned and fixed her—so evidently a country girl—with a supercilious indifference.

"Well, you might try," said one of them. "Got good references?"

"References?" repeated Minna blankly. She did not know what this meant.

"Oh, Mrs. Field ain't the kind to stick about references," spoke up the other, "she's that soft. Why, anybody could work her."

"I'll go there," said Minna. "Have you the address?" It was told to her.

"Lorin," she murmured. "Is that out of town?"

"Well, it's across the Bay."

"Across the Bay."

"Um. You're from the country, ain't you?"

"Yes. How—how do I get there? Is it far?"

"Well, you take the ferry at the foot of Market Street, and then the train on the other side. No, it ain't very far. Just ask any one down there. They'll tell you."

It was a chance; but Minna, after walking down to the ferry slips, found that the round trip would cost her twenty cents. If the journey proved fruitless, only a dime would stand between her and the end of everything. But it was a chance; the only one that had, as yet, presented itself. She made the trip.

And upon the street-railway cars, upon the ferryboats, on the locomotives and way-coaches of the local trains, she was reminded of her father's death, and of the giant power that had reduced her to her present straits, by the letters, P. and S. W. R. R. To her mind, they occurred everywhere. She seemed to see them in every direction. She fancied herself surrounded upon every hand by the long arms of the monster.

Minute after minute, her hunger gnawed at her. She could not keep her mind from it. As she sat on the boat, she found herself curiously scanning the faces of the passengers, wondering how long since such a one had breakfasted, how long before this other should sit down to lunch.

When Minna descended from the train, at Lorin on the other side of the Bay, she found that the place was one of those suburban towns, not yet become fashionable, such as may be seen beyond the outskirts of any large American city. All along the line of the railroad thereabouts, houses, small villas—contractors' ventures—were scattered, the advantages of suburban lots and sites for homes being proclaimed in seven-foot letters upon mammoth bill-boards close to the right of way.

Without much trouble, Minna found the house to which she had been directed, a pretty little cottage, set back from the street and shaded by palms, live oaks, and the inevitable eucalyptus. Her heart warmed at the sight of it. Oh, to find a little niche for herself here, a home, a refuge from those horrible city streets, from the rat of famine, with its relentless tooth. How she would work, how strenuously she would endeavour to please, how patient of rebuke she would be, how faithful, how conscientious. Nor were her pretensions altogether false; upon her, while at home, had devolved almost continually the care of the baby Hilda, her little sister. She knew the wants and needs of children.

Her heart beating, her breath failing, she rang the bell set squarely in the middle of the front door.

The lady of the house herself, an elderly lady, with pleasant, kindly face, opened the door. Minna stated her errand.

"But I have already engaged a girl," she said.

"Oh," murmured Minna, striving with all her might to maintain appearances. "Oh—I thought perhaps—" She turned away.

"I'm sorry," said the lady. Then she added, "Would you care to look after so many as three little children, and help around in light housework between whiles?"

"Yes, ma'am."

"Because my sister—she lives in North Berkeley, above here—she's looking for a girl. Have you had lots of experience? Got good references?"

"Yes, ma'am."

"Well, I'll give you the address. She lives up in North Berkeley."

She turned back into the house a moment, and returned, handing Minna a card.

"That's where she lives—careful not to *blot* it, child, the ink's wet yet—you had better see her."

"Is it far? Could I walk there?"

"My, no; you better take the electric cars, about six blocks above here."

When Minna arrived in North Berkeley, she had no money left. By a cruel mistake, she had taken a car going in the wrong direction, and though her error was rectified easily enough, it had cost her her last five-cent piece. She was now to try her last hope. Promptly it crumbled away. Like the former, this place had been already filled, and Minna left the door of the house with the certainty that her chance had come to naught, and that now she entered into the last struggle with life—the death struggle—shorn of her last pitiful defence, her last safeguard, her last penny.

As she once more resumed her interminable walk, she realised she was weak, faint; and she knew that it was the weakness of complete exhaustion, and the faintness of approaching starvation. Was this the end coming on? Terror of death aroused her.

"I *must*, I *must* do something, oh, anything. I must have something to eat."

At this late hour, the idea of pawning her little jacket occurred to her, but now she was far away from the city and its pawnshops, and there was no getting back.

She walked on. An hour passed. She lost her sense of direction, became confused, knew not where she was going, turned corners and went up by-streets without knowing why, anything to keep moving, for she fancied that so soon as she stood still, the rat in the pit of her stomach gnawed more eagerly.

At last, she entered what seemed to be, if not a park, at least some sort of public enclosure. There were many trees; the place was beautiful; well-kept roads and walks led sinuously and invitingly underneath the shade. Through the trees upon the other side of a wide expanse of turf, brown and sear under the summer sun, she caught a glimpse of tall buildings and a flagstaff. The whole place had a vaguely public, educational appearance, and Minna guessed, from certain notices affixed to the trees, warning the public against the picking of flowers, that she had found her way into the grounds of the State University. She went on a little further. The path she was following led her, at length, into a grove of gigantic live oaks, whose lower branches all but swept the ground. Here the grass was green, the few flowers in bloom, the shade very thick. A more lovely spot she had seldom seen. Near at hand was a bench, built around the trunk of the largest live oak, and here, at length, weak from hunger, exhausted to the limits of her endurance, despairing, abandoned, Minna Hooven sat down to enquire of herself what next she could do.

But once seated, the demands of the animal—so she could believe—became more clamorous, more insistent. To eat, to rest, to be safely housed against another night, above all else, these were the things she craved; and the craving within her grew so mighty that she crisped her poor, starved hands into little fists, in an agony of desire, while the tears ran from her eyes, and the sobs rose thick from her breast and struggled and strangled in her aching throat.

But in a few moments Minna was aware that a woman, apparently of some thirty years of age, had twice passed along the walk in front of the bench where she sat, and now, as she took more notice of her, she remembered that she had seen her on the ferry-boat coming over from the city.

The woman was gowned in silk, tightly corseted, and wore a hat of rather ostentatious smartness. Minna became convinced that the person was watching her, but before she had a chance to act upon this conviction she was surprised out of all countenance by the stranger coming up to where she sat and speaking to her.

"Here is a coincidence," exclaimed the new-comer, as she sat down; "surely you are the young girl who sat opposite me on the boat. Strange I should come across you again. I've had you in mind ever since."

On this nearer view Minna observed that the woman's face bore rather more than a trace of enamel and that the atmosphere about was impregnated with sachet. She was not otherwise conspicuous, but there was a certain hardness about her mouth and a certain droop of fatigue in her eyelids which, combined with an indefinite self-confidence of manner, held Minna's attention.

"Do you know," continued the woman, "I believe you are in trouble. I thought so when I saw you on the boat, and I think so now. Are you? Are you in trouble? You're from the country, ain't you?"

Minna, glad to find a sympathiser, even in this chance acquaintance, admitted that she was in distress; that she had become separated from her mother, and that she was indeed from the country.

"I've been trying to find a situation," she hazarded in conclusion, "but I don't seem to succeed. I've never been in a city before, except Bonneville."

"Well, it *is* a coincidence," said the other. "I know I wasn't drawn to you for nothing. I am looking for just such a young girl as you. You see, I live alone a good deal and I've been wanting to find a nice, bright, sociable girl who will be a sort of *companion* to me. Understand? And there's something about you that I like. I took to you the moment I saw you on the boat. Now shall we talk this over?"

Towards the end of the week, one afternoon, as Presley was returning from his club, he came suddenly face to face with Minna upon a street corner.

"Ah," he cried, coming toward her joyfully. "Upon my word, I had almost given you up. I've been looking everywhere for you. I was afraid you might not be getting along, and I wanted to see if there was anything I could do. How are your mother and Hilda? Where are you stopping? Have you got a good place?"

"I don't know where mamma is," answered Minna. "We got separated, and I never have been able to find her again."

Meanwhile, Presley had been taking in with a quick eye the details of Minna's silk dress, with its garniture of lace, its edging of velvet, its silver belt-buckle. Her hair was arranged in a new way and on her head was a wide hat with a flare to one side, set off with a gilt buckle and a puff of bright blue plush. He glanced at her sharply.

"Well, but—but how are you getting on?" he demanded.

Minna laughed scornfully.

"I?" she cried. "Oh, I've gone to hell. It was either that or starvation."

Presley regained his room at the club, white and trembling. Worse than the worst he had feared had happened. He had not been soon enough to help. He had failed again. A superstitious fear assailed him that he was, in a manner, marked; that he was foredoomed to fail. Minna had come—had been driven to this; and he, acting too late upon his tardy resolve, had not been able to prevent it. Were the horrors, then, never to end? Was the grisly spectre of consequence to forever dance in his vision? Were the results, the far-reaching results of that battle at the irrigating ditch to cross his path forever? When would the affair be terminated, the incident closed? Where was that spot to which the tentacle of the monster could not reach?

By now, he was sick with the dread of it all. He wanted to get away, to be free from that endless misery, so that he might not see what he could no longer help. Cowardly he now knew himself to be. He thought of himself only with loathing.

Bitterly self-contemptuous that he could bring himself to a

participation in such trivialties, he began to dress to keep his engagement to dine with the Cedarquists.

He arrived at the house nearly half an hour late, but before he could take off his overcoat, Mrs. Cedarquist appeared in the doorway of the drawing-room at the end of the hall. She was dressed as if to go out.

"My *dear* Presley," she exclaimed, her stout, over-dressed body bustling toward him with a great rustle of silk. "I never was so glad. You poor, dear poet, you are thin as a ghost. You need a better dinner than I can give you, and that is just what you are to have."

"Have I blundered?" Presley hastened to exclaim. "Did not Mr. Cedarquist mention Friday evening?"

"No, no, no," she cried; "it was he who blundered. *You* blundering in a social amenity! Preposterous! No; Mr. Cedarquist forgot that we were dining out ourselves to-night, and when he told me he had asked you here for the same evening, I fell upon the man, my dear, I did actually, tooth and nail. But I wouldn't hear of his wiring you. I just dropped a note to our hostess, asking if I could not bring you, and when I told her who you *were*, she received the idea with, oh, *empressement*. So, there it is, all settled. Cedarquist and the girls are gone on ahead, and you are to take the old lady like a dear, dear poet. I believe I hear the carriage. *Allons! En voiture!*"

Once settled in the cool gloom of the coupé, odorous of leather and upholstery, Mrs. Cedarquist exclaimed:

"And I've never really told you who you were to dine with; oh, a personage, really. Fancy, you will be in the camp of your dearest foes. You are to dine with the Gerard people, one of the Vice-Presidents of your *bête noir*, the P. and S. W. Railroad."

Presley started, his fists clenching so abruptly as to all but split his white gloves. He was not conscious of what he said in reply, and Mrs. Cedarquist was so taken up with her own endless stream of talk that she did not observe his confusion.

"Their daughter Honora is going to Europe next week; her mother is to take her, and Mrs. Gerard is to have just a few people to dinner—very informal, you know—ourselves, you and, oh, I don't know, two or three others. Have you ever seen Honora? The prettiest little thing, and will she be rich? Millions, I would not dare say how many. *Tiens. Nous voici.*"

The coupé drew up to the curb, and Presley followed Mrs. Cedarquist up the steps to the massive doors of the great house. In a confused daze, he allowed one of the footmen to relieve him of his hat and coat; in a daze he rejoined Mrs. Cedarquist in a room with a glass roof, hung with pictures, the art gallery, no doubt, and in a daze heard their names announced at the entrance of another room, the doors of which were hung with thick, blue curtains.

He entered, collecting his wits for the introductions and presentations that he foresaw impended.

The room was very large, and of excessive loftiness. Flat, rectagonal pillars of a rose-tinted, variegated marble, rose from the floor almost flush with the walls, finishing off at the top with gilded capitals of a Corinthian design, which supported the ceiling. The ceiling itself, instead of joining the walls at right angles, curved to meet them, a device that produced a sort of dome-like effect. This ceiling was a maze of golden involutions in very high relief, that adjusted themselves to form a massive framing for a great picture, nymphs and goddesses, white doves, golden chariots and the like, all wreathed about with clouds and garlands of roses. Between the pillars around the sides of the room were hangings of silk, the design—of a Louis Quinze type—of beautiful simplicity and faultless taste. The fireplace was a marvel. It reached from floor to ceiling; the lower parts, black marble, carved into crouching Atlases, with great muscles that upbore the superstructure. The design of this latter, of a kind of purple marble, shot through with white veinings, was in the same style as the design of the silk hangings. In its midst was a bronze escutcheon, bearing an undecipherable monogram and a Latin motto. Andirons of brass, nearly six feet high, flanked the hearthstone.

The windows of the room were heavily draped in sombre brocade and *écru* lace, in which the initials of the family were very beautifully worked. But directly opposite the fireplace, an extra window, lighted from the adjoining conservatory, threw a wonderful, rich light into the apartment. It was a Gothic window of stained glass, very large, the centre figures being armed warriors, Parsifal and Lohengrin; the one with a banner, the other with a swan. The effect was exquisite, the window a veritable masterpiece, glowing, flaming, and burning with a hundred tints and colours—opalescent, purple, wine-red, clouded pinks, royal blues, saffrons, violets so dark as to be almost black.

Under foot, the carpet had all the softness of texture of grass; skins (one of them of an enormous polar bear) and rugs of silk velvet were spread upon the floor. A Renaissance cabinet of ebony, many feet taller than Presley's head, and inlaid with ivory and silver, occupied one corner of the room, while in its centre stood a vast table of Flemish oak, black, heavy as iron, massive. A faint odour of sandalwood pervaded the air. From the conservatory near-by, came the splashing of a fountain. A row of electric bulbs let into the frieze of the walls between the golden capitals, and burning dimly behind hemispheres of clouded glass, threw a subdued light over the whole scene.

Mrs. Gerard came forward.

"This is Mr. Presley, of course, our new poet of whom we are all so proud. I was so afraid you would be unable to come. You have given me a real pleasure in allowing me to welcome you here."

The footman appeared at her elbow.

"Dinner is served, madame," he announced.

———

When Mrs. Hooven had left the boarding-house on Castro Street, she had taken up a position on a neighbouring corner, to wait for Minna's reappearance. Little Hilda, at this time hardly more than six years of age, was with her, holding to her hand.

Mrs. Hooven was by no means an old woman, but hard work had aged her. She no longer had any claim to good looks. She no longer took much interest in her personal appearance. At the time of her eviction from the Castro Street boarding-house, she wore a faded black bonnet, garnished with faded artificial flowers of dirty pink. A plaid shawl was about her shoulders. But this day of misfortune had set Mrs. Hooven adrift in even worse condition than her daughter.

Her purse, containing a miserable handful of dimes and nickels, was in her trunk, and her trunk was in the hands of the landlady. Minna had been allowed such reprieve as her thirty-five cents would purchase. The destitution of Mrs. Hooven and her little girl had begun from the very moment of her eviction.

While she waited for Minna, watching every street car and every approaching pedestrian, a policeman appeared, asked what she did, and, receiving no satisfactory reply, promptly moved her on.

Minna had had little assurance in facing the life struggle of the city. Mrs. Hooven had absolutely none. In her, grief, distress, the pinch of poverty, and, above all, the nameless fear of the turbulent, fierce life of the streets, had produced a numbness, an embruted, sodden, silent, speechless condition of dazed mind, and clogged, unintelligent speech. She was dumb, bewildered, stupid, animated but by a single impulse. She clung to life, and to the life of her little daughter Hilda, with the blind tenacity of purpose of a drowning cat.

Thus, when ordered to move on by the officer, she had silently obeyed, not even attempting to explain her situation. She walked away to the next street-crossing. Then, in a few moments returned, taking up her place on the corner near the boarding-house, spying upon the approaching cable cars, peeping anxiously down the length of the sidewalks.

Once more, the officer ordered her away, and once more, unprotesting, she complied. But when for the third time the policeman found her on the forbidden spot, he had lost his temper. This time when Mrs. Hooven departed, he had followed her, and when, bewildered, persistent, she had attempted to turn back, he caught her by the shoulder.

"Do you want to get arrested, hey?" he demanded. "Do you want me to lock you up? Say, do you, speak up?"

The ominous words at length reached Mrs. Hooven's comprehension. Arrested! She was to be arrested. The country-woman's fear of the Jail nipped and bit eagerly at her unwilling heels. She hurried off, thinking to return to her post after the policeman should have gone away. But when, at length, turning back, she tried to find the boarding-house, she suddenly discovered that she was on an unfamiliar street.

Unwittingly, no doubt, she had turned a corner. She could not retrace her steps. She and Hilda were lost.

"Mammy, I'm tired," Hilda complained.

Her mother picked her up.

"Mammy, where're we gowun, mammy?"

Where, indeed? Stupefied, Mrs. Hooven looked about her at the endless blocks of buildings, the endless procession of vehicles in the streets, the endless march of pedestrians on the sidewalks. Where was Minna; where was she and her baby to sleep that night? How was Hilda to be fed?

She could not stand still. There was no place to sit down; but one thing was left, walk.

Ah, that *via dolorosa* of the destitute, that *chemin de la croix* of the homeless. Ah, the mile after mile of granite pavement that *must* be, *must* be traversed. Walk they must. Move, they must; onward, forward, whither they cannot tell; why, they do not know. Walk, walk, walk with bleeding feet and smarting joints; walk with aching back and trembling knees; walk, though the senses grow giddy with fatigue, though the eyes droop with sleep, though every nerve, demanding rest, sets in motion its tiny alarm of pain. Death is at the end of that devious, winding maze of paths, crossed and recrossed and crossed again. There is but one goal to the *via dolorosa*; there is no escape from the central chamber of that labyrinth. Fate guides the feet of them that are set therein. Double on their steps though they may, weave in and out of the myriad corners of the city's streets, return, go forward, back, from side to side, here, there, anywhere, dodge, twist, wind, the central chamber where Death sits is reached inexorably at the end.

Sometimes leading and sometimes carrying Hilda, Mrs. Hooven set off upon her objectless journey. Block after block she walked, street after street. She was afraid to stop, because of the policemen. As often as she so much as slackened her pace, she was sure to see one of these terrible figures in the distance, watching her, so it seemed to her, waiting for her to halt for the fraction of a second, in order that he might have an excuse to arrest her.

Hilda fretted incessantly.

"Mammy, where're we gowun? Mammy, I'm tired." Then,

at last, for the first time, that plaint that stabbed the mother's heart:

"Mammy, I'm hungry."

"Be qui-ut, den," said Mrs. Hooven. "Bretty soon we'll hev der subber."

Passers-by on the sidewalk, men and women in the great six o'clock homeward march, jostled them as they went along. With dumb, dull curiousness, she looked into one after another of the limitless stream of faces, and she fancied she saw in them every emotion but pity. The faces were gay, were anxious, were sorrowful, were mirthful, were lined with thought, or were merely flat and expressionless, but not one was turned toward her in compassion. The expressions of the faces might be various, but an underlying callousness was discoverable beneath every mask. The people seemed removed from her immeasurably; they were infinitely above her. What was she to them, she and her baby, the crippled outcasts of the human herd, the unfit, not able to survive, thrust out on the heath to perish?

To beg from these people did not yet occur to her. There was no pride, however, in the matter. She would have as readily asked alms of so many sphinxes.

She went on. Without willing it, her feet carried her in a wide circle. Soon she began to recognise the houses; she had been in that street before. Somehow, this was distasteful to her; so, striking off at right angles, she walked straight before her for over a dozen blocks. By now, it was growing darker. The sun had set. The hands of a clock on the power-house of a cable line pointed to seven. No doubt, Minna had come long before this time, had found her mother gone, and had— just what had she done, just what *could* she do? Where was her daughter now? Walking the streets herself, no doubt. What was to become of Minna, pretty girl that she was, lost, houseless and friendless in the maze of these streets? Mrs. Hooven, roused from her lethargy, could not repress an exclamation of anguish. Here was misfortune indeed; here was calamity. She bestirred herself, and remembered the address of the boarding-house. She might inquire her way back thither. No doubt, by now the policeman would be gone home for the night. She looked about. She was in the district of modest residences, and a young man was coming toward her, carrying a new garden hose looped around his shoulder.

"Say, Meest'r; say, blease——"

The young man gave her a quick look and passed on, hitching the coil of hose over his shoulder. But a few paces distant, he slackened in his walk and fumbled in his vest pocket with his fingers. Then he came back to Mrs. Hooven and put a quarter into her hand.

Mrs. Hooven stared at the coin stupefied. The young man disappeared. He thought, then, that she was begging. It had come to that; she, independent all her life, whose husband had held five hundred acres of wheat land, had been taken for a beggar. A flush of shame shot to her face. She was about to throw the money after its giver. But at the moment, Hilda again exclaimed:

"Mammy, I'm hungry."

With a movement of infinite lassitude and resigned acceptance of the situation, Mrs. Hooven put the coin in her pocket. She had no right to be proud any longer. Hilda must have food.

That evening, she and her child had supper at a cheap restaurant in a poor quarter of the town, and passed the night on the benches of a little uptown park.

Unused to the ways of the town, ignorant as to the customs and possibilities of eating-houses, she spent the whole of her quarter upon supper for herself and Hilda, and had nothing left wherewith to buy a lodging.

The night was dreadful; Hilda sobbed herself to sleep on her mother's shoulder, waking thereafter from hour to hour, to protest, though wrapped in her mother's shawl, that she was cold, and to enquire why they did not go to bed. Drunken men snored and sprawled near at hand. Towards morning, a loafer, reeking of alcohol, sat down beside her, and indulged in an incoherent soliloquy, punctuated with oaths and obscenities. It was not till far along towards daylight that she fell asleep.

She awoke to find it broad day. Hilda—mercifully—slept. Her mother's limbs were stiff and lame with cold and damp; her head throbbed. She moved to another bench which stood in the rays of the sun, and for a long two hours sat there in the thin warmth, till the moisture of the night that clung to her clothes was evaporated.

A policeman came into view. She woke Hilda, and carrying her in her arms, took herself away.

"Mammy," began Hilda as soon as she was well awake; "Mammy, I'm hungry. I want mein breakfest."

"Sure, sure, soon now, leedle tochter."

She herself was hungry, but she had but little thought of that. How was Hilda to be fed? She remembered her experience of the previous day, when the young man with the hose had given her money. Was it so easy, then, to beg? Could charity be had for the asking? So it seemed; but all that was left of her sturdy independence revolted at the thought. *She* beg! *She* hold out the hand to strangers!

"Mammy, I'm hungry."

There was no other way. It must come to that in the end. Why temporise, why put off the inevitable? She sought out a frequented street where men and women were on their way to work. One after another, she let them go by, searching their faces, deterred at the very last moment by some trifling variation of expression, a firm set mouth, a serious, level eyebrow, an advancing chin. Then, twice, when she had made a choice, and brought her resolution to the point of speech, she quailed, shrinking, her ears tingling, her whole being protesting against the degradation. Every one must be looking at her. Her shame was no doubt the object of an hundred eyes.

"Mammy, I'm hungry," protested Hilda again.

She made up her mind. What, though, was she to say? In what words did beggars ask for assistance? She tried to remember how tramps who had appeared at her back door on Los Muertos had addressed her; how and with what formula certain mendicants of Bonneville had appealed to her. Then, having settled upon a phrase, she approached a whiskered gentleman with a large stomach, walking briskly in the direction of the town.

"Say, den, blease hellup a boor womun."

The gentleman passed on.

"Perhaps he doand hear me," she murmured.

Two well-dressed women advanced, chattering gayly.

"Say, say, den, blease hellup a boor womun."

One of the women paused, murmuring to her companion, and from her purse extracted a yellow ticket which she gave to Mrs. Hooven with voluble explanations. But Mrs. Hooven was confused, she did not understand. What could the ticket mean? The women went on their way.

The next person to whom she applied was a young girl of about eighteen, very prettily dressed.

"Say, say, den, blease hellup a boor womun."

In evident embarrassment, the young girl paused and searched in her little pocketbook.

"I think I have—I think—I have just ten cents here somewhere," she murmured again and again.

In the end, she found a dime, and dropped it into Mrs. Hooven's palm.

That was the beginning. The first step once taken, the others became easy. All day long, Mrs. Hooven and Hilda followed the streets, begging, begging. Here it was a nickel, there a dime, here a nickel again. But she was not expert in the art, nor did she know where to buy food the cheapest; and the entire day's work resulted only in barely enough for two meals of bread, milk, and a wretchedly cooked stew. Tuesday night found the pair once more shelterless.

Once more, Mrs. Hooven and her baby passed the night on the park benches. But early on Wednesday morning, Mrs. Hooven found herself assailed by sharp pains and cramps in her stomach. What was the cause she could not say; but as the day went on, the pains increased, alternating with hot flushes over all her body, and a certain weakness and faintness. As the day went on, the pain and the weakness increased. When she tried to walk, she found she could do so only with the greatest difficulty. Here was fresh misfortune. To beg, she must walk. Dragging herself forward a half-block at a time, she regained the street once more. She succeeded in begging a couple of nickels, bought a bag of apples from a vender, and, returning to the park, sank exhausted upon a bench.

Here she remained all day until evening, Hilda alternately whimpering for her bread and milk, or playing languidly in the gravel walk at her feet. In the evening, she started out again. This time, it was bitter hard. Nobody seemed inclined to give. Twice she was "moved on" by policemen. Two hours' begging elicited but a single dime. With this, she bought Hilda's bread and milk, and refusing herself to eat, returned to the bench—the only home she knew—and spent the night shivering with cold, burning with fever.

From Wednesday morning till Friday evening, with the exception of the few apples she had bought, and a quarter of a loaf of hard bread that she found in a greasy newspaper— scraps of a workman's dinner—Mrs. Hooven had nothing to eat. In her weakened condition, begging became hourly more difficult, and such little money as was given her, she resolutely spent on Hilda's bread and milk in the morning and evening.

By Friday afternoon, she was very weak, indeed. Her eyes troubled her. She could no longer see distinctly, and at times there appeared to her curious figures, huge crystal goblets of the most graceful shapes, floating and swaying in the air in front of her, almost within arm's reach. Vases of elegant forms, made of shimmering glass, bowed and courtesied toward her. Glass bulbs took graceful and varying shapes before her vision, now rounding into globes, now evolving into hour-glasses, now twisting into pretzel-shaped convolutions.

"Mammy, I'm hungry," insisted Hilda, passing her hands over her face. Mrs. Hooven started and woke. It was Friday evening. Already the street lamps were being lit.

"Gome, den, leedle girl," she said, rising and taking Hilda's hand. "Gome, den, we go vind subber, hey?"

She issued from the park and took a cross street, directly away from the locality where she had begged the previous days. She had had no success there of late. She would try some other quarter of the town. After a weary walk, she came out upon Van Ness Avenue, near its junction with Market Street. She turned into the avenue, and went on toward the Bay, painfully traversing block after block, begging of all whom she met (for she no longer made any distinction among the passers-by).

"Say, say, den, blease hellup a boor womun."

"Mammy, mammy, I'm hungry."

It was Friday night, between seven and eight. The great deserted avenue was already dark. A sea fog was scudding overhead, and by degrees descending lower. The warmth was of the meagerest, and the street lamps, birds of fire in cages of glass, fluttered and danced in the prolonged gusts of the trade wind that threshed and weltered in the city streets from off the ocean.

———

Presley entered the dining-room of the Gerard mansion with little Miss Gerard on his arm. The other guests had preceded them—Cedarquist with Mrs. Gerard; a pale-faced, languid young man (introduced to Presley as Julian Lambert) with Presley's cousin Beatrice, one of the twin daughters of Mr. and Mrs. Cedarquist; his brother Stephen, whose hair was straight as an Indian's, but of a pallid straw color, with Beatrice's sister; Gerard himself, taciturn, bearded, rotund, loud of breath, escorted Mrs. Cedarquist. Besides these, there were one or two other couples, whose names Presley did not remember.

The dining-room was superb in its appointments. On three sides of the room, to the height of some ten feet, ran a continuous picture, an oil painting, divided into long sections by narrow panels of black oak. The painting represented the personages in the *Romaunt de la Rose*, and was conceived in an atmosphere of the most delicate, most ephemeral allegory. One saw young chevaliers, blue-eyed, of elemental beauty and purity; women with crowns, gold girdles, and cloudy wimples; young girls, entrancing in their loveliness, wearing snow-white kerchiefs, their golden hair unbound and flowing, dressed in white samite, bearing armfuls of flowers; the whole procession defiling against a background of forest glades, venerable oaks, half-hidden fountains, and fields of asphodel and roses.

Otherwise, the room was simple. Against the side of the wall unoccupied by the picture stood a sideboard of gigantic size, that once had adorned the banquet hall of an Italian palace of the late Renaissance. It was black with age, and against its sombre surfaces glittered an array of heavy silver dishes and heavier cut-glass bowls and goblets.

The company sat down to the first course of raw Blue Point oysters, served upon little pyramids of shaved ice, and the two butlers at once began filling the glasses of the guests with cool Haut Sauterne.

Mrs. Gerard, who was very proud of her dinners, and never able to resist the temptation of commenting upon them to her guests, leaned across to Presley and Mrs. Cedarquist, murmuring, "Mr. Presley, do you find that Sauterne too cold? I always believe it is so *bourgeois* to keep such a delicate wine as Sauterne on the ice, and to ice Bordeaux or Burgundy— oh, it is nothing short of a crime."

"This is from your own vineyard, is it not?" asked Julian Lambert. "I think I recognise the bouquet."

He strove to maintain an attitude of *fin gourmet*, unable to refrain from comment upon the courses as they succeeded one another.

Little Honora Gerard turned to Presley:

"You know," she explained, "Papa has his own vineyards in southern France. He is so particular about his wines; turns up his nose at California wines. And I am to go there next summer. Ferrières is the name of the place where our vineyards are, the dearest village!"

She was a beautiful little girl of a dainty porcelain type, her colouring low in tone. She wore no jewels, but her little, undeveloped neck and shoulders, of an exquisite immaturity, rose from the tulle bodice of her first *décolleté* gown.

"Yes," she continued; "I'm to go to Europe for the first time. Won't it be gay? And I am to have my own *bonne*, and Mamma and I are to travel—so many places, Baden, Homburg, Spa, the Tyrol. Won't it be gay?"

Presley assented in meaningless words. He sipped his wine mechanically, looking about that marvellous room, with its subdued saffron lights, its glitter of glass and silver, its beautiful women in their elaborate toilets, its deft, correct servants; its array of tableware—cut glass, chased silver, and Dresden crockery. It was Wealth, in all its outward and visible forms, the signs of an opulence so great that it need never be husbanded. It was the home of a railway "Magnate," a Railroad King. For this, then, the farmers paid. It was for this that S. Behrman turned the screw, tightened the vise. It was for this that Dyke had been driven to outlawry and a jail. It was for this that Lyman Derrick had been bought, the Governor ruined and broken, Annixter shot down, Hooven killed.

The soup, *purée à la Derby*, was served, and at the same time, as *hors d'œuvres*, ortolan patties, together with a tiny sandwich made of browned toast and thin slices of ham, sprinkled over with Parmesan cheese. The wine, so Mrs. Gerard caused it to be understood, was Xeres, of the 1815 vintage.

———

Mrs. Hooven crossed the avenue. It was growing late. Without knowing it, she had come to a part of the city that experienced beggars shunned. There was nobody about. Block after block of residences stretched away on either hand, lighted, full of people. But the sidewalks were deserted.

"Mammy," whimpered Hilda. "I'm tired, carry me."

Using all her strength, Mrs. Hooven picked her up and moved on aimlessly.

Then again that terrible cry, the cry of the hungry child appealing to the helpless mother:

"Mammy, I'm hungry."

"Ach, Gott, leedle girl," exclaimed Mrs. Hooven, holding her close to her shoulder, the tears starting from her eyes. "Ach, leedle tochter. Doand, doand, doand. You praik my hairt. I cen't vind any subber. We got noddings to eat, noddings, noddings."

"When do we have those bread'n milk again, Mammy?"

"To-morrow—soon—py-and-py, Hilda. I doand know what pecome oaf us now, what pecome oaf my leedle babby."

She went on, holding Hilda against her shoulder with one arm as best she might, one hand steadying herself against the fence railings along the sidewalk. At last, a solitary pedestrian came into view, a young man in a top hat and overcoat, walking rapidly. Mrs. Hooven held out a quivering hand as he passed her.

"Say, say, den, Meest'r, blease hellup a boor womun."

The other hurried on.

———

The fish course was *grenadins* of bass and small salmon, the latter stuffed, and cooked in white wine and mushroom liquor.

"I have read your poem, of course, Mr. Presley," observed Mrs. Gerard. " 'The Toilers,' I mean. What a sermon you read us, you dreadful young man. I felt that I ought at once to 'sell all that I have and give to the poor.' Positively, it did stir me up. You may congratulate yourself upon making at least one convert. Just because of that poem Mrs. Cedarquist and I have started a movement to send a whole shipload of wheat to the starving people in India. Now, you horrid *réaction-naire*, are you satisfied?"

"I am very glad," murmured Presley.

"But I am afraid," observed Mrs. Cedarquist, "that we may be too late. They are dying so fast, those poor people. By the time our ship reaches India the famine may be all over."

"One need never be afraid of being 'too late' in the matter of helping the destitute," answered Presley. "Unfortunately, they are always a fixed quantity. 'The poor ye have always with you.' "

"How very clever that is," said Mrs. Gerard.

Mrs. Cedarquist tapped the table with her fan in mild applause.

"Brilliant, brilliant," she murmured, "epigrammatical."

"Honora," said Mrs. Gerard, turning to her daughter, at that moment in conversation with the languid Lambert, "Honora, *entends-tu, ma chérie, l'esprit de notre jeune Lamartine.*"

———

Mrs. Hooven went on, stumbling from street to street, holding Hilda to her breast. Famine gnawed incessantly at her stomach; walk though she might, turn upon her tracks up and down the streets, back to the avenue again, incessantly and relentlessly the torture dug into her vitals. She was hungry, hungry, and if the want of food harassed and rended her, full-grown woman that she was, what must it be in the poor, starved stomach of her little girl? Oh, for some helping hand now, oh, for one little mouthful, one little nibble! Food, food, all her wrecked body clamoured for nourishment; anything to numb those gnawing teeth—an abandoned loaf, hard, mouldered; a half-eaten fruit, yes, even the refuse of the gutter, even the garbage of the ash heap. On she went,

peering into dark corners, into the areaways, anywhere, everywhere, watching the silent prowling of cats, the intent rovings
of stray dogs. But she was growing weaker; the pains and
cramps in her stomach returned. Hilda's weight bore her to
the pavement. More than once a great giddiness, a certain
wheeling faintness all but overcame her. Hilda, however, was
asleep. To wake her would only mean to revive her to the
consciousness of hunger; yet how to carry her further? Mrs.
Hooven began to fear that she would fall with her child in
her arms. The terror of a collapse upon those cold pavements
glistening with fog-damp roused her; she must make an effort
to get through the night. She rallied all her strength, and
pausing a moment to shift the weight of her baby to the other
arm, once more set off through the night. A little while later
she found on the edge of the sidewalk the peeling of a banana. It had been trodden upon and it was muddy, but joyfully she caught it up.

"Hilda," she cried, " wake oop, leedle girl. See, loog den,
dere's somedings to eat. Look den, hey? Dat's goot, ain't it?
Zum bunaner."

But it could not be eaten. Decayed, dirty, all but rotting,
the stomach turned from the refuse, nauseated.

"No, no," cried Hilda, "that's not good. I can't eat it. Oh,
Mammy, please gif me those bread'n milk."

———

By now the guests of Mrs. Gerard had come to the entrées—Londonderry pheasants, escallops of duck, and *risso-
lettes à la pompadour*. The wine was Château Latour.

All around the table conversations were going forward
gayly. The good wines had broken up the slight restraint of
the early part of the evening and a spirit of good humour and
good fellowship prevailed. Young Lambert and Mr. Gerard
were deep in reminiscences of certain mutual duck-shooting
expeditions. Mrs. Gerard and Mrs. Cedarquist discussed a
novel—a strange mingling of psychology, degeneracy, and
analysis of erotic conditions—which had just been translated
from the Italian. Stephen Lambert and Beatrice disputed over
the merits of a Scotch collie just given to the young lady. The

scene was gay, the electric bulbs sparkled, the wine flashing back the light. The entire table was a vague glow of white napery, delicate china, and glass as brilliant as crystal. Behind the guests the serving-men came and went, filling the glasses continually, changing the covers, serving the entrées, managing the dinner without interruption, confusion, or the slightest unnecessary noise.

But Presley could find no enjoyment in the occasion. From that picture of feasting, that scene of luxury, that atmosphere of decorous, well-bred refinement, his thoughts went back to Los Muertos and Quien Sabe and the irrigating ditch at Hooven's. He saw them fall, one by one, Harran, Annixter, Osterman, Broderson, Hooven. The clink of the wine glasses was drowned in the explosion of revolvers. The Railroad might indeed be a force only, which no man could control and for which no man was responsible, but his friends had been killed, but years of extortion and oppression had wrung money from all the San Joaquin, money that had made possible this very scene in which he found himself. Because Magnus had been beggared, Gerard had become Railroad King; because the farmers of the valley were poor, these men were rich.

The fancy grew big in his mind, distorted, caricatured, terrible. Because the farmers had been killed at the irrigation ditch, these others, Gerard and his family, fed full. They fattened on the blood of the People, on the blood of the men who had been killed at the ditch. It was a half-ludicrous, half-horrible "dog eat dog," an unspeakable cannibalism. Harran, Annixter, and Hooven were being devoured there under his eyes. These dainty women, his cousin Beatrice and little Miss Gerard, frail, delicate; all these fine ladies with their small fingers and slender necks, suddenly were transfigured in his tortured mind into harpies tearing human flesh. His head swam with the horror of it, the terror of it. Yes, the People *would* turn some day, and turning, rend those who now preyed upon them. It would be "dog eat dog" again, with positions reversed, and he saw for one instant of time that splendid house sacked to its foundations, the tables overturned, the pictures torn, the hangings blazing, and Liberty, the red-handed Man in the Street, grimed with powder smoke, foul with the gutter, rush yelling, torch in hand, through every door.

———

At ten o'clock Mrs. Hooven fell.

Luckily she was leading Hilda by the hand at the time and the little girl was not hurt. In vain had Mrs. Hooven, hour after hour, walked the streets. After a while she no longer made any attempt to beg; nobody was stirring, nor did she even try to hunt for food with the stray dogs and cats. She had made up her mind to return to the park in order to sit upon the benches there, but she had mistaken the direction, and following up Sacramento Street, had come out at length, not upon the park, but upon a great vacant lot at the very top of the Clay Street hill. The ground was unfenced and rose above her to form the cap of the hill, all overgrown with bushes and a few stunted live oaks. It was in trying to cross this piece of ground that she fell. She got upon her feet again.

"Ach, Mammy, did you hurt yourself?" asked Hilda.

"No, no."

"Is that house where we get those bread'n milk?"

Hilda pointed to a single rambling building just visible in the night, that stood isolated upon the summit of the hill in a grove of trees.

"No, no, dere aindt no braid end miluk, leedle tochter."

Hilda once more began to sob.

"Ach, Mammy, please, *please*, I want it. I'm hungry."

The jangled nerves snapped at last under the tension, and Mrs. Hooven, suddenly shaking Hilda roughly, cried out:

"Stop, stop. Doand say ut egen, you. My Gott, you kill me yet."

But quick upon this came the reaction. The mother caught her little girl to her, sinking down upon her knees, putting her arms around her, holding her close.

"No, no, gry all so mudge es you want. Say dot you are hongry. Say ut egen, say ut all de dime, ofer end ofer egen. Say ut, poor, starfing, leedle babby. Oh, mein poor, leedle tochter. My Gott, oh, I go crazy bretty soon, I guess. I cen't hellup you. I cen't ged you noddings to eat, noddings, noddings. Hilda, we gowun to die togedder. Put der arms roundt me, soh, tighd, leedle babby. We gowun to die, we gowun to vind Popper. We aindt gowun to be hongry eny more."

"Vair we go now?" demanded Hilda.

"No places. Mommer's soh tiredt. We stop heir, leedle while, end rest."

Underneath a large bush that afforded a little shelter from the wind, Mrs. Hooven lay down, taking Hilda in her arms and wrapping her shawl about her. The infinite, vast night expanded gigantic all around them. At this elevation they were far above the city. It was still. Close overhead whirled the chariots of the fog, galloping landward, smothering lights, blurring outlines. Soon all sight of the town was shut out; even the solitary house on the hilltop vanished. There was nothing left but grey, wheeling fog, and the mother and child, alone, shivering in a little strip of damp ground, an island drifting aimlessly in empty space.

Hilda's fingers touched a leaf from the bush and instinctively closed upon it and carried it to her mouth.

"Mammy," she said, "I'm eating those leaf. Is those good?"

Her mother did not reply.

"You going to sleep, Mammy?" inquired Hilda, touching her face.

Mrs. Hooven roused herself a little.

"Hey? Vat you say? Asleep? Yais, I guess I wass asleep."

Her voice trailed unintelligibly to silence again. She was not, however, asleep. Her eyes were open. A grateful numbness had begun to creep over her, a pleasing semi-insensibility. She no longer felt the pain and cramps of her stomach, even the hunger was ceasing to bite.

———

"These stuffed artichokes are delicious, Mrs. Gerard," murmured young Lambert, wiping his lips with a corner of his napkin. "Pardon me for mentioning it, but your dinner must be my excuse."

"And this asparagus—since Mr. Lambert has set the bad example," observed Mrs. Cedarquist, "so delicate, such an exquisite flavour. How *do* you manage?"

"We get all our asparagus from the southern part of the

State, from one particular ranch," explained Mrs. Gerard. "We order it by wire and get it only twenty hours after cutting. My husband sees to it that it is put on a special train. It stops at this ranch just to take on our asparagus. Extravagant, isn't it, but I simply cannot eat asparagus that has been cut more than a day."

"Nor I," exclaimed Julian Lambert, who posed as an epicure. "I can tell to an hour just how long asparagus has been picked."

"Fancy eating ordinary market asparagus," said Mrs. Gerard, "that has been fingered by Heaven knows how many hands."

———

"Mammy, mammy, wake up," cried Hilda, trying to push open Mrs. Hooven's eyelids, at last closed. "Mammy, don't. You're just trying to frighten me."

Feebly Hilda shook her by the shoulder. At last Mrs. Hooven's lips stirred. Putting her head down, Hilda distinguished the whispered words:

"I'm sick. Go to schleep. . . . Sick. . . . Noddings to eat."

———

The dessert was a wonderful preparation of alternate layers of biscuit glacés, ice cream, and candied chestnuts.

"Delicious, is it not?" observed Julian Lambert, partly to himself, partly to Miss Cedarquist. "This *Moscovite fouetté*—upon my word, I have never tasted its equal."

"And you should know, shouldn't you?" returned the young lady.

———

"Mammy, mammy, wake up," cried Hilda. "Don't sleep so. I'm frightenedt."

Repeatedly she shook her; repeatedly she tried to raise the inert eyelids with the point of her finger. But her mother no longer stirred. The gaunt, lean body, with its bony face and sunken eye-sockets, lay back, prone upon the ground, the feet upturned and showing the ragged, worn soles of the shoes, the forehead and grey hair beaded with fog, the poor, faded bonnet awry, the poor, faded dress soiled and torn.

Hilda drew close to her mother, kissing her face, twining her arms around her neck. For a long time, she lay that way, alternately sobbing and sleeping. Then, after a long time, there was a stir. She woke from a doze to find a police officer and two or three other men bending over her. Some one carried a lantern. Terrified, smitten dumb, she was unable to answer the questions put to her. Then a woman, evidently a mistress of the house on the top of the hill, arrived and took Hilda in her arms and cried over her.

"I'll take the little girl," she said to the police officer. "But the mother, can you save her? Is she too far gone?"

"I've sent for a doctor," replied the other.

———

Just before the ladies left the table, young Lambert raised his glass of Madeira. Turning towards the wife of the Railroad King, he said:

"My best compliments for a delightful dinner."

———

The doctor who had been bending over Mrs. Hooven, rose.

"It's no use," he said; "she has been dead some time— exhaustion from starvation."

IX

O N DIVISION Number Three of the Los Muertos ranch the wheat had already been cut, and S. Behrman on a certain morning in the first week of August drove across the open expanse of stubble toward the southwest, his eyes searching the horizon for the feather of smoke that would mark the location of the steam harvester. However, he saw nothing. The stubble extended onward apparently to the very margin of the world.

At length, S. Behrman halted his buggy and brought out his field glasses from beneath the seat. He stood up in his place and, adjusting the lenses, swept the prospect to the south and west. It was the same as though the sea of land were, in reality, the ocean, and he, lost in an open boat, were scanning the waste through his glasses, looking for the smoke of a steamer, hull down, below the horizon. "Wonder," he muttered, "if they're working on Four this morning?"

At length, he murmured an "Ah" of satisfaction. Far to the south into the white sheen of sky, immediately over the horizon, he made out a faint smudge—the harvester beyond doubt.

Thither S. Behrman turned his horse's head. It was all of an hour's drive over the uneven ground and through the crackling stubble, but at length he reached the harvester. He found, however, that it had been halted. The sack sewers, together with the header-man, were stretched on the ground in the shade of the machine, while the engineer and separator-man were pottering about a portion of the works.

"What's the matter, Billy?" demanded S. Behrman reining up.

The engineer turned about.

"The grain is heavy in here. We thought we'd better increase the speed of the cup-carrier, and pulled up to put in a smaller sprocket."

S. Behrman nodded to say that was all right, and added a question.

"How is she going?"

"Anywheres from twenty-five to thirty sacks to the acre right along here; nothing the matter with *that* I guess."

"Nothing in the world, Bill."

One of the sack sewers interposed:

"For the last half hour we've been throwing off three bags to the minute."

"That's good, that's good."

It was more than good; it was "bonanza," and all that division of the great ranch was thick with just such wonderful wheat. Never had Los Muertos been more generous, never a season more successful. S. Behrman drew a long breath of satisfaction. He knew just how great was his share in the lands which had just been absorbed by the corporation he served, just how many thousands of bushels of this marvellous crop were his property. Through all these years of confusion, bickerings, open hostility and, at last, actual warfare he had waited, nursing his patience, calm with the firm assurance of ultimate success. The end, at length, had come; he had entered into his reward and saw himself at last installed in the place he had so long, so silently coveted; saw himself chief of a principality, the Master of the Wheat.

The sprocket adjusted, the engineer called up the gang and the men took their places. The fireman stoked vigorously, the two sack sewers resumed their posts on the sacking platform, putting on the goggles that kept the chaff from their eyes. The separator-man and header-man gripped their levers.

The harvester, shooting a column of thick smoke straight upward, vibrating to the top of the stack, hissed, clanked, and lurched forward. Instantly, motion sprang to life in all its component parts; the header knives, cutting a thirty-six foot swath, gnashed like teeth; beltings slid and moved like smooth flowing streams; the separator whirred, the agitator jarred and crashed; cylinders, augers, fans, seeders and elevators, drapers and chaff-carriers clattered, rumbled, buzzed, and clanged. The steam hissed and rasped; the ground reverberated a hollow note, and the thousands upon thousands of wheat stalks sliced and slashed in the clashing shears of the header, rattled like dry rushes in a hurricane, as they fell inward, and were caught up by an endless belt, to disappear into the bowels of the vast brute that devoured them.

It was that and no less. It was the feeding of some prodigious monster, insatiable, with iron teeth, gnashing and threshing into the fields of standing wheat; devouring always, never glutted, never satiated, swallowing an entire harvest, snarling and slobbering in a welter of warm vapour, acrid smoke, and blinding, pungent clouds of chaff. It moved belly-deep in the standing grain, a hippopotamus, half-mired in river ooze, gorging rushes, snorting, sweating; a dinosaur wallowing through thick, hot grasses, floundering there, crouching, grovelling there as its vast jaws crushed and tore, and its enormous gullet swallowed, incessant, ravenous, and inordinate.

S. Behrman, very much amused, changed places with one of the sack sewers, allowing him to hold his horse while he mounted the sacking platform and took his place. The trepidation and jostling of the machine shook him till his teeth chattered in his head. His ears were shocked and assaulted by a myriad-tongued clamour, clashing steel, straining belts, jarring woodwork, while the impalpable chaff powder from the separators settled like dust in his hair, his ears, eyes, and mouth.

Directly in front of where he sat on the platform was the chute from the cleaner, and from this into the mouth of a half-full sack spouted an unending gush of grain, winnowed, cleaned, threshed, ready for the mill.

The pour from the chute of the cleaner had for S. Behrman an immense satisfaction. Without an instant's pause, a thick rivulet of wheat rolled and dashed tumultuous into the sack. In half a minute—sometimes in twenty seconds—the sack was full, was passed over to the second sewer, the mouth reeved up, and the sack dumped out upon the ground, to be picked up by the wagons and hauled to the railroad.

S. Behrman, hypnotised, sat watching that river of grain. All that shrieking, bellowing machinery, all that gigantic organism, all the months of labour, the ploughing, the planting, the prayers for rain, the years of preparation, the heartaches, the anxiety, the foresight, all the whole business of the ranch, the work of horses, of steam, of men and boys, looked to this spot—the grain chute from the harvester into the sacks. Its volume was the index of failure or success, of riches or poverty. And at this point, the labour of the rancher ended. Here, at the lip of the chute, he parted company with his grain, and from here the wheat streamed forth to feed the world. The yawning mouths of the sacks might well stand for the unnumbered mouths of the People, all agape for food; and here, into these sacks, at first so lean, so flaccid, attenuated like starved stomachs, rushed the living stream of food, insistent, interminable, filling the empty, fattening the shrivelled, making it sleek and heavy and solid.

Half an hour later, the harvester stopped again. The men on the sacking platform had used up all the sacks. But S. Behrman's foreman, a new man on Los Muertos, put in an appearance with the report that the wagon bringing a fresh supply was approaching.

"How is the grain elevator at Port Costa getting on, sir?"

"Finished," replied S. Behrman.

The new master of Los Muertos had decided upon accumulating his grain in bulk in a great elevator at the tide-water port, where the grain ships for Liverpool and the East took on their cargoes. To this end, he had bought and greatly enlarged a building at Port Costa, that was already in use for that purpose, and to this elevator all the crop of Los Muertos was to be carried. The P. and S. W. made S. Behrman a special rate.

"By the way," said S. Behrman to his superintendent, "we're in luck. Fallon's buyer was in Bonneville yesterday. He's buying for Fallon and for Holt, too. I happened to run into him, and I've sold a ship load."

"A ship load!"

"Of Los Muertos wheat. He's acting for some Indian Famine Relief Committee—lot of women people up in the city—and wanted a whole cargo. I made a deal with him. There's about fifty thousand tons of disengaged shipping in San Francisco Bay right now, and ships are fighting for charters. I wired McKissick and got a long distance telephone from him this morning. He got me a barque, the 'Swanhilda.' She'll dock day after to-morrow, and begin loading."

"Hadn't I better take a run up," observed the superintendent, "and keep an eye on things?"

"No," answered S. Behrman, "I want you to stop down here, and see that those carpenters hustle the work in the ranch house. Derrick will be out by then. You see this deal is peculiar. I'm not selling to any middleman—not to Fallon's buyer. He only put me on to the thing. I'm acting direct with these women people, and I've got to have some hand in shipping this stuff myself. But I made my selling figure cover the price of a charter. It's a queer, mixed-up deal, and I don't fancy it much, but there's boodle in it. I'll go to Port Costa myself."

A little later on in the day, when S. Behrman had satisfied himself that his harvesting was going forward favourably, he reëntered his buggy and driving to the County Road turned southward towards the Los Muertos ranch house. He had not gone far, however, before he became aware of a familiar figure on horseback, jogging slowly along ahead of him. He recognised Presley; he shook the reins over his horse's back and very soon ranging up by the side of the young man passed the time of day with him.

"Well, what brings you down here again, Mr. Presley?" he observed. "I thought we had seen the last of you."

"I came down to say good-bye to my friends," answered Presley shortly.

"Going away?"

"Yes—to India."

"Well, upon my word. For your health, hey?"

"Yes."

"You *look* knocked up," asserted the other. "By the way," he added, "I suppose you've heard the news?"

Presley shrank a little. Of late the reports of disasters had followed so swiftly upon one another that he had begun to tremble and to quail at every unexpected bit of information.

"What news do you mean?" he asked.

"About Dyke. He has been convicted. The judge sentenced him for life."

For life! Riding on by the side of this man through the ranches by the County Road, Presley repeated these words to himself till the full effect of them burst at last upon him.

Jailed for life! No outlook. No hope for the future. Day after day, year after year, to tread the rounds of the same gloomy monotony. He saw the grey stone walls, the iron doors; the flagging of the "yard" bare of grass or trees—the cell, narrow, bald, cheerless; the prison garb, the prison fare, and round all the grim granite of insuperable barriers, shutting out the world, shutting in the man with outcasts, with the pariah dogs of society, thieves, murderers, men below the beasts, lost to all decency, drugged with opium, utter reprobates. To this, Dyke had been brought, Dyke, than whom no man had been more honest, more courageous, more jovial. This was the end of him, a prison; this was his final estate, a criminal.

Presley found an excuse for riding on, leaving S. Behrman behind him. He did not stop at Caraher's saloon, for the heat of his rage had long since begun to cool, and dispassionately, he saw things in their true light. For all the tragedy of his wife's death, Caraher was none the less an evil influence among the ranchers, an influence that worked only to the inciting of crime. Unwilling to venture himself, to risk his own life, the anarchist saloon-keeper had goaded Dyke and Presley both to murder; a bad man, a plague spot in the world of the ranchers, poisoning the farmers' bodies with alcohol and their minds with discontent.

At last, Presley arrived at the ranch house of Los Muertos. The place was silent; the grass on the lawn was half dead and over a foot high; the beginnings of weeds showed here and there in the driveway. He tied his horse to a ring in the trunk of one of the larger eucalyptus trees and entered the house.

Mrs. Derrick met him in the dining-room. The old look of uneasiness, almost of terror, had gone from her wide-open brown eyes. There was in them instead, the expression of one to whom a contingency, long dreaded, has arrived and passed. The stolidity of a settled grief, of an irreparable calamity, of a despair from which there was no escape was in her look, her manner, her voice. She was listless, apathetic, calm with the calmness of a woman who knows she can suffer no further.

"We are going away," she told Presley, as the two sat down at opposite ends of the dining table. "Just Magnus and myself—all there is left of us. There is very little money left; Magnus can hardly take care of himself, to say nothing of me. I must look after him now. We are going to Marysville."

"Why there?"

"You see," she explained, "it happens that my old place is vacant in the Seminary there. I am going back to teach— literature." She smiled wearily. "It is beginning all over again, isn't it? Only there is nothing to look forward to now. Magnus is an old man already, and I must take care of him."

"He will go with you, then," Presley said, "that will be some comfort to you at least."

"I don't know," she said slowly, "you have not seen Magnus lately."

"Is he—how do you mean? Isn't he any better?"

"Would you like to see him? He is in the office. You can go right in."

Presley rose. He hesitated a moment, then:

"Mrs. Annixter," he asked, "Hilma—is she still with you? I should like to see her before I go."

"Go in and see Magnus," said Mrs. Derrick. "I will tell her you are here."

Presley stepped across the stone-paved hallway with the glass roof, and after knocking three times at the office door pushed it open and entered.

Magnus sat in the chair before the desk and did not look up as Presley entered. He had the appearance of a man nearer eighty than sixty. All the old-time erectness was broken and bent. It was as though the muscles that once had held the back rigid, the chin high, had softened and stretched. A certain fatness, the obesity of inertia, hung heavy around the hips and abdomen, the eye was watery and vague, the cheeks and chin unshaven and unkempt, the grey hair had lost its forward curl towards the temples and hung thin and ragged around the ears. The hawk-like nose seemed hooked to meet the chin; the lips were slack, the mouth half-opened.

Where once the Governor had been a model of neatness in his dress, the frock coat buttoned, the linen clean, he now sat in his shirt sleeves, the waistcoat open and showing the soiled shirt. His hands were stained with ink, and these, the only members of his body that yet appeared to retain their activity, were busy with a great pile of papers,—oblong, legal documents, that littered the table before him. Without a moment's cessation, these hands of the Governor's came and went among the papers, deft, nimble, dexterous.

Magnus was sorting papers. From the heap upon his left hand he selected a document, opened it, glanced over it, then tied it carefully, and laid it away upon a second pile on his right hand. When all the papers were in one pile, he reversed the process, taking from his right hand to place upon his left, then back from left to right again, then once more from right to left. He spoke no word, he sat absolutely still, even his eyes did not move, only his hands, swift, nervous, agitated, seemed alive.

"Why, how are you, Governor?" said Presley, coming forward. Magnus turned slowly about and looked at him and at the hand in which he shook his own.

"Ah," he said at length, "Presley . . . yes."

Then his glance fell, and he looked aimlessly about upon the floor.

"I've come to say good-bye, Governor," continued Presley, "I'm going away."

"Going away . . . yes, why it's Presley. Good-day, Presley."

"Good-day, Governor. I'm going away. I've come to say good-bye."

"Good-bye?" Magnus bent his brows, "what are you saying good-bye for?"

"I'm going away, sir."

The Governor did not answer. Staring at the ledge of the desk, he seemed lost in thought. There was a long silence. Then, at length, Presley said:

"How are you getting on, Governor?"

Magnus looked up slowly.

"Why it's Presley," he said. "How do you do, Presley."

"Are you getting on all right, sir?"

"Yes," said Magnus after a while, "yes, all right. I am going away. I've come to say good-bye. No—" He interrupted himself with a deprecatory smile, "*you* said *that*, didn't you?"

"Well, you are going away, too, your wife tells me."

"Yes, I'm going away. I can't stay on . . ." he hesitated a long time, groping for the right word, "I can't stay on—on—what's the name of this place?"

"Los Muertos," put in Presley.

"No, it isn't. Yes, it is, too, that's right, Los Muertos. I don't know where my memory has gone to of late."

"Well, I hope you will be better soon, Governor."

As Presley spoke the words, S. Behrman entered the room, and the Governor sprang up with unexpected agility and stood against the wall, drawing one long breath after another, watching the railroad agent with intent eyes.

S. Behrman saluted both men affably and sat down near the desk, drawing the links of his heavy watch chain through his fat fingers.

"There wasn't anybody outside when I knocked, but I heard your voice in here, Governor, so I came right in. I wanted to ask you, Governor, if my carpenters can begin work in here day after to-morrow. I want to take down that partition there, and throw this room and the next into one. I guess that will be O. K., won't it? You'll be out of here by then, won't you?"

There was no vagueness about Magnus's speech or manner now. There was that same alertness in his demeanour that one sees in a tamed lion in the presence of its trainer.

"Yes, yes," he said quickly, "you can send your men here. I will be gone by to-morrow."

"I don't want to seem to hurry you, Governor."

"No, you will not hurry me. I am ready to go now."

"Anything I can do for you, Governor?"

"Nothing."

"Yes, there is, Governor," insisted S. Behrman. "I think now that all is over we ought to be good friends. I think I can do something for you. We still want an assistant in the local freight manager's office. Now, what do you say to having a try at it? There's a salary of fifty a month goes with it. I guess you must be in need of money now, and there's always the wife to support; what do you say? Will you try the place?"

Presley could only stare at the man in speechless wonder. What was he driving at? What reason was there back of this new move, and why should it be made thus openly and in his hearing? An explanation occurred to him. Was this merely a pleasantry on the part of S. Behrman, a way of enjoying to the full his triumph; was he testing the completeness of his victory, trying to see just how far he could go, how far beneath his feet he could push his old-time enemy?

"What do you say?" he repeated. "Will you try the place?"

"You—you *insist?*" inquired the Governor.

"Oh, I'm not insisting on anything," cried S. Behrman. "I'm offering you a place, that's all. Will you take it?"

"Yes, yes, I'll take it."

"You'll come over to our side?"

"Yes, I'll come over."

"You'll have to turn 'railroad,' understand?"

"I'll turn railroad."

"Guess there may be times when you'll have to take orders from me."

"I'll take orders from you."

"You'll have to be loyal to railroad, you know. No funny business."

"I'll be loyal to the railroad."

"You would like the place then?"

"Yes."

S. Behrman turned from Magnus, who at once resumed his seat and began again to sort his papers.

"Well, Presley," said the railroad agent: "I guess I won't see you again."

"I hope not," answered the other.

"Tut, tut, Presley, you know you can't make me angry."

He put on his hat of varnished straw and wiped his fat forehead with his handkerchief. Of late, he had grown fatter than ever, and the linen vest, stamped with a multitude of interlocked horseshoes, strained tight its imitation pearl buttons across the great protuberant stomach.

Presley looked at the man a moment before replying. But a few weeks ago he could not thus have faced the great enemy of the farmers without a gust of blind rage blowing tempestuous through all his bones. Now, however, he found to his surprise that his fury had lapsed to a profound contempt, in which there was bitterness, but no truculence. He was tired, tired to death of the whole business.

"Yes," he answered deliberately, "I am going away. You have ruined this place for me. I couldn't live here where I should have to see you, or the results of what you have done, whenever I stirred out of doors."

"Nonsense, Presley," answered the other, refusing to become angry. "That's foolishness, that kind of talk; though, of course, I understand how you feel. I guess it was you, wasn't it, who threw that bomb into my house?"

"It was."

"Well, that don't show any common sense, Presley," returned S. Behrman with perfect aplomb. "What could you have gained by killing me?"

"Not so much probably as you have gained by killing Harran and Annixter. But that's all passed now. You're safe from *me*." The strangeness of this talk, the oddity of the situation burst upon him and he laughed aloud. "It don't seem as though you could be brought to book, S. Behrman, by anybody, or by any means, does it? They can't get at you through the courts,—the law can't get you, Dyke's pistol missed fire for just your benefit, and you even escaped Caraher's six inches of plugged gas pipe. Just what are we going to do with you?"

"Best give it up, Pres, my boy," returned the other. "I guess there ain't anything can touch me. Well, Magnus," he said, turning once more to the Governor. "Well, I'll think over what you say, and let you know if I can get the place for you in a day or two. You see," he added, "you're getting pretty old, Magnus Derrick."

Presley flung himself from the room, unable any longer to witness the depths into which Magnus had fallen. What other scenes of degradation were enacted in that room, how much further S. Behrman carried the humiliation, he did not know. He suddenly felt that the air of the office was choking him.

He hurried up to what once had been his own room. On his way he could not but note that much of the house was in disarray, a great packing-up was in progress; trunks, half-full, stood in the hallways, crates and cases in a litter of straw encumbered the rooms. The servants came and went with armfuls of books, ornaments, articles of clothing.

Presley took from his room only a few manuscripts and note-books, and a small valise full of his personal effects; at the doorway he paused and, holding the knob of the door in his hand, looked back into the room a very long time.

He descended to the lower floor and entered the dining-room. Mrs. Derrick had disappeared. Presley stood for a long moment in front of the fireplace, looking about the room, remembering the scenes that he had witnessed there—the conference when Osterman had first suggested the fight for Railroad Commissioner and then later the attack on Lyman Derrick and the sudden revelation of that inconceivable treachery. But as he stood considering these things a door to his right opened and Hilma entered the room.

Presley came forward, holding out his hand, all unable to believe his eyes. It was a woman, grave, dignified, composed, who advanced to meet him. Hilma was dressed in black, the cut and fashion of the gown severe, almost monastic. All the little feminine and contradictory daintinesses were nowhere to be seen. Her statuesque calm evenness of contour yet re-mained, but it was the calmness of great sorrow, of infinite resignation. Beautiful she still remained, but she was older. The seriousness of one who has gained the knowledge of the world—knowledge of its evil—seemed to envelope her. The calm gravity of a great suffering past, but not forgotten, sat upon her. Not yet twenty-one, she exhibited the demeanour of a woman of forty.

The one-time amplitude of her figure, the fulness of hip and shoulder, the great deep swell from waist to throat were gone. She had grown thinner and, in consequence, seemed unusually, almost unnaturally tall. Her neck was slender, the outline of her full lips and round chin was a little sharp; her arms, those wonderful, beautiful arms of hers, were a little shrunken. But her eyes were as wide open as always, rimmed as ever by the thin, intensely black line of the lashes and her brown, fragrant hair was still thick, still, at times, glittered and coruscated in the sun. When she spoke, it was with the old-time velvety huskiness of voice that Annixter had learned to love so well.

"Oh, it is you," she said, giving him her hand. "You were good to want to see me before you left. I hear that you are going away."

She sat down upon the sofa.

"Yes," Presley answered, drawing a chair near to her, "yes, I felt I could not stay—down here any longer. I am going to take a long ocean voyage. My ship sails in a few days. But you, Mrs. Annixter, what are you going to do? Is there any way I can serve you?"

"No," she answered, "nothing. Papa is doing well. We are living here now."

"You are well?"

She made a little helpless gesture with both her hands, smiling very sadly.

"As you see," she answered.

As he talked, Presley was looking at her intently. Her dignity was a new element in her character and the certain slender effect of her figure, emphasised now by the long folds of the black gown she wore, carried it almost superbly. She conveyed something of the impression of a queen in exile. But she had lost none of her womanliness; rather, the contrary. Adversity had softened her, as well as deepened her. Presley saw that very clearly. Hilma had arrived now at her perfect maturity; she had known great love and she had known great grief, and the woman that had awakened in her with her affection for Annixter had been strengthened and infinitely ennobled by his death.

What if things had been different? Thus, as he conversed with her, Presley found himself wondering. Her sweetness, her beautiful gentleness, and tenderness were almost like palpable presences. It was almost as if a caress had been laid softly upon his cheek, as if a gentle hand closed upon his. Here, he knew, was sympathy; here, he knew, was an infinite capacity for love.

Then suddenly all the tired heart of him went out towards her. A longing to give the best that was in him to the memory of her, to be strong and noble because of her, to reshape his purposeless, half-wasted life with her nobility and purity and gentleness for his inspiration leaped all at once within him, leaped and stood firm, hardening to a resolve stronger than any he had ever known.

For an instant he told himself that the suddenness of this new emotion must be evidence of its insincerity. He was perfectly well aware that his impulses were abrupt and of short duration. But he knew that this was not sudden. Without realising it, he had been from the first drawn to Hilma, and all through these last terrible days, since the time he had seen her at Los Muertos, just after the battle at the ditch, she had obtruded continually upon his thoughts. The sight of her to-day, more beautiful than ever, quiet, strong, reserved, had only brought matters to a culmination.

"Are you," he asked her, "are you so unhappy, Hilma, that you can look forward to no more brightness in your life?"

"Unless I could forget—forget my husband," she answered, "how can I be happy? I would rather be unhappy in remembering him than happy in forgetting him. He was my whole world, literally and truly. Nothing seemed to count before I knew him, and nothing can count for me now, after I have lost him."

"You think now," he answered, "that in being happy again you would be disloyal to him. But you will find after a while—years from now—that it need not be so. The part of you that belonged to your husband can always keep him sacred, that part of you belongs to him and he to it. But you are young; you have all your life to live yet. Your sorrow need not be a burden to you. If you consider it as you should—as you *will* some day, believe me—it will only be a great help to you. It will make you more noble, a truer woman, more generous."

"I think I see," she answered, "and I never thought about it in that light before."

"I want to help you," he answered, "as you have helped me. I want to be your friend, and above all things I do not want to see your life wasted. I am going away and it is quite possible I shall never see you again, but you will always be a help to me."

"I do not understand," she answered, "but I know you mean to be very, very kind to me. Yes, I hope when you come back—if you ever do—you will still be that. I do not know why you should want to be so kind, unless—yes, of course— you were my husband's dearest friend."

They talked a little longer, and at length Presley rose.

"I cannot bring myself to see Mrs. Derrick again," he said. "It would only serve to make her very unhappy. Will you explain that to her? I think she will understand."

"Yes," answered Hilma. "Yes, I will."

There was a pause. There seemed to be nothing more for either of them to say. Presley held out his hand.

"Good-bye," she said, as she gave him hers.

He carried it to his lips.

"Good-bye," he answered. "Good-bye and may God bless you."

He turned away abruptly and left the room.

But as he was quietly making his way out of the house, hoping to get to his horse unobserved, he came suddenly upon Mrs. Dyke and Sidney on the porch of the house. He had forgotten that since the affair at the ditch, Los Muertos had been a home to the engineer's mother and daughter.

"And you, Mrs. Dyke," he asked as he took her hand, "in this break-up of everything, where do you go?"

"To the city," she answered, "to San Francisco. I have a sister there who will look after the little tad."

"But you, how about yourself, Mrs. Dyke?"

She answered him in a quiet voice, monotonous, expressionless:

"I am going to die very soon, Mr. Presley. There is no reason why I should live any longer. My son is in prison for life, everything is over for me, and I am tired, worn out."

"You mustn't talk like that, Mrs. Dyke," protested Presley, "nonsense; you will live long enough to see the little tad married." He tried to be cheerful. But he knew his words lacked the ring of conviction. Death already overshadowed the face of the engineer's mother. He felt that she spoke the truth, and as he stood there speaking to her for the last time, his arm about little Sidney's shoulder, he knew that he was seeing the beginnings of the wreck of another family and that, like Hilda Hooven, another baby girl was to be started in life, through no fault of hers, fearfully handicapped, weighed down at the threshold of existence with a load of disgrace. Hilda Hooven and Sidney Dyke, what was to be their histories? the one, sister of an outcast; the other, daughter of a convict. And he thought of that other young girl, the little Honora Gerard, the heiress of millions, petted, loved, receiving adulation from all who came near to her, whose only care was to choose from among the multitude of pleasures that the world hastened to present to her consideration.

"Good-bye," he said, holding out his hand.

"Good-bye."

"Good-bye, Sidney."

He kissed the little girl, clasped Mrs. Dyke's hand a moment with his; then, slinging his satchel about his shoulders by the long strap with which it was provided, left the house, and mounting his horse rode away from Los Muertos never to return.

Presley came out upon the County Road. At a little distance to his left he could see the group of buildings where once Broderson had lived. These were being remodelled, at length, to suit the larger demands of the New Agriculture. A strange man came out by the road gate; no doubt, the new proprietor. Presley turned away, hurrying northwards along the County Road by the mammoth watering-tank and the long wind-break of poplars.

He came to Caraher's place. There was no change here. The saloon had weathered the storm, indispensable to the new as well as to the old régime. The same dusty buggies and buckboards were tied under the shed, and as Presley hurried by he could distinguish Caraher's voice, loud as ever, still proclaiming his creed of annihilation.

Bonneville Presley avoided. He had no associations with the town. He turned aside from the road, and crossing the northwest corner of Los Muertos and the line of the railroad, turned back along the Upper Road till he came to the Long Trestle and Annixter's,—Silence, desolation, abandonment.

A vast stillness, profound, unbroken, brooded low over all the place. No living thing stirred. The rusted windmill on the skeleton-like tower of the artesian well was motionless; the great barn empty; the windows of the ranch house, cook house, and dairy boarded up. Nailed upon a tree near the broken gateway was a board, white painted, with stencilled letters, bearing the inscription:

"Warning. ALL PERSONS FOUND TRESPASSING ON THESE PREMISES WILL BE PROSECUTED TO THE FULLEST EXTENT OF THE LAW. By order P. and S. W. R. R."

As he had planned, Presley reached the hills by the head waters of Broderson's Creek late in the afternoon. Toilfully he climbed them, reached the highest crest, and turning about, looked long and for the last time at all the reach of the valley unrolled beneath him. The land of the ranches opened out forever and forever under the stimulus of that measureless range of vision. The whole gigantic sweep of the San Joaquin expanded Titanic before the eye of the mind, flagellated with heat, quivering and shimmering under the sun's red eye. It was the season after the harvest, and the great earth, the mother, after its period of reproduction, its pains of labour, delivered of the fruit of its loins, slept the sleep of exhaustion in the infinite repose of the colossus, benignant, eternal, strong, the nourisher of nations, the feeder of an entire world.

And as Presley looked there came to him strong and true the sense and the significance of all the enigma of growth. He seemed for one instant to touch the explanation of existence. Men were nothings, mere animalculæ, mere ephemerides that fluttered and fell and were forgotten between dawn and dusk. Vanamee had said there was no death. But for one second Presley could go one step further. Men were naught, death was naught, life was naught; FORCE only existed—FORCE that brought men into the world, FORCE that crowded them out of it to make way for the succeeding generation, FORCE that made the wheat grow, FORCE that garnered it from the soil to give place to the succeeding crop.

It was the mystery of creation, the stupendous miracle of re-creation; the vast rhythm of the seasons, measured, alternative, the sun and the stars keeping time as the eternal symphony of reproduction swung in its tremendous cadences like the colossal pendulum of an almighty machine—primordial energy flung out from the hand of the Lord God himself, immortal, calm, infinitely strong.

But as he stood thus looking down upon the great valley he was aware of the figure of a man, far in the distance, moving steadily towards the Mission of San Juan. The man was hardly more than a dot, but there was something unmistakably familiar in his gait; and besides this, Presley could fancy that he was hatless. He touched his pony with his spur. The man was Vanamee beyond all doubt, and a little later Presley, descending the maze of cow-paths and cattle-trails that led down towards the Broderson Creek, overtook his friend.

Instantly Presley was aware of an immense change. Vanamee's face was still that of an ascetic, still glowed with the rarefied intelligence of a young seer, a half-inspired shepherd-prophet of Hebraic legends; but the shadow of that great sadness which for so long had brooded over him was gone; the grief that once he had fancied deathless was, indeed, dead, or rather swallowed up in a victorious joy that radiated like sunlight at dawn from the deep-set eyes, and the hollow, swarthy cheeks. They talked together till nearly sundown, but to Presley's questions as to the reasons for Vanamee's happiness, the other would say nothing. Once only he allowed himself to touch upon the subject.

"Death and grief are little things," he said. "They are transient. Life must be before death, and joy before grief. Else there are no such things as death or grief. These are only negatives. Life is positive. Death is only the absence of life, just as night is only the absence of day, and if this is so, there is no such thing as death. There is only life, and the suppression of life, that we, foolishly, say is death. 'Suppression,' I say, not extinction. I do not say that life returns. Life never departs. Life simply *is*. For certain seasons, it is hidden in the dark, but is that death, extinction, annihilation? I take it, thank God, that it is not. Does the grain of wheat, hidden for certain seasons in the dark, die? The grain we think is dead *resumes again*; but how? Not as one grain, but as twenty. So all life. Death is only real for all the detritus of the world, for all the sorrow, for all the injustice, for all the grief. Presley, the good never dies; evil dies, cruelty, oppression, selfishness, greed—these die; but nobility, but love, but sacrifice, but generosity, but truth, thank God for it, small as they are, difficult as it is to discover them—these live forever, these are eternal. You are all broken, all cast down by what you have seen in this valley, this hopeless struggle, this apparently hopeless despair. Well, the end is not yet. What is it that remains after all is over, after the dead are buried and the hearts are broken? Look at it all from the vast height of humanity— 'the greatest good to the greatest numbers.' What remains? Men perish, men are corrupted, hearts are rent asunder, but what remains untouched, unassailable, undefiled? Try to find that, not only in this, but in every crisis of the world's life, and you will find, if your view be large enough, that it is *not* evil, but good, that in the end remains."

There was a long pause. Presley, his mind full of new thoughts, held his peace, and Vanamee added at length:

"I believed Angéle dead. I wept over her grave; mourned for her as dead in corruption. She has come back to me, more beautiful than ever. Do not ask me any further. To put this story, this idyl, into words, would, for me, be a profanation. This must suffice you. Angéle has returned to me, and I am happy. *Adios.*"

He rose suddenly. The friends clasped each other's hands.

"We shall probably never meet again," said Vanamee; "but if these are the last words I ever speak to you, listen to them, and remember them, because I know I speak the truth. Evil is short-lived. Never judge of the whole round of life by the mere segment you can see. The whole is, in the end, perfect."

Abruptly he took himself away. He was gone. Presley, alone, thoughtful, his hands clasped behind him, passed on through the ranches—here teeming with ripened wheat—his face set from them forever.

Not so Vanamee. For hours he roamed the country-side, now through the deserted cluster of buildings that had once been Annixter's home; now through the rustling and, as yet, uncut wheat of Quien Sabe! now treading the slopes of the hills far to the north, and again following the winding courses of the streams. Thus he spent the night.

At length, the day broke, resplendent, cloudless. The night was passed. There was all the sparkle and effervescence of joy in the crystal sunlight as the dawn expanded roseate, and at length flamed dazzling to the zenith when the sun moved over the edge of the world and looked down upon all the earth like the eye of God the Father.

At the moment, Vanamee stood breast-deep in the wheat in a solitary corner of the Quien Sabe rancho. He turned eastward, facing the celestial glory of the day and sent his voiceless call far from him across the golden grain out towards the little valley of flowers.

Swiftly the answer came. It advanced to meet him. The flowers of the Seed ranch were gone, dried and parched by the summer's sun, shedding their seed by handfuls to be sown again and blossom yet another time. The Seed ranch was no longer royal with colour. The roses, the lilies, the carnations, the hyacinths, the poppies, the violets, the mignonette, all these had vanished, the little valley was without colour; where once it had exhaled the most delicious perfume, it was now odourless. Under the blinding light of the day it stretched to its hillsides, bare, brown, unlovely. The romance of the place had vanished, but with it had vanished the Vision. It was no longer a figment of his imagination, a creature of dreams that advanced to meet Vanamee. It was Reality—it was Angéle in the flesh, vital, sane, material, who at last issued forth from the entrance of the little valley. Romance had vanished, but better than romance was here. Not a manifestation, not a dream, but her very self. The night was gone, but the sun had risen; the flowers had disappeared, but strong, vigorous, noble, the wheat had come.

In the wheat he waited for her. He saw her coming. She was simply dressed. No fanciful wreath of tube-roses was about her head now, no strange garment of red and gold enveloped her now. It was no longer an ephemeral illusion of the night, evanescent, mystic, but a simple country girl coming to meet her lover. The vision of the night had been beautiful, but what was it compared to this? Reality was better than Romance. The simple honesty of a loving, trusting heart was better than a legend of flowers, an hallucination of the moonlight. She came nearer. Bathed in sunlight, he saw her face to face, saw her hair hanging in two straight plaits on either side of her face, saw the enchanting fulness of her lips, the strange, balancing movement of her head upon her slender neck. But now she was no longer asleep. The wonderful eyes, violet blue, heavy-lidded, with their perplexing, oriental slant towards the temples, were wide open and fixed upon his.

From out the world of romance, out of the moonlight and the star sheen, out of the faint radiance of the lilies and the still air heavy with perfume, she had at last come to him. The moonlight, the flowers, and the dream were all vanished away. Angéle was realised in the Wheat. She stood forth in the sunlight, a fact, and no longer a fancy.

He ran forward to meet her and she held out her arms to him. He caught her to him, and she, turning her face to his, kissed him on the mouth.

"I love you, I love you," she murmured.

    .   .   .   .

Upon descending from his train at Port Costa, S. Behrman asked to be directed at once to where the bark "Swanhilda" was taking on grain. Though he had bought and greatly enlarged his new elevator at this port, he had never seen it. The work had been carried on through agents, S. Behrman having far too many and more pressing occupations to demand his presence and attention. Now, however, he was to see the concrete evidence of his success for the first time.

He picked his way across the railroad tracks to the line of warehouses that bordered the docks, numbered with enormous Roman numerals and full of grain in bags.

The sight of these bags of grain put him in mind of the fact that among all the other shippers he was practically alone in his way of handling his wheat. They handled the grain in bags; he, however, preferred it in the bulk. Bags were sometimes four cents apiece, and he had decided to build his elevator and bulk his grain therein, rather than to incur this expense. Only a small part of his wheat—that on Number Three division—had been sacked. All the rest, practically two-thirds of the entire harvest of Los Muertos, now found itself warehoused in his enormous elevator at Port Costa.

To a certain degree it had been the desire of observing the working of his system of handling the wheat in bulk that had drawn S. Behrman to Port Costa. But the more powerful motive had been curiosity, not to say downright sentiment. So long had he planned for this day of triumph, so eagerly had he looked forward to it, that now, when it had come, he wished to enjoy it to its fullest extent, wished to miss no feature of the disposal of the crop. He had watched it harvested, he had watched it hauled to the railway, and now would watch it as it poured into the hold of the ship, would even watch the ship as she cleared and got under way.

He passed through the warehouses and came out upon the dock that ran parallel with the shore of the bay. A great quantity of shipping was in view, barques for the most part, Cape Horners, great, deep sea tramps, whose iron-shod forefeet had parted every ocean the world round from Rangoon to Rio Janeiro, and from Melbourne to Christiania. Some were still in the stream, loaded with wheat to the Plimsoll mark, ready to depart with the next tide. But many others laid their great flanks alongside the docks and at that moment were being filled by derrick and crane with thousands upon thousands of bags of wheat. The scene was brisk; the cranes creaked and swung incessantly with a rattle of chains; stevedores and wharfingers toiled and perspired; boatswains and dock-masters shouted orders, drays rumbled, the water lapped at the piles; a group of sailors, painting the flanks of one of the great ships, raised an occasional chanty; the trade wind sang æolian in the cordages, filling the air with the nimble taint of salt. All around were the noises of ships and the feel and flavor of the sea.

S. Behrman soon discovered his elevator. It was the largest structure discernible, and upon its red roof, in enormous white letters, was his own name. Thither, between piles of grain bags, halted drays, crates and boxes of merchandise, with an occasional pyramid of salmon cases, S. Behrman took his way. Cabled to the dock, close under his elevator, lay a great ship with lofty masts and great spars. Her stern was toward him as he approached, and upon it, in raised golden letters, he could read the words "Swanhilda—Liverpool."

He went aboard by a very steep gangway and found the mate on the quarter deck. S. Behrman introduced himself.

"Well," he added, "how are you getting on?"

"Very fairly, sir," returned the mate, who was an Englishman. "We'll have her all snugged down tight by this time, day after to-morrow. It's a great saving of time shunting the stuff in her like that, and three men can do the work of seven."

"I'll have a look 'round, I believe," returned S. Behrman.

"Right–oh," answered the mate with a nod.

S. Behrman went forward to the hatch that opened down into the vast hold of the ship. A great iron chute connected this hatch with the elevator, and through it was rushing a veritable cataract of wheat.

It came from some gigantic bin within the elevator itself, rushing down the confines of the chute to plunge into the roomy, gloomy interior of the hold with an incessant, metallic roar, persistent, steady, inevitable. No men were in sight. The place was deserted. No human agency seemed to be back of

the movement of the wheat. Rather, the grain seemed im-
pelled with a force of its own, a resistless, huge force, eager,
vivid, impatient for the sea.

S. Behrman stood watching, his ears deafened with the roar
of the hard grains against the metallic lining of the chute. He
put his hand once into the rushing tide, and the contact
rasped the flesh of his fingers and like an undertow drew his
hand after it in its impetuous dash.

Cautiously he peered down into the hold. A musty odour
rose to his nostrils, the vigorous, pungent aroma of the raw
cereal. It was dark. He could see nothing; but all about and
over the opening of the hatch the air was full of a fine, impalpable dust that blinded the eyes and choked the throat and
nostrils.

As his eyes became used to the shadows of the cavern below him, he began to distinguish the grey mass of the wheat,
a great expanse, almost liquid in its texture, which, as the
cataract from above plunged into it, moved and shifted in
long, slow eddies. As he stood there, this cataract on a sudden
increased in volume. He turned about, casting his eyes upward toward the elevator to discover the cause. His foot
caught in a coil of rope, and he fell headforemost into the
hold.

The fall was a long one and he struck the surface of the
wheat with the sodden impact of a bundle of damp clothes.
For the moment he was stunned. All the breath was driven
from his body. He could neither move nor cry out. But, by
degrees, his wits steadied themselves and his breath returned
to him. He looked about and above him. The daylight in the
hold was dimmed and clouded by the thick chaff-dust thrown
off by the pour of grain, and even this dimness dwindled to
twilight at a short distance from the opening of the hatch,
while the remotest quarters were lost in impenetrable blackness. He got upon his feet only to find that he sunk ankle
deep in the loose packed mass underfoot.

"Hell," he muttered, "here's a fix."

Directly underneath the chute, the wheat, as it poured in,
raised itself in a conical mound, but from the sides of this
mound it shunted away incessantly in thick layers, flowing in
all directions with the nimbleness of water. Even as S. Behr-

man spoke, a wave of grain poured around his legs and rose rapidly to the level of his knees. He stepped quickly back. To stay near the chute would soon bury him to the waist.

No doubt, there was some other exit from the hold, some companion ladder that led up to the deck. He scuffled and waded across the wheat, groping in the dark with out-stretched hands. With every inhalation he choked, filling his mouth and nostrils more with dust than with air. At times he could not breathe at all, but gagged and gasped, his lips dis-tended. But search as he would, he could find no outlet to the hold, no stairway, no companion ladder. Again and again, staggering along in the black darkness, he bruised his knuckles and forehead against the iron sides of the ship. He gave up the attempt to find any interior means of escape and returned laboriously to the space under the open hatchway. Already he could see that the level of the wheat was raised.

"God," he said, "this isn't going to do at all." He uttered a great shout. "Hello, on deck there, somebody. For God's sake."

The steady, metallic roar of the pouring wheat drowned out his voice. He could scarcely hear it himself above the rush of the cataract. Besides this, he found it impossible to stay under the hatch. The flying grains of wheat, spattering as they fell, stung his face like wind-driven particles of ice. It was a veritable torture; his hands smarted with it. Once he was all but blinded. Furthermore, the succeeding waves of wheat, rolling from the mound under the chute, beat him back, swirling and dashing against his legs and knees, mounting swiftly higher, carrying him off his feet.

Once more he retreated, drawing back from beneath the hatch. He stood still for a moment and shouted again. It was in vain. His voice returned upon him, unable to penetrate the thunder of the chute, and horrified, he discovered that so soon as he stood motionless upon the wheat, he sank into it. Before he knew it, he was knee-deep again, and a long swirl of grain sweeping outward from the ever-breaking, ever-reforming pyramid below the chute, poured around his thighs, immobilising him.

A frenzy of terror suddenly leaped to life within him. The horror of death, the Fear of The Trap, shook him like a dry reed. Shouting, he tore himself free of the wheat and once more scrambled and struggled towards the hatchway. He stumbled as he reached it and fell directly beneath the pour. Like a storm of small shot, mercilessly, pitilessly, the unnumbered multitude of hurtling grains flagellated and beat and tore his flesh. Blood streamed from his forehead and, thickening with the powder-like chaff-dust, blinded his eyes. He struggled to his feet once more. An avalanche from the cone of wheat buried him to his thighs. He was forced back and back and back, beating the air, falling, rising, howling for aid. He could no longer see; his eyes, crammed with dust, smarted as if transfixed with needles whenever he opened them. His mouth was full of the dust, his lips were dry with it; thirst tortured him, while his outcries choked and gagged in his rasped throat.

And all the while without stop, incessantly, inexorably, the wheat, as if moving with a force all its own, shot downward in a prolonged roar, persistent, steady, inevitable.

He retreated to a far corner of the hold and sat down with his back against the iron hull of the ship and tried to collect his thoughts, to calm himself. Surely there must be some way of escape; surely he was not to die like this, die in this dreadful substance that was neither solid nor fluid. What was he to do? How make himself heard?

But even as he thought about this, the cone under the chute broke again and sent a great layer of grain rippling and tumbling toward him. It reached him where he sat and buried his hand and one foot.

He sprang up trembling and made for another corner.

"By God," he cried, "by God, I must think of something pretty quick!"

Once more the level of the wheat rose and the grains began piling deeper about him. Once more he retreated. Once more he crawled staggering to the foot of the cataract, screaming till his ears sang and his eyeballs strained in their sockets, and once more the relentless tide drove him back.

Then began that terrible dance of death; the man dodging, doubling, squirming, hunted from one corner to another, the wheat slowly, inexorably flowing, rising, spreading to every angle, to every nook and cranny. It reached his middle.

Furious and with bleeding hands and broken nails, he dug his way out to fall backward, all but exhausted, gasping for breath in the dust-thickened air. Roused again by the slow advance of the tide, he leaped up and stumbled away, blinded with the agony in his eyes, only to crash against the metal hull of the vessel. He turned about, the blood streaming from his face, and paused to collect his senses, and with a rush, another wave swirled about his ankles and knees. Exhaustion grew upon him. To stand still meant to sink; to lie or sit meant to be buried the quicker; and all this in the dark, all this in an air that could scarcely be breathed, all this while he fought an enemy that could not be gripped, toiling in a sea that could not be stayed.

Guided by the sound of the falling wheat, S. Behrman crawled on hands and knees toward the hatchway. Once more he raised his voice in a shout for help. His bleeding throat and raw, parched lips refused to utter but a wheezing moan. Once more he tried to look toward the one patch of faint light above him. His eye-lids, clogged with chaff, could no longer open. The Wheat poured about his waist as he raised himself upon his knees.

Reason fled. Deafened with the roar of the grain, blinded and made dumb with its chaff, he threw himself forward with clutching fingers, rolling upon his back, and lay there, moving feebly, the head rolling from side to side. The Wheat, leaping continuously from the chute, poured around him. It filled the pockets of the coat, it crept up the sleeves and trouser legs, it covered the great, protuberant stomach, it ran at last in rivulets into the distended, gasping mouth. It covered the face.

Upon the surface of the Wheat, under the chute, nothing moved but the Wheat itself. There was no sign of life. Then, for an instant, the surface stirred. A hand, fat, with short fingers and swollen veins, reached up, clutching, then fell limp and prone. In another instant it was covered. In the hold of the "Swanhilda" there was no movement but the widening ripples that spread flowing from the ever-breaking, ever-re-forming cone; no sound, but the rushing of the Wheat that continued to plunge incessantly from the iron chute in a prolonged roar, persistent, steady, inevitable.

CONCLUSION

THE "SWANHILDA" cast off from the docks at Port Costa two days after Presley had left Bonneville and the ranches and made her way up to San Francisco, anchoring in the stream off the City front. A few hours after her arrival, Presley, waiting at his club, received a despatch from Cedarquist to the effect that she would clear early the next morning and that he must be aboard of her before midnight.

He sent his trunks aboard and at once hurried to Cedarquist's office to say good-bye. He found the manufacturer in excellent spirits.

"What do you think of Lyman Derrick now, Presley?" he said, when Presley had sat down. "He's in the new politics with a vengeance, isn't he? And our own dear Railroad openly acknowledges him as their candidate. You've heard of his canvass."

"Yes, yes," answered Presley. "Well, he knows his business best."

But Cedarquist was full of another idea: his new venture—the organizing of a line of clipper wheat ships for Pacific and Oriental trade—was prospering.

"The 'Swanhilda' is the mother of the fleet, Pres. I had to buy *her*, but the keel of her sister ship will be laid by the time she discharges at Calcutta. We'll carry our wheat into Asia yet. The Anglo-Saxon started from there at the beginning of everything and it's manifest destiny that he must circle the globe and fetch up where he began his march. You are up with procession, Pres, going to India this way in a wheat ship that flies American colours. By the way, do you know where the money is to come from to build the sister ship of the 'Swanhilda'? From the sale of the plant and scrap iron of the Atlas Works. Yes, I've given it up definitely, that business. The people here would not back me up. But I'm working off on this new line now. It may break me, but we'll try it on. You know the 'Million Dollar Fair' was formally opened yesterday. There is," he added with a wink, "a Midway Pleasance in connection with the thing. Mrs. Cedarquist and our friend Hartrath 'got up a subscription' to construct a figure of California—heroic size—out of dried apricots. I assure you," he remarked with prodigious gravity, "it is a real work of art and quite a 'feature' of the Fair. Well, good luck to you, Pres. Write to me from Honolulu, and *bon voyage*. My respects to the hungry Hindoo. Tell him 'we're coming, Father Abraham, a hundred thousand more.' Tell the men of the East to look out for the men of the West. The irrepressible Yank is knocking at the doors of their temples and he will want to sell 'em carpet-sweepers for their harems and electric light plants for their temple shrines. Good-bye to you."

"Good-bye, sir."

"Get fat yourself while you're about it, Presley," he observed, as the two stood up and shook hands.

"There shouldn't be any lack of food on a wheat ship. Bread enough, surely."

"Little monotonous, though. 'Man cannot live by bread alone.' Well, you're really off. Good-bye."

"Good-bye, sir."

And as Presley issued from the building and stepped out into the street, he was abruptly aware of a great wagon shrouded in white cloth, inside of which a bass drum was being furiously beaten. On the cloth, in great letters, were the words:

"Vote for Lyman Derrick, Regular Republican Nominee for Governor of California."

*   *   *   *   *   *

The "Swanhilda" lifted and rolled slowly, majestically on the ground swell of the Pacific, the water hissing and boiling under her forefoot, her cordage vibrating and droning in the steady rush of the trade winds. It was drawing towards evening and her lights had just been set. The master passed Presley, who was leaning over the rail smoking a cigarette, and paused long enough to remark:

"The land yonder, if you can make it out, is Point Gordo, and if you were to draw a line from our position now through that point and carry it on about a hundred miles further, it would just about cross Tulare County not very far from where you used to live."

"I see," answered Presley, "I see. Thanks. I am glad to know that."

The master passed on, and Presley, going up to the quarter deck, looked long and earnestly at the faint line of mountains that showed vague and bluish above the waste of tumbling water.

Those were the mountains of the Coast range and beyond them was what once had been his home. Bonneville was there, and Guadalajara and Los Muertos and Quien Sabe, the Mission of San Juan, the Seed ranch, Annixter's desolated home and Dyke's ruined hop-fields.

Well, it was all over now, that terrible drama through which he had lived. Already it was far distant from him; but once again it rose in his memory, portentous, sombre, ineffaceable. He passed it all in review from the day of his first meeting with Vanamee to the day of his parting with Hilma. He saw it all—the great sweep of country opening to view from the summit of the hills at the head waters of Broderson's Creek; the barn dance at Annixter's, the harness room with its jam of furious men; the quiet garden of the Mission; Dyke's house, his flight upon the engine, his brave fight in the chaparral; Lyman Derrick at bay in the dining-room of the ranch house; the rabbit drive; the fight at the irrigating ditch, the shouting mob in the Bonneville Opera House.

The drama was over. The fight of Ranch and Railroad had been wrought out to its dreadful close. It was true, as Shelgrim had said, that forces rather than men had locked horns in that struggle, but for all that the men of the Ranch and not the men of the Railroad had suffered. Into the prosperous valley, into the quiet community of farmers, that galloping monster, that terror of steel and steam had burst, shooting athwart the horizons, flinging the echo of its thunder over all the ranches of the valley, leaving blood and destruction in its path.

Yes, the Railroad had prevailed. The ranches had been seized in the tentacles of the octopus; the iniquitous burden of extortionate freight rates had been imposed like a yoke of iron. The monster had killed Harran, had killed Osterman, had killed Broderson, had killed Hooven. It had beggared Magnus and had driven him to a state of semi-insanity after he had wrecked his honour in the vain attempt to do evil that good might come. It had enticed Lyman into its toils to pluck from him his manhood and his honesty, corrupting him and poisoning him beyond redemption; it had hounded Dyke from his legitimate employment and had made of him a high-wayman and criminal. It had cast forth Mrs. Hooven to starve to death upon the City streets. It had driven Minna to pros-titution. It had slain Annixter at the very moment when pain-fully and manfully he had at last achieved his own salvation and stood forth resolved to do right, to act unselfishly and to live for others. It had widowed Hilma in the very dawn of her happiness. It had killed the very babe within the mother's womb, strangling life ere yet it had been born, stamping out the spark ordained by God to burn through all eternity.

What then was left? Was there no hope, no outlook for the future, no rift in the black curtain, no glimmer through the night? Was good to be thus overthrown? Was evil thus to be strong and to prevail? Was nothing left?

Then suddenly Vanamee's words came back to his mind. What was the larger view, what contributed the greatest good to the greatest numbers? What was the full round of the circle whose segment only he beheld? In the end, the ultimate, final end of all, what was left? Yes, good issued from this crisis, untouched, unassailable, undefiled.

Men—motes in the sunshine—perished, were shot down in the very noon of life, hearts were broken, little children started in life lamentably handicapped; young girls were brought to a life of shame; old women died in the heart of life for lack of food. In that little, isolated group of human insects, misery, death, and anguish spun like a wheel of fire.

But the WHEAT *remained.* Untouched, unassailable, unde-filed, that mighty world-force, that nourisher of nations, wrapped in Nirvanic calm, indifferent to the human swarm, gigantic, resistless, moved onward in its appointed grooves. Through the welter of blood at the irrigation ditch, through the sham charity and shallow philanthropy of famine relief committees, the great harvest of Los Muertos rolled like a flood from the Sierras to the Himalayas to feed thousands of starving scarecrows on the barren plains of India.

Falseness dies; injustice and oppression in the end of everything fade and vanish away. Greed, cruelty, selfishness, and inhumanity are short-lived; the individual suffers, but the race goes on. Annixter dies, but in a far distant corner of the world a thousand lives are saved. The larger view always and through all shams, all wickednesses, discovers the Truth that will, in the end, prevail, and all things, surely, inevitably, resistlessly work together for good.

ESSAYS

Contents

THEORY AND REALITY

An Old Author and a New Writer Consider the Same Problem

THERE HAVE recently appeared two books, both dealing with the same very delicate sex problem, a problem so delicate in fact that it is almost impossible to consider the books critically. One of these books is by Mr. W. D. Howells and is called *A Parting and a Meeting*. The other is by Mrs. J. R. Jarboe of this city and is called *Robert Atterbury*. Each book has to do with the "ultimate physical relation of man and woman." A dangerous subject truly.

Mr. Howells touches it lightly, delicately, handling it with the greatest subtlety and finesse. Mrs. Jarboe rushes in where Mr. Howells fears to tread, grapples the subject by the throat, sledge-hammers at it, tears the veil from it boldly, uncompromisingly.

Mr. Howells tells a story; Mrs. Jarboe develops a theory. The *Parting and Meeting* is a little tale of how a certain young man of some seventy years ago attempted to prevail upon his sweetheart to join the Shakers with him and to live out the remainder of their lives keeping the relations of brother and sister. In a scene of exquisite delicacy and sympathetic insight, the girl refuses. The man joins the Shakers and the girl marries elsewhere. Sixty years afterward they meet, and though Roger is so old as to be almost in his dotage, he recovers intelligence enough to say, "I'm not so sure but I'd have done about as well to have gone with *you*, Chloe." That is all; this is the whole story, a touch, a suggestion, a hint.

According to Mrs. Jarboe's theory "there is no love which can justify marriage as it is at present understood. There is no law, no blessing of priest or church, which can render it anything but legalized prostitution. It is a crime against nature, against the race, against God." The author proposes as a remedy the Malthusian theory of restraint, a theory, beautiful upon paper but which practise and good political economists have long since demonstrated beyond question to be as delusive and impossible as the Ptolemaic system of astronomy. That the increase of the family after marriage should be restrained and limited is a fine and admirable ideal, but the idealists will close their eyes to the fact that men *and women* are after all only human. Even this word "human" is misleading. Is it not even truer that so-called humanity still is, and for countless generations will be, three-quarters animal, living and dying, eating and sleeping, mating and reproducing even as the animals; passing the half of each day's life in the performance of purely animal functions? This is lamentable, no doubt, but the grandest theory ever conceived by the mind of the most prodigious thinker is powerless to better the condition of the race, in this respect, as far as immediate results are concerned. There is no prospect for betterment except in the gradual evolution of the type through infinitely vast periods of time.

Mrs. Jarboe, however, does not apply her theory to her hero and heroine—Atterbury and Sara—even after all its elaborate development throughout the first part of the story. In their case the two young people made a virtue of necessity, since one was a consumptive and the other under the shadow of hereditary insanity.

In the case of two healthy, natural young people in real life, or in a good realistic novel, Mrs. Jarboe's fine-spun web of logic would have been rent at the first breath. The greater author of the *Parting and Meeting* knew his real life better. Chloe even refused to consider a union of her life with that of her lover's, conceived upon any such morbid, Utopian principles, and even Roger acknowledges its futility in admitting that, after all, he would have done wiser to have gone back with Chloe.

Mrs. Jarboe presents her subject unskilfully. However admirable her theory—*as* theory—may be, it is not clearly and convincingly expressed in the pages of *Robert Atterbury*. No matter what its purpose or how great a lesson it purposes to teach, the novel should *be* a novel; first and foremost, it should tell a real story, of real people and of real places.

In Mr. Howells's story, even the old chaise horse becomes a character, "making snatches at the foliage and from time to time champing thoughtfully on his bit as if he fancied he might have caught a leaf in his mouth," and Chloe and Roger are flesh and blood characters from first to last. It is what *they* do and what *they* say that interest the reader. In *Robert*

Atterbury, however, the people are little more than names and stand for nothing but the various mouthpieces for the author's theory. Chloe and Roger live and act by themselves, while Mrs. Jarboe shifts about the characters like a showman pulling the strings of his puppets. We forget Howells at once in the fortunes of his dramatis personæ. We cannot lose sight of the author of *Robert Atterbury* for a single instant.

The Wave, May 2, 1896

ZOLA AS A ROMANTIC WRITER

IT IS CURIOUS to notice how persistently M. Zola is misunderstood. How strangely he is misinterpreted even by those who conscientiously admire the novels of the "man of the iron pen." For most people Naturalism has a vague meaning. It is a sort of inner circle of realism—a kind of diametric opposite of romanticism, a theory of fiction wherein things are represented "as they really are," inexorably, with the truthfulness of a camera. This idea can be shown to be far from right, that Naturalism, as understood by Zola, is but a form of romanticism after all.

Observe the methods employed by the novelists who profess and call themselves "realists"—Mr. Howells, for instance. Howells's characters live across the street from us, they are "on our block." We know all about them, about their affairs, and the story of their lives. One can go even further. We ourselves are Mr. Howells's characters, so long as we are well behaved and ordinary and *bourgeois*, so long as we are not adventurous or not rich or not unconventional. If we are otherwise, if things commence to happen to us, if we kill a man or two, or get mixed up in a tragic affair, or do something on a large scale, such as the amassing of enormous wealth or power or fame, Mr. Howells cuts our acquaintance at once. He will none of us if we are out of the usual.

This is the real Realism. It is the smaller details of everyday life, things that are likely to happen between lunch and supper, small passions, restricted emotions, dramas of the reception-room, tragedies of an afternoon call, crises involving cups of tea. Every one will admit there is no romance here. The novel is interesting—which is after all the main point—but it is the commonplace tale of commonplace people made into a novel of far more than commonplace charm. Mr. Howells is not uninteresting; he is simply not romantic. But that Zola should be quoted as a realist, and as a realist of realists, is a strange perversion.

Reflect a moment upon his choice of subject and character and episode. The *Rougon-Macquart* live in a world of their own; they are not of our lives any more than are the Don Juans, the Jean Valjeans, the Ruy Blases, the Marmions, or the Ivanhoes. We, the *bourgeois*, the commonplace, the ordinary, have no part nor lot in the *Rougon-Macquart*, in *Lourdes*, or in *Rome*; it is not our world, not because our social position is different, but because we are *ordinary*. To be noted of M. Zola we must leave the rank and the file, either run to the forefront of the marching world, or fall by the roadway; we must separate ourselves; we must become individual, unique. The naturalist takes no note of common people, common in so far as their interests, their lives, and the things that occur in them are common, are ordinary. Terrible things must happen to the characters of the naturalistic tale. They must be twisted from the ordinary, wrenched out from the quiet, uneventful round of every-day life, and flung into the throes of a vast and terrible drama that works itself out in unleashed passions, in blood, and in sudden death. The world of M. Zola is a world of big things; the enormous, the formidable, the terrible, is what counts; no teacup tragedies here. Here Nana holds her monstrous orgies, and dies horribly, her face distorted to a frightful mask; Etienne Lantier, carried away by the strike of coal miners of *Le Voreux*, (the strike that is almost war), is involved in the vast and fearful catastrophe that comes as a climax of the great drama; Claude Lantier, disappointed, disillusioned, acknowledging the futility of his art after a life of effort, hangs himself to his huge easel; Jacques Lantier, haunted by an hereditary insanity, all his natural desires hideously distorted, cuts the throat of the girl he loves, and is ground to pieces under the wheels of his own locomotive; Jean Macquart, soldier and tiller of the fields, is drawn into the war of 1870, passes through the terrible scenes of Sedan and the Siege of Paris only to bayonet to death his truest friend and sworn brother-at-arms in the streets of the burning capital.

Everything is extraordinary, imaginative, grotesque even, with a vague note of terror quivering throughout like the vibration of an ominous and low-pitched diapason. It is all romantic, at times unmistakably so, as in *Le Rêve* or *Rome*, closely resembling the work of the greatest of all modern romanticists, Hugo. We have the same huge dramas, the same enormous scenic effects, the same love of the extraordinary, the vast, the monstrous, and the tragic.

Naturalism is a form of romanticism, not an inner circle of realism. Where is the realism in the *Rougon-Macquart*? Are such things likely to happen between lunch and supper? That Zola's work is not purely romantic as was Hugo's, lies chiefly in the choice of Milieu. These great, terrible dramas no longer happen among the personnel of a feudal and Renaissance nobility, those who are in the fore-front of the marching world, but among the lower—almost the lowest—classes; those who have been thrust or wrenched from the ranks who are falling by the roadway. This is not romanticism—this drama of the people, working itself out in blood and ordure. It is not realism. It is a school by itself, unique, somber, powerful beyond words. It is naturalism.

The Wave, June 27, 1896

THE "ENGLISH COURSES" OF THE
UNIVERSITY OF CALIFORNIA

IN THE "announcement of courses" published annually by the faculty of the University of California the reader cannot fail to be impressed with the number and scope of the hours devoted by the students to recitations and lectures upon the subject of "literature." At the head of this department is Professor Gayley (the same gentleman who is to edit the volumes of Shakespeare for Macmillan at the expense of the State of California.) Be pleased for a moment to consider these "literary" courses. They comprise "themes" written by the student, the subject chosen by the instructor and the matter found in text books and encyclopedias. They further include lectures, delivered by associate professors, who, in their turn have taken their information from text books and "manuals" written by other professors in other colleges. The student is taught to "classify." "Classification" is the one thing desirable in the eyes of the professors of "literature" of the University of California. The young Sophomore, with his new, fresh mind, his active brain and vivid imagination, with ideas of his own, crude, perhaps, but first hand, not cribbed from text books. This type of young fellow, I say, is taught to "classify," is set to work counting the "metaphors" in a given passage. This is actually true—tabulating them, separating them from the "similes," comparing the results. He is told to study sentence structure. He classifies certain types of sentences in De Quincey and compares them with certain other types of sentences in Carlyle. He makes the wonderful discovery—on suggestion from the instructor—that De Quincey excelled in those metaphors and similes relating to rapidity of movement. Sensation!

In his Junior and Senior years he takes up the study of Milton, of Browning, of the drama of the seventeenth and eighteenth centuries, English comedy, of advanced rhetoric, and of aesthetics. "Aesthetics," think of that! Here, the "classification" goes on as before. He learns to read Chaucer as it was read in the fourteenth century, sounding the final e; he paraphrases Milton's sonnets, he makes out "skeletons" and "schemes" of certain prose passages. His enthusiasm is about dead now; he is ashamed of his original thoughts and of those ideas of his own that he entertained as a Freshman and Sophomore. He has learned to write "themes" and "papers" in the true academic style, which is to read some dozen text books and encyclopedia articles on the subject, and to make over the results in his own language. He has reduced the writing of "themes" to a system. He knows what the instructor wants, he writes accordingly, and is rewarded by first and second sections. The "co-eds" take to the "classification" method even better than the young men. They thrive and fatten intellectually on the regime. They consider themselves literary. They write articles on the "Philosophy of Dante" for the college weekly, and after graduation they "read papers" to literary "circles" composed of post-graduate "co-eds," the professors' wives and daughters and a very few pale young men in spectacles and black cutaway coats. After the reading of the "paper" follows the "discussion," aided and abetted by cake and lemonade. This is literature! Isn't it admirable!

The young man, the whilom Sophomore, affected with original ideas, does rather different. As said, by the time he is a Junior or Senior, he has lost all interest in the "literary" courses. The "themes" must be written, however, and the best way is the easiest. This is how he oft-times goes about it: He knows just where he can lay his hands upon some fifty to a hundred "themes" written by the members of past classes, that have been carefully collected and preserved by enterprising students. It will go hard if he cannot in the pile find one upon the subject in hand. He does not necessarily copy it. He rewrites it in his own language. Do you blame him very much? Is his method so very different from that in which he is encouraged by his professor; viz., the cribbing—for it is cribbing—from text books? The "theme" which he rewrites has been cribbed in the first place.

The method of English instruction of the University of California often develops capital ingenuity in the student upon whom it is practiced. We know of one young man—a Senior—who found himself called upon to write four "themes," yet managed to make one—re-written four times—do for the four. This was the manner of it. The four "themes" called for were in the English, chemical, German and military courses respectively. The young fellow found a German treatise on the manufacture of gunpowder, translated it, made four copies, and by a little ingenuity passed it off in the four above named departments. Of course the thing is deplorable, yet how much of the blame is to be laid at the door of the English faculty?

The conclusion of the whole matter is that the literary courses of the University of California do not develop literary instincts among the students who attend them. The best way to study literature is to try to produce literature. It is original work that counts, not the everlasting compiling of facts, not the tabulating of metaphors, nor the rehashing of text books and encyclopedia articles.

They order this matter better at Harvard. The literary student at Cambridge has but little to do with lectures, almost nothing at all with text books. He is sent away from the lecture room and told to look about him and think a little. Each day he writes a theme, a page if necessary, a single line of a dozen words if he likes; anything, so it is original, something he has seen or thought, not read of, not picked up at second hand. He may choose any subject under the blue heavens from a pun to a philosophical reflection, only let it be his own. Once every two weeks he writes a longer theme, and during the last six weeks of the year, a still longer one, in six weekly installments. Not a single suggestion is offered as to subject. The result of this system is a keenness of interest that draws three hundred men to the course and that fills the benches at every session of the class. The class room work consists merely in the reading by the instructor of the best work done, together with his few critical comments upon it by the instructor in charge. The character of the themes produced under this system is of such high order that it is not rare to come across one of them in the pages of the first-class magazines of the day. There is no sufficient reason to suppose that the California collegians are intellectually inferior to those of the Eastern States. It is only a question of the means adopted to develop the material.

The Wave, November 28, 1896

AN OPENING FOR NOVELISTS

Great Opportunities for Fiction-Writers in San Francisco

THERE ARE CERTAIN cities in the world which are adaptable to the uses of the writer of fiction, and there are others which are not. Things can happen in some cities and the tale of them will be interesting; the same story laid in another city would be ridiculous. It is hard to say, why this is so, but a moment's review of the world's centers with this thought in mind will prove the truth of the statement beyond any shadow of doubt. Paris, London and Rome are "good material." Berlin, Vienna and Hamburg are not. Stories of New Orleans or of Constantinople could easily be made interesting, but no romancer has yet had the hardihood to attempt to write of Chicago or Buffalo. Imagine a novel of Chicago. The fact is very curious and the choice very arbitrary. There seems to be no rule applicable. A city need not necessarily be old, nor a seaport, nor "cosmopolitan," nor picturesque, nor beautifully built, nor large nor small. Any one who has the instinct for fiction can tell on the instant whether or not it is suitable as a background for a novel, a short story or a drama.

But consider San Francisco. It is not necessary to hesitate a moment. "Things can happen" in San Francisco. Kearny street, Montgomery street, Nob Hill, Telegraph Hill, of course Chinatown, Lone Mountain, the Poodle Dog, the Palace Hotel and the What Cheer House, the Barbary Coast, the Crow's Nest, the Mission, the Bay, the Bohemian Club, the Presidio, Spanish town, Fisherman's wharf.

There is an indefinable air about all these places that is suggestive of stories at once. You fancy the names would look well on a book's page. The people who frequent them could walk right into a novel or short story and be at home.

It occurs to me that there is perhaps one feature of the city that conduces to this effect, that is its isolation. Perhaps no great city of the world is so isolated as we are. Did you ever think of that? There is no great city to the north of us, to the south none nearer than Mexico, to the west is the waste of the Pacific, to the east the waste of the deserts. Here we are set down as a pin point in a vast circle of solitude. Isolation produces individuality, originality. The place has grown up independently. Other cities grow by accretion from without. San Francisco must grow by expansion from within; and so we have time and opportunity to develop certain unhampered types and characters and habits unbiased by outside influence, types that are admirably adapted to fictitious treatment.

It is a significant fact that the little that has been done in the way of gripping hold upon and impressing this life of ours between the covers of works of fiction has been done in the way of short stories. London had her Dickens, New Orleans her Cable, New York her Davis, Boston her Howells, Paris her Zola, but San Francisco still waits for her novelist. She will wait long, we believe. The conditions of our life are suited finely to the short story, but not as yet to the novel. We are growing and living, as it were, in spots, here a little and there a little, scattered bits of life and movement, quite independent of each other—short stories that are happening every day. But we are not settled enough yet for the novelist, who demands large, co-ordinated, broad and simple lines upon which to work, something far more unified than we can yet give him. But the short stories. There's the chance. Who shall be our Kipling? Where is the man that shall get at the heart of us, the blood and bones and fiber of us, that shall go a-gunning for stories up and down our streets and into our houses and parlors and lodging houses and saloons and dives and along our wharves and into our theaters; yes, and into the secretest chambers of our homes as well as our hearts?

Les Jeunes. Yes, there are Les Jeunes, and "The Lark" was delightful—delightful, fooling, but there's a graver note and a more virile to be sounded. Les Jeunes can do better than "The Lark." Give us stories now, give us men, strong, brutal men, with red-hot blood in 'em, with unleashed passions rampant in 'em, blood and bones and viscera in 'em, and women, too, that move and have their being, people that love and hate something better now than Vivettes and Perilles and Goups. They are here, these living men and women. Think of the short stories that are happening every hour of the time. Get hold of them, some of you younger writers, grip fast upon the life of them. It's the Life that we want, the vigorous, real thing, not the curious weaving of words and the polish of literary finish. Damn the "style" of a story, so long as we get the swing and rush and trample of the things that live. While you are rounding a phrase a sailor has been shanghaied down there along the water front; while you are sustaining a metaphor, another See Yup has been hatcheted yonder in Gambler's Alley; a man has time to be stabbed while you are composing a villanelle; the crisis of a life has come and gone while you have been niggling with your couplet. "Murder and sudden death," say you? Yes, but it's the life that lives; it's reality, it's the thing that counts. We don't want literature, we want life. We don't want fine writing, we want short stories. Kipling saw it here and Stevenson as they passed through—read the unwritten tales of us as they ran.

The tales are here. The public is here. A hundred clashing presses are hungry for you, future young story-writer of San Francisco, whoever you may be. Strike but the right note, and strike it with all your might, strike it with iron instead of velvet, and the clang of it shall go the round of the nations.

A qui le tour, who shall be our Kipling?

The Wave, May 22, 1897

FICTION IS SELECTION

To the man who has ever so modestly assumed the pose of a writer of fiction is given a certain experience which is usually trying, sometimes amusing, but that on rare occasions is profitable and entertaining to the last degree. People who wish him well give him "ideas" for stories, come to him with the remark "here's something you ought to make into a story," or "there's a character you ought to put into a book." More often than otherwise they clinch their recital with the remark: "This really happened, you know," as though it were any better for actually having happened. Take, for instance, a case like this: A very good friend of the writer's, a capital chap, but without the sense for fiction, tells him a yarn of a romantic elopement. As usual, he says, "this is something that actually happened, you know." Here is what actually happened: A young fellow is in love with a girl—parents on both sides opposed to the match—relentless. Young couple decide to elope—secret appointment at the gate at the bottom of the garden—carriage and horses there—start for the flight—pursuit—girl's brother on a horse (black for preference)—pistol shots exchanged—black horse of pursuing brother killed—down he goes with a hideous sliding clatter—next town is reached and marriage performed—subsequent reconciliation, etc., etc., etc. "Now isn't that a story for you?" he exclaims. "That actually happened at—" and he names the town and backs up his story with all manner of detail. "There's a story you ought to write," says he, in conclusion. No, indeed, not if the copy were paid for at the rate of twenty-five dollars per hundred words. The thing may have happened. There can be no doubt that such stories have happened. But the truth of a story in this sense of the word has nothing to do with its availability, from the point of view of good fiction. In a written tale it would not seem real. It would seem like a rehash of some tawdry yellow-covered romance of fifty or a hundred years ago. Fiction is what seems real, not what is real.

But for all this, the story writer must go to real life for his story. You can never think out, or invent or imagine a tale

that will be half so good as the things that have "really happened." The complications of real life are infinitely better,
stronger and more original than anything you can make up.
The only difference is in the matter of selection of details. The
story writer's position in regards to the life of the world is
like that of a maker of mosaics in front of a vast pile of tiny
many-colored blocks. He don't make the blocks nor color
them—the story writer does not invent nor imagine the parts
of his story. Writer and mosaicist alike select and combine.
The maker of a mosaic has a design in his brain, or, better
still, infinitely better, sees in the pile of little colored blocks in
front of him a certain little group or tiny heap that, by merest
accident, has tumbled into a design of its own. The design is
rough, very crude, the blocks do not fit together, and here
and there a green or blue or red block jars in the color
scheme. But, for all that, there is a suggestion of design there,
much more original than any design he could work out. Well,
he takes this group of blocks in hand, picks out and throws
away the red and the blue and the green that jar and fight,
trims off the edges of the blocks and makes them fit com-
pactly together; perhaps a gap or two is left. The whole vast
heap is at his command. Deftly he goes over it, picking out
here and there the blocks that he needs, a circular one here, a
triangular one there, now one of a bright vermillion, now one
of a sombre grey. Little by little he pieces together that crude
and rough design, gets everything to fit, everything to har-
monize; possibly he combines the first design with another;
possibly these two designs suggest a third still better; so he
proceeds. At last the final design is complete. A little polishing, a very little, for in roughness there is strength and in
sharp contrast, vividness; and there you are, a rounded whole,
a definite, compact and complete thing, taken out of and isolated from a formless heap and jumble of shape and colors.

There may be—in fact, there is—in the heap a hundred
and one other combinations of forms and shapes already arranged, "actually existing," made to hand, as it were, but the
designer over-passes them because these combinations have
been used by other designers before him, used so often that
there is no longer any originality or freshness in them.

Some one objects at this point: "What about imagination?

What about fancy? What about invention?" There is no such thing as imagination. What we elect to call imagination is mere combination of things not heretofore combined. The designer, before his heap of mosaic blocks, can only pick and choose. If he is daring enough, thoughtful enough, careful enough to combine two colors that have never before been combined, or two shapes never before fitted together, we call it "imagination." It is only observation, after all. The designer does not make his little blocks, does not color them. They are already made and colored for him. The fiction writer of the wildest and most untrammelled fancy cannot get away from real life. Imagination! There is no such thing; you can't imagine anything that you have not already seen and observed.

Like the skilled mosaic maker, any one with an eye accustomed to looking for short stories can run his glance over the heap of things we have elected to call life and here and there see combinations of form and color that are original, telling and worth working up. Such a one would not have given the elopement combination half a thought. The design may be in the heap, almost perfect as it lies; the story may have really happened; both are worthless for all that. Sometimes, however, the design does not exist at all except in your brain; you must go to your heap nevertheless. Here, for instance, is an "idea" for another kind of story. It has never happened, but it was told me by a man who has the fiction-sense rather keenly developed. Observe the difference between it and the other one of the elopement, but bear in mind that this last story is yet in its crude original state—needs, in fact, no end of handling and piecing and rearranging. It's a mere handful of blocks, so far. A Jew—sweats old clothes in a sordid basement—a wretched benighted man, squatting all day cross-legged in that sordid basement—has a wife no less sordid than himself. The Jew has no emotions, no fancies, no illusions. There is no poetry in the man. He sweats old clothes. Has not seen the country in fifteen or twenty years. However, in front of his shop stands a poplar tree—tall, very beautiful. Jew has a sort of blind, unreasoned attachment for the tree—looks at it in the evening after he is done with sweating old clothes—has watched its leaves come and go with the seasons—loves the tree, but don't know why—hardly knows that he does love the tree. All the starved poetry of the sordid man's life is centered about the tree. One day the tree is suddenly cut down—consternation—something gone out of the Jew's life—don't know exactly what—becomes morose and gloomy—goes from bad to worse—develops latent melancholia—insanity perhaps—quarrels with the sordid wife. All his peace of mind and little happiness gone—goes from worse to the worst of all—one day kills the sordid wife without knowing why—is adjudged insane and straight-jacketed in a sanitarium—would it all have happened if the tree had been left standing?

The Wave, September 11, 1897

PERVERTED TALES

The discovery of California by the editors of the Big Four Magazines of the East has had the lamentable result of crowding from their exalted places, heretofore so secure, a number of the world's most fascinating story-tellers. Their places have been filled from the ranks of that little army of youthful volunteers known as Les Jeunes. As a lamentable result old idols have been overthrown, old gods forgotten, and the children in the market place no longer dance to the tune of the old pipes. Where once the old favorite received a check, he now receives a printed form with veiled reference to availability, guarded allusions to the plans of the editor—and his story. With the view to stemming the perverse tide of popular favor—whose ebb and flow are not reducible to any known law—and, if only for a moment, sounding again the old notes once so compelling, the editors of this paper have secured for publication a few of these rejected tales and here submit them to the public of the West. Their genuineness is as Caesar's wife, and if internal evidence were wanting the opinions of experts in type-writing have been secured, which place their authenticity beyond fear and beyond reproach.

THE 'RICKSHA THAT HAPPENED.

By R——D K——G.

Ching-a-ring-a-ring ching-chaw
Ho, dinkum darkey.
> —The unedited diary of Bahlamooca Tah.

Jam yesterday and jam to-morrow
But never jam to-day.—Native Proverb.

"*Who's* all right? Rudyard! Who? *Rudyard!*"
> —Barrack-room ballad.

There was a man once—but that's another story. Person-ally, I do not believe much of this story, however, you may have it for what it is worth, to me it was worth five thousand dollars per thousand words.

A friend of mine, who is a *jinricksha* down by Benares, told me this tale one hot evening outside the Tiddledtypore gate. In the telling of it he spat reflectively and often into the moat. *Chaprassi simpkin peg*, as Mrs. Hawkseye says.

Mulligatawney, who is a private soldier and who dines with me at table d'hote on Thursdays, and who shares my box at the opera, says the tale is cheap at a gallon and a half of beer.

"Pwhat nex!" exclaimed Mulligatawney, when he heard it, shifting his quid to the other side of his mouth (we were at table). "It's *jaddoo*, that's phwat ut is. 'Tis flyin' in the face uv natoor to trifle with such brutil and licenshous soldiery as me and Orf-of-this an' Lear-eyed." Here he stole a silver spoon to hide his emotion. "*Choop*, sez oi to im," said Mulligatawney, filling himself another *jinricksha*, "*choop*, an' he chooped, like *ghairun* gone clane *dal-bat* an' *Kipiri* in hot weather. I waz only a recruity then. But I waz a corpril wanst. I was rejuced aftherwards, but I waz a corpril wanst," and he stared mournfully at the dying embers in the *jinricksha*.

We are a terrible bad lot out here in Indiana, but we can't help that. Here a man's whole duty is to lie *doggo* and not *ekka* more than once a week, and to pray for a war. Also he may keep a *jinricksha* in his stable if he can afford it. As that wonderful woman, Mrs. Hawkseye, says: "It better to *bustee* in a *jampanni* than to have your *jinricksha puckarowed*." But that's her affair.

Stepterfetchit had just come out from *home*. Now when a man comes out from home, if he is not *jinrickshaed* at the pier landing, he generally does one of three things (*jampanni chorah simpkin bungalow*), either he dies with swiftness, which is bad, or lives with swiftness, which is worse or marries, which is the worst of all. "A single man," says my friend Mulligatawney, "is an ornamint to the service." But as Lear-eyed observes, "when a mon is tewed wi' a lass he's *lokri* in a *bunder*, nothing but *dikh*," and he flung himself (seven foot four of British soldier), full length upon his *jinricksha*.

Stepterfetchit knew as much of Life (Life with a big L) as a weaning child, until I, who have seen everything worth seeing, and done everything worth doing, and have known everything worth knowing, from Indian magic to the cleaning of codfish, took him in hand. He began by contradicting his colonel, and went on from that to making love to Mrs. Hawkseye (till that lady told him he was a *bungalow*, with no more *pukaree* than a *dacoit*), and wound up by drinking too much *jinricksha* at his club.

Now, when a man takes to the *jinricksha* he is very likely to end at the *shroff*. So I spoke to the Major. You may hit a *marumutta* over the head at the beginning of your acquaintance, but you must not soap the tail of a kitten that belongs to a *Ryotwary*, unless you are prepared to prove it on his front teeth. It takes some men a life time to find this out, but the knowledge is useful. *Sempkin peg, do re mi fa, ching-a-ring-a-ring-ching-chaw*, but that's another story. We arrived—the Major and I—at Stepterfetchit's dak-bungalow on a red hot evening, when the heat blanketed the world like a hot towel round a swelled head. We nearly killed the *jinricksha* in getting there, but a mountain bred can *gawbry* more *jhil* than you would care to believe.

"Hark!" said the Major. We paused on the threshold and the silence of the Indian twilight gathered us in its hollow palms. We both heard a sound that came from Stepterfetchit's window. It was the ticking of an eight-day clock.

People write and talk lightly of blood running cold and of fear and all that sort of thing, but the real sensation is quite too terrible to be trifled with. As the Major and I heard the ticking of that eight-day clock, it is no lie to say that the *bhisti mussick* turned *shikary* in our *khitmatgar*. We were afraid. The Major entered the *bungalow* and I followed and *salaamed* the door behind me.

The *jinricksha* lay dead on the *charpoy* in Stepterfetchit's room. Stepterfetchit must have killed it hours before. "We came too late," groaned the Major. We made no attempt to keep from crying—I respected my self for that. But we gathered up the pieces of the *jinricksha* and sent them to Stepterfetchit's people at Home.

So now you know what I know of the Ricksha that never was.

Stepterfetchit is now a plate-layer somewhere down near Bareilly, on the line of the railroad, where the *Kharki* water tanks that the Rajah of Bathtub built out of stolen government money, when the commissariat bullock train was *puck-arowed* by Pathans, in the days of the old *budmash* Mahommud Dinare, and Mulligatawney is away annexing Burmah. When he heard of the affair he said:

"If a *punkah* is goin' to *ayah* niver loose your grip, but I waz a corpril wanst, I was rejuced aftherwards," which is manifestly unfair.

Mrs. Hawkseye says that a "*jinricksha* in the hand gathers no moss"—but that's another story.

THE GREEN STONE OF UNREST.

By S——N CR——E.

A Mere Boy stood on a pile of blue stones. His attitude was regardant. The day was seal brown. There was a vermillion valley containing a church. The church's steeple aspired strenuously in a direction tangent to the earth's center. A pale wind mentioned tremendous facts under its breath with certain effort at concealment to seven not-dwarfed poplars on an un-distant mauve hilltop.

The Mere Boy was a brilliant blue color. The effect of the scene was not un-kaleidoscopic.

After a certain appreciable duration of time the Mere Boy abandoned his regardant demeanor. The strenuously aspiring church steeple no longer projected itself upon his consciousness. He found means to remove himself from the pile of blue stones. He set his face valleyward. He proceeded.

The road was raw umber. There were in it wagon ruts. There were in it pebbles, Naples yellow in color. One was green. The Mere Boy allowed the idea of the green pebble to nick itself into the sharp edge of the disc of his Perception.

"Ah," he said, "a green pebble."

The rather pallid wind communicated another Incomprehensible Fact to the paranthine trees. It would appear that the poplars understood.

"Ah," repeated the Mere Boy, "a Green Pebble."

"Sho-o," remarked the wind.

The Mere Boy moved appreciably forward. If there were a thousand men in a procession and nine hundred and ninety-nine should suddenly expire, the one man who was remnant would assume the responsibility of the procession.

The Mere Boy was an abbreviated procession.

The blue Mere Boy transported himself diagonally athwart the larger landscape, printed in four colors, like a poster.

On the uplands were chequered squares made by fields, tilled and otherwise. Cloud-shadows moved from square to square. It was as if the Sky and Earth was playing a tremendous game of chess.

By and by the Mere Boy observed an Army of a Million Men. Certain cannon, like voluble but non-committal toads with hunched backs, fulminated vast hiccoughs at unimpassioned intervals. Their own invulnerableness was offensive.

An officer of blue serge waved a sword, like a picture in a school history. The non-committal toads pullulated with brief red pimples and swiftly relapsed to impassivity.

The line of the Army of a Million Men obnubilated itself in whiteness as a line of writing is blotted with a new blotter.

"Go teh blazes b'Jimminy," remarked the Mere Boy. "What yeh's shooting fur. They might be people in that field."

He was terrific in his denunciation of such negligence. He debated the question of his ir-removability.

"If I'm goin' teh be shot," he observed; "If I'm goin' teh be shot, b'Jimminy——"

*   *   *   *   *

A Thing lay in the little hollow.

The little hollow was green.

The Thing was pulpy white. Its eyes were white. It had blackish-yellow lips. It was beautifully spotted with red, like tomato stains on a rolled napkin.

The yellow sun was dropping on the green plain of the earth, like a twenty-dollar gold piece falling on the baize cloth of a gaming table.

The blue serge officer abruptly discovered the punctured Thing in the Hollow. He was struck with the ir-remediableness of the business.

"Gee," he murmured with interest. "Gee, it's a Mere Boy."

The Mere Boy had been struck with seventy-seven rifle bullets. Seventy had struck him in the chest, seven in the head. He bore close resemblance to the top of a pepper castor.

He was dead.

He was obsolete.

As the blue serge officer bent over him he became aware of a something in the Thing's hand.

It was a green pebble.

"Gee," exclaimed the blue serge officer. "A green pebble, gee."

The large Wind evolved a threnody with reference to the seven un-distant poplars.

A HERO OF TOMATO CAN.

By B——T H——TE.

Mr. Jack Oak-hearse calmly rose from the table and shot the bartender of Tomato Can, because of the objectionable color of his hair. Then Mr. Oak-hearse scratched a match on the sole of his victim's boot, lit a perfumed cigarette and strolled forth into the street of the camp to enjoy the evening air. Mr. Oak-hearse's face was pale and impassive, and stamped with that indefinable hauteur that marks the professional gambler. Tomato Can knew him to be a cool, desperate man. The famous Colonel Blue-bottle was reported to have made the remark to Miss Honorine-Sainte-Claire, when that leader of society opened the Pink Assembly at Toad-in-the-Hole, on the other side of the Divide, that he, Colonel Blue-bottle, would be everlastingly "—— ——ed if he didn't believe that that —— ——ed Oak-hearse would open a ——ed jack-pot on a pair of ——ed tens, ——ed if he didn't." To which Miss Ste.-Claire had responded:

"Fancy now."

On this occasion as Mr. Jack Oak-hearse stepped in the cool evening air of the Sierras from out of the bar of the hotel of Tomato Can, he drew from his breast pocket a dainty manicure set and began to trim and polish his slender, almost feminine finger nails, that had been contaminated with the touch of the greasy cards. Thus occupied he betook himself leisurely down the one street of Tomato Can, languidly dodging an occasional revolver bullet, and stepping daintily over the few unburied corpses that bore mute testimony to the disputatious and controversial nature of the citizens of Tomato Can. He arrived at his hotel and entered his apartments, gently waving aside the half-breed Mexican who attempted to disembowel him on the threshold. The apartment was crudely furnished as befitted the rough and ready character of the town of Tomato Can. The Wilton carpet on the floor was stained with spilt Moet and Chandon. The full-length portrait of Mr. Oak-hearse by Carolus Duran was punctured with bullet marks, while the teakwood escritoire, inlaid with buhl and jade, was encumbered with bowie knives, spurs and Mexican saddles.

Mr. Oak-hearse's valet brought him the London and Vienna papers. They had been ironed, and scented with orris root, and the sporting articles blue-penciled.

"Bill," said Mr. Oak-hearse, "Bill, I believe I told you to cut out all the offensive advertisements from my papers; I perceive, with some concern, that you have neglected it. Your punishment shall be that you will not brush my silk hat next Sunday morning."

The valet uttered an inarticulate cry and fell lifeless to the floor.

"It's better to stand pat on two pair than to try for a full hand," mused Mr. Oak-hearse, philosophically, and his long lashes drooped wearily over his cold steel-blue eyes, like velvet sheathing a poignard.

A little later the gambler entered the dining-room of the hotel in evening-dress, and wearing his cordon of the Legion of Honor. As he took his accustomed place at the table, he was suddenly aware of a lustrous pair of eyes that looked into his cold gray ones from the other side of the catsup bottle. Like all heroes, Mr. Jack Oak-hearse was not insensible to feminine beauty. He bowed gallantly. The lady flushed. The waiter handed him the menu.

"I will have a caviar sandwich," affirmed the gambler with

icy impassivity. The waiter next handed the menu to the lady, who likewise ordered a caviar sandwich.

"There is no more," returned the waiter. "The last one has just been ordered."

Mr. Oak-hearse started, and his pale face became even paler. A preoccupied air came upon him, and the lines of an iron determination settled upon his face. He rose, bowed to the lady, and calmly passed from the dining-room out into the street of the town and took his way toward a wooded gulch hard by.

When the waiter returned with the caviar sandwich he was informed that Mr. Oak-hearse would not dine that night. A triangular note on scented mauve paper was found at the office begging the lady to accept the sandwich from one who had loved not wisely but too many.

But the next morning at the head of the gulch on one of the largest pine trees the searchers found an ace of spades (marked) pinned to the bark with a bowie knife. It bore the following, written in pencil with a firm hand:

Here lies the body
of
JOHN OAK-HEARSE,
who was too much of a gentleman
to play a
Royal-flush
against a
Queen-full.

And so, pulseless and cold with a Derringer by his side and a bullet in his brain, though still as calm as in life lay he who had been at once the pest and the pride of Tomato Can.

VAN BUBBLES' STORY.

By R——D H——G D——S.

Young Charding-Davis had been a little unhappy all day long because on that particular morning the valet of his head serving man had made a mistake in the matter of his master's trousers, and it was not until he was breakfasting at Delmonico's some hours later that young Charding-Davis woke to the painful consciousness that he was wearing his serving-man's pants which were made by an unfashionable New York tailor. Young Charding-Davis himself ran over to London in his steam yacht once or twice a week to be fitted, so that the consequences of his serving-man's valet's mistake took away his appetite. The predicament troubled him so that he told the head cook about it, adding anxiously:

"What would you do about these trousers, Wallis?"

"I would keep 'em on, sir," said Wallis, touching his cap respectfully.

"That," said young Charding-Davis, with a sigh of relief, "is a good idea. Thank you, Wallis." Young Charding-Davis was so delighted at the novel suggestion that he tipped Wallis a little more generously than usual.

"Can you recommend a good investment for this," inquired Wallis, as he counted out the tip.

"Make a bid for the Pacific railroads," suggested young Charding-Davis, "or 'arrive' at the Savoy Hotel."

That night he went to dinner at the house of the Girl He Knew, and in honor of the occasion and because he thought it would please the Girl He Knew, young Charding-Davis put on a Yale sweater and football knickerbockers and the head-dress of feathers he had captured from a Soudanese Arab while acting as war correspondent for an English syndicate. Besides this, he wore some of his decorations and toyed gracefully with a golf-stick. During the dinner, while young Charding-Davis was illustrating a new football trick he had just patented, with the aid of ten champagne bottles and the Girl's pet skye terrier, a great and celebrated English diplomat leaned across the table over the center piece of orchids and live humming birds, and said:

"I say, Davis, tell us how you came by some of your decorations and orders. Most interesting and extraordinary, you know."

Young Charding-Davis tossed the skye-terrier into the air, and batted it thoughtfully the length of the room with his golf-stick, after the manner of Heavyflinger of the Harvard baseball nine. Then he twirled the golf-stick in his fingers as a Zulu *induna* twirls his *assegai*—he had learned the trick while shooting elephant on the Zambesi river in South Africa. Then he smiled with becoming modesty as he glanced carelessly at the alarm-clock that hung around his neck, suspended by the blue ribbon of the order of the Pshaw of Persia.

"Really, they are mere trifles," he replied, easily. "I would not have worn them only my serving man insists it is good form. The Cham of Tartary gave me this," he continued, lightly touching a nickel-plated apple-pie that was pinned upon the sweater, "for leaving the country in twenty-four hours, and this chest protector was presented me by the French Legation in Kamschatka for protecting a chest—but we'll let that pass," he said, enveloping himself with a smile of charming ingenuousness. "*This* is the badge of the Band of Hope to which I belong. I got this pie-plate from the Grand Mufti for conspicuous egoism in the absence of the enemy, and this Grand Army badge from a pawnbroker for four dollars. Then I have a few swimming medals for swimming across Whirlpool Rapids and a five-cent piece given me by Mr. Sage. I have several showcases full of other medals in my rooms. I'm thinking of giving an exhibition and reception, if I could get some pretty girls to receive with me. I've knocked about a bit, you know, and I pick them up here and there. I've crossed Africa two or three times, and I got up the late Greek war in order to make news for the New York papers, and I'm organizing an insurrection in South America for the benefit of a bankrupt rifle manufacturer who wants to dispose of some arms."

While Charding-Davis had been speaking young Van Bubbles, who was just out of the interior of Uganda, had been absent-mindedly drawing patterns in the tomato catsup he had spilled on the table-cloth.

"When I returned from Africa," he said, "this morning I had a curious experience." He fixed Charding-Davis with his glance for a moment, and then let it wander to a corner of the room and afterward drew it back and tied it to his chair leg. Charding-Davis grew a little pale, but he was too well bred to allow his feelings to overcome him. Young Van Bubbles continued:

"I met an old valet of mine on Fifth avenue, who has recently been engaged by the head serving man of one of New York's back-parlor heroes. He was wearing a pair of trousers which seemed to me strangely familiar, and when I spoke to him about the matter, broke down and confessed that he had caused his master's master to exchange trousers with him. You see the point of the story is," concluded young Van Bubbles, untieing his glance, and allowing it to stray toward Charding-Davis, who drove it away with his golf-stick, "that the back-parlor hero wore his valet's trousers to-day."

There was a silence.

"What an extraordinary story," murmured the diplomat.

"Quite so," said the Girl Charding-Davis Knew.

"Of course," added Van Bubbles, "I took the trousers from him. Here they are," he continued, dropping them on the table. "You see they were no more use to him. I thought, perhaps—" and once more his glance crept stealthily toward young Charding-Davis—"*you* might suggest a way out of the difficulty." He handed the trousers to Charding-Davis, saying: "Keep them, they are a mere trifle, and they may be of some interest to you."

The Girl Charding-Davis Knew saw the point of Van Bubbles' story at once. Charding-Davis tried to catch her eye, but she refused to look at him, and said to her father:

"Why won't he go away; tell him to go away, please."

On the steps outside the house young Charding-Davis reflected what next he should do. He strolled slowly homeward, and, as he came into his rooms, his head serving-man handed him two notes which had arrived in his absence. One was from the Most Beautiful Woman in New York offering him her hand and fortune; the other was written on the back of a ten thousand dollar check, and was from the Editor of the Greatest Paper in the World begging him to accept the vacant throne of the Nyam-Nyam of Khooinooristan in the capacity of Special Correspondent.

"I wonder now," said young Charding-Davis, "which of these offers I shall accept."

AMBROSIA BEER.

By A——E B——E.

Sterling Hallmark was one of the most prominent and en-thusiastic members of the Total Abstinence Union of San Francisco. His enthusiasm was not only of the passive de-scription. He took a delight in aiding the police in their raids upon the unlicensed beer halls of the Barbary Coast. He helped them break whisky and brandy flasks, and he himself often opened the spigots of the beer kegs and let the foaming liquid run out upon the sanded floor.

On the night of the thirtieth of February, 1868, Sterling Hallmark led the police in a furious attack upon the "Hole in the Wall," a notorious subterranean dive in the vicinity of Jackson street. The battle was short and decisive. The bar-tender and his assistants were routed and the victorious assailants turned their attention to the demolition of the un-savory resort. Bottles were broken, brandy flasks smashed, the contents of the decanters emptied. In the midst of the con-fusion Sterling Hallmark advanced with splendid intrepidity towards a large keg, bearing the inscription Ambrosia Beer, extra pale. He set his hand upon the spigot.

But at that moment a terrific crash rent the air. The frail building, in the cellar of which the "Hole in the Wall" was situated, collapsed because it was necessary it should do so at that precise instant for the purposes of this tale. The crazy edifice fell with a loud clatter and clouds of blinding dust.

When Sterling Hallmark recovered consciousness he was not for the moment aware of what had happened. Then he realized that he was uninjured, but that he was unmovably pinioned beneath a mass of debris, and that something was weighing heavily upon his chest. Looking up and around him he perceived in the dim light a ring of metal protruding from a dark object that lay upon his chest. As his senses ad-justed themselves to his environment he saw that the dark object was the keg of Ambrosia Beer, and that the ring of metal was the mouth of the spigot. The mouth of the spigot was directly in the line of his lips and not two inches distant from them. The terrible question that now confronted Sterling Hallmark was this, Had he opened that spigot before the collapse of the building, was the keg full or empty? He now found that by great exertion he could move his right arm so that his fingers could touch and clasp the spigot. A horrible fear came upon Sterling Hallmark, drops of cold perspiration bespangled his brow; he tried to cry out, but his voice failed him. His mouth was dry. A horrible thirst tortured him—a thousand fiends seemed shouting to him to open the spigot, unseen hands tugged at *his* free hand. He raised this hand to cover his eyes from the sight, but as he withdrew it again it dropped upon his breast two inches nearer the fatal spigot. At length the strain became too great to be borne, Sterling Hallmark became desperate. He laughed aloud in almost insensate glee.

"Ha, Ha!" exclaimed Sterling Hallmark.

He reached up and grasped the spigot and turned it with all his strength.

*   *   *   *   *

An hour later when the rescue party with axes and hatchets found their way into the cellar of the "Hole in the Wall," the foremost of them hauled out Sterling Hallmark.

"Thash a' ri' girlsh," screamed the unfortunate man as his rescuers tried to keep him on his feet. "Thash a' ri', I ne'r him feelsh sho 'appy, az-I-do-t'-ni'. Les op'n n'er li'l' bol, girlsh." The patrol wagon was rung for, and the raving inebriate was conveyed to the City Hall. The ride in the open air, however, had the effect of sobering him. He realized that he, Sterling Hallmark, temperance leader, had been *drunk*. He also realized that he could not stand the disgrace that would now inevitably follow him through life. He drew his revolver, and ere the policeman who accompanied him could interfere, had sent a bullet crashing through his brain.

*   *   *   *   *

A few moments after the patrol wagon had departed one of the rescue party discovered the keg labelled Ambrosia Beer, that had been rolled from the breast of Sterling Hallmark. With a few well-directed blows of his ax, he smashed in the head of the keg, and thrust his hand down to the bottom, groping about.

The interior of the keg was full of dust and rusty nailheads.

"Empty for over a year," he exclaimed, in tones of bitter disappointment.

I CALL ON LADY DOTTY.

FROM THE POLLY PARABLES
By AN——Y H——PE.

Like most women, Lady Dotty is in love with me—a little. Like most men, I am in love with Lady Dotty—a great deal.

Last Thursday afternoon at five o'clock, as I was strolling in St. James' Park (you may have remarked that I always stroll—in St. James' Park—on Thursday afternoons) it occurred to me to call on Lady Dotty. I forthwith presented myself at the house (it is by Van Burgh).

After I had waited some five minutes in the drawing-room Lady Dotty appeared.

"But I am not at home," she said on the threshold. "I am not at home, Mr. Carterer."

"Nor am I," I replied.

"And my husband is——"

"At home?"

"At his club."

"The brute," said I, "to leave you alone."

"There are others," she sighed, with half a glance at me. I had not called in a fortnight.

"I have languished in self-imposed solitude," I murmured with some gallantry.

"Why have you not been to see me in so long."

"My laundress——" I began.

"Your *laundress*, Mr. Carterer?"

"Refused to relent."

"You poor dear. Tea?"

"You are too kind," said I, with a bow.

Lady Dotty's maid, a delicious young creature named

Negligee, appeared with the tray and smoking cups and vanished.

Lady Dotty handed me my cup.

"Sit down," she ordered.

There was but one chair in the room. I sat down.

Lady Dotty—also sat down.

"Clarence is a beast," she said.

"Most husbands are."

"Sometimes they are not."

"When?"

"When they are other women's husbands."

"Wives," I remarked, "of other men are no less so."

"Why can't other men's wives marry other women's husbands," suggested Lady Dotty.

"The question is worthy of consideration," said I.

Negligee hurriedly entered at this point of our conversation.

"The husband of Madame," she exclaimed.

"Good heavens," said Lady Dotty.

I took my hat.

"Fly, Mr. Carterer," cried Lady Dotty.

"This way," murmured Negligee. "Follow me." She led me out into the dark hall, where the back stairs were.

"It is rather dark, sir. You were best to give me your hand."

"And my heart," I answered.

Our hands clasped.

It was, as Negligee remarked, rather dark.

The charming creature's face was close to mine.

"Were you ever kissed?" said I, boldly.

"I don't know how to kiss," said Negligee.

"We might put our heads together and find out how," I suggested.

As I say, Negligee is a delicious young creature. But a man never knows the usefulness of his watch until he is without it—to say nothing of his scarfpin.

FRANK NORRIS' WEEKLY LETTER

THE MOST ABIDING impression that one receives from a reading of "The Crisis" is one of regret. Here is a man whose immense public is assured, who is above the necessity of truckling, of bidding for popularity, whose subject is in a sense made to hand, already dramatic, picturesque, interesting; whose theme is enwoven with the career of the most lovable of great men, Lincoln, and yet who has thought it advisable to be cautious, to exercise an undue restraint, to use gray colors. So large a stage, so heroic a theme, so vast an audience, so boundless a popularity and such meager performance, such conservatism, such politeness, such decorum, such cautious holding to old ideas, to trite formulas, to accepted, time-honored, time-worn standards.

"The Crisis"—the very name implies vigorous action, and the handling of an epic phase of history with a powerful, unrestrained grip, and yet, always the repression of spontaneity, always from page to page, from chapter to chapter, the holding back of impulse. One expects the leap and finds instead only painful, painstaking clambering.

What—a war story and not one scene of battle struck off in the heat of blood! A tale of the death grapple of millions and not one inspiriting encounter. There is, to be sure, the episode in the nineteenth chapter, the capture of Camp Jackson by the Yankees, but how confusedly presented, how diffused the action; cut up into chapters, rendered in piece-meal, instead of en bloc.

It seems to me that this diffuseness, the scattering and partitioning of the drama, is the weakest point in Mr. Churchill's novel. Where is the grouping? Just what is the writer trying to show? Upon what peg does he hang his story? Up to what pivotal scene does he lead?

*   *   *

Just what is the crisis? Is it in the chapter called "The Crisis" (Chapter V. of Book II.)? If so, it is strangely out of place in the early part of the novel before the narrative is well begun. By the expression crisis, to just what does Mr.

Churchill refer? Is it the crisis in the life of the nation, or in the life of Virginia, or in the life of Abraham Lincoln? It is not clear. Not once in the book is there a single incisive stroke. The story does not seem to be "managed," constructed, arranged, plotted out.

The historical parts are for the most part distinct and unhinged from the fictitious. It is not an historical novel so much as historical events plus a novel.

And such a chance as he had! The story is laid in his native city, familiar to him as the palm of his hand. Yet there is little sense of background, of stage-setting. The place might as well have been New Orleans or Cincinnati. The reader does not see St. Louis. The time of the action is the most dramatic in the history of the country, and yet one misses the drama. It will be argued that in the course of the tale many of the grand scenes of history are included, many of the great figures of the time are introduced. But it is an open question whether this is the right method to be employed to reconstruct a period, to create the atmosphere of a phase.

Much, infinitely much more should have been attempted, or much less. Would not the idea of the civil war times have been more clearly, more forcibly presented by the working out in detail of a single theme, a single line, rather than by the synoptic description of the entire epoch from the time of the Lincoln-Douglas debates to the time of the President's assassination? Suppose Mr. Churchill had elected for his main theme the battle of Gettysburg, the surrender at Appomattox, or the tragedy of Ford's Opera House. Any one of these if worked out in detail would have implied and suggested the whole drama, the entire picture. It would have unified the book, solidified it, made it compact, direct, forceful and infinitely more interesting. No novelist that ever lived or will live could make a picture of the whole of the civil war in the compass of one, nor of one hundred volumes. Yet this is what the author of "The Crisis" sets out to do in 500 pages, and tell the story of Brice and Virginia at the same time.

And to consider now this part of the book—the love story of Virginia Carvel and Stephen Brice. There can be no question of Mr. Churchill's earnestness, no question of his "capacity for taking pains." Yet why in the face of these indubitable powers of his has he elected to sound again, for the hundreth time the old, old note—the story of the Northern man in love with the Southern girl, and the Southern girl responding to this affection in the end, after the usual period of hatred and defiance; the two continually at variance and separated by the violence of their patriotism—the one standing out for the nation and the other for state's sovereignty.

How often have we met these two, how wearisome are their misunderstandings, brought about in the same old way, carried on in the same old fashion, calmly and with dignity by the man, impulsively and hysterically by the girl, and ending in the trite reconciliation and in the girl's discovery of the Northern gentleman's heroism, which he carefully conceals from her and which the other characters in the book are as careful to proclaim. And the girl's father, or uncle, or guardian—it makes no difference so long as he is of the type of the Southern gentleman of the old school. In this case it is Colonel—of course, Colonel—Carvel. It needs not Mr. Christy's illustrations to know that he wears a slouch hat (even in the house in the presence of his daughter, punctiliously courteous though he is) and a goatee and a frock coat. We knew the Colonel long before we knew Mr. Churchill. We have known him ever since the publication—years ago—of the first novel of Southern life.

And Clarence Colfax. We know him, too—type of the young South, hot-headed, generous, worthless and courageous. The instant he comes upon the stage we know how he will end; how he will redeem a misspent life by unheard of courage on the battlefield. How he will be the rival and enemy of the hero and be pardoned and forgiven and saved by the latter's magnanimity. Hopper is an old friend, too, and, oh! the worn out, threadbare situation where he holds the Colonel's life in his hands and by this means hopes to force the heroine into accepting him as her husband!

*   *   *

So one closes the book with disappointment and a sense of wonder that Mr. Churchill, with all his earnestness, his ability for painstaking work, should have thought fit to truckle to the public with these bids for popularity, when his public to the extent of 200,000 readers was assured to him beforehand. Instead of a great, forceful, vivid story of a forceful, vivid time he has given us a "safe book" that may be read without fear and without reproach by the mildest young woman that ever "attended" a seminary. This for the description of Vicksburg:

"First there was a murderous assault and a still more murderous repulse. Three times the besiegers charged, sank their color staffs into the redoubts and three times were driven back. Then the blue army settled into the earth and folded into the ravines. Three days in that narrow space between the lines lay the dead and wounded suffering untold agonies in the moist heat. Then came a truce to bury the dead, to bring back what was left of the living."

"Murderous assault," "murderous repulse," "three times charged, three times driven back," " wounded suffering untold agonies," " what was left of the living," verbiage, empty phrases. Could Mr. Churchill have given us nothing better than this for Vicksburg? Vicksburg!

The best things in the book are the Lincoln portraits, especially the Lincoln of the debates, the Lincoln of the Freeport tavern, telling the story of the Quaker's apprentice and the rats. Then, after the great controversy, taking a child upon his knee and playing his jewsharp. One sees the rugged, human man of the people in these pictures; no heroics, no capitulations, no false colorings—just the plain, honest man he must have been. No doubt that Mr. Churchill has succeeded here. And the split between Colonel Carvel and Judge Whipple—admirably done; one sees and feels the inevitableness of it, understands it all plainly, with no less liking for either of the men.

*   *   *

Then, too, the scene where Brice, at first ashamed to be seen by Virginia in the crowd that are gaping at her as she stands talking to the Prince of Wales, rallies from this sense of false shame, "because of one whom he had known for the short space of one day. * * * Abraham Lincoln would not have blushed between honest clerks and farmers." There is something at once very boyish and very manly to this touch, thoroughly probable and true and persuasive.

But happy touches, be they never so many, do not make a good novel. In the end "The Crisis" is not interesting. It puts sentiment above sincerity. It puts the "small testament" into the hands of the wounded soldier, the fine speeches into the mouths of men and women laboring under great stress, it conceives of the hero as immaculate, of the heroine as without a flaw. It sacrifices truth to a false sense of beauty, and violates probability for the sake of stage effect.

On page 70 there is set forth a rather strenuous dialogue between Virginia and Clarence Colfax. He asks her to marry him and she answers that he must learn self-control.

"You must prove first that you are a man," she says. We are told that just here a doe ran out of the forest not twenty feet away; twenty feet, mind you. "But it" (our marriage) "has all been arranged," protests the young man.

"No one shall arrange that for me," replies Virginia promptly, and to avoid him (for he is supposed to step close to her at that) she leaps over the low fence railing, and "the doe fled into the forest whistling fearfully."

Now, just what has this doe got to do with the affair, "whistling fearfully," too? First it comes out of the forest, then it goes in again. Why? What is gained or proved or shown by this bobbing in and bobbing out of a doe? The doe came out of the forest. The doe goes back into the forest.

> The King of France with forty thousand men
> Marched up the hill and then marched down again.

New York, June 20

FRANK NORRIS' WEEKLY LETTER

I~T IS NOT~ more than a week ago since the present writer, in going through the daily batch of volunteer manuscripts submitted to a certain firm of New York publishers, came across a letter pinned to the typewritten draft of a novel. The letter was, in a way, a note and commentary upon the novel, and its writer declared with some vehemence, and more than once, that the events in the novel were true—were taken from real life—actually occurred, etc., etc. The inference was plain as paint. The author believed his story to be better by just so much, because the things in it were taken from actual life, were based on fact—must, therefore, be true to life. Now, here is the point. Is an event that is taken from actual life, true to life? Let us consider now. Suppose one had overlooked this author's letter, and had written to him to say that one of the faults of his story lay in the fact that it was not true to life. What a chance! How that author would have countered! How he would have forever demolished the critic, or the reader, with the one phrase, "But, sir, it actually happened." Therefore, it must be true.

Well, I say no. Let us talk about this Truth in Fiction, and with a certain provincial magistrate ask—in the name of American literature—"What is Truth?" A thing has actually happened; that is the proposition. Given to prove that it is not necessarily true when told as fiction—not necessarily true even when told with the most scrupulous adherence to fact, even when narrated with the meticulous science of the phonograph or pictured with the incontestable precision of the photograph.

*　　*　　*

Perhaps we will get a good grip of the problem at the outset if we make a difference, a wide difference, between Accuracy and Truth. A story can be accurate and yet lamentably—even wickedly—untrue. As, for instance, let us suppose that you have never seen a sheep, and that it devolves upon me to give you an idea of the animal—describe it, in fact. I go out into the fields and select a sheep. In size, build, habits, weight, wool-producing qualities and the like it is precisely like other sheep—but it is black. To you, then, I bring this sheep. I call your attention to the characteristics. I falsify nothing, conceal nothing. I present the creature fairly in every detail, in every particular. I am, in a word, accurate. But what is the result? To your notion all sheep are black, which is an untruth.

So that Accuracy is not necessarily Truth, and the novelist who relies upon the accurate presentation of a crisis in life, hoping by this means to create the impression of Truth, is leaning upon a broken reed.

For further—Life itself is not necessarily True—not necessarily True to life. I admit that this is much easier to assert than to prove, and the sound of it is that of a flippant paradox. Let us try an illustration or two. How many times—how almost invariably, especially with us stoical Anglo-Saxons—do men or women confronted suddenly with great tragedy or great joy fail to "rise to the occasion." How seldom is it that their actions or words at the moment are adequate, are interpretive of their emotions, give an expression of themselves. Mr. Davis tells of a condemned murderer who received the news of his pardon with the words:

"That's good. That's good."

*   *   *

Death-bed scenes are notoriously tame; heroic rescuers are most frequently silent at their work; the soldier receiving a mortal wound, when not struck unconscious, shouts "Gee!" and sits down suddenly with straddled legs. Wellington, at Waterloo, never cried "Up guards and at 'em!" Louis Napoleon's tame eagle refused to fly at the fortress of Ham; and Newton, when his little dog, by overturning a lamp, had irreparably destroyed fifty years of work, could only exclaim, "Ah, Flo, Flo, thou little knowest the ruin thou has wrought!" Suppose Newton had acted and spoken in proportion to the poignancy of his grief, what a noble, heroic strain of tragedy would have been given to the world. But if we all gave true expression to our feelings under stress there would be no need nor place for fiction.

And here comes the dividing line. Here stands the crux. Is

it too much to say that fiction can be truer than Life itself? I take it that we can say this and yet be well within conservatism. For fiction must not be judged by standards of real life, but both life and fiction referred to a third standard. The expression "true to life" is false, is inadequate, for life itself is not always true.

To what, then, should the truth of a novel be referred—to what standard? By what touchstone may we recognize the true metal?

*   *   *

Difficult question. Standards vary for different works of fiction. We must not refer Tolstoy to the same standard as Victor Hugo—the one a realist, the other a romanticist. We can conceive of no standard which would be large enough to include both, unless it would be one so vague, so broad, so formless as to be without value. Take the grand scene in Hernani. How would Tolstoy have done it? He would have brought it home as close to the reader as possible. Hugo has elevated it as far as he could in the opposite direction. Tolstoy would have confined himself to probabilities only. Hugo is confined by nothing save the limitations of his own imagination. The realist would have been accurate—only in this case he would not have chosen a black sheep. The romanticist aims at the broad truth of the thing—puts into his people's mouths the words they would have spoken if only they could have given expression to his thoughts.

Then the conclusion. Is it permissible to say that Accuracy is realism and Truth romanticism? I am not so sure, but I feel that we come close to a solution here. The divisions seem natural and intended. It is not difficult to be accurate, but it is monstrously difficult to be True; at best the romanticists can only aim at it, while on the other hand, mere accuracy as an easily obtainable result is for that reason less worthy.

*   *   *

Does Truth after all "lie in the middle"? And what school, then, is midway between the Realists and Romanticists, taking the best from each? Is it not the school of Naturalism, which strives hard for accuracy and truth? The nigger is out of the fence at last, but must it not be admitted that the author of the Debacle (not the author of La Terre and Fecondite) is up to the present stage of literary development the most adequate, the most satisfactory, the most just of them all?

New York, Aug. 2

Only two or three days ago I heard a story about a young man of letters that not only impressed me at the time, but has ever since been, as it were, a sort of obsession. The thing depressed me. I have not been able to get it out of my mind. It was not only because the story was sad in itself, but because there is every reason to believe—oh, let us say it is positively true—that there are hundreds of stories like this one of my young fellow working themselves out in every city in the union; more especially so in New York.

The story distinctly has a moral and for the sake of those beginners in letters who have yet to arrive—even for those whose "first book" is already published—the story shall be set down in this place.

*   *   *

The name of the young man does not matter, though he has been before the public. I doubt if there are one hundred people who would recall his name. He came of good people in Pennsylvania. His father was a lawyer in a small city, had been editor of the "city paper," and thence no doubt came the literary twist in our young man.

When he was twenty-two he wrote a novel. The novel was not great, but it was distinctly promising in that it was all his own. By some miraculous good fortune he had got started straight with his very first effort; had not been influenced by some favorite author, had not been Kiplingized or Davised or Anthony Hoped. This sort of thing happens oftener than you would suppose in little out of the way communities, where a boy will begin to write before he has, one may almost say, begun to read, and where there are no "literary" people to bother him and sidetrack him.

The stuff, then, was all his own. There was a fresh note in it that no one had ever heard before. Nothing astonishing about it, a book you would maybe yawn over, but it was his own. You can imagine, or I will ask you to understand, how carefully and with what meticulous nicety such a career, thus begun, should have been nurtured. Some writers work twenty

years before attaining to their own style, before becoming
original. But this young fellow was one of those country boys
who grow up unnoticed and are close enough to the soil to
get a good, vigorous growth early in life.

*   *   *

Well, his book was published by a New York firm and one
of the editors of this firm (who saw the promise in the work
and the prospects of a good investment in a potential genius
of the near future) sent for the young man to come to New
York and gave him a minor place on the editorial staff.

In New York the boy fell foul of a literary set first off. He
was invited to an "evening." There he met a few of the vast
army of "third-raters." Short-haired women and long-haired
men, minor poets whose opportunity in life is the blank space
left in the magazine between the end of an article and the
bottom of the page, authors who because of a story or two
printed in the Century or Harper's or Scribner's were considered to have "arrived"; book reviewers who hacked for the
literary weeklies and spoke of themselves as critics, and—
worst of all—a number of women who neither wrote nor
reviewed, but who "took an interest in young writers."
They took an interest in this boy of mine—some of them
had read his little book—and they fluttered and buzzed about
him.

He never knew the difference. He had never been in a large
city before and he thought this was the real thing. He
thought these people were the real literary force of New York,
and naturally enough he was flattered, dazed, confused. He
began to foregather with this set continually. He was made a
lion of when his book reached its little pinnacle of popularity—perhaps it sold 2,500 copies. The set kow-towed to
him and spoke of his book as a masterpiece. It was like Stevenson, they said, only with more polish. They said this for
an actual fact—Stevenson with more polish!—POLISH.

*   *   *

Then some of the women who "influenced" and some of
the half-baked "magazinists" took him in hand. Ah, they
understood his temperament. They could see where his forte

lay. Thus and thus he should write; the spiritual element (there was a healthy, sane animalism in the young man's book, a thing that hurt nobody and that he would modify in time)—the spiritual element was the great thing, the higher plane, the upward trend, and they quoted Walter Pater and Ruskin and Matthew Arnold, and by and by the boy began to think he saw his future in a different light. Began to think he really was Stevenson with more polish and that he must "strive for the spiritual" and "trend upward."

He learned the lingo of the "third-raters." He began to speak of certain books as "convincing" or "not convincing." He knew all about "catholicity of taste." He knew the difference between a metaphor and a simile and a "split infinitive" made him shudder.

In this spirit and with these surroundings to influence him he retired to himself for a few months and wrote his second book; wrote as those certain women of the set would have him write. The originality and unconventionality of his first book he looked upon as crudity—I suppose he said it "failed to convince."

*   *   *

His second book, of course, was a failure. His publisher would have none of it. Said it was "not the thing." The boy had the greatest difficulty in securing a publisher for it at all, and when it finally appeared it sold a few hundred copies, then stopped, and the real critics—the kind that do not appear in sets—hardly so much as noticed it.

The young fellow came back to the set to talk it over. Then, too, in his disappointment he wanted to be told again that he was "Stevenson with more polish."

But the set—the same women and magazinists and fakers who had ruined his one chance in life—could hardly find time to notice him now. When they did it was to tell him that he must strive to be more worthy of his better self, to find the "true note," his "individual medium of expression."

They hardly had time to say even this, however. A new little lion was among them—a Filipino poet with wild eyes and who looked like a fencing master.

*   *   *

The young man shouldered off, went by himself into a corner to think it over. His eyes were opened and he saw what these people had done to him. Saw the Great Mistake and that he had wasted his substance. He was eating husks with swine. He had sinned before heaven and the great good thing that had once been his he had allowed to be stripped from him, in return receiving a farrago of empty phrases.

He tried to pull out. He "arose and went to his father," but in his case it was too late. It was gone—the faint little spark that might, with care, have burst into a blaze. He could not now get back that fresh, untrammeled view of things that he had at first. His chance was gone and the light was dead within him.

He has gone back to Pennsylvania by now and is a law clerk in his father's office. He spends most of his time in serving papers and ruling forms and thinking how he will manage when his next chance comes.

It won't come again, however. But if he had kept away from literary sets and from the women who influence he would not have furnished a warning to the many others of his kind who are this very day going exactly the same gait.

New York, Aug. 22

Chicago American Literary Review, August 24, 1901

THE TRUE REWARD OF THE NOVELIST

NOT THAT ONE quarrels with the historical novel as such; not that one does not enjoy good fiction wherever found, and in whatever class. It is the method of attack of the latter-day copyists that one deplores—their attitude, the willingness of so very, very many of them to take off the hat to Fashion, and then hold the same hat for Fashion to drop pennies in.

Ah, but the man must be above the work or the work is worthless, and the man better off at some other work than that of producing fiction. The eye never once should wander to the gallery, but be always and with single purpose turned *inward* upon the work, testing it and retesting it that it rings true.

What one quarrels with is the perversion of a profession, the detestable trading upon another man's success. No one can find fault with those few good historical novels that started the fad. There was good workmanship in these, and honesty. But the copyists, the fakirs—they are not novelists at all, though they write novels that sell by the hundreds of thousands. They are business men. They find out—no, they allow *someone else* to find out—what the public wants, and they give it to the public cheap, and advertise it as a new soap is advertised. Well, they make money; and, if that is their aim—if they are content to prostitute the good name of American literature for a sliding scale of royalties—let's have done with them. They have their reward. But the lamentable result will be that these copyists will in the end so prejudice the people against an admirable school of fiction—the school of Scott—that for years to come the tale of historic times will be discredited and many a great story remain unwritten, and many a man of actual worth and real power hold back in the ranks for very shame of treading where so many fools have rushed in.

For the one idea of the fakir—the copyist—and of the public which for the moment listens to him, is Clothes, Clothes, Clothes, first, last and always Clothes. Not Clothes only in the sense of doublet and gown, but Clothes of speech,

Clothes of manners, Clothes of customs. Hear them expatiate over the fashion of wearing a cuff, over a trick of speech, over the architecture of a house, the archæology of armor and the like. It is all well enough in its way, but so easily dispensed with if there be flesh and blood underneath. Veronese put the people of his "Marriage at Cana" into the clothes of his contemporaries. Is the picture any less a masterpiece?

Do these Little People know that Scott's archæology was about one thousand years "out" in Ivanhoe, and that to make a parallel we must conceive of a writer describing Richelieu— say—in small clothes and a top hat? But is it not *Richelieu* we want, and *Ivanhoe*, not their clothes, their armor? And in spite of his errors Scott gave us a real Ivanhoe. He got beneath the clothes of an epoch and got the heart of it, and the spirit of it (different essentially and vitally from ours or from every other, the spirit of feudalism); and he put forth a masterpiece.

The Little People so very precise in the matter of buttons and "bacinets" do not so. Take the clothes from the people of their Romances and one finds only wooden manikins. Take the clothes from the epoch of which they pretend to treat and what is there beneath? It is only the familiar, well-worn, well-bethumbed nineteenth or twentieth century after all. As well have written of Michigan Avenue, Chicago, as "La Rue de la Harpe," "The Great North Road," or the "Appian Way."

It is a masquerade, the novel of the copyists; and the people who applaud them—are they not the same who would hold persons in respect because of the finery on their bodies? A poor taste, a cheap one; the taste of serving-men, the literature of chambermaids.

To approach the same subject by a different radius; why must the historical novel of the copyists always be conceived of in the terms of Romance? Could not the formula of Realism be applied at least as well, not the Realism of mere externals (the copyists have that), but the Realism of motives and emotions? What would we not give for a picture of the fifteenth century as precise and perfect as one of Mr. James's novels? Even if that be impossible the attempt, even though half-way successful, would be worth while, would be better than the wooden manikin in the tin-pot helmet and baggy hose. At least we should get somewhere, even if no further than Mr. Kingsley took us in *Hereward*, or Mr. Blackmore in *Lorna Doone*.

How about the business life and the student life, and the artisan life and the professional life, and above all, the home life of historic periods? Great Heavens! There was something else sometimes than the soldier life. They were not always cutting and thrusting, not always night riding, escaping, venturing, posing.

Or suppose that cut-and-thrust must be the order of the day, where is the "man behind," and the heart in the man and the spirit in the heart and the essential vital, elemental, all-important, true life within the spirit? We are all Anglo-Saxon enough to enjoy the sight of a fight, would go a block or so out of the way to see one, or be a dollar or so out of pocket. But let it not be these jointed manikins worked with a thread. At least let it be Mr. Robert Fitzsimmons or Mr. James Jeffries.

Clothes, paraphernalia, panoply, pomp and circumstance, and the copyist's public and the poor be-devilled, ink-corroded hack of an overdriven, underpaid reviewer on an inland paper speak of the "vivid coloring" and "the fine picture of a by-gone age"—it is easy to be vivid with a pot of vermilion at the elbow. Any one can scare a young dog with a false-face and a roaring voice, but to be vivid and use grays and browns, to scare the puppy with the lifted finger, that's something to the point.

The difficult thing is to get at the life immediately around you, the very life in which you move. No romance in it? No romance in *you*, poor fool. As much romance on Michigan avenue as there is realism in King Arthur's court. It is as you choose to see it. The important thing to decide is which formula is the best to help you grip the Real Life of this or any other age. Contemporaries always imagine that theirs is the prosaic day, and that chivalry and the picturesque died with their forbears. No doubt Merlin mourned for the old time of romance. Cervantes held that romance was dead. Yet most of the historical romances of the day are laid in Cervantes's time, or even after it.

Romance and Realism are constant qualities of every age,

day and hour. They are here today. They existed in the time of Job. They will continue to exist to the end of time, not so much in things as in the point of view of the people who see things.

The difficulty then is to get at the immediate life, immensely difficult, for you are not only close to the canvas, but are yourself part of the picture.

But the historic age is almost done to hand. Let almost anyone shut himself in his closet with a history and Violet LeDuc's *Dictionaire du Mobilier* and, given a few months' time, he can evolve an historical novel of the kind called popular. He need not know men—just clothes and the lingo, the "what-ho-without-there" gabble. But if he only chose he could find romance and adventure in Wall street or Bond street. But romance there does not wear the gay clothes and the showy accoutrements, and to discover it—the real romance of it—means hard work and close study, not of books, but of people and actualities.

Not only this, but to know the life around you, you must live—if not *among* people then *in* people. You must be something more than a novelist if you can, something more than just a writer. There must be that nameless sixth sense or sensibility in you that great musicians have in common with great inventors and great scientists, the thing that does not enter into the work, but that is back of it, the thing that would make of you a good *man* as well as a good novelist, the thing that differentiates the mere business man from the financier (for it is possessed of the financier and poet alike—so only they be big enough).

It is not genius, for genius is a lax, loose term so flippantly used that its expressiveness is long since lost. It is more akin to sincerity. And there once more we halt upon the great word—sincerity, sincerity, and again sincerity. Let the writer attack his historical novel with sincerity and he cannot then do wrong. He will see then the man beneath the clothes, and the heart beneath both, and he will be so amazed at the wonder of that sight that he will forget the clothes. His public will be small, perhaps, but he will have the better reward of the knowledge of a thing well done. Royalties on editions of hundreds of thousands will not pay him more to his satisfaction than that. To make money is not the province of a novelist. If he is the right sort he has other responsibilities, heavy ones. He of all men cannot think only of himself or for himself. And when the last page is written and the ink crusts on the pen-point and the hungry presses go clashing after another writer, the "new man" and the new fashion of the hour, he will think of the grim long grind of the years of his life that he has put behind him and of his work that he has built up volume by volume, sincere work, telling the truth as he saw it, independent of fashion and the gallery gods, holding to these with gripped hands and shut teeth—he will think of all this then, and he will be able to say: "I never truckled, I never took off the hat to Fashion and held it out for pennies. By God, I told them the truth. They liked it or they didn't like it. What had that to do with me? I told them the truth; I knew it for the truth then, and I know it for the truth now."

And that is his reward—the best that a man may know; the only one really worth the striving for.

World's Work, October 1901

NOVELISTS OF THE FUTURE

The Training They Need

IT SEEMS TO ME that a great deal could be said on this subject—a great deal that has not been said before. There are
so many novelists these latter days. So many whose works
show that they have had no training and it does seem that so
long as the fiction writers of the United States go fumbling
and stumbling along in this undisciplined fashion, governed
by no rule, observing no formula, setting for themselves no
equation to solve, that just so long shall we be far from that
desirable thing—an American school of fiction. Just now (let
us say that it is a pity) we have no school at all. We acknowledge no master, and we are playing at truant, incorrigible,
unmanageable, sailing paper boats in the creek behind the
schoolhouse, or fishing with bent pins in the pools and shallows of popular favor. That some catch goldfish there, is no
great matter, and is no excuse for the truancy. We are not
there for the goldfish, if you please, but to remain in the
school at work till we have been summoned to stand up in
our places and tell the master what we have learned.

There 's where we should be, and if we do not observe the
rules and conform to some degree of order, we should be
rapped on the knuckles or soundly clumped on the head, and
by vigorous discipline taught to know that formulas $(a-b)$
$(a+b)$ are important things for us to observe, and that each
and all of us should address ourselves with all diligence to
finding the value of x in our problems.

It is the class in the Production of Original Fiction which
of all the school contains the most truants. Indeed, its members believe that schooling is for them unnecessary. Not so
with the other classes. Not one single member of any single
one of them who does not believe that he must study first if
he would produce afterwards. Observe, there on the lower
benches, the assiduous little would-be carpenters and stonemasons; how carefully they con their tables of measurement,
their squares and compasses. "Ah, the toilers," you say, "the
grubby manual fellows—of course they must learn their
trade!"

Very well, then. Consider—higher up the class, on the very front row of benches—the Fine Arts row, the little painters and architects and musicians and actors of the future. See how painfully they study, and study and study. The little stonemason will graduate in a few months; but for these others of the Fine Arts classes, there is no such thing as graduation. For them there shall never be a diploma, signed and sealed, giving them the right to call themselves perfected at their work. All their lives they shall be students. In the vacations—maybe—they write, or build, or sing or act, but soon again they are back to the benches studying, studying always; working as never carpenter or stonemason worked. Now and then they get a little medal, a bit of gold and enamel, a bow of ribbon, that is all; the stonemason would disdain it, would seek it for the value of the metal in it. The Fine Arts people treasure it as the veteran treasures his cross.

And these little medals you—the truants, the bad boys of the paper boats and goldfish—you want them, too; you claim them and clamor for them. You who declare that no study is necessary for you; you who are not content with your catch of goldfish, you must have the bits of ribbon and enamel, too. Have you deserved them? Have you worked for them? Have you found the value of x in your equation? Have you solved the parenthesis of your problem? Have you even done the problem at all? Have you even glanced or guessed at the equation? The shame of it be upon you! Come in from the goldfish and go to work, or stay altogether at the fishing and admit that you are not deserving of the medal which the master gives as a reward of merit.

"But there are no books that we can study," you contest. "The architect and the musician, the painter and the actor—all of these have books ready to hand; they can learn from codified, systematized knowledge. For the novelist, where is there of cut-and-dried science that he can learn that will help him?"

And that is a good contention. No, there are no such books. Of all the arts, the art of fiction has no handbook. By no man's teaching can we learn the knack of putting a novel together in the best way. No one has ever risen to say, "Here is how the plan should be; thus and so should run the outline."

We must admit the fact, but neither does that excuse the goldfishing and the paper boat business. Some day the handbook may be compiled—it is quite possible—but meanwhile, and "faute de mieux," there is that which you may study better than all handbooks.

Observe, now. Observe, for instance, the little painter scholars. On the fly leaves of their school books they are making pictures—of what? Remember it, remember it and remember it—of the people around them. So is the actor, so the musician—all of the occupants of the Fine Arts bench. They are studying one another, quite as much as their books—even more, and they will tell you that it is the most important course in the curriculum.

You—the truant little would-be novelist—you can do this, quite as easily as they, and for you it is all the more important, for you must make up by the intimate knowledge of your fellows what you are forced to lack in the ignorance of forms. But you cannot get this knowledge out there behind the schoolhouse—hooking gold fish. Come in at the tap of the bell and, though you have no books, make pictures on your slate, pictures of the Fine Arts bench struggling all their lives for the foolish little medals, pictures of the grubby little boys in the stonemasons' corner, jeering the art classes for their empty toiling. The more you make these pictures, the better you shall do them. That is the kind of studying you can do, and from the study of your fellows you shall learn more than from the study of all the textbooks that ever will be written.

But to do this you must learn to sit very quiet, and be very watchful, and so train your eyes and ears that every sound and every sight shall be significant to you and shall supply all the deficiency made by the absence of textbooks.

This, then, to drop a very protracted allegory, seems to be the proper training of the novelist: The achieving less of an aggressive faculty of research, than of an attitude of mind—a receptivity, an acute sensitiveness. And this can be acquired.

But it cannot be acquired by shutting one's self in one's closet, by a withdrawal from the world, and that, so it would appear, is just the mistake so many would-be fiction-writers allow themselves. They would make of the art of the novelist an aristocracy, a thing exclusive, to be guarded from contact with the vulgar, humdrum, bread-and-butter business of life, to be kept unspotted from the world, considering it the result of inspirations, of exaltations, of subtleties and—above all things—of refinement, a sort of velvet-jacket affair, a studio hocus-pocus, a thing loved of women and of æsthetes.

What a folly! Of all the arts it is the most virile; of all the arts it will not, will not, will not flourish indoors. Dependent solely upon fidelity to life for existence, it must be practised in the very heart's heart of life, on the street corner, in the market place, not in the studios. God enlighten us! It is not an affair of women and æsthetes, and the muse of American fiction is no chaste, delicate, super-refined mademoiselle of delicate poses and "elegant" attitudinizings, but a robust, red-armed bonne-femme, who rough-shoulders her way among men and among affairs, who finds a healthy pleasure in the jostlings of the mob and a hearty delight in the honest, rough-and-tumble, Anglo-Saxon give-and-take knockabout that for us means life. Choose her, instead of the sallow, pale-faced statue-creature, with the foolish tablets and foolish, up-turned eyes, and she will lead you as brave a march as ever drum tapped to. Stay at her elbow and obey her as she tells you to open your eyes and ears and heart, and as you go she will show things wonderful beyond wonder in this great, new, blessed country of ours, will show you a life untouched, untried, full of new blood and promise and vigor.

She is a Child of the People, this muse of our fiction of the future, and the wind of a new country, a new heaven and a new earth is in her face and has blown her hair from out the fillets that the old world muse has bound across her brow, so that it is all in disarray. The tan of the sun is on her cheeks, and the dust of the highway is thick upon her buskin, and the elbowing of many men has torn the robe of her, and her hands are hard with the grip of many things. She is hail-fellow-well-met with everyone she meets, unashamed to know the clown and unashamed to face the king, a hardy, vigorous girl, with an arm as strong as a man's and a heart as sensitive as a child's.

Believe me, she will lead you far from the studios and the æsthetes, the velvet jackets and the uncut hair, far from the sexless creatures who cultivate their little art of writing as the fancier cultivates his orchid. Tramping along, then, with a stride that shall tax your best paces, she will lead you—if you are humble with her and honest with her—straight into a World of Working Men, crude of speech, swift of action, strong of passion, straight to the heart of a new life, on the borders of a new time, and there and only there, will you learn to know the stuff of which must come the American fiction of the future.

Boston Evening Transcript, November 27, 1901

THE NEED OF A LITERARY
CONSCIENCE

"Pᴵᴸᴀᴛᴇ ꜱᴀɪᴛʜ unto him: what is truth?" and it is of record
that he received no answer—and for very obvious reasons. For is it not a fact, that he who asks that question must
himself find the answer and that not even one sent from
Heaven can be of hope or help to him, if he is not willing to
go down into his own heart and into his own life to find it?

To sermonize, to elaborate a disquisition on nice distinctions of metaphysics is not appropriate here. But it is—so
one believes—appropriate to consider a certain very large
class of present day novelists of the United States who seldom
are stirred by that spirit of inquiry that for a moment disturbed the Roman, who do *not* ask what is truth, who do not
in fact care to be truthful at all, and who—and this is the
serious side of the business—are bringing the name of American literature perilously near to disrepute.

One does not quarrel for one instant with the fact that certain books of the writers in question have attained phenome-
nally large circulations. This is as it should be. There are very
many people in the United States, and compared with such a
figure as seventy million, a mere hundred thousand of books
sold is no great matter.

But here—so it seems—is the point. He who can address
a hundred thousand people is, no matter what his message
may be, in an important position. It is a large audience, one
hundred thousand, larger than any roofed building now
standing could contain. Less than one one hundredth part of
that number nominated Lincoln. Less than half of it won
Waterloo.

And it must be remembered that for every one person
who buys a book there are three who will read it and half a
dozen who will read what someone else has written about it,
so that the sphere of influence widens indefinitely, and the
audience that the writer addresses approaches the half-million
mark.

Well and good; but if the audience is so vast, if the influence is so far-reaching, if the example set is so contagious, it

becomes incumbent to ask, it becomes imperative to demand that the half-million shall be told the truth and not a lie.

And this thing called truth—"what is it?" says Pilate, and the average man conceives at once of an abstraction, a vague idea, a term borrowed from the metaphysicians, certainly nothing that has to do with practical, tangible, concrete work-a-day life.

Error! If truth is not an actual work-a-day thing, as concrete as the lamp-post on the corner, as practical as a cable-car, as real and homely and work-a-day and commonplace as a boot-jack, then indeed are we of all men most miserable and our preaching vain.

And truth in fiction is just as real and just as important as truth anywhere else—as in Wall Street, for instance. A man who does not tell the truth there and who puts the *un*-truth upon paper over his signature will be very promptly jailed. In the case of the Wall Street man the sum of money in question may be trivial, a hundred dollars, fifty dollars. But the untruthful novelist who starts in motion something like half a million dollars invokes not fear nor yet reproach. If truth in the matter of the producing of novels is not an elusive, intangible abstraction, what then is it? Let us get at the hard nub of the business, something we can hold in the hand. It is the thing that is one's own, the discovery of a subject suitable for fictitious narration that has never yet been treated, and the conscientious study of that subject and the fair presentation of results. Not a difficult matter it would appear, not an abstraction, not a philosophical kink. Newspaper reporters, who are not metaphysicians, unnamed, unrewarded, despised even and hooted and hounded, are doing this every day. They do it on a meagre salary, and they call the affair a "scoop." Is the standard of the novelist—he who is entrusted with the good name of his nation's literature—lower than that of a reporter?

"Ah, but it is so hard to be original," "ah, but it is so hard to discover anything new." Great Heavens! when a new life comes into the world for every tick of the watch in your pocket—a new life with all its complications, and with all the thousand and one other complications it sets in motion!

Hard to be original! when of all of those billion lives your own is as distinct, as individual, as "original," as though you were born out of season in the Paleozoic age and yours the first human face the sun ever shone upon.

Go out into the street and stand where the ways cross and hear the machinery of life work clashing in its grooves. Can the utmost resort of your ingenuity evolve a better story than any one of the millions that jog your elbow? Shut yourself in your closet and turn your eyes inward upon yourself—deep *into* yourself, down, down into the heart of you; and the tread of the feet upon the pavement is the systole and diastole of your own being—different only in degree. It is life; and it is that which you must have to make your book, your novel—life, not other people's novels.

Or look from your window. A whole Literature goes marching by, clamoring for a leader and a master hand to guide it. You have but to step from your doorway. And instead of this, instead of entering into the leadership that is yours by right divine, instead of this, you must toilfully, painfully endeavor to crawl into the armor of the chief of some other cause, the harness of the leader of some other progress.

But you will not fit into that panoply. You may never brace that buckler upon your arm, for by your very act you stand revealed as a littler man than he who should be chief—a littler man and a weaker; and the casque will fall so far over your face that it will only blind you, and the sword will trip you, and the lance, too ponderous, will falter in your grip, and all that life which surges and thunders behind you, will in time know you to be the false leader, and as you stumble will trample you in its onrush, and leave you dead and forgotten upon the road.

And just as a misconception of the truth makes of this the simplest and homeliest of things, a vagary, an abstraction and a bugbear, so it is possible that a misconception of the Leader creates the picture of a great and dreadful figure wrapped in majesty, solemn and profound. So that perhaps for very lack of self-confidence, for very diffidence, one shrinks from lifting the sword of him and from enduing one's forehead with the casque that seems so ponderous.

In other causes no doubt the leader must be chosen from the wise and great. In science and finance one looks to him to be a strong man, a swift and a sure man. But the literature that today shouts all in vain for its chief needs no such a one as this. Here the battle is not to the strong nor yet the race to the swift. Here the leader is no vast, stern being, profound, solemn, knowing all things, but, on the contrary, is as humble as the lowliest that follow after him. So that it need not be hard to step into that place of eminence. Not by arrogance, nor by assumption, nor by the achievement of the world's wisdom, shall you be made worthy of the place of high command. But it will come to you, if it comes at all, because you shall have kept yourself young and humble and pure in heart, and so unspoiled and unwearied and unjaded that you shall find a joy in the mere rising of the sun, a wholesome, sane delight in the sound of the wind at night, a pleasure in the sight of the hills at evening, shall see God in a little child and a whole religion in a brooding bird.

World's Work, December 1901

THE MECHANICS OF FICTION

W E APPROACH a delicate subject. And if the manner of approach is too serious it will be very like the 40,000 men of the king of France who marched terribly and with banners to the top of the hill with the meagre achievement of simply getting there. Of all the arts, as one has previously observed, that of novel writing is the least mechanical. Perhaps after all rightly so; still it is hard to escape some formality, some forms. There must always be chapter divisions, also a beginning and an end, which implies a middle, continuity, which implies movement, which in turn implies a greater speed or less, an accelerated, retarded or broken action; and before the scoffer is well aware he is admitting a multitude of set forms. No one who sets a thing in motion but keeps an eye and a hand upon its speed. No one who constructs but keeps watch upon the building, strengthening here, lightening there, here at the foundations cautious and conservative, there at the cornice fantastic and daring. In all human occupations, trades, arts or business, science, morals or religion, there exists 'way at the bottom a homogeneity and a certain family likeness, so that, quite possibly after all the discussion of the importance of the mechanics of fiction may be something more than mere speculative sophistry.

A novel addresses itself primarily to a reader, and it has been so indisputably established that the reader's time and effort of attention must be economized that the fact need not be mentioned in this place—it would not economize the reader's time nor effort of attention.

Remains then the means to be considered, or in other words: How best to tell your story.

It depends naturally upon the nature of the story. The formula which would apply to one would not be appropriate for another. That is very true, but at the same time it is hard to get away from that thing in any novel which, let us call, the pivotal event. All good novels have one. It is the peg upon which the fabric of the thing hangs, the nucleus around which the shifting drifts and currents must—suddenly—coagulate, the sudden releasing of the brake to permit for one instant the entire machinery to labor, full steam, ahead. Up to that point the action must lead; from it, it must decline.

But—and here one holds at least one mechanical problem—the approach, the leading up to this pivotal event must be infinitely slower than the decline. For the reader's interest in the story centres around it and once it is disposed of attention is apt to dwindle very rapidly—and thus back we go again to the economy proposition.

It is the slow approach, however, that tells. The unskilled, impatient of the tedium of meticulous elaboration, will rush at it in a furious gallop of short chapters and hurried episodes, so that he may come the sooner to the purple prose declamation and drama that he is sure he can handle with such tremendous effect.

Not so the masters. Watch them during the first third—say —of their novels. Nothing happens, or at least so you fancy. People come and go, plans are described, localities, neighborhoods; an incident crops up just for a second, for which you can see no reason, a note sounded that is puzzlingly inappropriate. The novel continues. There seems to be no progress; again that perplexing note, but a little less perplexing. By now we are well into the story. There are no more new people but the old ones come back again and again, and yet again; you remember them now after they are off the stage, you are more intimate with the two main characters. Then come a series of pretty incidents in which these two are prominent. The action still lags, but little by little you are getting more and more acquainted with these principal actors. Then perhaps comes the first acceleration of movement. The approach begins—ever so little—to rise, and that same note which seemed at first so out of tune sounds again and this time drops into place in the progression, beautifully harmonious, correlating the whole gamut. By now all the people are "on," by now all the groundwork is prepared. You know the localities so well that you could find your way about among them in the dark; hero and heroine are intimate acquaintances.

Now the action begins to increase in speed. The complication suddenly tightens, all along the line there runs a sudden alert. An episode far back there in the first chapter, an episode with its appropriate group of characters, is brought forward and coming suddenly to the front collides with the main line of development and sends it off upon an entirely unlooked for tangent. Another episode of the second chapter—let us suppose—all at once makes common cause with a more recent incident and the two produce a wholly unlooked for counter influence which swerves the main theme in still another direction and all this time the action is speeding faster and faster, the complication tightening and straining to the breaking point and then at last a 'motif' that has been in preparation ever since the first paragraph of the first chapter of the novel suddenly comes to a head, and in a twinkling the complication is solved with all the violence of an explosion and the catastrophe, the climax, the pivotal event fairly leaps from the pages with a rush of action that leaves you stunned, breathless and overwhelmed with the sheer power of its presentation. And there is a master-work of fiction.

Reading as the uninitiated do without an eye to the mechanics, without a consciousness of the wires and wheels and cogs and springs of the affair, it seems inexplicable that these great scenes of fiction—short as they are—some of them less than a thousand words in length—should produce so tremendous an effect by such few words, such simple language; and that sorely over-taxed word, "genius," is made to do duty as the explanation. But the genius is rare that in one thousand simple words, taken by themselves, could achieve the effect—for instance—of the fight aboard The Flying Scud in Stevenson's Wrecker. Taken by itself, the scene is hardly important except from the point of view of style and felicity of expression. It is the context of the story that makes it so tremendous, and because Osborne and Stevenson prepared for that very scene from the novel's initial chapter.

And it seems as if here in a phrase one could resume the whole system of fiction-mechanics—preparation of effect.

The unskilled will invariably attempt to atone for lack of such painstaking preparation for their "Grande Scenes" by hysteria, and by exclamation in presenting the catastrophe. They declaim, they shout, stamp, shake their fists and flood the page with sonorous adjectives, call upon heaven and upon God. They summon to their aid every broken down device to rouse the flaccid interest of the reader and conclusively, irretrievably and ignominiously fail. It is too late for heroic effort then, and the reader, uninterested in the character, unfamiliar with the locale, unattracted by any charm of "atmosphere," lays down the book unperturbed and forgets it before dinner.

Where is the fault? Is it not in defective machinery? The analogies are multitudinous. The liner with hastily constructed boilers will founder when she comes to essay the storm, and no stoking, however vigorous, no oiling, however eager, if delayed till then, will avail to aid her to ride through successfully. It is not the time to strengthen a wall when the hurricane threatens, prop and stay will not brace it then. Then the thing that tells is the plodding, slow, patient, brick-by-brick work, that only half shows down there at the foot half-hidden in the grass, obscure, unnoted. No genius is necessary for this sort of work, only great patience and a willingness to plod, for the time being.

No one is expected to strike off the whole novel in one continued fine frenzy of inspiration. As well expect the stone mason to plant his wall in a single day. Nor is it possible to lay down any rule of thumb, any hard and fast schedule in the matter of novel writing. But no work is so ephemeral, so delicate, so—in a word—artistic that it cannot be improved by systematizing.

There is at least one undisputably good manner in which the unskilled may order his work—besides the one of preparation already mentioned. He may consider each chapter as a unit, distinct, separate, having a definite beginning, rise, height and end, the action continuous, containing no break in time, the locality unchanged throughout—no shifting of the scene to another environment. Each chapter thus treated is a little work in itself, and the great story of the whole novel is told thus as it were in a series of pictures, the author supplying information as to what has intervened between the end of one chapter and the beginning of the next by suggestion or by actual résumé. As often as not the reader himself can fill up the gap by the context.

This may be over-artificial, and it is conceivable that there are times when it is necessary to throw artificiality to the winds. But it is the method that many of the greatest fiction writers have employed, and even a defective system is—at any rate in fiction—better than none.

Boston Evening Transcript, December 4, 1901

A PLEA FOR ROMANTIC FICTION

L ET US at the start make a distinction. Observe that one speaks of Romanticism and not of sentimentalism. One claims that the latter is as distinct from the former as is that other form of art which is called Realism. Romance has been often put upon and overburdened by being forced to bear the onus of abuse that by right should fall to sentiment; but the two should be kept very distinct, for a very high and illustrious place will be claimed for Romance, while sentiment will be handed down the scullery stairs.

Many people today are composing mere sentimentalism, and calling it and causing it to be called Romance, so that with those who are too busy to think much upon these subjects, but who none the less love honest literature, Romance too has fallen into disrepute. Consider now the cut-and-thrust stories. They are all labelled Romances, and it is very easy to get the impression that Romance must be an affair of cloaks and daggers, or moonlight and golden hair. But this is not so at all. The true Romance is a more serious business than this. It is not merely a conjurer's trick box, full of flimsy quackeries, tinsel and clap traps, meant only to amuse, and relying upon deception to do even that. Is it not something better than this? Can we not see in it an instrument, keen, finely tempered, flawless—an instrument with which we may go straight through clothes and tissues and wrappings of flesh down deep into the red living heart of things?

Is all this too subtle, too merely speculative and intrinsic, too "precieuse" and nice and "literary"? Devoutly one hopes the contrary. So much is made of so-called Romanticism in present day fiction, that the subject seems worthy of discussion, and a protest against the misuse of a really noble and honest formula of literature appears to be timely—misuse, that is, in the sense of limited use. Let us suppose for the moment that a Romance can be made out of the cut-and-thrust business. Good heavens, are there no other things that are romantic, even in this—falsely, falsely called—humdrum world of today? Why should it be that so soon as the novelist addresses himself—seriously—to the consideration of contemporary life he must abandon Romance and take up that harsh, loveless, colorless, blunt tool called Realism?

Now, let us understand at once what is meant by Romance and what by Realism. Romance—I take it—is the kind of fiction that takes cognizance of variations from the type of normal life. Realism is the kind of fiction that confines itself to the type of normal life. According to this definition, then, Romance may even treat of the sordid, the unlovely—as for instance, the novels of M. Zola. (Zola has been dubbed a Realist, but he is, on the contrary, the very head of the Romanticists.) Also, Realism, used as it sometimes is as a term of reproach, need not be in the remotest sense or degree offensive, but on the other hand respectable as a church, and proper as a deacon—as, for instance, the novels of Mr. Howells.

The reason why one claims so much for Romance, and quarrels so pointedly with Realism, is that Realism stultifies itself. It notes only the surface of things. For it Beauty is not even skin-deep, but only a geometrical plane, without dimensions of depth, a mere outside. Realism is very excellent so far as it goes, but it goes no farther than the Realist himself can actually see, or actually hear. Realism is minute, it is the drama of a broken teacup, the tragedy of a walk down the block, the excitement of an afternoon call, the adventure of an invitation to dinner. It is the visit to my neighbor's house, a formal visit, from which I may draw no conclusions. I see my neighbor and his friends—very, oh, such very! probable people—and that is all. Realism bows upon the doormat and goes away and says to me, as we link arms on the sidewalk: "That is life." And I say it is not. It is not, as you would very well see if you took Romance with you to call upon my neighbor.

Lately you have been taking Romance a weary journey across the water—ages and the flood of years—and haling her into the fubsy, musty, worm-eaten, moth-riddled, rust-corroded "Grandes Salles" of the Middle Ages and the Renaissance, and she has found the drama of a bygone age for you there. But would you take her across the street to your neighbor's front parlor (with the bisque fisher boy on the mantel and the photograph of Niagara Falls on glass hanging in the front window); would you introduce her there? Not you. Would you take a walk with her in Fifth avenue, or Beacon street, or Michigan avenue? No indeed. Would you choose her for a companion of a morning spent in Wall Street, or an afternoon in the Waldorf-Astoria? You just guess you would not.

She would be out of place, you say, inappropriate. She might be awkward in my neighbor's front parlor, and knock over the little bisque fisher boy. Well, she might. If she did, you might find underneath the base of the statuette, hidden away, tucked away—what? God knows. But something which would be a complete revelation of my neighbor's secretest life.

So you think Romance would stop in the front parlor and discuss medicated flannels and mineral waters with the ladies? Not for more than five minutes. She would be off up-stairs with you, prying, peeping, peering into the closets of the bedroom, into the nursery, into the sitting-room; yes, and into that little iron box screwed to the lower shelf of the closet in the library; and into those compartments and pigeon-holes of the "secretaire" in the study. She would find a heartache (may-be) between the pillows of the mistress's bed, and a memory carefully secreted in the master's deedbox. She would come upon a great hope amid the books and papers of the study table of the young man's room, and—perhaps—who knows—an affair, or, great heavens, an intrigue, in the scented ribbons and gloves and hairpins of the young lady's bureau. And she would pick here a little and there a little, making up a bag of hopes and fears, and a package of joys and sorrows—great ones, mind you—and then come down to the front door, and stepping out into the street, hand you the bags and package, and say to you—"That is Life!"

Romance does very well in the castles of the Middle Ages and the Renaissance chateaux, and she has the entrée there and is very well received. That is all well and good. But let us protest against limiting her to such places and such times. You will find her, I grant you, in the chatelaine's chamber and the dungeon of the man-at-arms; but, if you choose to look for her, you will find her equally at home in the brownstone house on the corner and in the office building downtown.

And this very day, in this very hour, she is sitting among the rags and wretchedness, the dirt and despair of the tenements of the East Side of New York.

"What?" I hear you say, "look for Romance—the lady of the silken robes and golden crown, our beautiful, chaste maiden of soft voice and gentle eyes—look for her among the vicious ruffians, male and female, of Allen street and Mulberry Bend?" I tell you she is there, and to your shame be it said that you will not know her in those surroundings. You, the aristocrats, who demand the fine linen and the purple in your fiction; you, the sensitive, the delicate, who will associate with your Romance only so long as she wears a silken gown. You will not follow her to the slums, for you believe that Romance should only amuse and entertain you, singing you sweet songs and touching the harp of silver strings with rosy-tipped fingers. If haply she should call to you from the squalor of a dive, or the awful degradation of a disorderly house, crying: "Look, listen! This, too, is life. These, too, are my children, look at them, know them and, knowing, help!" Should she call thus, you would stop your ears; you would avert your eyes, and you would answer, "Come from there, Romance. Your place is not there!" And you would make of her a harlequin, a tumbler, a sword dancer, when, as a matter of fact, she should be by right divine a teacher sent from God.

She will not always wear the robe of silk, the gold crown, the jewelled shoon, will not always sweep the silver harp. An iron note is hers if so she choose, and coarse garments, and stained hands; and, meeting her thus, it is for you to know her as she passes—know her for the same young queen of the blue mantle and lilies. She can teach you, if you will be humble to learn. Teach you by showing. God help you, if at last you take from Romance her mission of teaching, if you do not believe that she has a purpose, a nobler purpose and a mightier than mere amusement, mere entertainment. Let Realism do the entertaining with its meticulous presentation of teacups, rag carpets, wall paper and haircloth sofas, stopping with these, going no deeper than it sees, choosing the ordinary, the untroubled, the commonplace.

But to Romance belongs the wide world for range, and the unplumbed depths of the human heart, and the mystery of

sex, and the problems of life, and the black, unsearched
penetralia of the soul of man. You, the indolent, must not
always be amused. What matter the silken clothes, what matter the prince's houses? Romance, too, is a teacher, and if—
throwing aside the purple—she wears the camel's hair and
feeds upon the locusts, it is to cry aloud unto the people,
"Prepare ye the way of the Lord, make straight his path."

Boston Evening Transcript, December 18, 1901

FICTION WRITING AS A BUSINESS

T HE EXAGGERATED and exalted ideas of the unenlightened upon this subject are, I have found, beyond all reason and beyond all belief. The superstition that with the publication of the first book comes fame and affluence is as firmly rooted as that other delusion which asks us to suppose that "a picture in the Paris Salon" is the certificate of success, ultimate, final, definite.

One knows of course that, very naturally, the "Eben Holden" and "David Harum" and "Richard Carvel" fellows make fortunes, and that these are out of the discussion, but also one chooses to assume that the average, honest middle class author supports himself and even a family by the sale of his novels—lives on his royalties.

Royalties! why in the name of heaven were they called that, those microscopic sums that too, too often are less royal than beggarly? It has a fine sound, royalty. It fills the mouth. It can be said with an air—royalty. But there are plenty of these same royalties that will not pay the typewriter's bill.

Take an average case. No. That will not do, either, for the average published novel, I say it with my right hand raised, is, irretrievably, hopelessly and conclusively, a financial failure.

Take then an unusually lucky instance, literally a novel whose success is extraordinary, a novel which has sold 2500 copies. I repeat that this is an extraordinary success. Not one book out of fifteen will do as well. But let us consider it. The author has worked upon it for—at the very least—three months. It is published. Twenty-five hundred copies are sold. Then the sale stops. And by the word stop, one means cessation in the completest sense of the word. There are people— I know plenty of them—who suppose that when a book is spoken of as having stopped selling, a generality is intended, that merely a falling off of the initial demand has occurred. Error. When a book—a novel—stops selling, it stops with the definiteness of an engine when the fire goes out. It stops with a suddenness that is appalling, and thereafter not a copy, not one single, solitary copy is sold. And do not for an instant suppose that ever after the interest may be revived. A dead book can no more be resuscitated than a dead dog.

But to go back. The 2500 have been sold. The extraordinary, the marvellous has been achieved. What does the author get out of it, a royalty of ten per cent. Two hundred and fifty dollars. Two hundred and fifty dollars for three months' hard work. Roughly, less than twenty dollars a week, a little over $2.50 a day. An expert carpenter will easily make twice that, and the carpenter has infinitely the best of it in that he can keep that work up year in and year out, where the novelist must wait for a new idea, and the novel writer must then jockey and manœuvre for publication. Two novels a year is about as much as the writer can turn off and yet keep to a marketable standard. Even admitting that both the novels sell 2500 copies there is only $500 of profit. In the same time the carpenter has made his $1800, nearly four times as much. One may well ask the question: Is fiction writing a money-making profession?

The astonishing thing about the affair is that a novel may make a veritable stir, almost a sensation, and yet fail to sell very largely.

There is so and so's book. Everywhere you go you hear about it. Your friends have read it. It is in demand at the libraries. You don't pick up a paper that does not contain a review of the story in question. It is in the "Book of the Month" column. It is even, even—the pinnacle of achievement—in that shining roster, the list of best sellers for the week.

Why, of course the author is growing rich! Ah, at last he has arrived! No doubt he will build a country house out of his royalties. Lucky fellow, one envies him.

Catch him unawares and what is he doing? As like as not writing unsigned book reviews at five dollars a week, in order to pay his board bill—and glad of the chance.

It seems incredible. But one must remember this: That for every one person who buys a book, there will be six who will talk about it. And the half-thousand odd reviewers who are writing of the book do not buy it, but receive "editorial" copies from the publisher, upon which no royalty is paid.

I know it for an indisputable fact that a certain novel which

has even been called the best American novel of the nineteenth century, and which upon publication was talked about,
written about and even preached about, from the Atlantic to
the Pacific, took ten years in which to attain the sale of 10,000
copies. Even so famous, so brilliant an author as Harold Frederic did not at the first sell conspicuously. "That Lawton
Girl," "The Copperhead," "Seth's Brother's Wife," masterpieces though they are, never made money for the writer.
Each sold about two thousand copies. Not until "Theron
Ware" was published did Mr. Frederic reap his reward.

Even so great a name as that of George Meredith is not a
"sesame," and only within the last few years has the author of
"Evan Harrington" made more than five or six hundred dollars out of any one of his world famous books.

But of course there is another side. For one thing, the author is put to no expense in the composing of his novel. (It
is not always necessary to typewrite the manuscript.) The carpenter must invest much money in tools, must have a shop.
Shop rent, tools repaired or replaced cut into his $1800 of
profit. Or take it in the fine arts. The painter must have a
studio, canvases, models, brushes, a whole equipment; the
architect must have his draughting-room, the musician his instrument. But so far as initial expense is concerned, a half-
dollar will buy every conceivable necessary tool the novelist
may demand. He needs no office, shop, or studio rent; models are not required. The libraries of the city offer him a quiet
working-place if the home is out of the question. Nor, as one
has so often urged, is any expensive training necessary before
his money-earning capacity is attained. The architect must
buy instruction for many years. The painter must study in
expensive studios, the musician must learn in costly conser-
vatories, the singer must be taught by high-priced maestros.
Furthermore, it is often necessary for the aspirant to travel
great distances to reach the cities where his education is to be
furthered, almost invariably a trip to, and a residence in Europe is indispensable. It is a great undertaking and an expensive one to prepare for the professions named, and it takes
years of time, years during which the aspirant is absolutely
non-productive.

But the would-be novel writer may determine between

breakfast and dinner to essay the plunge, buy (for a few cents) ink and paper between dinner and supper, and have the novel underway before bedtime.

How much of an outlay of money does his first marketable novel represent? Practically nothing. On the other hand let us ask the same question of, say, the painter. How much money has he had to spend before he was able to paint his first marketable picture? To reach a total sum he must foot up the expenses of at least five years of instruction and study, the cost of living during that time, the cost of materials, perhaps even the price of a trip to Paris. Easily the sum may reach $5000. Fifty cents' worth of ink and paper do not loom large beside the figure.

Then there are other ways in which the fiction writer may earn money—by fiction. The novelist may look down upon the mere writer of short stories, or may even look down upon himself in the same capacity, but as a rule the writer of short stories is the man who has the money. It is much easier to sell the average short story than the average novel. Infinitely easier. And the short story of the usual length will fetch $100. One thousand people—think of it—one thousand people must buy copies of your novel before it will earn so much for you. It takes three months to complete the novel—the novel that earns the two hundred and fifty. But with ingenuity, the writer should be able to turn out six short stories in the same time, and if he has luck in placing them, there is six hundred dollars earned, more than twice the sum made by the novel. So that the novelist may eke out the alarming brevity of his semi-annual statements by writing and selling "short stuff."

Then—so far as the novel is concerned—there is one compensation, one source of revenue which the writer enjoys and which is, as a rule, closed to all others. Once the carpenter sells his piece of work it is sold for good and all. The painter has but one chance to make money from the sale of his picture. The architect receives payment for his design and there is the end. But the novelist—and one speaks now of the American—may sell the same work over many times. Of course, if the novel is a failure it is a failure and no more is said. But suppose it is a salable, readable, brisk bit of narrative, with a swift action and rapid movement. Properly managed this, under favorable conditions, might be its life history: First it is serialized either in the Sunday press or, less probably, in a weekly or monthly. Then it is made up into book form and sent over the course a second time. The original publisher sells sheets to a Toronto or Montreal house and a Canadian edition reaps a like harvest. It is not at all unlikely that a special cheap cloth edition may be bought and launched by some large retailer either of New York or Chicago. Then comes the paper edition, with small royalties it is true, but based upon an enormous number of copies, for the usual paper edition is an affair of tens of thousands. Next the novel crosses the Atlantic, and a small sale in England helps to swell the net returns, which again are added to—possibly—by the "colonial edition" which the English firm issues. Last of all comes the Tauchnitz edition, and with this (bar the improbable issuing of later special editions) the exploitation ceases. Eight separate times the same commodity has been sold, no one of the sales militating against the success of the other seven, the author getting his fair slice every time. Can any other trade, profession or art (excepting only that of the dramatist, which is, after all, a sister art) show the like? Even (speaking of the dramatist) there may be a ninth reincarnation of the same story and the creatures of the writer's pages stalk forth upon the boards in cloak and buskin.

And there are the indirect ways in which he may earn money. Some of his ilk there are who lecture. Nor are there found wanting those who read from their own works. Some write editorials or special articles in the magazines or newspapers with literary departments. But few of them have "princely" incomes.

Boston Evening Transcript, January 1, 1902

"THE LITERATURE OF THE WEST"

A Reply to W. R. Lighton

In the issue of the Transcript dated Dec. 28 Mr. William R. Lighton publishes an article under the title, "The Literature of the West." The contribution is important, the matter is carefully arranged and the points ingeniously brought out. Furthermore, Mr. Lighton writes from certain knowledge, and in this field is "one having authority."

One can but applaud his serious protest against the "red shirt" literature of Western life, his deprecation of the sensationalism that has been foisted upon the country and the conditions that prevail west of the Mississippi; but at the same time it may be permitted to take issue with some of his statements and to deny some of his conclusions.

In the first place, Mr. Lighton says: "The literature of the West has been only the literature of the mining camp and the cowboy." He deprecates this; he exclaims, "Will they (the people) never get enough of the Buffalo Bill style of entertainment, and think to ask how the West is really living?" and he calls for a saner, soberer literature, one that shall ignore the desperado, the cow puncher, the prospector and miner. He pleads for the fiction that shall picture the West as a quiet, well-ordered country wherein the people are peaceful, tranquil, rational and contented. He claims that the wild life is no longer the true life of the West.

But the West is yet in the transitional period. There was a time when the wild life was the only life. There will come a time when the quiet life will be the only life. But as yet the West is midway of the two extremes. It is true that the West is a place of banks, of schools, of policemen and law courts, but it is equally true that as yet the Desert is a tremendous immovable fact, that the Apache and the Sioux are just where they were when we found them seventy years ago, and that the expression of personal physical courage is more often and to a greater degree called upon in Arizona, Montana, Idaho, New Mexico and Nevada than anywhere else in the United States.

Understand the distinction; we are quite ready to relegate

the red shirt fellow with his stock lingo, his makeup, his swagger and his gallery plays, to the lumber room and the county jail. We are done with him. He was a characteristic once, but now he is only a very bad actor who dresses the part according to the illustrated weeklies, and who, "pour épater les bourgeois," wears "chaps" on the plains. We distinctly do not want him to speak of his local habitation as "these 'ere diggin's," or to address us as "pard," or to speak of death as the passing in of checks, or the kicking of the bucket. He would not be true to Western life.

But because of this, are we ready to accept as typical of our Far West the prosaic farming folk of Iowa or the city-bred gentleman of the office buildings of Denver or San Francisco, who pays his pew-rent regularly and who has never been out of whistling distance of a police officer? These would not be true to Western life. They exist, no question or doubt about it; so does the red-shirt man, but neither is characteristic.

Let us even concede Mr. Lighton's point that today in the West the undramatic, the unadventurous is oftenest to be met with, is in fact almost universal. That this is so is urged by Mr. Lighton as a reason for a calm, uneventful, sober-hued fiction. He says it is a true reflex of conditions.

It would seem so upon first consideration. But in the fictitious presentation of an epoch of a people, the writer must search for the idiosyncrasy, the characteristic, that thing, that feature, element or person that distinguishes the times or place treated of from all other times and all other places. He must address himself to the task of picturing the peculiarity, the specialized product of conditions that obtain in that locality and nowhere else. Thus if one were telling a story of a Southern plantation one would not choose as the main feature of the narrative a pirate captain of the Caribbean, but rather the typical planter. If the story were of Wall Street it would be inappropriate to introduce as chief actor a Maine Yankee.

One must observe the typical. It is all very well for Mr. Lighton to urge that the peaceable citizens, the city-bred men of the Denver office blocks, are in overwhelming majority to the cowboys, the miners, and frontiersmen. They are not typical of the West; the West did not produce them. They are in no way different from the peace loving, law-abiding citizens of New York or Chicago. Not so very different from the same class of man the world over.

New York produced the financier, Maine the trader, the South the planter, Boston the littérateur, Chicago the business man, but the product of the West from the very first and up to this very hour of writing has always been, through every varying condition, occupation or calling, the adventurer. You cannot get away from him. Long since he has put off the red shirt, he has even abandoned his revolver. Meet him and for all you would know he is a man of sober mind, decorous even, the kind to whom you would suppose adventures never came. A man who very possibly drinks little, who gambles less, who wears the bowler hat and pressed trousers of convention.

But scratch the surface ever so little and behold—there is the Forty-niner. There just beneath the veneer is the tough fibre of the breed, whose work since the beginning of the nineteenth century has been the subjugating of the West.

In all history I do believe there is no more splendid achievement than this conquering of the wilderness that began with Lewis and Clark and that—all asseveration to the contrary notwithstanding—still is going on. In years—centuries—to come, perhaps, these men, this epoch, this phase of our civilization will receive a just and adequate appreciation. The work these men have done—are yet doing—is nothing short of colossal. We who see it so continually, who are so close to the canvas are all too apt to underrate it. Remember that only sixty years ago this Western country was an unfenced wilderness, as untamed as the Arctic, unknown, unknowable, a region of terrors.

Other nations, other peoples, have put century after century to the reclaiming and subduing of their hinterlands. Some take as long as that to build one single cathedral. A scattering advance line of hard-grained, hard-riding, hard-working fellows, Anglo-Saxons, Americans, dash into this country, with its gigantic sweep of deserts, its inhospitable sands, its forbidding mountains, and in less than a generation have all but civilized it.

Then when the deserts are crossed by railroads, when the

sands are irrigated, when the mountains are mined, the cañons bridged, and the Indian driven off, when, in fact, the
country is rendered habitable, along comes the quiet unadventurous farmer and the city-bred fellow to settle in the
policed and protected country. And it is these men, cast
in a mould as common as the lamppost on the corner, that
Mr. Lighton would put forward as the typical, distinctive
Westerner.

Mr. Lighton permits himself a prophecy. He looks forward
to a writer who shall "offer to the world a Western book that
shall come from and relate to the prairies and their people,
for that is where the vital life of the West is throbbing. These
are the men and women who are to shape Western destiny. It
is in the mountains," he continues, "that Western men are
doing the theatrical things, keeping up the fire and fury of
morbid overwrought excitement, fancying themselves thrilled
with deep purposes, yet at the bottom irreclaimably narrow."

I do not believe the story of the West, the epic of this wonder work of the nineteenth century, will confine itself to any
one section. I do not believe that a chronicle of uneventful,
unperturbed life will truly present the character of the region.
No doubt there is beauty, poetry even, to be found, just as
Mr. Lighton claims, in the dull, prosaic farm labor of the
prairies. No doubt there are thousands upon thousands of
people beyond the Missouri who lead uneventful, unperturbed lives. No doubt of it. Equally there is no doubt that
simultaneously with the siege of Troy there was to be found
in the vast tracts of the old Greek world a quiet, beautiful
bucolic life. No doubt there were thousands of people who
never saw a spear hurled, except at the games. But the expression of the general life of that time, its idiosyncrasy, is not to
be found in bucolic verse, or unadventurous chronicle, but in
Homer's Iliad, an epic of strife, of conquest.

Exactly the same condition prevailed within the past half
century in the West as prevailed in Trojan times. It was the
beginning of an epoch, the dawn of a new civilization, and
the man of deeds, the man of action, the adventurer, the pioneer, was the great figure, the true figure.

Hector, however, had his Homer, Roland, Siegfried and
Robin Hood had their poets, but the conquerors of the West

have gone to their graves unsung, save in the traducing, falsifying dime-novels which have succeeded only in discrediting our one great chance for distinctive American literature. We had the material, Homer found no better, the heroes, the great fights, the play of unleashed, unfettered passionate humanity, and we let it all go, this national epic of America, the only one we shall ever have, to the wretched "Deadwood Dicks" and Buffalo Bills of the yellow backs, while we niggled and pottered and puddled about with a faked, half-baked imported semi-English school whose followers went to Florence and Rome for their backgrounds or to ante-revolutionary days for their characters, or who lied and tricked and strutted in Pathfinder and Leather-Stocking series.

We would not see it while it was working out its tremendous battle at our very doors, and now when the great fight is almost over—when even yet there may be a chance to note the passing phase by actual vision, and to speak first hand—now already there are many like Mr. Lighton who would have us forget our fighters and be ashamed of them as "sensational swashbucklers," putting forward instead the second generation, who, undisturbed, have sunk to the level of the commonplace, claiming that these are the true Westerners.

Mr. Lighton is justified in a prophecy. The Epic of the West will some day, in years to come, be written, but it will not confine itself to the prairie country, it will not deal with the present-day farmer of Iowa, nor the present-day merchant of Denver or San Francisco. It will be a universal theme that shall sing of no one locality but of the huge conglomerate West; and the true knight of the song shall be the fighter, rescued from the hands of the blackmailers and liars and set in his true place at last, dignified, heroic, indomitable, blood brother to Roland and Grettir the Strong, the one distinctive and romantic figure of American life.

Boston Evening Transcript, January 8, 1902

THE GREAT AMERICAN NOVELIST

O F ALL the overworked phrases of overworked book reviewers, the phrase, the "Great American Novelist," is beyond doubt worn the thinnest from much handling—or mishandling. Continually the little literary middlemen who come between the producers and the consumers of fiction are mouthing the words with a great flourish of adjectives, scareheading them in Sunday supplements or placarding them on posters, crying out, "Lo, he is here!" or "lo, there!" But the heathen rage and the people imagine a vain thing. The G. A. N. is either as extinct as the Dodo or as far in the future as the practical aeroplane. He certainly is not discoverable at the present.

The moment a new writer of fiction begins to make himself felt he is gibbeted upon this elevation—upon this *false*, insecure elevation, for the underpinning is of the flimsiest, and at any moment is liable to collapse under the victim's feet and leave him hanging in midair by head and hands, a fixture and a mockery.

And who is to settle the title upon the aspirant in the last issue? Who is to determine what constitutes the G. A. N.? Your candidate may suit *you*, but your neighbour may have a very different standard to which he must conform. It all depends upon what you mean by *Great*, what you mean by *American*. Shakespeare has been called great, and so has Mr. Stephen Phillips. Oliver Wendell Holmes was *American*, and so is Bret Harte. Who is to say?

And many good people who deplore the decay of American letters are accustomed to refer to the absence of a G. A. N. as though there were a Great English Novelist or a Great French Novelist. But do these two people exist? Ask any dozen of your friends to mention the Great English Novelist, and out of the dozen you will get at least a half-dozen different names. It will be Dickens or Scott or Thackeray or Bronte or Eliot or Stevenson, and the same with the Frenchman. And it seems to me that if a novelist were great enough to be universally acknowledged to be the Great one of his country, he would cease to belong to any particular geographical area and would become a heritage of the whole world; as for instance Tolstoi; when one thinks of him it is—is it not?—as a novelist first and as a Russian afterward.

But if one wishes to split hairs, one might admit that while the Great American Novelist is yet to be born, the possibility of *A*—note the indefinite article—*A* Great American Novel is not too remote for discussion. But such a novel will be sectional. The United States is a Union, but not a unit, and the life in one part is very, very different from the life in another. It is as yet impossible to construct a novel which will represent all the various characteristics of the different sections. It is only possible to make a picture of a single locality. What is true of the South is not true of the North. The West is different, and the Pacific Coast is a community by itself.

Many of our very best writers are working on this theory. Bret Harte made a study of the West as he saw it, and Mr. Howells has done the same for the East. Cable has worked the field of the Far South, and Eggleston has gone deep into the life of the Middle West.

But consider a suggestion. It is an argument on the other side, and to be fair one must present it. It is a good argument, and if based on fact is encouraging in the hope that the *Great* man may yet appear. It has been said that " what is true— vitally and inherently true—for any one man is true for all men." Accordingly, then, what is vitally true of the Westerner is true of the Bostonian—yes, and of the creole. So that if Mr. Cable, say, should only go *deep enough* into the hearts and lives of his creoles, he would at last strike the universal substratum and find the elemental thing that is common to the creole and to the Puritan alike—yes, and to the Cowboy and Hoosier and Greaser and Buckeye and Jay Hawker, and that, once getting hold of *that*, he could produce the Great American Novel that should be a picture of the entire nation.

Now, that is a very ingenious argument and sounds very plausible. But it won't do, and for this reason: If an American novelist should go so deep into the lives of the people of any one community that he would find the thing that is common to another class of people a thousand miles away, he would have gone *too* deep to be exclusively American. He would not only be American, but English as well. He would have sounded the world-note; he would be a writer not national, but international, and his countrymen would be all humanity, not the citizens of any one nation. He himself would be a heritage of the whole world, a second Tolstoi, which brings us back to the very place from which we started.

And the conclusion of the whole matter? That fiction is very good or very bad—there is no middle ground; that writers of fiction in their points of view are either limited to a circumscribed area or see humanity as a tremendous conglomerate whole; that it must be either Mary Wilkins or George Eliot, Edward Eggleston or William Shakespeare; that the others do not weigh very much in the balance of the world's judgment; and that the Great American Novel is not extinct like the Dodo, but mythical like the Hippogriff, and that the thing to be looked for is not the Great American Novelist, but the Great Novelist who shall also be an American.

The Responsibilities of the Novelist and Other Literary Essays,
New York: Doubleday, Page & Company, 1903

THE FRONTIER GONE AT LAST

HOW OUR RACE PUSHED IT WESTWARD AROUND THE
WORLD AND NOW MOVES EASTWARD AGAIN—THE
BROADER CONCEPTION OF PATRIOTISM AS THE AGE OF
CONQUEST ENDS

SUDDENLY WE have found that there is no longer any
Frontier. Until the day when the first United States ma-
rine landed in China we had always imagined that out yonder
somewhere in the West was the border land where civilization
disintegrated and merged into the untamed. Our skirmish line
was there, our posts that scouted and scrimmaged with the
wilderness, a thousand miles in advance of the steady march
of civilization.

And the Frontier has become so much an integral part of
our conception of things that it will be long before we shall
all understand that it is gone. We liked the Frontier; it was
romance, the place of the poetry of the Great March, the firing line where there was action and fighting, and where men
held each other's lives in the crook of the forefinger. Those
who had gone out came back with tremendous tales, and
those that stayed behind made up other and even more tremendous tales.

When we—we Anglo-Saxons—busked ourselves for the
first stage of the march, we began from that little historic
reach of ground in the midst of the Friesland swamps, and
we set our faces Westward, feeling no doubt the push of the
Slav behind us. Then the Frontier was Britain and the sober
peacefulness of land where are the ordered, cultivated English
farmyards of today was the Wild West for the Frisians of that
century; and for the little children of the Frisian peat cottages,
Hengist was the Apache Kid and Horsa Deadwood Dick—
freebooters, law-defiers, slayers-of-men, epic heroes, blood
brothers if you please to Boone and Bowie.

Then for centuries we halted and the van closed up with
the firing line and we filled all England and all Europe with
our clamor because for a while we seemed to have gone as far
Westward as it was possible; and the checked energy of the
race reacted upon itself, rebounded as it were, and back we

went to the Eastward again—crusading, girding at the Mohammedan, conquering his cities, breaking into his fortresses
with mangonel, siege engine and catapult—just as the boy
shut indoors finds his scope circumscribed and fills the whole
place with the racket of his activity.

But always, if you will recall it, we had a curious feeling
that we had not reached the ultimate West even yet, that there
was still a Frontier. Always that strange sixth sense turned our
heads toward the sunset; and all through the Middle Ages we
were peeking and prying at the Western horizon, trying to
reach it, to run it down, and the queer tales about Vineland
and that storm-driven Viking's ship would not down.

And then at last a naked savage on the shores of a little
island in what is now our West Indies, looking Eastward one
morning, saw the caravels, and on that day the Frontier was
rediscovered, and promptly a hundred thousand of the most
hardy rushed to the skirmish-line and went at the wilderness
as only the Anglo-Saxon can.

And then the skirmish-line decided that it would declare
itself independent of the main army behind and form an advance column of its own, a separate army corps, and no
sooner was this done then again the scouts went forward,
went Westward, pushing the Frontier ahead of them, scrim-
maging with the wilderness, blazing the way. At last they
forced the Frontier over the Sierra Nevada down to the edge
of the Pacific. And here it would have been supposed that the
Great March would have halted again as it did before the
Atlantic, that here at last the Frontier ended.

But on the first of May, eighteen hundred and ninety-eight,
a gun was fired in the Bay of Manila, still further Westward,
and in response the skirmish-line crossed the Pacific, still
pushing the Frontier before it. Then came a cry for help from
Legation Street in Peking and as the first boat bearing its con-
tingent of American marines took ground on the Asian shore,
the Frontier—at last after so many centuries, after so many
marches, after so much fighting, so much spilled blood, so
much spent treasure, dwindled down and vanished; for the
Anglo-Saxon in his course of empire had circled the globe
and had brought the new civilization to the old civilization,
had reached the starting point of history, the place from

which the migrations began. So soon as the marines landed there was no longer any West, and the equation of the horizon, the problem of the centuries for the Anglo-Saxon was solved.

So, lament it though we may, the Frontier is gone, an idiosyncrasy that has been with us for thousands of years, the one peculiar picturesqueness of our life is no more. We may keep alive for many years yet the idea of a Wild West, but the hired cowboys and paid rough riders of Mr. William Cody are more like "the real thing" than can be found today in Arizona, New Mexico or Idaho. Only the imitation cowboys, the college-bred fellows who "go out on a ranch" carry the revolver or wear the concho. The Frontier has become conscious of itself, acts the part for the Eastern visitor; and this self-consciousness is a sign, surer than all others, of the decadence of a type, the passing of an epoch. The Apache Kid and Deadwood Dick have gone to join Hengist and Horsa and the heroes of the Magnusson Saga.

But observe. What happened in the Middle Ages when for awhile we could find no Western Frontier? The race impulse was irresistible. March we must, conquer we must, and checked in the Westward course of empire we turned Eastward and expended the resistless energy that by blood was ours in conquering the Old World behind us.

Today we are the same race, with the same impulse, the same power and, because there is no longer a Frontier to absorb our overplus of energy, because there is no longer a wilderness to conquer and because we still must march, still must conquer, we remember the old days when our ancestors before us found the outlet for their activity checked and, rebounding, turned their faces Eastward, and went down to invade the Old World. So we. No sooner have we found that our path to the Westward has ended than, reacting Eastward, we are at the Old World again, marching against it, invading it, devoting our overplus of energy to its subjugation.

But though we are the same race, with the same impulses, the same blood-instincts as the old Frisian marsh people, we are now come into a changed time and the great word of our century is no longer War but Trade.

Or if you choose it is only a different word for the same

race-characteristic. The desire for conquest—say what you will—was as big in the breast of the most fervid of the Crusaders as it is this very day in the most peacefully-disposed of American manufacturers. Had the Lion-Hearted Richard lived today he would have become a "leading representative of the Amalgamated Steel Companies" and doubt not for one moment that he would have underbid his Manchester rivals in the matter of bridge girders. Had Mr. Andrew Carnegie been alive at the time of the preachings of Peter the Hermit he would have raised a company of *gens-d'armes* sooner than all of his brothers-in-arms, would have equipped his men better and more effectively, would have been first on the ground before Jerusalem, would have built the most ingenious siege engine and have hurled the first cask of Greek-fire over the walls.

Competition and conquest are words easily interchangeable, and the whole spirit of our present commercial crusade to the Eastward betrays itself in the fact that we cannot speak of it but in terms borrowed from the glossary of the warrior. It is a commercial "invasion," a trade " war," a "threatened attack" on the part of America; business is "captured," opportunities are "seized," certain industries are "killed," certain former monopolies are " wrested away." Seven hundred years ago a certain Count Baldwin, a great leader in the attack of the Anglo-Saxon Crusaders upon the Old World, built himself a siege engine which would help him enter the beleaguered city of Jerusalem. Jerusalem is beleaguered again today, and the hosts of the Anglo-Saxon commercial crusaders are knocking at the gates. And now a company named for another Baldwin—and for all we know a descendant of the count—leaders of the invaders of the Old World, advance upon the city, and, to help in the assault, build an engine— only now the engine is no longer called a *mangonel*, but a locomotive.

The difference is hardly of kind and scarcely of degree. It is a mere matter of names, and the ghost of Saladin watching the present engagement might easily fancy the old days back again.

So perhaps we have not lost the Frontier after all. A new phrase, reversing that of Berkeley's, is appropriate to the effect that "Eastward the course of commerce takes its way," and we must look for the lost battle-line not toward the sunset, but toward the East. And so rapid has been the retrograde movement that we must go far to find it, that scattered firing-line, where the little skirmishes are heralding the approach of the Great March. We must already go further afield than England. The main body, even to the reserves, are intrenched there long since, and even continental Europe is to the rear of the skirmishers.

Along about Suez we begin to catch up with them where they are deepening the great canal, and we can assure ourselves that we are fairly abreast of the most distant line of scouts only when we come to Khiva, to Samarcand, to Bokhara and the Trans-Baikal country.

Just now one hears much of the "American commercial invasion of England." But adjust the field glasses and look beyond Britain and search for the blaze that the scouts have left on the telegraph poles and mile posts of Hungary, Turkey, Turkey in Asia, Persia, Beloochistan, India and Siam. You'll find the blaze distinct and the road, though rough hewn, is easy to follow. Prophecy and presumption be far from us, but it would be against all precedent that the Grand March should rest forever upon its arms and its laurels along the Thames, the Mersey and the Clyde, while its pioneers and Frontiersmen are making roads for it to the Eastward.

Is it too huge a conception, too inordinate an idea to say that the American conquest of England is but an incident of the Greater Invasion, an affair of outposts preparatory to the real manœuvre that shall embrace Europe, Asia, the whole of the Old World? Why not? And the blaze is ahead of us, and every now and then from far off there in the countries that are under the rising sun we catch the faint sounds of the skirmishing of our outposts. One of two things invariably happens under such circumstances as these: either the outposts fall back upon the main body or the main body moves up to the support of its outposts. One does not think that the outposts will fall back.

And so goes the great movement, Westward, then Eastward, forward and then back. The motion of the natural forces, the elemental energies, somehow appear to be thus alternative—action first, then reaction. The tides ebb and flow again, the seasons have their slow vibrations, touching extremes at periodic intervals. Not impossibly, in the larger view, is the analogy applicable to the movements of the races. First Westward with the great migrations, now Eastward with the course of commerce, moving in a colossal arc measured only by the hemispheres, as though upon the equator a giant dial hand oscillated, in gradual divisions through the centuries, now marking off the Westward progress, now traveling proportionately to the reaction toward the East.

Races must follow their destiny blindly, but is it not possible that we can find in this great destiny of ours something a little better than mere battle and conquest, something a little more generous than mere trading and underbidding? Inevitably with constant change of environment comes the larger view, the more tolerant spirit, and every race movement, from the first step beyond the Friesland swamp to the adjustment of the first American theodolite on the Himalayan watershed, is an unconscious lesson in patriotism. Just now we cannot get beyond the self-laudatory mood, but is it not possible to hope that, as the progress develops, a new patriotism, one that shall include all peoples, may prevail? The past would indicate that this is a goal toward which we trend.

In the end let us take the larger view, ignoring the Frieslanders, the Anglo-Saxons, the Americans. Let us look at the peoples as a people and observe how inevitably as they answer the great Westward impulse the true patriotism develops. If we can see that it is so with all of them we can assume that it must be so with us, and may know that mere victory in battle as we march Westward, or mere supremacy in trade as we react to the East is not after all the great achievement of the races but patriotism. Not our selfish present-day conception of the word, but a new patriotism, whose meaning is now the secret of the coming centuries.

Consider then the beginnings of patriotism. At the very first, the seed of the future nation was the regard of family; the ties of common birth held men together and the first feeling of patriotism was the love of family. But the family grows, develops by lateral branches, expands and becomes the clan. Patriotism is the devotion to the clan, and the clansmen will fight and die for its supremacy.

Then comes the time when the clans, tired of the roving life of herders, halt a moment and settle down in a chosen spot, the tent becoming permanent evolves the dwelling house, and the encampment of the clan becomes at last a city. Patriotism now is civic pride, the clan absorbed into a multitude of clans is forgotten; men speak of themselves as Athenians not as Greeks, as Romans not as Italians. It is the age of cities.

The city extends its adjoining grazing fields, they include outlying towns, other cities, and finally the State comes into being. Patriotism no longer confines itself to the walls of the city, but is enlarged to encompass the entire province. Men are Hanoverians or Wurtemburgers not Germans; Scots or Welsh not English; are even Carolinians or Alabamans rather than Americans.

But the States are federated, pronounced boundaries fade, State makes common cause with State and at last the nation is born. Patriotism at once is a national affair, a far larger, broader, truer sentiment than that first huddling about the hearthstone of the family. The word "brother" may be applied to men unseen and unknown, and a countryman is one of many millions.

We have reached this stage at the present, but if all signs are true, if all precedent may be followed, if all augury may be relied on and the tree grow as we see the twig is bent, the progress will not stop here.

By war to the Westward the family fought its way upward to the dignity of the nation, by reaction Eastward the nation may in patriotic effect merge with other nations, and others and still others, peacefully, the bitterness of trade competition may be lost, the business of the nations seen as a friendly *quid pro quo*, give and take arrangement, guided by a generous reciprocity. Every century the boundaries are widening, patriotism widens with the expansion, and our countrymen are those of different race, even different nations.

Will it not go on, this epic of civilization, this destiny of the races, until at last and at the ultimate end of all, we who now arrogantly boast ourselves as Americans, supreme in conquest, whether of battle-ship or of bridge-building, may realize that the true patriotism is the brotherhood of man and know that the whole world is our nation and simple humanity our countrymen?

World's Work, February 1902

STORY-TELLERS vs. NOVELISTS

IT IS A THING accepted and indisputable that a story-teller is a novelist, but it has often occurred to one that the reverse is not always true and that the novelist is not of necessity a story-teller. The distinction is perhaps a delicate one, but for all that it seems to be decisive, and it is quite possible that with the distinction in mind a different judgment might be passed upon a very large part of present-day fiction. It would even be entertaining to apply the classification to the products of the standard authors.

The story-telling instinct seems to be a gift, whereas—we trend to the heretical—the art of composing novels—using the word in apposition to stories, long or short—may be an acquirement. The one is an endowment, the other an accomplishment. Accordingly throughout the following paragraphs the expression: novelists of composition, for the time being, will be used technically, and will be applied to those fiction-writers who have not the story-telling faculty.

It would not be fair to attempt a proof that the one is better or worse than the other. The difference is surely of kind and not of degree. One will only seek to establish the fact that certain eminent and brilliant novel-writers are quite bereft of a sense of fiction, that some of them have succeeded in spite of this deficiency, and that other novel-writers possessing this sense of fiction have succeeded *because* of it, and in spite of many drawbacks such as lack of training and of education.

It is a proposition which one believes to be capable of demonstration that every child contains in himself the elements of every known profession, every occupation, every art, every industry. In the five-year-old you may see glimpses of the soldier, trader, farmer, painter, musician, builder and so on to the end of the roster. Later, circumstances produce the atrophy of all of these instincts but one, and from that one specialized comes the career. Thus every healthy-minded child—no matter if he develops in later years to be financier or bootmaker—is a story-teller. As soon as he begins to talk he tells stories. Witness the holocausts and carnage of the leaden platoons of the nursery table, the cataclysms of the Grand Trans-Continental Play-room and Front-Hall Railroad system. This, though, is not real story-telling. The toys practically tell the story for him and are no stimulant to the imagination. However, the child goes beyond the toys. He dramatizes every object of his surroundings. The books of the library shelves are files of soldiers, the rugs are islets in the seaway of the floor, the easy-chair is a comfortable old gentleman holding out his arms, the sofa a pirate brig or a Baldwin locomotive, and the child creates of his surroundings an entire and complex work of fiction of which he is at one and the same time hero, author and public.

Within the heart of every mature human being, not a writer of fiction, there is the withered remains of a little story-teller who died very young. And the love of good fiction and the appreciation of a fine novel in the man of the world of riper years is—I like to think—a sort of memorial tribute which he pays to his little dead playmate of so very long ago, who died very quietly with his little broken tin locomotive in his hands on the cruel day when he woke to the realization that it had outlived its usefulness and its charm.

Even in the heart of some accepted and successful fiction-writer you shall find this little dead story-teller. These are the novelists of composition, whose sense of fiction, under stress of circumstances, has become so blunted that when come at last to full maturity and to the power of using the faculty, they can no longer command it. These are novelists rather of intellect than of spontaneous improvization; and all the force of their splendid minds, every faculty other than the lost fiction-faculty, must be brought into play to compensate for the lack. Some more than compensate for it, so prodigal in resource, so persistent in effort, so powerful in energy and in fertility of invention, that—as it were by main strength— they triumph over the other writer, the natural story-teller, from whose pen the book flows with almost no effort at all.

Of this sort—the novelists of intellect, in whom the born story-teller is extinct, the novelists of composition in a word—the great example, it would seem, is George Eliot. It was by taking thought that the author of "Romola" added to her stature. The result is superb, but achieved at what infinite pains, with what colossal labor—of head rather than of the heart! She did not *feel*, she *knew*, and to attain that knowledge, what effort had to be expended! Even all her art cannot exclude from her pages evidences of the labor, of the superhuman toil. And it was labor and toil for what? To get back, through years of sophistication, of solemn education, of worldly wisdom, back again to the point of view of the little lost child of the doll-house days.

But sometimes the little story-teller does not die, but lives on and grows with the man, increasing in favor with God, till at last he dominates the man himself and the play-room of the old days simply widens its walls till it includes the street outside, and the street beyond and other streets, the whole city, the whole world and the story-teller discovers a set of new toys to play with, and new objects of a measureless environment to dramatize about, and in exactly, *exactly* the same spirit in which he trundled his tin train through the halls and shouted boarding orders from the sofa he moves now through the world's play-room "making up stories"; only that now his heroes and his public are outside himself and he alone may play the author.

For him there is but little effort required. He has a *sense of fiction*. Every instant of his day he is dramatizing. The cable-car has for him a distinct personality. Every window in the residence quarters is an eye to the soul of the house behind. The very lamp-post on the corner, burning on through the night and through the storm, is a soldier, dutiful, vigilant in stress. A ship is Adventure. An engine a living brute; and the easy-chair of his library is still the same comfortable and kindly old gentleman holding out his arms.

The men and women of his world are not apt to be—to him—so important in themselves as in relation to the whirl of things in which he chooses to involve them. They cause events, or else events happen to them, and by an unreasoned instinct the story-teller preserves the consistencies (just as the child would not have run the lines of the hall railway across the sea-way of the floor between the rugs). Much thought is not necessary to him. Production is facile, a constant pleasure. The story runs from his pen almost of itself, it takes this shape or that, he knows not why, his people do this or that and by some blessed system of guess-work they are somehow always plausible and true-to-life. His work is haphazard, yet in the end and in the main tremendously probable. Devil-may-care, slipshod, melodramatic, but invincibly persuasive he uses his heart, his senses, his emotions, every faculty but that of the intellect. He does not *know*, he *feels*.

Dumas was this, and "The Three Musketeers," different from "Romola" in kind but not in degree, is just as superb as Eliot at her best. Only the Frenchman had a sense of fiction which the Englishwoman had not. Her novels are character studies, are portraits, are portrayals of emotions, or pictures of certain times and certain events, are everything you choose but they are not stories and no stretch of the imagination, no liberalness of criticism can make them such. She succeeded by dint of effort where the Frenchman—merely wrote.

George Eliot compensated for the defect artificially and succeeded eminently and conclusively, but there are not found wanting cases—in modern literature—where "novelists of composition" have *not* compensated beyond a very justifiable doubt, and where had they but rejoiced in a very small modicum of this dowry of the gods their work would have been—to one's notion—infinitely improved.

As for instance Tolstoi; incontestably great though he be, all his unquestioned power has never yet won for him that same vivid sense of fiction enjoyed by so (comparatively) unimportant a writer as the author of "Sherlock Holmes." And of the two, judged strictly upon their merits as *story-tellers*, one claims for Mr. Doyle the securer if not the higher place, despite the magnificent genius of the novelist.

In the austere Russian—gloomy, sad, acquainted with grief—the child died irrevocably long, long ago; and no power however vast, no wisdom however profound, no effort however earnest, can turn one wheel on the little locomotive of battered tin or send it one inch along the old right of way between the nursery and the front-room. One cannot but feel that the great author of "Anna Karenina" realizes as much as his readers the limitations that the loss of this untainted childishness imposes. The power was all his, the wonderful intellectual grip, but not the fiction spirit—the child's knack and love of "making up stories." Given *that*, plus the force already his own, and what a book would have been there! The perfect novel! No doubt, clearer than all others, the great Russian sees the partial failure of his work, and no doubt keener and deeper than all others sees that unless the child-vision and the child-pleasure be present to guide and to stimulate, the entrances of the kingdom must stay forever shut to those who would enter, storm they the gates never so mightily and beat they never so clamorously at the doors.

Whatever the end of fiction may be, whatever the reward and recompense bestowed, whatever object is gained by good work, the end will not be gained, nor the reward won, nor the object attained by force alone—by strength of will or of mind. Without the auxiliary of the little playmate of the old days the great doors that stand at the end of the road will stay forever shut. Look once, however, with the child's eyes, or for once touch the mighty valves with the child's hand and Heaven itself lies open with all its manifold wonders.

So that in the end, after all trial has been made and every expedient tested, the simplest way is the best and the humblest means the surest. A little child stands in the midst of the wise men and the learned, and their wisdom and their learning are set aside and they are taught that unless they become as one of these they shall in nowise enter into the Kingdom of Heaven.

World's Work, March 1902

THE NOVEL WITH A "PURPOSE"

AFTER YEARS of indoctrination and expostulation on the part of the artists, the people who read appear at last to have grasped this one precept—"the novel must not preach," but "the purpose of the story must be subordinate to the story itself." It took a very long time for them to understand this, but once it became apparent they fastened upon it with a tenacity comparable only to the tenacity of the American schoolboy to the date "1492." "The novel must not preach," you hear them say.

As though it were possible to write a novel without a purpose, even if it is only the purpose to amuse. One is willing to admit that this savors a little of quibbling, for "purpose" and purpose to amuse are two different purposes. But every novel, even the most frivolous, must have some reason for the writing of it, and in that sense must have a "purpose."

Every novel must do one of three things—it must (1) tell something, (2) show something or (3) prove something. Some novels do all three of these; some do only two; all must do at least one.

The ordinary novel merely tells something, elaborates a complication, devotes itself primarily to *things*. In this class comes the novel of adventure, such as "The Three Musketeers."

The second and better class of novel shows something, exposes the workings of a temperament, devotes itself primarily to the minds of human beings. In this class falls the novel of character, such as "Romola."

The third, and what we hold to be the best class, proves something, draws conclusions from a whole congeries of forces, social tendencies, race impulses, devotes itself not to a study of men but of man. In this class falls the novel with the purpose, such as "Les Miserables."

And the reason we decide upon this last as the highest form of the novel is because that, though setting a great purpose before it as its task, it nevertheless includes, and is forced to include, both the other classes. It must tell something, must narrate vigorous incidents and must show something, must penetrate deep into the motives and character of type-men, men who are composite pictures of a multitude of men. It must do this because of the nature of its subject, for it deals with elemental forces, motives that stir whole nations. These cannot be handled as abstractions in fiction. Fiction can find expression only in the concrete. The elemental forces, then, contribute to the novel with a purpose to provide it with vigorous action. In the novel, force can be expressed in no other way. The social tendencies must be expressed by means of analysis of the characters of the men and women who compose that society, and the two must be combined and manipulated to evolve the purpose—to find the value of x.

The production of such a novel is probably the most arduous task that the writer of fiction can undertake. Nowhere else is success more difficult; nowhere else is failure so easy. Unskilfully treated the story may dwindle down and degenerate into mere special pleading, and the novelist become a polemicist, a pamphleteer, forgetting that, although his first consideration is to prove his case, his *means* must be living human beings, not statistics, and that his tools are not figures, but pictures from life as he sees it. The novel with a purpose *is*, one contends, a preaching novel. But it preaches by telling things and showing things. Only, the author selects from the great storehouse of actual life the things to be told and the things to be shown, which shall bear upon his problem, his purpose. The preaching, the moralizing, is the result not of direct appeal by the writer, but is made—should be made—to the reader by the very incidents of the story.

But here is presented a strange anomaly, a distinction as subtle as it is vital. Just now one has said that in the composition of the kind of novel under consideration, the *purpose* is for the novelist the all-important thing, and yet it is impossible to deny that the *story*, as a mere story, is to the story writer the one great object of attention. How reconcile then these two apparent contradictions?

For the novelist, the purpose of his novel, the problem he is to solve, is to his story what the keynote is to the sonata. Though the musician cannot exaggerate the importance of the keynote, yet the thing that interests him is the sonata itself. The keynote simply coördinates the music, systematizes it, brings all the myriad little rebellious notes under a single harmonious code.

Thus, too, the purpose in the novel. It is important as an end and also as an ever-present guide. For the writer it is as important only as a note to which his work must be attuned. The moment, however, that the writer becomes really and vitally interested in his purpose his novel fails.

Here is the strange anomaly. Let us suppose that Hardy, say, should be engaged upon a story which had for purpose to show the injustices under which the miners of Wales were suffering. It is conceivable that he could write a story that would make the blood boil with indignation. But he himself, if he is to remain an artist, if he is to write his novel successfully, will, as a novelist, care very little about the iniquitous labor system of the Welsh coal mines. It will be to him as impersonal a thing as the key is to the composer of a sonata. As a man Hardy may or may not be vitally concerned in the Welsh coal miner. That is quite unessential. But as a novelist, as an artist, his sufferings must be for him a matter of the mildest interest. They are important, for they constitute his keynote. They are *not* interesting for the reason that the working out of his *story*, its people, episodes, scenes and pictures, is for the moment the most interesting thing in all the world to him, exclusive of everything else. Do you think that Mrs. Stowe was more interested in the slave question than she was in the writing of "Uncle Tom's Cabin"? Her book, her manuscript, the page-to-page progress of the narrative, were more absorbing to her than all the Negroes that were ever whipped or sold. Had it not been so that great purpose-novel never would have succeeded.

Consider the reverse,—"Fécondité" for instance. The purpose for which Zola wrote the book ran away with him. He really did care more for the depopulation of France than he did for his novel. Result—sermons on the fruitfulness of women, special pleading, a farrago of dry, dull incidents, overburdened and collapsing under the weight of a theme that should have intruded only indirectly.

This is preëminently a selfish view of the question, but it is assuredly the only correct one. It must be remembered that the artist has a double personality, himself as a man, and himself as an artist. But, it will be urged, how account for the artist's sympathy in his fictitious characters, his emotion, the actual tears he sheds in telling of their griefs, their deaths, and the like?

The answer is obvious. As an artist his sensitiveness is quickened because they are characters in his novel. It does not at all follow that the same artist would be moved to tears over the report of parallel catastrophes in real life. As an artist, there is every reason to suppose he would welcome the news with downright pleasure. It would be for him "good material." He would see a story in it, a good scene, a great character. Thus the artist. What he would do, how he would feel as a man is quite a different matter.

To conclude, let us consider one objection urged against the novel with a purpose by the plain people who read. For certain reasons, difficult to explain, the purpose novel always ends unhappily. It is usually a record of suffering, a relation of tragedy. And the plain people say, "Ah, we see so much suffering in the world, why put it into novels? We do not want it in novels."

One confesses to very little patience with this sort. "We see so much suffering in the world already!" Do they? Is this really true? The people who buy novels are the well-to-do people. They belong to a class whose whole scheme of life is concerned solely with an aim to avoid the unpleasant. Suffering, the great catastrophes, the social throes, that annihilate whole communities, or that crush even isolated individuals—all these are as far removed from them as earthquakes and tidal waves. Or, even if it were so, suppose that by some miracle these blind eyes were opened and the sufferings of the poor, the tragedies of the house around the corner, really were laid bare. If there is much pain in life, all the more reason that it should appear in a class of literature which, in its highest form, is a sincere transcription of life.

It is the complaint of the coward, this cry against the novel with a purpose, because it brings the tragedies and griefs of others to notice. Take this element from fiction, take from it the power and opportunity to prove that injustice, crime and inequality do exist and what is left? Just the amusing novels, the novels that entertain. The juggler in spangles with his balancing pole and gilt ball does this. You may consider the modern novel from this point of view. It may be a flippant paper-covered thing of swords and cloaks, to be carried on a railway journey and to be thrown out the window when read, together with the sucked oranges and peanut shells. Or it may be a great force, that works together with the pulpit and the universities for the good of the people, fearlessly proving that power is abused, that the strong grind the faces of the weak, that an evil tree is still growing in the midst of the garden, that undoing follows hard upon unrighteousness, that the course of Empire is not yet finished, and that the races of men have yet to work out their destiny in those great and terrible movements that crush and grind and rend asunder the pillars of the houses of the nations.

Fiction may keep pace with the Great March, but it will not be by dint of amusing the people. The muse is a teacher not a trickster. Her rightful place is with the leaders, but in the last analysis that place is to be attained and maintained not by cap-and-bells but because of a serious and sincere interest, such as inspires the great teachers, the great divines, the great philosophers, a well-defined, well-seen, courageously sought-for purpose.

World's Work, May 1902

A NEGLECTED EPIC

As I HAVE tried to point out once before in these pages, the Frontier has disappeared. The westward-moving course of empire has at last crossed the Pacific Ocean. Civilization has circled the globe and has come back to its starting point, the vague and mysterious East.

The thing has not been accomplished peacefully. From the very first it has been an affair of wars—of invasions. Invasions of the East by the West, and of raids north and south—raids accomplished by flying columns that dashed out from both sides of the main army. Sometimes even the invaders have fought among themselves, as for instance the Trojan War, or the civil wars of Italy, England and America; sometimes they have turned back on their tracks and, upon one pretext or another, reconquered the races behind them, as for instance Alexander's wars to the eastward, the Crusades, and Napoleon's Egyptian campaigns.

Retarded by all these obstacles, the march has been painfully slow. To move from Egypt to Greece took centuries of time. More centuries were consumed in the campaign that brought empire from Greece to Rome, and still more centuries passed before it crossed the Alps and invaded northern and western Europe.

But observe. Once across the Mississippi, the West—our Far West—was conquered in about forty years. In all the vast campaign from east to west here is the most signal victory, the swiftest, the completest, the most brilliant achievement— the wilderness subdued at a single stroke.

Now all these various fightings to the westward, these mysterious race-movements, migrations, wars and wanderings have produced their literature, distinctive, peculiar, excellent. And this literature we call epic. The Trojan War gave us the "Iliad," the "Odyssey" and the "Æneid"; the campaign of the Greeks in Asia Minor produced the "Anabasis"; a whole cycle of literature grew from the conquest of Europe after the fall of Rome—"The Song of Roland," "The Nibelungenlied,"

"The Romance of the Rose," "Beowulf," "Magnusson,"
"The Scotch Border Ballads," "The Poem of the Cid," "The
Heimskringla," "Orlando Furioso," "Jerusalem Delivered,"
and the like.

On this side of the Atlantic, in his clumsy, artificial way,
but yet recognized as a producer of literature, Cooper has
tried to chronicle the conquest of the eastern part of our
country. Absurd he may be in his ideas of life and character,
the art in him veneered over with charlatanism; yet the man
was solemn enough and took his work seriously, and his work
is literature.

Also a cycle of romance has grown up around the Civil
War. The theme has had its poets to whom the public have
been glad to listen. The subject is vast, noble; is in a word
epic, just as the Trojan War and the Retreat of the Ten Thousand were epic.

But when at last one comes to look for the literature that
sprang from and has grown up around the last great epic
event in the history of civilization, the event which in spite of
stupendous difficulties was consummated more swiftly, more
completely, more satisfactorily than any like event since the
westward migration began—I mean the conquering of the
West, the subduing of the wilderness beyond the Mississippi—What has this produced in the way of literature? The
dime novel! The dime novel and nothing else. The dime novel
and nothing better.

The Trojan War left to posterity the character of Hector;
the wars with the Saracens gave us Roland; the folklore of
Iceland produced Grettir; the Scotch border poetry brought
forth the Douglas; the Spanish epic the Cid. But the American epic, just as heroic, just as elemental, just as important
and as picturesque, will fade into history leaving behind no
finer type, no nobler hero than Buffalo Bill.

The young Greeks sat on marble terraces overlooking the
Ægean Sea and listened to the thunderous roll of Homer's
hexameter. In the feudal castles the minstrel sang to the
young boys, of Roland. The farm folk of Iceland to this very
day treasure up and read to their little ones hand-written
copies of the Gretla Saga chronicling the deeds and death
of Grettir the Strong. But the youth of the United States

learn of their epic by paying a dollar to see the "Wild West Show."

The plain truth of the matter is that we have neglected our epic—the black shame of it be on us—and no contemporaneous poet or chronicler thought it worth his while to sing the song or tell the tale of the West, because literature in the day when the West was being won was a cult indulged in by certain well-bred gentlemen in New England who looked eastward to the Old World, to the legends of England and Norway and Germany and Italy for their inspiration, and left the great, strong, honest, fearless, resolute deeds of their own countrymen to be defamed and defaced by the nameless hacks of the "yellow back" libraries.

One man,—who wrote "How Santa Claus Came to Simpson's Bar,"—one poet, one chronicler did, in fact, arise for the moment, who understood that wild, brave life and who for a time gave promise of bearing record of things seen.

One of the requirements of an epic—a true epic—is that its action must devolve upon some great national event. There was no lack of such in those fierce years after '49. Just that long and terrible journey from the Mississippi to the ocean is an epic in itself. Yet no serious attempt has ever been made by an American author to render into prose or verse this event in our history as "national" in scope, in origin and in results as the Revolution itself. The prairie schooner is as large a figure in the legends as the black ship that bore Ulysses homeward from Troy. The sea meant as much to the Argonauts of the fifties as it did to the ten thousand.

And the Alamo! There is a trumpet-call in the word; and only the look of it on the printed page is a flash of fire. But the very histories slight the deed, and to many an American, born under the same flag that the Mexican rifles shot to ribbons on that splendid day, the word is meaningless. Yet Thermopylae was less glorious, and in comparison with that siege the investment of Troy was mere wanton riot. At the very least the Texans in that battered adobe church fought for the honor of their flag and the greater glory of their country, not for loot or the possession of the person of an adulteress. Young men are taught to consider the Iliad, with its butcheries, its glorification of inordinate selfishness and vanity, as a classic. Achilles, murderer, egoist, ruffian and liar, is a hero. But the name of Bowie, the name of the man who gave his life to his flag at the Alamo, is perpetuated only in the designation of a knife. Crockett is the hero only of a "funny story" about a sagacious coon; while Travis, the boy commander who did what Gordon with an empire back of him failed to do, is quietly and definitely ignored.

Because we have done nothing to get at the truth about the West, because our best writers have turned to the old country folklore and legends for their inspiration, because "melancholy harlequins" strut in fringed leggings upon the street corners, one hand held out for pennies, we have come to believe that our West, our epic, was an affair of Indians, road agents and desperadoes, and have taken no account of the brave men who stood for law and justice and liberty, and for those great ideas died by the hundreds, unknown and unsung; died that the West might be subdued, that the last stage of the march should be accomplished, that the Anglo-Saxon should fulfil his destiny and complete the cycle of the world.

The great figure of our neglected epic, the Hector of our ignored Iliad, is not, as the dime novels would have us believe, a lawbreaker, but a lawmaker; a fighter, it is true, as is always the case with epic figures, but a fighter for peace, a calm, grave, strong man who hated the lawbreaker as the hound hates the wolf.

He did not lounge in barrooms; he did not cheat at cards; he did not drink himself to maudlin fury; he did not "shoot at the drop of the hat." But he loved his horse, he loved his friend, he was kind to little children; he was always ready to side with the weak against the strong, with the poor against the rich. For hypocrisy and pretence, for shams and subterfuges, he had no mercy, no tolerance. He was too brave to lie and too strong to steal. The odds in that lawless day were ever against him; his enemies were many and his friends were few; but his face was always set bravely against evil, and fear was not in him even at the end. For such a man as this could die no quiet death in a land where law went no further than the statute books and life lay in the crook of my neighbor's forefinger.

He died in defense of an ideal, an epic hero, a legendary

figure, formidable, sad. He died facing down injustice, dishonesty and crime; died "in his boots"; and the same world that has glorified Achilles and forgotten Travis finds none so poor to do him reverence. No literature has sprung up around him—this great character native to America. He is of all the world-types the one distinctive to us—peculiar, particular and unique. He is dead and even his work is misinterpreted and misunderstood. His very memory will soon be gone, and the American epic, which on the shelves of posterity should have stood shoulder to shoulder with the "Heimskringla" and the "Tales of the Nibelungen" and the "Song of Roland," will never be written.

World's Work, December 1902

THE RESPONSIBILITIES OF
THE NOVELIST

IT IS NOT here a question of the "unarrived," the "unpublished"; these are the care-free irresponsibles whose hours
are halcyon and whose endeavors have all the lure, all the
recklessness, of adventure. They are not recognized; they have
made no standards for themselves and if they play the *saltimbanque* and the charlatan nobody cares and nobody (except themselves) is affected.

But the writers in question are the successful ones who
have made a public and to whom some ten, twenty, or a
hundred thousand people are pleased to listen. You may believe if you choose that the novelist of all workers is independent, that he can write what he pleases, and that certainly,
certainly he should never "write down to his readers," that
he should never consult them at all.

On the contrary, I believe it can be proved that the successful novelist should be more than all others limited in the nature
and character of his work; more than all others he should
be careful of what he says; more than all others he should
defer to his audience; more than all others—more even than
the minister and the editor—he should "feel his public" and
watch his every word, testing carefully his every utterance,
weighing with the most relentless precision his every statement; in a word, possess a sense of his responsibilities.

For the novel is the great expression of modern life. Each
form of art has had its turn at reflecting and expressing its
contemporaneous thought. Time was when the world looked
to the architects of the castles and great cathedrals to truly
reflect and embody its ideals. And the architects—serious,
earnest men—produced such "expressions of contemporaneous thought" as the castle of Coucy and the church of Notre
Dame. Then with other times came other customs, and the
painters had their day. The men of the Renaissance trusted
Angelo and da Vinci and Velasquez to speak for them, and
trusted not in vain. Next came the age of the drama. Shakespeare and Marlowe found the value of x for the life and the
times in which they lived. Later on contemporary life had

been so modified that neither painting, architecture, nor drama was the best vehicle of expression, the day of the longer poems arrived, and Pope and Dryden spoke for their fellows.

Thus the sequence. Each age speaks with its own particular organ, and has left the Word for us moderns to read and understand. The castle of Coucy and the church of Notre Dame are the spoken words of the Middle Ages. The Renaissance speaks—and intelligibly—to us through the sibyls of the Sistine chapel and the Mona Liza. "Macbeth" and "Tamerlane" résumé the whole spirit of the Elizabethan age, while the "Rape of the Lock" is a wireless message to us straight from the period of the Restoration.

To-day is the day of the novel. In no other way and by no other vehicle is contemporaneous life so adequately expressed; and the critics of the twenty-second century, reviewing our times, striving to reconstruct our civilization, will look not to the painters, not to the architects nor dramatists, but to the novelists to find our idiosyncrasy.

I think this is true. I think if the matter could in any way be staticized, the figures would bear out the assumption. There is no doubt the novel will in time "go out" of popular favor as irrevocably as the long poem has gone, and for the reason that it is no longer the right mode of expression.

It is interesting to speculate upon what will take its place. Certainly the coming civilization will revert to no former means of expressing its thought or its ideals. Possibly music will be the interpreter of the life of the twenty-first and twenty-second centuries. Possibly one may see a hint of this in the characterization of Wagner's operas as the "Music of the Future."

This, however, is parenthetical and beside the mark. Remains the fact that to-day is the day of the novel. By this one does not mean that the novel is merely popular. If the novel was not something more than a simple diversion, a means of whiling away a dull evening, a long railway journey, it would not, believe me, remain in favor another day.

If the novel then is popular it is popular with a reason, a vital inherent reason; that is to say it is essential. Essential—to resume once more the proposition—because it expresses modern life better than architecture, better than painting, better than poetry, better than music. It is as necessary to the civilization of the twentieth century as the violin is necessary to Kubelik, as the piano is necessary to Paderewski, as the plane is necessary to the carpenter, the sledge to the blacksmith, the chisel to the mason. It is an instrument, a tool, a weapon, a vehicle. It is that thing which, in the hand of man, makes him civilized and no longer savage, because it gives him a power of durable, permanent expression. So much for the novel—the instrument.

Because it is so all-powerful to-day, the people turn to him who wields this instrument with every degree of confidence. They expect—and rightly—that results shall be commensurate with means. The unknown archer who grasps the bow of Ulysses may be expected by the multitude to send his shaft far and true. If he is not true nor strong he has no business with the bow. The people give heed to him only because he bears a great weapon. He himself knows before he shoots whether or no he is worthy.

It is all very well to jeer at the People and at the People's misunderstanding of the arts, but the fact is indisputable that no art that is not in the end understood by the People can live or ever did live a single generation. In the larger view, in the last analysis, the People pronounce final judgment. The People, despised of the artist, hooted, caricatured, and vilified, are after all, and in the main, the real seekers after Truth. Who is it after all, whose interest is liveliest in any given work of art? It is not now a question of *æsthetic* interest; that is the artist's, the amateur's, the cognoscenti's. It is a question of *vital* interest. Say what you will, Maggie Tulliver—for instance—is far more a living being for Mrs. Jones across the street than she is for your sensitive, fastidious, keenly critical artist, litterateur, or critic. The People—Mrs. Jones and her neighbors—take the life history of these fictitious characters, these novels, to heart with a seriousness that the æsthetic cult have no conception of. The cult consider them almost solely from their artistic sides. The People take them into their innermost lives. Nor do the people discriminate. Omnivorous readers as they are to-day, they make little distinction between Maggie Tulliver and the heroine of the last "popular novel." They do not stop to separate true from false, they do not care.

How necessary it becomes, then, for those who, by the

simple art of writing, can invade the heart's heart of thousands, whose novels are received with such measureless earnestness,—how necessary it becomes for those who wield such power to use it rightfully. Is it not expedient to act fairly? Is it not in Heaven's name essential that the People hear, not a lie, but Truth?

If the novel were not one of the most important factors of modern life, if it were not the completest expression of our civilization, if its influence were not greater than all the pulpits, than all the newspapers between the oceans, it would not be so important that its message should be true.

But the novelist to-day is the one who reaches the greatest audience. Right or wrong the People turn to him the moment he speaks, and what he says they believe.

For the million, Life is a contracted affair, is bounded by the walls of the narrow channel of affairs in which their feet are set. They have no horizon. They look to-day as they never have looked before, as they never will look again, to the writer of fiction to give them an idea of Life beyond their limits, and they believe him as they never have believed before and never will again.

This being so, is it not difficult to understand how certain of these successful writers of fiction—these favored ones into whose hands the gods have placed the great bow of Ulysses—can look so frivolously upon their craft? It is not necessary to specify. One speaks of those whose public is measured by "one hundred and fifty thousand copies sold." We know them, and because the gods have blessed us with wits beyond our deserving we know their work is false. But what of the "hundred and fifty thousand" who are not discerning and who receive this falseness as Truth, who believe this topsy-turvy picture of Life beyond their horizons is real and vital and sane?

There is no gauge to measure the extent of this malignant influence. Public opinion is made no one can say how, by infinitesimal accretions, by a multitude of minutest elements. Lying novels, surely, surely in this day and age of indiscriminate reading contribute to this more than all other influences of present-day activity.

The Pulpit, the Press, and the Novel—these indisputably are the great moulders of Public opinion and Public morals, to-day. But the Pulpit speaks but once a week; the Press is read with lightning haste and the morning news is wastepaper by noon. But the novel goes into the home to stay. It is read word for word, is talked about, discussed; its influence penetrates every chink and corner of the family.

Yet novelists are not found wanting who write for money. I do not think this is an unfounded accusation. I do not think it is asking too much of credulity. This would not matter if they wrote the Truth. But these gentlemen who are "in literature for their own pocket every time" have discovered that for the moment the People have confounded the Wrong with the Right, and prefer that which is a lie, to that which is true. "Very well then," say these gentlemen. "If they want a lie they shall have it"; and they give the People a lie in return for royalties.

The surprising thing about this is that you and I and all the rest of us do not consider this as disreputable, do not yet realize that the novelist has responsibilities. We condemn an editor who sells his editorial columns, and we revile the Pulpit attainted of venality. But the venal novelist,—he whose influence is greater than either the Press or Pulpit, —*him* we greet with a wink and the tongue in the cheek.

This should not be so. Somewhere the protest should be raised, and those of us who see the practice of this fraud should bring home to ourselves the realization that the selling of one hundred and fifty thousand books is a serious business. The People have a right to the Truth as they have a right to life, liberty, and the pursuit of happiness. It is *not* right that they be exploited and deceived with false views of life, false characters, false sentiment, false morality, false history, false philosophy, false emotions, false heroism, false notions of self-sacrifice, false views of religion, of duty, of conduct, and of manners.

The man who can address an audience of one hundred and fifty thousand people who—unenlightened—*believe what he says* has a heavy duty to perform, and tremendous responsibilities to shoulder; and he should address himself to his task not with the flippancy of the catch-penny juggler at the county fair, but with earnestness, with soberness, with a sense of his limitations, and with all the abiding sincerity that by the favor and mercy of the gods may be his.

The Critic, December 1902

Chronology

Southampton, England, at the end of the month. Advised that art instruction is superior in Paris, they leave for France the following month. Enrolls in August in Bouguereau atelier of the Julien Academy. Acquires a mastery of French and is absorbed in medieval French chronicles. Father returns to the United States in the fall.

1888   Continues studies in Paris and works on a monumental painting of the Battle of Crécy; mother and brother Charles return to the United States in the spring. Norris becomes something of a boulevardier.

1889   Writes article entitled "Clothes of Steel," tracing the history of the use of armor; mother submits it to San Francisco *Chronicle*, where it appears unsigned March 31 (his first publication). Returns from Paris in midyear and prepares for entrance examination to the University of California. Begins to write *Yvernelle: A Legend of Feudal France*, book-length narrative poem.

1890   Takes Berkeley entrance examination in the fall. Fails in mathematics, but is admitted to the literary program of the College of Letters. Takes courses principally in English, French, and history; during four years at Berkeley, contributes stories heavily indebted to Richard Harding Davis and Rudyard Kipling to the *Occident*, a student publication, and to the San Francisco *Argonaut*, the *Overland Monthly*, and the San Francisco *Wave*.

1891   Pledges Phi Gamma Delta; enters fully into undergraduate life. *Yvernelle* published in illustrated trade edition for Christmas by Lippincott; Mother advances $400 toward expense of publication.

1892   During 1892–93 academic year begins extensive reading of the works of Zola and is deeply engaged by courses in geology and zoology given by Joseph Le Conte, popularizer of ideas reconciling evolution and religion. Father undertakes in May a solitary trip around the world and then returns to Chicago rather than San Francisco.

1893   Contributes "Lauth" to the *Overland Monthly* in March, a story that owes much to Le Conte's beliefs. In October,

Sarah Collins, a charwoman, is murdered by her drunken husband in a San Francisco kindergarten; incident provides initial inspiration for *McTeague*.

1894   Completes fourth year at Berkeley but does not receive degree, having repeatedly failed the mathematics matriculation examination. Father sues mother for divorce; Mrs. Norris files countersuit; the settlement provides support only for her and Charles. Enters Harvard in the fall for a year; takes French, but devotes himself principally to English 22, a writing course; works on drafts of *Vandover and the Brute* and *McTeague* under the direction of Professor Lewis Gates, to whom *McTeague* is dedicated. The bulk of *Vandover and the Brute* completed by the end of the year.

1895   *McTeague* remains unfinished by the end of the term. Returns to San Francisco and signs contract with the San Francisco *Chronicle* to report the conflict between the Boers and the English in South Africa. Arrives in Cape Town in December; reaches Johannesburg in late December, just in time for the Jameson Raid, an abortive effort by English interests to seize the city from Boer control.

1896   Becomes ill in Johannesburg in early January shortly before being expelled from the Transvaal by the Boers; arrives in San Francisco in February. After recuperation, in April becomes staff member of the San Francisco *Wave*, a regional weekly initially sponsored by the Southern Pacific Railroad. For almost two years contributes short fiction, critical essays, feature stories, interviews, and reviews to *The Wave*, usually more than one contribution an issue and often anonymously or pseudonymously. Becomes associated with Les Jeunes, a group of San Francisco artists and bohemians led by Gelett Burgess and including Bruce Porter (the model for Vanamee in *The Octopus*). Meets Jeannette Black in the fall.

1897   Continues work at *The Wave*; relationship with Jeannette (described in autobiographical novel *Blix*) deepens. October, goes to Big Dipper Mine in the Sierras (managed by college friend Seymour Waterhouse) to revise and complete *McTeague*. Volume of short stories refused by New York publisher, who advises him to write an adventure novel. Begins writing *Moran of the Lady Letty* in early winter, a story of treasure-hunting in Lower California that features a strong, rough heroine.

1898 *Moran of the Lady Letty* appears in *The Wave* from January to April; S. S. McClure, upon reading it in serial form, calls him to New York in February to work for publishing firm of Doubleday & McClure as an editorial assistant; Norris is to be free to work on his own writings in the afternoons. March, meets with William Dean Howells, who offers to read *McTeague* in manuscript. Becomes acquainted with Lloyd Osbourne, writer and stepson of Robert Louis Stevenson, Mrs. Robert Louis Stevenson, and Katherine Herne, widow of the actor-playwright James A. Herne. Spanish-American War breaks out in April; sent to Cuba by *McClure's Magazine* as a reporter; meets fellow war correspondents Stephen Crane and Richard Harding Davis. Early July, views Battle of El Caney. August, becomes ill with fever and returns to San Francisco to recover. (Only two of his war reports published in his lifetime: "Comida," in the *Atlantic Monthly*, March 1899, and "With Lawton at El Caney," in the *Century*, June 1899.) *Moran of the Lady Letty* published by Doubleday & McClure in September, first book since *Yvernelle*. October, returns to New York, taking an apartment at 61 Washington Square South. Quickly completes *Blix* and begins work on *A Man's Woman*, adventure novel of Arctic exploration involving a strong-willed woman and an equally strong-willed explorer.

1899 *McTeague* published by Doubleday & McClure in February; revises the passage in which little August wets his pants in the Orpheum Theatre for the second printing. Novel elicits hostile reviews because of its "lurid" subject matter; Howells, however, pronounces it "altogether a remarkable book." (Made into the movie *Greed* by Erich von Stroheim in 1924.) Offers *Vandover and the Brute* to Doubleday & McClure, who decline it because of its even more troublesome contents. (*Vandover and the Brute* published in 1914 by Doubleday, Page, with a foreword by Charles Norris.) March, completes work on *A Man's Woman*; *Blix* begins to appear serially in the *Puritan*, a women's magazine. Plans a trilogy of novels, "The Epic of the Wheat"; describes it to Howells as, "First, a story of California (the producer), second, a story of Chicago (the distributor), third, a story of Europe (the consumer) and in each to keep to the idea of this huge, Niagara of wheat rolling from West to East." Leaves for San Francisco in early April to work up the background of the first novel of the trilogy, *The Octopus*, set in the San Joaquin Valley. Does research on the Mussel Slough Massacre (the principal historical event depicted in *The Octopus*) at the Mechanics' Institute Library and then spends several months on a ranch south of San Francisco. September, returns to New York; interviews Collis P. Huntington (the Shelgrim of *The Octopus*). *Blix* published by Doubleday & McClure in September. October, begins writing *The Octopus*.

1900   Begins the new year by accepting a position as special reader in the new firm of Doubleday, Page & Co., one of two publishing houses evolving out of Doubleday & McClure. Meets Hamlin Garland, who becomes a good friend. Marries Jeannette Black on February 12; they take up residence in The Anglesea, an apartment house at 60 Washington Square South. *A Man's Woman* published by Doubleday & McClure in February. In May, discovers and champions Theodore Dreiser's first novel, *Sister Carrie*, which Dreiser had submitted to the firm. Moves to small cottage in Roselle, New Jersey, in October. *The Octopus* completed in mid-December after over a year's writing.

1901   Gives up house in Roselle and travels to Chicago with Jeannette in the spring to do research on the second volume of "The Epic of the Wheat," *The Pit*, based on Joseph Leiter's attempt to corner the wheat market in 1897–98. *The Octopus*, published by Doubleday, Page in April, has largest sales of any book Norris published in his lifetime (33,000 copies of the trade edition). Early in the fall, after two months in San Francisco and three months in cabin at Greenwood Lake, New Jersey, returns to New York with Jeannette and rents apartment at 3605 Broadway, overlooking the Hudson River. Begins to write *The Pit*. Jeannette becomes pregnant. Stops working as reader for Doubleday, Page, supplementing book royalties by writing articles and stories for magazines and newspapers. Contributions include literary column for the *Chicago American* (May–Aug.) and occasional literary columns for the *Boston Evening Transcript* (Nov. 1901–Feb. 1902) and the monthly *World's Work* (from Oct. until his death). (Selection of short stories, *A Deal in Wheat*, published in 1903 by Doubleday, Page; second collection, *The Third Circle*, published in 1909.)

1902   Jeannette Norris, Jr., born on February 9. Completes *The Pit* in June and sells serial rights to *The Saturday Evening Post*. (Published by Doubleday, Page in 1903, *The Pit* is a bestseller; also produced successfully on Broadway by Channing Pollock in 1904.) Last of Norris's literary columns, "Salt and Sincerity," appears in *The Critic* from May to October. (A selected edition of Norris's criticism, *The Responsibilities of the Novelist and Other Literary Essays*, published by Doubleday, Page in 1903.) In July, leaves New York, dissatisfied with quality of literary life there; goes to San Francisco, where he plans a trip around the world in a tramp steamer with family to collect material for the last but never-written volume of "The Epic of the Wheat," *The Wolf*. In San Francisco, attends the hearing of old friend Dr. William Lawlor, appointed head of Glen Ellen Home for the Feebleminded by Governor Henry Gage and singled out for attack by Gage's political opponents; during hearing, defends Lawlor against a would-be assassin and is extolled by the press. The Norrises buy land for a homestead near Gilroy in the Santa Cruz Mountains, south of San Francisco. Jeannette undergoes surgery for appendicitis; Norris suffers attack of appendicitis one month later but does not go to the doctor immediately. Enters hospital on October 22, when pain becomes acute; operation reveals gangrene and peritonitis. Dies of peritonitis on October 25. Buried at Mountain View Cemetery in Oakland.

Note on the Texts

This volume contains three novels by Frank Norris, *Vandover and the Brute*, *McTeague*, and *The Octopus*, as well as a selection of his essays.

Frank Norris worked on drafts of both *Vandover and the Brute* and *McTeague* while he was a student in Lewis E. Gates's writing class at Harvard University, 1894–95. *Vandover* seems to have been completed, or nearly so, before he left Harvard in 1895; *McTeague* was not finished until several years later. Norris offered *Vandover* to Doubleday & McClure soon after they published *McTeague* in early 1899, but when they declined the novel, as did William Heinemann of London a little later, Norris apparently despaired of seeing it published and began lifting scenes from it for other novels. As the manuscript of *Vandover* has never come to light, the only authoritative text of the novel is that prepared by Norris's brother, the novelist Charles G. Norris, for the first edition of 1914, published by Doubleday, Page & Co., Garden City, New York. In the foreword to the 1914 edition (not included here), Charles Norris wrote that the publication of the work was delayed because the manuscript of the novel had been lost in the confusion of the San Francisco fire of 1906 and had not been recovered until 1913. However, in a 1930 conversation he told Franklin Walker (Frank Norris's biographer) that the manuscript had been held for several years by Norris's widow, Jeannette, and that the fire story was not authentic. He also told Walker that in preparing the novel for publication he had had to make some cuts, eliminating some of the strong language and a long chapter early in the novel in which Vandover is drunk. He also cut a description of the parlor that Frank Norris had used in *Blix* and added about 5,000 words of his own. Whatever the accuracy of Charles Norris's later recollections, the 1914 text, in the absence of any earlier document, is the sole authoritative text of *Vandover*.

The holograph manuscript of *McTeague*, which served as printer's copy for the first edition, survived intact into the

1920s. *The Argonaut Manuscript Limited Edition of Frank Norris' Work*, published in ten volumes by Doubleday, Doran in 1928, included a leaf of this manuscript (in a special envelope) in the first volume of each of the 245 sets of the edition. Thus the manuscript was widely dispersed, and, despite the efforts of James D. Hart and Joseph Katz in recent years, only some 100 leaves have been recovered. However, since Norris was a member of the New York firm of Doubleday & McClure in 1899 when *McTeague* was published, he probably saw the novel through the press with some care. (The surviving leaves of the manuscript support this belief.) Many reviewers of *McTeague* noted the strong subject matter—apparently the episode in the Orpheum Theatre (pp. 335–38 of this edition) that describes little August's incontinence was particularly controversial. Norris revised the passage for the second printing, making it an account of McTeague's searching for his hat. Because the revision apparently resulted from outside pressure, this volume prints the text of the first printing of *McTeague*.

The manuscript of *The Octopus* is not known to survive. The first edition of the novel, published by Doubleday, Page & Co., went through five printings in 1901. A number of minor textual alterations appeared in each, with by far the largest number in the second printing. Some of these alterations corrected typographical errors; some made stylistic changes—for example, "jumped high" was changed to "jumped fair" (975.35) and "clamouring machinery" to "bellowing machinery" (1070.32). The nature of these changes suggests that they originated with Norris. Therefore, the text of the fifth printing of the first edition of *The Octopus* is printed here.

The year following Norris's death in 1902, Doubleday, Page & Co. published *The Responsibilities of the Novelist and Other Literary Essays by Frank Norris*. That collection, which includes some of the essays printed here, appears to have been assembled by Jeannette Norris and her friend Isobel Strong. As Norris had no hand in preparing it and as its text frequently varies from the original publication in various magazines and newspapers, the collection has no authority. Therefore the texts included in this edition are those of the original periodical publications. The one exception is the essay "The Great American Novelist," which is cited in the *The Responsibilities of the Novelist* as having been syndicated for newspaper publication but for which no appearance other than *Responsibilities* has ever been found. Three paragraphs have been omitted from the *Boston Evening Transcript* text of "A Plea for Romantic Fiction." These paragraphs (which occurred following 1167.32 of this edition) describe women's education in America and bear no relation to the rest of the essay. Their presence is undoubtedly the result of an error in the *Transcript* editorial office. Internal subheads have been dropped from the *World's Work* text of "The True Reward of the Novelist."

The following are the sources of the texts of the essays included in this volume:

"Theory and Reality," San Francisco *Wave*, 15 (May 2, 1896), 8.

"Zola as a Romantic Writer," San Francisco *Wave*, 15 (June 27, 1896), 3.

"The 'English Courses' of the University of California," San Francisco *Wave*, 15 (November 28, 1896), 2–3.

"An Opening for Novelists," San Francisco *Wave*, 16 (May 22, 1897), 7.

"Fiction Is Selection," San Francisco *Wave*, 16 (September 11, 1897), 3.

"Perverted Tales," San Francisco *Wave*, 16 (December 25, 1897), 5–7.

"Frank Norris' Weekly Letter," *Chicago American Art and Literary Review*, June 22, 1901, p. 8.

"Frank Norris' Weekly Letter," *Chicago American Art and Literary Review*, August 3, 1901, p. 5.

"Frank Norris' Weekly Letter," *Chicago American Art and Literary Review*, August 24, 1901, p. 8.

"The True Reward of the Novelist," *World's Work*, 2 (October 1901), 1337–39.

"Novelists of the Future," *Boston Evening Transcript*, November 27, 1901, p. 14.

"The Need of a Literary Conscience," *World's Work*, 3 (December 1901), 1559–60.

"The Mechanics of Fiction," *Boston Evening Transcript*, December 4, 1901, p. 22.

"A Plea for Romantic Fiction," *Boston Evening Transcript*, December 18, 1901, p. 14.

"Fiction Writing as a Business," *Boston Evening Transcript*, January 1, 1902, p. 17.

" 'The Literature of the West,' " *Boston Evening Transcript*, January 8, 1902, p. 7.

"The Great American Novelist," *The Responsibilities of the Novelist* (New York: Doubleday, Page, 1903), pp. 85–89. (Listed in the bibliography of *Responsibilities* as syndicated January 19, 1903; this date, based on the correct dating of other syndicated essays misdated in the bibliography, is thought to be January 19, 1902.)

"The Frontier Gone At Last," *World's Work*, 3 (February 1902), 1728–31.

"Story-Tellers vs. Novelists," *World's Work*, 3 (March 1902), 1894–96.

"The Novel with a 'Purpose,' " *World's Work*, 4 (May 1902), 2117–19.

"A Neglected Epic," *World's Work*, 5 (December 1902), 2904–06.

"The Responsibilities of the Novelist," *The Critic*, 41 (December 1902), 537–40.

Doubleday & McClure, Norris's first publisher, as well as most American newspapers and magazines, followed American usage in spelling and punctuation. Norris's second publisher, Doubleday, Page & Co., adopted British usage in *The Octopus* and *Vandover and the Brute*, even though Norris himself preferred American style (as is revealed by the surviving manuscript leaves of *McTeague*). The spelling and punctuation of these first editions have been allowed to stand. Norris's essays in particular contain many variations in spelling and punctuation because of the different editorial practices of the journals in which the essays first appeared. These variations have also been retained.

This volume presents only the texts of these editions; it does not attempt to reproduce features of typographic design, such as the display capitalization of chapter openings. The texts are reproduced without change, except for the correction of typographical errors. Spelling, punctuation, and capitalization often are expressive features, and they are not altered, even when inconsistent or irregular. The following is a list of the typographical errors corrected, cited by page and line number: 25.21, governor"; 25.30, girl,'; 40.12, door:; 61.19, Victorine the cook; 62.15, mean?'; 90.16, Mr,; 108.12, *Cape Horner*; 108.30, *Cape Horner*; 131.5, Fremilt; 139.13, Beale, Jr.; 145.34, canes; 145.36, 'Did; 165.9, thestretcher; 185.19, firm; 205.1, *Lycanthropy-Mathesis*; 211.17, "Fifteen.; 225.13, *anything."*; 229.25, here; 229.25, here; 237.29, Steet; 245.12, fined; 287.7, junks; 298.22, waiscoats; 322.29, inacessible; 329.3, old; 329.7, "Parlors?"; 360.18, flat.; 364.35, past; 372.19, god-from-the machine; 387.38, Dokter; 401.37, Mechanic's; 410.31, It's; 420.27, "Parlors"; 445.35, went.; 446.23, flushing; 448.1, now?"; 460.26, "See,"; 470.3, tell?"; 491.29, murmumed; 492.25, if off; 498.18–19, McTeague's; 499.19, "Dentist"; 509.6, council; 517.16, looked; 526.12, jacknife; 587.24, Hoven's; 605.40, th n; 625.31, tumultous; 643.9, ful; 657.33, Derrick's; 670.22, *$5.00."*; 684.18, wall; 745.2, check; 769.20, corruscated; 774.39, Skeezichs; 810.24, reconnaisance; 818.15, S.W.; 825.40, Schiler; 867.25, han; 880.20, he; 916.16, him. ¶"I; 918.2, Guadlajara; 946.3, ususal; 947.1, popular; 947.36, again; 949.6, forebore; 969.36, hand,; 1015.32, Pharoahs; 1019.21, 'irrepressible; 1023.10, villifiers; 1089.31, "Right—oh,"; 1090.30, thick,; 1091.38, immobolising; 1106.38, Rougon Macquart; 1107.6, *ordinary*; 1107.38, *Réve*; 1110.4, the write; 1110.34, cribed; 1111.28, fill; 1112.26, Barbara; 1113.29, Jeunnes, and; 1114.6, had; 1117.11, untramelled; 1119.18, *intional*; 1120.15, im."; 1120.28, Stepterfechit; 1122.17, it's; 1123.11, square; 1123.14, canon; 1123.22, b'Jimminey; 1123.24, negligence,; 1123.31, beautifnlly; 1124.34, Sierra's; 1126.31, BUBBLE'S; 1127.15, Thank, you Wallis,"; 1127.24, knew; 1127.38, into air; 1128.40, contined:; 1129.3, o; 1129.10, to-day.; 1129.17, stealthy; 1129.24, father.; 1130.13, subteranean; 1131.6, Hallmark; 1131.14–15, insenstiate; 1131.16, Hallmark; 1131.22, girlish,'; 1131.23, keep on; 1131.26, to to; 1131.35, breast ef; 1132.9, wlth; 1132.29, long.; 1132.35, "Lady; 1133.4, down; 1135.17, But is; 1136.31, magnanimity,; 1141.16,

Ernani; 1153.39–40, outline?"; 1155.25, contry; 1167.1, window);
1198.29, even; 1198.31, "Fecondité"; 1202.3, Hemskringla,";
1205.11, "Hemskringla"; 1208.23–24, villified; 1208.38, Maggie-
Tulliver.

Notes

In the notes below, numbers refer to page and line of this volume (the line count includes chapter headings). No note is made for material found in a standard desk-reference book. Particularly useful as sources of information about the historical background, writing, and publication of Norris's novels and essays are Jesse S. Crisler, *A Critical and Textual Study of Frank Norris's "McTeague,"* unpublished dissertation, University of South Carolina, 1973; Jesse S. Crisler and Joseph R. McElrath, Jr., *Frank Norris: A Reference Guide* (Boston: G. K. Hall & Co., 1974); James D. Hart, *A Novelist in the Making: A Collection of Student Themes and the Novels "Blix" and "Vandover and the Brute"* (Cambridge, Mass.: Harvard University Press, 1970); Joseph Katz, "The Shorter Publications of Frank Norris: A Checklist," *Proof,* 3 (1973), 155–220; and Robert A. Morace, *A Critical and Textual Study of Frank Norris's Writings from the San Francisco "Wave,"* unpublished dissertation, University of South Carolina, 1976.

VANDOVER AND THE BRUTE

15.30   Van John] Vingt-et-un (or twenty-one or blackjack), a card game in which the winning hand is that closest to but not over twenty-one.

16.3   *Lampoon*] A Harvard undergraduate humor magazine.

20.5–6   one . . . state.] The Southern Pacific Railroad. Further indirect allusions to the Southern Pacific occur on 185.2–3, 206.4–6, and 240.14–16.

23.4–7   interesting . . . drug.] *The Wrecker* (1892), by Robert Louis Stevenson and Lloyd Osbourne.

24.13–14   California . . . Franklin.] One block south of the Norris family residence on Sacramento near Franklin.

25.13   cable in its slot] In the San Francisco cable-car system, power generated by steam kept a cable, slotted into the street, continually in motion; the driver attached his car to the moving cable with a gripping device.

32.2–3   IMPERIAL . . . Kearney] In the heart of the theater and restaurant district of San Francisco. Throughout both *Vandover and the Brute* and *McTeague,* Norris consistently spells Kearny Street as Kearney Street.

32.28   nickel-in-the-slot machines] Slot machines for candy or gum.

39.33   Palace Hotel] The principal San Francisco hotel, a huge structure on Market near Montgomery.

46.4−5   School . . . Market]   The San Francisco Art Association conducted a School of Design in rooms over the California Market, a large public market at California and Kearny. Norris attended the school at this
location.

49.11   *l'Art*]   A French art magazine with lavish illustrations.

49.11   Mechanics Library]   The Mechanics' Institute Library, a private
library much patronized by well-to-do San Franciscans.

52.16   Tivoli]   The Tivoli Opera House, on Ellis near Market, a popular
combination beer garden and theater.

53.30   czarina]   A brooch or pendant bearing a miniature portrait of the
Czarina Alexandra.

56.3−4   Marchand's . . . Poodle Dog]   Three fashionable restaurants of
the day.

59.27   Bohemian Club]   Originally a club for artists and writers, by the
1890s the Bohemian Club also included many prominent San Franciscans
from the professions and business.

59.37   *Chautauquan*]   A journal that had its origin in the Chautauqua
adult education movement of the 1870s.

61.19   Delphine]   The name "Victorine" appears here in the first edition
but it is clearly an error. See pp. 60.4−5, 28 and 61.2.

65.4   Mechanics' Fair]   The annual fair at the Mechanics' Institute was a
major event of the San Francisco season.

65.8−9   Cliff House]   A well-known restaurant overlooking the Pacific at
the western edge of San Francisco.

73.13   *'spotted toads'*]   Children born deformed by congenital syphilis.

78.38   fell]   Here meaning "hair."

86.28   Perrique]   More commonly "perique," a strong-flavored tobacco
from Louisiana.

87.4   patent log]   A mechanical device for determining the speed of a
ship.

108.7−8   fish horn]   Used originally by itinerant fish peddlers; thereafter,
any loud horn.

123.37−38   nine . . . twenty.]   This should be "nine thousand *seven*
hundred and twenty"—the correct balance; but since emending here would
not resolve the sums following, the passage has been reprinted as it originally
appeared.

136.3   "Midway Plaisance Music,"]   The Midway Plaisance was the principal entertainment street of the 1893 World's Columbian Exposition at Chicago.

153.16   nighthawks]   Cabs plying the city during the night.

166.17–19   some . . . lacking.]   Norris's depiction of an early symptom of paresis, a disease of the brain and nervous system caused by syphilitic infection. Vandover's physical and mental decline from this point on (including his lycanthropic hallucinations) tracks the late nineteenth-century description of paresis.

177.16–20   the story . . . him.]   *Ben Hur: A Tale of the Christ* (1880), by Lew Wallace (1827–1905).

182.35   Thursday . . . twelfth]   April 12 fell on a Thursday in 1894.

186.7   Mission]   The area south of Market near the old Mission Dolores.

199.2   Lick House]   A hotel at the corner of Montgomery and Sutter streets.

199.17   Cunarder]   A passenger ship of the Cunard Line.

201.37–38   Lotta's fountain]   One of San Francisco's most well-known landmarks, given to the city by Lotta Crabtree, a popular actress.

208.31   Sutro Baths]   Swimming pools, built by Adolph Sutro near the western edge of the city, which opened in March 1896.

211.27–212.2   On Vandover's . . . succession.]   In vingt-et-un, a player is permitted to "split" a pair into two separate hands and bet on each, as Ellis does here. Ellis then draws Van John or blackjack (a face card and an ace) on one of the hands, which requires double payment on the bet after Vandover goes over twenty-one.

232.27   Barbary Coast]   The red-light district of San Francisco, close to the dock area.

233.26   old Plaza]   Now Portsmouth Square, the original central square of San Francisco, at Kearny and Washington.

249.4–5   Black Crook]   An extremely popular musical extravaganza by Charles Barras (1826–73), originally produced in 1866 and still running in the 1890s.

256.19   gormed]   A variant of "gaumed," a dialect term for sticky or greasy.

257.20   *suz*]   A New England dialect exclamation of surprise.

McTEAGUE

263.4   Polk Street]   A street running from Market to San Francisco Bay, a block east of fashionable Van Ness Avenue.

263.9   steam beer]   A highly effervescent beer originating in San Francisco.

263.32   Placer County]   A mining area midway between Sacramento and Reno.

269.19   Cliff House]   See note 65.8–9.

270.11   B Street . . . bay]   A stop in Oakland on both the Southern Pacific Railroad and the East Bay trolley line.

281.18   rider of bicycles]   A new and fashionable form of transportation in the 1890s.

310.37   heads]   A group of small islands just outside the Golden Gate.

312.22   Mission]   See note 186.7.

316.23   Gotha truffle]   A German pastry dessert.

320.39   Goat Island]   The popular name for Yerba Buena Island.

326.21–22   fairy . . . ears.]   An allusion to Titania and Bottom in *A Midsummer Night's Dream*, Act III, Scene 1.

328.9   Orpheum]   The principal vaudeville theater of San Francisco, on O'Farrell near Powell.

331.13–14   Fauntleroy "costume"]   A costume featuring a lace collar and short velvet trousers, as worn by the title character in *Little Lord Fauntleroy* (1886), by Frances Hodgson Burnett (1849–1924).

335.32   Queen Charlottes]   Cream-filled pastries.

343.22   faro]   In faro, only two cards are dealt between the settling of bets.

401.7   Kearney]   See note 32.2–3.

401.37   Mechanics' Fair]   See note 65.4

404.2   picking waste]   Removing excess yarn from upholstery.

410.16   chest protector]   A garment to protect the chest from cold.

419.9   railroad strike]   A nationwide strike in June and July of 1895.

419.31   Chinese punk]   Chinese incense.

468.4   Whiskey and gum]   Whiskey in a mixer of hot water and sugar.

516.1   Plaza]   See note 233.26.

519.13   Kiralfy ballet]   A music hall troupe featuring young women in tights.

528.31   "monitors"]   High-pressure, swivel-mounted nozzles used in hydraulic mining.

531.7–8   a tall . . . gray]   Norris's self-portrait in the fall of 1897, when he was revising *McTeague* while a guest at Seymour Waterhouse's Placer County mine.

533.12   Burly drill]   More commonly "Burleigh" drill.

533.20   fitchered]   A mining term for a drill that is caught or hampered.

540.9–10   skunks . . . silver]   In what was commonly known as the "Crime of '73," Congress demonetized silver and thus lowered its price.

540.15   'contact']   The junction of two different kinds of rocks, often indicating the presence of gold ore.

540.15–16   country rocks]   Rocks containing mineral deposits.

540.28   color]   Particles of gold visible to the eye.

545.27   nitrate bed]   Sodium nitrate was in demand as a fertilizer at the time.

THE OCTOPUS

586.15   Pacific . . . Railroad]   Norris's fictional name for the Southern Pacific Railroad.

591.14   strike]   See note 419.9.

593.15   Jésus Tejéda]   Jesus Tejada was leader of a bandit gang that flourished in the Stockton area during the 1860s.

611.9   raven, like Elijah?]   1 Kings 17:4–6.

611.12–13   For . . . again]   Luke 15:24.

618.26   blue-stoning]   To treat with copper sulphate (in blue crystal form), an insecticide.

621.36–37   year . . . War!]   1877–78.

623.24–25   Marysville]   A small town about forty miles north of Sacramento.

625.13   "Sesame . . . Venice,"]   Both works by John Ruskin.

627.12–14   Terry . . . Ralson.]   David S. Terry (1823–89), lawyer and chief justice of the state supreme court; David C. Broderick (1820–59), San Francisco politician and United States senator killed by Terry in a duel; Edward D. Baker (1811–61), United States senator from Oregon and Union officer killed in the Civil War; James Lick (1796–1876), San Francisco financier and philanthropist; Juan Bautista Alvarado (1800–82), Mexican governor of California (1836–42); Joseph Emeric (1816–89), a wealthy Contra Costa rancher; Thomas O. Larkin (1802–58), wealthy California merchant of the Mexican period; William C. Ralston (1826–75), San Francisco banker and capitalist who died under mysterious circumstances after the failure of his bank.

627.20   Comstock boom] The Comstock Lode, a silver mine at Virginia City, Nevada, made millionaires of a number of miners after its discovery in 1859.

627.23–24   Dr. Glenn's . . . County] Hugh J. Glenn (1824–82) began the large-scale farming of wheat in California during the 1860s.

642.20   Queen's taste] To perfection.

691.23–31   'But . . . body.'] 1 Corinthians 15:35–44.

715.11   Gravelotte] A major Prussian victory, August 18, 1870, in the Franco-Prussian War.

715.29   Unzer Fritz] Karl Friedrich, King of Würtemburg (1823–91).

715.35   'Die Wacht am Rhein.'] A poem by Max Schneckenburger (1814–49), which, when set to music, became a patriotic song during the Franco-Prussian War.

734.16   'Snow Bound'] A popular long poem by John Greenleaf Whittier (1807–92).

738.6–7   'the voice . . . wilderness.'] Matthew 3:3.

740.26   grind] Joke.

749.30   'That . . . die,'] 1 Corinthians 15:36.

752.20   "As . . . Inclined,"] Alexander Pope, "Moral Essays" (1734), I, 150.

752.20–21   "Truth . . . Again,"] From "The Battle-Field," (1837), I, 25, by William Cullen Bryant (1794–1878).

752.21–22   "As for . . . Death,"] From Patrick Henry's (1736–99) speech to the Virginia Convention in 1775.

766.4   "farmer's satin."] A durable material (often wool) having a satin-like surface.

787.5–6   Fremont's . . . County.] The incident, which occurred in 1846 on what is now Fremont Peak, involved a small group of Americans and a Mexican force.

796.3–4   six . . . gas-pipe] Pipe filled with dynamite and used as a bomb.

804.33   Lotta's fountain] See note 201.37–38.

816.18–19   Million . . . Festival] Norris's name for the California Midwinter Exposition, held at San Francisco's Golden Gate Park in 1894.

817.18–19   Midway Plaisance] See note 136.3.

821.7   Young] Arthur Young (1741–1820), English writer on agricultural economics.

829.14   famine . . . India] There were major famines in Central India in 1897 and 1900.

831.9   caravels from Palos] Columbus sailed on his first voyage of discovery in 1492 from Palos de la Frontera in southwest Spain.

871.13–14   "Reading from Homer,"] A painting by Sir Lawrence Alma-Tadema (1836–1912), a popular English painter of classic subjects.

871.38–872.3   "The Toilers." . . . verse.] This account of the origin, nature, and success of Presley's poem is based on "The Man with the Hoe," by Edwin Markham (1852–1940). Markham's poem, which he wrote after seeing Millet's famous painting, appeared initially in the San Francisco *Examiner* in January 1899 and immediately attracted national attention.

873.35   gesabe] A Southwest dialect term for a cowboy, probably from the common Spanish phrase *quien sabe.*

878.31   aër-motor] A variation of aero-motor, a motor driven by wind power.

889.39–40   "Oh, Death . . . victory?"] 1 Corinthians 15:55.

895.37   Lick House] See note 199.2.

899.30   Cliff House] See note 65.8–9.

899.31   Sutro's Gardens] A public park adjoining the Sutro Baths, near the Cliff House; see also note 208.31.

899.32   Palace Hotel] See note 39.33.

901.32   wicker . . . baskets] Baskets that, when empty, fit into one another.

913.29   Dyke] This portion of the Dyke subplot is based on the noted California train robber Chris Evans.

956.19   Baldwin's . . . best] Matthias William Baldwin (1795–1866), manufacturer of locomotives.

1016.12   Czar] Alexander II of Russia was assassinated by a bomb in St. Petersburg in 1881.

1033.25   moth spots] Chloasma, patchy dark spots on the brow and cheeks. The physical description makes Shelgrim resemble Collis P. Huntington (1821–1900), one of the founders of the Southern Pacific and its president from 1890 to his death.

1040.31   Barbary Coast]   See note 232.27.

1048.21–22   *empressement*]   Eagerness.

1049.4–5   great house]   The mansion as described here resembles that of Mark Hopkins, one of the founders of the Southern Pacific, at California and Mason streets on Nob Hill.

1058.21   *Romaunt de la Rose*]   More commonly *Romance de la Rose*, an allegorical medieval poem.

1060.7   Xeres]   Sherry.

1061.16–17   'The poor . . . you.']   John 12:8.

1064.12–14   Sacramento . . . hill.]   Mrs. Hooven has wandered close to the summit of Nob Hill.

1071.13   Port Costa]   A major grain-shipping port during the 1880s and 1890s on Carquinez Strait, in Contra Costa County.

1085.35   'the greatest . . . numbers.']   The formula cited by the English philosopher Jeremy Bentham (1748–1832) as a guide to moral choice.

1095.5–6   'we're . . . more.']   The first line of a popular song, "How Are You Green-Backs" (1863), by E. Bowers, on the flooding of the country with paper currency during the Civil War.

1095.16–17   'Man . . . alone.']   Luke 4:4.

ESSAYS

1107.2–3   Jean . . . Ivanhoes.]   Heroes, respectively, of *Les Misérables* (1862) and *Ruy Blas* (verse drama, 1838) by Victor Hugo, and *Marmion, A Tale of Flodden Field* (narrative poem, 1808) and *Ivanhoe* (1819) by Sir Walter Scott.

1107.20–34   Here . . . capital.]   The *Rougon-Macquart* novels referred to are, in order, *Nana* (1880), *Germinal* (1885), *L'Oeuvre* (1886), *La Bête Humaine* (1890), *La Débâcle* (1892).

1107.38   *Le Rêve*]   Although in the *Rougon-Macquart* cycle, *Le Rêve* (1888) centers on the idyllic dreams of a young girl.

1113.29   Les Jeunes]   A group of artistic young San Franciscans who modeled themselves on bohemian groups in London and on the Continent.

1113.29   "The Lark"]   A literary magazine published by Les Jeunes from 1895 to 1897.

1113.36–37   Vivettes . . . Goups]   Vivette and Perilla were imaginary figures of refinement to whom many of the *Lark* essays were addressed; goops were boneless cartoon figures drawn by Gelett Burgess (1866–1951), a member of Les Jeunes, for the *Lark*.

1114.6   See Yup]   A San Francisco Chinese secret society.

1114.13   Kipling . . . Stevenson]   Norris refers to passages in Kipling's *American Notes* (1891) and Stevenson's *The Wrecker* (1892).

1119.2   *Big Four*]   *Harper's Monthly*, *Century*, *Scribner's*, and *Atlantic Monthly*.

1119.7   *Les Jeunes*]   See note 1113.29.

1119.21   THE 'RICKSHA THAT HAPPENED.]   A parody of Kipling's Indian stories.

1122.11   THE GREEN . . . UNREST.]   The first sentence recalls *Maggie: A Girl of the Streets* (1893), by Stephen Crane, but the rest of the piece parodies *The Red Badge of Courage* (1895).

1124.14   A HERO . . . CAN.]   A parody of Bret Harte's "The Outcasts of Poker Flat," from *The Luck of Roaring Camp and Other Sketches* (1870).

1126.31   VAN BUBBLES' STORY.]   A parody of Richard Harding Davis's *Van Bibber and Others* (1892) and a personal satire directed toward Davis's fame as a war correspondent.

1127.40   Heavyflinger]   An allusion to W. W. Heffelfinger, a famous Yale All-American football player of the early 1890s.

1130.1   AMBROSIA BEER.]   A parody of Ambrose Bierce's "One of the Missing," from *Tales of Soldiers and Civilians* (1891).

1132.6   I . . . DOTTY]   A parody of *The Dolly Dialogues* (1894), by Anthony Hope, the pseudonym of Sir Anthony Hope Hawkins (1863–1933).

1134.3   "The Crisis"]   By the popular American novelist Winston Churchill (1871–1947).

1139.4   New York publishers]   Doubleday, Page & Co.

1140.21   Mr. Davis]   Novelist and journalist Richard Harding Davis.

1142.2–3   Debacle . . . Fecondite]   Although all three of these novels are by Zola, *La Terre* was much attacked in America for its sexuality and *Fécondité* was frequently regarded as excessively polemical.

1148.19   "bacinets"]   Middle French term for lightweight helmets.

1148.24–25   "La Rue . . . Way."]   Respectively, main thoroughfares of medieval Paris and London and of ancient Rome.

1150.9–10   Violet . . . *Mobilier*]   More fully, *Dictionnaire du Mobilier Français*, by Eugène Emmanuel Viollet-le-Duc (1814–79).

1157.3   PILATE . . . truth?"]   John 18:38.

1161.3–6   40,000 . . . there.]   Norris alludes to the nursery rhyme that begins "The King of France went up the hill . . ."

1169.7   "Prepare . . . path."]   Mark 1:3.

1170.9–10   "Eben . . . Carvel"]   *Eben Holden* (1900), by Irving Bacheller (1859–1950); *David Harum* (1898), by Edward Westcott (1846–98); *Richard Carvel* (1899), by Winston Churchill (1871–1947).

1174.15   Tauchnitz]   A German publishing firm that produced cheap continental editions of works by English and American authors.

1175.2   *W. R. Lighton*]   A Kansas lawyer and author (1866–1916).

1183.7–8   United . . . China]   The Boxer Rebellion of mid-1900 had led the United States to send a detachment of marines to China for the relief of the U.S. Peking legation.

1185.13   concho]   Silver ornament worn on spurs.

1185.18   Magnusson Saga]   The collection of Icelandic sagas (1891–1905) edited by Eríkr Magnússon (1833–1913) and William Morris.

1186.24–30   certain . . . Baldwin]   Baldwin of Edessa (1058–1118), later King of Jerusalem, was a leader in the first Crusade and the fall of Jerusalem (1099); Matthias W. Baldwin (1795–1866) founded the great Baldwin Locomotive Company of Philadelphia.

1186.39–1187.1   new . . . way,"]   The line by Bishop George Berkeley (1695–1753), from his "Verses on the Prospect of Planting Arts and Learning in America," is "Westward the course of empire takes its way."

1201.4   As . . . pages,]   In "The Frontier Gone At Last," pages 1183–90 above.

1203.14–15   "How . . . Bar,"]   The story by Bret Harte, from his *Tales of the Argonauts* (1875).

1206.7–8   *saltimbanque*]   A mountebank or clown.

1208.28   Maggie Tulliver]   The heroine of George Eliot's *The Mill on the Floss* (1860).

CATALOGING INFORMATION

Norris, Frank, 1870–1902.
　　Novels and essays: Vandover and the brute;
　　McTeague; The octopus; Essays.
　　Ed. by Donald Pizer.

　　(The Library of America ; 33)
I. Title. II. Vandover and the brute. III. McTeague.
IV. The octopus. V. Essays. VI. Series.
PS2471　1986　　813'.4
ISBN 0-940450-40-2

This book is set in 10 point Linotron Galliard,
a face designed for photocomposition by Matthew Carter
and based on the sixteenth-century face Granjon. The paper
is acid-free Ecusta Nyalite and meets the requirements for perma-
nence of the American National Standards Institute. The binding
material is Brillianta, a 100% woven rayon cloth made by
Van Heek-Scholco Textielfabrieken, Holland. The com-
position is by Haddon Craftsmen, Inc., and The
Clarinda Company. Printing and binding
by R. R. Donnelley & Sons Company.
Designed by Bruce Campbell.

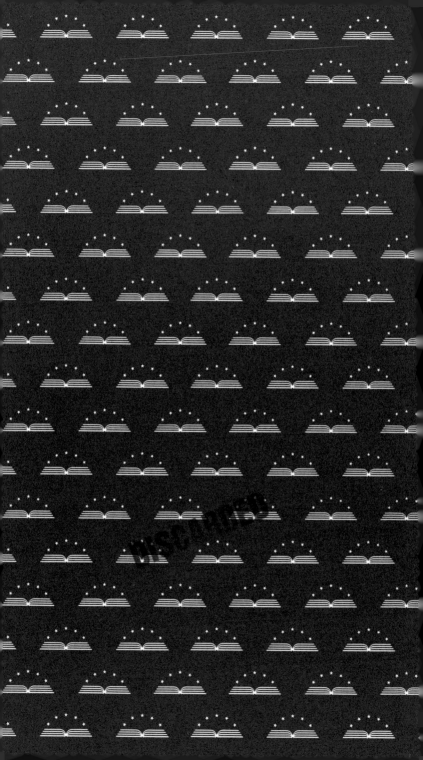